Lecture Notes in Computer Science 8784

Commenced Publication in 1973
Founding and Former Series Editors:
Gerhard Goos, Juris Hartmanis, and Jan van Leeuwen

Advanced Research in Computing and Software Science

Subline of Lectures Notes in Computer Science

Fabian Kuhn (Ed.)

Distributed Computing

28th International Symposium, DISC 2014
Austin, TX, USA, October 12-15, 2014
Proceedings

 Springer

Volume Editor

Fabian Kuhn
University of Freiburg
Department of Computer Science
79110 Freiburg, Germany
E-mail: kuhn@cs.uni-freiburg.de

ISSN 0302-9743   e-ISSN 1611-3349
ISBN 978-3-662-45173-1   e-ISBN 978-3-662-45174-8
DOI 10.1007/978-3-662-45174-8
Springer Heidelberg New York Dordrecht London

Library of Congress Control Number: 2014950904

LNCS Sublibrary: SL 1 – Theoretical Computer Science and General Issues

Typesetting: Camera-ready by author, data conversion by Scientific Publishing Services, Chennai, India

Printed on acid-free paper

Springer is part of Springer Science+Business Media (www.springer.com)

Preface

DISC, the International Symposium on Distributed Computing, is an international forum on the theory, design, analysis, implementation, and application of distributed systems and networks. DISC is organized in cooperation with the European Association for Theoretical Computer Science (EATCS).

This volume contains the papers presented at DISC 2014, the 28th International Symposium on Distributed Computing held during October 12–15, 2014, in Austin, TX. The volume also includes the citation for the 2014 Edsger W. Dijkstra Prize in Distributed Computing, and the 2014 Principles of Distributed Computing Doctoral Dissertation Award, both jointly sponsored by the EATCS Symposium on Distributed Computing (DISC) and the ACM Symposium on Principles of Distributed Computing (PODC). The Dijkstra Prize was awarded to K. Mani Chandy and to Leslie Lamport and it was presented at PODC 2014. The Principles of Distributed Computing Doctoral Dissertation Award was presented at DISC 2014 and it was given to Bernhard Haeupler.

In total, 151 regular papers and nine brief announcements were submitted to the symposium. Each submission was reviewed by at least three Program Committee members. For this task, the committee was assisted by about 180 external researchers. After reviewing the papers, the Program Committee made the final decisions in discussions carried out mostly over the Web, using EasyChair, from June 19 to July 10. The Program Committee accepted 34 submissions for regular presentations at DISC 2014. In addition, two closely related submissions were accepted as one merged paper, resulting in 35 regular papers presented at the symposium. Each presentation was accompanied by a paper of up to 15 pages in this volume. Revised and expanded versions of several selected papers will be considered for publication in a special issue of the journal *Distributed Computing*. Some of the regular submissions that were rejected, but generated substantial interest among the members of the Program Committee, were invited to be published as brief announcements. In total, 18 brief announcements appeared at DISC 2014. Each of the two-page brief announcements summarizes ongoing work or recent results, and it can be expected that these results will appear as full papers in later conferences or journals.

The best paper award of DISC 2014 was given to Ho-Lin Chen, Rachel Cummings, David Doty, and David Soloveichik for their paper "Speed Faults in Computation by Chemical Reaction Networks." The best student paper award of DISC 2014 was awarded to Merav Parter for her paper "Vertex Fault Tolerant Additive Spanners."

The program also consisted of two invited keynote lectures, presented by K. Mani Chandy from the California Institute of Technology and by Phil Bernstein from Microsoft Research. Abstracts of the invited lectures are included in these proceedings.

DISC 2014 was accompanied by two workshops: the Second Workshop on Biological Distributed Algorithms (BDA), organized by Yuval Emek and Nancy Lynch, and the Third Workshop on Advances on Distributed Graph Algorithms (ADGA), organized by Christoph Lenzen. BDA took place on October 11 and 12, ADGA on October 12. Additionally, on October 12, a sequence of tutorials was organized by Alessia Milani and Corentin Travers.

August 2014   Fabian Kuhn

Christian Schindelhauer   University of Freiburg, Germany
Boaz Patt-Shamir   Tel Aviv University, Israel
Jukka Suomela   Aalto University, Finland
Sébastien Tixeuil   UPMC Sorbonne University, France

Steering Committee

Marcos Aguilera   Microsoft Research, USA
Yehuda Afek   Tel Aviv University, Israel
Keren Censor-Hillel   Technion, Israel
Shlomi Dolev   Ben-Gurion University, Israel
Antonio Fernandez Anta
   (Chair)   IMDEA Networks, Spain
Fabian Kuhn   University of Freiburg, Germany
Achour Mostefaoui   University of Nantes, France

Organizing Committee

Chen Avin (Publicity)   Ben-Gurion University, Israel
Sebastian Daum
   (Publicity)   University of Freiburg, Germany
Mohamed Gouda
   (General Chair)   University of Texas, Austin, USA
Alessia Milani
   (Workshops/Tutorials) LaBRI, Bordeaux, France
Corentin Travers
   (Workshops/Tutorials) LaBRI, Bordeaux, France

Additional Reviewers

Abo Khamis, Mahmoud   Blin, Lelia
Afek, Yehuda   Bodlaender, Marijke
Akbari, Hoda   Bonomi, Silvia
Alistarh, Dan   Borokhovich, Michael
Alvaro, Peter   Boyle, Elette
Andoni, Alexandr   Brodsky, Alex
Arbel, Maya   Brown, Trevor
Asharov, Gilad   Cachin, Christian
Atrey, Pradeep   Calciu, Irina
Balasubramanian, Bharath   Canetti, Ran
Bannoura, Amir   Castañeda, Armando
Barenboim, Leonid   Censor-Hillel, Keren
Baruch, Mor   Charron-Bost, Bernadette
Bernard, Thibault   Chauhan, Himanshu

Organization

DISC, the International Symposium on Distributed Computing, is an annual forum for presentation of research on all aspects of distributed computing. It is organized in cooperation with the European Association for Theoretical Computer Science (EATCS). The symposium was established in 1985 as a biannual International Workshop on Distributed Algorithms on Graphs (WDAG). The scope was soon extended to cover all aspects of distributed algorithms and WDAG came to stand for International Workshop on Distributed Algorithms, becoming an annual symposium in 1989. To reflect the expansion of its area of interest, the name was changed to DISC (International Symposium on Distributed Computing) in 1998, opening the symposium to all aspects of distributed computing. The aim of DISC is to reflect the exciting and rapid developments in this field.

Program Committee Chair

Fabian Kuhn   University of Freiburg, Germany

Program Committee

James Aspnes	Yale University, USA
Hagit Attiya	Technion, Israel
Chen Avin	Ben-Gurion University, Israel
Shiri Chechik	Microsoft Research, USA
Faith Ellen	University of Toronto, Canada
Vijay Garg	University of Texas, Austin, USA
George Giakkoupis	Inria Rennes, France
Seth Gilbert	National University of Singapore
Rachid Guerraoui	EPFL, Switzerland
Bernhard Haeupler	Microsoft Research, USA
Danny Hendler	Ben-Gurion University, Israel
Majid Khabbazian	University of Alberta, Canada
Christoph Lenzen	MIT, USA
Victor Luchangco	Oracle Labs, USA
Dahlia Malkhi	Microsoft Research, USA
Thomas Moscibroda	Microsoft Research, China
Yoram Moses	Technion, Israel
Danupon Nanongkai	Brown University, Singapore
Andrzej Pelc	University of Québec, Canada
Jared Saia	University of New Mexico, USA
Thomas Sauerwald	University of Cambridge, UK

Chlebus, Bogdan
Cornejo, Alejandro
Dams, Johannes
Dani, Varsha
Daum, Sebastian
Dolev, Danny
Dolev, Shlomi
Eisenstat, David
Elsässer, Robert
Emek, Yuval
Fatourou, Panagiota
Feinerman, Ofer
Feldman, Ariel
Ferreira, Carla
Függer, Matthias
Gafni, Eli
Gelashvili, Rati
Ghaffari, Mohsen
Göös, Mika
Hadzilacos, Vassos
Hans, Sandeep
Hazay, Carmit
Hirvonen, Juho
Hoefer, Martin
Holzer, Stephan
Hua, Qiang-Sheng
Huang, Zengfeng
Huguenin, Kévin
Hung, Wei-Lun
Izraelevitz, Joseph
Izumi, Taisuke
Jakoby, Andreas
Jeż, Łukasz
Jurdzinski, Tomasz
Kallimanis, Nikolaos
Kantor, Erez
Katz, Jonathan
Kavitha, Telikepalli
Keidar, Idit
Keller, Barbara
Kesselheim, Thomas
Khabbazian, Majid
Khan, Maleq
Khunjush, Farshad
Kijima, Shuji

King, Valerie
Klonowski, Marek
Kobayashi, Yusuke
Kogan, Alex
Kopinsky, Justin
Korhonen, Janne H.
Korman, Amos
Kosowski, Adrian
Kowalski, Dariusz
Krinninger, Sebastian
Köhler, Sven
Lafourcade, Pascal
Lall, Ashwin
Lattanzi, Silvio
Lea, Doug
Lesani, Mohsen
Lev, Yossi
Lipmaa, Helger
Liu, Yujie
Lorch, Jacob
Mallmann-Trenn, Frederik
Marathe, Virendra
Masuzawa, Toshimitsu
Matsakis, Nick
Maurer, Alexandre
Mehrabian, Abbas
Michael, Maged
Milani, Alessia
Miller, Avery
Mittal, Neeraj
Mitton, Nathalie
Miyano, Eiji
Moir, Mark
Molla, Anisur Rahaman
Morrison, Adam
Moss, Eliot
Movahedi, Mahnush
Nagarajan, Viswanath
Narayanan, Lata
Newport, Calvin
Nisgav, Aviv
O'Neill, Adam
Ortolf, Christian
Oshman, Rotem
Palmieri, Roberto

Petit, Franck
Petrank, Erez
Pettie, Seth
Pinkas, Benny
Pop, Florin
Potop-Butucaru, Maria
Pourmiri, Ali
Radeva, Tsvetomira
Rajaraman, Rajmohan
Rawitz, Dror
Ribeiro Alves, David
Rinetzky, Noam
Riondato, Matteo
Robinson, Peter
Rodrigues, Luis
Rossbach, Chris
Ruppert, Eric
Rybicki, Joel
Saha, Barna
Sastry, Srikanth
Scalosub, Gabriel
Schmid, Stefan
Setty, Srinath
Sidford, Aaron
Shachnai, Hadas
Shah, Nihar
Stachowiak, Grzegorz
Stauffer, Alexandre
Sun, He
Tangwongsan, Kanat

Thaler, Justin
Timnat, Shahar
Thomas, Gael
Toueg, Sam
Tov, Roei
Trehan, Chhaya
Tristan, Jean-Baptiste
Vakilian, Ali
Viennot, Laurent
Wadia, Akshay
Weinstein, Omri
Welch, Jennifer
Wendeberg, Johannes
Widder, Josef
Wieder, Udi
Woelfel, Philipp
Wojciechowski, Paweł T.
Woods, Damien
Xiang, Lingxiang
Yamauchi, Yukiko
Yang, Hsin-Jung
Lee, Yin Tat
Young, Maxwell
Yu, Haifeng
Zadorojniy, Alexander
Zamani, Mahdi
Zhao, Kai
Zheng, Chaodong
Zhu, Leqi

Sponsoring Organizations

European Association for
Theoretical Computer Science

National Science Foundation

Oracle

DISC 2014 acknowledges the use of the EasyChair system for handling submissions, managing the review process, and compiling these proceedings.

The 2014 Edsger W. Dijkstra Prize in Distributed Computing

The Dijkstra Prize Committee has selected **Kanianthra Mani Chandy** and **Leslie Lamport** as the recipients of this year's Edsger W. Dijkstra Prize in Distributed Computing. The prize is given to them for their outstanding paper "Distributed Snapshots: Determining Global States of Distributed Systems", published in ACM Transactions on Computer Systems, Vol. 3, No. 1, 1985, pages 63–75.

The ACM-EATCS Edsger W. Dijkstra Prize in Distributed Computing is awarded for an outstanding paper on the principles of distributed computing, whose significance and impact on the theory and/or practice of distributed computing has been evident for at least a decade. The prize is sponsored jointly by the ACM Symposium on Principles of Distributed Computing (PODC) and the EATCS Symposium on Distributed Computing (DISC).

In their paper, Chandy and Lamport describe a distributed algorithm to record a consistent global state of an asynchronous distributed computation. Determining such a distributed snapshot is essential for several fundamental tasks and it is for example at the basis of solutions for termination or deadlock detection or to verify whether some other stable global property holds. Note that the inherent lack of a common clock or a global observer means that global states that are asynchronously recorded can be potentially inconsistent. The solution provided by Chandy and Lamport is extremely elegant and also remarkably simple, a fact that certainly also contributed to its success. The correctness proof is based on swapping of prerecording and postrecording events without affecting the correctness of the observed state. It is very significant that the recorded global state may not have been any of the global states that the system passed through in a real-time view of its execution.

The paper provides the first clear understanding of the definition of consistent global states in distributed systems. Consistent global states form the cornerstone of asynchronous distributed execution observation, and subsequent concepts such as those of the hugely popular vector clocks and concurrent common knowledge are based on consistent global states. Further, the paper demonstrates that the recorded state in the global snapshot is a valid equivalent state in the sense that an equivalent execution may very well pass through that state, even though the actual execution may not have. In fact, the possibility of the occurrence of the recorded state is indistinguishable from the possibility of the occurrence of the actual states that occurred in the distributed execution. This property led to the definition of global predicates on entire executions, as opposed to the definition of global predicates on individual observations of executions. Similarly, this spawned the important concept of isomorphism of executions.

In conclusion, the paper by Chandy and Lamport has had a profound and lasting impact on the theory and implementation of distributed algorithms and systems. It has led to concepts such as vector time, isomorphism of executions, global predicate detection, and concurrent common knowledge. Applications of the results of observing the system in consistent states include the development of vector clocks, checkpointing and message logging protocols, correct protocols for detecting stable properties such as distributed deadlocks and termination, mutual exclusion algorithms, garbage collection protocols, cache coherency and file coherency protocols in distributed replicated file systems, distributed debugging protocols, protocols for total message order and causal message order in group communication systems, global virtual time algorithms used particularly in parallel and distributed simulations of discrete event systems, and collaborative sessions and editing protocols in wide area systems and on the grid.

Dijkstra Prize Committee 2014

Lorenzo Alvisi	UT Austin, Texas, USA
Shlomi Dolev	Ben Gurion Univ., Israel
Rachid Guerraoui	EPFL, Switzerland
Idit Keidar	Technion, Israel
Fabian Kuhn (chair)	U. of Freiburg, Germany
Shay Kutten	Technion, Israel

The 2014 Principles of Distributed Computing Doctoral Dissertation Award

The Doctoral Dissertation Award Committee has awarded the Principles of Distributed Computing Doctoral Dissertation Award in Distributed Computing 2014 to **Dr. Bernhard Haeupler**. Dr. Bernhard Haeupler completed his thesis

"Probabilistic Methods for Distributed Information Dissemination"

on June 2013 under the co-supervision of Professors Jonathan Kelner, Muriel Médard, and David Karger at MIT. Bernhard Haeupler's thesis provides a sweeping multidisciplinary study of information dissemination in a network, making fundamental contributions to distributed computing and its connections to theoretical computer science and information theory. The thesis addresses an impressive list of topics to which Dr. Bernhard Haeupler contributed significantly. These topics include the design and analysis of gossip protocols overcoming the dependency to connectivity parameters such as conductance, the introduction of a completely new technique for analyzing the performance of network coding gossip algorithms, and new randomized protocols for multi-hop radio networks. These are just a few samples of the very many important contributions of Dr. Bernhard Haeupler's thesis, and the work in this dissertation is distinguished by an impressive combination of creativity, breadth, and technical skill.

The award is sponsored jointly by the ACM Symposium on Principles of Distributed Computing (PODC) and the EATCS Symposium on Distributed Computing (DISC). This award is presented annually, with the presentation taking place alternately at PODC and DISC. This year 2014 it will be presented at DISC, to be held in Austin, Texas, October 12–15, 2014.

Principles of Distributed Computing
Doctoral Dissertation Award Committee 2014

Yehuda Afek	Tel-Aviv Univ., Israel
James Aspnes	Yale University, USA
Pierre Fraigniaud (chair)	CNRS & U. Paris Diderot, France
Dariusz Kowalski	Univ. of Liverpool, UK
Gadi Taubenfeld	IDC Herzliya, Israel

DISC 2014 Invited Lecture:
Concurrent Computing over the Last 40 Years: What's Changed and What Hasn't

K. Mani Chandy

California Institute of Technology, USA

This talk looks at what has changed in concurrent computing over the last forty years, and what has not. The talk is from my personal, subjective point of view. The fundamental concepts developed by the giants of the field haven't changed. Many of these giants worked at, or spent parts of their sabbaticals at the University of Texas at Austin. The Dijkstra prize is named after one of these giants, Edsger Wybe Dijkstra. I'll show how the remarkable prescience of these pioneers has withstood the test of time. What has changed is the ease with which large concurrent systems can be set up and deployed. I'll share my experience in programming concurrent systems side-by-side with recent graduates who are almost 50 years younger than I am. Concurrency is the norm for them and they routinely deploy large systems with the Google App and Compute Engines or Amazon EC2 or other platforms. The research that is being reported at this conference will live on for decades because of the current and future crops of CS graduates.

DISC 2014 Invited Lecture:
Project Orleans, Distributed Virtual Actors for Programmability and Scalability

Phil Bernstein

Microsoft Research, USA

High-scale interactive services demand high throughput with low latency and high availability, difficult goals to meet with the traditional stateless three-tier architecture. The actor model makes it natural to build a stateful middle tier and achieve the required performance. However, popular actor implementations still pass many distributed systems problems to developers, such as reliability, location transparency, and distributed resource management. The Orleans programming model introduces the novel abstraction of virtual actors that addresses these problems, liberating developers from dealing with them. At the same time, it enables applications to attain high performance and scalability. This talk presents the Orleans programming model, distributed system mechanisms that support it, and several production applications that use Orleans and their performance. Information about Project Orleans can be found at http://research.microsoft.com/en-us/projects/orleans/

Table of Contents

Graph Distances and Routing

Radio Networks

Shared Memory

Dynamic and Social Networks

Relativistic Systems

Transactional Memory and Concurrent Data Structures

Distributed Graph Algorithms

Communication

Brief Announcements

Automatically Adjusting Concurrency to the Level of Synchrony

Pierre Fraigniaud[1], Eli Gafni[2], Sergio Rajsbaum[3], and Matthieu Roy[4]

[1] CNRS and University Paris Diderot, France
[2] Dpt. of Computer Science, UCLA, USA
[3] Instituto de Matemáticas, UNAM, Mexico
[4] LAAS-CNRS, CNRS and U. Toulouse, France

Abstract. The state machine approach is a well-known technique for building distributed services requiring high performance and high availability, by replicating servers, and by coordinating client interactions with server replicas using consensus. Indulgent consensus algorithms exist for realistic eventually partially synchronous models, that never violate safety and guarantee liveness once the system becomes synchronous. Unavoidably, these algorithms may never terminate, even when no processor crashes, if the system never becomes synchronous.

This paper proposes a mechanism similar to state machine replication, called *RC-simulation*, that can always make progress, even if the system is never synchronous. Using RC-simulation, the quality of the service will adjust to the current level of asynchrony of the network — degrading when the system is very asynchronous, and improving when the system becomes more synchronous. RC-simulation generalizes the state machine approach in the following sense: when the system is asynchronous, the system behaves as if $k + 1$ threads were running concurrently, where k is a function of the asynchrony.

In order to illustrate how the RC-simulation can be used, we describe a long-lived renaming implementation. By reducing the concurrency down to the asynchrony of the system, RC-simulation enables to obtain renaming quality that adapts linearly to the asynchrony.

1 Introduction

Problem Statement. The *state machine* approach (also called *active replication*) [33,37] is a well-known technique for building a reliable distributed system requiring high performance and high availability. In the state machine approach, a *consensus* algorithm is used by the replicas to simulate a *single* centralized state machine. The role of consensus is to ensure that replicas apply operations to the state machine in the same order. Paxos [34] is the most widely-used consensus protocol in this context. It maintains replica consistency even during highly asynchronous periods of the system, while rapidly making progress as soon as the system becomes stable.

The state machine approach is limited by the impossibility of solving consensus in an asynchronous system even if only one process can crash [22]. Indulgent [26] consensus algorithms such as Paxos, never violate safety (replicas

F. Kuhn (Ed.): DISC 2014, LNCS 8784, pp. 1–15, 2014.
© Springer-Verlag Berlin Heidelberg 2014

never decide different values), and they guarantee liveness (all correct replicas decide) once the system becomes synchronous [32]. However, while the system is in an asynchronous period, the state's machine progress is delayed. Moreover, any indulgent consensus algorithm has executions that never terminate, even when no processor crashes, due to the impossibility of [22], in case the system never becomes synchronous.

One may think that to achieve reliability in distributed systems, and to enforce cooperation among the replicas enabling the system to function as a whole despite the failure of some of its components, consensus is essential [23]. This is true in general, but not always. E.g., consensus is not essential for implementing replicated storage [7] (the dynamic case is discussed in [3]). Hence, the question of whether one can build a reliable distributed system that always makes progress, for some specific services at least, remains open. This is precisely the question we are interested in.

Summary of Results. In this paper, we provide a mechanism similar to state machine replication, but that can always make progress, even if the system is never synchronous. Using our mechanism, the quality of the service adjusts to the current level of asynchrony of the system – degrading when the system is very asynchronous, and improving when the system becomes more synchronous. The main contribution of this paper is the proof that such a mechanism exists. We call it the *reduced-concurrency simulation* (RC-simulation for short).

To be able to design such a mechanism, we had to come up with appropriate definitions of "quality" of a service, and of the "level of asynchrony" of the system. In the state machine approach, the service behaves as one single thread once the system becomes synchronous. This behavior is generalized through the RC-simulation, so that, when the level of asynchrony is k, then the system behaves as if $k + 1$ threads were running concurrently.

In order to illustrate, with a concrete example, how the RC-simulation is used to obtain a fault-tolerant service that always makes progress, we describe a long-lived renaming service. In this case, the quality of the service is manifested in terms of the output name space provided by the long-lived renaming service, the smaller the better. Thanks to the RC-simulation mechanism, a higher quality of service is obtained by reducing the concurrency down to the level of asynchrony of the system. In particular, if the system is synchronous, then the service behaves as if names were produced by a single server, giving to the clients names from a very small (optimal) space. If the system becomes more asynchronous, then the service behaves as if more servers were running concurrently, and hence it gives names from a larger space to the clients. Whatever the asynchrony of the system is, safety is never violated, in the sense that the names concurrently given to the clients are always pairwise distinct.

The formal setting we consider for deriving our results is the one of an asynchronous read/write shared memory system where any number of processes may fail by crashing. We are interested in *wait-free* algorithms [27]. For simplicity, we assume that snapshot operations are available, since they can be implemented wait-free [1], and we define level of asynchrony at this granularity. However, the definition can be easily adapted to the granularity of read/write operations. We also stress the fact that we picked this shared memory model, and we picked the specific renaming textbook algorithm in [9], as a proof of concept. Definitely, further work is needed to study other, more realistic shared memory and/or message passing models, as well as other services. Moreover, we have not tried to optimize the *efficiency* of our simulation, which is beyond the objective of this paper. The main outcome of the paper is a proof that it is *possible* to adapt the concurrency to the level of asynchrony in a generic way.

Related Work. Various partially synchronous models have been proposed to model real systems better. For instance, in [19,21], the relative processors speeds are bounded, and there are bounds on processing times and communication delays. In addition, some of these models allow the system to have an initial period where the bounds are not respected. However, it is assumed that, eventually, the system enters a *stable* period where the bounds do hold. More recently, partially synchronous systems enabling to study problems that are strictly weaker than consensus were considered in [2]. Also, there is work on progress conditions that adapt to the degree of synchrony in each run, e.g. [4] and references herein.

Although RC-simulation tackles different objectives, it is inspired by the *BG-simulation algorithm* [12]. The latter is used for deriving reductions between tasks defined in different models of distributed computing. Indeed, the BG-simulation allows a set of $t + 1$ processes, with at most t crash failures, to "simulate" a larger number n of processes, also with at most t failures. The first application of the BG-simulation algorithm was that there are no k-fault-tolerant algorithms for the n-process k-set-agreement problem [17], for any n. Borowsky and Gafni extended the BG-simulation algorithm to systems including set agreement variables [11]. Chaudhuri and Reiners later formalized this extension in [18], following the techniques of [36]. While the original BG-simulation works only for colorless tasks [12] (renaming and many other tasks are not colorless [14,29]), it can be extended to any task [24]. Other variants and extensions of the BG-simulation, together with additional applications, have appeared in [16,28,30,31,35].

At the core of the BG-simulation, and of our RC-simulation as well, is the *safe-agreement* abstraction, a weaker form of consensus that can be solved wait-free (as opposed to consensus). The safe-agreement abstraction was introduced in [10] as "non-blocking busy wait." Several variants are possible, including the wait-free version we use here (processes are allowed to output a special value $\perp$ that has not been proposed), and the variant that was used in the journal version [12]. Safe-agreement is reminiscent of the crusader problem [20]. A safe-agreement extension that supports adaptive and long-lived properties is discussed in [6]. Notice that we can apply our RC-simulation to renaming, which is not a colorless task (and hence cannot be used with the BG-simulation), because we use safe-agreement only to simulate threads consistently, as opposed to the BG-simulation, which uses safe-agreement for reductions between tasks.

A generalization of the state machine approach was presented in [25], where, instead of using consensus, it uses set agreement. In k-set agreement, instead of agreeing on a unique decision, the processes may agree on up to k different decisions. The paper [25] presents a state machine version with k-set agreement, where any number of processes can emulate k state machines of which at least one remains "highly available". This state machine version is not based on the BG-simulation, and is not dynamic, as opposed to our RC-simulation mechanism.

Renaming is a widely-studied problem that has many applications in distributed computing (see, e.g., the survey [15]). In long-lived renaming, the number of processes participating in getting or releasing a name can vary during the execution. When the number is small, the number of names in use should be small. An $f(k)$-renaming algorithm [8] is a renaming algorithm in which a process always gets a name in the range $\{1, \ldots, f(k)\}$, where k is the number of processes that participate in getting names. Notice that $f(k)$-renaming is impossible unless $f(k) \geq k$. Burns and Peterson [13] proved that long-lived $f(k)$-renaming is impossible in an asynchronous shared memory system using only reads and writes unless $f(k) \geq 2k-1$. They also gave the first long-lived $(2k-1)$-renaming algorithm in this model. for our example is from [9]. Finally, recall that indulgent algorithms progress only when synchrony is achieved. We refer to [5] for sensing fast that synchrony is on, and for solving renaming with an indulgent algorithm.

2   Reducing Concurrency

In this section, we describe the *reduced-concurrency* simulation, abbreviated in *RC-simulation* hereafter. At the core of the RC-simulation is the *safe-agreement mediated* simulation, or *SA-simulation* for short. The SA-simulation is the essential mechanism on top of which is implicitly built the well known BG-simulation [12]. We describe the SA-simulation explicitly in Section 2.2, and then explain in Section 2.3 how the RC-simulation is built on top of the SA-simulation in order to reduce concurrency. Hence, the contribution of this section is the complete description of the plain arrow on the left-hand side of Fig. 1, involving the notion of *partial asynchrony*, that we define next, in Section 2.1.

2.1   Partial Asynchrony

We are considering a distributed system composed of n crash-prone asynchronous processes. Each process p has a unique identity $Id(p) \in \{1, \ldots, n\}$. Processes communicate via a reliable shared memory composed of n multiple-reader single-writer registers, each process having the exclusive write-access to one of these n registers. For simplicity, by "read", we will actually mean an *atomic snapshot* of the entire content of the shared memory (recall that snapshots can be implemented wait-free using read/write registers [1]).

In the wait-free setting, the efficiency of the system can be altered by the asynchrony between the processes. To measure the amount of asynchrony experienced by the system, we introduce the novel notion of *partial asynchrony*. (See Fig. 1 for an illustration of the concepts defined hereafter). Let us consider a potentially infinite execution $\mathcal{E}$ of the system, and let p be a process.

A *blind interval* for p is a maximal time-interval during which p performs no snapshots. More precisely, let t_1 and t_2 with $t_2 > t_1$ be the times at which two

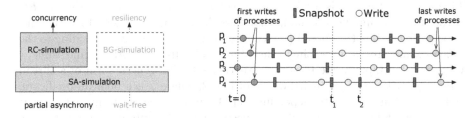

Fig. 1. RC- vs. BG-simulations (left), illustration of partial asynchrony (right)

consecutive snapshots performed by p occur in $\mathcal{E}$. The time-interval $I = (t_1, t_2)$ is called a blind time-interval for process p. If in addition we assume, w.l.o.g., that the first instruction of every process is a write, then the interval $[0, t)$ where t denotes the time at which process p performs its first snapshot, is also a blind interval for p. Thus, $\mathcal{E}$ can be decomposed into the sequence of consecutive blind intervals for a process p, where a snapshot by p is performed in between each of these intervals. In Fig. 1, each process performs four snapshots and five writes. Hence, there are five blind intervals for every process.

Definition 1. *The partial asynchrony experienced by process p in $\overset{\cdot}{\mathcal{E}}$ during a blind interval for p is the number of processes that do not perform any write during this time-interval. The partial asynchrony of p in $\mathcal{E}$ is the maximum, taken over all blind intervals I for p, of the partial asynchrony experienced by process p during I. Finally, the partial asynchrony of the system in $\mathcal{E}$ is the maximum, taken over all processes p, of the partial asynchrony of p in $\mathcal{E}$.*

On the right-hand side of Fig. 1, p_1 experiences a partial asynchrony of 1 because, p_4 is missing in the interval between its first two snapshots. The partial asynchrony of the whole execution is 2 because p_4 experiences a partial asynchrony of 2 in its blind interval (t_1, t_2) as both p_1 and p_3 are missing, but no processes experience a partial asynchrony of 3. For any non-negative integer k, an execution in which the partial asynchrony of the system is at most k is called k-partially asynchronous. In particular, an execution is 0-partially asynchronous if and only if all processes perform in lock steps. As another example, if the process p is much slower than all the other processes, then p experiences zero partial asynchrony. However, each of the $n-1$ other processes experiences a partial asynchrony of 1 caused by the slow process p. The general case is when the processes are subject to arbitrary delays, as illustrated in the example of Fig. 1. Then the larger the partial asynchrony experienced by a process p, the more asynchronous the system looks to p, and the more p may suffer from this asynchrony. Our objective is to limit the penalty incurred by the system because of asynchrony, by reducing the amount of concurrency.

2.2 The Safe-Agreement Mediated Simulation

The *safe-agreement mediated* simulation, or *SA-simulation* for short, is a generic form of execution of a collection $\mathcal{T}$ of *threads* by a system of n processes. Hence, let us first define the notion of thread.

Threads. A thread τ is a triple $(Id, A, value)$ where $Id = Id(\tau)$ is the *identity* of the thread τ, uniquely defining that thread, $A = A(\tau)$ is a set of instructions to be performed by the thread (typically, this set is the one corresponding to the code of some process executing a distributed wait-free algorithm), and $value = value(\tau)$ is an input value to this instruction set. The generic form of a thread code is described in the left-hand side of Fig. 2, where φ is a boolean predicate, and f is a function, both depending on A. In this generic form, a thread is thus a write, followed by a finite sequence of snapshot-write instructions. In the sequel, when we refer to an *instruction* of a thread, we precisely refer to such a snapshot-write instruction. The SA-simulation is an execution by n processes of the threads in a collection $\mathcal{T}$ of threads.

```
THREAD τ = (Id, A, value)
1:     view ← (Id, value)
2:     write(view)
3:     while φ(view) do
4:         view ← snapshot()
5:         write(view)
6:     decide f(view)
```

```
SA-SIMULATION of a collection T of threads.
1:     while true do
2:         view ← snapshot()
3:         if there exists an extendable thread τ ∈ T
4:             then perform next instruction of τ
```

Fig. 2. Generic code for threads (left), and code for SA-simulation (right)

For the sake of simplicity of the presentation, we assume that the threads are resident in memory when the simulation begins. Moreover, we also assume that each thread is either *available* or *non available*. Our simulation is concerned with simulating available threads. However a thread can be moved from non-available to available (not vice-versa), but such a move is not under the control of the system, and can be viewed as under the control of an adversary. This models the situation in which the system receives requests for executing threads, or for performing tasks, by abstracting away the input/output interface of the system with the outside world. Taking once again the example of long-lived renaming, a thread corresponding to the release of a name by a process can be made available only if a name has been acquired previously by this process, and two requests of names by a same process must be separated by a release name by the same process. Other than that, the adversary is entirely free to decide when processes request and release names.

SA-Simulation in a Nutshell. In essence, the SA-simulation relies on two notions: *extendability* and *agreement*. Roughly, a thread is *extendable* if it is not blocked, that is, if no processes are preventing others from performing the next instruction of the thread. Indeed, again roughly, performing an instruction of a thread requires some form of coordination among the processes, in order to decide which value to write, that is, to decide which view of the memory is consistent with a view that may have acquired a thread by snapshotting the memory. Since consensus is not possible to achieve in a wait-free environment [22], we will use weaker forms of agreement.

Let us present the general form of SA-simulation. The code of a process p performing SA-simulation of $\mathcal{T}$ is presented in Fig. 2. We assume a long-lived simulation, i.e., an infinite number of threads. Handling a finite number of threads just requires to change the condition in the while-loop of the SA-simulation, in order to complete the simulation when all (available) threads have been simulated. In what follows, we precisely explain how a process figures out whether there exists an extendable thread, and how it performs the next instruction of a thread. For this purpose, we first recall a core mechanism for performing a weak form of consensus: *safe-agreement*.

Safe-Agreement. Consider the following specification of *safe-agreement* (similar to [12]). Each process proposes a value, and must decide some output according to the following three rules: (1) *Termination*: every process that does not crash must decide a proposed value or $\bot$; (2) *Validity*: if not all processes crash, then at least one process must decide a value different from $\bot$; (3) *Agreement*: all processes that decide a value different from $\bot$ must decide the same value. The algorithm in Fig. 3 is a wait-free algorithm solving safe agreement, directly inspired from [6].

SAFE-AGREEMENT performed by process p proposing $v = value(p)$
1:    write $(Id(p), v)$
2:    snapshot memory, to get $view = \{(i_1, v_{i_1}), \ldots, (i_k, v_{i_k})\}$
3:    write $(Id(p), view)$
4:    snapshot memory, to get $setofview = \{(j_1, view_{j_1}), \ldots, (j_\ell, view_{j_\ell})\}$
5:    $minview \leftarrow \bigcap_{r=1}^{\ell} view_{j_r}$
6:    **if** for every i such that $(i, v_i) \in minview$ we have $view_i \in setofview$
7:    **then** decide minimum value w in $minview$
8:    **else** decide $\bot$

Fig. 3. Safe agreement

The Instruction Matrix. We explain now how processes decide whether there exist extendable threads. This is achieved thanks to the *virtual* shared data-structure displayed beside. Whenever a process p performs a snapshot of the memory, it gets a view of the current states of execution of all the threads. This view can be virtually represented by the instruction matrix M as displayed in the figure beside. The cell $M_{i,j}$ of the instruction matrix represents the status of the ith instruction of the jth thread (i.e., the

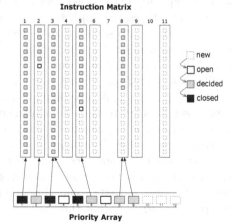

thread τ such that $Id(\tau) = j$). This status can be one of the following three states: (1) new: no processes have tried to perform this instruction yet, (2) open: at least one process is trying to perform this instruction, but the outcome of this instruction has not yet been decided, or (3) decided: the instruction has been performed, that is, an outcome has been decided for this instruction. A thread for which all cells are decided is said to be *fully executed* in the sense that all its instructions have been performed by the system. Of course, the SA-simulation executes the instructions of every thread in sequential order. That is, the column j of the instruction matrix corresponding to a thread that is available but not fully executed, consists in a (possibly empty) sequence of decided cells, immediately followed by a cell that is either open or new, immediately followed by a (possibly empty) sequence of cells in state new. The cell immediately following the (possibly empty) sequence of decided cells is called the *current instruction cell* of the thread. The instruction matrix enables to define formally the notion of extendability:

Definition 2. *A thread τ is* extendable *if it is available, not fully executed, and its current instruction cell is in state new.*

Note that the instruction matrix is an abstraction describing the execution status of the threads. It is not a data structure that is manipulated by the processes. Indeed, when a process performs the snapshot in SA-simulation, its view is the content of the whole memory, which contains the way the threads are progressing, including the number of snapshot-write instructions that have been already performed by each thread. In the SA-simulation, every process identifies some extendable thread τ, and aims at performing the next instruction of τ. Roughly, when a process tests whether there exists an extendable thread in SA-simulation, it tests all open cells in the instruction matrix using safe-agreement, and the answer is negative if and only if this process has decided $\perp$ for each of them. This mechanism is detailed next.

Performing Instruction. Recall that what we defined as an "instruction" of a thread is a snapshot followed by a write. Such a combination of snapshot-write appears explicitly in the generic form of a thread (cf. Fig. 2). The value written in memory by a thread is simply the view it gets during the last snapshot preceding the write. Hence, to simulate an instruction of a thread, the potentially many processes performing that instruction must agree on this view. This coordination is performed via safe-agreement.

There is one safe-agreement task associated to each cell (i, j) of the instruction matrix, $i, j \geq 1$. A process p aiming at simulating Instruction i of Thread j proposes its view to the safe-agreement of cell (i, j). By the specification of safe-agreement, it is guaranteed that, among all views proposed to this safe-agreement, only one of them with be outputted. (Not all processes may decide this view, but those ones decide $\perp$). If p outputs $\perp$, then p aborts this attempt to perform the instruction, and completes the while-loop of SA-simulation. Otherwise, i.e., if p outputs some view, then p writes this view for Thread j, to complete the write of that thread.

Safety and Liveness. We now establish the following lemma, which may have its interest on its own, but will also be later used to prove the correctness of our more refined RC-simulation. Let us define two crucial properties that are expected to be satisfied by a simulation of threads by a system of processes.

Safety: For every collection $\mathcal{T}$ of threads solving task T using a same algorithm A, the simulation of $\mathcal{T}$ by SA-simulation leads $\mathcal{T}$ to solve Task T.

Liveness: In any infinite execution of the SA-simulation on a finite collection $\mathcal{T}$ of threads in which t processes crash, with $0 \leq t < n$, all but at most t threads are fully executed.

Note that, in the definition of safety, the specification of a thread may depend on other threads: the consistency of the simulation is global. Also, the definition of liveness states that if t processes crash then at most t threads may be "blocked" by these t failures. Note however that the SA-simulation does not necessarily guarantee that all but t threads will eventually be executed if the collection of threads is infinite. Indeed, the SA-simulation does not avoid starvation. Starvation is a property addressed at a higher level of the simulation, depending on the policy for choosing which threads to execute among all extendable threads on top of the SA-simulation. For instance, BG-simulation selects the threads in an arbitrary manner, but executes these threads in a specific round-robin manner. Instead, RC-simulation, described later in this section, executes the threads in an arbitrary manner, but selects these threads in a specific manner to minimize concurrency. The following result states the basic properties of the SA-simulation.

Lemma 1. *The SA-simulation satisfies both the safety and liveness properties.*

2.3   The Reduced-Concurrency Simulation

In the SA-simulation, all available threads are potentially executed concurrently. We now show how to refine the simulation in order to execute concurrently as few threads as possible, while still remaining wait-free. For this purpose, we first refine the notion of available threads, by distinguishing two kinds of available threads. An available thread is *active* if it is not fully executed, and at least one cell of the column corresponding to that thread in the instruction matrix is either open or decided. An available thread that is not fully executed and not active is *pending*. In the SA-simulation, every process tries to make progress in any available extendable thread, including pending threads. Instead, in the RC-simulation described below, every process tries to make progress only for active extendable threads. It is only in the case where there are no more active extendable threads that the RC-simulation turns a pending thread into active. In this way, the number of active threads is not blowing up. Reducing the concurrency as much as possible however requires more work, and will be explained in detail in this section. One key ingredient in the RC-simulation is the *Priority Array*, described below.

The Priority Array. Similarly to the Instruction Matrix, the Priority Array is a *virtual* shared data-structure that enables to summarize the status of the different threads, as well as an instrument used to decide which thread to execute, and when (see the figure in Section 2.2). It is a linear array, in which the role of each cell is to point to a thread. As in the instruction matrix, there is a safe-agreement task associated to each cell of the priority array. This safe-agreement can be in one of the four following states: new, open, decided, and closed. For

$i \geq 1$, Cell i of the priority array is *new* if no processes have yet entered the safe-agreement program i (i.e., no processes have yet performed the first instruction of the ith Safe-Agreement). A cell is *open* if at least one process has entered Safe-Agreement i, but no value has yet been decided (all processes that exited the safe-agreement decided $\perp$). A cell is *decided* if at least one process has decided a value (different from $\perp$). Such a value is the identity of an available thread. Hence, a decided cell in the priority array is a pointer to an available thread. By construction, an active thread is an available thread pointed by a decided cell of the priority array. Finally, Cell i is *closed* if it is pointing to a fully executed thread. Initially, all cells of the priority array are in state new. The *head* of the priority array is defined as the cell with smallest index that is still in state new. We now have all the ingredients to describe the RC-simulation.

The RC-Simulation. The code of the RC-simulation is described in Fig. 4. The first instructions of RC-simulation are essentially the same as in the SA-simulation, with the unique modification that thread-instructions are only performed in active threads, while the SA-simulation is willing to advance any extendable thread.

RC-SIMULATION by processes p of an infinite collection $\mathcal{T}$ of threads.
```
1:    while true do
2:        view ← snapshot()
3:        (M, P) ← extract instruction matrix and priority array from view
4:        if there exists an active extendable thread τ ∈ T
5:        then perform next instruction of τ
6:        else view ← snapshot()
7:            (M', P') ← extract instruction matrix and priority array from view
8:            if (M', P') = (M, P), and there exists a pending thread
9:            then propose a pending thread to the head of the priority-array
```

Fig. 4. RC-simulation

Significant differences between the SA-simulation and the RC-simulation begin from the "else" Instruction. In particular, Instruction 8 compares the content of the memory at two different points in time. In the RC-simulation, a process p is willing to *open* a new thread, i.e., to move one available thread from the pending status to the active status, only if the memory has not changed between two consecutive snapshots of p (i.e., during a blind interval for p). More precisely, process p may open a new thread only if, in between two consecutive snapshots, the set of active threads has remained the same, and the instruction counters of these threads have remained the same. If that is the case, then p selects a thread τ among the pending threads (e.g., the one with smallest identity), and proposes τ for being opened. The role of the test in Instruction 8 will appear clearer later when we will analyze the number of threads that are simulated concurrently.

For opening a new thread τ, process p is proposing $Id(\tau)$ to the safe-agreement task at the head of the priority array. If p decides $\perp$ in this safe-agreement, then p initiates a new loop of RC-simulation. If p decides a value $j \neq \perp$ in this safe-agreement, then p tries to perform the first instruction of Thread j, which becomes active. Note that we may not have $j = Id(\tau)$ as other processes may have proposed different threads to this safe-agreement of the priority array. This holds even if the rule for selecting which thread to propose is deterministic (e.g., selecting the pending thread with smallest identity) because of the asynchrony between the processes, and because of the way threads become available. As for the general case, performing the first instruction of Thread j is mediated by Safe-Agreement $(1, j)$ of the Instruction Matrix. After this attempt to perform the first instruction of Thread j, process p starts a new loop of RC-simulation, independently from whether this attempt succeeded or not.

2.4   The Reduced-Concurrency Theorem

We first note that the RC-simulation satisfies the same safety and liveness conditions as the SA-simulation.

Lemma 2. *The RC-simulation satisfies both the safety and liveness properties.*

Assume now that all the threads in the collection $\mathcal{T}$ simulated by RC-simulation are performing the same wait-free algorithm A solving some task $T = (\mathcal{I}, \mathcal{O}, \Delta)$, such as renaming. Hence, the threads differ only in their identities, and, possibly, in their input data. The *performances* of Algorithm A, e.g., the number of names for renaming, may be affected by *point-contention*, i.e., by the maximum number of threads that are executed concurrently. For instance, a point-contention of 1 (that is, threads go one after the other) ensures perfect-renaming, while a point-contention of $k = |\mathcal{T}|$ may yield up to $2k - 1$ names. In this framework, RC-simulation helps, for it reduces the concurrency of the threads, down to partial asynchrony.

More specifically, let us consider an n-process system performing RC-simulation of a collection $\mathcal{T}$ of threads, all with same algorithm A solving task $T = (\mathcal{I}, \mathcal{O}, \Delta)$ wait-free. For every k, $0 \leq k < n$, if the partial asynchrony of the execution of the RC-simulation is at most k, then the performances of solving Task T mediated by the RC-simulation are the same as if the threads were executed with point-contention at most $k + 1$. This result can be summarized as follows.

$$\text{RC-simulation:} \quad k\text{-partial-asynchrony} \Longrightarrow (k+1)\text{-concurrency.}$$

In particular, if the partial asynchrony is 0 then threads are executed sequentially, one after the other. The following theorem formalizes these statements.

Theorem 1. *Let k, $0 \leq k < n$. For any execution of the RC-simulation:*

- *Bounded concurrency: Concurrency is at most partial-asynchrony plus 1. Specifically, if $k+1$ threads are executed concurrently by the system at time t, then at least one process p experienced a partial asynchrony at least k at some time $\leq t$.*
- *Adaptivity: Concurrency ultimately scales down with partial asynchrony. Specifically, if the partial asynchrony of the system is at most k after time t, then, eventually, the system will not execute more than $k + 1$ threads concurrently.*

Proof. To establish the theorem, we first observe a crucial property of the algorithm solving safe-agreement. This algorithm includes two write-instructions, and two snapshot-instructions. These instructions interleave in arbitrary manner among the different processes, but one can still say something interesting about this interleaving, in certain cases. The following behaviour is a common argument is the BG-simulation (see, e.g., [6,12]).

Claim. During the execution of the safe-agreement algorithm, if some process p decides $\perp$, then there exists a process $q \neq p$ such that q performed its first write before the first snapshot of p, and p performed its second snapshot before the second write of q.

In the situation of the statement of Claim 2.4, we say that q *blocked* p. Let us first prove the bounded concurrency property. Assume that $k + 1$ threads are executed concurrently by the system at time t. At this time t, let $i \geq 1$ be the largest index such that the ith cell of the priority array is not new (that is, the cell just before the head of the priority array at time t). Let p be the first process that performed a write instruction in the safe-agreement corresponding to that cell, turning the status of that cell from new to open. Process p did so because the instruction matrix as well as the priority array remained in identical states between its two previous snapshots in the RC-simulation. Let $t' \leq t$ be the time at which process p wrote in the ith cell of the priority array, turning it from new to open. Let t_1 and t_2, $t_1 < t_2 < t' \leq t$, be the respective times at which p performed its two snapshots in Instructions 2 and 6 of the RC-simulation leading p to access Cell i.

Let us examine the instruction matrix and the priority array between time t_1 and t_2 (both did not change in this time interval). Let k' be the number of threads concurrently executed at time t_2. Between time t_2 and t, some new threads, say x threads, $x \geq 0$, may have appeared (i.e., moved from pending to active), while some of the k' threads, say y, $y \geq 0$, may have disappeared (i.e., moved from active to fully executed). The former x corresponds to cells in the priority array that move from open to decided. The latter y corresponds to cells in the priority array that move from decided to closed. By definition, we have $k' + x - y = k + 1$, and thus $k' + x \geq k + 1$. Among the x threads, one thread may have been opened by p, when p initiates the safe-agreement of Cell i in the priority array. Now, since there were no extendable threads at time t_1, each of the k' threads has the cell of the instruction matrix corresponding to its current instruction in state open. Therefore, during time interval $[t_1, t_2]$, the total number of open cells equals at least $k' + x - 1$, where k' are open in the instruction matrix, and at least $x - 1$ are open in the priority array. Thus, during time interval $[t_1, t_2]$, the total number of open cells is at least k since $k' + x \geq k + 1$. Each of these cells corresponds to a safe-agreement for which no values are decided. In particular, p decided $\perp$ from each of these safe-agreements.

Let us fix one of these at least k safe-agreements. By Claim 2.4, process p was blocked by some process q which has not yet performed its second write at time t_2. Thus, to each of the at least k open cells in interval $[t_1, t_2]$ corresponds a distinct process which performed its first write (in the safe agreement of the cell) before time t_1, and had not yet performed its second write at time t_2. Hence, at least k processes performed no writes in the time interval $[t_1, t_2]$, which is the interval between two consecutive snapshots of process p. Therefore, the asynchrony experienced by process p at time $t_2 \leq t$ is at least k. This completed the proof of the bounded concurrency property.

Now remains to prove the adaptivity property. Let N be the number of threads that are concurrently executed at time t. By the same arguments as those exposed above, no threads are opened after time t until their number goes below $k + 1$. By the liveness property of Lemma 2, the number of thread concurrently executed after time t will thus decrease from N down to $k + 1$, which completes the proof of Theorem 1.   □

3   Application to Long-Lived Renaming

In this section, we use the RC-simulation for improving the performances of a classical long-lived renaming algorithm. Recall that the performances of an algorithm achieving renaming are typically measured in terms of the range of name-space, the tighter the better. In the context of this paper, the specification of long-lived renaming are rephrased as follows. Users perpetually request *names* to an n-process system such as described in Section 2.1, where a name is a nonnegative integer value in the range $[1, N]$ for some $N \geq n$ that is aimed to be as small as possible. Each user's request is performed by any one of the n processes, and all processes are eligible to receiving requests from users. Once a user has acquired a name, the user must eventually release it, and, as soon as a name has been released, it can be given to another user. At any point in time, all names that are currently acquired by users, and not yet released, must be pairwise distinct. We assume that a process p serving the request for a name by a user x does not serve any other request for names until the requested name has been acquired by x, and eventually released. The textbook renaming algorithm described in [9] is an adaptation to shared-memory system of the classical algorithm of [8] for renaming in message passing systems. It implements renaming with new names in the range $[1, 2n - 1]$. We show that, using RC-simulation, this range of names can be significantly reduced when the partial asynchrony is small, while the algorithm is shown not to adapt to partial asynchrony by itself.

Long-Lived Renaming in Presence of Bounded Partial-Asynchrony. In long-lived renaming, each process p requests a new name by invoking *ReqName(x)*, where x denotes the identifier of the user which queried p to get a name. Once p got a name for x, it can call *releaseName* for releasing that name. According to the specification of long-lived renaming stated above, for any process p, a sequence of such calls is correct if and only if *ReqName* and *releaseName* alternate in the sequence. As mentioned before, the renaming algorithm we use provides names in the range $[1, 2n-1]$. We first note that this range does not reduce much as a function of the asynchrony. For example, Observation 1 below shows that, even in case of partial asynchrony zero, i.e., even when the system performs in lock-steps, the range of names used by this renaming algorithm is still much larger than the ideal range $[1, n]$. We shall show in the next section that, instead, whenever mediated through the RC-simulation, this renaming algorithm uses a range of names that shrinks as the partial asynchrony decreases, up to $[1, n]$ for partial asynchrony zero.

Observation 1. *Even if the system is 0-partially asynchronous, there is an execution of the renaming algorithm in* [9] *for which the range of names is* $[1, \frac{3n}{2}]$.

RC-Simulation Mediated Long-Lived Renaming. In the following, we show that, through RC-simulation, the renaming algorithm of [9] adapts gracefully to partial asynchrony, while Observation 1 shows that the performances of this algorithm alone do not adapt to partial asynchrony. The result below is a corollary of Theorem 1. In particular, it shows that when the system is synchronous, or runs in lock-steps, the renaming algorithm mediated by the RC-simulation provides perfect renaming, using names in the range $[1, n]$. More generally, the mediation through RC-simulation of the renaming algorithm in [9] produces names in a range that grows linearly with partial asynchrony k.

Theorem 2. *If the system is k-partially asynchronous, for $0 \le k < n$, then the range of names provided by the renaming algorithm in* [9] *mediated by the RC-simulation is* $[1, n + k]$.

Acknowledgments. Supported by CONACYT-CNRS ECOS Nord, PAPIIT-UNAM, ANR-DISPLEXITY, INRIA- GANG, CNRS-PICS and RTRA STAE research grants.

References

1. Afek, Y., Attiya, H., Dolev, D., Gafni, E., Merritt, M., Shavit, N.: Atomic snapshots of shared memory. J. ACM 40(4), 873–890 (1993)
2. Aguilera, M.K., Delporte-Gallet, C., Fauconnier, H., Toueg, S.: Partial synchrony based on set timeliness. Distributed Computing 25(3), 249–260 (2012)
3. Aguilera, M.K., Keidar, I., Malkhi, D., Shraer, A.: Dynamic atomic storage without consensus. J. ACM 58(2), 7:1–7:32 (2011)
4. Aguilera, M.K., Toueg, S.: Adaptive progress: A gracefully-degrading liveness property. Distributed Computing 22(5-6), 303–334 (2010)
5. Alistarh, D., Gilbert, S., Guerraoui, R., Travers, C.: Generating fast indulgent algorithms. Theory Comput. Syst. 51(4), 404–424 (2012)
6. Attiya, H.: Adapting to point contention with long-lived safe agreement. In: Flocchini, P., Gąsieniec, L. (eds.) SIROCCO 2006. LNCS, vol. 4056, pp. 10–23. Springer, Heidelberg (2006)
7. Attiya, H., Bar-Noy, A., Dolev, D.: Sharing memory robustly in message-passing systems. J. ACM 42(1), 124–142 (1995)
8. Attiya, H., Bar-Noy, A., Dolev, D., Peleg, D., Reischuk, R.: Renaming in an asynchronous environment. Journal of the ACM 37(3), 524–548 (1990)
9. Attiya, H., Welch, J.: Distributed Computing Fundamentals, Simulations, and Advanced Topics, 2nd edn. John Wiley and Sons, Inc. (2004)
10. Borowsky, E., Gafni, E.: Generalized FLP impossibility result for t-resilient asynchronous computations. In: STOC 1993, pp. 91–100. ACM (1993)
11. Borowsky, E., Gafni, E.: The Implication of the Borowsky-Gafni Simulation on the Set-Consensus Hierarchy. Technical report, UCLA (1993)
12. Borowsky, E., Gafni, E., Lynch, N., Rajsbaum, S.: The BG distributed simulation algorithm. Distributed Computing 14(3), 127–146 (2001)
13. Burns, J.E., Peterson, G.L.: The ambiguity of choosing. In: PODC 1989, pp. 145–157. ACM (1989)

14. Castañeda, A., Imbs, D., Rajsbaum, S., Raynal, M.: Renaming is weaker than set agreement but for perfect renaming: A map of sub-consensus tasks. In: Fernández-Baca, D. (ed.) LATIN 2012. LNCS, vol. 7256, pp. 145–156. Springer, Heidelberg (2012)
15. Castañeda, A., Rajsbaum, S., Raynal, M.: The renaming problem in shared memory systems: An introduction. Comput. Sci. Rev. 5(3), 229–251 (2011)
16. Chandra, T., Hadzilacos, V., Jayanti, P., Toueg, S.: Wait-freedom vs. t-resiliency and the robustness of wait-free hierarchies (extended abstract). In: PODC 1994, pp. 334–343. ACM (1994)
17. Chaudhuri, S.: More choices allow more faults: Set consensus problems in totally asynchronous systems. Information and Computation 105(1), 132–158 (1993)
18. Chaudhuri, S., Reiners, P.: Understanding the Set Consensus Partial Order Using the Borowsky-Gafni Simulation (Extended Abstract). In: Babaoğlu, Ö., Marzullo, K. (eds.) WDAG 1996. LNCS, vol. 1151, pp. 362–379. Springer, Heidelberg (1996)
19. Cristian, F., Fetzer, C.: The timed asynchronous distributed system model. IEEE Trans. Parallel Distrib. Syst. 10(6), 642–657 (1999)
20. Dolev, D.: The byzantine generals strike again. J. of Algorithms 3(1), 14–30 (1982)
21. Dwork, C., Lynch, N., Stockmeyer, L.: Consensus in the presence of partial synchrony. J. ACM 35(2), 288–323 (1988)
22. Fischer, M., Lynch, N.A., Paterson, M.S.: Impossibility of Distributed Commit With One Faulty Process. Journal of the ACM 32(2) (April 1985)
23. Fischer, M.J.: The consensus problem in unreliable distributed systems (a brief survey). In: Karpinski, M. (ed.) FCT 1983. LNCS, vol. 158, pp. 127–140. Springer, Heidelberg (1983)
24. Gafni, E.: The extended BG-simulation and the characterization of t-resiliency. In: STOC 2009, pp. 85–92. ACM (2009)
25. Gafni, E., Guerraoui, R.: Generalized universality. In: Katoen, J.-P., König, B. (eds.) CONCUR 2011. LNCS, vol. 6901, pp. 17–27. Springer, Heidelberg (2011)
26. Guerraoui, R.: Indulgent algorithms. In: PODC, pp. 289–297. ACM (2000)
27. Herlihy, M.: Wait-free synchronization. ACM Trans. Program. Lang. Syst. 13(1), 124–149 (1991)
28. Herlihy, M., Ruppert, E.: On the existence of booster types. In: FOCS 2000, pp. 653–663. IEEE Computer Society (2000)
29. Imbs, D., Rajsbaum, S., Raynal, M.: The universe of symmetry breaking tasks. In: Kosowski, A., Yamashita, M. (eds.) SIROCCO 2011. LNCS, vol. 6796, pp. 66–77. Springer, Heidelberg (2011)
30. Imbs, D., Raynal, M.: Visiting Gafni's Reduction Land: From the BG Simulation to the Extended BG Simulation. In: Guerraoui, R., Petit, F. (eds.) SSS 2009. LNCS, vol. 5873, pp. 369–383. Springer, Heidelberg (2009)
31. Imbs, D., Raynal, M.: The multiplicative power of consensus numbers. In: PODC 2010, pp. 26–35. ACM (2010)
32. Keidar, I., Rajsbaum, S.: On the cost of fault-tolerant consensus when there are no faults: Preliminary version. SIGACT News 32(2), 45–63 (2001)
33. Lamport, L.: Time, clocks, and the ordering of events in a distributed system. Commun. ACM 21(7), 558–565 (1978)
34. Lamport, L.: The part-time parliament. ACM Trans. Comput. Syst. 16(2), 133–169 (1998)
35. Lo, W.-K., Hadzilacos, V.: On the power of shared object types to implement one-resilient Consensus. Distributed Computing 13(4), 219–238 (2000)
36. Lynch, N., Rajsbaum, S.: On the Borowsky-Gafni Simulation Algorithm. In: ISTCS 1996, pp. 4–15. IEEE Computer Society (June 1996)
37. Schneider, F.B.: Implementing Fault-Tolerant Services Using the State Machine Approach: A Tutorial. ACM Computing Surveys 22(4), 299–319 (1990)

Speed Faults in Computation
by Chemical Reaction Networks[*]

Ho-Lin Chen[1], Rachel Cummings[2], David Doty[2], and David Soloveichik[3]

[1] National Taiwan University, Taipei, Taiwan
holinc@gmail.com
[2] California Institute of Technology, Pasadena, California, USA
rachelc@u.northwestern.edu, ddoty@caltech.edu
[3] University of California, San Francisco, San Francisco, CA, USA
david.soloveichik@ucsf.edu

Abstract. Chemical reaction networks (CRNs) formally model chemistry in a well-mixed solution. Assuming a fixed molecular population size and bimolecular reactions, CRNs are formally equivalent to population protocols, a model of distributed computing introduced by Angluin, Aspnes, Diamadi, Fischer, and Peralta (PODC 2004). The challenge of fast computation by CRNs (or population protocols) is to ensure that there is never a bottleneck "slow" reaction that requires two molecules (agent states) to react (communicate), both of which are present in low ($O(1)$) counts. It is known that CRNs can be fast in expectation by avoiding slow reactions with high probability. However, states may be reachable (with low probability) from which the correct answer may only be computed by executing a slow reaction. We deem such an event a *speed fault*. We show that the problems decidable by CRNs guaranteed to avoid speed faults are precisely the *detection problems*: Boolean combinations of questions of the form "is a certain species present or not?". This implies, for instance, that no speed fault free CRN could decide whether there are at least two molecules of a certain species, although a CRN could decide this in "fast" expected time — i.e. speed fault free CRNs "can't count."

1 Introduction

Understanding the principles of molecular computation is essential to making sense of information processing in biological cellular regulatory networks. Further, in engineering of life-like devices (e.g. "wet robots" that can patrol the blood for cancer cells) we are rapidly approaching the point where we are limited by conceptual understanding: How molecular networks can be programmed

---

[*] The third, and fourth authors were supported by the Molecular Programming Project under NSF grants 0832824 and 1317694, the first author was supposed by NSC grant number 101-2221-E-002-122-MY3, the second author was supported by NSF grants CCF-1049899 and CCF-1217770, the third author was supported by a Computing Innovation Fellowship under NSF grant 1019343, NSF grants CCF-1219274 and CCF-1162589, and the fourth author was supported by NIGMS Systems Biology Center grant P50 GM081879.

F. Kuhn (Ed.): DISC 2014, LNCS 8784, pp. 16–30, 2014.

to process information and carry out computation subject to the natural constraints of aqueous chemistry is still not well-understood.

A foundational model of chemistry commonly used in natural sciences is that of chemical reaction networks (CRNs), i.e., (finite) sets of chemical reactions such as $A + B \rightarrow A + C$. Subject to discrete semantics (integer number of molecules) the model corresponds to a continuous time, discrete state, Markov process [12]. A state of the system is a vector of non-negative integers specifying the molecular counts of the species (e.g., A, B, C), a reaction can occur only when all its reactants are present, and transitions between states correspond to reactions (i.e., when the above reaction occurs the count of B is decreased by 1 and the count of C increased by 1). The transition rate is proportional to the product of the counts of the reactants. CRNs are widely used to describe natural biochemical systems such as the intricate cellular regulatory networks responsible for the information processing within cells. With recent advances in synthetic biology, CRNs are a promising language for the design of artificial biochemical networks. For example, the physical primitive of nucleic-acid strand displacement cascades provides concrete chemical implementations of arbitrary CRNs [4, 8, 16]. Thus, since in principle any CRN can be built, hypothetical CRNs with interesting behaviors are becoming of more than theoretical interest.

The importance of the CRN model is underscored by the observation that intimately related models repeatedly arise in theoretical computer science under different guises: e.g. vector addition systems [13], Petri nets [14], population protocols [1]. The connection to distributed computing models, in turn, resulted in novel insights regarding natural cellular regulatory networks [5].

Parallelism is a basic attribute of chemistry, and one that is of central importance in understanding molecular information processing. This kind of parallelism is both a blessing and a curse: it can be used to speed up computation, but we must be careful to avoid "race conditions" (reactions happening in an unintended order) which may lead to error.

Consider a very basic task: a chemical system (e.g. cell) responding to molecular signals present in very small quantities. More specifically, say the computation is to produce at least one molecule of Y if and only if there is at least one molecule of species A_1 and at least one molecule of species A_2. Consider the strategy shown in Fig 1(b). Intuitively, this corresponds to having receptors F that in order to activate need to bind both A_1 and A_2. By having n receptors F we can increase the rate of the first reaction, but if there is only one molecule of A_1, there will be at most one molecule of F' and thus the second reaction occurs at a rate independent of the amount of receptor. Thus this scheme is "not parallelizeable".[1]

---

[1] Bimolecular reaction rates scale inversely with the total volume, and it is impossible to fit arbitrarily many molecules in a fixed volume. While for large enough molecular counts we will run into this finite density constraint, we study the scaling of speed with molecular count before that point is reached. An alternate perspective is that our task is to compute as quickly as possible in volume sufficient to allow molecules of F to fill the volume with constant density [15].

A better strategy is to amplify the signal before taking the conjunction: e.g. Fig 1(c). Here the receptors release A_1 back upon interacting with it, and a single A_1 can interact with many receptors (converting them from F to F'). Intuitively, the more receptors F we have, the faster we'll get a large number of F''s, and the faster the Y will get produced via the second reaction. More specifically, observe that starting with $n > 0$ molecules of F, and a molecule of A_1 and A_2 each, the reachable states without Y are: for $0 \leq m \leq n$, $((n - m) F, m F', 1 A_1, 1 A_2)$. From any reachable state without Y, we can reach Y through a sequence of reaction executions where one of

the reactants is present in at least $\lfloor n^{1/2} \rfloor$ count,[2] and under stochastic chemical kinetics, the expected time to traverse this path is $O(1/n^{1/2})$ — decreasing with n.[3] Scheme Fig 1(d) is even faster: it can be shown that from any reachable state, the expected time to produce Y scales as $O(\log n/n)$.

Now consider a slightly different computational task: produce at least one molecule of Y if and only if there are at least 2 molecules of species A. The natural analog of Fig 1(b) fails to be deterministic: the reactions $A + F \to F'$, $A + F' \to Y$ suffer from a "race condition" where Y is never produced if both

Y iff [at least 1 molecule of A_1 and at least 1 molecule of A_2]

a) $A_1 + A_2 \to Y$

b) $A_1 + F \to F'$
    $A_2 + F' \to Y$

c) $A_1 + F \to F' + A_1$
    $A_2 + F' \to Y$

d) $A_1 + F_1 \to F_1'$
    $F_1' + F_1 \to F_1' + F_1'$
    $A_2 + F_2 \to F_2'$
    $F_2' + F_2 \to F_2' + F_2'$
    $F_1' + F_2' \to Y$

Y iff [at least 2 molecules of A]

e) $A + A \to Y$

f) $A + F \rightleftharpoons F'$
    $A + F' \to Y$

g) $A + F_1 \to F_1'$
    $F_1' + F_1 \to F_1' + F_1'$
    $A + F_2 \to F_2'$
    $F_2' + F_2 \to F_2' + F_2'$
    $F_1' + F_2' \to Y$

Fig. 1. Two molecular computation tasks: predicates "Is there at least 1 molecule of A_1 and at least one molecule of A_2?" (left), and "Are there at least 2 molecules of A?" (right). CRNs (a)-(d) compute the first predicate (left), and CRNs (e)-(g) compute the second (right). Parameter n is the initial amount of F, or F_1 and F_2 species which help in the computation. Informally the parallelizeable CRNs are those that produce the output faster with increasing n. Deterministic CRNs are those that compute correctly no matter what order the reactions happen to occur in. Other strategies (not shown) involve producing Y but consuming it if the predicate is not satisfied.

---

[2] If $m < \lfloor n^{1/2} \rfloor$, execute the first reaction $\lfloor n^{1/2} \rfloor - m$ times (resulting in $\lfloor n^{1/2} \rfloor$ molecules of F'), and then execute the second reaction. If $m \geq \lfloor n^{1/2} \rfloor$, execute the second reaction.

[3] The rate of a bimolecular reaction is proportional to the product of the counts of the reactants. Thus the expected time from the state with $m < \lfloor n^{1/2} \rfloor$ molecules of F' to reach the state with $\lfloor n^{1/2} \rfloor$ molecules of F' is proportional to $\sum_{i=m}^{\lfloor n^{1/2} \rfloor} 1/(n-i) \leq n^{1/2} \cdot 1/(n - n^{1/2}) = O(1/n^{1/2})$. Finally the rate of the second reaction when there are $\lfloor n^{1/2} \rfloor$ molecules of F' is proportional to $n^{1/2}$ and thus the expected time for it to fire is $O(1/n^{1/2})$ for a total expected time of $O(1/n^{1/2})$. Note that power $n^{1/2}$ was chosen in the analysis to ensure the optimal tradeoff between the rates of individual reaction executions and the total number of reaction executions.

molecules of A happen to react with F. This can be fixed by having the receptor F bind A reversibly[4] as in Fig. 1(f). However, this scheme is not parallelizeable for the same reason as (b).

The natural analog of the parallelizeable reaction scheme Fig 1(c) will not solve this task correctly at all: With reactions $A + F \rightarrow F' + A$, $A + F' \rightarrow Y$, even a single molecule of A will always lead to a Y.

Also problematic is the scheme shown in Fig 1(g) based on (d). While it is parallelizeable, it also suffers from a race condition that can result in an error. If the two molecules of A happen to react with different receptor types (F_1 and F_2) then Y will be produced. However, if both A's react with the same receptor type, Y will never be produced.

Informally, our main result is that no CRN is deterministic and parallelizeable at the same time for the "2 A problem" (or any computation that involves counting, rather than simply detecting the presence or absence of input species). Thus deterministic and parallelizeable must be disjoint in Fig. 1(right). Unlike the examples above, we allow a broader range of schemes that could produce and consume Y repeatedly but eventually converge on the presence or absence of Y as the output. In order to define "parallelizeable" formally, we introduce the notion of a "speed fault". A speed fault occurs if a state is reached such that to stabilize to the correct output from that state requires using a bimolecular reaction with both reactants bounded independently of n. Thus "deterministically parallelizeable" corresponds to speed fault free. Our main result is that the problems decidable by speed fault free CRNs are precisely the *detection problems*: Boolean combinations of questions of the form "is a certain species present or not?". Thus speed fault free CRNs "can't count."

The current work stems from the desire to understand fast deterministic computation in CRNs and population protocols. While sophisticated chemical algorithms and protocols have been developed to compute a large class of functions quickly and without error (see next section), most constructions are not deterministically fast in the same strong sense as they are deterministic. Indeed, deterministic computation is a worst case notion that intuitively ensures correctness no matter what unlucky sequence of reactions occurs. However, fast computation is defined with respect to large probability reaction sequences. Our definition captures the natural worst case notion of speed.[5]

Our positive result shows how any detection problem can be decided by a speed fault free CRN, and further shows that this computation is fast in the standard stochastic chemical kinetics model [12]. The largest part of this paper concerns the negative result that only detection problems can be computed by

---

[4] A reversible reaction $A + F \rightleftharpoons F'$ is simply syntactic sugar for two irreversible reactions $A + F \rightarrow F'$ and $F' \rightarrow A + F$.

[5] We observe that in the literature on computation in CRNs and population protocols it is almost never the case that computation is slow because the necessary sequence of reactions is too long – rather, slowdown is dominated by reaction bottlenecks where two low count species must react. Thus in this work we focus on this essential type of delay, captured in our notion of speed faults.

speed fault free CRNs (Section 4.2). The proof of the negative result consists of finding a worst-case reaction sequence that leads to a speed fault, assuming a non-detection problem is computed.

Absent speed-faults, the $O(1)$-count species must initiate cascades through intermediary large count species in order to "communicate." Consider the above "$2A$ problem." We can imagine isolating the two copies of A in "separate test tubes" and then use the symmetry between the two A molecules to make the system think that it's communicating with just one A (and thereby fail to detect the second A). To make this argument precise we develop a pumping technique which formally distinguishes species that can get arbitrarily large with increasing n from species whose counts are bounded by a constant[6]. We show that all large count species that can be encountered along a trajectory can be pumped to be *simultaneously* large. We then show that in the context of large counts of all pumpable species, reaction sequences can be decomposed into separate test tubes (parallel decomposition). A key part of the argument involves showing that the speed fault free CRN cannot detect small changes to pumpable species; for this we develop a new technique for performing surgery on reaction sequences.

2   Previous Work and Future Directions

Much related work in the distributed computing community is phrased in the language of population protocols rather than CRNs (e.g. [2]). While population protocols are equivalent to CRNs with exactly two reactants and two products, and thus a fixed population size, CRNs can naturally describe reactions that consume or produce net molecules. As a result CRNs can potentially explore an unbounded state space, and certain questions that are not natural for population protocols become germane for CRNs (for example: Turing universality). Because our negative result naturally applies to a changing population size, we phrase this paper in the language of CRNs.

CRNs have a surprisingly rich computational structure. If we allow the number of species and reactions to scale with the size of the input (i.e. we view CRNs as a non-uniform model of computation), then $\log s$ species can deterministically simulate space s-bounded Turing machines [6]. (These results are presented in a model called vector addition systems [13], but easily carry over.) Thus CRNs are a very powerful model of non-uniform computation. On the other hand, we ask what functions can be computed by a fixed CRN (i.e. fixed number of species and reactions, with input encoded in the initial molecular counts, which corresponds to a uniform model). In this setting, CRNs are not Turing universal, unless we allow for some probability of error [3, 15]. In attempting Turing universal computation, there will provably always be "race conditions" that lead to error if certain reactions occur in a (maybe unlikely but possible) malicious order. The fact that even such Turing universal computation is possible, and indeed can be

---

[6] Note that our pumping lemma is very different from a similarly called "pumping lemma" of ref. [2], which shows that how input can be increased without changing the output (thus pumping "input").

made "fast" is surprising since finite CRNs necessarily must represent binary data strings in a unary encoding, since they lack positional information to tell the difference between two molecules of the same species.

Deterministic computation of both predicates and functions has been exactly characterized, and corresponds to semilinear sets and functions [2, 7]. Angluin, Aspnes, and Eisenstat [2] showed that all semilinear predicates can be deterministically computed in expected $O(n \text{ polylog } n)$ "interactions" (molecules bumping into each other). In a volume of fixed size, with n molecules, there are an expected $\Theta(n^2)$ such interactions per unit time, which yields expected time $O((1/n)\text{polylog } n)$ — decreasing with n. Our results imply that when computing semilinear predicates other then the detection problems, it is always possible to reach a state (speed fault) from which the expected time to finish the computation is $\Omega(1)$ — independent of n. It is easy to reconcile the two results: in the construction of ref. [2], the probability that a speed fault is reached decreases with n, and thus the total expected time decreases with n as well. Our result implies that this is a necessary feature of any such construction, and is not simply due to insufficient cleverness of the researchers to avoid speed faults.

Other work showing the challenges in parallelizing CRNs include the investigation of running multiple copies of networks in parallel [9], and the inability of networks starting with only large count species to delay the production of any species [11].

While in this work we focused on parallelizable predicates, it remains to explore the class of parallelizable functions. For example, if the initial amount of A is the input and the final amount of B is the output, then we can think of the reaction $F + A \rightarrow 2B$ as deterministically computing $f(x) = 2x$. Clearly as the amount of F increases, the computation converges faster. On the other hand, we believe that computing division by 2 should not be possible without speed faults, although that remains to be shown.

Since the occurrence of a speed fault leads to a slow computational bottleneck, speed faults affect the tail bounds on the distribution of the computation time. Indeed, two CRNs may compute with the same fast expected time, but the one susceptible to speed faults will likely have a larger probability of taking significantly longer. It remains to rigorously draw out the connection between tail bounds and speed faults.

3 Preliminaries

3.1 Chemical Reaction Networks

If Λ is a finite set (in this paper, of chemical species), we write $\mathbb{N}^\Lambda$ to denote the set of functions $f : \Lambda \rightarrow \mathbb{N}$. Equivalently, we view an element $\mathbf{c} \in \mathbb{N}^\Lambda$ as a vector of $|\Lambda|$ nonnegative integers, with each coordinate "labeled" by an element of Λ. Given $S \in \Lambda$ and $\mathbf{c} \in \mathbb{N}^\Lambda$, we refer to $\mathbf{c}(S)$ as the *count of S in* $\mathbf{c}$. Let $|\mathbf{c}| = \|\mathbf{c}\|_\infty = \max_{S \in \Lambda} \mathbf{c}(S)$. We write $\mathbf{c} \leq \mathbf{c}'$ to denote that $\mathbf{c}(S) \leq \mathbf{c}'(S)$ for all $S \in \Lambda$, and $\mathbf{c} < \mathbf{c}'$ if $\mathbf{c} \leq \mathbf{c}'$ and $\mathbf{c} \neq \mathbf{c}'$. Since we view vectors $\mathbf{c} \in \mathbb{N}^\Lambda$ equivalently as multisets of elements from Λ, if $\mathbf{c} \leq \mathbf{c}'$ we say $\mathbf{c}$ is a *subset* of $\mathbf{c}'$. Given $\mathbf{c}, \mathbf{c}' \in \mathbb{N}^\Lambda$, we define the vector component-wise operations of addition $\mathbf{c} + \mathbf{c}'$, subtraction $\mathbf{c} - \mathbf{c}'$, and scalar multiplication $n\mathbf{c}$ for $n \in \mathbb{N}$. For a set $\Delta \subset \Lambda$, we view a vector $\mathbf{c} \in \mathbb{N}^{\Delta}$ equivalently as a vector $\mathbf{c} \in \mathbb{N}^{\Lambda}$ by assuming $\mathbf{c}(S) = 0$ for all $S \in \Lambda \setminus \Delta$. Write $\mathbf{c} \restriction \Delta$ to denote the vector $\mathbf{d} \in \mathbb{N}^{\Delta}$ such that $\mathbf{c}(S) = \mathbf{d}(S)$ for all $S \in \Delta$. Given $S_1, \ldots, S_k \in \Lambda$, $\mathbf{c} \in \mathbb{N}^{\Lambda}$, and $n_1, \ldots, n_k \in \mathbb{Z}$, we write $\mathbf{c} + \{n_1 S_1, \ldots, n_k S_k\}$ to denote vector addition of $\mathbf{c}$ with the vector $\mathbf{v} \in \mathbb{Z}^{\{S_1, \ldots, S_k\}}$ with $\mathbf{v}(S_i) = n_i$.

Given a finite set of chemical species Λ, a *reaction* over Λ is a triple $\alpha = \langle \mathbf{r}, \mathbf{p}, k \rangle \in \mathbb{N}^{\Lambda} \times \mathbb{N}^{\Lambda} \times \mathbb{R}^{+}$, specifying the stoichiometry (amount consumed/ produced) of the reactants and products, respectively, and the *rate constant* k. A reaction is *unimolecular* if it has one reactant and *bimolecular* if it has two reactants. For simplicity, in this paper we use $k = 1$ and the rate constant is omitted. For instance, given $\Lambda = \{A, B, C\}$, the reaction $A + 2B \to A + 3C$ is the pair $\langle (1, 2, 0), (1, 0, 3) \rangle$. A *(finite) chemical reaction network (CRN)* is a pair $N = (\Lambda, R)$, where Λ is a finite set of chemical *species*, and R is a finite set of reactions over Λ. A *state* of a CRN $N = (\Lambda, R)$ is a vector $\mathbf{c} \in \mathbb{N}^{\Lambda}$.

Given a state $\mathbf{c}$ and reaction $\alpha = \langle \mathbf{r}, \mathbf{p} \rangle$, we say that α is *applicable* to $\mathbf{c}$ if $\mathbf{r} \leq \mathbf{c}$ (i.e., $\mathbf{c}$ contains enough of each of the reactants for the reaction to occur). If α is applicable to $\mathbf{c}$, then write $\alpha(\mathbf{c})$ to denote the state $\mathbf{c} + \mathbf{p} - \mathbf{r}$ (i.e., the state that results from applying reaction α to $\mathbf{c}$). A finite or infinite sequence of reactions (α_i), where each $\alpha_i \in R$, is a *reaction sequence*. Given an initial state $\mathbf{c}_0$ and a reaction sequence (α_i), the induced *execution sequence* (or *path*) q is a finite or infinite sequence of states $q = (\mathbf{c}_0, \mathbf{c}_1, \mathbf{c}_2, \ldots)$ such that, for all $\mathbf{c}_i \in q$ $(i \geq 1)$, $\mathbf{c}_i = \alpha_i(\mathbf{c}_{i-1})$. If a finite execution sequence q starts with $\mathbf{c}$ and ends with $\mathbf{c}'$, we write $\mathbf{c} \Longrightarrow_q \mathbf{c}'$. We write $\mathbf{c} \Longrightarrow \mathbf{c}'$ if such an execution sequence exists and we say that $\mathbf{c}'$ is *reachable* from $\mathbf{c}$. We often abuse terminology and refer to reaction sequences and execution sequences (paths) interchangeably.

We will find ourselves frequently dealing with infinite sequences of states. The following technical lemma elucidates certain convenient properties of any such sequence and will be used repeatedly.

Lemma 3.1 (Dickson's Lemma [10]). *The set of states $\mathbb{N}^k$ is well-quasi-ordered. In particular, every infinite sequence $\mathbf{x}_0, \mathbf{x}_1, \ldots$ of states has an infinite nondecreasing subsequence $\mathbf{x}_{i_0} \leq \mathbf{x}_{i_1} \leq \ldots$, where $i_0 < i_1 < \ldots \in \mathbb{N}$, and every set $U \subseteq \mathbb{N}^k$ has a finite number of minimal elements.*

3.2 Stable Decidability of Predicates

We now review the definition of stable decidability of predicates introduced by Angluin, Aspnes, and Eisenstat [2]. Intuitively, some species "vote" for a YES/NO answer, and a CRN N is a stable decider if N is guaranteed to reach a consensus vote.

A *chemical reaction decider* (CRD) is a tuple $\mathcal{D} = (\Lambda, R, \Sigma, \Upsilon, \phi, \mathbf{s})$, where (Λ, R) is a CRN, $\Sigma \subseteq \Lambda$ is the *set of input species*, $\Upsilon \subseteq \Lambda$ is the set of *voters*, $\phi : \Upsilon \to \{\text{NO}, \text{YES}\}$ is the *(Boolean) output function*, and $\mathbf{s} \in \mathbb{N}^{\Lambda \setminus \Sigma}$ is the *initial context*. For the input vector $(n_1, \ldots, n_k) \in \mathbb{N}^k$, where $k = |\Sigma|$, we write the initial state as $\mathbf{i}(n_1, \ldots, n_k) \in \mathbb{N}^{\Lambda}$ defined by: $\mathbf{i}(n_1, \ldots, n_k) \restriction \Sigma = (n_1, \ldots, n_k)$

and $\mathbf{i}(n_1, \ldots, n_k) \upharpoonright (\Lambda \setminus \Sigma) = \mathbf{s}$. We extend ϕ to a partial function on states $\Psi : \mathbb{N}^\Lambda \dashrightarrow \{NO, YES\}$ as follows. $\Psi(\mathbf{c})$ is undefined if either $\mathbf{c}(X) = 0$ for all $X \in \Upsilon$, or if there exist $X_0, X_1 \in \Upsilon$ such that $\mathbf{c}(X_0) > 0$, $\mathbf{c}(X_1) > 0$, $\phi(X_0) = NO$ and $\phi(X_1) = YES$. Otherwise, there exists $b \in \{NO, YES\}$ such that $(\forall X \in \Upsilon)(\mathbf{c}(X) > 0$ implies $\phi(X) = b)$; in this case, the *output* $\Psi(\mathbf{c})$ of state $\mathbf{c}$ is b.

A state $\mathbf{o}$ is *output stable* if $\Psi(\mathbf{o})$ is defined and, for all $\mathbf{c}$ such that $\mathbf{o} \Longrightarrow \mathbf{c}$, $\Psi(\mathbf{c}) = \Psi(\mathbf{o})$. We call a whole CRD $\mathcal{D}$ *stable* if, for any initial state $\mathbf{i}$, there exists $b \in \{NO, YES\}$ such that, for every state $\mathbf{x}$ reachable from $\mathbf{i}$, there is an output stable state $\mathbf{o}$ reachable from $\mathbf{x}$ such that $\Psi(\mathbf{o}) = b$. If $\mathcal{D}$ is stable, then for some unique subset $S_0 \subseteq \mathbb{N}^k$ of inputs it always converges to output 0 and stays with that output, and for the remainder $S_1 = \mathbb{N}^k \setminus S_0$ it always converges to output 1 and stays with that output. We say that $\mathcal{D}$ *stably decides* the set S_1, or that $\mathcal{D}$ *stably decides* the predicate $\psi : \mathbb{N}^k \to \{0, 1\}$ defined by $\psi(\mathbf{x}) = 1$ iff $\mathbf{x} \in S_1$.

A set $A \subseteq \mathbb{N}^k$ is *linear* if $A = \{ \mathbf{b} + \sum_{i=1}^p n_i \mathbf{u}_i \mid n_1, \ldots, n_p \in \mathbb{N} \}$ for some constant vectors $\mathbf{b}, \mathbf{u}_1, \ldots, \mathbf{u}_p \in \mathbb{N}^k$. A is *semilinear* if it is a finite union of linear sets. The following theorem is due to Angluin, Aspnes, and Eisenstat [2]:

Theorem 3.2 ([2]). *A set $A \subseteq \mathbb{N}^k$ is stably decidable by a CRD if and only if it is semilinear.*

If a YES voter (or any other species, for that matter) cannot be produced by any sequence of reactions from a state $\mathbf{y}$, then it cannot be produced from any subset $\mathbf{y}' \leq \mathbf{y}$. The following lemma is useful when we want to argue the other way: that for certain species, beyond a certain value, *increasing* their counts cannot affect the ability or inability of the state to produce a YES voter. We say that a state $\mathbf{c}$ is *committed* if, for all states $\mathbf{z}$ such that $\mathbf{c} \Longrightarrow \mathbf{z}$, $\mathbf{z}(S) = 0$ for all YES-voting species S. In particular, all output-stable NO states are committed, and for stable CRDs, committed states are reachable only from inputs on which the predicate is false.[7]

Lemma 3.3. *For each CRD, there is a constant c such that, for all committed states $\mathbf{c}$, if $\mathbf{c}(S) > c$ for some $S \in \Lambda$, then for all $n \in \mathbb{Z}$, $\mathbf{c} + \{nS\}$ is also committed.*

4   Speed Fault Free CRDs

In this section we show our main result that speed fault free CRDs decide only "detection problems," i.e., detecting the presence or absence of a species, but not distinguishing between two different positive counts of it. To allow for "parallelization" of the computation, we introduce a "fuel" species F, whose count

---

[7] A committed state is not be output-stable NO if a state without any voters is reachable from it. The distinct notion of "committed" is useful because (unlike for output NO stability) the negation of committed is closed under superset (see the proof of Lemma 3.3), yet (like for output NO stability) reaching a committed state implies that the predicate value must be false.

is allowed to start arbitrarily large.[8] Increasing the amount of fuel species is analogous to increasing the amount of "receptor" in the introduction. We then formalize the concept of "speed fault free" discussed informally in the introduction. Briefly, a CRN experiences a speed fault if it reaches a state from which all paths to a correct state execute some reaction when the counts of all of its reactants are bounded by a constant (a "slow" reaction). Note that in the stochastic model, the expected time for such a reaction to occur is bounded below by a constant (independent of the amount of fuel).

Let $\mathcal{D} = (\Lambda, R, \Sigma, \Upsilon, \phi, \mathbf{s})$ be a stable CRD, where $\Sigma = \{A_1, \ldots, A_k\}$ are the input species and $\Lambda \setminus \Sigma$ contains a special "fuel" species F, with variable initial count n. The initial count of every other species in $\Lambda \setminus (\Sigma \cup \{F\})$ is $\mathbf{s}$ (unchanging with respect to n). Write the initial state of $\mathcal{D}$ with some number n_i of each input A_i and n molecules of F as $\mathbf{i}_n(n_1, \ldots, n_k)$.

Let $f \in \mathbb{N}$, let $\alpha \in R$ be a reaction and $\mathbf{x} \in \mathbb{N}^\Lambda$ be a state. We say that α occuring in state $\mathbf{x}$ is f-*fast* if at least one reactant has count at least f in $\mathbf{x}$. An execution sequence is called f-*fast* if all reactions in it are f-fast. [9]

Definition 4.1. *A stable CRD $\mathcal{D}$ is* speed fault free *if for all $n_1, \ldots, n_k$ and all $f \in \mathbb{N}$, for all sufficiently large n, for any state $\mathbf{x}$ such that $\mathbf{i}_n(n_1, \ldots, n_k) \Longrightarrow \mathbf{x}$, there is an output stable state $\mathbf{y}$ (which has the correct answer with respect to $n_1, \ldots, n_k$ by the stability of $\mathcal{D}$) such that $\mathbf{x} \Longrightarrow \mathbf{y}$ by an f-fast execution sequence.*

Definition 4.2. *A set $S \subseteq \mathbb{N}^k$ is a* simple detection set *if there is a $1 \le i \le k$ such that $S = \{ (x_1, \ldots, x_k) \in \mathbb{N}^k \mid x_i > 0 \}$. A set is a* detection set *if it is expressible as a combination of finite unions, intersections, and complements of simple detection sets.*

In other words, the predicate corresponding to a simple detection set S is a finite Boolean combination of questions of the form "is a certain species present?". The following theorem is the main result of this paper. We show each direction in two separate lemmas, Lemma 4.4 and Lemma 4.10.

Theorem 4.3. *The sets decidable by speed fault free CRDs are precisely the detection sets.*

4.1   Detection Problems Are Decidable by Speed Fault Free CRDs

This is the easier direction of Theorem 4.3. We give the intuition behind the proof here, and we do not formally define the model of stochastic chemical kinetics

---

[8] Allowing multiple fuel species $F_1, F_2, \ldots$ does affect our results since one of our reactions can be $F \to F_1 + F_2 \ldots$.

[9] It is worth noting that fast reaction sequences are not necessarily fast in the standard sense of stochastic kinetics, since although each reaction occurs quickly, it could be that there are a huge number of reactions in the sequence. Since our main result is a lower bound, this does not hurt the argument (and our upper bound result also shows that it is possible to decide detection problems quickly under the standard stochastic model).

used to prove the expected running time. See the full version of this paper for detailed definitions and the proof.

Lemma 4.4. *Every detection set is decidable by a speed fault free CRD. This CRD takes expected time $O(\log n / n)$ expected time to stabilize under the standard model of stochastic chemical kinetics with constant volume.*

Proof (sketch). To detect whether a species A is present or not, we may use "epidemic" reactions $A + F \rightarrow F_a$ and $F_a + F \rightarrow 2F_a$, where F votes NO and F_a votes YES. That is, if A encounters an F, then F changes state to F_a, and this information is "broadcast" throughout the population of F's. Since the sum $\mathbf{c}(F_a) + \mathbf{c}(F) = n$ is constant in any reachable state $\mathbf{c}$, the second bimolecular reaction always has a reactant with count $\geq n/2$ (hence that reaction is always $\frac{n}{2}$-fast), and the output-stable YES state is reached when all F's are converted to F_a. The extension to k input species just means that each F must store k bits, one for each input species. □

4.2   Speed Fault Free CRDs Decide Only Detection Problems

Before proceeding to the main argument, we need to develop some technical machinery. We first show that if a fast execution sequence is used to decrease the count of some species, then we can identify certain reactions that must necessarily occur (reaction extraction). We then develop a notion of pumping, which is used to identify species that can get arbitrarily large with increasing fuel. Finally, we show that reaction sequences in which one reactant is always pumpable can be decomposed into separate "test-tubes" (parallel decomposition). Finally we stitch these notions together to show that speed fault free CRDs cannot compute more than detection problems.

Reaction Extraction Lemma. Intuitively, the lemma below states that a fast reaction sequence that decreases certain species from high counts to low counts must contain reactions of a certain restricted form. These reactions will later be used to do "surgery" on fast reaction sequences, because they give a way to alter the count of certain species, by inserting or removing those reactions, while carefully controlling the effect these insertions and removals have on counts of other species.

Lemma 4.5. *Let $c_1, c_2 \in \mathbb{N}$ such that $c_2 > |\Lambda| \cdot c_1$, let $\mathbf{x}, \mathbf{y} \in \mathbb{N}^\Lambda$ such that $\mathbf{x} \Longrightarrow \mathbf{y}$ via c_2-fast reaction sequence q. Let $\Delta = \{D \in \Lambda | \mathbf{x}(D) \geq c_2, \mathbf{y}(D) \leq c_1\}$. Then there is an order on Δ, so that we may write $\Delta = \{D_1, D_2, \ldots, D_l\}$, such that, for all $i \in \{1, \ldots, l\}$, there is a reaction α_i of the form $D_i \rightarrow P_1 + \ldots + P_k$ or $D_i + S \rightarrow P_1 + \ldots + P_k$, such that $S, P_1, \ldots, P_k \notin \{D_1, \ldots, D_i\}$, and α_i occurs at least $\frac{c_2 - |\Lambda| \cdot c_1}{|R|}$ times in q in states $\mathbf{c}$ in which $\mathbf{c}(S) \geq c_2$.*

Lemma 4.5 is formally proved in the full version of this paper. Intuitively, to see such an ordering exists, it helps to think in reverse, first defining the last element D_l of the ordering. Consider the potential function $\Phi(\mathbf{c}) = \sum_{D \in \Delta} \mathbf{c}(D)$; then $\Phi(\mathbf{x})$ is large (at least $|\Delta| \cdot c_2$) and $\Phi(\mathbf{y})$ is small (at most $|\Delta| \cdot c_1$). On the path from $\mathbf{x}$ to $\mathbf{y}$, when Φ is between c_2 and $|\Delta| \cdot c_1$, it cannot get smaller by reactions of the form $D_i + D_j \to \ldots$, since $D_i, D_j \in \Delta$, or that reaction would not be c_2-fast. Therefore to get Φ down requires reactions with at most one reactant in Δ. Furthermore, if any product were in Δ, this would not decrease the value of Φ, hence some reaction must be of the desired form: consuming exactly one element of Δ. This element is D_l, the last in the ordering. Inductively defining an ordering on $\Delta \setminus \{D_l\}$ gives the entire ordering.

Pumpable Sets of Species. This section defines *pumpable* sets of species: species whose counts can be made arbitrarily large by increasing the amount of fuel (species F, see Definition 4.1) and proves some basic properties about them. For example, the fuel species F is trivially pumpable. If there is a reaction $F + A \to F' + A$, then F' is pumpable (if there is an A), because F can be arbitrarily large. To get a handle on the notion of speed fault free, we define pumping to enforce a certain kind of self-consistency (Π-friendly): you can pump without requiring any reactions where all reactants are not pumpable.

Let $\Pi \subseteq \Lambda$. If a reaction has at least one reactant in Π, say the reaction is Π-*friendly*. If $\mathbf{x} \Longrightarrow \mathbf{y}$ via a reaction sequence in which all reactions are Π-friendly, then we write $\mathbf{x} \Longrightarrow^{\Pi} \mathbf{y}$. Let $Z = (\mathbf{z}_1 \leq \mathbf{z}_2 \leq \mathbf{z}_3 \ldots)$, where each $\mathbf{z}_n \in \mathbb{N}^{\Lambda}$, be an infinite nondecreasing sequence of states. A set of species $\Pi \subseteq \Lambda$ is Z-*pumpable* if there exists a sequence of states $X = (\mathbf{x}_1, \mathbf{x}_2, \ldots)$ such that: (1) for all $P \in \Pi$ and $m \in \mathbb{N}$, $\mathbf{x}_m(P) \geq m$, and (2) for all $m \in \mathbb{N}$, there exists $n \in \mathbb{N}$ such that $\mathbf{z}_n \Longrightarrow^{\Pi} \mathbf{x}_m$.[10] Call such a sequence $(\mathbf{x}_m)$ a *pumping sequence* for Π. Π is *maximal Z-pumpable* if it is Z-pumpable and no strict superset of Π is Z-pumpable.

The next proposition shows that after pumping a maximal Π, all other species have bounded counts in all states reachable by Π-friendly paths. It is proven in the full version of this paper. Intuitively, it holds because if any other species $S \notin \Pi$ could get large via some reaction sequence r, then we could make the species in Π so large that we are able to hold some in reserve, then execute r, and then we would have S and all of Π large at the same time, contradicting the maximality of Π. We will use Proposition 4.6 repeatedly, but its most important consequence, intuitively, is that that the only way to get something outside of Π "large" is by executing a "slow" reaction (between two reactants not in Π).

Proposition 4.6. *Let $Z = (\mathbf{z}_1 \leq \mathbf{z}_2 \leq \ldots)$ be a infinite nondecreasing sequence of states, and let $\Pi \subseteq \Lambda$ be maximal Z-pumpable, with pumping sequence $(\mathbf{x}_m)$. Then there is a constant c such that, for all states $\mathbf{y}$ and $m, n \in \mathbb{N}$ such that $\mathbf{x}_m \Longrightarrow^{\Pi} \mathbf{y}$, then for all $S \in \Lambda \setminus \Pi$, $\mathbf{y}(S) < c$.*

---

[10] We can assume that $n \to \infty$ as $m \to \infty$. This is because $(\mathbf{z}_n)$ is a nondecreasing sequence, and so if $\mathbf{z}_n \Longrightarrow^{\Pi} \mathbf{x}_m$ for some $n, m \in \mathbb{N}$, then for all $n' > n$, there is a superset $\mathbf{x}'_m \geq \mathbf{x}_m$ such that $\mathbf{z}_{n'} \Longrightarrow^{\Pi} \mathbf{x}'_m$, and $\mathbf{x}'_m(S) \geq m$ for all $S \in \Pi$.

Parallel Decomposition. Intuitively, the following lemma shows that systems reacting by Π-friendly reactions can be effectively decomposed into separate non-interacting "test tubes" (in the context of a large excess of Π).[11] The following lemma is proved in the full version of this paper.

Lemma 4.7. *Suppose* $\mathbf{x}+\mathbf{y} \Longrightarrow^{\Pi} \mathbf{z}$. *Then there are* $\mathbf{p}, \mathbf{p}', \mathbf{p}'' \in \mathbb{N}^{\Pi}$, *and* $\mathbf{z}', \mathbf{z}'' \in \mathbb{N}^{\Lambda}$ *such that* $\mathbf{p}+\mathbf{x} \Longrightarrow^{\Pi} \mathbf{p}'+\mathbf{z}'$ *and* $\mathbf{p}+\mathbf{y} \Longrightarrow^{\Pi} \mathbf{p}''+\mathbf{z}''$, *where* $\mathbf{z}'+\mathbf{z}'' = \mathbf{z}$ *and* $\mathbf{p}' + \mathbf{p}'' = 2\mathbf{p}$.

Main Proof. Throughout this section, let $\mathcal{D} = (\Lambda, R, \Sigma, \Upsilon, \phi, \mathbf{s})$ be an arbitrary speed fault free CRD with $\Sigma = \{A_1, \ldots, A_k\}$ and fuel species F as in Definition 4.1. Supposing for the sake of contradiction that $\mathcal{D}$ decides some non-detection set, then there must exist some species A_i (assume without loss of generality that $i = 1$), and an input value $(n_1, n_2, \ldots, n_k) \in \mathbb{N}^k$, where $n_1 \geq 1$, with answer NO (without loss of generality) but input value $(n_1 + 1, n_2, \ldots, n_k)$ with answer YES. Let $\mathbf{i}_n$ be the above initial state with n_1 molecules of A_1, having n fuel molecules. We will show that for sufficiently large n, $\mathbf{i}_n + \{A_1\}$ is able to reach a state without YES-voting species, from which the only way to produce a YES voter is to execute a slow bimolecular reaction.

We now define two infinite sequences of states $(\mathbf{x}_m)$ and $(\mathbf{y}_m)$ used in the rest of the argument. Intuitively $(\mathbf{x}_m)$ makes "large" all species than can get large from $(\mathbf{i}_n)$, while $(\mathbf{y}_m)$ is a sequence of committed states reachable from $(\mathbf{x}_m)$ (but they have to be defined in a rather exacting way.) Let sequence $I = (\mathbf{i}_n)$ and let $\Pi \subseteq \Lambda$ be maximal I-pumpable with pumping sequence $(\mathbf{x}_m)$. In the full version of the paper we show that there is a $\mathbf{d} \in \mathbb{N}^{\Pi}$ such that $\mathbf{x}_m = \mathbf{x}_{m-1} + \mathbf{d}$. Define the sequence of output-stable NO states $(\mathbf{y}_m)$ inductively as follows. For the base case, let $\mathbf{y}_1$ be any output-stable NO state such that $\mathbf{x}_1 \Longrightarrow_{r_1} \mathbf{y}_1$; such a path r_1 must exist because $\mathcal{D}$ is stable. Inductively assume that $\mathbf{x}_{m-1} \Longrightarrow_{r_{m-1}} \mathbf{y}_{m-1}$. Then $\mathbf{x}_m = \mathbf{x}_{m-1} + \mathbf{d} \Longrightarrow_{r_{m-1}} \mathbf{y}_{m-1} + \mathbf{d}$. Let $f_m \in \mathbb{N}$ be the largest number such that there is a f_m-fast path p_m from $\mathbf{y}_{m-1} + \mathbf{d}$ to an output-stable NO state $\mathbf{y}_m$. Then let r_m be r_{m-1} followed by p_m.[12] By Proposition 4.6, once f is sufficiently large, any f-fast reaction sequence from $\mathbf{x}_m$ to $\mathbf{y}_m$ must be Π-friendly. Thus by reindexing $(\mathbf{x}_m)$ to start with a sufficiently large member of the sequence, we have that for all m, $\mathbf{x}_m \Longrightarrow^{\Pi} \mathbf{y}_m$.

By Dickson's Lemma there is an infinite nondecreasing subsequence $Y = (\mathbf{y}_{s_1}, \mathbf{y}_{s_2}, \ldots)$. Let $\Gamma = \{ S \in \Lambda \mid \lim_{n \to \infty} \mathbf{y}_{s_n}(S) = \infty \}$. By Proposition 4.6, $\Gamma \subseteq \Pi$ since $\mathbf{x}_{s_n} \Longrightarrow^{\Pi} \mathbf{y}_{s_n}$. Let $\Delta = \Pi \setminus \Gamma$. These are the species that are "large" in $(\mathbf{x}_m)$ but are bounded in Y. By further taking appropriate subsequences, we can ensure that each $\mathbf{y}_{s_n}(S) = \mathbf{y}_{s_{n+1}}(S)$ if $S \in \Lambda \setminus \Gamma$ and $\mathbf{y}_{s_n}(S) < \mathbf{y}_{s_{n+1}}(S)$ if $S \in \Gamma$.

---

[11] Note that in this way Π-friendly bimolecular reactions act somewhat analogously to unimolecular reactions: if $\mathbf{x} + \mathbf{y} \Longrightarrow \mathbf{z}$ by a sequence of unimolecular reactions, then $\mathbf{x} \Longrightarrow \mathbf{z}'$ and $\mathbf{y} \Longrightarrow \mathbf{z}''$ such that $\mathbf{z}' + \mathbf{z}'' = \mathbf{z}$.

[12] By the definition of speed fault free, $\lim_{m \to \infty} f_m = \infty$, since $\mathbf{x}_m$ and $\mathbf{y}_m$ for increasing m are reachable from input states $\mathbf{i}_n$ with increasing amounts of fuel.

Recall that a state is *committed* if it cannot produce a YES voter. The next lemma, formally proved in the full version of the paper, shows that changing counts of pumpable species (Π) by a "small" amount in $\mathbf{x}_m$, so long as m is sufficiently large, cannot change the ability of $\mathbf{x}_m$ to reach a committed state. Intuitively, later on $\mathbf{e}$ will represent a change in counts due to "processing" the extra copy of A_1 (the one that changes the correct answer in state $\mathbf{i}_n(n_1, \ldots, n_k)$ from NO to YES), and the following lemma will help us to derive a contradiction because the extra copy of A_1 should enable the production of a YES voter.

Lemma 4.8. *Let sequences* $(\mathbf{x}_m)$ *and* $(\mathbf{y}_m)$ *be as defined above. For all* $\epsilon \in \mathbb{N}$, *there exists* $\epsilon' \in \mathbb{N}$ *such that the following holds. For all* $\mathbf{e} \in \mathbb{Z}^\Pi$ *with* $|\mathbf{e}| \leq \epsilon$, *for infinitely many* m, *there exists* $\mathbf{e}_m \in \mathbb{Z}^\Gamma$ *with* $|\mathbf{e}_m| \leq \epsilon'$, *and* $m_2 < m$ *such that* $\mathbf{x}_m + \mathbf{e} \Longrightarrow^\Pi \mathbf{y}_{m_2} + \mathbf{e}_m$ *and* $\mathbf{y}_{m_2} + \mathbf{e}_m$ *is committed.*

Proof (sketch). We know that $\mathbf{x}_m \Longrightarrow_{r_m} \mathbf{y}_m$. Consider applying r_m to $\mathbf{x}_m + \mathbf{e}$ to get $\mathbf{y}_m + \mathbf{e}$. This may not work because it could drive some species negative, and the final state may not be committed. We use Lemma 4.5 to obtain an ordering $\Delta = \{D_1, \ldots, D_l\}$ such that we can add or remove from r_m reactions of the form $\alpha_i : D_i + S \to P_1 + \ldots + P_k$ where $S, P_1 \ldots, P_k$ are in $\Gamma \cup \{D_{i+1}, \ldots, D_l\}$. This gives a way to "fix" the count of D_i to make its count equal to its count in $\mathbf{y}_m$ by either removing α_i (to increase) or adding extra instances of α_i (to decrease), while affecting only species in Γ or "after" D_i (hence their counts will be fixed later). The counts of $D_1, \ldots, D_{i-1}$, which have already been fixed, are unaffected by the surgery to fix D_i, because they do not appear in α_i. When we are done, we have increased the "error" in species in Γ (corresponding to $\mathbf{e}_m \in \mathbb{Z}^\Gamma$ in the lemma statement), but by Lemma 3.3, $\mathbf{y}_m + \mathbf{e}_m$ is still committed. Unfortunately, we may be taking some species negative in the middle of the fixed path. To handle this, the full argument essentially relies on the definition of $\mathbf{y}_m$ iteratively defined by adding $\mathbf{d}$ to $\mathbf{y}_{m-1}$, and ends by reaching committed state $\mathbf{y}_{m_2} + \mathbf{e}_m$, for a smaller $m_2 < m$ (see full paper). $\square$

The next lemma uses Lemma 4.8 to show that, from state $\mathbf{x}_m + \mathbf{e}$, with $\mathbf{e} \in \mathbb{Z}^\Lambda$ "small," we can reach a committed state in which every species that can be "large", is actually large.

Lemma 4.9. *Let sequence* $(\mathbf{x}_m)$ *be as defined above. For all* $\epsilon \in \mathbb{N}$, *there exists* $c \in \mathbb{N}$ *and* $\Omega \subseteq \Lambda$ *such that the following holds. For all* $\mathbf{e} \in \mathbb{Z}^\Pi$ *such that* $|\mathbf{e}| \leq \epsilon$, *there exists an infinite sequence* $W_\mathbf{e} = (\mathbf{w}_n)$ *of states such that, for all* $n \in \mathbb{N}$, *there exists* $m_n \in \mathbb{N}$, *such that the following is true: (1)* $\mathbf{x}_{m_n} + \mathbf{e} \Longrightarrow^\Pi \mathbf{w}_n$, *(2)* $\mathbf{w}_n$ *is committed, (3) for all* $S \in \Omega$, $\mathbf{w}_n(S) \geq n$, *(4) for all* $S \in \Lambda \setminus \Omega$ *and all* $\mathbf{u}$ *such that* $\mathbf{w}_n \Longrightarrow^\Omega \mathbf{u}$, $\mathbf{u}(S) \leq c$, *and (5)* $\mathbf{w}_n$ *are nondecreasing.*

Lemma 4.9 is proven in the full version of this paper. Intuitively (albeit imprecisely), it follows by letting Ω be a maximal Y-pumpable set of species, where Y is the infinite sequence of committed states of the form $\mathbf{y}_{m_2} + \mathbf{e}_m$ shown to exist in Lemma 4.8. That is, while Π contains species that can simultaneously get large in state $\mathbf{x}_m$ starting from the initial state, and Γ contains species that happen to be large in the committed states $\mathbf{y}_{m_2} + \mathbf{e}_m$ reachable from $\mathbf{x}_m + \mathbf{e}$, Ω contains possibly more species than Γ: those that can get large, starting from states $\mathbf{y}_{m_2} + \mathbf{e}_m$.

The next lemma shows that speed fault free CRDs decide only detection problems. Lemma 4.10 is formally proved in the full version of this paper.

Lemma 4.10. $\mathcal{D}$ *is not speed fault free.*

Proof (sketch). Recall initial states $\mathbf{i}_n$ encode an input value making the predicate false, and $\mathbf{i}_n + \{A_1\}$ encode an input value making the predicate true. Let $\mathbf{e} = \mathbf{0}$ and consider the corresponding $W_0 = (\mathbf{w}_n)$. By Lemma 4.9 we have $\mathbf{i}_{n'} \Longrightarrow^{\Pi} \mathbf{x}_m \Longrightarrow^{\Pi} \mathbf{w}_n$. We can rewrite this path as $(\mathbf{i}_{n'} \setminus \{A_1\}) + \{A_1\} \Longrightarrow^{\Pi} \mathbf{w}_n$, and applying Lemma 4.7 obtain that there are $\mathbf{p}, \mathbf{p}' \in \mathbb{N}^{\Pi}$ such that: $\mathbf{p} + \{A_1\} \Longrightarrow^{\Pi} \mathbf{p}' + \mathbf{b}$, where $\mathbf{b} \le \mathbf{w}_n$. Call this path r. Since $\mathbf{b} \le \mathbf{w}_n$, it must be that $\mathbf{b}$ is committed even if any amount of Ω is added to it.

Let $\mathbf{e} = \mathbf{p}' - \mathbf{p} \in \mathbb{Z}^{\Pi}$ and consider the (different) sequence $W_{\mathbf{e}} = (\mathbf{w}_n)$ obtained using this $\mathbf{e}$ from Lemma 4.9. For all n, there is m such that $\mathbf{x}_m + \mathbf{e} \Longrightarrow^{\Pi} \mathbf{w}_n$ by some path p_n. Now, choose n large enough (so $\mathbf{x}_m \ge \mathbf{p}$) and add the extra molecule of A_1: $\mathbf{x}_m + \{A_1\} \Longrightarrow_r^{\Pi} \mathbf{x}_m + (\mathbf{p}' - \mathbf{p}) + \mathbf{b} = \mathbf{x}_m + \mathbf{e} + \mathbf{b} \Longrightarrow_{p_n}^{\Pi} \mathbf{w}_n + \mathbf{b}$. Because this state is reachable from a valid initial state with one extra molecule of A_1, we must be able to produce a YES voter from it. By assumption of a speed fault free CRD, this must be a fast path: for all f, there is an n such that $\mathbf{w}_n + \mathbf{b} \Longrightarrow \mathbf{z}_n$ by an f-fast path q_n, and $\mathbf{z}_n$ contains a YES voter. Is q_n Ω-friendly? If q_n is Ω-friendly then by Lemma 4.7 we can reach a YES voter solely from $\mathbf{w}_n$ or $\mathbf{b}$ given enough extra of species in Ω. This is a contradiction since both $\mathbf{w}_n$ and $\mathbf{b}$ are committed, even if any amount of Ω is added (by Lemma 3.3).

Thus q_n cannot be entirely Ω-friendly. Let α_n be the first reaction that is not Ω-friendly, and let $\mathbf{u}_n$ be the state immediately before this reaction occurs. If for all f, there is a q_n that is f-fast, it must be that $\mathbf{u}_n$ contains count f of some species X_n that is not in Ω (otherwise, α_n would be Ω-friendly). Consider $f > 2c$ where c is the constant from Lemma 4.9. Since the initial portion of q_n that leads to $\mathbf{u}_n$ is Ω-friendly, we have $\mathbf{w}_n + \mathbf{b} \Longrightarrow^{\Omega} \mathbf{u}_n$ and Lemma 4.7 applies. Consequently, $\exists \mathbf{o}, \mathbf{o}', \mathbf{o}'' \in \mathbb{N}^{\Omega}$ and $\mathbf{u}', \mathbf{u}'' \in \mathbb{N}^{\Lambda}$ such that $\mathbf{o} + \mathbf{w}_n \Longrightarrow^{\Omega} \mathbf{o}' + \mathbf{u}'_n$ and $\mathbf{o} + \mathbf{b} \Longrightarrow^{\Omega} \mathbf{o}'' + \mathbf{u}''_n$ and $\mathbf{u}'_n + \mathbf{u}''_n = \mathbf{u}_n$. Thus either $\mathbf{u}'_n$ or $\mathbf{u}''_n$ must contain at least $f/2$ of X_n. Since $\mathbf{w}_{n'}$ are nondecreasing and are larger than n' on Ω, for large enough n', $\mathbf{w}_{n'}$ from $W_{\mathbf{e}}$ exceeds $\mathbf{o} + \mathbf{w}_n$ and $\mathbf{w}_{n'}$ from W_0 exceeds $\mathbf{o} + \mathbf{b}$. But then we obtain a contradiction of condition (4) in Lemma 4.9. $\square$

Acknowledgements. We thank Damien Woods, Anne Condon, Chris Thachuk, Bonnie Kirkpatrick, Monir Hajiaghayi, and Ján Maňuch for useful discussions.

References

[1] Angluin, D., Aspnes, J., Diamadi, Z., Fischer, M., Peralta, R.: Computation in networks of passively mobile finite-state sensors. Distributed Computing 18, 235–253 (2006), Preliminary version appeared in PODC 2004

[2] Angluin, D., Aspnes, J., Eisenstat, D.: Stably computable predicates are semilinear. In: PODC 2006: Proceedings of the Twenty-fifth Annual ACM Symposium on Principles of Distributed Computing, pp. 292–299. ACM Press, New York (2006)

[3] Angluin, D., Aspnes, J., Eisenstat, D.: Fast computation by population protocols with a leader. Distributed Computing 21(3), 183–199 (2008); Preliminary version appeared in Dolev, S. (ed.) DISC 2006. LNCS, vol. 4167, pp. 61–75. Springer, Heidelberg (2006)

[4] Cardelli, L.: Strand algebras for DNA computing. Natural Computing 10(1), 407–428 (2011)

[5] Cardelli, L., Csikász-Nagy, A.: The cell cycle switch computes approximate majority. Scientific Reports 2 (2012)

[6] Cardoza, E., Lipton, R.J., Meyer, A.R.: Exponential space complete problems for Petri nets and commutative semigroups (preliminary report). In: STOC 1976: Proceedings of the 8th Annual ACM Symposium on Theory of Computing, pp. 50–54. ACM (1976)

[7] Chen, H.-L., Doty, D., Soloveichik, D.: Deterministic function computation with chemical reaction networks. Natural Computing (2013); Preliminary version appeared in DNA 2012. LNCS, vol. 7433, pp. 25–42. Springer, Heidelberg (2012)

[8] Chen, Y.-J., Dalchau, N., Srinivas, N., Phillips, A., Cardelli, L., Soloveichik, D., Seelig, G.: Programmable chemical controllers made from DNA. Nature Nanotechnology 8(10), 755–762 (2013)

[9] Condon, A., Hu, A., Maňuch, J., Thachuk, C.: Less haste, less waste: On recycling and its limits in strand displacement systems. Journal of the Royal Society Interface 2, 512–521 (2011); Preliminary version appeared in DNA 17 2011. LNCS, vol. 6937, pp. 84–99. Springer, Heidelberg (2011)

[10] Dickson, L.E.: Finiteness of the odd perfect and primitive abundant numbers with n distinct prime factors. American Journal of Mathematics 35(4), 413–422 (1913)

[11] Doty, D.: Timing in chemical reaction networks. In: SODA 2014: Proceedings of the 25th Annual ACM-SIAM Symposium on Discrete Algorithms, pp. 772–784 (January 2014)

[12] Gillespie, D.T.: Exact stochastic simulation of coupled chemical reactions. Journal of Physical Chemistry 81(25), 2340–2361 (1977)

[13] Karp, R.M., Miller, R.E.: Parallel program schemata. Journal of Computer and System Sciences 3(2), 147–195 (1969)

[14] Petri, C.A.: Communication with automata. Technical report, DTIC Document (1966)

[15] Soloveichik, D., Cook, M., Winfree, E., Bruck, J.: Computation with finite stochastic chemical reaction networks. Natural Computing 7(4), 615–633 (2008)

[16] Soloveichik, D., Seelig, G., Winfree, E.: DNA as a universal substrate for chemical kinetics. Proceedings of the National Academy of Sciences 107(12), 5393 (2008); Preliminary version appeared in DNA Computing. LNCS, vol. 5347, pp. 57–69. Springer, Heidelberg (2009)

Fault-Tolerant ANTS

Tobias Langner, Jara Uitto, David Stolz, and Roger Wattenhofer

ETH Zürich, Switzerland

Abstract. In this paper, we study a variant of the *Ants Nearby Treasure Search* problem, where n mobile agents, controlled by finite automata, search collaboratively for a treasure hidden by an adversary. In our version of the model, the agents may fail at any time during the execution. We provide a distributed protocol that enables the agents to detect failures and recover from them, thereby providing robustness to the protocol. More precisely, we provide a protocol that allows the agents to locate the treasure in time $\mathcal{O}(D + D^2/n + Df)$ where D is the distance to the treasure and $f \in \mathcal{O}(n)$ is the maximum number of failures.

1 Introduction

Ant colonies are a prime example of biological systems that are fault-tolerant. Removing some or even a large fraction of ants should not prevent the colony from functioning properly. In this paper we study the so-called *Ants Nearby Treasure Search (ANTS)* problem, a natural benchmark for ant-based distributed algorithms where n mobile agents try to efficiently find a food source at distance D from the nest. We present a novel distributed algorithm that can tolerate (up to) a constant fraction of ants being killed in the process.

In distributed computing, most algorithms can survive f crash faults by replication. Following this path, each ant can be made fault-tolerant by using $f + 1$ ants with identical behavior, making sure that at least one ant survives an orchestrated attack. However, since we allow $f \in \mathcal{O}(n)$ crash failures, we would be left with merely a constant number of fault-tolerant "super-ants", and a constant number of ants cannot find the food efficiently. As such we have to explore a smarter replication technique, where faulty ants have to be discovered and replaced in a coordinated manner.

In more detail, we study a variation of the ANTS problem, where the n agents are controlled by randomized finite state machines and are allowed to communicate by constant-sized messages with agents that share the same cell. The goal is to locate an adversarially hidden treasure. There is a simple lower bound of $\Omega(D + D^2/n)$ to locate the treasure [10]. This bound is based on the observation that at least one agent has to move to distance D, which takes time $\Omega(D)$, and that there are $\Omega(D^2)$ cells with distance at most D while a single agent can visit at most one new cell per round, which yields the $\Omega(D^2/n)$ term. In previous work, it was shown that the treasure can be located with randomized finite-state machines in optimal time in an asynchronous environment [8]. That approach, however, is rather fragile and requires the agents to be absolutely

F. Kuhn (Ed.): DISC 2014, LNCS 8784, pp. 31–45, 2014.

reliable. The failure of just a single agent can already result in not finding the treasure.

In the model of this paper, $f \in \mathcal{O}(n)$ of the agents can fail at any point in time. However, despite the presence of failures, we show that the treasure can be located efficiently, i.e., we find the treasure in time $\mathcal{O}(D + D^2/n + Df)$. In essence, we implement an error checking mechanism that detects if an agent died. As we keep track of the progress of the search by "remembering" which cells have been searched so far, we can then restart the search while avoiding to search cells that have already been searched.

1.1   Related Work

Searching the plane with n agents was introduced by Feinerman et al. In the original ANTS problem, the agents only communicate in the origin and thus search independently for a treasure [9, 10]. Moreover, the agents are controlled by randomized Turing machines and assuming knowledge of a constant approximation of n, the agents are able to locate the treasure in time $\mathcal{O}(D + D^2/n)$. This model was studied further by Lenzen et al., who investigated the effects of bounding the memory as well as the range of available probabilities of the agents [13]. Protocols in their models are robust by definition as the agents do not communicate outside of origin and thus the failure of an agent cannot affect any other agent.

The main differences between our model and theirs lie in the communication and computation capabilities of the agents. First, we use a significantly weaker computation model: our agents only use a constant amount of memory and are governed by finite automata. Second, our agents are allowed to communicate with each other during the execution. However, the communication is limited to constant sized-messages and only allowed between agents that share the same cell at the same time. The communication and computation model was originally introduced in a graph setting by Emek et al. [8].

Searching the plane is a special case of graph exploration. In the general version of the problem, the task is to visit all the nodes/edges by moving along the edges [1, 6, 7, 12, 16, 17]. In the finite case, it is known that a random walk visits all nodes in expected polynomial time [2]. In the infinite case, a random walk can take infinite time in expectation to reach a designated node.

Another closely related problem is the classic *cow-path* problem, where the task is to find food on a line. It is known that there is a deterministic algorithm with a constant competitive ratio. Furthermore, the spiral search is an optimal algorithm in the 2-dimensional variant [5]. The problem has also been studied in a multi-agent setting [14].

Searching graphs with finite state machines was studied earlier by Fraigniaud et al. [11]. Other work considering distributed computing by finite automata includes for example *population protocols* [3, 4].

1.2 Model

We investigate a variation of the *Ants Nearby Treasure Search (ANTS)* problem, where a set of mobile *agents* explore the infinite integer grid in order to locate a treasure positioned by an adversary. All agents are operated by randomized finite automata with a constant number of states and can communicate with each other through constant-size messages when they are located in the same cell. In contrast to [8] where the agents do not have to deal with robustness issues, our agents can fail at any time during the execution, thus making it much harder to develop correct algorithms for the ANTS problem. In all other aspects, our model is identical to the one of [8].

Consider a set $\mathcal{A}$ of n mobile agents that explore $\mathbb{Z}^2$. All agents start the execution in a dedicated grid cell – the *origin* (say, the cell with coordinates $(0,0) \in \mathbb{Z}^2$). The agents are able to determine whether they are located at the origin or not. The grid cells with either x or y-coordinate being 0 are denoted as *north/east/south/west-axis*, depending on the respective location.

We measure the *distance* $\mathrm{dist}(c, c')$ between two grid cells $c = (x, y)$ and $c' = (x', y')$ in $\mathbb{Z}^2$ with respect to the ℓ_1 norm (a.k.a. Manhattan distance), i.e., $|x - x'| + |y - y'|$. Two cells are called *neighbors* or *adjacent* if the distance between them is 1. In each execution step, an agent located in cell $(x, y) \in \mathbb{Z}^2$ can move to one of the four neighboring cells $(x, y+1), (x, y-1), (x+1, y), (x-1, y)$, or stay still. The four *position transitions* are denoted by the respective cardinal directions N, E, S, W, and the latter (stationary) position transition is denoted by P ("stay put"). We point out that the agents have a common sense of orientation, i.e., the cardinal directions are aligned with the corresponding grid axes for every agent in every cell.

The agents operate in a *synchronous environment*, meaning that the execution of all agents progresses in discrete rounds indexed by the non-negative integers. The runtime of a protocol is measured in the number of rounds that it takes the protocol to achieve its goal/terminate. We fix the duration of one round to be one time unit and thus can take the liberty to use the terms round and time interchangeably.

In comparison to the original ANTS problem, the communication and computational capabilities of our agents are more limited. An agent can only communicate with agents that are positioned in the same cell at the same time. This communication is restricted though: agent a positioned in cell c only senses for each state q whether there exists at least one agent $a' \neq a$ in cell c whose current state is q.

All agents are controlled by the same finite automaton. Formally, the agent's protocol $\mathcal{P}$ is specified by the 3-tuple $\mathcal{P} = \langle Q, s_0, \delta \rangle$, where Q is the finite set of *states*, $s_0 \in Q$ is the *initial state*, and $\delta : Q \times 2^Q \to 2^{Q \times \{N, S, E, W, P\}}$ is the *transition function*. At the beginning of the execution, each agent starts at the origin in the initial state s_0. Suppose that in round i, agent a is in state $q \in Q$ and positioned in cell $c \in \mathbb{Z}^2$. Then, the state $q' \in Q$ of agent a in round $i + 1$ and the corresponding movement $\tau \in \{N, S, E, W, P\}$ are dictated based on the transition function δ by picking the tuple (q', τ) uniformly at random from

$\delta(q, Q_a)$, where $Q_a \subseteq Q$ contains state $p \in Q$ if and only if there exists at least one agent $a' \neq a$ such that a' is in state p and positioned in cell c in round i. We assume that the application of the transition function and the corresponding movement occur instantaneously and simultaneously for all agents at the end of the round i.

Adversarial Failures. In contrast to previous work, the agents in our model are not immune to foreign influences and thus can fail at any time during the execution of their protocol. We consider an *adaptive off-line adversary* (sometimes also called omniscient adversary) that has access to all the parameters of the agents' protocol as well as to their random bits. Formally, the adversary specifies for each agent a the *failure time* $t^f(a)$ as the round at the end of which agent a fails. If the adversary does not fail a certain agent a at all, we set $t^f(a) = \infty$. If an agent a fails in round $r = t^f(a)$, then it is removed from the grid as well as the set $\mathcal{A}$; the agent cannot be observed anymore by other agents in any round $r' > r$ (failed agents do *not* leave a corpse behind).

Problem Statement. The goal of ANTS problem is to locate an adversarially hidden *treasure*, i.e., to bring at least one agent to the cell in which the treasure is positioned. The distance of the treasure from the origin is denoted by D while the maximum number of failures that the adversary may cause is denoted by f. We say that a protocol is $g(n)$-*robust* if it locates the treasure w.h.p. for some $f \in \Theta(g(n))$. A protocol that finds the treasure if (up to) a constant fraction of the agents fail is hence n-robust. The goal of this paper is to show that such an n-robust protocol indeed does exist. Therefore, we consider a scenario where $f = \alpha \cdot n$ for a constant α that will be determined later. The performance of a protocol is measured in terms of its runtime, which corresponds to the index of the round in which the treasure is found. Although we express the runtime complexity in terms of the parameters D, n, and f, we point out that neither of these parameters are known to the agents (who in general could not even store them in their constant memory).

2   An n-Robust Protocol

The goal of this section is to develop an n-robust protocol that solves the ANTS problem. In other words, we want to find a protocol that finds the treasure even if a constant fraction of the agents fails. During the remainder of the paper, we use a set of definitions which we shall introduce here. We refer to all cells in distance ℓ from the origin as *level* ℓ. We say that a cell c is *explored* in round r if it is visited by any agent in round r for the first time. Furthermore, a *configuration* of the agents is a function $C : \mathcal{A} \to \mathbb{Z}^2$ that maps each agent $a \in \mathcal{A}$ to a certain cell $c \in \mathbb{Z}^2$.

Giants. A key concept that will be used throughout this paper is the *giant*. A giant is a cluster of k agents that all perform exactly the same operations and always stay together during the execution of a protocol. If $k > f$, where we recall that f is the maximum number of agents that can fail, we can consider the cluster as a single (giant) agent that cannot be failed by the adversary.

As we design an n-robust protocol, all our giants will consist of $\alpha \cdot n$ agents for a constant $0 < \alpha < 1$. Observe that there can only be a constant number of giants. Since our protocol only requires a constant amount of giants, we proceed to explain how a protocol can create constantly many giants. Consider a protocol that requires g giants, each of size $\Theta(n)$, plus $\Theta(n)$ normal agents. At the beginning of the execution, each agent uniformly at random transitions to one of $g + 2$ distinct states, one state for each of the g giants and two additional states for the normal agents. By a simple Chernoff bound argument, it follows that the number of agents per giant is at least $n/(g+3)$ and the number of normal agents is at least $2n/(g + 3)$ w.h.p.[1] Hence, a protocol that relies on the survival of its g giants can tolerate $n/(g + 3) - 1$ failures and still operate correctly.

2.1 Overview

We describe a protocol that uses 10 giants, which can therefore tolerate up to $f = n/13 - 1$ failures by the above argument. The remaining agents (w.h.p. at least $2n/13$) will be called Explorers as their job is to explore cells in bulk. At any time during the execution, we are guaranteed to have at least $n/13$ surviving Explorers and we will denote this number by n_e.

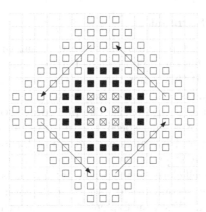

Fig. 1. This figures shows the ring of cells that is supposed to be explored by the ExpoSweep protocol in iteration 1 (crossed boxes), 2 (filled boxes) and 3 (empty boxes). The width of the ring increases by factor of (roughly) two in each iteration and the agents move further outwards.

Our protocol works iteratively and in each iteration, the Explorers explore all cells in a ring around the origin: The Explorers line up along the north axis on a

---

[1] We say that an event occurs *with high probability*, abbreviated by w.h.p., if the event occurs with probability at least $1 - n^{-\beta}$, where β is an arbitrarily large constant.

segment with a length that depends on the iteration. Then, all Explorers, together with the giants, perform a *sweep* around the origin by moving along the sides of a rectangle. If the exploration of a ring was not successful, meaning that at least one cell in the ring was not explored, the agents regroup and re-explore the ring. If the exploration was successful, the agents move further outwards to prepare for the exploration of the next ring. Then they approximately double the length of the segment (as long as possible) and start a new iteration. Figure 1 gives an illustration of the execution.

2.2 Basis Configuration

All four procedures presented in the following require that at their beginning, the agents form a special configuration, called a *basis*. All procedures also ensure that at their end, the agents are again in a basis. A basis consists of ten giants while all other (non-giant) agents serve as Explorers. An InnerGiant and a CollectGiant are positioned on the east, south, and west axis in the cell with distance d_1 from the origin. On the north axis, an InnerGiant, a StartGiant and a TriggerGiant reside in cell $(0, d_1)$ while an OuterGiant is in cell $(0, d_2)$ with $d_2 > d_1$. All Explorers are located somewhere along the cells between d_1 and d_2 on the north axis. If the parameters are relevant in the context, we write (d_1, d_2)-basis or (d_1)-basis if the second parameter is not relevant (or not known explicitly). See Figure 2 for an illustration.

2.3 Compacting a Segment

The goal of the COMPACT procedure is to ensure that the Explorers occupy a contiguous segment of cells on the north-axis between InnerGiant and OuterGiant (unless failures occur). If this is not the case, they are compacted towards the origin to form a contiguous, yet shorter, segment.

Let the agents be in a (d_1, d_2)-basis. The procedure COMPACT is started by the StartGiant, which moves with speed $1/2$ (it stays put every second round) towards the OuterGiant and instructs each group of Explorers that it meets to start repeated *compacting steps*. A compacting step consists of two rounds. First, the Explorer moves one cell closer to the origin. If that cell is empty, it stays there and does nothing in the second round, otherwise it moves back to its previous cell in the second round. When an Explorer moves onto the cell containing the InnerGiant, it moves back and *stops* compacting. The same happens if an Explorer moves onto a cell with at least one stopped Explorer.

When the StartGiant has reached the OuterGiant, it instructs the OuterGiant to perform compacting steps as well. Then, the StartGiant waits two rounds and then moves back towards the InnerGiant with speed $1/2$ until it arrives there (without further instructing Explorers on the way).

Analysis. The duration of a COMPACT execution is defined as the time between the StartGiant moving away from the InnerGiant and returning to the InnerGiant again. Observe that if the agents start COMPACT from a (d_1, d_2)-basis, they form a (d_1, d_2')-basis at the end for some $d_2' \leq d_2$. Let $E_b = (n_d)_{d_1 < d < d_2}$ and $E_e = (n_d)_{d_1 < d < d_2'}$ be the sequences of the counts of Explorers on the cells $(0, d)$ at the beginning and the end of the execution of COMPACT, respectively. Further, we denote by $S|_0$ the sub-sequence of the sequence S where each 0-element is removed. Then the following lemma establishes the correctness of COMPACT.

Lemma 1. *If no failures occur during a* COMPACT *execution, then* $E_e = E_b|_0$.

Proof. Let us call the set of Explorers that occupy the same cell at the beginning of a COMPACT execution a *team* and let us index the teams by $1, 2, \ldots, k$ according to increasing distances from the origin. Observe that during COMPACT, the Explorers of a fixed team behave (and move) identically and thus it suffices to examine the individual teams.

By design, team i never overtakes team $i - 1$ and moreover only meets team $i - 1$ if the latter has already stopped. Team i only stops in a cell that does not contain another stopped team and therefore no two teams will end up at the same cell at the end of the execution. As a team only stops in the cell directly next to the cell that contains either a stopped team or the InnerGiant, the teams will occupy a contiguous segment of cells outwards from the InnerGiant. As the OuterGiant also performs compacting steps, it will end up directly adjacent to the outermost team. Thus, all cells between cell $(0, d_1)$ and $(0, d_2')$ are occupied by the teams 1 to k in that order and the claim follows.   □

As an agent moves one step towards the origin every two rounds unless it has reached the cell in which it will stop, all agents have stopped in their target position when the StartGiant arrives back at the InnerGiant.

2.4   Searching a Ring

In this section we introduce the procedure SEGSWEEP (segment sweep) which aims to search all cells in a ring, i.e., a set of consecutive levels. As all our procedures, SEGSWEEP requires the agents to be in a basis. Let the agents be in a (d_1, d_2)-basis.

A SEGSWEEP consists of four QSWEEPs (quarter sweep), one for each quarter-plane, that are executed subsequently. Figure 2 gives an illustration of the different steps of a single QSWEEP. The first QSWEEP (of the north-east quarter-plane) is initiated by the StartGiant which starts moving north towards the OuterGiant along the north axis and while passing the Explorers tells them to diagonally move towards the east-axis by alternatingly moving east and south. As soon as the StartGiant starts moving north, the TriggerGiant moves diagonally towards the east-axis and will meet the east-InnerGiant and east-CollectGiant in cell $(d_1, 0)$. When the TriggerGiant arrives at cell $(d_1, 0)$ in round r, it stops there and instructs the CollectGiant to move outwards (east).

The CollectGiant moves to cell $(d_1 + 1, 0)$ to receive the Explorers that are exploring distance $d_1 + 1$ and thus should arrive in cell $(d_1 + 1, 0)$ soon. Now we have to distinguish two cases. Either at least one Explorer arrives in round $r + 3$ (the Explorer in distance $d + 1$ starts moving towards the east-axis one

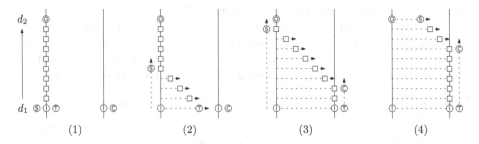

Fig. 2. This figure illustrates different stages of a QSWEEP. The two (perpendicular) axes between which the QSWEEP is performed are aligned parallel to each other for the sake of clarity. (1) shows the (d_1, d_2)-basis while in (2) the StartGiant (S) has already sent on their way several Explorers ($\square$) and the TriggerGiant (T). In (3), the TriggerGiant has reached the CollectGiant (C) on the second axis which is now on the way to collect the incoming Explorers and in (4) the StartGiant has reached the OuterGiant (O) on the first axis and is now en route towards meeting the CollectGiant on the second axis.

round later than the Explorer in distance d and has to visit two more cells before arriving there) which means that the search of the north-east quarter-plane in distance $d_1 + 1$ was successful or no Explorer arrives in round $r + 3$, which means that the search was not successful because the team of Explorers was failed. In both cases, the CollectGiant moves one cell outwards in round $r + 4$ to receive the Explorers of level $d_1 + 2$ which are bound to arrive there in round $r + 6$. The CollectGiant continues to move a cell outwards every three rounds and whenever a group of Explorers meet the CollectGiant, they stop in the respective cell.

When the StartGiant arrives at the OuterGiant on the north-axis, the Outer-Giant moves inwards (south) and when it arrives at the InnerGiant, it becomes a CollectGiant and stays put. The StartGiant then moves diagonally towards the east-axis and will meet the (moving) CollectGiant in cell $(d_2, 0)$ to notify it that the QSWEEP is complete upon which the CollectGiant becomes an OuterGiant and stays put. Now the StartGiant moves inwards (west) until it meets the east-InnerGiant and the TriggerGiant. The configuration of the agents is now identical (apart from a 90°-rotation) to the configuration before the first QSWEEP and thus QSWEEPs of the south-east, south-west, and north-west quarter-plane can be performed in an analogous fashion.

When the StartGiant arrives at the north-axis for the second time, the last of the four QSWEEPs is finished. On its way back towards the InnerGiant, the StartGiant now observes whether each cell between the OuterGiant and the InnerGiant contains at least one Explorer. If this is the case, the StartGiant enters a special *complete* state, which, as we will later show, implies that all levels ℓ with $d_1 \leq \ell \leq d_2$ have been explored. Otherwise, the StartGiant enters a special *incomplete* state, meaning that at least one level might not have been explored completely.

Analysis. We say that a SEGSWEEP *begins* in the round in which the StartGiant starts moving towards the OuterGiant from the cell containing the InnerGiant and TriggerGiant. The SEGSWEEP *ends* when the StartGiant arrives back at the InnerGiant on the north-axis after the fourth QSWEEP.

Our agents operate in an adversarial environment and thus we need to show that the SEGSWEEP procedure works correctly independent of failures of the agents. Here, that means that all (surviving) agents end up in a (d_1)-basis after a SEGSWEEP and that if the StartGiant enters the complete state, a ring was completely explored. To see the former, note that the design of the procedure ensures that, regardless of potential failures, each Explorer is stopped by a CollectGiant when crossing an axis and the StartGiant and CollectGiant will meet in the cell in distance d'_2 on every axis. All other giants are in their original position and thus, after four QSWEEPs, the agents are again in a (d_1)-basis. The following two lemmas are essential for the correctness of the procedure.

Consider a single execution of SEGSWEEP that starts from a (d_1, d_2)-basis. We call the execution *successful* if at the end, all levels ℓ with $d_1 \leq \ell \leq d_2$ have been explored.

Lemma 2. *If the StartGiant is in the complete state at the end of a* SEGSWEEP, *then the* SEGSWEEP *was successful.*

Proof. Observe that the StartGiant can only enter the complete state if, at the end of a SEGSWEEP, each cell between InnerGiant and OuterGiant contains at least one Explorer. The design of the procedure ensures that an Explorer can only end up in cell $(0, d)$ for $d_1 < d < d'_2$ at the end of a SEGSWEEP if it has started the SEGSWEEP in cell $(0, d)$ and in between explored all cells of level d (and in passing almost all cells of level $d + 1$). As level d_1 and d'_2 are explored by TriggerGiant and StartGiant, the claim follows.   □

Lemma 3. *If no agent failed during a* COMPACT *execution and the subsequent* SEGSWEEP, *then the* SEGSWEEP *was successful.*

Proof. The COMPACT execution ensures that before the first QSWEEP all cells between InnerGiant and OuterGiant contain at least one Explorer. If no agent fails, all these Explorers will end up in the same cell at the end of the fourth QSWEEP by design of the procedure. Hence, the StartGiant will observe at least one Explorer in each cell between InnerGiant and OuterGiant and thus enter the complete state. The claim then follows from Lemma 2.   □

2.5 Shifting the Segment

In this section, we introduce the procedure SHIFT, an additional building block that allows the agents to move further outwards from the origin. Its concept is similar to the giant movement during a SEGSWEEP. SHIFT assumes that all agents form a (d_1, d_2)-basis for some $d_1 < d_2$ and transforms it into a (d_2+1, d_3)-basis for some $d_3 > d_2 + 1$.

The StartGiant moves north towards the OuterGiant and sends the TriggerGiant away to move diagonally to the cell $(d_1, 0)$ on the east-axis, where an InnerGiant/CollectGiant reside. When the TriggerGiant arrives at there, it stays put and sends the two other giants to move outwards (east) with speed $1/3$. When the StartGiant arrives at the OuterGiant, it moves one cell further outwards (to cell $(0, d_2 + 1)$) and then also moves diagonally towards the east-axis. As the speed of the two giants moving outwards on the east-axis is $1/3$, they will meet the diagonally moving StartGiant in cell $(0, d_2 + 1)$ and stop there. The StartGiant moves inwards (west) until meeting the TriggerGiant in cell $(0, d_1)$. This process is repeated three times to move the InnerGiant/CollectGiant on the other axis outwards to the cell in distance $d_2 + 1$ from the origin.

When the StartGiant has returned to the north-axis and meets the TriggerGiant in cell $(0, d_1)$, it first sends the TriggerGiant and InnerGiant north in order to stop in cell $(0, d_2 + 1)$, which is one cell outwards of the cell currently occupied by the OuterGiant. Then it moves north with speed $1/2$ and whenever it meets a group of Explorers, it instructs them to move north until they find an empty cell. Whenever the OuterGiant observes an Explorer in its cell, it moves one cell north to make sure that it always marks the outermost cell. When the StartGiant arrives at the cell containing the TriggerGiant/InnerGiant, it stops. Now the agents form a $(d_2 + 1, d_3)$-basis for some $d_3 > d_2 + 1$.

2.6   Uniform Splitting

In this section, we introduce the procedure UNISPLIT (uniform splitting) to line up the agents properly for the SEGSWEEP procedure. Before we go into the implementation details of UNISPLIT, we briefly explain a few important aspects we have to take into account with the design. First, we do not want the *size* of any segment, i.e., the distance between d_1 and d_2 in a (d_1, d_2)-basis to be much larger than the distance to the treasure D. Since it takes at least time linear in the size of the segment to line the agents up, we might end up using a lot of time lining up unnecessarily many Explorers.

Second, we want to explore the grid as fast as possible. Therefore, we want to line up the Explorers as quickly as possible while maintaining the first property mentioned above. Since we are interested in the asymptotic runtime and the memory bounds are constant, we choose an exponential approach. In other words, we double the segment size after every sweep, as long as there are enough agents available.

Third, we observe that if some level in the SEGSWEEP is explored with a single Explorer, it only takes the adversary one failure to force our protocol to repeat the whole segment. Therefore, as long as we are using segment sizes that are sub-linear to the number of agents, it makes sense to use many agents per level. Thus, the aim of UNISPLIT is to split the agents along the segment uniformly.

Doubling the Segment Size. Assume that the agents form a (d_1, d_2)-basis. As before, we call all Explorers residing in the same cell a team. To double the segment size, the agents perform the following. The TriggerGiant moves north with speed $1/2$ instructing all the cells containing Explorers to perform a *split*. Each Explorer a tosses a fair coin and if the coin shows head, a moves north with speed 1 until it finds the first cell without an Explorer (if the coin shows tail, they stay put). To ensure that the OuterGiant marks the end of the segment, it always moves north whenever it sees an Explorer. When the TriggerGiant reaches the OuterGiant, it turns around and moves back to the InnerGiant. Once the TriggerGiant reaches the InnerGiant, the agents again form a (d_1)-basis.

We refer to the process of doubling the segment size to as a *pass* of UNISPLIT. Notice that the segment size k does not necessarily double, i.e., it might be that the new size is $k' \le 2k$, if some cells contained less than two Explorers. In addition, there might be empty cells along the segment due to unfortunate coin tosses or failures. As the next step, we show that the size of the segment grows by a constant factor in every pass with high probability as long as the team size distribution is "good enough". The key to prove this property is to treat the splitting process as a balls-into-bins experiment.

Consider the situation after the jth pass of UNISPLIT. The coin tosses performed by the agents so far assign to each agent a bit-sequence of length j. As there are 2^j different possible bit-sequences, one can model our setting as follows: Each of the n agents throws a single ball into the bin corresponding to its bit-sequence while there are 2^j bins altogether. The following lemma establishes that only a constant fraction of the bins is empty w.h.p.

Lemma 4. *Consider a balls-into-bins experiment where $m \ge 4$ balls are thrown uniformly at random into 2^j bins for an integer j with $0 < j < \log m$. Let Z^j be the number of empty bins at the end of the experiment. We have $Z^j < 2/e \cdot 2^j$ w.h.p.*

Proof. Let us first consider the case where $j \le \kappa \log \log m$ for some $\kappa \ge 2$ to be determined later. Then the number of bins is $\mathcal{O}(\log^\kappa m)$ and the expected number of balls per bin is $\Omega(m/\log^\kappa m)$. Observe that the probability that a fixed bin is empty is $(1 - 1/2^j)^m \le e^{-m/2^j}$. By the union bound, the probability that there exists an empty bin is at most $\sum_{i=1}^{2^j} e^{-m/2^j} \in e^{-\Omega(m/\log^\kappa m)}$. Thus we get $\Pr[Z^j \ge 2/e \cdot 2^j] \le \Pr[Z^j \ge 0] \in e^{-\Omega(m/\log^\kappa m)} \subset o(m^{-\beta})$ for any $\beta > 0$.

Now consider the case where $j > \kappa \log \log m$. Let Z_i^j be the indicator random variable for the event that bin i of 2^j is empty and we have $Z^j = \sum_{i=1}^{2^j} Z_i^j$. A well-known result from balls-into-bins is that instead of dissecting the dependencies between the loads of different bins, one can approximate the scenario well by modeling the load of each bin by an *independent* Poisson random variable [15]. We will denote all random variables derived from this approximation with a tilde and the ones corresponding to the exact scenario without.

Let $\tilde{B}_i^j$ be the random variable indicating the number of balls in bin i and observe that $\Pr[\tilde{B}_i^j = r] = e^{-\mu}\mu^r/(r!)$ for $\mu = m/2^j$ as $\tilde{B}_i^j$ has a Poisson distribution with parameter μ where we observe that $\mu > 1$. Let $\tilde{Z}_i^j$ be the indicator random variable for the event that $\tilde{B}_i^j = 0$ and observe that $\mathbb{E}[\tilde{Z}_i^j] = \Pr[\tilde{B}_i^j = 0] = e^{-\mu} < 1/e$. Let $\tilde{Z}^j = \sum_{i=1}^{2^j} \tilde{Z}_i^j$ be the random variable for the total number of empty bins and by linearity of expectation we get $\mathbb{E}[\tilde{Z}^j] < 2^j/e$. As the $\tilde{Z}_i^j$ are independent by assumption, we can use a Chernoff bound to get $\Pr[\tilde{Z}^j \ge 2/e \cdot 2^j] \le \Pr[\tilde{Z}^j \ge 2\mathbb{E}[\tilde{Z}^j]] \le e^{-2^j/(3e)}$. Observe that since $m \ge 4$,

$\kappa \geq 2$, and $j > \kappa \log \log m$, it holds that $\kappa \log m \leq \log^\kappa m$ and we get

$$\Pr[\tilde{Z}^j \geq 2/e \cdot 2^j] = e^{-\log^\kappa m/(3e)} \leq e^{-\kappa \log m/(3e)} < m^{-\kappa/(3e)} \ .$$

We can now use a result from [15] stating that any event that takes place with probability p in the Poisson approximation takes place with probability at most $pe\sqrt{m}$ in the exact case where m is the number of balls thrown. Hence, we get for the exact case $\Pr[Z^j \geq 2/e \cdot 2^j] < \sqrt{m}e \cdot m^{-\kappa/(3e)} \leq m^{-\beta}$ for any $\beta > 0$ and a large enough value of κ. □

Lemma 5. *Let E be any subset of (surviving) Explorers of size n_e. After the jth iteration of* UniSplit *for $0 < j < \log(n_e)$, the Explorers in E are members of $\Omega(2^j)$ different teams w.h.p.*

Proof. Lemma 4 states that after the jth iteration there are at most $2/e \cdot 2^j$ empty bins w.h.p. Thus there are at least $(e-2)/e \cdot 2^j \in \Omega(2^j)$ many non-empty bins w.h.p., which the Explorers in E must occupy. The claim follows. □

Recall that n_e, the minimum number of surviving Explorers, is guaranteed to be $\Theta(n)$. Thus, Lemma 5 implies that no matter which subset of Explorers the adversary lets survive, these Explorers will be members of $\Omega(2^j)$ different teams after the jth pass of UniSplit for $0 < j < \log(n_e)$ w.h.p.

Corollary 6. *The number of teams after the jth pass of* UniSplit *is $\Omega(2^j)$ for $0 < j < \log(n_e)$ w.h.p.*

2.7 Putting Everything Together

In this section we explain how we can connect the procedures presented in the previous section in order to obtain the n-robust protocol ExpoSweep (exponential sweep) for the ANTS-problem.

The protocol starts with all agents located at the origin. Then the agents create the 10 giants required by SegSweep as described earlier. Now, the agents ensure that the StartGiant, InnerGiant, and TriggerGiant, are located in cell $(0,1)$, the OuterGiant in cell $(0,3)$, and an InnerGiant/CollectGiant-pair on the east-, south-, west-axis in the cell with distance 1 to the origin. Observe that this configuration is a $(1,3)$-basis. Then the agents iteratively perform the protocol described in Algorithm 1.

It is easy to verify that all the aforementioned subroutines of our protocol only require a constant amount of states and therefore, the total number of states required by our protocol is also a constant.

3   Runtime

We begin the runtime analysis by bounding the time needed for any SegSweep in terms of distance to the treasure.

Algorithm 1. EXPOSWEEP

---

1. The StartGiant triggers the execution of COMPACT as described in Section 2.3.
2. The StartGiant triggers the execution of SEGSWEEP as described in Section 2.4. When the SEGSWEEP is finished, there are two cases: If the StartGiant enters the incomplete state, go to step 2. Otherwise, proceed to step 3.
3. The StartGiant triggers the execution of SHIFT as described in Section 2.5.
4. The StartGiant triggers the execution of UNISPLIT as described in Section 2.6.

Lemma 7. *If the treasure has not been found at the start of iteration i of SEG-SWEEP and the agents form a (d_1, d_2)-basis, then $d_1 < D$ and $d_2 \leq 2D$.*

Proof. Observe that the agents only move to a (d_1)-basis after SEGSWEEP has explored all levels $\ell < d_1$, and hence, $d_1 < D$. Assume for contradiction that $d_2 > 2D$. Since d_2 can at most double in UNISPLIT, there must have been a pass of UNISPLIT that started from a (d'_1, d'_2) basis, where $d'_1 \leq D \leq d'_2$. Since UNISPLIT is only performed after a successful execution of SEGSWEEP, the treasure must have already been found.   □

Lemma 8. *Any iteration i of EXPOSWEEP before the treasure was found lasts at most $\mathcal{O}(D)$ rounds.*

Proof. By Lemma 7, $d_2 \leq 2D$ for any (d_1, d_2)-basis at the start of iteration i. By looking at the details of the EXPOSWEEP protocol, we first observe that the time complexity of COMPACT is clearly $\mathcal{O}(D)$ since the time needed is bounded simply by the time it takes the StartGiant to move from InnerGiant to OuterGiant and back. Second, it is easy to see that each QSWEEP takes at most $\mathcal{O}(D)$ rounds to finish. Since searching a ring consists of four QSWEEPs, the second step of our protocol takes $\mathcal{O}(D)$ rounds. A similar argument holds for the SHIFT procedure. The time complexity of step 4 is again bounded by the time that it takes the TriggerGiant to move back and forth a distance of at most $d_2 \leq 2D$ and thus, the claim follows.   □

Now we can combine the previous results to establish the total runtime of the EXPOSWEEP protocol.

Theorem 9. *The runtime of the EXPOSWEEP protocol is $\mathcal{O}(D + D^2/n + Df)$ for $f = n/13$ w.h.p.*

Proof. By Lemma 8 we know that the furthest level that is searched by the EXPOSWEEP protocol is $\mathcal{O}(D)$. As the failure of a single agent can cause at most one repetition of a EXPOSWEEP iteration, the maximum time that it takes the EXPOSWEEP protocol to recover from the failure of an agent is $\mathcal{O}(D)$. Thus, we can account for all failure-induced runtime costs by an additional term of $\mathcal{O}(Df)$. In the remainder of the proof, we will therefore only bound the runtime of EXPOSWEEP iterations without any failures.

Let us first examine the case when $D \in o(n)$, which means that the Explorers are still performing splits when the treasure is in range. Consider the ith iteration of EXPOSWEEP. Using Corollary 6, we can bound the maximum distance explored by the preceding iterations from below by $d(i) = \sum_{j=0}^{i-1} \Omega(2^j) = \Omega(2^i)$. The treasure will be explored in the smallest iteration i' such that $d(i') \geq D$. Observe that $i' \in c \log D$ for some constant $c > 0$. As iteration i explores at most level $d(i) + 2^i \in \mathcal{O}(2^i)$, we can bound the time required to complete iterations 1 to i' by

$$\sum_{i=0}^{c \log D} \mathcal{O}(2^i) \in \mathcal{O}(D) .$$

Now let us consider the case when $D \in \Omega(n)$. By Corollary 6, we know that after $\mathcal{O}(\log n)$ iterations of EXPOSWEEP, there are $\Omega(n)$ teams of Explorers. Hence, the treasure will be discovered after $\mathcal{O}(D/n)$ additional iterations. By Lemma 8, any iteration takes at most $\mathcal{O}(D)$ rounds. The total runtime is therefore

$$\sum_{i=0}^{c \log D} \mathcal{O}(2^i) + \sum_{i=c \log D+1}^{\mathcal{O}(D/n)} \mathcal{O}(D) = \mathcal{O}(D^2/n) .$$

Including the $\mathcal{O}(Df)$ term for the runtime costs caused by agent failures yields the theorem.   □

4   Conclusion

In this work we presented an algorithm that solves the ANTS problem in time $\mathcal{O}(D+D^2/n+Df)$ while tolerating $f \in \mathcal{O}(n)$ failures during the execution w.h.p. Our algorithm uses a combination of a constant number of fault-tolerant giants and $\Theta(n)$ Explorer agents, working together. The few "expensive" giants are used to manage the algorithm such that it is fault-tolerant, and the many "cheap" Explorers are responsible for solving the problem efficiently. It is an interesting open question whether one can solve the ANTS problem in a fault-tolerant way without making use of classic replication, and we conjecture that this is not the case, i.e., that some structure like giants is necessary to solve the ANTS problem in the presence of failures.

References

1. Albers, S., Henzinger, M.: Exploring Unknown Environments. SIAM Journal on Computing 29, 1164–1188 (2000)
2. Aleliunas, R., Karp, R.M., Lipton, R.J., Lovasz, L., Rackoff, C.: Random Walks, Universal Traversal Sequences, and the Complexity of Maze Problems. In: Proceedings of the 20th Annual Symposium on Foundations of Computer Science (SFCS), pp. 218–223 (1979)
3. Angluin, D., Aspnes, J., Diamadi, Z., Fischer, M.J., Peralta, R.: Computation in Networks of Passively Mobile Finite-State Sensors. Distributed Computing, 235–253 (March 2006)
4. Aspnes, J., Ruppert, E.: An Introduction to Population Protocols. In: Garbinato, B., Miranda, H., Rodrigues, L. (eds.) Middleware for Network Eccentric and Mobile Applications, pp. 97–120. Springer (2009)

5. Baeza-Yates, R.A., Culberson, J.C., Rawlins, G.J.E.: Searching in the Plane. Information and Computation 106, 234–252 (1993)
6. Deng, X., Papadimitriou, C.: Exploring an Unknown Graph. Journal of Graph Theory 32, 265–297 (1999)
7. Diks, K., Fraigniaud, P., Kranakis, E., Pelc, A.: Tree Exploration with Little Memory. Journal of Algorithms 51, 38–63 (2004)
8. Emek, Y., Langner, T., Uitto, J., Wattenhofer, R.: Solving the ANTS Problem with Asynchronous Finite State Machines. In: Esparza, J., Fraigniaud, P., Husfeldt, T., Koutsoupias, E. (eds.) ICALP 2014, Part II. LNCS, vol. 8573, pp. 471–482. Springer, Heidelberg (2014)
9. Feinerman, O., Korman, A.: Memory Lower Bounds for Randomized Collaborative Search and Implications for Biology. In: Aguilera, M.K. (ed.) DISC 2012. LNCS, vol. 7611, pp. 61–75. Springer, Heidelberg (2012)
10. Feinerman, O., Korman, A., Lotker, Z., Sereni, J.S.: Collaborative Search on the Plane Without Communication. In: Proceedings of the 31st ACM Symposium on Principles of Distributed Computing (PODC), pp. 77–86 (2012)
11. Fraigniaud, P., Ilcinkas, D., Peer, G., Pelc, A., Peleg, D.: Graph Exploration by a Finite Automaton. Theoretical Computer Science 345(2-3), 331–344 (2005)
12. Förster, K.-T., Wattenhofer, R.: Directed Graph Exploration. In: Baldoni, R., Flocchini, P., Binoy, R. (eds.) OPODIS 2012. LNCS, vol. 7702, pp. 151–165. Springer, Heidelberg (2012)
13. Lenzen, C., Lynch, N., Newport, C., Radeva, T.: Trade-offs between Selection Complexity and Performance when Searching the Plane without Communication. In: Proceedings of the 33rd Symposium on Principles of Distributed Computing, PODC (2014)
14. López-Ortiz, A., Sweet, G.: Parallel Searching on a Lattice. In: Proceedings of the 13th Canadian Conference on Computational Geometry (CCCG), pp. 125–128 (2001)
15. Mitzenmacher, M., Upfal, E.: Probability and Computing: Randomized Algorithms and Probabilistic Analysis. Cambridge University Press, New York (2005)
16. Panaite, P., Pelc, A.: Exploring Unknown Undirected Graphs. In: Proceedings of the 9th Annual ACM-SIAM Symposium on Discrete Algorithms (SODA), pp. 316–322 (1998)
17. Reingold, O.: Undirected Connectivity in Log-Space. Journal of the ACM (JACM) 55, 17:1–17:24 (2008)

Task Allocation in Ant Colonies

Alejandro Cornejo[1], Anna Dornhaus[2], Nancy Lynch[3], and Radhika Nagpal[1]

[1] Harvard University
School of Engineering and Applied Sciences
[2] University of Arizona
Ecology and Evolutionary Biology
[3] Massachusetts Institute of Technology
CSAIL

Abstract. In this paper we propose a mathematical model for studying the phenomenon of division of labor in ant colonies. Inside this model we investigate how simple task allocation mechanisms can be used to achieve an optimal division of labor.

We believe the proposed model captures the essential biological features of division of labor in ant colonies and is general enough to study a variety of different task allocation mechanisms. Within this model we propose a distributed randomized algorithm for task allocation that imposes only minimal requirements on the ants; it uses a constant amount of memory and relies solely on a primitive binary feedback function to sense the current labor allocation. We show that with high probability the proposed algorithm converges to a near-optimal division of labor in time which is proportional to the logarithm of the colony size.

1 Introduction

Task allocation in ant colonies is the process used by individual ant workers in a colony to select which task to perform in order to ensure the survival of the colony. Depending on the species the tasks typically include things like collecting food, feeding and caring for the offspring and defending the nest against intruders or parasites. The number of individuals allocated to each task varies over time in response to changes in the demand for different tasks.

From a biology perspective, there is an extensive body of empirical work studying the phenomenon of division of labor in ant colonies across different ant species [1–5]. Biologists have also proposed a number of individual behaviors that could produce the collective division of labor [1, 6–9]. It has been suggested that ant workers might select tasks based on different features, including their age [10, 11], body size [12, 13], genetic background [14], position in the nest [13, 15, 16], nutrition [17], in response to signals from other ants [10, 18], or by comparing internal response thresholds to the need to perform a particular task [19–21].

Most of these works were born out of a desire to understand what are the algorithms that may be used by ants, and not to compare the performance of

F. Kuhn (Ed.): DISC 2014, LNCS 8784, pp. 46–60, 2014.
© Springer-Verlag Berlin Heidelberg 2014

different algorithms. In addition, although in biology there is much work on optimization, there is not a tradition of explicitly separating the system model, the problem statement, and the algorithm being considered. This has made it difficult to generalize the results across different insect species. Most of the modeling studies do not attempt to compare how well different strategies perform, and obtaining any empirical observations for this purpose would be extremely hard (if not impossible). As a result, despite the wealth of empirical results, the trade-offs between different division of labor strategies remain poorly understood.

Our contributions are twofold. First, we describe a very general mathematical formulation for the problem of task allocation in ant colonies. Second, we propose a distributed algorithm that solves the task allocation problem efficiently and imposing only minimal assumptions on the capabilities of the individual ants. The algorithm we propose is modeled after a common strategy thought to be used by ants.

The model for task allocation proposed in this paper is meant to provide a rigorous theoretical framework under which new and existing mechanisms for division of labor can be formulated, studied and compared. In particular it allows modeling ant colonies consisting of workers that have different characteristics and formulate strategies that have different notions about of what is an optimal task allocation.

The randomized distributed algorithm for task allocation we propose requires constant memory with respect to the colony size, and assumes that ants can only sense the need for a particular task through a primitive binary feedback function. In more detail, we assume that each ant can use the information available in the environment (including sensing pheromones or other signaling methods between ants) to determine whether a particular task requires more workers or not. We show that using only this information and a constant amount of memory, ants can converge to a near-optimal task allocation with high probability, in a number of steps which is logarithmic in the size of the colony.

1.1 Related Work

As we argued before, from a biology standpoint there is a large body of work studying division of labor in ant colonies [1–5]. However existing models do not address the question of how well task allocation performs, and it is difficult to quantitatively compare the different proposed strategies.

We are not the first to leverage the tools of distributed computation to understand social insects and model biological processes. In particular the problem of ants foraging for food was recently studied in the distributed computing community [22–25]. In more detail, by modeling the environment as an infinite two-dimensional grid, upper [22] and lower [23] bounds were provided for the problem of ants collaboratively foraging for food on the environment without using communication. These bounds were recently generalized and improved in [25]

In a different vein, the parallels between the process of sensory organ pre-cursor selection in the fruit fly and the problem of finding a maximal independent set have been used to design novel bio-inspired algorithms for fundamental problems in distributed computation [26].

The problem of task allocation is an important and well-studied topic in computer science, particularly in the distributed computing community. One of the oldest incarnations, is that of multiprocessor scheduling [27, 28], a recent survey is available in [29]. Another related problem is that of the centralized k-server problem in which a collection of requests must be assigned to servers [30], distributed versions of this problem have also been considered [31].

The general formulation of task allocation considers some number p of processors that must cooperatively perform n tasks. The existing literature covers a great number of variants of this problem, processors and tasks might be identical or different; tasks might arrive online or may be known to the processors in advance; all processors may not be able to perform all tasks, or tasks may have to be performed in a certain order; processors may be susceptible to fail-stop (or other) failures; processors may communicate through shared memory, message passing, or may not rely on communication; etc. A recent and thorough review on the problem of distributed task allocation is available in [32].

There are several subtle differences between existing distributed task allocation algorithms and the task allocation algorithm for ant colonies that we consider. Namely the algorithm we consider only uses constant memory, does not require that ants to be capable of sensing the demand of each task or to estimate global parameters (like the size of the colony). A more fundamental difference between the problem statements is that the number of tasks we consider is a small constant with respect to the number of ants, and we are concerned with the allocation of proportions of workers to different tasks and not the allocation of individual workers to specific tasks.

2   System Model

We start by describing a mathematical model for the task allocation problem in ant colonies. For the sake of simplicity, throughout our discussion we use the term *energy* loosely without specifying the unit; however, any energy unit can be used (e.g., Joule) as long as it is used consistently throughout the definitions.

Task Allocation Problem

The task allocation problem concerns a set A of ants, and a set T of tasks. The size of an ant colony $|A|$ depends on the species and varies slowly through the lifetime of the colony, but can be considered fixed during short time intervals. Depending on the ant species typical colony sizes range from 10 to millions; in some species, each colony goes through this entire range through its lifetime. The number of tasks $|T|$ and their typical energy requirements also depend on the ant species considered. However the number of tasks performed by a particular species is constant and is not a function of the size of the colony.

For a task $\tau \in T$, a time $t \in \mathbb{R}_{\geq 0}$ and an ant $a \in A$ we define the following quantities.

- $d(\tau, t)$ is the energy demand for task τ at time t. This "demand" reflects how much work is currently needed in this task, and can be determined by environmental conditions, the colony size, the fraction of brood (ant offspring) vs workers, etc; although we do not attempt to uncover the relationship between the demand and these parameters.
- $e(\tau, a, t)$ is the energy that ant a can supply to task τ at time t when it is engaged in this task. This captures the effectiveness of an ant at a specific task, and may be determined by its morphological characteristics, as well its previous experience.

Task Assignment

A task assignment is a function y that assigns at each time t and for each ant $a \in A$ either one task $\tau \in T$ or no task. Formally $y(a, t) \in T \cup \{\bot\}$.

Given an assignment y we define $Y(\tau, t)$ as the set of ants assigned to task $\tau \in T$, and $I(t)$ is the set of ants that are not assigned to any task at time t. Formally that is:

$$Y(\tau, t) = \{a \in A : y(a, t) = \tau\}$$
$$I(t) = \{a \in A : y(a, t) = \bot\}$$

Thus by definition at any time t we have that $A = I(t) \cup \bigcup_{\tau \in T} Y(\tau, t)$. We will say an ant is *idle* at time t if it belongs to the set $I(t)$[1].

For succinctness we define the energy supply and the energy need at each task (both are defined in terms of a task assignment).

- $w(\tau, t) = \sum_{a \in Y(\tau, t)} e(\tau, a, t)$ is the energy supplied to task τ at time t, and it is the sum of the energy supplied by the individual ants assigned to task τ at time t.
- $q(\tau, t) = d(\tau, t) - w(\tau, t)$, if negative represents a surplus of energy at task τ, if positive represents a deficit of energy at task τ, and if zero then the task τ is in equilibrium.

A *satisfying* task assignment is one where no task has an energy deficit, formally at time t a *satisfying* task assignment is one where $q(\tau, t) \le 0$ for all $\tau \in T$. We say a task allocation problem is satisfiable if it has at least one satisfying task assignment.

We are mostly interested in satisfiable task allocation problems where the energy available at the colony far exceeds the energy demands of the tasks. This is likely consistent with what has been observed in real ant colonies [4], where even during periods where tasks have a very high demand (such as nest

---

[1] We believe this formulation is superior to the alternative of considering an additional "idle task", since task allocation algorithms will need to deal with this task differently, and it would unnecessarily complicate the definition of the demand and effectiveness functions to account for the "idle task".

migration) an important fraction of the ants remain idle where the rest perform the tasks necessary for the survival of the colony.

Ideally, we would like to find task assignments that achieve equilibrium for every task (i.e., where the energy demand equals the energy supply). However due to rounding issues this is not always possible, even when restricted to satisfiable task allocation problems. For instance, consider the case where the energy demand for each task is an odd number and the energy that can be exerted by each ant on any task is an even number. In this case, regardless of the number of ants assigned to each task, no task can be at equilibrium.

For this reason, we instead seek task assignments that minimize the squared difference between the energy demands and the energy supplied. Formally, an *optimal* task assignment is one that minimizes $\sum_{\tau \in T} q(\tau, t)^2$. Clearly a task assignment where all tasks are at equilibrium is optimal, but the opposite need not be true.

3   Restricted System Model

The model described in Section 2 was intentionally defined to be as broad as possible. This decision was made with the purpose of allowing others to study different kinds of task allocation algorithms and ant behaviors.

The following sections refine this broad model by imposing some additional restrictions. The algorithm we describe in Section 4 considers this restricted version.

Complexity of individual variation. Variation of the individual ant workers in the colony is captured by the parameter $e(\tau, a, t)$. This parameter can model complex effects such as a particular ant being worst at a task because of its physical characteristics, or an ant getting better at a particular task through experience. Unfortunately capturing even the simplest forms of individual variations in the colony using this parameter quickly results in an intractable task allocation formulation.

For instance, consider the case where, for each ant $a \in A$, the parameter $e(\tau, a, t)$ is the same for every task $\tau \in T$ and for every time $t \in \mathbb{R}_{\geq 0}$. In other words, the effectiveness of an ant does not depend on the task it performs and does not vary through time, but different ants may have different levels of effectiveness. This is the simplest form for the parameter $e(\tau, a, t)$ that still allows each individual in the colony to have a different level effectiveness.

In this case, even if we assume a centralized full-information setting, the problem of finding an optimal assignment of ants to tasks can be shown to be NP-complete. This remains true even if there are only wo tasks with equal demand since the set partition problem, known to be NP-complete [33], can be reduced to the task allocation problem. In general this problem is also hard to approximate and thus finding near-optimal solutions remains NP-hard [34]

The problem can be made tractable by placing additional restrictions, for instance by limiting the possible values of the demand for each task or the restricting different levels of effectiveness of ants. Regardless, real ant colonies may not converge on optimal or even near-optimal solutions, as long as the solutions they have arrived at through the evolutionary process allow colonies to survive and do better than their competitors.

For the above reasons, and in an effort to consider algorithms that more closely resemble those used by real ant colonies, in this paper we restrict our attention to task allocation problems without individual variation. There is empirical biological evidence that supports this decision: at least in some ant species [3], variation in task-specific efficiency among workers is not utilized by colonies. In other words, worker allocation to tasks in some cases is unrelated to their ability to perform them particularly well.

Concretely in the rest of the paper we assume that $e(\tau, a, t)$ is known and constant for all $\tau \in T, a \in A$ and $t \in \mathbb{R}^+$. Therefore for simplicity throughout the rest of the paper we will assume that both the energy demand $d(\tau, t)$ and energy supply $w(\tau, t)$ are measured in ant units.

Synchronous task allocation. For the purposes of this paper we will assume that time proceeds in synchronous lock-step rounds $i = 1, 2, \ldots$. A task allocation algorithm is a program that runs locally at each ant to produce a task assignment. During each round $i \in \mathbb{R}$, every ant $a \in A$ works at task $y(a, i)$. Before transitioning to the next round each ant may communicate with other ants, sense different parameters of the environment and perform some local computation to decide on what task to work on at the next round. The next section describes in detail exactly which environmental parameters are capable of sensing and/or communicating.

4   Allocation through Binary Feedback

In this section we propose and analyze a randomized distributed algorithm for task allocation that requires only a very primitive binary feedback function. In particular the algorithm we describe does not require that ants know the size of the colony $|A|$, the energy demand $d(\tau, i)$ of a task $\tau \in T$, or the energy supplied $w(\tau, i)$ to a task $\tau \in T$.

Instead, we assume that through local communication and by sensing their environment and their own state, each ant can determine for each round i and for each task $\tau \in T$ whether τ has too few or too many ants assigned to it. In other words, ants can determine only whether a task has a deficit or surplus of energy, but they are not able to quantify it. Specifically we assume that at each round i and for each task $\tau \in T$ ants can sense only a binary feedback function $f(\tau, i)$ where:

$$f(\tau, i) = \begin{cases} +1 & q(\tau, i) \geq 0, \\ -1 & q(\tau, i) < 0. \end{cases}$$

Recall that $q(\tau, i) = d(\tau, i) - w(\tau, i)$ is the difference between the energy demand for task τ at round i and the energy supplied for task τ at round i. Therefore the feedback function f is positive when the demand is greater than or equal to the energy supply, and is negative otherwise. Alternative feedback functions that do not distinguish sharply between having a surplus or deficit of energy are discussed in Section 5.

This restricted binary feedback model prevents the colony from trying to reach a perfect allocation in expectation in a single step, and thus the colony must rely on a progressive refinement strategy. Moreover, this binary feedback function does not provide enough information for the colony to determine if the demand is matched exactly by the energy supplied to that task, and having oscillations of the energy supply around the demand is inevitable.

4.1   Algorithm Description

This subsection describes a randomized distributed algorithm that relies only on the aforementioned binary feedback function to converge to a near-optimal task allocation.

Ants executing the algorithm can be in one of the five states RESTING, FIRSTRESERVE, SECONDRESERVE, TEMPWORKER and COREWORKER, they maintain a task $currentTask \in T \cup \{\bot\}$ and a table ϱ of potentials for each task $\tau \in T$. Initially ants start in the RESTING state with $currentTask = \bot$ and a potential of zero for every task $\forall \tau \in T, \varrho[\tau] = 0$. The paragraphs below describe each state in detail as well as the role of the potential table ϱ and the task $currentTask$.

Ants in the RESTING state are idle and use the potential table ϱ to choose a $currentTask$ and to determine when to start working (i.e., transition to a working state). The potential for every task is a two bit value $\{0, 1, 2, 3\}$ which is updated based on the output of the binary feedback function; specifically tasks with a deficit get their potential increased, and tasks with a surplus get a potential of zero. The $candidateList$ is defined as those tasks potential of 3, and with constant probability ants in the RESTING state will choose a task from the $candidateList$ uniformly at random and transition to the TEMPWORKER state. This is in the same spirit of the response-threshold strategies proposed by biologists [20].

Ants in the TEMPWORKER state and COREWORKER state work on the task specified by $currentTask$ (ants in all other states are idle). Specifically, ants in the TEMPWORKER state transition to the FIRSTRESERVE state if there is a surplus of energy in $currentTask$, and otherwise transition to the COREWORKER state. Ants in the COREWORKER state transition to the TEMPWORKER state if there is a surplus of energy in $currentTask$, and otherwise remain in the CORE-WORKER state. The result is that when there is a surplus of energy all ants in the TEMPWORKER state will become idle before any ants in the COREWORKER state.

Ants in the FIRSTRESERVE state and SECONDRESERVE are state idle, but unlike ants in the RESTING state (which are also idle) if they start working they

---

Algorithm 1. Binary-Threshold Algorithm

---

state ← RESTING, $currentTask \leftarrow \perp$, $\varrho[\tau] = 0, \forall \tau \in T$ ▷ Initialize
case state = RESTING

$$\forall \tau \in T, \varrho[\tau] \leftarrow \begin{cases} 0 & \text{if } f(\tau, i) < 0 \\ \max(\varrho[\tau] + 1, 3) & \text{if } f(\tau, i) > 0 \end{cases}$$

     candidateList ← $\{\tau \in T \mid \varrho[\tau] = 3\}$
     if candidateList $\neq \varnothing$ **then**
         with probability $\frac{1}{2}$ **do**
             $\forall \tau \in T, \varrho[\tau] \leftarrow 0$
             $currentTask \leftarrow$ random task from candidateList
             state ← TEMPWORKER
         end with
     end if
case state = FIRSTRESERVE
     if $f(currentTask, i) < 0$ **then**
         state ← RESTING
     else
         with probability $\frac{1}{2}$ **do**
             state ← TEMPWORKER
         otherwise
             state ← SECONDRESERVE
         end with
     end if
case state = SECONDRESERVE
     if $f(currentTask, i) < 0$ **then**
         state ← RESTING
     else
         state ← TEMPWORKER
     end if
case state = TEMPWORKER
     if $f(currentTask, i) < 0$ **then**
         state ← FIRSTRESERVE
     else
         state ← COREWORKER
     end if
case state = COREWORKER
     if $f(currentTask, i) < 0$ **then**
         state ← TEMPWORKER
     end if
end case

---

will do so at the task they were last working on. Ants in the FIRSTRESERVE state transition to the RESTING state if there is a surplus of energy in *currentTask*, and otherwise they transition to the TEMPWORKER state with constant probability or join the SECONDRESERVE state. Ants in the SECONDRESERVE state transition to the RESTING state if there is a surplus of energy *currentTask*, and otherwise transition to the TEMPWORKER state. Having two reserve states, one with a deterministic transition and the other with a probabilistic transition, allow us to recruit ants only from the reserved states instead of the entire idle population, which prevents big oscillations. Indeed, biologists [35–39] have provided compelling evidence that ants prefer to work on tasks they have become experienced in.

We remark that two reserve states is the minimum required for our recruitment process to work. The requirement that the potential of a task to reaches three before a resting ant starts working guarantees that resting ants do not start working on a task until ants in the reserved states for that task have already started working.

The number of bits of memory required by the algorithm to store the *state*, the *currentTask* and the potential table ϱ is $3 + \log_2 |T| + 2|T| \in \Theta(|T|)$, which is linear on the number of tasks and independent of the colony size $|A|$.

For simplicity whenever ants make a decision with constant probability, we will assume they make the decision with probability $\frac{1}{2}$ (i.e., as if each ant was flipping an independent unbiased coin). However by changing only the constants in the different lemmas and propositions, the same analysis works if ants are using any other constant probability.

4.2   Algorithm Analysis

Before describing the properties satisfied by the proposed algorithm we introduce some additional notation. For a round i we denote with REST_i, FIRST_i, SECOND_i, TEMP_i and CORE_i the set of ants that at the beginning of round i are in the state RESTING, FIRSTRESERVE, SECONDRESERVE, TEMPWORKER and COREWORKER respectively. Additionally for a round i and a task τ we denote with $\text{FIRST}_i(\tau)$, $\text{SECOND}_i(\tau)$, $\text{TEMP}_i(\tau)$ and $\text{CORE}_i(\tau)$ the set of ants that at the beginning of round i have τ as their *currentTask* and are in the state FIRSTRESERVE, SECONDRESERVE, TEMPWORKER and COREWORKER state respectively.

For the energy supplied by the colony to converge to the energy demanded by a task we must require that the demand remains "constant" for a sufficiently long period of time. Specifically, the demand of task τ is constant at a round i iff $d(\tau, i - 1) = d(\tau, i) = d(\tau, i + 1)$. Similarly, the demand for a task τ is constant during an interval $[i, i+k]$ iff for all $j \in [i, i+k]$ the demand for task τ is constant at round j.

Proof roadmap. In the following paragraphs we outline the steps used to prove that the proposed algorithms converges quickly to a near-optimal allocation.

First, we show (Lemma 1) that given an interval of constant demand where the number of ants in the colony is sufficient to satisfy the demand, then as long as no task has too big a surplus during the interval, then the probability that none of the tasks with a deficit becomes satisfied during the interval is exponentially small in the interval length.

Next (Lemma 4) we show that in an interval of constant demand, once a task transitions from having a deficit of ants to having a surplus of ants, this transition will keep happening every two or three rounds during that interval. We refer to these transitions as *oscillations*. We also show that each time an oscillation happens, with constant probability it is a constant fraction smaller than the previous oscillation in the interval.

We leverage the previous result to show (Lemma 5) that in an interval of constant demand with oscillations, the probability that by the end of the interval the size of the oscillations is greater than one ant is exponentially small on the interval length.

Finally we show (Theorem 6) that during an interval of constant demand of logarithmic length, with high probability by the end of the interval the number of workers assigned to each task only differs from the demand by at most one ant. Due to space constraints we only outline the proofs.

Informally, the following lemma shows that during an interval of constant demand and given sufficiently many ants, then if a set of tasks is satisfied without surplus and a set of tasks is unsatisfied, then it is likely that an additional task will become satisfied.

Lemma 1. Fix a constant $\varepsilon \in (0,1)$ and let $k \in \Theta(\log \frac{1}{\varepsilon})$.

If the demands for all tasks are constant during the interval $[i, i+k]$, and $|A| \geq \sum_{\tau \in T} (d(\tau, i) + 1)$, and there is a set of tasks $C \subseteq T$ such that $\forall \tau \in T \setminus C$ $d(\tau, i) > w(\tau, i)$ and $\forall \tau \in C, \forall j \in [i, i+k]$ $d(\tau, j) \leq w(\tau, j) \leq d(\tau, j) + 1$, then
$$\Pr\left[\forall \tau \in T \setminus C, \forall j \in [i, i+k]\, w(\tau, j) < d(\tau, j)\right] \leq \varepsilon.$$

The proof of this lemma argues that given the conditions assumed, then in order for all task to remain unsatisfied during the entire interval, at least one ant must repeatedly decide not to work at any task, despite the fact that there are tasks that need work; and the probability of this happening is exponentially small on the interval length.

For the remaining part of the analysis we will make use of Hoeffding's inequality. In addition we will also leverage the following proposition, which can be shown easily as a consequence of Hoeffding's inequality.

Proposition 2. Let $X_1, \ldots, X_k$ be independent random variables where $\Pr[X_i = 1] = \Pr[X_i = 0] = \frac{1}{2}$ and let $X = \sum_{i=1}^{k} X_i$. If $k \geq 2$ then $\Pr\left[\frac{1}{8}k \leq X \leq \frac{7}{8}k\right] \geq \frac{1}{2}$.

To simplify the analysis we introduce the following definition.

Definition 1. An *oscillation* happens for task τ at round i if $f(\tau, i) < 0$ and $f(\tau, i+1) > 0$.

Observe that if the demand for task τ is constant at round i and an oscillation occurs for task τ at round i, then the fact that $f(\tau, i) < 0$ implies that $d(\tau, i) < |\mathrm{CORE}_i(\tau) \cup \mathrm{TEMP}_i(\tau)|$ and the algorithm guarantees that by round $i + 1$ any temporary worker becomes idle and only core workers remain. This together with $f(\tau, i+1) > 0$ implies that $|\mathrm{CORE}_i(\tau)| < d(\tau, i)$. This is summarized in the next proposition.

Proposition 3. If there is an oscillation for task τ at round i and the demand for τ was constant at round i then $|\mathrm{CORE}_i(\tau)| < d(\tau, i) \leq |\mathrm{CORE}_i(\tau) \cup \mathrm{TEMP}_i(\tau)|$.

Observe that during an oscillation of task τ at round i the ants in $\mathrm{TEMP}_i(\tau)$ transition between working and being idle, while the ants in $\mathrm{CORE}_i(\tau)$ keep working through the oscillation, and there are never more than $\mathrm{CORE}_i(\tau) \cup \mathrm{TEMP}_i(\tau)$ ants working during the oscillation. Therefore given an oscillation for task τ at round i we say $|\mathrm{TEMP}_i(\tau)|$ is the *magnitude* of the oscillation, $|\mathrm{CORE}_i(\tau)|$ is the *low-value* of the oscillation, and $|\mathrm{CORE}_i(\tau) \cup \mathrm{TEMP}_i(\tau)|$ is the *high-value* of the oscillation.

The next lemma shows that if an oscillation happens during an interval of constant demand, it will happen again in two or three rounds. Moreover with constant probability the magnitude of the oscillation will become a constant fraction smaller than the previous oscillation by either increasing the low-value or decreasing the high-value.

Lemma 4. If there is an oscillation for task τ at round i and the demand for τ is constant during the interval $[i, i+4]$ then:
1. $\mathrm{SECOND}_{i+2}(\tau) \subseteq \mathrm{TEMP}_i(\tau)$ and if $|\mathrm{TEMP}_i(\tau)| \geq 2$ then with probability at least $\frac{1}{2}$ we have $\frac{1}{8}|\mathrm{TEMP}_i(\tau)| \leq |\mathrm{SECOND}_{i+2}(\tau)| \leq \frac{7}{8}|\mathrm{TEMP}_i(\tau)|$.
2. There is an oscillation for task τ either at
   a) round $i+2$ where $\mathrm{TEMP}_{i+2} = \mathrm{TEMP}_i(\tau) \setminus \mathrm{SECOND}_{i+2}(\tau)$ and $\mathrm{CORE}_{i+2}(\tau) = \mathrm{CORE}_i(\tau)$, or
   b) round $i + 3$ where $\mathrm{TEMP}_{i+3} = \mathrm{SECOND}_{i+2}(\tau)$ and $\mathrm{CORE}_{i+3}(\tau) = \mathrm{TEMP}_i(\tau) \cup \mathrm{CORE}_i(\tau) \setminus \mathrm{SECOND}_{i+2}(\tau)$.

The proof follows through a straightforward but detailed analysis of the state transitions made by the ants on the different states of the algorithm during the interval, relying on Proposition 2 to show that the magnitude of oscillations decreases by a constant fraction with constant probability.

The next lemma shows that given an interval with a constant demand and where the number of resting ants is greater than the number of ants required by a particular task, then the probability that the magnitude of the oscillations does not converge to one is exponentially small in the interval length.

Lemma 5. Fix $\varepsilon \in (0, 1)$ and let $k \in \Theta(\log |A| + \log \frac{1}{\varepsilon})$. If the demand for task τ is constant in the interval $[i, i+k]$ with oscillations for task τ at round i and $i + k$ then $\Pr\left[|\mathrm{TEMP}_{i+k}(\tau)| > 1\right] \leq \varepsilon$.

This lemma can be shown as a consequence of the results of Lemma 4 and following a standard concentration of measure argument.

We are finally ready to prove the main theorem of this paper. Namely, we show that if the colony has enough ants to satisfy the demand, then during an interval with a length which is logarithmic on the colony size and linear on the number of tasks, the probability that the difference between the energy supplied to each task, and the energy required by each task, is greater than one for any task, is exponentially small on the size of the colony.

Theorem 6. *Fix $\varepsilon \in (0,1)$ and let $k \in \Theta(|T|(\log \frac{1}{\varepsilon} + \log |A| + \log |T|))$.*
If demand is constant for all tasks in the interval $[i, i+k]$ and $|A| \geq \sum_{\tau \in T}(1 + d(\tau, i))$, then $\Pr[\forall \tau \in T \, d(\tau, i+k) - w(\tau, i+k)| \leq 1] \geq 1 - \varepsilon$.

To prove this theorem we go through a case analysis, showing that unless the work supplied by the colony has converged to be within one ant of the demand for every task, an additional task will converge after at most $\Theta(\log |A| + \log \frac{1}{\varepsilon})$; the additive $\log |T|$ term is a result of a union bound over the probability of not converging for each task.

Given that in real ant colonies we expect $|T|$ to be a constant, then by letting $\varepsilon = 1/|A|$ we get the following corollary.

Corollary 1. *Let $k \in \Theta(\log |A|)$. If the demand is constant for all tasks in the interval $[i, i+k]$ and the number of ants is enough to satisfy the demand, then with high probability ants converge to an allocation where $|d(\tau, i+k) - w(\tau, i+k)| \leq 1$.*

5 Conclusions and Future Work

We've shown that given certain assumptions, a fairly simple task allocation algorithm can achieve near-optimal performance in time which is logarithmic on the colony size. The assumptions we had to make were that individual workers did not differ in their ability to perform tasks, that workers could sense whether each task required more workers or not, and that workers use a small amount of memory about recently performed tasks and task demand. No sophisticated communication or sensing, nor long-term memory were required. Interestingly, we also argued that once variation among workers (in ability to perform tasks) is introduced, the task allocation problem becomes NP-hard. This may be the reason that such variation, when it is not correlated with clear categorizing factors such as body size, is not always optimally utilized by ants [3].

It is inherent in our algorithm, and probably any algorithm that does not allow ants to measure precisely how many workers are needed to fulfill a task, that the number of workers engaged in a task fluctuates around the optimum. In other words, the algorithm does not reach an optimal allocation immediately, but approaches it over time. Our model assumes that workers go through three stages between being fully uncommitted and idle (RESTING) and fully committed and working on a task (COREWORKER). These stages introduces some resistance in workers to being too frequently reallocated among different tasks, and thus reduces oscillations.

As future work, we would like to explore different, weaker binary feedback functions. For instance, one could consider a binary function which is only correct with probability $1 - \gamma$ for some $\gamma < \frac{1}{2}$. An alternative binary feedback function could return accurate values when the difference between the demand and the supply is different by a significant mount, but returns random values when the energy supply and demand are close to being in equilibrium. We conjecture that with little modifications the same algorithm would perform well in these circumstances, but it would provide slightly weaker guarantees (bigger oscillations) and require a more technical analysis.

In this paper the role of communication has been abstracted and is captured by the binary feedback function. We would also like to explore possible mechanisms by which said function could be implemented using explicit means of communication, such as pheromone or other signaling mechanisms.

What are the effects of varying the number of tasks on the properties of the algorithm. Specifically, the memory requirements of the proposed algorithm are linear in the number of tasks, and so is its convergence time. Can either of these be decreased to be logarithmic on the number of tasks?

References

[1] Camazine, S.: Self-organization in biological systems. Princeton University Press (2003)

[2] Seeley, T.D.: The wisdom of the hive: the social physiology of honey bee colonies. Harvard University Press (2009)

[3] Dornhaus, A.: Specialization does not predict individual efficiency in an ant. PLoS Biology 6(11), e285 (2008)

[4] Dornhaus, A., et al.: Why do not all workers work? Colony size and workload during emigrations in the ant Temnothorax albipennis. Behavioral Ecology and Sociobiology 63(1), 43–51 (2008)

[5] Pinter-Wollman, N., et al.: How is activity distributed among and within tasks in Temnothorax ants? Behavioral Ecology and Sociobiology 66(10), 1407–1420 (2012)

[6] Beekman, M., Sumpter, D.J.T., Ratnieks, F.L.W.: Phase transition between disordered and ordered foraging in Pharaoh's ants. Proceedings of the National Academy of Sciences 98(17), 9703–9706 (2001)

[7] Sumpter, D., Pratt, S.: A modelling framework for understanding social insect foraging. Behavioral Ecology and Sociobiology 53(3), 131–144 (2003)

[8] Myerscough, M.R., Oldroyd, B.P.: Simulation models of the role of genetic variability in social insect task allocation. Insectes Sociaux 51(2), 146–152 (2004)

[9] Lanan, M.C., et al.: The trail less traveled: individual decision-making and its effect on group behavior. PloS One 7(10), e47976 (2012)

[10] Robinson, G.E.: Regulation of division of labor in insect societies. Annual Review of Entomology 37(1), 637–665 (1992)

[11] Seid, M.A., Traniello, J.F.A.: Age-related repertoire expansion and division of labor in Pheidole dentata (Hymenoptera: Formicidae): a new perspective on temporal polyethism and behavioral plasticity in ants. Behavioral Ecology and Sociobiology 60(5), 631–644 (2006)

[12] Wilson, E.O.: Caste and division of labor in leaf-cutter ants (Hymenoptera: Formicidae: Atta). Behavioral Ecology and Sociobiology 7(2), 157–165 (1980)

[13] Jandt, J.M., Dornhaus, A.: Spatial organization and division of labour in the bumblebee Bombus impatiens. Animal Behaviour 77(3), 641–651 (2009)

[14] Robinson, G.E., Grozinger, C.M., Whitfield, C.W.: Sociogenomics: social life in molecular terms. Nature Reviews Genetics 6(4), 257–270 (2005)

[15] Sendova-Franks, A.B., Franks, N.R.: Spatial relationships within nests of the ant Leptothorax unifasciatus and their implications for the division of labour. Animal Behaviour 50(1), 121–136 (1995)

[16] Tofts, C., Franks, N.R.: Doing the right thing: ants, honeybees and naked mole-rats. Trends in Ecology & Evolution 7(10), 346–349 (1992)

[17] Toth, A.L., Robinson, G.E.: Worker nutrition and division of labour in honeybees. Animal Behaviour 69(2), 427–435 (2005)

[18] Gordon, D.M.: The organization of work in social insect colonies. Complexity 8(1), 43–46 (2002)

[19] Weidenmüller, A.: The control of nest climate in bumblebee (Bombus terrestris) colonies: interindividual variability and self reinforcement in fanning response. Behavioral Ecology 15(1), 120–128 (2004)

[20] Bonabeau, E., Theraulaz, G., Deneubourg, J.-L.: Quantitative study of the fixed threshold model for the regulation of division of labour in insect societies. Proceedings of the Royal Society of London. Series B: Biological Sciences 263(1376), 1565–1569 (1996)

[21] Ravary, F., et al.: Individual experience alone can generate lasting division of labor in ants. Current Biology 17(15) (2007)

[22] Feinerman, O., et al.: Collaborative search on the plane without communication. In: Proceedings of the 2012 ACM Symposium on Principles of Distributed Computing, pp. 77–86. ACM (2012)

[23] Feinerman, O., Korman, A.: Memory lower bounds for randomized collaborative search and implications for biology. In: Aguilera, M.K. (ed.) DISC 2012. LNCS, vol. 7611, pp. 61–75. Springer, Heidelberg (2012)

[24] Korman, A.: Theoretical distributed computing meets biology. In: Proceedings of the 4th International Workshop on Theoretical Aspects of Dynamic Distributed Systems, p. 7. ACM (2012)

[25] Lenzen, C., Lynch, N., Newport, C., Radeva, T.: Trade-offs between Selection Complexity and Performance when Searching the Plane without Communication. In: Proceedings of the 2012 ACM Symposium on Principles of Distributed Computing. Springer (2014)

[26] Afek, Y., et al.: A biological solution to a fundamental distributed computing problem. Science 331(6014), 183–185 (2011)

[27] Liu, C.L., Layland, J.W.: Scheduling algorithms for multiprogramming in a hard-real-time environment. Journal of the ACM (JACM) 20(1), 46–61 (1973)

[28] Dertouzos, M.L., Mok, A.K.: Multiprocessor online scheduling of hard-real-time tasks. IEEE Transactions on Software Engineering 15(12), 1497–1506 (1989)

[29] Davis, R.I., Burns, A.: A survey of hard real-time scheduling for multiprocessor systems. ACM Computing Surveys (CSUR) 43(4), 35 (2011)

[30] Fiat, A., Rabani, Y., Ravid, Y.: Competitive k-server algorithms. In: Proceedings of the 31st Annual Symposium on Foundations of Computer Science, pp. 454–463. IEEE (1990)

[31] Bartal, Y., Rosen, A.: The distributed k-server problem-a competitive distributed translator for k-server algorithms. In: Proceedings of the 33rd Annual Symposium on Foundations of Computer Science, pp. 344–353. IEEE (1992)

[32] Georgiou, C., Shvartsman, A.A.: Cooperative Task-Oriented Computing: Algorithms and Complexity. Synthesis Lectures on Distributed Computing Theory 2(2), 1–167 (2011)

[33] Garey Michael, R., Johnson, D.S.: Computers and Intractability: A guide to the theory of NP-completeness. WH Freeman & Co., San Francisco (1979)

[34] Shmoys, D.B., Tardos, É.: An approximation algorithm for the generalized assignment problem. Mathematical Programming 62(1-3), 461–474 (1993)

[35] Deneubourg, J.-L., et al.: Self-organization mechanisms in ant societies (II): learning in foraging and division of labor. In: From Individual to Collective Behavior in Social Insects, p. 177 (1987)

[36] Merkle, D., Middendorf, M.: Dynamic polyethism and competition for tasks in threshold reinforcement models of social insects. Adaptive Behavior 12(3-4), 251–262 (2004)

[37] Plowright, R.C., Plowright, C.M.S.: Elitism in social insects: a positive feedback model. In: Interindividal Behavioral Variability in Social Insects, pp. 419–431 (1988)

[38] Theraulaz, G., Bonabeau, E., Denuebourg, J.N.: Response threshold reinforcements and division of labour in insect societies. Proceedings of the Royal Society of London. Series B: Biological Sciences 265(1393), 327–332 (1998)

[39] Tripet, F., Nonacs, P.: Foraging for Work and Age-Based Polyethism: The Roles of Age and Previous Experience on Task Choice in Ants. Ethology 110(11), 863–877 (2004)

Communication-Efficient Randomized Consensus

Dan Alistarh[1], James Aspnes[2], Valerie King[3], and Jared Saia[4]

[1] Microsoft Research, Cambridge, UK
dan.alistarh@microsoft.com
[2] Yale University, Department of Computer Science
aspnes@cs.yale.edu
[3] University of Victoria, Simons Institute for the Theory of Computing, Berkeley,
Institute for Advanced Study, Princeton
val@cs.uvic.ca
[4] University of New Mexico, Department of Computer Science
saia@cs.unm.edu

Abstract. We consider the problem of consensus in the challenging *classic* model. In this model, the adversary is adaptive; it can choose which processors crash at any point during the course of the algorithm. Further, communication is via asynchronous message passing: there is no known upper bound on the time to send a message from one processor to another, and all messages and coin flips are seen by the adversary.

We describe a new randomized consensus protocol with expected message complexity $O(n^2 \log^2 n)$ when fewer than $n/2$ processes may fail by crashing. This is an almost-linear improvement over the best previously known protocol, and within logarithmic factors of a known $\Omega(n^2)$ message lower bound. The protocol further ensures that no process sends more than $O(n \log^3 n)$ messages in expectation, which is again within logarithmic factors of optimal. We also present a generalization of the algorithm to an arbitrary number of failures t, which uses expected $O(nt + t^2 \log^2 t)$ total messages. Our protocol uses messages of size $O(\log n)$, and can therefore scale to large networks.

Our approach is to build a message-efficient, resilient mechanism for aggregating individual processor votes, implementing the message-passing equivalent of a weak shared coin. Roughly, in our protocol, a processor first announces its votes to small groups, then propagates them to increasingly larger groups as it generates more and more votes. To bound the number of messages that an individual process might have to send or receive, the protocol progressively increases the weight of generated votes. The main technical challenge is bounding the impact of votes that are still "in flight" (generated, but not fully propagated) on the final outcome of the shared coin, especially since such votes might have different weights. We achieve this by leveraging the structure of the algorithm, and a technical argument based on martingale concentration bounds. Overall, we show that it is possible to build an efficient message-passing implementation of a shared coin, and in the process (almost-optimally) solve the classic consensus problem in the asynchronous message-passing model.

1 Introduction

Consensus [28, 29] is arguably the most well-studied problem in distributed computing. The FLP impossibility result [21], showing that consensus could not be achieved

F. Kuhn (Ed.): DISC 2014, LNCS 8784, pp. 61–75, 2014.

deterministically in an asynchronous message-passing system with even one crash failure, sparked a flurry of research on overcoming this fundamental limitation, either by adding timing assumptions, e.g. [19], employing failure detectors, e.g. [17], or by relaxing progress conditions to allow for *randomization*, e.g. [13]. A significant amount of research went into isolating time and space complexity bounds for randomized consensus in the shared-memory model, e.g. [4, 5, 9, 10, 12, 15, 20], developing elegant and technically complex tools in the process. As a result, the time complexity of consensus in asynchronous shared memory is now well characterized: the tight bound on total number of steps is $\Theta(n^2)$ [12], while the individual step bound is $\tilde{\Theta}(n)$ [5].[1]

Somewhat surprisingly, the complexity of randomized consensus in the other core model of distributed computing, the *asynchronous message-passing model*, is much less well understood. In this model, communication is via full-information, asynchronous message passing: there is no known upper bound on the time to send a message from one processor to another, and all messages are seen by the adversary. Further, as in the shared memory model, the adversary is adaptive; it can choose which processors crash at any point during the course of the algorithm. We refer to this as the *classic* model.

While simulations exist [11] allowing shared-memory algorithms to be translated to message-passing, their overhead is at least linear in the number of nodes. It is therefore natural to ask if message-efficient solutions for randomized consensus can be achieved, and in particular if quadratic shared-memory communication cost for consensus can be also achieved in message-passing systems against a strong, adaptive adversary.

In this paper, we propose a new randomized consensus protocol with expected message complexity $O(n^2 \log^2 n)$ against a strong (adaptive) adversary, in an asynchronous message-passing model in which less than $n/2$ processes may fail by crashing. This is an almost-linear improvement over the best previously known protocol. Our protocol is also *locally-efficient*, ensuring that no process sends or receives more than expected $O(n \log^3 n)$ messages, which is within logarithmic factors of the linear lower bound [12]. We also provide a generalization to an arbitrary number of failures $t < n/2$, which uses $O(nt + t^2 \log^2 t)$ messages.

Our general strategy is to construct a **message-efficient weak shared coin**. A weak shared coin with parameter $\delta > 0$ is a protocol in which for each possible return value ± 1, there is a probability of at least δ that all processes return that value. We then show that this shared coin can be used in a message-efficient consensus protocol modeled on a classic shared-memory protocol of Chandra [16].

Since early work by Bracha and Rachman [15], implementations of weak shared coins for shared-memory systems with an adaptive adversary have generally been based on voting. If the processes between them generate n^2 votes of ± 1, then the absolute value of the sum of these votes will be at least n with constant probability. If this event occurs, then even if the adversary hides $\Theta(n)$ votes by crashing processes, the total vote seen by the survivors will still have the same sign as the actual total vote.

Such algorithms can be translated to a message-passing setting directly using the classic Attiya-Bar-Noy-Dolev (ABD) simulation [11]. The main idea of the simulation is that a write operation to a register is simulated by distributing a value to a majority of the processes (this is possible because of the assumption that a majority of the processes do not fail). Any subsequent read operation contacts a majority of the processes, and

---

[1] We consider a model with n processes, $t < n/2$ of which may fail by crashing. The $\tilde{\Theta}$ notation hides logarithmic factors.

because the majorities overlap, this guarantees that any read sees the value of previous writes.

The obvious problem with this approach is that its message complexity is high: because ABD uses $\Theta(n)$ messages to implement a write operation, and because each vote must be written before the next vote is generated if we are to guarantee that only $O(n)$ votes are lost, the cost of this direct translation is $\Theta(n^3)$ messages. Therefore, the question is whether this overhead can be eliminated.

Our Approach. To reduce both total and local message complexity, we employ two new ingredients.

The first is an algorithmic technique to reduce the message complexity of distributed vote counting by using a binary tree of process groups called **cohorts**, where each leaf corresponds to a process, and each internal node represents a cohort consisting of all processes in the subtree. Instead of announcing each new vote to all participants, new ± 1 votes are initially only announced to small cohorts at the bottom of the tree, but are propagated to increasingly large cohorts as more votes are generated. As the number of votes grows larger, the adversary must crash more and more processes to hide them. This generalizes the one-crash-one-vote guarantee used in shared-memory algorithms to a many-crashes-many-votes approach.

At the same time, this technique renders the algorithm message-efficient. Given a set of generated votes, the delayed propagation scheme ensures that each vote accounts for exactly one update at the leaf, $1/2$ updates (amortized) at the 2-neighborhood, and in general, $1/2^i$ (amortized) updates at the ith level of the tree. Practically, since the ith level cohort has 2^i members, the propagation cost of a vote is exactly one message per tree level. In total, that is $\log n$ messages per vote, amortized.

A limitation of the above scheme is that a fast process might have to generate all the $\Theta(n^2)$ votes itself in order to decide, which would lead to high individual message complexity. The second technical ingredient of our paper is a procedure for assigning increasing weight to a processes' votes, which reduces individual complexity. This general idea has previously been used to reduce individual work for shared-memory randomized consensus [5,7,10]; however, we design and analyze a new weighting scheme that is customized for our vote-propagation mechanism.

In our scheme, each process doubles the weight of its votes every $4n \log n$ votes, and we run the protocol until the total reported variance—the sum of the squares of the weights of all reported votes—exceeds $n^2 \log n$. Intuitively, this allows a process running alone to reach the threshold quickly, reducing per-process message complexity. This significantly complicates the termination argument, since a large number of generated votes, of various weights, could be still making their way to the root at the time when a process first notices the termination condition. We show that, with constant probability, this drift is not enough to influence the sign of the sum, by carefully bounding the weight of the extra votes via the structure of the algorithm and martingale concentration bounds. We thus obtain a constant-bias weak shared coin. The bounds on message complexity follow from bounds on the number of votes generated by any single process or by all the processes together before the variance threshold is reached.

We convert the shared coin construction into a consensus algorithm via a simple framework inspired by Chandra's shared-memory consensus protocol [16], which in turn uses ideas from earlier consensus protocols of Chor, Israeli, and Li [18] and Aspnes and Herlihy [9]. Roughly, we associate each of the two possible decision values with a message-passing implementation of a max register [6, 8], whose value is incremented by the "team" of processes obtaining that value from the shared coin. If a process sees that its own team has fallen behind, it switches to the other team, and once one of the max register's values surpasses the other by two, the corresponding team wins. Ties are broken (eventually) by having processes that do not observe a clear leader execute a weak shared coin. This simple protocol maintains the asymptotic complexity of the shared coin in expectation.

Finally, we present a more efficient variant of the protocol for the case where $t = o(n)$, based on the observation that we can "deputize" a subset of $2t + 1$ of the processes to run the consensus protocol, and broadcast their result to all n processes. The resulting protocol has total message complexity $O(nt + t^2 \log^2 t)$, and $O(n + t \log^3 t)$ individual message complexity.

Overall, we show that it is possible to build message-efficient weak shared coins and consensus in asynchronous message-passing systems. Our vote counting construction implements a message-efficient, asynchronous approximate trigger counter [25], which may be of independent interest. An interesting aspect of our constructions is that message sizes are small: since processes only communicate vote counts, messages only require $O(\log n)$ bits of communication.

2 System Model and Problem Statement

We consider the standard asynchronous message-passing model, in which n processes communicate with each other by sending messages through channels. We assume that there are two uni-directional channels between any pair of processes. Communication is *asynchronous*, in that messages can be arbitrarily delayed by a channel, and in particular may be delivered in arbitrary order. However, we assume that messages are not corrupted by the channel.

Computation proceeds in a sequence of *steps*. At each step, a process checks incoming channels for new messages, then performs local computation, and sends new messages. A process may become *faulty*, in which case it ceases to perform local computation and to send new messages. A process is *correct* if it takes steps infinitely often during the execution. We assume that at most $t < n/2$ processes may be faulty during the execution.

Message delivery and process faults are assumed to be controlled by a *strong (adaptive)* adversary. At any time during the computation, the adversary can examine the entire state of the system (in particular, the results of process coinflips), and decide on process faults and messages to be delivered.

The *(worst-case) message complexity* of an algorithm is simply the maximum, over all adversarial strategies, of the total number of messages sent by processes running the algorithm. Without loss of generality, we assume that the adversary's goal is to maximize the message complexity of our algorithm.

In the *(binary) randomized consensus* problem, each process starts with an input in $\{0, 1\}$, and returns a decision in $\{0, 1\}$. A correct protocol satisfies *agreement*: all processes that return from the protocol choose the same decision, *validity*: the decision must equal some process's input, and *probabilistic termination*: every non-faulty process returns after a finite number of steps, with probability 1.

3   Related Work

The first shared-memory protocol for consensus was given by Chor, Israeli, and Li [18] for a weak adversary model, and is based on a race between processors to impose their proposals. Abrahamson [1] gave the first wait-free consensus protocol for a strong adversary, taking exponential time. Aspnes and Herlihy [9] gave the first polynomial-time protocol, which terminates in $O(n^4)$ expected total steps. Subsequent work, e.g. [4, 10, 15, 30], continued to improve upper and lower bounds for this problem, until Attiya and Censor [12] showed a tight $\Theta(n^2)$ bound on the total number of steps for asynchronous randomized consensus. In particular, their lower bound technique implies an $\Omega(t(n-t))$ total message complexity lower bound and a $\Omega(t)$ individual message complexity lower bound for consensus in the asynchronous message-passing model. Our $(n/2 - 1)$-resilient algorithms match both lower bounds within logarithmic factors, while the t-resilient variant matches the first lower bound within logarithmic factors.

To our knowledge, the best previously known upper bound for consensus in asynchronous message-passing requires $\Theta(n^3)$ messages. This is obtained by simulating the elegant shared-memory protocol of Attiya and Censor-Hillel [12], using the simulation from [11]. A similar bound can be obtained by applying the same simulation to an $O(n)$-individual-work algorithm of Aspnes and Censor [7].

In the message passing model, significant work has focused on the problem of Byzantine agreement, which is identical to consensus except that the adversary *controls* up to t processes, and can cause them to deviate arbitrarily from the protocol. In 1983, Fischer, Lynch and Patterson [21] showed that no deterministic algorithm could solve consensus, and hence Byzantine agreement, in the classic model. In the same year, Ben-Or gave a randomized algorithm for Byzantine agreement which required an expected exponential communication rounds and number of messages [13]. His algorithm tolerated $t < n/5$. Subsequent work extended this idea in two directions: to solve message-passing Byzantine agreement faster and with higher resilience, and to solve agreement wait-free, in asynchronous shared-memory tolerating crash failures.

Resilience against Byzantine faults was improved to $t < n/3$ in 1984 by Bracha [14]. However, the communication rounds and number of messages remained exponential in expectation. This resilience is the best possible for randomized Byzantine agreement [24]. In 2013, King and Saia gave the first algorithm for Byzantine agreement in the classic model with expected polynomial communication rounds and number of messages [26]. Their algorithm required in expectation $O(n^{2.5})$ communication rounds, $O(n^{6.5})$ messages, and $O(n^{7.5})$ bits sent. It tolerated $t < n/500$. Unfortunately, local computation time was exponential. In 2014, the same authors achieved polynomial computation time. However, the new algorithm required expected $O(n^3)$ communication rounds, $O(n^7)$ messages, and $O(n^8)$ bits sent. Further, the resilience decreased to $t < 0.000028n$ [27].

4   A Message-Passing Max Register

To coordinate the recording of votes within a group, we use a message-passing max register [6]. The algorithm is adapted from [8], and is in turn based on the classic ABD implementation of a message-passing register [11]. The main change from [8] is that we allow for groups consisting of $g < n$ processes. Recall that a max register maintains a value v, which is read using the *MaxRead* operation, and updated using the *MaxUpdate* operation. A $MaxUpdate(u)$ operation changes the value only if u is higher than the current value v.

Description. We consider a group G of g processes, which implement the max register R collectively. Each process p_i in the group maintains a current value estimate v_i locally. The communicate procedure [11] broadcasts a request to all processes in the group G, and waits for at least $\lceil g/2 \rceil$ replies.[2]

To perform a MaxRead, the process communicates a $MaxRead(R)$ request to all other processes, setting its value v_i to be the maximum value received. Before returning this value, the process communicates a $MaxReadACK(R, v_i)$ message. All processes receiving such a message will update their current estimate of R, if this value was less than v_i. If it receives at least $\lceil g/2 \rceil$ replies, the caller returns v_i as the value read. This ensures that, if a process p_i returns v_i, no other process may later return a smaller value for R.

A MaxUpdate with input u is similar to a MaxRead: the process first communicates a $MaxUpdate(R, u)$ message to the group, and waits for at least $\lceil g/2 \rceil$ replies. Process p_i sets its estimate v_i to the maximum between u and the maximum value received in the first round, before communicating this value once more in a second broadcast round. Again, all processes receiving this message will update their current estimate of R, if necessary. The algorithm ensures the following properties.

Lemma 1. *The max register algorithm above implements a linearizable max register. If the communicate procedure broadcasts to a group G of processes of size g, then the message complexity of each operation is $O(g)$, and the operation succeeds if at most $\lfloor g/2 \rfloor$ processes in the group are faulty.*

5 The Weak Shared Coin Algorithm

We now build a message-efficient asynchronous weak shared coin. Processes generate random votes, whose weight increases over time, and progressively communicate them to groups of nodes of increasing size. This implements a shared coin with constant bias, which in turn can be used to implement consensus.

Vote Propagation. The key ingredient is a message-efficient construction of an approximate asynchronous vote counter, which allows processes to maintain an estimate of the total number of votes generated, and of their sum and variance. The distributed vote counter is structured as a binary tree, where each process is associated with a leaf. Each subtree of height h is associated with a *cohort* of 2^h processes, corresponding to its leaves. To each such subtree s, we associate a max register R_s, implemented as described above, whose value is maintained by all the processes in the corresponding cohort. For example, the value at each leaf is only maintained by the associated process, while the root value is tracked by all processes.

The max register R_s corresponding to the subtree rooted at s maintains three values: the *count*, an estimate of the number of votes generated in the subtree, *total*, an estimate

---

[2] Since $t < n/2$ processes may crash, and g may be small, a process may block while waiting for replies. This only affects the progress of the protocol, but not its safety. Our shared coin implementation will partition the n processes into max register groups, with the guarantee that some groups always make progress.

```
 1  Let K = n² log₂ n
 2  Let T = 4n log₂ n
 3  count ← 0
 4  var ← 0
 5  total ← 0
 6  for k ← 1, 2, ..., ∞ do
 7  │   Let wₖ = 2^⌊(k−1)/T⌋
 8  │   Let vote = ±wₖ with equal probability
 9  │   count ← count + 1
10  │   var ← var + wₖ²
11  │   total ← total + vote
12  │   Write ⟨count, var, total⟩ to max register for my leaf
13  │   for j ← 1 ... log₂ n do
14  │   │   if 2ʲ does not divide k then
15  │   │   │   break
16  │   │   Let s be my level-j ancestor, with children s_ℓ and s_r
17  │   │   in parallel do
        │   │       /* read left and right counts                       */
18  │   │   │   ⟨count_ℓ, var_ℓ, total_ℓ⟩ ← ReadMax(s_ℓ)
19  │   │   │   ⟨count_r, var_r, total_r⟩ ← ReadMax(s_r)
        │   │       /* update the parent                                 */
20  │   │   WriteMax(s, ⟨count_ℓ + count_r, var_ℓ + var_r, total_ℓ + total_r⟩)
21  │   if n divides k then
22  │   │   ⟨count_root, var_root, total_root⟩ ← ReadMax(root)
        │   │       /* if the root variance exceeds the threshold        */
23  │   │   if var_root ≥ K then
24  │   │   │   return sgn(total_root)          /* return sign of root total */
```

Algorithm 1: Shared coin using increasing votes

of the sum of generated votes, and *var*, an estimate of the variance of the generated votes. Values are ordered only by the first component. Practically, the implementation is identical to the max register described in the previous section, except that whenever sending the *count*, processes also send the associated *total* and *var*. Processes always adopt the tuple of maximum *count*. If a process receives two tuples with the same *count* but different *total/var* components, they adopt the one with the maximum total.

A process maintains max register estimates for each subtree it is part of. Please see Algorithm 1 for the pseudocode. In the kth iteration of the shared coin, the process generates a new vote with weight $\pm w_k$ chosen as described in the next paragraph. After generating the vote, the process will propagate its current set of votes up to level r, the highest power of two which divides k (line 15). At each level from 1 (the leaf's parent) up to r, the process reads the max registers left and right children, and updates the $\langle count, total, var \rangle$ of the parent to be the sum of the corresponding values at the child max registers (lines 17–20).

If n divides k, then the process also checks the count at the root. If the root variance count is greater than the threshold of K votes, the process returns the sign of the root total as its output from the shared coin. Otherwise, the process continues to generate votes.

Vote Generation. Each process generates votes with values $\pm w_k$ in a series of epochs, each epoch consisting of $T = 4n \log_2 n$ loop iterations. Within each epoch, all votes have the same weight, and votes are propagated up the tree of max registers using the schedule described above. At the start of a new epoch, the weight of the votes doubles. This ensures that only $O(\log n)$ epochs are needed until a single process can generate enough variance by itself to overcome the offsets between the observed vote and the generated vote due to delays in propagation up the tree.

Because votes have differing weights, we track the total variance of all votes included in a max register in addition to their number, and continue generating votes until this total variance exceeds a threshold $K = n^2 \log_2 n$, at which point the process returns the sign of the root total (line 24).

6   Algorithm Analysis

We prove that the algorithm in Section 5 implements a correct weak shared coin. We first analyze some of the properties of the tree-based vote counting structure. For simplicity, we assume that the number of processes n is a power of two. Due to space constraints, the complete argument is given in the full version of the paper [3].

Vote Propagation. The algorithm is based on the idea that, as processes take steps, counter values for the cohorts get increased, until, eventually, the root counter value surpasses the threshold, and processes start to return. We first provide a way of associating a set of generated votes to each counter value.

We say that a process p_i counts a number x_i of (consecutive) locally-generated votes to node s if, after generating the last such vote, process p_i updates the max register at s in its loop iteration. We prove that this procedure has the following property:

Lemma 2. *Consider a subtree rooted at node s with ℓ leaves, corresponding to member processes $q_1, q_2, \ldots, q_\ell$. Let $x_1, x_2, \ldots, x_\ell$ be the number of votes most recently counted by processes $q_1, q_2, \ldots, q_\ell$ at node s, respectively. Then the value of the* count *component of the max register at s is at least $\sum_{m=1}^{\ell} x_m$.*

Proof Strategy. The proof can be divided into three steps. The first shows that the coin construction offers a good approximation of the generated votes, i.e. the total vote U^t observed in the root max register at any time t is close to the actual total generated vote V^t at the same time. The second step shows that when the threshold K is crossed at some time t, the **common votes total** $|V^t|$ is likely to be far away from 0. The last step shows that, for any subsequent time t', the combination of the approximation slack $U^{t'} - V^{t'}$ and any **extra votes** $V^{t'} - V^t$ observed by a particular process at time t' will not change the sign of the total vote.

The first step involves a detailed analysis of what votes may be omitted from the visible total combined with an extension of the Azuma-Hoeffding inequality [10]; the second step requires use of a martingale Central Limit Theorem [23, Theorem 3.2]; the last follows from an application of Kolmogorov's inequality. (For background on martingales, we point the reader to [22].) We begin by stating a few technical claims.

Lemma 3. *Fix some execution of Algorithm 1, let n_i be the number of votes generated by process p_i during this execution, and let w_{n_i} be the weight of the n_i-th vote. Then*

1. $\sum_{i=1}^{n} \sum_{j=1}^{n_i} w_j^2 \leq \frac{K+2n^2}{1-8n/T} = O(n^2 \log n)$.
2. $w_{n_i} \leq \sqrt{1 + \frac{4K+8n^2}{T-8n}} = O(\sqrt{n})$.
3. *For all* j, $n_j = O(n \log^2 n)$.
4. $\sum_i w_{n_i}^2 \leq n + \frac{4K+8n^2}{T-8n} = O(n)$.
5. $\sum_i n_i = O(n^2 \log n)$.

For any adversary strategy $\mathcal{A}$, let $\tau_{\mathcal{A}}$ be a stopping time corresponding to the first time t at which $U^{\text{root}}[t].\text{var} \geq K$. We will use a martingale Central Limit Theorem to show that $V^{\text{root}}[\tau_{\mathcal{A}}].\text{total}$ converges to a normal distribution as n grows, when suitably scaled. This will then be used to show that all processes observe a population of common votes whose total is likely to be far from zero. The notation $X \xrightarrow{p} Y$ means that X converges in probability to Y, and $Y \xrightarrow{d} Y$ means that X converges in distribution to Y. We show that the following convergence holds.

Lemma 4. *Let $\{\mathcal{A}_n\}$ be a family of adversary strategies, one for each number of processes $n \in \mathbb{N}$. Let $\tau_n = \tau_{\mathcal{A}_n}$ be as above. Then*

$$\frac{V^{\text{root}}[\tau_n].\text{total}}{\sqrt{K}} \xrightarrow{d} N(0,1). \tag{1}$$

Once this is established, for each subtree s and time t_s, let $D^s[t_s] = V^s[t_s].\text{total} - U^s[t_s].\text{total}$ be the difference between the generated votes in s at time t_s and the votes reported to the max register corresponding to s at time t_s. Let s_ℓ and s_r be the left and right subtrees of s, and let t_{s_ℓ} and t_{s_r} be the times at which the values added to produce $U^s[t_s].\text{total}$ were read from these subtrees. Recursing over all proper subtrees of s, we obtain that

$$D^s[t_s] = V^s[t_s].\text{total} - U^s[t_s].\text{total} = \sum_{s'} \left(V^{s'}[t_{\text{parent}(s')}].\text{total} - V^{s'}[t_{s'}].\text{total} \right),$$

where s' ranges over all proper subtrees of s.

To bound this sum, we consider each (horizontal) layer of the tree separately, and observe that the missing interval of votes $\left(V^{s'}[t_{\text{parent}(s')}].\text{total} - V^{s'}[t_{s'}].\text{total} \right)$ for each subtree s in layer h consists of at most 2^h votes by each of at most 2^h processes. For each process p_i individually, the variance of its 2^h heaviest votes, using Lemma 3, is at most $2^h \left(1 + (4/T) \sum_{j=1}^{n_i} w_j^2 \right)$. If we sum the total variance of at most 2^h votes from all processes, we get at most

$$2^h \left(n^2 + (4/T) \sum_{i=1}^{n} \sum_{j=1}^{n_i} w_j^2 \right) \leq 2^h \left(n^2 + \frac{K + 2n^2}{1 - 8n/T} \right),$$

again using Lemma 3.

We would like to use this bound on the total variance across all missing intervals to show that the sum of the total votes across all missing intervals is not too large. Intuitively, if we can apply a bound to the total variance on a particular interval, we expect the Azuma-Hoeffding inequality to do this for us. But there is a complication in that the total variance for an interval may depend in a complicated way on the actions taken by the adversary during the interval. So instead, we attack the problem indirectly, by adopting a different characterization of the relevant intervals of votes and letting the adversary choose between them to obtain the actual intervals that contributed to $D^{\text{root}}[t]$. We will use the following extended version of the classic Azuma-Hoeffding inequality [10]:

Lemma 5 ([10, Theorem 4.5]). *Let* $\{S_0, \mathcal{F}_0\}$, $0 \le i \le n$ *be a zero-mean martingale with difference sequence* $\{X_i\}$. *Let* w_i *be measurable* $\mathcal{F}_{i-1}$, *and suppose that for all* i, $|X_i| \le w_i$ *with probability 1; and that there exists a bound* W *such that* $\sum_{i=1}^n w_i^2 \le W$ *with probability 1. Then for any* $\lambda > 0$,

$$\Pr\left[S_n \ge \lambda\right] \le e^{-\lambda^2/2W}. \tag{2}$$

Fix an adversary strategy. For each subtree s, let $X_1^s, X_2^s, \ldots$ be the sequence of votes generated in s. For each s, t, and W, let $Y_i^{tsW} = X_i^s$ if (a) at least t votes have been generated by all processes before X_i^s is generated, *and* (b) $\sum_{j<i}(Y_i^{tsW})^2 + (X_i^s)^2 \le W$. Otherwise, let Y_i^{tsW} be 0. If we let $\mathcal{F}_i$ be generated by all votes preceding X_i^s, then the events (a) and (b) are measurable $\mathcal{F}_i$, so $\{Y_i^{tsW}, \mathcal{F}_i\}$ forms a martingale. Furthermore, since only the sign of Y_i^{tsW} is unpredictable, we can define $w_i = (Y_i^{tsW})^2$ to fit Lemma 5. From (b), we have that $\sum w_i^2 \le W$ always. It follows that, for any $c > 0$,

$$\Pr\left[\sum_i Y_i^{tsW} \ge \sqrt{2cW \ln n}\right] \le e^{-c \ln n} = n^{-c}.$$

There are polynomially many choices for the parameters t, s, and W. Union bounding over all such choices shows that, for c sufficiently large, with high probability $\sum_i Y_i^{tsW}$ is bounded by $\sqrt{2cW \ln n}$ for all such intervals. We now use this to show the following.

Lemma 6. *For any adversary strategy and sufficiently large* n, *with probability* $1 - o(1)$, *it holds that at all times* t,

$$\left|V^{\text{root}}[t].\text{total} - U^{\text{root}}[t].\text{total}\right| \le 6n\sqrt{\log_2 n}.$$

Proof. We are trying to bound $D^{\text{root}}[t] = \sum_s (V^s[t_{\text{parent}(s)}] - V^s[t_s])$, where s ranges over all proper subtrees of the tree and for each s of size 2^h, the interval $(t_s, t_{\text{parent}(s)}]$ includes at most 2^h votes for each process.

Suppose that for each t, s, W, it holds that $Y^{tsW} \le \sqrt{9W \ln n}$. By the preceding argument, each such event fails with probability at most $n^{-9/2}$. There are $O(n^2 \log n)$ choices for t, $O(n)$ choices for s, and $O(n^2 \log n)$ choices for W, so taking a union bound over all choices of Y^{tsW} not occurring shows that this event occurs with probability $O(n^{-1/2} \log^2 n) = o(1)$.

If all Y^{tsW} are bounded, then it holds deterministically that

$$
\sum_s (V^s[t_{\text{parent}(s)}] - V^s[t_s]) = \sum_{h=0}^{\log_2 n - 1} \sum_{s,|s|=2^h} (V^s[t_{\text{parent}(s)}] - V^s[t_s])
$$

$$
= \sum_{h=0}^{\log_2 n - 1} \sum_{s,|s|=2^h} Y^{t_s s W_s} \leq \sum_{h=0}^{\log_2 n - 1} \sum_{s,|s|=2^h} \sqrt{2cW_s \ln n}
$$

$$
= \sqrt{2c \ln n} \sum_{h=0}^{\log_2 n - 1} \sum_{s,|s|=2^h} \sqrt{W_s} \leq \sqrt{9 \ln n} \sum_{h=0}^{\log_2 n - 1} \sum_{s,|s|=2^h} \sqrt{W_s},
$$

where W_s is the total variance of the votes generated by s in the interval $(t_s, t_{\text{parent}(s)}]$.

Note that this inequality does not depend on analyzing the interaction between voting and when processes read and write the max registers. For the purposes of computing the total offset we are effectively allowing the adversary to choose what intervals it includes retrospectively, after carrying out whatever strategy it likes for maximizing the probability that any particular values Y^{tsW} are too big.

Because each process i in s generates at most 2^h votes, and each such vote has variance at most $w_{n_i}^2$, we have

$$
W_s \leq 2^h \sum_{i \in s} w_{n_i}^2.
$$

Furthermore, the subtrees at any fixed level h partition the set of processes, so applying Lemma 3 gives

$$
\sum_{s,|s|=2^h} W_s \leq \sum_{s,|s|=2^h} 2^h \sum_{i \in s} w_{n_i}^2 = 2^h \sum_i w_{n_i}^2 \leq 2^h \left(n + \frac{4K + 8n^2}{T - 8n} \right).
$$

By concavity of square root, $\sum \sqrt{x_i}$ is maximized for non-negative x_i constrained by a fixed bound on $\sum \sqrt{x_i}$ by setting all x_i equal. Setting all $n/2^h$ values W_s equal gives the following upper bound.

$$
W_s \leq \frac{2^h}{n} \cdot 2^h \left(n + \frac{4K + 8n^2}{T - 8n} \right) = 2^{2h} \left(1 + \frac{4K + 8n^2}{Tn - 8n^2} \right), \text{ and thus}
$$

$$
\sqrt{W_s} \leq 2^h \sqrt{1 + \frac{4K + 8n^2}{Tn - 8n^2}},
$$

which gives the bound

$$\sqrt{9\ln n}\sum_{h=0}^{\log_2 n-1}\sum_{s,|s|=2^h}\sqrt{W_s}\le\sqrt{9\ln n}\sum_{h=0}^{\log_2 n-1}2^h\sqrt{1+\frac{4K+8n^2}{Tn-8n^2}}$$

$$=\sqrt{9\ln n\left(1+\frac{4K+8n^2}{Tn-8n^2}\right)}\sum_{h=0}^{\log_2 n-1}2^h=3(n-1)\sqrt{\ln n}\sqrt{1+\frac{4K+8n^2}{Tn-8n^2}}$$

$$=3(n-1)\sqrt{\ln n}\sqrt{1+\frac{\log_2 n+2}{\log_2 n-2}}\le 6n\sqrt{\log_2 n},$$

when n is sufficiently large. The last step uses the fact that for $K=n^2\log n$ and $T=4n\log n$, the value under the radical converges to 2 in the limit, and $3\sqrt{2/\ln 2}<6$.

For the last step of the proof, we need to show that the **extra votes** that arrive after K variance has been accumulated are not enough to push $V^{\text{root}}[t]$ close to the origin. For this, we use Kolmogorov's inequality, a martingale analogue to Chebyshev's inequality, which says that if we are given a zero-mean martingale $\{S_i,\mathcal{F}_i\}$ with bounded variance, then $\Pr[\exists i\le n:|S_i|\ge\lambda]\le\frac{\lambda^2}{\text{Var}[S_n]}$.

Consider the martingale $S_1,S_2,\dots$ where S_i is the sum of the first i votes after $V^{\text{root}}[i].\text{var}$ first passes K. Then from Lemma 3,

$$\text{Var}[S_i]\le\frac{K+2n^2}{1-8n/T}-K=\frac{8K(n/T)+2n^2}{1-8n/T}=\frac{8n^2+2n^2}{1-2/(\log_2 n)}=O(n^2).$$

So for any fixed c, the probability that $|S_i|$ exceeds cK for any i is $O(1/\log n)=o(1)$.

Final Argument. From Lemma 4, we have that the total common vote $V^{\text{root}}[\tau_n].\text{total}$ converges in distribution to $N(0,1)$ when scaled by $\sqrt{K}=n\sqrt{\log_2 n}$. In particular, for any fixed constant c, there is a constant probability $\pi_c>0$ that for sufficiently large n, $\Pr\left[V^{\text{root}}[\tau_n]\ge cn\sqrt{\log_2 n}\right]\ge\pi_c$.

Let c be 7. Then with probability $\pi_7-o(1)$, all of the following events occur:

1. The common vote $V^{\text{root}}[\tau_n].\text{total}$ exceeds $7n\sqrt{\log_2 n}$;
2. For any i, the next i votes have sum $o(n\sqrt{\log_2 n})$;
3. The vote $U^{\text{root}}[t].\text{total}$ observed by any process differs from $V^{\text{root}}[t].\text{total}$ by at most $6n\sqrt{\log_2 n}$.

If this occurs, then every process observes, for some t, $U^{\text{root}}[t].\text{total}\ge 7n\sqrt{\log_2 n}-6n\sqrt{\log_2 n}-o(n\sqrt{\log n})>0$. In other words, all processes return the same value $+1$ with constant probability for sufficiently large n. By symmetry, the same is true for -1. We have therefore constructed a weak shared coin with constant agreement probability.

Theorem 1. *Algorithm 1 implements a weak shared coin with constant bias, message complexity $O(n^2\log^2 n)$, and with a bound of $O(n\log^3 n)$ on the number of messages sent and received by any one process.*

Proof. We have just shown that Algorithm 1 implements a weak shared coin with constant bias, and from Lemma 3 we know that the maximum number of votes generated by any single process is $O(n \log^2 n)$. Because each process communicates with a subtree of 2^h other processes every 2^{-h} votes, each level of the tree contributes $\Theta(1)$ amortized outgoing messages and incoming responses per vote, for a total of $\Theta(\log n)$ messages per vote, or $O(n \log^3 n)$ messages altogether.

In addition, we must count messages received and sent by a process p as part of the max register implementation. Here for each process q in p's level-h subtree, p may incur $O(1)$ messages every 2^h votes generated by q. Each such process q generates at most $O(n \log^2 n)$ votes, and there are 2^h such processes q. So p incurs a total of $O(n \log^2 n)$ votes from its level-h subtree. Summing over all $\log n$ levels gives the same $O(n \log^3 n)$ bound on messages as for max-register operations initiated by p.

This gives the final bound of $O(n \log^3 n)$ messages per process. Applying the same reasoning to the total vote bound from Lemma 3 yields the bound of $O(n^2 \log^2 n)$ on total message complexity.

7   Consensus Protocol and Extension for General t

Consensus. We now describe how to convert a message-efficient weak shared coin into message-efficient consensus. We adapt a shared-memory consensus protocol, due to Chandra [16], which, like many shared-memory consensus protocols has the **early binding** property identified by Aguilera and Toueg [2] as necessary to ensure correctness of a consensus protocol using a weak shared coin.

Chandra's protocol uses two arrays of bits to track the speed of processes with preference 0 or 1. The mechanism of the protocol is similar to previous protocols of Chor, Israeli, and Li [18] and Aspnes and Herlihy [9]: if a process observes that the other team has advanced beyond it, it adopts that value, and if it observes that all processes with different preferences are two or more rounds behind, it decides on its current preference secure in the knowledge that they will switch sides before they catch up. The arrays of bits effectively function as a max register, so it is natural to replace them with two max registers $m[0]$ and $m[1]$, initially set to 0, implemented as in Section 4. The complete description, pseudocode, and proof are given in the full version of the paper [3].

Theorem 2. *Let* SharedCoin$_r$, *for each* r, *be a shared coin protocol with constant agreement parameter, individual message complexity* $T_1(n)$, *and total message complexity* $T(n)$. *Then the algorithm described above implements a consensus protocol with expected individual message complexity* $O(T_1(n) + n)$ *and total message complexity* $O(T(n) + n^2)$.

Extension for General t. We can decrease the message complexity of the protocol by taking advantage of values of $t = o(n)$. The basic idea is to reduce message complexity by "deputizing" a set of $2t+1$ processes to run the protocol described above and produce an output value, which they broadcast to all other participants. For this, we fix processes $p_1, \ldots, p_{2t+1}$ to be the group of processes running the consensus protocol, which we call the *deputies*. When executing an instance of the protocol, each process first sends a *Start* message to the deputies. If the process is a deputy, it waits to receive *Start* notifications from $n - t$ processes. Upon receiving these notifications, the process runs the consensus algorithm described above, where the only participants are processes $p_1, \ldots, p_{2t+1}$. Upon completing this protocol, each deputy broadcasts a $\langle Result, value \rangle$ message to all processes, and returns the decided value. If the process is not a deputy, then it simply waits for a *Result* message from one of the deputies, and returns the corresponding value. Correctness follows from the previous arguments.

Theorem 3. *Let $n, t > 0$ be parameters such that $t < n$. The algorithm described above implements randomized consensus using $O(nt + t^2 \log^2 t)$ expected total messages, and $O(n + t \log^3 t)$ expected messages per process.*

8 Conclusions and Future Work

We have described a randomized algorithm for consensus with expected message complexity $O(n^2 \log^2 n)$ that tolerates $t < n/2$ crash faults; this algorithm also has the desirable property that each process sends and receives expected $O(n \log^3 n)$ messages on average, and message size is logarithmic. We also present a generalization that uses expected $O(nt + t^2 \log^2 t)$ messages.

Two conspicuous open problems remain. The first is whether we can close the remaining poly-logarithmic gap for the message cost of consensus in the classic model. Second, can we use techniques from this paper to help close the gap for message-cost of Byzantine agreement in the classic model? To the best of our knowledge, the current lower bound for message cost of Byzantine agreement is $\Omega(n^2)$, while the best upper bound is $O(n^{6.5})$ — a significant gap.

References

1. Abrahamson, K.: On achieving consensus using a shared memory. In: Proceedings of the Seventh Annual ACM Symposium on Principles of Distributed Computing, PODC 1988, pp. 291–302. ACM, New York (1988)
2. Aguilera, M.K., Toueg, S.: The correctness proof of Ben-Or's randomized consensus algorithm. Distributed Computing 25(5), 371–381 (2012)
3. Alistarh, D., Aspnes, J., King, V., Saia, J.: Communication-efficient randomized consensus (2014), Full version available at http://www.cs.yale.edu/homes/aspnes/papers/disc2014-submission.pdf
4. Aspnes, J.: Lower bounds for distributed coin-flipping and randomized consensus. J. ACM 45(3), 415–450 (1998)
5. Aspnes, J., Attiya, H., Censor, K.: Randomized consensus in expected $O(n \log n)$ individual work. In: PODC 2008: Proceedings of the Twenty-Seventh ACM Symposium on Principles of Distributed Computing, pp. 325–334 (August 2008)
6. Aspnes, J., Attiya, H., Censor-Hillel, K.: Polylogarithmic concurrent data structures from monotone circuits. J. ACM 59(1), 2 (2012)
7. Aspnes, J., Censor, K.: Approximate shared-memory counting despite a strong adversary. ACM Transactions on Algorithms 6(2), 1–23 (2010)
8. Aspnes, J., Censor-Hillel, K.: Atomic snapshots in $O(\log^3 n)$ steps using randomized helping. In: Afek, Y. (ed.) DISC 2013. LNCS, vol. 8205, pp. 254–268. Springer, Heidelberg (2013)
9. Aspnes, J., Herlihy, M.: Fast randomized consensus using shared memory. Journal of Algorithms 11(3), 441–461 (1990)

10. Aspnes, J., Waarts, O.: Randomized consensus in expected $O(n \log^2 n)$ operations per processor. SIAM J. Comput. 25(5), 1024–1044 (1996)

11. Attiya, H., Bar-Noy, A., Dolev, D.: Sharing memory robustly in message-passing systems. J. ACM 42(1), 124–142 (1995)

12. Attiya, H., Censor, K.: Tight bounds for asynchronous randomized consensus. J. ACM 55(5), 20:1–20:26 (2008)

13. Ben-Or, M.: Another advantage of free choice (extended abstract): Completely asynchronous agreement protocols. In: Proceedings of the Second Annual ACM Symposium on Principles of Distributed Computing, PODC 1983, pp. 27–30. ACM, New York (1983)

14. Bracha, G.: An asynchronous [(n - 1)/3]-resilient consensus protocol. In: PODC 1984: Proceedings of the Third Annual ACM Symposium on Principles of Distributed Computing, pp. 154–162. ACM, New York (1984)

15. Bracha, G., Rachman, O.: Randomized consensus in expected O(n²log n) operations. In: Toueg, S., Spirakis, P.G., Kirousis, L.M. (eds.) WDAG 1991. LNCS, vol. 579, pp. 143–150. Springer, Heidelberg (1992)

16. Chandra, T.D.: Polylog randomized wait-free consensus. In: Proceedings of the Fifteenth Annual ACM Symposium on Principles of Distributed Computing, Philadelphia, Pennsylvania, USA, May 23-26, pp. 166-175 (1996)

17. Chandra, T.D., Toueg, S.: Unreliable failure detectors for reliable distributed systems. J. ACM 43(2), 225–267 (1996)

18. Chor, B., Israeli, A., Li, M.: On processor coordination using asynchronous hardware. In: Proceedings of the Sixth Annual ACM Symposium on Principles of Distributed Computing, PODC 1987, pp. 86–97. ACM, New York (1987)

19. Dwork, C., Lynch, N., Stockmeyer, L.: Consensus in the presence of partial synchrony. J. ACM 35(2), 288–323 (1988)

20. Fich, F., Herlihy, M., Shavit, N.: On the space complexity of randomized synchronization. J. ACM 45(5), 843–862 (1998)

21. Fischer, M.J., Lynch, N.A., Paterson, M.S.: Impossibility of distributed consensus with one faulty process. J. ACM 32(2), 374–382 (1985)

22. Grimmett, G.R., Stirzaker, D.R.: Probability and Random Processes. Oxford University Press (2001)

23. Hall, P., Heyde, C.: Martingale Limit Theory and Its Application. Academic Press (1980)

24. Karlin, A., Yao, A.: Probabilistic lower bounds for byzantine agreement and clock synchronization. Unpublished manuscript

25. Keralapura, R., Cormode, G., Ramamirtham, J.: Communication-efficient distributed monitoring of thresholded counts. In: Proceedings of the 2006 ACM SIGMOD International Conference on Management of Data, SIGMOD 2006, pp. 289–300. ACM, New York (2006)

26. King, V., Saia, J.: Byzantine agreement in polynomial expected time. In: Proceedings of the ACM Symposium on Theory of Computing, STOC (2013)

27. King, V., Saia, J.: Faster agreement via a spectral method for detecting malicious behavior. In: Proceedings of the ACM-SIAM Symposium on Discrete Algorithms (SODA) (2014)

28. Lamport, L., Shostak, R., Pease, M.: The byzantine generals problem. ACM Trans. Program. Lang. Syst. 4(3), 382–401 (1982)

29. Pease, M., Shostak, R., Lamport, L.: Reaching agreement in the presence of faults. J. ACM 27(2), 228–234 (1980)

30. Saks, M., Shavit, N., Woll, H.: Optimal time randomized consensus - making resilient algorithms fast in practice. In: Proc. of the 2nd ACM Symposium on Discrete Algorithms (SODA), pp. 351–362 (1991)

Tight Bound on Mobile Byzantine Agreement

François Bonnet[1], Xavier Défago[1],
Thanh Dang Nguyen[1], and Maria Potop-Butucaru[2]

[1] School of Information Science, JAIST, Japan
[2] Université Pierre & Marie Curie (UPMC) – Paris 6, France

Abstract. This paper investigates the problem of Byzantine Agreement in a synchronous system where malicious agents can move from process to process, corrupting their host. Earlier works on the problem are based on biased models which, as we argue in the paper, give an unfair advantage either to the correct processes or to the adversary controlling the malicious agents. Indeed, the earlier studies of the problem assume that, after a malicious agent has left a process, that process, said to be cured, is able to instantly and accurately detect the fact that it was corrupted in earlier rounds, and thus can take local actions to recover a valid state (Garay's model). We found no justification for that assumption which clearly favors correct processes. Under that model, an algorithm is known for $n > 4t$, where n is the number of processes and t the maximum number of malicious agents. The tightness of the bound is unknown. In contrast, more recent work on the problem remove the assumption on detection and assume instead that a malicious agent may have left corrupted messages in the send queue of a cured process. As a result, the adversary controlling the malicious agents can corrupt the messages sent by cured processes, as well as those sent by the newly corrupted ones, thus doubling the number of effective faults. Under that model, which favors the malicious agents, the problem can be solved if and only if $n > 6t$. In this paper, we refine the latter model to avoid the above biases. While a cured process may send messages (based on a state corrupted by the malicious agent), it will behave correctly in the way it sends those messages: i.e., send messages according to the algorithm. Surprisingly, in this model we could derive a new non-trivial tight bound for Byzantine Agreement. We prove that at least $5t+1$ processors are needed in order to tolerate t mobile Byzantine agents and provide a time optimal algorithm that matches this lower bound, altogether with a formal specification of the problem.

1 Introduction

New emergent distributed systems such as P2P, overlay networks, social networks or clouds are inherently vulnerable to faults, insider attacks, or viruses. Faults and attacks cannot be predicted accurately, may affect different parts of a system, and may occur at any moment of its execution. In this work, we investigate the case where transient state corruptions, which can be abstracted as malicious "agents," can move through the network and corrupt the nodes they occupy.

F. Kuhn (Ed.): DISC 2014, LNCS 8784, pp. 76–90, 2014.
© Springer-Verlag Berlin Heidelberg 2014

This models the situation where, as soon as a faulty node is repaired (e.g., by software rejuvenation), another one becomes compromised. For more than two decades, the main case study problem in this context was Byzantine Agreement. Briefly stated, it requires processors, some of which malicious, that start the computation with an initial value to decide on the same value. When faults are mobile the problem is known as Mobile Byzantine Agreement and requires special attention for preserving agreement once it has been reached.

Related work. Byzantine Agreement, introduced by Lampport *et al.* [12,16], has been studied for decades in static distributed systems under different aspects (e.g., *possibility, complexity, cost*) in various models (from synchronous [12,16,17] to asynchronous [5,13], from authenticated [8] to anonymous [14]) with different methodologies (deterministic [12, 16], probabilistic [3, 9]). In all these works, faults are stationary. That is, they do not change their original location during the computation.

Santoro *et al.* [19,20], and later Schmid *et al.* [22], investigate the agreement problem in dynamic transmission failure models for both complete and arbitrary networks. These models assume that different communication links may randomly fail at different times. Santoro and Widmayer [19] study the k-agreement problem, where the system reaches a k-agreement if, in finite time, k processes choose the same value, either 0 or 1, with $k > \lceil n/2 \rceil$,[1] where n is the total number of processes.

Based on the bivalent argument of Fischer *et al.* [10], they state that ($\lceil n/2 + 1 \rceil$)-agreement is impossible in a synchronous system if at each time there is one processor whose messages may be corrupted. Although not explicitly stated, the impossibility applies to the mobile Byzantine model. Thus, work on Mobile Byzantine Agreement typically rely on the assumption that at least one process remains uncorrupted for $\Omega(n)$ rounds of communication.

Mobile Byzantine Agreement, introduced by Reischuk [18], has regained much attention recently. Research on the problem, in synchronous systems, follows two main directions: constrained or unconstrained mobility.

Constrained mobility. This direction, studied by Buhrman *et al.* [4], considers that malicious agents move from one node to another only when protocol messages are sent (similar to how viruses would propagate). In that model, they prove a tight bound for Mobile Byzantine Agreement ($n > 3t$, where t is the maximal number of simultaneously faulty processes) and propose a time optimal protocol that matches this bound.

Unconstrained mobility. In this direction, which includes the work in this paper, the mobility of malicious agents is *not* constrained by message exchanges [1,11,15,18,21].

Reischuk [18] proposed a first sub-optimal solution under an additional hypothesis on the stability/stationarity of malicious agents for a given period of time. Later, Ostrovsky and Yung [15] introduced the notion of an adversary that

---

[1] If $k \leq \lceil n/2 \rceil$ the k-agreement problem is trivial.

can inject and distribute faults in the system at a constant rate in every round and proposed solutions (mixing randomization and self-stabilization) for tolerating the attacks of mobile viruses. Then, Garay [11] and, more recently, Banu et al. [1] and Sasaki et al. [21] consider, in their model, that processes execute synchronous rounds composed of three phases: *send, receive, compute*. Between two consecutive rounds, malicious agents can move from one host to another, hence the set of faulty processes has a bounded size although its membership can change from one round to the next. Garay's model is particular in that, a process has a limited ability to detect its own infection after the fact. More precisely, during the first round following the leave of the malicious agent, a process enters a state, called *cured*, during which it can take preventive actions to avoid sending messages that are based on a corrupted state. Under this assumption, Garay [11] proposes an algorithm that solves Mobile Byzantine Agreement provided that $n > 6t$.

Notice that Garay's model advantages the cured processes since they have the possibility of miraculously detecting the leave of malicious agents. In the same model, Banu et al. [1] propose a Mobile Byzantine Agreement algorithm for $n > 4t$. However, to the best of our knowledge, the tightness of the bound remains an open question.

Sasaki et al. [21] investigate the problem in a different model where processes do not have this ability to detect when malicious agents move. This is similar to our model with the subtle difference that cured processes have *no control* on the messages they send. That is, messages are computed in the previous round (i.e., when the process was still faulty) and the cured process cannot control the buffer where these messages are stored, even though the process is no longer faulty. It follows that a cured process may behave as a malicious one for one additional round. They propose tight bounds for Mobile Byzantine Agreement in arbitrary networks if $n > 6t$ and the degree of the network is $d > 4t$. This work extends the tight bounds ($n > 3t$ and $d > 2t$) for Byzantine Agreement of Dolev [7] in arbitrary networks with static faults.

Motivation. Analyzing the results proposed in [1,11,21], it is clear that there is a gap between how these models capture the power of malicious agents or cured processes. Garay's model [11] is biased toward the cured processes, whereas the model of Sasaki et al. [21] favors the malicious agent, as it can control the send buffer of a cured process even though it is no longer hosted by the process. Our research fills the gap by avoiding these biases; similarly to Sasaki's model [21], a cured process may send corrupted messages, but only computed based on the corrupted state left by a malicious agent. In particular, a malicious agent can corrupt neither the code nor the identity of the process it occupies, and a cured process always executes a correct code which ensures, for instance, that it will send the same message to all of its neighbors.

The difference between the three models are subtle (see Fig. 1) but they have important consequences (Table 1). Figure 1 depicts the effects of a malicious agent on a process. Red areas correspond to the steps controlled by the malicious agent. In Sasaki's model [21] (Fig. 1b), a single malicious agent can corrupt a process for two rounds even though it occupies the process only for a single round. In Garay's model [11] (Fig. 1a) a cured process is aware of its current state (cured), which is represented in green. In our model (Fig 1c; defined in Sect. 2) malicious nodes have the same power as in Garay's model, but the cured processes may send messages with corrupted content as in Sasaki's model.

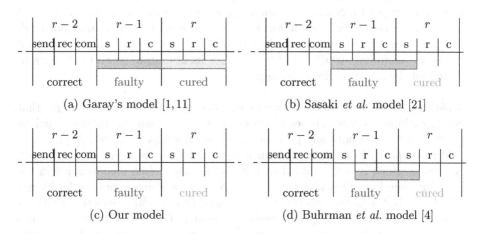

(a) Garay's model [1, 11]   (b) Sasaki *et al.* model [21]

(c) Our model   (d) Buhrman *et al.* model [4]

Fig. 1. Graphical representation of the various fault models

Table 1. Lower and upper bounds for Byzantine Agreement with mobile faults

Model	Impossibility result	Possibility result	Byzantine vs Cured Game
Garay [11]	open question	$n > 6t$	Advantaged Cured
Banu *et al.* [1]	open question	$n > 4t$	Advantaged Cured
Sasaki *et al.* [21]	$n \leq 6t$	$n > 6t$	Advantaged Byzantine Agent
This paper	$n \leq 5t$	$n > 5t$	No one advantaged
Buhrman *et al.* [4]	$n \leq 3t$	$n > 3t$	Virus like propagation

Contribution. In this model we prove a tight bound for the agreement problem. We prove in Section 3 that the problem has no solution if the size of the network is $n < 5t$ (where t is an upper bound on the number of faulty agents) and propose an algorithm that matches this bound in Section 4. We also formalize the Mobile Byzantine Agreement problem in Section 2.2. Following the results proved in [11], our solution is also asymptotically time optimal.

2 Model and Definitions

2.1 System Model

Processes. We consider a synchronous message-passing system consisting of n processes $p_0, p_1, \ldots, p_{n-1}$ where $\Pi = \{0, \ldots, n-1\}$ denotes the set of process indices. Each process is an automaton whose state evolves following the execution of its local algorithm. All processes execute the same algorithm.

The network is fully connected: all pairs of processes are directly linked with a reliable bidirectional channel; *i.e.* there is no loss, duplication, or alteration of messages. The system evolves in synchronous rounds and all processes start simultaneously at round 0. There is a round counter accessible to the algorithm executed by each process. Each round consists of three steps; *send, receive,* and *compute.* Based on its current local state, a process (1) computes and *sends* a message to all processes (including itself); (2) *receives* messages sent by all processes (including itself); and (3) *computes* its new state based on its current state and the set of received message.

Mobile malicious agents. Faults are represented by malicious mobile agents that can move from process to process between rounds. There are at most t malicious agents, with $t < n$, and any process can be occupied by an agent. A process is said to be *faulty* in a given round if it is occupied by an agent in that round. A process which is not occupied by a malicious agent, but was occupied in the previous round is called a *cured* process. A process which is neither faulty nor cured is called a *correct* process. $\mathcal{F}_r$, $\mathcal{C}o_r$, and $\mathcal{C}u_r$ denote respectively the set of faulty, correct, and cured processes at round r. For ease of writing, we also consider the combined sets of correct/cured processes as the set of non-faulty processes $\mathcal{C}_r = \mathcal{C}o_r \cup \mathcal{C}u_r = \Pi \setminus \mathcal{F}_r$.

Malicious agents are mobile and can move between the compute step of a round and the send step of the next round (Figure 1c). The behavior of a faulty process is controlled by the malicious agent. In particular, the agent can corrupt the local state of its host process, and force it to send arbitrary messages (potentially different messages to different processes). However, a malicious agent cannot corrupt the identify of that process (*i.e.*, it cannot send messages using another identity), and is unable to modify the code of the algorithm (*i.e.*, the process resumes executing the correct algorithm after the malicious agent moves away). So, as suggested in [4], we assume a secure, tamper-proof read-only memory where the identity and the code are stored.

While it is possible for each non-faulty process to rejuvenate its code at the beginning of each round, local variables may still be corrupted (and of course cannot be recovered). Therefore, in the case of cured processes the computation may be performed using a corrupted state.

Comparison with previous models. As explained in Section 1 and graphically depicted in Figure 1, the above model differs from Garay's [11] and Sasaki's [21] as follows. In Sasaki's model [21], a single malicious agent can corrupt a process for more than a round although occupying this process only for a round. In our model, once the malicious agent leaves a process, that process will execute the correct code even though the computation will be performed on a corrupted state. Differently from the Garay's model [11], where a cured process has the knowledge of its cured state and exploits it in the algorithm, in our model processes can not access and exploit this knowledge.

Notation. In the formal definitions and proofs, var_i^r denotes the value of variable *var* in process p_i at the end of round r. We also use the notation $\#_w(\mathcal{W})$ to refer to the number of occurrences of w in tuple $\mathcal{W}$.

2.2   Mobile Byzantine Agreement Problem

We now formally define the Mobile Byzantine Agreement problem introduced first by Garay *et al.* [11] and refined most recently by Sasaki *et al.* [21]. The definition presented here is stronger than the definition proposed by Sasaki [21] (see discussion below).

Each initially-correct process p_i has an initial value w_i. All processes must *decide*[2] a value *dec* such that the following properties hold:

1. *BA-Termination*: Eventually, all non-faulty processes during a round terminate the round with a non-bottom decided value.

$$\exists r, \quad \forall r' > r \quad \forall i \in \mathcal{C}_{r'} \quad dec_i^{r'} \neq \bot$$

2. *BA-Agreement*: No two non-faulty processes decide different values:

$$\forall r, r' \quad \forall i \in \mathcal{C}_r \quad \forall j \in \mathcal{C}_{r'} \quad \left(dec_i^r \neq \bot \wedge dec_j^{r'} \neq \bot \right) \Rightarrow \left(dec_i^r = dec_j^{r'} \right)$$

3. *BA-Validity*: If all initially-correct processes propose the same value w, correct processes can decide only w.

$$\forall w \quad (\forall i \in \mathcal{C}o_0 \quad w_i = w) \Rightarrow (\forall r \quad \forall i \in \mathcal{C}_r \quad dec_i^r \in \{\bot, w\})$$

Note that specification of Mobile Byzantine Agreement given in this section is actually stronger than the definition proposed by Sasaki *et al.* [21]. They differ in two important aspects. Firstly, where we require that, after some time, all non-faulty processes decide a value at every round, their definition requires a decision only from processes that are not faulty infinitely often. Secondly, where we allow non-faulty processes to decide only on a unique non-bottom value, Sasaki's algorithm [21] allows the variable storing the decision to take arbitrary values for a finite number of rounds. In other words, our specification requires *perpetual* consistency whereas Sasaki's algorithm ensures *eventually* consistency.

We now state two lemmas, proved in earlier models [11,19], which also apply to our model. The first lemma states a necessary condition. That condition is however not sufficient; as explained previously, a bound on the number of faults is also required.

Lemma 1 (stated in [11]; formal proof derivable from [19]). *Mobile Byzantine Agreement requires that at least one process remains uncorrupted for $\Omega(n)$ rounds of communication.*

Lemma 2 (from [11]). *Every Mobile Byzantine Agreement protocol requires $\Omega(n)$ rounds in its worst case execution.*

---

[2]   We use a terminology consistent with the classical definition of Byzantine agreement. However, the action "decide" does not in itself guarantee a permanent decision. Indeed, due to the mobility of the malicious agents, non-faulty processes must *re-decide* the decision at the end of each round.

3   Upper Bound on the Number of Faulty Processes

In this section, we prove that, in the presence of t malicious mobile agents, Mobile Byzantine Agreement cannot be solved with $5t$ processes or less, even if some process remains uncorrupted forever.

Sasaki *et al.* [21] proved a similar result by reduction from a well-known existing bound. From the classical bound ($n \leq 3t$) on synchronous Byzantine agreement, they could obtain their bound ($n \leq 6t$) by considering both faulty and cured processes as Byzantine.

However, we cannot use the same approach because, in sharp contrast with Sasaki's model [21] and as explained in Section 2, in our model, the adversary cannot entirely control cured processes.

Theorem 1. *There is no deterministic algorithm that solves Mobile Byzantine Agreement in a synchronous five-process system in the presence of a single mobile Byzantine agent (even with a permanently correct process).*

Proof. The proof is by contradiction. Given a system consisting of five processes $\{p_0, \ldots, p_4\}$, where at least one is permanently correct, let us suppose that there exists an algorithm that can solve the BA problem in the presence of a single malicious mobile agent. Suppose that, in this algorithm, processes send the same message to all processes.[3] Note that, during an execution, nothing prevents a faulty processes from sending different messages to other processes.

General idea. We consider three executions of this algorithm. In executions E^0 and E^1, all correct processes propose the same value; 0 and 1 respectively. The BA properties imply that, eventually, non-faulty processes respectively decide 0 and 1 in these two executions. The third execution, called E^{01}, brings a contradiction: some processes decide 0 while others decide 1.

The three executions are represented on Figure 2. Red (resp. light red) arrows correspond to corrupt messages sent by faulty (resp. cured) processes. The values proposed by correct processes appear on the left. Non-correct processes do not have proposed values since they may have been corrupted by the malicious agent. Vertical dashed lines separate successive rounds.

For each execution, we choose the process occupied by the single malicious agent. As required, there is at least one process which is permanently non-faulty in each execution.

Executions E^0 and E^1. In execution E^0, the malicious agent alternates between processes p_0 and p_1. In execution E^1, it alternates between processes p_2 and p_3. Processes p_2, p_3, and p_4 are initially correct and propose 0 in E^0, while processes p_0, p_1, and p_4 are initially correct and propose 1 in E^1.

---

[3] If not the case, we can trivially define an algorithm that satisfies this property by combining the set of sent messages into a single message.

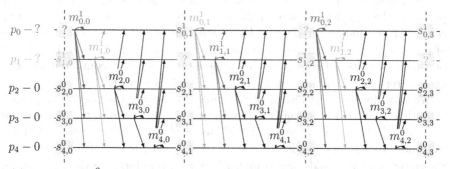

(a) Execution E^0 where initially-correct processes p_2, p_3, and p_4 propose value 0.

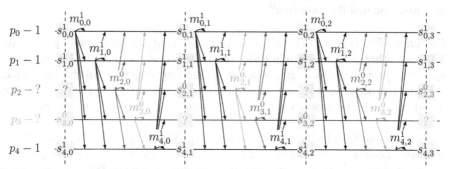

(b) Execution E^1 where initially-correct processes p_0, p_1, and p_4 propose value 1.

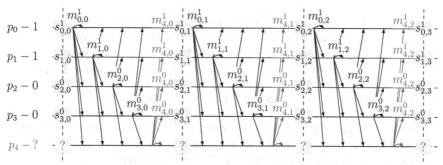

(c) Execution E^{01} where initially-correct processes p_0 and p_1 propose value 1 while initially-correct processes p_2 and p_3 propose value 0. Process p_4 is faulty and sends different messages to each process.

Fig. 2. Three executions leading to a contradiction of the existence of a BA protocol in a 5-process system with one mobile malicious agent. (Legend: Arrows correspond to messages exchanged between processes. Gray boxes contain the new local state computed by each process at the end of each round, which is then used to send message in the following round. Red indicates actions taken by the faulty processes while light red refers to actions taken by cured processes. Vertical dashed line separate successive rounds.)

For non-faulty processes, the messages sent during these executions are computed by the algorithm based on the local states of processes. For correct processes (*i.e.*, excluding cured ones), let us denote by $s^0_{i,r}$ (resp. $s^1_{i,r}$) the local state of process p_i at the beginning of the round r in execution E^0 (resp. E^1). Based on this local state, let $m^0_{i,r}$ (resp., $m^1_{i,r}$) denote the message computed and sent by a correct process p_i at round r in execution E^0 (resp., E^1).

We now define the behavior of the malicious agent. For the faulty process p_i (either p_0 or p_1) at round r of execution E^0, we choose that p_i sends the message $m^1_{i,r}$ (*i.e.*, the message it would have sent at the same round in E^1) and we choose that p_i updates its local state to $s^1_{i,r+1}$ at the end of the round (*i.e.*, the same state it would have computed in E^1). Similarly we choose that the faulty process p_i (either p_2 or p_3) at round r of execution E^1 sends the message $m^0_{i,r}$ and updates its state to $s^0_{i,r+1}$.

Execution E^{01}. In execution E^{01}, the malicious agent always occupies process p_4. The four other processes are initially (and forever) correct. As in E^0, processes p_2 and p_3 propose 0. As in E^1, processes p_0 and p_1 propose 1. In this execution, the faulty process p_4 does not send the same message to all processes. At any round, p_4 sends the message $m^1_{4,r}$ to p_0 and p_1, but sends $m^0_{4,r}$ to p_3 and p_4.

Indistinguishability. In the sequel, we prove the following claim: E^0 and E^{01} are indistinguishable for p_2 and p_3, and similarly E^1 and E^{01} for p_0 and p_1. This can be proven by induction on the round number, using the following predicate $\mathcal{P}(r)$ for $r \geq 0$:

$$
\mathcal{P}(r) = \begin{cases}
p_0 \text{ starts round } r \text{ in } E^1 \text{ and } E^{01} \text{ with the same local state} \\
p_1 \text{ starts round } r \text{ in } E^1 \text{ and } E^{01} \text{ with the same local state} \\
p_2 \text{ starts round } r \text{ in } E^0 \text{ and } E^{01} \text{ with the same local state} \\
p_3 \text{ starts round } r \text{ in } E^0 \text{ and } E^{01} \text{ with the same local state}
\end{cases}
$$

The proof is only for p_0. The proofs for p_1, p_2, and p_3 are identical.

- *Case $r = 0$.* p_0 proposes the same value in E^1 and E^{01} and therefore starts round 0 with the same initial local state, namely $s^0_{0,0}$.
- *Case $r \geq 0$.* Let us suppose that predicate $\mathcal{P}(r)$ is true.
  - p_0 is correct in E^1 and E^{01} and, by induction hypothesis, starts round r with the same local state. Therefore p_0 necessarily sends the same message, namely $m^1_{0,r}$, to all processes in round r of both E^1 and E^{01}. Similarly, p_1 sends the same message $m^1_{1,r}$ to all processes in round r of both E^1 and E^{01}.
  - p_2 is correct in E^0 and E^{01} and, by induction hypothesis, starts round r with the same local state. Therefore p_2 necessarily sends the same message, namely $m^0_{2,r}$, to all processes in round r of both E^0 and E^{01}. Considering execution E^1, there are two cases to consider; (1) p_2 is faulty during round r and then, by construction, the malicious agent forces p_2 to send the message $m^0_{2,r}$; (2) p_2 is cured during round r, which means

that it was faulty in the previous round and the malicious agent forced p_2 to start round r in the local state $s_{2,r}^0$ which implies that p_2 still sends the message $m_{2,r}^0$. In all cases, p_2 sends the same message in round r of both E^1 and E^{01}.

Similarly, p_3 sends the same message $m_{3,r}^0$ to all processes in round r of both E^1 and E^{01}.

- p_4 is faulty in E^{01}. By construction, in each round, it sends to p_0 the same message as in E^1. It means that p_4 sends the same message, namely $m_{4,r}^0$, to p_0 in round r of both E^1 and E^{01}.

Process p_0 receives the same messages from all processes in round r of E^1 and E^{01}. Since p_0 is correct in both executions, it computes the same new local state and starts round $r + 1$, which prove $\mathcal{P}(r + 1)$.

Thus by induction, the predicate $\mathcal{P}(r)$ is true for all rounds and therefore the claim holds. Since p_0 and p_1 eventually decide 1 in E^1, they also decide 1 in E^{01}. Similarly, since p_2 and p_3 eventually decide 0 in E^0, they also decide 0 in E^{01}. Contradiction.

When $n \leq 5t$, the proof of Theorem 1 can be generalized by replacing any process appearing in the proof by a group of processes of size at most t.

Corollary 1. *There is no deterministic algorithm that solves the Mobile Byzantine Agreement problem in a synchronous n-process system in the presence of t mobile byzantine agent if $n \leq 5t$ (even with a permanently correct process).*

4 Algorithm for Mobile Byzantine Agreement

Given a system with t malicious mobile agents, we introduce an algorithm that solves Mobile Byzantine Agreement under the following two conditions: (1) there are at least $5t + 1$ processes in total, and (2) at least one process remains uncorrupted for $3n$ consecutive rounds (see Lemma 1).

Algorithm 1. BA algorithm (code for p_i with proposed value w_i)

```
1   Function MBA(w_i):
2   │   v_i ← w_i;

3   │   for s = 0 to n − 1 do
4   │   │   begin round // proposing round r = 3s
5   │   │   │   v_i ← propose(v_i);
6   │   │   │   dec_i ← ⊥;
7   │   │   end round

8   │   │   begin round // collecting round r = 3s + 1
9   │   │   │   SV_i ← collect(v_i);
10  │   │   │   dec_i ← ⊥;
11  │   │   end round

12  │   │   begin round // deciding round r = 3s + 2
13  │   │   │   v_i ← decide(s, SV_i);
14  │   │   │   dec_i ← ⊥;
15  │   │   end round
16  │   end for

17  │   dec_i ← v_i;

18  │   for r = 3n to ∞ do
19  │   │   begin round // maintaining round
20  │   │   │   send dec_i to all processes;
21  │   │   │   dec_i ← the value received at least n − 2t times;
22  │   │   end round
23  │   end for

24  Function propose(v):
25  │   PV[1..n] ← [⊥, ..., ⊥];
26  │   send v to all processes;
27  │   foreach j ∈ Π do
28  │   │   if v_j received from j then PV[j] ← v_j;
29  │   if ∃w ≠ ⊥, #_w(PV) ≥ n − 2t then return w;
30  │   return ⊥;

31  Function collect(v):
32  │   SV[1..n] ← [⊥, ..., ⊥];
33  │   send v to all processes;
34  │   foreach j ∈ Π do
35  │   │   if v_j received from j then SV[j] ← v_j;
36  │   return SV;

37  Function decide(s, SV):
38  │   EV[1..n][1..n] ← [[⊥, ..., ⊥], ..., [⊥, ..., ⊥]];
39  │   send SV to all processes;
40  │   foreach j ∈ Π do
41  │   │   if SV_j received from j then EV[j] ← SV_j;

42  │   RV[1..n] ← [⊥, ..., ⊥];
43  │   foreach j ∈ Π do
44  │   │   if ∃w ≠ ⊥, #_w(EV[·][j]) > 2t then RV[j] ← w;

45  │   if ∃w ≠ ⊥, #_w(RV) > 3t then return w;
46  │   else
47  │   │   c ← s mod n;
48  │   │   if ∃w ≠ ⊥, #_w(EV[c][·]) > 2t then return w;
49  │   │   return 0;
```

4.1   Description of the Algorithm

The algorithm builds upon earlier ones [1, 11, 21] but contains some important improvements; (i) a clear separation between the deciding and the maintaining parts, (ii) a simplification of the code of the algorithm, and (iii) additional code in order to satisfy our stricter BA-Agreement property. The algorithm (lines $1-23$) consists of two main parts:

1. Deciding part: processes execute $3n$ rounds to agree on a value.
2. Maintaining part: processes execute the same round forever to keep the decided value.

Maintaining part (lines $18-23$) This part is simple and repeats forever from round $3n$. The goal is to allow cured processes to recover the decided value from correct ones, since that value may have been corrupted by the malicious agent. All processes exchange their current decided values *dec* and update their variable *dec* to the value that has been received at least $n-2t$ times. During each of these rounds, there must be at least $n-2t$ correct processes according to the model. If all of them send the same value (which is guaranteed by the algorithm), all non-faulty processes receive $n-2t$ messages containing this same value and thus decide accordingly.

Deciding part (lines $3-16$) This part is complex and consists of n phases of 3 rounds each. The goal is to guarantee that, at the end of round $3n-1$, all non-faulty processes have the same value v and therefore decide it (line 17). During the first $3n$ rounds, v may take different non-bottom values, which is why processes cannot decide in earlier rounds.[4]

This part uses the rotating coordinator paradigm. Recall that, in each round, there are at least $n-t$ non-faulty processes, and at least $n-2t$ correct ones. Each of the n phases are divided into 3 rounds:

- Proposing round; all non-faulty processes (at least $n-t$) end the round with at most one non-bottom value v. Consequently, it guarantees that the (at least $n-2t$) correct processes of the next round start with at most one non-bottom value v.
- Collecting round; processes exchange the values computed in the previous round and store them in array SV (the set of received values).
- Deciding round; processes try to agree on the same value v using the rotating coordinator paradigm. If the coordinator of the current round is correct during the entire phase, non-faulty processes are guaranteed to terminate the phase with the same value. Such a coordinating round exists since, by assumption, there is one process which is correct for at least $3n$ rounds.
  In the deciding round, processes exchange the array SV computed during the previous round. Based on the arrays they received, each process computes

---

[4] This is different from previous papers as already mentioned in Section 2.

a new[5] array RV (the vector of reconstructed values). For each non-faulty process, both SV and RV contain "almost" the same values ($SV = RV$ if all processes are correct), but, as it appears in the proof, these two arrays are necessary to guarantee the correctness of our algorithm.

After the phase corresponding to a correct coordinator, all non-faulty processes have the same value v. This property will continue during all subsequent phases even if the corresponding coordinators are faulty (in fact lines $46 - 49$ will not be executed anymore as shown in the proof).

Additional code (lines 6, 10, 14) Usually, the variable *dec* is initialized to $\perp$ at the beginning of an algorithm. However, this value may be corrupted for any process that becomes faulty during the execution. To satisfy the BA-Agreement property, it is therefore necessary for each non-faulty process to re-initialize its variable *dec* to $\perp$ at the end of each of the first $3n$ round.

4.2   Proof of the Algorithm

Due to page limitations, the proof of the algorithm appears in [2]. We only state here the final theorem.

Theorem 2. *Algorithm 1 solves Mobile Byzantine Agreement in a synchronous n-process system in the presence of t mobile Byzantine agents provided that $n \geq 5t + 1$ and that at least one process remains uncorrupted.*

5   Conclusion and Discussion

We proposed a new model for Mobile Byzantine Agreement, that balances the power of correct and malicious agents. In our model, a process cannot detect its own infection and cannot instantly recover its state after the malicious agent moves away. Hence, our model gives less power to correct processes than Garay's model [11]. Recall that, in this model, a cured process can magically detect the leave of the malicious agent. In contrast, in our model, a cured process (a process that has been infected by a malicious agent) will not behave maliciously after the agent left it. That is, a cured process may send corrupted messages (computed based on a corrupted state) but it will send the same corrupted message to all neighbors. In this respect, our model gives less power to the Byzantine agents than Sasaki's model [21] where a Byzantine agent can prepare messages and control the sending of these messages even after it left that process. In our model, we prove that there is no protocol for Mobile Byzantine Agreement in synchronous networks with $n \leq 5t$. We propose then a tight algorithm which can tolerate t mobile Byzantine agents with at least $5t + 1$ processes.

In the following, we list several open questions and non trivial research directions in this area. The next step in our research is the study on the feasibility

---

[5] Technically, as in [21], it is possible to use the same variable for both SV and RV. We choose to use two different names for the clarity of the proof.

of Mobile Byzantine Agreement on arbitrary topologies. Another interesting direction would be to decrease, via randomization, the time complexity of the algorithm.

Notice that, even though our model has a self-stabilization flavor, our work is different in several aspects from the self-stabilizing Byzantine agreement of [6]. Note that in the case of self-stabilizing Byzantine agreement the studied model assumes that the Byzantine set is fixed. That is, it does not change during the execution. Also it is assumed, as in all self-stabilizing algorithms, that the system eventually becomes coherent (i.e. the communication network and a sufficient fraction of nodes is not faulty for sufficient long time period for the pre-conditions for convergence of the protocol to hold). More specifically, in self-stabilization it is assumed that during the convergence period the system does not suffer additional perturbations. In our case the system is permanently stressed due to the mobility of the Byzantine nodes. Note also that the problem solved in [6] is different since it allows the output of inconsistent decision values during transient periods.

In our model, a malicious agent can move anywhere in the network, and likely most work on the subject, we considered a fully connected topology. Sasaki *et al.* [21] have considered the case of different topologies. An interesting line of work is to generalize to arbitrary topologies, and also to consider when the mobility of the malicious agents is constrained by a, possibly different, topology.

Finally, to the best of our knowledge, so far no investigation of Mobile Byzantine Agreement has been done in anonymous settings or networks where node identities are not unique. In these contexts, algorithms based on a coordinator are not applicable.

Acknowledgments. This research was supported in part by JSPS KAKENHI Grant Number 26330020 and 26870228.

References

1. Banu, N., Souissi, S., Izumi, T., Wada, K.: An improved byzantine agreement algorithm for synchronous systems with mobile faults. International Journal of Computer Applications 43(22), 1–7 (2012)
2. Bonnet, F., Défago, X., Nguyen, T.D., Potop-Butucaru, M.: Tight bound on mobile byzantine agreement. Research Report IS-RR-2014-004, Japan Advanced Institute of Science and Technology (JAIST) (May 2014)
3. Bracha, G.: An o(log n) expected rounds randomized byzantine generals protocol. Journal of the ACM 34(4), 910–920 (1987)
4. Buhrman, H., Garay, J.A., Hoepman, J.H.: Optimal resiliency against mobile faults. In: Proceedings of the 25th International Symposium on Fault-Tolerant Computing (FTCS 1995), pp. 83–88 (1995)
5. Correia, M., Veronese, G.S., Lung, L.C.: Asynchronous byzantine consensus with $2f + 1$ processes. In: Proceedings of the 25th ACM Symposium on Applied Computing, SAC 2010, pp. 475–480 (2010)
6. Daliot, A., Dolev, D.: Self-stabilizing Byzantine agreement. In: Proc. 25th ACM Symp. on Principles of Distributed Computing (PODC 2006), pp. 143–152 (2006)

7. Dolev, D.: The byzantine generals strike again. Journal of Algorithms 3(1), 14–30 (1982)
8. Dolev, D., Fischer, M.J., Fowler, T.R., Lynch, N.A., Strong, H.R.: An efficient algorithm for byzantine agreement without authentication. Information and Control 52(3), 257–274 (1982)
9. Feldman, P., Micali, S.: An optimal probabilistic protocol for synchronous byzantine agreement. SIAM Journal on Computing 26(4), 873–933 (1997)
10. Fischer, M.J., Lynch, N.A., Paterson, M.S.: Impossibility of distributed consensus with one faulty process. Journal of the ACM 32(2), 374–382 (1985)
11. Garay, J.A.: Reaching (and maintaining) agreement in the presence of mobile faults. In: Tel, G., Vitányi, P. (eds.) WDAG 1994. LNCS, vol. 857, pp. 253–264. Springer, Heidelberg (1994)
12. Lamport, L., Shostak, R., Pease, M.: The byzantine generals problem. ACM Transactions on Programming Languages and Systems 4(3), 382–401 (1982)
13. Martin, J.P., Alvisi, L.: Fast byzantine consensus. IEEE Transactions on Dependable and Secure Computing 3(3), 202–215 (2006)
14. Okun, M., Barak, A.: Efficient algorithms for anonymous byzantine agreement. Theory of Computing Systems 42(2), 222–238 (2008)
15. Ostrovsky, R., Yung, M.: How to withstand mobile virus attacks (extended abstract). In: Proceedings of the 10th Annual ACM Symposium on Principles of Distributed Computing (PODC 1991), pp. 51–59 (1991)
16. Pease, M., Shostak, R., Lamport, L.: Reaching agreement in the presence of faults. Journal of the ACM 27(2), 228–234 (1980)
17. Raynal, M.: Fault-tolerant Agreement in Synchronous Message-passing Systems. Synthesis Lectures on Distributed Computing Theory. Morgan & Claypool Publishers (2010)
18. Reischuk, R.: A new solution for the byzantine generals problem. Information and Control 64(1-3), 23–42 (1985)
19. Santoro, N., Widmayer, P.: Time is not a healer. In: Cori, R., Monien, B. (eds.) STACS 1989. LNCS, vol. 349, pp. 304–313. Springer, Heidelberg (1989)
20. Santoro, N., Widmayer, P.: Majority and unanimity in synchronous networks with ubiquitous dynamic faults. In: Pelc, A., Raynal, M. (eds.) SIROCCO 2005. LNCS, vol. 3499, pp. 262–276. Springer, Heidelberg (2005)
21. Sasaki, T., Yamauchi, Y., Kijima, S., Yamashita, M.: Mobile byzantine agreement on arbitrary network. In: Baldoni, R., Nisse, N., van Steen, M. (eds.) OPODIS 2013. LNCS, vol. 8304, pp. 236–250. Springer, Heidelberg (2013)
22. Schmid, U., Weiss, B., Keidar, I.: Impossibility results and lower bounds for consensus under link failures. SIAM Journal on Computing 38(5), 1912–1951 (2009)

Unbeatable Consensus[*]

Armando Castañeda[1], Yannai A. Gonczarowski[2], and Yoram Moses[3]

[1] Universidad Nacional Autónoma de México (UNAM), México
armando@cs.technion.ac.il
[2] The Hebrew University of Jerusalem and Microsoft Research, Israel
yannai@gonch.name
[3] Technion — Israel Institute of Technology, Israel
moses@ee.technion.ac.il

Abstract. The *unbeatability* of a consensus protocol, introduced by Halpern, Moses and Waarts in [15], is a stronger notion of optimality than the accepted notion of early stopping protocols. Using a novel knowledge-based analysis, this paper derives the first practical unbeatable consensus protocols in the literature, for the standard synchronous message-passing model with crash failures. These protocols strictly dominate the best known protocols for uniform and non-uniform consensus, in some case beating them by a large margin. The analysis provides a new understanding of the logical structure of consensus, and of the distinction between uniform and nonuniform consensus. Finally, the first (early stopping and) unbeatable protocol that treats decision values "fairly" is presented. All of these protocols have very concise descriptions, and are shown to be efficiently implementable.

Keywords: Consensus, uniform consensus, optimality, knowledge.

1 Introduction

Following [16], we say that a protocol P is a ***worst-case optimal*** solution to a decision task S in a given model if it solves S, and decisions in P are always taken no later than the *worst-case* lower bound for decisions in this problem, in that model. Here we consider standard synchronous message-passing models with n processes and at most $t < n$ crash failures per run; it will be convenient to denote the number of *actual* failures in a given run by f. Processes proceed in a sequence of synchronous rounds. The very first consensus protocols were worst-case optimal, deciding in exactly $t + 1$ rounds in all runs [6,20]. It was soon realized, however, that they could be strictly improved upon by ***early stopping*** protocols [5], which are also worst-case optimal, but can often decide much faster than the original ones. This paper presents a number of consensus protocols that are not only worst-case optimal and early stopping, but furthermore cannot be strictly improved upon, and are thus optimal in a much stronger sense.

In benign failure models it is typically possible to define the behaviour of the environment (i.e., the adversary) in a manner that is independent of the protocol,

---

[*] A full version of this paper with complete proofs is available on arXiv.org [2]. Part of the results of this paper were announced in [1].

F. Kuhn (Ed.): DISC 2014, LNCS 8784, pp. 91–106, 2014.
© Springer-Verlag Berlin Heidelberg 2014

in terms of a pair $\alpha = (\vec{v}, \mathsf{F})$ consisting of a vector $\vec{v}$ of initial values and a failure pattern F. (A formal definition is given in Section 2.) A failure model $\mathcal{F}$ is identified with a set of (possible) failure patterns. For ease of exposition, we will think of such a pair $\alpha = (\vec{v}, \mathsf{F})$ as a particular *adversary*. In a synchronous environment, a deterministic protocol P and an adversary α uniquely define a run $r = P[\alpha]$. With this terminology, we can compare the performance of different decision protocols solving a particular task in a given context $\gamma = (\vec{\mathsf{V}}, \mathcal{F})$, where $\vec{\mathsf{V}}$ is a set of possible vectors of initial values. A decision protocol Q **dominates** a protocol P in γ, denoted by $Q \preceq_\gamma P$ if, for all adversaries α and every process i, if i decides in $P[\alpha]$ at time m_i, then i decides in $Q[\alpha]$ at some time $m_i' \le m_i$. Moreover, we say that Q **strictly dominates** P if $Q \preceq_\gamma P$ and $P \not\preceq_\gamma Q$. I.e., if Q dominates P and for some $\alpha \in \gamma$ there exists a process i that decides in $Q[\alpha]$ *strictly before* it does so in $P[\alpha]$. In the crash failure model, the early-stopping protocols of [5] strictly dominate the original protocols of [20], in which decisions are always performed at time $t + 1$. Nevertheless, these early stopping protocols may not be optimal solutions to consensus. Following [16] a protocol P is said to be an **all-case optimal** solution to a decision task S in a context γ if it solves S and, moreover, it dominates every protocol P' that solves S in γ. Dwork and Moses presented all-case optimal solutions to the *simultaneous* variant of consensus [9]. For the standard (*eventual*) variant of consensus, in which decisions are not required to occur simultaneously, Moses and Tuttle showed that no all-case optimal solution exists [18]. Consequently, Halpern, Moses and Waarts in [15] initiated the study of a natural notion of optimality that is achievable by eventual consensus protocols:

Definition 1 (Halpern, Moses and Waarts). *A protocol P is an* **unbeatable** *solution to a decision task S in a context γ if P solves S in γ and no protocol Q solving S in γ strictly dominates P.*[1]

Halpern, Moses and Waarts observed that for every consensus protocol P there exists an unbeatable protocol Q_P that dominates P. Moreover, they showed a two-step transformation that defines such a protocol Q_P based on P. This transformation and the resulting protocols are based on a notion of *continual* common knowledge that is computable, but not efficiently: in the resulting protocol, each process executes exponential time (PSPACE) local computations in every round. The logical transformation is not applied in [15] to an actual protocol. As an example of an unbeatable protocol, they present a particular protocol, called $P0_{\text{opt}}$, and argue that it is unbeatable in the crash failure model. Unfortunately, as we will show, $P0_{\text{opt}}$ is in fact beatable. This does not refute the general analysis and transformation defined in [15]; they remain correct. Rather, the fault is in an unsound step in the proof of optimality of $P0_{\text{opt}}$ (Theorem 6.2 of [15]), in which an inductive step is not explicitly detailed, and does not hold.

---

[1] All-case optimal protocols are called *"optimal in all runs"* in [9]. They are termed *"optimum"* in [15], while unbeatable protocols are simply called *"optimal"* there. We prefer the term *unbeatable* because "optimal" is used very broadly, and inconsistently, in the literature.

The main contributions of this paper are:

1. A knowledge-based analysis is applied to the classical consensus protocol, and is shown to yield solutions that are optimal in a much stronger sense than all previous solutions. Much simpler and more intuitive than the framework used in [15], it illustrates how the knowledge-based approach can yield a structured approach to the derivation of efficient protocols.

2. OPT_0, the first explicit unbeatable protocol for nonuniform consensus is presented. It is computationally efficient, and its unbeatability is established by way of a succinct proof. Moreover, OPT_0 is shown to strictly dominate the $P0_{\text{opt}}$ protocol from [15], proving that the latter is in fact beatable.

3. An analysis of uniform consensus gives rise to U-OPT_0, the first explicit unbeatable protocol for uniform consensus. The analysis used in the design of U-OPT_0 sheds light on the inherent difference and similarities between the uniform and nonuniform variants of consensus in this model.

4. Early stopping protocols for consensus are traditionally one-sided, preferring to decide on 0 (or on 1) if possible. deciding on a predetermined value (say, 0) if possible, we present an An unbeatable (and early stopping) majority consensus protocol OPT_{Maj} is presented, that prefers the *majority* value.

5. We identify the notion of a *hidden path* as being crucial to decision in the consensus task. If a process identifies that no hidden path exists, then it can decide. In the fastest early-stopping protocols, a process decides after the first round in which it does not detect a new failure. By deciding based on the nonexistence of a hidden path, our unbeatable protocols can stop up to $t - 3$ rounds faster than the best early stopping protocols in the literature.

We now sketch the intuition behind, our unbeatable consensus protocols.

In the standard version of consensus, every process i starts with an initial value $v_i \in \{0, 1\}$, and the following properties must hold in every run r:

(Nonuniform) **Consensus:**

> **Decision:** Every correct process must decide on some value,
> **Validity:** If all initial values are v then the correct processes decide v, and
> **Agreement:** All correct processes decide on the same value.

The connection between knowledge and distributed computing was proposed in [14] and has been used in the analysis of a variety of problems, including consensus (see [10] for more details and references). In this paper, we employ simpler techniques to perform a more direct knowledge-based analysis. Our approach is based on a simple principle recently formulated by Moses in [19], called the *knowledge of preconditions* principle (**KoP**), which captures an essential connection between knowledge and action in distributed and multi-agent systems. Roughly speaking, the **KoP** principle says that if C is a necessary condition for an action α to be performed by process i, then $K_i(C)$ — i knowing C — is a necessary condition for i performing α. E.g., it is not enough for a client to have positive credit in order to receive cash from an ATM; the ATM must *know* that the client has positive credit.

Problem specifications typically state or imply a variety of necessary conditions. In the crash failure model studied in this paper, we will say that a process is *active* at time m in a given run, if it does not crash before time m. For $v \in \{0, 1\}$, we denote by $\mathsf{decide}_i(v)$ the action of i deciding v, and use $\bar{v}$ as shorthand for $1 - v$.

Lemma 1. *Consensus implies the following necessary conditions for* $\mathsf{decide}_i(v)$ *in the crash failure model:*

(a) "at least one processes had initial value v*" (we denote this by* $\exists v$*), and*

(b) "no currently active process has decided, or is currently deciding, $\bar{v}$*" (we denote this by* $\mathsf{no\text{-}decided}(\bar{v})$*).*

Both parts follow from observing that if i decides v at a point where either (a) or (b) does not hold, then the execution can be extended to a run in which i (as well as j, for (b)) is correct (does not crash), and this run violates **Validity** for (a) or **Agreement** for (b).

Given Lemma 1, **KoP** implies that $K_i \exists v$ and $K_i \mathsf{no\text{-}decided}(\bar{v})$ are also necessary conditions for $\mathsf{decide}_i(v)$. In this paper, we will explore how this insight can be exploited in order to design efficient consensus protocols. Indeed, our first unbeatable protocol will be one in which, roughly speaking, the rule for $\mathsf{decide}_i(0)$ will be $K_i \exists 0$, and the rule for $\mathsf{decide}_i(1)$ will be $K_i \mathsf{no\text{-}decided}(0)$. As we will show, if the rule for $\mathsf{decide}_i(0)$ is $K_i \exists 0$, then $\mathsf{no\text{-}decided}(0)$ reduces to the fact $\mathsf{not\text{-}known}(\exists 0)$, which is true at a given time if $K_j \exists 0$ holds for no currently-active process j. Thus, $K_i \mathsf{no\text{-}decided}(0)$ — our candidate rule for deciding 1 — then becomes $K_i \mathsf{not\text{-}known}(\exists 0)$. While $K_i \exists 0$ involves the knowledge a process has about initial values, $K_i \mathsf{not\text{-}known}(\exists 0)$ is concerned with i's knowledge about the knowledge of others. We will review the formal definition of knowledge in the next section, in order to turn this into a rigorous condition.

Converting the above description into an actual protocol essentially amounts to providing concrete tests for when these knowledge conditions hold. It is straightforward to show (and quite intuitive) that in a full-information protocol $K_i \exists 0$ holds exactly if there is a message chain from some process j whose initial value is 0, to process i. To determine that $\mathsf{not\text{-}known}(\exists 0)$, a process must have proof that no such chain can exist. Our technical analysis identifies a notion of a *hidden path* with respect to i at a time m, which implies that a message chain could potentially be communicating a value unbeknownst to i. It is shown that hidden paths are key to evaluating whether $K_i \mathsf{not\text{-}known}(\exists 0)$ holds. In fact, it turns out that hidden paths are key to obtaining additional unbeatable protocols in the crash failure model. We present two such protocols; one is a consensus protocol in which a process that sees a majority value can decide on this value, and the other is an unbeatable protocol for the *uniform* variant of consensus. In uniform consensus, any two processes that decide must decide on the same value, even if one (or both) of them crash soon after deciding.

This paper is structured as follows: The next section reviews the definitions of the synchronous crash-failure model and of knowledge in this model. Section 3 presents OPT_0, our unbeatable consensus protocol, proves its unbeatability, and shows that it beats the protocol $P0_{opt}$ of [15]. It then derives an unbeatable consensus protocol, OPT_{Maj}, that treats 0 and 1 in a balanced way. Both unbeatable protocols decide in no more than $f + 1$ rounds in runs in which f processes actually fail but they can decide much earlier than that. Section 4 studies uniform consensus, and derives U-OPT_0, an unbeatable protocol for uniform consensus. Finally, Section 5 concludes with a discussion. Due to lack of space, proofs are not presented here. For a full version of this paper see [2]

2 Preliminary Definitions

Our model of computation is the standard synchronous message-passing model with benign crash failures. A system has $n \geq 2$ processes denoted by Procs $= \{1, 2, \ldots, n\}$. Each pair of processes is connected by a two-way communication link, and each message is tagged with the identity of the sender. They share a discrete global clock that starts out at time 0 and advances by increments of one. Communication in the system proceeds in a sequence of *rounds*, with round $m + 1$ taking place between time m and time $m + 1$. Each process starts in some *initial state* at time 0, usually with an *input value* of some kind. In every round, each process first performs a local computation, and performs local actions, then it sends a set of messages to other processes, and finally receives messages sent to it by other processes during the same round. We consider the local computations and sending actions of round $m + 1$ as being performed at time m, and the messages are received at time $m + 1$.

A faulty process fails by *crashing* in some round $m \geq 1$. It behaves correctly in the first $m - 1$ rounds and sends no messages from round $m + 1$ on. During its crashing round m, the process may succeed in sending messages on an arbitrary subset of its links. At most $t \leq n - 1$ processes fail in any given execution.

It is convenient to consider the state and behaviour of processes at different (process-time) nodes, where a **node** is a pair $\langle i, m \rangle$ referring to process i at time m. A **failure pattern** describes how processes fail in an execution. It is a layered graph F whose vertices are nodes $\langle i, m \rangle$ for $i \in$ Procs and $m \geq 0$. Such a vertex denotes process i and time m. An edge has the form $(\langle i, m-1 \rangle, \langle j, m \rangle)$ and it denotes the fact that a message sent by i to j in round m would be delivered successfully. Let Crash(t) denote the set of failure patterns in which all failures are crash failures, and no more than t crash failures occur. An **input vector** describes the initial values that the processes receive in an execution. The only inputs we consider are initial values that processes obtain at time 0. An input vector is thus a tuple $\vec{v} = (v_1, \ldots, v_n)$ where v_j is the input to process j. We think of the input vector and the failure pattern as being determined by an external scheduler, and thus a pair $\alpha = (\vec{v}, F)$ is called an *adversary*.

A **protocol** describes what messages a process sends and what decisions it takes, as a deterministic function of its local state at the start of a round and the messages received during a round. We assume that a protocol P has access to the values of n and t, typically passed to P as parameters.

A **run** is a description of an infinite behaviour of the system. Given a run r and a time m, we denote by $r_i(m)$ the **local state** of process i at time m in r, and the **global state** at time m is defined to be $r(m) = \langle r_1(m), r_2(m), \ldots, r_n(m) \rangle$. A protocol P and an adversary α uniquely determine a run, and we write $r = P[\alpha]$.

Since we restrict attention to benign failure models and focus on decision times and solvability in this paper, it is sufficient to consider *full-information protocols* (*fip's* for short), defined below [4]. There is a convenient way to consider such protocols in our setting. With an adversary $\alpha = (\vec{v}, \mathsf{F})$ we associate a **communication graph** $\mathcal{G}_\alpha$, consisting of the graph F extended by labelling the initial nodes $\langle j, 0 \rangle$ with the initial states v_j according to α. Every node $\langle i, m \rangle$ is associated with a subgraph $\mathcal{G}_\alpha(i, m)$ of $\mathcal{G}_\alpha$, which we think of as i's view at $\langle i, m \rangle$. Intuitively, this graph will represent all nodes $\langle j, \ell \rangle$ from which $\langle i, m \rangle$ has heard, and the initial values it has seen. Formally, $\mathcal{G}_\alpha(i, m)$ is defined by induction on m. $\mathcal{G}_\alpha(i, 0)$ consists of the node $\langle i, 0 \rangle$, labelled by the initial value v_i. Assume that $\mathcal{G}_\alpha(1, m), \ldots, \mathcal{G}_\alpha(n, m)$ have been defined, and let $J \subseteq \mathsf{Procs}$ be the set of processes j such that $j = i$ or $e_j = (\langle j, m \rangle, \langle i, m+1 \rangle)$ is an edge of F. Then $\mathcal{G}_\alpha(i, m+1)$ consists of the node $\langle i, m+1 \rangle$, the union of all graphs $\mathcal{G}_\alpha(j, m)$ with $j \in J$, and the edges $e_j = (\langle j, m \rangle, \langle i, m+1 \rangle)$ for all $j \in J$. We say that (j, ℓ) is *seen* by $\langle i, m \rangle$ if (j, ℓ) is a node of $\mathcal{G}_\alpha(i, m)$. Note that this occurs exactly if the failure pattern F allows a (Lamport) message chain from $\langle j, \ell \rangle$ to $\langle i, m \rangle$.

A full-information protocol P is one in which at every node $\langle i, m \rangle$ of a run $r = P[\alpha]$ the process i constructs $\mathcal{G}_\alpha(i, m)$ after receiving its round m nodes, and sends $\mathcal{G}_\alpha(i, m)$ to all other processes in round $m+1$. In addition, P specifies what decisions i should take at $\langle i, m \rangle$ based on $\mathcal{G}_\alpha(i, m)$. Full-information protocols thus differ only in the decisions taken at the nodes. Let $\mathsf{d}(i, m)$ be status of i's decision at time m (either '$\perp$' if it is undecided, or a concrete value 'v'). Thus, in a run $r = P[\alpha]$, we define the local state $r_i(m) = \langle \mathsf{d}(i, m), \mathcal{G}_\alpha(i, m) \rangle$ if i does not crash before time m according to α, and $r_i(m) = \odot$, an uninformative "crashed" state, if i crashes before time m.

For ease of exposition and analysis, all of our protocols are full-information. However, in fact, they can all be implemented in such a way that any process sends any other process a total of $O(f \log n)$ bits throughout any execution (as shown in [2]).

2.1   Knowledge

Our construction of unbeatable protocols will be assisted and guided by a knowledge-based analysis, in the spirit of [10,14]. Runs are dynamic objects, changing from one time point to the next. E.g., at one point process i may be undecided, while at the next it may decide on a value. Similarly, the set of initial values that i knows about, or has seen, may change over time. In general, whether a process "knows" something at a given point can depend on what is true in other runs in which the process has the same information. We will therefore consider the truth of facts at *points* (r, m)—time m in run r, with respect to a set of runs R (which we call a **system**). We will be interested in systems of the form $R_P = R(P, \gamma)$ where P is a protocol and $\gamma = \gamma(\mathsf{V}^n, \mathcal{F})$ is the set of all adversaries that assign initial values from V and failures according to $\mathcal{F}$. We will write $(R, r, m) \models A$ to state that fact A holds, or is satisfied, at (r, m) in the system R.

The truth of some facts can be defined directly. For example, the fact $\exists v$ will hold at (r, m) in R if some process has initial value v in $(r, 0)$. We say that *(satisfaction of)* a fact A is **well-defined in** R if for every point (r, m) with $r \in R$ we can determine whether or not $(R, r, m) \models A$. Satisfaction of $\exists v$ is thus well defined. Moreover, any boolean combination of well-defined facts is also well defined. We will write $K_i A$ to denote that **process** i **knows** A, and define:

Definition 2 (Knowledge). *Suppose that A is well defined in R. Define that* $(R, r, m) \models K_i A$ *iff* $(R, r', m) \models A$ *holds for all $r' \in R$ with $r_i(m) = r'_i(m)$.*

Thus, if A is well defined in R then Definition 2 makes $K_i A$ well defined in R. Note that what a process knows or does not know depends on its local state. The definition can then be applied recursively, to define the truth of $K_j K_i A$ etc. Knowledge has been used to study a variety of problems in distributed computing. In particular, we now formally define $(R, r, m) \models$ not-known($\exists 0$) to hold iff $(R, r, m) \not\models K_j \exists 0$ holds for every process j that does not crash by time m in r. We will make use of the following fundamental connection between knowledge and actions in distributed systems. A fact A is a **necessary condition** for process i performing action σ (e.g. deciding on an output value) in R if $(R, r, m) \models A$ whenever i performs σ at a point (r, m) of R.

Theorem 1 (Knowledge of Preconditions, [19]). *Let $R_P = R(P, \gamma)$ be the set of runs of a deterministic protocol P. If A is a necessary condition for i performing σ in R_P, then so is $K_i A$.*

3   Unbeatable Consensus

We start with the standard version of consensus defined in the Introduction, and consider the crash failure context $\gamma_{cr}^t = \langle V^n, \text{Crash}(t) \rangle$, where $V = \{0, 1\}$ — initial values are binary bits. Every protocol P in this setting determines a system $R_P = R(P, \gamma_{cr}^t)$. Recall that Lemma 1 establishes necessary conditions for decision in consensus. Based on this, Theorem 1 yields:

Lemma 2. *Let P be a consensus protocol for γ_{cr}^t and let $R_P = R(P, \gamma_{cr}^t)$. Then both $K_i \exists v$ and $K_i$no-decided($\bar{v}$) are necessary conditions for* decide$_i$(v) *in R_P.*

An analysis of knowledge for *fips* in the crash failure model was first performed by Dwork and Moses in [9]. The following result is an immediate consequence of that analysis. Under the full-information protocol, we have:

Lemma 3 (Dwork and Moses [9]). *Let P be a fip in γ_{cr}^t and let $r \in R_P = R(P, \gamma_{cr}^t)$. For all processes i, j, $(R_P, r, t+1) \models K_i \exists v$ iff $(R_P, r, t+1) \models K_j \exists v$.*

Of course, a process that does not know $\exists 0$ must itself have an initial value of 1. Hence, based on Lemma 3, it is natural to design a *fip*-based consensus protocol that performs decide$_i$(0) at time $t + 1$ if $K_i \exists 0$, and otherwise performs decide$_i$(1). (In the very first consensus protocols, all decisions are performed at time $t + 1$ [20].) Indeed, one can use Lemma 3 to obtain a strictly better protocol, in which decisions on 0 are performed sooner:

> **Protocol P_0** (for an undecided process i at time m):
>   **if** $K_i \exists 0$ **then** decide$_i(0)$
>   **elseif** $m = t + 1$ **then** decide$_i(1)$

Notice that in a *fip* consensus protocol, it is only necessary to describe the rules for decide$_i(0)$ and decide$_i(1)$, since in every round a process sends all it knows to all processes. Since $K_i \exists 0$ is a necessary condition for decide$_i(0)$, the protocol P_0 decides on 0 as soon as any consensus protocol can. In the early 80's Dolev suggested a closely related protocol B (standing for *"Beep"*) for γ_{cr}^t, in which processes decide 0 and broadcast the existence of a 0 when they see a 0, and decide 1 at $t + 1$ otherwise [7]; for all adversaries, it performs the same decisions at the same times as P_0. Halpern, Moses and Waarts show in [15] that for every consensus protocol P in γ_{cr}^t there is an unbeatable consensus protocol Q dominating P. Our immediate goal is to obtain an unbeatable consensus protocol dominating P_0. To this end, we make use of the following.

Lemma 4. *If $Q \preceq P_0$ is a consensus protocol, then* decide$_i(0)$ *is performed in Q exactly when $K_i \exists 0$ first holds.*

We can now formalize the discussion in the Introduction, showing that if decisions on 0 are performed precisely when $K_i \exists 0$ first holds, then no-decided(0) reduces to not-known($\exists 0$).

Lemma 5. *Let P be a fip, in which* decide$_i(0)$ *is performed in P exactly when $K_i \exists 0$ first holds, and let $R_P = R(P, \gamma_{cr}^t)$. Then $(R_P, r, m) \models K_i$no-decided(0) iff $(R_P, r, m) \models K_i$not-known($\exists 0$) for all $r \in R_P$ and $m \geq 0$.*

The proof of Lemma 5 is fairly immediate: If $(R_P, r, m) \not\models K_i$not-known($\exists 0$) then there is a run r' of R_P such that both $r_i(m) = r_i'(m)$ and $(R_P, r', m) \models K_j \exists 0$ for some correct process j; therefore, process j decides 0 in r'. The other direction follows directly from the decision rule for 0. We can now define a *fip* consensus protocol in which 0 is defined as soon as its necessary condition $K_i \exists 0$ holds, and 1 is decided as soon as possible, given the rule for deciding 0:

> **Protocol OPT_0** (for an undecided process i at time m):
>   **if** $K_i \exists 0$ **then** decide$_i(0)$
>   **elseif** $K_i$not-known($\exists 0$) **then** decide$_i(1)$

We can show that OPT_0 is, indeed, an unbeatable protocol:

Theorem 2. OPT_0 *is an unbeatable consensus protocol in γ_{cr}^t.*

3.1   Testing for Knowing that Nobody Knows

OPT_0 is not a standard protocol, because its actions depend on tests for process i's knowledge. (It is a *knowledge-based program* in the sense of [10].) In order to turn it into a standard protocol, we need to replace these by explicit tests on the processes' local states. The rule for $\mathsf{decide}_i(0)$ is easy to implement. By Lemma 3(a), $K_i \exists 0$ holds exactly if i's local state contains a time 0 node that is labelled with value 0. The rule $K_i\mathsf{not\text{-}known}(\exists 0)$ for performing $\mathsf{decide}_i(1)$ holds when i knows that no active process knows $\exists 0$, and we now characterize when this is true. A central role in our analysis will be played by process i's knowledge about the contents of various nodes in the communication graph. Recall that local states $r_i(m)$ in fip's are communication graphs of the form $\mathcal{G}_\alpha(i, m)$; we abuse notation and write $\theta \in r_i(m)$ (respectively, $(\theta, \theta') \in r_i(m)$) if θ is a node of $\mathcal{G}_\alpha(i, m) = r_i(m)$ (respectively, if (θ, θ') is an edge of $\mathcal{G}_\alpha(i, m) = r_i(m)$); in this case, we say that θ is **seen** by $\langle i, m \rangle$. We now make the following definition:

Definition 3 (Revealed). *Let $r \in R_P = R(P, \gamma_{\mathrm{cr}}^t)$ for a fip protocol P. We say that **node $\langle j', m' \rangle$ is revealed to $\langle i, m \rangle$ in r** if either (1) $\langle j', m' \rangle \in r_i(m)$, or (2) for some process i' such that $\langle i', m' \rangle \in r_i(m)$ it is the case that $(\langle j', m' - 1 \rangle, \langle i', m' \rangle) \notin r_i(m)$. We say that **time m' is revealed to $\langle i, m \rangle$ in r** if $\langle j', m' \rangle$ is revealed to $\langle i, m \rangle$ for all processes j'.*

Intuitively, if node $\langle j', m' \rangle$ is revealed to $\langle i, m \rangle$ then i has proof at time m that $\langle j', m' \rangle$ can not carry information that is not known at $\langle i, m \rangle$ but may be known at another node $\langle j, m \rangle$ at the same time. This because either i sees $\langle j', m' \rangle$ at that point—this is part (1)—or i has proof that j' crashed before time m', and so its state there was ☺, and j' did not send any messages at or after time m'. It is very simple and straightforward from the definition to determine which nodes are revealed to $\langle i, m \rangle$, based on $r_i(m) = \mathcal{G}_\alpha(i, m)$. Observe that if a node $\langle j', m' \rangle$ is revealed to $\langle i, m \rangle$, then i knows at m what message could have been sent at $\langle j', m' \rangle$: If $\langle j', m' \rangle \in r_i(m)$ then $r_{j'}(m')$ is a subgraph of $r_i(m)$, while if $(\langle j', m' - 1 \rangle, \langle i', m' \rangle) \notin r_i(m)$ for some node $\langle i', m' \rangle \in r_i(m)$, then j' crashed before time m' in r, and so it sends no messages at time m'. Whether and when a node $\langle j', m' \rangle$ is revealed to i depends crucially on the failure pattern. If i receives a message from j' in round $m' + 1$, then $\langle j', m' \rangle$ is immediately revealed to $\langle i, m' + 1 \rangle$. If this message is not received by $\langle i, m' + 1 \rangle$, then $\langle j', m' + 1 \rangle$ — the successor of $\langle j', m' \rangle$ — becomes revealed (as being crashed, i.e. in state ☺) to $\langle i, m' + 1 \rangle$. But in general $\langle j', m' \rangle$ can be revealed to i at a much later time than $m' + 1$, (A simple instance of this is when $K_i \exists 0$ first becomes true at a time $m > 1$; this happens when $\langle j, 0 \rangle$ with $v_j = 0$ is first revealed to i.)

Suppose that some time $k \leq m$ is revealed to $\langle i, m \rangle$. Then, in a precise sense, process i at time m has all of the information that existed in the system at time k (in the hands of processes that had not crashed by then). In particular, if this information does not contain an initial value of 0, then nobody can know $\exists 0$ at or after time m. We now formalize this intuition and show that revealed nodes can be used to determine when a process can know $\mathsf{not\text{-}known}(\exists 0)$.

Lemma 6. *Let P be a fip and let $r \in R_P = R(P, \gamma_{\mathrm{cr}}^t)$. For every node $\langle i, m \rangle$, it is the case that $(R_P, r, m) \models K_i\mathsf{not\text{-}known}(\exists 0)$ exactly if both (1) $(R_P, r, m) \not\models K_i \exists 0$ and (2) some time $k \leq m$ is revealed to $\langle i, m \rangle$ in r.*

Based on Lemma 6, we now obtain a standard unbeatable consensus protocol for γ_{cr}^t that implements OPT_0:

Protocol $\text{OPT}_0^{\text{std}}$ (for an undecided process i at time m):

> **if** i has seen a time-0 node with initial value 0 **then** decide$_i$(0)
> **elseif** some time $k \leq m$ is revealed to $\langle i, m \rangle$ **then** decide$_i$(1)

We emphasize that $\text{OPT}_0^{\text{std}}$ (and thus also OPT_0), and all the following protocols, can be implemented efficiently. The protocol only uses information about the existence of 0 and about the rounds at which processes crash. It can therefore be implemented in such a way that any process sends a total of $O(f \log n)$ bits (see [2]) in every run, and executes $O(n)$ local steps in every round.

The formulation of $\text{OPT}_0^{\text{std}}$, in addition to facilitating an efficient implementation, also makes the worst-case stopping time of $\text{OPT}_0^{\text{std}}$ and OPT_0 apparent.

Lemma 7. *In* $\text{OPT}_0^{\text{std}}$ *(and thus also* OPT_0*), all decisions are made by time* $f + 1$ *at the latest.*[2]

It is interesting to compare OPT_0 with efficient early-stopping consensus protocols [3,5,12,15]. Let's say that ***the sender set repeats at*** $\langle i, m \rangle$ in run r if i hears from the same set of processes in rounds $m-1$ and m. If this happens then, for every $\langle j, m-1 \rangle \notin r_i(m)$, we are guaranteed that $(\langle j, m-2 \rangle, \langle i, m-1 \rangle) \notin r_i(m)$. Thus, all nodes at time $(m-1)$ are revealed to $\langle i, m \rangle$. Indeed, in a run in which f failures actually occur, the sender set will repeat for every correct process by time $f + 1$ at the latest. Efficient early stopping protocols typically decide when the sender set repeats. Indeed, the protocol $P0_{\text{opt}}$ that was claimed by [15] to be unbeatable does so as well, with a slight optimization. Writing $\forall 1$ to stand for "all initial values are 1", $P0_{\text{opt}}$ is described as follows:

Protocol $P0_{\text{opt}}$ (for an undecided process i at time m) [15] :

> **if** $K_i \exists 0$ **then** decide$_i$(0)
> **elseif** $K_i \forall 1$ or $m \geq 2$ and the sender set repeats at $\langle i, m \rangle$ **then** decide$_i$(1)

OPT_0 and $P0_{\text{opt}}$ differ only in the rule for deciding 1. But OPT_0 strictly beats $P0_{\text{opt}}$, and sometimes by a wide margin. If $t = \Omega(n)$ then it can decide faster by a *ratio* of $\Omega(n)$. Indeed, we can show:

Lemma 8. *If* $3 \leq t \leq n - 2$, *then* OPT_0 *strictly dominates* $P0_{\text{opt}}$. *Moreover, there exists an adversary for which* decide$_i$(1) *is performed after 3 rounds in* OPT_0, *and after* $t + 1$ *rounds in* $P0_{\text{opt}}$.

3.2   Hidden Paths and Agreement

It is instructive to examine the proof of Lemma 6 (see [2]) and consider when an active process i is undecided at $\langle i, m \rangle$ in OPT_0. This occurs if both $\neg K_i \exists 0$ and, in addition, for every $k = 0, \ldots, m$ there is at least one node $\langle j_k, k \rangle$ that is not revealed to $\langle i, m \rangle$. We call the sequence of nodes $\langle j_0, 0 \rangle, \ldots, \langle j_m, m \rangle$ a ***hidden path w.r.t.*** $\langle i, m \rangle$. Such a hidden path implies that all processes $j_0, \ldots, j_m$

---

[2] In all our protocols, a process can stop at the earlier of one round after deciding and time $t + 1$.

have crashed. Roughly speaking, $\exists 0$ could be relayed along such a hidden path without i knowing it (see Fig. 1). More formally, its existence means that there is

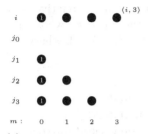 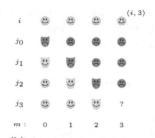 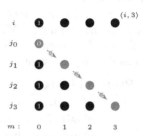

(a) All nodes seen (directly or indirectly) by $\langle i, 3 \rangle$. The initial value is shown for all seen time-0 nodes. Notably, both $\neg K_i \exists 0$ and $\neg K_i \neg \exists 0$ hold at time $m = 3$.

(b) The state of each node, according to the information held by $\langle i, 3 \rangle$: ☺=seen by all; ☺=seen, may have crashed; ●=revealed, seen by none; ☻=hidden: may have been seen by others.[3]

(c) A run that is possible according to the information held by $\langle i, 3 \rangle$;[4] in this run, $K_{j_3} \exists 0$ holds at time $m = 3$. Therefore, $\neg K_i$not-known($\exists 0$) at time $m = 3$. $\langle i, 3 \rangle$ is therefore undecided in OPT_0.

Fig. 1. A hidden path $\langle j_0, 0 \rangle, \ldots, \langle j_3, 3 \rangle$ w.r.t. $\langle i, 3 \rangle$ implies $\neg K_i$not-known($\exists 0$) at 3

a run, indistinguishable at $\langle i, m \rangle$ from the current one, in which $v_{j_0} = 0$ and this fact is sent from each j_k to j_{k+1} in every round $k+1 \leq m$. In that run process j_m is active at time m and $K_{j_m} \exists 0$, and that is why $K_i$not-known($\exists 0$) *does not* hold. Hidden paths are implicit in many lower bound proofs for consensus in the crash failure model [5,9], but they have never before been captured formally. Clearly, hidden paths can relay more than just the existence of a value of 0. In a protocol in which some view can prove that the state is univalent in the sense of Fischer, Lynch and Paterson [11], a hidden path from a potentially pivotal state can keep processes from deciding on the complement value. Our analysis in the remainder of the paper provides additional cases in which unbeatable consensus is obtained when hidden paths can be ruled out.

3.3 Majority Consensus

Can we obtain other unbeatable consensus protocols? Clearly, the symmetric protocol OPT_1, obtained from OPT_0 by reversing the roles of 0 and 1, is unbeatable and neither dominates, nor is dominated by, OPT_0. Of course, OPT_0 and OPT_1 are extremely biased, each deciding on its favourite value if at all possible, even if it appears as the initial value of a single process. One may argue

---

[3] For simplicity, in this example every node seen by $\langle i, 3 \rangle$ is also seen by all other nodes in the view of $\langle i, 3 \rangle$. In other words, there exists no node $\langle j, m' \rangle$ that is in state ☻ according to the information held by $\langle i, 3 \rangle$, i.e. both $\langle j, m' \rangle$ is seen by $\langle i, 3 \rangle$, and i has indirectly learnt by time 3 that j has in fact crashed at m'.

[4] In this run, the state of both $\langle j_0, 0 \rangle$ and $\langle j_1, 1 \rangle$, according to the information held by $\langle j_3, 3 \rangle$, is ☻, as defined in Footnote 3.

that it is natural, and may be preferable in many applications, to seek a more balanced solution, in which minority values are not favoured. Fix $n > 0$ and define the fact "Maj $= 0$" to be true if at least $n/2$ initial values are 0, while "Maj $= 1$" is true if strictly more than $n/2$ values are 1. Finally, relative to a node $\langle i, m \rangle$, we define $Maj\langle i, m \rangle \triangleq 0$ if at least half of the processes whose initial value is known to i at time m have initial value 0; $Maj\langle i, m \rangle \triangleq 1$ otherwise. Consider the following protocol:

Protocol OPT_{Maj} (for an undecided process i at time m):

if $K_i(\text{Maj} = 0)$	**then** decide$_i$(0)
elseif $K_i(\text{Maj} = 1)$	**then** decide$_i$(1)
elseif some time $k \leq m$ is revealed to $\langle i, m \rangle$ **then** decide$_i$($Maj\langle i, m \rangle$).	

We note that whether $K_i(\text{Maj} = 0)$ (resp. $K_i(\text{Maj} = 1)$) holds can be checked efficiently: it holds exactly if i has seen at least (resp. strictly more than) $n/2$ time-0 nodes with initial value 0 (resp. 1).

Theorem 3. *If $t > 0$, then OPT_{Maj} is an unbeatable consensus protocol. In particular, in a run in which $f \leq t$ failures actually occur, all decisions are performed by time $f + 1$, at the latest.*

The proof of Theorem 3 formalizes the following idea. Suppose that i sees fewer than a full majority of either value at $\langle i, m \rangle$ and has a hidden path. Then i considers it possible that the node $\langle j_1, 1 \rangle$ in the hidden path may have seen either a full majority of 0's or a full majority of 1's, and this information may reach an active node $\langle j_m, m \rangle$. Decision is thus impossible in this case, and decisions are made when no hidden path w.r.t. $\langle i, m \rangle$ is possible. Thus, OPT_{Maj} is an unbeatable consensus protocol that satisfies an additional "fairness" property:

Majority Validity: For $v \in \{0, 1\}$, if more than half of the processes are both correct and have initial value v, then no process decides $\bar{v}$ in r.

4   Unbeatable Uniform Consensus

It is often of interest to consider *uniform* consensus [3,8,13,17,21,22] in which we replace the **Agreement** condition of consensus by:

Uniform Agreement: The processes that decide in a given run must all decide on the same value.

This forces correct processes and faulty ones to act in a consistent manner. Requiring uniformity makes sense only in a setting where failures are benign, and all processes that decide do so according to the protocol. Uniformity may be desirable when elements outside the system can observe decisions, as in distributed databases when decisions correspond to commitments to values.

Under crash failures, a process generally does not know whether or not it is correct. Indeed, so long as it has not seen t failures, the process may (for all it knows) crash in the future. As a result, while $K_i \exists 0$ is a necessary condition for decide$_i$(0) as before, it cannot be a *sufficient* condition for decision in any uniform consensus protocol. This is because a process starting with 0 immediately decides 0 with this rule, and may immediately crash. If all other processes have initial value 1, all other decisions can only be on 1. Of course, $K_i \exists 0$ is still a necessary condition for deciding 0, but it is *not* sufficient. Denote by $\exists$correct(v) the fact "some *correct* process knows $\exists$v". We show the following:

Lemma 9. $K_i \exists$correct(v) *is a necessary condition for i deciding* v *in any protocol solving Uniform Consensus.*

There is a direct way to test whether $K_i \exists$correct(v) holds, based on $r_i(m)$:

Lemma 10. *Let* $r \in R_P = R(P, \gamma_{cr}^t)$ *and assume that i knows of* ***d*** *failures at* (r, m). *Then* $(R_P, r, m) \models K_i \exists$correct(v) *iff at least one of* *(a)* $m > 0$ *and* $(R_P, r, m-1) \models K_i \exists$v, *or (b)* $(R_P, r, m) \models K_i(K_j \exists$v *held at time* $m-1)$ *holds for at least* $(\boldsymbol{t}-\boldsymbol{d})$ *distinct processes* j.

By Lemma 3, at time $\boldsymbol{t}+1$ the conditions $K_i \exists$v and $K_i \exists$correct(v) are equivalent. As in the case of consensus, we note that if $K_i \exists 0$ (equivalently, $K_i \exists$correct(0)) does not hold at time $\boldsymbol{t}+1$, then it never will. We thus phrase the following *beatable* algorithm, analogous to P_0, for Uniform Consensus; in this protocol, $K_i \exists$correct(0) (the necessary condition for deciding 0 in uniform consensus) replaces $K_i \exists 0$ (the necessary condition in consensus) as the decision rule for 0. The decision rule for 1 remains the same. Note that $K_i \exists$correct(0) can be efficiently checked, by applying the test of Lemma 10.

Protocol U-P_0 (for an undecided process i at time m):
    if $K_i \exists$correct(0) **then** decide$_i$(0)
    elseif $m = \boldsymbol{t}+1$ **then** decide$_i$(1).

Following a similar line of reasoning to that leading to OPT$_0$, we obtain an unbeatable uniform consensus protocol:

Protocol U-OPT$_0$ (for an undecided process i at time m):
    if $K_i \exists$correct(0)   **then** decide$_i$(0)
    elseif $\neg K_i \exists 0$ and some time $k \leq m$ is revealed to $\langle i, m \rangle$ **then** decide$_i$(1).

Recall that whether $K_i \exists$correct(0) holds can be checked efficiently via the characterization in Lemma 10.

Theorem 4. U-OPT$_0$ *is an unbeatable* ***uniform*** *consensus protocol in which all decisions are made by time* $f+2$ *at the latest, and if* $f \geq \boldsymbol{t}-1$, *then all decisions are made by time* $f+1$ *at the latest.*

Hidden paths again play a central role. Indeed, as in the construction of OPT$_0$ from P_0, the construction of U-OPT$_0$ from U-P_0 involves some decisions on 1 being moved earlier in time, by means of the last condition, checking the absence of a hidden path. (Decisions on 0 cannot be moved any earlier, as they are taken as soon as the necessary condition for deciding 0 holds.) Observe that the need to obtain $K_i \exists$correct(v) rather than $K_i \exists$v concisely captures the essential distinction between uniform consensus and nonuniform consensus. The fact that the same condition — the existence of a hidden path — keeps a process i from knowing that no active j can know $K_j \exists \mathsf{correct}(\mathsf{v})$, as well as keeping i from knowing that no j knows $K_j \exists \mathsf{v}$, explains why the bounds for both problems, and their typical solutions, are similar.

Proving the unbeatability of U-OPT_0 is more challenging than proving it for OPT_0. Intuitively, this is because gaining that an initial value of 0 that is known by a nonfaulty process does not imply that some process has already decided on 0. As a result, the possibility of dominating U-OPT_0 by switching 0 decisions to 1 decisions needs to be explicitly rejected. This is done by employing reachability arguments essentially establishing the existence of the continual common knowledge conditions of [15].

The fastest early-stopping protocol for uniform consensus in the literature, opt-EDAUC of [3] (a similar algorithm is in [8]), also stops in $\min(f+2,\, t+1)$ rounds at the latest. Similarly to Lemma 8, not only does U-OPT_0 strictly dominate opt-EDAUC, but furthermore, there are adversaries against which U-OPT_0 decides in 1 round, while opt-EDAUC decides in $t+1$ rounds:

Lemma 11. *If $2 \le t \le n-2$, then U-OPT_0 strictly dominates the opt-EDAUC protocol of [3]. Moreover, there exists an adversary for which $\mathsf{decide}_i(1)$ is performed after 1 round in U-OPT_0, and after $t+1$ rounds in opt-EDAUC.*

5   Discussion

It is possible to consider variations on the notion of unbeatability. One could, for example, compare runs in terms of the time at which the last correct process decides. We call the corresponding notion ***last-decider unbeatability***.[5] This neither implies, nor is implied by, the notion of unbeatability studied so far in this paper. None of the consensus protocols in the literature is last-decider unbeatable. In fact, all of our protocols are also last-decider unbeatable:

Theorem 5. *The protocols OPT_0 and $\mathrm{OPT}_{\mathsf{Maj}}$ are also last-decider unbeatable for consensus, while U-OPT_0 is last-decider unbeatable for uniform consensus.*

We note that Lemmas 8 and 11 show that our protocols beat the previously-known best ones by a large margin w.r.t. last-decider unbeatability as well.

Unbeatability is a natural optimality criterion for distributed protocols. It formalizes the intuition that a given protocol cannot be strictly improved upon, which is significantly stronger than saying that it is worst-case optimal, or even early stopping. All of the protocols that we have presented have a very concise and intuitive description, and are efficiently implementable; thus, unbeatability is attainable at a modest price. Crucially, our unbeatable protocols can decide much faster than previously known solutions to the same problems.

---

[5] This notion was suggested to us by Michael Schapira; we thank him for the insight.

Acknowledgements. Armandon Castañeda was supported in part by an Aly Kaufman Fellowship at the Technion. Yannai Goczarowski was supported in part by ISF grant 230/10, by the Google Inter-university center for Electronic Markets and Auctions, by the European Research Council under the European Community's Seventh Framework Programme (FP7/2007-2013) / ERC grant agreement no. [249159] and by an Adams Fellowship of the Israeli Academy of Sciences and Humanities. Yoram Moses is the Israel Pollak Academic chair at the Technion; his work was supported in part by ISF grant 1520/11.

References

1. Castañeda, A., Gonczarowski, Y.A., Moses, Y.: Brief announcement: Pareto-optimal solutions to consensus and set consensus. In: PODC, pp. 113–115 (2013)
2. Castañeda, A., Gonczarowski, Y.A., Moses, Y.: Unbeatable consensus (September 2014), http://arXiv.org
3. Charron-Bost, B., Schiper, A.: Uniform consensus is harder than consensus. J. Algorithms 51(1), 15–37 (2004)
4. Coan, B.: A communication-efficient canonical form for fault-tolerant distributed protocols. In: Proc. 5th ACM Symp. on Principles of Distributed Computing, pp. 63–72 (1986)
5. Dolev, D., Reischuk, R., Strong, H.R.: Early stopping in Byzantine agreement. Journal of the ACM 34(7), 720–741 (1990)
6. Dolev, D., Strong, H.R.: Requirements for agreement in a distributed system. In: Schneider, H.J. (ed.) Distributed Data Bases, pp. 115–129. North-Holland (1982)
7. Dolev, D.: Beep protocols (personal communication)
8. Dutta, P., Guerraoui, R., Pochon, B.: The time-complexity of local decision in distributed agreement. SIAM J. Comput. 37(3), 722–756 (2007)
9. Dwork, C., Moses, Y.: Knowledge and common knowledge in a Byzantine environment: crash failures. Information and Computation 88(2), 156–186 (1990)
10. Fagin, R., Halpern, J.Y., Moses, Y., Vardi, M.Y.: Reasoning about Knowledge. MIT Press (2003)
11. Fischer, M.J., Lynch, N.A., Paterson, M.S.: Impossibility of distributed consensus with one faulty processor. Journal of the ACM 32(2), 374–382 (1985)
12. Gafni, E., Guerraoui, R., Pochon, B.: The complexity of early deciding set agreement. SIAM J. Comput. 40(1), 63–78 (2011)
13. Hadzilacos, V.: On the relationship between the atomic commitment and consensus problems. In: Simons, B., Spector, A. (eds.) Fault-Tolerant Distributed Computing. LNCS, vol. 448, pp. 201–208. Springer, Heidelberg (1990)
14. Halpern, J.Y., Moses, Y.: Knowledge and common knowledge in a distributed environment. Journal of the ACM 37(3), 549–587 (1990), a preliminary version appeared in PODC (1984)
15. Halpern, J.Y., Moses, Y., Waarts, O.: A characterization of eventual byzantine agreement. SIAM J. Comput. 31(3), 838–865 (2001)
16. Herlihy, M., Moses, Y., Tuttle, M.R.: Transforming worst-case optimal solutions for simultaneous tasks into all-case optimal solutions. In: PODC, pp. 231–238 (2011)
17. Keidar, I., Rajsbaum, S.: A simple proof of the uniform consensus synchronous lower bound. Inf. Process. Lett. 85(1), 47–52 (2003)

18. Moses, Y., Tuttle, M.R.: Programming simultaneous actions using common knowledge. Algorithmica 3, 121–169 (1988)
19. Moses, Y.: Knowledge and Distributed Coordination (in preparation)
20. Pease, M., Shostak, R., Lamport, L.: Reaching agreement in the presence of faults. Journal of the ACM 27(2), 228–234 (1980)
21. Raynal, M.: Optimal early stopping uniform consensus in synchronous systems with process omission failures. In: SPAA, pp. 302–310. ACM Press (2004)
22. Wang, X., Teo, Y.M., Cao, J.: A bivalency proof of the lower bound for uniform consensus. Inf. Process. Lett. 96(5), 167–174 (2005)

Reliable Broadcast
with Respect to Topology Knowledge*

Aris Pagourtzis, Giorgos Panagiotakos, and Dimitris Sakavalas

School of Electrical and Computer Engineering
National Technical University of Athens, 15780 Athens, Greece
pagour@cs.ntua.gr, {gpanagiotakos,sakaval}@corelab.ntua.gr

Abstract. We study the Reliable Broadcast problem in incomplete networks against a Byzantine adversary. We examine the problem under the *locally bounded adversary model* of Koo (2004) and the *general adversary model* of Hirt and Maurer (1997) and explore the tradeoff between the level of topology knowledge and the solvability of the problem.

We refine the local pair-cut technique of Pelc and Peleg (2005) in order to obtain impossibility results for every level of topology knowledge and any type of corruption distribution. On the positive side we devise protocols that match the obtained bounds and thus, exactly characterize the classes of graphs in which Reliable Broadcast is possible.

Among others, we show that Koo's Certified Propagation Algorithm (CPA) is *unique* against locally bounded adversaries in ad hoc networks, that is, it can tolerate as many local corruptions as any other non-faulty algorithm; this settles an open question posed by Pelc and Peleg. We also provide an adaptation of CPA against general adversaries and show its uniqueness. To the best of our knowledge this is the first optimal algorithm for Reliable Broadcast in generic topology ad hoc networks against general adversaries.

1 Introduction

A fundamental problem in distributed networks is Reliable Broadcast (Byzantine Generals), in which the goal is to distribute a message correctly despite the presence of Byzantine faults. That is, an adversary may control several nodes and be able to make them deviate from the protocol arbitrarily by blocking, rerouting, or even altering a message that they should normally relay intact to specific nodes. In general, agreement problems have been primarily studied under the threshold adversary model, where a fixed upper bound t is set for the number of corrupted players and broadcast can be achieved if and only if $t < n/3$, where n is the total number of players. The Broadcast problem has been extensively studied in complete networks under the threshold adversary

---

* Work supported by ALGONOW project of the Research Funding Program THALIS, co-financed by the European Union (European Social Fund – ESF) and Greek national funds through the Operational Program "Education and Lifelong Learning" of the National Strategic Reference Framework (NSRF).

F. Kuhn (Ed.): DISC 2014, LNCS 8784, pp. 107–121, 2014.

model mainly in the period from 1982, when it was introduced by Lamport, Shostak and Pease [11], to 1998, when Garay and Moses [5] presented the first fully polynomial Broadcast protocol optimal in resilience and round complexity.

The case of Reliable Broadcast under a threshold adversary in incomplete networks has been studied to a much lesser extent, in a study initiated in [1,2,10], mostly through protocols for Secure Message Transmission which, combined with a Broadcast protocol for complete networks, yield Broadcast protocols for incomplete networks. Naturally, connectivity constraints are required to hold in addition to the $n/3$ bound. Namely, at most $t < c/2$ corruptions can be tolerated, where c is network connectivity, and this bound is tight[1].

In the case of an honest dealer, particularly meaningful in wireless networks, the impossibility threshold of $n/3$ does not hold; for example, in complete networks with an honest dealer the problem becomes trivial regardless of the number of corrupted players. However, in incomplete networks the situation is different. A small number of traitors (corrupted players) may manage to block the entire protocol if they control a critical part of the network, e.g. if they form a separator of the graph. It therefore makes sense to define criteria (or parameters) depending on the structure of the graph, in order to bound the number or restrict the distribution of traitors that can be tolerated.

An approach in this direction is to consider topological restrictions on the adversary's corruption capacity. We will first focus on local restrictions, the importance of which comes, among others, from the fact that they may be used to derive criteria which can be employed in *ad hoc* networks. Such a paradigm is the *t-locally bounded adversary model*, introduced in [9], in which at most a certain number t of corruptions are allowed in the neighborhood of every node.

The locally bounded adversarial model is particularly meaningful in real-life applications and systems. For example, in social networks it is more likely for an agent to have a quite accurate estimation of the maximum number of malicious agents that may appear in its neighborhood, than having such information, as well as knowledge of connectivity, for the whole network. In fact, this scenario applies to all kinds of networks, where each node is assumed to be able to estimate the number of traitors in its close neighborhood. It is also natural for these traitor bounds to vary among different parts of the network. Motivated by such considerations, in this work we will introduce a generalization of the *t*-locally bounded model.

1.1   Related Work

Considering *t*-locally bounded adversaries, Koo [9] proposed a simple, yet powerful protocol, namely the *Certified Propagation Algorithm* (CPA) (a name coined by Pelc and Peleg in [14]), and applied it to networks of specific topology. CPA is based on the idea that a set of $t+1$ neighbors of a node always contain an honest one. Pelc and Peleg [14] considered the *t*-locally bounded model in generic graphs and gave a sufficient topological condition for CPA to achieve Broadcast. They also provided an upper bound on the number of corrupted players t that can be locally tolerated in order to achieve Broadcast by any protocol, in terms of an appropriate graph parameter; they left the deduction of tighter bounds as an open problem. To this end, Ichimura and Shigeno [8] proposed an efficiently computable graph parameter which implies a more tight, but not exact, characterization of the class of graphs on which CPA achieves Broadcast. It had remained open until very recently to derive a tight parameter revealing the maximum number of traitors that can be locally tolerated by CPA in a graph G with dealer D. Such a parameter is implicit in the work of Tseng *et al.* [16], who gave a necessary and sufficient condition for CPA Broadcast. Finally, in [12] such a graph parameter was presented explicitly, together with an efficient 2-approximation algorithm for computing its value.

A more general approach regarding the adversary structure was initiated by Hirt and Maurer in [7] where they studied the security of multiparty computation protocols with respect to an *adversary structure*, i.e. a family of sets of players, such that the adversary may entirely corrupt any set in the family. This line of work has yielded results on Broadcast against a general adversary in complete networks [4] but, to the best of our knowledge, the case of Broadcast against general adversaries in incomplete networks has not been studied as such.[1] A study on the related problem of Iterative Approximate Byzantine Consensus against general adversaries can be seen in [15] where a similar model for the *ad hoc* case is considered.

1.2 Our Results

In this work we study the tradeoff between the level of topology knowledge and the solvability of the problem, under various adversary models.

We first consider a natural generalization of the t-locally bounded model, namely the *non-uniform t-locally bounded model* which subsumes the (uniform) model studied so far. The new model allows for a varying bound on the number of corruptions in each player's neighborhood. We address the issue of locally resilient Broadcast in the non-uniform model. We present a new necessary and sufficient condition for CPA to be t-locally resilient by extending the notion of *local pair cut* of Pelc and Peleg [14] to the notion of *partial local pair cut*. Note that although equivalent conditions exist [16,12], the simplicity of the new condition allows to settle the open question of CPA Uniqueness [14] in the affirmative: we show that if any *safe* (non-faulty) algorithm achieves Broadcast in an *ad hoc* network then so does CPA. We next prove that computing the validity of the condition is NP-hard and observe that the latter negative result also has a positive aspect, namely that a polynomially bounded adversary is unable to design an optimal attack unless $P = NP$.

We next shift focus on networks of known topology and devise an optimal resilience protocol, which we call *Path Propagation Algorithm* (PPA). Using PPA we prove that a topological condition which was shown in [14] to be necessary

---

[1] Some related results are implicit in [10], but in the problem studied there, namely Secure Message Transmission, additional secrecy requirements are set which are out of the scope of our study.

for the existence of a Broadcast algorithm is also sufficient. Thus, we manage to exactly characterize the class of networks for which there exists a solution to the Broadcast problem. On the downside, we prove that it is NP-hard to compute an essential decision rule of PPA, rendering the algorithm inefficient. However, we are able to provide an indication that probably no efficient protocol of optimal resilience exists, by showing that efficient algorithms which behave exactly as PPA w.r.t. decision do not exist if P $\neq$ NP.

We then take one step further, by considering a hybrid between *ad hoc* and known topology networks: each node knows a part of the network, namely a connected subgraph containing itself. We propose a protocol for this setting as well, namely the *Generalized Path Propagation Algorithm* (GPPA). We use GPPA to show that this *partial knowledge* model allows for Broadcast algorithms of increased resilience.

Finally, we study the general adversary model and show that an appropriate adaptation of CPA is unique against general adversaries in *ad hoc* networks. To the best of our knowledge this is the first algorithm for Reliable Broadcast in generic topology *ad hoc* networks against a general adversary. We show an analogous result for known topology networks, which however can be obtained implicitly from [10] as mentioned above.

We conclude by discussing how to extend our results to the case of a corrupted dealer by simulating Broadcast protocols for complete networks.

A central tool in our work is a refinement of the local pair-cut technique of Pelc and Peleg [14] which proves to be adequate for the exact (in most cases) characterization of the class of graphs for which Broadcast is possible for any level of topology knowledge and type of corruption distribution. A useful by-product of practical interest is that the refined cuts can be used to determine the exact subgraph in which Broadcast is possible.

For clarity we have chosen to present our results for the *t*-local model first (Sections 3,4,5), for which proofs and protocols are somewhat simpler and more intuitive, and then for the more involved general adversary model (Section 6).

2   Problem and Model Definition

In this paper we address the problem of *Reliable Broadcast with an honest dealer* in generic (incomplete) networks. As we will see in Section 6, this case essentially captures the difficulty of the general problem, where even the dealer may be corrupted. The problem definition follows.

Reliable Broadcast with Honest Dealer. The network is represented by a graph $G = (V, E)$, where V is the set of players, and E represents authenticated channels between players. We assume the existence of a designated honest player, called the *dealer*, who wants to broadcast a certain value $x_D \in X$, where X is the initial input space, to all players. We say that a distributed protocol achieves Reliable Broadcast if by the end of the protocol every honest player has *decided* on x_D, i.e. if it has been able to deduce that x_D is the value originally sent by the dealer and output it as its own decision.

The problem is trivial in complete networks; we will consider the case of incomplete networks here. For brevity we will refer to the problem as the Broadcast problem.

We will now formally define the adversary model by generalizing the notions originally developed in [9,14]. We will also define basic notions and terminology that we will use throughout the paper. We refer to the participants of the protocol by using the terms *node* and *player* interchangeably.

Corruption function. Taking into account that each player might be able to estimate her own upper bound on the corruptions of its neighborhood, as discussed earlier, we introduce a model in which the maximum number of corruptions in each player's neighborhood may vary from player to player. We thus generalize the standard t-locally bounded model [9] in which a uniform upper bound on the number of local corruptions was assumed. Here we consider $t : V \to \mathbb{N}$ to be a *corruption function* over the set of players V.

Non-Uniform t-Locally Bounded Adversary Model. The network is represented by a graph $G = (V, E)$. One player $D \in V$ is the dealer (sender). A corruption function $t : V \to \mathbb{N}$ is also given, implying that an adversary may corrupt at most $t(u)$ nodes in the neighborhood $\mathcal{N}(u)$ of each node $u \in V$. The family of t-*local* sets plays an important role in our study since it coincides with the family of admissible corruption sets.

Definition 1 (t-local set). *Given a graph $G = (V, E)$ and a function $t : V \to \mathbb{N}$ a t-local set is a set $C \subseteq V$ for which $\forall u \in V$, $|\mathcal{N}(u) \cap C| \leq t(u)$. For $V' \subseteq V$ a t-local w.r.t. V' set is a set $C \subseteq V$ for which $\forall u \in V'$, $|\mathcal{N}(u) \cap C| \leq t(u)$.*

Uniform vs Non-Uniform Model. Obviously the original t-locally bounded model corresponds to the special case of t being a constant function. Hereafter we will refer to the original t-locally bounded model as the *Uniform Model* as opposed to the *Non-Uniform Model* which we introduce here.

In our study we will often make use of node-cuts which separate some players from the dealer, hence, node-cuts that do not include the dealer. From here on we will simply use the term *cut* to denote such a node-cut. The notion of t-*local pair cut* was introduced in [14] and is crucial in defining the bounds for which correct dissemination of information in a network is possible.

Definition 2 (t-local pair cut). *Given a graph $G = (V, E)$ and a function $t : V \to \mathbb{N}$, a pair of t-local sets C_1, C_2 s.t. $C_1 \cup C_2$ is a cut of G is called a t-local pair cut.*

The next definition extends the notion of t-local pair cut and is particularly useful in describing capability of achieving Broadcast in networks of unknown topology (*ad hoc* networks) where each player's knowledge of the topology is limited in its own neighborhood.

Definition 3 (t-partial local pair cut). *Let C be a cut of G, partitioning $V \setminus C$ into sets $A, B \neq \emptyset$ s.t. $D \in A$. C is a t-partial local pair cut (t-plp cut) if there exists a partition $C = C_1 \cup C_2$ where C_1 is t-local and C_2 is t-local w.r.t. B.*

In the uniform model the *Local Pair Connectivity* ($\mathrm{LPC}(G, D)$) [14] parameter of a graph G with dealer D, was defined to be the minimum integer t s.t. G has a t-local pair cut. To define the corresponding notion in the non-uniform model we need to define a (partial) order among corruption functions. Nevertheless, for reasoning about our results it suffices to consider the following decision problem:

Definition 4 (pLPC). *Given a graph G, a dealer D and a corruption function t determine whether there exists a t-plp cut in G.*

Definition 5 (t-locally resilient algorithm). *An algorithm which achieves Broadcast for any t-local corruption set in graph G with dealer D is called t-locally resilient for (G, D).*

Definition 6 (safe / t-locally safe algorithm). *A Broadcast algorithm which never causes an honest node to decide on an incorrect value, is called* safe. *A Broadcast algorithm which never causes an honest node to decide on an incorrect value under any t-local corruption set, is called t-locally safe.*

3   Ad Hoc Networks

3.1   Certified Propagation Algorithm (CPA)

The Certified Propagation algorithm [9] uses only local information and thus is particularly suitable for *ad hoc* networks. CPA is probably the only Broadcast algorithm known up to now for the t-locally bounded model, which does not require knowledge of the network topology. We use a modification of the original CPA that can be employed under the non-uniform t-locally bounded adversary model. Namely a node v, upon reception of $t(v) + 1$ messages with the same value x from $t(v) + 1$ distinct neighbors, decides on x, sends it to all neighbors and terminates. It can easily be proven by induction that CPA is a t-locally safe Broadcast algorithm.

3.2   CPA Uniqueness in *Ad Hoc* Networks

Based on the above definitions we can now prove the *CPA uniqueness conjecture* for *ad hoc* networks, which was posed as an open problem in [14]. The conjecture states that no algorithm can locally tolerate more corrupted nodes than CPA in networks of unknown topology.

We consider only the class of *t-locally safe* Broadcast algorithms. We assume the *ad hoc* network model, as described e.g. in [14]. In particular we assume that nodes know only their own labels, the labels of their neighbors and the label of the dealer. We call a distributed Broadcast algorithm that operates under these assumptions an *ad hoc Broadcast algorithm*.

Theorem 1 (Sufficient Condition). *Given a graph G, a corruption function t and a dealer D, if no t-plp cut exists, then CPA is t-locally resilient for (G, D).*

Proof. Suppose that no t-plp cut exists in G. Let T be the corruption set; clearly $T \cup N(D)$ is a cut on G as defined before (i.e. not including node D). Since T is t-local and $T \cup N(D)$ is not a t-plp cut there must exist $u_1 \in V \setminus (T \cup \mathcal{N}(D) \cup D)$ s.t. $|N(u_1) \cap (N(D) \setminus T)| \geq t(u_1) + 1$. Since u_1 is honest it will decide on the dealer's value x_D. Let us now use the same argument inductively to show that every honest node will eventually decide on the correct value x_D through CPA. Let $C_k = (N(D) \setminus T) \cup \{u_1, u_2, ..., u_{k-1}\}$ be the set of the honest nodes that have decided until a certain round of the protocol. Then $C_k \cup T$ is a cut. Since T is t-local, by the same argument as before there exists a node u_k s.t. $|C_k \cap N(u_k)| \geq t(u_k) + 1$ and u_k will decide on x_D. Eventually all honest players will decide on x_D. Thus CPA is t-locally resilient in G.

Theorem 2 (Necessary Condition). *Let $\mathcal{A}$ be a t-locally safe ad hoc Broadcast algorithm. Given a graph G, a corruption function t and a dealer D, if a t-plp cut exists, then $\mathcal{A}$ is not t-locally resilient in (G, D).*

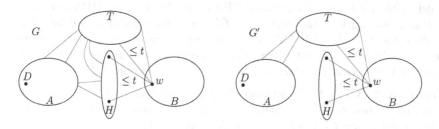

Fig. 1. Graphs G and G'

Proof. Assume that there exists a t-plp cut $C = T \cup H$ in graph G with dealer D with T being the t-local set of the partition and H the t-local w.r.t. to B set (Figure 1). Let G' be a graph that results from G if we remove some edges that connect nodes in $A \cup T \cup H$ with nodes in H so that the set H becomes t-local in G' (e.g. we can remove all edges that connect nodes in $A \cup T \cup H$ with nodes in H). Note that the existence of a set of edges that guarantees such a property is implied by the fact that H is t-local w.r.t. B.

The proof is by contradiction. Suppose that there exists a t-locally safe Broadcast algorithm $\mathcal{A}$ which is t-locally resilient in graph G with dealer D. We consider the following executions σ and σ' of $\mathcal{A}$:

Execution σ is on the graph G with dealer D, with dealer's value $x_D = 0$, and corruption set T; in each round, all players in T perform the actions that perform in the respective round of execution σ' (where T is a set of honest players).

Execution σ' is on the graph G' with dealer D, with dealer's value $x_D = 1$, and corruption set H; in each round, all players in H perform the actions that perform in the respective round of execution σ (where H is a set of honest players).

Note that T, H are admissible corruption sets in G, G' respectively due to their t-locality. It is easy to see that $H \cup T$ is a cut which separates D from B in both G

and G' and that actions of every node of this cut are identical in both executions σ, σ'. Consequently, the actions of any honest node $w \in B$ must be identical in both executions. Since, by assumption, algorithm $\mathcal{A}$ is t-locally resilient on G with dealer D, w must decide on the dealer's message 0 in execution σ on G with dealer D, and must do the same in execution σ' on G' with dealer D. However, in execution σ' the dealer's message is 1. Therefore $\mathcal{A}$ makes w decide on an incorrect message in (G', D). This contradicts the assumption that $\mathcal{A}$ is locally safe.

We can show that if we drop the requirement for t-local safety, then the theorem does not hold. Intuitively, the reason is that an *ad hoc* protocol that assumes certain topological properties for the network may be t-locally resilient in a family of graphs that have the assumed topological properties. Indeed, Pelc and Peleg [14] introduced another algorithm for the uniform model, the *Relaxed Propagation Algorithm* (RPA) which uses knowledge of the topology of the network and they proved that there exists a graph G'' with dealer D for which RPA is 1-locally resilient and CPA is not. So if we use RPA in an *ad hoc* setting assuming that the network is G'' then this algorithm will be t-locally resilient for (G'', D) while CPA will not. Non-t-local safety of RPA can easily be shown. This shows that there exists non-safe algorithms of higher resilience than CPA. The next corollary is immediate from Theorems 1,2.

Corollary 1 (CPA Uniqueness). *Given a graph G and dealer D, if there exists an ad hoc Broadcast algorithm which is t-locally resilient in (G, D) and t-locally safe, then CPA is t-locally resilient in (G, D).*

3.3 Hardness of pLPC

Ichimura and Shigeno in [8] prove that the *set splitting* problem, known as NP-hard [6], can be reduced to the problem of computing the minimum integer t such that a t-local pair cut exists in a graph G. By generalizing the notion of the t-local pair cut to that of t-plp cut and defining the pLPC problem analogously one can use a nearly identical proof to that of [8] and show that the pLPC problem is NP-hard. For completeness the proof is given in the full version[2].

Theorem 3. pLPC *is* NP-*hard.*

Therefore, computing the necessary and sufficient condition for CPA to work is NP-hard. Observe that this negative result also has a positive aspect, namely that a polynomially bounded adversary is unable to always compute an optimal attack unless P = NP.

4   Known Topology Networks

4.1   The Path Propagation Algorithm

Considering only safe Broadcast algorithms, the uniqueness of CPA in the *ad hoc* model implies that an algorithm that achieves Broadcast in cases where

---

[2] All omitted proofs are deferred to the full version.

CPA does not, must operate under a weaker model e.g., assuming additional information on the topology of the network. It thus makes sense to consider the setting where players have full knowledge of the topology of the network. In this section we propose the *Path Propagation Algorithm* (PPA) and show that is of optimal resilience in the full-knowledge model. For convenience we will use the following notions: a set $S \subseteq V \setminus D$ is called a *cover* of a set of paths $\mathcal{P}$ if and only if $\forall p \in \mathcal{P}$, $\exists s \in S$ s.t. $s \in p$ (s is a node of p). With $tail(p)$ we will denote the last node of path p. The description of PPA follows.

Protocol 1: *Path Propagation Algorithm (PPA)*

Input (for each node v): graph G, dealer D, $t(v) = \max$ #corruptions in $N(v)$.
Message format: pair (x, p), where $x \in X$ (message space), and p is a path of G (message's propagation trail).

Code for D: send message (x_D, D) to all neighbors, decide on x_D and terminate.
Code for $v \neq D$: upon reception of (x, p) from node u **do:**

    if $(v \in p) \vee (tail(p) \neq u)$ **then discard** the message
    else send $(x, p||v)$ [3] to all neighbors.

    if decision$(v) \neq \bot$ **then send** message $(\text{decision}(v), v)$ to all neighbors.

function decision(v)
    (* *dealer propagation rule* *)
    if $v \in \mathcal{N}(D)$ and v receives (x_D, D) **then return** x_D.
    (* *honest path propagation rule* *)
    if v receives $(x, p_1), \ldots, (x, p_n) \wedge \nexists\ t$-local cover of $\{p_1, \ldots, p_n\}$
    then return x **else return** $\bot$.

The correctness of the honest path propagation rule is trivial: if a path is entirely corruption free, then value x, which is relayed through that path, is correct. Checking whether $tail(p) \neq u$ we ensure that at least one corrupted node will be included in a faulty path. Observe that each player can check the validity of the honest path propagation rule only if it has knowledge of the corruption function t and the network's topology.

4.2   A Necessary and Sufficient Condition

We will now show that the non-existence of a t-local pair cut is a sufficient condition for PPA to achieve Broadcast in the t-locally bounded model in networks of known topology (proof omitted).

---

[3] By $p||v$ we denote the path consisting of path p and node v, with the last node of p connected to v.

Theorem 4 (Sufficiency). *Given a graph G with dealer D and corruption function t, if no t-local pair cut exists in (G, D) then all honest players will decide through PPA on x_D.*

Using the same arguments as in the proof of the necessity of condition $t < LPC(G, D)$ [14] it can be seen that the non-existence of a t-local pair cut is a necessary condition for any algorithm to achieve Broadcast under the non-uniform model.

Theorem 5 (Necessity). *Given a graph G with dealer D and corruption function t, if there exists a t-local pair cut in (G, D) then there is no t-locally resilient algorithm for (G, D).*

Thus the non-existence of a t-local pair cut proves to be a necessary and sufficient condition for the existence of a t-locally resilient algorithm in both the uniform and the non-uniform model. Therefore PPA is of optimal resilience.

4.3   On the Hardness of Broadcast in Known Networks

In order to run PPA we have to be able to deduce whether a corruption-free path exists among a set of paths broadcasting the same value. Formally, given a graph $G(V, E)$, a set of paths $\mathcal{P}$ and a node u (the one that executes decision(u)) we need to determine whether there exists a t-local cover T of $\mathcal{P}$. We call this problem the Local Path Cover Problem, $LPCP(G, D, u, t, \mathcal{P})$ and show that is NP-hard (proof omitted).

Theorem 6. *It is* NP-*hard to compute $LPCP(G, D, u, t, \mathcal{P})$.*

The above theorem implies that PPA may not be practical in some cases, since its decision rule cannot be always checked efficiently. It remains to show whether any other algorithm which has the same resilience as PPA can be efficient. The following theorem provides an indication that the answer is negative, by showing that algorithms which behave exactly as PPA w.r.t. decision are unlikely to be efficient (proof omitted).

Theorem 7. *Assuming* P $\neq$ NP, *no safe fully polynomial protocol Π can satisfy the following: for any graph G, dealer D, corruption function t, and admissible corruption set C executing protocol Π_C, a node u decides through PPA on a value x iff u will decide on x by running Π on (G, D, t, C, Π_C).*

5   Partial Knowledge

Until now we have presented optimal resilience algorithms for Broadcast in two extreme cases, with respect to the knowledge over the network topology: the *ad hoc* model and the full-knowledge model. A natural question arises: is there any algorithm that works well in settings where nodes have partial knowledge of the topology?

To address this question we devise a new, generalized version of PPA that can run with partial knowledge of the topology of the network. More specifically we assume that each player v only has knowledge of the topology of a certain connected subgraph G_v of G which includes v. Namely if we consider the family $\mathcal{G}$ of connected subgraphs of G we use the *topology view function* $\gamma : V \to \mathcal{G}$, where $\gamma(v)$ represents the subgraph over which player v has knowledge of the topology. We also define the *joint view* of a set S as the subgraph $\gamma(S)$ of G with node-set $V(\gamma(S)) = \bigcup_{u \in S} V(\gamma(u))$ and edge-set $E(\gamma(S)) = \bigcup_{u \in S} E(\gamma(u))$. We will call an algorithm which achieves Broadcast for any t-local corruption set in graph G with dealer D and view function γ, (γ, t)-*locally resilient* for (G, D).

Now given a corruption function t and a view function γ we define the Generalized Path Propagation Algorithm (GPPA) to work exactly as PPA apart from a natural modification of the path propagation rule.

Generalized path propagation rule: Player v receives the same value x from a set $\mathcal{P}$ of paths that are completely inside $\gamma(v)$ and is able to deduce (from the topology) that no t-local cover of $\mathcal{P}$ exists.

Remark. Note that GPPA generalizes both CPA and PPA. Indeed, if $\forall v \in V$, $\gamma(v) = \mathcal{N}(v)$, then GPPA$(G, D, t, \gamma)$ coincides with CPA(G, D, t). If, on the other hand, $\forall v \in V$, $\gamma(v) = G$ then GPPA(G, D, t, γ) coincides with PPA(G, D, t). We also notice that, quite naturally, as γ provides more information for the topology of the graph, resilience increases, with CPA being of minimal resilience in this family of algorithms, and PPA achieving maximal resilience.

To prove necessary and sufficient conditions for GPPA being t-locally resilient we need to generalize the notion of t-plp cut as follows:

Definition 7 (type 1 (γ, t)-partial local pair cut). *Let C be a cut of G, partitioning $V \setminus C$ into sets $A, B \neq \emptyset$ s.t. $D \in A$. C will be called a type 1 (γ, t)-partial local pair cut (plp1 cut) if there exists a partition $C = C_1 \cup C_2$ s.t. C_1 is t-local and C_2 is t-local in the graph $\gamma(B)$.*

Definition 8 (type 2 (γ, t)-partial local pair cut). *Let C be a cut of G, partitioning $V \setminus C$ into sets $A, B \neq \emptyset$ s.t. $D \in A$. C will be called a type 2 (γ, t)-partial local pair cut (plp2 cut) if there exists a partition $C = C_1 \cup C_2$ s.t. C_1 is t-local and $\forall u \in B$, $C_2 \cap N(u)$ is t-local in the graph $\gamma(u)$.*

We can now show the following two theorems. The proofs build on the techniques presented for CPA and PPA and are omitted.

Theorem 8 (sufficient condition). *Let t be corruption function and γ be a view function, if no (γ, t)-plp2 cut exists in G with dealer D then GPPA(G, D, t, γ) is (γ, t)-locally resilient for G, D.*

Theorem 9 (necessary condition). *Let t be a corruption function, γ be a view function and $\mathcal{A}$ be a t-locally safe ad hoc Broadcast algorithm. If a (γ, t)-plp1 cut exists in graph G with dealer D, then $\mathcal{A}$ is not (γ, t)-locally resilient for G, D.*

One can argue that increased topology knowledge implies increased resilience for GPPA compared to CPA; for example, the sufficient condition of GPPA holds in settings where the sufficient condition of CPA does not hold. An overview of our results concerning the t-local model with respect to the level of topology knowledge appears in Figure 2.

Notice that the reason for which GPPA is not optimal is that nodes in $\gamma(v)$ do not share their knowledge of topology. An optimal resilience protocol would probably include exchange of topological knowledge among players.

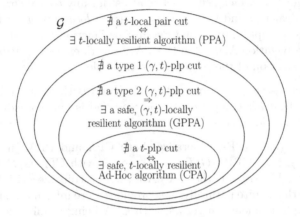

Fig. 2. Overview of conditions concerning the existence of t-locally resilient algorithms with respect to the level of topology knowledge. Note that $\mathcal{G}$ refers to the family of pairs (G, D).

6   General Adversary

Hirt and Maurer in [7] study the security of multiparty computation protocols with respect to an *adversary structure*, that is, a family of subsets of the players; the adversary is able to corrupt one of these subsets. More formally, a structure $\mathcal{Z}$ for the set of players V is a monotone family of subsets of V, i.e. $\mathcal{Z} \subseteq 2^V$, where all subsets of Z are in $\mathcal{Z}$ if $Z \in \mathcal{Z}$. Let us now redefine some notions that we have introduced in this paper in order to extend our results to the case of a general adversary. We will call an algorithm that achieves Broadcast for any corruption set $T \in \mathcal{Z}$ in graph G with dealer D, $\mathcal{Z}$-*resilient*. We next generalize the notion of a t-local pair cut.

Definition 9 ($\mathcal{Z}$-pair cut). *A cut C of G for which there exists a partition $C = C_1 \cup C_2$ and $C_1, C_2 \in \mathcal{Z}$ is called a $\mathcal{Z}$-pair cut of G.*

Known Topology Networks. We adapt PPA in order to address the Broadcast problem under a general adversary. The Generalized $\mathcal{Z}$-PPA algorithm can be obtained by a modification of the path propagation rule of PPA (Protocol 1).

$\mathcal{Z}$-*PPA Honest Path Propagation Rule*: player v receives value x from a set $\mathcal{P}$ of paths and is able to deduce that for any $T \in \mathcal{Z}$, T is not a cover of $\mathcal{P}$.

Moreover, the following theorems can be easily shown using essentially the same proofs as for Theorems 4, and 5 and replacing the notion of t-local pair cut with that of $\mathcal{Z}$-pair cut.

Theorem 10 (Sufficiency). *Given a graph G, dealer D, and an adversary structure $\mathcal{Z}$, if no $\mathcal{Z}$-pair cut exists, then all honest players will decide on x_D through $\mathcal{Z}$-PPA.*

Theorem 11 (Necessity). *Given a graph G, dealer D, and an adversary structure $\mathcal{Z}$, if there exists a $\mathcal{Z}$-pair cut then there is no $\mathcal{Z}$-resilient Broadcast algorithm for (G, D).*

Ad Hoc Networks. Since in the *ad hoc* model the players know only their own labels, the labels of their neighbors and the label of the dealer it is reasonable to assume that a player has only local knowledge on the actual adversary structure $\mathcal{Z}$. Specifically, given the actual adversary structure $\mathcal{Z}$ we assume that each player v knows only the *local adversary structure* $\mathcal{Z}_v = \{A \cap \mathcal{N}(v) : A \in \mathcal{Z}\}$.

As in known topology networks, we can describe a generalized version $\mathcal{Z}$-CPA of CPA, which is an *ad hoc* Broadcast algorithm for the general adversary model. In particular, we modify the propagation rule of CPAin the following way.

$\mathcal{Z}$-*CPA Propagation Rule*: if a node v is not a neighbor of the dealer, then upon receiving the same value x from all its neighbors in a set $N \subseteq \mathcal{N}(v)$ s.t. $N \notin \mathcal{Z}_v$, it decides on value x.

In order to argue about the topological conditions which determine the effectiveness of $\mathcal{Z}$-CPA we generalize the notion of partial t-local pair cut.

Definition 10 ($\mathcal{Z}$-partial pair cut). *Let C be a cut of G partitioning $V \setminus C$ into sets $A, B \neq \emptyset$ s.t. $D \in A$. C is a $\mathcal{Z}$-partial pair cut ($\mathcal{Z}$-pp cut) if there exists a partition $C = C_1 \cup C_2$ with $C_1 \in \mathcal{Z}$ and $\forall u \in B$, $\mathcal{N}(u) \cap C_2 \in \mathcal{Z}_u$.*

Analogously to CPA Uniqueness, we can now prove $\mathcal{Z}$-CPA Uniqueness in the general adversary model (proofs omitted).

Theorem 12 (Sufficient Condition). *Given a graph G, dealer D, and an adversary structure $\mathcal{Z}$, if no $\mathcal{Z}$-pp cut exists, then $\mathcal{Z}$-CPA is $\mathcal{Z}$-resilient.*

Theorem 13 (Necessary Condition). *Let $\mathcal{A}$ be a safe ad hoc Broadcast algorithm. Given a graph G, dealer D, and an adversary structure $\mathcal{Z}$, if a $\mathcal{Z}$-pp cut exists then $\mathcal{A}$ is not $\mathcal{Z}$-resilient for G, D.*

Complexity of $\mathcal{Z}$-CPA. Regarding the computational complexity of $\mathcal{Z}$-CPA one can observe that it is polynomial if and only if for every player v there exists a polynomial (w.r.t. the size of G) algorithm $\mathcal{B}$ which given a set $S \subseteq \mathcal{N}(v)$ decides whether $S \in \mathcal{Z}_v$. Since $\mathcal{Z}$-CPA is clearly polynomial in round complexity and communication complexity, if such an algorithm $\mathcal{B}$ exists, $\mathcal{Z}$-CPA is fully polynomial.

Dealer Corruption. We have studied the problem of Broadcast in the case where the dealer is honest. In order to address the general case in which the dealer may also be corrupted one may observe that for a given adversary structure $\mathcal{Z}$ and graph G, $\mathcal{Z}$-resilient Broadcast in *ad hoc* networks can be achieved if the following conditions both hold:

1. $\not\exists Z_1, Z_2, Z_3 \in \mathcal{Z}$ s.t. $Z_1 \cup Z_2 \cup Z_3 = V$.
2. $\forall v \in V$ there does not exist a $\mathcal{Z}$-pp cut for G with dealer v.

Condition 1 was proved by Hirt and Maurer [7] sufficient and necessary for the existence of secure multiparty protocols in complete networks. $\mathcal{Z}$-resilient Broadcast in the general case where the network is incomplete can be achieved by simulating any protocol for complete graphs (e.g. the protocol presented in [4]) as follows: each one-to-many transmission is replaced by an execution of $\mathcal{Z}$-CPA. It is not hard to see that the conjunction of the above two conditions is necessary and sufficient for Broadcast in incomplete networks in the case of corrupted dealer. Analogously, the same result holds in networks of known topology, if we replace Condition 2 with the corresponding $\mathcal{Z}$-pair cut condition. Naturally, the above observations hold also in the special case of a locally bounded adversary.

7   Open Questions

Necessary and sufficient criteria for Broadcast on known topology and ad-hoc networks are NP-hard to compute. It remains open to define and study meaningful approximation objectives.

We conjecture that in the known topology locally bounded setting no safe, fully polynomial algorithm can achieve optimal resilience. We have provided an indication towards proving this in Subsection 4.3.

Regarding the partial knowledge model discussed in Section 5, GPPA is not of optimal resilience. Devising such an algorithm would be of great interest. One direction towards this, is to consider discovering the network topology under a Byzantine adversary, as studied in [13,3].

In the *ad hoc* general adversary setting, we proved that $\mathcal{Z}$-CPA is unique, thus having optimal resilience. We conjecture that it is also unique w.r.t. polynomial time complexity, i.e., if a safe protocol achieves Broadcast in polynomial time then so does $\mathcal{Z}$-CPA.

References

1. Dolev, D.: The byzantine generals strike again. J. Algorithms 3(1), 14–30 (1982)
2. Dolev, D., Dwork, C., Waarts, O., Yung, M.: Perfectly secure message transmission. J. ACM 40(1), 17–47 (1993), http://doi.acm.org/10.1145/138027.138036
3. Dolev, S., Liba, O., Schiller, E.M.: Self-stabilizing byzantine resilient topology discovery and message delivery - (extended abstract). In: Gramoli, V., Guerraoui, R. (eds.) NETYS 2013. LNCS, vol. 7853, pp. 42–57. Springer, Heidelberg (2013)
4. Fitzi, M., Maurer, U.M.: Efficient byzantine agreement secure against general adversaries. In: Kutten, S. (ed.) DISC 1998. LNCS, vol. 1499, pp. 134–148. Springer, Heidelberg (1998)

5. Garay, J.A., Moses, Y.: Fully polynomial byzantine agreement for $n > 3t$ processors in $t + 1$ rounds. SIAM J. Comput. 27(1), 247–290 (1998)
6. Garey, M.R., Johnson, D.S.: Computers and Intractability: A Guide to the Theory of NP-Completeness. W. H. Freeman (1979)
7. Hirt, M., Maurer, U.M.: Complete characterization of adversaries tolerable in secure multi-party computation (extended abstract). In: Burns, J.E., Attiya, H. (eds.) PODC 1997, pp. 25–34. ACM (1997)
8. Ichimura, A., Shigeno, M.: A new parameter for a broadcast algorithm with locally bounded byzantine faults. Inf. Process. Lett. 110(12-13), 514–517 (2010)
9. Koo, C.Y.: Broadcast in radio networks tolerating byzantine adversarial behavior. In: Chaudhuri, S., Kutten, S. (eds.) PODC 2004, pp. 275–282. ACM (2004)
10. Kumar, M.V.N.A., Goundan, P.R., Srinathan, K., Rangan, C.P.: On perfectly secure communication over arbitrary networks. In: Proceedings of the Twenty-first Annual Symposium on Principles of Distributed Computing, PODC 2002, pp. 193–202. ACM, New York (2002), http://doi.acm.org/10.1145/571825.571858
11. Lamport, L., Shostak, R.E., Pease, M.C.: The byzantine generals problem. ACM Trans. Program. Lang. Syst. 4(3), 382–401 (1982)
12. Litsas, C., Pagourtzis, A., Sakavalas, D.: A graph parameter that matches the resilience of the certified propagation algorithm. In: Cichoń, J., Gębala, M., Klonowski, M. (eds.) ADHOC-NOW 2013. LNCS, vol. 7960, pp. 269–280. Springer, Heidelberg (2013)
13. Nesterenko, M., Tixeuil, S.: Discovering network topology in the presence of byzantine faults. IEEE Trans. Parallel Distrib. Syst. 20(12), 1777–1789 (2009)
14. Pelc, A., Peleg, D.: Broadcasting with locally bounded byzantine faults. Inf. Process. Lett. 93(3), 109–115 (2005)
15. Tseng, L., Vaidya, N.: Iterative approximate byzantine consensus under a generalized fault model. In: Frey, D., Raynal, M., Sarkar, S., Shyamasundar, R.K., Sinha, P. (eds.) ICDCN 2013. LNCS, vol. 7730, pp. 72–86. Springer, Heidelberg (2013)
16. Tseng, L., Vaidya, N.H., Bhandari, V.: Broadcast using certified propagation algorithm in presence of byzantine faults. CoRR abs/1209.4620 (2012)

Evacuating Robots via Unknown Exit in a Disk

Jurek Czyzowicz[1,5], Leszek Gąsieniec[2], Thomas Gorry[2],
Evangelos Kranakis[3,*], Russell Martin[2], and Dominik Pajak[4,**]

[1] Département d'informatique, Université du Québec en Outaouais, Canada
[2] Department of Computer Science, University of Liverpool, Liverpool, UK
[3] School of Computer Science, Carleton University, Ottawa, Canada
[4] INRIA Bordeaux Sud-Ouest, 33405 Talence, France

Abstract. Consider k mobile robots inside a circular disk of unit radius. The robots are required to evacuate the disk through an unknown exit point situated on its boundary. We assume all robots having the same (unit) maximal speed and starting at the centre of the disk. The robots may communicate in order to inform themselves about the presence (and its position) or the absence of an exit. The goal is for all the robots to evacuate through the exit in minimum time.

We consider two models of communication between the robots: in *non-wireless* (or *local*) *communication* model robots exchange information only when simultaneously located at the same point, and *wireless communication* in which robots can communicate one another at any time.

We study the following question for different values of k: what is the optimal evacuation time for k robots? We provide algorithms and show lower bounds in both communication models for $k = 2$ and $k = 3$ thus indicating a difference in evacuation time between the two models. We also obtain almost-tight bounds on the asymptotic relation between evacuation time and team size, for large k. We show that in the local communication model, a team of k robots can always evacuate in time $3 + \frac{2\pi}{k}$, whereas at least $3 + \frac{2\pi}{k} - O(k^{-2})$ time is sometimes required. In the wireless communication model, time $3 + \frac{\pi}{k} + O(k^{-4/3})$ always suffices to complete evacuation, and at least $3 + \frac{\pi}{k}$ is sometimes required. This shows a clear separation between the local and the wireless communication models.

1   Introduction

Consider a team of mobile robots inside an environment represented by a circular disk of unit radius. The robots need to find an exit being a point at an unknown position on the boundary of the disk in order to evacuate through this point. The exit is recognized when visited by a robot. The robots may communicate in order to exchange the knowledge about the presence (or the absence) of the exit

---

* Research Supported in Part by NSERC Discovery Grant.
** Research Supported by the LaBRI under the "Mobilité junior" Program 2013, and by the CNRS LIA LIRCO.

F. Kuhn (Ed.): DISC 2014, LNCS 8784, pp. 122–136, 2014.
© Springer-Verlag Berlin Heidelberg 2014

acquired through their previous movements. We consider two communication models. In the *non-wireless* (or *local*) model, communication is possible between robots which arrive at the same point (in the environment) at the same moment, while the *wireless* model allows broadcasting a message by a robot, which is instantly acquired by other robots, independently of their current positions in the environment. The robots start at the centre of the disk and they can move with a speed not exceeding their maximum velocity (which is the same for all robots). The objective is to plan the movements of all robots, which result in the shortest worst-case time needed for all robots to evacuate.

1.1 Related Work

Mobile agents are autonomous entities traveling within geometric or graph-modeled environments. Besides *mobility*, agents possess the ability to *perceive* the environment, *compute*, and *communicate* among themselves. They collaborate in order to perform tasks assigned to them. When agents operate in geometric environments (then they are usually called robots) their performance is measured by the geometric distance travelled, most often disregarding their computing, communicating and environment-perceiving activities.

When the geometric environment is not known in advance by the mobile robots, in many papers their task consisted in exploring the environment[1,2,13,17]. The coordination of exploration between multiple robots has been mainly studied by the robotics community [10,25,26]. However even if the main objective assigned to the robots is different from exploration, often part of their activity is devoted to the recognition or mapping of the terrain and/or the position of the robots within it [20,22,24]. When the map of the environment is known to the robots, a lot of research was devoted to search games, when the searchers usually try to minimize the time to find an immobile or a moving hider [3,4,21]. The literature of the case of mobile fugitives, often known as cops and robbers or pursuit-evasion games is particularly rich [12,15], with numerous variations related to the type of environment, speed of evasion and pursuit, robots visibility and many others [23]. The searching for a motionless point target in the simple environment presented in our paper has some similarities with the lost at sea problem, [16,18], the cow-path problem [8,9], and with the plane searching problem [5,6].

The problem of evacuation has been studied for grid polygons from the perspective of constructing centralized evacuation plans, resulting in the fastest possible evacuation from the rectilinear environment [14]. Previously, [7] considered evacuation planning as earliest-arrival flows with multiple sources giving the first algorithm strongly polynomial in input/output size.

Evacuation in a distributed setting, when the mobile robots (know the simple environment but not the exit positions) has been recently asked in [11] for the case of a line. They proved that evacuation of multiple uniform agents is as hard as the cow-path problem. Evacuation of two robots without wireless communication was discussed with the research group of M. Yamashita during the visit of the second co-author at Kyushu University [19]. The discussion focused on laying the foundations for the lower bound presented in this paper and seeking ways to improve the respective upper bound. However, the main objective of our problem is to find a compromise between, on one hand, spreading sufficiently the robots so that they can find the exit point fast in parallel, and, on the other hand, not to spread them too far so that, when one robot finds the exit, the escape route to it of the other robots is not too long.

1.2   Preliminaries

The environment is a disk of unit radius. The robots start their movement at the centre of the disk. We assume that the perception device of the robot permits to recognize a boundary point of the environment when the robot arrives there. Similarly, we assume that a robot recognizes the presence of other robots at the same position as well the fact that the robot is currently at the exit point. We also assume that the robots are labeled, i.e. they may execute different algorithms. Each such algorithm instructs the robot to make the moves with a speed not exceeding its maximal speed. In particular, the algorithm may ask the robot to move towards the centre of the disk or a chosen point on its boundary or to follow the boundary clockwise or counterclockwise. The movement may be changed when the perception mechanism allows the robot to acquire some knowledge about the environment (e.g. the exit point, boundary point, a meeting point with another robot). The robots are allowed to stay motionless at the same point. If A and B are points on the perimeter of the disk, by $\widehat{AB}$ we will denote arc from A to B in the clockwise direction and by AB we will denote the cord connecting A and B. The length of $\widehat{AB}$ will be denoted by $|\widehat{AB}|$ and the length of AB will be denoted by $|AB|$.

1.3   Outline and Results of the Paper

In Section 2 we consider the evacuation problem for two robots, while Section 3 analyzes the case of three robots. Section 4 proves tight asymptotic bounds for k robots. Each section is divided into two parts consisting of the analysis for the non-wireless and wireless models, respectively. The complexity details corresponding to the three sections are in Table 1.

Table 1. Upper and Lower bounds for $k \geq 2$ robots

Model	Bound	$k = 2$	$k = 3$	$k \geq 4$
Non-wireless	Upper	~5.74 (Th 1)	~5.09 (Th 8)	$3 + \frac{2\pi}{k} < 4.58$ (Th 8)
	Lower	~5.199 (Th 2)	~4.519 (Th 5)	$3 + \frac{2\pi}{k} - O(k^{-2})$ (Th 9)
Wireless	Upper	~4.83 (Th 3)	~4.22 (Th 6)	$3 + \frac{\pi}{k} + O(k^{-4/3})$ (Th 10)
	Lower	~4.83 (Th 4)	~4.159 (Th 7)	$3 + \frac{\pi}{k} > 3.785$ (Th 11)

These results establish a clear separation between the non-wireless and the wireless communication models. Due to lack of space the detail of missing proofs of some theorems and lemmas are deferred to the full version of the paper.

2   Two Robots

Consider a disk centered at K. Two robots, say r_1, r_2, start at K moving with constant speed, say 1, searching for an exit located at an unknown point on the perimeter of the disk. In the sequel we prove upper and lower bounds for the two robot case in the non-wireless and wireless cases.

2.1   Non-wireless Communication

Algorithm $\mathcal{A}_1$ indicates the robot trajectory for evacuation without wireless communication.

Algorithm $\mathcal{A}_1$ [for two robots without wireless communication]

1. Both robots move to an arbitrary point A on the perimeter.
2. At A the robots move along the perimeter of the disk in opposite directions; robot r_1 moves counter-clockwise and robot r_2 moves clockwise until one of the two robots, say r_1, finds the exit at B.
3. Now robot r_1 is at point B and r_2 is at point C (symmetric to B). Robot r_1 chooses a point D such that the length of the chord BD is equal to the length of the arc $\widehat{CD}$ and moves towards D.
4. Since the length of the chord BD is equal to the length of the arc $\widehat{CD}$, both robots arrive at D at the same time. Robot r_1 has knowledge about the location of the exit thus both robots can now follow the straight line DB and exit.

In the following theorem we give a bound on the worst-case evacuation time of algorithm $\mathcal{A}_1$.

Theorem 1. *There is an algorithm for evacuating the robots from an unknown exit located on the perimeter of the disk which takes time $1 + \alpha/2 + 3\sin(\alpha/2)$, where the angle α satisfies the equation $\cos(\alpha/2) = -1/3$. It follows that the evacuation algorithm takes time ~ 5.74.*

Proof. (Theorem 1) We calculate the time required until both robots from algorithm $\mathcal{A}_1$ reach the exit. Denote $x = |\widehat{BA}| = |\widehat{AC}|$, $y = |BD| = |\widehat{CD}|$ and $\alpha = |\widehat{BD}|$. According to the definition of the above algorithm $\mathcal{A}_1$ the total time required is $f(\alpha) = 1 + x + 2y$. Observe that $\alpha = 2x + y$, and $y = 2\sin(\alpha/2)$, because y is a chord of the angle α. By substituting x and y in the definition of the function f we can express the evacuation time as a function of the angle α as follows. $f(\alpha) = 1 + \frac{\alpha - y}{2} + 2y = 1 + \frac{\alpha}{2} + \frac{3y}{2} = 1 + \frac{\alpha}{2} + 3\sin(\alpha/2)$. Now we

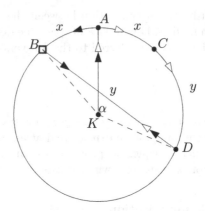

Fig. 1. Evacuation of two robots without wireless communication

differentiate with respect to α and we obtain: $\frac{df(\alpha)}{d\alpha} = \frac{1}{2} + \frac{3}{2}\cos(\alpha/2)$. It is easy to see that this derivative equals 0 for the maximum of function $f(\alpha)$, which yields as value for α the solution of $\cos(\alpha/2) = -1/3$. This proves Theorem 1.

We remark however that algorithm $\mathcal{A}_1$ is not optimal. Suppose that we modify algorithm $\mathcal{A}_1$ by making the robot arriving at point D on Fig. 1 walk along a small segment z from D towards K and back, before continuing the circular arc following D (similarly for the other robot arriving at the point symmetric to D). Our experiments show that, for sufficiently small length of such segment z, the maximum cost of 5.74 may be slightly reduced.

In the sequel we state and prove a lower bound.

Theorem 2. *It takes at least* $3 + \frac{\pi}{4} + \sqrt{2}$ *(~ 5.199) time units for two robots to evacuate from an unknown exit located in the perimeter of the disk.*

Proof. (Theorem 2) At the beginning, both robots are located at the center K of the disk. It takes at least 1 time unit for both of them to move to the perimeter of the disk.

In less than an additional $\pi/4$ time units the two robots cover at most a length of $\pi/2$ of the perimeter. The main idea is to observe, that until that time of the movement we can always construct a square $ABCD$ with sides equal to $\sqrt{2}$ whose all vertices are not yet visited by neither of the two robots. The vertices represent positions where an adversary can place an exit. Using an adversary argument it can be shown that an additional $2 + \sqrt{2}$ time units are required for robot evacuation. We give details of this argument in the following two lemmas.

Lemma 1. *For any $\epsilon > 0$, at time $1 + \frac{\pi}{4} - \epsilon$ there exists a square inscribed in the disk none of whose vertices has been explored by a robot.*

Proof. (Lemma 1) The proof is easily derived by rotating a square inscribed in the disk continuously for an angle of $\pi/2$. More precisely assume on the contrary that such an inscribed square does not exist. Consider a partition of

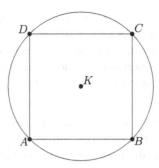

Fig. 2. Forming a square $ABCD$ of positions not yet explored by the robots

perimeter of the disk into four arcs of length $\pi/2$, E_1, E_2, E_3, E_4. Any point $e_1 \in E_1$ uniquely defines an inscribed square with vertices $e_1 \in E_1, e_2 \in E_2, e_3 \in E_3, e_4 \in E_4$. Moreover for a different $e_1' \in E_1$, $e_1' \neq e_1$ vertices of the inscribed square $\{e_1', e_2', e_3', e_4'\}$ are different $e_i' \neq e_i$ for all $i \in 1, 2, 3, 4$. By the assumption, for any $e_1 \in E_1$ at least one of the vertices $\{e_1, e_2, e_3, e_4\}$ of the inscribed square has to be explored (denote it by e^*). Thus for any e_1 we can identify an explored vertex $e^*(e_1)$. Since for different e_1, the inscribed square is different then the function $e^*(e_1)$ is an injection. Thus the image of the function $e^*(e_1)$ is a set of length $\pi/2$ of explored points. But such set does not exist because at time $1 + \pi/4 - \epsilon$ the total length of the set of explored points less than $\pi/2$. Therefore we obtain a contradiction at time $1 + \frac{\pi}{4} - \epsilon$ that an inscribed square, none of whose vertices has been explored by a robot, does exist.

Lemma 2. *For any square inscribed in the disk none of whose vertices has been explored by a robot it takes more than $2 + \sqrt{2}$ time to evacuate both robots from a vertex of the square.*

Proof. (Lemma 2) Take the square $ABCD$ with unexplored vertices. Consider any evacuation algorithm $\mathcal{A}$. We allow the algorithm to place the robots on arbitrary positions of the disk (possibly also on vertices of the square). The adversary can run the algorithm with undefined position of the exit and place the exit depending on the behaviour of the robots. The adversary will run the algorithm from perspective of a fixed robot r and will place the exit at a some point P. The placement of the exit at point P in time t is possible if robot r has no information whether the exit is located in P. Formally we say that a point P is *unknown* to robot r at time t if for any time moment $t' \in [0, t]$ robot r is at distance more than t' from P. This means that even if other robot started at P it could not meet r at any time in the interval $[0, t]$. Take a robot r and the first time moment t when the third vertex of the square is visited by a robot. Consider two cases

    Case 1. $\sqrt{2} \leq t < 2$.

    Denote the vertex visited by r in time t by A. The adversary places the exit in the antipodal point C. Observe that point C is unknown to r at time t. This is because if r was at distance at most t' from C at some time $t' \in [0, t]$ then it would be at distance $2 - t'$ from A and would reach A no sooner than at time 2, which is a contradiction as $t < 2$. Thus placement of the exit in C cannot affect movement of r until time t. Therefore, the adversary can place the exit in C and the evacuation time in this case will be at least $t + 2 \geq 2 + \sqrt{2}$.

Case 2. $2 \leq t$.

Time moment t is the first time when three vertices of the square are explored (it is possible that in t both robots explore a new vertex). Therefore, at time t, some robot r has knowledge about at most three vertices. The adversary simply places the exit in the vertex unknown to r and the evacuation time of r will be at least $t + \sqrt{2} \geq 2 + \sqrt{2}$.

Observe that t cannot be smaller than $\sqrt{2}$ because within time t at least one robot has to traverse at least one side of the square. This proves Lemma 2.

Clearly, the proof of Theorem 2 is an immediate consequence of Lemmas 1 and 2.

2.2   Wireless Communication

Algorithm $\mathcal{A}_2$ indicates the robot trajectory for evacuation with wireless communication.

Algorithm $\mathcal{A}_2$ [for two robots with wireless communication]
1. Both robots move to an arbitrary point A on the perimeter.
2. At A the robots start moving along the perimeter of the disk in opposite directions: robot r_1 moves counter-clockwise and robot r_2 moves clockwise until one of the robots, say r_1, finds the exit at B.
3. Robot r_1 notifies r_2 using wireless communication about the location of the exit and robot r_2 takes the shortest chord to B.

Theorem 3. *There is an algorithm for evacuating two robots from an unknown exit located on the perimeter of the disk which takes time at most $1 + \frac{2\pi}{3} + \sqrt{3}$.*

Proof. (Theorem 3) Consider the maximum evacuation time of algorithm $\mathcal{A}_2$. If the angular distance between A and B equals x, then the length of the chord taken by the robot r_2 equals to $c(x) = 2\sin(\pi - x)$ (see Figure 3). Thus the evacuation time T satisfies $T \leq \max_{0 \leq x \leq \pi}\{1 + x + 2\sin(\pi - x)\} = \max_{0 \leq x \leq \pi}\{1 + x + 2\sin x\}$. The function $f(x) = 1 + x + 2\sin x$ in the interval $[0, \pi]$ is maximized at the point $x^* = 2\pi/3$ and $f(x^*) = 1 + 2\pi/3 + \sqrt{3}$. This proves Theorem 3.

We now state the main lower bound.

Theorem 4. *For any algorithm it takes at least $1 + \frac{2\pi}{3} + \sqrt{3}$ time in the worst case for two robots to evacuate from an unknown exit located in the perimeter of the disk.*

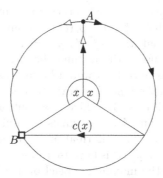

Fig. 3. Evacuation of two robots with wireless communication

3 Three Robots

In this section we analyze evacuation time for three robots in both non-wireless and wireless models.

3.1 Non-wireless Communication

The first lemma provides a lower bound which is applicable for any k robots in the non-wireless model.

Lemma 3. *For any $k \geq 3$ and $1 < \alpha < 2$, it takes in the worst case at least $\min\left\{3 + \frac{\alpha\pi}{k}, 3 + 2\sin\left(\pi - \frac{\alpha\pi}{2}\right)\right\}$ time to evacuate from an unknown exit located on the perimeter of the disk in the model without wireless communication.*

Proof. (Lemma 3) Take any evacuation algorithm $\mathcal{A}$. Denote by $\mathcal{A}_r^p(t)$ the position of robot r in time t if the exit is located at point p. Since we are considering the worst case, we need to show that there exists a point p^* on the perimeter such that if the exit is located at p^* then the evacuation time of the algorithm $\mathcal{A}$ is at least $3 + \frac{2\pi}{k} - O(k^{-2})$. Consider the following three time intervals: $I_1 = [0, 1), I_2 = \left[1, 1 + \frac{\alpha\pi}{k}\right), I_3 = \left[1 + \frac{\alpha\pi}{k}, 3\right)$. Since algorithm $\mathcal{A}$ is deterministic, the robots will follow a fixed trajectory, independent of the location of the exit until finding the exit or being notified about it by some other robot. Denote these trajectories by $p_1(t), p_2(t), \ldots p_k(t)$. Consider two cases:

Case 1. There exists a robot r and time $t^* \in I_3$ such that point $p = p_r(t^*)$ of the trajectory of the robot r is on the perimeter of the disk.

We will argue that the adversary can place the exit at point p^* being antipodal of p. We need to prove that if the exit is at point p^* then until time t^* robot r will be unaware of the location of the exit and will follow the trajectory $p_r(t)$. Consider the trajectory followed by robot r in algorithm $\mathcal{A}$ if the exit is at point p^*. Robot r is following the trajectory $p_r(t)$ until finding the exit or being notified about it. We want to show that robot r cannot be notified about the exit until time t^*. Assume on the contrary that $1 \leq t' < t^*$ is the first moment in time when r

either discovered the exit or met a robot carrying information about the location of the exit. Thus we have that $\mathcal{A}_r^{p^*}(t) = p_r(t)$,   for all $t \in [0, t']$. First note that since $p = p_r(t^*)$ we have that $dist(\mathcal{A}_r^{p^*}(t'), p^*) = dist(p_r(t'), p^*) > t' - 1$. The last inequality is true because if the distance between $p_r(t')$ and p^* would be at most $t' - 1$ then the distance to p would be at least $3 - t'$ (because p and p^* are antipodal) and robot r following trajectory $p_r(t)$ would not be able to reach p until time t^* (recall $t^* < 3$), which is a contradiction since $p_r(t^*) = p$. Now observe that in algorithm $\mathcal{A}$ if the exit is located at p^* then for any time moment $t' \leq 3$, any robot carrying information about the location of the exit is at distance at most $t' - 1$ from p^* (it is because robots can exchange informations only when they meet and the maximum speed of a robot is 1). Thus it is not possible that robot r in time t' obtain the information about the exit by meeting another robot. It is also not possible that $p_r(t') = p^*$, because robot r following trajectory $p_r(t)$ would not be able to reach p until time t^*. Thus such t' does not exist and we have: $\mathcal{A}_r^{p^*}(t) = p_r(t)$,   for all $t \in [0, t^*]$. In time moment t^* robot r following algorithm $\mathcal{A}$ is at distance 2 from the exit located at p^*. Thus the total evacuation time is at least $t^* + 2 \geq 3 + \alpha\pi/k$, since $t^* \geq 1 + \alpha\pi/k$ (because $t^* \in I_3$).

Case 2. None of the trajectories $p_1(t), p_2(t), \ldots p_k(t)$ in the interval I_3 is equal to a point on the perimeter.

In this case we consider robots following the trajectories $p_1(t), p_2(t), \ldots, p_k(t)$ in the time interval $[0, 3)$. We need the following lemma.

Lemma 4. *If a perimeter of a disk whose subset of total length $u + \epsilon > 0$ has not been explored for some $\epsilon > 0$ and $\pi \geq u > 0$, there exist two unexplored boundary points between which the distance along the perimeter is at least u.*

The set of points U on the perimeter of the disk that were not visited by any robot following such trajectories satisfies $|U| \geq 2\pi - \alpha\pi$ because in this case robots can explore the perimeter only in time interval I_2 of length $\alpha\pi/k$. Thus by Lemma 4 there exists a pair of unexplored points at distance at least $2\pi - \alpha\pi - \epsilon$ for any $\epsilon > 0$. The chord connecting these two points has length at least $2\sin(\pi - \alpha\pi/2 - \epsilon/2)$. Take this chord and denote its endpoints by u_1 and u_2. The adversary can run the algorithm $\mathcal{A}$ until moment t' when one of the points u_1, u_2 is visited and the adversary can place the exit in the other one. Note that until moment t' robots are following trajectories $p_r(t)$ because none of the robots has any information about the exit, thus $t' \geq 3$. Now the first robot that visited one of the points u_1, u_2 still needs to travel at least $2\sin(\pi - \alpha\pi/2 - \epsilon/2)$ because the exit is on the other end of the chord. Thus exploration time is in this case at least $3 + 2\sin(\pi - \alpha\pi/2 - \epsilon/2)$. We showed that the worst case time of evacuation T for any correct algorithm satisfies $T \geq \min\left\{3 + \frac{\alpha\pi}{k}, 3 + 2\sin\left(\pi - \frac{\alpha\pi}{2} - \frac{\epsilon}{2}\right)\right\}$, for any $\epsilon > 0$. The claim of the lemma follows by passing to the limit as $\epsilon \to 0$.

Theorem 5. *It takes at least 4.519 time in the worst case to evacuate three robots from an unknown exit located in the perimeter of the disk in the model without wireless communication.*

Proof. (Theorem 5) We have by Lemma 3 that the evacuation time T of any evacuation algorithm $\mathcal{A}$ satisfies $T \geq \min\{3 + \frac{\alpha\pi}{k}, 3 + 2\sin(\pi - \alpha\pi/2)\}$ for any $k \geq 3$. To prove the statement we numerically find such α that $\frac{\alpha\pi}{3} = 2\sin\left(\pi - \frac{\alpha\pi}{2}\right)$. If we set $\alpha = 1.408$, we obtain $T \geq \min\left\{3 + \frac{\alpha\pi}{3}, 3 + 2\sin\left(\pi - \frac{\alpha\pi}{2}\right)\right\} > 4.519$. This proves Theorem 5.

3.2 Wireless Communication

We have three robots r_1, r_2, r_3 and consider the following algorithm.

Algorithm $\mathcal{A}_3$ [for three robots with wireless communication]

1. Robot r_1 moves to an arbitrary point A of the perimeter, robots r_2 and r_3 move together to the point B at angle $y = 4\pi/9 + 2\sqrt{3}/3 - 401/300$ in the clockwise direction to the radius taken by robot r_1.
2. Robot r_1 moves in the counter-clockwise direction. Robot r_2 moves in the clockwise direction. Robot r_3 moves in the counter-clockwise direction for time y. Then r_3 moves towards the center. Then r_3 moves towards the perimeter at angle $\pi - y/2$ in the clockwise direction to radius RB.
3. A robot that discovers the exit sends notification to other robots.
4. Upon receiving notification a robot walks to the exit using the shortest path.

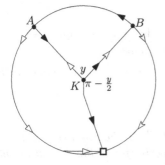

Fig. 4. Evacuation of three robots with wireless communication

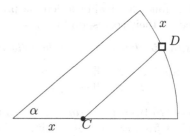

Fig. 5. $|CD| = \sqrt{1 - 2x\cos(\alpha - x) + x^2}$

The upper bound is proved in the following theorem.

Theorem 6. *It is possible to evacuate three robots from an unknown exit located on the perimeter of the disk in time at most* $\frac{4\pi}{9} + \frac{2\sqrt{3}+5}{3} + \frac{1}{600} < 4.22$ *in the model with wireless communication.*

The lower bound is proved in the following theorem.

Theorem 7. *Any algorithm takes at least* $1 + \frac{2}{3}\arccos\left(-\frac{1}{3}\right) + \frac{4\sqrt{2}}{3} \sim 4.159$ *time in the worst case for three robots to evacuate from an unknown exit located in the perimeter of the disk.*

4 k Robots

We prove asymptotically tight bounds for k robots in both the non-wireless and wireless models.

4.1 Non-wireless Communication

The trajectory of the robots is given in algorithm $\mathcal{A}_4$.

Algorithm $\mathcal{A}_4$ [for k robots with wireless communication]

1. The k robots "spread" at equal angles $2\pi/k$ and they all reach the perimeter of the disk in time 1.
2. Upon reaching the perimeter, they all move clockwise along the perimeter for $2\pi/k$ time units.
3. In one time unit, all robots move to the center of the disk. Since at least one robot has found the exit it can inform the remaining robots.
4. In one additional time unit all robots move to the exit.

Theorem 8. *It is possible to evacuate k robots from an unknown exit located on the perimeter of the disk in time $3 + \frac{2\pi}{k}$ in the model with local communication.*

Proof. (Theorem 8) Clearly the algorithm $\mathcal{A}_4$ is correct and attains the desired upper bound.

The following technical lemma provides bounds on the sin and cos functions based on their corresponding Taylor series expansions.

Lemma 5. *For any $x \geq 0$ the following bound on values of $\sin x$ and $\cos x$ hold:*

(1) $\sin x \geq x - x^3/3!$
(2) $\cos x \leq 1 - x^2/2! + x^4/4!$

Theorem 9. *It takes time at least $3 + \frac{2\pi}{k} + O(k^{-2})$ in the worst case to evacuate k robots from an unknown exit located on the perimeter of the disk in the model without wireless communication.*

Proof. (Theorem 9) We have by Lemma 3 that the evacuation time T of any evacuation algorithm $\mathcal{A}$ satisfies $T \geq \min\{3 + \frac{\alpha\pi}{k}, 3 + 2\sin(\pi - \alpha\pi/2)\}$. If we set $\alpha = 2k/(k+1)$ then taking into account Lemma 5 we obtain:

$$T \geq \min\left\{3 + \frac{\pi}{k+1}, 3 + 2\sin\left(\frac{\pi}{k+1}\right)\right\} \geq 3 + \frac{\pi}{k+1} - \frac{\pi^3}{3!(k+1)^3}$$

$$= 3 + \frac{\pi}{k} - \frac{\pi}{k(k+1)} - \frac{\pi^3}{3!(k+1)^3} = 3 + \frac{\pi}{k} - O(k^{-2}),$$

This proves the theorem.

For $k \geq 3$ robots we conjecture that the time T required to find a exit on the perimeter of a disk is exactly $3 + \frac{2\pi}{k}$.

4.2   Wireless Communication

The trajectory of the robots is given in algorithm $\mathcal{A}_5$.

Algorithm $\mathcal{A}_5$ [for k robots with wireless communication]

1. Divide the team of robots into two groups: Group G_α of size $k_\alpha = \lceil k^{2/3} \rceil$, and Group G_β of size $k_\beta = k - k_\alpha$.
2. Assign a continuous arc $\widehat{AB}$ of length $\pi - 2\sqrt{\pi}k^{-1/3}$ to group G_α and remaining part of the perimeter denoted by $\widehat{BA}$ (of length $\pi + 2\sqrt{\pi}k^{-1/3}$) to group G_β.
3. Divide arcs $\widehat{AB}$ and $\widehat{BA}$ equally between members of groups. Each robot belonging to G_α is assigned an arc of length $a_\alpha = |\widehat{AB}|/k_\alpha$. Each robot from group G_β receives an arc of length $a_\beta = |\widehat{BA}|/k_\beta$.
4. Each robot goes from the center to the perimeter and explores an assigned arc. Extremal robots from group G_α when exploring the assigned arcs go towards each other (see Figure 6). All other robots explore assigned arcs is any direction. A robot that discovers the exit sends notification to all other robots using wireless communication.
5. Upon receiving a notification about the position of the discovered exit, a robot takes the shortest chord to the exit.
6. Robots from group G_β after finishing exploration of their arcs start moving towards the center.

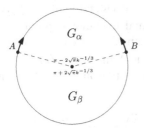

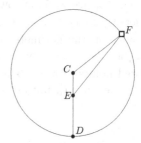

Fig. 6. Extremal (leftmost and rightmost) robots from group G_α are moving towards the interior of the arc $\widehat{AB}$

Fig. 7. $|DE| + |EF| < |DC| + |CF|$

Theorem 10. *If $k \geq 100$ then it is possible to evacuate k robots from an unknown exit located in the perimeter of the disk in time $3 + \frac{\pi}{k} + O(k^{-4/3})$, in the model with wireless communication.*

Proof. (Theorem 10) Consider the evacuation time of the algorithm $\mathcal{A}_5$. Note that since $k \geq 100$ then $k - \lceil k^{2/3} \rceil \geq \lceil k^{2/3} \rceil$ implying that $a_\alpha > a_\beta$. Thus robots from G_β finish exploration first and start going towards the center while robots from G_α are still exploring (point 6. in the pseudocode). We will show an upper bound on evacuation time T of the algorithm. Consider two cases:

Case 1. The exit is located within the arc $\widehat{AB}$.

Consider the evacuation time T_β of robots from group G_β. Observe that since $\epsilon > 1$, then $a_\alpha < 1$ thus the exit is discovered while robots from G_β are walking towards the center (before they reach the center). Robots from G_β start moving towards the center at time $1 + a_\beta$. At some time t' satisfying $2 + a_\beta > t' > 1 + a_\beta$ the exit is discovered by a robot from group G_α. Consider a trajectory taken by a robot r from group G_β starting from time $1 + a_\beta$. If r would simply walk to the center and then from the center to the exit (location of the exit would be known by the time when r reaches the center). The time would be not more than $3 + a_\beta$. By the triangle inequality the path taken by robot r acting according to the algorithm is shorter (see Figure 7). Thus the evacuation time T_β for robots belonging to team G_β is at most

$$T_\beta \leq 3 + a_\beta \leq 3 + \frac{\pi + 2\sqrt{\pi}k^{-1/3}}{k - k_\alpha}$$

$$= 3 + \frac{\pi + 2\sqrt{\pi}k^{-1/3}}{k} + \frac{(\pi + 2\sqrt{\pi}k^{-1/3})\lceil k^{2/3}\rceil}{k(k - \lceil k^{2/3}\rceil)} = 3 + \frac{\pi}{k} + O(k^{-4/3}).$$

Consider now the evacuation time of robots from group G_α. Assume that the exit is discovered at time $1 + x$ for some $0 \leq x \leq a_\alpha$. Since the extremal robots from group G_α are walking towards each other at the time moment $1 + x$ two arcs of length x has been explored starting from each endpoint of arc $\widehat{AB}$. Thus the distance on the perimeter between extremal unexplored points of arc $\widehat{AB}$ is $\pi - 2\sqrt{\pi}k^{-1/3} - 2x$. Hence the maximum length of a chord connecting two unexplored points of arc $\widehat{AB}$ in this moment is $2\sin((\pi - 2\sqrt{\pi}k^{-1/3} - 2x)/2)$. Therefore the time T_α until evacuation of all robots from group G_α is at most

$$T_\alpha \leq \max_{0 \leq x \leq a_\alpha} \left\{ 1 + x + 2\sin\left(\frac{\pi - 2\sqrt{\pi}k^{-1/3} - 2x}{2}\right) \right\}$$

$$= \max_{0 \leq x \leq a_\alpha} \left\{ 1 + x + 2\cos\left(\sqrt{\pi}k^{-1/3} + x\right) \right\}.$$

The function $f(x) = 1 + x + 2\cos(\sqrt{\pi}k^{-1/3} + x)$ has derivative $f'(x) = 1 - 2\cos(\sqrt{\pi}k^{-1/3} + x)$. For $k \geq 100$ we have that $2\sqrt{\pi}k^{-1/3} + a_\alpha \leq \pi/6$. Thus $\cos(\sqrt{\pi}k^{-1/3} + x) \leq 1/2$ for all $x \in [0, a_\alpha]$, which implies that the function $f(x)$ is non-decreasing in the considered set. In order to find the maximum it is sufficient to consider its value at the extremal point a_α.

$$T_\alpha \leq 1 + a_\alpha + 2\sin(\pi/2 - (\sqrt{\pi}k^{-1/3} + a_\alpha))$$

$$= 1 + \frac{\pi - 2\sqrt{\pi}k^{-1/3}}{\lceil k^{2/3}\rceil} + 2\cos\left(\sqrt{\pi}k^{-1/3} + \frac{\pi - 2\sqrt{\pi}k^{-1/3}}{\lceil k^{2/3}\rceil}\right)$$

$$\leq 1 + \frac{\pi - 2\sqrt{\pi}k^{-1/3}}{\lceil k^{2/3} \rceil} + 2 - \left(\sqrt{\pi}k^{-1/3} + \frac{\pi - 2\sqrt{\pi}k^{-1/3}}{\lceil k^{2/3} \rceil} \right)^2$$

$$+ \left(\sqrt{\pi}k^{-1/3} + \frac{\pi - 2\sqrt{\pi}k^{-1/3}}{\lceil k^{2/3} \rceil} \right)^4 / 12$$

$$\leq 3 + O(k^{-4/3})$$

Thus in this case the evacuation time $T \leq \max\{T_\alpha, T_\beta\} \leq 3 + \frac{\pi}{k} + O(k^{-4/3})$.

Case 2. The exit is located within arc $\widehat{BA}$.

Each robot from group G_β explores an arc of length $(\pi + 2\sqrt{\pi}k^{-1/3})/(k - k_\alpha)$. Thus time until the exit is discovered is at most $1 + (\pi + 2\sqrt{\pi}k^{-1/3})/(k - \lceil k^{2/3} \rceil)$. Since we are in the wireless communication model, each robot is notified immediately and needs additional time at most 2 to go to the exit. Thus the total evacuation time in this case is at most

$$T \leq 3 + \frac{\pi + 2\sqrt{\pi}k^{-1/3}}{k - k^{2/3} - 1}$$

$$= 3 + \frac{\pi + 2\sqrt{\pi}k^{-1/3}}{k} + \frac{(\pi + 2\sqrt{\pi}k^{-1/3})(k^{2/3} + 1)}{k(k - k^{2/3} - 1)}$$

$$= 3 + \frac{\pi}{k} + O(k^{-4/3})$$

This completes the proof of Theorem 10.

Lemma 6. *For any $k \geq 2$ and x satisfying $\pi/k \leq x < 2\pi/k$ and any evacuation algorithm it takes time at least $1 + x + 2\sin(xk/2)$ to evacuate from an unknown exit located in the perimeter of the disk.*

Theorem 11. *It takes at least $3 + \frac{\pi}{k}$ time in the worst case to evacuate $k \geq 2$ robots from an unknown exit located on the perimeter of the disk in the model with wireless communication.*

Proof. (Theorem 11) This is a direct consequence of Lemma 6 where $x = \pi/k$. □

5   Conclusion

We studied the evacuation problem for k robots in a disk of unit radius and provided several algorithms in both non-wireless and wireless communication models for $k = 2$ and $k = 3$ robots. For the case of k robots we were able to give asymptotically tight bounds thus indicating a clear separation between the non-wireless and the wireless communication models. There are many interesting open questions. An interesting challenge would be to tighten our bounds or even determine optimal algorithms for $k = 2, 3$ robots. Another interesting class of problems is concerned with evacuation from more than one exit, or with robots having distinct maximal speeds. Finally, the geometric domain being considered, the starting positions of the robots, as well as the communication model provide challenging variants of the questions considered in this paper.

References

1. Albers, S., Henzinger, M.R.: Exploring Unknown Environments. SIAM J. Comput. 29(4), 1164–1188 (2000)
2. Albers, S., Kursawe, K., Schuierer, S.: Exploring unknown environments with obstacles. Algorithmica 32, 123–143 (2002)
3. Alpern, S., Gal, S.: The theory of search games and rendezvous. Int. Series in Operations research and Management Science, vol. 55. Kluwer Academic Publishers (2002)
4. Alpern, S., Fokkink, R., Gąsieniec, L., Lindelauf, R., Subrahmanian, V.S(eds.): Search Theory, A Game Theoretic Approach. Springer (2013)
5. Baeza-Yates, R.A., Culberson, J.C., Rawlins, G.J.E.: Searching in the Plane. Inf. Comput. 106(2), 234–252 (1993)
6. Baeza-Yates, R.A., Schott, R.: Parallel Searching in the Plane. Comput. Geom. 5, 143–154 (1995)
7. Baumann, N., Skutella, M.: Earliest Arrival Flows with Multiple Sources. Math. Oper. Res. 34(2), 499–512 (2009)
8. Beck, A.: On the linear search Problem. Naval Res. Logist. 2, 221–228 (1964)
9. Bellman, R.: An optimal search problem. SIAM Rev. 5, 274 (1963)
10. Burgard, W., Moors, M., Stachniss, C., Schneider, F.E.: Coordinated multi-robot exploration. IEEE Transactions on Robotics 21(3), 376–386 (2005)
11. Chrobak, M., Gąsieniec, L., Gorry, T., Martin, R.: Evacuation problem on the line (in preparation)
12. Chung, T.H., Hollinger, G.A., Isler, V.: Search and pursuit-evasion in mobile robotics. Autonomous Robots 31(4), 299–316 (2011)
13. Deng, X., Kameda, T., Papadimitriou, C.H.: How to learn an unknown environment. In: Proc. 32nd Symp. on Foundations of Computer Science, pp. 298–303 (1991)
14. Fekete, S., Gray, C., Kröller, A.: Evacuation of Rectilinear Polygons. In: Wu, W., Daescu, O. (eds.) COCOA 2010, Part I. LNCS, vol. 6508, pp. 21–30. Springer, Heidelberg (2010)
15. Fomin, F.V., Thilikos, D.M.: An annotated bibliography on guaranteed graph searching. Theoretical Computer Science 399(3), 236–245 (2008)
16. Gluss, B.: An alternative solution to the "lost at sea" problem. Naval Research Logistics Quarterly 8(1), 117–122 (1961)
17. Hoffmann, F., Icking, C., Klein, R., Kriegel, K.: The polygon exploration problem. SIAM J. Comp. 31, 577–600 (2001)
18. Isbell, J.: Pursuit Around a Hole. Naval Research Logistics Quarterly 14(4), 569–571 (1967)
19. Kijima, S., Yamashita, M., Yamauchi, Y.: Private communication (2013)
20. Kleinberg, J.M.: On-line Search in a Simple Polygon. In: SODA, pp. 8–15 (1994)
21. Lidbetter, T.: Hide-and-seek and Other Search Games, PhD Thesis. London School of Economics (2013)
22. Mitchell, J.S.B.: Geometric shortest paths and network optimization. In: Handbook of Computational Geometry, pp. 633–702 (2000)
23. Nahin, P.: Chases and Escapes: The Mathematics of Pursuit and Evasion. Princeton University Press, Princeton (2007)
24. Papadimitriou, C.H., Yannakakis, M.: Shortest paths without a map. Theor. Comput. Sci. 84, 127–150 (1991)
25. Thrun, S.: A Probabilistic On-Line Mapping Algorithm for Teams of Mobile Robots. I. J. Robotic Res. 20(5), 335–363 (2001)
26. Yamauchi, B.: Frontier-Based Exploration Using Multiple Robots. In: Agents, pp. 47–53 (1998)

Randomized Pattern Formation Algorithm for Asynchronous Oblivious Mobile Robots*

Yukiko Yamauchi and Masafumi Yamashita

Faculty of Information Science and Electrical Engineering, Kyushu University, Japan
{yamauchi,mak}@inf.kyushu-u.ac.jp

Abstract. We present a randomized pattern formation algorithm for asynchronous oblivious (i.e., memory-less) mobile robots that enables formation of any target pattern. As for deterministic pattern formation algorithms, the class of patterns formable from an initial configuration I is characterized by the symmetricity (i.e., the order of rotational symmetry) of I, and in particular, every pattern is formable from I if its symmetricity is 1. The randomized pattern formation algorithm ψ_{PF} we present in this paper consists of two phases: The first phase transforms a given initial configuration I into a configuration I' such that its symmetricity is 1, and the second phase invokes a deterministic pattern formation algorithm ψ_{CWM} by Fujinaga et al. (DISC 2012) for asynchronous oblivious mobile robots to finally form the target pattern.

There are two hurdles to overcome to realize ψ_{PF}. First, all robots must simultaneously stop and agree on the end of the first phase, to safely start the second phase, since the correctness of ψ_{CWM} is guaranteed only for an initial configuration in which all robots are stationary. Second, the sets of configurations in the two phases must be disjoint, so that even oblivious robots can recognize which phase they are working on. We provide a set of tricks to overcome these hurdles.

Keywords: Mobile robot, pattern formation, randomized algorithm.

1 Introduction

Consider a distributed system consisting of anonymous, asynchronous, oblivious (i.e., memory-less) mobile robots that do not have access to a global coordinate system and are not equipped with communication devices. We investigate the problem of forming a given pattern F from *any* initial configuration I, whose goal is to design a distributed algorithm that works on each robot to navigate it so that the robots as a whole eventually form F from any I. Besides the theoretical interest how the robots with extremely weak capability can collaborate, the fact that self-organization is a key property desired for autonomous distributed systems motivates our work. However, a stream of papers [2–7] have showed that

* This work was supported by a Grant-in-Aid for Scientific Research on Innovative Areas "Molecular Robotics" (No. 24104003 and No. 24104519) of The Ministry of Education, Culture, Sports, Science, and Technology, Japan.

F. Kuhn (Ed.): DISC 2014, LNCS 8784, pp. 137–151, 2014.

the problem is not solvable by a deterministic algorithm, intuitively because the symmetry among robots cannot be broken by a deterministic algorithm. Specifically, let $\rho(P)$ be the (geometric) symmetricity of a set P of points, where $\rho(P)$ is defined as the number of angles θ (in $[0, 2\pi)$) such that rotating P by θ around the center of the smallest enclosing circle of P produces P itself.[1] Then F is formable from I by a deterministic algorithm, if and only if $\rho(I)$ divides $\rho(F)$, which suggests us to explore a *randomized solution*.

This paper presents a randomized pattern formation algorithm ψ_{PF}. Algorithm ψ_{PF} is *universal* in the sense that for any given target pattern F, it forms F from *any* initial configuration I (not only from I such that $\rho(I)$ divides $\rho(F)$). We however need the following assumptions; the number of robots $n \geq 5$, and both I and F do not contain multiplicities. The idea behind ψ_{PF} is simple and natural; first the symmetry breaking phase realized by randomized algorithm ψ_{SB} translates I into another configuration I' such that $\rho(I') = 1$ with probability 1 if $\rho(I) > 1$, and then the second phase invokes the (deterministic) pattern formation algorithm ψ_{CWM} in [5], which forms F from any initial configuration I' such that $\rho(I') = 1$.[2] Since randomization is a traditional tool to break symmetry, one might claim that ψ_{PF} is trivial. It is not the case at all, mainly because our robots are asynchronous. We return to this issue later in this section, after a brief introduction of our robot model.

In the literature [2–7], the robots are modeled by points on a two dimensional Euclidean plane. Each robot repeats a Look-Compute-Move cycle, where it obtains the positions of other robots (in Look phase), computes the curve to a next position with a pattern formation algorithm (in Compute phase), and moves along the curve (in Move phase). We assume that the execution of each cycle ends in finite time. Each robot has no access to the global x-y coordinate system; it has its own x-y local coordinate system, and the robots' positions in Look phase and the curve to its next position in Compute and Move phases are given in its x-y local coordinate system. The x-y local coordinate systems are all right-handed. The robots are oblivious in the sense that the algorithm is a function of the robots' positions (in its x-y local coordinate system) observed in the preceding Look phase. We assume discrete time $0, 1, \ldots$, and introduce three types of asynchrony. In the *fully-synchronous* (FSYNC) model, robots execute Look-Compute-Move cycles synchronously at each time instance. In the *semi-synchronous* (SSYNC) model, once activated, robots execute Look-Compute-Move cycles synchronously. We do not make any assumption on synchrony for the *asynchronous* (ASYNC) model.

A crucial assumption here is that a robot can sense the position of another robot, but cannot sense its velocity. In the SSYNC (and hence FSYNC) model, a robot never observe moving robots by definition, while in the ASYNC model, a robot does but cannot tell which of them are moving. This is an essential difficulty in designing a randomized algorithm for the ASYNC model. In this

---

[1] That is, P is rotational symmetry of order $\rho(P)$.

[2] Of course we can also use the pattern formation algorithm in [2] since it keeps the terminal agreement of ψ_{SB} (i.e., the leader), during the formation.

paper, we devise a trick to overcome this problem. Specifically, in order for ψ_{CWM} to start working in safe, in the terminal configuration of ψ_{SB} all robots must simultaneously stop and agree on the end of the symmetry breaking phase. We solve the symmetricity breaking problem in two phases: The *randomized leader election* phase and the *termination agreement* phase. In the randomized leader election phase, robots randomly select the leader on the largest empty circle, which is the largest circle centered at the center of the smallest enclosing circle of robots and contains no robot in its interior. The robots on the largest empty circle move by randomly selected small distance along the circumference of the largest empty circle, and when they break the symmetry, some of the robots enter the interior of the largest empty circle to form a new largest empty circle. They repeat this random selection phase until the system reaches a configuration where exactly one robot is on the current largest empty circle. We call this robot the leader. At this point, some robots may be still circulating on the previous largest empty circles. Now, the problem is to check the termination of these random movements when we have the leader. The leader defines a static destination point for each of these robots, such that they cannot reach by their small random movement. The randomly moving robots should start deterministic new movement. Eventually, all these robots stop and the leader moves closer to the the center of the smallest enclosing circle so that the robots agree the termination. Finally, robots start a pattern formation phase.

Related Works. The pattern formation problem in FSYNC model and SSYNC model was first investigated by Suzuki and Yamashita [6, 7]. First, they showed that any target pattern formable by non-oblivious robots in the FSYNC model is formable by oblivious robots in the SSYNC model, except point formation of two robots. They also showed that point formation of two robots is unsolvable in the SSYNC model, while there is a trivial solution in the FSYNC model. Second, they characterized the formable patterns by non-oblivious robots in the FSYNC model. A necessary and sufficient condition to from a target pattern F from a given initial configuration I is $\rho(I)|\rho(F)$. Later, ASYNC model was introduced by Flocchini et al. [3]. Since we cannot apply pattern formation algorithms for the FSYNC or SSYNC model to the ASYNC model, the pattern formation problem in the ASYNC model has been an open problem. Dieudonné et al. proposed a universal pattern formation algorithm with a unique leader for more than three oblivious robots in the ASYNC model [2]. Fujinaga et al. presented an embedded pattern formation algorithm for oblivious robots in the ASYNC model, where each robot obtains an embedded target pattern in its local coordinate system [4]. Their algorithm is based on a minimum weight perfect matching between the target points and the positions of robots, which is called *clockwise matching*. Finally, Fujinaga et al. presented a pattern formation algorithm for oblivious robots in the ASYNC model that uses the embedded pattern formation algorithm [5]. Cieliebak et al. presented a gathering algorithm for more than two oblivious robots in the ASYNC model [1].

All these papers investigate robots with deterministic algorithms. To the best of our knowledge, randomized symmetricity breaking is a new notion which works as a fundamental preprocessing for many tasks of robots.

2   System Model

Let $R = \{r_1, r_2, \ldots, r_n\}$ be a set of anonymous robots in a two-dimensional Euclidean plane. Each robot r_i is a point and does not have any identifier, but we use r_i just for description.

A *configuration* is a set of positions of all robots at a given time. In the ASYNC model, when no robot observes a configuration, the configuration does not affect the behavior of any robots. Hence, we consider the sequence of configurations, in each of which at least one robot executes a Look phase. In other words, without loss of generality, we consider discrete time $1, 2, \ldots$. A robot starting a Look-Compute-Move cycle at time t obtains the positions of other robots at time $t' \geq t$ (Look phase), computes a curve to the next location (Compute phase), and starts moving along the curve at time $t'' \geq t'$ (Move phase). The Move phase finishes at some time $t''' \geq t''$. Let $p_i(t)$ (in the global coordinate system Z_0) be the position of r_i ($r_i \in R$) at time t ($t \geq 0$). $P(t) = \{p_1(t), p_2(t), \ldots, p_n(t)\}$ is a configuration of robots at time t. The robots initially occupy distinct locations, i.e., $|P(0)| = n$.

The robots do not agree on the coordinate system, and each robot r_i has its own x-y *local coordinate system* denoted by $Z_i(t)$ such that the origin of $Z_i(t)$ is its current position.[3] We assume each local coordinate system is right-handed, and it has an arbitrary unit distance. For a set of points P (in Z_0), we denote by $Z_i(t)[P]$ the positions of $p \in P$ observed in $Z_i(t)$.

An algorithm is a function, say ψ, that returns a curve to the next location in the two-dimensional Euclidean plane when given a set of positions. Each robot has an independent private source of randomness and an algorithm can use it to generate a random rational number. A robot is *oblivious* in the sense that it does not remember past cycles. Hence, ψ uses only the observation in the Look phase of the current cycle.

In each Move phase, each robot moves at least $\delta > 0$ (in the global coordinate system) along the computed curve, or if the length of the curve is smaller than δ, the robot stops at the destination. However, after δ, a robot stops at an arbitrary point of the curve. All robots do not know this minimum moving distance δ. During movement, a robot always proceeds along the computed curve without stopping temporarily. We call this assumption *strict progress property*.

An execution is a sequence of configurations, $P(0), P(1), P(2), \ldots$. The execution is not uniquely determined even when it starts from a fixed initial configuration. Rather, there are many possible executions depending on the activation schedule of robots, execution of phases, and movement of robots. The *adversary*

---

[3] During a Move phase, we assume that the origin of the local coordinate system of robot r_i is fixed to the position where the movement starts, and when the Move phase finishes, the origin is the current position of r_i.

can choose the activation schedule, execution of phases, and how the robots move and stop on the curve. We assume that the adversary knows the algorithm, but does not know any random number generated at each robot before it is generated. Once a robot generates a random number, the adversary can use it to control all robots.

Pattern Formation. A target pattern F is given to every robot r_i as a set of points $Z_0[F] = \{Z_0[p] | p \in F\}$. We assume that $|Z_0[F]| = n$. In the following, as long as it is clear from the context, we identify $p \in F$ with $Z_0[p]$ and write, for example, "F is given to r_i" instead of "$Z_0[F]$ is given to r_i." It is enough emphasizing that F is not given to a robot in terms of its local coordinate system.

Let $\mathbb{T}$ be a set of all coordinate systems, which can be identified with the set of all transformations, rotations, uniform scalings, and their combinations. Let $\mathcal{P}_n$ be the set of all patterns of n points. For any $P, P' \in \mathcal{P}_n$, P is *similar* to P', if there exists $Z \in \mathbb{T}$ such that $Z[P] = P'$, denoted by $P \simeq P'$.

We say that algorithm ψ forms pattern $F \in \mathcal{P}_n$ from an initial configuration I, if for any execution $P(0)(= I), P(1), P(2), \ldots$, there exists a time instance t such that $P(t') \simeq F$ for all $t' \geq t$.

For any $P \in \mathcal{P}_n$, let $C(P)$ be the smallest enclosing circle of P, and $c(P)$ be the center of $C(P)$. Formally, the *symmetricity* $\rho(P)$ of P is defined by

$$\rho(P) = \begin{cases} 1 & \text{if } c(P) \in P, \\ |\{Z \in \mathbb{T} : P = Z[P]\}| & \text{otherwise.} \end{cases}$$

We can also define $\rho(P)$ in the following way [6]: P can be divided into regular k-gons centered at $c(P)$, and $\rho(P)$ is the maximum of such k. Here, any point is a regular 1-gon with an arbitrary center, and any pair of points $\{p, q\}$ is a regular 2-gon with its center $(p + q)/2$.

For any configuration P $(c(P) \notin P)$, let $P_1, P_2, \ldots, P_{n/\rho(P)}$ be a decomposition of P into the above mentioned regular $\rho(P)$-gons centered at $c(P)$. Yamashita and Suzuki [7] showed that even when each robot observes P in its local coordinate system, all robots can agree on the order of P_i's such that the distance of the points in P_i from $c(P)$ is no greater than the distance of the points in P_{i+1} from $c(P)$, and each robot is conscious of the group P_i it belongs to. We call the decomposition $P_1, P_2, \ldots, P_{n/\rho(P)}$ ordered by this condition the *regular $\rho(P)$-decomposition* of P.

A point on the circumference of $C(P)$ is said to be "on circle $C(P)$" and "the interior of $C(P)$" ("the exterior", respectively) does not include the circumference. We denote the interior (exterior, respectively) of $C(P)$ by $Int(C(P))$ $(Ext(C(P)))$. We denote the radius of $C(P)$ by $r(P)$. Given two points p and p' on $C(P)$, we denote the arc from p to p' in the clockwise direction by $arc(p, p')$. When it is clear from the context, we also denote the length of $arc(p, p')$ by $arc(p, p')$. The largest empty circle $L(P)$ of P is the largest circle centered at $c(P)$ such that there is no robot in its interior, hence there is at least one robot on its circumference.

Algorithm with Termination Agreement. A robot is *static* when it is not in a Move phase, i.e., in a Look phase or a Compute phase, or not executing a cycle. A configuration is *static* if all robots are static. Because robots in the ASYNC model cannot recognize static configurations, we further define station-ary configurations. A configuration P is *stationary* for an algorithm ψ, if in any execution starting from P, configuration does not change.

We say algorithm ψ guarantees termination agreement if in any execution $P(0), P(1), \ldots$ of ψ, there exists a time instance t such that $P(t)$ is a stationary configuration, in $P(t')$ $(t' \geq t)$, ψ outputs $\emptyset$ at any robot, and all robots know the fact. Specifically, $\psi(Z'[P(t')]) = \emptyset$ in any local coordinate system Z'. This property is useful when we compose multiple algorithms to complete a task.

3   Randomized Pattern Formation Algorithm

The idea of the proposed universal pattern formation algorithm is to translate a given initial configuration I with $\rho(I) > 1$ into a configuration I' with $\rho(I') = 1$ with probability 1, and after that the robots start the execution of a pattern formation algorithm. We formally define the problem.

Definition 1. The symmetricity breaking problem *is to change a given initial configuration I into a stationary configuration I' with $\rho(I') = 1$.*

In Section 3.1, we present a randomized symmetricity breaking algorithm ψ_{SB} with termination agreement. In the following, we assume $n \geq 5$ and I and F do not contain any multiplicities. Additionally, we assume that for a given initial configuration I, no robot occupies $c(I)$, i.e., $c(I) \cap I = \emptyset$.[4] Due to the page limitation, we omit the pseudo code of ψ_{SB}.

In Section 3.2, we present a randomized universal pattern formation algorithm ψ_{PF}, that uses ψ_{SB} and a pattern formation algorithm ψ_{CWM} [5] with slight modification.

3.1   Randomized Symmetricity Breaking Algorithm ψ_{SB}

In the proposed algorithm ψ_{SB}, robots elect a single leader that occupies a point nearest to the center of the smallest enclosing circle. Clearly, the symmetricity of such configuration is one.

We use a sequence of circles to show the progress of ψ_{SB}. In configura-tion P, let $C_i(P)$ be the circle centered at $c(P)$ with radius $r(P)/2^i$. Hence, $C_0(P) = C(P)$. We denote the radius of $C_i(P)$ by γ_i. We call the infinite set of circles $C_0(P), C_1(P), \ldots$ the set of *binary circles*. Because ψ_{SB} keeps the small-est enclosing circle of robots unchanged during any execution, we use C_i instead of $C_i(P)$. We call C_i the *front circle* if C_i is the largest binary circle in $L(P)$ including the circumference of $L(P)$, and we call C_{i-1} the *backward circle* (Fig. 1). We denote the number of robots in C_i and on C_i by n_i. Hence, if the current front circle C_i is the largest empty circle, n_i is the number of robots on C_i, otherwise it is smaller than the number of robots on C_i.

---

[4] If there is a robot on $c(I)$, we move the robot by some small distance from $c(I)$ to satisfy the conditions of the terminal configuration of ψ_{SB}.

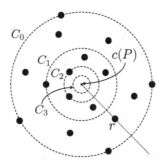

Fig. 1. The set of binary circles and radial track of r, where C_0 is the smallest enclosing circle, C_1 is the backward circle, and C_2 is the front circle

Recall that all local coordinate systems are right handed. Hence, all robots agree on the clockwise direction on each binary circle. For C_i ($i \geq 0$) and a robot r on C_i, we call the next robot on C_i in its clockwise direction *predecessor*, denoted by $pre(r)$, and the one in the counter-clockwise direction *successor*, denoted by $suc(r)$. When there are only two robots r and r' on C_i, $pre(r) = suc(r) = r'$. We say r is neighboring to r' if $r' = pre(r)$ or $r' = suc(r)$. For example, in Fig. 2(a), $pre(r_0)$ is r_1, $suc(r_0)$ is r_7, and r_1 and r_7 are neighbors of r_0.

During an execution of the proposed algorithm, robot r moves to an inner binary circle along a half-line starting from the center of the smallest enclosing circle and passing r's current position. We call this half-line the *radial track* of r (Fig. 1). When r moves from a point on C_i to C_{i+1} along its radial track, we say r *proceeds to C_{i+1}*.

Algorithm ψ_{SB} first sends each robot to its inner nearest binary circle along its radial track if the robot is not on any binary circle. Hence, the current front circle is also the largest empty circle.

Then, ψ_{SB} probabilistically selects at least one robot on the current front circle C_i, and make them proceed to C_{i+1}. These selected robots repeat the selection on C_{i+1}. By repeating this, the number of robots on a current front circle reaches 1 with probability 1. The single robot on the front circle is called the *leader*.

We will show the detailed selection procedure on each front circle. We have two cases depending on the positions of robots when the selection of a front circle C_i starts. One is the *regular polygon case* where robots on C_i form a regular n_i-gon, and the other is the *non-regular polygon case* where n_i robots on C_i form a non-regular polygon.

Selection in the Regular Polygon Case. When robots on the current front circle C_i form a regular n_i-gon (i.e., for all robot r on C_i, $arc(suc(r), r) = 2\pi\gamma_i/n_i$), it is difficult to select some of the robots. Especially, when the symmetricity of the current configuration is n_i, it is impossible to deterministically select some of the robots. In a regular n_i-gon case, ψ_{SB} makes these robots randomly circulate on C_i. Then, a robot that do not catch up with its predecessor and caught by its successor is selected and proceeds to C_{i+1}.

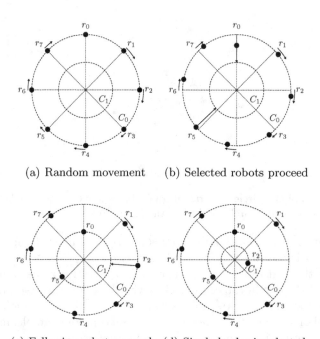

(a) Random movement   (b) Selected robots proceed

(c) Following robot proceeds (d) Single leader is selected

Fig. 2. Random selection

First, if robot r on C_i finds that the robots on C_i form a regular n_i-gon, r randomly selects "stop" or "move." If it selects "move," it generates a random number v in $(0..1]$, and moves $v(1/4)(2\pi\gamma_i/n_i)$ along C_i in the clockwise direction (Fig. 2(a)). This procedure ensures that the regular n_i-gon is broken with probability 1. When r finds that the regular n_i-gon is broken, r stops.

Uniform moving direction ensures the following invariants:

1. Once r finds that it is caught by $suc(r)$, i.e., the following inequality holds, r never leave from $suc(r)$.

$$Caught(r) = arc(suc(r), r) \leq 2\pi\gamma_i/n_i$$

2. Once r finds that it missed $pre(r)$, i.e., the following inequality holds, r never catch up with $pre(r)$.

$$Missing(r) = 2\pi\gamma_i/n_i < arc(r, pre(r)) \leq (5/4)(2\pi\gamma_i/n_i)$$

We say robot r is *selected* if it finds that the following predicate holds.

$$Selected(r) = Caught(r) \wedge Missing(r)$$

Then, a selected robot proceeds to C_{i+1} (Fig. 2(b)). Since no two neighboring robots satisfy *Selected* at a same time, while *Selected*(r) holds at r, $suc(r)$ and

$pre(r)$ wait for r to proceed to C_1. Even when $n_i = 2$, when they are not in the symmetric position, just one of the two robots becomes selected. Note that other robots cannot check whether r is selected or not in the ASYNC model because they do not know whether r has observed the configuration and found that $Selected(r)$ holds.

Observation 1. *During the above random movement on the current front circle C_i, $(3/4)(2\pi\gamma_i/n_i) \le arc(r, pre(r)) \le (5/4)(2\pi\gamma_i/n_i)$ holds at each robot r on C_i. Let $r' = pre(r)$ and $r'' = suc(r)$ for r on C_i. If r becomes selected and proceeds to C_{i+1}, then $arc(suc(r'), r') > (5/4)(2\pi\gamma_i/n_i)$ and $arc(r'', pre(r'')) > (5/4)(2\pi\gamma_i/n_i)$ hold thereafter even when robots move.*

After some selected robots proceed to C_{i+1}, other robots might be still moving on C_i and may become selected later. However, in the ASYNC model, no robot can determine which robot is moving on C_i. For the robots on C_{i+1} to ensure that no more robot will join C_{i+1}, ψ_{SB} makes some of the non-selected robots on C_i proceed to C_{i+1}. The robots on C_i are classified into three types, rejected, following, and undefined.

The predecessor and the successor of a selected robot are classified into *rejected*, and each rejected robot stays on C_i. All robots can check whether robot r is rejected or not with the following condition:

$Rejected(r) =$
$(arc(r, pre(r)) > (5/4)(2\pi\gamma_i/n_i)) \lor (arc(suc(r), r) > (5/4)(2\pi\gamma_i/n_i)).$

Non-rejected robot r becomes *following* if r finds that at least one of the following three conditions hold:

$FollowPre(r) = \neg Rejected(r) \land Rejected(pre(r)) \land Caught(r)$
$FollowSuc(r) = \neg Rejected(r) \land Rejected(suc(r)) \land Missing(r)$
$FollowBoth(r) = \neg Rejected(r) \land Rejected(pre(r)) \land Rejected(suc(r)).$

Hence, we have

$Following(r) = FollowPre(r) \lor FollowSuc(r) \lor FollowBoth(r).$

Intuitively, the predecessor and the successor of a following robot never become selected nor following. Algorithm ψ_{SB} makes each following robot proceed to C_{i+1} (Fig. 2(c)).

Finally, robots on C_i that are neither selected, rejected nor following are classified into *undefined*.

Note that $Rejected(r)$ implies $\neg Selected(r)$ and $\neg Following(r)$. Additionally, $Selected(r)$ and $Following(r)$ may hold at a same time.

Eventually, all robots on C_i recognize their classification from selected, following, and rejected. We can show that once a robot finds its classification, it never changes. Then, selected robots and following robots leave C_i and only rejected robots remain on C_0. During the random selection phase, n_i does not change

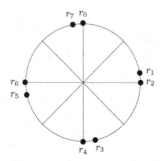

Fig. 3. Non-regular case. All robots are rejected, and no robot proceeds to C_1 with the two conditions *Rejected* and *Following*.

since robots moves in $Int(C_i) \cup C_i$. Hence, all robots can check whether a robot r on C_i is rejected or not with $Rejected(r)$, and the robots on C_{i+1} agree that no more robot proceeds to C_{i+1}. These robots start a new (random) selection on C_{i+1}.

Consider the case where $i = 0$. When $n = 5$, the length of the random movement is largest, and each robot circulates at most $\pi/10$. Hence, no two robots form a diameter. Additionally, ψ_{SB} guarantees that no two neighboring robots leave C_0. Hence, ψ_{SB} keeps C_0 during the random selection. In the same way, when $n \geq 5$, the random selection does not change C_0.

Selection for non-regular polygon case. When robots on the current front circle C_i does not form a regular n_i-gon, ψ_{SB} basically follows the random selection. Thus, robots do not circulate on C_i randomly, but check their classification with the three conditions.

Because robots do not form a regular n_i-gon on C_i, there exists a robot r on C_i that satisfies $arc(suc(r), r) < 2\pi\gamma_i/n_i$. However, there exists many positions of n_i robots on C_i where all such robot r are also rejected, i.e., $arc(r, pre(r)) > (5/4)(2\pi\gamma_i/n_i)$, from which no robot becomes selected nor following (Fig. 3).

In this case, we add one more condition $NRSelected(r)$. We say r satisfies $NRSelected(r)$ when r is on the front circle C_i, all robots on C_i do not satisfy *Selected* nor *Following*, and $arc(r, pre(r)) > (5/4)(2\pi\gamma_i/n_i)$ and $arc(suc(r), r) \leq 2\pi\gamma_i/n_i$ hold. We note that no two neighboring robots satisfies $NRSelected$. Robot r proceeds half way to C_{i+1}, and waits for all robots satisfying $NRSelected$ to proceed.[5] Robots in between C_i and C_{i+1} can reconstruct the non-regular polygon on C_i with their radial tracks and after all robots satisfied $NRSelected$ leaves C_i, the robots in $Ext(C_{i+1}) \cap Int(C_i)$ proceeds to C_{i+1}. Note that during a random selection, no robot on C_i satisfies $NRSelected$.

We consider one more exception case for initial configurations where robots form a non-regular polygon on C_0. In this case, each robot r first examines $NRSelected(r)$. If proceeding all robots satisfying $NRSelected$ changes C_0, the successor of such robot proceeds to C_1 instead of them. Assume that r is one

---

[5] Otherwise, r cannot distinguish how many robots satisfied $NRSelected$.

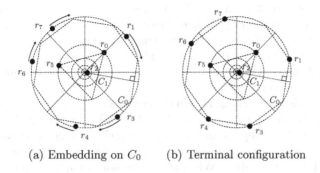

(a) Embedding on C_0 (b) Terminal configuration

Fig. 4. Stopping rejected robots when the leader is first generated on C_2. (a) The leader embeds a regular octagon on C_0 by its position on C_4. (b) After all robots C_0 have reached the corners of embedded polygons, r_L proceeds to C_5.

of such robots satisfying $NRSelected(r)$. Because C_0 is broken after all robots satisfying $NRSelected$ proceeds, in the initial configuration $arc(r, pre(r)) = \pi\gamma_0$. Otherwise, there exists a rejected robot that does not satisfy $NRSelected$ in the initial configuration. Hence, proceeding $suc(r)$ does not change C_0.

After that, robots on C_i determine their classification by using *Rejected*, *Following*, and following robots proceed to C_{i+1}. Eventually all following robots leave C_i, and only rejected robots remain on C_i.

Termination Agreement. By repeating the above procedure on each binary circle, with probability 1, only one robot reaches the inner most binary circle, with all other robots rejected (Fig. 2(d)). We say this robot is selected as a single leader. However, rejected robots may be still moving on the binary circles. Thus, the leader robot starts a new phase to stop all rejected robots, so that the terminal configuration is stationary.

Let r_L be the single leader and C_i be the front circle for $R \setminus \{r_L\}$ (this implies the leader is selected during the random selection on C_i). Intuitively, r_L checks the termination of C_{i-j} ($i - j \geq 0$) when r_L is on C_{i+j+2}. Given a current observation, all robots on C_{i-j} are expected to move at most $(1/4)(2\pi\gamma_{i-j}/n_{i-j})$ from corners of some regular n_{i-j}-gon. Hence, there exists an embedding of regular n_{i-j}-gon onto C_{i-j} so that its corners does not overlap these expected tracks. If there is no such embedding, then randomized selection has not been executed on C_{i-j}, and r_L embeds an arbitrary regular n_{i-j}-gon on C_{i-j}. Robot r_L shows the embedding by its position on C_{i+j+2}, i.e., r_L's radial track is the perpendicular bisector of an edge of the regular n_{i-j}-gon (Fig. 4(a)).

Then, ψ_{SB} makes robots on C_{i-j} occupy distinct corners of the regular n_{i-j}-gon. The target points of these robots are determined by the clockwise matching algorithm [4]. We restrict the matching edges before we compute the clockwise matching. Specifically, we use arcs on C_{i-j} instead of direct edges, and direction of each matching edge (from a robot to its destination position) is always in the clockwise direction. Note that under this restriction, the clockwise matching algorithm works correctly on C_{i-j}.[6] The robots on C_{i-j} has to start a new movement with fixed target positions. Because robots can agree the clockwise matching irrespective of their local coordinate systems, r_L can check whether robots on C_{i-j} finish the random movement.

Then, r_L calculates its next position on C_{i+j+3} in the same way for robots on C_{i-j-1}, and moves to that point.

The leader finishes checking all binary circles on C_{2i+2}, then it proceeds to C_{2i+3} to show the termination of ψ_{SB} (See Fig. 4(b)). However, ψ_{SB} carefully moves robots on C_0 to keep the smallest enclosing circle. When there are just two robots on C_0, then the random selection has not been executed on C_0, and r_L does not check the embedding. When there are more than three robots, there is at least one robot that can move toward its destination with keeping the smallest enclosing circle, and ψ_{SB} first moves such a robot.

For any configuration P satisfying the following two conditions, ψ_{SB} outputs $\emptyset$ at any robot irrespective of its local coordinate system. Hence, such configuration P is a stationary configuration of ψ_{SB}.

1. P contains a single leader on the front circle, denoted by C_b.
2. All other robots are in $Ext(C_k) \cup C_k$, satisfying $b \geq 2k + 3$.

Clearly, ψ_{SB} guarantees terminal agreement among all robots.

Algorithm ψ_{SB} guarantees the reachability to a terminal configuration with probability 1, and the terminal configuration is deterministically checkable by any robots in its local coordinate system.

3.2   Randomized Pattern Formation Algorithm ψ_{PF}

We present a randomized pattern formation algorithm ψ_{PF}. Algorithm ψ_{PF} executes ψ_{SB} when the configuration does not satisfy the two conditions of the terminal configuration of ψ_{SB}. When the current configuration satisfies the two terminal conditions of ψ_{SB}, ψ_{PF} starts a pattern formation phase.

Fujinaga et al. proposed a pattern formation algorithm ψ_{CWM} in the ASYNC model, which uses the clockwise minimum weight perfect matching between the robots and an embedded target pattern [5]. The embedding of the target pattern is determined by the robots on the largest empty circle. Additionally, when there is a single robot on the largest empty circle, ψ_{CWM} keeps this robot the nearest robot to the center of the smallest enclosing circle during any execution. We use this property to separate the configurations that appears executions of ψ_{SB} and those of ψ_{CWM}.

---

[6] Algorithm ψ_{CWM} [4] reconstructs a clockwise matching from all minimum weight perfect matchings between robots and target points, i.e., for a set of overlapping edges, ψ_{CWM} selects some of them in a "clockwise" manner. The critical assumption is that the number of robots is equal to the number of target points. When ψ_{SB} uses ψ_{CWM}, it restricts the direction of edges when considering the set of all minimum weight matchings. Because the number of target points is larger than the number of robots, without this restriction, a robot in the middle point of two target points may increase the number of target points.

Algorithm ψ_{PF} uses ψ_{CWM} after ψ_{SB} terminates, however, to compose ψ_{SB} and ψ_{CWM}, we modify the terminal configuration of ψ_{SB} to keep the leader showing the termination of ψ_{SB}. Let P be a given terminal configuration of ψ_{SB}, and the single leader be r_L on the front circle C_L. Given a target pattern F, let $F_1, F_2, \ldots, F_{n/\rho(F)}$ be the regular $\rho(F)$-decomposition of F. Then, ψ_{CWM} embeds F so that $f \in F_1$ lies on the radial track of r_L, and $r(F) = r(P)$. When $c(F) \in F$, ψ_{CWM} also perturbs this target point. Let F' be this embedding.

Then, ψ_{PF} first moves r_L as follows: Let $L(F')$ be the largest empty circle of F' and $\ell(F')$ be its radius. Let k $(k > 0)$ be an integer such that C_k be the largest binary circle in $L(F')$. If C_{2k+3} is in C_L, r_L proceeds to C_{2k+3}. When C_{2k+3} is in $Ext(C_L)$, r_L does not move. Then, ψ_{PF} starts the execution of ψ_{CWM}. After $R \setminus \{r_L\}$ reach their destination positions, r_L moves to its target point along its radial track.

4   Correctness

Let I be an initial configuration where robots form a regular n-gon. We first show that ψ_{SB} randomly selects at least one and at most $n/2$ robots and C_0 does not change by robots' random movement on C_0.

Lemma 1. *Starting from an initial configuration I where the robots form a regular n-gon, with probability 1, any execution of ψ_{SB} in the ASYNC model reaches a configuration where at least one robot is selected, and until then ψ_{SB} does not change the smallest enclosing circle of robots.*

Proof. Let $P(0), P(1), \ldots$ be an arbitrary execution of ψ_{SB} in the ASYNC model where the robots form a regular n-gon in $P(0)(= I)$.

Because $n \geq 5$ and each robot moves at most $(1/4)(2\pi\gamma_0/n)$ when it observes a regular n-gon configuration, the random movement does not produce a neighboring robots that satisfies $arc(r, suc(r)) > \pi\gamma_0$ until some robot proceeds to C_1. Hence, the random circulation of robots does not change C_0.

We consider the worst behavior of the adversary against ψ_{SB}, that is, the adversary always tries to keep the regular n-gon of robots.

As adversary activates some robots, eventually ψ_{SB} outputs a moving distance larger than 0 at some robot. This robot starts its Move phase in finite time. The adversary has no choice other than to activate other robots so that all robots move with keeping a regular n-gon.

We first consider the case where $(1/4)(2\pi\gamma_0/n) \geq \delta$. With probability $n\delta/\pi\gamma_0$, a robot, say r, outputs a moving distance smaller than the (unknown) minimum moving distance δ. Even when all robots start their move phases with keeping regular n-gon, r stops while the adversary cannot stop other robots, and the adversary have no choice to activate r again to keep the regular n-gon. Let $P(t)$ be a configuration where r stops while other robots are moving. With probability $1/2$, ψ_{SB} outputs "stop" at r. Then, because of the strict progress property, in $P(t + 1)$, the robots do not keep a regular n-gon. When r is activated after $P(t + 1)$, r becomes selected.

Assume that a robot r is in a Compute phase, while all other robots are moving. The adversary has no choice to stop all robots, because in the same way as the above discussion, ψ_{SB} outputs "stop" with probability $1/2$ and the regular n-gon is probabilistically broken. Hence, all robots stop at least once in every $(1/4)(2\pi\gamma_0/n)$ distance, and at least with probability $n\delta/\pi\gamma_0$, the regular n-gon is broken. Consequently, ψ_{SB} defeats the adversary and breaks the initial regular n-gon with probability 1.

When $(1/4)(2\pi\gamma_0/n) < \delta$, ψ_{SB} always outputs moving distance smaller than δ, and the above discussion also holds.   □

A selected robot r proceeds to C_1 and while $Selected(r)$ holds, $Selected$ and $Following$ do not hold at its neighbors, and the neighbors become rejected after r proceeds. We have the same property for any following robot. Eventually, all robots recognize their classification and selected and following robots reach C_1.

Lemma 2. *No two neighboring robots in $P(0)$ enters the interior of C_0 in the randomized selection on C_0.*

From Lemma 2, the smallest enclosing circle does not change during any execution of ψ_{SB} when $n \geq 5$.

Then, We obtain the following theorem.

Theorem 2. *Starting from an initial configuration I, where robots form a regular n-gon, with probability 1, the system reaches a configuration where C_0 contains only rejected robots.*

The rejected robots on C_0 do not become selected nor following even when robots on C_1 moves, because n_0 does not change and all robots can check their states with the predicate $Rejected$. Hence, robots on C_1 start a new random selection phase. We obtained the base case. Clearly, Theorem 2 holds for the robots on any front circle.

Corollary 1. *Starting from a configuration where the robots on the front circle C_i form a regular polygon, with probability 1, the system reaches a configuration where at least one and at most half of these robots reach C_{i+1}, and C_i contains only rejected robots.*

In the same way as randomized selection, we have the following corollary for deterministic selection.

Corollary 2. *Starting from a configuration where the robots on the front circle C_i form a non-regular polygon, the system eventually reaches a configuration where at least one and at most $(n_i - 3)$ of these robots reach C_{i+1}, and C_i contains only rejected robots.*

From Corollary 1 and Corollary 2, we have the following theorem.

Theorem 3. *With probability 1, the system reaches a configuration where only one robot is on the front circle, and all robots in the backward circle are rejected.*

Then, ψ_{SB} makes the leader check whether the robots on each binary circle C_i have stopped by embedding a regular n_i-gon so that robots on C_i starts a new deterministic movement to reach the corners of the regular n_i-gon. The system eventually reaches a terminal configuration of ψ_{SB} with probability 1.

Theorem 4. *Starting from any arbitrary configuration with $n \geq 5$ robots, the system reaches a terminal configuration of ψ_{SB} with probability 1.*

From a static terminal configuration of ψ_{SB}, robots execute ψ_{CWM}, and we have the following theorem.

Theorem 5. *Algorithm ψ_{PF} forms any target pattern from any initial configuration with probability 1.*

5   Conclusion

We present a randomized pattern formation algorithm for oblivious robots in the ASYNC model. The proposed algorithm consists of a randomized symmetricity breaking algorithm and a pattern formation algorithm proposed by Fujinaga et al. [5]. One of our future directions is to extend our results to the robots with limited visibility, where oblivious robots easily increase the symmetricity [8].

Acknowledgment. We would like to thank Miss Zhe Qu for the discussion with us about the topic of this paper.

References

1. Cieliebak, M., Flocchini, P., Prencipe, G., Santoro, N.: Distributed computing by mobile robots: Gathering. SIAM J. of Comput. 41(4), 829–879 (2012)
2. Dieudonné, Y., Petit, F., Villain, V.: Leader election problem versus pattern formation problem. In: Lynch, N.A., Shvartsman, A.A. (eds.) DISC 2010. LNCS, vol. 6343, pp. 267–281. Springer, Heidelberg (2010)
3. Flocchini, P., Prencipe, G., Santoro, N., Widmayer, P.: Arbitrary pattern formation by asynchronous, anonymous, oblivious robots. Theor. Comput. Sci. 407, 412–447 (2008)
4. Fujinaga, N., Ono, H., Kijima, S., Yamashita, M.: Pattern formation through optimum matching by oblivious CORDA robots. In: Lu, C., Masuzawa, T., Mosbah, M. (eds.) OPODIS 2010. LNCS, vol. 6490, pp. 1–15. Springer, Heidelberg (2010)
5. Fujinaga, N., Yamauchi, Y., Kijima, S., Yamashita, M.: Asynchronous pattern formation by anonymous oblivious mobile robots. In: Aguilera, M.K. (ed.) DISC 2012. LNCS, vol. 7611, pp. 312–325. Springer, Heidelberg (2012)
6. Suzuki, I., Yamashita, M.: Distributed anonymous mobile robots: Formation of geometric patterns. SIAM J. on Comput. 28(4), 1347–1363 (1999)
7. Yamashita, M., Suzuki, I.: Characterizing geometric patterns formable by oblivious anonymous mobile robots. Theor. Comput. Sci 411, 2433–2453 (2010)
8. Yamauchi, Y., Yamashita, M.: Pattern formation by mobile robots with limited visibility. In: Moscibroda, T., Rescigno, A.A. (eds.) SIROCCO 2013. LNCS, vol. 8179, pp. 201–212. Springer, Heidelberg (2013)

A Theoretical Foundation for Scheduling and Designing Heterogeneous Processors for Interactive Applications

Shaolei Ren[1], Yuxiong He[2], and Kathryn S. McKinley[2]

[1] Florida International University, Miami, FL
[2] Microsoft Research, Redmond, WA

Abstract. To improve performance and meet power constraints, vendors are introducing heterogeneous multicores that combine high performance and low power cores. However, choosing which cores and scheduling applications on them remain open problems. This paper presents a scheduling algorithm that provably minimizes energy on heterogeneous multicores and meets latency constraints for interactive applications, such as search, recommendations, advertisements, and games. Because interactive applications must respond quickly to satisfy users, they impose multiple constraints, including average, tail, *and* maximum latency. We introduce SEM (Slow-to-fast, Energy optimization for Multiple constraints), which minimizes energy by choosing core speeds and how long to execute jobs on each core. We prove SEM minimizes energy without *a priori* knowledge of job service demand, satisfies multiple latency constraints simultaneously, and only migrates jobs from slower to faster cores. We address practical concerns of migration overhead and congestion. We prove optimizing energy for *average* latency requires homogeneous cores, whereas optimizing energy for *tail* and *deadline* constraints requires heterogeneous cores. For interactive applications, we create a formal foundation for scheduling and selecting cores in heterogeneous systems.

1 Introduction

Power constraints are forcing computer architects to turn to heterogeneous multicore hardware to improve performance. For instance, smartphones are shipping with Qualcomm's Snapdragon and ARM's Cortex-A15 [15], which include high performance and low power cores with the same instruction set, called big/little and Asymmetric Multicore Processors (AMP). Design principles for selecting cores in heterogeneous system and scheduling algorithms that optimize their energy consumption, however, remain open problems. This paper presents a scheduling algorithm that provably minimizes energy on heterogeneous processors serving interactive applications. We prove and establish scheduling insights and design principles with practical implications for heterogeneous core selection.

Interactive applications are latency-sensitive. Examples include serving web pages, games, search, advertising, recommendations, and mobile applications. Since interactive applications must be responsive to attract and please users, they

F. Kuhn (Ed.): DISC 2014, LNCS 8784, pp. 152–166, 2014.
© Springer-Verlag Berlin Heidelberg 2014

must meet *latency* requirements. Furthermore, they must be energy efficient. In data centers, energy is an increasingly higher fraction of total costs [19], and 1% energy saving may translate to millions of dollars. On mobile, energy efficiency translates directly into longer battery life and happier users.

Prior schedulers that optimize for energy efficiency and heterogeneity have major limitations. (1) They often predict demand for each request, scheduling high demand jobs to high performance fast cores and other jobs to low power slow cores [1,9,11,36,38,40]. Unfortunately, the service demand of individual requests in interactive applications is usually unknown and difficult to predict [23]. (2) For unknown service demand, prior work only optimizes for a *single simple* latency constraint [23,35,37], such as average latency or maximum latency, and is inadequate for two reasons. First, many applications strive for consistency by reducing tail latency (e.g., 95th- and 99th-percentile) or variance [13,17], which average and maximum latency do not model. Second, some applications *require* a combination of low average, tail, and worst-case latencies [12,16]. For example, search, finance applications, ads, and commerce have customer requirements and expectations for average and tail latency [12,13,17].

This paper shows how to optimize energy efficiency of interactive workloads subject to multiple latency constraints by exploiting heterogeneous multicores, addressing the aforementioned challenges as follows.

Unknown service demand. Instead of predicting individual job demand, we exploit the service demand *distribution* measured online or offline, which changes slowly over time [23,26]. We schedule incoming jobs to appropriate cores without knowing their individual service demands.

Multiple latency constraints. The scheduling literature typically optimizes for average or maximum latency only. To generalize and combine latency constraints, we use L_p norms [2–5,18,25,31,39]. The L_p norms encapsulate maximum latency ($p \to \infty$) and average latency ($p = 1$) as special cases. Optimizing for larger values of p places more emphasis on the latency of longer jobs. Appropriate values of p effectively mitigate unfairness and extreme outliers for long jobs [2,5]. Optimizing the L_1 and L_2 norms together reduce latency variance, which makes latency more *predictable* and improves user experience [32].

This paper presents an optimal algorithm that minimizes energy on heterogeneous processors given a demand distribution and latency constraints. We quantitatively characterize the optimal schedule and the ratio of fast to slow core speeds in a heterogeneous system. We present an *optimal* scheduling algorithm, called SEM (Slow-to-fast, Energy optimization for Multiple constraints). Given a service demand distribution, SEM schedules interactive jobs on heterogeneous multicore processors to minimize energy consumption while simultaneously satisfying multiple L_p norm latency constraints.

We show *an optimal schedule migrates jobs from slower to faster cores.* Ideally, we want to schedule high demand (long) jobs on fast cores to meet latency requirements and short jobs on slow cores to save energy *without* a prior knowledge of service demand. SEM exploits this observation by scheduling short jobs

on energy efficient slow cores where they complete with high probability and
then migrating long jobs to fast cores to meet the latency constraints.

We show *more heterogeneity is desirable for higher p*, where p is the L_p norm
moment and the heterogeneity degree is the ratio of the fastest to slowest core
speed. Given a single average latency constraint ($p = 1$), the energy optimal
schedule requires a homogeneous processor. For all other latency constraints
($p > 1$) and multiple constraints, the optimal schedule requires heterogeneous
processors.

We show *bounds on the ratio of the fastest and slowest core speeds for an
optimal heterogeneous processor*. The result indicates that the more heterogeneous workload is and/or the less power additional core performance consumes,
the more heterogeneous the hardware needs to be. Our result provides a formal
and quantitative guide for selecting core speeds while designing heterogeneous
processors. For practical choices of p and measured service load distributions,
the ratio ranges from two to eight. Systems with this degree of heterogeneity are
thus quite practical to assemble from current server, client, and mobile cores.

Due to space constraints, we state the theorems and intuitions here and refer
readers elsewhere for the proofs [27]. We leave to future work experimental evaluation of energy. Our own prior work exploits the slow-to-fast insight to optimize
performance (not energy) of interactive applications [26]. We achieved substantial performance improvements in simulation and on real systems by configuring
Simultaneous Multi-Threading (SMT) hardware as a dynamic heterogeneous
multicore [26]. No prior work presents an optimal algorithm or theory for energy
efficiency under multiple latency constraints, nor provides guidelines for selecting core speeds. This work is the first formal analysis to deliver these properties
for scheduling interactive workloads on heterogeneous multicore processors for
energy minimization subject to multiple latency constraints.

2   Job, Processor, and Scheduling Models

This section and Table 1 describe our job, processor, and scheduling model.

Job model. We focus on CPU intensive interactive services such as search, ads,
finance option pricing, games, and serving dynamic web page content [6,19,40].
Each interactive service request is a *job*. Each job has *work w* (service demand),
which represents the number of CPU cycles the job takes to complete. Since it
is often impossible to accurately predict a job's service demand [23], we model
w as a discrete random variable whose value is unknown until the job completes.
We divide the service demand into N units (also called "bins" in this paper)
and the *size* of the i-th bin is denoted by w_i, which we obtain by measuring the
distribution of work for the application. The choice of "bin" sizes is determined
by the measurement accuracy, and our model is not restricted to any particular
choices. The job service demand w follows a distribution that only takes values
out of the set $\mathcal{W} = \{\tilde{w}_1, \tilde{w}_2, \cdots, \tilde{w}_N\}$, where we define $\tilde{w}_i = \sum_{j=1}^{i} w_j$, for $i =
1, 2, \cdots, N$. This assumption is not restrictive. In practice, a job's service demand
cannot be continuous and is typically grouped into a finite number of bins [35].

Table 1. Symbols and definitions

	Definition		Definition
w	CPU service demand	x_i	Speed of core i
w_i	Size of the i-th demand bin	$z(x)$	Power consumption
f_i	Probability of demand $\tilde{w}_i = \sum_{j=1}^{i} w_j$	$e(x)$	Energy function
F_i	Cumulative distribution	L_p	L_p norm with moment p
F_i^c	Complementary cumulative distribution	$\tilde{D}(p)$	L_p norm latency constraint

Let $\{f_1, f_2, \cdots, f_N\}$ and $\{F_0, F_1, \cdots, F_N\}$ be the probability distribution and cumulative distribution of the job's service demand, respectively: $f_i = \Pr(w = \tilde{w}_i)$ and $F_i = \sum_{j=1}^{i} f_j$, for $i = 1, 2, \cdots, N$. While the service demand of any single job is unknown *a priori*, we assume the aggregate service demand distribution of jobs is measured with online or offline profiling as in previous work [23].

Processor model. We adopt a standard processor model. With speed $x > 0$, a core will consume a power of $z(x)$. Correspondingly, the energy consumption per unit work is $e(x) = z(x)/x$. The processing time for a unit work increases linearly with respect to the inverse of core speed. Given a particular application, the effective speed x and power $z(x)$ can be obtained by system measurements. Consequently, the effective speed x may differ from the clock rate of CPU and both clock speed an power may vary depending on the application [14, 20].

We assume the energy function $e(x)$ is continuously differentiable, increasing, and strictly convex in $x \geq 0$. This assumption is validated extensively by both analytical models and measurement studies [14, 23, 35]. In practice, if a slower core consumes more power and thus energy than a fast one, it wont be built. Because of CMOS circuit characteristics, energy is well approximated as $e(x) = b \cdot x^{\alpha-1} + c$ for core speed x, where the power exponent $\alpha \geq 2$ and static energy $c \geq 0$ [8, 23]. We concentrate on heterogeneous multicores which consists of multiple diverse cores, but our approach applies to cores with multiple speeds realized with DVFS.

We refer to the core executing the i-th bin of a job's demand as core i, for $i = 1, 2, \cdots, N$. We denote the core speed and power consumption of core i by x_i and $z_i = z(x_i)$, respectively. The energy consumption per unit work of core i is given by $e_i = e(x_i) = z(x_i)/x_i$. Two cores i and j may be equivalent in some cases, i.e., $x_i = x_j$, for $i, j = 1, 2, \cdots, N$. For example, one core will execute multiple bins when demand for this core differs between two or more jobs.

2.1 Scheduling Objective —Energy

Our scheduling objective is minimize average energy on a heterogeneous processor when scheduling interactive jobs that are subject to multiple latency constraints. The scheduler determines the core speeds x_i for each bin $i = 1, 2, \cdots, N$. We express the average energy consumption of a job as

$$\bar{e}(\mathbf{x}) = \sum_{i=1}^{N} \left[\sum_{j=1}^{i} z_j \cdot \frac{w_j}{x_j} \right] \cdot f_i = \sum_{i=1}^{N} [1 - F_{i-1}] \cdot e(x_i) \cdot w_i, \tag{1}$$

where $e_i = e(x_i) = z(x_i)/x_i$ is the energy per unit work consumed by core i and $\mathbf{x} = (x_1, x_2, \cdots, x_N)$ is a vector expression. The term "$\sum_{j=1}^{i} z_j \cdot \frac{w_j}{x_j}$" represents the energy consumption of a job with a service demand of $\sum_{j=1}^{i} w_j$ (which occurs with a probability of f_i), and hence we have the average energy consumption as $\sum_{i=1}^{N} \left[\sum_{j=1}^{i} z_j \cdot \frac{w_j}{x_j} \right] \cdot f_i$. Equivalently, we can rewrite the average energy consumption as $\sum_{i=1}^{N} [1 - F_{i-1}] \cdot e(x_i) \cdot w_i$, where $(1 - F_{i-1})$ is the probability that the i-th bin of the service demand is processed (i.e., the probability that a job has at least a service demand of $\sum_{j=1}^{i} w_j$).

2.2   Scheduling Constraints —Latency

Many prior studies mainly focused on *single* and *simple* latency constraints, such as maximum latency (deadline) or average latency [23, 35]. Motivated by recent work that addresses latency requirements in contexts such as load balancing [2, 25], we introduce the L_p norm to generalize latency constraints. For concision, we sometimes abbreviate the L_p norm with L_p. Specifically, given the core speeds $\mathbf{x} = (x_1, x_2, \cdots, x_N)$, we mathematically express the L_p norm for latency as follows

$$D(p) = \left[\sum_{i=1}^{N} (t_i)^p \cdot f_i \right]^{\frac{1}{p}} = \left\{ \sum_{i=1}^{N} \left[\sum_{j=1}^{i} \frac{w_j}{x_j} \right]^p \cdot f_i \right\}^{\frac{1}{p}}, \tag{2}$$

where $p \geq 1$ and $t_i = \sum_{j=1}^{i} \frac{w_j}{x_j}$ is the latency of a job with a service demand of $\tilde{w}_i = \sum_{j=1}^{i} w_j$. The L_p norm for latency generalizes over maximum and average latency. Given $p = \infty$, L_∞ is maximum latency and given $p = 1$, L_1 is average latency. Intuitively, larger values of p emphasize optimizing the latency of longer jobs, effectively mitigating unfairness and extreme outliers for long jobs [2, 5].

Latency variance determines the *predictability* of a scheduling algorithm [32] and depends on the L_2 and L_1 through the simple expression $L_2 - L_1$. For average latency and latency variance, we can apply various techniques, such as Chebyshev inequality, to bound tail distributions and estimate high-percentile latency. Thus, simultaneously considering multiple L_p latency constraints, such as the L_1 and L_2 norms, well characterizes requirements on interactive applications [2–4, 25].

This paper focuses on interactive applications where the actual demand of individual jobs is unknown and hence all jobs have the same latency constraints, e.g., all web pages have similar latency constraints, since users will abandon the browser if responses are too slow. Differentiated services for different jobs are beyond the scope of this paper and could be interesting future work.

3   Problem Formulation and Algorithm

This section formalizes the energy minimization problem and presents the SEM scheduling algorithm, which minimizes energy subject to latency constraints.

The inputs to SEM are the probability distribution of service demand f_i, the size of each service demand bin w_i, and energy consumption per unit work $e(x)$ in terms of the processing speed x. SEM outputs the optimal job schedule, which prescribes a sequence of core speeds $x_1, x_2, \cdots, x_N$, where x_i is the core speed to process the i-th service demand bin. An incoming job with unknown service demand will execute on the prescribed sequence of core speeds until completion. For example, given an application that has jobs with service demands of $1, 2, 5$, or 10 (units of work) and some probability distribution, then there are 4 service demand bins with the following sizes: $w_1 = 1, w_2 = 2 - 1 = 1, w_3 = 5 - 2 = 3, w_4 = 10 - 5 = 5$. Given a set of L_p latency constraints, SEM determines the optimal core speed x_i for executing each service demand bin w_i. For example, $x_1 = 1$ GHz, $x_2 = x_3 = 1.5$ Ghz, and $x_4 = 3$ GHz. This scheduling plan is determined offline and then used in deployment. In deployment, when a job arrives, it's service demand is unknown. SEM first processes the job on a 1 GHz core. If the job does not completed after 1 unit of work, SEM migrates the job to a 1.5 GHz core. If the job does not completed after processing another $w_2 + w_3 = 4$ units of work, SEM migrate it to a 3GHz core, and continue processing the job until it completes. Formally, this problem is stated as follows.

$$\mathbf{P1}: \min_{\mathbf{x}} \sum_{i=1}^{N} \{[1 - F_{i-1}] \cdot e(x_i) \cdot w_i\} \tag{3}$$

$$s.t., \quad \left\{ \sum_{i=1}^{N} \left[\sum_{j=1}^{i} \frac{w_j}{x_j} \right]^{p_k} f_i \right\}^{\frac{1}{p_k}} \leq \tilde{D}(p_k), \tag{4}$$

$$\text{for } k = 1, 2, \cdots, K,$$

$$\mathbf{x} \succeq \mathbf{0}, \tag{5}$$

where $\succeq$ is an element-wise operator, constraining all the core speeds to be non-negative. This formulation assumes that the core speeds $x_1, x_2, \cdots, x_N$ can be continuously chosen from any non-negative values. In other words, here core speeds are unconstrained. (Section 6 shows how to handle the limited numbers of core speeds available in practice.) The objective function in (3) minimizes the average energy of all jobs. The latency constraints in (4) are imposed with K different norms where $1 \leq p_1 < p_2 < \cdots < p_K \leq \infty$. Note that imposing a tail latency constraint of L_∞ excludes outlier jobs, e.g., for 95-percentile latency, the 5% longest jobs are excluded by the L_∞ norm.

This **P1** formulation is a convex optimization problem. The latency constraints in Inequality (4) are convex because L_p norms are convex when $p \geq 1$. The speed constraints in Inequality (5) are linear. A linear combination of the energy consumption per unit work $e(x)$ is strictly convex in terms of the processing speed x due to CMOS characteristics [23]. The objective function in (3) is also convex. Since **P1** is convex, there exist efficient algorithms that find the globally optimal solution, which we denote as $\mathbf{x}^*$.

We derive the solution to **P1** using a primal-dual iterative approach. A companion technical report presents the algorithm and its proof [27]. We set a threshold ϵ as a stopping criterion such that the iteration stops once the difference of the L_2 norm between two consecutively iterated values is below the threshold. The iterative approach has a iteration-complexity bounded by $\mathcal{O}(1\backslash\epsilon^2)$ [22].

Note that we analytically derive the solution to **P1** instead of using a convex solver. The analytical form exposes important properties of the optimal solution and has implications for hardware core choices that we discuss in Section 4 and Section 5. These properties cannot be derived using a convex solver.

Further note that we only compute an optimal schedule *once* offline for any given job service demand distribution and heterogeneous system. Our online scheduler simply applies the precomputed optimal schedule, executing a job on each core speed for the precomputed specified optimal time, until the job completes. Therefore, the computational overhead in deployment is negligible.

4   An Optimal Schedule Migrates from Slow to Fast Cores

Under the optimal schedule, core speeds monotonically increase as hardware processes more of the job's work. In other words, *an optimal scheduler need only migrate a job from slower to faster cores.* Theorem 1 formalizes this property. While prior studies [23, 26, 35, 37] show to use the "slow to fast" property under the maximum latency constraint in different contexts such as DVFS, in contrast, Theorem 1 is the first formal result that applies it to the more general case of *any* latency norm constraint and with *multiple* latency norm constraints.

Theorem 1. *The optimal core speeds that solve **P1** satisfy* $0 < x_1^* \leq x_2^* \leq \cdots \leq x_N^*$. *If only the L_1 latency constraint is imposed, then* $x_1^* = x_2^* = \cdots = x_N^*$.

Proof. The technical report contains the proof [27]. ∎

Theorem 1 tells us, without a priori knowledge of each job's service demand, an optimal schedule first processes a job on a slow core. If the job does not complete within some time interval (because it is long), SEM migrates it to faster cores. Thus, a short job completes on slower cores to save energy while a long job uses faster cores to meet the latency constraints. Consequently, the average energy consumption is minimized while satisfying latency constraints.

The intuition behind Theorem 1 is that long jobs have a greater impact on latency constraints. In particular, the latency norm constraint specified by Equation (2) is mostly dominated by long jobs (the larger p_k, the more dominated by long jobs, which can be seen by taking the partial derivative of (2) with respect to the latency experienced by jobs with various demands). In the extreme case, when $p_k \to \infty$, only the maximum latency incurred by the longest jobs is important. Thus, we want to process the long jobs fast enough to meet the latency constraints. On the other hand, processing short jobs using slower cores saves energy without penalizing the latency constraints.

If only the average latency constraint ($p = 1$) is considered, Theorem 1 reduces to a special case where $x_1^* = x_2^* = \cdots = x_N^*$, i.e., the optimal schedule uses a homogeneous processor. Intuitively, this reduction holds because delaying short and long jobs have the same impact on the L_1 norm. More formally, the technical report [27] derives that $e(x_i)x_i^2$ is the same for all $i = 1, 2, \cdots, N$ and hence, homogeneous speeds are optimal when only satisfying the L_1 norm latency constraint. For all other latency constraints ($p > 1$) and multiple constraints, the optimal energy-efficient schedule requires heterogeneous processors.

5   Implications for Cores in a Heterogeneous System

This section analyzes how latency constraints, workload characteristics, and core power/performance characteristics effect core choices in a heterogeneous system.

5.1   Effect of Latency Constraints on Heterogeneity

Given Theorem 1, a key question is what core speeds to include in a heterogeneous system. In practice, the fastest cores are limited by physics and the software will be tuned such that the fastest core speed can satisfy the most demanding jobs. We therefore exploit this theorem to select the remaining lower power cores by investigating the ratio of the fastest x_N^* to the slowest x_1^* speed. We define this ratio as the *degree of heterogeneity* , giving a formal quantitative guideline for selecting core speeds in a heterogeneous processor. Our analysis shows that *more heterogeneity is desired for larger p in the L_p norm constraint.*

We derive this result using a widely-used class of energy functions [23] expressed in the form $e(x) = b \cdot x^{\alpha-1}$, where $b > 0$ and $\alpha \geq 2$ (corresponding to a power function of $z(x) = b \cdot x^\alpha$ [23]). The lack of a closed-form expression of the optimal core speeds $\mathbf{x}^*$ makes it prohibitive to derive the exact value of the degree of heterogeneity. We instead exploit monotonicity to derive upper and lower bounds, using Theorem 2 to show that degree of heterogeneity is monotonically increasing in $p \geq 1$.

Theorem 2. *Given $e(x) = b \cdot x^{\alpha-1}$ and one L_p latency constraint, then the degree of heterogeneity $\frac{x_N^*}{x_1^*}$ increases with increasing p for $p \geq 1$.*

Proof. The technical report contains the proof [27].   ■

Theorem 2 proves that as $p \geq 1$ increases, the optimal degree of heterogeneity also increases; the latency constraint thus imposes the optimal choice of core speeds. More precisely, given two different values of p, we can select two different latency constraints, under which the corresponding minimum core speeds are the same using the optimal job schedule. Under a latency constraint with a larger p value, long jobs require faster cores, because larger values of p place a more stringent requirement on the latency of longer jobs. Thus, if p increases, so does x_N^*/x_1^*. Furthermore, we prove a lemma in the technical report [27] that the degree of heterogeneity is a constant for a given p regardless of latency constraints, which establishes *hardware requires more heterogeneity for larger p.*

5.2   How Much Heterogeneity Is Desirable?

This section explores how much heterogeneity is desirable. We use Theorem 2 to derive both upper and lower bounds on degree of heterogeneity in Theorem 3.

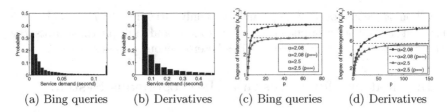

(a) Bing queries   (b) Derivatives   (c) Bing queries   (d) Derivatives

Fig. 1. (a) (b) Service demand distributions of Bing and Financial derivative workloads. Most jobs are short, but long jobs are not negligible. (c) (d) Degree of heterogeneity as a function of p given one L_p constraint and power model: $z(x) = 21 \cdot x^\alpha$.

This result delivers quantitative guidance for selecting the cores in heterogeneous multicore processors for interactive applications.

Theorem 3. *Given* $e(x) = b \cdot x^{\alpha-1}$ *and* K L_p *latency constraints specified by* $1 \le p_1 \le p_2 \le \cdots \le p_K \le \infty$, *then the degree of heterogeneity* $\frac{x_N^*}{x_1^*}$ *satisfies:*

$$1 \le \frac{x_N^*}{x_1^*} \le \left(\frac{1}{f_N}\right)^{\frac{1}{\alpha}} \tag{6}$$

where f_N *is the probability that a job has the maximum service demand of* $\tilde{w}_N$.

We call a latency constraint dominant *if and only if satisfying it ensures that all the other latency constraints, if any, are also satisfied under the optimal schedule. Thus, the dominant latency constraint is the most stringent requirement. When average latency is dominant, the first inequality above becomes an equality:* $x_N^*/x_1^* = 1$. *When maximum latency is dominant, the second inequality becomes equality:* $\frac{x_N^*}{x_1^*} = \left(\frac{1}{f_N}\right)^{\frac{1}{\alpha}}$.

Proof. The technical report contains the proof [27].   ∎

Theorem 3 has two interesting implications.

1. Workload heterogeneity prefers hardware heterogeneity. The upper bound on the degree of heterogeneity increases as f_N decreases (i.e., with fewer long jobs). When the workload is homogeneous, all jobs have the same service demand and $f_N = 1$. In this case, Theorem 3 indicates that $x_N^*/x_1^* = 1$ and homogeneous hardware is optimal. For a heterogeneous workload where f_N is small, the value of x_N^*/x_1^* may become very large. When slow cores complete short jobs, they save energy, whereas with the optimal schedule, the fastest processors process long jobs to satisfy the maximum latency constraint without incurring too much average energy, since f_N is small.

2. Core power and performance influences on hardware heterogeneity. When the speed of a core increases, so does its power consumption. We observe from (6) that the upper bound on the degree of heterogeneity decreases with α. A larger α indicates power consumption grows faster than core speed and hence using fast cores will significantly increases average energy consumption and degree of heterogeneity will be smaller.

Example We consider two example interactive workloads, Bing web search and Monte Carlo financial pricing (see elsewhere for details [26]). They illustrate how latency constraints, workload, and core performance and power characteristics affect the desired heterogeneity. Figure 1(a) and Figure 1(b) show the distributions of service demand for the two applications, measured in terms of the job processing time on an Intel i7-2600 Sandy Bridge core. The demand spike in Figure 1(a) occurs because the search engine caps job processing time at 120 ms and returns the top results found so far. Search engines often cap query processing time and return partial results to tradeoff quality and response time [17].

Figure 1(c) and 1(d) show how the degree of heterogeneity (Y-axis x_n^*/x_1^*) changes as a function of p in L_p with Bing and financial applications, respectively, when we can choose any core speed. We normalize speed to an i7-2600 Sandy Bridge core and use the power model: $z(x) = 21 \cdot x^\alpha$, because $z(1) = 21W$ is the power consumption of the i7-2600 Sandy Bridge core. Blue and red lines represent the cases of $\alpha = 2.08$ (a lower energy cost for performance) and $\alpha = 2.5$ (a higher energy cost for performance) respectively.

Figure 1(c) and 1(d) confirm Theorems 2 and 3. (1) When p increases, the degree of heterogeneity increases and has an upper bound, as predicted. In particular, a homogeneous processor is optimal in terms of energy consumption when $p = 1$ (average latency), whereas the maximum degree of heterogeneity is desirable when $p = \infty$ (a deadline). (2) The degree of heterogeneity decreases with larger α because faster cores consume proportionally more energy. (3) Comparing Figure 1(c) and 1(d) shows financial derivative pricing requires a higher degree of heterogeneity than Bing web search given the same p because the longest jobs are rarer in derivatives (f_N is smaller). The rarer the long jobs, the faster the fastest core we can choose without compromising average energy because the prolific short jobs execute on the slowest low power cores.

6   Discrete Core Speeds, Migration, and Congestion

This section extends SEM to address the following practical considerations: (1) a limited selection of core speeds, (2) job migration overhead, and (3) congestion due to multiple jobs competing for the same core(s).

Discrete core speeds Given a set of core speeds, $0 < s_1 \leq s_2 \leq \cdots \leq s_M$, we formulate our problem as follows:

$$\mathbf{P2}: \min_{\mathbf{x}} \sum_{i=1}^{N} \{[1 - F_{i-1}] \cdot e(x_i) \cdot w_i\} \tag{7}$$

$$s.t., \text{ Constraint (4)} \tag{8}$$

$$x_i \in \{s_1, s_2, \cdots, s_M\}, i = 1, 2, \cdots, N. \tag{9}$$

P2 is a combinatorial optimization problem, which is notoriously difficult to solve [37]. We use an efficient branch-and-bound algorithm to produce solutions arbitrarily close-to-optimal. A greedy solution finds a schedule that will consume more energy than the optimal schedule (i.e., the upper bound), whereas the job schedule obtained by replacing "$x_i \in \{s_1, s_2, \cdots, s_M\}$" with $x_i \in [s_1, s_M]$ and then using convex optimization will produce an average energy consumption that is less than the optimal schedule (i.e., the lower bound). By iteratively finding and refining the upper and lower bounds until the gap becomes sufficiently small, we identify a schedule arbitrarily close to the optimal schedule [7]. The technical report contains the details of the solution and the derivation [27].

P2 is an NP-hard problem, even if only the maximum latency constraint is considered [37]. Without specifying the maximum number of iterations, the proposed algorithm may iterate up to M^N times, enumerating all the possible solutions in the worst case. Nevertheless, the beauty of branch-and-bound algorithm is that it typically converges much faster, which we also observe. In fact, with an appropriately-set stopping criterion, the number of iterations required for convergence is upper bounded, and in practice, the actual number of iterations is typically even much smaller than the upper bound. The complete analysis of convergence rate is beyond our scope, and interested readers are referred to the literature [7].

Moreover, as we discussed in Section 3, we only compute an optimal schedule *once* offline for any given job service demand distribution and heterogeneous processor. Our online scheduler simply applies the precomputed optimal schedule. Therefore, the computational overhead in deployment is negligible.

Migration overhead. Migrating a job from one core to another incurs overhead from copying job state and warming up caches. Our experiments show that job migration overheads are fairly small on both web search [17] and interactive finance applications. One migration is less than 50 microseconds, less than 0.1% of the maximum latency requirement in the order of 100 milliseconds. Moreover, a job can only migrate up to $Q - 1$ times, where Q is the number of different core speeds. Because Q is very small ($2 \sim 4$) in practice and many short jobs completed on slow cores, SEM often does not incur much migration overhead.

To extend our solution when migration costs are high, e.g., migrating a job between two servers, we describe a heuristic approach to incorporate migration overhead in the analytical model. This approach is conservative and assumes worst-case migration overhead. More specifically, let τ^o represent the migration overhead, quantified by the time during which a core cannot process any work. In the worst case, a job with a demand of $\tilde{w}_i = \sum_{j=1}^{i} w_j$ may migrate up to $(i-1)$ times, for $i = 1, 2, \cdots, N$. Thus, the new worst-case latency constraint becomes

$$\left\{ \sum_{i=1}^{N} \left[\sum_{j=1}^{i} \frac{w_j}{x_j} + (i-1) \cdot \tau^o \right]^{p_k} f_i \right\}^{\frac{1}{p_k}} \leq \tilde{D}(p_k). \qquad (10)$$

By neglecting the constant energy consumption incurred by the migration process in the worst case, we reformulate the energy minimization problem **P2** by replacing the latency constraint (8) with (10) to account for the migration overhead. The solution can be found in a similar way following our preceding analysis.

Congestion. We briefly discuss how to apply SEM as a building block when congestion or queuing delay results in multiple jobs demanding the same core at the same time. A key observation is that the presence of congestion may cause a violation in the latency constraints if we directly apply SEM. To satisfy the desired latency that includes both processing delay and queueing delay, we can impose a more stringent constraints for the processing delay which, if *appropriately* chosen and after adding the queueing delay, will satisfy the total latency constraints. To choose the appropriate L_p norm constraint to handle this delay, we propose integral control to dynamically adjust the processing delay constraint based on the difference between the observed latency and the target latency (latency constraint). The control function is expressed as

$$\tilde{D}_i(p_k) = \tilde{D}_{i-1}(p_k) + V \cdot d_i(p_k), \text{ for } k = 1, 2, \cdots, K,$$

where $i = 1, 2, \cdots$ represents time steps, $\tilde{D}_i(p_k)$ is the output of the integral controller at time i representing the augmented L_p norm constraint on the processing delay. $V > 0$ defines the ratio of the control adjustment to the control error and $d_i(p_k)$ is the difference between the target and observed latency. Thus, if the observed latency is greater than the constraint, $d_i(p_k) < 0$, a more stringent processing delay constraint, $\tilde{D}_i(p_k)$, will be imposed for the next time step, and vice versa.

Finally, note that using the above method to address congestion will not alter the value of p. Thus, our slow to fast scheduling insight and the quantitative upper and lower bounds on the ratio of fast to slow core speeds still hold.

7   Related Work

Heterogeneous multicore processors. As computer architects face the end of Dennard scaling, they are turning to heterogeneous multicore processors, which combine high performance but high power cores with lower power and lower performance cores to meet a variety of performance objectives, i.e., throughput, energy, power, etc. To effectively utilize these systems, a scheduler must match jobs to an appropriate core. Four types of schedulers have been proposed to allocate jobs or parts of jobs to different cores. (1) With known or predicted resource demand, incoming jobs are scheduled to the most appropriate core [9,11,38]. (2) With known performance requirements, latency-sensitive applications such as games or videos are processed by fast cores, whereas latency-tolerant applications such as background services are processed by slow cores [15,24,28]. (3) With known job characteristics, complementary job allocation is applied to maximize the server utilization while avoiding resource bottlenecks (e.g., memory-intensive jobs and CPU-intensive jobs are allocated to the same server [34]). (4) If a single job has different phases [21,29,30], such as parallel phases and sequential phases, schedulers map the sequential phase on a high-performance core and the parallel phase on a number of energy-efficient cores.

L_p norms and multiple latencies Because the L_p norms are a general class of constraints, researchers have applied them in various contexts, such as minimizing the total latency via online load balancing [5, 31] and multi-user scheduling of wireless networks [39]. Our study considers multiple L_p norm latency constraints simultaneously for individual interactive services. Prior work mainly considers multiple latency constraints to provide differentiated performance guarantees to different traffic classes [10,33], whereas we exploit the diversity of demand within the requests, without requiring knowledge about the demand of any individual request, to meet constraints for a variety of interactive applications.

Latency sensitive and real-time scheduling. Related work also considers exploiting heterogeneous processors and DVFS to improve energy-efficiency for latency-sensitive and real-time jobs [1,23,35–37]. Some of them [1,36,38,40] assume that the service demand of each job is either known or accurately predicted, which is not available for many applications. Other studies on DVFS and real-time systems assume unknown service demand [23, 35, 37], but they consider a hard deadline as the only latency constraint. Our prior work [26] studies scheduling interactive workloads on a heterogeneous processor for quality/throughput maximization (not energy minimization) subject to a single deadline constraint. While it also leverages the "slow to fast" insight, it always uses fast cores first whenever they are available for performance optimization. In contrast, SEM starts jobs on slow cores and migrates them to fast cores along the execution to minimize energy. Moreover, this prior work [26] does not address multiple latency constraints and it does not deliver quantitative insights for selecting cores in heterogeneous processors. To the best of our knowledge, we offer the first formal analysis to characterize the optimal schedule and hardware design for scheduling latency-sensitive jobs on heterogeneous processors with multiple latency constraints without requiring a priori knowledge of the service demand of each individual job.

8   Conclusion

This paper presents an efficient scheduling algorithm for interactive jobs on heterogeneous processors subject to multiple latency constraints expressed in the form of L_p norms and optimizes energy. We introduce the SEM scheduling which advances the existing research in two key ways. (1) The SEM algorithm does not rely on the service demand of each individual job, which is difficult and even impossible to obtain in many interactive applications such as web search. (2) The SEM algorithm explicitly incorporates multiple L_p norm latency constraints which, compared to prior work, more accurately characterize the explicit and implicit multiple service level agreements on the latency of interactive applications. We prove that an optimal schedule only migrates jobs from slower to faster cores. Moreover, we quantify how to select cores in heterogeneous hardware for interactive applications. The more the system needs to limit outliers, the more heterogeneous the hardware needs to be. The more heterogeneous the workload service demand is, the less power additional performance costs and the more heterogeneous the hardware needs to be.

References

1. Albers, S., Müller, F., Schmelzer, S.: Speed scaling on parallel processors. In: SPAA (2007)
2. Anand, S., Garg, N., Kumar, A.: Resource augmentation for weighted flow-time explained by dual fitting. In: SODA (2012)
3. Azar, Y., Epstein, A.: Convex programming for scheduling unrelated parallel machines. In: STOC (2005)
4. Azar, Y., Epstein, L., Richter, Y., Woeginger, G.J.: All-norm approximation algorithms. In: Penttonen, M., Schmidt, E.M. (eds.) SWAT 2002. LNCS, vol. 2368, pp. 288–297. Springer, Heidelberg (2002)
5. Bansal, N., Pruhs, K.: Server scheduling in the l_p norm: A rising tide lifts all boat. In: STOC (2003)
6. Bornholt, J., Mytkowicz, T., McKinley, K.S.: The model is not enough: Understanding energy consumption in mobile devices. In: Hot Chips (2012)
7. Boyd, S., Ghosh, A., Magnani, A.: Branch and bound methods (2003), http://www.stanford.edu/class/ee392o/bb.pdf
8. Brooks, D., Bose, P., Schuster, S., Jacobson, H., Kudva, P., Buyuktosunoglu, A., Wellman, J., Zyuban, V., Gupta, M., Cook, P.: Power-aware microarchitecture: Design and modeling challenges for next generation microprocessors. In: Micro (2000)
9. Cao, T., Blackburn, S.M., Goa, T., McKinley, K.S.: The yin and yang of power and performance for asymmetric hardware and managed software. In: ISCA (2012)
10. Chao, H.J., Uzun, N.: An atm queue manager handling multiple delay and loss priorities. IEEE/ACM Trans. Networking 3, 652–659 (1995)
11. Chen, J., John, L.K.: Efficient program scheduling for heterogeneous multi-core processors. In: DAC (2009)
12. Dean, J., Barroso, L.A.: The tail at scale. CACM 56(2), 74–80 (2013)
13. DeCandia, G., Hastorun, D., Jampani, M., Kakulapati, G., Lakshman, A., Pilchin, A., Sivasubramanian, S., Vosshall, P., Vogels, W.: Dynamo: Amazon's highly available key-value store. In: SOSP (2007)
14. Esmaeilzadeh, H., Cao, T., Xi, Y., Blackburn, S.M., McKinley, K.S.: Looking back on the language and hardware revolutions: Measured power, performance, and scaling. In: ASPLOS (2011)
15. Greenhalgh, P.: Big.LITTLE processing with ARM Cortex-A15 & Cortex-A7. ARM Whitepaper (September 2011)
16. Harchol-Balter, M.: The effect of heavy-tailed job size distributions on computer system design. In: Applications of Heavy Tailed Distributions in Economics (1999)
17. He, Y., Elnikety, S., Larus, J., Yan, C.: Zeta: Scheduling interactive services with partial execution. In: SOCC (2012)
18. Im, S., Moseley, B.: An online scalable algorithm for minimizing l_k-norms of weighted flow time on unrelated machines. In: SODA (2011)
19. Janapa Reddi, V., Lee, B.C., Chilimbi, T., Vaid, K.: Web search using mobile cores: Quantifying and mitigating the price of efficiency. In: ISCA (2010)
20. Kotla, R., Devgan, A., Ghiasi, S., Keller, T., Rawson, F.: Characterizing the impact of different memory-intensity levels. In: WWC (2004)

21. Kumar, R., Farkas, K.I., Jouppi, N.P., Ranganathan, P., Tullsen, D.M.: Single-ISA heterogeneous multi-core architectures: The potential for processor power reduction. In: MICRO (2003)
22. Lan, G., Lu, Z., Monteiro, R.D.: Primal-dual first-order methods with $\mathcal{O}(1\backslash\epsilon)$ iteration-complexity for cone programming. Mathematical Programming 126(1), 1–29 (2011)
23. Lorch, J.R., Smit, A.J.: Improving dynamic voltage scaling algorithms with PACE. In: SIGMETRICS (2001)
24. Nathuji, R., Isci, C., Gorbatov, E.: Exploiting platform heterogeneity for power efficient data centers. In: ICAC (2007)
25. Pruhs, K.: Competitive online scheduling for server systems. In: SIGMETRICS (2007)
26. Ren, S., He, Y., Elnikety, S., McKinley, K.S.: Exploiting processor heterogeneity in interactive systems. In: ICAC (2013)
27. Ren, S., He, Y., McKinley, K.S.: A theoretical foundation for scheduling and designing heterogeneous processors for interactive applications. Tech. Rep. TR-2014-101. Microsoft Research (2014)
28. Srinivasan, S., Iyer, R., Zhao, L., Illikkal, R.: HeteroScouts: Hardware assist for OS scheduling in heterogeneous CMPs. In: SIGMETRICS (2011)
29. Suleman, M.A., Mutlu, O., Qureshi, M.K., Patt, Y.N.: Accelerating critical section execution with asymmetric multi-core architectures. In: ASPLOS (2009)
30. Suleman, M.A., Patt, Y.N., Sprangle, E., Rohillah, A., Ghuloum, A., Carmean, D.: Asymmetric chip multiprocessors: Balancing hardware efficiency and programmer efficiency. TR-HPS-2007-001 (2007)
31. Suri, S., Tóth, C.D., Zhou, Y.: Selfish load balancing and atomic congestion games. In: SPAA (2004)
32. Wierman, A., Harchol-Balter, M.: Classifying scheduling policies with respect to higher moments of conditional response time. In: SIGMETRICS (2005)
33. Xie, Y., Yang, T.: Cell discarding policies supporting multiple delay and loss requirements in atm networks. In: Globecom (1997)
34. Xiong, W., Kansal, A.: Energy efficient data intensive distributed computing. IEEE Data Eng. Bull. (2011)
35. Xu, R., Xi, C., Melhem, R., Moss, D.: Practical PACE for embedded systems. In: EMSOFT (2004)
36. Yao, F.F., Demers, A.J., Shenker, S.J.: A scheduling model for reduced CPU energy. In: FOCS (1995)
37. Yuan, W., Nahrstedt, K.: Energy-efficient CPU scheduling for multimedia applications. ACM Trans. Computer Systems 24(3), 292–331 (2006)
38. Yun, H., Wu, P.-L., Arya, A., Kim, C., Abdelzaher, T.F., Sha, L.: System-wide energy optimization for multiple DVS components and real-time tasks. Real-Time Systems 47(5), 489–515 (2011)
39. Zeng, W., Ng, C., Medard, M.: Joint coding and scheduling optimization in wireless systems with varying delay sensitivities. In: SECON (2012)
40. Zhu, Y., Reddi, V.J.: High-performance and energy-efficient mobile web browsing on big/little systems. In: HPCA (2013)

Vertex Fault Tolerant Additive Spanners[*]

Merav Parter

Department of Computer Science and Applied Mathematics,
The Weizmann Institute, Rehovot, Israel
merav.parter@weizmann.ac.il

Abstract. A *fault-tolerant* structure for a network is required to continue functioning following the failure of some of the network's edges or vertices. In this paper, we address the problem of designing a *fault-tolerant* additive spanner, namely, a subgraph H of the network G such that subsequent to the failure of a single vertex, the surviving part of H still contains an *additive* spanner for (the surviving part of) G, satisfying $\text{dist}(s, t, H \setminus \{v\}) \leq \text{dist}(s, t, G \setminus \{v\}) + \beta$ for every $s, t, v \in V$. Recently, the problem of constructing fault-tolerant additive spanners resilient to the failure of up to f-*edges* has been considered [8]. The problem of handling *vertex* failures was left open therein. In this paper we develop new techniques for constructing additive FT-spanners overcoming the failure of a single vertex in the graph. Our first result is an FT-spanner with additive stretch 2 and $O(n^{5/3})$ edges. Our second result is an FT-spanner with additive stretch 6 and $O(n^{3/2})$ edges. The construction algorithm consists of two main components: (a) constructing an FT-clustering graph and (b) applying a modified path-buying procedure suitably adopted to failure prone settings. Finally, we also describe two constructions for *fault-tolerant multi-source additive spanners*, aiming to guarantee a bounded additive stretch following a vertex failure, for every pair of vertices in $S \times V$ for a given subset of sources $S \subseteq V$. The additive stretch bounds of our constructions are 4 and 8 (using a different number of edges).

1 Introduction

An (α, β)-spanner H of an unweighted undirected graph G is a spanning subgraph satisfying for every pair of vertices $s, t \in V$ that $\text{dist}(s, t, H) \leq \alpha \cdot \text{dist}(s, t, G) + \beta$. When $\beta = 0$, the spanner is termed a *multiplicative* spanner and when $\alpha = 1$ the spanner is *additive*. Clearly, additive spanners provide a much stronger guarantee than multiplicative ones, especially for long distances. Constructions of additive spanners with *small* number of edges are currently known for $\beta = 2, 4, 6$ with $O(n^{3/2}), \widetilde{O}(n^{7/5})$ and $O(n^{4/3})$ edges respectively

---

[*] Recipient of the Google European Fellowship in distributed computing; research is supported in part by this Fellowship. Supported in part by the Israel Science Foundation (grant 894/09), the I-CORE program of the Israel PBC and ISF (grant 4/11), the United States-Israel Binational Science Foundation (grant 2008348), the Israel Ministry of Science and Technology (infrastructures grant), and the Citi Foundation.

F. Kuhn (Ed.): DISC 2014, LNCS 8784, pp. 167–181, 2014.

[1,2,5,11,14,15]. This paper considers a network G that may suffer single *vertex* failure events, and looks for fault tolerant additive spanners that maintain their additive stretch guarantee under failures. Formally, a subgraph $H \subseteq G$ is a β-additive FT-spanner iff for every $(s,t) \in V \times V$ and for every failing vertex $v \in V$, $\text{dist}(s,t,H \setminus \{v\}) \leq \text{dist}(s,t,G \setminus \{v\}) + \beta$. As a motivation for such structures, consider a situation where it is required to lease a subnetwork of a given network, which will provide short routes from every source s and every target t with additive stretch 2. In a failure-free environment one can simply lease a 2-additive spanner H_0 of the graph with $\Theta(n^{3/2})$ edges. However, if one of the vertices in the graph fails, some $s-t$ routes in $H_0 \setminus \{v\}$ might be significantly longer than the corresponding route in the surviving graph $G \setminus \{v\}$. Moreover, s and t are not even guaranteed to be connected in $H_0 \setminus \{v\}$. One natural approach towards preparing for such eventuality is to lease a larger set of links, i.e., an additive FT-spanner.

The notion of fault-tolerant spanners for general graphs was initiated by Chechik at el. [10] for the case of multiplicative stretch. Specifically, [10] presented algorithms for constructing an f-vertex fault tolerant spanner with multiplicative stretch $(2k-1)$ and $O(f^2 k^{f+1} \cdot n^{1+1/k} \log^{1-1/k} n)$ edges. A randomized construction attaining an improved tradeoff for vertex fault-tolerant spanners was then presented in [13]. Constructions of fault-tolerant spanners with *additive* stretch resilient to *edge* failures were recently given by Braunschvig at el. [8]. They establish the following general result. For a given n-vertex graph G, let H_1 be an ordinary additive $(1, \beta)$ spanner for G and H_2 be a fault tolerant $(\alpha, 0)$ spanner for G resilient against up to f edge faults. Then $H = H_1 \cup H_2$ is a $(1, \beta(f))$ additive fault tolerant spanner for G (for up to f edge faults) for $\beta(f) = O(f(\alpha + \beta))$. In particular, fixing the number of H edges to be $O(n^{3/2})$ and the number of faults to $f = 1$ yields an additive stretch of 14. Hence, in particular, there is no construction for additive stretch < 14 and $o(n^2)$ edges. In addition, note that these structures are resilient only to *edge* failures as the techniques of [8] cannot be utilized to protect even against a single vertex failure event. Indeed, the problem of handling *vertex* failures was left open therein.

In this paper, we make a first step in this direction and provide additive FT-structures resilient to the failure of a single *vertex* (and hence also edge) event. Our constructions provide additive stretch 2 and 6 and hence provide an improved alternative also for the case of a single edge failure event, compared to the constructions of [8].

The presented algorithms are based upon two important notions, namely, *replacement paths* and the *path-buying procedure*, which have been studied extensively in the literature. For a source s, a target vertex t and a failing vertex $v \in V$, a *replacement path* is the shortest $s-t$ path $P_{s,t,v}$ that does not go through v. The vast literature on *replacement paths* (cf. [7,16,19,21]) focuses on *time-efficient* computation of the these paths as well as their efficient maintenance in data structures (a.k.a *distance oracles*).

Fault-resilient structures that preserve exact distances for a given subset of sources $S \subseteq V$ have been studied in [17], which defines the notion of an FT-MBFS structure $H \subseteq G$ containing the collection of all replacement paths $P_{s,t,v}$ for every pair $(s,t) \in S \times V$ for a given subset of sources S and a failing vertex $v \in V$. Hence, FT-MBFS structures preserve the exact $s - t$ distances in $G \setminus \{v\}$ for every failing vertex v, for every source $s \in S$.

It is shown in [17] that for every graph G and a subset S of sources, there exists a (poly-time constructible) 1-edge (or vertex) FT-MBFS structure H with $O(\sqrt{|S|} \cdot n^{3/2})$ edges. This result is complemented by a matching lower bound showing that for sufficiently large n, there exist an n-vertex graph G and a source-set $S \subseteq V$, for which every FT-MBFS structure is of size $\Omega(\sqrt{|S|} \cdot n^{3/2})$. Hence *exact* FT-MBFS structures may be rather expensive. This last observation motivates the approach of resorting to *approximate* distances, in order to allow the design of a sparse subgraph with properties resembling those of an FT-MBFS structure.

The problem of constructing *multiplicative approximation replacement paths* $\widetilde{P}_{s,t,v}$ (i.e., such that $|\widetilde{P}_{s,t,v}| \leq \alpha \cdot |P_{s,t,v}|$) has been studied in [3,9,6]. In particular its *single source* variant has been studied in [4,18]. In this paper, we further explore this approach. For a given subset of sources S, we focus on constructions of subgraphs that contain an *approximate* BFS structure with additive stretch β for every source $s \in S$ that are resistant to a single vertex failure.

Indeed, the construction of additive sourcewise FT-spanners provides a key building block of additive FT-spanner constructions (in which bounded stretch is guaranteed for all pairs). We present two constructions of sourcewise spanners with different stretch-size tradeoffs. The first construction ensures an additive stretch 4 with $\widetilde{O}(\max\{n \cdot |S|, (n/|S|)^3\})$ edges and the second construction guarantees additive stretch 8 with $\widetilde{O}(\max\{n \cdot |S|, (n/|S|)^2\})$. As a direct consequence of these constructions, we get an additive FT-spanner with stretch 6 and $\widetilde{O}(n^{3/2})$ edges and an additive sourcewise FT-spanner with additive stretch 8 and $\widetilde{O}(n^{4/3})$ for at most $O(n^{1/3})$ sources.

Our constructions employ a modification of the *path-buying* strategy, which was originally devised in [5] to provide 6-additive spanners with $O(n^{4/3})$ edges. Recently, the path-buying strategy was employed in the context of pairwise spanners, where the objective is to construct a subgraph $H \subseteq G$ that satisfies the bounded additive stretch requirement only for a *subset* of pairs [12]. The high-level idea of this procedure as follows. In an initial clustering phase, a suitable clustering of the vertices is computed, and an associated subset of edges is added to the spanner. Then comes a path-buying phase, where they consider an appropriate sequence of paths, and decide whether or not to add each path into the spanner. Each path P has a *cost*, given by the number of edges of p not already contained in the spanner, and a *value*, measuring P's help in satisfying the considered set of constraints on pairwise distances. The considered path P is added to the spanner iff its value is sufficiently larger than its cost. In our adaptation to the FT-setting, an FT-clustering graph is computed first, providing every vertex with a sufficiently *high* degree (termed hereafter a *heavy* vertex) *two* clusters to which it belongs. Every cluster consists of a center vertex v connected via a star to a subset of its heavy neighbors. In our design not all replacement paths are candidates to be bought in the path-buying procedure. Let $\pi(s,t)$ be an $s-t$ shortest-path between a source s and a heavy vertex t (in our constructions, all heavy vertices are clustered). We divide the failing events on $\pi(s,t)$ into two classes depending on the position of the failing vertex on $\pi(s,t)$ with respect to the least common ancestor (LCA) $\ell(s,t)$ of t's cluster members in the BFS tree rooted at s. Specifically, a vertex fault $\pi(s,t)$ that occurs on $\ell(s,t)$ is handled *directly* by adding the last edge of the corresponding replacement path to the spanner. Vertex failures that occur strictly below the LCA, use the shortest-path $\pi(s,x)$ between s and some member x in the cluster of t whose failing vertex v does not appear on its $\pi(s,x)$ path. The approximate replacement path will follow $\pi(s,x)$ and then use the intercluster path between x and t. The main technicality is when concerning the complementary case when that failing events occur strictly above $\ell(s,t)$. These events are further divided into two classes depending on the structure of their replacement path. Some of these replacement paths would again be handled directly by collecting their last edges into the structure and only the second type paths would be candidate to be bought by the path-buying procedure. Essentially, the structure of these paths and the cost and value functions assigned to them would guarantee that the resulting structure is sparse, and in addition, that paths that were not bought have an alternative safe path in the surviving part of the structure.

Contributions. This paper provides the first constructions for additive spanners resilient upon single vertex failure. In addition, it provides the first additive FT-structures with stretch guarantee as low as 2 or 6 and with $o(n^2)$ edges.

The main technical contribution of our algorithms is in adapting the path-buying strategy to the vertex failure setting. Such an adaptation has been initiated in [18] for the case of a *single-source* s and a single *edge* failure event. In this paper, we extend this technique in two senses: (1) dealing with many sources and (2) dealing with *vertex* failures. In particular, [18] achieves a construction of single source additive spanner with $O(n^{4/3})$ edges resilient to a single *edge* failure. In this paper, we extend this construction to provide a multiple source additive spanners resilient to a single vertex failure, for $O(n^{1/3})$ sources, additive stretch 8 and $\widetilde{O}(n^{4/3})$ edges. In summary, we show the following.

Theorem 1 (2-additive FT-spanner). *For every n-vertex graph $G = (V,E)$, there exists a (polynomially constructible) subgraph $H \subseteq G$ of size $\widetilde{O}(n^{5/3})$ such that $\mathrm{dist}(s,t,H \setminus \{v\}) \leq \mathrm{dist}(s,t,G \setminus \{v\}) + 2$ for every $s,t,v \in V$.*

Theorem 2 (6-additive FT-spanner). *For every n-vertex graph $G = (V,E)$, there exists a (polynomially constructible) subgraph $H \subseteq G$ of size $\widetilde{O}(n^{3/2})$ such that $\mathrm{dist}(s,t,H \setminus \{v\}) \leq \mathrm{dist}(s,t,G \setminus \{v\}) + 6$ for every $s,t,v \in V$.*

Theorem 3 (8-additive sourcewise FT-spanner). *For every n-vertex graph $G = (V,E)$ and a subset of sources $S \subset V$ where $|S| = \widetilde{O}(n^{1/3})$, there exists a (polynomially constructible) subgraph $H \subseteq G$ of size $\widetilde{O}(n^{4/3})$ such that $\mathrm{dist}(s,t,H \setminus \{v\}) \leq \mathrm{dist}(s,t,G \setminus \{v\}) + 8$ for every $s \in S$ and $t,v \in V$.*

2   Preliminaries

Notation. Given a graph $G = (V, E)$, a vertex pair s, t and an edge weight function $W : E(G) \to \mathbb{R}^+$, let $SP(s, t, G, W)$ be the set of $s - t$ shortest-paths in G according to the edge weights of W. Throughout, we make use of (an arbitrarily specified) weight assignment W that guarantees the uniqueness of the shortest paths[1]. Hence, $SP(s, t, G', W)$ contains a single path for every $s, t \in V$ and for every subgraph $G' \subseteq G$, we override notation and let $SP(s, t, G, W)$ be the unique $s - t$ path in G according to W. When the shortest-path are computed in G, let $\pi(s, t) = SP(s, t, G, W)$. To avoid cumbersome notation, we may omit W and simply refer to $\pi(s, t) = SP(s, t, G, W)$. For a subgraph $G' \subseteq G$, let $V(G')$ (resp., $E(G')$) denote the vertex set (resp. edge set) in G'.

For a given source node s, let $T_0(s) = \bigcup_{t \in V} \pi(s, t)$ be a shortest paths (or BFS) tree rooted at s. For a set $S \subseteq V$ of source nodes, let $T_0(S) = \bigcup_{s \in S} T_0(s)$ be a union of the single source BFS trees. For a vertex $t \in V$ and a subset of vertices $V' \in V$, let $T(t, V') = \bigcup_{u \in V'} \pi(u, t)$ be the union of all $\{t\} \times V'$ shortest-paths (by the uniqueness of W, $T(t, V')$ is a subtree of $T_0(t)$). Let $\Gamma(v, G)$ be the set of v's neighbors in G. Let $E(v, G) = \{(u, v) \in E(G)\}$ be the set of edges incident to v in the graph G and let $\deg(v, G) = |E(v, G)|$ denote the degree of node v in G. For a given graph $G = (V, E)$ and an integer $\Delta \leq n$, a vertex v is Δ-*heavy* if $\deg(v, G) \geq \Delta$, otherwise it is Δ-*light*. When Δ is clear from the context, we may omit it and simply refer to v as *heavy* or *light*. For a graph $G = (V, E)$ and a positive integer $\Delta \leq n$, let $V_\Delta = \{v \mid \deg(v, G) \geq \Delta\}$ be the set of Δ-heavy vertices in G. (Throughout, we sometimes simplify notation by omitting parameters which are clear from the context.) For a subgraph $G' = (V', E') \subseteq G$ (where $V' \subseteq V$ and $E' \subseteq E$) and a pair of vertices $u, v \in V$, let $\text{dist}(u, v, G')$ denote the shortest-path distance in edges between u and v in G'. For a path $P = [v_1, \ldots, v_k]$, let $\text{LastE}(P)$ be the last edge of P, let $|P|$ denote its length and let $P[v_i, v_j]$ be the subpath of P from v_i to v_j. For paths P_1 and P_2, denote by $P_1 \circ P_2$ the path obtained by concatenating P_2 to P_1. For "visual" clarity, the edges of these paths are considered throughout, to be directed away from the source node s. Given an $s - t$ path P and an edge $e = (x, y) \in P$, let $\text{dist}(s, e, P)$ be the distance (in edges) between s and y on P. In addition, for an edge $e = (x, y) \in T_0(s)$, define $\text{dist}(s, e) = i$ if $\text{dist}(s, x, G) = i - 1$ and $\text{dist}(s, y, G) = i$. A vertex w is a *divergence point* of the $s - v$ paths P_1 and P_2 if $w \in P_1 \cap P_2$ but the next vertex u after w (i.e., such that u is closer to v) in the path P_1 is not in P_2.

Basic Tools. We consider the following graph structures.

Definition 1 ((α, β, S)-AMBFS FT-spanners). *A subgraph $H \subseteq G$ is an (α, β, S) FT-AMBFS (approximate multi-BFS) structure with respect to S if for every $(s, t) \in S \times V$ and every $v \in V$, $\text{dist}(s, t, H \setminus \{v\}) \leq \alpha \cdot \text{dist}(s, t, G \setminus \{v\}) + \beta$.*

---

[1] The role of the weights W is to perturb the edge weights by letting $W(e) = 1 + \epsilon$ for a random infinitesimal $\epsilon > 0$.

Definition 2 ((α, β) FT-spanners). *A subgraph $H \subseteq G$ is an (α, β) FT-spanner if it is an (α, β, V) FT-AMBFS structure for G with respect to V.*

Throughout, we restrict attention to the case of a single vertex fault. When $\alpha = 1$, H is termed (β, S) additive FT-spanner. In addition, in case where $S = V$, H is an β-additive FT-spanner.

FT-Clustering Graph. A subset $Z \subseteq V$ is an *FT-center* set for V if every Δ-*heavy* vertex v has at least two neighbors in Z, i.e., $|\Gamma(v, G) \cap Z| \geq 2$. For every heavy vertex $v \in V_\Delta$, let $Z(v) = \{z_1(v), z_2(v)\}$ be two arbitrary neighbors of v in Z. The clustering graph $G_\Delta \subseteq G$ consists of the edges connecting the Δ-heavy vertices v to their two representatives in Z as well as all edges incident to the Δ-light vertices. Formally,

$$G_\Delta = \bigcup_{v \in V_\Delta} \{(v, z_1(v)), (v, z_2(v))\} \cup \bigcup_{v \notin V_\Delta} E(v, G).$$

The Δ-*heavy* vertices are referred hereafter as *clustered*, hence every missing edge in $G \setminus G_\Delta$ is incident to a clustered vertex.

For every center vertex $z \in Z$, let C_z be the cluster consisting of z and all the Δ-heavy vertices it represents, i.e., $C_z = \{z\} \cup \{v \in V_\Delta \mid z \in Z(v)\}$. Note that every center z is connected via a star to each of the vertices in its cluster C_z, hence the diameter of each cluster C_z in G_Δ is 2.

For a failing vertex v and a heavy vertex t, let $z_v(t) \in Z(t) \setminus \{v\}$ be a cluster center of t in $G \setminus \{v\}$. In particular, if $z_1(t) \neq v$, then $z_v(t) = z_1(t)$, else $z_v(t) = z_2(t)$. Let $C_v(t)$ be the cluster centered at $z_v(t)$. Note that since every heavy vertex has two cluster centers $z_1(t)$ and $z_2(t)$, we have the guarantee that at least one of them survives the single vertex fault event. The next observation summarizes some important properties of the clustering graph.

Observation 4. *(1) $|E(G_\Delta)| = O(\Delta \cdot n)$.*
(2) Every missing edge is incident to a clustered vertex in V_Δ.
(3) The diameter of every cluster C_z is 2.
(4) There exists an FT-center set $Z \subseteq V$ of size $|Z| = \tilde{O}(n/\Delta)$.

Obs. 4(4) follows by a standard hitting set argument.

Replacement Paths. For a source s, a target vertex t and a vertex $v \in G$, a *replacement path* is the shortest $s - t$ path $P_{s,t,v} \in SP(s, t, G \setminus \{v\})$ that does not go through v.

Observation 5. *Every path $P_{s,t,v}$ contains at most $3n/\Delta$ Δ-heavy vertices.*

New-Ending Replacement Paths. A replacement path $P_{s,t,v}$ is called *new-ending* if its last edge is different from the last edge of the shortest path $\pi(s, t)$. Put another way, a new-ending replacement path $P_{s,t,v}$ has the property that once it diverges from the shortest-path $\pi(s, t)$ at the vertex b, it joins $\pi(s, t)$ again only at the final vertex t. It is shown in [17] that for a given graph G and a set S of source vertices, a structure $H \subseteq G$ containing a BFS tree rooted at each $s \in S$ plus the last edge of each new-ending replacement path $P_{s,t,v}$ for every $(s,t) \in S \times V$ and every $v \in V$, is an FT-MBFS structure with respect to S. Our algorithms exploit the structure of new-ending replacement paths to construct (β, S)-additive FT-structure. Essentially, a key section in our analysis concerns with collecting the last edges from a subset of new-ending replacement paths as well as bounding the number of new-ending paths $P_{s,t,v}$ whose detour segments intersect with $\pi(s', t) \setminus \{t\}$ for some other source $s' \in S$.

The basic building block. Our constructions of β-additive FT-spanners, for $\beta \geq 2$, consist of the following two building blocks: (1) an FT-clustering graph G_Δ for some parameter Δ, and (2) an $(\beta - 2, Z)$-additive FT-spanner where Z is an FT-center set (i.e., cluster centers) for the vertices.

Lemma 1. *Let $\beta \geq 2$ and $H = G_\Delta \cup H_{\beta-2}(Z)$ where Z is an FT-center set for V_Δ. Then H is an β-additive FT-spanner.*

Proof: Consider vertices $u_1, u_2, u_3 \in V$. Let $P \in SP(u_1, u_2, G \setminus \{u_3\})$ be the $u_1 - u_2$ replacement path in $G \setminus \{u_3\}$ and let (x, y) be the last missing edge on $P \setminus H$ (i.e., closest to u_2). Since $G_\Delta \subseteq H$, by Obs. 4(2), y is a clustered vertex. Let $z = z_{u_3}(y)$ be the cluster center of y in $G \setminus \{u_3\}$, and consider the following $u_1 - u_2$ path $P_3 = P_1 \circ P_2$ where $P_1 \in SP(u_1, z, H \setminus \{u_3\})$ and $P_2 = (z, y) \circ P[y, u_2]$. Clearly, $P_3 \subseteq H \setminus \{u_3\}$, so it remains to bound its length. Since $H_{\beta-2}(Z) \subseteq H$, it holds that $|P_1| \leq \mathrm{dist}(u_1, z, G \setminus \{u_3\}) + \beta - 2$. Hence,

$$
\begin{aligned}
\mathrm{dist}(u_1, u_2, H \setminus \{u_3\}) \leq |P_3| &= |P_1| + |P_2| \\
&\leq \mathrm{dist}(u_1, z, G \setminus \{u_3\}) + \beta - 2 + \mathrm{dist}(y, u_2, G \setminus \{u_3\}) \\
&\leq \mathrm{dist}(u_1, y, G \setminus \{u_3\}) + \mathrm{dist}(y, u_2, G \setminus \{u_3\}) + \beta + 1 \\
&\leq |P| + \beta = \mathrm{dist}(u_1, u_2, G \setminus \{u_3\}) + \beta \ ,
\end{aligned}
$$

where the second inequality follows by the triangle inequality using the fact that the edge (z, y) exists in $H \setminus \{u_3\}$. The lemma follows. ∎

3 Additive Stretch 2

We begin by considering the case of additive stretch 2. We make use of the construction of FT-MBFS structures presented in [17].

Fact 6 ([17]). *There exists a polynomial time algorithm that for every n-vertex graph $G = (V, E)$ and source set $S \subseteq V$ constructs an FT-MBFS structure $H_0(S)$ from each source $s_i \in S$, tolerant to one edge or vertex failure, with a total number of $O(\sqrt{|S|} \cdot n^{3/2})$ edges.*

Set $\Delta = \lceil n^{2/3} \rceil$ and let Z be an FT-center set for V_Δ as given by Obs. 4(4). Let $H_0(Z)$ be an FT-MBFS structure with respect to the source set Z as given by Fact 6. Then, let $H = G_\Delta \cup H_0(Z)$. Thm. 1 follows by Lemma 1, Obs. 4 and Fact 6.

4 Sourcewise Additive FT-Spanners

In this section, we present two constructions of $(4, S)$ and $(8, S)$ additive FT-spanners with respect to a given source set $S \subseteq V$. The single source case (where $|S| = 1$) is considered in [18], which provides a construction of a single source FT-spanner[2] with $O(n^{4/3})$ edges and additive stretch 4. The current construction increases the stretch to 8 to provide a bounded stretch for $\widetilde{O}(n^{1/3})$ sources with the same order of edges, $\widetilde{O}(n^{4/3})$.

4.1 Sourcewise Spanner with Additive Stretch 4

Lemma 2. *There exists a subgraph $H_4(S) \subseteq G$ with $\widetilde{O}(\max\{|S| \cdot n, (n/|S|)^3\})$ edges satisfying $\mathrm{dist}(s, t, H_4(S) \setminus \{v\}) \leq \mathrm{dist}(s, t, G \setminus \{v\}) + 4$ for every $(s, t) \in S \times V$ and $v \in V$.*

The following notation is useful in our context. Let $\mathcal{C} = \{C_z \mid z \in Z\}$ be the collection of clusters corresponding to the FT-centers Z. For a source $s \in S$ and a cluster $C_z \in \mathcal{C}$ rooted at FT-center $z \in Z$, let $\mathrm{LCA}(s, C_z)$ be the least common ancestor (LCA) of the cluster vertices of C_z in the BFS tree $T_0(s)$ rooted at s. Let $\pi(s, C_z)$ be the path connecting s and $\mathrm{LCA}(s, C_z)$ in $T_0(s)$.

Algorithm Cons4SWSpanner for Constructing $H_4(S)$ Spanner

Step (0): Replacement-path definition. For every $(s, t) \in S \times V$ and every $v \in V$, let $P_{s,t,v} = SP(s, t, G \setminus \{v\}, W)$.

Step (1): Clustering. Set $\Delta = |S|$ and let $Z \subseteq V$ be an FT-center set of size $\widetilde{O}(n/\Delta)$ (by Obs. 4(4) such set exists). Let $\mathcal{C} = \{C_z \mid z \in Z\}$ be the collection of $|Z|$ clusters. For a heavy vertex t, let $C_1(t), C_2(t)$ be its two clusters in $\mathcal{C}$ corresponding to the centers $z_1(t)$ and $z_2(t)$ respectively.

Step (2): Shortest-path segmentation. For every $(s, t) \in S \times V_\Delta$, the algorithm uses the first cluster of t, $C_1(t)$, to segment the path $\pi(s, t)$. Define

$$\pi^{far}(s, t) = \pi(s, \ell(s, t)) \setminus \{\ell(s, t)\} \text{ and } \pi^{near}(s, t) = \pi(\ell(s, t), t) \setminus \{\ell(s, t)\},$$

where $\ell(s, t) = \mathrm{LCA}(s, C_1(t))$ is the LCA of the cluster $C_1(t)$ in the tree $T_0(s)$. Hence, $\pi(s, t) = \pi^{far}(s, t) \circ \ell(s, t) \circ \pi^{near}(s, t)$. The algorithm handles separately vertex faults in the near and far segments. Let $V^{near}(s, t) = V(\pi^{near}(s, t))$ and $V^{far}(s, t) = V(\pi^{far}(s, t))$.

Step (3): Handling faults in the cluster center and the LCA. Let $E^{local}(t) = \{\mathrm{LastE}(P_{s,t,v}) \mid s \in S, v \in \{z_1(t), \mathrm{LCA}(s, C_1(t))\}\}$ and $E^{local} = \bigcup_{t \in V_\Delta} E^{local}(t)$, be the last edges of replacement-paths protecting against the failure of the primary cluster center $z_1(t)$ and the least common ancestor $\mathrm{LCA}(s, C_1(t))$.

---

[2] The construction of [18] supports a single edge failure, yet, it can be modified to overcome a single vertex failure as well.

Step (4): Handling far vertex faults $V^{far}(s,t)$. A replacement path $P_{s,t,v}$ is *new-ending* if its last edge is not in $(T_0(S) \cup G_\Delta)$. For a new-ending path $P_{s,t,v}$, let $b_{s,t,v}$ be the unique divergence point of $P_{s,t,v}$ from $\pi(s,t)$ (in the analysis we show that such point exists). Let $D_{s,t,v} = P_{s,t,v}[b_{s,t,v}, t]$ denote the detour segment and let $D^+_{s,t,v} = D_{s,t,v} \setminus \{b_{s,t,v}\}$ denote the detour segment excluding the divergence point. For every clustered vertex t, let $\mathcal{P}^{far}(t)$ be the collection of new-ending $s - t$ paths protecting against vertex faults in the far segments, i.e., $\mathcal{P}^{far}(t) = \{P_{s,t,v} \mid s \in S, \texttt{LastE}(P_{s,t,v}) \notin T_0(S) \text{ and } v \in V^{far}(s,t)\}$.

The algorithm divides this set into two subsets $\mathcal{P}^{far}_{dep}(t)$ and $\mathcal{P}^{far}_{indep}(t)$ depending on the structure of the partial detour segment $D^+_{s,t,v}$. A new-ending path $P_{s,t,v}$ is *dependent* if $D^+_{s,t,v}$ intersects $\pi(s',t) \setminus \{t\}$ for some $s' \in S$, i.e., for a dependent path $P_{s,t,v}$, it holds that

$$V(D^+_{s,t,v}) \cap V(T(t,S)) \neq \{t\} . \tag{1}$$

Otherwise, it is *independent*. Let

$$\mathcal{P}^{far}_{dep}(t) = \{P_{s,t,v} \in \mathcal{P}^{far}(t) \mid s \in S, v \in V^{far}(s,t) \text{ and } V(D^+_{s,t,v}) \cap V(T(t,S)) \neq \{t\}\}$$

be the set of all $S \times \{t\}$ dependent paths and let $\mathcal{P}^{far}_{indep}(t) = \mathcal{P}^{far} \setminus \mathcal{P}^{far}_{dep}(t)$ be the set of independent paths.

Step (4.1): Handling dependent *new-ending paths.* The algorithm simply takes the last edges $E^{far}_{dep}(t)$ of all dependent replacement paths where $E^{far}_{dep}(t) = \{\texttt{LastE}(P) \mid P \in \mathcal{P}^{far}_{dep}(t)\}$. (In the analysis section, we show that the $E^{far}_{dep}(t)$ sets are sparse.) Let $E^{far}_{dep} = \bigcup_{t \in V_\Delta} E^{far}_{dep}(t)$.

Step (4.2): Handling independent *new-ending paths.* The algorithm employs a modified *path-buying* procedure on the collection $\mathcal{P}^{far}_{indep} = \bigcup_{t \in V_\Delta} \mathcal{P}^{far}_{indep}(t)$ of new-ending independent paths. The paths of $\mathcal{P}^{far}_{indep}$ are considered in some arbitrary order. A path $P \in \mathcal{P}^{far}_{indep}$ is bought, if it improves the pairwise cluster distances in some sense. Starting with

$$G_0 = T_0(S) \cup G_\Delta \cup E^{local} \cup E^{far}_{dep} , \tag{2}$$

at step $\tau \geq 0$, the algorithm is given $G_\tau \subseteq G$ and considers the path $P_\tau = P_{s,t,v}$. Let $e = (x, y)$ be the first missing edge on $P_\tau \setminus E(G_\tau)$ (where x is closer to s). Note that since $G_\Delta \subseteq G_0$, both x and t are clustered. Recall that for a clustered vertex u and a failing vertex v, $C_v(u)$ is the cluster of u centered at $z_v(u) = Z(u) \setminus \{v\}$. For every cluster C, let $V_f(C)$ be the collection of vertices appearing on the paths $\pi(s,C) = \pi(s, \texttt{LCA}(s,C))$ for every $s \in S$ excluding the vertices of the clusters. That is,

$$V_f(C) = \bigcup_{s \in S} V(\pi(s,C)) \setminus C. \tag{3}$$

The path P_τ is added to G_τ resulting in $G_{\tau+1} = G_\tau \cup P_\tau$, only if

$$\text{dist}(x, t, P_\tau) < \text{dist}(C_v(x), C_v(t), G_\tau \setminus V_f(C_v(t))). \tag{4}$$

Let $\tau' = |\mathcal{P}_{indep}^{far}|$ be the total number of independent paths considered to be bought by the algorithm. Then, the algorithm outputs $H_4(S) = G_{\tau'}$. This completes the description of the algorithm.

Analysis. Throughout the discussion, we consider a $P_{s,t,v}$ paths of clustered vertices $t \in V_\Delta$. A path $P_{s,t,v}$ is a new-ending path, if $\text{LastE}(P_{s,t,v}) \notin G_0$ (see Eq. (2)). Let $b_{s,t,v}$ be the first divergence point of $P_{s,t,v}$ and $\pi(s,t)$.

Lemma 3. *For every vertex* $u \in P_{s,t,v}$ *such that* $\text{LastE}(P_{s,t,v}[s, u]) \notin T_0(S)$*, it holds that: (a)* $v \in \pi(s, u)$*.   (b)* $V(P_{s,t,v}[b_{s,t,v}, u]) \cap V(\pi(s, u)) = \{b_{s,t,v}, u\}$*.*

The next claim shows that a new-ending $P_{s,t,v}$ path whose last edge is not in G_0 (see Eq. (2)), protecting against faults in the near segment, has a good approximate replacement $\widetilde{P}_{s,t,v}$ in $T_0 \cup G_\Delta$.

Lemma 4. *If* $\text{LastE}(P_{s,t,v}) \notin G_0$ *and* $v \in \pi^{near}(s, t)$*, then* $\text{dist}(s, t, (G_0 \cup G_\Delta) \setminus \{v\}) \leq \text{dist}(s, t, G \setminus \{v\}) + 4$*.*

For every new-ending path $P_{s,t,v}$, recall that $D_{s,t,v}^+ = D_{s,t,v} \setminus \{b_{s,t,v}\}$. Let (x, y) be the first missing in $P_{s,t,v} \setminus E(T_0(S))$ (where x is closer to y). The following auxiliary claims are useful.

Lemma 5. *For every vertex* $u \in P_{s,t,v}$ *such that* $\text{LastE}(P_{s,t,v}[s, u]) \notin (T_0(S) \cup G_\Delta \cup E^{local})$*, it holds that: (a)* $C_v(u) = C_1(u)$*. (b)* $P_{s,t,v}[x, t] \subseteq D_{s,t,v}^+$*.*

Corollary 1. *Let* $t \in V_\Delta$*. For every* $P_{s,t,v} \in \mathcal{P}_{indep}^{far}(t)$*,* $P_{s,t,v}[x, t] \cap V_f(C_v(t)) = \emptyset$ *where* x *is the first vertex of* $D_{s,t,v}^+$*.*

In the full version, we show that $H_4(S)$ is a $(4, S)$ FT-spanner. We proceed with the size analysis.

Lemma 6. *For every* $t \in V_\Delta$*,* $|E^{local}(t)| = O(|S|)$*, hence* $|E^{local}| = O(|S| \cdot n)$*.*

Bounding the number of last edges in $E_{dep}^{far}(t)$*.* We now turn to bound the number of edges added due to step (4.1), i.e., the last edges of new-ending *dependent* paths $P_{s,t,v}$ protecting against the faults in the far segment $\pi^{far}(s, t)$. To bound the number of edges in $E_{dep}^{far}(t)$, consider the partial BFS tree rooted at t, $T(t, S) \subseteq T_0(T)$, whose leaf set is contained in the vertex set S where $T(t, S) = \bigcup_{s \in S} \pi(s, t)$. It is convenient to view this tree as going from the leafs towards the root, where the root t is at the bottom and the leafs are on the top of the tree. Let $V^+ = S \cup \{u \in T(t, S) \mid \deg(u, T(t, S)) \geq 3\}$, be the union of S and the vertices with degree at least 3 in the tree $T(t, S)$. We have that $|V^+| < 2|S|$. A pair of vertices $x, y \in V^+$ is *adjacent* if their shortest-path $\pi(x, y)$ is contained in the tree $T(t, S)$ and it is free from any other V^+ vertex, i.e, $\pi(x, y) \subseteq T(t, S)$ and $\pi(x, y) \cap V^+ = \{x, y\}$. Let $\Pi(V^+) = \{\pi(x, y) \mid x, y \in V^+ \text{ and } x, y \text{ are adjacent }\}$ be the collection of paths between adjacent pairs.

Observation 7. (1) $T(t, S) = \Pi(V^+)$. (2) $\Pi(V^+)$ consists of at most $2|S| + 1$ paths $\pi(x, y)$ (i.e., there are at most $2|S|$ adjacent pairs).

We now show the following.

Lemma 7. For every $t \in V_\Delta$, $|E_{dep}^{far}(t)| = O(|S|)$.

We first claim that every two dependent replacement paths with the same divergence point have the same last edge.

Lemma 8. For every two dependent paths $P_{s_1, t, v_1}, P_{s_2, t, v_2} \in \mathcal{P}_{dep}^{far}(t)$, if $b_{s_1, t, v_1} = b_{s_2, t, v_2}$ then $\text{LastE}(P_{s_1, t, v_1}) = \text{LastE}(P_{s_2, t, v_2})$.

Since our goal is to bound the number of last edges of the new ending dependent paths $\mathcal{P}_{dep}^{far}(t)$, to avoid double counting, we now restrict attention to $\mathcal{Q}^{far}(t)$, a collection of representative paths in $\mathcal{P}_{dep}^{far}(t)$ each ending with a distinct new edge from $E_{dep}^{far}(t)$. Formally, for each new edge $e \in E_{dep}^{far}(t)$, let $P(e)$ be an arbitrary path in $\mathcal{P}_{dep}^{far}(t)$ satisfying that $\text{LastE}(P(e)) = e$. Let $\mathcal{Q}^{far}(t) = \{P(e), e \in E_{dep}^{far}(t)\}$ (hence $|\mathcal{Q}^{far}(t)| = |E_{dep}^{far}(t)|$). From now on, we aim towards bounding the cardinality of $\mathcal{Q}^{far}(t)$. Let $\text{DP} = \{b_{s,t,v} \mid P_{s,t,v} \in \mathcal{Q}^{far}(t)\}$ be the set of divergence points of the new ending paths in $\mathcal{Q}^{far}(t)$. By Lemma 8, it holds that in order to bound the cardinality of $\mathcal{P}_{dep}^{far}(t)$, it is sufficient to bound the number of distinct divergence points. To do that, we show that every path $\pi(x, y)$ of two adjacent vertices $x, y \in V^+$, contains at most one divergence point in $\text{DP} \setminus V^+$.

Lemma 9. $|\pi(x, y) \cap (\text{DP} \setminus V^+)| \leq 1$ for every $\pi(x, y) \in \Pi(V^+)$.

Proof: Assume, towards contradiction, that there are two divergence points b_{s_1, t, v_1} and b_{s_2, t, v_2} on some path $\pi(x, y)$ for two adjacent vertices $x, y \in V^+$. For ease of notation, let $P_i = P_{s_i, t, v_i}$, $b_i = b_{s_i, t, v_i}$, $D_i = D_{s_i, t, v_i}$ and $D_i^+ = D_i \setminus \{b_i\}$ for $i \in \{1, 2\}$. Without loss of generality, assume the following: (1) y is closer to t than x and (2) b_2 is closer to t than b_1. By construction, the vertices s_1 and s_2 are in the subtree $T(x) \subseteq T(t, S)$. For an illustration see Fig. 1. We now claim that the failing vertices v_1, v_2 occur on $\pi(y, t)$. Since D_1^+ and D_2^+ are vertex disjoint with $\pi(y, t) \setminus \{t\}$, it would imply that both detour segments D_1 and D_2 are free from the failing vertices and hence at least one of the two new edges $\text{LastE}(P_1), \text{LastE}(P_2)$ could have been avoided. We now focus on v_1 and show that $v_1 \in \pi(y, t)$, the exact same argumentation holds for v_2. Since P_1 is a new-ending *dependent* path, by Eq. (1), there exists some source $s_3 \in s \setminus \{s_1\}$ satisfying that $(D_1^+ \cap \pi(s_3, t)) \setminus \{t\} \neq \emptyset$. Let $w \in (D_1^+ \cap \pi(s_3, t)) \setminus \{t\}$ be the first intersection point (closest to s_1). See Fig. 1 for schematic illustration. We first claim that s_3 is not in the subtree $T(x) \subseteq T(t, S)$ rooted at x. To see why this holds, assume, towards contradiction, that $s_3 \in T(x)$. It then holds that the replacement path P_1 has the following form $P_1 = \pi[s_1, x] \circ \pi(x, b_1) \circ P_1[b_1, w] \circ P_1[w, t]$. Recall, that since $b_1 \in \text{DP} \setminus V^+$, $b_1 \neq x$ and also $b_1 \neq w$. Since $P_1[x, w]$ goes through b_1, by the optimality of P_1, it holds that

$$\text{dist}(x, w, G \setminus \{v_1\}) > \text{dist}(b_1, w, G \setminus \{v_1\}) . \tag{5}$$

On the other hand, the path $\pi(s_3, t)$ has the following form: $\pi(s_3, t) = \pi(s_3, w) \circ \pi(w, x) \circ \pi(x, b_1) \circ \pi(b_1, t)$. Hence, $\pi(w, b_1)$ goes through x. Since the failing vertex $v_1 \in \pi(b_1, t)$ is not in $\pi(w, b_1)$, by the optimality of $\pi(w, b_1)$, we get that $\mathrm{dist}(w, b_1, G \setminus \{v_1\}) > \mathrm{dist}(x, w, G \setminus \{v_1\})$, leading to contradiction with Ineq. (5). Hence, we conclude that $s_3 \notin T(x)$ (in particular this implies that $s_3 \neq s_2$). Note that $\pi(w, t)$ is a segment of $\pi(s_3, t)$ and hence it is contained in the tree $T(t, S)$. Since P_1 is a new-ending path (i.e., $\mathtt{LastE}(P_1) \notin T(t, S)$), we have that $P_1[w, t] \neq \pi(w, t)$ are distinct $w - t$ paths. We next claim that the failing vertex v_1 must occur on $\pi(w, t)$ and hence also on $\pi(s_3, t)$. To see this, observe that if $\pi(w, t)$ would have been free from the failing vertex v_1, then it implies that $\pi(w, t) = SP(w, t, G \setminus \{v_1\}) = P_1[w, t]$, contradiction as $\mathtt{LastE}(P_1) \neq \mathtt{LastE}(\pi(w, t))$. Finally, we show that $v_1 \in \pi(y, t)$. By the above, the failing vertex v_1 is common to both paths $\pi(s_1, t)$ and $\pi(s_3, t)$, i.e., $v_1 \in \pi(s_1, t) \cap \pi(s_3, t)$. By the definition of the path $\pi(x, y)$, all its internal vertices u have degree 2 and hence $(\pi(x, y) \cap \pi(s_3, t)) \setminus \{y\} = \emptyset$, concluding that $v_1 \in \pi(y, t)$. By the same argumentation, it also holds that v_2 is in $\pi(y, t)$. As the detours D_1 and D_2 are vertex disjoint with $\pi(y, t) \setminus \{t\}$, it holds that they are free from the two failing vertices, i.e., $v_1, v_2 \notin D_1 \cup D_2$. Since $P_1, P_2 \in \mathcal{Q}^{far}(t)$, it holds that $\mathtt{LastE}(P_1) \neq \mathtt{LastE}(P_2)$, and hence there are two $b_1 - t$ distinct shortest paths in $G \setminus \{v_1, v_2\}$, given by D_1 and $\pi(b_1, b_2) \circ D_2$. By optimality of these paths, they are of the same lengths. Again, we end with contradiction to the uniqueness of the weight assignment W. The claim follows. ∎

By Lemma 8 there are at most $|V^+|$ replacement paths with divergence point in V^+. By Lemma 9, there is at most one divergence point on each segment $\pi(x, y)$ of an adjacent pair (x, y). Combining with Obs. 7(2), we get $|E^{far}(t)| = |\mathcal{Q}^{far}(t)| = O(|S|)$. The lemma follows. ∎

In the full version, we complete the size analysis and proves Lemma 2, by bounding the number of edges added by the path-buying procedure of Step (4.2).

4.2   Sourcewise Spanner with Additive Stretch 8

In this section, we present Alg. $\mathtt{Cons8SWSpanner}$ for constructing a sourcewise additive FT-spanner with additive stretch 8. The size of the resulting spanner is smaller (in order) than the $H_4(S)$ spanner of Alg. $\mathtt{Cons4SWSpanner}$, at the expense of larger stretch. The algorithm is similar in spirit to Alg. $\mathtt{Cons4SWSpanner}$ and the major distinction is in the path-buying procedure of step (4.2).

Lemma 10. *There exists a subgraph $H_8(S) \subseteq G$ with $\widetilde{O}(\max\{|S| \cdot n, (n/|S|)^2\})$ edges s.t. $\mathrm{dist}(s, t, H_8(S) \setminus \{v\}) \leq \mathrm{dist}(s, t, G \setminus \{v\}) + 8$ for every $(s, t) \in S \times V$ and every $v \in V$.*

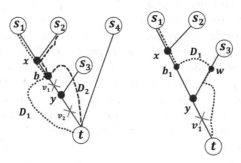

Fig. 1. Schematic illustration of new-ending dependent paths. Shown is the tree $T(t, S)$ with the root t at the bottom and leaf set is contained in the set of sources S. (a) The two replacement paths have the same divergence point b, hence one of the new last edges is redundant. (b) A new-ending $s_1 - t$ dependant path P_{s_1,t,v_1} with a divergence point $b_1 \in \pi(x, y)$ intersects with $\pi(s_3, t)$ at the vertex $w \notin \{b_1, t\}$. Since $P_{s_1,t,v}$ is a new-ending path (i.e., its last edges is not on $T(t, S)$), the failing vertex v must occur on the path $\pi(w, t)$. Hence $v_1 \in \pi(s_1, t) \cap \pi(s_3, t)$, implying that $v_1 \in \pi(y, t)$. Since this holds for any new-ending path with a divergence point in $\pi(x, y)$, we get that only one new edge from all these paths is needed.

Algorithm Cons8SWSpanner for constructing $H_8(S)$ spanner

Step (0-4.1): Same as in Alg. Cons4SWSpanner. Let E^{local}, E^{far}_{dep} be the set of last edges obtained at the end of step (3) and set (4.1) respectively. Let $\mathcal{P}^{far}_{indep}$ be the set of new-ending independent paths.

Step (4.2): Handling independent *new-ending paths.* Starting with G_0 as in Eq. (2), the paths of $\mathcal{P}^{far}_{indep}$ are considered in an arbitrary order. At step τ, we are given $G_\tau \subseteq G$ and consider the path $P_\tau = P_{s,t,v}$. Let $D_\tau = P_\tau \setminus \pi(s, t)$ be the detour segment of P_τ (since $\pi(s, t) \subseteq T_0(S)$ is in G_0, all missing edges of P_τ occur on its detour segment).

    To decide whether P_τ should be added to G_τ, the number of pairwise cluster "distance improvements" is compared to the number of new edges added due to P_τ. To do that we compute the set $\mathtt{ValSet}(P_\tau)$ containing all pairs of clusters that achieves a better distance if P_τ is bought. The value and cost of P_τ are computed as follows. Let $\mathtt{Val}(P_\tau) = |\mathtt{ValSet}(P_\tau)|$ as the number of distance improvements as formally defined later. We next define a key vertex $\phi_\tau \in V_\Delta$ on the path P_τ.

Definition 3. *Let $\phi_{s,t,v}$ (or ϕ_τ for short) be the last vertex on P_τ (closest to t) satisfying that: (N1) $\mathtt{LastE}(P_\tau[s, \phi_\tau]) \notin G_\tau$, and (N2) $v \in \pi^{near}(s, \phi_\tau) = \pi(\ell, \phi_\tau) \setminus \{\ell\}$ where $\ell = \mathtt{LCA}(s, C_v(\phi_\tau))$.*
If there is no vertex on P_τ that satisfies both (N1) and (N2), then let ϕ_τ be the first vertex incident to the first missing edge on $P_\tau \setminus E(G_\tau)$ (i.e., such that $P_\tau[s, \phi_\tau]$ is the maximal prefix that is contained in G_τ).

Let $Q_\tau = P_\tau[\phi_\tau, t]$ and define $\text{Cost}(P_\tau) = |E(Q_\tau) \setminus E(G_\tau)|$ be the number of edges of Q_τ that are missing in the current subgraph G_τ. Thus $\text{Cost}(P_\tau)$ represents the increase in the size of the spanner G_τ if the procedure adds Q_τ. Our algorithm attempts to buy only the suffix Q_τ of P_τ when considering P_τ. We now define the set $\text{ValSet}(P_\tau) \subseteq \mathcal{C} \times \mathcal{C}$ which contains a collection *ordered* cluster pairs. Let $C_1(\tau) = C_v(\phi_\tau)$ and $C_2(\tau) = C_v(t)$ be the clusters of ϕ_τ and t in $G_\Delta \setminus \{v\}$. Let $\kappa = \text{Cost}(P_\tau)$. The candidate P_τ is said to be *cheap* if $\kappa \leq 4$, otherwise it is *costly*. The definition of $\text{ValSet}(P_\tau)$ depends on whether or not the path is cheap. In particular, if P_τ is cheap, then let $\text{ValSet}(P_\tau) = \{(C_1(\tau), C_2(\tau))\}$ only if

$$\text{dist}(\phi_\tau, t, P_\tau) < \text{dist}(C_1(\tau), C_2(\tau), G_\tau \setminus V_f(C_2(\tau))) , \qquad (6)$$

where $V_f(C_2(\tau))$ is as given by Eq. (3), and let $\text{ValSet}(P_\tau) = \emptyset$ otherwise. Alternatively, if P_τ is costly, we do the following.

Definition 4. *Let* $U_{s,t,v} = \{u_{3\ell+1} \mid \ell \in \{0, \ldots, \lfloor(\kappa - 1)/3\rfloor\}\} \subseteq Q_\tau$ *be some representative endpoints of missing edges on* Q_τ *satisfying that*

$$\text{LastE}(Q_\tau[\phi_\tau, u_\ell]) \notin G_\tau \text{ for every } u_\ell \in U_{s,t,v} \text{ and } \text{dist}(u_\ell, u_{\ell'}, Q_\tau) \geq 3$$

for every $u_\ell, u_{\ell'} \in U_{s,t,v}$.

Define

$$\begin{aligned} \text{ValSet}_1(P_\tau) = \{(C_1(\tau), C_\ell) \mid C_\ell = C_v(u_\ell), u_\ell \in U_{s,t,v} \qquad (7)\\ \text{and } \text{dist}(\phi_\tau, u_\ell, P_\tau) < \text{dist}(C_1(\tau), C_\ell, G_\tau \setminus V_f(C_\ell))\} \end{aligned}$$

and

$$\begin{aligned} \text{ValSet}_2(P_\tau) = \{(C_\ell, C_2(\tau)) \mid C_\ell = C_v(u_\ell), u_\ell \in U_{s,t,v} \qquad (8)\\ \text{and } \text{dist}(u_\ell, t, P_\tau) < \text{dist}(C_\ell, C_2(\tau), G_\tau \setminus V_f(C_2(\tau)))\} \end{aligned}$$

Let $\text{ValSet}(P_\tau) = \text{ValSet}_1(P_\tau) \cup \text{ValSet}_2(P_\tau)$. The subpath Q_τ is added to G_τ resulting in $G_{\tau+1}$ only if

$$\text{Cost}(P_\tau) \leq 4 \cdot \text{Val}(P_\tau) , \qquad (9)$$

where $\text{Val}(P_\tau) = |\text{ValSet}(P_\tau)|$. (Note that when P_τ is cheap, Eq. (9) holds iff Eq. (6) holds.) The output of Alg. Cons8SWSpanner is the subgraph $H_8(S) = G_{\tau'}$ where $\tau' = |\mathcal{P}_{indep}^{far}|$. This completes the description of the algorithm. In the full version, we analyze the algorithm and prove Lemma 10.

Additive stretch 6 (for all pairs). Thm. 2 follows immediately by Lemma 2. This should be compared with the single source additive FT-spanner $H_4(\{s\})$ of [18] and the (all-pairs, non FT) 6-additive spanner, both with $O(n^{4/3})$ edges.

Acknowledgment. I am very grateful to my advisor, Prof. David Peleg, for many helpful discussions and for reviewing this paper.

References

1. Aingworth, D., Chekuri, C., Indyk, P., Motwani, R.: Fast estimation of diameter and shortest paths (without matrix multiplication). SIAM J. Comput. 28(4), 1167–1181 (1999)
2. Knudsen, M.B.T.: Additive Spanners: A Simple Construction. In: Ravi, R., Gørtz, I.L. (eds.) SWAT 2014. LNCS, vol. 8503, pp. 277–281. Springer, Heidelberg (2014)
3. Baswana, S., Sen, S.: Approximate distance oracles for unweighted graphs in expected $O(n^2)$ time. ACM Trans. Algorithms 2(4), 557–577 (2006)
4. Baswana, S., Khanna, N.: Approximate Shortest Paths Avoiding a Failed Vertex: Optimal Size Data Structures for Unweighted Graph. In: STACS, pp. 513–524 (2010)
5. Baswana, S., Kavitha, T., Mehlhorn, K., Pettie, S.: Additive spanners and (α, β)-spanners. ACM Trans. Algo. 7, A.5 (2010)
6. Bernstein, A.: A nearly optimal algorithm for approximating replacement paths and k shortest simple paths in general graphs. In: Proc. 21st ACM-SIAM Symp. on Discrete Algorithms (2010)
7. Bernstein, A., Karger, D.: A nearly optimal oracle for avoiding failed vertices and edges. In: Proc. 41st ACM Symp. on Theory of Computing, pp. 101–110 (2009)
8. Braunschvig, G., Chechik, S., Peleg, D.: Fault tolerant additive spanners. In: Golumbic, M.C., Stern, M., Levy, A., Morgenstern, G. (eds.) WG 2012. LNCS, vol. 7551, pp. 206–214. Springer, Heidelberg (2012)
9. Chechik, S., Langberg, M., Peleg, D., Roditty, L.: f-sensitivity distance oracles and routing schemes. Algorithmica 63, 861–882 (2012)
10. Chechik, S., Langberg, M., Peleg, D., Roditty, L.: Fault-tolerant spanners for general graphs. In: STOC, pp. 435–444 (2009)
11. Chechik, S.: New Additive Spanners. In: SODA (2013)
12. Cygan, M., Grandoni, F., Kavitha, T.: On Pairwise Spanners. In: STACS, pp. 209–220 (2013)
13. Dinitz, M., Krauthgamer, R.: Fault-tolerant spanners: better and simpler. In: PODC, pp. 169–178 (2011)
14. Dor, D., Halperin, S., Zwick, U.: All-pairs almost shortest paths. SIAM J. Computing 29(5), 1740–1759 (2000)
15. Elkin, M., Peleg, D.: $(1 + \varepsilon, \beta)$-Spanner Constructions for General Graphs. SIAM Journal on Computing 33(3), 608–631 (2004)
16. Grandoni, F., Williams, V.V.: Improved Distance Sensitivity Oracles via Fast Single-Source Replacement Paths. In: FOCS (2012)
17. Parter, M., Peleg, D.: Sparse Fault-tolerant BFS trees. In: Bodlaender, H.L., Italiano, G.F. (eds.) ESA 2013. LNCS, vol. 8125, pp. 779–790. Springer, Heidelberg (2013)
18. Parter, M., Peleg, D.: Fault Tolerant Approximate BFS Structures. In: SODA (2014)
19. Roditty, L., Zwick, U.: Replacement paths and k simple shortest paths in unweighted directed graphs. ACM Trans. Algorithms (2012)
20. Thorup, M., Zwick, U.: Spanners and emulators with sublinear distance errors. In: SODA, pp. 802–809 (2006)
21. Weimann, O., Yuster, R.: Replacement paths via fast matrix multiplication. In: FOCS (2010)
22. Woodruff, D.P.: Lower bounds for additive spanners, emulators, and more. In: FOCS, pp. 389–398 (2006)
23. Woodruff, D.P.: Additive spanners in nearly quadratic time. In: Abramsky, S., Gavoille, C., Kirchner, C., Meyer auf der Heide, F., Spirakis, P.G. (eds.) ICALP 2010. Part I. LNCS, vol. 6198, pp. 463–474. Springer, Heidelberg (2010)

Close to Linear Space Routing Schemes

Liam Roditty and Roei Tov

Department of Computer Science, Bar Ilan University, Ramat-Gan, Israel
liamr@macs.biu.ac.il, roei81@gmail.com

Abstract. Let $G = (V, E)$ be an unweighted undirected graph with n-vertices and m-edges, and let $k > 2$ be an integer. We present a routing scheme with a poly-logarithmic header size, that given a source s and a destination t at distance Δ from s, routes a message from s to t on a path whose length is $O(k\Delta + m^{1/k})$. The total space used by our routing scheme is $\tilde{O}(mn^{O(1/\sqrt{\log n})})$, which is almost linear in the number of edges of the graph. We present also a routing scheme with $\tilde{O}(n^{O(1/\sqrt{\log n})})$ header size, and the same stretch (up to constant factors). In this routing scheme, the routing table of *every* $v \in V$ is at most $\tilde{O}(kn^{O(1/\sqrt{\log n})} deg(v))$, where $deg(v)$ is the degree of v in G. Our results are obtained by combining a general technique of Bernstein [6], that was presented in the context of dynamic graph algorithms, with several new ideas and observations.

1 Introduction

In [20] Thorup and Zwick presented the notion of *distance oracle*. Given a graph $G = (V, E)$ with n-vertices and m-edges, the goal is to produce, after a preprocessing phase, a compact data structure, named distance oracle, that can answer quickly distance queries between any pair of vertices in the graph. Thorup and Zwick showed that for any integer $k \geq 1$ it is possible to construct a $O(kn^{1+1/k})$ space distance oracle in $\tilde{O}(mn^{1/k})$ time. Queries are answered in $O(k)$ time and returns an estimated distance with multiplicative stretch of $2k - 1$. Wulff-Nilsen [22] showed that distance oracles of large stretch can be build in linear time. Recently, Wulff-Nilsen [23] showed, using a clever query algorithm, that the query time of Thorup and Zwick can be reduced from $O(k)$ to $O(\log k)$. Even more recently, Chechik [8] showed that the query time of Thorup and Zwick can be reduced to $O(1)$.

Compact routing schemes can be viewed as a distributed implementation of distance oracle. The graph is a distributed network, and a distributed algorithm runs on processors (nodes). Each node in the graph has a routing table. A message that is sent from a source to a destination has a header that contains the name of the destination and possibly some additional information. When a node receives a message, it first checks if it is the message destination, and if not, then based on the header information and its own routing table it chooses the link on which it forwards the message. The stretch of a routing scheme is the worst ratio between the length of a path on which a message is routed and the distance in the network between the source and the destination.

F. Kuhn (Ed.): DISC 2014, LNCS 8784, pp. 182–196, 2014.
© Springer-Verlag Berlin Heidelberg 2014

Thorup and Zwick [19] showed that their distance oracle can be implemented distributively with a slightly worse stretch. They showed a routing scheme for any integer $k > 1$, in which every vertex has a routing table of size at most $\tilde{O}(n^{1/k})$, and messages are sent over routes with multiplicative stretch of $4k - 5$. Routing schemes for general graphs have a long history that spans from the end of the 1980's ([9], [11], [5], [4]) until very recently ([1] and [7]). In [19] Thorup and Zwick give a detailed description of the previous results. Recently, Abraham and Gavoille [1] showed a routing scheme with multiplicative stretch of 2 and additive stretch of 1-stretch. The routing tables in each vertex are of size at most $\tilde{O}(n^{3/4})$. More recently Chechik [7] improved the $4k - 5$ stretch and showed a routing scheme with routing tables in each vertex of size at most $\tilde{O}(n^{1/k} \log D)$, where D is the diameter, and stretch $(4 - \alpha)k - \beta$, for some absolute constants $\alpha, \beta > 0$.

Common to all the results mentioned so far is that they are only meaningful in dense graphs. The space bound has no connection to the number of edges of the graph. In sparse graphs with $m = \tilde{O}(n)$ the required space for distance oracles or routing tables is significantly larger than the size of the input. In many real world networks $m = \tilde{O}(n)$, and thus in order to make the results applicable for implementation it is important to study also sparse graphs.

Indeed, sparse graphs were the subject of several recent studies on distance oracles. Sommer, Verbin, and Yu [18] obtained lower bounds, that hold even for sparse graphs $(m = \tilde{O}(n))$, on the three-way tradeoff between space, stretch and query time. Pătraşcu and Roditty [13] showed that for weighted graphs with $m = n^2/\alpha$, there exist a stretch 2-distance oracle with size of $O(n^2/\alpha^{1/3})$. This result was extended by Pătraşcu, Thorup and Roditty [14] that obtained for any fixed positive integers k and ℓ, stretches $\alpha = 2k + 1 \pm \frac{2}{\ell}$, using $\tilde{O}(m^{1+2/(\alpha+1)})$ space and $O(k+\ell)$ query time. Porat and Roditty [17] showed that in unweighted graphs for any $\varepsilon > 0$ they can construct a data structure of size $O(nm^{1-\varepsilon/(4+2\varepsilon)})$, that returns $1 + \varepsilon$ stretch in $O(m^{1-\varepsilon/(4+2\varepsilon)})$ time. Agarwal and Godfrey [3] extended and improved [17] for weighted undirected graphs. Although there was quite intensive work on distance oracles and other distance data structures for sparse graphs, there were no real advances in routing schemes over sparse graphs. Moreover, in many practical scenarios what we are really interested in is a routing scheme and not a centralized data structure.

Agarwal, Godfrey and Har-Peled showed in [2] that for any $1 \leq \alpha \leq n$ there is a distance oracle that returns stretch 2 with $O(m + n^2/\alpha)$ space and stretch 3 with $O(m + n^2/\alpha^2)$ space both with a query of $O(\alpha m/n)$. This is also mentioned by Pătraşcu and Roditty in [13]. It is straightforward to use these ideas to obtain a distance data structure of size $\tilde{O}(m)$, query of $O(m^{1/k} + k)$ and stretch $4k - 5$.

In this paper we show that it is possible to obtain a routing scheme with similar properties. More specifically, we present a routing scheme with a poly-logarithmic header size, that given a source s and a destination t at distance Δ from s, routes a message from s to t on a path whose length is $O(k\Delta + m^{1/k})$. The total space used by our routing scheme is $\tilde{O}(mn^{O(1/\sqrt{\log n})})$. We then show that if we are willing to pay the non-standard price of a header of size $\tilde{O}(n^{O(1/\sqrt{\log n})})$, then it is possible to obtain a routing scheme with a worst case bound on the routing table size of *every* $v \in V$. The bound is $\tilde{O}(kn^{O(1/\sqrt{\log n})}deg(v))$, where $deg(v)$ is the degree of v in G. The stretch is same, up to a constant factor.

Routing schemes and centralized distance data structures are closely related, and the current state-of-the-art for centralized distance data structures is a natural barrier for routing schemes. Therefore, it is unlikely that one can design routing scheme with near to linear space and constant stretch, that avoids the additive term of $O(m^{1/k})$, without getting a similar result for centralized distance data structure, which will be an important breakthrough.

We obtain our results using a general technique that was presented by Bernstein [6] in the context of dynamic graph algorithms. Roughly speaking, he showed that using ideas of Thorup and Zwick from [21] it is possible to represent a $(1 + \varepsilon)$-approximation of almost all distances of every unweighted undirected graph, using a very sparse weighted graph with small unweighted diameter. We show that using several new ideas together with a new look on Bernstein's result it is possible to obtain a routing scheme with close to linear total space.

We then show that using a greedy partition algorithm it is possible to partition the graph vertices such that the routing data will be distributed between the vertices in a way that is proportional to their degree. This allows us together with more ideas to obtain a bound on the routing table of every vertex.

The rest of this paper is organized as follows. In the next section we present some preliminaries that are needed throughout the paper. In Section 3 we formally present a distance data structure with $O(m^{1/k}+k)$ query and $\tilde{O}(m)$ space, which we aim in the later sections to implement in a distributed manner. In Section 4 we present our poly-logarithmic size header routing scheme with a close to linear total space. In Section 5 we show that with a header of size $\tilde{O}(n^{O(1/\sqrt{\log n})})$ we can get for every $v \in V$ a routing table of size $\tilde{O}(kn^{O(1/\sqrt{\log n})}deg(v))$.

2 Preliminaries

Basic definitions. Let $G = (V, E)$ be an n-vertices m-edges undirected unweighted graph. For every $u, v \in V$, let $d(u, v)$ be the length of the shortest path between u and v. Let $deg(u)$ be the degree of u in G. For every $u \in V$, let $id(u)$ be a unique identifier from the set $\{1, \ldots, n\}$. Given a vertex $u \in V$, the distance of an edge (x, y) from u is $\min\{d(u, x), d(u, y)\}$. Let $e_1 = (x_1, y_1)$ and $e_2 = (x_2, y_2)$ be two edges at distance ℓ from u. Ties are broken as follows. For $i \in \{1, 2\}$ assume, wlog, that $d(u, x_i) = \ell$, and that $id(x_i) < id(y_i)$ if $d(u, y_i) = \ell$. If $x_1 \neq x_2$, then e_1 is closer than e_2, if and only if $id(x_1) < id(x_2)$. If $x_1 = x_2$, then e_1 is closer than e_2, if and only if $id(y_1) < id(y_2)$. Let $E(u, \ell)$ be the ℓ closest edges of u. Let $V(E(u, \ell))$ be the endpoints of the edges of $E(u, \ell)$. Let $r_u^\ell \geq 0$ be the largest distance between u and a vertex $w \in V(E(u, \ell))$ that satisfies the following: there is no other vertex $w' \notin V(E(u, \ell))$ such that $d(u, w) = d(u, w')$. We omit the superscript and write r_u in cases that the meaning is clear from the context.

Lemma 1. *For every* $x \in V(E(u, \ell))$ *it holds that* $d(u, x) \le r_u + 1$. *Moreover,* *if* $(x, y) \in E(u, \ell)$ *then it cannot be that both* $d(u, x)$ *and* $d(u, y)$ *equal* $r_u + 1$.

Proof. We start with the first part of the lemma. Assume towards a contradiction that there exists an edge $(x, y) \in E(u, \ell)$, such that, wlog, $d(u, x) > r_u + 1$. It follows that the edge (x, y) is at distance of at least $r_u + 1$. Let (x', y') be any edge such that, wlog, $d(u, x') = r_u$. Since by the definition (x', y') is closer to u than (x, y), we get that $(x', y') \in E(u, \ell)$. This implies that all vertices at distance $r_u + 1$ from u must be in $V(E(u, \ell))$, a contradiction to the maximality of r_u.

Let $(x, y) \in E(u, \ell)$, such that $d(u, x) = r_u + 1$ and $d(u, y) = r_u + 1$. Again the edge (x, y) is at distance $r_u + 1$, and the same contradiction as before is followed. □

For every set $A \subseteq V$ and every vertex $u \in V$, let $p_A(u)$ be the closest vertex to u from A, where ties are broken in favor of the vertex with the smaller identifier. Notice that by this definition, if v is on a shortest path between u and $p_A(u)$, then $p_A(u) = p_A(v)$.

We will also use a restricted variant of the classical Breadth-First-Search (BFS) algorithm. In particular, if the edges of vertex u are ordered by the indices of their other endpoints, it is straightforward to have a variant of the BFS algorithm that gets a source s and an additional integer parameter ℓ and outputs the ℓ edges that are closest to s as well as the distance of s from each vertex of $V(E(s, \ell))$ in $O(\ell)$ time.

Distance oracles. A distance oracle is a succinct data structure that supports efficient distance queries. In their seminal result Thorup and Zwick [20] showed that there is a data structure of size $O(kn^{1+1/k})$ that returns a $(2k - 1)$ multiplicative approximation (stretch) of the distances of an undirected weighted graph in $O(k)$ time. Their data structure is constructed as follows. Let $k \ge 1$ and let $A_0, A_1, \ldots, A_k$ be sets of vertices, such that $A_0 = V$, $A_k = \emptyset$ and A_i is formed by picking each vertex of A_{i-1} independently with probability $n^{-1/k}$ (w.h.p $A_{k-1} \ne \emptyset$). For every $u \in V$, let $p_i(u) = p_{A_i}(u)$. The *bunch* of $u \in V$ is

$$B(u) = \cup_{i=0}^{k-1} \{v \in A_i \setminus A_{i+1} \mid d(u, v) < d(u, p_{i+1}(u))\},$$

where $d(u, p_k(u)) = \infty$.

They showed that the expected size of every bunch is $O(kn^{1/k})$ or $\tilde{O}(kn^{1/k})$ in the worst case (with a deterministic sampling technique). The cluster of $w \in A_i \setminus A_{i+1}$ is:

$$C(w) = \{u \in V \mid d(u, w) < d(u, p_{i+1}(u))\}.$$

It follows from this definition that if $u \in C(w)$ and v is on a shortest path between u and w then $v \in C(w)$. Thus, there is a shortest paths tree $T_C(w)$ that spans the cluster $C(w)$. Thorup and Zwick showed that for every pair of vertices $u, v \in V$ there is a vertex w such that $u, v \in C(w)$ and the distance between u

and v using only the edges of $T_C(w)$ is at most $(2k-1)d(u,v)$. Such a vertex w can be found in $O(k)$ time.

Throughout the paper, when referring to distance oracle and clusters, we refer to the work of Thorup and Zwick that we have just described.

Routing schemes. A routing scheme is a distributed algorithm that runs on processors (nodes) in a network as the one defined above. Each node in the network has a routing table. A message that is sent from a source to a destination has a header that contains the name of the destination and possibly some additional information. When a node receives a packet, it first checks if it is the packet destination, and if not, then based on the header information and its own routing table it chooses the link on which it forwards the packet. We assume a node is allowed to change the header of a message during the routing. The stretch of a routing scheme is the worst ratio between the length of a path on which a message is routed and the distance in the network between the source and the destination. If for every pair $s, t \in V$ the message is sent over a path of length at most $\alpha d(s,t) + \beta$ then we say that the routing scheme has a multiplicative stretch of α and an additive stretch of β. In this paper we consider name-dependent routing schemes. In such schemes during the preprocessing phase, in which the routing tables are constructed, the nodes get also an additional short label that becomes part of their name. For a detailed review of routing scheme the reader is referred to [19] and the references therein.

Our model is the standard model for routing scheme as described by Peleg and Upfal [16]. We are given a connected undirected graph $G = (V, E)$. The nodes are given a unique initial ids of $O(\log n)$ bits, $V = \{1, \ldots, n\}$. The nodes represent the processors of the network and the edges represent bidirectional links between the vertices. A vertex can communicate directly only with its neighbours. A vertex v has $deg(v)$ ports numbered from 1 to $deg(v)$. An edge is a pair $((u, i), (v, j))$. When vertex u sends a message to its neighbour v, it uploads it on port i, and v downloads it from port j. Usually, we ignore the ports and assume we simply send a message over the edge (u, v). Additionally, we assume that the processors work in the CONGEST synchronized model [15]. In this model in each round every vertex (processor) can send a message of poly-log bits to each of its neighbors. This assumption is required since in our routing schemes the source first checks whether the destination is in its near neighbourhood.

In our routing schemes, we use the following two results as building blocks. The first is due to Thorup and Zwick [19] and, independently, Fraigniaud and Gavoille [12]. They showed that given a tree it is possible to route between every pair of vertices on a shortest path (in the tree) using only the labels of the pair and no additional information. The labels are of size $O(\log^2 n/\log \log n)$ and each link on the path is obtained in constant time. The second result is a general compact routing scheme for weighted undirected graphs. Thorup and Zwick [19] showed that based on their distance oracle [20] it is possible to get a compact routing scheme. In this routing scheme the source chooses a cluster to route on locally based on its own cluster, bunch and the label of the destination.

As a result of that, the stretch is $4k - 5$ and not $2k - 1$ as in the distance oracle. The label of every vertex is of size $o(k \log^2 n)$ and the routing table is of size $\tilde{O}(n^{1/k})$.

3   A Distance Data Structure with Almost Linear Space

In this section we present a distance oracle with $\tilde{O}(m)$ space, $O(m^{1/k} + k)$ query time, and $4k - 5$ multiplicative stretch, where k is an integer greater than 1. This generalizes a simple result from [13]. A similar result is also presented in [2].

The data structure is constructed as follows. In the first step a set $E' \subset E$ of size $O(m^{1-1/k} \log m)$ that hits[1] the $m^{1/k}$ closest edges of every vertex is formed deterministically [10]. The set $A \subseteq V$ is the set of all endpoints of edges in E'. For each vertex $v \in V$ we compute $p_A(u)$, the closest vertex to u from the set A. We compute the distance between every pair of vertices in A, and form a complete graph H whose vertices are the vertices of A and the weights of its edges are the corresponding distances between the vertices in G. Finally, we construct the distance oracle of Thorup and Zwick for H with parameter $k - 1$. A pseudo-code of this construction is presented in Algorithm 1.

The query algorithm works as follows. Let $u, v \in V$. At the first stage we check if $V(E(u, m^{1/k}))$ and $V(E(v, m^{1/k}))$ intersect. If they do then we can obtain almost the exact distance. If not, then we query the distance oracle of Thorup and Zwick for an approximation of $d(p_A(u), p_A(v))$ and return $d(u, p_A(u)) + \hat{d}(p_A(u), p_A(v)) + d(p_A(v), v)$ as an estimation. A pseudo-code of the query is presented in Algorithm 2.

Algorithm 1. Preprocess-Distances$((V, E), k)$

E' hits all the sets $E(u, m^{1/k})$, for every $u \in V$;
$A \leftarrow V(E')$;
foreach $u \in V$ **do**
  $\llcorner$ compute $p_A(u)$ and $d(u, p_A(u))$;
foreach $u, v \in A$ **do**
  $\llcorner$ compute $d_G(u, v)$;
let $H = (A, A \times A, w)$,
  where $w(u, v) = d_G(u, v)$, for every $u, v \in A \times A$;
$DO_H \leftarrow \texttt{ThorupZwickDO}(H, k - 1)$;

Next, we prove the following:

Theorem 1. *Let $k > 1$ be an integer. The data structure described above outputs a $(4k - 5)$-approximation of the distance between every pair of vertices in $O(m^{1/k} + k)$ time. The size of the data structure is $\tilde{O}(m)$.*

---

[1] An edge set E' hits edge sets $E_1, E_2, \ldots, E_p$, if the intersection between E' and any E_i $(1 \le i \le p)$ is non-empty.

Algorithm 2. Query(u, v)

---

if $V(E(u, m^{1/k})) \cap V(E(v, m^{1/k})) \neq \emptyset$ then

    ⌊ return $\min_{w \in V(E(u, m^{1/k})) \cap V(E(v, m^{1/k}))} \{d(u, w) + d(w, v)\}$;

else

    ⌊ $\hat{d}(p_A(u), p_A(v)) \leftarrow QueryDO_H(p_A(u), p_A(v))$;

    ⌊ return $d(u, p_A(u)) + \hat{d}(p_A(u), p_A(v)) + d(p_A(v), v)$;

Proof.

Space: Every vertex saves its closest vertex from the set A, at a total cost of $O(n)$. For the graph H, that has $\tilde{O}(m^{1-1/k})$ vertices, we create a distance oracle with parameter $k - 1$. Thus, the cost of this is $\tilde{O}(m^{(1-1/k)(1+1/(k-1))}) = \tilde{O}(m)$.

Query: The incident edges of every vertex are ordered by the identifiers of their other endpoint. Therefore, it is straightforward to compute the $m^{1/k}$ closest edges of a given vertex in $O(m^{1/k})$ time. In the same time bound we can check, by using a hash table, if $V(E(u, m^{1/k}))$ and $V(E(v, m^{1/k}))$ intersect. If there is no intersection then we query the distance oracle of Thorup and Zwick at a cost of $O(k)$.

Approximation: Let P be a shortest path between u and v. Assume first that $V(E(u, m^{1/k})) \cap V(E(v, m^{1/k})) \neq \emptyset$.

Let $w = \arg\min_{w \in V(E(u, m^{1/k})) \cap V(E(v, m^{1/k}))} \{d(u, w) + d(w, v)\}$. If $w \in P$ then the exact distance is returned. Thus, assume that $w \notin P$. There is a vertex $u' \in V(E(u, m^{1/k})) \cap P$ such that $d(u, u') = r_u$. Similarly, there is a vertex $v' \in V(E(v, m^{1/k})) \cap P$ such that $d(v, v') = r_v$. Since the intersection is not on a vertex from P it must be that $d(u, v) \geq r_u + r_v + 1$. On the other hand from Lemma 1 we have that $d(u, w) \leq r_u + 1$ and $d(v, w) \leq r_v + 1$. Thus, $d(u, w) + d(v, w) \leq d(u, v) + 1$. Consider now the case that $V(E(u, m^{1/k})) \cap V(E(u, m^{1/k})) = \emptyset$. In this case we query the distance oracle of Thorup and Zwick for a $2(k-1)-1$ approximation of the distance between $p_A(u)$ and $p_A(v)$. From Lemma 1 we know that $d(u, p_A(u)) \leq r_u$ and $d(v, p_A(v)) \leq r_v$. Thus, $d(p_A(u), p_A(v)) \leq d(u, v) + r_u + r_v \leq 2d(u, v)$. The total estimated distance is at most $r_u + (2k - 3) \cdot 2d(u, v) + r_v \leq (4k - 5)d(u, v)$. $\qquad\square$

4 A Routing Scheme with an Almost Linear Total Space

Our goal is to implement the distance data structure described above in a distributed manner. There are two obvious obstacles. The first obstacle is to implement the query phase given a source u and a destination v. In a distributed implementation the query is done only on the source side, thus it is not possible to obtain the set $V(E(v, m^{1/k}))$ of the destination. The second and the more serious obstacle is that the distance oracle of Thorup and Zwick is constructed for the graph H and not for the input graph G. The edges of the graph H are virtual edges that correspond to paths in G and not edges. Thus, edges on a path of H cannot be used directly for routing and should be translated into their corresponding paths in G.

In this section we show that it is possible to overcome these obstacles and present a routing scheme that requires a total space of $\tilde{O}(m \cdot n^{O(1/\sqrt{\log n})})$. Given a source and a destination after a query phase of $O(m^{1/k})$ messages the routing is done on a path of stretch $O(k)$. Our routing scheme uses a header of poly-logarithmic size.

For the sake of simplicity we present our routing scheme in two stages. In the first stage we assume that all the virtual edges in the graph H, that correspond to shortest paths in G, have at most h edges, where h is a parameter to be fixed later. The total space needed for this routing scheme is $\tilde{O}(mh)$. In the second stage we show that using the ideas of Bernstein [6] it is possible to obtain a new weighted graph with small hop-diameter. We then use this new graph together with our routing scheme to deal with the case that the graph H has virtual edges that correspond to arbitrarily long shortest paths in G.

4.1   A Routing Scheme for Virtual Edges of Bounded Weight

Let $G = (V, E)$ be an unweighted undirected graph. In the preprocessing step we compute a hitting set $E' \subset E$ of size $O(m^{1-1/k} \log m)$ that hits the $m^{1/k}$ closest edges of every vertex as before. Let $A = V(E')$. We compute for each $v \in A$, a shortest path tree $T(v)$ that contains all vertices $u \in V$ such that $p_A(u) = v$. For each such tree, we construct its own tree compact routing scheme using either [19] or [12], to enable routing between every vertex u and its closest vertex $p_A(u)$ using a shortest path (notice that tree routing scheme is mainly needed for the harder case of routing from $p_A(u)$ to u). At u we store the following information: $p_A(u)$, $d(u, p_A(u))$, the label of u in the routing scheme of $T(p_A(u))$, r_u and the last edge in $E(u, m^{1/k})$. The label of u is denoted with $label(u)$ and contains the following information: u, $p_A(u)$ and the label of u in the tree routing scheme of the tree $T(p_A(u))$.

As before we have a weighted graph $H = (A, A \times A)$, where the weight of an edge is the distance between its endpoints in G. In this case we assume all edges in H has a weight of at most h. We construct for H the compact routing scheme of [19]. This allows us to route between vertices of A using a path of H. An edge (x, y) of H is a virtual edge and not a physical edge of G, thus, it cannot be used directly to transfer a message between x and y. Let $P = \{x = x_1, x_2, \ldots, x_\ell = y\}$ be the shortest path that corresponds to the edge (x, y) in H. In order to route from x to y using P, we save at node x_i in a translation table HT_{x_i} for the entry (x, y), the vertex x_{i+1}, the successor of x_i in P. A pseudo-code of this preprocessing phase is presented in Algorithm 3.

We now turn to describe how to route a message from a source u to a destination v. First, u checks whether v is in $V(E(u, m^{1/k}))$, and if it is, then the routing is done on a shortest path. In the CONGEST model it is relatively straightforward to obtain, in a distributed manner, the set $V(E(u, m^{1/k}))$ at u. We can assume also that u has less than $m^{1/k}$ neighbors, since in our model u knows all its ports with their other endpoints so in such a case u can check locally if v

---

Algorithm 3. Preprocess-Routing(G, k, h)

E' hits all the sets $E(u, m^{1/k})$, for every $u \in V$;
$A \leftarrow V(E')$;
foreach $u \in V$ **do**
 compute and store $p_A(u)$, $d(u, p_A(u))$, r_u and the last edge in
 $E(u, m^{1/k})$, at u;
 initialize hash table HT_u;
foreach $u \in A$ **do**
 Compute $T(u)$ and a tree routing scheme for it;
let $H = (A, A \times A, w)$, where $w(u, v) = d_G(u, v) \leq h$, for every
$u, v \in A \times A$;
compute routing scheme for H with parameter $k - 1$;
foreach (u, v) *that is in some tree of the routing scheme* **do**
 Let $P = \{u = v_1, \dots, v_\ell = v\}$ be a shortest path in G;
 foreach $v_i \in P \setminus \{v_\ell\}$ **do** $HT_{v_i}(u, v) \leftarrow v_{i+1}$;

---

is in $V(E(u, m^{1/k}))$. The process of computing $V(E(u, m^{1/k}))$ is initiated by u which sends a message to all its neighbors saying its distance from u is 0. The message contains also r_u, the last edge (x, y) in $E(u, m^{1/k})$ (which is stored at u) and v. Upon receiving a message from u for the first time, a vertex w sets its distance from u to be the distance in the message plus 1. If either $d(u, w) < r_u$ or $d(u, w) = r_u$ and $id(w) < id(x)$, then w sends the message with its distance to all its neighbors. If $id(w) = id(x)$, then w sends the message with its distance only to those neighbors w' of w that satisfy $id(w') \leq id(y)$. If $d(u, w) = r_u$ and $id(w) > id(x)$ or $d(u, w) > r_u$ then w does not send any message. During this process if v is found then a connection between u and v is established on a shortest path. We pay for this process by adding the additive term $O(m^{1/k})$ to the bound on the total length of the routing path. Notice that, in contrast to the situation in the centralized model, we cannot obtain the set $V(E(v, m^{1/k}))$, thus we cannot check for an intersection. As we shall see later in Lemma 2, this only affects the multiplicative stretch of the routing scheme by a constant factor.

Consider the case that $v \notin V(E(u, m^{1/k}))$. Let $u' = p_A(u)$ and $v' = p_A(v)$. Notice that u' is stored at u and v' is part of the label of v. The message is sent from u to u' using the tree routing scheme of $T(u')$. Then, from u' to v', the message is sent using the routing scheme of the graph H. Finally, from v' to v the message is sent using the tree routing scheme of $T(v')$. The routing scheme of H produces a routing path from u' to v' with edges of H. Let (x, y) be an edge of H and assume that the message should be sent from x to y on the way to v' by the routing scheme of H. Thus, there is a shortest path $P = \{x = x_1, x_2, \dots, x_\ell = y\}$ in G that corresponds to (x, y) with at most h edges (recall that h is a parameter to be fixed later). Our routing algorithm will send the message over the path P starting from x and towards y as a temporary target. At x_i the next edge on the shortest path to y is obtained from $HT_{x_i}(x, y)$. When the message reaches

y, we use the routing scheme of H to obtain the next virtual edge to route on, until v' is reached.

Lemma 2. *Let $k > 2$ be an integer. The routing scheme described above uses $\tilde{O}(mh)$ space. It routes a message from a source u to a destination v, at distance Δ from u, over a path of length at most $(16k - 33)\Delta + O(m^{1/k})$. The header size is poly-logarithmic.*

Proof. The graph H has $\tilde{O}(m^{1-1/k})$ vertices, thus, the space required for the routing scheme of H with parameter $k - 1$ is $\tilde{O}(m^{(1-1/k)(1+1/(k-1))}) = \tilde{O}(m)$. This means that the number of edges of H that participate in the routing scheme is $\tilde{O}(m)$. Each such edge has a corresponding shortest path with at most h edges in G. Thus, the total cost for storing the information needed for routing between endpoints of virtual edges is $\tilde{O}(mh)$. It is argued above that the query phase generates $O(m^{1/k})$ messages which are reflected in the additive stretch, thus it is only left to show that the multiplicative stretch is $16k - 33$. We bound first the distance between $p_A(u) = u'$ and $p_A(v) = v'$. Since $v \notin V(E(u, m^{1/k}))$ it follows that $d(u, u') \leq d(u, v)$. Also, since v' is the closest vertex to v from A it follows that $d(v, v') \leq d(u, v) + d(u, u') \leq 2d(u, v)$ and that $d(u', v') \leq 4d(u, v)$. Recall that for any $k > 1$, the routing scheme Thorup and Zwick has stretch of $4k - 5$. Thus, the length of the routing path is bounded by $d(u, u') + (4(k - 1) - 5)d(u', v') + d(v, v')$, which is at most $d(u, v) + (4(k - 1) - 5)4d(u, v) + 2d(u, v) = (16k - 33)d(u, v)$, and the stretch is $16k - 33$. At any stage the header includes only the label of v and possibly the current endpoint of a virtual edge that the message is headed to, all of poly-logarithmic size.   □

4.2   Virtual Edges with Unbounded Weight

We now show how to deal with the case that the edges of H have an unbounded weight. We use a very nice observation of Bernstein [6], which is based on the following lemma of Thorup and Zwick:

Lemma 3 ([21]). *Let $G = (V, E)$ be an unweighted undirected graph. Let $G' = \cup_{w \in V} T_C(w)$ be the union of the clusters tree of [20] distance oracle with parameter k'. For every $u, v \in V$ there is a path in G' of length at most $(1+\varepsilon)d(u, v) + O((1/\varepsilon)^{k'})$.*

Bernstein [6] extended the above lemma and showed that there is a path $\hat{P}(x, y)$ between x and y in G' with stretch $(1 + \varepsilon)$, that can be characterized using a set $N(x, y)$ of $\tilde{O}(k' \cdot s)$ special vertices from $\hat{P}(x, y)$, where $s = (4/\varepsilon)^{k'}$.

Let $x, y \in V$ and let $c \leq d(x, y)$, where $c = \Theta((1/\varepsilon)^{k'})$ [2]. We consider distance oracle with parameter k' [3] as defined in Lemma 3, and show how to construct

---

[2] We require a lower bound on the distance between x and y to neglect the additive factor of the stretch in Lemma 3, so we have a $1 + \varepsilon$ multiplicative stretch.

[3] Note we use here the following standard notations $C(\cdot)$, $T_C(\cdot)$ and $p_i(\cdot)$, as defined in the preliminaries, with respect to the distance oracle of Lemma 3.

$\hat{P}(x,y)$ and its corresponding set $N(x,y)$. Let $P(x,y) = \{x = x_0, x_1, \ldots, x_t = y\}$ be a shortest path between x and y in G. Let $r = \lfloor d(x,y)/s \rfloor$. The path $\hat{P}(x,y)$ and the set $N(x,y)$ are constructed as follows. The path $P(x,y)$ is divided into at most $s+1$ intervals each of size at least r. Consider the first interval. Let $r(1)$ be the index such that $x_{r(1)-1}$ is the furthest vertex on $P(x,y)$ that is still in $C(x)$. The path $\hat{P}(x,y)$ goes from x to $x_{r(1)-1}$ on $T_C(x)$ and then uses the edge $(x_{r(1)-1}, x_{r(1)})$. The vertices $x_{r(1)-1}$ and $x_{r(1)}$ are added to the set $N(x,y)$. Assume $r(1) \leq r$ now let $x_{r(2)-1}$ be the furthest vertex on $P(x,y)$ that is still in $C(p_1(x_{r(1)}))$. The path $\hat{P}(x,y)$ goes from $x_{r(1)}$ to $x_{r(2)-1}$ on $T_C(p_1(x_{r(1)}))$ and then uses the edge $(x_{r(2)-1}, x_{r(2)})$. The vertices $x_{r(2)-1}$ and $x_{r(2)}$ are added to the set $N(x,y)$. The path $\hat{P}(x,y)$ goes from $x_{r(2)}$ to $x_{r(3)-1}$ on $T_C(p_2(x_{r(2)}))$ and then uses the edge $(x_{r(3)-1}, x_{r(3)})$. We stop this process when we reach $x_{r(i)}$ such that $r(i) > r$ and pass to the vertex $x_{r(i)}$ in the beginning of the next interval. We repeat this process for each interval until we reach an interval that contains y.

Bernstein [6] showed that for each interval we add $\tilde{O}(k')$ vertices to $N(x,y)$, so the total size of $N(x,y)$ is $\tilde{O}(k' \cdot s)$. He also showed that the length of $\hat{P}(x,y)$ has a multiplicative stretch of $1 + \varepsilon$ in the length of $P(x,y)$. Notice that given the set $N(x,y)$ and G' it is possible to construct the path $\hat{P}(x,y)$.

In the preprocessing we also compute a union of clusters G' of Thorup and Zwick distance oracle with parameter $k' = \sqrt{\log n / \log(4/\varepsilon)} = O(\sqrt{\log n})$ on G. For each of these clusters we compute a tree routing scheme. The size of the union of these clusters together with the tree routing schemes is $O(n^{1+O(1/\sqrt{\log n})})$.

Consider an edge (x,y) of H that is part of the compact routing scheme of H. If the weight of (x,y) is at most $c = \Theta(n^{(1/\sqrt{\log n})})$ we treat it in the same manner as before. If the weight is larger than c we construct the set $N(x,y)$. The size of $N(x,y)$ is $\tilde{O}(sk') = O(n^{O(1/\sqrt{\log n})})$.

Let $\hat{P}(x,y)$ be the $(1 + \varepsilon)$ path that corresponds to the set $N(x,y) = \{x = x_1, x_2, \ldots, x_\ell = y\} \subset \hat{P}(x,y)$. We will use the set $N(x,y)$ to send the message from x to y on $\hat{P}(x,y)$. By the way $N(x,y)$ was constructed it follows that for every two consecutive vertices $x_i, x_{i+1} \in N(x,y)$ either $(x_i, x_{i+1}) \in E$ or there is a vertex w such that $x_i, x_{i+1} \in C(w)$. A vertex $x_i \in N(x,y)$ saves in $HT_{x_i}(x,y)$ the vertex x_{i+1}, and if $(x_i, x_{i+1}) \notin E$ then also the vertex w and the label of x_{i+1} in the tree routing scheme of $T_C(w)$. There are $\tilde{O}(m)$ virtual edges. Each virtual edge with weight larger than c has $O(n^{O(1/\sqrt{\log n})})$ vertices in its special set. We add information to $HT_{x_i}(x,y)$ only if $x_i \in N(x,y)$ and (x,y) is a virtual edge of weight larger than c, therefore, the total additional space required is $\tilde{O}(mn^{O(1/\sqrt{\log n})})$.

The routing of a message from x to y is relativity straightforward using this additional information . Let vertex x' be the vertex that is saved at $HT_x(x,y)$. If there is an edge (x,x') in G we send the message from x to x' using this edge. If there is no such an edge then a vertex w is saved at $HT_x(x,y)$ together with the label of x' in the tree routing scheme of $T_C(w)$. We route to x' using the tree routing scheme of $T_C(w)$. At x' we continue in the same manner until we reach y. Since the weight of (x,y) is at least c, the message is routed from x to y on a path of length at most $(1 + \varepsilon)d(x,y)$.

From the above discussion and from Lemma 2 we conclude the following theorem:

Theorem 2. *Let $k > 2$ be an integer and $\varepsilon > 0$. There is a routing scheme that uses $\tilde{O}(mn^{O(1/\sqrt{\log n})})$ total space and poly-logarithmic headers, that given a source s and a destination t at distance Δ from s, routes a message from s to t on a path of length at most $(1 + \varepsilon)(16k - 33)\Delta + O(m^{1/k})$.*

5 A Routing Scheme with a Worst-Case Bound on the Routing Tables

In the routing scheme of Section 4 vertices may store an arbitrarily large portion of the routing information. In this section we present a routing scheme with a non-standard header size of $\tilde{O}(n^{O(1/\sqrt{\log n})})$. However, every vertex $v \in V$ stores routing information of size $\tilde{O}(kn^{O(1/\sqrt{\log n})}deg(v))$.

The following theorem summarize the properties of our new routing scheme.

Theorem 3. *Given an unweighed undirected graph, a source s and a destination t at distance Δ from s, we route from s to t on a path of length at most $O(k\Delta + m^{1/k})$ with header size of $\tilde{O}(n^{O(1/\sqrt{\log n})})$. Every $v \in V$ saves routing information of size $\tilde{O}(kn^{O(1/\sqrt{\log n})}deg(v))$.*

Proof. In the routing scheme of Section 4 we have the following types of data stored at every $v \in V$:

Type-1: Every $v \in V$ participates in the tree routing scheme of the tree rooted at $p_A(v)$. The cost per vertex is poly-logarithmic.

Type-2: Every $v \in V$ participates in tree routing schemes for clusters of a Thorup and Zwick distance oracle for G with parameter $\sqrt{\log n / \log(4/\varepsilon)} = O(\sqrt{\log n})$. The cost per vertex is $O(n^{O(1/\sqrt{\log n})})$.

Type-3: Every $v \in A$ participates in tree routing schemes for clusters of Thorup and Zwick distance oracle for H with parameter $k - 1$. The cost per vertex is $\tilde{O}(km^{1/k})$.

Type-4: Every $v \in V$ that is part of the shortest path that corresponds to a small virtual edge or in the special set of a large virtual edge has an entry in HT_v for that edge.

In every $v \in V$ the cost for storing data of types 1 and 2 is less than our desired bounded of $\tilde{O}(kn^{O(1/\sqrt{\log n})}deg(v))$. The problem is with the cost for storing data of types 3 and 4. In the new routing scheme we will divide the data of these types among several vertices.

We route a message from source s to destination t as follows. At s we check if $t \in V(E(s, m^{1/k}))$, and if it is we send the message on a shortest path to t. If $t \notin V(E(s, m^{1/k}))$ then we route the message from s to $p_A(s)$ using the tree routing scheme of $p_A(s)$, and from $p_A(t)$ to t using the tree routing scheme of $p_A(t)$. In our new routing scheme the routing from $p_A(s)$ to $p_A(t)$ is done in a new way to avoid the cost of storing data of types 3 and 4.

In the routing scheme presented in Section 4 routing between vertices $s, t \in A$ is done using the scheme of [19] as follows[4]. At s we have a list of every $w \in A$ such that $s \in C(w)$[5] with the label of s in the tree routing scheme of $T_C(w)$. The label of t contains the vertices $p_0(t), \ldots, p_{k-1}(t)$ and the label of t in the tree routing schemes of $T_C(p_j(t))$, for every $0 \leq j \leq k-1$. We look for the minimal j for which $s \in C(p_j(t))$ and route from s to t using the tree routing scheme of $T_C(p_j(t))$. The edges of $T_C(p_j(t))$ are virtual edges, hence, to actually route over G we also have to translate virtual edges as described in Section 4.

The graph H is a clique therefore for every $s \in C(w)$ there is a virtual edge between s and w in H. In s we store the translation information for every edge (s, w) such that $s \in C(w)$. If $d(s, w) \leq c$ we save the exact shortest path in G that corresponds to (s, w) and if $d(s, w) > c$ then we save the set $N(s, w)$. The size of the data saved at s is $\tilde{O}(km^{1/k}n^{O(1/\sqrt{\log n})})$ since s is in at most $\tilde{O}(km^{1/k})$ clusters and the shortest path or the special set that corresponds to (s, w) is of size $O(n^{O(1/\sqrt{\log n})})$. Using this information we can route from s to $p_j(t)$, where j is the minimal index for which $s \in C(p_j(t))$. Note that the routing table of s is of size $\tilde{O}(km^{1/k}n^{O(1/\sqrt{\log n})})$ which is still too high. We will show how to handle it later. Now, we still need to show how to route from $p_j(t)$ to t.

Next, we prove an important property for the virtual edges between w and t when $t \in C(w)$ and also $p_j(t) = w$, for some $j \in [0, k-1]$.

Lemma 4. *Let $t, t' \in A$ and let $w, w' \in A_j$ (recall that A_j is a set in the sampling sets of the distance oracle) such that $w = p_j(t)$, $w' = p_j(t')$ and $j \in [0, k-1]$. Let P and P' be the shortest paths in G that correspond to (w, t) and (w', t'), respectively. The paths P and P' are vertex disjoint.*

Proof. Assume on the contrary that $P \cap P' \neq \emptyset$ and let $z \in P \cap P'$. Assume, $id(w) < id(w')$ and $d(z, w) \leq d(z, w')$[6]. This implies that $d(t', z) + d(z, w) \leq d(t', z) + d(z, w')$. Since z is on shortest paths between t' and w' and between t' and w it follows that $d(t', w) \leq d(t', w')$. But then we reach to a contradiction since $w' = p_j(t')$ which means that either $d(t', w') < d(t', w)$ or $d(t', w') = d(t', w)$ and $id(w') < id(w)$. $\square$

Let $j \in [0, k-1]$, and let $A_j = \{w_1, w_2, \ldots, w_\ell\}$. For $w \in A_j$, let $R(w) = \{v \in V \mid \exists t \text{ s.t. } p_j(t) = w, d(w, v) + d(v, t) = d(w, t)\}$.

From Lemma 4 it follows that $R(w) \cap R(w') = \emptyset$, for every $w, w' \in A_j$. Moreover, if $v \in V$ belongs to $R(w)$ then there is a shortest path between v and w in G such that every vertex on this path is also in $R(w)$. Therefore, for every $w \in A_j$ we can use the set $R(w)$ to define a shortest path tree $T_R(w)$ that is rooted at w and spans $R(w)$. For every $T_R(w)$ we compute a tree routing scheme. The total storage required from a vertex $v \in V$ to all these trees is $O(k)$.

---

[4] For simplicity we use their stretch $(4k-3)$-routing scheme and not the $(4k-5)$-routing scheme.

[5] Since this proof only considers the distance oracle for H and in order to keep a clean presentation of this proof, we avoid extra notation for the distance oracle for H. e.g. we use here $C(w)$ and not $C^H(w)$, A_i and not A_i^H, etc.

[6] Notice that case that $d(z, w) > d(z, w')$ is identical.

Given a pair $s, t \in A$ we route from s to t as follows. We look for the minimal index j for which $s \in C(p_j(t))$ and route from s to $p_j(t)$ using the virtual edge and its translation information that is saved at s. We add this information to the header of the message. Then, at every intermediate vertex we route to the next vertex on the routing path using the path information saved at the header. In case that the message has to be sent between two special vertices we use the same mechanism as in Section 4. When the message reaches $p_j(t)$ we use the tree routing scheme of $T_R(p_j(t))$ to route from $p_j(t)$ to t.

By doing so we avoid the cost of storing data of type 4. The cost of storing data of type 3 at vertices of A is increased to $\tilde{O}(km^{1/k}n^{O(1/\sqrt{\log n})})$. Next, we show how to modify the preprocessing such that this data is distributed among the vertices of G. We then show how to route messages between vertices of A using the distributed information.

We will have the following greedy process over the vertices of A. Let $F = A$. For every $v \in F$, compute $E(v, m^{1/k})$ and pick the vertex v with minimal r_v. Remove v from F and mark it. Remove from F every vertex u such that $V(E(v, m^{1/k})) \cap V(E(u, m^{1/k})) \neq \emptyset$. These vertices are *not* marked. Store at every such u the translation information of the virtual edge (u, v). We repeat on this process by keep on picking a vertex of minimal radius from F, until F gets empty. We denote by D all the vertices that were marked during this process.

For every $u \in A \setminus D$ we do not store any data of type 3. The data of type 3 of every $v \in D$ is of size $\tilde{O}(km^{1/k}n^{O(1/\sqrt{\log n})})$. We distribute this data among the vertices of $V(E(v, m^{1/k}))$, such that every vertex of v will get a portion of the data that is proportional to its degree. From the way D was created it follows that for every $u \in V$ there is at most one vertex $v \in D$ such that $u \in V(E(v, m^{1/k}))$. Thus, every $u \in V$ cannot get a data of type 3 from two different vertices of D.

Now given a pair $s, t \in A$, the routing from s to t works as follows. If $s \in D$, then at a cost of $O(m^{1/k})$ messages we query the vertices of $V(E(s, m^{1/k}))$ for the minimal index j such that $s \in C(p_j(t))$. The data that is needed to route from s to $p_j(t)$ is sent from the vertex of $V(E(s, m^{1/k}))$ that contains it to s. This data is added to the header of the message as before, and the message is routed to $p_j(t)$ using it. Routing from $p_j(t)$ to t is done using the tree routing scheme of $T_R(p_j(t))$.

Consider now the case that $s \notin D$. In this case, s first computes $V(E(s, m^{1/k}))$ and check if $t \in V(E(s, m^{1/k}))$. If it is, then the routing is done using a shortest path. If it is not, then since $s \notin D$ there is a vertex $s' \in D$ such that $V(E(s, m^{1/k})) \cap V(E(s', m^{1/k})) \neq \emptyset$ and $r_{s'} \leq r_s$. We stored at s the data needed to translate the virtual edge (s, s'). We add this data to the header and route to s'. The length of the shortest path between s and s' is at most $2r_s$ and since $d(s, t) \geq r_s$ we get that $d(s, s') \leq 2d(s, t)$. The virtual edge is translated to a path of length at most $(1 + \varepsilon)d(s, s')$. The message is sent from s to s' on a path of length at most $(1 + \varepsilon)2d(s, t)$ and from s' to t on a path of length at most $(4(k - 1) - 3)(d(s, t) + d(s, s'))$. Thus, the total length of the path from s to t is $O(k)d(s, t)$.

References

1. Abraham, I., Gavoille, C.: On approximate distance labels and routing schemes with affine stretch. In: Peleg, D. (ed.) DISC 2011. LNCS, vol. 6950, pp. 404–415. Springer, Heidelberg (2011)
2. Agarwal, R., Godfrey, B., Har-Peled, S.: Faster approximate distance queries and compact routing in sparse graphs. CoRR abs/1201.2703 (2012)
3. Agarwal, R., Godfrey, P.B.: Distance oracles for stretch less than 2. In: SODA, pp. 526–538 (2013)
4. Awerbuch, B., Bar-Noy, A., Linial, N., Peleg, D.: Improved routing strategies with succinct tables. J. Algorithms 11(3), 307–341 (1990)
5. Awerbuch, B., Peleg, D.: Routing with polynomial communication-space trade-off. SIAM J. Discrete Math. 5(2), 151–162 (1992)
6. Bernstein, A.: Fully dynamic (2 + epsilon) approximate all-pairs shortest paths with fast query and close to linear update time. In: FOCS, pp. 693–702. IEEE Computer Society (2009)
7. Chechik, S.: Compact routing schemes with improved stretch. In: Fatourou, P., Taubenfeld, G. (eds.) PODC, pp. 33–41. ACM (2013)
8. Chechik, S.: Approximate distance oracles with constant query time. In: STOC (2014)
9. Cowen, L.: Compact routing with minimum stretch. In: Tarjan, R.E., Warnow, T. (eds.) SODA, pp. 255–260. ACM/SIAM (1999)
10. Dor, D., Halperin, S., Zwick, U.: All-pairs almost shortest paths. SIAM J. Comput. 29(5), 1740–1759 (2000)
11. Eilam, T., Gavoille, C., Peleg, D.: Compact routing schemes with low stretch factor (extended abstract). In: Coan, B.A., Afek, Y. (eds.) PODC, pp. 11–20. ACM (1998)
12. Fraigniaud, P., Gavoille, C.: Routing in trees. In: Orejas, F., Spirakis, P.G., van Leeuwen, J. (eds.) ICALP 2001. LNCS, vol. 2076, pp. 757–772. Springer, Heidelberg (2001)
13. Patrascu, M., Roditty, L.: Distance oracles beyond the thorup-zwick bound. In: FOCS, pp. 815–823. IEEE Computer Society (2010)
14. Patrascu, M., Roditty, L., Thorup, M.: A new infinity of distance oracles for sparse graphs. In: FOCS, pp. 738–747 (2012)
15. Peleg, D.: Distributed Computing: A Locality-sensitive Approach. Society for Industrial and Applied Mathematics, Philadelphia (2000)
16. Peleg, D., Upfal, E.: A trade-off between space and efficiency for routing tables. J. ACM 36(3), 510–530 (1989)
17. Porat, E., Roditty, L.: Preprocess, set, query! In: Demetrescu, C., Halldórsson, M.M. (eds.) ESA 2011. LNCS, vol. 6942, pp. 603–614. Springer, Heidelberg (2011)
18. Sommer, C., Verbin, E., Yu, W.: Distance oracles for sparse graphs, pp. 703–712 (2009)
19. Thorup, M., Zwick, U.: Compact routing schemes. In: SPAA, pp. 1–10 (2001)
20. Thorup, M., Zwick, U.: Approximate distance oracles. J. ACM 52(1), 1–24 (2005)
21. Thorup, M., Zwick, U.: Spanners and emulators with sublinear distance errors. In: SODA, pp. 802–809. ACM Press (2006)
22. Wulff-Nilsen, C.: Approximate distance oracles with improved preprocessing time. In: SODA, pp. 202–208 (2012)
23. Wulff-Nilsen, C.: Approximate distance oracles with improved query time. In: Khanna, S. (ed.) SODA, pp. 539–549. SIAM (2013)

Near-Optimal Distributed Tree Embedding[*]

Mohsen Ghaffari[1] and Christoph Lenzen[2]

[1] Massachusetts Institute of Technology
ghaffari@csail.mit.edu
[2] MPI for Informatics
Campus E1 4, 66123 Saarbrücken
clenzen@mpi-inf.mpg.de

Abstract. *Tree embeddings* are a powerful tool in the area of graph approximation algorithms. Essentially, they transform problems on general graphs into much easier ones on trees. Fakcharoenphol, Rao, and Talwar (FRT) [STOC'04] present a probabilistic tree embedding that transforms n-node metrics into (probability distributions over) trees, while *stretching* each pairwise distance by at most an $O(\log n)$ factor in expectation. This $O(\log n)$ stretch is optimal.

Khan et al. [PODC'08] present a distributed algorithm that implements FRT in $O(\text{SPD} \log n)$ rounds, where SPD is the *shortest-path-diameter* of the weighted graph, and they explain how to use this embedding for various distributed approximation problems. Note that SPD can be as large as $\Theta(n)$, even in graphs where the hop-diameter D is a constant. Khan et al. noted that it would be interesting to improve this complexity. We show that this is indeed possible.

More precisely, we present a distributed algorithm that constructs a tree embedding that is essentially as good as FRT in $\tilde{O}(\min\{n^{0.5+\varepsilon}, \text{SPD}\}+D)$ rounds, for any constant $\varepsilon > 0$. A lower bound of $\tilde{\Omega}(\min\{n^{0.5}, \text{SPD}\} + D)$ rounds follows from Das Sarma et al. [STOC'11], rendering our round complexity near-optimal.

1 Introduction and Related Work

Metric embeddings are a versatile technique in centralized approximation algorithms. Given an arbitrary metric space on n points—i.e., a weighted graph on n nodes with distances being the metric—metric embeddings transform it into a "nicer" metric space while incurring only a small *distortion*. A basic example is Bourgain's theorem [5], which shows that it is possible to embed into ℓ_2 with $O(\log n)$ distortion. The general approach for using metric embeddings in approximation algorithms is as follows: (1) using the embedding, transform the given problem instance to one in a more convenient metric space (i.e., nicer graph); (2) solve the simpler problem; (3) transform the solution back to one of the original instance. See [14, 18] for surveys.

Tree embeddings are a particularly useful branch of metric embeddings, which "transform" general graphs into trees. This is especially attractive, because finding solutions

---

[*] This work was supported by AFOSR contract number FA9550-13-1-0042, NSF award 0939370-CCF, NSF award CCF-1217506, NSF award CCF-AF-0937274, and DFG funding Le 3107/1-1. The first author is also thankful for the support of Simons Award for graduate students in Theoretical Computer Science (number 31872).

F. Kuhn (Ed.): DISC 2014, LNCS 8784, pp. 197–211, 2014.

on trees is often quite easy, if not trivial. Not surprisingly, the approach has a caveat: one cannot hope for a small distortion when (deterministically) embedding into a tree; for example, transforming an n-node cycle to any tree will incur an $\Omega(n)$ distortion on at least one edge. But not all the hope is lost, as there is still the option of embedding probabilistically. Indeed, a beautiful line of work [1–3,9] shows this to be feasible, obtaining successively better distortions, and ending with the algorithm of Fakcharoenphol, Rao, and Talwar (FRT) [9], which achieves $O(\log n)$ distortion. More precisely, the FRT algorithm maps any n-point metric into a tree drawn from a certain probability distribution so that each pairwise distance is *stretched* by a factor $O(\log n)$ in expectation. The trees in the support of this distribution have some further desirable properties, which make them even more helpful in many applications, e.g., they are *hierarchically separated trees* [9]. This $O(\log n)$ distortion is existentially optimal, as demonstrated by graph families such as expander graphs and diamond graphs [3].

The fact that graph problems are often easier on trees is not particular to centralized algorithms. Hence, it is natural to expect that *tree embeddings* should be helpful in distributed algorithms as well. Actualizing this intuition, Khan et al. [15] showed how to implement FRT distributedly and use it to get distributed approximation algorithms for a number of graph problems. The distributed tree embedding of Khan et al. works in $O(\mathrm{SPD}\log n)$ rounds of the CONGEST model, where SPD denotes the *shortest-path-diameter*. CONGEST is the standard model for distributed computation, in which each node can send one B-bit size message per round to each of its neighbors; typically, $B = O(\log n)$. The *shortest-path-diameter* SPD is the minimum integer $h \in \mathbb{N}^+$ such that for any pair of nodes v and u, there is a least-weight path between v and u that has at most h hops. Note that SPD can be much larger than the hop diameter D, up to factor $\Theta(n)$; see, e.g., Figure 1.

Khan et al. noted that it would be interesting to improve the round complexity. This is particularly intriguing in light of the developments in the general area of distributed approximation algorithms. On the lower bound side, an elegant sequence of papers [7, 8, 21] show $\tilde{\Omega}(D + \sqrt{n})$ rounds to be necessary for a wide range of (approximation) problems, including those for which tree embeddings can be useful. Here, D is the hop diameter of the network graph. On the upper bound side, in the last couple of years approximation algorithms with round complexity $\tilde{O}(D + \sqrt{n})$, or close to it, have been developed for a number of different graph problems [11–13,16,17,19]. Consequently, it is intriguing to ask

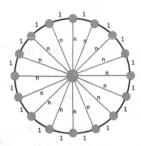

Fig. 1. An example where $D = 2$ and SPD $\approx n/2$. Numbers on edges show their weights.

"Is there an $\tilde{O}(D + \sqrt{n})$-round tree embedding algorithm?"

We consider answering this question important as a positive result would add tree embeddings to the set of our $\tilde{O}(D + \sqrt{n})$-round tools and extend the range of problems in the $\tilde{O}(D + \sqrt{n})$-round category to those which can be solved via tree embedding.

1.1 Our Contribution

We show that there is a distributed algorithm that provides a probabilistic tree embedding that is essentially as good as FRT—i.e., with only a constant factor larger stretch— in almost $\tilde{O}(D + \sqrt{n})$ rounds.

> **Theorem 1 (INFORMAL).** *For any $\varepsilon > 0$, a probabilistic tree embedding with expected stretch of $O(\log n / \varepsilon)$ can be computed in $\tilde{O}(\min\{n^{0.5+\varepsilon}, \text{SPD}\} + D)$ rounds of the* **CONGEST** *model.*

The formal version specifying how the embedding is represented distributedly is presented in Theorem 22. As mentioned, this result is near-optimal in both stretch and round complexity: the former must be $\Omega(\log n)$ [3], and we show in the full version of this paper that [7] yields that the latter must be $\tilde{\Omega}(\min\{\sqrt{n}, \text{SPD}\} + D)$.

1.2 Overview

Here, we explain the key ideas of our construction. For brevity, the description of FRT is deferred to Section 3.

FRT = Least Elements (LE) Lists: Given a weighted graph $G = (V, E, W)$, computing FRT's probabilistic tree embedding of G boils down to the following: (1) choose a permutation π of V uniformly at random; (2) for each node $v \in V$ and each distance d, find the node w within distance d of v that appears first in the permutation π. For each node v, this generates a list of nodes with one entry for each distance d. Note that the π-indices of the nodes in the list are decreasing as a function of d. The list can be compressed by only keeping the entry

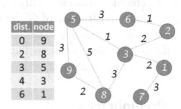

Fig. 2. The LE list for node 9. Nodes are labeled randomly, edges by their weights.

with the minimum distance d for each node w in the list. The compressed lists are called Least Elements (LE) lists [6]. See Figure 2 for an example.

Distributed LE-list Computation: Khan et al. [15] present a neat method for computing LE lists distributedly. Their algorithm runs in iterations; in each iteration, each node sends its whole current (compressed) list to its neighbors. Initially, each list contains only the node itself at distance 0. In each round, each node updates its lists using the received ones and the distances from the sending neighbors. After at most SPD iterations, we get the correct LE lists. A key observation of [15] is that, due to the random order π, in each iteration, each list will contain at most $O(\log n)$ entries, with high probability (w.h.p.). Thus, each of the at most SPD iterations can be performed in $O(\log n)$ rounds, which translates to a total of $O(\text{SPD} \log n)$ rounds.

A Strawman Idea: LE lists can be determined easily if we have all-to-all distances. Since we know how to get a multiplicative approximation of all-to-all distances in time close to $\tilde{O}(D + \sqrt{n})$ [16], a natural idea is to use these approximates to construct an

FRT-like embedding. However, this idea does not go far, mainly because multiplicative approximates do not satisfy (any approximation of) the triangle inequality.

Our Approach In a Nutshell: We construct a *virtual* graph G' whose distances approximate those of G and has shortest-path diameter $S_{G'}$ at most $\tilde{O}(\sqrt{n})$. Note that distances in a graph always satisfy the triangle inequality, which enables us to apply the FRT construction. However, since G' is a virtual graph, we cannot readily use the algorithm by Khan et al. [15] to achieve a time complexity of $\tilde{O}(S_{G'}) = \tilde{O}(\sqrt{n})$.

We resolve this by entangling the construction of G' with the computation of LE lists. More concretely, we pick the first $\Theta(\sqrt{n})$ nodes in the random order π of FRT, call them S, and find factor $\varrho = O(1/\varepsilon)$ approximations of distances among nodes of S. This part uses the spanner construction of Baswana and Sen [4] and its adaptation in [16]. We set the G'-distances among S equal to these approximations by adding direct virtual edges of the corresponding weight, while the original edges of G are added to G' with weight raised by factor ϱ. As now the approximated distances between nodes in S are *exact* G'-distances, we can directly compute the G'-LE lists of the nodes in S. Here it is crucial that the nodes in S are prioritized by π, implying that their lists will only contain nodes in S. Furthermore, for any pair of nodes for which a least-weight path has at least roughly $\sqrt{n}\log n$ hops, w.h.p. one such path has a node from S within its first $O(\sqrt{n}\log n)$ hops. Thus, it suffices to run the LE list computation, jump-started with the complete lists on S, only for $\tilde{O}(\sqrt{n})$ iterations. The fact that we have entangled the (random) construction of G' with the (random) permutation π of FRT creates some probabilistic dependency issues. However, by opening up the analysis of FRT and the LE list computation, we show that this does affect neither the stretch nor the running time by more than factor 2.

2   Preliminaries

Model: The network is represented by a connected, simple, and weighted graph $G = (V, E, W)$ of $n := |V|$ nodes, with edge weights $W : E \to \mathbb{N}$ bounded polynomially in n. Initially each node knows the weights of its incident edges. We use the CONGEST model [20]: communication occurs in synchronous rounds, where in each round $B = O(\log n)$ bits can be sent in each direction of each edge.

Each node independently picks an $O(\log n)$-bit *identifier* (*ID* in short), uniformly at random. These are the identifiers that we will use in the remainder of the paper. We use random IDs because they readily give us a uniformly random ordering π of the nodes. We use notation $v < w$ to mean that the random ID of node v is smaller than that of node w. It is easy to see that, with high probability, the random ID picked by each node is unique, and we assume throughout the paper that this holds true. Here, we use the phrase "with high probability" (w.h.p.) to indicate that an event occurs with probability at least $1 - 1/n^c$, for an arbitrary constant $c > 0$ fixed in advance.

Graph-Theoretic Notations:
- For a node v, denote the set of its neighbors by $\mathcal{N}(v)$.
- For a path $p = (v_0, \ldots, v_h)$, define its length $\ell(p) := h$ and its weight $W(p) := \sum_{i=1}^{h} W(v_{i-1}, v_i)$.

- For $v, w \in V$, denote by P_{vw} the set of all paths starting at v and ending at w.
- The hop distance of $v, w \in V$ is defined as $\mathrm{hd}(v, w) := \min_{p \in P_{vw}}\{\ell(p)\}$.
- The (hop) diameter of G is $D := \max_{v,w \in V}\{\mathrm{hd}(v, w)\}$.
- The (weighted) distance of $v, w \in V$ is given by $\mathrm{wd}(v, w) := \min_{p \in P_{vw}}\{W(p)\}$.
- The weighted diameter of G is $\mathrm{WD} := \max_{v,w \in V}\{\mathrm{wd}(v, w)\}$.
- The shortest-path diameter of G is $\mathrm{SPD} := \max_{v,w \in V}\{\min\{\ell(p)|\ p \in P_{vw} \wedge W(p) = \mathrm{wd}(v, w)\}\}$.

For brevity, we use the conventions that "diameter" denotes the hop diameter, but "distance" refers to *weighted* distances. When talking of graphs other than G, we subscript the above notations by the respective graph.

3   Recap: FRT, Least Element Lists, and Spanners

3.1   The FRT Probabilistic Tree Embedding

Given a weighted graph $G = (V, E, W)$, FRT randomly constructs a tree $T = (V_T, E_T, W_T)$ such that there is a mapping $\mathfrak{M}$ from V to leaves of T, and for each pair of nodes $u, v \in V$, we have

- $\mathrm{wd}(u, v) \leq \mathrm{wd}_T(\mathfrak{M}(v), \mathfrak{M}(v))$, and
- $\mathbb{E}[\mathrm{wd}_T(\mathfrak{M}(v), \mathfrak{M}(u))] \in O(\mathrm{wd}(u, v) \log n)$.

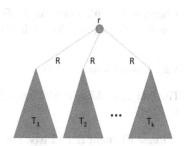

Fig. 3. FRT's recursion

FRT–An Intuitive Description: The construction can be viewed as a tree of hierarchical decompositions. The key decomposition step is as follows: Pick $R \in [\mathrm{WD}/4, \mathrm{WD}/2]$ uniformly at random. For each node w, define its (exclusive) ball

$$B(w) := \{v \in V \mid \mathrm{wd}(v, w) \leq R \wedge \forall w' \in V : \mathrm{wd}(v, w') \leq R \Rightarrow w \leq w'\}.$$

Recall from Section 2 that the notation $w \leq w'$ means w has a smaller random ID compared to w'. We recursively create a tree embedding T_i for each subgraph of G induced by a nonempty ball $B(w)$. Finally, add a root node r and connect the roots of trees T_i to r via edges of weight R.

FRT–A Formal Description: The whole structure of the FRT tree can be succinctly described as follows. Choose a uniformly random $\beta \in [1, 2)$. Denote by $L := \lceil \log \mathrm{WD} \rceil + 1$ the maximum level of the tree. For each $v \in V$ and each $i \in \{0, \ldots, L\}$, let node $v_i \in V$ minimize the ID among the set $\{w \in V \mid \mathrm{wd}(v, w) \leq \beta 2^{i-1}\}$. Note that v_i is a function[1] of v. In particular, $v_0 = v$ and $v_L = \min V$ is the first node in the order π. The node set V_T of the tree is $\{(v_i, \ldots, v_L) \mid v \in V \wedge i \in \{0, \ldots, L\}\}$. Note that each different sequence $(v_i, \ldots, v_L)$ starting with v_i denotes a distinct "copy" of $v_i \in V$. For each tree node $(v_i, \ldots, v_L)$ with $i < L$, its parent is the tree node $(v_{i+1}, \ldots, v_L)$, and the weight of the edge connecting them is $\beta 2^i$. Finally, we have $\mathfrak{M}(v) := (v_0, \ldots, v_L)$. Thus, the node set V is mapped to the leaf set of the tree. Figure 4 shows an example.

---

[1] A better notation might be $c_i(v)$, indicating that this is the level i center of node v. However, for brevity we write $v_i = c_i(v)$.

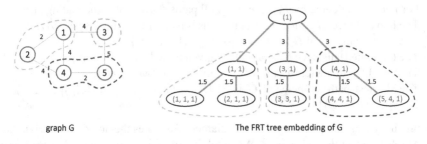

Fig. 4. A simple example of an FRT tree

The fact that, for each $v, w \in V$, $\mathrm{wd}(v, w) \leq \mathrm{wd}_T(\mathfrak{M}(v), \mathfrak{M}(w))$ can be easily verified. The main result of Fakcharoenphol, Rao, and Talwar [10] is the probabilistic upper bound.

Theorem 2 ([10], Theorem 2). *For the embedding described above, it holds for each $v, w \in V$ that $\mathbb{E}[d_T(\mathfrak{M}(v), \mathfrak{M}(w))] \in O(\log n) \cdot \mathrm{wd}(v, w)$.*

3.2   Least Element Lists

The FRT embedding can be implicitly encoded via a data structure called *Least Element lists* [6].

Least Element (LE) Lists: For each node v, its LE list is

$$L_v := \{(w, \mathrm{wd}(v, w)) \in V \times \mathbb{N}_0 \mid \nexists u \in V : (u < w \wedge \mathrm{wd}(v, u) \leq \mathrm{wd}(v, w))\}.$$

Given the LE lists, each node v can easily compute the nodes v_i, for $i \in \{1, \ldots, L\}$, from its LE list L_v. This is because, for any given distance d, node v can recover the node of smallest ID within distance d as the node w of smallest ID satisfying that $(w, \mathrm{wd}(v, w)) \in L_v$ and $\mathrm{wd}(v, w) \leq d$. Moreover, these lists allow us to determine the next hop on a least-weight path from v to v_i locally.

Observation 3. *If $(w, \mathrm{wd}(v, w)) \in L_v$ for $w \neq v$, then $u \in \mathcal{N}(v)$ exists such that $(w, \mathrm{wd}(v, w) - W(v, u)) \in L_u$. Hence, if for each $w \in V$, $w \neq v$, s.t. $(w, \mathrm{wd}(v, w)) \in L_v$ we choose $p_v(w) \in \mathcal{N}(v)$ with $(w, \mathrm{wd}(v, w) - W(v, p_v(w))) \in L_{p_v(w)}$, then the edges $(v, p_v(w))$ form a shortest-path tree rooted at w.*

3.3   Distributed Computation of Least Element Lists

Next, we explain the distributed algorithm of Khan et al. [15] for computing LE lists:

---

1. Each $v \in V$ initializes $L_v^{(0)} := \{(v,0)\})$. Set $i := 0$.
2. All nodes v do the following *iteration* in parallel:
   (a) Send $L_v^{(i)}$ to all neighbors.
   (b) Set $L_v^{(i+1)} := L_v^{(i)}$.
   (c) For all $w \in \mathcal{N}(v)$ and $(u,d) \in L_w^{(i)}$, set $L_v^{(i+1)} := L_v^{(i+1)} \cup \{(u, d + W(v,w))\}$.
   (d) Scan $L_v^{(i+1)}$ in ascending order of distances (i.e., second entries) and delete each entry for which the ID (i.e., the first entry) is not smaller than all IDs previously encountered in the scan.
   (e) Set $i := i + 1$.
   while $\exists v \in V$ so that $L_v^{(i)} \neq L_v^{(i-1)}$.
3. Each $v \in V$ returns $L_v^{(i)} = L_v$.

From the definition of LE lists, the following observations regarding this algorithm are straightforward.

Observation 4. *If $(w, \mathrm{wd}(v,w)) \in L_v$, then $(w, \mathrm{wd}(v,w))$ is not deleted from $L_v^{(i)}$ during its scan.*

Observation 5. *For $i \in \mathbb{N}_0$, suppose $(w, \mathrm{wd}(v,w)) \in L_v$ and $(w, \mathrm{wd}(u,w)) \in L_u^{(i)}$ for $u \in \mathcal{N}(v)$ on a least-weight path from v to w. Then $(w, \mathrm{wd}(v,w))) \in L_v^{(i+1)}$.*

Observations 3, 4, and 5 essentially imply the following, which is shown in the full version.

Lemma 6. *The above algorithm computes correct LE lists. It terminates after at most* SPD $+1$ *iterations.*

Remark 7. If node $v \in V$ also memorizes which neighbor sent the (first) message causing it to insert an entry into L_v, the least-weight paths indicated by the respective pointers have minimal hop count, and the trees implied by Observation 3 have minimal depth (which is bounded by SPD).

The remaining analysis boils down to showing that the lists are always short, i.e., have $O(\log n)$ entries w.h.p. We remark that our analysis fixes a technical issue with the one in [15]. However, the key idea is the same; see the full version for details.

Lemma 8 ([15], Lemma 5). *For each $v \in V$ and each $i \in \mathbb{N}_0$, $|L_v^{(i)}| \in O(\log n)$ w.h.p.*

Theorem 9. *The LE lists can be computed within $O(\mathrm{SPD} \log n)$ rounds w.h.p.*

3.4 Spanners and Skeletons

In our algorithm, we will make use of known techniques for constructing spanners and skeletons. Here, we briefly review these tools. We note that the description is adapted to best suit our application.

For $\varrho \geq 1$, a (multiplicative) ϱ-spanner of a graph $H = (V_H, E_H, W_H)$ is a graph $H_S = (V_H, E_S, W_S)$ with $E_S \subseteq E_H$, $W_S(e) = W_H(e)$ for all $e \in E_S$, and $\mathrm{wd}_{H_S}(v, w) \leq \varrho \, \mathrm{wd}_H(v, w)$ for all $v, w \in V_H$. Ideally, we want both ϱ and $|E_S|$ to be as small as possible.

We will make use of a spanner construction on a certain virtual graph. For $S \subseteq V$, the h-hop S-skeleton of G is defined as the weighted graph $G_{S,h} := (S, E_{S,h}, W_{S,h})$ with $E_{S,h} := \{\{s, t\} \in \binom{S}{2} \mid \mathrm{hd}(s, t) \leq h\}$ and $W_{S,h}(s, t) := \min\{W(p) \mid p \in P_{st} \wedge \ell(p) \leq h\}$ for each $\{s, t\} \in E_{S,h}$. In words, the graph has node set S and $\{s, t\}$ is an edge iff s and t are in hop distance at most h; the weight of this edge then is the minimum weight of an s-t path of at most h hops.

For the purposes of this paper, we consider the special case that each node is sampled into S independently with probability $1/\sqrt{n}$ and that $h := c\sqrt{n} \log n$ for a sufficiently large constant c. In this case, the skeleton preserves weighted distances.

Lemma 10 ([16], Lemma 4.6). *If nodes are sampled into S with independent probability $1/\sqrt{n}$ and $h := c\sqrt{n} \log n$ for a sufficiently large constant c, then $\mathrm{wd}_{G_{S,h}}(s, t) = \mathrm{wd}(s, t)$ for all $s, t \in S$ w.h.p.*

The hop-distance h up to which we need to explore paths in G to "find" the edges in $E_{G_{S,h}}$ is in $\tilde{O}(\sqrt{n})$. Furthermore, because $|S| \in \tilde{O}(\sqrt{n})$, $G_{S,h}$ can be encoded using $\tilde{O}(n)$ bits. We can further reduce this to $\tilde{O}(n^{0.5+\varepsilon})$ bits by constructing a spanner of $G_{S,h}$, sacrificing a factor of $O(1/\varepsilon)$ in the accuracy of the distances.

Theorem 11 ([16], Theorem 4.10). *Suppose nodes are sampled into S independently with probability $1/\sqrt{n}$ and $h := c\sqrt{n} \log n$ for a sufficiently large constant c. Then, for any $k \in \mathbb{N}$, w.h.p. a $(2k - 1)$-spanner of $G_{S,h}$ can be computed and made known to all nodes in $\tilde{O}(n^{1/2+1/(2k)} + D)$ rounds. Furthermore, for each $s, t \in S$, there is a unique $p \in P_{st}$ of weight $W(p) \leq (2k - 1) \, \mathrm{wd}(s, t)$ so that each node on p knows that it is on p as well as which of its neighbors is the next node on p (as a function of the ID of t).*

This is achieved by simulating the Baswana-Sen spanner construction [4] on $G_{S,h}$ using a truncated version of the multi-source Bellman-Ford algorithm. For details and proofs we refer to [16].

4   Fast Distributed Tree Embedding

In this section, we explain our algorithm. We first give an intuitive explanation of what our key ideas are. Then, we present the algorithm and its correctness, running time, and approximation analysis.

4.1   Key Ideas

When computing LE lists according to the algorithm by Khan et al. [15], information spreads along least-weight paths. For most of the nodes, however, the induced shortest-path trees (cp. Observation 3) will be fairly shallow: Let S be the set of nodes which their ID is in the first $1/\sqrt{n}$ fraction of range of possible IDs. Recall from Section 2 that we assign IDs uniformly and independently at random. Thus, $\Pr[v \in S] = 1/\sqrt{n}$.

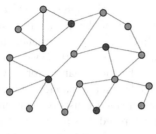
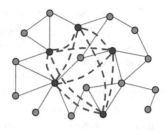

Graph G   Virtual Graph G'

Fig. 5. Virtual graph construction. Red nodes are in S, i.e., their ID is in the top $1/\sqrt{n}$ fraction of the ID range. Dotted red lines indicate virtual edges in G', whose weights are the ϱ-approximation of their endpoints' distance in G. Green edges show edges from G that are not connecting two nodes from S. In G', their weight is by factor ϱ larger than in G. Hence, for each $s, t \in S$, the virtual edge $\{s, t\}$ is a least-weight path from s to t in G'.

When following a least-weight path, w.h.p. one will encounter a node in S after at most $O(\sqrt{n} \log n)$ hops. Such a node will never have any entries corresponding to nodes of larger IDs. By the union bound and Observation 3, we get that the trees rooted at nodes in $V \setminus S$ have depth $O(\sqrt{n} \log n)$ w.h.p.

Observation 12. *Let S be the set of nodes with ID in the first $1/\sqrt{n}$ fraction of the ID range. For each $v \in V \setminus S$, the depth of a shortest-path tree rooted at v whose nodes are the set $\{w \in V \mid (v, \mathrm{wd}(w, v)) \in L_w\}$ is $O(\sqrt{n} \log n)$ w.h.p.*

For nodes in S, there is no such guarantee. In fact, if a graph contains a very light path of $n - 1$ hops and otherwise only edges of large weight, it is certain that the tree rooted at the minimum-ID node has depth $\Omega(n)$, even if the hop diameter D is very small. Nonetheless, the property that on any path a node from S will be encountered within $O(\sqrt{n} \log n)$ hops w.h.p. still applies. Hence, once the LE lists of the nodes in S are determined, the algorithm from the Section 3.3 will complete after $O(\sqrt{n} \log n)$ additional iterations w.h.p.

Observation 13. *If for some $i \in \mathbb{N}_0$ and all $s \in S$ it holds that $L_s^{(i)} = L_s$, then $L_v^{(i')} = L_v$ for all $v \in V$ and $i' \in i + O(\sqrt{n} \log n)$ w.h.p.*

In summary, the problem boils down to computing the LE lists for the small subset $S \subset V$ quickly. We do not know how to do this exactly in sublinear time, i.e., $\tilde{o}(n)$ rounds. Consequently, we will make use of approximation. Recall that, since the IDs are uniformly random, S is a uniformly random subset of V containing each node with independent probability $1/\sqrt{n}$. This is exactly the precondition required in the skeleton and spanner constructions given by Lemma 10 and Theorem 11. Thus, in $\tilde{O}(n^{1/2+\varepsilon} + D)$ rounds, we can make ϱ-approximate distances, for $\varrho \in O(1/\varepsilon)$, between nodes in S global knowledge. More precisely, these approximations are induced by the distance metric of a spanner of the $O(\sqrt{n} \log n)$-hop S-skeleton. Hence, we can compute *exact* LE lists of this spanner locally. Using these lists instead of those for G *approximately* preserves distances.

Next, we want to use these lists and Observation 13 to complete the computation of LE lists for the remaining set $V \setminus S$ quickly. However, unfortunately we did not compute

LE lists for G. To address this issue, we consider the virtual graph $G' = (V, E', W')$, where $E' := E \cup \binom{S}{2}$, and $W'(e')$ is the distance of s and t in the spanner iff $e' = \{s, t\}$ for some $s, t \in S$ and $W(e') = \varrho W(e)$ otherwise. In G', the spanner distances between $s, t \in S$ are the exact distances, and for any $v, w \in V$, $\mathrm{wd}(v, w) \leq \mathrm{wd}_{G'}(v, w) \leq \varrho \, \mathrm{wd}(v, w)$. Intuitively, without distorting distances by more than factor ϱ, we have ensured that the LE lists of nodes in S we determined from the spanner are their *exact* LE lists in G', and by Observation 13, we can compute the LE lists of nodes in $V \setminus S$ quickly. Finally, we would like to argue that the computed lists are those of an FRT embedding of G', and because G' satisfies that $\mathrm{wd}(v, w) \leq \mathrm{wd}_{G'}(v, w) \leq \varrho \, \mathrm{wd}(v, w)$ w.h.p., the overall expected distortion is $O(\varrho \log n)$ in expectation.

Is it that simple? Almost, but not quite. The issue with the above simplistic reasoning is that it ignores dependencies. Since G' depends on S, the permutation of V induced by the ranks is not independent of the topology of G', and therefore it is not obvious that the bound on the expected distortion of the FRT algorithm applies. Similarly, the statement of Lemma 8 that (intermediate) LE lists are w.h.p. of size $O(\log n)$ relies on the independence of the permutation from the topology of G'. Both of these issues can be resolved, by arguing about S and $V \setminus S$ separately; the total orders the IDs induce on S and $V \setminus S$, respectively, are independent of what nodes are in S and thus the topology of G'.

4.2 Our Algorithm: Constructing the Virtual Graph G' and Computing its LE Lists

Here we describe our algorithm. This algorithm uses a parameter $k \in \mathbb{N}$ that can be set arbitrarily. For our main result, one should think of k as $k = \lceil 1/\varepsilon \rceil$.

---

1. Construct any BFS tree, determine its depth $\hat{D} \in \Theta(D)$ and n (the latter by aggregation on the tree), and make these values known to all nodes.
2. Put the nodes whose random ID is in the first $1/\sqrt{n}$ fraction of the ID range in set S.
3. Set $h := c\sqrt{n} \log n$ for a sufficiently large constant c and $\rho := 2k - 1$. Construct a ρ-spanner $\tilde{G}$ of $G_{S,h}$ in $\tilde{O}(n^{1/2+1/(2k)} + D)$ rounds, using the algorithm given by Theorem 11.
4. Define the virtual graph $G' := (V, E', W')$ as follows:
   - $E' := E \cup \binom{S}{2}$.
   - For each $s, t \in S$, set $W'(s, t) := W_{\tilde{G}}(s, t)$.
   - For each $e \in E' \setminus \binom{S}{2}$, set $W(e') := \rho W(e)$.
5. Each $s \in S$ locally computes L_v^S, its LE list for the metric on S induced by distances in $\tilde{G}$.
6. Each node $s \in S$ initializes $L_s^{(0)} := L_s^S$. Nodes $v \in V \setminus S$ initialize $L_v^{(0)} := \{(v, 0)\}$. The algorithm from Section 3.3 is run on G, however with the lists $L_v^{(0)}$ initialized as just specified.
7. Return the computed lists.

4.3 Correctness Analysis

We first show that the algorithm computes the desired LE lists.

Lemma 14. *W.h.p.,* $\mathrm{wd}_{\tilde{G}}(s,t) = \mathrm{wd}_{G'}(s,t)$ *for all* $s,t \in \mathcal{S}$.

Proof. Theorem 11 guarantees that w.h.p., $\tilde{G}$ is a ρ-spanner of $G_{\mathcal{S},h}$. By Lemma 10, w.h.p. $\mathrm{wd}_{G_{\mathcal{S},h}}(s,t) = \mathrm{wd}(s,t)$ for all $s,t \in \mathcal{S}$. In the following, we condition on both events occuring. Therefore, for any $s,t \in \mathcal{S}$,

$$\mathrm{wd}_{G'}(s,t) \leq \mathrm{wd}_{\tilde{G}}(s,t) \leq \rho\, \mathrm{wd}_{G_{\mathcal{S},h}}(s,t) = \rho\, \mathrm{wd}(s,t).$$

It remains to prove that $\mathrm{wd}_{G'}(s,t) \geq \mathrm{wd}_{\tilde{G}}(s,t)$. To this end, consider any path $p = (v_0 = s, v_1, \ldots, v_{\ell(p)} = t)$ in G'. It decomposes into subpaths $p = p_1 \circ p_2 \circ \ldots \circ p_m$ (for some $m \leq \ell(p)$) so that each p_i, $i \in \{1, \ldots, m\}$, starts and ends at a node in $\mathcal{S}$ and all its internal nodes are in $V \setminus \mathcal{S}$. Therefore, either $p_i = (s_i, t_i)$ for some $s_i, t_i \in \mathcal{S}$ and $W'(p_i) = \mathrm{wd}_{\tilde{G}}(s_i, t_i)$, or $p_i = (s_i, \ldots, t_i)$ consists of edges from E only. The latter implies that

$$W'(p_i) = \rho W(p_i) \geq \rho\, \mathrm{wd}(s_i, t_i) = \rho\, \mathrm{wd}_{G_{\mathcal{S},h}}(s_i, t_i) \geq \mathrm{wd}_{\tilde{G}}(s_i, t_i).$$

Thus, in both cases, $W'(p_i) \geq \mathrm{wd}_{\tilde{G}}(s_i, t_i)$. By repeated application of the triangle inequality ($\mathrm{wd}_{\tilde{G}}$ is a metric), we conclude that

$$\mathrm{wd}_{\tilde{G}}(s,t) \leq \sum_{i=1}^{m} \mathrm{wd}_{\tilde{G}}(s_i, t_i) \leq \sum_{i=1}^{m} W'(p_i) = W'(p).$$

As p was an arbitrary s-t path in G', we conclude that $\mathrm{wd}_{G'}(s,t) \geq \mathrm{wd}_{\tilde{G}}(s,t)$. $\qquad\square$

Corollary 15. *W.h.p., the LE lists computed locally in Step 5 are the LE lists for* G' *of nodes in* $\mathcal{S}$.

Corollary 16. *W.h.p., the above algorithm returns LE lists for the graph* G' *specified in Step 4.*

4.4 Running Time Analysis

Clearly, the first step of the algorithm requires $O(D)$ rounds. The other steps that do not solely consist of local computations are Steps 3 and 6. By Theorem 11, the time complexity of Step 3 is $\tilde{O}(n^{1/2+1/(2k)} + D)$ w.h.p. Hence, it remains to analyze the time complexity of Step 6.

Lemma 17. *Step 6 of the above algorithm performs* $O(\sqrt{n}\log n)$ *iterations of the LE list algorithm w.h.p.*

The proof appears in the full version; essentially, the lemma follows from the fact that on each path, a node from $\mathcal{S}$ is encountered every $O(\sqrt{n}\log n)$ hops w.h.p.

Due to this lemma, it is sufficient to show that in each iteration, the lists contain $O(\log n)$ entries w.h.p.

Lemma 18. *For each iteration of the LE list algorithm during Step 6, all lists have* $O(\log n)$ *entries w.h.p.*

Proof. For each node $v \in V$ and each index $i \in \mathbb{N}_0$, we split its list $L_v^{(i)}$ into two parts. The head of the list $H_v^{(i)}$ consists of entries (s, d) with $s \in S$ and its tail $T_v^{(i)}$ consists of entries (v, d) with $v \in V \setminus S$. Consider the following virtual graph:

 - Take a copy of G'.
 - Add a copy of each node in S and connect it to the original by a 0-weight edge.
 - Connect each copy of a node $s \in S$ to each original node $t \in S \setminus \{s\}$ by an edge of weight $W'(s, t)$.

Now initialize, for each $s \in S$, $L_{s'}^{(0)} := \{(s, 0)\}$, where s' is the copy of s. For all original nodes $v \in V$, set $L_v^{(0)} := \emptyset$. Observe that

 (i) after one iteration of the LE list algorithm, each original node has the same head $H_v^{(0)}$ as according to the initialization in Step 6 of the algorithm;
 (ii) no message from a copy of a node ever causes a change in the lists in later rounds; and
 (iii) the permutation of S induced by the IDs is uniform and independent of the topology.

The third observation implies that Lemma 8 applies,[2] i.e., the list heads have $O(\log n)$ entries w.h.p. The first two observations imply that the list heads are identical to those of the iterations of the LE list algorithm performed in Step 6 (shifted by one round). Hence, $|H_v^{(i)}| \in O(\log n)$ w.h.p. for all nodes $v \in V$ and rounds i.

Now consider the list tails. Suppose the list construction algorithm was run on G, but with $L_s^{(0)} := \emptyset$ for all $s \in S$. Since the ranks induce a uniformly random permutation on $V \setminus S$ (that is independent of G), Lemma 8 applies and, in each iteration, the respective lists have $O(\log n)$ entries w.h.p. We claim that the tails $T_v^{(i)}$, $v \in V$, $i \in \mathbb{N}_0$, are always prefixes of these lists. This follows because if an entry of an (intermediate) head list causes deletion of an entry from a tail list, it can never happen that the deleted entry would affect neighbors' lists in future iterations (the head entry causing the deletion always takes precedence).

To complete the proof, for each iteration i we take the union bound over all nodes and the events that the head and tail lists are short, implying that, w.h.p., $|L_v^{(i)}| = |H_v^{(i)}| + |T_v^{(i)}| \in O(\log n)$ for all nodes $v \in V$. $\qquad\square$

We summarize the result on LE list computation for G':

Theorem 19. *W.h.p., the algorithm computes the LE lists of the virtual graph G' defined in Step 5 and (if suitably implemented) terminates in* $\tilde{O}(n^{1/2+1/(2k)} + D)$ *rounds.*

4.5 Approximation Analysis

So far, we have shown that our algorithm computes LE lists for G' and does so fast. However, we cannot apply Theorem 2 to show that these LE lists represent a virtual

---

[2] Technically speaking, we use a slightly more general version of the lemma, in which a subset of the nodes may be anonymous; the reasoning remains identical. Here, all nodes but the copies of nodes in S are anonymous.

tree sampled from the (distribution of trees given by) the FRT embedding. Since the construction of G' depends on the choice of $\mathcal{S}$, and this choice depends on the random IDs, G' and the permutation on V induced by the IDs are not independent. We now adapt the analysis of [10] to our setting and show how to remedy the probabilistic dependencies created by our algorithm. In the following, denote by T the FRT tree specified by the LE lists on G'.

Lemma 20. *For each* $v, u \in V$, $\mathbb{E}[\mathrm{wd}_T(\mathfrak{M}(v), \mathfrak{M}(u))] \in O(\log n) \cdot \mathrm{wd}_{G'}(v, u)$.

Proof (Sketch). For any $\mathcal{S} \subset V$, denote by $\mathcal{E}_{\mathcal{S}}$ the event that $\mathcal{S}$ is the set of the nodes with random IDs in the first $1/\sqrt{n}$ fraction of the ID range. It suffices to show that

$$\mathbb{E}[\mathrm{wd}_T(\mathfrak{M}(v), \mathfrak{M}(u)) \mid \mathcal{E}_{\mathcal{S}}] \in O(\log n) \cdot \mathrm{wd}_{G'}(v, u).$$

We condition on $\mathcal{E}_{\mathcal{S}}$ and an arbitrary outcome of the spanner construction (which uses independent randomness); this fixes G'. Note that the total orders the IDs induce on each of the sets $\mathcal{S}$ and $V \setminus \mathcal{S}$, respectively, are still uniformly random and *independent* of G'.

Fix $u, v \in V$. We say w *settles* u and v on level i, iff it is the node with the smallest ID so that

$$\min\{\mathrm{wd}_{G'}(w, v), \mathrm{wd}_{G'}(w, u)\} \leq \beta 2^{i-1}. \tag{1}$$

We say w *cuts* u and v on level i, iff it settles them on level i and also

$$\beta 2^{i-1} \leq \max\{\mathrm{wd}_{G'}(w, v), \mathrm{wd}_{G'}(w, u)\}. \tag{2}$$

It is not hard to show that if $(v_{i+1}, \ldots, v_L)$ is the least common ancestor of v and u, then $\mathrm{wd}_T(\mathfrak{M}(v), \mathfrak{M}(u)) < \beta 2^{i+1} < 2^{i+2}$ and either v_i or u_i cuts v and u. Hence, if we denote by $\mathcal{E}_{w,i}$ the event that $w \in V$ cuts u and v on level i, we have that

$$\mathbb{E}[\mathrm{wd}_T(\mathfrak{M}(v), \mathfrak{M}(u)) \mid \mathcal{E}_{\mathcal{S}}] < \sum_{w \in V} \sum_{i=1}^{L} P[\mathcal{E}_{w,i}] \cdot 2^{i+2}$$

$$= \sum_{w \in \mathcal{S}} \sum_{i=1}^{L} P[\mathcal{E}_{w,i}] \cdot 2^{i+2} + \sum_{w \in V \setminus \mathcal{S}} \sum_{i=1}^{L} P[\mathcal{E}_{w,i}] \cdot 2^{i+2}.$$

Both sums are handled analogously; let us consider only the first one here. Sort the nodes $w \in \mathcal{S}$ in ascending order w.r.t. $\min\{\mathrm{wd}_{G'}(w, v), \mathrm{wd}_{G'}(w, u)\}$ and let w_k be the kth node in this order. We rewrite $P[\mathcal{E}_{w_k,i}]$ as

$P[(1)$ and (2) for w_k and $i] \cdot P[w_k$ settles u and v on level $i \mid (1)$ and (2) for w and $i]$.

As the random order on $\mathcal{S}$ is uniform and independent of G', the second, conditional probability is $1/k$. Concerning the first probability, recall that (1) and (2) hold exactly if $\beta 2^{i-1} \in [\mathrm{wd}_{G'}(w, v), \mathrm{wd}_{G'}(w, u)]$. Here, w.l.o.g. we have assumed that $\mathrm{wd}_{G'}(w, v) < \mathrm{wd}_{G'}(w, u)$. Computation shows that

$$\sum_{i=1}^{L} P[(1) \text{ and } (2) \text{ for } w_k \text{ and } i] \cdot 2^{i+2} = \int_{\mathrm{wd}_{G'}(w,v)}^{\mathrm{wd}_{G'}(w,u)} 2^3 \, dx$$

$$= 8(\mathrm{wd}_{G'}(w, u) - \mathrm{wd}_{G'}(w, v)) \leq 8 \, \mathrm{wd}_{G'}(v, u),$$

where in the final step we applied the triangle inequality. We conclude that

$$\sum_{w \in W} \sum_{i=1}^{L} P[\mathcal{E}_{w,i}] \cdot 2^{i+2} \leq \sum_{k=1}^{|W|} \frac{8}{k} \cdot \mathrm{wd}_{G'}(v, u)$$
$$< 8H_n \cdot \mathrm{wd}_{G'}(v, u) \in O(\log n) \cdot \mathrm{wd}_{G'}(v, u).$$

Full proofs of the lemma and the statements below are given in the full version. As distances in G' are w.h.p. at most by factor $O(\log n/\varepsilon)$ larger than in G, we conclude that the embedding given by the LE lists for G' is also good for G.

Corollary 21. *For each $v, u \in V$, we have that $\mathbb{E}[\mathrm{wd}_T(\mathfrak{M}(v), \mathfrak{M}(u))] \in O(k \log n) \cdot \mathrm{wd}(v, u)$.*

We arrive at our main result, which was informally stated in Theorem 1.

Theorem 22. *For any $0 < \varepsilon \leq 1$, it is possible to sample from a distribution of probabilistic tree embeddings with expected stretch $O(\log n/\varepsilon)$ in $\tilde{O}(\min\{n^{0.5+\varepsilon}, \mathrm{SPD}\} + D)$ rounds w.h.p. in the $\mathsf{CONGEST}$ model. The computed embedding is given distributedly, in the form of corresponding LE lists. Moreover, if not all least-weight paths in G induced by the LE lists have $\tilde{O}(\sqrt{n})$ hops, the subtree of the virtual tree induced by the set S of nodes whose (uniformly random) ID is in the first $1/\sqrt{n}$ fraction of the ID range is known to all nodes, and for each edge $\{s, t\}$ in this subtree there is a unique s-t-path in G whose weight does not exceed the weight of the virtual edge and whose nodes know that they are on this path.*

We remark that instead of just constructing the tree embedding in form of the LE lists, this result also makes sure that the embedding can be used for approximation algorithms efficiently. For instance, it is essential that we can, e.g., select a root-leaf path in the virtual tree and map it back to a corresponding path in G in $\tilde{O}(\min\{n^{0.5+\varepsilon}, \mathrm{SPD}\} + D)$ rounds. Note that this operation is very basic, as it will be required whenever seeking to connect two leaves in different subtrees. Reconstructing such a path hop by hop using LE lists may take SPD time, which is too slow if $\mathrm{SPD} \gg \sqrt{n}$. Fortunately, if SPD is large, for each path all but a prefix of $\tilde{O}(\sqrt{n})$ hops corresponds to a route in the constructed skeleton spanner, and the additional information collected during the spanner construction stage is sufficient to quickly determine the remaining edges in G by announcing the (endpoints of) the subpath in the skeleton spanner to all nodes.

References

1. Alon, N., Karp, R.M., Peleg, D., West, D.: A graph-theoretic game and its application to the k-server problem. SIAM J. Comput. 24(1), 78–100 (1995)
2. Bartal, Y.: Probabilistic approximation of metric spaces and its algorithmic applications. In: Proc. of the Symp. on Found. of Comp. Sci. (FOCS), pp. 184–193 (1996)
3. Bartal, Y.: On approximating arbitrary metrices by tree metrics. In: Proc. of the Symp. on Theory of Comp. (STOC), pp. 161–168 (1998)
4. Baswana, S., Sen, S.: A simple and linear time randomized algorithm for computing sparse spanners in weighted graphs. Random Structures and Algorithms 30(4), 532–563 (2007)

5. Bourgain, J.: On Lipschitz embedding of finite metric spaces in Hilbert space. Israel Journal of Mathematics 52(1-2), 46–52 (1985)
6. Cohen, E.: Size-estimation framework with applications to transitive closure and reachability. Journal of Computer and System Sciences 55(3), 441–453 (1997)
7. Das Sarma, A., Holzer, S., Kor, L., Korman, A., Nanongkai, D., Pandurangan, G., Peleg, D., Wattenhofer, R.: Distributed verification and hardness of distributed approximation. In: Proc. of the Symp. on Theory of Comp. (STOC), pp. 363–372 (2011)
8. Elkin, M.: Unconditional lower bounds on the time-approximation tradeoffs for the distributed minimum spanning tree problem. In: Proc. of the Symp. on Theory of Comp. (STOC), pp. 331–340 (2004)
9. Fakcharoenphol, J., Rao, S., Talwar, K.: A tight bound on approximating arbitrary metrics by tree metrics. In: Proc. of the Symp. on Theory of Comp. (STOC), pp. 448–455 (2003)
10. Fakcharoenphol, J., Rao, S., Talwar, K.: A tight bound on approximating arbitrary metrics by tree metrics. Journal of Computer and System Sciences 69(3), 485–497 (2004)
11. Ghaffari, M.: Near-optimal distributed approximation of minimum-weight connected dominating set. In: Esparza, J., Fraigniaud, P., Husfeldt, T., Koutsoupias, E. (eds.) ICALP 2014, Part II. LNCS, vol. 8573, pp. 483–494. Springer, Heidelberg (2014)
12. Ghaffari, M., Kuhn, F.: Distributed minimum cut approximation. In: Afek, Y. (ed.) DISC 2013. LNCS, vol. 8205, pp. 1–15. Springer, Heidelberg (2013)
13. Holzer, S., Wattenhofer, R.: Optimal distributed all pairs shortest paths and applications. In: The Proc. of the Int'l Symp. on Princ. of Dist. Comp. (PODC), pp. 355–364 (2012)
14. Indyk, P., Matousek, J.: Low-distortion embeddings of finite metric spaces. In: Handbook of Discrete and Computational Geometry, vol. 37, p. 46 (2004)
15. Khan, M., Kuhn, F., Malkhi, D., Pandurangan, G., Talwar, K.: Efficient distributed approximation algorithms via probabilistic tree embeddings. In: The Proc. of the Int'l Symp. on Princ. of Dist. Comp. (PODC), pp. 263–272 (2008)
16. Lenzen, C., Patt-Shamir, B.: Fast routing table construction using small messages: Extended abstract. In: Proc. of the Symp. on Theory of Comp. (STOC), pp. 381–390 (2013)
17. Lenzen, C., Patt-Shamir, B.: Improved distributed steiner forest construction. In: The Proc. of the Int'l Symp. on Princ. of Dist. Comp. (PODC) (2014)
18. Matoušek, J.: Lectures on discrete geometry, vol. 212. Springer (2002)
19. Nanongkai, D.: Distributed approximation algorithms for weighted shortest paths. In: Proc. of the Symp. on Theory of Comp. (STOC) (to appear, 2014)
20. Peleg, D.: Distributed Computing: A Locality-sensitive Approach. Society for Industrial and Applied Mathematics, Philadelphia (2000)
21. Peleg, D., Rubinovich, V.: A near-tight lower bound on the time complexity of distributed MST construction. In: Proc. of the Symp. on Found. of Comp. Sci. (FOCS), pp. 253–261 (1999)

Deterministic Leader Election
in Multi-hop Beeping Networks[*]
(Extended Abstract)

Klaus-Tycho Förster, Jochen Seidel, and Roger Wattenhofer

Computer Engineering and Networks Laboratory,
ETH Zurich, 8092 Zurich, Switzerland
{foklaus,seidelj,wattenhofer}@ethz.ch

Abstract. We study deterministic leader election in multi-hop radio networks in the beeping model. More specifically, we address explicit leader election: One node is elected as the leader, the other nodes know its identifier, and the algorithm terminates at some point with the network being quiescent. No initial knowledge of the network is assumed, i.e., nodes know neither the size of the network nor their degree, they only have a unique identifier. Our main contribution is a deterministic explicit leader election algorithm in the synchronous beeping model with a run time of $O(D \log n)$ rounds. This is achieved by carefully combining a fast local election algorithm with two new techniques for synchronization and communication in radio networks.

1 Introduction

Distributed computing and wireless communication are prime application areas for randomization, as randomized algorithms are often both simpler and more efficient than their deterministic counterparts. However, in some cases the randomized algorithm is only of Monte Carlo nature, i.e., with some probability the algorithm fails. This is a problem if the randomized algorithm is used as a starting point for other (deterministic and Las Vegas) algorithms, as the algorithm as a whole can also not provide any guarantees anymore. A classic example for such a basic problem is leader election, which is often used to as a first step for other wireless algorithms. We would argue in this paper that leader election deserves to be understood deterministically as well, and we present a new algorithm that solves leader election in the wireless beeping model – our algorithm is slower than the fastest known randomized algorithm, but the overhead is bearable.

The beeping model has emerged as an alternative to the traditional radio network model. The beeping model is binary, in a synchronous time step nodes can only choose to beep or not to beep. If a node is beeping, it does not get any feedback regarding other nodes. On the other hand, if a node is silent, it will

---

[*] The full version of this paper is available at
http://disco.ethz.ch/publications/DISC2014-leader.pdf

F. Kuhn (Ed.): DISC 2014, LNCS 8784, pp. 212–226, 2014.
© Springer-Verlag Berlin Heidelberg 2014

learn whether all its neighbors are also silent, or whether at least one neighbor is beeping. The beeping model was introduced to the distributed computing community by Cornejo and Kuhn [7] shortly after it was implemented [8].

In this model, we deterministically solve leader election: All the nodes in the multi-hop network have to agree on a single leader. As leader election is impossible without nodes having unique identifiers [1], we assume that each node is equipped with a unique ID. We want our algorithm to be uniform, i.e., apart from their ID, nodes have no knowledge about any global or local network properties (e.g., the network size, or their degree).

Our main result is an algorithm that deterministically solves the leader election problem in $O(D \log n)$ time, where D is the diameter of the network and n is the number of nodes. Once a leader is elected, all nodes in the network know the leader's ID, and the network is quiescent. We achieve this task by carefully combining several methods.

1.1 Overview

First, we describe a Campaigning algorithm (Section 3) that can be compared to one iteration of a real word political campaign: Every node is equipped with a candidate leader and attempts to convince its neighborhood that this candidate would make a great leader. The idea is that, if enough campaigns are performed, everyone will be convinced of the same leader, since her influence spreads at least one hop per iteration. In other words, we would like to perform multiple campaigns, one after another.

As it turns out, in the beeping model ensuring that the next algorithm starts synchronized is a non-trivial task. We thus develop a technique that allows us to sequentially execute algorithms (Section 4) and apply it to the Campaigning algorithm (Section 4.3).

The third method establishes a "back-channel" (Section 5) that directs messages towards a specific node, in our case the current candidate leaders. This allows the last remaining candidate to detect its election and turn the network quiescent. Our main result is now obtained by executing the Campaigning algorithm multiple times sequentially, while at the same time using the back-channel to notify the global leader when its successful election is detected. Lastly, we briefly sketch how our algorithm can be extended to include a simple synchronized wake-up protocol (Section 6).

1.2 Related Work

Leader election is one of the fundamental problems in distributed computing, often used as the first step for solving a myriad of other problems in networks. As such, the problem was studied over decades in various communication and network models [17].

In radio networks, communication takes usually place in synchronous rounds, and nodes may either transmit or listen in every round. If a node transmits, it cannot hear incoming messages, but the message is sent to all its neighbors at once. If a node listens, it receives messages from all its neighbors, but the message obtained depends on the model of collision detection. Should collision detection be available, then a node can separate between no message sent, exactly one message sent, or a collision of multiple messages. With no collision detection available nodes can only distinguish between exactly one message sent to it or just noise.

Leader election in radio networks was first considered in single-hop radio networks, followed by the study of multi-hop radio networks. We start with a short coverage of the single-hop case:

For deterministic algorithms in single-hop radio networks, the run time highly depends on the availability of collision detection: With collision detection, it is $\Theta(\log n)$ [3,12,13,19], while without collision detection, it is $\Theta(n \log n)$ [6]. A similar case can be made for randomized algorithms in single-hop radio networks: With collision detection, the expected run time is $\Theta(\log \log n)$ [20]. The expected run time goes to $O(\log n)$ if w.h.p. is desired. Should no collision detection be available, then the run time increases to $\Theta(\log n)$ in the expected case [2,16], and to $\Theta(\log^2 n)$ w.h.p. [14].

We would argue that the study of leader election in multi-hop radio networks can be divided into the following fields for related work to our results. One can consider (1) radio networks with or (2) without collision detection, and (3) the beeping model. Second, the used algorithms can be either deterministic or randomized. We refer to [4,10,15] for an extended overview of these areas.

For deterministic algorithms, Kowalski and Pelc [15] displayed the discrepancy between models with and without collision detection. They showed that if collision detection is available, the runtime is $\Theta(n)$, while without collision detection, there is a lower bound of $\Omega(n \log n)$. Their $O(n)$ algorithm with collision detection relies on a careful combination of multiple innovative techniques, e.g., remote token elimination and distributed fuzzy-degree clustering. In contrast to the model in this paper, they require messages of logarithmic size, collision detection, and the knowledge of an upper bound polynomial in the number of identifiers. Our algorithm can be simulated therein since their model is strictly stronger. Asymptotically, we achieve a better run time for graphs with a diameter $D \in o(n/\log n)$, cf. [10].

For randomized algorithms in radio networks without collision detection, Chlebus, Kowalski, and Pelc [4] broke the $\Omega(n \log n)$ barrier: They present a randomized algorithm with $O(n)$ expected time and prove a lower bound of $\Omega(n)$. Furthermore, they give a deterministic algorithm for the model without collision detection with a run time of $O(n \log^{3/2} n \sqrt{\log \log n})$. They use logarithmic size messages and also assume that an upper bound on the network size is known.

Finally, Ghaffari and Haeupler [10] considered randomized leader election in the beeping model. Their algorithm runs in $O((D + \log n \log \log n) \cdot \min(\log \log n, \log n/D))$ time. To choose the random starting set of candidates, they rely on knowledge of n, while we assume our algorithms to be uniform. To cope with overlapping transmissions, they present a sophisticated technique using superimposed codes. We deem our overhead of $O(\log n)$ in the worst case bearable.

To the best of our knowledge, no results are published for deterministic leader election in the beeping model.

The authors of [10] also consider a variant of the beeping model in which only a subset $S \subseteq V$ of the nodes wakes up in round 0 [11]. We adapt our algorithm to this setting in Section 6. The difficulty is to allow nodes that are being woken up by neighbors to synchronize their execution with that of nodes that are already awake. The related wake-up problem, where nodes may also activate spontaneously and no collision detection is available was studied in its own right, for single-hop [9] as well as multi-hop [5] networks. In [18] the goal is to activate the whole network if exactly one node is active initially.

2   Preliminaries

Network Model. The network is modeled as a connected undirected graph $G = (V, E)$ with node set V and edge set E. We denote by D the diameter of G, and by n the number of nodes in V. All nodes $u \in V$ have a unique identifier (ID), denoted by $\mathrm{id}(u)$, from the range $\{1, 2, \ldots, O(n^\gamma)\}$, with $\gamma \geq 1$ being a constant. We denote by $l(v)$ the *length* of u's identifier in bits, i.e., $l(u) = \lceil \log_2(\mathrm{id}(u)) \rceil$. The *neighborhood* $\mathcal{N}(u)$ of u is the set $\{u\} \cup \{v : (u, v) \in E\}$. In a similar fashion, the *d-neighborhood* $\mathcal{N}(u, d)$ of a node u contains all nodes with a distance of at most d to u, e.g., $\mathcal{N}(u, 1) = \mathcal{N}(u)$.

Beeping Model. We consider one of the most basic communication models, the synchronous beeping model: All nodes start synchronized[1] in round 0, and communication between nodes proceeds in synchronous rounds, where messages are transmitted via the edges of the network. In every round, each node may choose to either *beep* or *listen* to incoming messages. If a node v beeps, the beep will be transmitted to all nodes in $\mathcal{N}(v)$. Otherwise, if v listens, then the message received by v in a round is defined as follows: (i) if no node in $\mathcal{N}(v)$ beeps, then v receives a 0 (*silence*), and (ii) if one or more nodes in $\mathcal{N}(v)$ beeps, then v receives a 1 (*beep*).

Uniform Algorithms. We only consider uniform algorithms. That is, unless mentioned otherwise, the input for a node v consists of only $\mathrm{id}(v)$ (but not the value of γ). Note that neither n, nor D, nor any upper bounds on those network parameters, can be inferred from the value $\mathrm{id}(v)$ (or $l(v)$) of a single node v. Nodes also do not have any knowledge about the network topology, e.g., the IDs of their neighbors, or even their own degree. Moreover, we require that in every network the algorithm reaches a quiescent state, i.e., a state in which no node transmits beeps anymore.

3   Convincing Your Neighbors

In this section, we give an algorithm called Campaigning that can be compared to a political campaign at a word of mouth level. Everyone is convinced that

---

[1] In Section 6 we also handle the case in which only a subset of the nodes wakes up.

either she herself is a good candidate, or that she knows the name of a good candidate. If you know a better candidate than all of your neighbors and their neighbors, you will try to convince your direct neighbors. However, if they are aware that a better candidate is out there — they will ignore your conversion attempts. Some candidates might reach a good deal of local followers, but only a globally best candidate can guarantee to spread her sphere of influence all the time.

The algorithm `Campaigning` can be seen as one iteration of this process, where nodes exchange information only with their local neighborhood. The general idea is that after D iterations are performed, *"There can be only one!"*[2], and all nodes will be convinced of the same leader. Hence, the candidates of the different nodes do not have to be unique, e.g., the algorithm works with just one candidate for all nodes or n different candidates.

We have to reach a state where nodes can transmit information to their neighbors, without other nodes disturbing them, since beeps do not encode relevant further information. Particular challenges arise from the facts that the algorithm has to be uniform, i.e., that n is not known, and that we are confined to the restricted beeping model. E.g., one cannot just "beep the identifier" and then proceed with another part of the algorithm, since any receiving node will hear all its neighbors – and cannot distinguish if all sent a beep or just one.

The main idea is to first reach local consensus on the longest identifier, then to agree locally on the highest identifier, and finally, to let those with the locally highest identifier transmit their identifier to their neighbors. To reach a state of local consensus, we turn some nodes into buffer-nodes that no longer participate. Therefore, we divide our algorithm into three separate procedures `campaign_longest_id`, `campaign_highest_id`, and `campaign_transmit_id`.

We first give an overview of the three procedures in Subsection 3.1, followed by a detailed mode of operations for `Campaigning` in Subsection 3.2. The full version also contains a pseudo code description of our algorithm. We conclude by stating correctness and run time results in Subsection 3.3.

3.1   Overview of the Procedures

Every node v gets as input an id, referred to as *campaigning-identifier*, that is stored in v's variable id_{in}. Also, all nodes start in an *active* role, but can change to be *passive* or *inactive* during the algorithm. Active nodes might convince their neighbors at the end and passive nodes might receive a new candidate, but it can be necessary to turn nodes inactive to let them act as local separators.

After the first procedure, `campaign_longest_id`, exactly those nodes v with the *longest* id_{in} in their 2-neighborhood are still active. If a node v is not active, but has an active neighbor w, then v turns passive, since it is interested in the campaigning-identifier of w. Nodes not fulfilling either of these requirements turn inactive. Furthermore, to separate clusters of active nodes with campaigning-identifiers of different length, the procedure creates buffers of inactive nodes

---

[2] Connor MacLeod, 1985. In *Highlander*.

between them. Thus, inside a cluster, all active campaigning-identifiers are of equal length, allowing each cluster to agree on a common starting time for the following procedure.

The second procedure `campaign_highest_id` mimics the first procedure, but now for the *highest* instead of the *longest* identifier. After `campaign_highest_id`, exactly those nodes v with the highest id_{in} in their 2-neighborhood remain active. The buffer of inactive nodes is extended to separate active nodes with different campaigning-identifiers. Hence, in the third procedure `campaign_transmit_id`, all still active nodes can convince their passive neighbors unhindered.

3.2 Details of the Algorithm

In this subsection, we describe the algorithm `Campaigning` and each of its three procedures for a node $v \in V$. We describe the algorithm from the perspective of a single node v. The input campaigning-identifier for v is stored in id_{in}, and the length of id_{in} in bits is stored in the variable l_{in}. Furthermore, v initializes the variables $role \leftarrow active$, $l_{out} \leftarrow l_{in}$, and $id_{out} \leftarrow id_{in}$. Then, the node v executes `campaign_longest_id`, `campaign_highest_id`, `campaign_transmit_id`, and the output of node v is id_{out}. Should a node become inactive at any time, i.e., if $role = inactive$, then the algorithm immediately terminates and the value currently stored in id_{out} is returned as v's output.

Each procedure consist of *phases*, which are divided into three rounds each. For ease of notation, we call the rounds in one phase *slots*, i.e., slot 0, slot 1, and slot 2. Conceptually, the first two slots 0 and 1 of each phase are used to transmit data, while slot 2 will exclusively be used for notification signals from active nodes. Recall that v *hears* a beep only if some node $u \in \mathcal{N}(v)$, $u \neq v$ transmits a beep, i.e., v does not hear beeps of itself.

campaign_longest_id. The length of `campaign_longest_id` may vary; at the end of the procedure, node v stores the number of elapsed phases in l_{out} if at the end of the procedure v is active or passive. Node v starts by beeping in slots 0 and 1 for the first $l_{in} - 1$ phases. Then, v listens in slot 0, and beeps received in slot 0 are relayed in slot 1. If v relays at least one beep, it turns passive. Should a beep be heard in the next slot 2, the node v turns inactive. Otherwise, already in phase l_{in} there was no beep to relay. In that case, if a (relayed) beep is received in slot 1, then v turns inactive. Else v beeps in slot 2 of that phase and finishes the procedure as active. Should after phase l_{in} a beep be heard in slot 1, the passive relaying node v turns inactive as well. Should there be a phase where the passive node v hears no beeps in slot 0,1, it either *i*) turns inactive if no beep is heard in slot 2, or *ii*) finishes the procedure as passive if a beep is heard in slot 2.

campaign_highest_id. This procedure consists of l_{out} phases, and we denote the current phase of node v by p.

If v is passive at the beginning of phase p, then beeps heard in slot 0 are relayed in slot 1. Should no beep be heard in slot 0, but a beep is heard in slot

1, v turns inactive. Also, if no beep is heard in slot 2 of phase $l_{out}(v)$, then v turns inactive.

We denote by the positions $1, \ldots, l_{in}$ the bits of id_{in}, starting from the most significant bit. If v is active at the beginning of phase p, then v beeps in slots 0 and 1 if position p in id_{in} is a 1 bit. Else, when a beep is heard in slot 0 or 1, v turns passive. If the current phase is l_{out} and v is still active, then v beeps in slot 2.

campaign_transmit_id. Much like `campaign_highest_id`, this procedure consists of l_{out} phases. An active node v uses the l_{out} phases to transmit the l_{out} bits of id_{in}, whereas passive nodes store the l_{out} received bits in id_{out}.

3.3   Convincing via `Campaigning`

We can now state some important properties of the algorithm `Campaigning`, which will be used in the next sections to prove our main result. For formal proofs please refer to the full version of this paper; here we restrict ourselves to presenting the necessary key ideas. We begin with the following correctness lemma, which essentially states that nodes may only adopt identifiers from their neighborhood, i.e., identifiers spread only locally and no new identifiers are created.

Lemma 1 *Let v be a node that just finished algorithm* `Campaigning`$(id_{in}(v))$. *Then* $id_{out}(v) \leq \max_{w \in \mathcal{N}(v,1)} id_{in}(w)$ *and* $\exists x \in \mathcal{N}(v,1)$ *s.t.* $id_{out}(v) = id_{in}(x)$.

The proof to Theorem 1 consists of a careful case distinction based on the node's *role* in the `Campaigning` algorithm. In Theorem 2, we show that the influence of a potential leader will spread one hop per round. This is crucial for the whole leader election process, since it will be extended later on to show that D executions of the algorithm suffice to convince all nodes of the leader.

Theorem 2. *Execute algorithm* `Campaigning`$(\text{id}_{in}(v))$ *for* $\forall v \in V$. *Let* $v' \in V$ *be a node with* $\text{id}_{in}(v') = \max_{w \in \mathcal{N}(v',3)} \text{id}_{in}(w)$. *Then for all nodes* $u \in \mathcal{N}(v',1)$ *holds:* $\text{id}_{out}(u) = \text{id}_{in}(v')$.

The above theorem is established by observing that a node v with a locally highest campaigning-identifier (i.e., the highest id_{in} in $\mathcal{N}(v,3)$) remains active, its neighbors do not turn inactive, and thus the campaigning-identifier is propagated one hop. Finally, Theorem 3 states that the run time of `Campaigning` depends only on the largest campaigning-identifier length in the 1-neighborhood.

Theorem 3. *Execute algorithm* `Campaigning`$(\text{id}_{in}(v))$ *for* $\forall v \in V$. *The run time for each node v is* $O(\max_{w \in \mathcal{N}(v,1)} l_{in}(w))$ *rounds.*

This is true since the maximum run time of a node is completely determined after `campaign_longest_id` has finished. Recall that all identifiers are at most in $O(n^\gamma)$, and hence the run time is bounded by $O(\log n)$ rounds. Since Lemma 1 ensures that no new identifiers are created in the network, we obtain the following corollary.

Corollary 4. *Let* $\max_{v \in V} l_{in}(v) \in O(\log n)$. *It holds that the run time of algorithm* `Campaigning`$(id_{in}(v))$ *is* $O(\log n)$ *rounds for* $\forall v \in V$.

4 Convincing Your Network

We would like to apply the campaigning method presented in the previous section to propagate the highest ID further. In other words, we need to execute `Campaigning` multiple times in succession. This task would be easy if there was some kind of global synchronization in order to guarantee that all nodes can start the next invocation of the campaigning algorithm at the same time. However, since the node labels have different lengths, so does each campaign. To overcome this obstacle, we design a generic approach to sequentially execute arbitrarily many algorithms in the beeping model. The key ingredient in our approach is the following *balanced counter* technique.

4.1 Balanced Counters

We present a method that enables the network to manage a balanced counter for every node u. At every node u, our balanced counter technique stores an integer value denoted by *counter*. To manipulate *counter* the two methods `increment` and `reset`, which instruct the counter to increment its value by one or reset it to zero, respectively, are provided. Our goal is to satisfy the following *balancing property*: For any two neighboring nodes u, v *participating*, i.e., not currently resetting their counters, the *counter* values of u and v shall differ by at most 1.

Note that transmitting the whole counter value in every round is not feasible due to the limited nature of the communication means the nodes have at their disposal. However, it turns out that transmitting the *counter* value modulo 3 suffices to ensure the balancing property. The transmission technique we use requires three reserved rounds, and allows a node to determine whether their neighbors have a lower counter value than themselves. The idea is now that nodes refrain from incrementing the counter as long as there are neighbors that are still behind.

We describe the balanced counter technique from the perspective of some node u using a state machine. Each node may be in one of the following states: COUNT, RESET-NOTIFY, or RESET-WAIT, and we denote u's current state by *state*. If *state* = COUNT, then u is considered to be a *participating* node, and either `increment` or `reset` may be invoked at u. In the other two states those operations are not available to u. The only allowed state transitions for node u are

1. COUNT $\rightarrow$ RESET-NOTIFY if no node $v \in \mathcal{N}(u)$ is in RESET-WAIT,
2. RESET-NOTIFY $\rightarrow$ RESET-WAIT if no node $v \in N(u)$ is in COUNT, and
3. RESET-WAIT $\rightarrow$ COUNT if no node $v \in N(u)$ is in RESET-NOTIFY.

Communication of the balanced counter technique is subdivided into phases indexed by the positive integers. Each individual phase consists of 6 rounds; to avoid confusion we use the term slot to refer to the individual rounds within a phase. The role of the first three slots $(0, 1, 2)$ is to transmit the counter increments, whereas the last three slots $(3, 4, 5)$ are used to transmit the node's current state. We now give a detailed description of the balanced counter technique; the full version also includes a pseudo-code description.

Initially, the state of u is COUNT, and $counter = 0$. In each phase, the operation at node u is as follows:

1. If $state =$ COUNT, then u beeps in slot $counter$ (mod 3) and in slot 3;
2. If $state =$ RESET-NOTIFY, then u beeps in slot 4; and
3. If $state =$ RESET-WAIT, then u beeps in slot $counter$ (mod 3) and in slot 5.

Node u listens in all slots in which it does not beep.

Increment. The purpose of this operation is to increment $counter$ by one without violating the balancing property. When `increment` is invoked at node u, then u waits for the first phase in which no beep is received in slot $counter - 1$ (mod 3) (note that u never transmits in slot $counter - 1$ (mod 3)). Node v increments $counter$ by 1 at the end of that phase and returns from the `increment` operation.

Reset. The purpose of this operation is to reset node u's value of $counter$ to zero in accord with neighboring nodes $v \in N(u)$, while allowing nodes v to proceed participating before invoking `reset` themselves. Specifically, when `reset` is invoked at node u, then u successively transitions (1) from COUNT to RESET-NOTIFY, thereby setting $counter \leftarrow 0$, (2) from RESET-NOTIFY to RESET-WAIT, and eventually (3) from RESET-WAIT back to COUNT. In this process u respects the aforementioned restrictions for state transitions, utilizing the transmissions in slots 3 to 5. In particular, the aforementioned transition (i), $1 \leq i \leq 3$, is consummated in the first phase in which no beep is received in slot $2 + i$.

An inductive argument can be used to establish the following lemma; a formal proof is presented in the full version of this paper.

Lemma 5 *The balanced counter technique satisfies the balancing property.*

4.2   Balanced Executions

Consider two algorithms $\mathcal{A}$ and $\mathcal{B}$ that shall be simulated sequentially. To achieve our goal, we intend to simulate the execution of $\mathcal{A}$ and $\mathcal{B}$ in the network. In $\mathcal{A}$'s simulation, the balanced counter is used as a round counter. Since the round counter satisfies the balancing property, it is ensured that the simulations performed by neighboring nodes progress at the same rate. When at some node u the simulation of $\mathcal{A}$ terminates, the round counter is reset by u. Node u then waits until its round counter returns to the COUNT state and thereupon starts the simulation of $\mathcal{B}$.

One needs to ensure that when round r of $\mathcal{A}$ (or $\mathcal{B}$) is simulated at node u, then u can determine whether one of its neighbors transmitted a beep in round $r - 1$ of the simulation. To that end, we extend each phase of the counter technique by three additional slots and reserve the first 6 slots (0–5) for the balanced counter technique. Consider a phase p and a node u currently simulating algorithm $\mathcal{A}$, and denote by r the *counter* value for node u at the beginning of phase p. The three new slots (6–8) are used to transmit and receive the beeps emitted during the simulation as follows.

Assuming that $\mathcal{A}$ did not terminate in round $r - 1$, the goal in phase p is to simulate $\mathcal{A}$'s round r. Node u simulates round r of algorithm $\mathcal{A}$ utilizing slot $r \pmod 3 + 6$ to replace $\mathcal{A}$'s access to the communication channel, where beeps received in slot $(r - 1 \pmod 3) + 6$ replace the beeps received by v in the simulation if node u listened in round $r - 1$ of $\mathcal{A}$. Moreover, in slot $r - 1 \pmod 3$, node u re-transmits a beep if u beeped in the last simulated round $r - 1$ under $\mathcal{A}$. If u incremented the counter to the value r in the current phase, i.e., the counter progressed from $r - 1$ to r, then v invokes **increment** again. Note that **increment** may delay incrementing r for several phases; in that case, the same round r of $\mathcal{A}$ is simulated in phase p multiple times, and if the beeps received in slot $r - 1$ change, then so does the simulated execution of $\mathcal{A}$'s round r.

Otherwise, if $\mathcal{A}$ terminated its execution in the previous round $r - 1$, the goal is to safely start the simulation of the next algorithm $\mathcal{B}$ at node u. To that end, node u invokes the **reset** operation. However, the simulated execution of the next algorithm $\mathcal{B}$ (possibly using u's output of $\mathcal{A}$ as input) only starts once u continues participating in the balanced counter, i.e., when $state = \textsc{Count}$.

In the full paper we explain how to exploit the balanced counter property to obtain the following correctness lemma. It essentially states that the balanced execution technique behaves as if global synchronization was used to start the algorithms one after the other.

Lemma 6 *Let $A = (\mathcal{A}_1, \ldots, \mathcal{A}_k)$ be a finite sequence of algorithms. Denote, for every $v \in V$, by $\hat{o}_1(v)$ the output produced at v by $\mathcal{A}_1$ when executed on G. For $i > 1$ and for every $v \in V$, denote by $\hat{o}_i(v)$ the output produced at v by $\mathcal{A}_i$ when executed on G, where the input to every $u \in V$ for $\mathcal{A}_i$ is specified as $\hat{o}_{i-1}(u)$.*

It holds that for every node v, the output $o(v)$ produced at v when using the balanced execution technique for A is $o(v) = \hat{o}_k(v)$.

4.3   Leader Election through Campaigning

We now have the tools available to design a non-quiescent leader election algorithm. Utilizing the balanced execution technique, every node executes the **Campaigning** algorithm sequentially, again and again. For every node u, the input to the first invocation of **Campaigning** is $id(u)$, and the input to every following invocation of **Campaigning** is the output of the previous one. In the following we refer to this basic protocol as the **Restless-LE** (for leader election) algorithm. It is immediate from the design of **Restless-LE**, that the network will never reach a quiescent state — for instance, the balanced counter technique never ceases to transmit. The following lemma states that **Restless-LE** obtains the desired result after at most D invocations of **Campaigning**.

Lemma 7 *If the network G executes* `Restless-LE`, *then for every node $u \in V$, the output produced at u by the D-th invocation of* `Campaigning` *is* $\max_{v \in V} \text{id}(v)$.

Utilizing the balanced execution technique, Theorem 7 can be obtained by inductively applying Theorems 1 and 2 for D times. Simulating D invocations of `Campaigning` takes $O(D \log n)$ rounds, as is stated in Theorem 8. The proofs to both Theorems 7 and 8 appear in the full version.

Theorem 8. *If the network G executes* `Restless-LE`, *then for every node $u \in V$, the D-th invocation of* `Campaigning` *terminates after* $O(D \log n)$ *rounds.*

Note that the network never reaches quiescence since the balanced counter technique continues to beep even after the D-th invocation of `Campaigning` has terminated. Moreover, without knowledge of D, node u has no means to decide when sufficiently many campaigns have been run.

5   Terminating and Achieving Quiescence

It seems that in the previous section we robbed Peter to pay Paul: We obtained `Restless-LE` which finds a leader in time $O(D \log n)$, but now our algorithm does not achieve quiescence, nor does a node know when to terminate. These two flaws could be considered a major drawback if one wishes to use the leader election algorithm as a foundation for another algorithm, since it is unclear when the latter can be started. To overcome this obstacle we implement an overlay network protocol that executes concurrently to the `Campaigning` invocations. The overlay network we establish on top of the original communication graph resembles the layers of an onion with the elected leader at its core. Utilizing the overlay network, we then describe how candidates detect whether the leader election process has terminated. Causing all non-elected nodes to terminate is now achieved by sending a broadcast message.

In order to form the overlay network, each node u keeps track of one additional variable *depth* taking values from the set $\{0, 1, 2\}$, initially set to 0. We say that a path $p = (u_1, \ldots, u_k)$, $(u_{i-1}, u_i) \in E$ for $2 \leq i \leq k$, is a *downward overlay path* if for all $i \geq 2$ it holds that $depth(u_i) = depth(u_{i-1})+1 \pmod 3$, and we denote the length k of a path p by $length(p)$. Conversely, we say that p is an *upward overlay path* if p reversed is a downward overlay path. One can think of downward overlay paths as leading away from the network's core, whereas upward overlay paths lead towards it. Note that initially, all overlay paths consist of only a single node. The general idea is to relay beeps along upward and downward overlay paths. Before extending the `Restless-LE` algorithm to utilize the overlay network, thus obtaining the quiescent terminating leader election algorithm `Quiescent-LE` in Section 5.1, we describe the operation of our overlay network technique in more detail. Note that in the full version of this paper we include a pseudo-code representation of the overlay network technique.

Every round r of the leader election algorithm is replaced by phases consisting of 10 slots, one single slot and three triplets of slots. The single slot is reserved to execute the non-terminating leader election algorithm we obtained in Section 4.3. For clarity, we refer to the first slot triplet as *control* slots, to the second triplet as *up channel* slots, and to the last triplet as *down channel* slots. The control slots, up channel slots, and down channel slots are numbered from 0 to 2 (e.g., up channel slot 2 is the last slot in the second triplet of slots in a phase). While the role of the control slots is to establish the overlay network, the up and down channel slots are used to transmit beeps to nodes with smaller and higher depth, respectively.

More specifically, in every phase p, node u listens in the up channel $depth - 1$ (mod 3) and in the down channel $depth + 1$ (mod 3). If a beep is received in one of those slots, then in the following phase $p + 1$, u beeps in the up channel $depth$ or in the down channel $depth$, correspondingly. The overlay network further provides the two operations beep_depth and join, which are implemented as follows. When beep_depth is invoked by node u, then u transmits a beep in control slot $depth$. The corresponding join operation causes u to listen in the three control slots; node u then sets $depth \leftarrow i + 1$ (mod 3), where i denotes the index of the first control slot in which a beep was received, thereby joining the overlay network of one of its neighbors that invoked beep_depth.

5.1   Quiescent Leader Election

In this section, we describe the Quiescent-LE algorithm that utilizes the overlay network technique in conjunction with the Restless-LE algorithm. Formation of the overlay network is tightly coupled with Restless-LE and the invocations of Campaigning therein. Namely, whenever an invocation of Campaigning at node u returns a new ID x, node u joins the overlay network of a neighbor that transmitted x to u. Nodes that are currently being convinced of a new leader emit a signal into the upward channel of neighboring nodes, thus ensuring that no candidate terminates unless a consensus on the leader's ID has been reached.

In particular, for a node u in phase p, denote by σ the state in which the last Campaigning invocation that terminated for node u was upon termination. Denote further by $last\_role$, $last\_in$, and $last\_out$ the values of the corresponding variables $role$, id_{in} and id_{out} in σ. In phase p a node u is called a *candidate* if $last\_in = \mathrm{id}(u)$, and we say that node c is the candidate of u if $last\_in = \mathrm{id}(c)$. The idea is now to utilize the overlay network so that nodes may join the overlay network of their corresponding candidate. This is accomplished by setting the $depth$ variable accordingly whenever the value of $last\_out$ changes.

In Quiescent-LE, the operation of node u is as follows (please refer to the full version for a pseudo-code description). If $last\_role = active$, then u invokes beep_depth, thus allowing nodes $v \in \mathcal{N}(u)$ to set their depth. Correspondingly, u invokes join if its candidate has changed (i.e., if $last\_role = passive$), in order to assign a new value to its depth variable. In any case, if $last\_role \neq active$, then node u beeps in all three up channel slots in contrast to the normal up channel operation. A candidate that has not received a beep through the up channel for 18 consecutive rounds emits a signal in the down channel, thus instructing nodes to terminate.

Theorem 9. *The uniform algorithm* Quiescent-LE *terminates after* $O(D \log n)$ *rounds at every node. Every node returns the same output* $\max_{v \in V} \mathrm{id}(v)$.

The proof to our main result, namely, the above Theorem 9, is based on the concept of coalitions that form around potential leader nodes. All nodes inside a coalition share the same potential leader and form an onion layer network with the potential leader at its core. Eventually, the coalition Z corresponding to the highest identifier z overrules every other. In particular, coalition Z extends its borders by one step in every Campaigning invocation. This is crucial in order to ensure proper formation of the onion layer network, which in turn guarantees that the leader node (with identifier z) can safely issue the terminating signal. We refer to the full version of this paper for an extensive proof.

6   Synchronized Wake-Up Protocol

Note that one may also study a variant of the beeping model (see, e.g., [11]) in which only a subset $S \subseteq V$ of the nodes wakes up in round 0. Nodes in $V \setminus S$ are initially *asleep*, and wake up only if they receive a beep from one of their neighbors. In particular, such a node is no longer considered asleep. We briefly discuss how our algorithm can be extended to include a wake-up protocol.

Every original slot in a phase of Quiescent-LE is replaced by two slots, where the first slot takes the role of the corresponding original slot, and in the second slot a node is always silent. Additionally, the phase is preceded by another two slots, referred to as wake-up slots. Consider an asleep node u. As soon as u receives a beep, it enters an intermediate *snooze* state, and if u receives a beep in the next round as well, then it turns *awake*. Otherwise, snoozing nodes turn awake after receiving two beeps consecutively. A node that just turned awake enters the protocol after the wake-up slots, thus aligning its execution with awake neighbors. That is, the first round in which u participates corresponds to the first original slot of Quiescent-LE. Note that in particular, due to the balanced execution technique, node u postpones the progress of awake neighboring nodes. Lastly, a node u that is awake beeps in both wake-up slots whenever u starts a phase of Quiescent-LE that coincides with the beginning of a balanced execution phase, and remains silent in the wake-up slots otherwise.

7   Conclusion

We described a deterministic uniform leader election algorithm in the beeping model that achieves quiescence after $O(D \log n)$ rounds. There are three main ingredients to our algorithm:

1. A Campaigning algorithm that propagates the locally highest identifier one hop per invocation.
2. A technique to sequentially execute arbitrarily many algorithms in the beeping model, based on a simple balanced counter approach.
3. An overlay network, based on the onion layer principle.

Our algorithm is obtained by using the sequential execution technique (2.) to execute the `Campaigning` method (1.) multiple times, one after the other. In its first invocation, the algorithm essentially creates a 2-hop independent set containing at least one node. The independent nodes are potential leaders and transmit their identifier to their neighbors. In subsequent invocations, potential leaders correspond to clusters of nodes with the same campaigning-identifier. When clusters touch, the cluster C having the larger campaigning-identifier wins, and the neighboring clusters shrink as bordering nodes join C. This yields a non-quiescent uniform algorithm `Restless-LE` for leader election, where the leader is not informed about her successful election.

If the diameter D was known to all nodes, then termination could be achieved by stopping after the Dth invocation of `Campaigning`. However, we want our algorithm to be uniform. We create an onion layer overlay network (3.) in order to achieve uniformity and quiescence. Potential leaders form the core of an onion, and nodes in a cluster are layered according to their distance to the core. Since the cluster of the eventual leader grows in each step, eventually all nodes will be part of a single cluster. The onion layer principle can now be used to establish a communication channel from outer layers towards the core and vice versa. When the cluster stops growing, the leader is informed about her successful election, in turn allowing her to issue a termination signal to all nodes. Lastly, we explain how the algorithm can be extended to handle the synchronous wake-up situation described in [11].

References

1. Angluin, D.: Local and global properties in networks of processors (extended abstract). In: STOC, pp. 82–93 (1980)
2. Bar-Yehuda, R., Goldreich, O., Itai, A.: On the time-complexity of broadcast in multi-hop radio networks: An exponential gap between determinism and randomization. J. Comput. Syst. Sci. 45(1), 104–126 (1992)
3. Capetanakis, J.: Tree algorithms for packet broadcast channels. IEEE Transactions on Information Theory 25(5), 505–515 (1979)
4. Chlebus, B.S., Kowalski, D.R., Pelc, A.: Electing a leader in multi-hop radio networks. In: Baldoni, R., Flocchini, P., Binoy, R. (eds.) OPODIS 2012. LNCS, vol. 7702, pp. 106–120. Springer, Heidelberg (2012)
5. Chrobak, M., Gasieniec, L., Kowalski, D.R.: The wake-up problem in multihop radio networks. SIAM J. Comput. 36(5), 1453–1471 (2007)
6. Clementi, A.E.F., Monti, A., Silvestri, R.: Distributed broadcast in radio networks of unknown topology. Theor. Comput. Sci. 302(1-3), 337–364 (2003)
7. Cornejo, A., Kuhn, F.: Deploying wireless networks with beeps. In: Lynch, N.A., Shvartsman, A.A. (eds.) DISC 2010. LNCS, vol. 6343, pp. 148–162. Springer, Heidelberg (2010)
8. Flury, R., Wattenhofer, R.: Slotted programming for sensor networks. In: IPSN, pp. 24–34 (2010)
9. Gasieniec, L., Pelc, A., Peleg, D.: The wakeup problem in synchronous broadcast systems. SIAM J. Discrete Math. 14(2), 207–222 (2001)
10. Ghaffari, M., Haeupler, B.: Near optimal leader election in multi-hop radio networks. In: SODA, pp. 748–766 (2013)

11. Ghaffari, M., Haeupler, B.: Near optimal leader election in multi-hop radio networks. CoRR, abs/1210.8439v2 (April 2014)
12. Greenberg, A.G., Winograd, S.: A lower bound on the time needed in the worst case to resolve conflicts deterministically in multiple access channels. J. ACM 32(3), 589–596 (1985)
13. Hayes, J.F.: An adaptive technique for local distribution. IEEE Transactions on Communications 26(8), 1178–1186 (1978)
14. Jurdzinski, T., Stachowiak, G.: Probabilistic algorithms for the wake-up problem in single-hop radio networks. Theory Comput. Syst. 38(3), 347–367 (2005)
15. Kowalski, D.R., Pelc, A.: Leader election in ad hoc radio networks: A keen ear helps. Journal of Computer and System Sciences 79(7), 1164–1180 (2013)
16. Kushilevitz, E., Mansour, Y.: An $\Omega(D \log(N/D))$ lower bound for broadcast in radio networks. SIAM J. Comput. 27(3), 702–712 (1998)
17. Lynch, N.A.: Distributed Algorithms. Morgan Kaufmann (1996)
18. Pelc, A.: Activating anonymous ad hoc radio networks. Distributed Computing 19(5-6), 361–371 (2007)
19. Tsybakov, B.S., Mikhailov, V.A.: Free synchronous packet access in a broadcast channel with feedback. Probl. Inf. Transm. 14(4), 259–280 (1978)
20. Willard, D.E.: Log-logarithmic selection resolution protocols in a multiple access channel. SIAM J. Comput. 15(2), 468–477 (1986)

Who Are You?
Secure Identities in Ad Hoc Networks

Seth Gilbert[1], Calvin Newport[2], and Chaodong Zheng[1,*]

[1] Department of Computer Science, National University of Singapore, Singapore
{gilbert,chaodong}@comp.nus.edu.sg
[2] Department of Computer Science, Georgetown University, United States
cnewport@cs.georgetown.edu

Abstract. *Sybil attacks* occur when malicious users create multiple fake
identities to gain an advantage over honest users. Wireless ad hoc networks
are particularly vulnerable to these attacks because the participants are
not known in advance, and they use an open and shared communication
medium. In this paper, we develop algorithms that thwart sybil attacks in
multi-channel wireless ad hoc networks using *radio resource testing* strategies. In particular, we describe and analyze new anti-sybil algorithms that
guarantee, with high probability, that each honest device accepts a set of
trusted and unforgeable identities that include all other honest devices and
a bounded number of fake (sybil) identities. The proposed algorithms provide trade-offs between time complexity and sybil bounds. We also note
that these algorithms solve, as subroutines, two problems of independent
interest in this anonymous wireless setting: Byzantine consensus and network size estimation.

1 Introduction

Imagine the following scenario: A group of independent wireless devices is activated in a single hop wireless network. Some of them are honest while others
are malicious. The honest devices are provided with no information regarding
the size of the network or the identities of the other devices. The goal is to solve
some standard distributed computing problem; e.g., the honest devices may need
to reach agreement, vote on a proposal, simulate a shared object, or establish a
fair schedule to share a limited resource.

Intuitively, this *anonymous wireless network* scenario seems hopeless. Honest
devices are provided with no advance information on network size or participants,
and there is no obvious way to distinguish honest from malicious devices. Thus,
malicious devices can commence a *sybil attack* [8] in which they create many
fake identities (also called *sybil identities*, or *sybils*) to bias a given distributed
algorithm. For example, when running a consensus algorithm that depends on

* This research is supported by MOE2011-T2-2-042 "Fault-tolerant Communication
Complexity in Wireless Networks" from the Singapore MOE AcRF-2, by NSF grant
CCF 1320279, and by the Ford Motor Company University Research Program.

F. Kuhn (Ed.): DISC 2014, LNCS 8784, pp. 227–242, 2014.

a majority vote, the malicious devices could create enough sybil identities to ensure they control a majority of voters.

This paper proves–perhaps surprisingly–that this scenario is not hopeless. We describe and analyze new algorithms that allow honest devices to constrain the number of sybil identities to an asymptotically optimal limit. Our results answer open questions regarding sybil resistance in ad hoc networks and provide a general foundation for establishing trusted computing in the increasingly untrustworthy world of wireless networking.

Radio Resource Testing. Thwarting a sybil attack typically relies on some combination of additional external information (see, e.g., [22, 23]), *computational resource tests* (see, e.g., [2, 9, 15]), and/or *radio resource tests* (see, e.g., [12, 13, 16–19]). In this paper, we adopt the radio resource testing approach. In particular, we leverage two assumptions: (a) each malicious device has a single radio which can only tune into a single channel at a time; and (b) the total number of real malicious devices, t, is less than c, the total number of available channels. The first assumption derives from the idea that the adversary has the same hardware available as the honest devices (and, notably, hardware similar to standard wireless devices today). The second assumption is unavoidable: when dealing with wireless communication, if the malicious users can send and receive over *all* channels of the relevant spectrum band simultaneously, then they can *jam* on every channels, preventing all communication; in this case, most non-trivial problems become impossible to solve.

Given these assumptions, devices can *test* potential identities by requiring them to participate on certain channels at certain times. Because malicious devices are limited in the number of channels they can use concurrently, if these tests are constructed carefully, they can limit the number of identities each malicious device can convincingly maintain.

The networking community recognizes this radio resource testing approach as practical, as most real world wireless devices have access to many more channels than they can use simultaneously, and it does not require additional information or detailed assumptions on computational capabilities. Typically, however, existing anti-sybil protocols that use radio resource tests either: (a) rely on a central trusted base station (e.g., [12]); (b) combine radio resource testing with other resource constraints or outside information (e.g., [18]); or (c) require time complexity that grows with the number of sybil identities (e.g., [19]), allowing the malicious devices to potentially swamp the system with never-ending tests. In this paper, by contrast, we present fully distributed algorithms that reduce the number of sybils to an asymptotically optimal limit, without a centralized base station, using only radio resource tests, and with provable time complexity guarantees that are expressed with respect to the actual number of devices.

Results. We consider a single hop wireless network consisting of $c > 1$ channels. We divide time into synchronous slots and assume that the n devices (or *nodes*) are activated simultaneously. At most $t \leq \min\{n, c\}/\alpha$ of these devices are malicious, where $\alpha \geq 1$ is a sufficiently large constant. Honest devices do not know n or t in advance. We assume standard collision rules: if multiple devices send on the same channel during the same slot, the messages are lost due to a collision, which can be detected at the receivers' end. Collisions further complicate our task as: (a) malicious devices can intentionally jam; and (b) honest devices must deal with contention resolution even without knowledge of the network size. We also assume the availability of standard asymmetric cryptographic primitives. This allows devices to generate unique public/private key pairs and use their public keys as identities. Because devices can sign their messages with their private keys, these identities are unforgeable. The challenge in our setting, therefore, is to prevent the malicious devices from creating *too many* sybil identities. The algorithms described below are randomized and their guarantees hold with high probability (i.e., with probability at least $1 - 1/n^\beta$ for any $\beta \geq 1$).

We begin by describing and analyzing a basic algorithm named SIMPLESY-BILSIEVE. This algorithm terminates in $O(n \lg^2 n \cdot \max\{1, n/c\})$ time. It provides each honest node with a set of unforgeable identities that includes all other honest nodes and no more than $O(t \cdot \max\{1, n/c\})$ sybil identities. Notice, when c is larger than n, the time complexity is $O(n \lg^2 n)$ and the number of sybil identities is bounded at an (asymptotically) optimal $O(t)$.[1] On the other extreme, when c is small compared to n, the time complexity grows to $O(n^2 \lg^2 n)$ and the sybil bound grows to $O(n)$. In settings where c is large or $O(n)$ sybils is tolerable, this basic algorithm is sufficient. On the other hand, in many settings, such as large networks, it might be preferable to obtain an optimal $O(t)$ bound on the number of sybils, even when $c < n$.

Motivated by this goal, we next present an augmented algorithm that we call SYBILSIEVE. This algorithm offers the same bound on the number of sybils as the basic algorithm, but is a factor of n slower. In exchange for this extra time, however, the algorithm provides two new strong guarantees: (a) all honest nodes terminate simultaneously (hence providing barrier synchronization); and (b) all honest nodes agree on the same estimate of n that is within a constant factor of the actual count.

We conclude by introducing our final (and strongest) algorithm which we call SYBILSIEVE². This algorithm builds on the useful guarantees of SYBILSIEVE to reduce the number of sybil identities to an optimal $O(t)$, even for $c < n$. Similar to SYBILSIEVE, it also runs in $O(n^2 \lg^2 n \cdot \max\{1, n/c\})$ time. Notice, these three algorithms provide users with trade-offs between time complexity and sybil resistance.

Lastly, we note that as a subcomponent of SYBILSIEVE², we develop an algorithm for solving Monte Carlo Byzantine consensus[2] in a sybil-prone environment. Both this consensus subroutine, and the synchronization and network size estimation implemented by SYBILSIEVE, may be of independent interest, as they simplify the bootstrapping of more advanced protocols in this setting.

---

[1] $O(t)$ sybil identities is clearly asymptotically optimal as the malicious nodes could behave honestly.

[2] The consensus protocol maintains its safety properties with high probability, but not with probability one.

2 Related Work

Sybil Attacks. The term "sybil attack" was coined by Douceur [8] in the context of peer-to-peer systems. As previously mentioned, one classical defense against sybil attacks is resource testing: each client must prove that it has a sufficient quantity of some resource; as long as each user, both honest and malicious, has approximately the same quantity of that resource, we can use resource testing to thwart sybil attacks. Cryptographic puzzles (e.g., brute force decryption, invert hash function) [2,9,15] are a standard example of computational resource tests.

In wireless networks, radio resource testing is a natural approach, and several variants have been explored in [17, 19]. Recently, by combining radio resource tests with other resource testing techniques, Mónica [18] succeeds in accomplishing the seemingly impossible: providing an algorithm that can be used to construct sybil-free quorums in ad hoc wireless networks. Nevertheless, their approach relies on multiple resource restrictions (both computational and radio), and makes several limiting assumptions (e.g., knowledge of network size and sender-side collision detection). Another recent approach for repelling sybil attacks is developed by Klonowski et al. [16]. Their approach only requires simple cryptographic tools (mostly one-way functions and pseudorandom number generators), and works in single channel environment. However, the proposed algorithm needs prior knowledge of network size, and requires running time that is proportional to the number of sybil identities created.

We have previously explored the idea of radio resource testing in the context of wireless devices downloading data from a *centralized* base station [12]. The resulting SYBILCAST protocol showed how a centralized base station can continuously test for sybil identities while at the same time servicing data requests. In this paper, there is no longer any fixed base station, hence we develop a novel uncoordinated, distributed implementation of radio resource tests which is at the heart of the SIMPLESYBILSIEVE protocol. In [12], we study the on-going process of nodes downloading data from the base station, and hence, we allow devices to enter the network at different times. In this paper, by contrast, we focus on solving one-shot distributed computing problems, and we therefore assume that devices begin the protocol simultaneously.

Aside from resource testing, other approaches to coping with sybil attacks exist as well. Pre-distributing credentials or signed certificates is perhaps the simplest approach (e.g., see the survey in [14,19]). Researchers have also leveraged radio fingerprinting techniques (e.g., using signal strength patterns to uniquely identify radios) to detect fake identities (e.g., see [7,20]). Another notable alternative relies on relationships among users in social networks (e.g., see [22,23]).

Consensus. Consensus is a fundamental problem in distributed computing (see e.g., [3]). Ad hoc and anonymous networks are a particularly challenging environment in which to achieve consensus, and there exist several papers that attempt to address it [1, 4, 5, 10]. Unfortunately, these papers do not consider sybil attacks. Recently, work by Golebiewski et al. [13] shows how to achieve fair leader election in spite of sybil attacks. Their approach is similar to [16], discussed earlier, and can potentially be used to solve consensus. (Note, though, that they assume knowledge of the network size.) In this paper, we solve (as subroutine) Monte Carlo Byzantine consensus in unknown and anonymous wireless ad hoc networks.

3 Model and Problem

We assume a single hop wireless network (i.e., a complete network) consisting of n devices (called *nodes* in the following) and $c > 1$ communication channels. To simplify calculations, we assume c is a power of 2. (If not, we can round down.) We divide time into synchronous *slots* and assume all nodes start in the same slot. In each slot, each node can participate on one of the c available channels. It can then decide to send or receive. We assume a sending node cannot receive, and vice versa (i.e., the channel is half-duplex). When a single node u sends on a channel k during a slot r, all nodes receiving on channel k during slot r receive u's message. If multiple nodes send on channel k during slot r, then all nodes receiving on channel k detect a collision. Finally, we assume nodes have access to standard asymmetric cryptography primitives; i.e., they can generate public/private key pairs and use them to encrypt/decrypt, and sign/verify messages. We assume nodes cannot break the cryptographic system.

Adversary model. We allow some nodes to suffer Byzantine failure. In particular, a faulty node can: (a) try to create sybil identities; (b) cause collisions (i.e., jam) on a channel by broadcasting noise; and/or (c) try to spoof messages (i.e., pretend to be some other *real honest* nodes). Notice, honest nodes that detect a collision cannot tell if it originates from jamming or multiple messages being sent concurrently. We assume a bound t on the maximum number of faulty nodes. More specifically, the algorithms we consider require that $t \leq \min\{n, c\}/\alpha$, for a constant $\alpha \geq 1$. We assume that honest nodes do *not* know n or t, but they know c and α. The faulty nodes, on the other hand, are aware of all parameters. We also allow the faulty nodes to collude, and adapt to past execution history. Therefore, we sometimes refer to them collectively as a single adaptive malicious entity named *Eve* that can use up to t channels per slot.

Problem statement. The goal of our sybil-thwarting algorithm is for each honest node to construct a set of trusted and unforgeable identities that includes: (a) a unique identity for each honest node, and (b) a bounded number of sybil identities. We assume that each honest node generates a unique public/private key pair at the beginning of an execution and uses its public key as its identity. Each node can subsequently sign its messages with its private key, confirming the identity of their sender (so that malicious nodes cannot spoof messages on behalf of an honest node). The challenge, therefore, is to minimize the number of sybil identities accepted by honest nodes, while simultaneously trying to minimize the time complexity. In this paper, we study randomized algorithms and require that their guarantees hold with high probability (w.h.p.).

4   The SimpleSybilSieve Algorithm

We begin by presenting the SimpleSybilSieve algorithm which introduces our core strategies for defeating sybil attacks. Notice, throughout this section, we assume $\alpha \geq 6$; and throughout the paper, we use δ to denote a small constant.

4.1   Protocol Description

The first issue that needs to be resolved is the unknown number of nodes, and we estimate it in the usual manner: the protocol proceeds in epochs, where in epoch i, we assume there are $n_i = 2^i$ nodes in total. In addition, in epoch i, we use $n_i/2$ channels; if $c < n_i/2$, then we simulate the $n_i/2$ needed channels using $n_i/(2c)$ slots for each "round" of the protocol.

At a high level, nodes have two tasks during each epoch: (a) check whether the current estimation of n is accurate; and (b) if the estimation is (roughly) correct, use the results of uncoordinated radio resource tests to spot honest identities and eliminate sybils. To achieve these goals, in each round, each honest node will broadcast or listen–each with probability $1/2$–on a random channel that is chosen from $[1, n_i/2]$.

Honest nodes count the number of silent rounds in each epoch to determine the accuracy of the current estimation. If the estimate is too small, there is nothing Eve can do to make it look correct, as the honest nodes alone generate enough contention on each channel to prevent too many silent rounds. Once the estimate is correct, by contrast, Eve cannot make the good estimate look bad, because she can only jam a limited number of channels simultaneously.

Once an honest node believes the current estimate is correct, it will re-examine the messages it has received during the current epoch to determine which identities to accept. More specifically, an honest node accepts an identity if it has heard that identity sufficiently many times in the current epoch. Since the number of radios Eve has is limited, the number of sybils she can successfully create in one epoch is limited as well.

We now describe each honest node's behavior in more detail. In epoch i, there are $an_i \lg n_i$ rounds, where $a > 0$ is some sufficiently large constant. In each round, every node will go to a random channel that is chosen uniformly from $[1, n_i/2]$. Then, each node will broadcast or listen, each with probability $1/2$. If a node chooses to broadcast, it will broadcast its identity (i.e., its public key). If a node chooses to listen, it will record whether it has heard silence (i.e., nothing), noise, or a packet from another identity.

After each epoch, for every node: if at least $\gamma_1 = (1-\delta)(1-1/\alpha)e^{-1/2} = \Theta(1)$ fraction of rounds were silent, among the rounds that it chose to listen, the node will terminate (without accepting any new identities). Otherwise, if at least $\gamma_2 = (1-\delta)(1-4/\alpha)e^{-2} = \Theta(1)$ fraction of slots were silent, where $\gamma_2 < \gamma_1$, then the node accepts every identity from which it has received at least $a\gamma_2(\lg n_i)/2$ messages. This procedure is summarized in Fig. 4.1.

Pseudocode of SimpleSybilSieve executed at node u:

1: Generate asymmetric key pair. Let k_p^u be u's public key, and k_o^u be u's private key.
2: $ids \leftarrow \emptyset$.   ▷ Set containing identities that u accepts.
3: **for** (every epoch $i \geq 1$) **do**
4:    $n_i \leftarrow 2^i$, $count_{listen} \leftarrow 0$, $count_{silent} \leftarrow 0$.
5:    $ids_{count} \leftarrow \emptyset$.   ▷ ids_{count} is a dictionary structure with value being an integer.
6:    **for** (every round $1 \leq j \leq an_i \lg n_i$) **do**
7:       $ch \leftarrow \texttt{random}(n_i/2)$.   ▷ $\texttt{random}(x)$ returns a random value from $[1, x]$.
8:       **for** (every slot $1 \leq k \leq \max\{1, n_i/2c\}$) **do**   ▷ Simulate one round with multiple slots.
9:          **if** $(\lfloor (ch - 1)/c \rfloor = k - 1)$ **then**
10:             **if** $(\texttt{random}(2) = 1)$ **then**   ▷ Broadcast with probability $1/2$.
11:                $\texttt{broadcast}(\langle k_p^u \rangle, ((ch - 1) \bmod c) + 1)$. ▷ $\texttt{broadcast}(m, h)$ broadcasts m on h.
12:             **else**   ▷ Listen with probability $1/2$.
13:                $count_{listen} \leftarrow count_{listen} + 1$.
14:                $msg \leftarrow \texttt{listen}(((ch - 1) \bmod c) + 1)$. ▷ $\texttt{listen}(h)$ means listen on channel h.
15:                **if** $(msg \neq nil$ **and** $msg \neq noise)$ **then**   ▷ Node has heard a message.
16:                   Let k_p^v be the public key inside msg.
17:                   **if** $(k_p^v \notin ids_{count})$ **then** $ids_{count}[k_p^v] \leftarrow 1$.
18:                   **else** $ids_{count}[k_p^v] \leftarrow ids_{count}[k_p^v] + 1$.
19:             **else if** $(msg = nil)$ **then**   ▷ Node has heard a silent round.
20:                $count_{silent} \leftarrow count_{silent} + 1$.
21:    **if** $(count_{silent}/count_{listen} \geq (1 - \delta)(1 - 1/\alpha)e^{-1/2})$ **then return** ids.
22:    **else if** $(count_{silent}/count_{listen} \geq (1 - \delta)(1 - 4/\alpha)e^{-2})$ **then**
23:       **for** (every identity k_p^v in ids_{count}) **do**
24:          **if** $(ids_{count}[k_p^v] \geq a(1 - \delta)(1 - 4/\alpha) \lg n_i/(2e^2))$ **then** $ids \leftarrow ids \bigcup \{k_p^v\}$.

Fig. 1. Pseudocode of SimpleSybilSieve

4.2 Analysis

In this subsection, we sketch the proof that every honest node will terminate at epoch $\lfloor \lg n \rfloor + O(1)$ and accept all other honest nodes. We will also show that there are at most $O(t \cdot \max\{1, n/c\})$ sybil identities that are accepted by honest nodes. Full proofs are provided in the full version of the paper [11].[3]

Termination and Correctness. To begin with, we argue that no honest nodes will accept any identities or terminate before (or during) epoch $\lg(n/(g \lg n))$, where g is a positive constant. The claim follows via standard coupon collector analysis as, in these epochs, the number of broadcasting honest nodes exceeds the number of used channels, creating contention and preventing silent rounds.

Lemma 1. *For any epoch i where $1 \leq i \leq \lg(n/(g \lg n))$, for some constant $g > 1$: w.h.p. honest nodes will hear only noisy rounds, and hence will not accept any identities during epoch i or terminate at the end of epoch i.*

We continue to consider epochs from $\lg(n/(g \lg n))$ to epoch $\lfloor \lg n \rfloor$. For these epochs, we claim that all honest nodes will still not terminate, since they will not hear enough silent rounds.

---

[3] If not otherwise stated, full proofs for lemmas and theorems in other parts the paper are provided in [11] as well.

Lemma 2. *For any epoch i where $\lg(n/(g\lg n)) \leq i \leq \lfloor\lg n\rfloor$, w.h.p. no honest nodes will terminate after epoch i.*

We then claim that every honest node will accept all other honest nodes during epoch $\lfloor\lg n\rfloor$, i.e., each honest node will hear from all the other honest nodes sufficiently often in that epoch.

Lemma 3. *Every honest node will accept all other honest nodes during epoch $\lfloor\lg n\rfloor$, w.h.p.*

Lastly, we show all honest nodes will terminate at most two epochs later.

Lemma 4. *All honest nodes will terminate no later than the end of epoch $\lfloor\lg n\rfloor + 2$, w.h.p.*

Constraining Sybil Identities. We now show SIMPLESYBILSIEVE can ensure the total number of sybil identities that are accepted by any honest nodes is at most $O(t \cdot \max\{1, n/c\})$. Firstly, we identify the epochs in which honest nodes can potentially accept sybil identities.

Lemma 5. *Honest nodes will accept sybil identities only between epoch $\lfloor\lg n\rfloor - 1$ and epoch $\lfloor\lg n\rfloor + 1$, w.h.p.*

Any earlier, there are too few channels (and too much contention); any later, there are too many channels. At this point, we can also summarize honest nodes' behavior as follows: (a) for every epoch before and including $\lfloor\lg n\rfloor$, no honest nodes will terminate; (b) during epoch $\lfloor\lg n\rfloor - 1$ to epoch $\lfloor\lg n\rfloor + 1$, honest nodes may accept identities, which include other honest nodes and sybil identities; (c) by the end of epoch $\lfloor\lg n\rfloor$, every honest node must have accepted all other honest nodes; and (d) some (or all) honest nodes may terminate after epoch $\lfloor\lg n\rfloor + 1$, and all remaining will terminate after epoch $\lfloor\lg n\rfloor + 2$.

In the following key technical lemma, we show for every epoch i where $\lfloor\lg n\rfloor - 1 \leq i \leq \lfloor\lg n\rfloor + 1$, at most $O(t \cdot \max\{1, n/c\})$ sybil identities will be accepted by honest nodes. The intuition is as follows: in each round in these epochs, each honest node will, in expectation, broadcast its identity $\Theta(1)$ times. On the other hand, Eve can broadcast an identity at most $O(t \cdot \max\{1, n/c\})$ times in every round, each of which we call a broadcast round-channel combination. This implies Eve can advocate an identity at most $O(t \cdot \max\{1, n/c\})$ times faster than honest nodes. Since each honest node's broadcast rate allows itself to be accepted $O(1)$ times (by other honest nodes) in each of these three epochs, we know Eve can successfully create at most $O(t \cdot \max\{1, n/c\})$ sybil identities in each of these three epochs. One tricky point in the proof is to carefully analyze the (in)dependence relationship between multiple broadcast round-channel combinations, and then apply Chernoff bounds accordingly.

Lemma 6. *For epoch i where $\lfloor\lg n\rfloor - 1 \leq i \leq \lfloor\lg n\rfloor + 1$, w.h.p. at most $\frac{2(1+\delta)e^2 \cdot e^{-(n-t)/n_i}}{(1-\delta)(1-4/\alpha)} \cdot t \cdot \max\{1, n_i/2c\} = O(t \cdot \max\{1, n/c\})$ sybil identities will be accepted by honest nodes in that epoch.*

Based on the above six lemmas, we can immediately obtain the following theorem which states the key guarantees provided by SIMPLESYBILSIEVE.

Theorem 1. *For any $t \le \min\{n, c\}/\alpha$ where $\alpha \ge 6$, SIMPLESYBILSIEVE terminates in $O(n \lg^2 n \cdot \max\{1, n/c\})$ slots, and guarantees the following, w.h.p.: (a) there are at most $O(t \cdot \max\{1, n/c\})$ sybil identities accepted by the honest nodes, collectively; and (b) every honest node accepts all other honest nodes.*

5   The SybilSieve Algorithm

Our goal is to build on the foundation provided by SIMPLESYBILSIEVE to get an optimal $O(t)$ bound on the number of sybil identities for all values of c (not just when $c > n$). An obstacle, however, is that nodes executing SIMPLESYBILSIEVE do not necessarily terminate at the same time. This makes it difficult to use SIMPLESYBILSIEVE in a more involved anti-sybil strategy. To address this problem, we present an improved version of SIMPLESYBILSIEVE that we call SYBILSIEVE. This new algorithm offers the same sybil bounds as SIMPLESYBILSIEVE, but is slower. In exchange for the extra time, it guarantees that all nodes terminate at the same time and share a common constant-factor estimate of n (both of which will prove to be useful for our final algorithm).

At the core of SYBILSIEVE is a consensus primitive named SYBILSENSUS. Nodes execute SYBILSENSUS at the end of each epoch to decide whether or not to terminate. This ensures nodes stop simultaneously. Nodes then use the epoch number (when they stop) to derive their common estimate of the network size.

For ease of presentation, we define the following notation: (a) let H denote the set of honest nodes; (b) for any honest node u, let ids_u (or just ids when there is no ambiguity) denote the set of identities it has already accepted; and (c) for any protocol, if all honest nodes start executing it simultaneously, then we say we have a *synchronized execution* of it. We also note here, in the reminder of the paper, we assume $\alpha \ge 256$.

5.1   SybilSensus: A Consensus Building Block

SYBILSENSUS is a wireless variant of the Byzantine consensus algorithm described in [21], with sybil attacks taken into consideration. Before presenting it, we first briefly discuss a broadcast primitive named CONSISTBCST, which is an implementation of the authenticated broadcast (i.e., *Echo Broadcast*) algorithm from [21]. CONSISTBCST is used in SYBILSENSUS.

CONSISTBCST. Consistent broadcast ensures consistency among the messages that are accepted by honest nodes. In particular, it enforces: (a) if an honest node broadcasts a message, then all honest nodes will eventually *accept* that message; (b) if Eve sends a message on behalf of an honest node (i.e., Eve is spoofing), then no honest nodes will accept that message; and (c) if an honest node accepts a message, then all honest nodes will eventually accept that message. When sybil attacks are present, in our context, consistent broadcast should also guarantee: (d) if Eve sends a message on behalf of a sybil identity that is not accepted by any honest nodes, then no honest nodes will accept it.

CONSISTBCST is a typical implementation of Echo Broadcast [21]: initially, the sender broadcasts the message to everyone; everyone who receives the message directly from u, or who receives enough "echo" messages, send an "echo" message repeating the initial message; finally, everyone who receives enough total copies of the message accepts it. In our context, the protocol is modified as follows: (a) a node only processes messages that are properly signed from other identities that it has already accepted; (b) the protocol is parametrized to operate based on an estimated network size, and the guarantees will only hold if this estimate is within a constant (multiplicative) factor of being correct; and (c) the guarantees hold only if the number of sybil identities that are accepted by the honest nodes is not too large. Due to space constraint, more detailed description and analysis of CONSISTBCST are provided in the full version of the paper.

SYBILSENSUS. We now describe the SYBILSENSUS protocol, which solves a variant of consensus in which nodes agree on a set of items (instead of on a single value). Initially, in SYBILSIEVE, we use SYBILSENSUS only to solve traditional (binary) consensus, where nodes agree on whether or not to terminate; later, in SYBILSIEVE^2, we will use the more general version to agree on the set of identities. It operates under the assumption that we have a reasonable network size estimation, and that there are only a limited number of sybil identities present.

Each execution of SYBILSENSUS at an honest node u requires three parameters: (a) a set of items, denoted as I_u; (b) an estimation of n, denoted as $\hat{n}$; and (c) a set of identities that is currently accepted by u, denoted as ids_u.

When the protocol terminates, each node outputs a new set S_u. These sets should agree: every node should output the same set. The validity condition has two parts. First, if an item x is in the input set I_u for every honest node u, then x is in the output set. Second, if an item x is *not* in the input set I_u for any honest node u, then x is *not* in the output set.

An execution of SYBILSENSUS consists of $\hat{f} + 1$ phases, where $\hat{f} = \hat{n}/3 - 1$. During the execution of SYBILSENSUS, nodes will use CONSISTBCST to broadcast messages. In phase i, an honest node u will decide whether to broadcast messages, and the contents of the messages, based on the following rules: (a) in phase one, for every item x in I_u, u will broadcast a message which is a concatenation of its identity and x; and (b) in any phase $i \geq 2$, for every item x that has appeared in at least $\hat{f} + i - 1$ different accepted messages before the start of phase i, u will broadcast a message which is a concatenation of its identity and x. On the other hand, during each phase, honest nodes will also record items that have appeared in accepted messages. By the end of these $\hat{f} + 1$ phases, for every item x that has appeared in at least $2\hat{f} + 1$ different accepted messages, u will add it to S_u. Finally, SYBILSENSUS returns S_u as the return value. The pseudocode of SYBILSENSUS is available in [11].

In the following lemma, we show SYBILSENSUS leads to consensus.

Lemma 7. *If honest nodes perform a synchronized execution of* SYBILSENSUS *with the same $\hat{n}$, then* SYBILSENSUS *guarantees: all honest nodes finish executing* SYBILSENSUS *simultaneously, and each outputs a set S containing zero or more items. Moreover, if: (a) $n/16 \le \hat{n} \le n$; (b) $|(\bigcup_{u \in H} ids_u) \setminus H| \le \hat{f} = \hat{n}/3 - 1$; (c) $\forall u \in H$ we have $H \subseteq ids_u$; and (d) there are at most $O(n)$ differently named items that are initially in some honest nodes' sets I. Then,* SYBILSENSUS *further guarantees:*

- *(Agreement) Every honest node outputs the same set S, w.h.p.*
- *(Validity) For any item x that is initially in every honest node's set I, after the execution of* SYBILSENSUS*, $\forall u \in H$ we have $x \in S_u$, w.h.p. Similarly, for any item x that is initially not in any honest nodes' I, after the execution of* SYBILSENSUS*, $\forall u \in H$ we have $x \notin S_u$, w.h.p.*

In the special cases where network size estimation is not accurate and honest nodes have not accepted each other yet, SYBILSENSUS can still provide "parial" validity for binary consensus. This property is stated in the lemma below and will later be shown to be useful for SYBILSIEVE.

Lemma 8. *If: (a) honest nodes perform a synchronized execution of* SYBILSENSUS *with the same $\hat{n}$; (b) $|(\bigcup_{u \in H} ids_u) \setminus H| \le \hat{f} = \hat{n}/3 - 1$; and (c) each honest node's initial I is an empty set. Then, all honest nodes will finish executing* SYBILSENSUS *simultaneously, and each outputs an empty set, w.h.p.*

We note here, when it is known that there are only a limited number of accepted sybil identities, SYBILSENSUS can directly be used as a consensus protocol. Otherwise, in an unknown and anonymous environment, nodes need to run sybil-resistant node discovery protocol (such as SYBILSIEVE) as a preliminary step (in order to limit the number of accepted sybil identities).

5.2   Maintaining Synchrony

With SYBILSENSUS in hand, we can now present the SYBILSIEVE protocol. SYBILSIEVE is similar to SIMPLESYBILSIEVE, with the key difference being termination: at the end of each epoch, nodes run SYBILSENSUS to decide whether to terminate or not; the input to SYBILSENSUS depends on whether the termination condition under the SIMPLESYBILSIEVE protocol is met. In particular, an input set contains a singleton item *term* if and only if the termination condition is met under the SIMPLESYBILSIEVE protocol. A node terminates after current epoch only if all nodes have agreed to terminate. The pseudocode of SYBILSIEVE is available in [11].

In the following lemma, we claim that SYBILSIEVE guarantees all honest nodes will terminate after the same epoch (and hence obtain the same estimate of network size). The key intuition behind it is: (a) for every epoch before $\lfloor \lg n \rfloor$, although trusted identities are not fully established, Lemma 8 ensures honest nodes will not incorrectly terminate; and (b) starting from epoch $\lfloor \lg n \rfloor$, the conditions which allow SYBILSENSUS to act like a consensus protocol are met, hence all honest nodes will not terminate after epoch $\lfloor \lg n \rfloor$ due to the validity property, and will all terminate simultaneously either after epoch $\lfloor \lg n \rfloor + 1$ or after epoch $\lfloor \lg n \rfloor + 2$ due to the agreement (or validity) property.

Lemma 9. *All honest nodes will finish executing* SYBILSIEVE *simultaneously, either after epoch* $\lfloor \lg n \rfloor + 1$ *or after epoch* $\lfloor \lg n \rfloor + 2$, *w.h.p.*

Combining Lemma 9 and our analysis in Subsection 4.2, we immediately have the following theorem which states the key guarantees SYBILSIEVE can provide.

Theorem 2. *For any* $t \leq \min\{n, c\}/\alpha$ *where* $\alpha \geq 256$, SYBILSIEVE *terminates in* $O(n^2 \lg^2 n \cdot \max\{1, n/c\})$ *slots, and guarantees the following after protocol execution, w.h.p.: (a) there are at most* $O(t \cdot \max\{1, n/c\})$ *sybil identities accepted by the honest nodes, collectively; (b) every honest node accepts all other honest nodes; and (c) all honest nodes terminate simultaneously and have the same estimate of network size which is either* $2^{\lfloor \lg n \rfloor}$ *or* $2^{\lfloor \lg n \rfloor + 1}$.

6   The SybilSieve² Algorithm

In this section we describe our final algorithm, SYBILSIEVE², which provides the strongest sybil bounds. This algorithm first runs SYBILSIEVE. It takes advantage of the synchronous termination and network size estimation of SYBILSIEVE to then run a sybil-reduction phase that guarantees no more than $O(t)$ sybil identities. The final time complexity is $O(n^2 \lg^2 n \cdot \max\{1, n/c\})$, which is n times slower than SIMPLESYBILSIEVE.

In more detail, the SYBILSIEVE² protocol contains three parts. The first part, as mentioned, executes SYBILSIEVE. The second part executes our consensus algorithm, SYBILSENSUS, so that honest nodes agree on a common set of accepted identities. The third part uses repeated instances of a variant of our previously developed centralized anti-sybil algorithm [12], rotating who plays the role of base station, and reduces the number of sybil identities to the (asymptotically) optimal $O(t)$. We now describe the second and third part of SYBILSIEVE² in more detail, and then conclude with our final theorem statement.

Second Part of SYBILSIEVE². After the execution of SYBILSIEVE, honest nodes may have accepted different sets of sybil identities. This creates difficulties for the third part of SYBILSIEVE². Hence, honest nodes first run SYBILSENSUS to reach agreement on which identities to accept.

We will refer to the list of identities that an honest node accepts after the execution of SYBILSIEVE as a *pre-list*; and we refer to the list of identities that an honest node accepts after the execution of the second part of SYBILSIEVE² as a *common-list*.

For each honest node u, the second part of SYBILSIEVE^2 is an execution of SYBILSENSUS with an input set containing $\Theta(n)$ items: each denotes one identity that is in u's pre-list. (In particular, each item's name is the corresponding identity's public key.) On the other hand, SYBILSENSUS's input for estimation on network size is $\hat{n}_u/2$, where $\hat{n}_u$–which is either $2^{\lfloor \lg n \rfloor}$ or $2^{\lfloor \lg n \rfloor+1}$ due to Theorem 2–is the estimation on network size obtained by u during the first part of SYBILSIEVE^2. The return value of SYBILSENSUS is u's common-list.

The following lemma shows SYBILSENSUS ensures all honest nodes will obtain same common-list, which contains all honest nodes, and $O(n)$ sybil identities.

Lemma 10. *After the execution of the second part of* SYBILSIEVE^2, *w.h.p. all honest nodes will obtain same common-list which contains all honest nodes and at most* $0.0667n = O(n)$ *sybil identities.*

We note here, Lemma 10 also reveals another important corollary: *by appending* SYBILSENSUS *after* SYBILSIEVE, *honest nodes can reach consensus anonymously with no prior knowledge of other participants, w.h.p.* This effectively solves the Byzantine consensus problem in unknown and anonymous wireless networks, with sybil attacks and other malicious behavior present.

Third Part of SYBILSIEVE^2. In the last part of the SYBILSIEVE^2 protocol, honest nodes will execute many repetitions of a variant of the SYBILCAST [12] protocol, and reduce the total number of sybil identities to $O(t)$.

Due to Lemma 10, after the second part of SYBILSIEVE^2, all honest nodes will agree on a same common-list, which includes all honest nodes and at most $O(n)$ sybil identities. At the beginning of the third part of SYBILSIEVE^2, honest nodes will sort this common-list according to some pre-defined order (e.g., dictionary order). Then, honest nodes will repeatedly execute the SYBILCAST variant, with identities in the common-list taking turns (in order) playing the role of "base station." (Note that this requires the honest nodes to agree on a common list of identities.) In each repetition, the "base station" verifies the identities and broadcasts a list which contains the identities it believes are honest. When all repetitions are done, honest nodes accept identities that are considered to be honest in at least a majority of repetitions. The pseudocode of the general structure of part three of SYBILSIEVE^2 is available in the full version of the paper.

Each execution of the variant of SYBILCAST consists of three phases: the dissemination phase, the collection phase, and the verification phase. In the dissemination phase, the "base station" will disseminate different random binary strings, called seeds, to every other identity in the common-list, which instructs them as to which channels to listen on. In the collection phase, the base station will broadcast many one-time random binary strings, called nonces; other nodes, on the other hand, will hop among channels according to the sequence defined by its seed, and collect nonces. Finally, in the verification phase, nodes will send the nonces they have collected during the preceding collection phase back to the base station. The base station will add identities that can provide sufficient nonces to its *rep-list*, and then broadcast the rep-list.

During the last part of SYBILSIEVE[2], in each repetition in which an honest node is playing as the base station, SYBILCAST ensures there are at most $O(t)$ sybil identities in the rep-list. On the other hand, Eve is only playing as the base station (via her sybil identities) in at most a small constant fraction of all repetitions. Since honest nodes only accept an identity if that identity has appeared in the rep-list in a large constant fraction of all repetitions, we know in total at most $O(t)$ sybil identities will be accepted by honest nodes.

We conclude by stating the key guarantees SYBILSIEVE[2] can provide in the following theorem:

Theorem 3. *For any $t \leq \min\{n, c\}/\alpha$ where $\alpha \geq 256$, SYBILSIEVE[2] terminates in $O(n^2 \lg^2 n \cdot \max\{1, n/c\})$ slots, and guarantees the following, w.h.p.: (a) there are at most $O(t)$ sybil identities accepted by the honest nodes, collectively; (b) every honest node accepts all other honest nodes; and (c) all honest nodes terminate simultaneously and have same estimation on network size which is either $2^{\lfloor \lg n \rfloor}$ or $2^{\lfloor \lg n \rfloor + 1}$.*

7   Discussion

In this paper, we develop new algorithms that can effectively thwart sybil attacks in multi-channel ad hoc wireless networks. They allows wireless devices to securely and reliably establish identities in unknown and anonymous environment. These protocols can also serve as building blocks for other protocols.

Although our algorithm can achieve consensus in unknown and anonymous networks only *with high probability*, we suspect it is impossible to solve this problem with probability one. For deterministic algorithms, in recent work by Delporte-Gallet et al. [6], the authors show that synchronous Byzantine agreement is unsolvable if the number of distinct identifiers is less than $3t$, where t is the number of Byzantine nodes. Since it is hard for deterministic algorithms to break symmetry in our setting, this seems to imply consensus is impossible, here, for deterministic algorithms. As for randomized algorithms, with small probability, nodes may end up with same coins and hence fail to generate sufficient identities. In fact, under our model, even if nodes indeed generate unique identities, the fact that Eve can potentially keep jamming one honest node (with some small probability) and isolate it from the remaining honest nodes also seems to imply that consensus cannot always be guaranteed.

References

1. Alchieri, E.A.P., Bessani, A.N., da Silva Fraga, J., Greve, F.: Byzantine consensus with unknown participants. In: Baker, T.P., Bui, A., Tixeuil, S. (eds.) OPODIS 2008. LNCS, vol. 5401, pp. 22–40. Springer, Heidelberg (2008)
2. Aspnes, J., Jackson, C., Krishnamurthy, A.: Exposing computationally-challenged Byzantine impostors. Tech. rep., Yale University Department of Computer Science
3. Attiya, H., Welch, J.: Distributed Computing: Fundamentals, Simulations, and Advanced Topics. Wiley (2004)

4. Chockler, G., Demirbas, M., Gilbert, S., Lynch, N., Newport, C., Nolte, T.: Consensus and collision detectors in radio networks. Distributed Computing 21(1), 55–84 (2008)
5. Delporte-Gallet, C., Fauconnier, H., Tielmann, A.: Fault-tolerant consensus in unknown and anonymous networks. In: 29th IEEE International Conference on Distributed Computing Systems, pp. 368–375 (2009)
6. Delporte-Gallet, C., Fauconnier, H., Guerraoui, R., Kermarrec, A.-M., Ruppert, E., Tran-The, H.: Byzantine agreement with homonyms. In: Proceedings of the 30th Annual ACM SIGACT-SIGOPS Symposium on Principles of Distributed Computing, pp. 21–30. ACM, New York (2011)
7. Demirbas, M., Song, Y.: An rssi-based scheme for sybil attack detection in wireless sensor networks. In: Proceedings of the 2006 International Symposium on World of Wireless, Mobile and Multimedia Networks, pp. 564–570. IEEE Computer Society, Washington D.C. (2006)
8. Douceur, J.R.: The sybil attack. In: Druschel, P., Kaashoek, F., Rowstron, A. (eds.) IPTPS 2002. LNCS, vol. 2429, pp. 251–260. Springer, Heidelberg (2002)
9. Dwork, C., Naor, M.: Pricing via processing or combatting junk mail. In: Brickell, E.F. (ed.) CRYPTO 1992. LNCS, vol. 740, pp. 139–147. Springer, Heidelberg (1993)
10. Fusco, E.G., Pelc, A.: Communication complexity of consensus in anonymous message passing systems. In: Fernàndez Anta, A., Lipari, G., Roy, M. (eds.) OPODIS 2011. LNCS, vol. 7109, pp. 191–206. Springer, Heidelberg (2011)
11. Gilbert, S., Newport, C., Zheng, C.: Who are you? secure identities in ad hoc networks. Tech. rep. National University of Singapore (2014)
12. Gilbert, S.L., Zheng, C.: Sybilcast: Broadcast on the open airwaves. In: Proceedings of the 25th Annual ACM Symposium on Parallelism in Algorithms and Architectures, pp. 130–139. ACM, New York (2013)
13. Gołębiewski, Z., Klonowski, M., Koza, M., Kutyłowski, M.: Towards fair leader election in wireless networks. In: Ruiz, P.M., Garcia-Luna-Aceves, J.J. (eds.) ADHOC-NOW 2009. LNCS, vol. 5793, pp. 166–179. Springer, Heidelberg (2009)
14. Hoffman, K., Zage, D., Nita-Rotaru, C.: A survey of attack and defense techniques for reputation systems. ACM Computing Survey 42(1), 1:1–1:31 (2009)
15. Klonowski, M., Koza, M.: Countermeasures against sybil attacks in wsn based on proofs-of-work. In: Proceedings of the 6th ACM Conference on Security and Privacy in Wireless and Mobile Networks, pp. 179–184. ACM, New York (2013)
16. Klonowski, M., Koza, M., Kutyłowski, M.: Repelling sybil-type attacks in wireless ad hoc systems. In: Steinfeld, R., Hawkes, P. (eds.) ACISP 2010. LNCS, vol. 6168, pp. 391–402. Springer, Heidelberg (2010)
17. Mónica, D., Leitão, J., Rodrigues, L., Ribeiro, C.: On the use of radio resource tests in wireless ad-hoc networks. In: Proceedings of the 3rd Workshop on Recent Advances on Intrusion-Tolerant Systems, pp. F21–F26 (2009)
18. Mónica, D., Leitão, J., Rodrigues, L., Ribeiro, C.: Observable non-sybil quorums construction in one-hop wireless ad hoc networks. In: 2010 IEEE/IFIP International Conference on Dependable Systems and Networks, pp. 31–40 (2010)
19. Newsome, J., Shi, E., Song, D., Perrig, A.: The sybil attack in sensor networks: Analysis & defenses. In: Proceedings of the 3rd International Symposium on Information Processing in Sensor Networks, pp. 259–268. ACM, New York (2004)

20. Piro, C., Shields, C., Levine, B.N.: Detecting the sybil attack in mobile ad hoc networks. In: Securecomm and Workshops, pp. 1–11 (2006)
21. Srikanth, T., Toueg, S.: Simulating authenticated broadcasts to derive simple fault-tolerant algorithms. Distributed Computing 2(2), 80–94 (1987)
22. Yu, H., Gibbons, P., Kaminsky, M., Xiao, F.: Sybillimit: A near-optimal social network defense against sybil attacks. In: 2008 IEEE Symposium on Security and Privacy, pp. 3–17 (2008)
23. Yu, H., Kaminsky, M., Gibbons, P., Flaxman, A.: Sybilguard: Defending against sybil attacks via social networks. IEEE/ACM Transactions on Networking 16(3), 576–589 (2008)

Approximate Local Sums and Their Applications in Radio Networks

Zhiyu Liu and Maurice Herlihy

Department of Computer Science
Brown University
zhiyu_liu@brown.edu, mph@cs.brown.edu

Abstract. Although any problem in a radio network can be solved using broadcast algorithms, some problems can be solved substantially more efficiently by more specialized algorithms. This paper presents two new approximate algorithms for the *local sum* problem, in which each node computes a $(1 \pm \epsilon)$-approximation to the sum of the values held by its incoming neighbors (nodes that have outgoing edges to the node). We propose algorithms both with and without collision detection, as well as for the beeping model, with round complexity $O(\frac{\log^2 n + \log n \log m}{\epsilon^2})$, where n is the number of nodes and the value held by each node is a real number in $\{0\} \cup [1, m]$. We then show how these algorithms can be used as building blocks to construct applications such as approximate random walk distribution, PageRank, and global sum.

Keywords: radio networks, algorithms, model with collision detection, model without collision detection, beeping model, local sum, random walk, PageRank.

1 Introduction

Broadcasting problems [6] [3] are a class of extensively studied, fundamental problems in radio networks. In broadcasting problems, each message that needs to be broadcast is considered as a piece of abstract information, such that the only way for a node in a network to receive a message is to hear the message directly. Imagine there are a clique of n nodes, each having a message to broadcast to others. Because of the existence of message collisions in radio networks, a node cannot hear more than one message at a time, and hence any broadcast algorithm has to take $\Omega(n)$ rounds to let a node collect all messages.

However, in many applications, the information that a node needs to collect can be expressed as a function of some neighbors' values, such as the sum of numbers held by some neighbors, the highest temperature in a district, or the distribution of some items. It is possible that a node can get an accurate approximation to such numerical information, using a specialized algorithm substantially faster than the $\Omega(n)$ bound. A key to achieving this is usually to let the node communicate with others in a clever way, such that it can reveal the information by interpreting its communication history. For example, it is well

F. Kuhn (Ed.): DISC 2014, LNCS 8784, pp. 243–257, 2014.

known that a node in a radio network can get a good approximation of the number of its neighbors in only $O(\log n)$ rounds, using techniques similar to the famous Decay procedure [3], such as [13].

In this paper, we show a non-trivial generalization of the idea in [13] to efficiently solve the *approximate local sum problem*, in which each node has an input value and is asked to get an accurate enough approximation to the sum of the inputs of its incoming neighbors (nodes that have outgoing edges to the node). More specifically, we propose a randomized $(1 \pm \epsilon)$ approximate local sum algorithm with round complexity $O(\frac{\log^2 n + \log n \log m}{\epsilon^2})$ for both the model with collision detection and the beeping model, where n is the number of nodes and the input of each node is a real number in $\{0\} \cup [1, m]$[1]. Solving problems in radio networks without the help of collision detection is usually harder and more costly. However, by some subtle modifications to our algorithm, we manage to design an approximate local sum algorithm for the model without collision detection, with the same round complexity.

These approximate local sum algorithms turn out to be useful for some important applications. We show how to use them as building blocks to approximate the distribution of a random walk in a radio network. Suppose a random walk in a radio network starts with an initial distribution $x^0 = (x_1^0, ..., x_n^0)$ at time 0, where x_k^i denotes node k's value in the distribution x^i at time i. We present an algorithm, by which each node k computes an $(1 \pm \epsilon)$ approximation of x_k^t in $O(\frac{t^3}{\epsilon^2} \log(tn) \log(\frac{tn \cdot max}{\epsilon \cdot min}))$ rounds with high probability, where min and max are known upper bound and lower bound on x_k^t, respectively. We then show how this algorithm in turn can be used to solve approximate PageRank and approximate global sum in a radio network.

The paper is organized as follows. Section 2 shows the related work. The radio network models and the local sum problem are defined formally in Section 3. In Section 4, we present the approximate local sum algorithm for both the model with collision detection and the beeping model. In Section 5, we show the approximate local sum algorithm for the model without collision detection. Then in Section 6, we describe how to use the approximate local sum algorithms as building blocks to construct algorithms for approximate random walk distribution, PageRank, and global sum. Due to space limits, we only present in the appendix a proof sketch of the approximate local sum algorithm for both the model with collision detection and the beeping model. The complete version of that proof and the proofs for other results are deferred to the full version of this paper.

2   Related Work

The local broadcasting problem has been extensively studied in the setting of single-hop radio networks since the late 1970s (e.g. [5] [4] [14] [21]). In this prob-

---

[1] In fact, our algorithm works for input range $\{0\} \cup [min, max]$, for any positive numbers min and max, by simply scaling inputs from $[min, max]$ to $[1, m] = [1, \frac{max}{min}]$ by dividing them by min.

lem, a clique of n nodes (or k of the n nodes) need to exchange their messages with each other. When n is unknown to the nodes, a natural solution is to first estimate the value of n, as Greenberg et al. [13] proposed. Their estimating protocol is the following. In round i, each node broadcasts a signal with probability 2^{-i}. The protocol stops in round j, when no collision occurs for the first time. It can be proved that the expectation of 2^j is roughly $0.9n$. The estimating technique in [13] is analogous to the well-known Decay strategy [3], which has been widely used to solve different broadcasting, conflict resolution, wakeup problems (e.g. [8] [17] [9] [12] [11] [10] [16]) in radio networks.

It is easy to see that estimating n is actually a special case of estimating the local sum of a clique of nodes, where each node has input value 1. The idea behind our approximate local sum algorithms can be thought of as a generalization of the technique in [13]. While the estimating protocol in [13] gives a constant-factor approximation to n in a single-hop network (since a constant-factor approximation to n is usually good enough for efficiently solving broadcasting and conflict resolution problems), our local sum algorithms, with the help of Chernoff bounds, can compute arbitrarily close approximations to the local sums of all nodes in a multi-hop network. As the informal descriptions of our algorithms show in Sections 4 and 5, accurately approximating local sums, especially in multi-hop radio networks without the help of collision detection, is much more complicated and it requires some non-trivial, subtle modifications in order to keep the complexities of our algorithms as small as $O(\frac{\log^2 n + \log n \log m}{\epsilon^2})$ (note that in the local broadcasting problem in multi-hop radio networks, it takes $\Omega(\log^2 n)$ for some node to receive even a single message from a neighbor [12]). To the best of our knowledge, our algorithms are the first to accurately approximate local sums in the radio network models with and without collision detection.

Besides the two classical radio network models—the models with and without collision detection, we also consider the beeping model [7], which has drawn a lot of attention recently (e.g. [1] [15]). The beeping model is a model where nodes have extremely weak communication power.

One important application of our approximate local sum algorithms is to approximate PageRank [19] in a radio network. The random walk-based method we use to solve approximate PageRank was first proposed by Avrachenkov et al. [2]. Sarma et al. [20] showed how to use this method to approximate PageRank in the classical CONGEST model, in which no collisions exist, while we solve the problem in radio network models, in which collisions exist.

3   Local Sum Problem in Radio Networks

A multi-hop radio network is modeled as a directed graph $G = (V, E)$ consisting of $n = |V|$ nodes, where node k can receive messages from node ℓ if edge $(\ell, k) \in E$ (we call k an *outgoing neighbor* of ℓ and ℓ an *incoming neighbor* of k). Nodes communicate in synchronous *rounds*. In each round, a node k either *broadcasts* a single message of size $O(\log n)$ to all outgoing neighbors, or *listens* for messages from its incoming neighbors. If k listens in a round and only one of its incoming neighbors broadcast a message, v receives that message. If k listens while all its incoming neighbors are also listening, k receives nothing. If k listens while two or more incoming neighbors broadcast, a *collision* occurs and k cannot receive those messages. In the paper, we consider two different models with respect to collision detection. In the *model with collision detection*, node k receives a special "collision message" $\perp$ when k listens and two or more incoming neighbors are broadcasting. In the *model without collision detection*, k receives nothing when such a collision occurs. In other words, in the model without collision detection, nodes cannot distinguish a collision from a silence.

We also consider the *beeping model* [7], in which each message is just a beep signal. When a node k listens, it has only binary feedback: if no incoming neighbors are broadcasting, k receives nothing; if one or more incoming neighbors are broadcasting, k receives a beep.

In the *local sum* problem, each node k has an input v_k, a real number in $\{0\} \cup [1, m]$. Let $N(k)$ denote the set of k's incoming neighbors. The goal is to let each node k compute its local sum $sum_k = \sum_{\ell \in N(k)} v_\ell$, which is in the range $\{0\} \cup [1, nm]$. Given an arbitrarily small positive $\epsilon < 1$, a value s is said to be a $(1 \pm \epsilon)$ approximation of sum_k, if $(1 - \epsilon)sum_k \le s \le (1 + \epsilon)sum_k$.

4 Approximate Local Sum with Collision Detection

Figure 1 shows Algorithm 1, a $(1 \pm \epsilon)$ approximate local sum algorithm that works for the radio network model with collision detection. Since each message in Algorithm 1 is just a beep signal, Algorithm 1 also works for the beeping model.

The algorithm has two parts. In the first part, called the *preprocessing stage* (Lines 3-13), node k estimates the maximum input contributed by any incoming neighbor. There are $\log nm$ preprocessing phases (Line 3), where preprocessing phase i is concerned with the range $[2^i, 2^{i+1})$. In each round of preprocessing phase i, if its input is in that range, node k broadcasts a signal with probability $1/2$ (Line 6). In every other round, it listens for a message (or collision) (Lines 8-10). At the end of the preprocessing stage, the node's $flag$ variable holds the highest range where it received a signal. With high probability, the highest input contributed by any incoming neighbor lies within $[2^{flag}, 2^{flag+1})$.

In the main part of the algorithm (Lines 14-29), node k computes s, a $(1+\epsilon)$-approximation of the local sum. This part proceeds in a sequence of $\log mn + 1$ phases (Line 14), and each phase encompasses $\Theta(\frac{\log n}{\epsilon^2})$ rounds (Lines 16-25). Node k keeps track of r, the number of rounds in the current phase in which node k listens (Line 22), and c, the number of rounds in the current phase in which it listens but receives nothing (Line 23). In each round of phase i, if the input v_k of node k satisfies $v_k < 2^i$, then node k broadcasts with probability $1 - (1 - \frac{1}{2^i})^{v_k}$ (Lines 18-19), and otherwise it listens (Lines 20-23). In phases where $v_k \ge 2^i$, the node just listens (Line 18). Each time the node listens, it increments r, and each time it fails to receive a signal, it increments c. At the end node k: input v_k

```
1     s = 0;
2     flag = 0;
3     for i = 1 to log nm
4         for j = 1 to Θ(log n)
5             draw δ from [0, 1] uniformly at random;
6             if (2^i ≤ v_k < 2^{i+1} and δ < ½)
7                 broadcast a signal in this round;
8             else
9                     listen in this round;
10                    if (receive a signal) flag = i; end if
11            end if
12        end for
13    end for
14    for i = 1 to log nm + 1
15        c = r = 0;
16        for j = 1 to Θ(log n / ε²)
17            draw δ from [0, 1] uniformly at random;
18            if (v_k < 2^i and δ > (1 − 1/2^i)^{v_k})
19                broadcast a signal in this round;
20            otherwise
21                    listen in this round;
22                    r = r + 1;
23                    if (receive nothing in this round) c = c + 1; end if
24            end if
25        end for
26        if (both i > flag and c/r > 1/6 hold for the first time)
27            solve s for c/r = (1 − 1/2^i)^s;
28        end if
29    end for
30    return s;
```

Fig. 1. Algorithm 1: a $(1 \pm \epsilon)$ approximate local sum algorithm for the radio network model with collision detection and the beeping model

of each phase, node k checks whether it can compute the estimate s. If this phase is the first satisfying the condition at line 26, node k computes s, by solving the equation at line 27. After that, the node will not recompute s, but it continues to broadcast with the probabilities shown until the algorithm completes.

Here is an informal sketch why this algorithm works. First, consider phase i where every input $v_k < 2^i$. In each of the $\Theta(\frac{\log n}{\epsilon^2})$ rounds (Line 16) of phase i, node k broadcasts its input v_k with probability $1 - (1 - \frac{1}{2^i})^{v_k}$, and with the complementary probability, $(1 - \frac{1}{2^i})^{v_k}$, it listens without broadcasting. If node k listens, it will hear nothing from its incoming neighbors (because they are also listening) with probability

$$\prod_{v_\ell \in N(k)} \left(1 - \frac{1}{2^i}\right)^{v_\ell} = \left(1 - \frac{1}{2^i}\right)^{sum_k}.$$

Recall that r is the number of rounds in phase i in which the node listens, and c the number of those rounds in which it receives nothing, so $\frac{c}{r}$ is an approximation of $(1 - \frac{1}{2^i})^{sum_k}$. If sum_k is roughly in the range $[2^{i-1}, 2^i)$, $(1 - \frac{1}{2^i})^{sum_k}$ will be a constant greater than $\frac{1}{6}$. While for a smaller $i' \leq i - 2$, such that $sum_k \geq 2^{i'+1}$, $(1 - \frac{1}{2^{i'}})^{sum_k}$ will be less than $\frac{1}{e^2}$, a constant less than $\frac{1}{6}$. Therefore, if node k listens in $\Theta(\frac{\log n}{\epsilon^2})$ rounds in each phase, we can prove by the Chernoff bound [18] that with high probability node k finds $\frac{c}{r} > \frac{1}{6}$ for the first time at Line 26 in phase i, such that sum_k is in the range $[2^{i-1}, 2^i)$ or $[2^i, 2^{i+1})$ (see Lemma 4). In fact, we can prove that $\frac{c}{r}$ in this phase will be a $(1 \pm \epsilon)$-approximation of $(1 - \frac{1}{2^i})^{sum_k}$ with high probability. Moreover, consider the strictly decreasing function $f(s) = (1 - \frac{1}{2^i})^s$ as in the right hand side of the equation at Line 27. We will see that for s roughly in the range $[2^{i-1}, 2^{i+1})$, the slope $f'(s)$ is steep enough that a $(1 \pm \epsilon)$ multiplicative error on $f(s)$ will induce only a $(1 \mp \Theta(\epsilon))$ multiplicative error on s. Therefore, we can conclude that the solution s to the equation[2] at Line 27 is a $(1 \pm \epsilon)$ approximation of the local sum sum_k with high probability.

We call attention to some subtle aspects of Algorithm 1. First, if v_k is much bigger than 2^i in phase i, then node k will listen with very small probability $(1 - \frac{1}{2^i})^{v_k}$ in a round in phase i. If so, node k will not listen for sufficiently many rounds in phase i to get an accurate enough approximation. The preprocessing stage addresses this problem by having each node tell its outgoing neighbors the range in which its input lies. As mentioned, at the end of the preprocessing phase, node k will have $flag = i_{max}$ with high probability, such that the biggest value among the inputs of its incoming neighbors is in the range $[2^{i_{max}}, 2^{i_{max}+1})$. Recall that we can accurately approximate sum_k in a phase i when sum_k is in the range $[2^{i-1}, 2^{i+1})$. Hence, it suffices to let node k compute s in phase i when sum_k is in the range $[2^{i-1}, 2^i)$. Note that $sum_k \geq 2^i$ in the first i_{max} phases. That is, only in some phase $i \geq flag + 1$ is sum_k in the range $[2^{i-1}, 2^i)$ and only then does computing s yield a good approximation of sum_k. By testing whether $i > flag$ at Line 26, we prevent node k from computing s in the first $flag$ phases. This condition holds for neighbors of node k as well, so node k knows that each of its outgoing neighbors ℓ has a value of $flag$ (which we call $flag_\ell$ here to distinguish it from k's $flag$) such that $2^{flag_\ell} \geq sum_\ell \geq v_k$, so node ℓ also does not compute s in the first $flag_\ell$ rounds. It follows that node k does not have to broadcast messages in phases i, when $2^i < v_k$. That is why we have $v_k < 2^i$ as a condition at Line 18. By doing so, node k can always listen in the first $\lfloor \log v_k \rfloor$ phases, avoiding the risk that it listens with a very small probability, when $\left(1 - \frac{1}{2^i}\right)^{v_k}$ is very small at Line 18.

---

[2] In fact, it suffices to let node k compute a $(1 \pm \Theta(\epsilon))$ approximate solution to the equation, instead of an accurate one. Since $f(x)$ is strictly decreasing and its slope is steep enough, node k can efficiently get an approximate solution by binary search.

Second, for node k, there can be $\Theta(\log nm)$ phases between phase 1 and phase i^*, where $2^{i^*-1} \leq sum_k < 2^{i^*}$. Thus, even if we use the Chernoff bound to show that in each phase $i < i^*$, $\frac{c}{r} \leq \frac{1}{6}$ at Line 26 with probability $1 - O(\frac{1}{n^a})$ for some constant a, we would end up showing that $\frac{c}{r} \leq \frac{1}{6}$ in all phases $i < i^*$ with probability $1 - O(\frac{\log mn}{n^a})$. When m is extremely large, probability $1 - O(\frac{\log mn}{n^a})$ is not considered high probability. One way to improve the probability of success is to increase the number of rounds in each phase, but doing so will increase the round complexity of the algorithm. Fortunately, we can avoid these costs with the help of the *flag* variable: node k needs to consider $\frac{c}{r}$ only in phases $i > flag$. As Lemma 3 shows, there are only $O(\log n)$ rounds in between phase *flag* and phase i^* and hence node k can succeed with probability $1 - O(\frac{\log n}{n^a})$, which is still high probability.

Theorem 1. *All nodes in Algorithm 1 compute $(1 \pm \epsilon)$ approximations of their local sums with probability $1 - O(\frac{1}{n})$ in $O(\frac{\log^2 n + \log n \log m}{\epsilon^2})$ rounds.*

5   Approximate Local Sum without Collision Detection

Figure 2 shows Algorithm 2, a way to modify Algorithm 1 to work in the radio network model without collision detection. Each node k first sets $v'_k = 4v_k$ (Line 3) and computes a $(1 + \epsilon)$ approximation s of $sum'_k = \sum_{\ell \in N(k)} v'_\ell = \sum_{\ell \in N(k)} (4v_\ell) = 4sum_k$ in order to finally get $s/4$, a $(1 + \epsilon)$ approximation of sum_k. Note that $v'_k \in \{0\} \cup [4, 4m]$ and $sum'_k \in \{0\} \cup [4, 4nm]$.

The preprocessing stage (Lines 4–14) is modified as follows. First, node k may send messages in any preprocessing phase i if $v'_k \geq 2^i$ (Line 7), while in Algorithm 1, it can only send messages in preprocessing round i if $2^i \leq v_k < 2^{i+1}$. (In fact, $v_k \geq 2^i$ also works for Algorithm 1, but we think $2^i \leq v_k < 2^{i+1}$ is easier for readers to understand the high-level idea of the algorithm.) Second, instead of sending a message with probability $\frac{1}{2}$ in each of the $\Theta(\log n)$ rounds in preprocessing phase i, node k sends a message with probability $(\frac{1}{2})^j$ (Line 7) in the jth round.

The main part of the algorithm is modified as follows. In phase i, node k temporarily sets $v'_k = 2^{i+3}$ if $v_k > 2^{i+3}$ (Line 17). Second, node k now has three choices in a round: with probability $(1 - \frac{1}{2^i})^{v'_k}$ (line 20), it listens; with probability $\frac{v'_k}{2^i}(1 - \frac{1}{2^i})^{v'_k - 1}$ (Line 24), it sends a message "1"; otherwise (Line 26), it sends a message "2+". Third, c now counts the number of rounds in a phase i in which it listens and receives a message "1" (line 23). Finally, the condition under which s is computed is changed (Line 31) and node k chooses the solution s that is greater than 2^i (Line 32).

The high-level idea of Algorithm 2 is as follows. Suppose no node changes its v'_k at Line 17, i.e., $v'_k \leq 2^{i+3}$. To better understand the algorithm, let us assume that each v'_k is an integer. Then, we can think of node k as a simulation of a collection of v'_k nodes, each with input value 1: with probability $(1 - \frac{1}{2^i})^{v'_k}$, all the v'_k nodes listen, simulated by node k listening in this round with the same

---

node k: input v_k

```
1     s = 0;
2     flag = 0;
3     v'_k = 4v_k;
4     for i = 1 to log nm
5         for j = 1 to Θ(log n)
6             draw δ from [0,1] uniformly at random;
7             if (v'_k ≥ 2^i and δ < (½)^j)
8                 broadcast a signal in this round;
9             else
10                listen in this round;
11                if (receive a signal) flag = i; end if
12            end if
13        end for
14    end for
15    for i = 1 to log nm + 1
16        c = r = 0;
17        v'_k = min{4v_k, 2^{i+3}}
18        for j = 1 to Θ(log n / ε²)
19            draw δ from [0,1] uniformly at random;
20            if (δ < (1 - 1/2^i)^{v'_k})
21                listen in this round;
22                r = r + 1;
23                if (receive a message "1") c = c + 1; end if
24            else if ( (1 - 1/2^i)^{v'_k} ≤ δ < (1 - 1/2^i)^{v'_k} + v'_k/2^i (1 - 1/2^i)^{v'_k - 1} )
25                    broadcast a message "1" in this round;
26                else
27                    broadcast a message "2+";
28                end if
29            end if
30        end for
31        if (both i > flag - 3 and c/r > 2(1 - 1/2^i)^{2^{i+2} - 1} hold for the first time)
32            solve s for c/r = s/2^i (1 - 1/2^i)^{s-1} and s > 2^i;
33    end for
34    return s/4;
```

Fig. 2. Algorithm 2: a $(1 \pm \epsilon)$ approximate local sum algorithm for the radio network model without collision detection

probability (Lines 20-21); with probability $\frac{v'_k}{2^i}(1 - \frac{1}{2^i})^{v'_k - 1}$, only one of them sends a message, simulated by node k sending a message "1" with the same probability(Lines 24-25); otherwise, two or more nodes send messages, simulated by node k sending a message "2+" (Lines 26-27) . Thus, if node k listens in a round in phase i, it will receive a single massage "1" with probability

$$\sum_{\ell \in N(k)} \left(\frac{v_\ell'}{2^i} \left(1 - \frac{1}{2^i} \right)^{v_\ell' - 1} \left(1 - \frac{1}{2^i} \right)^{sum_k' - v_\ell'} \right) = \sum_{\ell \in N(k)} \left(\frac{v_\ell'}{2^i} \left(1 - \frac{1}{2^i} \right)^{sum_k' - 1} \right)$$

$$= \frac{sum_k'}{2^i} \left(1 - \frac{1}{2^i} \right)^{sum_k' - 1}.$$

Note that this equation holds even if v_ℓ''s are not integers. Hence, we know that $\frac{c}{r}$ is an approximation of $\frac{sum_k'}{2^i}(1 - \frac{1}{2^i})^{sum_k' - 1}$, which can be used to compute an approximation of sum_k'.

If sum_k' is roughly in the range $[2^{i+1}, 2^{i+2})$, $\frac{sum_k'}{2^i}(1 - \frac{1}{2^i})^{sum_k' - 1}$ will be a constant greater than $2(1 - \frac{1}{2^i})^{2^{i+2} - 1}$ in phase i, while in any phase $i' \leq i - 2$, $\frac{sum_k'}{2^{i'}}(1 - \frac{1}{2^{i'}})^{sum_k' - 1}$ will be less than $2(1 - \frac{1}{2^{i'}})^{2^{i'+2} - 1}$. Suppose m is polynomial in n. As in Algorithm 1, if node k listens in $\Theta(\frac{\log n}{\epsilon^2})$ rounds in each phase, we can prove by the Chernoff bound and the union bound that with high probability node k finds $\frac{c}{r} > 2(1 - \frac{1}{2^i})^{2^{i+2} - 1}$ for the first time in phase i at Line 31, such that sum_k' is roughly in the range $[2^{i+1}, 2^{i+2})$ (or $[2^{i+2}, 2^{i+3})$). Moreover, the function $f(s) = \frac{s}{2^i}(1 - \frac{1}{2^i})^{s-1}$ is strictly decreasing when $s > 2^i$, and if s is roughly in the range $[2^{i+1}, 2^{i+3})$, the slope $f'(s)$ is steep enough[3] that a $(1 \pm \epsilon)$ multiplicative error on $f(s)$ will incur only a $(1 \mp \Theta(\epsilon))$ multiplicative error on s. It follows that the unique solution s at Line 32 will be a $(1 \pm \epsilon)$ approximation of sum_k' with high probability.

However, m can be superpolynomial in n, in which case the "high probability" guarantee above by the union bound will break, as there are $\Theta(\log nm)$ phases. As in Algorithm 1, the preprocessing stage deals with this situation. We can prove that after the preprocessing stage, node k has $i_{max} - flag = O(\log n)$ with probability $1 - O(\frac{1}{n^2})$, where i_{max} is the integer such that the maximum value among its incoming neighbors' v_ℓ''s is in the range $[2^{i_{max}}, 2^{i_{max}+1})$. Unlike Algorithm 1, Algorithm 2 does not guarantee that $flag = i_{max}$, since making $flag = i_{max}$ is too costly without the help of collision detection. Fortunately, we will show that $i_{max} - flag = O(\log n)$ is good enough. The reason for computing $flag$ in Algorithm 2 is similar to that in Algorithm 1: node k knows that it does not need to compute s in the first $flag - 3$ rounds, since only in phase $i > flag - 3$ can sum_k' be in the range $[2^{i+1}, 2^{i+2})$. Given $i_{max} - flag = O(\log n)$, we can prove that $i^* - flag = O(\log n)$, for i^* such that sum_k' is in the range $[2^{i^*+1}, 2^{i^*+2})$. Thus, there are only $O(\log n)$ rounds from phase $flag - 2$ to phase i^*. As in Algorithm 1, we can prove by the Chernoff bound that $\frac{c}{r}$ is "very close to" its expected value in each phase $i \in [flag - 2, i^*]$ with probability $1 - O(\frac{1}{n^a})$, so we can prove that $\frac{c}{r}$ is always "very close to" its expected values in all these phases with probability $1 - O(\frac{\log n}{n^a})$. This implies that Algorithm 2 succeeds with high probability.

---

[3] If s is in the range $[2^{i-1}, 2^{i+1})$, the slope may be too flat that a small error on $f(s)$ can induce a very large error on s. That is why we scaled sum_k' to $[4, 4nm]$, assuring $sum_k' \in (2^{i+1}, 2^{i+3})$ for some i.

There is one more point to consider. If v'_k is much bigger than 2^i in phase i, then node k will listen in a round with very small probability $(1 - \frac{1}{2^i})^{v'_k}$, as in Algorithm 1. However, since an outgoing neighbor ℓ's *flag* is only close to, but not necessarily equal to ℓ's i_{max} in Algorithm 2, we cannot simply let node k listen all the time in phase i, as it does in Algorithm 1 at Line 18 when $v_k \geq 2^i$. This is because otherwise, node ℓ may compute a wrong $s \approx (sum'_\ell - v'_k)$ in some phase $i \in [flag - 2, i_{max} - 1]$. Therefore, we let node k set $v'_k = 2^{i+3}$ when v'_k is too big, assuring that node k can listen in $\Theta(\frac{\log n}{\epsilon^2})$ rounds in phase i with high probability. On the other hand, setting $v'_k = 2^{i+3}$ guarantees that with high probability any outgoing neighbor ℓ will have a value of $\frac{c}{r}$ not bigger than a value close to $\frac{2^{i+3}}{2^i}(1 - \frac{1}{2^i})^{2^{i+3}-1}$. Thus, node ℓ will have $\frac{c}{r} < 2(1 - \frac{1}{2^i})^{2^{i+2}-1}$ with high probability at Line 31 and hence it will not compute s in this phase.

Theorem 2. *All nodes in Algorithm 2 compute $(1 \pm \epsilon)$ approximations of their local sums with probability $1 - O(\frac{1}{n})$ in $O(\frac{\log^2 n + \log n \log m}{\epsilon^2})$ rounds.*

6   Applications in Computing Random Walk Distributions

6.1   Approximate Random Walk Distribution Algorithm

Suppose a random walk in a radio network starts with an initial distribution $x^0 = (x^0_1, ..., x^0_n)$ at time 0, where x^i_k denotes the value of node k at time i, for any $1 \leq k \leq n$ and any $1 \leq i \leq t$ (Note that $\sum_k x^i_k$ doesn't have to be 1). The goal is to let each node k compute an approximation of x^t_k, its own value in the random walk distribution x^t at time t.

We assume that each node k knows Δ_k, the number of k's outgoing neighbors. We also assume that a lower bound min on $\min_k x^t_k$ and an upper bound max on $\sum_k x^0_k$ are known to all nodes. In Figure 3, we present Algorithm 3 that computes an $(1 \pm \epsilon)$ approximation of x^t_k for each node k. Algorithm 3 uses Algorithm 1 (or Algorithm 2, depending on the radio network model) as a building block.

Each node k in Algorithm 3 takes as input $v^0_k = x^0_k$, its value at time 0. At time i, for each $1 \leq i \leq t$, node k uses the approximate local sum algorithm[4] $\mathcal{A}$ at Line 4 to distribute v^{i-1}_k evenly to its outgoing neighbors and get its local sum v^i_k, which turns out to be a good approximation of x^i_k. Finally, node k outputs v^t_k, a $(1 \pm \epsilon)$ approximation of x^t_k.

To reduce the round complexity of Algorithm 3, we restrict $\mathcal{A}$ for input range $[\frac{\epsilon \cdot min}{3tn^2}, max]$. However, v^{i-1}_k may be smaller than $\frac{\epsilon \cdot min}{3tn}$. Also, since $\mathcal{A}$ can introduce errors on the values of nodes, v^{i-1}_k may exceed its upper bound max. Therefore, we let node k modify v^{i-1}_k if necessary at Lines 2 and 3, such that v^{i-1}_k/Δ is always within $\mathcal{A}$'s input range at Line 4. In the appendix, we prove that Line 2 will only reduce but not increase errors while Line 3 will introduce at most a $\epsilon/2$ relative error to v^t_k at the end of Algorithm 3. We also prove that

---

[4] As we mentioned earlier, $\mathcal{A}$ works for input range $[\frac{\epsilon \cdot min}{3tn^2}, max]$ by simply scaling each input in the range to $[1, \frac{3tn^2 \cdot max}{\epsilon \cdot min}]$.

node k: input $v_k^0 = x_k^0$

Let $\mathcal{A}$ be an $(1 \pm \frac{\epsilon}{3t})$ approximate local sum algorithm in Figure 1 for input range $[\frac{\epsilon \cdot min}{3tn^2}, max]$, where Lines 4 and 16 in Figure 1 consist of $\Theta(\log(tn))$ and $\Theta(\frac{9t^2 \log(tn)}{\epsilon^2})$ iterations instead, respectively.

```
1    for i = 1 to t
2        if (v_k^{i-1} > max) v_k^{i-1} = max; end if;
3        if (v_k^{i-1} < ε·min/3tn) v_k^{i-1} = ε·min/3tn; end if;
4        run A with input v_k^{i-1}/Δ_k, and get the return value v_k^i;
5    end for
6    return v_k^t
```

Fig. 3. Algorithm 3: a $(1 \pm \epsilon)$ approximation algorithm for x^t

the amount of errors accumulated over time will not go beyond $\pm \epsilon x_k^t$ and hence Algorithm 3 is a $(1 \pm \epsilon)$ approximate algorithm for x_k^t, as stated in the following theorem.

Theorem 3. *Algorithm 3 computes a $(1 \pm \epsilon)$ approximation of x_k^t for every node k with probability $1 - O(\frac{1}{n})$ in $O(\frac{t^3}{\epsilon^2} \log(tn) \log(\frac{tn \cdot max}{\epsilon \cdot min}))$ rounds.*

6.2   Applications: PageRank and Global Sum

An immediate application of Algorithm 3 is to approximate the PageRank values for nodes in a radio network. In the PageRank problem, a small constant c, called *reset probability*, is fixed. The goal is to compute the stationary distribution π that satisfies

$$\pi = \pi((1-c)P + \frac{c}{n}E),$$

where E is a matrix whose entries are all 1's, and each entry p_{kl} of P is $\frac{1}{\Delta_k}$ if node ℓ is an outgoing neighbor of k, and 0 otherwise. Recall that Δ_k is the number of k's outgoing neighbors. As [2] pointed out, we can rewrite the above equation as

$$\pi = \left(\frac{c}{n}\right)\underline{1}^T \sum_{t=0}^{\infty}(1-c)^k P^k.$$

This implies we can compute the PageRank as follows. Each node k starts with a uniform input value $x_k^0 = \frac{c}{n}$. At time i, node k distributes $\frac{x_k^{t-1}}{1-c}$ according to P and receives its value x_k^t. Thus we have $\pi_k = \sum_{t=0}^{\infty} x_k^t$. Since $\pi \geq \frac{c}{n}$, it is easy to prove that $\pi_k' = \sum_{t=0}^{T} x_k^t$ is a $(1 - \frac{\epsilon}{2})$ approximation of π_k, where $T = \frac{a \log(\frac{n}{\epsilon c})}{c}$, for a large enough constant a. Therefore, we can run Algorithm 3 for

$(1 \pm \epsilon')$ approximation to simulate this procedure from time 0 to time T, where $\epsilon' = \epsilon/3$ and the input range of the local sum algorithm $\mathcal{A}$ in Algorithm 3 is $[\frac{\epsilon \frac{c}{n}}{3Tn^2}, n \cdot \frac{c}{n}] = [\frac{\epsilon c^2}{3an^3 \log(\frac{n}{\epsilon c})}, c]$. Given that the relative error is in the range $[(1 - \frac{\epsilon}{2})(1 - \epsilon'), (1 - \epsilon')] \in [(1 - \epsilon), (1 - \epsilon/3)]$ with high probability, It is trivial to prove the following theorem.

Theorem 4. *Each node k in a radio network can compute a $(1 \pm \epsilon)$ approximation of its PageRank value π_k in $O\big(\frac{T^3}{\epsilon^2} \log(Tn) \log\big(\frac{Tn}{\epsilon}\big)\big)$ rounds with probability $1 - O(\frac{1}{n})$, where $T = \frac{\log(\frac{n}{\epsilon c})}{c}$.*

Another application of Algorithm 3 is to let each node in a radio network compute an $(1 \pm \epsilon)$ approximation of the global sum, the sum of the inputs of all nodes.

Assume that an upper bound T_ϵ on a mixing time of a random walk on a connected radio network is known to all nodes. More specifically, every node knows that the random walk distribution x^{T_ϵ} at time T_ϵ is a $(1 \pm \frac{\epsilon}{6})$ approximation of the stationary distribution π, where ϵ is a small enough constant.

Suppose each node k in the global sum problem has an input $v_k \in \{0\} \cup [1, m]$. To approximate the global sum, each node k first runs Algorithm 3 for $(1 \pm \frac{\epsilon}{6})$ approximation with input 1 for T_ϵ time steps, and receives a return value a_k. Then, node k runs Algorithm 3 for $(1 \pm \frac{\epsilon}{6})$ approximation again for T_ϵ time steps, now with its input v_k, and receives a return value b_k. It is easy to see that the global sum $S \approx \frac{\pi_k b_k n}{\pi_k a_k} = \frac{b_k n}{a_k}$, and more specifically $\frac{b_k n}{a_k}$ is a $(1 \pm \epsilon)$ approximation of S with high probability, as stated in the following theorem.

Theorem 5. *Each node k in a radio network can compute a $(1 \pm \epsilon)$ approximation of the global sum in $O\big(\frac{T_\epsilon^3}{\epsilon^2} \log(T_\epsilon n) \log\big(\frac{T_\epsilon nm}{\epsilon}\big)\big)$ rounds with probability $1 - O(\frac{1}{n})$.*

References

1. Afek, Y., Alon, N., Bar-Joseph, Z., Cornejo, A., Haeupler, B., Kuhn, F.: Beeping a maximal independent set. In: Peleg, D. (ed.) DISC 2011. LNCS, vol. 6950, pp. 32–50. Springer, Heidelberg (2011)
2. Avrachenkov, K., Litvak, N., Nemirovsky, D., Osipova, N.: Monte carlo methods in pagerank computation: When one iteration is sufficient. SIAM J. Numer. Anal. 45(2), 890–904 (2007)
3. Bar-Yehuda, R., Goldreich, O., Itai, A.: On the time-complexity of broadcast in radio networks: An exponential gap between determinism randomization. In: Proceedings of the Sixth Annual ACM Symposium on Principles of Distributed Computing, PODC 1987, pp. 98–108. ACM, New York (1987)
4. Capetanakis, J.: Generalized tdma: The multi-accessing tree protocol. IEEE Transactions on Communications 27(10), 1476–1484 (1979)
5. Capetanakis, J.: Tree algorithms for packet broadcast channels. IEEE Trans. Inf. Theor. 25(5), 505–515 (2006)
6. Chlamtac, I., Kutten, S.: On broadcasting in radio networks–problem analysis and protocol design. IEEE Transactions on Communications 33(12), 1240–1246 (1985)

7. Cornejo, A., Kuhn, F.: Deploying wireless networks with beeps. In: Lynch, N.A., Shvartsman, A.A. (eds.) DISC 2010. LNCS, vol. 6343, pp. 148–162. Springer, Heidelberg (2010)

8. Czumaj, A., Rytter, W.: Broadcasting algorithms in radio networks with unknown topology. In: Proceedings of the 44th Annual IEEE Symposium on Foundations of Computer Science, pp. 492–501 (2003)

9. Gasieniec, L., Peleg, D., Xin, Q.: Faster communication in known topology radio networks. In: Proceedings of the Twenty-fourth Annual ACM Symposium on Principles of Distributed Computing, PODC 2005, pp. 129–137. ACM, New York (2005)

10. Gąsieniec, L., Pelc, A., Peleg, D.: The wakeup problem in synchronous broadcast systems (extended abstract). In: Proceedings of the Nineteenth Annual ACM Symposium on Principles of Distributed Computing, PODC 2000, pp. 113–121. ACM, New York (2000)

11. Ghaffari, M., Haeupler, B., Khabbazian, M.: Randomized broadcast in radio networks with collision detection. In: Proceedings of the 2013 ACM Symposium on Principles of Distributed Computing, PODC 2013, pp. 325–334. ACM, New York (2013)

12. Ghaffari, M., Haeupler, B., Lynch, N., Newport, C.: Bounds on contention management in radio networks. In: Aguilera, M.K. (ed.) DISC 2012. LNCS, vol. 7611, pp. 223–237. Springer, Heidelberg (2012)

13. Greenberg, A.G., Flajolet, P., Ladner, R.E.: Estimating the multiplicities of conflicts to speed their resolution in multiple access channels. J. ACM 34(2), 289–325 (1987)

14. Hayes, J.F.: An adaptive technique for local distribution. IEEE Transactions on Communications 26(8), 1178–1186 (1978)

15. Huang, B., Moscibroda, T.: Conflict resolution and membership problem in beeping channels. In: Afek, Y. (ed.) DISC 2013. LNCS, vol. 8205, pp. 314–328. Springer, Heidelberg (2013)

16. Jurdziński, T., Stachowiak, G.: Probabilistic algorithms for the wakeup problem in single-hop radio networks. In: Bose, P., Morin, P. (eds.) ISAAC 2002. LNCS, vol. 2518, pp. 535–549. Springer, Heidelberg (2002)

17. Kowalski, D.R., Pelc, A.: Broadcasting in undirected ad hoc radio networks. In: Proceedings of the Twenty-second Annual Symposium on Principles of Distributed Computing, PODC 2003, pp. 73–82. ACM, New York (2003)

18. Mitzenmacher, M., Upfal, E.: Probability and computing - randomized algorithms and probabilistic analysis. Cambridge University Press (2005)

19. Page, L., Brin, S., Motwani, R., Winograd, T.: The pagerank citation ranking: Bringing order to the web. Technical report. Stanford University (1999)

20. Das Sarma, A., Molla, A.R., Pandurangan, G., Upfal, E.: Fast distributed pagerank computation. In: Frey, D., Raynal, M., Sarkar, S., Shyamasundar, R.K., Sinha, P. (eds.) ICDCN 2013. LNCS, vol. 7730, pp. 11–26. Springer, Heidelberg (2013)

21. Tsybakov, B.S., Mikhailov, V.A.: Free synchronous access of packets to a broadcast feedback channel. Problems Inform. Transmission 14(4), 259–280 (1978)

A   Proof of Algorithm 1

Fact 6 *For $|t| = 1$ and for any $n > 1$, it holds that $e^t(1 - \frac{1}{n}) \leq (1 + \frac{t}{n})^n \leq e^t$. More specifically, for all positive integers i, it holds that $\frac{1}{2e} \leq \frac{1}{e}(1 - \frac{1}{2^i}) \leq (1 - \frac{1}{2^i})^{2^i} \leq \frac{1}{e}$.*

It is easy to verify that Algorithm 1 always correctly returns $s = 0$ for node k when $sum_k = 0$. If $sum_k > 0$, we can prove the correctness of the algorithm by the following lemmas.

Lemma 1. *Let i_{max} be the maximum integer such that there is an incoming neighbor ℓ of node k with $v_\ell \in [2^{i_{max}}, 2^{i_{max}+1})$. Then after the preprocessing stage, node k has $flag = i_{max}$ with probability $1 - O(\frac{1}{n^2})$.*

Lemma 2. *In phase i, for each $1 \leq i \leq \log nm + 1$, node k listens in $\Theta(\frac{\log n}{\epsilon^2})$ rounds with probability $1 - O(\frac{1}{n^3})$.*

Lemma 3. *Suppose $2^{i^*-1} \leq sum_k < 2^{i^*}$ for some $1 \leq i^* \leq \log nm + 1$. Then with probability $1 - O(\frac{1}{n^2})$, node k will find $i \leq flag$ or $\frac{c}{r} \leq \frac{1}{6}$ at line 26 in the first $i^* - 2$ phases.*

Proof. Let i_{max} be the maximum integer such that there is an incoming neighbor ℓ of node k with $v_\ell \geq 2^{i_{max}}$. Obviously $i_{max} < i^*$. By lemma 1, node k will find $flag = i_{max}$ after the preprocessing stage with probability $1 - O(\frac{1}{n^2})$ and hence it will find $i \leq flag$ in the first i_{max} phases with with probability $1 - O(\frac{1}{n^2})$.

Now consider phase i', for $i_{max} < i' \leq i^* - 2$. Suppose node k listens in $\frac{d \log n}{\epsilon^2}$ rounds in phase i', for some constant d. We know that node k receives no signal with probability $(1 - \frac{1}{2^{i'}})^{sum_k} < (1 - \frac{1}{2^{i'}})^{2^{i^*-1}} \leq \frac{1}{e^2}$ in a round of phase i' when it listens. By the Chernoff bound, if node k listens in $r = \frac{d \log n}{\epsilon^2}$ rounds in phase i^* for a large enough constant d, say $d \geq 9/(\frac{e^2}{6} - 1)^2$, we know $\Pr[c \geq \frac{1}{6}r] \leq \Pr[c \geq (1 + (\frac{e^2}{6} - 1))\frac{r}{e^2}] \leq e^{-d \log n(\frac{e^2}{6} - 1)^2/3} \leq \frac{1}{n^3}$. Combining this result and Lemma 2, we can conclude that node k finds $\frac{c}{r} < \frac{1}{6}$ at the end of phase i' with probability $1 - O(\frac{1}{n^3})$.

Since node k has at most $n - 1$ incoming neighbors, each having an input less than $2^{i_{max}+1}$, we know that $2^{i^*-1} \leq sum_k < 2^{i_{max}+1}(n - 1)$ and hence $\log \frac{2^{i^*-1}}{2^{i_{max}+1}} \leq \log n$. That is to say, there are at most $\log n$ phases between phase i_{max} and phase $i^* - 1$. Therefore, we can conclude in all phases between phase i_{max} and phase $i^* - 2$, node k cannot find $\frac{c}{r} > \frac{1}{6}$ will probability at least $1 - O(\frac{\log n}{n^3}) \geq 1 - O(\frac{1}{n^2})$. This completes the proof. $\square$

Lemma 4. *Suppose $2^{i^*-1} \leq sum_k < 2^{i^*}$ for some $1 \leq i^* \leq \log nm + 1$. Then with probability $1 - O(\frac{1}{n^2})$, node k will find both $i' > flag$ and $\frac{c}{r} > \frac{1}{6}$ for the first time at line 26 in phase i', where $i' = i^* - 1$ or $i' = i^*$.*

Lemma 5. *Node k returns a $(1 + \epsilon)$ approximation of sum_k with probability $1 - O(\frac{1}{n^2})$.*

Proof. If $sum_k = 0$, then it is easy to see that none of its incoming neighbors will broadcast a message and hence node k will always successfully return $s = 0$. Now consider $2^{i^*-1} \leq sum_k < 2^{i^*}$ for some $1 \leq i^* \leq \log nm + 1$. Suppose node k finds both $i' > flag$ and $\frac{c}{r} > \frac{1}{6}$ for the first time in phase i', where $i' = i^* - 1$ or $i' = i^*$. Then we know that all incoming neighbors of node k have inputs smaller than $2^{i'}$. Also suppose node k listens in $\frac{d \log n}{\epsilon^2}$ rounds in phase i', for a constant d. Thus at the end of phase i', node k has $r = \frac{d \log n}{\epsilon^2}$ and $\mathrm{E}[c] = \frac{d \log n}{\epsilon^2}(1 - \frac{1}{2^{i'}})^{sum_k} > \frac{d \log n}{\epsilon^2}(1 - \frac{1}{2^{i'}})^{2^{i^*}} \geq \frac{d \log n}{\epsilon^2}(1 - \frac{1}{2^{i^*-1}})^{2^{i^*}} \geq \frac{d \log n}{(2e)^2 \epsilon^2} = \frac{d' \log n}{\epsilon^2}$, for a constant $d' = \frac{d}{4e^2}$. Again, by the Chernoff bound, $\Pr[c \geq (1 + \frac{1}{4}\epsilon)\mathrm{E}[c]] \leq e^{-\frac{\mathrm{E}[c]\epsilon^2}{4^2 \times 3}} = e^{-d' \log n/48}$. If d and d' are large enough, we have $e^{-d' \log n/48} < \frac{1}{n^2}$ and hence $\Pr[\frac{c}{r} < (1 + \frac{1}{4}\epsilon)(1 - \frac{1}{2^{i'}})^{sum_k}] = \Pr[c < (1 + \frac{1}{4}\epsilon)\mathrm{E}[c]] \geq 1 - \frac{1}{n^2}$. Similarly, we can prove that $\Pr[\frac{c}{r} > (1 - \frac{1}{4}\epsilon)(1 - \frac{1}{2^{i'}})^{sum_k}] \geq 1 - \frac{1}{n^2}$. Therefore, $\Pr[(1 - \frac{1}{4}\epsilon)(1 - \frac{1}{2^{i'}})^{sum_k} < \frac{c}{r} < (1 + \frac{1}{4}\epsilon)(1 - \frac{1}{2^{i'}})^{sum_k}] \geq 1 - \frac{2}{n^2}$.

Now we analyze the accuracy of s computed at line 27 in phase i'. Note that $f(s) = (1 - \frac{1}{2^{i'}})^s$ is a strictly decreasing function. Also note that $2^{i'-1} \leq sum_k < 2^{i'+1}$. Thus, $f((1+\epsilon)sum_k) = (1 - \frac{1}{2^{i'}})^{(1+\epsilon)sum_k} = (1 - \frac{1}{2^{i'}})^{\epsilon sum_k}(1 - \frac{1}{2^{i'}})^{sum_k} \leq (1 - \frac{1}{2^{i'}})^{\epsilon 2^{i'-1}}(1 - \frac{1}{2^{i'}})^{sum_k} \leq (\frac{1}{e})^{\epsilon/2}(1 - \frac{1}{2^{i'}})^{sum_k} < (\frac{1}{2e})^{\epsilon/4}(1 - \frac{1}{2^{i'}})^{sum_k} < (1 - \frac{1}{4}\epsilon)(1 - \frac{1}{2^{i'}})^{sum_k}$. Similarly, we can prove that $f((1 - \epsilon)sum_k) = (1 - \frac{1}{2^{i'}})^{(1-\epsilon)sum_k} > (1 + \frac{1}{4}\epsilon)(1 - \frac{1}{2^{i'}})^{sum_k}$. Therefore, if $(1 - \frac{1}{4}\epsilon)(1 - \frac{1}{2^{i'}})^{sum_k} < (1 - \frac{1}{2^{i'}})^s < (1 + \frac{1}{4}\epsilon)(1 - \frac{1}{2^{i'}})^{sum_k}$, we can conclude that the s computed at line 27 satisfies $(1 - \epsilon)sum_k < s < (1 + \epsilon)sum_k$. That is, with probability at least $1 - \frac{2}{n^2}$, node k will have $(1 - \frac{1}{4}\epsilon)(1 - \frac{1}{2^{i'}})^{sum_k} < \frac{c}{r} < (1 + \frac{1}{4}\epsilon)(1 - \frac{1}{2^{i'}})^{sum_k}$ at the end of phase i' and hence it will get a s which is a $(1 + \epsilon)$ approximation of sum_k. Combining this with Lemma 2 and Lemma 4, we can conclude that node k returns a $(1 + \epsilon)$ approximation of sum_k with probability $1 - O(\frac{1}{n^2})$. □

It is easy to see that Algorithm 1 finishes in $O(\log nm \cdot \frac{\log n}{\epsilon^2}) = O(\frac{\log^2 n + \log n \log m}{\epsilon^2})$ rounds. Combining Lemma 5 and the union bound, we immediately prove Theorem 1.

Radio Network Lower Bounds Made Easy*

Calvin Newport

Georgetown University
Washington, DC
cnewport@cs.georgetown.edu

Abstract. Theoreticians have studied distributed algorithms in the synchronous radio network model for close to three decades. A significant fraction of this work focuses on lower bounds for basic communication problems such as *wake-up* (symmetry breaking among an unknown set of nodes) and *broadcast* (message dissemination through an unknown network topology). In this paper, we introduce a new technique for proving this type of bound, based on reduction from a probabilistic hitting game, that simplifies and strengthens much of this existing work. In more detail, in this single paper we prove new expected time and high probability lower bounds for wake-up and global broadcast in single and multi-channel versions of the radio network model both with and without collision detection. In doing so, we are able to reproduce results that previously spanned a half-dozen papers published over a period of twenty-five years. In addition to simplifying these existing results, our technique, in many places, also improves the state of the art: of the eight bounds we prove, four strictly strengthen the best known previous result (in terms of time complexity and/or generality of the algorithm class for which it holds), and three provide the first known non-trivial bound for the case in question. The fact that the same technique can easily generate this diverse collection of lower bounds indicates a surprising unity underlying communication tasks in the radio network model—revealing that deep down, below the specifics of the problem definition and model assumptions, communication in this setting reduces to finding efficient strategies for a simple game.

1 Introduction

In this paper, we introduce a new technique for proving lower bounds for basic communication tasks in the radio network model. We use this technique to unify, simplify, and in many cases strengthen the best known lower bounds for two particularly important problems: wake-up and broadcast.

The Radio Network Model. The radio network model represents a wireless network as a graph $G = (V, E)$, where the nodes in V correspond to the wireless devices and the edges in E specify links. Executions proceed in synchronous rounds.

---

* This work is supported in part by NSF grant number CCF 1320279 and the Ford Motor Company University Research Program.

F. Kuhn (Ed.): DISC 2014, LNCS 8784, pp. 258–272, 2014.

In each round, each node can choose whether or not to broadcast messages to its neighbors in G. If multiple neighbors of a given node broadcast during the same round, however, the messages are lost due to collision. This model was first introduced by Chlamtac and Kutten [4], who used it to study centralized algorithms. Soon after, Bar-Yehuda et al. [2,3] introduced the model to the distributed algorithms community where variations have since been studied in a large number of subsequent papers; e.g., [1,20,18,21,13,19,6,10,11,17,9,12,8,7,15,14].

Two of the most investigated problems in the radio network model are *wake-up* (basic symmetry breaking among an unknown set of participants in a single hop network) and *broadcast* (propagating a message from a source to all nodes in an unknown multihop network). Lower bounds for these problems are important because wake-up and/or broadcast reduce to most useful communication tasks in this setting, and therefore capture something fundamental about the cost of distributed computation over radio links.

Our Results. In this paper, we introduce a new technique (described below) for proving lower bounds for wake-up and broadcast in the radio network model. We use this technique to prove new expected time and high probability lower bounds for these two problems in the single and multiple channel versions of the radio network model both with and without collision detection. In doing so, we reproduce in this single paper a set of existing results that spanned a half-dozen papers [23,20,18,13,9,7] published over a period of twenty-five years. Our technique simplifies these existing arguments and establishes a (perhaps) surprising unity among these diverse problems and model assumptions. Our technique also strengthens the state of the art. All but one of the results proved in this paper improve the best known existing result by increasing the time complexity and/or generalizing the class of algorithms for which the bound holds (many existing bounds for these problems hold only for *uniform* algorithms that require nodes to use a pre-determined sequence of independent broadcast probabilities; all of our lower bounds, by contrast, hold for all randomized algorithms). In several cases, we prove the first known bound for the considered assumptions.

The full set of our results with comparisons to existing work are described in Figure 1. Here we briefly mention three highlights (in the following, n is the network size and D the network diameter). In Section 6, we significantly simplify Willard's seminal $\Omega(\log \log n)$ bound for expected time wake-up with collision detection [23]. In addition, whereas Willard's result only holds for uniform algorithms, our new version holds for all algorithms. In Section 7, we prove the first tight bound for high probability wake-up with multiple channels and the first known expected time bound in this setting. And in Section 9, we prove that Kushilevitz and Mansour's oft-cited $\Omega(D \log (n/D))$ lower bound for expected time broadcast [20] *still holds* even if we assume multiple channels and/or collision detection—opening an unexpected gap with the wake-up problem for which these assumptions improve the achievable time complexity.

Our Technique. Consider the following simple game which we call *k-hitting*. A *referee* secretly selects a target set $T \subseteq \{1, 2, ..., k\}$. The game proceeds in rounds.

In each round, a *player* (represented by a randomized algorithm) generates a proposal P. If $|P \cap T| = 1$, the player wins. Otherwise, it moves on to the next round. In Section 3, we leverage a useful combinatorial result due to Alon et al. [1] to prove that this game requires $\Omega(\log^2 k)$ rounds to solve with high probability (w.r.t. k), and $\Omega(\log k)$ rounds in expectation. (Notice, you could propose the sets of a (k, k)-*selective family* [5] to solve this problem deterministically, but this would require $\Omega(k)$ proposals in the worst-case.)

These lower bounds are important because in this paper we show that this basic hitting game reduces to solving wake-up and broadcast under all of the different combinations of model assumptions that we consider. In other words, whether or not you are solving wake-up or broadcast, assuming multiple channels or a single channel, and/or assuming collision detection or no collision detection, if you can solve the problem quickly you can solve this hitting game quickly. Our lower bounds on the hitting game, therefore, provide a fundamental speed-limit for basic communication tasks in the radio network model.

The trick in applying this method is identifying the proper reduction argument for the assumptions in question. Consider, for example, our reduction for wake-up with a single channel and no collision detection. Assume some algorithm $\mathcal{A}$ solves wake-up with these assumptions in $f(n)$ rounds, in expectation. As detailed in Section 5, we can use $\mathcal{A}$ to define a player that solves the k-hitting game in $f(k)$ rounds with the same probability—allowing the relevant hitting game lower bound to apply. Our strategy for this case is to have the player simulate $\mathcal{A}$ running on all k nodes in a network of size k. For each round of the simulation, it proposes the ids of the nodes that broadcast, then simulates all nodes receiving nothing. This is not necessarily a valid simulation of $\mathcal{A}$ running on k nodes: *but it does not need to be*. What we care about are the simulated nodes with ids in T: the (unknown to the player) target set for this instance of the hitting game. The key observation is that in the *target execution* where only the nodes in T are active, they will receive nothing until the first round where one node broadcasts alone—solving wake-up. In the player's simulation, these same nodes are also receiving nothing (by the the player's fixed receive rule) so they will behave the same way. This will lead to a round of the simulation where only one node from T (and perhaps other nodes outside of T) broadcast. The player will propose these ids, winning the hitting game.

These reductions get more tricky as we add additional assumptions. Consider, for example, what happens when we now assume collision detection. Maintaining consistency between the nodes in T in the player simulation and the target execution becomes more complicated, as the player must now correctly simulate a collision event whenever two or more nodes from T broadcast—even though the player *does not know* T. Adding multiple channels only further complicates this need for consistency. Each bound in this paper, therefore, is built around its own clever method for a hitting game player to correctly simulate a wake-up or broadcast algorithm in such a way that it wins the hitting game with the desired efficiency. These arguments are simple to understand and sometimes surprisingly elegant once identified, but can also be elusive before they are first pinned down.

	Existing (exp. | high)	This Paper (exp. | high)
wake-up	$\Omega(\log n) \mid \Omega(\log^2 n)$ [18,13]	$\Omega(\log n) \mid \Omega(\log^2 n)$ (*)
wake-up/cd	$\Omega(\log \log n) \mid \Omega(\log n)$ [23]	$\Omega(\log \log n) \mid \Omega(\log n)$ (*)
wake-up/mc	? | $\Omega(\frac{\log^2 n}{C \log \log n} + \log n)$ [9,7]	$\Omega(\frac{\log n}{C} + 1) \mid \Omega(\frac{\log^2 n}{C} + \log n)$ (*)
wake-up/cd/mc	$\Omega(1) \mid$?	$\Omega(1) \mid \Omega(\frac{\log n}{\log C} + \log \log n)$
broadcast	$\Omega(D \log (n/D))$ [20]	$\Omega(D \log (n/D))$
broadcast/cd/mc	?	$\Omega(D \log (n/D)$

Fig. 1. This table summarizes the expected time (exp.) and high probability (high) results for wake-up and broadcast in the existing literature as well as the new bounds proved in this paper. In these bounds, n is the network size, C the number of channels, and D the network diameter. In the problem descriptions, "cd" indicates the collision detection assumption and "mc" indicates the multiple channels assumption. In the existing results we provide citation for the paper(s) from which the results derive and use "?" to indicate a previously open problem. In all cases, the new results in this paper simplify the existing results. We marked some of our results with "(*)" to indicate that the existing results assumed the restricted *uniform* class of algorithms. All our algorithms hold for all randomized algorithms, so any result marked by "(*)" is strictly stronger than the existing result. We do not separate expected time and high probability for the broadcast problems as the tight bounds are the same for both cases.

Roadmap. A full description of our results and how they compare to existing results is provided in Figure 1. In addition, before we prove each bound in the sections that follow, we first discuss in more detail the relevant related work. In Section 2, we formalize our model and the two problems we study. In Section 3, we formalize the hitting games at the core of our technique then bound from below their complexity. In Section 4, we detail a general simulation strategy that we adopt in most of our wake-up bounds (by isolating this general strategy in its own section we reduce redundancy). Sections 5 to 8 contain our wake-up lower bounds, and Section 9 contains our broadcast lower bound. (We only need one section for broadcast as we prove that the same result holds for all assumptions considered in this paper.)

2 Model and Problems

In this paper we consider variants of the standard *radio network model*. This model represents a radio network with a connected undirected graph $G = (V, E)$ of diameter D. The $n = |V|$ nodes in the graph represent the wireless devices and the edges in E capture communication proximity. In more detail, executions in this model proceed in synchronous rounds. In each round, each node can choose to either *transmit* a message or *receive*. In a given round, a node $u \in V$ can receive a message from a node $v \in V$, if and only if the following conditions hold: (1) u is receiving and v is transmitting; (2) v is u's neighbor in G; and (3) v is the *only* neighbor of u transmitting in this round. The first condition captures the half-duplex nature of the radio channel and the second condition captures message collisions. To achieve the strongest possible lower bounds, we assume nodes are provided unique ids from $[n]$. In the following, we say an algorithm is *uniform* if (active) nodes use a predetermined sequence of independent broadcast probabilities to determine whether or not to broadcast in each round, up until they first receive a message. A uniform algorithm, for example, cannot select its broadcast probability in a given round based on the outcome of a coin flip during a previous round. This prohibits, among other strategies, allowing nodes to change their behavior based on whether or not they previously chose to broadcast (e.g., as in [21]).

In the *collision detection* variant of the radio network model, a receiving node u can distinguish between silence (no neighbor is transmitting) and collision (two or more neighbors are transmitting) in a given round. In this paper, to achieve the strongest possible lower bounds, when studying single hop networks we also assume that a transmitter can distinguish between broadcasting alone and broadcasting simultaneously with one or more other nodes. In the *multichannel* variant of the radio network model, we use a parameter $\mathcal{C} \geq 1$ to indicate the number of orthogonal communication channels available to the nodes. When $\mathcal{C} > 1$, we generalize the model to require each node to choose in each round a single channel on which to participate. The communication rules above apply separately to each channel. In other words, a node u receives a message from v on channel c in a given round, if and only if in this round: (1) u receives on c and v transmits on c; (2) v is a neighbor of u; and (3) no other neighbor of u transmits on c.

We study both *expected time* and *high probability* results, where we define the latter to mean probability at least $1 - \frac{1}{n}$. We define the notation $[i, j]$, for integers $i \leq j$, to denote the range $\{i, i + 1, ..., j\}$, and define $[i]$, for integer $i > 0$, to denote $[1, i]$.

Problems. The *wake-up* problem assumes a single hop network consisting of *inactive* nodes. At the beginning of the execution, an arbitrary subset of these nodes are *activated* by an adversary. Inactive nodes can only listen, while active nodes execute an arbitrary randomized algorithm. We assume that active nodes have no advance knowledge of the identities of the other active nodes. The problem is solved in the first round in which an active node broadcasts alone (therefore *waking up* the listening inactive nodes). When considering a model with collision detection, we still require that an active node broadcasts alone to solve the problem (e.g., to avoid triviality, we assume that the inactive nodes need to receive a message to wake-up, and that simply detecting a collision is not sufficient[1]). When considering multichannel networks, we assume the inactive nodes are all listening on the same known *default* channel (say, channel 1). To solve the problem, therefore, now requires that an active node broadcasts alone on the default channel.

The *broadcast* problem assumes a connected multihop graph. At the beginning of the execution, a single *source* node u is provided a message m. The problem

---

[1] Without this restriction, the problem is trivially solved by just having all active nodes broadcast in the first round.

is solved once every node in the network has received m. We assume nodes do not have any advance knowledge of the network topology. As is standard, we assume that nodes are inactive (can only listen) until they first receive m. As in the wake-up problem, detecting a collision alone is not sufficient to activate an inactive node, and in multichannel networks, we assume inactive nodes all listen on the default channel.

3 The k-Hitting Game

The k-hitting game, defined for some integer $k > 1$, assumes a player that faces off against an referee. At the beginning of the game, the referee secretly selects a target set $T \subseteq \{1, ..., k\}$. The game then proceeds in rounds. In each round, the player generates a proposal $P \subseteq \{1, ..., k\}$. If $|P \cap T| = 1$, then the player wins the game. Otherwise, the player moves on to the next round learning no information other than the fact that its proposal failed. We formalize both entities as probabilistic automata and assume the player does not know the referee's selection and the referee does not know the player's random bits. Finally, we define the restricted k-hitting game to be a variant of the game where the target set is always of size two.

A Useful Combinatorial Result. Before proving lower bounds for our hitting game we cite an existing combinatorial result that will aid our arguments. To simplify the presentation of this result, we first define some useful notation. Fix some integer $\ell > 0$. Consider two sets $A \subseteq \{1, 2, ..., \ell\}$ and $B \subseteq \{1, 2, ...\ell\}$. We say that A hits B if $|A \cap B| = 1$. Let an ℓ-family be a family of non-empty subsets of $\{1, 2, ..., \ell\}$. The size of an ℓ-family $\mathscr{A}$, sometimes noted as $|\mathscr{A}|$, is the number of sets in $\mathscr{A}$. Fix two ℓ-families $\mathscr{A}$ and $\mathscr{B}$. We say $\mathscr{A}$ hits $\mathscr{B}$, if for every $B \in \mathscr{B}$ there exists an $A \in \mathscr{A}$ such that A hits B. Using this notation, we can now present the result:

Lemma 1 ([1,15]). *There exists a constant $\beta > 0$, such that for any integer $\ell > 1$, these two results hold:*

1. *There exists an ℓ-family $\mathscr{R}$, where $|\mathscr{R}| \in O(\ell^8)$, such that for every ℓ-family $\mathscr{H}$ that hits $\mathscr{R}$, $|\mathscr{H}| \in \Omega(\log^2 \ell)$.*
2. *There exists an ℓ-family $\mathscr{S}$, where $|\mathscr{S}| \in O(\ell^8)$, such that for every $H \subseteq \{1, 2, ..., \ell\}$, H hits at most a $(\frac{1}{\beta \log(\ell)})$-fraction of the sets in $\mathscr{S}$.*

The first result from this lemma was proved in a 1991 paper by Alon et al. [1]. It was established using the probabilistic method and was then used to prove a $\Omega(\log^2 n)$ lower bound on centralized broadcast solutions in the radio network model. The second result is a straightforward consequence of the analysis used in [1], recently isolated and proved by Ghaffari et al. [15].

Lower Bounds for the k-Hitting Game. We now prove lower bounds on our general and restricted k-hitting games. These results, which concern probabilities, leverage Lemma 1, which concerns combinatorics, in an interesting way which depends on the size of $\mathscr{R}$ and $\mathscr{S}$ being polynomial in ℓ.

Theorem 1. *Fix some player $\mathcal{P}$ that guarantees, for all $k > 1$, to solve the k-hitting game in $f(k)$ rounds, in expectation. It follows that $f(k) \in \Omega(\log k)$.*

Proof. Fix any $k > 1$. Let β and $\mathcal{S}$ be the constant and ℓ-family provided by the second result of Lemma 1 applied to $\ell = k$. The lemma tells us that for any $P \subseteq [k]$, P hits at most a $(\frac{1}{\beta \log k})$-fraction of the sets in $\mathcal{S}$. It follows that for any k-family $\mathcal{H}$, such that $|\mathcal{H}| < \frac{\beta \log k}{2}$, $\mathcal{H}$ hits less than half the sets in $\mathcal{S}$.

We now use these observations to prove our theorem. Let $\mathcal{P}$ be a k-hitting game player. Consider a referee that selects the target set by choosing a set T from $\mathcal{S}$ with uniform randomness. Let $\mathcal{H}$ be the first $\lfloor \frac{\beta \log k}{2} \rfloor - 1$ proposals generated by $\mathcal{P}$ in a given instance of the game. By our above observation, this sequence of proposals hits less than half the sets in $\mathcal{S}$. Because the target set was chosen from $\mathcal{S}$ with randomness that was uniform and independent of the randomness used by $\mathcal{P}$ to generate its proposals, it follows that the probability that $\mathcal{H}$ hits the target is less than $1/2$. To conclude, we note that $f(k)$ must therefore be larger than $\lfloor \frac{\beta \log k}{2} \rfloor - 1 \in \Omega(\log k)$, as required by the theorem.

Theorem 2. *Fix some player $\mathcal{P}$ that guarantees, for all $k > 1$, to solve the k-hitting game in $f(k)$ rounds with probability at least $1 - \frac{1}{k}$. It follows that $f(k) \in \Omega(\log^2 k)$.*

Proof. Fix any $\ell > 1$. Let $\mathcal{R}$ be the ℓ-family provided by the first result of Lemma 1 applied to this value. Let $t = |\mathcal{R}|$. We know from the lemma that $t \in O(\ell^8)$.

To achieve our bound, we will consider the behavior of a player $\mathcal{P}$ in the k-hitting game for $k = t + 1$. As in Theorem 1, we have our referee select its target set by choosing a set from $\mathcal{R}$ with uniform randomness. (Notice, in this case, our referee is actually making things *easier* for the player by restricting its choices to only the values in $[\ell]$ even though the game is defined for the value set $[k]$, which is larger. As we will show, this advantage does not help the player much.)

Let $c \log^2(\ell)$, for some constant $c > 0$, be the exact lower bound from the first result of Lemma 1. Let $\mathcal{H}$ be the first $\lfloor c \log^2(\ell) \rfloor - 1$ proposals generated by $\mathcal{P}$ in a given instance of the game. Lemma 1 tells us that there is at least one set $R \in \mathcal{R}$ that $\mathcal{H}$ does not hit. Because the target set was chosen from $\mathcal{R}$ with randomness that was uniform and independent of the randomness used by $\mathcal{P}$, it follows that the probability that $\mathcal{H}$ misses the target is at least $1/t$ (recall that t is the size of $\mathcal{R}$). Inverting this probability, it follows that the probability that $\mathcal{P}$ wins the game with the proposals represented by $\mathcal{H}$ is less than or equal to $1 - \frac{1}{t} = 1 - \frac{1}{k-1} < 1 - \frac{1}{k}$. It follows that $f(k)$ must be larger than $|\mathcal{H}|$ and therefore must be of size at least $c \log^2(\ell) \in \Omega(\log^2(\ell))$. To conclude the proof, we note that $k \in O(\ell^8)$, from which it follows that $\ell \in \Omega(k^{1/8})$ and therefore that $\log^2(\ell) \in \Omega(\log^2 k)$, as required by the theorem.

The below theorem is proved similar to Theorem 2. The details can be found in the full version of this paper [22].

Theorem 3. *Fix some player $\mathcal{P}$ that guarantees, for all $k > 1$, to solve the restricted k-hitting game in $f(k)$ rounds with probability at least $1 - \frac{1}{k}$. It follows that $f(k) \in \Omega(\log k)$.*

4 Simulation Strategy

Most of our bounds for the *wake-up* problem use a similar simulation strategy. To reduce redundancy, we define the basics of the strategy and its accompanying notation in its own section. In more detail, the *wake-up simulation strategy*, defined with respect to a wake-up algorithm $\mathcal{A}$, is a general strategy for a k-hitting game player to generate proposals based on a local simulation of $\mathcal{A}$. The strategy works as follows. The player simulates $\mathcal{A}$ running on all k nodes in a k-node network satisfying the same assumptions on collision detection and channels assumed by $\mathcal{A}$. For each simulated round, the player will generate one or more proposals for the hitting game. In more detail, at the beginning of a new simulated round, the player simulates the k nodes running $\mathcal{A}$ up until the point that they make a broadcast decision. At this point, the player applies a *proposal rule* that transforms these decisions into one or more proposals for the hitting game. The player then makes these proposals, one by one, in the game. If none of these proposals wins the hitting game, then the player most complete the current simulated round by using a *receive rule* to specify what each node receives; i.e., silence, a message, or a collision (if collision detection is assumed by $\mathcal{A}$). In other words, a given application of the wake-up simulation strategy is defined by two things: a definition of the *proposal rule* and *receive rule* used by the player to generate proposals from the simulation, and specify receive behavior in the simulation, respectively.

To analyze a wake-up simulation strategy for a given instance of the k-hitting game with target set T, we define the *target execution* for this instance to be the execution that would result if $\mathcal{A}$ was run in a network where only the nodes corresponding to T were active and they used the same random bits as the player uses on their behalf in the simulation. We say the simulation strategy is *consistent* with its target execution through a given round, if the nodes corresponding to T in the simulation behave the same (e.g., send and receive the same messages) as the corresponding nodes in the target execution through this round.

5 Lower Bounds for Wake-Up

We begin by proving tight lower bounds for both expected and high probability solutions to the wake-up problem in the most standard set of assumptions used with the radio network model: a single channel and no collision detection. As explained below, our bounds are tight and generalize the best know previous bounds, which hold only for uniform algorithms, to now apply to all randomized algorithms. (We note that a preliminary version of our high probability bound below appeared as an aside in our previous work on structuring multichannel radio networks [8]).

In terms of related work, the *decay* strategy introduced Bar-Yehuda et al. [3] solves the wake-up problem in this setting with high probability in $O(\log^2 n)$ rounds and in expectation in $O(\log n)$ rounds. In 2002, Jurdzinski and Stachowiak [18] proved the necessity of $\Omega\left(\frac{\log n \log(1/\epsilon)}{\log\log n + \log\log(1/\epsilon)}\right)$ rounds to solve wake-up with probability at least $1 - \epsilon$, which proves decay optimal within a $\log\log n$ factor. Four years later, Farach-Colton et al. [13] removed the $\log\log n$ factor by applying linear programming techniques. As mentioned, these existing bounds only apply to uniform algorithms in which nodes use a predetermined sequence of broadcast probabilities. (Section 3.1 of [13] claims to extend their result to a slightly more general class of uniform algorithms in which a node can choose a uniform algorithm to run based on its unique id.)

Theorem 4. *Let $\mathcal{A}$ be an algorithm that solves wake-up with high probability in $f(n)$ rounds in the radio network model with a single channel and no collision detection. It follows that $f(n) \in \Omega(\log^2 n)$.*

Proof. Fix some wake-up algorithm $\mathcal{A}$ that solves wake-up in $f(n)$ rounds with high probability in a network with one channel and no collision detection. We start by defining a wake-up simulation strategy that uses $\mathcal{A}$ (see Section 4). In particular, consider the *proposal rule* that has the player propose the id of every node that broadcasts in the current simulated round, and the *receive rule* that always has all nodes receive nothing.

Let $\mathcal{P_A}$ be the k-hitting game player that uses this simulation strategy. We argue that $\mathcal{P_A}$ solves the k-hitting game in $f(k)$ rounds with high probability in k. To see why, notice that for a given instance of the hitting game with target T, $\mathcal{P_A}$ is consistent with the target execution until the receive rule of the first round in which exactly one node in T broadcasts. (In all previous rounds, $\mathcal{P_A}$ correctly simulates the nodes in T receiving nothing, as its receive rule has all nodes always receive nothing.) Assume $\mathcal{A}$ solves wake-up in round r in the target execution. It follows that r is the first round in which a node in T broadcasts alone in this execution. By our above assumption, $\mathcal{P_A}$ is consistent with the target execution up to the application of the receive rule in r. In particular, it is consistent when it applies the proposal rule for simulated round r. By assumption, this proposal will include exactly one node from T—winning the hitting game.

We assumed that $\mathcal{A}$ solves wake-up in $f(n)$ rounds with high probability in n. Combined with our above argument, it follows that $\mathcal{P_A}$ solves the k-hitting game in $f(k)$ rounds with high probability in k. To complete our lower bound, we apply a contradiction argument. In particular, assume for contradiction that there exists a wake-up algorithm $\mathcal{A}$ that solves wake-up in $f(n) \in o(\log^2 n)$ rounds, with high probability. The hitting game player $\mathcal{P_A}$ defined above will therefore solve k-hitting in $o(\log^2 n)$ rounds with high probability. This contradicts Theorem 2.

Theorem 5. *Let $\mathcal{A}$ be an algorithm that solves wake-up in $f(n)$ rounds, in expectation, in the radio network model with a single channel and no collision detection. It follows that $f(n) \in \Omega(\log n)$.*

Proof (Idea). It is sufficient to apply the same argument as in Theorem 4. The only change is in the final contradiction argument, where we simply replace $\log^2 n$ with $\log n$, and now contradict Theorem 1.

6   Lower Bounds for Wake-Up with Collision Detection

We prove tight lower bounds for expected and high probability bounds on the wake-up problem in the radio network model with collision detection. In terms of related work, a seminal paper by Willard [23] describes a wake-up algorithm (he called the problem "selection resolution," but the definition in this setting is functionally identical) which solves the problem in $O(\log \log n)$ rounds, in expectation. He also proved the result tight with an $\Omega(\log \log n)$ lower bound for uniform algorithms. As Willard himself admits, his lower bound proof is mathematically complex. Below, we significantly simplify this bound and generalize it to hold for all algorithms. From a high-probability perspective, many solutions exist in folklore for solving wake-up (and related problems) in $O(\log n)$ rounds. Indeed, leveraging collision detection, wake-up can be solved *deterministically* in $O(\log n)$ rounds (e.g., use the detector to allow the active nodes to move consistently through a binary search tree to identify the smallest active id). The necessity of $\Omega(\log n)$ rounds seems also to exist in folklore.

We begin with our high probability result. Our simulation strategy is more difficult to deploy here because the player must now somehow correctly simulate the collision detection among the nodes in the (unknown) target set T. To overcome this difficulty, we apply our solution to networks in which only two nodes are activated and then achieve a contradiction with our lower bound on *restricted* hitting. The details of this proof are deferred to the full version [22].

Theorem 6. *Let $\mathcal{A}$ be an algorithm that solves wake-up with high probability in $f(n)$ rounds in the radio network model with a single channel and collision detection. It follows that $f(n) \in \Omega(\log n)$.*

We now simplify and strengthen Willard's bound of $\Omega(\log \log n)$ rounds for expected time wake up. At the core of our result is a pleasingly simple but surprisingly useful observation: if you can solve wake-up in t rounds with collision detection, you can then use this strategy to solve the hitting game in 2^t rounds by simulating (carefully) all possible sequences of outcomes for the collision detector behavior in a t round execution. Solving the problem in $o(\log \log n)$ rounds (in expectation) with collision detection, therefore, yields a hitting game solution that requires only $2^{o(\log \log k)} = o(\log k)$ rounds (in expectation), contradicting Theorem 1—our lower bound on expected time solutions to the hitting game.

Theorem 7. *Let $\mathcal{A}$ be an algorithm that solves wake-up in $f(n)$ rounds, in expectation, in the radio network model with a single channel and collision detection. It follows that $f(n) \in \Omega(\log \log n)$.*

Proof. Fix some algorithm $\mathcal{A}$ that solves wake-up in $f(n)$ rounds, in expectation, in this setting. We start by defining a player $\mathcal{P}_{\mathcal{A}}$ that simulates $\mathcal{A}$ to solve k-hitting in no more than $2^{f(k)+1}$ rounds, in expectation. Our player will use a variant of the simulation strategy defined in Section 4 and used in the preceding proofs, and we will, therefore, adopt much of the terminology of this approach (with some minor modifications). In more detail, in this variant, $\mathcal{P_A}$ will run a different fixed-length simulation of $\mathcal{A}$, starting from round 1, to generate each of its guesses in the hitting game. Most of these simulations will *not* be consistent with the relevant target execution. We will show, however, that in the case that the target execution solves wake-up, at least one such simulation is consistent and will therefore win the game.

In more detail, for a given k, let $B_{f(k)}$ be a full rooted binary tree of depth $f(k)$. We define a tree node labeling ℓ, such that for every non-root node u, $\ell(u) = 0$ if u is a left child of its parent and $\ell(u) = 1$ if u is a right child (by some consistent orientation). Let d be the depth function (i.e., $d(u)$ is the depth of u in the tree with $d(root) = 0$). Finally, let $p(u)$ return the $d(u)$-bit binary string defined by the sequence of labels (by ℓ) on the path that descends from the root to u (including u). For example, if the path from the root to u goes from the root to its right child v, then from v to its left child u, $p(u) = 10$.

Our player $\mathcal{P_A}$, when playing the k-hitting game, generate one guess for each node in $B_{f(k)}$. Fix some such node u. To generate a guess for u, the player first executes a $d(u)$-round simulation of $\mathcal{A}$, running on all k nodes in a k-node network, using $p(u)$ to specify collision detector behavior (in a manner described below). After it simulates these $d(u)$ full rounds, it then simulates just enough of round $d(u) + 1$ to determine the simulated nodes' broadcast decisions in this round. The player proposes the id of the nodes that choose to broadcast in this final partial round. (When generating a guess for the root node, the player simply proposes the nodes that broadcast in the first round.)

In more detail, for each round $r \leq d(u)$ of the simulation for tree node u, if the rth bit of $p(u)$ is 0, the player simulates all nodes detecting silence, and if the bit is 1, it simulates all nodes detecting a collision. As a final technicality, let κ be the random bits provided to the player to resolve its random choices. We assume that for each simulated node i, the players uses the same bits from κ for i in each of its simulations. We do not, therefore, assume independence between different simulations.

Consider the target execution of $\mathcal{A}$ for a given instance of the hitting game with target set T and random bits κ. Assume that the target execution defined for these bits and target set solves wake-up in some round $r \leq f(k)$. Notice that in every round $r' < r$, there are only two possible behaviors: (1) no nodes broadcast (and all nodes therefore receive and detect nothing); and (2) two or more nodes broadcast (and all nodes therefore detect a collision). By definition, there exists a node u in $B_{f(k)}$ such that $p(u)$ is a binary string of length $r - 1$, where for each bit position i in the string, $i = 0$ if no nodes broadcast in that round of the target execution, and $i = 1$ if two or more nodes broadcast in that round of the target execution. It follows that the first $r - 1$ rounds of the simulation associated with tree node u are consistent with the target execution. Because exactly one node from T broadcasts in round r of the target execution, and the u-simulation is consistent through round $r - 1$, then this same single node from T will broadcast in the simulated beginning of round r. The player's proposal associated with u will therefore win the hitting game.

Pulling together the pieces, by assumption, the target execution for a given T and κ solves wake-up in $f(k)$ rounds, in expectation. It follows that our player solves k-hitting with the same probability. The number of guesses required to solve the problem in this case is bounded by the number of nodes in $B_{f(k)}$ (as there is one guess per node), which is $2^{f(k)+1} - 1$. We can now conclude with our standard style of contradiction argument. Assume for contradiction that there exists an algorithm $\mathcal{A}$ that solves wake-up with a single channel and collision detection in $f(n) \in o(\log \log n)$ rounds, in expectation. It follows that $\mathcal{P_A}$ wins the k-hitting game in $2^{f(k)+1} \in o(\log k)$ rounds, in expectation. This contradicts Theorem 1.

7   Lower Bounds for Wake-Up with Multiple Channels

In recent years, theoreticians have paid increasing attention to multichannel versions of the radio network model (e.g., [10,11,17,9,12,8,7]). These investigations are motivated by the reality that most network cards allow the device to choose its channel from among multiple available channels. From a theoretical perspective, the interesting question is how to leverage the parallelism inherent in multiple channels to improve time complexity for basic communication problems. Daum et al. [7], building on results from Dolev et al. [9], prove a lower bound of $\Omega\left(\frac{\log^2 n}{\mathcal{C}\log\log n} + \log n\right)$ rounds for solving wake-up with high probability and uniform algorithms in a network with $\mathcal{C}$ channels. A lower bound for expected-time solutions was left open. The best known upper bound solves the problem in $O\left(\frac{\log^2 n}{\mathcal{C}} + \log n\right)$ rounds with high probability and in $O\left(\frac{\log n}{\mathcal{C}} + 1\right)$ rounds in expectation [7].

In the theorems that follow, we prove new lower bounds that match the best known upper bounds. These bounds close the $\log\log n$ gap that exists with the best known previous results, establish the first non-trivial expected time bound, and strengthen the results to hold for all algorithms. To prove our high probability bound, both terms in the sum are tackled separately. To prove the first term, we show that a player can simulate an algorithm using $\mathcal{C}$ channels by making $\mathcal{C}$ proposals for each simulated round—one for each channel—to test if T has an isolated broadcast on any channel. The second term uses a reduction from the restricted hitting game. The expected time result adopts a similar strategy as the first term. The proofs for these theorems are deferred to the full version [22].

Theorem 8. *Let $\mathcal{A}$ be an algorithm that solves wake-up with high probability in $f(n,\mathcal{C})$ rounds in the radio network model with $\mathcal{C} \geq 1$ channels. It follows that for every $\mathcal{C} \geq 1$, $f(n,\mathcal{C}) \in \Omega(\log^2 n/\mathcal{C} + \log n)$.*

Theorem 9. *Let $\mathcal{A}$ be an algorithm that solves wake-up in $f(n,\mathcal{C})$ rounds, in expectation, in the radio network model with $\mathcal{C} \geq 1$ channels. It follows that for every $\mathcal{C} \geq 1$, $f(n,\mathcal{C}) \in \Omega(\log n/\mathcal{C} + 1)$.*

8   Lower Bound for Wake-Up with Collision Detection and Multiple Channels

The final combination of model parameters to consider for wake-up is collision detection *and* multiple channels. No non-trivial upper or lower bounds are currently known for this case. We rectify this omission by proving below that $\Omega(\log n / \log \mathcal{C} + \log \log n)$ rounds are necessary to solve this problem with high probability in this setting. Notice, this bound represents an interesting split with the preceding multichannel results (which assume no collision detection), as the speed-up is now logarithmic in $\mathcal{C}$ instead of linear. On the other hand, the $\log^2 n$ term in the previous case is replaced here with a faster $\log n$ term. Collision detection, in other words, seems to be powerful enough on its own that adding extra channels does not yield much extra complexity gains. We do not consider an expected time result for this setting. This is because even *without* collision detection, the best known upper bound for multichannel networks [7] approaches $O(1)$ time (which is trivially optimal) quickly as the number of channels increases. The proof for the below theorem, which combines techniques from both Section 6 and Section 7, is deferred to the full version[22].

Theorem 10. *Let $\mathcal{A}$ be an algorithm that solves wake-up with high probability in $f(n, \mathcal{C})$ rounds in the radio network model with $\mathcal{C} \geq 1$ channels and collision detection. It follows that for every $\mathcal{C} \geq 1$, $f(n, \mathcal{C}) \in \Omega(\log n / \log \mathcal{C} + \log \log n)$.*

9   Lower Bound for Global Broadcast

We now turn our attention to proving a lower bound for global broadcast. The tight bound for this problem is $\Theta(D \log (n/D) + \log^2 n)$ rounds for a connected multihop network of size n with diameter D. The lower bound holds for expected time solutions and the matching upper bounds hold with high probability [3,19,6]. The $\log^2 n$ term was established in [1], where it was shown to hold even for centralized algorithms, and the $D \log (n/D)$ term was later proved by Kushilevitz and Mansour [20]. Below, we apply our new technique to reprove (and significantly simplify) the $\Omega(D \log (n/D))$ lower bound for expected time solutions to global broadcast. (We do not also reprove the $\Omega(\log^2 n)$ term because this bound is proved using the same combinatorial result from [1] that provides the mathematical foundation for our technique. To reprove the result of [1] using [1] is needlessly circular.)

Perhaps surprisingly, we show that this bound holds even if we allow multiple channels and collision detection, both of which are assumptions that break the original lower bound from [20]. Notice, this indicates a interesting split with the wake-up problem for which these assumptions *improve* the achievable time complexity.

It is important to remind the reader at this point that the definition of collision detection we consider in this paper *does not* allow a collision to activate a node. Instead, activation still requires that a node receive a message. Once activated, however, nodes can use collision detection to speed up or otherwise simplify contention management. The assumption that collisions *can* activate nodes (essentially) reduces the problem to the less well-studied *synchronous start* variation in which all nodes activate in round 1 (if collisions can activate nodes then the source can instigate a wave of collisions that activates the entire network quickly). Recent work solved the synchronous start broadcast problem in $O(D + \text{polylog}(n))$ rounds using collision detection [16]. The problem's complexity without collision detection remains open.

Returning to our result, the proof details for the theorem below are deferred to the full version of this paper [22]. The intuition, however, is straightforward to describe. Given n nodes, we can construct a network consisting of D ordered *layers* each containing n/D nodes. Imagine that only a subset of the nodes in each layer are connected to the next layer. The only way to advance the message from one layer to the next, therefore, is to isolate a single node from this unknown set of connected nodes. Accordingly, it is not hard to reduce our hitting game to this task, reducing the challenge of broadcast to solving D sequential instances of the (n/D)-hitting game, where each instance requires $\Omega(\log(n/D))$ rounds.

Theorem 11. *Let $\mathcal{A}$ be an algorithm that solves global broadcast in $f(n, \mathcal{C}, D)$ rounds, in expectation, in the radio network model with collision detection, $\mathcal{C} \geq 1$ channels, and a network topology with diameter D. It follows that for every $\mathcal{C}, D \geq 1$, $f(n, \mathcal{C}, D) \in \Omega(D \log(n/D))$.*

Acknowledgments. The author acknowledges Mohsen Ghaffari for his helpful conversations regarding the combinatorial results from [1,15]. The author also acknowledges Sebastian Daum and Fabian Kuhn for their feedback on early applications of this technique to the wake-up problem.

References

1. Alon, N., Bar-Noy, A., Linial, N., Peleg, D.: A Lower Bound for Radio Broadcast. Journal of Computer and System Sciences 43(2), 290–298 (1991)
2. Bar-Yehuda, R., Goldreigch, O., Itai, A.: On the Time-Complexity of Broadcast in Multi-Hop Radio Networks: An Exponential Gap between Determinism and Randomization. In: Proceedings of the ACM Conference on Distributed Computing (1987)
3. Bar-Yehuda, R., Goldreigch, O., Itai, A.: On the Time-Complexity of Broadcast in Multi-Hop Radio Networks: An Exponential Gap between Determinism and Randomization. Journal of Computer and System Sciences 45(1), 104–126 (1992)
4. Chlamtac, I., Kutten, S.: On Broadcasting in Radio Networks–Problem Analysis and Protocol Design. IEEE Transactions on Communications 33(12), 1240–1246 (1985)
5. Clementi, A.E.F., Monti, A., Silvestri, R.: Distributed Broadcast in Radio Networks of Unknown Topology. Theoretical Computer Science 302(1-3) (2003)
6. Czumaj, A., Rytter, W.: Broadcasting algorithms in radio networks with unknown topology. Journal of Algorithms 60, 115–143 (2006)

7. Daum, S., Gilbert, S., Kuhn, F., Newport, C.: Leader Election in Shared Spectrum Radio Networks. In: Proceedings of the ACM Conference on Distributed Computing. ACM (2012)
8. Daum, S., Kuhn, F., Newport, C.: Efficient Symmetry Breaking in Multi-Channel Radio Networks. In: Aguilera, M.K. (ed.) DISC 2012. LNCS, vol. 7611, pp. 238–252. Springer, Heidelberg (2012)
9. Dolev, S., Gilbert, S., Guerraoui, R., Kuhn, F., Newport, C.: The Wireless Synchronization Problem. In: Proceedings of the ACM Conference on Distributed Computing (2009)
10. Dolev, S., Gilbert, S., Guerraoui, R., Newport, C.: Gossiping in a Multi-channel Radio Network. In: Pelc, A. (ed.) DISC 2007. LNCS, vol. 4731, pp. 208–222. Springer, Heidelberg (2007)
11. Dolev, S., Gilbert, S., Guerraoui, R., Newport, C.: Secure Communication Over Radio Channels. In: Proceedings of the ACM Conference on Distributed Computing (2008)
12. Dolev, S., Gilbert, S., Khabbazian, M., Newport, C.: Leveraging Channel Diversity to Gain Efficiency and Robustness for Wireless Broadcast. In: Proceedings of the ACM Conference on Distributed Computing (2011)
13. Farach-Colton, M., Fernandes, R.J., Mosteiro, M.A.: Lower Bounds for Clear Transmissions in Radio Networks. In: Correa, J.R., Hevia, A., Kiwi, M. (eds.) LATIN 2006. LNCS, vol. 3887, pp. 447–454. Springer, Heidelberg (2006)
14. Ghaffari, M., Haeupler, B.: Near Optimal Leader Election in Multi-Hop Radio Networks (2013)
15. Ghaffari, M., Haeupler, B., Khabbazian, M.: A Bound on the Throughput of Radio Networks. CoRR (ArXiv), abs/1302.0264 (February 2013)
16. Ghaffari, M., Haeupler, B., Khabbazian, M.: Randomized Broadcast in Radio Networks with Collision Detection. In: Proceedings of the ACM Conference on Distributed Computing (2013)
17. Gilbert, S., Guerraoui, R., Kowalski, D., Newport, C.: Interference-Resilient Information Exchange. In: Proceedings of the IEEE International Conference on Computer Communications (2009)
18. Jurdziński, T., Stachowiak, G.: Probabilistic Algorithms for the Wakeup Problem in Single-Hop Radio Networks. In: Bose, P., Morin, P. (eds.) ISAAC 2002. LNCS, vol. 2518, pp. 535–549. Springer, Heidelberg (2002)
19. Kowalski, D., Pelc, A.: Broadcasting in Undirected Ad Hoc Radio Networks. Distributed Computing 18(1), 43–57 (2005)
20. Kushilevitz, E., Mansour, Y.: An $\Omega(D\backslash\log(N/D))$ Lower Bound for Broadcast in Radio Networks. SIAM Journal on Computing 27(3), 702–712 (1998)
21. Moscibroda, T., Wattenhofer, R.: Maximal Independent Sets in Radio Networks. In: Proceedings of the ACM Conference on Distributed Computing (2005)
22. Newport, C.: Radio Network Lower Bounds Made Easy. CoRR (ArXiv), abs/1405.7300 (May 2014)
23. Willard, D.: Log-Logarithmic Selection Resolution Protocols in a Multiple Access Channel. SIAM Journal on Computing 15(2), 468–477 (1986)

On Correctness of Data Structures under Reads-Write Concurrency*

Kfir Lev-Ari[1], Gregory Chockler[2], and Idit Keidar[1]

[1] EE Department, Technion, Israel
[2] CS Department, Royal Holloway, UK

Abstract. We study the correctness of shared data structures under reads-write concurrency. A popular approach to ensuring correctness of read-only operations in the presence of concurrent update, is read-set validation, which checks that all read variables have not changed since they were first read. In practice, this approach is often too conservative, which adversely affects performance. In this paper, we introduce a new framework for reasoning about correctness of data structures under reads-write concurrency, which replaces validation of the entire read-set with more general criteria. Namely, instead of verifying that all read shared variables still hold the values read from them, we verify abstract conditions over the shared variables, which we call *base conditions*. We show that reading values that satisfy some base condition at every point in time implies correctness of read-only operations executing in parallel with updates. Somewhat surprisingly, the resulting correctness guarantee is not equivalent to linearizability, and is instead captured through two new conditions: *validity* and *regularity*. Roughly speaking, the former requires that a read-only operation never reaches a state unreachable in a sequential execution; the latter generalizes Lamport's notion of regularity for arbitrary data structures, and is weaker than linearizability. We further extend our framework to capture also linearizability. We illustrate how our framework can be applied for reasoning about correctness of a variety of implementations of data structures such as linked lists.

1 Introduction

Motivation Concurrency is an essential aspect of computing nowadays. As part of the paradigm shift towards concurrency, we face a vast amount of legacy sequential code that needs to be parallelized. A key challenge for parallelization is verifying the correctness of the new or transformed code. There is a fundamental tradeoff between generality and performance in state-of-the-art approaches to correct parallelization. General purpose methodologies, such as transactional memory [13,23] and coarse-grained locking, which do not take into account the

---

* This work was partially supported by the Intel Collaborative Research Institute for Computational Intelligence (ICRI-CI), by the Israeli Ministry of Science, by a Royal Society International Exchanges Grant, and by the Randy L. and Melvin R. Berlin Fellowship in the Cyber Security Research Program.

F. Kuhn (Ed.): DISC 2014, LNCS 8784, pp. 273–287, 2014.
© Springer-Verlag Berlin Heidelberg 2014

inner workings of a specific data structure, are out-performed by hand-tailored fine-grained solutions [19]. Yet the latter are notoriously difficult to develop and verify. In this work, we take a step towards mitigating this tradeoff.

It has been observed by many that correctly implementing concurrent modifications of a data structure is extremely hard, and moreover, contention among writers can severely hamper performance [21]. It is therefore not surprising that many approaches do not allow write-write concurrency; these include the *read-copy-update (RCU)* approach [18], flat-combining [12], coarse-grained readers-writer locking [8], and pessimistic software lock-elision [1]. It has been shown that such methodologies can perform better than ones that allow write-write concurrency, both when there are very few updates relative to queries [18] and when writes contend heavily [12]. We focus here on solutions that allow only read-read and read-write concurrency.

A popular approach to ensuring correctness of read-only operations in the presence of concurrent updates, is *read-set validation*, which checks that no shared variables have changed since they were first read. In practice, this approach is often too conservative, which adversely affects performance. For example, when traversing a linked list, it suffices to require that the last read node is connected to the rest of the list; there is no need to verify the values of other traversed nodes, since the operation no longer depends on them. In this paper, we introduce a new framework for reasoning about correctness of concurrent data structures, which replaces validation of the entire read-set with more general conditions: instead of verifying that all read shared variables still hold the values read from them, we verify abstract conditions over the variables. These are captured by our new notion of *base conditions*.

Roughly speaking, a *base condition* of a read-only operation at time t, is a predicate over shared variables, (typically ones read by the operation), that determines the local state the operation has reached at time t. Base conditions are defined over sequential code. Intuitively, they represent invariants the read-only operation relies upon in sequential executions. We show that the operation's correctness in a concurrent execution depends on whether these invariants are preserved by update operations executed concurrently with the read-only one. We capture this formally by requiring each state in every read-only operation to have a *base point* of some base condition, that is, a point in the execution where the base condition holds. In the linked list example – it does not hurt to see old values in one section of the list and new ones in another section, as long as we read every next pointer consistently with the element it points to. Indeed, this is the intuition behind the famous hand-over-hand locking (lock-coupling) approach [20,3].

Our framework yields a methodology for verifiable reads-write concurrency. In essence, it suffices for programmers to identify base conditions for their sequential data structure's read-only operations. Then, they can transform their sequential code using means such as readers-writer locks or RCU, to ensure that read-only operations have base points when run concurrently with updates.

It is worth noting that there is a degree of freedom in defining base conditions. If coarsely defined, they can constitute the validity of the entire read-set, yielding coarse-grained synchronization as in snapshot isolation and transactional memories. Yet using more precise observations based on the data structure's inner workings can lead to fine-grained base conditions and to better concurrency. Our formalism thus applies to solutions ranging from validation of the entire read-set [9], through multi-versioned concurrency control [5], which has read-only operations read a consistent snapshot of their entire read-set, to fine-grained solutions that hold a small number of locks, like hand-over-hand locking.

Overview of Contributions This paper makes several contributions that arise from our observation regarding the key role of base conditions. We observe that obtaining base points of base conditions guarantees a property we call *validity*, which specifies that a concurrent execution does not reach local states that are not reachable in sequential ones. Intuitively, this property is needed in order to avoid situations like division by zero during the execution of the operation. To incorporate read-time order, we restrict base point locations to ones that follow all operations that precede the read-only operation, and precedes ones that ensue it. Somewhat surprisingly, this does not suffice for the commonly-used correctness criterion of *linearizability (atomicity)* [14] or even *sequential consistency* [15] (discussed in the full paper [17]). Rather, it guarantees a correctness notion weaker than linearizability, similar to Lamport's *regularity* semantics for registers, which we extend here for general objects for the first time.

In Section 2, we present a formal model for shared memory data structure implementations and executions, and define correctness criteria. Section 3 presents our methodology for achieving regularity and validity: We formally define the notion of a base condition, as well as base points, which link the sequentially-defined base conditions to concurrent executions. We assert that base point consistency implies validity, and that the more restricted base point condition, which we call *regularity base point consistency*, implies regularity (formal proofs appear in the full paper). We proceed to exemplify our methodology for a standard linked list implementation, in Section 4 (see the full paper for more examples). In Section 5 we turn to extend the result for linearizability. We define a condition on update operations, namely, having a *single visible mutation point (SVMP)*, which along with regularity base point consistency ensures linearizability.

We note that we see this paper as the first step in an effort to simplify reasoning about fine-grained concurrent implementations. It opens many directions for future research, which we overview in Section 6. Due to space considerations, some formal definitions and proofs are deferred to the full paper, as is our result about sequential consistency.

Comparison with Other Approaches The regularity correctness condition was introduced by Lamport [16] for registers. To the best of our knowledge, the regularity of a data structure as we present in this paper is a new extension of the definition.

Using our methodology, proving correctness relies on defining a base condition for every state in a given sequential implementation. One easy way to do so is to define base conditions that capture the entire read-set, i.e., specify that there is a point in the execution where all shared variables the operation has read hold the values that were first read from them. But often, such a definition of base conditions is too strict, and spuriously excludes correct concurrent executions. Our definition generalizes it and thus allows for more parallelism in implementations.

Opacity [11] defines a sufficient condition for validity and linearizability, but not a necessary one. It requires that every transaction see a consistent snapshot of all values it reads, i.e., that all these values belong to the same sequentially reachable state. We relax the restriction on shared states busing base conditions.

Snapshot isolation [4] guarantees that no operation ever sees updates of concurrent operations. This restriction is a special case of the possible base points that our base point consistency criterion defines, and thus also implies our condition for the entire read-set.

We prove that the SVMP condition along with regularity base point consistency suffices for linearizability. There are mechanisms, for example, transactional memory implementations [9], for which it is easy to see that these conditions hold for base conditions that capture the entire read-set. Thus, the theorems that we prove imply, in particular, correctness of such implementations.

In this paper we focus on correctness conditions that can be used for deriving a correct data structure that allows reads-write concurrency from a sequential implementation. The implementation itself may rely on known techniques such as locking, RCU [18], pessimistic lock-elision [1], or any combinations of those, such as RCU combined with fine-grained locking [2]. There are several techniques, such as flat-combining [12] and read-write locking [8], that can naturally expand such an implementation to support also write-write concurrency by adding synchronization among update operations.

Algorithm designers usually prove linearizability of by identifying a serialization point for every operation, showing the existence of a specific partial ordering of operations [7], or using rely-guarantee reasoning [24]. Our approach simplifies reasoning – all the designer needs to do now is identify a base condition for every state in the existing sequential implementation, and show that it holds under concurrency. This is often easier than finding and proving serialization points, as we exemplify. In essence, we break up the task of proving data structure correctness into a generic part, which we prove once and for all, and a shorter, algorithm-specific part. Given our results, one does not need to prove correctness explicitly (e.g., using linearization points or rely-guarantee reasoning, which typically result in complex proofs). Rather, it suffices to prove the much simpler conditions that read-only operations have base points and updates have an SVMP, and linearizability follows from our theorems. Another approach that simplifies verifiable parallelization is to re-write the data structure using primitives that guarantee linearizability such as LLX and SCX [6]. Whereas the latter focuses on non-blocking concurrent data structure implementations using their primitive, our work is focused on reads-write concurrency, and does not restrict the implementation; in particular, we target lock-based implementations as well as non-blocking ones.

2   Model and Correctness Definitions

We consider a shared memory model where each process performs a sequence of operations on shared data structures. The data structures are implemented using a set $X = \{x_1, x_2, ...\}$ of shared variables. The shared variables support atomic read and write operations (i.e., are atomic registers), and are used to implement more complex data structures. The values in the x_i's are taken from some domain $\mathcal{V}$.

2.1   Data Structures and Sequential Executions

A *data structure implementation* (algorithm) is defined as follows:

- A set of states, $\mathcal{S}$, were a *shared state* $s \in \mathcal{S}$ is a mapping $s : X \rightarrow \mathcal{V}$, assigning values to all shared variables. A set $\mathcal{S}_0 \subseteq \mathcal{S}$ defines *initial states*.
- A set of operations representing methods and their parameters. For example, $find(7)$ is an operation. Each *operation op* is a state machine defined by:
  - A set of local states $\mathcal{L}_{op}$, which are usually given as a set of mappings l of values to local variables. For example, for a local state l, $l(y)$ refers to the value of the local variable y in l. $\mathcal{L}_{op}$ contains a special initial local state $\perp \in \mathcal{L}_{op}$.
  - A deterministic transition function $\tau_{op}(\mathcal{L}_{op} \times \mathcal{S}) \rightarrow Steps \times \mathcal{L}_{op} \times \mathcal{S}$ where $step \in Steps$ is a transition label, which can be *invoke*, $a \leftarrow read(x_i)$, $write(x_i, v)$, or *return(v)* (see the full paper for more details). Note that there are no atomic read-modify-write steps. Invoke and return steps interact with the application while read and write steps interact with the shared memory.

  We assume that every operation has an isolated state machine, which begins executing from local state $\perp$.

For a transition $\tau(l, s) = \langle step, l', s' \rangle$, l determines the step. If *step* is an invoke, return, or write step, then l' is uniquely defined by l. If *step* is a read step, then l' is defined by l and s, specifically, $read(x_i)$ is determined by $s(x_i)$. Since only write steps can change the content of shared variables, $s = s'$ for invoke, return, and read steps.

For the purpose of our discussion, we assume the entire shared memory is statically allocated. This means that every read step is defined for every shared state in $\mathcal{S}$. One can simulate dynamic allocation in this model by writing to new variables that were not previously used. Memory can be freed by writing a special value, e.g., "invalid", to it.

A state consists of a local state l and a shared state s. By a slight abuse of terminology, in the following, we will often omit either shared or local component of the state if its content is immaterial to the discussion. A *sequential execution of an operation* is an alternating sequence of steps and states with transitions being according to τ. A *sequential execution of a data structure* is a sequence of operation executions that begins in an initial state; see the full paper for a formal definition. A *read-only operation* is an operation that does not perform write steps in any execution. All other operations are *update operations*.

A state is *sequentially reachable* if it is reachable in some sequential execution of a data structure. By definition, every initial state is sequentially reachable. The *post-state* of an invocation of operation o in execution μ is the shared state of the data structure after o's return step in μ; the *pre-state* is the shared state before o's invoke step. Recall that read-only operations do not change the shared state and execution of update operations is serial. Therefore, every pre-state and post-state of an update operation in μ is sequentially reachable. A state st' is sequentially reachable from a state st if there exists a sequential execution fragment that starts at st and ends at st'.

In order to simplify the discussion of initialization, we assume that every execution begins with a dummy (initializing) update operation that does not overlap any other operation.

2.2   Correctness Conditions for Concurrent Data Structures

A *concurrent execution fragment of a data structure* is a sequence of interleaved states and steps of different operations, where state consists of a set of local states $\{l_i, ..., l_j\}$ and a shared state s_k, where every l_i is a local state of a pending operation. A *concurrent execution of a data structure* is a concurrent execution fragment of a data structure that starts from an initial shared state. Note that a sequential execution is a special case of concurrent execution. An example of a concurrent execution is detailed in the full paper.

A *single-writer multiple-reader (SWMR) execution* is one in which update operations are not interleaved; read-only operations may interleave with other read-only operations and with update operations. In the remainder of this paper we discuss only SWMR executions.

For an execution σ of data structure ds, the *history* of σ, denoted H_σ, is the subsequence of σ consisting of the invoke and return steps in σ (with their respective return values). For a history H_σ, *complete(H_σ)* is the subsequence obtained by removing pending operations, i.e., operations with no return step, from H_σ. A history is *sequential* if it begins with an invoke step and consists of an alternating sequence of invoke and return steps.

A data structure's correctness in sequential executions is defined using a *sequential specification*, which is a set of its allowed sequential histories.

Given a correct sequential data structure, we need to address two aspects when defining its correctness in concurrent executions. As observed in the definition of opacity [11] for memory transactions, it is not enough to ensure serialization of completed operations, we must also prevent operations from reaching undefined states along the way. The first aspect relates to the data structure's external behavior, as reflected in method invocations and responses (i.e., histories):

Linearizability and Regularity A history H_σ is *linearizable* [14] if there exists H'_σ that can be created by adding zero or more return steps to H_σ, and there is a sequential permutation π of complete(H'_σ), such that: (1) π belongs to the sequential specification of ds; and (2) every pair of operations that are not interleaved in σ, appear in the same order in σ and in π. A data structure ds is *linearizable*, also called *atomic*, if for every execution σ of ds, H_σ is linearizable.

We next extend Lamport's regular register definition [16] for SWMR data structures (we do not discuss regularity for MWMR executions, which can be defined similarly to [22]). A data structure ds is *regular* if for every execution σ of ds, and every read-only operation $ro \in H_\sigma$, if we omit all other read-only operations from H_σ, then the resulting history is linearizable.

Validity The second correctness aspect is ruling out bad cases like division by zero or access to uninitialized data. It is formally captured by the following notion of *validity*: A data structure is *valid* if every local state reached in an execution of one of its operations is sequentially reachable. We note that, like opacity, validity is a conservative criterion, which rules out bad behavior without any specific data structure knowledge. A data structure that does not satisfy validity may be correct, but proving that requires care.

3   Base Conditions, Validity and Regularity

3.1   Base Conditions and Base Points

Intuitively, a base condition establishes some link between the local state an operation reaches and shared variables the operation has read before reaching this state. It is given as a predicate Φ over shared variable assignments. Formally:

Definition 1 (Base Condition). Let l be a local state of an operation op. A predicate Φ over shared variables is a *base condition* for l if every sequential execution of op starting from a shared state s such that $\Phi(s) = true$, reaches l.

For completeness, we define a base condition for $step_i$ in an execution μ to be a base condition of the local state that precedes $step_i$ in μ.

Consider a data structure consisting of an array of elements v and a variable $lastPos$, whose last element is read by the function $readLast$. An example of an execution fragment of $readLast$ that starts from state s_1 (depicted in Figure 1) and the corresponding base conditions appear in Algorithm 1. The $readLast$ operation needs the value it reads from $v[tmp]$ to be consistent with the value of $lastPos$ that it reads into tmp because if $lastPos$ is newer than $v[tmp]$, then $v[tmp]$ may contain garbage. The full paper details base conditions for every possible local state of $readLast$.

The predicate $\Phi_3 : lastPos = 1 \wedge v[1] = 7$ is a base condition of l_3 because l_3 is reachable from any shared state in which $lastPos = 1$ and $v[1] = 7$ (e.g., s_2 in Figure 1), by executing lines 1-2.

We now turn to define base points of base conditions, which link a local state with base condition Φ to a shared state s where $\Phi(s)$ holds.

(a) s_1 (b) s_2

Fig. 1. Two shared states satisfying the same base condition $\Phi_3 : lastPos = 1 \wedge v[1] = 7$

local state	base condition	Function $readLast()$
$l_1 : \{\}$	$\Phi_1 : true$	$tmp \leftarrow \textbf{read}(lastPos)$
$l_2 : \{tmp = 1\}$	$\Phi_2 : lastPos = 1$	$res \leftarrow \textbf{read}(v[tmp])$
$l_3 : \{tmp = 1, res = 7\}$	$\Phi_3 : lastPos = 1 \wedge v[1] = 7$	$\textbf{return}(res)$

Algorithm 1. The local states and base conditions of readLast when executed from s_1. The shared variable $lastPos$ is the index of the last updated value in array v. See Algorithm 2 for corresponding update operations.

Definition 2 (Base Point). Let μ be a concurrent execution, ro be a read-only operation executed in μ, and Φ_t be a base condition of the local state and step at index t in μ. An execution fragment of ro in μ has a *base point* for point t with Φ_t, if there exists a sequentially reachable post-state s in μ, called a *base point of t*, such that $\Phi_t(s)$ holds.

Note that together with Definition 1, the existence of a base point s implies that t is reachable from s in all sequential runs starting from s.

We say that a data structure ds satisfies *base point consistency* if every point t in every execution of every read-only operation ro of ds has a base point with some base condition of t.

The possible base points of read-only operation ro are illustrated in Figure 2. To capture real-time order requirements we further restrict base point locations.

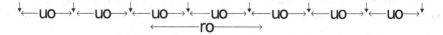

Fig. 2. Possible locations of ro's base points

Definition 3 (Regularity Base Point). A base point s of a point t of ro in a concurrent execution μ is a *regularity base point* if s is the post-state of either an update operation executed concurrently with ro in μ or of the last update operation that ended before ro's invoke step in μ.

The possible regularity base points of a read-only operation are illustrated in Figure 3. We say that a data structure ds satisfies *regularity base point consistency* if it satisfies base point consistency, and every return step t in every execution of every read-only operation ro of ds has a regularity base point with a base condition of t. Note, in particular, that the base point location is only restricted for the return step, since the return value is determined by its state.

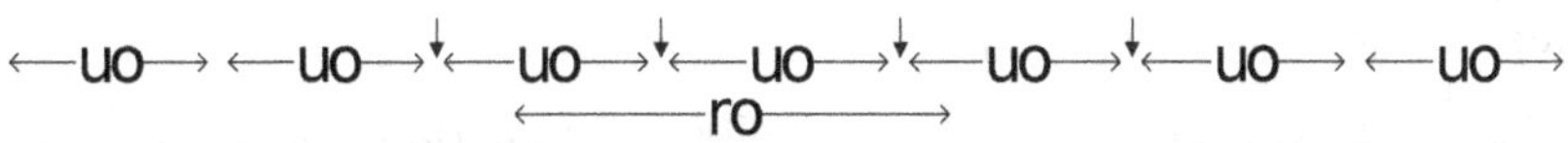

Fig. 3. Possible locations of *ro*'s regularity base points

Function *writeSafe(val)*
   $i \leftarrow \mathbf{read}(lastPos)$
   $\mathbf{write}(v[i+1], val)$
   $\mathbf{write}(lastPos, i+1)$

Function *writeUnsafe(val)*
   $i \leftarrow \mathbf{read}(lastPos)$
   $\mathbf{write}(lastPos, i+1)$
   $\mathbf{write}(v[i+1], val)$

Algorithm 2. Unlike *writeUnsafe*, *writeSafe* ensures a regularity base point for every local state of *readLast*; it guarantees that any concurrent *readLast* operation sees values of *lastPos* and *v*[*tmp*] that occur in the same sequentially reachable post-state. It also has a single visible mutation point (as defined in Section 5), and hence linearizability is established.

In Algorithm 2 we see two versions of an update operation: *writeSafe* guarantees the existence of a base point for every local state of *readLast* (Algorithm 1), and *writeUnsafe* does not. As shown in the full paper, *writeUnsafe* can cause a concurrent *readLast* operation interleaved between its two write steps to see values of *lastPos* and *v*[*lastPos*] that do not satisfy *readLast*'s return step's base condition, and to return an uninitialized value.

3.2   Deriving Correctness from Base Points

In the full paper we prove the following theorems:

Theorem 1 (Validity). *If a data structure ds satisfies base point consistency, then ds is valid.*

Theorem 2 (Regularity). *If a data structure ds satisfies regularity base point consistency, then ds is regular.*

4   Using Our Methodology

We now demonstrate the simplicity of using our methodology. Based on Theorems 1 and 2 above, the proof for correctness of a data structure (such as a linked list) becomes almost trivial. We look at three linked list implementations: Algorithm 3, which assumes managed memory (i.e., automatic garbage collection), an algorithm that uses RCU methodology, and an algorithm based on hand-over-hand locking (the latter two are deferred to the full paper for space limitations).

For Algorithm 3, we first prove that the listed predicates are indeed base conditions, and next prove that it satisfies regularity base point consistency. By doing so, and based on Theorem 2, we get that the algorithm satisfies both validity and regularity.

Function *remove(n)*
  $p \leftarrow \bot$
  $next \leftarrow \mathbf{read}(head.next)$
  while $next \neq n$
    $p \leftarrow next$
    $next \leftarrow \mathbf{read}(p.next)$
  $\mathbf{write}(p.next, n.next)$

Function *insertLast(n)*
  $last \leftarrow readLast()$
  $\mathbf{write}(last.next, n)$

Base conditions:

$\Phi_1 : true$

$\Phi_2 : head \overset{*}{\Rightarrow} n$
$\Phi_3 : head \overset{*}{\Rightarrow} n$

Function *readLast()*
  $n \leftarrow \bot$
  $next \leftarrow \mathbf{read}(head.next)$
  while $next \neq \bot$
    $n \leftarrow next$
    $next \leftarrow \mathbf{read}(n.next)$
  $\mathbf{return}(n)$

Algorithm 3. A linked list implementation in a memory-managed environment. For simplicity, we do not deal with boundary cases: we assume that a node can be found in the list prior to its deletion, and that there is a dummy head node.

Consider a linked list node stored in local variable n (we assume the entire node is stored in n, including the value and *next* pointer). Here, $head \overset{*}{\Rightarrow} n$ denotes that there is a set of shared variables $\{head, n_1, ..., n_k\}$ such that $head.next = n_1 \wedge n_1.next = n_2 \wedge ... \wedge n_k = n$, i.e., that there exists some path from the shared variable $head$ to n. Note that n is the only element in this predicate that is associated with a specific read value. We next prove that this defines base conditions for Algorithm 3.

Lemma 3. *In Algorithm 3, Φ_i defined therein is a base condition of the i-th step of* readLast.

Proof. For Φ_1 the claim is vacuously true. For Φ_2, let l be a local state where *readLast* is about to perform the second read step in *readLast*'s code, meaning that $l(next) \neq \bot$. Note that in this local state both local variables n and $next$ hold the same value. Let s be a shared state in which $head \overset{*}{\Rightarrow} l(n)$. Every sequential execution from s iterates over the list until it reaches $l(n)$, hence the same local state where $n = l(n)$ and $next = l(n)$ is reached.

For Φ_3, Let l be a local state where *readLast* has exited the while loop, hence $l(n).next = \bot$. Let s be a shared state such that $head \overset{*}{\Rightarrow} l(n)$. Since $l(n)$ is reachable from $head$ and $l(n).next = \bot$, every sequential execution starting from s exits the while loop and reaches a local state where $n = l(n)$ and $next = \bot$. $\square$

Lemma 4. *In Algorithm 3, if a node n is read during concurrent execution μ of* readLast, *then there is a shared state s in μ such that n is reachable from* head *in s and* readLast *is pending.*

Proof. If n is read in operation *readLast* from a shared state s, then s exists concurrently with *readLast*. The operation *readLast* starts by reading *head*, and it reaches n.

Thus, n must be linked to some node n' at some point during *readLast*. If n was connected (or added) to the list while n' was still reachable from the head, then there exists a state where n is reachable from the head and we are done. Otherwise, assume n is added as the next node of n' at some point after n' is already detached from the list. Nodes are only added via *insertLast*, which is not executed concurrently with any *remove* operation. This means nodes cannot be added to detached elements of the list. A contradiction.   □

The following lemma, combined with Theorem 2 above, guarantees that Algorithm 3 satisfies regularity.

Lemma 5. *Every local state of* readLast *in Algorithm 3 has a regularity base point.*

Proof. We show regularity base points for predicates Φ_i, proven to be base points in Lemma 3.

The claim is vacuously true for Φ_1. We now prove for Φ_2 and $\Phi_3 : head \overset{*}{\Rightarrow} n$. By Lemma 4 we get that there is a shared state s where $head \overset{*}{\Rightarrow} n$ and *readLast* is pending. Note that n's next field is included in s as part of n's value. Since both update operations - *remove* and *insertLast* - have a single write step, every shared state is a post-state of an update operation. Specifically this means that s is a sequentially reachable post-state, and because *readLast* is pending, s is one of the possible regularity base points of *readLast*.   □

5   Linearizability

We first show that regularity base point consistency is insufficient for linearizability. In Figure 4 we show an example of a concurrent execution where two read-only operations ro_1 and ro_2 are executed sequentially, and both have regularity base points. The first operation, ro_1, reads the shared variable *first name* and returns Joe, and ro_2 reads the shared variable *surname* and returns Doe. An update operation uo updates the data structure concurrently, using two write steps. The return step of ro_1 is based on the post-state of uo, whereas ro_2's return step is based on the pre-state of uo. There is no sequential execution of the operations where ro_1 returns Joe and ro_2 returns Doe.

Thus, an additional condition is required for linearizability. We suggest *single visible mutation point (SVMP)*, which adds a restriction regarding the behaviour of update operations. A data structure that satisfies SVMP and regularity base point consistency is linearizable.

The SVMP condition is related to the number of *visible mutation points* an execution of an update operation has. Intuitively, a visible mutation point in an execution of an update operation is a write step that writes to a shared variable that might be read by a concurrent operation. A more formal definition ensues.

Let α be an execution fragment of op starting from shared state s. We define α^t as the shortest prefix of α including t steps of op, and we denote by $steps_{op}(\alpha)$ the subsequence of α consisting of the steps of op in α. We say that α^t and

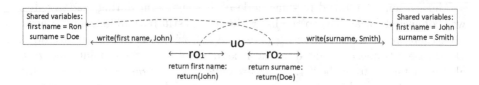

Fig. 4. Every local state of ro_1 and ro_2 has a regularity base point, and still the execution is not linearizable. If ro_1 and ro_2 belong to the same process, then the execution is not even sequentially consistent (see the full paper).

α^{t-1} are *indistinguishable* to a concurrent read-only operation ro if for every concurrent execution μ_t starting from s and consisting only of steps of ro and α^t, and concurrent execution μ_{t-1} starting from s and consisting only of steps of ro and α^{t-1}, $steps_{ro}(\mu_t) = steps_{ro}(\mu_{t-1})$. In other words, ro's executions are not unaffected by the t'th step of op.

If α^t and α^{t-1} are indistinguishable to a concurrent read-only operation ro, then point t is a *silent point* for ro in α. A point that is not silent is a *visible mutation point* for ro in α.

Definition 4 (SVMP condition). A data structure ds satisfies the SVMP condition if for each update operation uo of ds, in every execution of uo from every sequentially reachable shared state, uo has at most one visible mutation point, for all possible concurrent read-only operations ro of ds.

Note that a read-only operation may see mutation points of multiple updates. Hence, if a data structure satisfies the SVMP condition and not base point consistency, it is not necessarily linearizable. For example, in Figure 5 we see two sequential single visible mutation point operations, and a concurrent read-only operation ro that counts the number of elements in a list. Since ro only sees one element of the list, it returns 1, even though there is no shared state in which the list is of size 1. Thus, the execution is not linearizable or even regular.

Intuitively, if a data structure ds satisfies the SVMP condition, then all of its shared states are sequentially reachable post-states. If ds also satisfies regularity base point consistency, then the visible mutation point condition guarantees that the order among base points of non-interleaved read-only operations preserves the real time order among those operations.

In Algorithm 3, the remove operation has a single visible mutation point, which is the step that writes to $p.next$. Thus, from Theorem 6 below, this implementation is linearizable. The theorem is proven in the full paper.

Theorem 6 (Linearizability). *If data structure ds satisfies SVMP and regularity base point consistency, then ds is linearizable.*

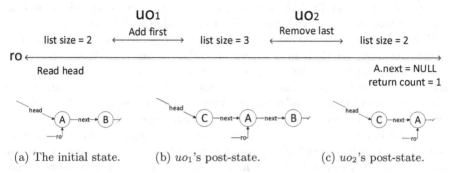

(a) The initial state.   (b) uo_1's post-state.   (c) uo_2's post-state.

Fig. 5. Every update operation has a single visible mutation point, but the execution is not linearizable

6   Conclusions and Future Directions

We introduced a new framework for reasoning about correctness of data structures in concurrent executions, which facilitates the process of verifiable parallelization of legacy code. Our methodology consists of identifying base conditions in sequential code, and ensuring regularity base points for these conditions under concurrency. This yields two essential correctness aspects in concurrent executions – the internal behaviour of the concurrent code, which we call validity, and the external behaviour, in this case regularity, which we have generalized here for data structures. Linearizability is guaranteed if the implementation further satisfies the SVMP condition.

We believe that this paper is only the tip of the iceberg, and that many interesting connections can be made using the observations we have presented. For a start, a natural expansion of our work would be to consider also multi-writer data structures. Another interesting direction to pursue is to use our methodology for proving the correctness of more complex data structures than the linked lists in our examples.

Currently, using our methodology involves manually identifying base conditions. It would be interesting to create tools for suggesting a base condition for each local state. One possible approach is to use a dynamic tool that identifies likely program invariants, as in [10], and suggests them as base conditions. Alternatively, a static analysis tool can suggest base conditions, for example by iteratively accumulating read shared variables and omitting ones that are no longer used by the following code (i.e., shared variables whose values are no longer reflected in the local state).

Another interesting direction for future work might be to define a synchronization mechanism that uses the base conditions in a way that is both general purpose and fine-grained. A mechanism of this type will use default conservative base conditions, such as verifying consistency of the entire read-set for every local state, or two-phase locking of accessed shared variables. In addition, the mechanism will allow users to manually define or suggest finer-grained base conditions. This can be used to improve performance and concurrency, by validating the specified base condition instead of the entire read-set, or by releasing locks when the base condition no longer refers to the value read from them.

From a broader perspective, we showed how correctness can be derived from identifying inner relations in a sequential code, (in our case, base conditions), and maintaining those relations in concurrent executions (via base points). It may be possible to use similar observations in other models and contexts, for example, looking at inner relations in synchronous protocol, in order to derive conditions that ensure their correctness in asynchronous executions.

And last but not least, the definitions of internal behaviour correctness can be extended to include a weaker conditions than validity, (which is quiet conservative). These weaker conditions will handle local states in concurrent executions that are un-reachable via sequential executions but still satisfy the inner correctness of the code.

Acknowledgements. We thank Naama Kraus, Dahlia Malkhi, Yoram Moses, Dani Shaket, Noam Shalev, and Sasha Spiegelman for helpful comments and suggestions.

References

1. Afek, Y., Matveev, A., Shavit, N.: Pessimistic software lock-elision. In: Aguilera, M.K. (ed.) DISC 2012. LNCS, vol. 7611, pp. 297–311. Springer, Heidelberg (2012)
2. Arbel, M., Attiya, H.: Concurrent updates with rcu: Search tree as an example. In: Proceedings of the 2014 ACM Symposium on Principles of Distributed Computing, PODC 2014, pp. 196–205. ACM, New York (2014)
3. Bayer, R., Schkolnick, M.: Concurrency of Operations on B-trees. In: Readings in Database Systems, pp. 129–139. Morgan Kaufmann Publishers Inc., San Francisco (1988)
4. Berenson, H., Bernstein, P., Gray, J., Melton, J., O'Neil, E., O'Neil, P.: A critique of ansi sql isolation levels. SIGMOD Rec. 24(2), 1–10 (1995)
5. Bernstein, P.A., Hadzilacos, V., Goodman, N.: Concurrency Control and Recovery in Database Systems. Addison-Wesley Longman Publishing Co., Inc., Boston (1986)
6. Brown, T., Ellen, F., Ruppert, E.: Pragmatic primitives for non-blocking data structures. In: PODC, pp. 13–22 (2013)
7. Chockler, G., Lynch, N., Mitra, S., Tauber, J.: Proving atomicity: An assertional approach. In: Fraigniaud, P. (ed.) DISC 2005. LNCS, vol. 3724, pp. 152–168. Springer, Heidelberg (2005)
8. Courtois, P.J., Heymans, F., Parnas, D.L.: Concurrent control with "readers" and "writers". Commun. ACM 14(10), 667–668 (1971)
9. Dice, D., Shalev, O., Shavit, N.: Transactional locking ii. In: Dolev, S. (ed.) DISC 2006. LNCS, vol. 4167, pp. 194–208. Springer, Heidelberg (2006)
10. Ernst, M.D., Cockrell, J., Griswold, W.G., Notkin, D.: Dynamically discovering likely program invariants to support program evolution. In: Proceedings of the 21st International Conference on Software Engineering, ICSE 1999, pp. 213–224. ACM, New York (1999)

11. Guerraoui, R., Kapalka, M.: On the correctness of transactional memory. In: Proceedings of the 13th ACM SIGPLAN Symposium on Principles and Practice of Parallel Programming, PPoPP 2008, pp. 175–184. ACM, New York (2008)
12. Hendler, D., Incze, I., Shavit, N., Tzafrir, M.: Flat combining and the synchronization-parallelism tradeoff. In: Proceedings of the 22nd ACM Symposium on Parallelism in Algorithms and Architectures, SPAA 2010, pp. 355–364. ACM, New York (2010)
13. Herlihy, M., Moss, J.E.B.: Transactional memory: Architectural support for lock-free data structures. SIGARCH Comput. Archit. News 21(2), 289–300 (1993)
14. Herlihy, M.P., Wing, J.M.: Linearizability: A correctness condition for concurrent objects. ACM Trans. Program. Lang. Syst. 12(3), 463–492 (1990)
15. Lamport, L.: How to make a multiprocessor computer that correctly executes multiprocess programs. IEEE Trans. Comput. 28(9), 690–691 (1979)
16. Lamport, L.: On interprocess communication. Part ii: Algorithms. Distributed Computing 1(2), 86–101 (1986)
17. Lev-Ari, K., Chockler, G., Keidar, I.: On correctness of data structures under reads-write concurrency. Tech. Rep. CCIT 866, EE, Technion (August 2014)
18. McKenney, P.E., Slingwine, J.D.: Read-copy update: Using execution history to solve concurrency problems. In: Parallel and Distributed Computing and Systems (1998)
19. Moir, M., Shavit, N.: Concurrent data structures. In: Metha, D., Sahni, S. (eds.) Handbook of Data Structures and Applications, pp. 47-14–47-30. Chapman and Hall/CRC Press (2007)
20. Samadi, B.: B-trees in a system with multiple users. Inf. Process. Lett. 5(4), 107–112 (1976)
21. Scherer III, W.N., Scott, M.L.: Advanced contention management for dynamic software transactional memory. In: Proceedings of the Twenty-fourth Annual ACM Symposium on Principles of Distributed Computing, PODC 2005, pp. 240–248. ACM, New York (2005)
22. Shao, C., Welch, J.L., Pierce, E., Lee, H.: Multiwriter consistency conditions for shared memory registers. SIAM J. Comput. 40(1), 28–62 (2011)
23. Shavit, N., Touitou, D.: Software transactional memory. In: Proceedings of the Fourteenth Annual ACM Symposium on Principles of Distributed Computing, PODC 1995, pp. 204–213. ACM, New York (1995)
24. Vafeiadis, V., Herlihy, M., Hoare, T., Shapiro, M.: Proving correctness of highly-concurrent linearisable objects. In: Proceedings of the Eleventh ACM SIGPLAN Symposium on Principles and Practice of Parallel Programming, PPoPP 2006, pp. 129–136. ACM, New York (2006)

Solo-Fast Universal Constructions
for Deterministic Abortable Objects*

Claire Capdevielle, Colette Johnen, and Alessia Milani

Univ. Bordeaux, LaBRI, UMR 5800, F-33400 Talence, France
firstname.lastname@labri.fr

Abstract. In this paper we study efficient implementations for deterministic abortable objects. Deterministic abortable objects behave like ordinary objects when accessed sequentially, but they may return a special response *abort* to indicate that the operation failed (and did not take effect) when there is contention.

It is impossible to implement deterministic abortable objects only with read/write registers [3]. Thus, we study *solo-fast* implementations. These implementations use stronger synchronization primitives, e.g., CAS, only when there is contention. We consider interval contention.

We present a non-trivial solo-fast universal construction for deterministic abortable objects. A universal construction is a method for obtaining a concurrent implementation of any object from its sequential code. The construction is *non-trivial* since in the resulting implementation a failed process can cause only a finite number of operations to abort. Our construction guarantees that operations that do not modify the object always return a legal response and do not use CAS. Moreover in case of contention, at least one writing operation succeeds. We prove that our construction has asymptotically optimal space complexity for objects whose size is constant.

1 Introduction

With the raise of multicore and many core machines efficient concurrent programming is a major challenge. Linearizable shared objects are central in concurrent programming; They provide a convenient abstraction to simplify the design of concurrent programs. But implementing them is complex and expensive when strong progress conditions are required, e.g. wait-freedom (every process completes its operations in a finite number of steps) [10]. The complexity originates in executions where processes execute concurrent operations. Obstruction-freedom was proposed to circumvent this difficulty by allowing an operation to never return in case of contention [11]. This separation between correctness and progress let devise simpler and more efficient algorithms. In fact any obstruction free object can be implemented using only read/write registers.

---

* This work was partially supported by the ANR project DISPLEXITY (ANR-11-BS02-014). This study has been carried out in the frame of "the Investments for the future" Programme IdEx Bordeaux CPU (ANR-10-IDEX-03-02).

F. Kuhn (Ed.): DISC 2014, LNCS 8784, pp. 288–302, 2014.

On the other hand, as pointed out by Attiya et al. in [3], ideally shared objects should always return the control, and when this happens the caller should know if the operation took place or not. This behavior is formalized in the notion of *deterministic abortable object* proposed by Hadzilacos and Toueg [9]. A deterministic abortable object ensures that if several processes contend to operate on it, it may return a special response *abort* to indicate that the operation failed. And it assures that an operation that aborts does not take effect. Operations that do not abort return a response which is legal w.r.t. the sequential specification of the object.

In this paper we study efficient implementations for deterministic abortable objects. Attiya et al. proved that it is impossible to implement deterministic abortable objects only with read/write registers [3]. Thus, we study implementations that use only read/write registers when there is no contention and use stronger synchronization primitives, e.g., Compare and Swap (CAS), when contention occurs. These implementations are called *solo-fast* and are expected to take advantage of the fact that in practice contention is rare.

The notion of solo-fast was defined in [3] for *step contention* : There is step contention when the steps of a process are interleaved with the steps of another process. In the same paper, they prove a linear lower bound on the space complexity of solo-fast implementations of obstruction-free objects. This result also holds for deterministic abortable objects.

We consider an asynchronous shared-memory system where processes communicate through linearizable shared objects and can fail by crashing, i.e. ; a process can stop taking steps while executing an operation. In this model, we study the possibility that deterministic abortable objects can be implemented efficiently if a process is allowed to use strong synchronization primitives even in absence of step contention, provided that its operation is concurrent with another one. This notion of contention is called *interval contention* [1]. Step contention implies interval contention, the converse is not true. We only consider implementations where a crashed process can cause only a finite number of concurrent operations to abort. This property, called *non-triviality*, is formally defined in [2].

Our results. First we prove a linear lower bound on the space complexity of solo-fast implementations of abortable objects for our weaker notion of solo-fast. To prove our result we adapt the notion of pertubable object presented in [14] to abortable objects and we prove that a k-CAS abortable register is perturbable according to our definition.

Then, we present a solo-fast universal construction for deterministic abortable objects, called NSUC. A *universal construction* [10] is a methodology for automatically transform any sequential object in a concurrent one. An implementation resulting from our universal construction is solo-fast and has asymptotically optimal space complexity if the implemented object has constant size. The NSUC algorithm guarantees that operations that do not modify the object always return a legal response. Also in case of contention, at least one writing operation succeeds to modify the object. In particular, writing operations are applied one at the time. Each process makes a local copy of the object and computes the new state locally. We associate a sequence number with each state. A process that wants to modify the ith state has to compete to win the $i + 1$th sequence number. A process that does not experience contention uses only read/write registers, while a CAS register is used in case of contention to decide the new state. It may happen that (at most) one process p behaves as if it was running solo, while other processes were competing for the same sequence number. In this case, we use a lightweight helping mechanism to avoid inconsistency : any other process acquires the state proposed by p as its new state. If it succeeds to apply it, it notifies the process p that its state has been applied. Then the helping process aborts. We ensure that if a process crashes while executing an operation, then it can cause at most two operations per process to abort. Our construction uses $O(n)$ read/write registers and $n + 1$ CAS registers. Also it keeps at most $2n + 1$ versions of the object.

Related work. Attiya et al. were the first to propose the idea of shared objects that in case of contention return a fail response [3]. Few variants of these objects have been proposed [2,3,9]. The ones proposed in [2,3] differ from deterministic abortable objects in the fact that when a fail response is returned the caller does not know if the operation took place or not.

A universal construction for deterministic abortable objects is presented in [9]. This construction can be easily transformed into solo-fast by using the solo-fast consensus object proposed in [3], but it has unbounded space complexity, since it stores all the operations performed on the object. Also operations that only read the state of the object modify the representation of the implemented object and may fail by returning abort.

Several universal constructions have been proposed for ordinary wait-free concurrent objects. A good summary can be found in [5]. These constructions could be transformed in solo-fast by replacing the strong synchronization primitives they use with their solo-fast counterpart. To the best of our knowledge no solo-fast LL/SC or CAS register exist. Luchangco et al. presented a fast-CAS register [15] whose implementation ensures that no strong synchronization primitive is used in execution without contention. But, in case of contention, concurrent operations can leave the system in a state such that a successive operation will use strong synchronization primitives even if running solo. So, their implementation is not solo-fast. Even using the solo-fast consensus object by Attiya at al, which has $\Theta(n)$ space complexity, we cannot easily modify existing universal constructions while ensuring all the good properties of our solution.

Abortable objects behave similarly to transactional memory [12]. Transactional memory enables processes to synchronize via in-memory transactions. A transaction can encapsulate any piece of sequential code. This generality costs a greater overhead as compared to abortable objects. Also transactional memory is not aware of the sequential code embedded in a transaction. A hybrid approach between transactional memory and universal constructions has been presented by Crain *et al.* [6]. Their solution assumes that no failures occur. In addition they use a linked list to store all committed transactions. Thus, their solution has unbounded space complexity. Finally, the NSUC algorithm ensures *multi-version permissiveness* and *strong progressiveness* proposed for transactional memory respectively in [16] and in [8] when conflicts are at the granularity of the entire implemented object.

Paper organization. In Section 2 we present our model and preliminaries. In Section 3 we prove the lower bound on the space complexity. In Section 4 we present our solo-fast universal construction. Finally, a sketch of the correctness proof of our construction is given in Section 5.

2   Preliminaries

We consider an asynchronous shared memory system, in which n processes $p_1 \ldots p_n$ communicate through shared objects, such as read/write registers and CAS objects. Every object has a type that is defined by a quadruple (Q, O, R, Δ), where Q is a set of states, O is a set of invocations, R is a set of responses, and $\Delta \subseteq Q \times O \times Q \times R$ is the sequential specification of the type. A tuple (s, op, s', res) in Δ means that if type T is in state s when $op \in O$ is invoked, then T can change its state to s' and return the response res.

For each type $T = (Q, O, R, \Delta)$, we consider the deterministic abortable counterpart of T as defined in [9] and denoted T^{da}. T^{da} is equal to $(Q, O, R^{da}, \Delta^{da})$ where $R^{da} = R \cup \{\bot\}$ for some $\bot \notin R$, and, for every tuple (s, op, s', res) in Δ, the sequential specification Δ^{da} contains the following two tuples: (s, op, s', res) and $(s, op, s, \bot)$. These two tuples of Δ^{da} correspond to op completing normally, and op aborting without taking effect.

A universal construction is a method to transform any sequential object into a linearizable concurrent object. It takes as input the sequential code of an operation and its arguments. The algorithm that implements this method is a sequence of operations on shared objects provided by the system, called *base objects*. To avoid confusion between the base objects and the implemented ones, we reserve the term operation for the objects being implemented and we call *primitives* the operations on base objects. We say that an operation of an implemented object is performed and that a primitive is applied to a base object.

In the following, we consider that for any given base object o the set of its primitives is either *historyless* or not. Let o be a base object that supports two operations f and f'. Following [7], we say that f overwrites f' on o, if applying f' and then f results in the same state of o as applying just f, using the same input parameters (if any) in both cases. A set of primitives is called *historyless* if all the primitives in the set that may change the state of the object overwrite each other; we also require that each such operation overwrites itself. A primitive/operation is a *writing* primitive/operation if its application may change the state of the object. Otherwise it is a *read-only* primitive/operation.

A step of a process consists of a primitive applied to a base object and possibly some local computation. A configuration specifies the value of each base object and the state of each process at some point in time. A step e by a process p is *enabled* at a given configuration C, if p is about to apply e at C. In

an *initial configuration*, all base objects have their initial values and all processes are in their initial states. An *execution* is a (possibly infinite) sequence
$C_i, \phi_i, C_{i+1}, \phi_{i+1}, \ldots, \phi_{j-1}, C_j$ of alternating configurations (C_k) and steps (ϕ_k),
where the application of ϕ_k to configuration C_k results in configuration C_{k+1}, for
each $i \leq k < j$. For any configuration C, for any finite execution α ending with
C and any execution α' starting at C, the execution $\alpha\alpha'$ is the concatenation of
α and α'; in this case α' is called an extension of α. An execution α is q-free if
no step in α is applied by the process q.

The *execution interval* of an operation starts with an invocation and terminates
when a response is returned. An invocation without a matching response is a *pending* operation. Two operations op and op' are *concurrent* in a execution α, if they
are both pending in some finite prefix of α. This implies that their intervals overlap.
An operation op *precedes* an operation op' in α if the response of op precedes the invocation of op' in α. An operation experiences *interval contention* in an execution
α if it is concurrent with at least another operation in α.

Processes may experience *crash failures*. For any given execution α, if a process
p does not fail in α, we say that p is *correct* in α.

Properties of the implemented object. We consider universal constructions that
guarantee that all implementations resulting by their application are wait-free
[10], linearizable [13], *non-trivial* and *non-trivial solo-fast*. *Wait-free* implementations ensure that in every execution, each correct process completes its operation in a finite number of steps. *Linearizability* ensures that for every execution α
and for every operation that completes and some of the uncompleted operations
in α, there is some point within the execution interval of the operation called
its linearization point, such that the response returned by the operation in α is
the same as the response it would return if all these operations were executed
serially in the order determined by their linearization points.

Informally, an implementation of an object is *non-trivial* if for any given
execution α every operation that aborts is concurrent with some other operation
in α, and an operation that remains incomplete, due to a crash, does not cause
infinitely many other operations to abort. A more formal definition can be found
in [2].

Finally, an implementation is said *non-trivial solo-fast* if for any given execution α a process p applies some non-historyless primitives while performing an
instance of an operation op, only if op is concurrent with some other operation in
α; and an operation that remains incomplete, due to a crash, does not justify the
application of non-historyless primitives by infinitely many other operations.

3   Lower Bound

In the following we adapt the definition of perturbable objects presented in [3]
and originally proposed in [14] to deterministic abortable objects.

Definition 1. *A deterministic abortable object O is perturbable for n processes,
if for every linearizable and non-trivial implementation of O there is an operation*

instance op_n by process p_n, such that for any p_n-free execution $\alpha\lambda$ where some process $p_l \neq p_n$ applies no step in λ and no process applies more than a single step in λ, there is an extension of α, γ, consisting of steps by p_l, such that the first response $res \neq \bot$, that p_n returns when repeatedly performing op_n solo after $\alpha\lambda$ is different from the first response $res' \neq \bot$ it returns when repeatedly performing op_n solo after $\alpha\gamma\lambda$.

By adjusting the proof of Lemma 4.7 in [14], in [4] we prove that the set of deterministic abortable objects which are perturbable is not empty. In particular, we prove that the k-valued deterministic abortable CAS is perturbable. A k-valued deterministic abortable CAS is the type (Q, O, R, Δ), where $Q = \{1, 2, .., k\}$, $O = \{Read, CAS(u, v) \text{ with } u, v \in \{1, 2, .., k\}\}$, $R = \{1, 2, .., k\} \cup \{true, false, \bot\}$ and $\forall s, u, v \in \{1, 2, .., k\}$ $\Delta = \{(s, Read, s, s)\} \cup \{(s, CAS(s, v), v, true)\} \cup \{(s, CAS(u, v), s, false) \text{ with } u \neq s\} \cup \{(s, Read, s, \bot)\} \cup \{(s, CAS(u, v), s, \bot)\}$.

In the following we prove that any non-trivial solo-fast implementation of a deterministic abortable object that is perturbable has space complexity in $\Omega(n)$. The proof is similar to the proof of Theorem 4 in [3]. This proof does not directly apply because we consider a notion of solo-fast which is weaker than the one assumed in [3].

The following definition is needed for our proof.

Definition 2. *A base object o is covered after an execution α if the set of primitives applied to o in α is historyless, and there is a process that has, after α, an enabled step e about to apply a writing primitive to o. We also say that e covers o after α.*
An execution α is k-covering if there exists a set of processes $\{p_{j_1}, ..., p_{j_k}\}$, called, covering set, such that each process in the covering set has an enabled writing step that covers a distinct base object after α.

Theorem 1. *Let A be an n-process non-trivial solo-fast implementation of a perturbable deterministic abortable object. The space complexity of A is at least $n - 1$.*

Proof. To prove the theorem we construct an execution which is p_n-free and $(n-1)$-covering. The proof goes by induction. The empty execution is vacuously a 0-covering execution and it is p_n-free. Assume that α_i, for $i < n - 1$, is an i-covering execution with covering set $\{p_{j_1}, ..., p_{j_i}\}$ and is p_n-free. Let λ_i be the execution fragment that consists of the writing steps by processes $p_{j_1}...p_{j_i}$ that are enabled after α_i, arranged in some arbitrary order.

Let $p_{j_{i+1}}$ be a process not in $\{p_n, p_{j_1}, ..., p_{j_i}\}$. Since $i < n - 1$, this process exists. Because of the non-triviality of the solo-fast property process $p_{j_{i+1}}$ applies only historyless primitives after a finite number of its own steps when executing solo after α_i. Let δ be the shortest execution by $p_{j_{i+1}}$ when executing solo after α_i such that $p_{j_{i+1}}$ applies only historyless primitives (if any) after $\alpha_i\delta$ if still running solo. $\alpha_i' = \alpha_i\delta$ is p_n-free and the writing steps of processes $p_{j_1}...p_{j_i}$ are enabled at the configuration immediately after α_i'.

By Definition 1, there is an extension of α_i', γ, by $p_{j_{i+1}}$ such that the first response different than abort returned to p_n when repeatedly executing op_n respectively after $\alpha_i'\lambda_i$ and $\alpha_i'\gamma\lambda_i$ is different. We claim that γ contains a writing step that accesses a base object not covered after α_i' . We assume otherwise to obtain a contradiction. Since all steps in λ_i and γ apply primitives from a historyless set, every writing primitive applied to a base object in γ is overwritten by some event in λ_i. Thus, the values of all base objects are the same after $\alpha_i'\lambda_i$ and after $\alpha_i'\gamma\lambda_i$. This implies that op_n must return the same response after both $\alpha_i'\lambda_i$ and $\alpha_i'\gamma\lambda_i$, which is a contradiction.

We denote γ' the shortest prefix of γ at the end of which $p_{j_{i+1}}$ has an enabled writing step about to access an object not covered after α_i'. We define α_{i+1} to be $\alpha_i'\gamma'$. α_{i+1} is a p_n-free execution and it is $(i+1)$-covering. This latter property is true because at the configuration immediately after α_{i+1} processes $\{p_{j_1}, ..., p_{j_i}, p_{j_{i+1}}\}$ have enabled writing steps that cover distinct base objects. It follows that A has an $(n-1)$-covering execution. $\square$

4   A Non-trivial Solo-Fast Universal Construction (NSUC)

The NSUC algorithm uses single writer multi reader (SWMR) registers and *Compare&Swap* registers (CAS). A register R stores a value from some set and supports a read primitive which returns the value of R, and a write primitive which writes a value into R. A CAS object supports the primitive $CAS(c, e, v)$ and $Read(c)$, If the value of c matches the expected value e, then $CAS(c, e, v)$ writes the new value v into c and returns $true$ (the CAS succeeds). Otherwise, CAS returns $false$ and does not modify the state of the CAS (the CAS fails). $Read(c)$ returns the value in c and it does not modify its state.

In the following we describe the shared variables used by our universal construction.

- An array A of n SWMR registers. Each register contains a sequence number. In particular, process p_i announces its intention to change the current state of the shared object, by writing into location $A[i]$ the sequence number that will be associated with the new state if p_i succeeds its operation. Initially, $A[j] = 0$ for $j = 1..n$.
  An array F of n SWMR registers. The process p_i writes $< sv, \sigma >$ in $F[i]$ if it has detected that it is the first process to announce its intention to define a state for the sequence number sv. σ is a pointer to the state proposed by p_i for the sequence number sv. Initially, $F[j] =< 0, \bot >$ for $j = 1..n$.
- An array OS of n SWMR registers. If there is no contention process p_i writes $< sv, s >$ into $OS[i]$ where s is the pointer to the new state of the shared object computed by p_i while executing its operation and sv is the associated sequence number. Initially, $OS[j] =< 0, \bot >$ for $j = 1..n$.
- A CAS register OC. It is used in case of contention to decide the new state of the object among the ones proposed by the concurrent operations. If a process p_i detects contention, it tries to change the value of OC into a tuple $< sv, id, s >$ where id is the identifier of the process that proposes the state

pointed by s and associated with the sequence number sv. id may be different than i if process p_i detects that another process p_{id} is the first one to propose a new state for sv. p_i then helps the other process to apply its operation. Initially, $OC = <0, 0, \sigma>$ where σ is the pointer to the initial state of the shared object.

- An array S of n CAS registers. Before trying to update the CAS register OC, a process writes the sequence number stored in OC into S. Precisely, if the value of OC is $<sv, i, s>$, $S[i]$ will be set to sv. This is necessary to ensure that a process is always aware that its operation succeeded even if its operation was completed by another (helping) process. Thus, if $S[i] = sv$ process i knows that its operation which computed the state associated with sv succeeded. Initially, $S[j] = 0$ for $j = 1..n$.

At any configuration, the tuple with the highest sequence number stored either in the CAS register OC or in the array OS contains the pointer to the current state of the implemented object.

NSUC Description

In the following, unless explicitly stated, all line numbers refer to Algorithm 1.

When a process p_i wants to execute an operation op on an object of type T, it first gets the current state of the object and the corresponding sequence number and stores them locally in variables $state$ and seq respectively (line 1). Then, p_i locally applies op to the read state (line 2). The NSUC algorithm assumes a function $APPLY_T(s, op, arg)$ that returns the response matching the invocation of the operation op on a type T in a sequential execution of op with input arg applied to the state of the object pointed by s. $APPLY_T(s, op, arg)$ also returns a pointer to the new state of the object.

If op is a read-only operation, p_i immediately returns the response (lines 3 to 5). We suppose to know a priori if an operation is read-only. Then, p_i checks if some other process is concurrently executing a writing operation on it. This is done by reading the other entries of the array A and looking for sequence numbers greater than or equal to $sv + 1$.

Three cases can be distinguished :

- **lines 10 to 11.** A sequence number greater than $sv + 1$ is found. This implies that some other process already decided the state for $sv + 1$, so p_i aborts.
- **lines 13 to 17.** All the sequence numbers read by p_i are smaller than $sv + 1$. Then, p_i writes its computed new state together with the associated sequence number ($<sv + 1, newState>$) into the register $F[i]$ (line 14) and checks again for concurrent operations (line 15). Consider the case where again all the sequence numbers read by p_i in the announce array A are smaller than $sv + 1$ (the other case will be studied below). Any other process competing for $sv + 1$ will discover that p_i was the first process to propose a state for $sv + 1$ and then it will abort its own operation, after helping p_i to

complete its operation (lines 21 to 24). Finally, p_i writes its new state into the read/write register $OS[i]$ and returns the response of the operation (lines 16-17). The state of the object associated with $sv + 1$ is the one proposed by p_i.

```
 1 < seq, state >← STATE() ;                          //Find the object state
 2 < newState, res >← APPLY_T(state, op, arg);
 3 if op is read-only then
 4 |   return res
 5 end
 6 seq ← seq + 1;
 7 A[i] ← seq;                        //The process announces its intention
 8 id_new ← i;
 9 seq_A ← LEVEL_A(i);
10 if seq_A > seq then      //A state is already decided for seq value
11 |   return ⊥
12 end
13 if seq_A < seq then                          //The process is alone
14 |   F[i] ←< seq, newState >;
15 |   if LEVEL_A(i) < seq then          //The process is still alone
16 |   |   OS[i] ←< seq, newState >;
17 |   |   return res
18 |   end
19 else                               //There is interval contention
20 |   < id_F, newState_F >←WHOS_FIRST(seq);
21 |   if newState_F ≠ ⊥ then          //Presence of a first process
22 |   |   newState ← newState_F;
23 |   |   id_new ← id_F;
24 |   end
25 end
26 < seq_OC, id_OC, state_OC >←READ(OC);
27 while seq_OC < seq do
28 |   if (seq_OC ≠ 0) then OLD_WIN(seq_OC, id_OC);
29 |   CAS(OC, < seq_OC, id_OC, state_OC >, < seq, id_new, newState >);
30 |   < seq_OC, id_OC, state_OC >←READ(OC);
31 end
32 if (seq_OC = seq ∧ id_OC ≠ i) ∨ (seq_OC > seq ∧ READ(S[i]) ≠ seq) then
33 |   res ← ⊥;
34 end
35 return res
```

Algorithm 1: NSUC - Code for process p_i to apply operation op with the input arg on the implemented object

- **lines 20 to 35.**p_i reads $sv+1$ in one of the other entries. So, it detects that another process is concurrently trying to decide the state for this sequence number. If the detection is done on line 13, then p_i checks the presence of a process p_j competing for $sv+1$ and which has seen no contention (i.e. p_j has written its proposal in $F[j]$) in line 14. If this process exists, p_i will help p_j to apply its new state of the object (lines 21 to 24). In particular, since there is contention p_i will try to write state computed by p_j into the CAS register OC (lines 26 to 31). Then it will return abort (lines 32 to 35). Otherwise p_i continues to compete for its own proposal. It tries to write the proposed state into OC (lines 26 to 31) until a decision is taken for $sv+1$. If a process (p_i or a helper) succeeds to perform a CAS in OC with p_i's proposal then p_i returns the response of its own operation (line 35). Otherwise it aborts. We have a similar behavior if a process detects the contention on line 15.

---

1 $seq_{max} \leftarrow 0$; $\sigma_{max} \leftarrow \perp$;
2 for $j = 1..n$ **do**
3 $< seq_{OS}, \sigma > \leftarrow OS[j]$;
4   **if** $seq_{OS} > seq_{max}$**then** $seq_{max} \leftarrow seq_{OS}$; $\sigma_{max} \leftarrow \sigma$; **end**
5 end
6 $< seq_{OC}, id_{OC}, \sigma_{OC} > \leftarrow READ(OC)$;
7 if $seq_{OC} < seq_{max}$ **then return** $< seq_{max}, \sigma_{max} >$ **end**
8 return $< seq_{OC}, \sigma_{OC} >$

Algorithm 2: function $STATE()$

$STATE$ returns a pointer to the current state of the shared object and its sequence number.

---

1 $seq_{max} \leftarrow 0$;
2 for $j = 1..n \mid j \neq i$ **do**
3 $seq_A \leftarrow A[j]$;
4   **if** $seq_{max} < seq_A$ **then** $seq_{max} \leftarrow seq_A$; **end**
5 end
6 return seq_{max}

Algorithm 3: function $LEVEL_A(i)$

$LEVEL_A(i)$ returns the highest sequence number written into the announce array A by a process other than p_i.

---

1 for $j = 1..n$ **do**
2 $< seq_F, \sigma_F > \leftarrow F[j]$;
3   **if** $seq_F = sv$ **then return** $< j, \sigma_F >$ **end**
4 end
5 return $< 0, \perp >$

Algorithm 4: function $WHOS\_FIRST(sv)$

For a given sequence number sv, $WHOS\_FIRST(sv)$ returns the tuple (j, σ) where j is the first process (if any) to propose a new state for sv and σ is a pointer to the proposed state.

---

1   $seq_S \leftarrow READ(S[id_{OC}])$;
2   **if** $seq_{OC} > seq_S$ **then** $CAS(S[id_{OC}], seq_S, seq_{OC})$ **end**

Algorithm 5: function $OLD\_WIN((seq_{OC}, id_{OC})$

OLD_WIN tries to write seq_{OC} in the CAS $S[id_{OC}]$ if $S[id_{OC}]$'s value is smaller than seq_{OC}. This ensures that a slow process p whose operation succeeded to modify the CAS OC is aware that its operation was successfully executed. In fact, it may happen that p did not take steps while another process completed its operation and, then another operation overwrote its changes by writing into OC. p can recover the status of its operation checking into its location in S and then it can return the correct response.

Complexity

Let t be the worst case step complexity to perform an operation on the sequential implementation of the object (i.e. the time complexity of the function $APPLY_T$). By inspecting the pseudocode it is simple to see that the step complexity of the functions $STATE$, $LEVEL_A$ and $WHOS\_FIRST$ is in $O(n)$. Also the step complexity of the function OLD_WIN is $O(1)$. We establish that a process can repeat the loop (lines 27 to 31 of the Algorithm 1) at most n times. Thus, the step complexity of our construction is $O(n + t)$. Since the execution of every operation includes the execution of the functions $STATE$ and $APPLY_T$, the step complexity of the NSUC construction is in $\Theta(n + t)$.

Let s be the size of the sequential representation of the object. The NSUC algorithm stores at most $2n + 1$ sequential representations of the object (n in the array F, n in the array OS and 1 in OC). So the space complexity of NSUC algorithm is in $O(ns)$.

5   Proof Sketch of NSUC

In this section we sketch the ideas behind the correctness of our construction. The complete proof can be found in [4]. In the following all the line numbers refer to Algorithm 1 unless otherwise stated.

Wait-freedom. A process p stays in the loop (lines 27 to 31) only if another process q succeeds the CAS at line 29 with a sequence number smaller than the seq value of p when executing line 27, in between the last read of OC by p and the last application of the CAS primitive to OC by p. After its CAS, q exits the loop and its operation is terminated.

The sequence numbers written in the CAS object OC and in the register $OS[i]$ $\forall i = 1..n$ are increasing. Then the next operation of q will have a sequence number greater than or equal to seq (from line 1 and from the pseudocode of the function STATE). So, process q can prevent p to exit the loop at most once. This implies the next theorem.

Theorem 2. *Every invocation of an operation by a correct process returns after a finite number of its own steps.*

Deterministic Abortable Object. Roughly speaking, the next theorem states that an operation that aborts does not modify the state of the object.

Theorem 3. *Let op be an operation instance executed by a process p in an execution α such that op aborts. Let sv be the sequence number computed by p at lines 1 and 6 of Algorithm 1 while executing op. The tuple with the sequence number sv and the corresponding pointer to the state computed by p will never be written either into OC or into OS.*

By inspecting the pseudocode of NSUC algorithm, a process p can abort only on line 11 or line 33. If op completes succesfully it defines the sv-th state of the object. If p aborts on line 11, it did not write into the shared register OS or any CAS. So, consider the case where process p aborts on line 33. According to line 32, one of the two following conditions has to be verified.

Either, the process p reads in OC a pointer to the state corresponding to the sequence number sv and the process identifier associated with this sequence number is different than p. This means that another operation has succeeded to define the sv-th state of the object. We complete the proof by proving that each sequence number is associated with a single state.

Or the process p reads in OC a sequence number greater than sv. We prove that if a state corresponding to a sequence number v has been written into OC So, a state $< sv, i, state >$ has been defined for the sv-th sequence number and it has been overwritten. We prove that before the overwritting of the tuple $< sv, i, state >$ in OC a process has written in $S[i]$ the sequence number sv, in order to notify process i that the state it proposed for sv has been applied. Therefore, process p aborts only if $S[p] \neq sv$. This means that the state computed by p while executing op has not been associated with sv.

Non-triviality. In its first steps, a process p executing an operation op computes sv, the sequence number associated with the state it will define if op succeeds. To compute sv, (line 1) p reads the greatest sequence number associated with a state of the object and it increments this value by one (line 6). Then, p announces its intention to define the sv-th state by writing sv in a shared register $A[p]$ (line 7). p may abort its operation op only if it detects (by reading A) an operation op' with a sequence number greater than or equal to sv. We prove that op is concurrent with op'.

Also, we prove that if op aborts, at the configuration immediately after it aborts the sv-th state has been defined. As the sequence number written in CAS OC and OS are increasing, if process p executes a new operation, this latter will be associated with a greater sequence number than sv. An operation does not change its sequence number. Thus, for any operation op' that does not complete, process p will eventually only execute operations whose sequence number are greater than the sequence number of op'. Thus, op' cannot cause the abort of these latter operations. In particular, we prove that an operation that does not complete can cause the abort of at most two operations per process.

Theorem 4. *The universal construction NSUC is non-trivial.*

Non-trivial solo-fast. Similarly to the non-trivial property, we prove that during the execution of an operation a process applies some no-histoyless primitives only if this operation is concurrent with another one. Also, an operation op that does not complete can cause a process to apply no-histoyless primitives for only 2 consecutive operations.

Theorem 5. *The universal construction NSUC is non-trivial solo-fast.*

Linearizability. For any given execution α we construct a permutation π of the high-level operations in α such that π respects the sequential specification of the object and the real-time order between operations. Since the operations that abort do not change the state of the object and return a special response *abort*, they do not impact on the response returned by the other operations and on the state computed by writing operations. Thus, in the following we discuss how to create the permutation without taking into account aborted operations; then we put aborted operations in π respecting their real-time order.

First, we order all writing operations according to the ascending order on the sequence number associated with them. Secondly, we consider each read-only operation in the order in which its reponse occurs in α. A read-only operation that returns the state of the object corresponding to the sequence number k is placed immediately before the writing operation with sequence number $k + 1$ or at the end of the linearization if this latter write does not exist.

By inspecting the pseudocode it is simple to see that the total order defined by the sequence numbers respects the real-time order between writing operations. Also a read-only operation r that starts after the response of a successful writing operation w with sequence number i, will return a state of the object whose sequence number is greater than or equal to i. Thus r follows w in π. Similarly, consider two read-only operations op and op'. If op precedes op' in α, the sequence number of op' is greater than or equal to the sequence number of op, then op' is not ordered before op in π.

Theorem 6. *The universal construction NSUC is linearizable.*

6   Conclusion

We have studied solo-fast implementations of deterministic abortable objects. We have investigated the possibility for those implementations to have a better space complexity than linear if relaxing the constraints for a process to use strong synchronization primitives.

We have proved that solo-fast implementations of some deterministic abortable objects have space complexity in $\Omega(n)$ even if we allow a process to use strong synchronization primitives in absence of step contention, provided that its operation is concurrent with another one. To prove our result we consider only non-trivial implementations, that is implementations where a crashed process can cause only a finite number of concurrent operations to abort.

Then, we have presented a non trivial solo-fast universal construction for deterministic abortable objects. Any implementation resulting from our construction is *wait-free, non-trivial* and *non-trivial solo-fast* : without interval contention, an operation uses only read/write registers; and a failed process can abort at most two operations per process. Similarly at most two operations per process use strong synchronization primitives being concurrent with a failed operation. Moreover, in case of contention our universal construction ensures that at least one writing operation succeeds to modify the object. Finally, a process that executes a read-only operation does not apply strong synchronization primitives and the operation always returns a legal response.

If t is the worst time complexity to perform an operation on the sequential object, then $\Theta(t + n)$ is the worst step complexity to perform an operation on the resulting object. If the sequential object has size s, then the resulting object implementation has space complexity in $O(ns)$. This is asymptotically optimal if the implemented object has constant size. On the other hand to prove our lower bound we consider base objects accessed via a set of historyless primitives, e.g., read/write registers. Thus, it does not imply that n CAS objects are needed to implement a non trivial solo-fast universal construction for deterministic abortable objects. The possibility to design this universal construction using $O(n)$ read/write registers but just a constant number of CAS objects is an open problem.

References

1. Afek, Y., Stupp, G., Touitou, D.: Long lived adaptive splitter and applications. Distributed Computing 15(2), 67–86 (2002)
2. Aguilera, M.K., Frolund, S., Hadzilacos, V., Horn, S.L., Toueg, S.: Abortable and query-abortable objects and their efficient implementation. In: The 26th ACM Symposium on Principles of Distributed Computing (PODC 2007), pp. 23–32 (2007)
3. Attiya, H., Guerraoui, R., Hendler, D., Kuznetsov, P.: The complexity of obstruction-free implementations. J. ACM 56(4), 24:1–24:33 (2009)
4. Capdevielle, C., Johnen, C., Alessia, M.: Solo-fast universal constructions for deterministic abortable objects. Tech. Rep. 1480-14. LaBRI, Univ. de Bordeaux, France (May 2014), http://labri.fr/~johnen/
5. Chuong, P., Ellen, F., Ramachandran, V.: A universal construction for wait-free transaction friendly data structures. In: The 22nd ACM Symposium on Parallelism in Algorithms and Architectures (SPAA 2010), pp. 335–344 (2010)
6. Crain, T., Imbs, D., Raynal, M.: Towards a universal construction for transaction-based multiprocess programs. Theor. Comput. Sci. 496, 154–169 (2013)

7. Fich, F., Herlihy, M., Shavit, N.: On the space complexity of randomized synchronization. J. ACM 45(5), 843–862 (1998)
8. Guerraoui, R., Kapalka, M.: The semantics of progress in lock-based transactional memory. In: The 36th ACM SIGPLAN-SIGACT Symposium on Principles of Programming Languages (POPL 2009), pp. 404–415 (2009)
9. Hadzilacos, V., Toueg, S.: On deterministic abortable objects. In: The 2013 ACM Symposium on Principles of Distributed Computing (PODC 2013), pp. 4–12 (2013)
10. Herlihy, M.: Wait-free synchronization. ACM Trans. Program. Lang. Syst. 13(1), 124–149 (1991)
11. Herlihy, M., Luchangco, V., Moir, M.: Obstruction-free synchronization: Double-ended queues as an example. In: The 23rd International Conference on Distributed Computing Systems (ICDCS 2003), pp. 522–529 (2003)
12. Herlihy, M., Moss, J.E.B.: Transactional memory: Architectural support for lock-free data structures. In: The 20th Annual International Symposium on Computer Architecture (ISCA 1993), pp. 289–300 (1993)
13. Herlihy, M., Wing, J.M.: Linearizability: A correctness condition for concurrent objects. ACM Transactions on Programming Languages and Systems 12(3), 463–492 (1990)
14. Jayanti, P., Tan, K., Toueg, S.: Time and space lower bounds for nonblocking implementations. SIAM J. Comput. 30(2), 438–456 (2000)
15. Luchangco, V., Moir, M., Shavit, N.N.: On the uncontended complexity of consensus. In: Fich, F.E. (ed.) DISC 2003. LNCS, vol. 2848, pp. 45–59. Springer, Heidelberg (2003)
16. Perelman, D., Fan, R., Keidar, I.: On maintaining multiple versions in STM. In: The 29th ACM Symposium on Principles of Distributed Computing (PODC 2010), pp. 16–25 (2010)

Space Bounds for Adaptive Renaming[*]

Maryam Helmi, Lisa Higham, and Philipp Woelfel

University of Calgary
Department of Computer Science
Calgary, T2N1N4 Alberta, Canada

Abstract. We study the space complexity of implementing long-lived and one-shot adaptive renaming from multi-reader multi-writer registers, in an asynchronous distributed system with n processes. In an $f(k)$-*adaptive renaming algorithm* each participating process gets a distinct name, in the range $\{1, \ldots, f(k)\}$ provided k processes participate.

We show that any obstruction-free long-lived $f(k)$-adaptive renaming object requires m registers, where $m \leq n - 1$ is the largest integer such that $f(m) \leq n - 1$. This implies a lower bound of $n - c$ registers for long-lived $(k+c)$-adaptive renaming, which is tight. We also prove a lower bound of $\lfloor \frac{n}{c+1} \rfloor$ registers for implementing any obstruction-free one-shot $(k+c)$-adaptive renaming.

We also provide one-shot renaming algorithms, e.g., a wait-free one-shot $(\frac{3k^2}{2})$-adaptive one from $\lceil \sqrt{n} \rceil$ registers, and an obstruction-free one-shot $f(k)$-adaptive renaming algorithm from only $\lceil f^{-1}(n) \rceil$ registers.

1 Introduction

Networks with a large number of processes, such as the Internet, provide services that are typically used by only a small number of processes simultaneously. This is problematic if the time or space used by the service is a function of the size of the name-space of the processes that could use it. The time or space consumed by such applications can be significantly diminished by having each process that wants to use the application first acquire a temporary name from a name space that is adequate to distinguish all the participants, but much smaller than the name-space of the network, and then return the temporary name to the pool when it is finished with the service. This is the role of a shared renaming object. A related application of the renaming object is in operating systems where processes repeatedly acquire and release names that correspond to a limited number of resources [10]. Renaming is an important tool in distributed computing [5] because it enhances the practicality and usefulness of network services. A renaming object may be even more useful if the time and space resources it consumes is a reasonable function of the actual number of processes that are currently either holding, acquiring, or releasing a name.

With an adaptive renaming object, each of the n processes can perform a getName() and return a name in a small domain $\{1, \ldots, f(k)\}$ where $f: \{1, \ldots, n\} \to \mathbb{N}$ is a function

[*] This research was undertaken, in part, thanks to funding from the Canada Research Chairs program, the Discovery Grants program of the Natural Sciences and Engineering Research Council of Canada (NSERC), and Alberta Innovates Technology Futures (AITF).

F. Kuhn (Ed.): DISC 2014, LNCS 8784, pp. 303–317, 2014.

of the number of participants, k. The step complexity of deterministic and randomized algorithms has been studied extensively in asynchronous systems (see e.g., [2–4,8,11]). However, there are no previous results on the space complexity of adaptive renaming. Because renaming seems to require that participants discover information about each other, adaptive renaming appears related to $f(k)$-adaptive collect. Attiya, Fich and Kaplan [6], proved that $\Omega(f^{-1}(n))$ multi-reader multi-writer registers are required for $f(k)$-adaptive collect. In this case, like renaming, k is total contention, but unlike renaming, $f(k)$ is the step complexity.

Suppose you have m shared registers available to construct a renaming object for a system with n processes. First we would like to know under what additional conditions such an implementation exists, and when it does, how best to use the m registers. Suppose, when there are k participants, the acquired names are in the range $\{1,\ldots,f(k)\}$. Will $f(k) = k^c$ for a small constant c suffice for the application? Must $f(k)$ be closer to k, say within a constant? Perhaps it should even be exactly k (*tight* adaptive renaming)? Does the application need to permit processes to repeatedly acquire and release a name (*long-lived* renaming), or do processes get a name at most once (*one-shot* renaming)? How strong a progress guarantee is required? Is the number of participants usually less than some bound b much smaller than n? If so, is there still some significant likelihood that the number of participants is somewhat bigger than b, or is there confidence that the bound b is never, or only very rarely, exceeded? In the rare cases when there are a large number of participants, can the system tolerate name assignments from a very large name space?

In order to study the space complexity implication for these questions, we first generalize the adaptive renaming definition. A *one-shot b-bounded $f(k)$-adaptive renaming object* supports the operation getName(), which returns a name x, and satisfies: 1) no two participating processes acquire the same x, 2) when the number of participants, k, is at most b, $x \in \{1,\ldots,f(k)\}$. A *long-lived b-bounded $f(k)$-adaptive renaming object* supports the operation relName() as well as getName() and satisfies the same two requirements, where the participating processes are those that last executed getName() without a subsequent relName(). The special case when $f(k) = k$ is called *tight* renaming. Our goal is to determine the relationships between b, $f(k)$, and m for one-shot versus long-lived, and wait-free versus obstruction-free implementations of adaptive renaming objects from multi-reader/multi-writer registers.

In this paper we show:

- Let m be the largest integer such that $f(m) \leq n-1$ and $m \leq n-1$. At least m registers are required to implement any obstruction-free long-lived m-bounded $f(k)$-adaptive renaming object.
- At least $\lfloor \frac{n}{c+1} \rfloor$ registers are required to implement any obstruction-free one-shot $(k+c)$-adaptive renaming object where, c is a non-negative integer constant.
- For any $m \leq n$, there is a wait-free one-shot $(m-1)$-bounded $(k(k+1)/2)$-adaptive renaming algorithm implemented from m bounded registers. When $k \geq m$, the returned names are in the range $\{1,\ldots,n+\frac{m(m-1)}{2}\}$.
- For any $m \leq n$, there is a obstruction-free one-shot $(m-1)$-bounded k-adaptive renaming algorithm implemented from $m+1$ bounded registers. When $k \geq m$, the returned names are in the range $\{1,\ldots,n+m-1\}$.

Corollaries of these results include a wait-free one-shot $(\frac{3k^2}{2})$-adaptive renaming algorithm that uses only $\lceil\sqrt{n}\rceil$ registers, an obstruction-free one-shot $f(k)k$-adaptive renaming algorithm that uses only $\lceil f^{-1}(n)\rceil$ registers, as well as a tight space bound of $n - c$ registers for long-lived $(k + c)$-adaptive renaming for any integer constant $c \geq 0$.

Our lower bound proofs use covering techniques first introduced by Burns and Lynch [9]. The main challenge is to exploit the semantics of the renaming object to force the processes to write to a large number of registers. In the lower bound for the one-shot case, we first build an execution in which some processes are poised to write to (*cover*) a set of registers. Then we argue that if enough new processes take steps after this, at least one of them must become poised to write to a register not already covered, since, otherwise, the covering processes can obliterate all the traces of the new processes, causing some getName() to return an incorrect result. For the lower bound for the long-lived case, we exploit that fact that processes can perform getName() and relName() repeatedly to build a long execution where, in each inductive step either another register is covered or an available name is used up without being detected by other processes.

2 Preliminaries

This section describes our model of computation and the notation, vocabulary and general techniques used in this paper. Previous work by many researchers (for example [7,9,12,13,15,16]) have collectively developed notation, vocabulary and techniques that serve to make our description of results and presentation of proofs precise, concise and clear. Much of the terminology presented in this section is borrowed or adapted from this previous research.

Our computational model is an asynchronous shared memory system consisting of n processes $\mathcal{P} = \{p_1, \ldots, p_n\}$ and m shared registers $\mathcal{R} = \{R_1, \ldots, R_m\}$. The processes each execute code (possibly, nondeterministic) that can access their own private registers as well as shared registers. Each shared register supports two operations, read and write. Each such operation happens atomically in memory. Processes can only communicate via those operations on shared registers. The algorithm is *deterministic* if each processes code is deterministic.

A *configuration* C is a tuple $(s_1, \ldots, s_n, v_1, \ldots, v_m)$, denoting that process p_i, $1 \leq i \leq n$, is in state s_i, and register r_j, $1 \leq j \leq m$, has value v_j. Configurations will be denoted by capital letters, and the initial configuration is denoted C^*. A *schedule* σ is a sequence of process identifiers. An *execution* $(C; \sigma)$ is a sequence of steps that starts at configuration C where at each step, the next process p_i indicated in the schedule σ, performs the next operation in its program. The final configuration of the execution $(C; \sigma)$ is denoted $\sigma(C)$. A configuration, C, is *reachable* if there exists a finite schedule, σ, such that $\sigma(C^*) = C$. If σ and π are finite schedules then $\sigma\pi$ denotes the concatenation of σ and π. Let P be a set of processes, and σ a schedule. We say σ is *P-only* if only identifiers of processes in P appear in σ. If the set P contains only one process, p, then we say σ is *p-only*. We denote the set of processes that appear in schedule σ by $\text{procs}(\sigma)$.

We say process p *covers* register r in a configuration C, if there is a choice available to p such that in its next step, it writes to register r. A set of processes P covers a set of registers R if for every register $r \in R$ there is a process $p \in P$ such that p covers r. Consider a process set P that covers the register set R in configuration C. If π_P is a permutation of P, where all processes in P that cover a register in R appear before all processes that don't cover a register in R, then the execution $(C; \pi_P)$ is called a *block-write* by P to R. Two configurations $C_1 = (s_1, \ldots, s_n, v_1, \ldots, v_m)$ and $C_2 = (s'_1, \ldots, s'_n, v'_1, \ldots, v'_m)$ are *indistinguishable* to process p_i if $s_i = s'_i$ and $v_j = v'_j$ for $1 \leq j \leq n$. If S is a set of processes, and for every process $p \in S$, C_1 and C_2 are indistinguishable to p, then for any S-only schedule σ, $\sigma(C_1)$ and $\sigma(C_2)$ are indistinguishable to p.

A deterministic implementation of a method is *wait-free* if for any reachable configuration C and any process p, p completes its method call in a finite number of its own steps, regardless of the steps taken by other processes. A deterministic implementation of a method is *obstruction-free* if for any reachable configuration C and any process p, there is a finite p-only schedule σ, such that p finishes its method call in execution (C, σ). The notion of obstruction-free progress is extended to non-deterministic implementations by only requiring that there is some finite sequence of choices available to p such that under these choices p finishes its method call. More precisely, a non-deterministic implementation of a method satisfies *non-deterministic solo-termination*, if for any reachable configuration C and any process p, there is a finite p-only schedule σ, and a set of choices available to p, such that p finishes its method call in execution (C, σ) given those choices.

For a renaming algorithm, process p *participates* in execution E if it takes steps during E. It participates in configuration C if p has started a getName operation and has not completed the following relName (x). A process is called *idle*, if it does not participate. A configuration C is called *quiescent*, if $\forall p \in \mathcal{P}$, p is idle in C. We say process p *owns* name x in execution E, if p has completed a getName operation which returned name x and p has not started relName (x).

3   A Space Lower Bound for Long-Lived Loose Renaming Objects

Let m be the largest integer such that $f(m) \leq n - 1$. We prove that at least m registers are required for obstruction-free long-lived $f(k)$-adaptive renaming in our system. The proof relies on two lemmas. Lemma 1 says that there is no reachable configuration in which $n - m$ of the processes own names in the range $\{1, \ldots, n - 1\}$, while all of the other m processes are idle and unaware of any of the processes with names. The intuition for this proof is simple: Suppose there is such a configuration. Then we let each of the m idle processes get a name. The result is that these m processes and the $n - m$ invisible ones all hold names from $\{1, \ldots, n-1\}$, so they cannot all be distinct. Lemma 2 provides the core of the lower bound argument. It says that for any reachable configuration in which fewer than $n - m$ processes own names in the range $\{1, \ldots, n-1\}$, while all of the other m processes are idle and unaware of the processes with names, there is an execution starting from that configuration in which either m distinct registers are written, or one more name is owned, and the unnamed processes are again idle and still unaware of the processes with names. Since the initial configuration has no processes with names, and all processes are idle, we can apply Lemma 2 repeatedly until either we have covered m registers or we reach a configuration in which $n - m - 1$ processes own names in the range $\{1, \ldots, n-1\}$. Since, according to Lemma 1, we cannot get beyond an $(n-m-1)$-named configuration, we must eventually cover m registers, completing the proof. We will see, in the formal proof, that the result applies even when the renaming implementation is m-bounded.

The definitions and lemmas that follow refer to any obstruction-free implementation from shared registers of a long-lived $f(k)$-adaptive renaming object. For a configuration C and a set of processes Q, we say Q is *invisible* in C, if there is a reachable quiescent configuration D such that C and D are indistinguishable to all processes in $\overline{Q}$. If the set Q contains only one process q, then we say process q is invisible. Configuration C is called ℓ-*named*, if there is a set Q of ℓ processes, such that in C every process in Q owns a name in $\{1,\ldots,n-1\}$ and Q is invisible.

Lemma 1. *For the largest integer m satisfying $f(m) \leq n-1$, there is no reachable $(n-m)$-named configuration.*

The full proof is omitted due to space constraints.

The intuition for Lemma 2 is as follows. Recall that in an ℓ-named configuration, ℓ processes have names, the $n - \ell$ others are idle and unaware of the presence of the named processes, and no register is covered. Starting from this configuration we select one process at a time from the set of idle processes and let it execute until either it covers a register not already covered, or it gets a name without covering a new register. We continue this construction as long as the selected process covers a new register. If we reach m processes we are done. Otherwise, we reached a configuration in which one more process holds a name. Furthermore, we can obliterate the trace of this process with the appropriate block write, and then let all non-idle process complete their getName() method. This takes us to an $(\ell+1)$-named configuration.

Lemma 2. *Let m be the largest integer such that $f(m) \leq n-1$. For any $0 \leq \ell \leq n-m$ and any reachable ℓ-named configuration C, there exists a schedule σ, where $|\mathrm{procs}(\sigma)| \leq m$, and either*
- *in configuration $\sigma(C)$ at least m distinct registers are covered; or*
- *configuration $\sigma(C)$ is $(\ell+1)$-named.*

Proof. Let C be an ℓ-named configuration, and let Q be the set of ℓ processes that are invisible in C and D the quiescent configuration that is indistinguishable from C for all processes in $\overline{Q}$. First, we inductively construct a sequence of schedules $\delta_0, \delta_1, \ldots$ until we have constructed δ_{last} such that in $\delta_{last}(C)$ either
a) m registers are covered, or,
b) $(\ell+1)$ processes own names in $\{1,\ldots,n-1\}$.

We maintain the invariant that for each $i \in \{0,\ldots,last\}$ in configuration $\delta_i(C)$, a set P_i of i processes covers a set R_i of i distinct registers, $P_i \cap Q = \emptyset$, and all processes in $\overline{P_i}$ are idle in execution $(C;\delta_i)$. Let δ_0 be the empty schedule. Then in configuration $\delta_0(C) = C$, no register is covered, so the invariant is true for $P_0 = R_0 = \emptyset$.

Now consider $i \geq 0$. If a) or b) holds for δ_i, we let $last = i$ and are done. Otherwise, since in $\delta_i(C)$ a set R_i of i distinct registers is covered, we have $i < m$. We construct δ_{i+1} as follows. Select $p \in \overline{P_i \cup Q}$. Let γ be the shortest p-only schedule such that either
1) p does a complete getName() in execution $(\delta_i(C);\gamma)$, or
2) in configuration $\gamma(\delta_i(C))$, p covers a register $r \notin R_i$.

Let δ_{i+1} be $\delta_i\gamma$. First assume case 1) happens. Then because Q is invisible to p, in $(\delta_i(C);\gamma)$ p becomes aware of at most the $i < m$ other processes in P_i. Since $f(m) \leq n-1$, p gets a name in $\{1,\ldots,n-1\}$, and thus in configuration $\delta_{i+1}(C)$ all processes in $Q\cup\{p\}$ own names in $\{1,\ldots,n-1\}$ and $|Q\cup\{p\}| = \ell+1$. So condition b) is achieved, the construction stops and $\delta_{last} = \delta_{i+1}$.

Now suppose case 2) happens. If $i+1 = m$, then condition a) is achieved, the construction stops and $\delta_{last} = \delta_{i+1}$. Otherwise, the invariant remains satisfied for $R_{i+1} = R_i \cup \{r\}$ and $P_{i+1} = P_i \cup \{p\}$. Clearly, after at most m steps either a) or b) is achieved.

Now, using schedule δ_{last} we construct schedule σ. If $\delta_{last}(C)$ satisfies a), let $\sigma = \delta_{last}$ and the lemma holds. Hence, suppose that $\delta_{last}(C)$ satisfies b). Let α be the P_{last-1}-only schedule such that in execution $(\delta_{last}\pi_{P_{last-1}}(C);\alpha)$ every process $q \in P_{last-1}$ completes its pending getName() operation and performs a complete relName(). During execution $(C;\delta_{last})$ only registers in R_{last-1} were written and in configuration $\delta_{last}(C)$, P_{last-1} covers these registers. Because $\delta_{last} = \delta_{last-1}\gamma$ for some p-only postfix γ of δ_{last}, after a block write by P_{last-1}, configurations $\delta_{last}\pi_{P_{last-1}}(C)$ and $\delta_{last-1}\pi_{P_{last-1}}(C)$ are indistinguishable to $\overline{Q\cup\{p\}}$. Since C and D are indistinguishable to $\overline{Q}$, configurations $\delta_{last-1}\pi_{P_{last-1}}(C)$ and $\delta_{last-1}\pi_{P_{last-1}}(D)$ are also indistinguishable to $\overline{Q}$. So, configurations $\delta_{last}\pi_{P_{last-1}}(C)$ and $\delta_{last-1}\pi_{P_{last-1}}(D)$ are indistinguishable to $\overline{Q\cup\{p\}}$. Hence, configurations $\delta_{last}\pi_{P_{last-1}}\alpha(C)$ and $\delta_{last-1}\pi_{P_{last-1}}\alpha(D)$ are indistinguishable to $\overline{(Q\cup\{p\})}$. Since $\delta_{last-1}\pi_{P_{last-1}}\alpha(D)$ is quiescent, configuration $\delta_{last}\pi_{P_{last-1}}\alpha(C)$ is an $(\ell+1)$-named configuration. Therefore, the lemma holds for $\sigma = \delta_{last}\pi_{P_{last-1}}\alpha$. □

Theorem 3. *Let m the the largest integer such that $f(m) \leq n-1$. Any obstruction-free implementation of a long-lived m-bounded $f(k)$-adaptive renaming object requires at least m registers.*

Proof. Let $C_0 = C^*$, and note that C_0 is a reachable 0-named configuration. We iteratively construct a sequence of schedules $\sigma_0, \sigma_1, \ldots, \sigma_{last}$ as follows: If $0 \leq i \leq n-m$ and C_i is a reachable i-named configuration, we apply Lemma 2 to obtain a schedule σ_i, $|procs(\sigma_i)| \leq m$, such that $C_{i+1} = \sigma_i(C_i)$ is either an $(i+1)$-named configuration, or in C_{i+1} at least m distinct registers are covered. In the latter case we let $last = i+1$ and finish the iterative construction. By Lemma 1, the iterative construction ends eventually, as no $(n-m)$-named configuration C_{n-m} exists. Hence, there is a reachable configuration C_{last}, $last < n-m$, in which m registers are covered, and in particular the implementation uses at least m registers. □

Corollary 4. *Let $c \in \{1,\ldots,n-1\}$ and $b = \lfloor \frac{n-1}{c} \rfloor$. Any obstruction-free implementation of a long-lived b-bounded $(c \cdot k)$-adaptive renaming object requires at least b registers.*

4   A Space Lower Bound for One-shot Additive Loose Renaming

Proving space lower bounds for one-shot renaming is more difficult, since we cannot obtain a covering of registers by letting processes repeatedly get and release names. Therefore we study almost tight one-shot renaming objects, where the name space is only an additive constant term larger than the contention. We refer to one-shot $(k + c)$-renaming object as an additive loose renaming object, where k is the number of participants and $c \geq 0$ is an integer constant. For the case $c = 0$, it is called an adaptive tight renaming object.

We prove a lower bound of $\lfloor \frac{n}{c+1} \rfloor$ registers for one-shot obstruction-free additive loose renaming objects. Since in the $(k + c)$-renaming problem a process is allowed to return a name in the range $\{1, \ldots, c+1\}$ when it runs alone, there is no incentive for having a $(k + c)$-renaming object in a system with $n \leq c + 1$. Hence in our proofs we assume $c \leq n - 2$.

We consider an arbitrary obstruction-free one-shot $(k + c)$-adaptive renaming algorithms. Our lower bound proof relies on two lemmas. Lemma 5 says that there are at most c processes in the system, which do not write to any register while completing a getName() call in a solo-execution. The reason is that if there are $c + 1$ such processes, then then we can let all of them run in such a way that they remain invisible, and get names in $\{1, \ldots, c+1\}$. If we run any other process afterwards, it also gets a names in $\{1, \ldots, c+1\}$, contradicting name distinctness.

Lemma 5. *Let $c \leq n - 2$, and for any process p, let σ_p denote a p-only schedule such that p performs a complete getName() in execution $(C^*; \sigma_p)$. There are at most c processes q that do not write to any register in execution $(C^*; \sigma_q)$.*

The straight-forward proof of this lemma is omitted due to space restrictions.

In Lemma 6, we extend this idea by partitioning processes into sets of size $c + 1$ and then constructing an execution such that in each such set, there must be at least one process that writes to a register not previously written.

Lemma 6. *Let $c \in \{0, \ldots, n-2\}$, $k \in \{1, \ldots, \lfloor \frac{n}{c+1} \rfloor\}$, $B_k = \{p_1, \ldots, p_{(c+1)k}\}$, and $\widehat{B}_k = \{p_{c+2}, \ldots, p_{(c+1)k}\}$ (and thus $\widehat{B}_1 = \emptyset$). There exists a B_k-only schedule σ_k and a $\widehat{B}_k$-only schedule $\widehat{\sigma}_k$, such that for $C_k = \sigma_k(C^*)$ and $\widehat{C}_k = \widehat{\sigma}_k(C^*)$ we have*
a) *in configuration C_k, there is a set R_k of k distinct registers covered by B_k;*
b) *$\widehat{\sigma}_k$ is the subsequence of σ_k constructed by removing from σ_k all occurrences of processes in $\{p_1, \ldots, p_{c+1}\}$; and*
c) *C_k and $\widehat{C}_k$ are indistinguishable to $\mathcal{P} - \{p_1, \ldots, p_{c+1}\}$.*

Proof. The proof proceeds by induction on k. For the base case, $k = 1$, by Lemma 5, there is a process $p \in \{p_1, \ldots, p_{c+1}\}$ and a p-only schedule σ_p such that during the execution $(C^*; \sigma_p)$ process p performs a complete getName() and writes to a register. Let σ_1 be the shortest prefix of σ_p such that p covers a register in $\sigma_1(C^*)$, and let r be the register covered. Then the lemma is true for $R_1 = \{r\}$ and the empty schedule $\widehat{\sigma}_1$.

Suppose that a), b), and c) are true for $k \geq 1$. Let A be the set of processes $\{p_{(c+1)k+1}, \ldots, p_{(c+1)(k+1)}\}$. Let α be an A-only schedule such that in execution $(C_k; \alpha)$, every process $p \in A$ performs a complete getName(). First suppose there is a process $q \in A$ that writes during $(C_k; \alpha)$ to a register that is not in R_k. Let α' be the shortest prefix of α such that in $\alpha'(C_k)$ some process $q \in A$ covers a register $r \notin R_k$. Set $\sigma_{k+1} = \sigma_k \alpha'$, $\widehat{\sigma}_{k+1} = \widehat{\sigma}_k \alpha'$, and $R_{k+1} = R_k \cup \{r\}$. By the induction hypothesis, $C_k = \sigma_k(C^*)$ and $\widehat{\sigma}_k(C^*) = \widehat{C}_k$ are indistinguishable to $\mathcal{P} - \{p_1, \ldots, p_{c+1}\}$, so $C_{k+1} = \sigma_{k+1}(C^*) = \alpha'(C_k)$

and $\widehat{C}_{k+1} = \widehat{\sigma}_{k+1}(C^*) = \alpha'(\widehat{C}_k)$ are also indistinguishable to $\mathcal{P} - \{p_1, \ldots, p_{c+1}\}$. Moreover, in C_k all registers in R_k are covered, so in C_{k+1} all registers in R_{k+1} are covered, and the inductive hypothesis follows.

It remains to prove that there is a process $q \in A$ that writes during $(C_k; \alpha)$ to a register that is not in R_k. By way of contradiction, assume that each process $p \in A$ writes only to R_k during $(C_k; \alpha)$. Since processes in A do not distinguish C_k from $\widehat{C}_k$, where only processes in $\widehat{B}_k$ are participants, processes in A must return names of value at most $|\widehat{B}_k| + |A| + c \le (c+1)k + c$ in execution $(C_k; \alpha)$. Let π_{B_k} be a permutation of B_k such that $(\pi_{B_k}; \alpha(C_k))$ is a block-write to R_k. Let β be a B_k-only schedule such that each process $p \in B_k$ completes its getName() in execution $(\alpha \pi_{B_k}(C_k); \beta)$. Since no process in B_k distinguishes $\alpha \pi_{B_k}(C_k)$ from $\pi_{B_k}(C_k)$, processes in B_k return names of value at most $|B_k| + c \le (c+1)k + c$ during $(\alpha \pi_{B_k}(C_k); \beta)$. We showed above, that also all processes in A return names of value at most $(c+1)k + c$ in $(C_k; \alpha)$ and thus in $(\alpha \pi_{B_k}(C_k); \beta)$. Hence, in that execution all processes in $B_k \cup A$ return names in $\{1, \ldots, (c+1)k + c\}$. This contradicts name distinctness because $|B_k \cup A| = (c+1)k + c + 1$.   □

Maximizing k in Lemma 6 provides space lower bounds for one shot additive loose renaming objects and for tight renaming objects.

Theorem 7. *For any constant integer $c \ge 0$, any obstruction-free implementation of a one-shot $(k+c)$-adaptive renaming object for a system with n processes requires at least $\lfloor \frac{n}{c+1} \rfloor$ registers. In particular, adaptive tight renaming for n processes requires at least n registers.*

5 One-shot $(m-1)$-Bounded Renaming Algorithms

This section contains two different one-shot renaming algorithms using only shared registers. These algorithms are simplified by assuming that there is a scan operation available in the system, which atomically returns the complete contents of all the m registers. Later we show how to remove this assumption.

In our proofs, a *register configuration* is a tuple $(v_1, \ldots, v_m)$, denoting that register $R[i]$, $1 \le i \le m$, has value v_i. The proofs focus on just the sub-sequence of register configurations produced by an execution. Specifically, given an execution $E = (C^*; \sigma)$, let *write schedule* $\widehat{\sigma}$ denote the sub-sequence of σ that produces write steps in $(C^*; \sigma)$. Execution E gives rise to the sequence of *register configurations* $\Gamma_E = C_0, C_1, \ldots$ such that the i-th step of $\widehat{\sigma}$ is a write that changes register configuration C_{i-1} to register configuration C_i and $C_0 = C^*$. For any scan operation s in E, define $index(s) = i$, if s occurs in E between C_i and C_{i+1} in Γ_E. Notice that the view returned by a scan with index i is equal to C_i. A register configuration $C = (v_1, \ldots, v_m)$ is *consistent* if $v_1 = \cdots = v_m$ in which case we say v_1 is the *content* of C. Let C_i and C_j be register configurations in the sequence $\Gamma_E = C_0, C_1, \ldots$ such that $i \le j$. *Interval* (C_i, C_j) denotes the sub-sequence of steps in execution E that begins at register configuration C_i and ends at register configuration C_j in Γ_E.

A local variable x in these algorithms is denoted by x_p when it is used in the method call invoked by process p.

shared: $\mathcal{R} = R[1,\ldots,m]$: array of multi-writer multi-reader registers, initialized to $\perp$;

local: An array $r[0,\ldots,m-1]$; pos initialized to 0; S initialized to $\{id\}$;

Function getName
1 **repeat**
2     $R[pos].\text{write}(S)$
3     $r[0,\ldots,m-1] := \mathcal{R}.\text{scan}$
4     $S := \bigcup_{i=0}^{m-1} r[i] \cup S$
5     $pos := (pos+1) \bmod m$
6 **until**
$(|S| \geq m) \vee (r[0] = r[1] = \cdots = r[m-1] = S)$
7 **if** $|S| \leq m-1$ **then**
8   **return** $(|S|(|S|-1))/2 + rank(id,S)$
9 **else**
10   **return** $m(m-1)/2 + id$
11 **end**

Fig. 1. $(m-1)$-Bounded $(k(k+1)/2)$-Adaptive Renaming

5.1 Wait-Free One-shot $(m-1)$-Bounded $(k(k+1)/2)$-Adaptive Renaming

In the algorithm presented in Fig. 1, each process maintains a set of the processes, S, that it knows are participating including itself, and alternately executes write and scan operations. In the write operation, it writes S to the next register after where it last wrote, in cyclic order through the m registers. After each of its scan operations, it updates S to all the processes it sees in the scan together with the processes already in its set. The process stops with an assigned name when either its scan shows exactly its own set, S, in every register, or S has grown to size at least m. If $|S|$ is less than m, its name is based on $|S|$ and its rank in S, where $rank(id,S) = |\{i|(i \in S) \wedge (i \leq id)\}|$. If $|S|$ is m or greater, it returns a safe but large name. The correctness of this algorithm relies on the fact that if any two processes return names based on a set of size $s < m$, then they have the same set. The main component of the proof is to establish this fact.

Observation 8. *For any* write *operation with value S by process p, $p \in S$.*

Lemma 9. *For any execution E, let C_0 be a consistent register configuration with content $\widehat{S}$. For any register configuration C following C_0 in E, define $\mathcal{R}_C = \{R \in \mathcal{R} | \widehat{S} \not\subseteq R\}$. Then there exists a one-to-one function $f_C : \mathcal{R}_C \to \mathcal{P}$ satisfying, $\forall R \in \mathcal{R}_C$, $f_C(R) \in R$ and $f_C(R)$ performs at least one* write *in Interval (C_0, C).*

Proof. Let $C_0, C_1, \ldots$ be the sequence of register configurations that arises from E starting at C_0. We prove the lemma by induction on the indices of this sequence. The base case $k = 0$, is trivially true since set $\mathcal{R}_{C_0}$ is the empty set.

Suppose that the induction hypothesis is true for $k-1 \geq 0$. Let the write step between C_{k-1} and C_k be the operation, w, by process p, into register $R[j]$ with value V. Let s be the most recent scan operation by p preceding w if it exists.

If $\widehat{S} \subseteq V$, then $\mathcal{R}_{C_k} = \mathcal{R}_{C_{k-1}} \setminus \{R[j]\}$. Define $f_{C_k}(R) = f_{C_{k-1}}(R)$, $\forall R \in \mathcal{R}_{C_k}$. Since $f_{C_{k-1}}$ satisfies the induction hypothesis, and $\mathcal{R}_{C_k} \subseteq \mathcal{R}_{C_{k-1}}$, f_{C_k} also satisfies the induction hypothesis.

Now consider the case $\widehat{S} \not\subseteq V$. So $\mathcal{R}_{C_k} = \mathcal{R}_{C_{k-1}} \cup \{R[j]\}$. We first show that s happens before C_0 or it does not exist. Suppose, for the purpose of contradiction, that $0 \leq index(s) \leq k-1$. We have $\forall i, 0 \leq i \leq m-1, \widehat{S} \not\subseteq R[i]$ in configuration $C_{index(s)}$, since otherwise, by Line 4, $\widehat{S} \subseteq V$. Thus $|\mathcal{R}_{C_{index(s)}}| = m$. By the induction hypothesis, $f_{C_{index(s)}}$ selects a distinct process from each register in $\mathcal{R}_{C_{index(s)}}$, implying, by Line 4, that the size of S_p at least m. Hence p would have stopped in Line 6 before performing any write operation. Therefore s happens before C_0 or s does not exist, and consequently any write by p before w happens before C_0. On the other hand, $\forall R \in \mathcal{R}_{C_{k-1}}, f(R)$ performs a write during Interval (C_0, C_{k-1}) implying p is not in $\{f(R)|R \in \mathcal{R}_{C_{k-1}}\}$. By Observation 8, $p \in V$ and p performs a write after C_0. Therefore by defining $f_{C_k}(R) = f_{C_{k-1}}(R)$, $\forall R, R \in (\mathcal{R}_{C_{k-1}} \setminus \{R[j]\})$ and $f_{C_k}(R[j]) = p$, the induction hypothesis holds for k.   □

Lemma 10. *For any execution E, let $\widehat{S}_p$ and $\widehat{S}_q$ be the value of S_p and S_q in Line 7 for p and q when they have completed the repeat loop. If $|\widehat{S}_p| = |\widehat{S}_q| < m$ then $\widehat{S}_p = \widehat{S}_q$.*

Proof. Let C_p and C_q be the consistent register configurations that resulted in $\widehat{S}_p$ and $\widehat{S}_q$ respectively and assume, without loss of generality, that C_p precedes C_q in Γ_E. By Line 6, $R[0] = \cdots = R[m-1] = \widehat{S}_q$ in C_q. Thus in C_q, either $\forall i, 0 \leq i \leq m-1, \widehat{S}_p \subseteq R[i]$ or $\forall i, 0 \leq i \leq m-1, \widehat{S}_p \not\subseteq R[i]$.

For the first case, by Line 4, $\widehat{S}_p \subseteq \widehat{S}_q$ and since $|\widehat{S}_p| = |\widehat{S}_q|$, $\widehat{S}_p = \widehat{S}_q$. For the latter case, set $\mathcal{R}_{C_q}$ has size m. By Lemma 9, there is a distinct process $f_{C_q}(R)$ in each register in $\mathcal{R}_{C_q}$. So there are at least m distinct processes in $\widehat{S}_q$ contradicting $|\widehat{S}_q| < m$.   □

Lemma 11. *The names returned by any two distinct processes are distinct.*

Proof. Let $\widehat{S}_p$ and $\widehat{S}_q$ be the values of S_p and S_q in Line 7. If $|\widehat{S}_p| \geq m$ and $|\widehat{S}_q| \geq m$, the names returned by p and q in Line 10 are distinct because $p \neq q$. If $|\widehat{S}_p| < m$ and $|\widehat{S}_q| \geq m$, then, by Line 8, the name returned by p is at most $(m-1)(m-2)/2 + (m-1) = m(m-1)/2$ and, by Line 10, the name returned by q is bigger than $m(m-1)/2$. If $|\widehat{S}_p| < m$ and $|\widehat{S}_q| < m$, both processes return at Line 8. First suppose $l = |\widehat{S}_p| < |\widehat{S}_q|$. Then the name returned by p is at most $(l+1)(l)/2$ and the name returned by q is at least $(l+1)(l)/2 + 1$. If $|\widehat{S}_p| = |\widehat{S}_q|$, by Lemma 10, $\widehat{S}_p = \widehat{S}_q$. Therefore $rank(p, \widehat{S}_p) \neq rank(q, \widehat{S}_q)$. Thus, in all cases the names returned by p and q are distinct.   □

Observation 12. *Set $\{p\}$ is written by p before any other write of any set $V \supseteq \{p\}$.*

Lemma 13. *Let k be the number of participating processes. Then, any name returned by any process p, is in the range $\{1, \ldots, \frac{k(k+1)}{2}\}$, if $k < m$ and in the range $\{1, \ldots, n + \frac{m(m-1)}{2}\}$, if $k \geq m$.*

Proof. By Observation 12, $\forall q \in S_p$, q performs at least one write before p returns. Thus, $\forall q \in S_p$, q is a participating process. Hence, $|S_p| \leq k$. If $k < m$, then $|S_p| < m$. Therefore, process p returns in Line 8, and the name is in the range $\{1, \ldots, \frac{k(k+1)}{2}\}$. If $k \geq m$, then p returns either in Line 8 or in Line 10. Therefore the name is in the range $\{1, \ldots, \frac{m(m-1)}{2} + n\}$.   □

Intuitively, we see that there is a finite bound, say B, on the number of times any process can execute Line 2 because, either a process continues to write the same set and thus terminates at Line 8, or it keeps updating its set with new values, in which case it eventually terminates at Line 10 because its set is large. The formal proof of this is omitted due to page constraints.

The atomic scan in Line 3 is replaced with a linearizable implementation, using the standard double collect technique [1]. A process obtains a *view* of $\mathcal{R}$ by reading $R[1]$ through $R[m]$ consecutively. It repeatedly gets a view until it obtains two identical consecutive views, and the scan returns this view. In order to guarantee linearizability of the scan method, processes augment the values they write to $\mathcal{R}$ with sequence numbers. Since there can be only a finite number of write operations to $\mathcal{R}$, the scan method based on double collects is wait-free. Moreover, each process increments its sequence number at most B times, and thus sequence numbers can be stored in bounded registers. Thus, Lemmas 11 and 13, and the observed bound B yield the following result.

Theorem 14. *For any $m \geq 1$, there is a wait-free one-shot $(m-1)$-bounded $(k(k+1)/2)$-adaptive renaming algorithm implemented from m bounded registers. Additionally, when $k \geq m$, the returned names are in the range $\{1, \ldots, n + \frac{m(m-1)}{2}\}$.*

Setting $m = \lceil \sqrt{n} \rceil$ we have,

Corollary 15. *There is a wait-free one-shot $(3k^2)/2$-adaptive renaming algorithm implemented from $\lceil \sqrt{n} \rceil$ bounded registers.*

5.2   Obstruction-Free $(m-1)$-Bounded k-Adaptive Renaming

Algorithm Description. Pseudo-code for the algorithm is found in Fig. 2. A *naming set* is a set of ordered pairs where each pair is a process id and a proposed name such that each process id occurs in at most one pair in the set. Let S be a naming set. In our algorithm and the analysis we use the following notation:

- $Procs(S) = \{x | (x, y) \in S\}$,
- $Names(S) = \{y | (x, y) \in S\}$,
- if $(p, n) \in S$, then $name(p, S)$ is n; otherwise $name(p, S)$ is equal to 0.

Each register R stores either the value $\bot$ (the initial value), or an ordered triple $(set, writer, proposal)$. In the latter case, set is a naming set, $writer$ is a process id and $proposal$ is a positive integer less than m. Each process p maintains a naming set S_p and alternates between write and scan until it terminates with a name for itself. Each scan returns a view, which is the content of all registers. Each write by p writes a triple consisting of its set S_p, its id p, and its proposed name $name_p$, to some register $R[j]$. Process p uses its preceding scan and its previous value of S_p to determine the new value of S_p, $name_p$ and j.

Function Update describes how p constructs S_p in three steps. In the first step (Lines 18-22), p creates a naming set based only on the *writer*s and *proposal*s of each register in its view. If the view contains a *writer* with more than one *proposal*, p chooses one pair arbitrarily. In the second step (Lines 23-31), p augments its naming set with additional pairs for processes that are not *writer*s in its view but occur in the union of all naming sets in its view. The main issue occurs when there is some process that is

shared: $\mathcal{R} = R[1, \ldots, m]$: array of multi-writer multi-reader registers, initialized to $\bot$;
local: An array $r[1, \ldots, m]$; pos initialized to 1; S initialized to $\emptyset$; $proposed$ initialized to 1.

Function getName

1 **repeat**
2     $R[pos].\text{write}(S, id, proposed)$
3     $r[1, \ldots, m] := \mathcal{R}.\text{scan}$
4     $S := Update(S, r[1, \ldots, m])$
5     $proposed = \min\{i \in \mathbb{N} | i \notin Names(S)\}$
6   **if** $\exists i, \text{ s.t. } (r[i].writer = id) \wedge (r[i] \neq (S, id, proposed))$ **then**
7        $pos := \max\{i | (r[i].writer = id) \wedge (r[i] \neq (S, id, proposed))\}$
8   **else if** $\exists j, \text{ s.t. } r[j] \neq (S, id, proposed)$ **then**
9        $pos := j$
10   **end**
11 **until** $(|S| + 1 \geq m) \vee (r[1] = r[2] = \cdots = r[m] = (S, id, proposed))$
12 **if** $|S| + 1 < m$ **then**
13   **return** $proposed$
14 **else**
15   **return** $m - 1 + id$
16 **end**

Function Update

17 $S_{new} = \emptyset$
18 **for all**
    $w \in \{r[i].writer | 1 \leq i \leq m\} \setminus \{id\}$ **do**
19   Let $j \in \{1, \ldots, m\}$ such that $r[j].writer = w$
20     $name_w := r[j].proposal$
21     $S_{new} := S_{new} \cup \{(w, name_w)\}$
22 **end**
23 **for** $\forall p \in Procs(\bigcup_{i=1}^{m} r[i].set) \setminus Procs(S_{new})$ **do**
24   **if** $\exists i, j, (i < j) \wedge (r[i].writer = r[j].writer) \wedge (p \in Procs(r[j].set))$ **then**
25        $name_p := name(p, r[j].set)$
26   **else**
27   Let $j \in \{1, \ldots, m\}$ s.t. $p \in Procs(r[j].set)$
28        $name_p := name(p, r[j].set)$
29   **end**
30     $S_{new} := S_{new} \cup \{(p, name_p)\}$
31 **end**
32 **for** $\forall p \in Procs(S) \setminus Procs(S_{new})$ **do**
33     $S_{new} := S_{new} \cup \{(p, name(p, S))\}$
34 **end**
35 **return** S_{new}

Fig. 2. $(m-1)$-Bounded k-Adaptive Renaming

paired with more that one name in two or more naming sets from different registers. In this case, if there are two such registers with the same *writer* then, p chooses the pair which occurs in the register with bigger index. Otherwise, p picks one pair arbitrarily. Finally (Lines 32-34), p adds any pair (q, n_q) such that q exists in the previous version of S_p and is not yet added. Observe that S_p is a naming set.

Line 5 describes how p sets $name_p$— It chooses for $name_p$ the smallest integer that is not paired by some other process in S_p.

Lines 6-10 describe how p sets j— If there is any register with *writer* component equal to p but with content different from $(S_p, p, name_p)$ then p writes to register $R[j]$ where j is the biggest index amongst these registers. Otherwise it writes to some register whose content is different than $(S_p, p, name_p)$. Process p continues until either in some scan, all registers contain the same information that p has written or $|S_p|$ is larger than $m - 1$. In the first case p returns $name_p$ and in the second case it returns $m + p - 1$.

Overview of Proof. Once a process p terminates with name $n_p < m - 1$, the pair (*writer*, *proposal*) of every register is equal to (p, n_p). The core idea is that after p terminates, every register that is overwritten with the wrong name for p or no name for p, has a distinct *writer* component. Therefore, if a subsequent scan by another process, say q, does not include the correct name for p, the set of processes in that scan is large and q terminates with a name larger than m. If the set of processes in the scan is not large, then there is some writer that is in the *writer* component of at least 2 registers. In that case, we prove that for any such pair of registers with the same writer, the correct name for p is in the register with the larger index. In this way, the algorithm ensures that process q keeps (p, n_p) in its naming set, and discards incorrect names for p.

Let p be a process that has terminated and returned name n_p. Define $last_p$ to be the last scan by p. For any register configuration D following register configuration $C_{index(last_p)}$, define a set of registers $W_p(D) = \{R \in \mathcal{R} \mid (R.writer \neq p) \wedge ((p, n_p) \notin R.set)\}$ and a set of processes $\rho_p(D) = \bigcup_{R \in W_p(D)} \{R.writer\}$.

Lemma 16. *Let E be an execution starting in the initial configuration and ending in configuration C, and suppose $(R[1], \ldots, R[m]) = (v_1, \ldots, v_m)$ in configuration C. If there are two integers i and j such that $i < j$, $v_i.writer = v_j.writer = p$ and $v_i \neq v_j$, then the last write of v_i to $R[i]$ happens before the last write of v_j to $R[j]$.*

Due to space constraints, the proof of this lemma is omitted.

Lemma 17. *Consider an execution E in which process p's* getName() *call returns name $n_p \leq m - 1$. Let $\Gamma_E = C_0, C_1, \ldots$ be the sequence of register configurations that arise from E. Then for any register configuration C_k where $k \geq index(last_p)$,*

   i) $|W_p(C_k)| = |\rho_p(C_k)|$;

   ii) $\forall q \in \rho_p(C_k)$, q performs a write *in the interval $(C_{index(last_p)}, C_k)$; and*

   iii) for any $q \in \mathcal{P}$ and any write schedule $\sigma_k = \alpha_1 q \alpha_2 q \alpha_3$, where $\sigma_k(C_{index(last_p)}) = C_k$, if v is the value written by q in the one step execution $(\alpha_1 q \alpha_2(C_{index(last_p)}), q)$, then $(p, n_p) \in v.set$.

Proof. We prove the lemma by induction on k. Since $n_p \leq m - 1$, p returns in Line 13. Therefore the condition $r[1] = \cdots = r[m] = (S_p, p, n_p)$ held when p last executed Line 11. Hence, condition $R[1] = \cdots = R[m] = (S_p, p, n_p)$ held in $C_{index(last_p)}$. Therefore the lemma holds for the base case $k = index(last_p)$ because $W_p(C_{index(last_p)}) = \rho_p(C_{index(last_p)}) = \emptyset$ and $\sigma_{index(last_p)}$ is the empty schedule.

Suppose that the lemma holds for $k - 1 \geq index(last_p)$. Let w be the write that changes register configuration C_{k-1} to C_k, and let x be the process that performs w. Then clearly $x \neq p$, since p has performed its last write before $C_{index(last_p)}$. Suppose w puts value (S_x, x, n_x) into register R, and let s be x's scan operation that precedes w if it exists.

We first show that if $C_{index(last_p)}$ precedes $C_{index(s)}$ in Γ_E, then $(p, n_p) \in S_x$. If in $C_{index(s)}$, there exists an i such that $R[i].writer = p$, then by Line 21, $(p, n_p) \in S_x$. Otherwise suppose, in $C_{index(s)}$, there is a process u and indices i, j, $i < j$, such that $r[i].writer = r[j].writer = u$. Then there exist two writes by u, one, say w_1, to $R[i]$ with value $r[i]$ and another one, say w_2, to register $R[j]$ with value $r[j]$, and both w_1 and w_2 occur in Interval $(C_{index(last_p)}, C_{index(s)})$. If $r[i] \neq r[j]$ then by Lemma 16, w_1 precedes w_2 in E and by the induction hypothesis (iii), $(p, n_p) \in r[j].set$. If $r[i] = r[j]$ then again by induction hypothesis (iii), $(p, n_p) \in r[j].set$. In either case, Line 24 evaluates to true.

Hence by Line 25, $(p, n_p) \in S_x$. Finally, if $\forall i \neq j$, $r[i].writer \neq r[j].writer$, then by the for-loop (Lines 18-22), $|S_x| \geq m - 1$. Hence, the presumed write w by x cannot happen.

If $(p, n_p) \in S_x$ then, $W_p(C_k) = W_p(C_{k-1}) \setminus \{R\}$. Therefore (i) and (ii) are trivially true. Since $(p, n_p) \in S_x$, (iii) is true for $\sigma_k = \sigma_{k-1} x$.

If $(p, n_p) \notin S_x$ then, as proved above, $C_{index(s)}$ precedes $C_{index(last_p)}$ in Γ_E or s does not exist. Since for all $q \in \rho_p(C_{k-1})$, q performs a write during $(C_{index(last_p)}, C_{k-1})$ and the most recent operation before w by x happens before $C_{index(last_p)}$ or there is no operation before w, $x \notin \rho_p(C_{k-1})$. Thus, $W_p(C_k) = W_p(C_{k-1}) \cup \{R\}$. Since the most recent operation before w by x happens before $C_{index(last_p)}$, there is no write schedule $\alpha_1 x \alpha_2 x \alpha_3$ satisfying $\alpha_1 x \alpha_2 x \alpha_3(C_{index(last_p)}) = C_k$. Therefore (iii) remains true.   □

Lemma 18. *Let p and q be two distinct processes that have terminated in execution E and returned names n_p and n_q respectively. Suppose that $C_{index(last_p)}$ precedes $C_{index(last_q)}$ in Γ_E. If $n_p, n_q \leq m - 1$, then $|W_p(C_{index(last_q)})| = 0$.*

Proof. Since $n_q \leq m - 1$, q returns in Line 13. Hence $C_{index(last_q)}$ is consistent with content (S_q, q, n_q). Therefore, $|W_p(C_{index(last_q)})| \in \{0, m\}$. By Lemma 17, $|W_p(C_{index(last_q)})| = |\rho_p(C_{index(last_q)})|$. Since in $C_{index(last_q)}$, $R.writer = q$ for all $R \in \mathcal{R}$, $|\rho_p(C_{index(last_q)})| \leq 1$, and thus $|W_p(C_{index(last_q)})| \leq 1$. Therefore $|W_p(C_{index(last_q)})| = 0$.
□

Lemma 19. *The names returned by any two distinct processes and are distinct.*

Proof. (Sketch.) Let n_p and n_q be the names returned by p and q, respectively. Let $\widehat{S}_p$ (respectively, $\widehat{S}_q$) be the value of S_p (respectively, S_q) when p (respectively, q) executes Line 12. The cases: $|\widehat{S}_p|, |\widehat{S}_q| \geq m - 1$ and $|\widehat{S}_p| < m - 1$ and $|\widehat{S}_q| \geq m - 1$ are straightforward, with proofs similar to the corresponding cases in the proof of Lemma 11. Consider the case $|\widehat{S}_p|, |\widehat{S}_q| < m - 1$ implying $n_p, n_q \leq m - 1$. Without loss of generality assume that $C_{index(last_p)}$ precedes $C_{index(last_q)}$ in Γ_E. By Lemma 18, $|W_p(C_{index(last_q)})| = 0$. Thus, $(p, n_p) \in \widehat{S}_q$. Therefore $proposed_q \neq n_p$ in Line 5.   □

Observation 20. *Let $\widehat{S}_p$ be the value of S_p created by Update in Line 5 following p's scan operation scan$_p$ in Line 3. Then $\forall q \in Procs(\widehat{S}_p)$, q performs at least one write before scan$_p$.*

Lemma 21. *Suppose that k is the number of participating processes. Then, any name returned by any process p, is in the range $\{1, \ldots, k\}$, if $k \leq m - 1$ and in the range $\{1, \ldots, n + m - 1\}$, if $k \geq m$.*

The proof of Lemma 21 is straightforward. It is omitted due to space constraints.

Theorem 22. *For any $m \geq 2$ there is an obstruction-free $(m - 1)$-bounded k-adaptive renaming algorithm implemented from $m + 1$ bounded registers such that when $k \geq m - 1$ the returned names are in the range $\{1, \ldots, n + m - 1\}$.*

Proof. There is an obstruction-free implementation of m-component snapshot objects from $m + 1$ bounded registers [14]. Since our algorithm in Fig. 2 is deterministic we can replace the atomic scan registers with a linearizable scan. By Lemma 21 and Lemma 19, the algorithm solves $(m-1)$-bounded k-adaptive renaming. Thus, it suffices to prove that the algorithm is obstruction-free.

If p runs alone then the value of S_p computed in Line 4 and $proposed_p$ computed in Line 5 remain the same. Therefore after m `write` operations all registers contain $(S_p, p, proposed_p)$. Therefore, in the m-th iteration of the repeat-until loop (Line 11) evaluates to true and p stops. $\qquad\square$

References

1. Afek, Y., Attiya, H., Dolev, D., Gafni, E., Merritt, M., Shavit, N.: Atomic snapshots of shared memory. J. of the ACM 40(4), 873–890 (1993)
2. Afek, Y., Merritt, M.: Fast, wait-free (2k-1)-renaming. In: Proc. of 18th PODC, pp. 105–112 (1999), J. of the ACM
3. Alistarh, D., Aspnes, J., Gilbert, S., Guerraoui, R.: The complexity of renaming. In: Proc. of 52nd FOCS, pp. 718–727 (2011)
4. Alistarh, D., Attiya, H., Gilbert, S., Giurgiu, A., Guerraoui, R.: Fast randomized test-and-set and renaming. In: Lynch, N.A., Shvartsman, A.A. (eds.) DISC 2010. LNCS, vol. 6343, pp. 94–108. Springer, Heidelberg (2010)
5. Attiya, H., Bar-Noy, A., Dolev, D., Peleg, D., Reischuk, R.: Renaming in an asynchronous environment. J. of the ACM 37(3), 524–548 (1990)
6. Attiya, H., Fich, F., Kaplan, Y.: Lower bounds for adaptive collect and related objects. In: Proc. of 23rd PODC, pp. 60–69 (2004)
7. Attiya, H., Welch, J.: Distributed Computing: Fundamentals, Simulations and Advanced Topics. John Wiley Interscience (2004)
8. Brodsky, A., Ellen, F., Woelfel, P.: Fully-adaptive algorithms for long-lived renaming. Journal of Distributed Computing 24(2), 119–134 (2011)
9. Burns, J., Lynch, N.: Bounds on shared memory for mutual exclusion. Journal of Information and Computation 107(2), 171–184 (1993)
10. Burns, J., Peterson, G.: The ambiguity of choosing. In: Proc. of 8th PODC, PODC 1989, pp. 145–157 (1989), J. of the ACM
11. Ellen, F., Woelfel, P.: An optimal implementation of fetch-and-increment. In: Afek, Y. (ed.) DISC 2013. LNCS, vol. 8205, pp. 284–298. Springer, Heidelberg (2013)
12. Fich, F., Herlihy, M., Shavit, N.: On the space complexity of randomized synchronization. J. of the ACM, 843–862 (1998)
13. Fich, F., Ruppert, E.: Hundreds of impossibility results for distributed computing. Distributed Computing 16(2-3), 121–163 (2003)
14. Giakkoupis, G., Helmi, M., Higham, L., Woelfel, P.: An $O(\sqrt{n})$ space bound for obstruction-free leader election. In: Afek, Y. (ed.) DISC 2013. LNCS, vol. 8205, pp. 46–60. Springer, Heidelberg (2013)
15. Helmi, M., Higham, L., Pacheco, E., Woelfel, P.: The space complexity of long-lived and one-shot timestamp implementations. J. of the ACM 61(1), 7–27 (2014)
16. Lynch, N.: Distributed Algorithms. Morgan Kaufmann (1996)

Lower Bounds for Structuring Unreliable Radio Networks*

Calvin Newport

Georgetown University
Washington, DC
cnewport@cs.georgetown.edu

Abstract. In this paper, we study lower bounds for randomized solutions to the maximal independent set (MIS) and connected dominating set (CDS) problems in the dual graph model of radio networks—a generalization of the standard graph-based model that now includes unreliable links controlled by an adversary. We begin by proving that a natural geographic constraint on the network topology is required to solve these problems efficiently (i.e., in time polylogarthmic in the network size). In more detail, we prove that in the absence of this constraint, for a network of size n: every MIS algorithm now requires $\Omega(n^{1-\epsilon})$ rounds to solve the problem, for any constant $\epsilon, 0 < \epsilon \leq 1$, and every CDS algorithm that provides a reasonable approximation of a minimum CDS now requires $\Omega(\sqrt{n}/\log n)$ rounds. We then prove the importance of the assumption that nodes are provided advance knowledge of their reliable neighbors (i.e, neighbors connected by reliable links). In more detail, we prove that in the absence of this assumption, for any CDS algorithm that guarantees a $g(n)$-approximation of a minimum CDS in $f(n)$ rounds, it follows that $g(n) + f(n) = \Omega(n)$. This holds even if we assume the geographic constraint and the weakest possible adversary controlling the unreliable links. Finally, we show that although you can efficiently build an MIS without advance neighborhood knowledge, this omission increases the problem's dependence on the geographic constraint. When both constraints are missing, every MIS algorithm now requires $\Omega(n)$ rounds, even if we assume the weakest possible adversary. Combined, these results answer an open question by proving that the efficient MIS and CDS algorithms from [2] are optimal with respect to their dual graph model assumptions. They also provide insight into what properties of an unreliable network enable efficient local computation.

1 Introduction

This paper proves four new lower bounds on the maximal independent set (MIS) and connected dominating set (CDS) problems in radio networks with unreliable links. These bounds establish the necessary model assumptions for building

---

* This work is supported in part by NSF grant number CCF 1320279 and the Ford Motor Company University Research Program.

F. Kuhn (Ed.): DISC 2014, LNCS 8784, pp. 318–332, 2014.

structures efficiently in this dynamic setting. In doing so, they also prove that the MIS and CDS algorithms of [2] are optimal with respect to their assumptions. As emphasized in previous studies (e.g., [11,14,2]), these two problems are important in the radio setting as they provide clusterings and routing backbones, respectively, both of which are useful to higher-level applications.

The Dual Graph Model. Theoreticians have studied distributed algorithms in radio network models since the 1980s. Most of this existing work assumes static models in which receive behavior depends on a fixed set of deterministic rules. This property is true, for example, of both the popular graph-based [3,1] and signal-strength [15] models. We argue that it is important, however, to also study radio network models that are more dynamic and less predictable. This type of model uncertainty can abstract the complex behavior observed in real wireless networks [17], and therefore improve the likelihood that properties proved in the theory setting will remain satisfied in a practical deployment. Our call for dynamic radio network models, in other words, is an attempt to help close the gap between theory and practice.

In a recent series of papers motivated by this argument, we study distributed computation in a dynamic radio network environment that we call the *dual graph* model [10,9,2,6,7]. This model generalizes the well-studied graph-based models [3,1] to now include two topology graphs. The first graph captures *reliable* links that are present in every round of the computation[1] and the second captures *unreliable* links that come and go as determined by a (bounded) adversary. The collision rules in each round are the same as in the standard graph-based models.

Results. In previous work [2], we studied the MIS and CDS problems in the dual graph model with an adaptive adversary and the following two strong assumptions: (1) a natural geographic constraint holds with respect to the dual graphs (see Section 2); and (2) the nodes are provided the ids of their reliable neighbors (i.e., neighbors in the reliable link graph) at the beginning of the execution. Under these assumptions, we described randomized MIS and CDS algorithms that are efficient, which we define in the following to mean time polylogarthmic in the network size. Furthermore, the CDS algorithm guarantees a structure that is a constant-approximation of a minimum CDS in the network. We note that in the standard graph-based model *without* unreliable links, the best known solutions to these problems are also polylogarthmic [14], indicating that the above assumptions enable algorithms to minimize the impact of unreliability.

In this paper, we explore the necessity of these two assumptions. We begin by proving that the geographic constraint is required to efficiently build an

---

[1] Notice, a more general approach to modeling unreliability would be to assume a single graph that changes from round to round. The dual graph model assumes the same reliable sub-graph is present in each each round because it enables more natural and simple definitions of standard problems; e.g., to define *broadcast*, we can simply say the message gets to all nodes connected to the source in the reliable sub-graph, and to define structuring algorithms, we can require that the structures to be correct with respect to this sub-graph—definitions that are complicated without this stability.

MIS or CDS in the dual graph model. In more detail, in Section 3.1 we prove that without this assumption, every randomized MIS algorithm now requires $\Omega(n^{1-\epsilon}/\log n)$ rounds to solve the problem in a network of size n, for any constant $\epsilon, 0 < \epsilon \leq 1$. We then prove, in Section 3.2, that any randomized CDS algorithm that guarantees to provide at least a $o(\sqrt{n})$-approximation of the minimum CDS now requires $\Omega(\sqrt{n}/\log n)$ rounds to solve the problem. In both cases, these results hold even when we weaken the adversary from the offline adaptive adversary assumed in [2] (which knows the nodes' random bits) to the weaker online adaptive adversary (which does not know these bits). Note that these lower bounds are exponentially worse than what is possible with the geographic constraint—underscoring its importance.

To prove our MIS lower bound, we show that any algorithm that works efficiently in this setting must work in a ring with a (non-geographic) unreliable link topology that allows a clever adversary to prevent many segments of the ring from receiving any messages. The nodes in these isolated segments must then make an MIS decision based only on their id and the ids of their neighbors (which, by assumption, they are provided). By repurposing a key combinatorial result due to Linial [13], we are able to show that for a particular method of assigning ids to the ring, it is likely that some isolated segments will make mistakes. To prove the CDS result, we use simulations of the algorithm in question to carefully build a challenging (non-geographic) dual graph network and id assignment in which it is likely that either the CDS is too large (leading to a bad approximation) or is not connected (violating correctness).

We proceed by exploring the necessity of the second assumption which provides nodes advance knowledge of their reliable neighbors. We emphasize that for structuring problems, nodes need *some* way to distinguish reliable links from unreliable links, as the problem definitions require that the structures be correct with respect to the reliable link graph (see Section 2). They do not, however, necessarily require advance knowledge of their reliable neighbors. With this in mind, we study what happens when we replace this advance knowledge assumption with a *passive* alternative that simply labels messages received from a reliable neighbor as reliable—leaving it up to the algorithm to discover these nodes.

We prove in Section 4.1 that the advance knowledge assumption is necessary to efficiently solve the CDS problem. In more detail, we prove that with a geographic constraint, the weakest possible adversary (a static adversary that never changes the unreliable links it includes), but only passive neighborhood knowledge, for any randomized CDS algorithm that guarantees to construct a $g(n)$-approximation of the minimum CDS in $f(n)$ rounds, it follows that $g(n) + f(n) = \Omega(n)$. We then turn our attention to the MIS problem. In Section 4.2, we first show that the MIS solution from [2] still works with passive knowledge—identifying a gap with respect to the CDS problem. We then prove, however, that the switch to passive knowledge *increases* the dependence of any MIS solution on the assumption of a geographic constraint. In particular, we prove that with the passive neighborhood knowledge, the static adversary, and no geographic constraint, every randomized MIS algorithm now requires $\Omega(n)$ rounds to solve the problem.

In both bounds, we rely on a static adversary that adds unreliable links between all nodes in all rounds. In such a network, only one node can successfully send a message in a given round (if any two nodes send, there will be a collision everywhere), but any successful message will be received by all nodes in the network. The key to the arguments is the insight that a received message is only useful if it comes from a reliable neighbor, and therefore, in each round, at most a small fraction of the network receives useful information. If we run the algorithm for a sufficiently small number of rounds, a significant fraction of nodes will end up making an MIS or CDS decision without *any* knowledge of their reliable neighborhood (as they did not receive any useful messages and we assume no advance knowledge of reliable neighbors). Our bounds use reductions from hard guessing games to careful network constructions to prove that many nodes are subsequently likely to guess wrong.

Implications. In addition to proving the algorithms from [2] optimal, our lower bounds provide interesting general insight into what enables efficient local computation in an unreliable environment. They show us, for example, that geographic network topology constraints are crucial—without such constraints, the MIS and CDS problems cannot be solved efficiently in the dual graph model, even with strong assumptions about neighborhood knowledge. Though existing structuring results in other radio network models all tend to use similar constraints (e.g., [11,14]), to the best of our knowledge this is the first time they are shown to be *necessary* in a radio setting. Our lower bounds also identify an interesting split between the MIS and CDS problems, which are typically understood to be similar (building an MIS is often a key subroutine in CDS algorithms). In particular, the MIS problem can still be solved efficiently with passive neighborhood knowledge, but the CDS problem cannot. Our intuition for this divide, as highlighted by the details of our proof argument (see Section 4.1), is that a CDS's requirement for reliable connectivity necessitates, in the absence of advance neighborhood knowledge, a sometimes laborious search through a thicket of unreliable links to find the small number of reliable connections needed for correctness.

Related Work. The dual graph model was introduced independently by Clementi et al. [4] and Kuhn et al. [10], and has since been well-studied [9,2,6,7]. In [2], we presented an MIS and CDS algorithm that both require $O(\log^3 n)$ rounds, for a network of size n and the strong assumptions described above. It was also shown in [2], that an efficient CDS solution is *impossible* if provided imperfect advance neighborhood knowledge (i.e., a list of reliable neighbors that can contain a small number of mistakes). In the classical graph-based radio network model [3,1], which does not include unreliable edges, the best known MIS algorithm requires $O(\log^2 n)$ rounds [14] (which is tight [8,5]), and assumes a similar geographic constraints as in [2] (and which we prove necessary in the dual graph model in this paper). Strategies for efficiently building a CDS once you have an MIS in the classical radio network model (with geographic constraints) are well-known in folklore. It is sufficient, for example, to simply connect all MIS nodes within 3 hops, which can be accomplished in this setting in $O(\log^2 n)$ rounds with a bounded randomized flood (see [2] for more discussion). Finally, we note that the dual graph model combined with the geographic constraint defined below is similar to the quasi-unit disk graph model [12]. The key difference, however, is that the dual graph model allows the set of unreliable links selected to change from round to round.

2   Model and Problems

The *dual graph* model describes a synchronous multihop radio network with both reliable and unreliable links. In more detail, the model describes the network topology with two graphs on the same vertex set: $G = (V, E)$ and $G' = (V, E')$, where $E \subseteq E'$. The $n = |V|$ nodes in V correspond to the wireless devices and the edges describe links. An *algorithm* in this model consists of n randomized *processes*. An execution of an algorithm in a given network (G, G') begins with an adversary assigning each process to a node in the graph. This assignment is unknown to the processes. To simplify notation, we use the terminology *node u*, with respect to an execution and vertex u, to refer to the process assigned to node u in the graph in the execution. Executions then proceed in synchronous rounds. In each round r, each node decides whether to transmit a message or receive based on its randomized process definition. The communication topology in this round is described by the edges in E (which we call the *reliable* links) plus *some subset* (potentially empty) of the edges in $E' \setminus E$ (which we call the *unreliable* links). This subset, which can change from round to round, is determined by a bounded adversary (see below for the adversary bounds we consider).

Once a topology is fixed for a given round, we use the standard communication rules for graph-based radio network models. That is, we say a node u receives a message m from node v in round r, if and only if: (1) node u is receiving; (2) node v is transmitting m; and (3) v is the only node transmitting among the neighbors of u in the communication topology *fixed by the adversary for r*. Notice, the dual graph model is a strict generalization of the classical graph-based radio network model (they are equivalent when $G = G'$).

Network Assumptions. To achieve the strongest possible lower bounds, we assume nodes are assigned unique ids from $[n]$ (where we define $[i]$, for any integer $i > 0$, to be the sequence $\{1, 2, ..., i\}$). Structuring algorithms often require constraints on the network topology. In this paper, we say a dual graph (G, G') satisfies the *geographic constraint*, if there exists some constant $\gamma \geq 1$, such that we can embed the nodes in our graph in a Euclidean plane with distance function d, and $\forall u, v \in V$, $u \neq v$: if $d(u, v) \leq 1$ then (u, v) is in G, and if $d(u, v) > \gamma$, (u, v) is not in G'. This constraint says that close nodes can communicate, far away nodes cannot, and for nodes in the *grey zone* in between, the behavior is controlled by the adversary.

We consider two assumptions about nodes' knowledge regarding the dual graph. The *advance* neighborhood knowledge assumption provides every node

u, at the beginning of the execution, the ids of its neighbors in G (which we also call u's *reliable* neighbors). This assumption is motivated by the real world practice of providing wireless algorithms a low-level neighbor discovery service. The *passive* neighborhood knowledge assumption, by contrast, labels received messages at a node u with a "reliable" tag if and only if the message was sent by a reliable neighbor. This assumption is motivated wireless cards' ability to measure the signal quality of received packets.

Adversary Assumptions There are different assumptions that can be used to bound the adversary that decides in the dual graph model which edges from $E'\backslash E$ to include in the communication topology in each round. Following the classical definitions of adversaries in randomized analysis, in this paper we consider the following three types: (1) the *offline adaptive* adversary, which when making a decision on which links to include in a given round r, can use knowledge of the network topology, the algorithm being executed, the execution history through round $r-1$, and the nodes' random choices for round r; (2) the *online adaptive* adversary, which is a weaker version of the offline adaptive variant that no longer learns the nodes' random choices in r before it makes its link decisions for r; and (3) a *static* adversary, which includes the same set of unreliable links in every round. In this paper, when we refer to the "⟨*adversary type*⟩ *dual graph model*", we mean the dual graph model combined with adversaries that satisfy the ⟨*adversary type*⟩ constraints.

The MIS and CDS Problems. Fix some undirected graph $H = (V, E)$. We say $S \subseteq V$ is a *maximal independent set* (MIS) of H if it satisfies the following two properties: (1) $\forall u, v \in S$, $u \neq v$: $\{u, v\} \notin E$ (no two nodes in S are neighbors in H); and (2) $\forall u \in V \setminus S$, $\exists v \in S$: $\{u, v\} \in E$ (every node in H is either in S or neighbors a node in S). We say $C \subseteq V$ is a *connected dominating set* (CDS) of H if it satisfies property 2 from the MIS definition (defined now with respect to C), and C is a connected subgraph of H.

In this paper, we assume the structuring algorithms used to construct an MIS or CDS run for a fixed number of rounds then have each node output a 1 to indicate it joins the set and a 0 to indicate it does not (that is, we consider Monte Carlo algorithms). It simplifies some of the lower bounds that follow to exactly specify how a node makes its decision to output 1 and 0. With this in mind, in this paper, we assume that at the end of a fixed-length execution, the algorithm provides the nodes a function that each node will use to map the following information to a probability $p \in [0, 1]$ of joining the relevant set: (1) the node's id; (2) the ids of the node's neighbors (in the advance neighborhood knowledge setting); and (3) the node's message history (which messages it received and in what rounds they were received). The node then outputs 1 with probability p and 0 with probability $1 - p$. For a given algorithm $\mathcal{A}$, we sometimes use the notation $\mathcal{A}.out$ to reference this function.

We say a structuring algorithm $\mathcal{A}$ *solves the MIS problem in* $f(n)$ *rounds* if it has each node output after $f(n)$ rounds, for network size n, and this output is a correct MIS with respect to G (the reliable link graph) with at least constant probability. We say an algorithm $\mathcal{A}$ *solves the CDS problem in $f(n)$ rounds and provides a $g(n)$-approximation* if it has each node output after $f(n)$ rounds, it guarantees that this output is a correct CDS with respect to G, *and* it guarantees the size of the CDS is within a factor of $g(n)$ of the size of the minimum-sized CDS for G, for network size n, also with at least constant probability.

3   The Necessity of Geographic Constraints

We begin by proving that the geographic constant is necessary to efficiently solve the MIS and CDS problem in the dual graph model. In both bounds we assume an online adaptive adversary, which is weaker than the offline adaptive adversary assumed in [2]—strengthening our results.

3.1   MIS Lower Bound

We prove that without the geographic constraint every MIS solution requires a time complexity that is arbitrarily close to $\Omega(n/\log n)$ rounds. This is exponentially worse than the $O(\log^3 n)$-round solution possible with this constraint. Our proof argument begins by introducing and bounding an abstract game that we call *selective ring coloring*. This game is designed to capture a core difficulty of constructing in MIS in this unreliable setting. We then connect this game to the MIS problem using a reduction argument.

The Selective Ring Coloring Game. The (g, n)-*selective ring coloring game* is defined a function $g : \mathbb{N} \to \mathbb{N}$ and some integer $n > 0$. The game is played between a player and a referee (both formalized as randomized algorithms) as follows. Let $t(n)$ be the set containing all $\frac{n!}{(n-3)!}$ ordered triples of values from $[n]$. In the first round, the player generates a mapping $C : t(n) \to \{1, 2, 3\}$ that assigned a color from $\{1, 2, 3\}$ to each triple in $t(n)$. Also during the first round, the referee assigns unique ids from $[n]$ to a ring of size n. In particular, we define the ring as the graph $R = (V, E)$, where $V = \{u_1, u_2, ..., u_n\}$, and $E = \{\{u_i, u_{i+1}\} \mid 1 \le i < n\} \cup \{u_n, u_1\}$. Let $\ell : V \to [n]$ be the bijection describing the referee's assignment of ids to this ring. The player and referee have no interaction during this round—their decisions regarding C and ℓ are made independently.

At the beginning of the second round, the player sends the referee C and the referee sends the player ℓ. Consider the coloring that results when we color each u_i in the ring with color $C(\ell(u_i^{CC}), \ell(u_i), \ell(u_i^{C}))$, where u_i^{CC} and u_i^{C} are u_i's counterclockwise and clockwise neighbors, respectively. Notice, it is possible that this graph suffers from some coloring violations. This brings us to the third round. In the third round, the player generates a set S containing up to $g(n)$ ids from $[n]$. It sends this set of *exceptions* to the referee. The referee considers the coloring of the nodes left in R once the exceptions and their incident edges are removed from the graph. If any coloring violations still remain, the referee declares that the player *loses*. Otherwise, it declares that the player *wins*.

A Lower Bound for Selective Ring Coloring. We now prove a fundamental limit on solutions to the selective ring coloring game. In particular, we prove that to win the game with constant probability requires a value of $g(n)$ that is close to n. To prove this lower bound we will make use of a useful combinatorial result established in Linial's seminal proof of the necessity of $\Omega(\log^* n)$ rounds to constant-color a ring in the message passing model. This result concerns the following graph definition which captures relationships between possible t-neighborhoods of a ring with ids from $[m]$:

Definition 1. *Fix two integers t and m, where $t > 0$ and $m > 2t+1$. We define the undirected graph $B_{t,m} = (V_{t,m}, E_{t.m})$ as follows:*

- $V_{t.m} = \{(x_1, x_2, ..., x_{2t+1}) \mid \forall i, j \in [2t+1] : x_i \in [m], i \neq j \Rightarrow x_i \neq x_j\}$.
- $E_{t,m} = \{\{v_1, v_2\} \mid v_1 = (x_1, ..., x_{2t+1}), v_2 = (y, x_1, ..., x_{2t}), y \neq x_{2t+1}\}$.

Notice that in the context of the message passing model, each node $(x_1, x_2, ..., x_{2t+1})$ in $B_{t,m}$ represents a potential *view* of a *target* node x_{t+1} in an execution, where *view* describes what ids a given node in the ring learns in a t round execution in this model; i.e., its id, and the id of nodes within t hops in both directions. The following result (adapted from Theorem 2.1 of [13]) bounds the chromatic number of $B_{t,m}$.

Lemma 1 (From [13]). *Fix two integers t and m, where $t > 0$ and $m > 2t+1$, and consider the graph $B_{t,m}$. It follows: $\chi(B_{t,m}) = \Omega(\log^{(2t)} m)$, where $\log^{(2t)} m$ is the $2t$ times iterated logarithm of m.*

We use this lemma in a key step in our following multi-step proof of the need for close to n exceptions to win selective ring coloring.

Lemma 2. *Let $\mathcal{P}$ be a player that guarantees to solve the (g, n)-selective ring coloring game with constant probability, for all n. It follows that for every constant $\epsilon, 0 < \epsilon \leq 1$: $g(n) = \Omega(n^{1-\epsilon})$.*

Proof. Assume for contradiction that for some constant ϵ that satisfies the constraints of the lemma statement, some $g(n) = o(n^{1-\epsilon})$, and some player $\mathcal{P}$ that guarantees for all n to win the (g, n)-selective ring coloring game with constant probability.

We start by describing a referee that will give $\mathcal{P}$ trouble. In more detail, to define ℓ, the referee first assigns i to node u_i, for all $i \in [n]$. It then partitions the ring with this preliminary assignment into consecutive sequences of nodes each of length $f(n) = n^{\epsilon/5}$. Finally, for each partition, it takes the ids assigned to nodes in the partition and permutes them with uniform randomness. We emphasize that the permutation in each partition is independent. We reference the $n/f(n)$ partitions[2] of R as $P_1, P_2, ..., P_{n/f(n)}$. We use $I_1, I_2, ..., I_{n/f(n)}$ to describe the corresponding ids in each partition.

---

[2] For simplicity of notation, we assume $f(n)$ and $n/f(n)$ are whole numbers. We can handle the other case through the (notationally cluttered) use of ceilings and floors.

To understand the effectiveness of this strategy we start by exploring the difficulty of correctly coloring these partitions. Intuitively, we note that a 1-round coloring algorithm in the message passing model needs more than a constant number of colors to guarantee to correctly color all permutations of a non-constant-sized partition. This intuition will provide the core of our upcoming argument that many of our referee's random id assignments generate coloring violations for any given C provided by $\mathcal{P}$. To formalize this intuition we leverage the result from Linial we established above. To do so, fix some P_i. Let b be a bijection from $[\|P_i\|]$ to I_i. Next consider $B^b_{1,f(n)}$, which we define the same as $B_{1,f(n)}$, except we now relabel each vertex (x, y, z) as $(b(x), b(y), b(z))$. By Lemma 1, we know that $\chi(B_{1,f(n)}) = \Omega(\log^{(2)} f(n))$. Clearly, this same result still holds for $\chi(B^b_{1,f(n)})$ (as we simply transformed the labels). Notice, because $f(n) = \omega(1)$, it follows that for sufficiently large n, $\chi(B^b_{1,f(n)})$ is strictly larger than 3. Fix this value of n for the remainder of this proof argument.

We now consider a specific instance of our game with $\mathcal{P}$, our referee, and our fixed value of n. Focus as above on partition P_i. Let C be the coloring function produced by the player and ℓ the assignment produced by our referee. Because we just established that the chromatic number of $B^b_{1,f(n)}$ is larger than 3, if we color this graph with C (which uses only three colors), there are (at least) two neighbors $v_1 = (x_1, x_2, x_3)$ and $v_2 = (y, x_1, x_2)$ in the graph that are colored the same.

It follows that if ℓ happens to assign the sequence of ids y, x_1, x_2, x_3 to four consecutive nodes in P_i, C will color x_1 and x_2 the same, creating a coloring violation.[3] We can now ask what is the probability that this bad sequence of ids is chosen by ℓ? This probability is crudely lower bounded by $|I_i|^{-4} = f^{-4}(n)$. We can now expand our attention to the total number of partitions with coloring violations. To do so, we define the following indicator variables to capture which partitions have coloring violations:

$$\forall j \in [n/f(n)], X_j = \begin{cases} 1 & \text{if } P_j \text{ has a coloring violation w.r.t. } C \text{ and } \ell, \\ 0 & \text{else.} \end{cases}$$

We know from above that for any particular j, $\Pr[X_j = 1] > f^{-4}(n)$. It follows directly from our process for defining ℓ that this probability is independent for each X_j. If $Y = X_1 + X_2 + \ldots + X_{n/f(n)}$ is the total number of coloring violations, therefore, by linearity of expectation, and the fact that $f(n) = n^{\epsilon/5}$, the following holds:

$$\mathbb{E}[Y] = \mathbb{E}[X_1] + \mathbb{E}[X_2] + \ldots + \mathbb{E}[X_{n/f(n)}] > \frac{n}{f^5(n)} = n^{1-\epsilon}.$$

A straightforward application of Chernoff tells us that Y is within a constant factor of this expectation with high probability in n. We are now ready to pull

---

[3] A subtlety in this step is that we need $|P_i| = f(n) \geq 4$. If this is not true for the value of n fixed above we can just keep increasing this value until it becomes true.

together the pieces to reach our contradiction. We have shown that with high probability our referee strategy, combined with player $\mathcal{P}$, generates at least $n^{1-\epsilon}$ coloring violations, with high probability. We assumed, however, that $g(n) = o(n^{1-\epsilon})$. It follows (for sufficiently large n) that with high probability, the player will not have enough exceptions to cover all the coloring violations. His success probability, therefore, is sub-constant. This contradicts our assumption that the player wins with at least constant probability for this definition of g.

Connecting Selective Ring Coloring to the MIS Problem. Our next step is to connect the process of building an MIS in our particular wireless model to achieving efficient solutions to the ring coloring game we just bounded. At a high-level, this argument begins by noting that if you can build an MIS fast then you can three color a ring fast. It then notes this if you can three-color a ring fast in our online adaptive model, then you can do so with an adversary that ends up forcing many partitions in the ring to decide without receiving a message (and therefore, base their decision only on the ids of their reliable neighbors). To conclude the proof, we show that the coloring generated by this function can be used to win the selective ring coloring game. The faster the original MIS algorithm works, the smaller the g for which it can solve selective ring coloring. The proof details for the below lemma can be found in the full version [16].

Lemma 3. *Let $\mathcal{A}$ be an algorithm that solves the MIS problem in $g(n)$ rounds, for some polynomial g, in the online adaptive dual graph model with a network size of n, advance neighborhood knowledge, but no geographic constraint. It follows that there exists a player $\mathcal{P}_\mathcal{A}$ that solves the (g', n)-selective coloring game with some constant probability p', where $g'(n) = O(g(n) \cdot \log n)$.*

Our final theorem follows directly from Lemmata 2 and 3:

Theorem 1. *Let $\mathcal{A}$ be an algorithm that solves the MIS problem in $f(n)$ rounds in the online adaptive dual graph model with a network size of n, advance neighborhood knowledge, and no geographic constraint. It follows that for every constant ϵ, $0 < \epsilon \leq 0$, $f(n) = \Omega(n^{1-\epsilon}/\log n)$.*

As an immediate corollary to the above, we note that the family of functions described by $\Omega(n^{1-\epsilon}/\log n)$ is equivalent to the family described by $\Omega(n^{1-\epsilon})$, allowing for the omission of the $\log n$ divisor if desired in describing the bound.

3.2   CDS Lower Bound

We now prove the necessity of the geographic constraint for the CDS problem. In particular, we prove that in the absence of this constraint, any CDS algorithm that guarantees a reasonable approximation now requires $\Omega(\sqrt{n}/\log n)$ rounds. This is worse than the $O(\log^3 n)$ solution that provides a $O(1)$-approximation that is possible with this constraint. Unlike our lower bound in the previous section, we do not use a reduction argument below. We instead deploy the more traditional strategy of using the definition of a fixed algorithm to construct a network in which the algorithm performs poorly.

Theorem 2. *Let $\mathcal{A}$ be an algorithm that solves the CDS problem in $f(n)$ rounds and provides a $o(\sqrt{n})$-approximation in the online adaptive dual graph model with a network size of n, advance neighborhood knowledge, and no geographic constraint. It follows that $f(n) = \Omega(\sqrt{n}/\log n)$.*

Proof. Assume for contradiction that there exists some algorithm $\mathcal{A}$ that achieves an $o(\sqrt{n})$-approximation in $f(n) \leq \sqrt{n}/(2\log n)$ rounds with (at least) constant probability p. Our proof proceeds in two steps. During the first step, we use the definition of $\mathcal{A}$ to construct a challenging dual graph network $(G_\mathcal{A}, G'_\mathcal{A})$ and assignment of ids to nodes in that network. The second step describes and analyzse an online adaptive adversary that causes $\mathcal{A}$, with sufficiently high probability, to either violate correctness or produce (at best) an $\Omega(\sqrt{n})$-approximation of the minimum CDS when run in this network with these id assignments. This yields the needed contradiction.

Beginning with the first step, we fix $k = \sqrt{n}$ (assume for simplicity that $\sqrt{n}$ is a whole number, the proof easily extends to fractional values, but at the expense of increased notational cluttering). To construct our dual graph $(G_\mathcal{A}, G'_\mathcal{A})$, we first fix $G'_\mathcal{A}$ to be the complete graph over all n nodes. (It is here we potentially violate the geographic constraint.) To define $G_\mathcal{A}$, we partition the set $I = [n]$ of unique ids from 1 to n into sets $C_1, C_2, ..., C_k$ of size k. We will now create a subgraph of size k in $G_\mathcal{A}$ for each C_h and assign ids from C_h to these nodes. In particular, for each id partition C_h, let $i_0 \in C_h$ be the smallest id in C_h. We add a node to $G_\mathcal{A}$ and assign it id i_0. We call this the *core* node for C_h. Moving forward in our process, let $C'_h = C_h \setminus \{i_0\}$. We call C'_h a *point set*.

We must now add nodes corresponding to the ids in point set C'_h. To do so, for each $i \in C'_h$, we define p_i^h to be the probability that i joins the CDS as defined by the function $\mathcal{A}.out$ applied to id i, neighbor set $C'_h \setminus \{i\}$, and an empty message history (see Section 2). We call each such p^h value a *join probability*. How we add nodes to the graph associated with point set C'_h depends on the join probability values. In more detail, we consider two cases:

Case 1: $\forall i \in C'_h : p_i^h \geq 1/2$. In this case, we add a clique of size $k-1$ to the graph. We then assign the ids in C'_h to nodes in this clique arbitrarily. Finally, we choose one $i \in C'_h$ to act as a *connector*, and connect the node with this id to the core node for C_h that we previously identified. Notice, the neighbor set for i is different now than it was when we calculated p_i^h, but for all other nodes with ids in C'_h, the neighbor sets are the same.

Case 2: $\exists i \in C'_h : p_i^h < 1/2$. In this case, we add a clique of size $k-2$ to the graph, then add an edge from a single *connector* node in the clique to a new node, that we call the *extender*, then connect the extender to our previously identified core node for this set. Let i be the id from C'_h for which the property that defines this case holds. We assign this id to the connector. We then assign the ids from $C'_h \setminus \{i\}$ to the clique and extender nodes arbitrarily. Notice, in this case, the node with the id i is the *only* id in C'_h for which its neighbor set is the same here as it was when its join probability was calculated.

We repeat this behavior for every set C_h, $h \in [k]$. Finally, to ensure our graph is connected, we add edges between all ℓ core nodes to form a clique.

Having now used the definition of $\mathcal{A}$ to define a specific reliable link graph $G_{\mathcal{A}}$, and an id assignment to this graph, consider the behavior of $\mathcal{A}$ when executed in $(G_{\mathcal{A}}, G'_{\mathcal{A}})$, with this specfied id assignment, and an online adaptive adversary that behaves as follows in each round r. By definition, the adversary knows the probability that each node in the network will broadcast in this round, so it can therefore calculate $\mathbb{E}[B_r]$, the expected value of B_r, the actual number of broadcasters in round r. If $\mathbb{E}[B_r] \geq b \log n$, for a constant $b > 0$ we will fix later, then the adversary includes all edges in the network for r, and otherwise it includes *no* extra edges from $G'_{\mathcal{A}} \setminus G_{\mathcal{A}}$.

Notice, this is the same online adaptive adversary strategy we used in the proof of Lemma 3, and as in that proof, a standard Chernoff analysis tells us that for any constant $c \geq 1$, there exists a constant b that guarantees that with probability at least $1 - n^{-c}$, in any round in which more than $\log n$ nodes broadcast, all edges from $G'_{\mathcal{A}}$ are included in the network by the adversary. If we combine this property with the observation that no node in $G_{\mathcal{A}}$ neighbors more than one set C'_h (by "neighbors C_h" we mean neighbors at least one node in C_h), it follows that with this same high probability no more than $\log n$ point sets include a node that receives a message in any given round.

At this point, we remind ourselves of our assumption that $f(n) \leq \sqrt{n}/(2 \log n)$. If our communication bound from above holds, it would then hold that in $f(n)$ rounds, at least half of the $\sqrt{n}$ point sets received no messages. Moving forward, assume this property holds. Let us consider what will happen when the nodes in these *silent* point sets decide whether or not to join the CDS by using the probabilities specified by $\mathcal{A}.out$ applied to their neighborhood ids and an empty message history.

There are two possibilities. The first possibility is that half or more of these silent points sets fell under Case 1 from our above procedure. For each such point set, there are $\sqrt{n} - 2$ nodes that will now join the CDS with probability at least $1/2$ (i.e., the nodes in C'_h with the exception of the connector). The expected number of nodes that join from this point set is therefore at least $\frac{\sqrt{n}-2}{2}$. (Key in this result is the fact that these nodes are in silent sets, which means they have received *no* messages, and therefore their behavior is based on an independent coin flip weighted according to the probability returned by $\mathcal{A}.out$.) Given that we have at least $\sqrt{n}/2$ such silent point sets, the total expected number of nodes that join is in $\Omega(n)$ (by linearity of expectation). A Chernoff bound concentrates this expectation around the mean and provides that with high probability in n, the total number of nodes that join is within a constant factor of this linear expectation.

The second possibility is that half or more of these silent point sets fall under Case 2. For each such silent point set, the connector node *does not join* with probability at least $1/2$. Notice, if the connector does not join, then its point set is disconnected from the rest of the network, and therefore, the overall CDS is not correct. Because there are at least $\sqrt{n}/2$ silent point sets in this case that are violating correctness with probability at least $1/2$, the probability that this CDS is correct is exponentially small in n.

We are left to combine the probabilities of the relevant events. We have shown that with high probability, a $f(n)$-round execution of $\mathcal{A}$ in $(G_\mathcal{A}, G'_\mathcal{A})$, with our above adversary strategy, concludes with at least half of the point sets having received no messages. If this event occurs, then there are two possibilities analyzed above concerning whether these silent point sets mainly fall under Case 1 or 2 from our graph construction procedure. We proved that the first possibility leads to a $\Omega(\sqrt{n})$-approximation with high probability (as with this probability, $\Omega(n)$ nodes join in a network where $O(\sqrt{n})$ nodes is sufficient to form a CDS), and the second possibility leads to a lack of connectivity with (very) high probability. A union bound on either of these two events (many silent sets and bad performance given many silent sets) failing yields a sub-constant probability. This probability, however, upper bounds the probability of the algorithm satisfying the theorem. This provides our contradiction.

4   The Necessity of Advance Neighborhood Knowledge

In this section we explore the importance of advance neighborhood knowledge by proving new lower bounds for the MIS and CDS problems when provided the weaker assumption of passive neighborhood knowledge.

4.1   CDS Lower Bound

In this section, we prove that any CDS solution requires both the geographic constraint *and* advance neighborhood knowledge. In more detail, we prove below that if we assume the geographic constraint but only passive neighborhood knowledge, any CDS algorithm now requires either a slow time complexity or a bad approximation factor (formally, these two values must add to something linear in the network size). Our bound reduces k-isolation, a hard guessing game, to the CDS problem.

The k-Isolation Game. The game is defined for an integer $k > 0$ and is played by a player $\mathcal{P}$ modeled as a synchronous randomized algorithm. At the beginning of the game, a *referee* chooses a target value $t \in [k]$ with uniform randomness. The player $\mathcal{P}$ now proceeds in rounds. In each round, the player can guess a single value $i \in [k]$ by sending it to referee. If $i = t$, the player wins. Otherwise, it is told it did not win and continues to the next round. Once again, the straightforward probabilistic structure of the game yields a straightforward bound:

Lemma 4. *Fix some $k > 1$ and $r \in [k]$. No player can win the k-isolation game in r rounds with probability better than r/k.*

Connecting Isolation to the CDS Problem. We now reduce this isolation game to CDS construction. To do so, we show how to use a CDS algorithm to construct an isolation game player that simulates the algorithm in a barbell network (two cliques connected by a single edge) with the bridge nodes indicating the target. The proof details for the below theorem can be found in the full version [16].

Theorem 3. *Let $\mathcal{A}$ be an algorithm that solves the CDS problem in $f(n)$ rounds and provides a $g(n)$-approximation in the static dual graph model with a network of size n, passive neighborhood knowledge, and the geographic constraint. It follows that $g(n) + f(n) = \Omega(n)$.*

4.2   MIS Lower Bound

It is straightforward to show that the MIS algorithm from [2] still works if we replace the advance neighborhood knowledge assumption with its passive alternative (the algorithm uses this knowledge only to discard messages it receives from unreliable neighbors). We prove below, however, that the passive assumption increases the fragility of any MIS solution. In particular, we show that when we switch from advance to passive, the bound from Section 3.1 now increases to $\Omega(n)$ and still holds even with a static adversary. As before, we use a reduction argument from a hard guessing game.

The k-Bit Revealing Game. The game is defined for an integer $k > 0$ and is played by a player $\mathcal{P}$ modeled as a synchronous randomized algorithm. At the beginning of the game, a *referee* generates a sequence κ of k bits, where each bit is determined with uniform and independent randomness. In the following, we use the notation $\kappa[i]$, for $i \in [k]$, to refer to the ith bit in this sequence. The player $\mathcal{P}$ now proceeds in rounds. In each round, it can request a value $i \in [k]$, and the adversary will respond by returning $\kappa[i]$. At the end of any round (i.e., after the bit is revealed), the player can decide to guess κ by sending the referee a sequence $\hat{\kappa}$ of k bits. If $\hat{\kappa} = \kappa$, the player wins; otherwise it loses. We say a player $\mathcal{P}$ solves the k-bit revealing game in $f(k)$ rounds with probability p, if with probability p it wins the game by the end of round $f(k)$. Given the well-behaved probabilistic structure of this game, the following bound is straightforward to establish.

Lemma 5. *Fix some $k > 1$ and $t \in [k]$. No player can solve the k-bit revealing game in t rounds with probability $p > 2^{-(k-t)}$.*

Connecting Bit Revealing to the MIS Problem. We now reduce our bit revealing game to the more complex task of building an MIS in a non-geographic static dual graph network. In particular, we will show how to use an MIS algorithm to solve the bit revealing game by having a player simulate the algorithm in a carefully constructed dual graph network. In this network, we partition nodes into sets, such that we can match these sets to bits, and use the MIS decisions of nodes in a given set to guess the corresponding bit in the revealing game. The proof details for the below theorem can be found in the full version [16].

Theorem 4. *Let $\mathcal{A}$ be an algorithm that solves the MIS problem in $f(n)$ rounds in the static dual graph model with a network of size n, passive neighborhood knowledge, and no geographic constraint. It follows that $f(n) = \Omega(n)$.*

References

1. Bar-Yehuda, R., Goldreich, O., Itai, A.: On the Time-Complexity of Broadcast in Multi-Hop Radio Networks: An Exponential Gap between Determinism and Randomization. Journal of Computer and System Sciences 45(1), 104–126 (1992)
2. Censor-Hillel, K., Gilbert, S., Kuhn, F., Lynch, N., Newport, C.: Structuring Unreliable Radio Networks. In: Proceedings of the ACM Conference on Distributed Computing (2011)
3. Chlamtac, I., Kutten, S.: On Broadcasting in Radio Networks–Problem Analysis and Protocol Design. IEEE Transactions on Communications 33(12), 1240–1246 (1985)
4. Clementi, A., Monti, A., Silvestri, R.: Round Robin is Optimal for Fault-Tolerant Broadcasting on Wireless Networks. Journal of Parallel and Distributed Computing 64(1), 89–96 (2004)
5. Farach-Colton, M., Fernandes, R.J., Mosteiro, M.A.: Lower Bounds for Clear Transmissions in Radio Networks. In: Correa, J.R., Hevia, A., Kiwi, M. (eds.) LATIN 2006. LNCS, vol. 3887, pp. 447–454. Springer, Heidelberg (2006)
6. Ghaffari, M., Haeupler, B., Lynch, N., Newport, C.: Bounds on Contention Management in Radio Networks. In: Aguilera, M.K. (ed.) DISC 2012. LNCS, vol. 7611, pp. 223–237. Springer, Heidelberg (2012)
7. Ghaffari, M., Lynch, N., Newport, C.: The Cost of Radio Network Broadcast for Different Models of Unreliable Links. In: Proceedings of the ACM Conference on Distributed Computing (2013)
8. Jurdziński, T., Stachowiak, G.: Probabilistic Algorithms for the Wakeup Problem in Single-Hop Radio Networks. In: Bose, P., Morin, P. (eds.) ISAAC 2002. LNCS, vol. 2518, pp. 535–549. Springer, Heidelberg (2002)
9. Kuhn, F., Lynch, N., Newport, C., Oshman, R., Richa, A.: Broadcasting in Unreliable Radio Networks. In: Proceedings of the ACM Conference on Distributed Computing (2010)
10. Kuhn, F., Lynch, N., Newport, C.: Brief Announcement: Hardness of Broadcasting in Wireless Networks with Unreliable Communication. In: Proceedings of the ACM Conference on Distributed Computing (2009)
11. Kuhn, F., Moscibroda, T., Wattenhofer, R.: Initializing Newly Deployed Ad Hoc and Sensor Networks. In: Proceedings of the International Conference on Mobile Computing and Networking (2004)
12. Kuhn, F., Wattenhofer, R., Zollinger, A.: Ad-Hoc Networks Beyond Unit Disk Graphs. In: Proceedings of the International Workshop on the Foundations of Mobile Computing (2003)
13. Linial, N.: Locality in Distributed Graph Algorithms. SIAM Journal on Computing 21(1), 193–201 (1992)
14. Moscibroda, T., Wattenhofer, R.: Maximal Independent Sets in Radio Networks. In: Proceedings of the ACM Conference on Distributed Computing (2005)
15. Moscibroda, T., Wattenhofer, R.: The Complexity of Connectivity in Wireless Networks. In: Proceedings of the IEEE International Conference on Computer Communications (2006)
16. Newport, C.: Lower Bounds for Structuring Unreliable Radio Networks. Full version available on ArXiv and the author's publication web site: http://cs.georgetown.edu/~cnewport/publications.html
17. Newport, C., Kotz, D., Yuan, Y., Gray, R.S., Liu, J., Elliott, C.: Experimental Evaluation of Wireless Simulation Assumptions. Simulation 83(9), 643–661 (2007)

Random Walks on Evolving Graphs
with Recurring Topologies*

Oksana Denysyuk and Luís Rodrigues

INESC-ID, Instituto Superior Técnico, Universidade de Lisboa
{oksana.denysyuk,ler}@ist.utl.pt

Abstract. In this paper we consider dynamic networks that can change over time. Often, such networks have a repetitive pattern despite constant and otherwise unpredictable changes. Based on this observation, we introduce the notion of a ρ-*recurring family* of a dynamic network, which has the property that the dynamic network frequently contains a graph in the family, where frequently means at a rate $0 < \rho \leq 1$. Using this concept, we reduce the analysis of max-degree random walks on dynamic networks to the case for static networks. Given a dynamic network with a ρ-recurring family $\mathcal{F}$, we prove an upper bound of $O\left(\rho^{-1}\hat{t}_{hit}(\mathcal{F}) \log n\right)$ on the hitting and cover times, and an upper bound of $O\left(\rho^{-1}(1 - \hat{\lambda}(\mathcal{F}))^{-1} \log n\right)$ on the mixing time of random walks, where n is the number of nodes, $\hat{t}_{hit}(\mathcal{F})$ is upper bound on the hitting time of graphs in $\mathcal{F}$, and $\hat{\lambda}(\mathcal{F})$ is upper bound on the second largest eigenvalue of the transition matrices of graphs in $\mathcal{F}$. These results have two implications. First, they yield a general bound of $O\left(\rho^{-1}n^3 \log n\right)$ on the hitting time and cover time of a dynamic network (ρ is the rate at which the network is connected); this result improves on the previous bound of $O\left(\rho^{-1}n^5 \log^2 n\right)$ [3]. Second, the results imply that dynamic networks with recurring families preserve the properties of random walks in their static counterparts. This result allows importing the extensive catalogue of results for static graphs (cliques, expanders, regular graphs, etc.) into the dynamic setting.

1 Introduction

In this paper we consider dynamic networks that can change over time. These networks abstract many important systems, such as mobile networks, where nodes may change neighbors as they move; and peer-to-peer networks, where nodes may connect or disconnect due to churn. A dynamic network is modeled as an *evolving graph*, which is a sequence of graphs $\mathcal{G} = \{G_i\}$ over n nodes, each graph representing a snapshot of the system at a given instant.

Much recent work has considered dynamic networks, by proposing and analyzing new algorithms [11,17,24] and by deriving new complexity bounds [18,26]. Because of their generality, dynamic networks are not only of theoretical importance, but also

---

* This work was partially supported by Fundação para a Ciência e Tecnologia (FCT) via the project PEPITA (PTDC/EEI-SCR/2776/2012) and via the INESC-ID multi-annual funding through the PIDDAC Program fund grant, under project PEst-OE/EEI/LA0021/2013.

F. Kuhn (Ed.): DISC 2014, LNCS 8784, pp. 333–345, 2014.
© Springer-Verlag Berlin Heidelberg 2014

of practical relevance. At the same time, this generality makes it hard to derive strong results, which has motivated new properties that constrain the behavior of dynamic networks. Unfortunately, existing properties are either too restrictive or hard to evaluate in practice (see Section 2).

We propose a new and intuitive approach to study dynamic networks, by looking at families of graphs that recur frequently in the dynamic network. Informally, a ρ-*recurring family* of an evolving graph $\mathcal{G}$ is a family $\mathcal{F}$ of (static) graphs such that, with frequency ρ, some graph in $\mathcal{F}$ appears in the sequence $\mathcal{G}$. For example, if $\rho = 1/2$, then half of the graphs in the sequence $\mathcal{G}$ belong to $\mathcal{F}$; note that it is possible that no individual graph in $\mathcal{F}$ recurs with frequency $1/2$. Also note that the other half of the graphs in the sequence $\mathcal{G}$ may be completely arbitrary and even contain a different recurring family.

Every evolving graph has a trivial 1-recurring family, the family of all graphs. But real networks may have other more interesting recurring families because, by their own nature, these networks tend to preserve certain topological characteristics. For example, nodes in a peer-to-peer network may keep a constant number of neighbors [28]; such network has graphs with constant degree as a recurring family. Also, numerous dynamic networks build and maintain global structures, such as overlay rings [32] or routing trees [31]; in these examples, the recurring families are graphs with the required ring or tree structures. Table 1 has more examples of recurring families in various contexts.

In this paper, we focus on the study of random walks. Due to their simplicity, locality, low overhead, and correct operation under topology changes, random walks have been recently used in different types of dynamic networks for a number of applications: querying, searching, routing, topology maintenance, etc. [4,13,15,30,27].

We show that recurring families can be used to reduce the analysis of random walks in dynamic networks—which are complex—to the simpler case of static networks—which are well understood. Specifically, we give upper bounds on the behavior of random walks in dynamic networks based on similar bounds in static networks, given a recurring family.

In this study, we make two assumptions. First, we assume an *oblivious* adversary controlling the dynamic network; that is, the evolution of the graph is independent of the position of the random walk. Without this assumption, the adversary can degenerate the random walk, causing it to oscillate forever between two nodes (see Section 3). Second, we assume a *max-degree* random walk: at each node, the probability of transitioning to each neighbor is $1/d_{max}$, where d_{max} is the maximum degree of the graph. For nodes with degree $d < d_{max}$, there is a probability of $1 - d/d_{max}$ of remaining at the node. Max-degree random walks are a well-behaved variant of *simple* random walks—which choose each neighbor uniformly at random—but simple random walks can have an erratic behavior in dynamic networks [3] (e.g., their cover time can be exponential).

Our main result states that, if $\mathcal{F}$ is a ρ-recurring family of an evolving graph $\mathcal{G}$, then a max-degree random walk on $\mathcal{G}$ has hitting time and cover time of $O\left(\rho^{-1}\hat{t}_{hit}(\mathcal{F})\log n\right)$ and mixing time of $O\left(\rho^{-1}(1-\hat{\lambda}(\mathcal{F}))^{-1}\log n\right)$, where $\hat{t}_{hit}(\mathcal{F})$ is an upper bound on the hitting time of graphs in $\mathcal{F}$, and $\hat{\lambda}(\mathcal{F})$ is an upper bound on the second largest eigenvalue of the transition matrices of graphs in $\mathcal{F}$. To prove these results, we consider the *homogeneous* Markov Chains of the graphs in the recurring family, and relate these chains to the *time non-homogeneous* Markov Chain of the random walk on the dynamic network. Specifically, using arguments from matrix analysis, we analyze the transition matrices in the recurring family and obtain bounds on the algebraic properties (eigenvalues, etc.) for each matrix considered as a homogeneous Markov chain. We then relate the product of the matrices in the recurring family to the product of all matrices in the non-homogeneous chain, and map the bounds to the original dynamic network.

The obtained bounds are nearly tight and have two important implications. First, they reduce the known gap between the complexity of random walks in dynamic and static networks. In particular, in static networks, the cover time has a general upper bound of $O(n^3)$ [2][1], but in dynamic networks, the previously known bound was much higher: $O(\rho^{-1} n^5 \log^2 n)$ [3], where ρ is the frequency with which the network is connected. We reduce this gap to just a $\log n$ factor: by using the trivial ρ-recurring family of all connected graphs, we obtain a general bound of $O(\rho^{-1} n^3 \log n)$.

Second, these results imply that dynamic networks with ρ-recurring families preserve the random-walk properties of their static counterparts. It is thus possible to import the extensive catalogue of results for random walks on static graphs to the dynamic setting. For instance, it is known that random walks are especially efficient on certain families of graphs, such as expanders. For expanders, hitting time is $O(n)$, cover time is $O(n \log n)$ and mixing time is $O(\log n)$. Thus, in evolving graphs where expanders appear frequently, we can derive stronger bounds. We say that evolving graph $\mathcal{G}$ has a ρ-recurring expander if fraction ρ of the graphs in $\mathcal{G}$ are expanders. Then, it follows that, for $\mathcal{G}$, hitting time is $O(\rho^{-1} n \log n)$, cover time is $O(\rho^{-1} n \log n)$, and mixing time is $O(\rho^{-1} \log n)$, respectively.

In summary, this paper makes the following contributions:

- we introduce a novel property of evolving graphs, which we call a *ρ-recurring family*;
- using recurring families, we derive new bounds for a random walk on an evolving graph;
- we show that random walks on evolving graphs with recurring families preserve the properties of their static counterparts;
- we argue that our bounds are nearly tight and improve upon previously known bounds.

Paper Organization. The remainder of this paper is organized as follows. Section 2 discusses related work. Section 3 states the model and Section 4 defines the problem addressed in this paper. In Section 5 we state the main results and in Section 6 we discuss their implications. In Section 7 we sketch the proofs. Finally, Section 8 presents the conclusions and outlines directions for future work.

---

[1] More precisely, [2] proves an $O(nm)$ cover time bound of a *simple* random walk on a graph with n nodes and m edges. It can be shown that the *max-degree* random walk on a graph is equivalent to a simple random walk on the graph, augmented with sufficiently many self-loops, such that the degree of each node is d_{max}. In such augmented graph $m \leq n^2$; thus, [2] implies an $O(n^3)$ cover time bound for the max-degree random walk (we defer the complete proof to the full version of the paper).

2 Related Work

Dynamic Networks. There is a growing interest in the study of graphs that evolve over time, representing a variety of dynamic networks. Different models of dynamic networks have been proposed, each capturing specific features of some concrete scenario. Random changes of links are considered in [8]. In [9], the authors propose a model of a dynamic network where the existence of an edge in a round stochastically depends on its existence in the previous round. Adversarial networks have also received attention [8,24,16,26], representing a worst-case scenario where link changes are controlled by an adversary that tries to slow down communication. This last model covers the widest range of different network behaviors; therefore, we adopt it for our study.

Different properties have been proposed to analyze algorithms in such networks. For an extensive discussion, we refer the interested reader to [7] and [25]. In [24], the authors propose an elegant concept of T-interval connectivity and use it to study token dissemination. Evolving graph $\mathcal{G}$ is T-interval connected if, for every T consecutive rounds, there exists a connected spanning subgraph of $\mathcal{G}$ that does not change. T-interval connectivity is a strong property and may be too restrictive for some real world scenarios. Moreover, we focus on random walks, and this property is not well-suited for this problem, because the behavior of a random walk is not governed by a stable spanning subgraph. For example, a lollipop graph has cover time of $\Theta(n^3)$, despite having a line as a spanning subgraph, which has a cover time of $\Theta(n^2)$. Here, the existence of the line does not help the cover time of the lollipop. By contrast, we show that recurring families closely relate to the behavior of random walks in the evolving graph. In fact, our results imply that T-interval connectivity is not necessary for the random walk to make fast progress, as long as the evolving graph forms good topologies often enough.

Another popular property of the dynamic network is its *dynamic diameter* [11,24,26], which is the worst-case number of rounds required to route a piece of information from any given node to all other nodes. Intuitively, the concept of dynamic diameter is useful in the study of information spreading. Unfortunately, however, the dynamic diameter is hard to estimate in a real network, which is a practical drawback.

A number of other papers study information spreading in dynamic networks, e.g., [17,18]. Our paper differs from these works because it proposes and uses a different property to study dynamic networks (recurring families) and it focuses on a different problem, random walks.

Random Walks. Much work has considered random walks on static graphs, with the proposal of bounds for many families of graphs. For a comprehensive survey please refer to [29]. More recently, there has been growing interest in random walks in dynamic settings. In [10] the authors study random walks on a graph that evolves by adding new node with random or preferential connections to existing nodes. Since the graph grows, one never visits all nodes, and so the usual notions of hitting, cover, and mixing times (which we consider) do not apply.

In [13], the authors consider connected randomly evolving graphs where, in each round, the set of edges for a node is chosen uniformly at random. The authors show that the random walk on such evolving graph is essentially a random walk on a clique:

each transition can be seen as a random choice of a list of neighbors and then a random choice of an item in the list. Thus, the cover time of such graph is $O(n \log n)$. This result does not apply to adversarial evolving graphs (which we consider). For example, if an adversary chooses a sparse random graph and never changes it, then the cover time of such graph is $O(n^2 \log n)$ [21].

To our knowledge, [3] is the first paper to address randoms walks on adversarial evolving graphs. The authors show that the behavior of a *simple* random walk on evolving graphs can differ significantly from the static case. In particular, the cover time of a simple random walk can be exponential as demonstrated by an example of a dynamic star over nodes $0, \ldots, n-1$, where in round t the center of the star is node t mod $(n-1)$, and the remaining nodes are leaves. In addition, all nodes have self-loops, allowing the random walk to remain at one node for several rounds. Notice that node $n-1$ is never at the center of the star. The only way the walk can reach node $n-1$ is by staying at some leaf for $n-2$ rounds until this leaf becomes a center of the star (if the walk moves to the center too soon, the process starts over, because the center will itself be a leaf again in the next round). The probability that the random walk stays at a leaf for $n-2$ consecutive rounds is $\frac{1}{2^{(n-2)}}$; hence, the cover time is $\Omega\left(2^n\right)$. Additionally, [3] gives a $O\left(\rho^{-1} d_{max}^2 n^3 \log^2 n\right)$ [3] bound on the cover time of a max-degree random walk on $\mathcal{G}$, where ρ is the fraction of connected graphs $\mathcal{G}$ and d_{max} is the maximum degree of any graph in $\mathcal{G}$. The result of [3] implies the general bound of $O\left(\rho^{-1} n^5 \log^2 n\right)$ for any evolving graph. We improve this result to the nearly tight $O(\rho^{-1} n^3 \log n)$. Our results also give stronger bounds on evolving graphs with structure, as we later explain.

Random walks in dynamic networks are also considered in [11], which studies simple random walks on connected *regular* evolving graphs. Note that the results of [11] also apply to *max-degree* random walks on any connected evolving graph. The authors formally discuss the notion of mixing time in a dynamic network and give a $O((1 - \lambda)^{-1} \log n)$ bound where λ is an upper bound on the second largest (in absolute value) eigenvalue of *all* transition matrices of graphs in $\mathcal{G}$. This result is weaker than ours for two reasons. First, it considers only mixing time and not hitting nor cover times. Second, the bound in [11] is governed by the *worst* graph appearing in the entire evolving graph, whereas our bounds are governed by the good graphs that appear frequently. The authors of [11] also propose an algorithm for distributed computation of a random walk that runs in $O(\sqrt{t_{mix}\tau})$ rounds where t_{mix} is the mixing time and τ is the dynamic diameter of the evolving graph. The analysis of the running time of this algorithm can benefit from our new results on the mixing time in dynamic networks with structure (which we explain later).

3   Evolving Graph Model

We consider an undirected network with a fixed set V of n nodes, where edges between nodes may change over time. Execution proceeds in synchronous rounds, where in each round an adversary chooses the set of links connecting pairs of nodes. An execution generates an evolving graph, which is a sequence $\mathcal{G} = G_1, G_2, \ldots$ of graphs over nodes V, where G_t is a snapshot of the evolving graph in round t. We omit reference to V when it is clear from the context.

Definition 1 (ρ**-Recurring Family**). *Given an evolving graph $\mathcal{G} = G_1, G_2, \ldots$ and a number $0 < \rho \leq 1$, a ρ-recurring family $\mathcal{F}$ of $\mathcal{G}$ is a family of graphs such that, for every $M \geq 1$, at least $\lfloor \rho M \rfloor$ elements in $G_1, \ldots, G_M$ are in $\mathcal{F}$.*

Intuitively, this definition requires that, with frequency at least ρ, the graphs in a ρ-recurring family appear in $\mathcal{G}$. The definition can be weakened to require the frequency ρ to hold only for sufficiently large M; the results in this paper can be easily modified to work with this weaker definition.

Note that every evolving graph has a 1-recurring family, the family of all (including disconnected) graphs on V. Also, if $\mathcal{F}$ is a ρ-recurring family of $\mathcal{G}$ then we can add any graphs to $\mathcal{F}$ and still have a ρ-recurring family of $\mathcal{G}$. Generally, we are interested in small recurring families, because our bounds are based on the worst graph in the family.

The paper focuses on random walks on $\mathcal{G}$. We assume an *oblivious adversary* that determines the evolving graph without knowledge of the random walk. Without this assumption, an adaptive adversary could degenerate the random walk using a simple strategy: in odd rounds, the adversary provides the current position v_i of the random walk with a single edge to some fixed node v_j. In even rounds the adversary provides v_j with a single edge to v_i. Under this strategy, the random walk oscillates between v_i and v_j forever. Such a random walk never converges (it has infinite mixing time, hitting time, etc).

4 Random Walk Definition

We assume that, in round one, a random walk starts at some node of a given evolving graph and, in each round, it moves from a node to one of its neighbors with certain probability. We consider a max-degree random walk: at every node, we move to a given neighbor with fixed probability $1/d_{max}$, where d_{max} is the maximum degree of the graph or an upper bound on the maximum degree (if d_{max} is unknown, we can let $d_{max} = n$); with probability $1 - d/d_{max}$ we do not move, where d is the node degree. The max-degree random walk can be seen as a simple random walk on a graph augmented with self-loops so that every node has the same degree d_{max}. We further make the standard assumption of an aperiodic random walk; this can be ensured, for example, by avoiding bipartite graphs or by assuming that all nodes have self-loops.

Max-degree aperiodic random walks are attractive for two reasons. First, in steady state, it is easy to show that every node has equal probability; this property is useful for applications that require fairness, such as fair token circulation [20]. Second, the random walk avoids the poor exponential behavior that simple random walks may exhibit [3].

We are interested in the following asymptotic properties of the random walk, which are natural extensions of the properties of random walks on static graphs. Given evolving graph $\mathcal{G}$:

- Hitting time $t_{hit}(\mathcal{G})$ is the maximal expected number of rounds before the random walk visits some node of $\mathcal{G}$;
- Cover time $t_{cov}(\mathcal{G})$ is the expected number of rounds before the random walk visits every node of $\mathcal{G}$ at least once;

- Mixing time $t_{mix}(\mathcal{G})$ is the expected number of rounds before reaching the steady state distribution of the random walk on $\mathcal{G}$ (if such distribution exists).

5 Statement of the Main Results

We now state the upper bounds on the hitting time, cover time, and mixing time of random walks on evolving graphs, based on the properties of a recurring family of that graph. The graph will generally have many recurring families; the bounds apply to each of them.

For a family $\mathcal{F}$ of graphs, let $\hat{t}_{hit}(\mathcal{F})$ be an upper bound on the hitting time of the graphs in $\mathcal{F}$ and $\hat{\lambda}(\mathcal{F})$ be an upper bound on the second largest eigenvalue of the transition matrices of the graphs in $\mathcal{F}$. Our main results are the following:

Theorem 2. *Let $\mathcal{G}$ be an evolving graph over n nodes and $\mathcal{F}$ be a ρ-recurring family of $\mathcal{G}$. The hitting time and cover time of a max-degree random walk on $\mathcal{G}$ are bounded by*

$$t_{hit}(\mathcal{G}) \leq t_{cov}(\mathcal{G}) = O\left(\rho^{-1}\hat{t}_{hit}(\mathcal{F})\log n\right).$$

Theorem 3. *Let $\mathcal{G}$ be an evolving graph over n nodes and $\mathcal{F}$ be a ρ-recurring family of $\mathcal{G}$. The mixing time of a max-degree random walk on $\mathcal{G}$ is bounded by*

$$t_{mix}(\mathcal{G}) = O\left(\rho^{-1}(1-\hat{\lambda}(\mathcal{F}))^{-1}\log n\right).$$

The bounds on cover time and mixing time are tight in the sense that there is an evolving graph that matches the bounds; meanwhile, the bounds on hitting time are within $\log n$ factor from the optimal. Specifically, take an evolving graph $\mathcal{G}$ that is a static expander, that is $\mathcal{G} = G, G, \dots$ where G is an expander. Then $\mathcal{G}$'s hitting time is $\Theta(n)$, its cover time is $\Theta(n \log n)$, and its mixing time is $O\left((1 - \hat{\lambda}(\{G\}))^{-1}\log n\right)$. We see that the cover and mixing times match Theorems 2 and 3, while the hitting time is within a $\log n$ factor.

Thus, the behavior of the random walk on evolving graphs can be studied via its recurring families. Doing so allows importing the results on static graphs to the dynamic setting. We next give several applications of this idea.

6 Implications

General Bound. In some cases, little is known about the topology of the dynamic network $\mathcal{G}$; its changes over time can be arbitrary and unpredictable. However, if we only know that there exists some $\rho > 0$ such that, for every $M \geq 1$, $\mathcal{G}$ is connected in at least ρM rounds, we can apply our results to obtain non-trivial bounds[2]. For such $\mathcal{G}$, we can take the ρ-recurring family of all connected graphs and obtain the following result:

---

[2] If $\mathcal{G}$ does not remain connected for any fraction ρ of rounds, its mixing, hitting, and cover times can be infinite.

Theorem 4. *Let $\mathcal{G}$ be an evolving graph such that, for every $M \geq 1$, $\mathcal{G}$ is connected in at least ρM rounds. Then, the hitting time and cover time of a max-degree random walk on $\mathcal{G}$ are bounded by*
$$t_{cov}(\mathcal{G}) = O\left(\rho^{-1} n^3 \log n\right).$$
This theorem improves on the cover time bound of $O\left(\rho^{-1} n^5 \log^2 n\right)$ in [3]. The proof is by direct application of Theorem 2.

Relevant ρ-Recurring Families. We can model many dynamic networks by evolving graphs with structure. For instance, many mobile ad hoc networks have cliques as recurring families. Cliques have excellent mixing and hitting times of only $\Theta(1)$ and $\Theta(n)$. However, unfavorable topologies can emerge frequently, such as lollipop and barbell graphs, which have poor mixing and hitting times of $\Theta(n^3)$. If $\mathcal{G}'$ forms a clique at least a fraction $\rho > 0$ of the time—we say that $\mathcal{G}'$ has a ρ-recurring clique—then even if $\mathcal{G}'$ has frequent lollipops and barbell graphs, our results show that its behavior is governed by the good topologies. Here, the ρ-recurring clique provides an intuitive example: when the network forms a clique, the random walk can jump to any node, irrespective of the remaining rounds. It is thus easy to see that the random walk quickly covers the network. Theorems 2 and 3 yield a bound of $O(\rho^{-1} n \log n)$ on the cover and hitting times of $\mathcal{G}'$ and a bound of $O(\rho^{-1} \log n)$ on the mixing time. By contrast, the result in [11], which is governed by the worst graphs in $\mathcal{G}'$, yields a much looser bound of $O(n^3 \log n)$ on the mixing time (and no results on hitting and cover time). With a little more work, we can further improve the bounds of Theorems 2 and 3 using the same proof techniques, to obtain tight bounds for all metrics, as stated in the following theorem:

Theorem 5. *If evolving graph $\mathcal{G}$ has a ρ-recurring clique, then the mixing time of a max-degree random walk on $\mathcal{G}$ is $O(\rho^{-1})$, the hitting time is $O(\rho^{-1} n)$, and the cover time is $O(\rho^{-1} n \log n)$.*

Expander graphs are another important recurring family in many dynamic networks. For instance, some unstructured peer-to-peer overlays seek to maintain good expansion properties [28]. Our results imply that an evolving graph with ρ-recurring bounded-degree expander has $O(\rho^{-1} n \log n)$ cover time and $O(\rho^{-1} \log n)$ mixing time. Thus, regardless of arbitrary topologies generated during transition periods, a random walk on such evolving graph preserves the properties of its good static topologies.

In Table 1 we illustrate more implications of our results. All the graphs in the table have $(d_{max} - d_{min}) < c$, for some constant c. This property minimizes the difference between simple and max-degree random walks, allowing us to use the bounds for simple random walks in static graphs (the intuition is that adding bounded holding probabilities does not change the asymptotic behavior of the random walk).

Unions as ρ-Recurring Families. We further note that a recurring family $\mathcal{F}$ can be defined as a union of multiple well-known families of graphs. As an example, consider a network arranged in a ring in which one fixed link is intermittent (e.g., it may be an unstable link in a radio network). We can model such network as an evolving graph. When the link is present, the graph is a ring; when the link is absent, the graph is a chain. We may have no information about what fraction ρ of the time the graph is a ring or chain, making it impossible to apply our results to either ring or chain. However,

Table 1. New bounds obtained from Theorems 2, 3, and 5, for a max-degree random walk on evolving graphs, with the corresponding recurring families

ρ-recurring family	occurrence in dynamic networks	cover time	mixing time	static ref
cliques	mobile ad-hoc networks mesh networks	$O(\rho^{-1}n\log n)$	$O(\rho^{-1})$	[14]
regular and nearly regular	structured overlays(rings) unstructured overlays	$O(\rho^{-1}n^2\log n)$	$O(\rho^{-1}n^2\log n)$	[22]
2-dim grids	sensor networks	$O(\rho^{-1}n\log^2 n)$	$O(\rho^{-1}n\log n)$	[12]
bound.degree trees	routing overlays	$O(\rho^{-1}n^2\log n)$	$O(\rho^{-1}n^2\log n)$	[5]
d-regular expanders	unstructured overlays	$O(\rho^{-1}n\log n)$	$O(\rho^{-1}\log n)$	[6]

we can take the ρ-recurring family to contain *both* the ring and chain, and in this case $\rho = 1$. Then, Theorems 2 and 3 give strong bounds of $O\left(n^2\log n\right)$ on the hitting and cover times, and of $O\left(n^2\log n\right)$ on the mixing time. In this example, the intermittent link was fixed, but the example carries through identically even if the intermittent link varies over time.

7 Proofs

In this section we sketch the proofs of the main results. Due to space constraints, the complete proofs have been deferred to the full version of the paper.

Preliminaries and Main Technique. Let $\mathcal{G} = G_1, G_2, \ldots$ be an evolving graph; in each round t, A_{G_t} denotes the transition probability matrix of the random walk on G_t. If $\mathbf{p}_t = (p_1, p_2, \ldots, p_n)$ is the probability distribution on the nodes in round t, then, the probability distribution on the nodes in round $t + 1$ is calculated by $\mathbf{p}_{t+1} = \mathbf{p}_t A_{G_t}$. Hence, the random walk on $\mathcal{G}$ can be modeled as a stochastic process that holds the Markov property, i.e., each transition of the random walk depends only on its current position and the transition probabilities in a given round. This kind of stochastic processes is known in the literature as *time non-homogeneous* Markov chains [23].

We model the random walk on evolving graphs as a time non-homogeneous Markov chain and work with products of stochastic matrices. For conciseness, we denote by $\mathcal{G}_{\rho,\mathcal{F}}$ an evolving graph $\mathcal{G}$ with a ρ-recurring family $\mathcal{F}$. In the analysis of $\mathcal{G}_{\rho,\mathcal{F}}$, we rely on the common algebraic properties of the stochastic matrices of graphs in $\mathcal{F}$. We then use the fact that, for any $M > 0$, in a set of M matrices, there are at least ρM matrices with those properties, to obtain the overall bounds.

For the mixing time we use the well known relation to the second largest eigenvalue. For the hitting and cover times, we bound the spectral radii of principal submatrices (i.e., matrices resulting from deleting an i-the row and an i-th column). The bound on the spectral radii of the principal submatrices is related to the hitting time of the *homogeneous* Markov chain.

Below we summarize the notation used in our proofs.

Notation

- $\|\mathbf{v}\|_p = \sqrt[p]{\sum_{i=1}^n |v_i|^p}$ for some vector $\mathbf{v} = (v_1, \ldots, v_n)$.
- $\lambda_1(A) \geq \lambda_2(A) \geq \ldots \geq \lambda_n(A)$ are eigenvalues of square matrix A.
- $\lambda(A) = \max\{|\lambda_2(A)|, |\lambda_n(A)|\}$.
- $\hat{\lambda}(\mathcal{F}) = \max_{G \in \mathcal{F}} \lambda(A_G)$, where A_G is the transition matrix of a max-degree random walk on G.
- $\delta(A) = \max_i |\lambda_i(A)|$ is spectral radius of matrix A.
- $\left\|\mathbf{v} - \mathbf{w}\right\|_{TV} = \max_{X \in \Omega} |\mathbf{v}(X) - \mathbf{w}(X)|$ denotes the total variation of two probability measures $\mathbf{v}$ and $\mathbf{w}$ over Ω.
- $t_{hit}(G)$ is the hitting time of graph G.
- $\hat{t}_{hit}(\mathcal{F})$ denotes upper bound on the hitting times of all graphs in family $\mathcal{F}$.
- $\mathcal{G}_{\rho,\mathcal{F}}$ denotes an evolving graph $\mathcal{G}$ with a ρ-recurring family $\mathcal{F}$.

Recall that we make the standard aperiodicity assumption. Moreover, as a result of using the max-degree strategy, the transition probability matrices A_{G_t}, in each round t, are symmetric and doubly stochastic (i.e., every row sums to one and every column sums to one). Therefore, each A_{G_t} has eigenvector $\frac{\mathbf{i}}{n} = \left(\frac{1}{n}, \frac{1}{n}, \ldots\right)$ with a corresponding eigenvalue $\lambda_1(A_{G_t}) = 1$.

Also, since the matrices A_{G_t} are real symmetric with all entries $0 \leq a_{i,j} \leq 1$, for any $i, j \leq n$, all eigenvalues of A_{G_t} are real (see e.g. [19]). In particular, $-1 < \lambda_n(A_{G_t}) \leq \ldots \leq \lambda_1(A_{G_t}) \leq 1$ (the strict inequality follows from aperiodicity). Also, when G_t is connected, $\lambda(A_{G_t}) = \max\{|\lambda_2(A_{G_t})|, |\lambda_n(A_{G_t})|\} < 1$. Hence, if the evolving graph is connected in sufficiently many rounds, the resulting time non-homogeneous Markov chain is ergodic and has unique stationary distribution $\pi = \frac{\mathbf{i}}{n}$.

Mixing Time. We start by bounding the mixing time. The *convergence rate* of the Markov chain is the rate at which the chain approaches stationary distribution. For *homogeneous* chains, the spectral gap of the transition matrix, i.e. the difference between the largest and the second largest eigenvalues in absolute value, defines the convergence rate to the stationary distribution [1].

The following Lemma 6 bounds the convergence rate of a max-degree random walk on an evolving graph in any given round t.

Lemma 6. *If $\mathbf{p}_t = (p_1, \ldots, p_n)$ is a probability distribution on nodes of G_t, then*

$$\left\|\mathbf{p}_{t+1} - \frac{\mathbf{i}}{n}\right\|_2^2 \leq \lambda^2(A_{G_t}) \left\|\mathbf{p}_t - \frac{\mathbf{i}}{n}\right\|_2^2.$$

The following Lemma 7 establishes the monotonicity property of distribution p_t: whenever G_t belongs to $\mathcal{F}$, the random walk on $\mathcal{G}_{\rho,\mathcal{F}}$ gets closer to the stationary distribution at a known rate, while never moving away from the stationary distribution in the remaining rounds.

Lemma 7. *Consider a max-degree random walk on $\mathcal{G}_{\rho,\mathcal{F}}$. Let $\hat{\lambda}(\mathcal{F})$ denote an upper bound on the second largest (in absolute value) eigenvalues of the stochastic matrices of all graphs in $\mathcal{F}$ (i.e., $\forall_{G \in \mathcal{F}} \lambda(A_G) \leq \hat{\lambda}(\mathcal{F})$). It holds that*

$$\left\|\mathbf{p}_{t+1} - \frac{\mathbf{i}}{n}\right\|_2^2 \leq \left(\hat{\lambda}(\mathcal{F})\right)^{2\rho t} \left\|\mathbf{p}_1 - \frac{\mathbf{i}}{n}\right\|_2^2.$$

We are now ready to prove the bound on the mixing time in Theorem 3. We use the standard definition of the mixing time via the total variation distance to the steady state distribution (e.g., [1]):

$$t_{mix} = min \left\{ t: \left\| \mathbf{P}_t - \pi \right\|_{TV} < \tfrac{1}{4} \right\}.$$

This definition gives the expected value of minimal random time at which the random walk has the stationary distribution.

We use the standard method of bounding the total variation distance via the 2-norm distance to the steady state distribution.

By taking $t = O\left(\rho^{-1} (1 - \hat{\lambda}(\mathcal{F}))^{-1} \log n \right)$ and applying Lemma 7, we show that after t rounds, the total variation distance is less than $\tfrac{1}{4}$.

Hitting Time and Cover Time. We take an arbitrary node j and remove the corresponding row and column from matrix A_{G_t}. Let A' be the resulting matrix. Lemma 8 connects the largest eigenvalue of A' to the largest eigenvalue of the fundamental matrix $(\mathbb{I} - A')^{-1}$.

Lemma 8. *Let A_{G_t} be the transition probability matrix of a max-degree random walk on graph G_t. Let A' be an $(n-1) \times (n-1)$ matrix resulting from deleting the j-th row and j-th column from A_{G_t}, for some $1 \leq j \leq n$. And let $\mathbb{I}$ be an $(n-1) \times (n-1)$ identity matrix. Then,*

$$\lambda_1 (A') = 1 - \frac{1}{\lambda_1 \left((\mathbb{I} - A')^{-1} \right)}.$$

The following lemma uses Lemma 8 to connect the spectral radius of A' to the hitting time of the deleted node j.

Lemma 9. *Let A_{G_t} be the transition probability matrix of a max-degree random walk on graph G_t. Let A' be an $(n-1) \times (n-1)$ matrix resulting from deleting the j-th row and j-th column from A_{G_t}, for some $1 \leq j \leq n$. Then,*

$$\delta(A') \leq \begin{cases} \left(1 - \frac{1}{t_{hit}(G_t)}\right) & \text{if } G_t \text{ is connected} \\ 1 & \text{otherwise.} \end{cases}$$

We now sketch the proof of Theorem 2. We take an arbitrary node i and remove the corresponding rows and columns from the matrices $A_{G_1}, A_{G_2}, \ldots$. We use the bounds on the spectral radii of these submatrices, given in Lemma 9, to obtain the bound on the spectral radius of the product of those submatrices. Then, we relate the spectral radius of the product to the hitting time of the deleted node i. The cover time is obtained by the union bound over all n nodes.

8 Conclusions

We have introduced the notion of a ρ-recurring family of evolving graphs, which has the property that the evolving graph frequently contains a graph in the family. We believe that recurring families is a natural and powerful concept to understand many real dynamic networks.

We have studied max-degree random walks and, using the concept of recurring families, derived bounds on hitting, cover, and mixing times of an evolving graph with a ρ-recurring family $\mathcal{F}$. These results imply that dynamic networks with recurring families preserve the properties of random walks in their static counterparts. This allows importing the extensive catalogue of results for static graphs into the dynamic setting.

We believe that ρ-recurring families may be useful to study other problems in dynamic networks, such as rumour spreading, information dissemination, and token circulation. We leave this as future work.

Acknowledgements. The authors are grateful to Fabian Kuhn and the anonymous referees for their valuable feedback on the previous versions of the paper.

References

1. Aldous, D., Fill, J.A.: Reversible Markov Chains and Random Walks on Graphs. Unpublished (1995)
2. Aleliunas, R., Karp, R.M., Lipton, R.J., Lovász, L., Rackoff, C.: Random walks, universal traversal sequences, and the complexity of maze problems. In: 20th Annual Symposium on Foundations of Computer Science, FOCS 1979, pp. 218–223 (1979)
3. Avin, C., Koucký, M., Lotker, Z.: How to explore a fast-changing world (cover time of a simple random walk on evolving graphs). In: Aceto, L., Damgård, I., Goldberg, L.A., Halldórsson, M.M., Ingólfsdóttir, A., Walukiewicz, I. (eds.) ICALP 2008, Part I. LNCS, vol. 5125, pp. 121–132. Springer, Heidelberg (2008)
4. Bar-Yossef, Z., Friedman, R., Kliot, G.: Rawms - random walk based lightweight membership service for wireless ad hoc networks. ACM Trans. Comput. Syst. 26(2), 1–66 (2008)
5. Brightwell, G., Winkler, P.: Extremal cover times for random walks on trees. Journal of Graph Theory 14(5), 547–554 (1990)
6. Broder, A.Z., Karlin, A.R.: Bounds on the cover time. J. Theoretical Probab. 2, 101–120 (1988)
7. Casteigts, A., Flocchini, P., Quattrociocchi, W., Santoro, N.: Time-varying graphs and dynamic networks. International Journal of Parallel, Emergent and Distributed Systems 27(5), 387–408 (2012)
8. Clementi, A.E.F., Pasquale, F., Monti, A., Silvestri, R.: Communication in dynamic radio networks. In: Proceedings of the Twenty-sixth Annual ACM Symposium on Principles of Distributed Computing, PODC 2007, pp. 205–214. ACM, New York (2007)
9. Clementi, A.E.F., Macci, C., Monti, A., Pasquale, F., Silvestri, R.: Flooding time in edge-markovian dynamic graphs. In: PODC 2008, pp. 213–222. ACM, New York (2008)
10. Cooper, C., Frieze, A.: Crawling on simple models of web graphs. Internet Mathematics 1, 57–90 (2003)
11. Das Sarma, A., Molla, A.R., Pandurangan, G.: Fast distributed computation in dynamic networks via random walks. In: Aguilera, M.K. (ed.) DISC 2012. LNCS, vol. 7611, pp. 136–150. Springer, Heidelberg (2012)
12. Dembo, A., Peres, Y., Rosen, J., Zeitouni, O.: Cover times for brownian motion and random walks in two dimensions. Annals of Mathematics 160(2), 433–464 (2004)
13. Dolev, S., Schiller, E., Welch, J.L.: Random walk for self-stabilizing group communication in ad hoc networks. IEEE Transactions on Mobile Computing 5, 893–905 (2006)
14. Feige, U.: A tight lower bound on the cover time for random walks on graphs. Random Struct. Algorithms 6, 433–438 (1995)

15. Gkantsidis, C., Mihail, M., Saberi, A.: Random walks in peer-to-peer networks: algorithms and evaluation. Perform. Eval. 63, 241–263 (2006)
16. Haeupler, B.: Analyzing network coding gossip made easy. In: Proceedings of the 43rd Annual ACM Symposium on Theory of Computing, STOC 2011, pp. 293–302. ACM, New York (2011)
17. Haeupler, B., Karger, D.: Faster information dissemination in dynamic networks via network coding. In: Proceedings of the 30th Annual ACM SIGACT-SIGOPS Symposium on Principles of Distributed Computing, PODC 2011, pp. 381–390. ACM, New York (2011)
18. Haeupler, B., Kuhn, F.: Lower bounds on information dissemination in dynamic networks. In: Aguilera, M.K. (ed.) DISC 2012. LNCS, vol. 7611, pp. 166–180. Springer, Heidelberg (2012)
19. Horn, R.A., Johnson, C.R.: Matrix analysis. Cambridge University Press, New York (1986)
20. Ikeda, S., Kubo, I., Okumoto, N., Yamashita, M.: Fair circulation of a token. IEEE Transactions on Parallel and Distributed Systems 13(4), 367–372 (2002)
21. Jonasson, J.: On the cover time for random walks on random graphs. Comb. Probab. Comput. 7(3), 265–279 (1998)
22. Kahn, J.D., Linial, N., Nisan, N., Saks, M.E.: On the cover time of random walks on graphs. Journal of Theoretical Probability 2(1), 121–128 (1989)
23. Kirkland, S.: Nonhomogeneous matrix products. World Scientific, River Edge (2002)
24. Kuhn, F., Lynch, N., Oshman, R.: Distributed computation in dynamic networks. In: Proceedings of the 42nd ACM Symposium on Theory of Computing, STOC 2010, pp. 513–522. ACM, New York (2010)
25. Kuhn, F., Oshman, R.: Dynamic networks: Models and algorithms. SIGACT News 42(1), 82–96 (2011)
26. Kuhn, F., Oshman, R., Moses, Y.: Coordinated consensus in dynamic networks. In: Proceedings of the 30th Annual ACM SIGACT-SIGOPS Symposium on Principles of Distributed Computing, PODC 2011, pp. 1–10. ACM, New York (2011)
27. Law, C., Siu, K.-Y.: Distributed construction of random expander networks. In: Twenty-Second Annual Joint Conference of the IEEE Computer and Communications, INFOCOM 2003, vol. 3, pp. 2133–2143. IEEE Societies (2003)
28. Leitao, J., Pereira, J., Rodrigues, L.: Hyparview: A membership protocol for reliable gossip-based broadcast. In: In IEEE/IFIP International Conference on Dependable Systems and Networks, DSN 2007, pp. 419–428. IEEE Computer Society (2007)
29. Lovász, L.: Random walks on graphs: A survey (1993)
30. Massoulié, L., Le Merrer, E., Kermarrec, A.-M., Ganesh, A.: Peer counting and sampling in overlay networks: random walk methods. In: Proceedings of the Twenty-fifth Annual ACM Symposium on Principles of Distributed Computing, PODC 2006, pp. 123–132. ACM, New York (2006)
31. Perkins, C.E., Royer, E.M.: Ad-hoc on-demand distance vector routing. In: Proceedings of the Second IEEE Workshop on Mobile Computer Systems and Applications, WMCSA 1999, pp. 90–100. IEEE Computer Society, Washington, DC (1999)
32. Stoica, I., Morris, R., Karger, D., Frans Kaashoek, M., Balakrishnan, H.: Chord: A scalable peer-to-peer lookup service for internet applications. In: Proceedings of the 2001 Conference on Applications, Technologies, Architectures, and Protocols for Computer Communications, SIGCOMM 2001, pp. 149–160. ACM, New York (2001)

Randomized Rumor Spreading
in Poorly Connected Small-World Networks

Abbas Mehrabian[1,*] and Ali Pourmiri[2]

[1] Department of Combinatorics and Optimization, University of Waterloo,
Waterloo, Ontario, Canada
amehrabi@uwaterloo.ca
[2] Max Planck Institute for Informatics, Saarbrücken, Germany
pourmiri@mpi-inf.mpg.de

Abstract. The Push-Pull protocol is a well-studied round-robin rumor spreading protocol defined as follows: initially a node knows a rumor and wants to spread the rumor to all nodes in a network quickly. In each round, every informed node sends the rumor to a random neighbor, and every uninformed node contacts a random neighbor and gets the rumor from her if she knows it. We analyze the behavior of this protocol on random k-trees, a class of power law graphs which are small-world and have large clustering coefficients, built as follows: initially we have a k-clique. In every step a new node is born, a random k-clique of the current graph is chosen, and the new node is joined to all nodes of the k-clique. When $k > 2$ is fixed, we show that if initially a random node is aware of the rumor, then with probability $1 - o(1)$ after $\mathcal{O}\left((\log n)^{(k+3)/(k+1)} \cdot \log\log n \cdot f(n)\right)$ rounds the rumor propagates to $n - o(n)$ nodes, where n is the number of nodes and $f(n)$ is any slowly growing function. When $k = 2$, the previous statement holds for $\mathcal{O}\left(\log^2 n \cdot \log\log n \cdot f(n)\right)$ many rounds. Since these graphs have polynomially small conductance, vertex expansion $\mathcal{O}(1/n)$ and constant treewidth, these results demonstrate that Push-Pull can be efficient even on poorly connected networks.

On the negative side, we prove that with probability $1 - o(1)$ the protocol needs at least $\Omega\left(n^{(k-1)/(k^2+k-1)}/f^2(n)\right)$ rounds to inform all nodes. This exponential dichotomy between time required for informing *almost all* and *all* nodes is striking. Our main contribution is to present, for the first time, a natural class of random graphs in which such a phenomenon can be observed. Our technique for proving the upper bound successfully carries over to a closely related class of graphs, the random k-Apollonian networks, for which we prove an upper bound of $\mathcal{O}\left((\log n)^{(k^2-3)/(k-1)^2} \cdot \log\log n \cdot f(n)\right)$ rounds for informing $n - o(n)$ nodes with probability $1 - o(1)$, when $k > 2$ is a constant.

Keywords: randomized rumor spreading, push-pull protocol, random k-trees, random k-Apollonian networks.

* Supported by the Vanier Canada Graduate Scholarships program. Part of this work was done while the author was visiting Monash University, Australia.

F. Kuhn (Ed.): DISC 2014, LNCS 8784, pp. 346–360, 2014.
© Springer-Verlag Berlin Heidelberg 2014

1   Introduction

Randomized rumor spreading is an important primitive for information dissemination in networks and has numerous applications in network science, ranging from spreading information in the WWW and Twitter to spreading viruses and diffusion of ideas in human communities (see [5, 10–12, 19]). A well studied rumor spreading protocol is the *Push-Pull protocol*, introduced by Demers, Greene, Hauser, Irish, Larson, Shenker, Sturgis, Swinehart, and Terry [9]. Suppose that one node in a network is aware of a piece of information, the 'rumor.' The protocol proceeds in rounds. In each round, every *informed* node contacts a random neighbor and sends the rumor to it ('pushes' the rumor), and every *uninformed* nodes contacts a random neighbor and gets the rumor if the neighbor possibly knows it ('pulls' the rumor). Note that this is a synchronous protocol, e.g. a node that receives a rumor in a certain round cannot send it on in the same round.

A point to point communication network can be modelled as an undirected graph: the nodes represent the processors and the links represent communication channels between the nodes. Studying rumor spreading has several applications to distributed computing in such networks, of which we mention just two. The first is in broadcasting algorithms: a single processor wants to broadcast a piece of information to all other processors in the network (see [25] for a survey). There are at least three advantages to the Push-Pull protocol: it is simple (each node makes a simple local decision in each round; no knowledge of the global topology is needed; no state is maintained), scalable (the protocol is independent of the size of network: it does not grow more complex as the network grows) and robust (the protocol tolerates random node/link failures without the use of error recovery mechanisms, see [15]). A second application comes from the maintenance of databases replicated at many sites, e.g., yellow pages, name servers, or server directories. There are updates injected at various nodes, and these updates must propagate to all nodes in the network. In each round, a processor communicate with a random neighbor and they share any new information, so that eventually all copies of the database converge to the same contents. See [9] for details. Other than the aforementioned applications, rumor spreading protocols have successfully been applied in various contexts such as resource discovery [24], load balancing [3], data aggregation [28], and the spread of computer viruses [2].

We only consider simple, undirected and connected graphs. For a graph G, let $\Delta(G)$ and $\mathrm{diam}(G)$ denote the maximum degree and the diameter of G, respectively, and let $\deg(v)$ denote the degree of a vertex v. Most studies in randomized rumor spreading focus on the *runtime* of this protocol, defined as the number of rounds taken until a rumor initiated by one vertex reaches all other vertices. It is clear that $\mathrm{diam}(G)$ is a lower bound for the runtime of the protocol. We say an event happens *with high probability (whp)* if its probability approaches 1 as n goes to infinity. Feige, Peleg, Raghavan and Upfal [15] showed that for an n-vertex G, whp the rumor reaches all vertices in $\mathcal{O}(\Delta(G) \cdot (\mathrm{diam}(G) + \log n))$ rounds. This protocol has been studied on many graph classes such as complete graphs [27], Erdős-Réyni random graphs [14, 15, 17], random regular graphs [1, 18], and hypercube graphs [15]. For most of these classes it turns out that whp the runtime is $\mathcal{O}(\mathrm{diam}(G) + \log n)$, which does not depend on the maximum degree.

Randomized rumor spreading has recently been studied on real-world networks models. Doerr, Fouz, and Friedrich [10] proved an upper bound of $\mathcal{O}(\log n)$ for the runtime on preferential attachment graphs, and Fountoulakis, Panagiotou, and Sauerwald [19] proved the same upper bound (up to constant factors) for the runtime on the giant component of random graphs with given expected degrees (also known as the Chung-Lu model) with power law degree distribution.

The runtime is closely related to the *expansion profile* of the graph. Let $\Phi(G)$ and $\alpha(G)$ denote the conductance and the vertex expansion of a graph G, respectively. After a series of results by various scholars, Giakkoupis [22, 23] showed that for any n-vertex graph G, the runtime of the Push-Pull protocol is $\mathcal{O}\left(\min\{\Phi(G)^{-1} \cdot \log n, \alpha(G)^{-1} \cdot \log^2 n\}\right)$. It is known that whp preferential attachment graphs and random graphs with given expected degrees have conductance $\Omega(1)$ (see [6, 30]). So it is not surprising that rumors spread fast on these graphs. Censor-Hillel, Haeupler, Kelner, and Maymounkov [4] presented a different rumor spreading protocol that whp distributes the rumor in $\mathcal{O}(\mathrm{diam}(G) + \mathrm{polylog}(n))$ rounds on any connected n-vertex graph, which seems particularly suitable for poorly connected graphs.

1.1 Our Contribution

We study the Push-Pull protocol on random k-trees, a class of random graphs defined as follows.

Definition 1 (Random k-tree process [20][1]). *Let k be a positive integer. Build a sequence $G(0)$, $G(1)$, ... of random graphs as follows. The graph $G(0)$ is just a clique on k vertices. For each $1 \leq t \leq n$, $G(t)$ is obtained from $G(t-1)$ as follows: a k-clique of $G(t-1)$ is chosen uniformly at random, a new vertex is born and is joined to all vertices of the chosen k-clique. The graph $G(n)$ is called a random k-tree on $n + k$ vertices.*

Sometimes it is convenient to view this as a 'random graph evolving in time.' In this interpretation, in every round $1, 2, \ldots$, a new vertex is born and is added to the evolving graph, and $G(t)$ denotes the graph at the end of round t. Observe that $G(t)$ has $k + t$ many vertices and $kt + 1$ many k-cliques.

The definition of random k-trees enjoys a 'the rich get richer' effect, as in the preferential attachment scheme. Think of the number of k-cliques containing any vertex v as the 'wealth' of v (note that this quantity is linearly related to $\deg(v)$). Then, the probability that the new vertex attaches to v is proportional to the wealth of v, and if this happens, the wealth of v increases by $k - 1$. On the other hand, random k-trees have much larger clustering coefficients than preferential attachment graphs, as all neighbors of each new vertex are joined to each other. It is well-known that real-world networks tend to have large clustering coefficients (see, e.g., [32, Table 1]).

---

[1] Note that this process is different from the random k-tree process defined by Cooper and Uehara [8] which was further studied in [7].

Gao [20] showed that whp the degree sequence of $G(n)$ asymptotically follows a power law distribution with exponent $2 + \frac{1}{k-1}$. The diameter of $G(n)$ is $\mathcal{O}(\log n)$ whp. It is not hard to verify that the clustering coefficient of $G(n)$ is at least $1/2$, as opposed to preferential attachment graphs and random graphs with given expected degrees, whose clustering coefficients are $o(1)$ whp. As per these properties, random k-trees serve as more realistic models for real-world networks.

On the other hand, whp a random k-tree on $n + k$ vertices has conductance $\mathcal{O}\left(\log n \cdot n^{-1/k}\right)$ and vertex expansion $\mathcal{O}(k/n)$. Therefore we can not resort to existing results linking the runtime to expansion properties to show rumors spread fast in these graphs. Another interesting structural property of a random k-tree is its *treewidth* (see [29] for a comprehensive survey). Gao [21] proved that many random graph models, including Erdös-Réyni random graphs with expected degree $\omega(\log n)$ and preferential attachment graphs with out-degree greater than 11, have treewidth $\Theta(n)$, whereas all random k-trees have treewidth k by construction.[2]

In conclusion, distinguishing features of random k-trees, such as high clustering coefficient, polynomially bad expansion and tree-like structure (due to a small treewidth), inspired us to study randomized rumor spreading on this unexplored random environment. Our first main contribution is the following theorem.

Theorem 1. *Let $k > 2$ be constant and let $f(n) = o(\log \log n)$ be an arbitrary function going to infinity with n. If initially a random vertex of an $(n + k)$-vertex random k-tree knows a rumor, then with high probability after $\mathcal{O}\left((\log n)^{\frac{k+3}{k+1}} \cdot \log \log n \cdot f(n)\right)$ rounds of the* Push-Pull *protocol, $n - o(n)$ vertices will know the rumor. If $k = 2$, then the previous statement holds for $\mathcal{O}\left(\log^2 n \cdot \log \log n \cdot f(n)^{3/2}\right)$ rounds.*

We give a high-level sketch of the proof of Theorem 1. Let $m = o(n)$ be a suitably chosen parameter, and note that $G(m)$ is a subgraph of $G = G(n)$. Consider the connected components of $G - G(m)$. Most vertices born later than round m have relatively small degree, so most these components have a small maximum degree (and logarithmic diameter) thus the rumor spreads quickly inside each of them. A vertex $v \in V(G(m))$ typically has a large degree, but this means that there is a high chance that v has a neighbor x with small degree, which quickly receives the rumor from v and spreads it (or vice versa). We build an almost-spanning tree T of $G(m)$ with logarithmic height, such that for every edge uv of T, one of u and v have a small degree, or u and v have a common neighbor with a small degree. Either of these conditions implies the rumor is exchanged quickly between u and v. This tree T then works as a 'highway system' to spread the rumor among the vertices of $G(m)$ and from them to the components of $G - G(m)$.

---

[2] According to [21], not much is known about the treewidth of a preferential attachment graph with out-degree between 3 and 11.

The main novelty in this proof is how the almost-spanning tree is built and used (using small degree vertices for fast rumor transmission between high degree vertices has also been used in previous papers, e.g. [10] and [19]). Our second main contribution is the following theorem, which gives a polynomial lower bound for the runtime.

Theorem 2. *Let $f(n) = o(\log \log n)$ be an arbitrary function going to infinity with n. Suppose that, initially, one vertex in the random k-tree, $G(n)$, knows the rumor. Then, with high probability, the* Push-Pull *protocol needs at least $n^{(k-1)/(k^2+k-1)} f(n)^{-2}$ rounds to inform all vertices of $G(n)$.*

We give a high-level sketch of the proof of Theorem 2. A *barrier* in a graph is a subset D of edges of size $\mathcal{O}(1)$, whose deletion disconnects the graph. If both endpoints of every edge of a barrier D have very large degrees, then the protocol needs a very large time to pass the rumor through D. For proving Theorem 2, we prove the random k-tree has a barrier whp. The main novelty in this proof is introducing and using the notion of a barrier.

It is instructive to contrast Theorems 1 and 2. The former implies that if you want to inform almost all the vertices, then you just need to wait for a polylogarithmic number of rounds. The latter implies that, however, if you want to inform each and every vertex, then you have to wait for polynomially many rounds. This is a striking phenomenon and the main message of this paper is to present, for the first time, a natural class of random graphs in which this phenomenon can be observed. In fact, in many applications, such as epidemics, viral marketing and voting, it is more appealing to inform 99 percent of the vertices very quickly instead of waiting a long time until everyone gets informed.

It is worth mentioning that bounds for the number of rounds to inform *almost all* vertices have already appeared in the literature, see for instance [11, 19]. In particular, for power-law Chung-Lu graphs with exponent $\in (2,3)$, it is shown in [19] that whp after $\mathcal{O}(\log \log n)$ rounds the rumor spreads in $n - o(n)$ vertices, but to inform *all* vertices of the giant component $\Theta(\log n)$ rounds are necessary and sufficient. This result also shows a great difference between the two cases, however in both cases the required time is quite small.

A closely related class of graphs is the class of *random k-Apollonian networks*, introduced by Zhang, Comellas, Fertin, and Rong [33]. Their construction is very similar to the construction of random k-trees, with just one difference: if a k-clique is chosen in a certain round, it will never be chosen again. It is known that whp random k-Apollonian networks exhibit a power law degree distribution and large clustering coefficient [31, 34] and have logarithmic diameter [7]. The proof of the following theorem is similar to the proof of Theorem 1 and is thus omitted from this abstract.

Theorem 3. *Let $k > 2$ be constant and let $f(n) = o(\log \log n)$ be an arbitrary function going to infinity with n. Assuming that initially a random vertex of an $(n+k)$-vertex random k-Apollonian network knows a rumor, with high probability after $\mathcal{O}\left((\log n)^{(k^2-3)/(k-1)^2} \cdot \log \log n \cdot f(n)\right)$ rounds of the* Push-Pull *protocol, at least $n - o(n)$ vertices will know the rumor.*

For the rest of the paper, k is a constant larger than 1, and the asymptotics are for n going to infinity. Preliminaries and connections with urn models appear in Section 2. Theorems 1 and 2 are proved in Sections 3 and 4, respectively.

2   Preliminaries

We will need some definitions and results from urn theory (see, e.g., [26] for a general introduction).

Definition 2 (Pólya-Eggenberger urn). *Start with W_0 white and B_0 black balls in an urn. In every step a ball is drawn from the urn uniformly at random, the ball is returned to the urn, and s balls of the same color are added to the urn. Let* $\mathrm{Polya}(W_0, B_0, s, n)$ *denote the distribution of the number of white balls right after n draws.*

Proposition 1. *Let $X = \mathrm{Polya}(a, b, k, n)$, $w = a+b$ and let $c \geqslant (a+b)/k$. Then* $\mathbf{Pr}\left[X = a\right] \leqslant \left(\frac{c}{c+n}\right)^{a/k}$ *and*

$$\mathbf{E}\left[X^2\right] = \left(a + \frac{a}{w}\,kn\right)^2 + \frac{abk^2 n(kn + w)}{w^2(w + k)}\,.$$

Definition 3 (Generalized Pólya-Eggenberger urn). *Let $\alpha, \beta, \gamma, \delta$ be non-negative integers. We start with W_0 white and B_0 black balls in an urn. In every step a ball is drawn from the urn uniformly at random and returned to the urn. Additionally, if the ball is white, then δ white balls and γ black balls are returned to the urn; otherwise, i.e. if the ball is black, then β white balls and α black balls are returned to the urn. Let* $\mathrm{Polya}\left(W_0, B_0, \begin{bmatrix} \alpha & \beta \\ \gamma & \delta \end{bmatrix}, n\right)$ *denote the distribution of the number of white balls right after n draws.*

Note that Pólya-Eggenberger urns correspond to the matrix $\begin{bmatrix} s & 0 \\ 0 & s \end{bmatrix}$. The following proposition follows from known results.

Proposition 2. *Let $X = \mathrm{Polya}\left(W_0, B_0, \begin{bmatrix} \alpha & 0 \\ \gamma & \delta \end{bmatrix}, n\right)$ and let r be a positive integer. If $\gamma, \delta > 0$, $\alpha = \gamma + \delta$, and $r\delta \geqslant \alpha$, then we have*

$$\mathbf{E}\left[X^r\right] \leqslant \left(\frac{\alpha n}{W_0 + B_0}\right)^{r\delta/\alpha} \prod_{i=0}^{r-1}(W_0 + i\delta) + \mathcal{O}\left(n^{(r-1)\delta/\alpha}\right)\,.$$

Proposition 3. *Suppose that in $G(j)$ vertex x has $A > 0$ neighbors, and is contained in B many k-cliques. Conditional on this, the degree of x in $G(n + j)$ is distributed as*

$$A + \left(\mathrm{Polya}\left(B, kj + 1 - B, \begin{bmatrix} k & 0 \\ 1 & k - 1 \end{bmatrix}, n\right) - B\right) \Big/ (k - 1)\,.$$

Proof. We claim that $\text{Polya}\left(B, kj+1-B, \begin{bmatrix} k & 0 \\ 1 & k-1 \end{bmatrix}, n\right)$ is the total number of k-cliques containing x in $G(n+j)$. At the end of round j, there are B many k-cliques containing x, and $kj+1-B$ many k-cliques not containing x. In each subsequent round $j+1, \ldots, j+n$, a random k-clique is chosen and k new k-cliques are created. If the chosen k-clique contains x, then $k-1$ new k-cliques containing x are created, and 1 new k-clique not containing x is created. Otherwise, i.e. if the chosen k-clique does not contain x, then no new k-cliques containing x is created, and k new k-cliques not containing x are created. Hence $\text{Polya}\left(B, kj+1-B, \begin{bmatrix} k & 0 \\ 1 & k-1 \end{bmatrix}, n\right)$ is exactly the total number of k-cliques containing x in $G(n+j)$. Hence the number of k-cliques that are created in rounds $j+1, \ldots, j+n$ and contain x is $\text{Polya}\left(B, kj+1-B, \begin{bmatrix} k & 0 \\ 1 & k-1 \end{bmatrix}, n\right) - B$, and the proof follows by noting that every new neighbor of x creates $k-1$ new k-cliques containing x. □

Combining Propositions 2 and 3 we obtain the following lemma.

Lemma 1. *Let $1 \leqslant j \leqslant n$ and let q be a positive integer. Let x denote the vertex born in round j. Conditional on any $G(j)$, the probability that x has degree greater than $k + q(n/j)^{(k-1)/k}$ in $G(n)$ is $\mathcal{O}\left(q\sqrt{q}\exp(-q)\right)$.*

3   Proof of Theorem 1

Once we have the following lemma, our problem reduces to proving a structural result for random k-trees. The proof is along the lines of that of [15, Theorem 2.2].

Lemma 2. *Let G be an n-vertex graph and let $\Sigma \subseteq V(G)$ with $|\Sigma| = n - o(n)$ be such that for every pair of vertices $u, v \in \Sigma$ there exists a (u,v)-path $uu_1u_2 \ldots u_{l-1}v$ such that $l \leqslant \chi$ and for every $0 \leqslant i \leqslant l-1$ we have $\min\{\deg(u_i), \deg(u_{i+1})\} \leqslant \tau$ (where we define $u_0 = u$ and $u_l = v$). If a random vertex in G knows a rumor, then whp after $6\tau(\chi + \log n)$ rounds of the Push-Pull protocol, at least $n - o(n)$ vertices will know the rumor.*

Let $f(n) = o(\log\log n)$ be an arbitrary function going to infinity with n, and

$$m = \left\lceil \frac{n}{f(n)^3(\log n)^2} \right\rceil$$

if $k = 2$, and

$$m = \left\lceil \frac{n}{f(n)(\log n)^{2k/(k^2-1)}} \right\rceil$$

if $k > 2$. Finally, let $q = \lceil 4\log\log n \rceil$ and let

$$\tau = 2k + q(n/m)^{1-1/k} . \tag{1}$$

An argument similar to the proof of Lemma 4 gives that whp a random k-tree on $n+k$ vertices has diameter $\mathcal{O}(\log n)$. Theorem 1 thus follows from Lemma 2 and the following structural result, which we prove in the rest of this section.

Lemma 3. *Let G be an $(n + k)$-vertex random k-tree. Whp there exists $\Sigma \subseteq V(G)$ satisfying the conditions of Lemma 2 with τ defined in (1) and $\chi = \mathcal{O}(\log n + \operatorname{diam}(G))$.*

For the rest of this section, G is an $(n + k)$-vertex random k-tree. Recall from Definition 1 that $G = G(n)$, where $G(0), G(1), \ldots$, is the random k-tree process. Consider the graph $G(m)$, which has $k + m$ vertices and $mk + 1$ many k-cliques. For an edge e of $G(m)$, let $N(e)$ denote the number of k-cliques of $G(m)$ containing e. We define a spanning forest F of $G(m)$ as follows: for every $1 \leqslant t \leqslant m$, if the vertex x born in round t is joined to the k-clique C, then in F, x is joined to a vertex $u \in V(C)$ such that

$$N(xu) = \max_{v \in V(C)} N(xv).$$

Note that F has k trees and the k vertices of $G(0)$ lie in distinct trees. Think of these trees as rooted at these vertices. The tree obtained from F by merging these k vertices is the 'highway system' described in the sketch of the proof of Theorem 1. Informally speaking, the proof is divided into three parts: first, we show that this tree has a small height (Lemma 4), second, we show that each edge in this tree quickly exchanges the rumor with a reasonably large probability (Lemma 6), and finally we show that almost all vertices in $G - G(m)$ have quick access to and from F (Lemma 7). Let LOG denote the event 'each tree in F has height $\mathcal{O}(\log n)$.'

Lemma 4. *With high probability LOG happens.*

Proof. We inductively define the notion of *draft* for vertices and k-cliques of $G(m)$. The draft of the vertices of $G(0)$ as well as the k-clique they form equals 0. The draft of every k-clique equals the maximum draft of its vertices. Whenever a new vertex is born and is joined to a k-clique, the draft of the vertex equals the draft of the k-clique plus one. It is easy to see that if $xy \in E(G(m))$ and x is born later than y, then $\operatorname{draft}(x) \geqslant \operatorname{draft}(y) + 1$. In particular, if x is a vertex of F with distance h to the root, then $\operatorname{draft}(x) \geqslant h$. Hence we just need to show that whp the draft of each k-clique is $\mathcal{O}(\log n)$.

We define an auxiliary tree whose vertices are the k-cliques of $G(m)$. Start with a single vertex corresponding to $G(0)$. Whenever a new vertex x is born and is joined to a k-clique C, k new k-cliques are created. In the auxiliary tree, add these to the set of children of C. The depth of each vertex in this auxiliary tree equals the draft of its corresponding k-clique, as defined above. The height of this auxiliary tree is stochastically less than or equal to the height of a random k-ary recursive tree (see [13, Section 1.3.3] for the definition), whose height is $\mathcal{O}(\log n)$ whp, as proved in [13, Theorem 6.47]. □

We prove Lemma 3 conditional on the event LOG. In fact, we prove it for any $G(m)$ that satisfies LOG. Let G_1 be an arbitrary instance of $G(m)$ that satisfies LOG. All randomness in the following refers to rounds $m+1, \ldots, n$. The following deterministic lemma, whose proof appears at the end of the section, will be used in the proof of Lemma 6.

Lemma 5. *Assume that $k > 2$ and $xy \in E(F)$ and suppose that x is born later than y. If the degree of x in G_1 is greater than $2k - 2$, then $N(xy) \geqslant (k^2 - 1)/2$.*

A vertex of G is called *modern* if it is born later than the end of round m, and is called *traditional* otherwise. In other words, vertices of G_1 are traditional and vertices of $G - G_1$ are modern. We say edge $uv \in E(G)$ is *fast* if at least one of the following is true: $\deg(u) \leqslant \tau$, or $\deg(v) \leqslant \tau$, or u and v have a common neighbor w with $\deg(w) \leqslant \tau$. For an edge $uv \in E(F)$, let $p_S(uv)$ denote the probability that uv is not fast, and let p_S denote the maximum of p_S over all edges of F.

Lemma 6. *We have $p_S = o(1/(f(n) \log n))$.*

Proof. Let $xy \in E(F)$ be arbitrary. By symmetry we may assume that x is born later than y. First, suppose that $k > 2$. By Lemma 5, at least one of the following is true: vertex x has less than $2k - 1$ neighbors in G_1, or $N(xy) \geqslant (k^2 - 1)/2$. So we may consider two cases.

- Case 1: vertex x has less than $2k - 1$ neighbors in G_1. In this case vertex x lies in at most $k^2 - 2k + 2$ many k-cliques of G_1. Assume that x has A neighbors in G_1 and lies in B many k-cliques in G_1. Let

$$X = \text{Polya}\left(B, km + 1 - B, \begin{bmatrix} k & 0 \\ 1 & k - 1 \end{bmatrix}, n - m \right) .$$

  Then by Proposition 3 the degree of x is distributed as $A + (X - B)/(k-1)$. By Proposition 2,

$$\mathbf{E}\left[X^q\right] \leqslant (1 + o(1)) \left(\frac{k(n - m)}{km + 1} \right)^{\frac{q(k-1)}{k}} \prod_{i=0}^{q-1} (B + i(k - 1))$$

$$\leqslant (1 + o(1)) \left(\frac{n}{m} \right)^{\frac{q(k-1)}{k}} (k - 1)^q \prod_{i=0}^{q-1} (k + i)$$

$$\leqslant (k - 1)^q (k + q)! \left(\frac{n}{m} \right)^{\frac{q(k-1)}{k}} ,$$

  where we have used $B \leqslant k(k - 1)$ for the second inequality. Therefore,

$$\mathbf{Pr}\left[\deg(x) > 2k + q(n/m)^{\frac{k-1}{k}} \right] \leqslant \mathbf{Pr}\left[X \geqslant (k - 1)q(n/m)^{\frac{k-1}{k}} \right]$$

$$\leqslant \frac{\mathbf{E}\left[X^q\right]}{(k - 1)^q q^q (n/m)^{\frac{q(k-1)}{k}}} = \mathcal{O}\left(\frac{(k + q)^{k+q}\sqrt{q}}{q^q \exp(k + q)} \right) = o\left(\frac{1}{f(n) \log n} \right) .$$

- Case 2: $N(xy) \geqslant (k^2 - 1)/2$. In this case we bound from below the probability that there exists a modern vertex w that is adjacent to x and y and has degree at most τ. We first bound from above the probability that x

and y have no modern common neighbors. For this to happen, none of the k-cliques containing x and y must be chosen in rounds $m+1, \ldots, n$. This probability equals $\mathbf{Pr}\left[\text{Polya}(N(xy), mk + 1 - N(xy), k, n - m) = N(xy)\right]$. Since $N(xy) \geqslant (k^2 - 1)/2$, by Proposition 1 we have

$$\mathbf{Pr}\left[\text{Polya}(N(xy), mk + 1 - N(xy), k, n - m) = N(xy)\right] \leqslant \left(\frac{m+1}{n+1}\right)^{\frac{k^2-1}{2k}},$$

which is $o\left(1/(f(n)\log n)\right)$.

Now, assume that x and y have a modern common neighbor w. If there are multiple such vertices, choose the one that is born first. Since w appears later than round m, by Lemma 1,

$$\mathbf{Pr}\left[\deg(w) > k + q(n/m)^{(k-1)/k}\right] = \mathcal{O}\left(q\sqrt{q}\exp(-q)\right) = o\left(\frac{1}{f(n)\log n}\right).$$

The proof for $k = 2$ is very similar to the argument for Case 2 above: note that in this case we have $N(xy) \geqslant 1$ for all edges $xy \in E(F)$, and we have

$$\mathbf{Pr}\left[\text{Polya}(1, 2m, 2, n - m) = 1\right] \leqslant \sqrt{\frac{m+1}{n+1}} = \mathcal{O}\left(\sqrt{\frac{m}{n}}\right) = o\left(\frac{1}{f(n)\log n}\right). \quad \square$$

Enumerate the k-cliques of G_1 as $C_1, \ldots, C_{mk+1}$. Then choose $r_1 \in C_1, \ldots,$ $r_{mk+1} \in C_{mk+1}$ arbitrarily, and call them the *representative vertices*. Starting from G_1, when modern vertices are born in rounds $m+1, \ldots, n$ until G is formed, every clique C_i 'grows' to a random k-tree with a random number of vertices, which is a subgraph of G. Enumerate these subgraphs as $H_1, \ldots, H_{mk+1}$, and call them the *pieces*. More formally, $H_1, \ldots, H_{mk+1}$ are induced subgraphs of G such that a vertex v is in $V(H_j)$ if and only if every path connecting v to a traditional vertex intersects $V(C_j)$. In particular, $V(C_j) \subseteq V(H_j)$ for all $j \in \{1, \ldots, mk+1\}$. Note that the H_j's may intersect as a traditional vertex may lie in more than one C_j, however every modern vertex lies in a unique piece.

A traditional vertex is called *nice* if it is connected to some vertex in $G(0)$ via a path of fast edges. Since F has height $\mathcal{O}(\log n)$ and each edge of F is fast with probability at least $1 - p_S$, the probability that a given traditional vertex is not nice is $\mathcal{O}(p_S \log n)$ by the union bound. A piece H_j is called *nice* if all its modern vertices have degrees at most τ, and the vertex r_j is nice. A modern vertex is called *nice* if it lies in a nice piece. A vertex/piece is called *bad* if it is not nice.

Lemma 7. *The expected number of bad vertices is $o(n)$.*

Proof. The total number of traditional vertices is $k + m = o(n)$ so we may just ignore them in the calculations below. Let $\eta = nf(n)/m = o(\log^3 n)$. Say piece H_j is *sparse* if $|V(H_j)| \leqslant \eta + k$. We first bound the expected number of modern vertices in non-sparse pieces. Observe that the number of modern vertices in each piece is distributed as $X = (\text{Polya}(1, km, k, n - m) - 1)/k$. Using Proposition 1 we get $\mathbf{E}\left[X^2\right] \leqslant 2kn^2/m^2$. By the second moment method, for every $t > 0$ we have

$$\mathbf{Pr}\left[X \geqslant t\right] \leqslant \frac{\mathbf{E}\left[X^2\right]}{t^2} \leqslant \frac{2kn^2}{m^2t^2}.$$

The expected number of modern vertices in non-sparse pieces is thus at most

$$\sum_{i=0}^{\infty}(2^{i+1}\eta)(km+1)\,\mathbf{Pr}\left[2^i\eta < X \leqslant 2^{i+1}\eta\right] \leqslant \sum_{i=0}^{\infty}(2^{i+1}\eta)(km+1)\frac{2kn^2}{m^2\eta^2 2^{2i}}$$

$$\leqslant \mathcal{O}\left(\frac{n^2}{m\eta}\right)\sum_{i=0}^{\infty}2^{-i} = \mathcal{O}\left(\frac{n^2}{m\eta}\right),$$

which is $o(n)$.

We now bound the expected number of modern vertices in sparse bad pieces. For bounding this from above we find an upper bound for the expected number of bad pieces, and multiply by η. A piece H_j can be bad in two ways:

(1) the representative vertex r_j is bad: the probability of this is $\mathcal{O}\left(p_S \log n\right)$. Therefore, the expected number of pieces that are bad due to this reason is $\mathcal{O}\left(mkp_S \log n\right)$, which is $o(n/\eta)$ by Lemma 6.

(2) there exists a modern vertex in H_j with degree greater than τ: the probability that a given modern vertex has degree greater than τ is $\mathcal{O}\left(q\sqrt{q}\exp(-q)\right)$ by Lemma 1. So the average number of modern vertices with degree greater than τ is $\mathcal{O}\left(nq\sqrt{q}\exp(-q)\right)$. Since every modern vertex lies in a unique piece, the expected number of pieces that are bad because of this reason is bounded by $\mathcal{O}\left(nq\sqrt{q}\exp(-q)\right) = o(n/\log^3 n)$.

So the expected number of bad pieces is $o(n/\eta + n/\log^3 n)$. and the expected number of modern vertices in sparse bad pieces is $o(n + \eta n/\log^3 n) = o(n)$. $\square$

We now prove Lemma 3, which concludes the proof of Theorem 1.

Proof (of Lemma 3). Let Σ denote the set of nice modern vertices. By Lemma 7 and using Markov's inequality, we have $|\Sigma| = n - o(n)$ whp. Let $\{a_1, \ldots, a_k\}$ denote the vertex set of $G(0)$. Using an argument similar to the proof of Lemma 6, it can be proved that given $1 \leqslant i < j \leqslant k$, the probability that edge a_ia_j is not fast is $o(1)$. Since the total number of such edges is a constant, whp all such edges are fast. Let u and v be nice modern vertices, and let r_u and r_v be the representative vertices of the pieces containing them, respectively. Since the piece containing u is nice, there exists a (u, r_u)-path whose vertices except possibly r_u all have degrees at most τ. The length of this path is at most diam(G). Since r_u is nice, for some $1 \leqslant i \leqslant n$ there exists an (r_u, a_i)-path in F consisting of fast edges. By appending these paths we find a (u, a_i)-path with length at most diam$(G) + \mathcal{O}(\log n)$ such that for every pair of consecutive vertices in this path, one of them has degree at most τ. Similarly, for some $1 \leqslant j \leqslant n$ there exists a (v, a_j)-path of length $\mathcal{O}(\log n + \text{diam}(G))$, such that one of every pair of consecutive vertices in this path has degree at most τ. Since the edge a_ia_j is fast, we can build a (u, v)-path of length $\mathcal{O}(\log n + \text{diam}(G))$ of the type required by Lemma 2, and this completes the proof. $\square$

Proof (of Lemma 5). Assume that x is joined to $u_1, \ldots, u_k$ when it is born. Also assume that $v_1, v_2, \ldots, v_{k-1}, \ldots$ are the neighbors of x that are born later than x, in the order of birth. Let Ψ denote the number of pairs (u_j, C), where $u_j \in V(G_1)$ and C is a k-clique in G_1 such that $\{x, u_j\} \subseteq V(C)$. Consider the round in which vertex x is born and is joined to $u_1, \ldots, u_k$. For every $j \in \{1, \ldots, k\}$, the vertex u_j is contained in $k - 1$ new k-cliques, so in this round Ψ increases by $k(k - 1)$. For each $i \in \{1, \ldots, k - 1\}$, consider the round in which vertex v_i is born. This vertex is joined to x and $k - 1$ neighbors of x. At this round x has neighbor set $\{u_1, \ldots, u_k, v_1, \ldots, v_{i-1}\}$. Thus at least $k - i$ of the u_j's are joined to v_i in this round. Each vertex u_j that is joined to v_i in this round is contained in $k - 1$ new k-cliques, so in this round Ψ increases by at least $(k - i)(k - 1)$. Consequently, we have $\Psi \geqslant k(k - 1) + \sum_{i=1}^{k-1}(k - i)(k - 1) = (k^2 - 1)k/2$. By the pigeonhole principle, there exists some $\ell \in \{1, \ldots, k\}$ such that the edge xu_ℓ is contained in at least $(k^2 - 1)/2$ many k-cliques, and this completes the proof. □

4 Proof of Theorem 2

Definition 4 (s-barrier). *A pair $\{C_1, C_2\}$ of disjoint k-cliques in a connected graph is an s-barrier if (i) the set of edges between C_1 and C_2 is a cut-set, i.e. deleting them disconnects the graph, and (ii) the degree of each vertex in $V(C_1) \cup V(C_2)$ is at least s.*

Observe that if G has an s-barrier, then for any starting vertex, whp the Push-Pull protocol needs at least $\Omega(s)$ rounds to inform all vertices.

Lemma 8. *The graph $G(n)$ has an $\Omega(n^{1-1/k})$-barrier with probability $\Omega(n^{1/k-k})$.*

Proof. Let $u_1, \ldots, u_k$ be the vertices of $G(0)$, and let $v_1, \ldots, v_k$ be the vertices of $G(k) - G(0)$ in the order of appearance. We define two events: Event A is that for every $1 \leqslant i \leqslant k$, when v_i appears, it attaches to $v_1, v_2, \ldots, v_{i-1}, u_i, u_{i+1}, \ldots, u_k$; and for each $1 \leqslant i, j \leqslant k$, u_i and v_j have no common neighbor in $G(n) - G(k)$. Event B is that all vertices of $G(k)$ have degree $\Omega(n^{(k-1)/k})$ in $G(n)$. Note that if A and B both happen, then the pair $\{u_1 u_2 \ldots u_k, v_1 v_2 \ldots v_k\}$ is an $\Omega(n^{(k-1)/k})$-barrier in $G(n)$. Hence to prove the lemma it suffices to show $\mathbf{Pr}[A] = \Omega(n^{1/k-k})$ and $\mathbf{Pr}[B|A] = \Omega(1)$.

For A to happen, first, the vertices $v_1, \ldots, v_k$ must choose the specific k-cliques, which happens with constant probability. Moreover, the vertices appearing after round k must not choose any of the $k^2 - 1$ many k-cliques that contain both u_i's and v_j's. Since $1 - y \geqslant e^{-y-y^2}$ for every $y \in [0, 1/4]$,

$$\mathbf{Pr}\,[A] = \Omega(\mathbf{Pr}\,[\mathrm{Polya}(k^2 - 1, 2, k, n - k) = k^2 - 1])$$

$$= \Omega\left(\prod_{i=0}^{n-k-1}\left(\frac{2+ik}{k^2+1+ik}\right)\right)$$

$$\geqslant \Omega\left(\prod_{i=0}^{4k-1}\left(\frac{2+ik}{k^2+1+ik}\right)\prod_{i=4k}^{n-k-1}\left(1-\frac{k^2-1}{ik}\right)\right)$$

$$\geqslant \Omega\left(\exp\left(-\sum_{i=4k}^{n-k-1}\left\{\frac{k^2-1}{ik}+\left(\frac{k^2-1}{ik}\right)^2\right\}\right)\right)$$

which is $\Omega(n^{1/k-k})$ since $\sum_{i=4k}^{n-k-1}\frac{k^2-1}{ik} \leqslant (k - 1/k)\log n + \mathcal{O}(1)$ and moreover $\sum_{i=4k}^{n-k-1}\left(\frac{k^2-1}{ik}\right)^2 = \mathcal{O}(1)$.

Conditional on A and using an argument similar to that in the proof of Proposition 3, the degree of each of the vertices $u_1, \ldots, u_k, v_1, \ldots, v_k$ in $G(n)$ is at least $k + (\mathrm{Polya}(1, 1, \begin{bmatrix} k & 0 \\ 1 & k-1 \end{bmatrix}, n-k)-1)/(k-1)$. By [16, Proposition 16], there exists $\delta > 0$ such that

$$\mathbf{Pr}\left[\mathrm{Polya}(1, 1, \begin{bmatrix} k & 0 \\ 1 & k-1 \end{bmatrix}, n - k) < \delta n^{(k-1)/k}\right] < 1/(2k + 1)\,.$$

By the union bound, the probability that all vertices $u_1, \ldots, u_k, v_1, \ldots, v_k$ have degrees at least $\delta n^{(k-1)/k}/(k-1)$ is at least $1/(2k+1)$, hence $\mathbf{Pr}\,[B|A] \geqslant 1/(2k+1) = \Omega(1)$.   □

Let $f(n) = o(\log\log n)$ be a function going to infinity with n, and let $m = \left\lceil f(n)n^{1-k/(k^2+k-1)} \right\rceil$. (Note that the value of m is different from that in Section 3, although its role is somewhat similar.) Consider the random k-tree process up to round m. Enumerate the k-cliques of $G(m)$ as $C_1, \ldots, C_{mk+1}$. Starting from $G(m)$, when new vertices are born in rounds $m+1, \ldots, n$ until $G = G(n)$ is formed, every clique C_i 'grows' to a random k-tree with a random number of vertices, which is a subgraph of G. Enumerate these subgraphs as $H_1, \ldots, H_{mk+1}$, and call them the *pieces*. We say a piece is *moderate* if its number of vertices is between $n/(mf(n))$ and $nf(n)/m$. Note that the number of vertices in a piece has expected value $\Theta(n/m)$. The following lemma is proved by showing this random variable does not deviate much from its expected value.

Lemma 9. *With high probability, there are $o(m)$ non-moderate pieces.*

Proof (of Theorem 2). Consider an alternative way to generate $G(n)$ from $G(m)$: first, we determine how many vertices each piece has, and then we expose the structure of the pieces. Let Y denote the number of moderate pieces. By Lemma 9 we have $Y = \Omega(m)$ whp. We prove the theorem conditional on $Y = y$, where $y = \Omega(m)$ is otherwise arbitrary. Note that after the sizes of the pieces are exposed, what happens inside each piece in rounds $m + 1, \ldots, n$ is mutually independent from other pieces. Let H be a moderate piece with n_1 vertices. By Lemma 8, the probability that H has an $\Omega(n_1^{1-1/k})$-barrier is $\Omega(n_1^{1/k-k})$. Since $n/(mf(n)) \leqslant n_1 \leqslant nf(n)/m$, the probability that H has a $\Omega((n/(mf(n)))^{1-1/k})$-barrier is $\Omega((nf(n)/m)^{1/k-k})$. Since there are $y = \Omega(m)$ moderate pieces in total, the probability that no moderate piece has an $\Omega\left((n/(mf(n)))^{1-1/k}\right)$-barrier is at most $(1 - \Omega((nf(n)/m)^{1/k-k}))^y \leqslant \exp(-\Omega(f(n))) = o(1)$, which means whp there exists an $\Omega\left(n^{(k-1)/(k^2+k-1)}f(n)^{-2}\right)$-barrier in $G(n)$, as required. $\qquad\square$

References

1. Berenbrink, P., Elsässer, R., Friedetzky, T.: Efficient randomised broadcasting in random regular networks with applications in peer-to-peer systems. In: Proc. 27th Symp. Principles of Distributed Computing (PODC), pp. 155–164 (2008)
2. Berger, N., Borgs, C., Chayes, J., Saberi, A.: On the spread of viruses on the Internet. In: Proc. 16th Symp. Discrete Algorithms (SODA), pp. 301–310 (2005)
3. Boyd, S., Ghosh, A., Prabhakar, B., Shah, D.: Randomized gossip algorithms. IEEE Transactions on Information Theory 52(6), 2508–2530 (2006)
4. Censor-Hillel, K., Haeupler, B., Kelner, J.A., Maymounkov, P.: Global computation in a poorly connected world: Fast rumor spreading with no dependence on conductance. In: 44th Symp. Theory of Computing (STOC), pp. 961–970 (2012)
5. Chierichetti, F., Lattanzi, S., Panconesi, A.: Rumor spreading in social networks. In: Albers, S., Marchetti-Spaccamela, A., Matias, Y., Nikoletseas, S., Thomas, W. (eds.) ICALP 2009, Part II. LNCS, vol. 5556, pp. 375–386. Springer, Heidelberg (2009)
6. Chung, F.R.K., Lu, L., Vu, V.H.: The spectra of random graphs with given expected degrees. Internet Mathematics 1(3), 257–275 (2003)
7. Cooper, C., Frieze, A.: The height of random k-trees and related branching processes. arXiv 1309.4342v2 [math.CO] (2013)
8. Cooper, C., Uehara, R.: Scale free properties of random k-trees. Mathematics in Computer Science 3(4), 489–496 (2010)
9. Demers, A., Greene, D., Hauser, C., Irish, W., Larson, J., Shenker, S., Sturgis, H., Swinehart, D., Terry, D.: Epidemic algorithms for replicated database maintenance. In: Proc. 6th Symp. Principles of Distributed Computing (PODC), pp. 1–12 (1987)
10. Doerr, B., Fouz, M., Friedrich, T.: Social networks spread rumors in sublogarithmic time. In: Proc. 43rd Symp. Theory of Computing (STOC), pp. 21–30 (2011)
11. Doerr, B., Fouz, M., Friedrich, T.: Asynchronous rumor spreading in preferential attachment graphs. In: Fomin, F.V., Kaski, P. (eds.) SWAT 2012. LNCS, vol. 7357, pp. 307–315. Springer, Heidelberg (2012)
12. Doerr, B., Fouz, M., Friedrich, T.: Why rumors spread so quickly in social networks. Commun. ACM 55(6), 70–75 (2012)
13. Drmota, M.: Random trees: An interplay between combinatorics and probability. Springer, Wien (2009)
14. Elsässer, R.: On the communication complexity of randomized broadcasting in random-like graphs. In: Proceedings of the 18th ACM Symposium on Parallelism in Algorithms and Architectures, SPAA 2006, pp. 148–157 (2006)
15. Feige, U., Peleg, D., Raghavan, P., Upfal, E.: Randomized broadcast in networks. Random Struct. Algorithms 1(4), 447–460 (1990)

16. Flajolet, P., Dumas, P., Puyhaubert, V.: Some exactly solvable models of urn process theory. In: 4th Colloquium on Mathematics and Computer Science Algorithms, Trees, Combinatorics and Probabilities, pp. 59–118. Discrete Math. Theor. Comput. Sci. Proc., AG, Assoc. Discrete Math. Theor. Comput. Sci., Nancy (2006)

17. Fountoulakis, N., Huber, A., Panagiotou, K.: Reliable broadcasting in random networks and the effect of density. In: Proc. 29th IEEE Conf. Computer Communications (INFOCOM), pp. 2552–2560 (2010)

18. Fountoulakis, N., Panagiotou, K.: Rumor spreading on random regular graphs and expanders. In: Serna, M., Shaltiel, R., Jansen, K., Rolim, J. (eds.) APPROX and RANDOM 2010. LNCS, vol. 6302, pp. 560–573. Springer, Heidelberg (2010)

19. Fountoulakis, N., Panagiotou, K., Sauerwald, T.: Ultra-fast rumor spreading in social networks. In: 23th Symp. Discrete Algorithms (SODA), pp. 1642–1660 (2012)

20. Gao, Y.: The degree distribution of random k-trees. Theor. Comput. Sci. 410(8-10), 688–695 (2009)

21. Gao, Y.: Treewidth of Erdős-Rényi random graphs, random intersection graphs, and scale-free random graphs. Discrete Applied Mathematics 160(4-5), 566–578 (2012)

22. Giakkoupis, G.: Tight bounds for rumor spreading with vertex expansion. In: Proc. 25th Symp. Discrete Algorithms (SODA), pp. 801–815 (2014)

23. Giakkoupis, G.: Tight bounds for rumor spreading in graphs of a given conductance. In: 28th International Symposium on Theoretical Aspects of Computer Science (STACS 2011), vol. 9, pp. 57–68 (2011)

24. Harchol-Balter, M., Leighton, F.T., Lewin, D.: Resource discovery in distributed networks. In: Proc. 18th Symp. Principles of Distributed Computing (PODC), pp. 229–237 (1999)

25. Hedetniemi, S.M., Hedetniemi, S.T., Liestman, A.L.: A survey of gossiping and broadcasting in communication networks. Networks 18(4), 319–349 (1988)

26. Johnson, N.L., Kotz, S.: Urn models and their application: An approach to modern discrete probability theory. Wiley Series in Probability and Mathematical Statistics. John Wiley & Sons, New York (1977)

27. Karp, R., Schindelhauer, C., Shenker, S., Vöcking, B.: Randomized Rumor Spreading. In: 41st Symp. Foundations of Computer Science (FOCS), pp. 565–574 (2000)

28. Kempe, D., Dobra, A., Gehrke, J.: Gossip-based computation of aggregate information. In: 44th Symp. Foundations of Computer Science (FOCS), pp. 482–491 (2003)

29. Kloks, T.: Treewidth: Computations and Approximations. Springer (1994)

30. Mihail, M., Papadimitriou, C.H., Saberi, A.: On certain connectivity properties of the internet topology. In: Proc. 44th Symp. Foundations of Computer Science (FOCS), pp. 28–35 (2003)

31. Mungan, M.: Comment on "apollonian networks: Simultaneously scale-free, small world, Euclidean, space filling, and with matching graphs". Phys. Rev. Lett. 106, 029802 (2011)

32. Watts, D.J., Strogatz, D.H.: Collective dynamics of 'small-world' networks. Nature 393, 440–442 (1998)

33. Zhang, Z., Comellas, F., Fertin, G., Rong, L.: High-dimensional Apollonian networks. J. Phys. A 39(8), 1811–1818 (2006)

34. Zhou, T., Yan, G., Wang, B.H.: Maximal planar networks with large clustering coefficient and power-law degree distribution. Phys. Rev. E 71, 046141 (2005)

Making Sense
of Relativistic Distributed Systems

Seth Gilbert[1] and Wojciech Golab[2],*

[1] National University of Singapore
seth.gilbert@comp.nus.edu.sg
[2] University of Waterloo
wgolab@uwaterloo.ca

"Time is an illusion."
—Albert Einstein

Abstract. Linearizability, a widely-accepted correctness property for shared objects, is grounded in classical physics. Its definition assumes a total temporal order over invocation and response events, which is tantamount to assuming the existence of a global clock that determines the time of each event. By contrast, according to Einstein's theory of relativity, there can be no global clock: time itself is relative. For example, given two events A and B, one observer may perceive A occurring before B, another may perceive B occurring before A, and yet another may perceive A and B occurring simultaneously, with respect to local time.

Here, we generalize linearizability for relativistic distributed systems using techniques that do not rely on a global clock. Our novel correctness property, called *relativistic linearizability*, is instead defined in terms of causality. However, in contrast to standard "causal consistency," our interpretation defines relativistic linearizability in a manner that retains the important *locality* property of linearizability. That is, a collection of shared objects behaves in a relativistically linearizable way if and only if each object individually behaves in a relativistically linearizable way.

1 Introduction

Distributed computing theory is deeply intertwined with physics, particularly the fundamental concepts of space and time. A distributed computation is often described as a collection of events, each of which occurs at a specific place and time. The ordering of events lies at the heart of many proposed correctness properties. Most notably, Herlihy and Wing's widely-accepted linearizability property [14] for shared objects relies on a totally ordered collection of operation invocations and responses. This total order over events induces a partial "happens before" order over the underlying operations, which are regarded as executing over intervals of time. Linearizability requires that these operations behave as though

---

* Author supported in part by the Natural Sciences and Engineering Research Council of Canada (NSERC), Discovery Grants Program.

F. Kuhn (Ed.): DISC 2014, LNCS 8784, pp. 361–375, 2014.

they were executed one at a time, in some sequence consistent with the "happens before" partial order. This ordering creates the illusion that each operation takes effect instantaneously, despite executing over a longer interval.

Herlihy and Wing's definition (see Section 3), as well as the method they propose for proving linearizability, weave together a number of mathematical building blocks—partial orders, total orders, representation invariants and abstraction functions. Underlying these convenient abstractions are two fundamental assumptions: (1) events can be totally ordered according to an irreflexive, transitive temporal relation; (2) the states of the "base objects" used to construct the implemented object can be observed simultaneously. While these assumptions are in line with classical or Newtonian physics, Einstein's theory of relativity tells us that both time and simultaneity are in fact relative [8]. That is, two events may occur in opposite orders from the perspectives of two observers, and two events that appear simultaneous to one observer may not be simultaneous to another observer. Intuitively, these phenomena occur because the speed of light in a vacuum appears the same to all observers irrespective of their relative motion or the motion of the light source. As a result, assumptions (1) and (2) break in a relativistic distributed system where components may move relative to each other at high speeds.

Correctness properties generally fall into two categories: those that assume totally ordered events, and those based upon some notion of causality. Properties in the first category lack a precise interpretation in a relativistic environment, whereas properties in the second category lack the important property of *locality*. Locality, also known as composability, states that a collection of consistent objects is, *collectively*, consistent. For building larger systems, locality is critical: with it, you can use a collection of well-designed (i.e., consistent) objects to build a larger system that continues to behave as you would expect it to. By contrast, without locality, it is difficult to reason about systems of many shared objects.

Thus, neither of the two categories of known correctness properties is ideal for specifying the behavior of distributed systems in a relativistic setting—a problem of growing importance in light of ongoing endeavors to establish a human colony on Mars [1], and construct an interplanetary Internet [15]. Consider for example a hypothetical key-value storage system for inter-planetary data sharing, and suppose that scientists using the system insist on always seeing the latest version of the data. How can the desired behavior of get and put operations on key-value pairs be specified without referring to a global clock or sacrificing locality?

In this paper, we define *relativistic linearizability*—a generalization of linearizability for relativistic distributed systems. We then: (1) present four candidate definitions of relativistic linearizability that do not rely on global clocks; (2) prove that these definitions form a hierarchy, and that only one provides locality; (3) describe special cases in which different levels of our hierarchy collapse; and (4) discuss techniques for constructing relativistically linearizable objects.

2   Related Work

In this section, we overview the role of time and causality in correctness properties of shared objects. In his seminal paper on inter-process communication [16], Lamport considers a model where events are related by an irreflexive partial order called "precedes," denoted →. Lamport considers two cases. In one case, the set of events corresponds to the set of points in Einstein's four-dimensional spacetime continuum and → is the "happens before" relation of special relativity: event A happens before event B if a pulse of light emitted at A may be observed at B, and hence A may influence or even cause B. In the second case, called the *global-time* model, events are totally ordered according to real-valued tags, which are most naturally interpreted as timestamps from a global clock. An operation on an object can thus be regarded as an interval of time.

Lamport defines several correctness conditions for read-write registers, i.e., safe, regular, and atomic. These definitions are grounded in the global-time model, in that they refer to "overlap" among operation. For example, a read operation on a safe register may return any value if the read operation overlaps (i.e., is concurrent with) a write. In principle, this definition could be generalized to the relativistic model; such a generalization is not stated explicitly in [16].

Herlihy and Wing's *linearizability* property generalizes Lamport's notion of the atomic register to arbitrary typed shared objects [14]. Linearizability is a local property, meaning that an execution involving a collection of objects is linearizable if and only if for each object the "sub-execution" of only that object is linearizable. The technique proposed for proving linearizability assumes that the states of the underlying objects can be observed simultaneously, i.e., by defining an *abstraction function* that maps the joint state of the underlying objects to a set of possible states of the abstract type. Alternatively, linearizability can be proved by showing that each operation takes effect at some *linearization point* (see, e.g., [10,11]), which is tantamount to the assumption of a global clock.

Strong linearizability is a specialized form of linearizability that simplifies the analysis of randomized algorithms [11]. Informally, strong linearizability ensures that linearization points are determined at runtime whereas linearizability only requires that such points can be found after an execution is observed. Strong linearizability is a local property, similar to linearizability.

Causal consistency is another commonly proposed correctness condition [2,9,19]. It states that operations must appear to take effect in some total order that extends a particular "causally precedes" relation. Specifically, two operations are causally ordered if they are executed by the same processor, or if one reads a value written by the other, or by way of a transitive relationship involving a third operation. In fact (see Section 4), an execution can be causally consistent even when operations appear to take effect in a total order that disagrees with the "happens before" partial order of relativity, and hence causal consistency is not a local property. As a result, compositions of causally consistent objects require additional synchronization to preserve causal consistency. In practice this is achieved using dependency tracking mechanisms, which increase latency and limit scalability when the number of dependencies is large [4,19]. The overhead is especially high in systems that track all *potential* causal dependencies represented by the "happens before" relation of special relativity. Alternatively, a system may track only a subset of such dependencies that are declared explicitly by applications. The drawback of this approach is that causal relationships among interactions of different users are not always known to an application.

Eventual consistency is a popular correctness property for key-value storage systems [7,21,22]. Informally, a system is eventually consistent if clients agree on the latest value of an object if, for a sufficient length of time, there are no updates to the object and no failures. Eventual consistency is a local property and can be formalized without reference to global clocks [6,23], but it is not suitable for all applications because it allows clients to observe arbitrarily stale or out-of-order data. In contrast to strongly consistent systems, such as conventional relational databases, eventually consistent storage systems can remain available for both reading and updating even in the presence of network partitions [5,20].

3 Model

We consider a distributed message passing model with a fixed number N of processors denoted $\mathcal{P} = \{p_1, p_2, ..., p_N\}$. Processors may fail by crashing permanently and the message channels between them may drop and reorder messages. The system is relativistic in the sense that processors may be in motion at high speeds relative to one another. As a result, relativistic effects such as time dilation and length contraction may be observed as stipulated by Einstein's theory of relativity [8]. This implies that processors cannot in general agree on a global clock, on the order in which events occur globally, or on whether two events occurred simultaneously.

An execution is modeled as a history $H = (E, <_E)$ where E is a finite set of *events* and $<_E$ is an irreflexive partial order over E. Events are points in Einstein's four-dimensional spacetime and represent primitive actions such as sending a message, receiving a message, or performing some local computation. The partial order $<_E$ is the "happens before" relation of relativity, as in Lamport's general model [16,17]. That is, $e_1 <_E e_2$ means that it is possible for a hypothetical pulse of light originating at event e_1 to reach event e_2. The *light cone* of event e_1 is the set of events in H that may be influenced by e_1, namely $\{e_2 \in E \mid e_1 <_E e_2\}$. For example, a message receive event is always in the light cone of the corresponding message send event. We refer to H as a *classic history* in the special case when $<_E$ is a total order. Informally, H is classic when each pair of events occurs sufficiently close in space or far apart in time so that one event in the pair is in the light cone of the other.

Although the events occurring in a history $H = (E, <_E)$ are in general only partially ordered, a particular observer perceives them as occurring in some total order in terms of local time [8]. In this context, "perceives" means that the local time at which an event occurs is calculated by taking into account the propagation time of light from the position of the event to the observer, rather than merely the time when such light might reach the observer. E.g., a human observer on Earth who sees a solar flare eruption on the surface of the sun at local time t perceives this eruption as occurring roughly at local time t less eight minutes. Local time is defined within a specific *frame of reference* [8], which is a coordinate system that captures the observer's motion (i.e., velocity, rotation) in space.

In this paper, we focus specifically on distributed systems that simulate shared *objects*, such as key-value pairs, using a message passing protocol. We model such objects similarly to Herlihy and Wing [14]. Processors interact with objects by executing *operations* that read and modify the state of exactly one object, and produce a return value. A processor initiates an operation by executing a single event, usually sending a message, called an *invocation*. The operation is terminated when the same processor executes another event, usually receiving a message, called a *response*. An invocation of operation *op* by processor p on object X is denoted $(\textsc{In}, p, X, op)$. A response of this operation with return value *ret* is denoted $(\textsc{Re}, p, X, ret)$. A response is *matching* with respect to an invocation if both refer to the same processor and object. An *operation execution* (or op-ex) comprises an invocation and its matching response, if it exists. For any history $H = (E, <_E)$, an op-ex *ox* is *pending* if it lacks a matching response, and is *complete* otherwise. If *ox* is complete, then its invocation precedes its matching response in the happens before partial order $<_E$. We denote by $\text{compl}(H)$ the subsequence of H comprising the events of complete op-ex's in H.

Given histories $H = (E, <_E)$ and $H' = (E', <_{E'})$, we say that H *is a subhistory of* H', denoted $H \subseteq H'$, if $E \subseteq E'$ and $<_E \subseteq <_{E'}$. Given history H and object X, we denote by $H|X$ the subhistory of H comprising the events in E applied to X and the corresponding subset of $<_E$. For processor p, we denote by $H|p$ the subhistory comprising events applied at processor p and the corresponding subset of $<_E$. Two histories H and H' are *equivalent* if for every processor p, $H|p = H'|p$. We assume that every history H is *well-formed*: for every processor p, if $H|p$ is non-empty, then the events in $H|p$ are totally ordered and form an alternating sequence of invocations and responses, starting with an invocation.

For any given history $H = (E, <_E)$, Lamport [16] defines two temporal relations over pairs of operation executions, ox_1 and ox_2 in H: $ox_1 \longrightarrow_H ox_2$ denotes that ox_1 is complete and its response happens before the invocation of ox_2; and $ox_1 \dashrightarrow_H ox_2$ denotes that the invocation of ox_1 happens before some event of ox_2. If $ox_1 \longrightarrow_H ox_2$ holds then $ox_1 \dashrightarrow_H ox_2$ holds as well, but the converse is not true. Relation $\longrightarrow_H$ is an irreflexive partial order, but $\dashrightarrow_H$ is not a partial order as it lacks transitivity. We say that H is *sequential* if every pair of distinct op-ex's is related by $\longrightarrow_H$.

The correct behavior of an object in a sequential history can be captured succinctly as a *type* $\tau = (\mathcal{S}, s_{init}, \mathcal{O}, \mathcal{R}, \delta)$ where $\mathcal{S}$ is the set of states, $s_{init} \in \mathcal{S}$ is the initial state, $\mathcal{O}$ is a set of operation types, $\mathcal{R}$ is the set of responses, and $\delta : \mathcal{S} \times \mathcal{O} \to \mathcal{S} \times \mathcal{R}$ is a (one-to-many) state transition mapping. Specifically, if a processor applies an operation of type *ot* to an object of type τ that is in state s, then the object may return a response r and change its state to s' if and only if $(s', r) \in \delta(s, ot)$. For a sequential history H, we say that an object

X *conforms* to its type $\tau = (\mathcal{S}, s_{init}, \mathcal{O}, \mathcal{R}, \delta)$ in H if $H|X$ is consistent with some sequence of transitions of δ starting from state s_{init}, in the following sense: letting ot_i and ret_i denote the operation type and response of the i'th operation execution on X in $H|X$ (according to the order $\longrightarrow_H$) and letting $k = |H|X|$, there exists a sequence $\langle s_0, s_1, s_2, ..., s_k \rangle$ of states in $\mathcal{S}$ such that $s_0 = s_{init}$, and $(s_i, ret_i) \in \delta(s_{i-1}, ot_i)$ holds for all $i \leq k$. We say that H is *legal* if for every object X accessed in H, X conforms to its type in H.

4 Defining Relativistic Linearizability

Our goal is to devise a correctness property for shared objects that is general enough to encompass relativistic distributed systems, and yet retains the principal advantages of linearizability—the illusion that operation executions take effect instantaneously, and the locality property. We present several candidate definitions of *relativistic linearizability* that refer to the "happens before" temporal relation described in Section 3, but do not rely on the existence of a global clock. We establish precise relationships between these candidate definitions and also prove that some (but not all) of them achieve locality.

Causality-based correctness properties for shared objects have been previously considered (see Section 2). These definitions are suitable for a relativistic environment and do not require a global clock. However, it is well known that causal consistency lacks the locality property of linearizability. As an example, Figure 1 illustrates causal consistency in an execution involving two processors, p and q, interacting with two objects, X and Y. Both objects have integer-valued states initialized to 0. Short solid arrows indicate the responses of reads, whereas long solid arrows denote the "causally precedes" partial order [2]. The op-ex's applied to X are by themselves causally consistent because they can be regarded as taking effect in the following order: $q.\text{read}(X)$, $p.\text{write}(X, 1)$, $p.\text{read}(X, 1)$. An analogous comment holds for Y. However, it is easily seen that the entire execution is not causally consistent—there is no total order over the op-ex's that extends the "causally precedes" relation and in which every read returns the value assigned by the last write. (This example is similar to Theorem 2.)

As we show in the remainder of the paper, locality is in fact attainable in correctness properties based upon causality. In other words, the absence of locality

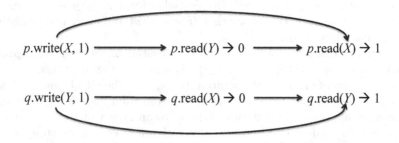

Fig. 1. Example of an execution in which causal consistency is not local

in Figure 1 is a side-effect of how causality is used in the definition of causal consistency, rather than a fundamental weakness of causality itself. A hint of the problem is the absence of causal relationships between p's operations in the top half of Figure 1 and q's operations in the bottom half. By contrast, the partial order used to define linearizability is an interval order, which in this case would guarantee that either p.write$(X, 1)$ happens before q.read(X) or q.write$(Y, 1)$ happens before p.read(Y). In the former case $H|X$ is not linearizable, and in the latter case $H|Y$ is not linearizable, hence locality holds trivially.

The key insight underlying our definitions of relativistic linearizability is that causality is most naturally interpreted as the "happens before" relation of rela- tivity, which captures all possible dependencies among events. Accordingly, the main technical challenge lying ahead is to decide how exactly this partial or- der should be used to constrain the total order in which operation executions must appear to take effect. Before continuing further, we first restate Herlihy and Wing's definition in the context of our relativistic model. Such a rephrasing is necessary because Herlihy and Wing model operation executions explicitly as intervals of time whose endpoints are totally ordered, and hence their definition lacks an obvious counterpart in our relativistic model.

Definition 1. *For any classic history $H = (E, <_E)$, we say that H is lineariz- able if there exists a classic history $H' = (E', <_{E'})$ such that:*

L1 $H \subseteq H'$;

L2 *there exists a set M of matching responses for a subset of operation execu- tions that are pending in H such that $E' = E \cup M$ and $<_{E'} = <_E \cup (E \times M)$ (i.e., H' is obtained from H by "appending" the matching responses in M);*

L3 *compl(H') is equivalent to some legal sequential history S; and*

L4 $\longrightarrow_S$ *extends* $\longrightarrow_H$.

The sequential history S referred to by property L3 is called a linearization of H.

Definition 1 assumes that $<_E$ is a total order (since H is classic), and hence the partial order $\longrightarrow_H$ is an interval order over the time intervals corresponding to operation executions, as in [14]. Since we adopt Lamport's more general def- inition of $\longrightarrow$ rather than using interval orders explicitly, in our model one can in principle obtain a definition of relativistic linearizability from Definition 1 by simply removing the restriction that H is classic:

Definition 2 (R0-linearizability). *For any history $H = (E, <_E)$, we say that H is R0-linearizable if and only if it satisfies Definition 1 generalized to arbitrary histories. The corresponding linearization S is called an R0-linearization of H.*

Although Definition 2 is very natural and meets our goal of avoiding global clocks, we found dealing with it difficult as it requires reasoning directly about partially ordered events. Moreover, as we show later on in Theorem 2, R0- linearizability lacks locality. As a result, we explore an alternative approach in which an arbitrary history H is first reduced to a classic history.

Specifically, consider how H might be perceived by an observer in a particular frame of reference where events are totally ordered in terms of local time. Such a frame of reference can be described as a coordinate system with the observer positioned at the origin, but for our purposes it is more convenient to reason directly about events and local time. Thus, we model a frame of reference as a total order over events that extends the "happens before" partial order:

Definition 3. *For any history $H = (E, <_E)$, a total order $<_T$ over E is called feasible with respect to H (or H-feasible for short) if and only if $<_E \subseteq <_T$. Furthermore, H_T denotes the classic history $(E, <_T)$ and $\longrightarrow_T$ denotes $\longrightarrow_{H_T}$.*

Lemma 1. *For any history $H = (E, <_E)$, suppose that E contains events e_1, e_2 such that neither $e_1 <_E e_2$ nor $e_2 <_E e_1$. Then there exist H-feasible total orders $<_T$ and $<_{T'}$ such that $e_1 <_T e_2$ and $e_2 <_{T'} e_1$.*

Note that Definition 3 is more general than necessary to accommodate all possible frames of reference in special relativity. That is, for every history H and every frame of reference F there exists a corresponding H-feasible total order $<_T$, meaning that events in F are ordered in terms of local time identically to $<_T$. However, not every H-feasible $<_T$ corresponds to a frame of reference. Consider for example the hypothetical scenario of a train passing through a station, where an observer standing on the station platform perceives the train getting struck by three lightning bolts simultaneously: one at the front of the train (event A), one in the middle of the train (event B), and one at the rear of the train (event C). A passenger who is stationary with respect to the train (i.e., on the train) instead perceives A occurring first, then B, then C, and a passenger on a different train passing the station in the opposite direction perceives C first, then B, then A. In Einstein's theory of special relativity, which considers non-accelerating frames of reference and ignores gravitational effects, there is no frame of reference in which an observer perceives B occurring before *both* A and C as that would require the "plane of simultaneity" to intersect twice in spacetime with the line along which A, B and C are positioned. In contrast, such a total order (e.g., B then A then C) is feasible according to Definition 3.

We now present our candidate definitions of relativistic linearizability, called R1, R2 and R3. Loosely speaking (i.e., ignoring the technicality discussed in the previous paragraph), R1 states that H appears linearizable in some frame of reference, R2 states that H appears linearizable in every frame of reference, and R3 states that H is not only linearizable in every frame of reference but all observers furthermore agree on a common linearization.

Definition 4 (R1-linearizability). *For any history $H = (E, <_E)$, we say that H is R1-linearizable if and only if there exists an H-feasible total order $<_T$ such that the history $H_T = (E, <_T)$ is linearizable. Any linearization of H_T is called an R1-linearization of H.*

Definition 5 (R2-linearizability). *For any history $H = (E, <_E)$, we say that H is R2-linearizable if and only if for every H-feasible total order $<_T$, the history*

$H_T = (E, <_T)$ *is linearizable. Any linearization* S *of any such* H_T *is called an* R2-linearization of H.

Definition 6 (R3-linearizability). *For any history* $H = (E, <_E)$, *we say that* H *is* R3-linearizable *if and only if there exists an R1-linearization* S *of* H *such that for every* H-feasible total order $<_T$, *the history* $H_T = (E, <_T)$ *is linearizable, and moreover* S *is a linearization of* H_T. *Any such history* S *is called an* R3-linearization *of* H.

The properties R0-R3 form a hierarchy, as stated in Theorem 1.

Theorem 1. *For any history* $H = (E, <_E)$, *if* H *is R3-linearizable then* H *is R2-linearizable; if* H *is R2-linearizable then* H *is R1-linearizable; and if* H *is R1-linearizable then* H *is R0-linearizable.*

Proof (sketch). The relationships among R1, R2 and R3 follow from Definitions 4–6. Next, suppose that H is R1-linearizable and let $<_T$ be any H-feasible total order. Since $\longrightarrow_T$ extends $\longrightarrow_H$ it follows that H is also R0-linearizable.

Next, in Theorems 2–4 we separate R0 and R1 against R2 and against R3 in terms of locality.

Theorem 2. *R0-linearizability and R1-linearizability are not local properties.*

Proof (sketch). The analysis is analogous to the earlier argument that causal consistency is not local, and also uses the history illustrated in Figure 1.

Theorem 3. *R2-linearizability is a local property.*

Proof. Consider an arbitrary history $H = (E, <_E)$ over some set of objects $X_0, X_1, \ldots, X_k$. Suppose that $H|X_i$ is R2-linearizable for every object X_i. We must show that for every H-feasible total order $<_T$, the classic history $H_T = (E, <_T)$ is linearizable. Since linearizability is local, it suffices to show that $H_T|X_i$ is linearizable for every object X_i. Choose an arbitrary i and consider the histories $H|X_i = (E_i, <_{E_i})$ and $H_T|X_i = (E_i, <_{T_i})$, where E_i is the subset of E pertaining to X_i, $<_{E_i}$ is the subset of $<_E$ pertaining to E_i, and $<_{T_i}$ is the subset of $<_T$ pertaining to E_i. Since $<_T$ is H-feasible, it follows that $<_E \subseteq <_T$ and hence $<_{E_i} \subseteq <_{T_i}$. Furthermore, since $<_{T_i}$ is a total order over E_i, it follows that $<_{T_i}$ is $H|X_i$-feasible. Since we assume that $H|X_i$ is R2-linearizable, this implies that $H_T|X_i$ is linearizable, as wanted.

For R3-linearizability, we can proceed similarly to Theorem 2 by constructing a history $H = (E, <_E)$ containing operation executions whose events are not related at all by $<_E$. However, to aid discussion later on in Section 5 we apply a different proof technique that relies on relative motion between the processors that execute operations. The scenario is presented in Figure 2 as a two-dimensional Minkowski diagram where the horizontal axis represents time and the vertical axis represents one dimension of space. The thinner dashed lines indicate hypothetical rays of light, which according to special relativity follow

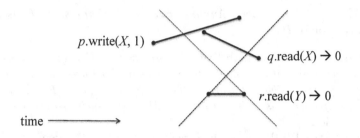

$p.\mathrm{write}(X, 1)$

$q.\mathrm{read}(X) \rightarrow 0$

$r.\mathrm{read}(Y) \rightarrow 0$

time $\longrightarrow$

Fig. 2. Example of an execution in which R3-linearizability is not local

straight paths in spacetime and are shown at a 45° angle from the horizontal axis. The thicker solid lines with round endpoints indicate operation executions. The partial order $<_E$ can be interpreted as follows: if event e_1 appears to the left of point e_2 in the diagram, and the hypothetical line from e_1 to e_2 is angled less than 45° from the horizontal axis (i.e., e_2 is in the light cone of e_1), then $e_1 <_E e_2$.

Theorem 4. *R3-linearizability is not a local property.*

Proof. Consider the history $H = (E, <_E)$ illustrated in Figure 2, where X and Y are integer-valued read/write register objects initialized to 0. Let ox_p, ox_q, and ox_r denote p's, q's and r's operation executions. Let I_i and R_i denote the invocation and response of ox_i for $i \in \{p, q, r\}$.

Since $I_p <_E R_q$ and $I_q <_E R_p$, it follows that $H|X$ has exactly one R3-linearization S_X in which $ox_q \longrightarrow_{S_X} ox_p$. And since there is only one op-ex on Y in H, $H|Y$ is trivially R3-linearizable. We will show that H is not R3-linearizable. Suppose otherwise. Let S be an R3-linearization of H. Since S_X is the only R3-linearization of $H|X$, it follows that $ox_q \longrightarrow_S ox_p$. Next, consider ox_p and ox_r. Since R_p is not related to I_r in $<_E$, there exists an H-feasible total order $<_{T'}$ such that $R_p <_{T'} I_r$, hence $ox_p \longrightarrow_S ox_r$. Finally, consider ox_r and ox_q. Since R_r is not related to I_q in $<_E$, there exists an H-feasible total order $<_{T''}$ such that $R_r <_{T''} I_q$, hence $ox_r \longrightarrow_S ox_q$. Thus, $ox_q \longrightarrow_S ox_p$, $ox_p \longrightarrow_S ox_r$, and $ox_r \longrightarrow_S ox_q$, which contradicts $\longrightarrow_S$ being irreflexive and transitive. $\qquad\blacksquare$

5   Proof Techniques

Proving that a history satisfies one of our interpretations R1-R3 of relativistic linearizability amounts to reasoning about conventional linearizability in one or more frames of reference. R1 is the easiest property to prove in that it suffices to fix one frame of reference, e.g., where one of the processors is stationary, and to reason about the partial order of operations executions in that frame of reference. At the same time, R1 lacks locality (see Theorem 2). R2 is superior in that regard, but requires reasoning about all possible frames of reference.

To bridge the gap between R1 and R2, we characterize in Definitions 7–10 a condition under which R1 implies R2 (see Theorem 5). Informally, the condition (Definition 10) requires that the order of operation executions in an R1-linearization S of a history H reflects the direction of the $\dashrightarrow_H$ relation (see Definitions 7 and 8), or else if two operations are not related by $\dashrightarrow_H$ then they and any other operation executions positioned between them in S must commute (Definition 9). This ensures that for any H-feasible total order $<_T$ a linearization of H_T can be obtained by permuting groups of consecutive operations in S.

Definition 7. *For any history $H = (E, <_E)$, and any distinct operation executions ox, ox' in H, we say that ox and ox' are:*

- *strongly connected in H if $ox \dashrightarrow_H ox'$ and $ox' \dashrightarrow_H ox$*
- *weakly connected in H if either $ox \dashrightarrow_H ox'$ or $ox' \dashrightarrow_H ox$ (but not both)*
- *connected in H if they are strongly or weakly connected in H*
- *disconnected in H if they are not connected in H*

(Recall: $ox \dashrightarrow_H ox'$ means the invoc. of ox happens before some event of ox'.)

Definition 8. *A history $H = (E, <_E)$ is called connected if every pair of operation executions in H is connected. Otherwise, H is called disconnected.*

Definition 9. *For any shared object type $\tau = (S, s_{init}, O, R, \delta)$, an operation type $ot \in O$ is called read-only if for every state $s \in S$, $\delta(s, ot) = (s, r)$ for some response r. (I.e., executing ot always causes a trivial state transition.)*

Definition 10. *For any history $H = (E, <_E)$, an R1-linearization S of H is called R2-conducive if for every pair of op-ex's ox, ox' the following hold:*

1. *if ox and ox' are weakly connected and $ox \dashrightarrow_H ox'$, then $ox \longrightarrow_S ox'$; and*
2. *if ox and ox' are disconnected then both are executions of read-only operation types, and all operation executions that appear between ox and ox' in S are also of read-only operation types.*

Theorem 5. *Let $H = (E, <_E)$ be any history and suppose that S is an R2-conducive R1-linearization of H. Then H is R2-linearizable. Furthermore, if H is connected then S itself is an R2-linearization of H.*

Proof. Let $<_T$ be any H-feasible total order. First, we will show that $H_T = (E, <_T)$ is linearizable, hence H is R2-linearizable. If S itself is a linearization of H_T then we are done, so suppose otherwise. Since S is an R1-linearization, it is a legal sequential history, and so it follows that $\longrightarrow_S$ does not extend $\longrightarrow_T$. That is, S contains op-ex's ox and ox' such that $ox \longrightarrow_S ox'$ and $ox' \longrightarrow_T ox$.
Case A: ox and ox' are strongly connected. This contradicts $ox' \longrightarrow_T ox$.
Case B: ox and ox' are weakly connected. Then $ox \dashrightarrow_H ox'$ or $ox' \dashrightarrow_H ox$ but not both. Since $ox' \longrightarrow_T ox$ it follows that $ox' \dashrightarrow_H ox$, and hence $ox' \longrightarrow_S ox$ since S is R2-conducive. This contradicts $ox \longrightarrow_S ox'$.
Case C: ox and ox' are disconnected. Since S is R2-conducive, this implies that ox and ox' both have read-only operation types, and similarly for any operation executions $ox_1, ox_2, ..., ox_k$ that appear between ox and ox' in S. Transform S to S' by permuting $ox, ox_1, ox_2, ..., ox_k, ox'$ so that they appear in any order that

extends $\longrightarrow_T$. We will show that S' is also an R1-linearization of H, hence by applying the transformation repeatedly we can eliminate Case C entirely.

Note that the transformation from S to S' may break the R2-conducive property, particularly clause 1 of Definition 10 for one or more op-ex pairs in $ox, ox_1, ox_2, ..., ox_k, ox'$. This is not a problem for two reasons. First, although we use R2-conduciveness in Case B, we never return to this case for such a pair of op-ex's because the transformation arranges them in S' consistently with $\longrightarrow_T$. Second, the R2-linearization we are constructing need not itself be R2-conducive.

Since S' is a permutation of S, it suffices to show that S' is legal and that $\longrightarrow_{S'}$ extends $\longrightarrow_H$. Since S' is obtained from S by permuting consecutive operation executions of read-only types, S' is legal because S is legal. Next, suppose for contradiction that $\longrightarrow_{S'}$ does not extend $\longrightarrow_H$. That is, $\longrightarrow_{S'}$ orders two op-ex's differently than $\longrightarrow_H$. Since $\longrightarrow_S$ extends $\longrightarrow_H$, it follows that these two op-ex's are in the subset $ox, ox_1, ox_2, ..., ox_k, ox'$, which are permuted in the transformation from S to S'. This contradicts the fact that by construction S' orders these operation executions consistently with $\longrightarrow_T$, hence with $\longrightarrow_H$.

Finally, we must show that if H is connected then S is an R2-linearization of H. Following earlier parts of the proof we see that if H is connected then Case C does not apply, whereas Cases A and B both lead to contradictions. Thus, S itself must be a linearization of H_T no matter how $<_T$ is chosen, as wanted.

Since R2 is a local property, when applying Theorem 5 to deduce R2 from R1 it suffices to consider each object in isolation. This result is captured as follows:

Corollary 1. *Let $H = (E, <_E)$ be an R1-linearizable history over some set of objects $X_1, X_2, ..., X_k$. Suppose for each object X_i that $H|X_i$ has an R2-conducive R1-linearization. Then H is R2-linearizable.*

Proof. By Theorem 5, each $H|X_i$ is R2-linearizable, and so by Theorem 3 H is R2-linearizable.

Similarly to Theorem 5, it is possible also to deduce R3 from R2 under special conditions, as stated in Lemma 2 and Theorem 6.

Lemma 2. *For any history $H = (E, <_E)$, if H is R3-linearizable then H is connected.*

Proof (sketch). If H is disconnected then two op-ex's in H may linearize in opposite orders in different frames of reference (Lemma 1), which precludes R3.

Theorem 6. *Let $H = (E, <_E)$ be any history and suppose that S is an R2-conducive R1-linearization of H. If H is connected then H is R3-linearizable.*

Proof. If H is connected then it follows directly from Theorem 5 that S is an R2-linearization of H. Furthermore, S is by definition R2-conducive. We will show that S is also an R3-linearization of H, as wanted. Let $<_T$ be any H-feasible total order and consider $H_T = (E, <_T)$. Suppose for contradiction that S is not a linearization of H_T. Since S is an R1-linearization, it is a legal sequential history, and so it must be the case that $\longrightarrow_S$ does not extend $\longrightarrow_T$. That is, S contains operation executions ox and ox' such that $ox \longrightarrow_S ox'$ and $ox' \longrightarrow_T ox$. If ox and ox' are strongly or weakly connected then we derive a contradiction as in Cases A and B in the proof of Theorem 5. Otherwise ox and ox' are disconnected, which contradicts H being connected.

In contrast to Theorem 5, Corollary 1 has no analog in the context of deducing R3 from R1. That is, if H is R3-linearizable then one can show that for each object X_i the history $H|X_i$ has an R2-conducive R1-linearization, but in general it is not possible to compose these R1-linearizations to form an R2-conducive R1-linearization of H itself, which could be used to deduce that H is R3-linearizable using Theorem 6.

Although Theorem 6 asserts that connectedness combined with the property of being R2-conducive are sufficient to obtain R3 from R1, it does not promise R3 locality. In cases where locality is needed, it can be achieved by defining the relativistic counterpart of linearization points.

Definition 11. *Let $H = (E, <_E)$ be a history. A* linearization point *for an op-ex ox in H is an event e in spacetime (not necessarily in E) where: (i) the invocation of ox happens before e; and (ii) if ox is complete, then e happens before the repsonse of ox.*

Theorem 7. *Let $H = (E, <_E)$ be a history and let L be a set of linearization points for the op-ex's in H. Suppose that all the linearization points are distinct and totally ordered by the happens before relation of relativity, and let $\longrightarrow_L$ denote the corresponding total order on operation executions in H. Then H has an R3-linearization S such that $\longrightarrow_S \subseteq \longrightarrow_L$ if and only for each object X_i accessed in H the subhistory $H|X_i$ has an R3-linearization S_i such that $\longrightarrow_{S_i} \subseteq \longrightarrow_L$.*

Proof. If H has an R3-linearization S such that $\longrightarrow_S \subseteq \longrightarrow_L$, then for each object X_i, $S_i = S|X_i$ is an R3-linearization of $H|X_i$; furthermore $\longrightarrow_{S_i} \subseteq \longrightarrow_S \subseteq \longrightarrow_L$ by construction. Conversely, if for each object X_i the subhistory $H|X_i$ has an R3-linearization S_i such that $\longrightarrow_{S_i} \subseteq \longrightarrow_L$, then the sequential histories S_i can be composed into an R3-linearization S of H by ordering op-ex's according to $\longrightarrow_L$. $\qquad\blacksquare$

Theorem 7 yields a recipe for constructing a restricted class of R3-linearizations that provide locality. However, choosing linearization points in our relativistic model is strictly harder than in Herlihy and Wing's classic model because we must ensure that they are totally ordered in the happens before relation of relativity. Thus the linearization points of all objects must be defined jointly, whereas in conventional linearizability it suffices to define them for each object individually. In that sense linearization points themselves lack locality in our relativistic model.

6   Discussion and Conclusions

Our results demonstrate that linearizability can be defined precisely in a relativistic environment without sacrificing locality. In particular, we established in

Theorem 3 that the R2-linearizability property is local. As such, we consider R2 the most natural definition of relativistic linearizability. Since R2 captures the idea that the linearization order is relative, like time and distance, we propose that R2 be referred to as *Einstein-linearizability* or *E-linearizability* for short.

Although we favor R2, properties R1 and R3 offer other advantages despite lacking locality. R1 is strictly weaker than R2 in our hierarchy (see Theorems 1, 2 and 3), and therefore is easier to prove for a given history H. Specifically, to prove R1 it suffices to consider only a single H-feasible total order, whereas R2 and R3 refer to all such orders. On the other hand, R3 is easier to reason about than R2 in that all possible observers perceive a common linearization.

In Section 5, we described techniques for inferring R2 from R1 and R3 from R1 under special conditions. Our technique for inferring R2 from R1 requires that if the events of two operation executions ox, ox' are causally related in any way then in a given frame of reference ox cannot be linearized before ox' unless some event of ox precedes some event of ox' in the happens before partial order of relativity (see clause 1 of Definition 10). This requirement holds even if the two op-ex's are concurrent in Herlihy and Wing's sense with respect to local time. Furthermore, disconnected operations must commute (see clause 2 of Definition 10). Deducing R3 from R1 further requires that all operation executions be connected. R3 becomes local if we restrict our attention to linearizations constructed specifically by defining linearization points (see Theorem 7).

Many known implementations of shared objects in message passing systems satisfy R1-linearizability. These include key-value storage systems whose replication protocols can be configured to use majority quorums, such as Amazon's Dynamo key-value store [7], the ABD simulation of read-write registers [3], as well as any system that uses Paxos state machine replication [18]. Furthermore, these systems satisfy both our R2-conducive and connected properties, and so it is possible to reason about their behavior by deducing R3 from R1 via Theorem 6. In fact, a Paxos-replicated state machine can be used to obtain a fault-tolerant R3-linearizable implementation of any shared object type. On the other hand, quorum-based replication in general does not guarantee connectedness since it does not require that read quorums overlap with each other. (Overlap is needed only to detect read-write and write-write conflicts.) For example, with five-way replication read operations could access only two replicas provided that writes access four replicas, and hence some pairs of reads may be disconnected. In that case R3-linearizability is not attainable but Theorem 5 can be used to prove that such systems satisfy R2-linearizability since clause 2 of Definition 10 accommodates disconnected reads.

Acknowledgements. Theorems 2 and 3 are joint work with Jonathan Z.Y. Hay and Y.C. Tay. Parts of these results have been presented previously in their keynote talk [13] and Hay's final year project [12].

References

1. Mars One, http://www.mars-one.com/
2. Ahamad, M., Neiger, G., Burns, J.E., Kohli, P., Hutto, P.W.: Causal memory: Definitions, implementation, and programming. Distr. Comp. 9(1), 37–49 (1995)

3. Attiya, H., Bar-Noy, A., Dolev, D.: Sharing memory robustly in message-passing systems. J. ACM 42(1), 124–142 (1995)
4. Bailis, P., Fekete, A., Ghodsi, A., Hellerstein, J.M., Stoica, I.: The potential dangers of causal consistency and an explicit solution. In: Proc. of the 5th ACM Symposium on Cloud Computing (2012)
5. Brewer, E.A.: Towards robust distributed systems (Invited Talk). In: Proc. of the 19th Symposium on Principles of Distributed Computing (2000)
6. Burckhardt, S., Gotsman, A., Yang, H.: Understanding eventual consistency. Microsoft Research Technical Report MSR-TR-2013-39 (2013)
7. De Candia, G., Hastorun, D., Jampani, M., Kakulapati, G., Lakshman, A., Pilchin, A., Sivasubramanian, S., Vosshall, P., Vogels, W.: Dynamo: Amazon's highly available key-value store. In: Proc. of the 21st ACM Symposium on Operating Systems Principles (2007)
8. Einstein, A.: The Meaning of Relativity, 6th edn. Taylor & Francis (2003)
9. Friedman, R., Vitenberg, R., Chockler, G.: On the composability of consistency conditions. Inf. Process. Lett. 86(4), 169–176 (2003)
10. Golab, W., Hadzilacos, V., Hendler, D., Woelfel, P.: RMR-efficient implementations of comparison primitives using read and write operations. Distr. Comp. 25(2), 109–162 (2012)
11. Golab, W., Higham, L., Woelfel, P.: Linearizable implementations do not suffice for randomized distributed computation. In: Proc. of the 43rd ACM Symposium on Theory of Computing, pp. 373–382 (2011)
12. Hay, J.Z.Y.: Using local time to reconstruct memory models for parallel computation. Final year project. National University of Singapore (2012)
13. Hay, J.Z.Y., Tay, Y.C.: Memory consistency for parallel systems: A reformulation without global time (keynote address). In: Proc. National Conference on High Performance Computing & Simulation (2013)
14. Herlihy, M., Wing, J.M.: Linearizability: A correctness condition for concurrent objects. ACM TOPLAS 12(3), 463–492 (1990)
15. Jackson, J.: The interplanetary internet. IEEE Spectrum (2005)
16. Lamport, L.: On interprocess communication, Part I: Basic formalism and Part II: Algorithms. Distributed Computing 1(2), 77–101 (1986)
17. Lamport, L.: Time, clocks, and the ordering of events in a distributed system. Commun. ACM 21(7), 558–565 (1978)
18. Lamport, L.: The part-time parliament. ACM Trans. Comput. Syst. 16(2), 133–169 (1998)
19. Lloyd, W., Freedman, M.J., Kaminsky, M., Andersen, D.G.: Don't settle for eventual: scalable causal consistency for wide-area storage with COPS. In: Proc. 23rd ACM Symposium on Operating Systems Principles, pp. 401–416 (2011)
20. Lynch, N., Gilbert, S.: Brewer's conjecture and the feasibility of consistent, available, partition-tolerant web services. ACM SIGACT News 33(2), 51–59 (2002)
21. Terry, D., Petersen, K., Spreitzer, M., Theimer, M.: The case for non-transparent replication: Examples from Bayou. IEEE Data Engineering Bull. 21(4), 12–20 (1998)
22. Vogels, W.: Eventually consistent. ACM Queue 6(6), 14–19 (2008)
23. Zhu, Y., Wang, J.: Client-centric consistency formalization and verification for system with large-scale distributed data storage. Future Gener. Comput. Syst. 26(8), 1180–1188 (2010)

Safety of Live Transactions in Transactional Memory: TMS is Necessary and Sufficient

Hagit Attiya[1], Alexey Gotsman[2], Sandeep Hans[1], and Noam Rinetzky[3]

[1] Technion - Israel Institute of Technology, Israel
[2] IMDEA Software Institute, Spain
[3] Tel Aviv University, Israel

Abstract. One of the main challenges in stating the correctness of transactional memory (TM) systems is the need to provide guarantees on the system state observed by *live* transactions, i.e., those that have not yet committed or aborted. A TM correctness condition should be weak enough to allow flexibility in implementation, yet strong enough to disallow undesirable TM behavior, which can lead to run-time errors in live transactions. The latter feature is formalized by *observational refinement* between TM implementations, stating that properties of a program using a concrete TM implementation can be established by analyzing its behavior with an abstract TM, serving as a specification of the concrete one.

We show that a variant of *transactional memory specification* (*TMS*), a TM correctness condition, is equivalent to observational refinement for the common programming model in which local variables are rolled back upon a transaction abort and, hence, is the weakest acceptable condition for this case. This is challenging due to the nontrivial formulation of TMS, which allows different aborted and live transactions to have different views of the system state. Our proof reveals some natural, but subtle, assumptions on the TM required for the equivalence result.

1 Introduction

Transactional memory (TM) eases the task of writing concurrent applications by letting the programmer designate certain code blocks as *atomic*. TM allows developing a program and reasoning about its correctness as if each atomic block executes as a *transaction*—in one step and without interleaving with others—even though in reality the blocks can be executed concurrently. Figure 1 shows how atomic blocks are used to manipulate several shared *transactional objects* X, Y and Z, access to which is mediated by the TM.

```
result := abort;
while (result == abort) {
    result := atomic {
        x := X.read();
        y := Y.read();
        z := 42 / (x - y);
        Z.write(z); } }
```

Fig. 1. TM usage

The common approach to stating TM correctness is through a *consistency condition* that restricts the possible TM executions. The main subtlety of formulating such a condition is the need to provide guarantees on the state of transactional objects observed by *live* transactions, i.e., those that have not yet committed or aborted. Because live transactions can always be aborted, one might think it unnecessary to provide any guarantees for them, as done by common database consistency conditions [1]. However, in the setting of transactional memory, this is often unsatisfactory. For example, in Figure 1 the programmer may rely on the fact that $X \neq Y$, and, correspondingly, make sure

F. Kuhn (Ed.): DISC 2014, LNCS 8784, pp. 376–390, 2014.

that every committing transaction preserves this invariant. If we allow the transaction to read values of X and Y violating the invariant (counting on it to abort later, due to inconsistency), this will lead to the program *faulting* due to a division by zero.

The question of which TM consistency condition to use is far from settled, with several candidates having been proposed [2–5]. An ideal condition should be weak enough to allow flexibility in TM implementations, yet strong enough to satisfy the intuitive expectations of the programmer and, in particular, to disallow undesirable behaviors such as the one described above. *Observational refinement* [6, 7] allows formalizing the programmer's expectations and thereby evaluating consistency conditions systematically. Consider two TM implementations—a *concrete* one, such as an efficient TM, and an *abstract* one, such as a TM executing every atomic block atomically. Informally, the concrete TM *observationally refines* the abstract one for a given programming language if every behavior a user can observe of any program P in this language using the concrete TM can also be observed when P uses the abstract TM instead. This allows the programmer to reason about the behavior of P (e.g., the preservation of the invariant $X \neq Y$) using the expected intuitive semantics formalized by the abstract TM; the observational refinement relation implies that the conclusions (e.g., the safety of the division in Figure 1) will carry over to the case when P uses the concrete TM.

In prior work [8] we showed that a variant of the *opacity* condition [2] is equivalent to observational refinement for a particular programming language and, hence, is the weakest acceptable consistency condition for this language. Roughly speaking, a concrete TM implementation is in the opacity relation with an abstract one if for any sequence of interactions with the concrete TM, dubbed a *history*, there exists a history of the abstract TM where: (i) the actions of every separate thread are the same as in the original history; and (ii) the order of non-overlapping transactions present in the original history is preserved. However, our result considered a programming language in which local variables modified by a transaction are not rolled back upon an abort. Although this assumption holds in some situations (e.g., Scala STM [9]), it is non-standard and most TM systems do not satisfy it. In this paper, we consider a variant of *transactional memory specification (TMS)* [5], a condition weaker than opacity,[1] and show that, under some natural assumptions on the TM, it is equivalent to observational refinement for a programming language in which local variables do get rolled back upon an abort.

This result is not just a straightforward adjustment of the one about opacity to a more realistic setting: TMS weakens opacity in a nontrivial way, which makes reasoning about its relationship with observational refinement much more intricate. In more detail, the key feature of opacity is that the behavior of *all* transactions in a history of the concrete TM, including aborted and live ones, has to be justified by a single history of the abstract TM. TMS relaxes this requirement by requiring only committed transactions in the concrete history to be justified by a single abstract one obeying (i)–(ii) above; every response obtained from the TM in an aborted or live transaction may be justified by a separate abstract history. The constraints on the choice of the abstract history are subtle: on one hand, somewhat counter-intuitively, TMS allows it to include transactions that aborted in the concrete history, with their status changed to committed, and exclude some that committed; on the other hand, this is subject to certain carefully chosen constraints. The flexibility in the choice of the abstract history is meant to al-

---

[1] The condition we present here is actually called TMS1 in [5, 10]. These papers also propose another condition, TMS2, but it is stronger than opacity [10] and therefore not considered here.

low the concrete TM implementation to perform as many optimizations as possible. However, it is not straightforward to establish that this flexibility does not invalidate observational refinement (and hence, the informal guarantees that programmers expect from a TM) or that the TMS definition cannot be weakened further.

Our results ensure that this is indeed the case. Informally, if local variables are not rolled back when transactions abort, threads can communicate to each other the observations they make inside aborted transactions about the state of transactional objects. This requires the TM to provide a consistent view of this state across all transactions, as formalized by the use of a single abstract history in opacity. However, if local variables are rolled back upon an abort, no information can leak out of an uncommitted transaction, possibly apart from the fact that the code in the transaction has faulted, stopping the computation. To get observational refinement in this case we only need to make sure that a fault in the transaction occurring with the concrete TM could be reproduced with the abstract one. For this it is sufficient to require that the state of transactional objects seen by every live transaction can be justified by some abstract history; different transactions can be justified by different histories.

Technically, we prove that TMS is sufficient for observational refinement by establishing a nontrivial property of the set of computations of a program, showing that a live transaction cannot notice the changes in the committed/aborted status of transactions concurrent with it that are allowed by TMS (Lemma 1, Section 6.1). Proving that TMS is necessary for observational refinement is challenging as well, as this requires us to devise multiple programs that can observe whether the subtle constraints governing the change of transaction status in TMS are fulfilled by the TM. We have identified several closure properties on the set of histories produced by the abstract TM required for these results to hold. Although intuitive, these properties are not necessarily provided by an arbitrary TM, and our results demonstrate their importance.

To concentrate on the core goal of this paper, the programming language we consider does not allow explicit transaction aborts or transaction nesting and assumes a static separation of transactional and non-transactional shared memory. Extending our development to lift these restrictions is an interesting avenue for future work. Also, due to space constraints, we defer some of the proofs to [11, Appendix D].

2   Programming Language Syntax

We consider a language where a program $P = C_1 \parallel \cdots \parallel C_m$ is a parallel composition of **threads** C_t, $t \in \mathsf{ThreadID} = \{1, \ldots, m\}$. Every thread $t \in \mathsf{ThreadID}$ has a set of **local variables** $\mathsf{LVar}_t = \{x, y, \ldots\}$ and threads share a set of **global variables** $\mathsf{GVar} = \{g, \ldots\}$, all of type integer. We let $\mathsf{Var} = \mathsf{GVar} \uplus \biguplus_{t=1}^{m} \mathsf{LVar}_t$ be the set of all program variables. Threads can also access a transactional memory, which manages a fixed collection of **transactional objects** $\mathsf{Obj} = \{o, \ldots\}$, each with a set of **methods** that threads can call. For simplicity, we assume that each method takes one integer parameter and returns an integer value, and that all objects have the same set of methods $\mathsf{Method} = \{f, \ldots\}$. The syntax of commands C is standard: C can be of the forms

$$c \mid C; C \mid \mathtt{while}\,(b)\,\mathtt{do}\,C \mid \mathtt{if}\,(b)\,\mathtt{then}\,C\,\mathtt{else}\,C \mid x := \mathtt{atomic}\,\{C\} \mid x := o.f(e)$$

where b and e denote Boolean and integer expressions over local variables, left unspecified. The syntax includes **primitive commands** c from a set PComm, sequential composition, conditionals, loops, `atomic` blocks and object method invocations. Primitive commands execute atomically, and they include assignments to local and global variables and a special `fault` command, which stops the execution of the program in an error state. Thus, `fault` encodes illegal computations, such as division by zero.

An **atomic block** $x :=$ `atomic` $\{C\}$ executes C as a **transaction**, which the TM can **commit** or **abort**. The system's decision is returned in the local variable x, which gets assigned distinguished values committed or aborted. We do not allow programs in our language to abort a transaction explicitly and forbid nested atomic blocks and, hence, nested transactions. We also assume that a program can invoke methods on transactional objects only inside atomic blocks and access global variables only outside them. Local variables can be accessed in both cases; however, threads cannot access local variables of other threads. Due to space constraints, we defer the formalisation of the rules on variable accesses to [11, Appendix A]. When we later define the semantics of our programming language, we mandate that, if a transaction is aborted, local variables are rolled back to the values they had at its start, and hence, the values written to them by the transaction cannot be observed by the following non-transactional code.

3   Model of Computations

To define the notion of observational refinement for our programming language and the TMS consistency condition, we need a formal model for program computations. To this end, we introduce *traces*, which are certain finite sequences of *actions*, each describing a single computation step (we do not consider infinite computations).

Definition 1. *Let* Actionld *be a set of action identifiers. A **TM interface action** ψ has one of the following forms:*

Request actions	Matching response actions	
$(a, t, \text{txbegin})$	(a, t, OK)	$(a, t, \text{aborted})$
$(a, t, \text{txcommit})$	$(a, t, \text{committed})$	$(a, t, \text{aborted})$
$(a, t, \text{call } o.f(n))$	$(a, t, \text{ret}(n')\, o.f)$	$(a, t, \text{aborted})$

where $a \in$ Actionld, $t \in$ ThreadID, $o \in$ Obj, $f \in$ Method *and* $n, n' \in \mathbb{Z}$. *A **primitive action** χ has the form (a, t, c), where $c \in$ PComm *is a primitive command. We use φ to range over actions of either type.*

TM interface actions denote the control flow of a thread t crossing the boundary between the program and the TM: **request** actions correspond to the control being transferred from the former to the latter, and **response** actions, the other way around. A txbegin action is generated upon entering an `atomic` block, and a txcommit action when a transaction tries to commit upon exiting an `atomic` block. Actions call and ret denote a call to and a return from an invocation of a method on a transactional object and are annotated with the method parameter or return value. The TM may abort a transaction at any point when it is in control; this is recorded by an aborted response action.

A **trace** τ is a finite sequence of actions satisfying certain natural well-formedness conditions (stated informally due to space constraints; see [11, Appendix B]): every action in τ has a unique identifier; no action follows a `fault`; request and response actions are properly matched; for every thread t, $\tau|_t$ cannot contain a request action immediately followed by a primitive action; actions denoting the beginning and end of transactions are properly matched; call and ret actions occur only inside transactions; and commands in τ do not access local variables of other threads and do not access global variables when inside a transaction. We denote the set of traces by Trace. A *history* is a trace containing only TM interface actions; we use H, S to range over histories. We specify the behavior of a TM implementation by the set of possible interactions it can have with programs: a ***transactional memory*** $\mathcal{T}$ is a set of histories that is prefix-closed and closed under renaming action identifiers.

We denote irrelevant expressions by _ and use the following notation: $\tau(i)$ is the i-th element of τ; $\tau|_t$ is the projection of τ onto actions of the form $(\_, t, \_)$; $|\tau|$ is the length of τ; $\tau_1 \tau_2$ is the concatenation of τ_1 and τ_2. We say that an action φ is in τ, denoted by $\varphi \in \tau$, if $\tau = \_\varphi\_$. The empty sequence of actions is denoted ε.

A ***transaction*** T is a nonempty trace such that it contains actions by the same thread, begins with a txbegin action and only its last action can be a committed or an aborted action. A transaction T is: ***committed*** if it ends with a committed action, ***aborted*** if it ends with aborted, ***commit-pending*** if it ends with txcommit, and ***live***, in all other cases. We refer to this as T's ***status***. A transaction T is ***completed*** if it is either committed or aborted, and ***visible*** if it contains a txcommit action. A transaction T is ***in a trace*** τ, written $T \in \tau$, if $\tau|_t = \tau_1 T \tau_2$ for some t, τ_1 and τ_2, where either T is completed or τ_2 is empty. We denote the set of all transactions in τ by $\text{tx}(\tau)$ and use self-explanatory notation for various subsets of transactions: committed(τ), aborted(τ), pending(τ), live(τ), visible(τ). For $\varphi \in \tau$, the ***transaction of*** φ ***in*** τ, denoted txof(φ, τ), is the subsequence of τ comprised of all actions that are in the same transaction in τ as φ (undefined if φ does not belong to a transaction).

4   Transactional Memory Specification (TMS)

In this section we define the TMS [5] correctness condition in our setting. TMS was originally formulated using I/O automata; here we define it in a different style appropriate for our goals (we provide further comparison in Section 7). Since threads may communicate through global variables outside of transactions, they may observe the *real-time order* between non-overlapping transactions in a history. Therefore, this order is a crucial building block in the TMS definition, as is common in consistency conditions for shared-memory concurrency, such as opacity [2] or linearizability [12].

Definition 2. *Let $\psi = (\_, t, \_)$ and $\psi' = (\_, t', \_)$ be two actions in a history H; ψ is **before** ψ' **in the real-time order** in H, denoted by $\psi \prec_H \psi'$, if $H = H \psi H_2 H_2' \psi' H_3$ and either (i) $t = t'$ or (ii) $(\_, t', \text{txbegin}) \in H_2' \psi'$ and either $(\_, t, \text{committed}) \in \psi H_2$ or $(\_, t, \text{aborted}) \in \psi H_2$. A transaction T is **before** an action ψ' **in the real-time order** in H, denoted by $T \prec_H \psi'$, if $\psi \prec_H \psi'$ for every $\psi \in T$. A transaction T is **before** a transaction T' **in the real-time order** in H, denoted by $T \prec_H T'$, if $T \prec_H T'(1)$.*

The following *opacity relation* [2,8] $H \sqsubseteq_{\text{op}} S$ ensures that S is a permutation of H preserving the real-time order.

Definition 3. *A history H is in the **opacity relation** with a history S, denoted by $H \sqsubseteq_{\text{op}} S$, if $\forall \psi, \psi'. (\psi \in S \iff \psi \in H) \land (\psi \prec_H \psi' \implies \psi \prec_S \psi')$.*

Given a history H of program interactions with a concrete TM, TMS requires us to justify the behavior of all committed transactions in H by a single history S of the abstract TM, and to justify each response action ψ inside a transaction in H by an abstract history S_ψ. As we show in this paper, the existence of such justifications ensures that TMS implies observational refinement between the two TMs: the behavior of a program during some transaction in the history H of the program's interactions with the concrete TM can be reproduced when the program interacts with the abstract TM according to the history S or S_ψ. Below we use this insight when explaining the rationale for key TMS features.

The history S_ψ used to justify a response action ψ includes the transaction of ψ and a subset of transactions from H whose actions justify the response ψ. The following notion of a *possible past* of a history $H = H_1\psi$ defines all sets of transactions from H that can form S_ψ. Note that, if a transaction selected by this definition is aborted or commit-pending in H, its status is changed to committed when constructing S_ψ, as formalized later in Definition 5. Informally, the response ψ is given as if all the transactions in its possible past have taken effect and all the others have not. We first give the formal definition of a possible past, and then explain it using an example.

Definition 4. *A history $H_\psi = H_1'\psi$ is a **possible past** of a history $H = H_1\psi$, where ψ is a response action that it is not a committed or aborted action, if:*

(i) H_1' is a subsequence of H_1;

(ii) H_ψ is comprised of the transaction of ψ and some of the visible transactions in H: $\mathrm{tx}(H_\psi) \subseteq \{\mathrm{txof}(\psi, H)\} \cup \mathrm{visible}(H)$.

(iii) for every transaction $T \in H_\psi$, out of all transactions preceding T in the real-time order in H, the history H_ψ includes exactly the committed ones:

$$\forall T \in \mathrm{tx}(H_\psi).\, \forall T' \in \mathrm{tx}(H).\, T' \prec_H T \implies$$
$$(T' \in \mathrm{tx}(H_\psi) \iff T' \in \mathrm{committed}(H)).$$

We denote the set of possible pasts of H by $\mathrm{TMSpast}(H)$.

We explain the definition using the history H of the trace shown in Figure 2; one of its possible pasts H_ψ consists of the transactions T_1, T_4 and T_5. According to (ii), the transaction of ψ (T_5 in Figure 2) is always included into any possible past, and live transactions are excluded: since they have not made an attempt to commit, they should not have an effect on ψ. Out of the visible transactions in H, we are allowed to select which ones to include (and, hence, treat as committed), subject to (iii): if we include a transaction T then, out of all transactions preceding T in the real-time order in H, we have to include exactly the committed ones. For example, since T_4 and T_5 are included in H_ψ, T_1 must also be included and T_3 must not. This condition is necessary for TMS to imply observational refinement. Informally, T_3 cannot be included into H_ψ because, in a program producing H, in between T_3 aborting and T_5 starting, thread t_2 could have communicated to thread t_3 the fact that T_3 has aborted, e.g., using a global variable g, as illustrated in Figure 2. When executing ψ, the code in T_5 may thus expect that T_3 did not take effect; hence, the result of ψ has to reflect this, so that the code behavior is preserved when replacing the concrete TM by an abstract one in observational refinement. This is a key idea used in our proof that TMS is necessary for observational refinement (Section 6.2). In contrast to T_3, we can include T_4 into H_ψ even if it is aborted or commit-pending. Since our language does not allow accessing global variables inside transactions, there is no way for the code in T_5 to find out about the status of T_4 from thread t_2, and hence, this code will not notice if the status of

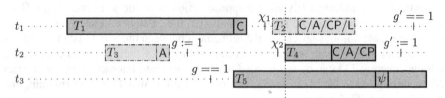

Fig. 2. Transactions T_1, T_4 and T_5 form one possible past of the history H of the trace shown. Allowed status of transactions in H is denoted as follows: committed – C, aborted – A, commit-pending – CP, live – L. The transaction T_5 executes only primitive actions after ψ in the trace.

T_4 is changed to committed when replacing the concrete TM by an abstract one in observational refinement. For similar reasons, we can exclude T_2 from H_ψ even if it is committed. This idea is used in our proof that TMS is sufficient for observational refinement (Section 6.1).

Before giving the definition of TMS, we introduce operations used to change the status of transactions in a possible past of a history to committed. *Suffix commit completion* below converts commit-pending transactions into committed; then *completed possible past* defines a possible past with all transactions committed.

Definition 5. *A history H^c is a **suffix completion** of a history $H\psi$ if $H^c = H\psi H'$, every action in H' is either* committed *or* aborted, *and every transaction in H^c except possibly that of ψ, is completed. It is a **suffix commit completion** of H if H' consists of* committed *actions only. The sets of suffix completions and suffix commit completions of H are denoted* comp(H) *and* ccomp(H), *respectively.*

*A history H^c_ψ is a **completed possible past** of a history $H = H_1\psi$, if H^c_ψ is a suffix commit completion of a history obtained from a possible past $H'_1\psi$ of H by replacing all the* aborted *actions in H'_1 by* committed *actions. The set of completed possible pasts of H is denoted* cTMSpast(H):

$$\mathsf{cTMSpast}(H_1\psi) = \{H^c_\psi \mid \exists H'_1 . H'_1\psi \in \mathsf{TMSpast}(H_1\psi) \wedge H^c_\psi \in \mathsf{ccomp}(\mathsf{com}(H'_1)\psi)\},$$

where $|\mathsf{com}(H'_1)| = |H'_1|$ *and*

$$\mathsf{com}(H'_1)(i) = (\text{if } (H'_1(i) = (a, t, \mathsf{aborted})) \text{ then } (a, t, \mathsf{committed}) \text{ else } H'_1(i)).$$

For example, one completed possible past of the history in Figure 2 consists of the transactions T_1, T_4 and T_5, with the status of the latter changed to committed if it was previously aborted or commit-pending. Note that a history H has a suffix completion only if H is of the form $H = H_1\psi$ where all the transactions in $H_1\psi$, except possibly that of ψ, are commit-pending or completed. Also, cTMSpast($H_1\psi$) $\neq \emptyset$ only if ψ is a response action.

The following definition of the *TMS relation* between TMs matches a history H arising from a concrete TM with a similar history S of an abstract TM. As part of this matching, we require that S preserves the real-time order of H. As in Definition 4(iii), this requirement is necessary to ensure observational refinement between the TMs: preserving the real-time order is necessary to preserve communication between threads when replacing the concrete TM with the abstract one.

Definition 6. *A history H is in the **TMS relation** with TM $\mathcal{T}$, denoted $H \sqsubseteq_{\text{tms}} \mathcal{T}$, if:*

(i) *$\exists H^c \in \text{comp}(H|_{\neg\text{live}})$, $S \in \mathcal{T}$. $H^c|_{\text{com}} \sqsubseteq_{\text{op}} S$, where $\cdot|_{\neg\text{live}}$ and $\cdot|_{\text{com}}$ are the projections to actions by transactions that are not live and by committed transactions, respectively; and*

(ii) *for every response action ψ such that it is not a committed or aborted action and $H = H_1\psi H_2$, we have $\exists H_\psi^c \in \text{cTMSpast}(H_1\psi)$. $\exists S_\psi \in \mathcal{T}$. $H_\psi^c \sqsubseteq_{\text{op}} S_\psi$.*

*A TM $\mathcal{T}_C$ is in the **TMS relation** with a TM $\mathcal{T}_A$, denoted by $\mathcal{T}_C \sqsubseteq_{\text{tms}} \mathcal{T}_A$, if $\forall H \in \mathcal{T}_C$. $H \sqsubseteq_{\text{tms}} \mathcal{T}_A$.*

5 Observational Refinement

Our main result relates TMS to *observational refinement*, which we introduce in this section. This requires defining the semantics of the programming language, i.e., the set of traces that computations of programs produce. Due to space constraints, we defer its formal definition to [11, Appendix C] and describe only its high-level structure. A **state** of a program records the values of all its variables: $s \in \text{State} = \text{Var} \to \mathbb{Z}$. The semantics of a program $P = C_1 \parallel \cdots \parallel C_m$ is given by the set of traces $[\![P, \mathcal{T}]\!](s) \subseteq \text{Trace}$ it produces when executed with a TM $\mathcal{T}$ from an initial state s. To define this set, we first define the set of traces $[\![P]\!](s) \subseteq \text{Trace}$ that a program can produce when executed from s with the behavior of the TM unrestricted, i.e., considering all possible values the TM can return to object method invocations and allowing transactions to commit or abort arbitrarily. We then restrict to the set of traces produced by P when executed with $\mathcal{T}$ by selecting those traces that interact with the TM in a way consistent with $\mathcal{T}$: $[\![P, \mathcal{T}]\!](s) = \{\tau \mid \tau \in [\![P]\!](s) \wedge \text{history}(\tau) \in \mathcal{T}\}$, where $\text{history}(\cdot)$ projects to TM interface actions. The definition of $[\![P]\!](s)$ follows the intuitive semantics of our programming language. In particular, it mandates that local variables be rolled back upon a transaction abort and includes traces corresponding to incomplete program computations into $[\![P]\!](s)$.

We can now define *observations* and *observational refinement*. Informally, given a trace τ of a client program, we consider observable: (i) the sequence of actions performed outside transactions in τ; (ii) the per-thread sequence of actions in τ excluding uncommitted transactions; and (iii) whether a τ ends with `fault` or not. Then observational refinement between a concrete TM $\mathcal{T}_C$ and an abstract one $\mathcal{T}_A$ states that every observable behavior of a program P using $\mathcal{T}_C$ can be reproduced when P uses $\mathcal{T}_A$. Hence, any conclusion about its observable behavior that a programmer makes assuming $\mathcal{T}_A$ will carry over to $\mathcal{T}_C$. Since our notion of observations excludes actions performed inside aborted or live transactions other than faulting, the programmer cannot make any conclusions about them. But, crucially, the programmer can be sure that, if a program is non-faulting under $\mathcal{T}_A$, it will stay so under $\mathcal{T}_C$. An action $\varphi \in \tau$ is **transactional** if $\varphi \in T$ for some $T \in \tau$, and **non-transactional** otherwise. We denote by $\tau|_{\text{trans}}$ and $\tau|_{\neg\text{trans}}$ the projections of τ to transactional and non-transactional actions.

Definition 7. *The **thread-local observable behavior** of thread t in a trace τ, denoted by $\text{observable}_t(\tau)$, is $\lightning$ if $\tau|_t$ ends with a `fault` action, and $(\tau|_t)|_{\text{obs}}$ otherwise, where $\cdot|_{\text{obs}}$ denotes the projection to non-transactional actions and actions by committed transactions. A TM $\mathcal{T}_C$ **observationally refines** a TM $\mathcal{T}_A$, denoted by $\mathcal{T}_C \preceq \mathcal{T}_A$, if for every program P, state s and trace $\tau \in [\![P, \mathcal{T}_C]\!](s)$ we have: (i) $\exists \tau' \in [\![P, \mathcal{T}_A]\!](s)$. $\tau'|_{\neg\text{trans}} = \tau|_{\neg\text{trans}}$; and (ii) $\forall t. \exists \tau_t' \in [\![P, \mathcal{T}_A]\!](s)$. $\text{observable}_t(\tau_t') = \text{observable}_t(\tau)$.*

6   Main Result

The main result of this paper is that the TMS relation is equivalent to observational refinement for abstract TMs that enjoy certain natural closure properties. Their formulation relies on the following notions.

A history H_a is an ***immediate abort extension of a history*** H if H is a subsequence of H_a, and whenever $\psi \in H_a$ and $\psi \notin H$ we have: (i) $\psi = (\_,\_,\text{txbegin})$ or $\psi = (\_,\_,\text{aborted})$, (ii) if $\psi = (\_,t,\text{txbegin})$ then $H_a = H_a' \psi (\_,t,\text{aborted})\_$, where $H_a' \in \{\varepsilon, \_(\_,\_,\text{committed}), \_(\_,\_,\text{aborted})\}$, and (iii) if $\psi = (\_,\_,\text{aborted})$ then there exists $\psi' \notin H$ such that $H_a = \_\psi'\psi\_$. We denote by $\text{addab}(H)$ the set of all immediate abort extensions of H. Informally, a history $H_a \in \text{addab}(H)$ is an extension of H with transactions that abort immediately after their invocation. Note that the added transactions are placed either right before other transactions begin or right after they complete.

A history H_c is a ***non-interleaved completion*** of a history H if H is a subsequence of H_c, $\text{pending}(H_c) = \emptyset$ and whenever $\psi \in H_c$ and $\psi \notin H$ we have $H_c = \_(\_,t,\text{txcommit})\,\psi\_$ and either $\psi = (\_,t,\text{committed})$ or $\psi = (\_,t,\text{aborted})$. We denote the set of non-interleaved completions of H by $\text{nicomp}(H)$. Informally, $H' \in \text{nicomp}(H)$ completes each commit-pending transaction in H by adding a committed or aborted action at its end.

The required closure properties are formulated as follows:

CLP1 A TM $\mathcal{T}$ is ***closed under immediate aborts*** if whenever $H \in \mathcal{T}$ and $\text{aborted}(H) = \emptyset$, we also have $H' \in \mathcal{T}$ for any history $H' \in \text{addab}(H)$.

CLP2 A TM $\mathcal{T}$ is ***closed under removing transaction responses*** if whenever $H_1(\_,t,\text{aborted})H_2 \in \mathcal{T}$ or $H_1(\_,t,\text{committed})H_2 \in \mathcal{T}$ for H_2 not containing actions by t, we also have $H_1 H_2 \in \mathcal{T}$.

CLP3 A TM $\mathcal{T}$ is ***closed under removing live and aborted transactions*** if whenever $H \in \mathcal{T}$, we also have $H' \in \mathcal{T}$ for any history H' which is a subsequence of H such that $\text{committed}(H') = \text{committed}(H)$, $\text{pending}(H') = \text{pending}(H)$, $\text{live}(H') \subseteq \text{live}(H)$ and $\text{aborted}(H') \subseteq \text{aborted}(H)$.

CLP4 A TM $\mathcal{T}$ is ***closed under completing commit-pending transactions*** if whenever $H \in \mathcal{T}$, we have $\text{nicomp}(H) \cap \mathcal{T} \neq \emptyset$.

These properties are satisfied by the expected TM specification that executes every transaction atomically [8].

Theorem 1. *Let $\mathcal{T}_C$ and $\mathcal{T}_A$ be transactional memories.*
  (i) If $\mathcal{T}_A$ satisfies CLP1 and CLP2, then $\mathcal{T}_C \sqsubseteq_{\text{tms}} \mathcal{T}_A \implies \mathcal{T}_C \preceq \mathcal{T}_A$.
  (ii) If $\mathcal{T}_A$ satisfies CLP3 and CLP4, then $\mathcal{T}_C \preceq \mathcal{T}_A \implies \mathcal{T}_C \sqsubseteq_{\text{tms}} \mathcal{T}_A$.

6.1   Proof of Theorem 1(i) (Sufficiency)

Let us fix a program $P = C_1 \parallel \ldots \parallel C_m$ and a state s. As we have noted before, the main subtlety of TMS lies in justifying the behavior of a live transaction under $\mathcal{T}_C$ by a history of $\mathcal{T}_A$ where the committed/aborted status of some transactions is changed, as formalized by the use of cTMSpast in Definition 6(ii). Correspondingly, the most challenging part of the proof is to show that a trace from $[\![P, \mathcal{T}_C]\!](s)$ with a fault inside a live transaction can be transformed into a trace with the fault from $[\![P, \mathcal{T}_A]\!](s)$. The following lemma describes the first and foremost step of this transformation: given a trace $\tau \in [\![P]\!](s)$ with a live transaction and a history $H_\psi^c \in \mathsf{cTMSpast}(\mathrm{history}(\tau))$, the lemma converts τ into another trace from $[\![P]\!](s)$ that contains the same live transaction, but whose history of non-aborted transactions is H_ψ^c. In other words, this establishes that the live transaction cannot notice changes in the committed/aborted status of other transactions done by $\mathsf{cTMSpast}$. Let $\tau|_{\neg\mathsf{abortedtx}}$ be the projection of τ excluding aborted transactions.

Lemma 1 (Live transaction insensitivity). *Let $\tau = \tau_1 \psi \tau_2 \in [\![P]\!](s)$ be such that ψ is a response action by thread t_0 that is not a committed or aborted action and τ_2 is a sequence of primitive actions by thread t_0. For any $H_\psi^c \in \mathsf{cTMSpast}(\mathrm{history}(\tau))$ there exists $\tau_\psi \in [\![P]\!](s)$ such that $\mathrm{history}(\tau_\psi)|_{\neg\mathsf{abortedtx}} = H_\psi^c$ and $\tau_\psi|_{t_0} = \tau|_{t_0}$.*

Proof. We first show how to construct τ_ψ and then prove that it satisfies the required properties. We illustrate the idea of its construction using the trace τ in Figure 2. Let $\mathrm{history}(\tau) = H_1 \psi$. Since $H_\psi^c \in \mathsf{cTMSpast}(H)$, by Definition 5 there exist histories H_1', H_1'', and H^{cc} such that

$$H_1' \psi \in \mathsf{TMSpast}(H_1 \psi) \;\wedge\; H_1'' = \mathrm{com}(H_1') \;\wedge\; H_\psi^c = H_1'' \psi H^{cc} \in \mathsf{ccomp}(H_1'' \psi).$$

Recall that, for the τ in Figure 2, $H_1' \psi$ consists of the transactions T_1, T_4 and T_5. Then H_1'' is obtained from H_1' by changing the last action of T_4 to committed if it was aborted; H_ψ^c is obtained by completing T_4 with a committed action if it was commit-pending. The trickiness of the proof comes from the fact that just mirroring these transformations on τ may not yield a trace of the program P: for example, if T_4 aborted, the code in thread t_2 following T_4 may rely on this fact, communicated to it by the TM via a local variable. Fortunately, we show that it is possible to construct the required trace by erasing certain suffixes of every thread and therefore getting rid of the actions that could be sensitive to the changes of transaction status, such as those following T_4. This erasure has to be performed carefully, since threads can communicate via global variables: for example, the value written by the assignment to g' in the code following T_4 may later be read by t_1, and, hence, when erasing the the former, the latter action has to be erased as well. We now explain how to truncate τ consistently.

Let ψ^b be the last txbegin action in $H_1' \psi$; then for some traces τ_1^b and τ_2^b we have $\tau = \tau_1^b \psi^b \tau_2^b \psi \tau_2$. For the τ in Figure 2, ψ^b is the txbegin action of T_4. Our idea is, for every thread other than t_0, to erase all its actions that follow the last of its transactions included into $H_1' \psi$ or its last non-transactional action preceding ψ^b, whichever is later. Formally, for every thread t, let τ_t^I denote the prefix of $\tau|_t$ that ends with the last TM interface action of t in $H_1' \psi$, or ε if no such action exists. For example, in Figure 2, $\tau_{t_1}^I$ and $\tau_{t_2}^I$ end with the last TM interface actions of T_1 and T_4, respectively. Similarly, let τ_t^N denote the prefix of $\tau|_t$ that ends in the last non-transactional action of t in τ_t^b, or ε if no such action exists. For example, in Figure 2, $\tau_{t_1}^N$ and $\tau_{t_2}^N$ end with χ_1 and χ_2, respectively. Let $\tau_{t_0} = \tau|_{t_0}$ and for each $t \neq t_0$ let τ_t be τ_t^I, if $|\tau_t^N| < |\tau_t^I|$, and τ_t^N, otherwise. We then let the truncated trace τ' be the subsequence of τ such that $\tau'|_t = \tau_t$ for each t. Thus, for the τ in Figure 2, in the corresponding trace τ' the actions of t_1 end with χ_1 and those of t_2 with the last action of T_4; note that this erases both operations on g'. To construct τ_ψ from τ', we mirror the transformations of H_1' into H_1'' and H_ψ^c. Let τ'' be defined by $|\tau''| = |\tau'|$ and

$$\tau''(i) = (\mathrm{if}\ (\tau'(i) = (a, t, \mathsf{aborted}) \wedge \tau'(i) \in H_1'))\ \mathrm{then}\ (a, t, \mathsf{committed})\ \mathrm{else}\ \tau'(i)).$$

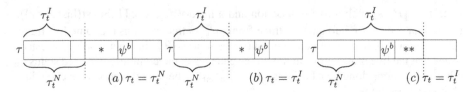

Fig. 3. Cases in the proof of Lemma 1. * all actions by t are transactional; ** all actions by t come from a single transaction, started before or by ψ^b.

Then we let $\tau_\psi = \tau'' H^{cc}$.

We first prove that $\tau_\psi|_{t_0} = \tau|_{t_0}$. Let $T = \mathsf{txof}(\psi, H_1\psi)$; then by Definition 4(ii), $T \in H_1'\psi$. Hence, by Definition 4(iii) we have

$$\forall T'. \, T' \prec_{H_1'\psi} T \iff T' \prec_{H_1\psi} T \wedge T' \in \mathsf{committed}(H_1\psi), \tag{1}$$

so that $(H_1'\psi)|_{t_0}$ does not contain aborted transactions and $\tau''|_{t_0} = \tau'|_{t_0} = \tau|_{t_0}$. Besides, $H^{cc}|_{t_0} = \varepsilon$ and, hence, $\tau_\psi|_{t_0} = \tau''|_{t_0} = \tau|_{t_0}$.

We now sketch the proof that $\tau_\psi \in [\![P]\!](s)$, appealing to the intuitive understanding of the programming language semantics. To this end, we show that τ' and then τ'' belong to $[\![P]\!](s)$. We start by analyzing how the trace $\tau|_t$ is truncated to τ_t for every thread $t \neq t_0$. Let us make a case split on the relative positions of τ_t^N, τ_t^I and ψ^b in τ. There are three cases, shown in Figure 3. Either $\tau_t = \tau_t^N$ (a, thread t_1 in Figure 2) or $\tau_t = \tau_t^I$ (b, c). In the former case, ψ^b has to come after the end of τ_t^N. In the latter case, either ψ^b comes after the end of τ_t^I (b) or is its last action or precedes the latter (c, thread t_2 in Figure 2).

By the choice of τ_t^N, in (a) and (b) the fragment of τ in between the end of τ_t^N and ψ^b can contain only those actions by t that are transactional (T_2 in Figure 2). By the choice of τ_t^I and ψ^b, in (c) the fragment of τ in between ψ^b and the end of τ_t^I cannot contain a txbegin action by t; hence, by the choice of τ_t^N it can contain only those actions by t that are transactional. Furthermore, these have to come from a single transaction, started either by ψ^b or before it (T_4 in Figure 2). Finally, by the choice of ψ^b the actions of t_0 following ψ^b are transactional and come from the transaction of ψ, also started either by ψ^b or before it (T_5 in Figure 2). Given this analysis, the transformation from τ to τ' can be viewed as a sequence of two: (i) erase all actions following ψ^b, except those in some of transactions that were already ongoing at this time; (ii) erase some suffixes of threads containing only transactional actions. Since transactional actions do not access global variables, they are not affected by the actions of other threads. Furthermore, as we noted in Section 5, $[\![P]\!](s)$ includes incomplete program computations. This allows us to conclude that $\tau' \in [\![P]\!](s)$.

We now show that τ'' is valid, again referring to cases (a-c). Let $T = \mathsf{txof}(\psi^b, H_1\psi)$; then $T \in H_1'\psi$ by the choice of ψ^b and by Definition 4(iii) we get (1). Hence, for threads t falling into cases (a) or (b), $\tau'|_t$ does not contain aborted transactions that are also in $H_1'\psi$. For threads t falling into case (c), an aborted transaction by t included into $H_1'\psi$ can only be the last one in $\tau'|_t$. Finally, above we established that $(H_1'\psi)|_{t_0}$ does not contain aborted transactions. Hence, transactions in τ' whose status is changed from aborted to committed when switching to τ'' do not have any actions following them in τ'. Furthermore, $[\![P]\!](s)$ allows committing or aborting transactions arbitrarily. This allows us to conclude that $\tau'' \in [\![P]\!](s)$. For the same reason, we get $\tau_\psi \in [\![P]\!](s)$.

Finally, we show that $\mathsf{history}(\tau_\psi)|_{\neg\mathsf{abortedtx}} = H^c_\psi$. It is sufficient to show that $\mathsf{history}(\tau'')|_{\neg\mathsf{abortedtx}} = H''_1\psi$; since $\tau_\psi = \tau''H^{cc}$ and H^{cc} contains only committed actions, this would imply

$$\mathsf{history}(\tau_\psi)|_{\neg\mathsf{abortedtx}} = \mathsf{history}(\tau''H^{cc})|_{\neg\mathsf{abortedtx}} =$$
$$\mathsf{history}(\tau'')|_{\neg\mathsf{abortedtx}}H^{cc} = H''_1\psi H^{cc} = H^c_\psi.$$

By the choice of τ^I_t for $t \neq t_0$, every transaction in $(H'_1\psi)|_t$ is also in τ^I_t. Hence, $H'_1\psi$ is a subsequence of $\mathsf{history}(\tau')$. By the definition of τ'' and H''_1, $H''_1\psi$ is a subsequence of $\mathsf{history}(\tau'')$. Then since $H''_1\psi$ does not contain aborted transactions, $H''_1\psi$ is a subsequence of $\mathsf{history}(\tau'')|_{\neg\mathsf{abortedtx}}$.

Thus, to prove $\mathsf{history}(\tau'')|_{\neg\mathsf{abortedtx}} = H''_1\psi$ it remains to show that every non-aborted transaction in $\mathsf{history}(\tau'')$ is in $H''_1\psi$. Since the construction of τ'' from τ' changes the status of only those transactions that belong to $H'_1\psi$, it is sufficient to show that every non-aborted transaction in $\mathsf{history}(\tau')$ is in $H'_1\psi$. Here we only consider the case when such a transaction is by a thread $t \neq t_0$ and $\tau'|_t = \tau^N_t \neq \varepsilon$; we cover the other cases in [11, Appendix D]. Let χ^N_t be the last action in τ^N_t and $T = \mathsf{txof}(\psi^b, H_1\psi) \in H'_1\psi$. Then by Definition 4(iii) we get (1). Since χ^N_t comes before ψ^b in $H_1\psi$, any transaction T' in $\tau'|_t$ is such that $T' \prec_{H_1\psi} T$, which together with (1) implies the required. This concludes the proof that $\mathsf{history}(\tau'')|_{\neg\mathsf{abortedtx}} = H''_1\psi$. $\square$

We now give the other lemmas necessary for the proof. Definition 6 matches a history of $\mathcal{T}_C$ with one of $\mathcal{T}_A$ using the opacity relation, possibly after transforming the former with cTMSpast. The following lemma is used to transform a trace of P accordingly. The lemma shows that, if we consider only traces where aborted transactions abort immediately (i.e., are of the form $(\_, \_, \mathsf{txbegin})(\_, \_, \mathsf{aborted}))$, then the opacity relation implies observational refinement with respect to observing non-transactional actions and thread-local trace projections. This result is a simple adjustment of the one about the sufficiency of opacity for observational refinement to our setting [8, Theorem 16] (it was proved in [8] for a language where local variables are *not* rolled back upon a transaction abort; this difference, however, does not matter if aborted transactions abort immediately).

Lemma 2. *Consider* $\tau \in [\![P]\!](s)$ *such that all the aborted transactions in* τ *abort immediately. Let S be such that* $\mathsf{history}(\tau) \sqsubseteq_{\mathsf{op}} S$. *Then there exists* $\tau' \in [\![P]\!](s)$ *such that* $\mathsf{history}(\tau') = S$, $\tau|_{\neg\mathsf{trans}} = \tau'|_{\neg\mathsf{trans}}$ *and* $\forall t. \tau'|_t = \tau|_t$.

Let $\tau|_{\neg\mathsf{abortact}}$ be the trace obtained from τ by removing all actions inside aborted transactions, so that every such transaction aborts immediately. We can benefit from Lemma 2 because local variables are rolled back if a transaction aborts, and, hence, applying $\cdot|_{\neg\mathsf{abortact}}$ to a trace preserves its validity.

Proposition 1. $\forall \tau. \tau \in [\![P]\!](s) \implies \tau|_{\neg\mathsf{abortact}} \in [\![P]\!](s)$.

Finally, Definition 6 matches only histories of committed transactions, but the histories of the traces in Lemma 2 also contain aborted transactions. Fortunately, the following lemma allows us to add empty aborted transactions into the abstract history while preserving the opacity relation.

Lemma 3. *Let H be a history where all aborted transactions abort immediately and S be such that $H|_{\neg\text{abortedtx}} \sqsubseteq_{\text{op}} S$. There exists a history $S' \in \text{addab}(S)$ such that $H \sqsubseteq_{\text{op}} S'$.*

Definition 6(i), Proposition 1 and Lemmas 2 and 3 can be used to prove that the TMS relation preserves non-transactional actions and thread-local observable behavior of threads whose last action is not a `fault`.

Lemma 4. *If $\mathcal{T}_C \sqsubseteq_{\text{tms}} \mathcal{T}_A$ and $\mathcal{T}_A$ satisfies CLP1 and CLP2, then*

$$\forall \tau \in [\![P, \mathcal{T}_C]\!](s). \exists \tau' \in [\![P, \mathcal{T}_A]\!](s). (\tau'|_{\neg\text{trans}} = \tau|_{\neg\text{trans}}) \wedge (\forall t. (\tau'|_t)|_{\text{obs}} = (\tau|_t)|_{\text{obs}}).$$

Proof of Theorem 1(i). Given Lemma 4, we only need to establish the preservation of faults inside transactions. Consider $\tau_0 \in [\![P, \mathcal{T}_C]\!](s)$ such that $\tau_0 = \tau_1 \psi \tau_2 \chi$, where $\chi = (\_, t_0, \texttt{fault})$ is transactional and ψ is the last TM interface action by thread t_0. Then $\tau_2|_{t_0}$ consists of transactional actions and thus does not contain accesses to global variables. Hence, $\tau = \tau_1 \psi (\tau_2|_{t_0}) \chi \in [\![P, \mathcal{T}_C]\!](s)$. By our assumption, $\mathcal{T}_C \sqsubseteq_{\text{tms}} \mathcal{T}_A$. Then there exists $H_\psi^c \in \text{cTMSpast}(\text{history}(\tau))$ and $S \in \mathcal{T}_A$ such that $H_\psi^c \sqsubseteq_{\text{op}} S$. By Lemma 1, for some trace τ_ψ we have $\tau_\psi \in [\![P]\!](s)$, $\text{history}(\tau_\psi)|_{\neg\text{abortedtx}} = H_\psi^c$ and $\tau_\psi|_{t_0} = \tau|_{t_0}$. By Proposition 1, $\tau_\psi|_{\neg\text{abortact}} \in [\![P]\!](s)$. Using Lemma 3, we get a history S' such that $\text{history}(\tau_\psi|_{\neg\text{abortact}}) \sqsubseteq_{\text{op}} S'$ and $S' \in \text{addab}(S)$. Since $S \in \mathcal{T}_A$ and $\mathcal{T}_A$ is closed under immediate aborts (CLP1), we get $S' \in \mathcal{T}_A$. Hence, by Lemma 2, for some $\tau' \in [\![P, \mathcal{T}_A]\!](s)$ we have $\tau'|_{t_0} = \tau_\psi|_{t_0} = \tau|_{t_0} = \_\chi$, as required. $\square$

6.2   Proof Sketch for Theorem 1(ii) (Necessity)

Consider $\mathcal{T}_C$ and $\mathcal{T}_A$ such that $\mathcal{T}_C \preceq \mathcal{T}_A$ and $\mathcal{T}_A$ satisfies the closure conditions stated in the theorem. To show that for any $H_0 \in \mathcal{T}_C$ we have $H_0 \sqsubseteq_{\text{tms}} \mathcal{T}_A$, we have to establish conditions (i) and (ii) from Definition 6. We sketch the more interesting case of (ii), in which $H_0 = H_1 \psi H_2 = HH_2 \in \mathcal{T}_C$, where ψ is a response action by a thread t_0 that is not a committed or aborted action. We need to find $H^c \in \text{cTMSpast}(H)$ and $S \in \mathcal{T}_A$ such that $H^c \sqsubseteq_{\text{op}} S$.

To this end, we construct a program P_H (as we explain further below) where every thread t performs the sequence of transactions specified in $H|_t$. The program monitors certain properties of the TM behavior, e.g., checking that the return values obtained from methods of transactional objects in committed transactions correspond to those in H and that the real-time order between actions includes that in H. If these properties hold, thread t_0 ends by executing the `fault` command. Let s be a state with all variables set to distinguished values. We next construct a trace $\tau \in [\![P_H, \mathcal{T}_C]\!](s)$ such that $\text{history}(\tau) = H$ and t_0 faults in τ. By Definition 7, there exists $\tau' \in [\![P_H, \mathcal{T}_A]\!](s)$ such that t_0 faults in τ'. However, the program P_H is constructed so that t_0 can fault in τ' only if the properties of the TM behaviour the program monitors hold, and thus H is related to $\text{history}(\tau')$ in a certain way. This relationship allows us to construct $H^c \in \text{cTMSpast}(H)$ from H and $S \in \mathcal{T}_A$ from $\text{history}(\tau')$ such that $H^c \sqsubseteq_{\text{op}} S$.

In more detail, thread t_0 in P_H monitors the return status of every transaction and the return values obtained inside the atomic blocks corresponding to transactions committed in $H|_{t_0}$ and the (live) transaction of ψ. If there is a mismatch with $H|_{t_0}$, this is recorded in a special local variable. At the end of the transaction of ψ, t_0 checks the variable and faults if the TM behavior matched $H|_{t_0}$. This construction is motivated by the fact that faulting is the only observation Definition 7 allows us to make about the behavior of the live transaction of ψ. Since the definition does not correlate actions by threads t other than t_0 between τ and τ', such threads monitor TM behavior differently: if there is a mismatch with $H|_t$, a thread t faults immediately. Since a trace can have at most one `fault` and t_0 faults in τ', this ensures that any committed transaction in τ' behaves as in H.

To check whether an execution of P_H complies with the real-time order in H, for each transaction in H, we introduce a global variable g, which is initially 0 and is set to 1 by the thread executing the transaction right after the transaction completes, by a command following the corresponding atomic block. Before starting a transaction, each thread checks whether all transactions preceding this one in the real-time order in H have finished by reading the corresponding g variables. Thread t_0 records the outcome in the special local variable checked at the end; all other threads fault upon detecting a mismatch.

Let $H' = \text{history}(\tau')$. This construction of P_H allows us to infer that: (i) the projection of $H'|_{t_0}$ to committed transactions and $\text{txof}(\psi, H')$ is equal to the corresponding projection of $H|_{t_0}$; (ii) for all other threads t a similar relationship holds for the prefix of $H'|_t$ ending with the last transaction preceding $\text{txof}(\psi, H')$ in the real-time order; (iii) the real-time order in H' includes that in H. Transactions concurrent with $\text{txof}(\psi, H')$ in H' may behave differently from H. However, checks done by P_H inside these transactions ensure that, if such a transaction T is visible in H', then the return values inside T match those in H. The checks on the global variables g done right before T also ensure that all transactions preceding T in the real-time order in H commit or abort in H' as prescribed by H. This relationship between H and H' allows us to establish the requirements of Definition 6(ii). $\square$

7 Related Work

When presenting TMS [5], Doherty et al. discuss why it allows programmers to think only of serial executions of their programs, in which the actions of a transaction appear consecutively. This discussion—corresponding to our sufficiency result—is informal, since the paper lacks a formal model for programs and their semantics. Most of it explains how Definition 6(i) ensures the correctness of committed transactions. The discussion of the most challenging case of live transactions—corresponding to Definition 6(ii) and our Lemma 1—is one paragraph long. It only roughly sketches the construction of a trace with an abstract history allowed by TMS and does not give any reasoning for why this trace is a valid one, but only claims that constraints in Definition 6(ii) ensure this. This reasoning is very delicate, as indicated by our proof of Lemma 1, which carefully selects which actions to erase when transforming the trace. Moreover, Doherty et al. do not try to argue that TMS is the weakest condition possible, as we established by our necessity result.

Another TM consistency condition, weaker than opacity but incomparable to TMS, is *virtual world consistency* (*VWC*) [3]. Like TMS, VWC allows every operation in a live or aborted transaction to be justified by a separate abstract history. However, it places different constraints on the choice of abstract histories, which do not take into account the real-time order between actions. Because of this, VWC does not imply observational refinement for our programming language: taking into account the real-time order is necessary when threads can communicate via global variables outside transactions.

Our earlier paper [8] laid the groundwork for relating TM consistency and observational refinement, and it includes a detailed comparison with related work on opacity and observational refinement. The present paper considers a much more challenging case of a language where local variables are rolled back upon an abort. To handle this case, we developed new techniques, such as establishing the live transaction insensitivity property (Lemma 1) to prove sufficiency and proposing monitor programs for the nontrivial constraints used in the TMS definition to prove necessity. Similarly to [8] and other papers using observational refinement to study consistency conditions [13, 14], we reformulate TMS so that it is not restricted to a particular abstract TM $\mathcal{T}_A$. This generality, not allowed by the original TMS definition, has two benefits. First, our reformulation can be used to compare two TM implementations, e.g., an optimized and an unoptimized one. Second, dealing with the general definition forces us to explicitly state the closure properties required from the abstract TM, rather than having them follow implicitly from its atomic behavior.

Acknowledgements. We thank Mohsen Lesani, Victor Luchangco and the anonymous reviewers for comments that helped us improve the paper. This work was supported by EU FP7 project ADVENT (308830).

References

1. Papadimitriou, C.H.: The serializability of concurrent database updates. J. ACM 26, 631–653 (1979)
2. Guerraoui, R., Kapalka, M.: On the correctness of transactional memory. In: PPOPP, pp. 175–184 (2008)
3. Imbs, D., Raynal, M.: Virtual world consistency: A condition for STM systems (with a versatile protocol with invisible read operations). Theor. Comput. Sci. 444, 113–127 (2012)
4. Attiya, H., Hans, S., Kuznetsov, P., Ravi, S.: Safety of deferred update in transactional memory. In: ICDCS (2013)
5. Doherty, S., Groves, L., Luchangco, V., Moir, M.: Towards formally specifying and verifying transactional memory. Formal Aspects of Computing 25, 769–799 (2013)
6. He, J., Hoare, C., Sanders, J.: Prespecification in data refinement. Information Processing Letters 25, 71–76 (1987)
7. He, J., Hoare, C., Sanders, J.: Data refinement refined. In: Robinet, B., Wilhelm, R. (eds.) ESOP 1986. LNCS, vol. 213, pp. 187–196. Springer, Heidelberg (1986)
8. Attiya, H., Gotsman, A., Hans, S., Rinetzky, N.: A programming language perspective on transactional memory consistency. In: PODC, pp. 309–318 (2013)
9. Scala STM Expert Group: Scala STM quick start guide (2012), http://nbronson.github.io/scala-stm/quick_start.html
10. Lesani, M., Luchangco, V., Moir, M.: Putting opacity in its place. In: WTTM (2012)
11. Attiya, H., Gotsman, A., Hans, S., Rinetzky, N.: Safety of live transactions in transactional memory: Tms is necessary and sufficient. Technical Report CS-2014-02, Technion (2014)
12. Herlihy, M., Wing, J.M.: Linearizability: A correctness condition for concurrent objects. ACM Transactions on Programming Languages and Systems 12, 463–492 (1990)
13. Gotsman, A., Yang, H.: Liveness-preserving atomicity abstraction. In: Aceto, L., Henzinger, M., Sgall, J. (eds.) ICALP 2011, Part II. LNCS, vol. 6756, pp. 453–465. Springer, Heidelberg (2011)
14. Filipović, I., O'Hearn, P., Rinetzky, N., Yang, H.: Abstraction for concurrent objects. In: Castagna, G. (ed.) ESOP 2009. LNCS, vol. 5502, pp. 252–266. Springer, Heidelberg (2009)

Decomposing Opacity

Mohsen Lesani and Jens Palsberg

Computer Science Department
University of California, Los Angeles
{lesani,palsberg}@ucla.edu

Abstract. Transactional memory (TM) algorithms are subtle and the TM correctness conditions are intricate. Decomposition of the correctness condition can bring modularity to TM algorithm design and verification. We present a decomposition of opacity called markability as a conjunction of separate intuitive invariants. We prove the equivalence of opacity and markability. The proofs of markability of TM algorithms can be aided by and mirror the algorithm design intuitions. As an example, we prove the markability and hence opacity of the TL2 algorithm. In addition, based on one of the invariants, we present lower bound results for the time complexity of TM algorithms.

1 Introduction

A transactional memory (TM) [24, 36] is a concurrent object that encapsulates and manages accesses to an array of memory locations. The clients of a TM are transactions, sequences of accesses to the encapsulated locations. A transactional processing system is the composition of a TM and a set of client transactions. While the clients issue the invocation events, the TM issues the response events. Researchers have proposed several TM correctness conditions including opacity [20], VWC [25], TMS1 and TMS2 [13], and DU-opacity [2] that characterize the required safety conditions on TM response events.

Considering strength of the promised safety properties, designing a correct TM is an art. TM algorithms whether in software [9, 11, 12, 15, 23, 35], hardware [1, 7, 22, 37] or hybrid [8, 10, 26, 31, 32] are subtle and prone to bugs [30]. Thus, verification of TM algorithms by model checking [4–6, 16–18, 33], invariant generation [14] and theorem proving [28] has been a topic of recent attention. Verifying a complicated monolithic condition for a realistic specification of a TM algorithm can be a formidable problem. Can the correctness condition of TM be stated as a conjunction of simpler intuitive conditions? In other words, is there an meaningful decomposition of the correctness condition? What are the separate invariants that the TM designers should maintain? Decomposition of the correctness condition enhances the understanding of the correctness and brings modularity to the algorithm design. It showcases different aspects of correctness and helps designers concentrate on maintaining one aspect at a time. More importantly, separation has obvious benefits of modularity and scalability for verification. Furthermore, it supports studying the time complexity and performance of TM algorithms.

F. Kuhn (Ed.): DISC 2014, LNCS 8784, pp. 391–405, 2014.
© Springer-Verlag Berlin Heidelberg 2014

We decompose opacity to separate intuitive invariants. We define that an execution history is markable if there is a specific ordering relation on the set of transactions and read operations called marking such that three invariants are satisfied. We prove that markability is required and sufficient for opacity. At a high level, the first invariant called write-observation requires that each read operation returns the most current value. The second invariant called read-preservation requires that the read location is not overwritten in the interval that the location is read and the transaction takes effect. The third invariant is the well-known real-time-preservation property. We show that the marking relation for the TL2 algorithm [11] can be defined using the execution order and the linearization order of method calls on the used synchronization objects and proofs of markability can be aided by and mirror the algorithm design intuitions. We prove markability and hence opacity of TL2. Finally, inspired by the read-preservation invariant, we present lower bound results for the time complexity of a class of TM algorithms.

In the following sections, we first introduce the notion of markability and present the marking of TL2 as an example. We then formally define markability, and present the marking theorem that states the equivalence of opacity and markability. Next, we formally state the marking relation of TL2 and state that TL2 is markable and hence opaque. Finally, we present our lower bound results for the time complexity of TM algorithms.

2   Write-observation and Read-preservation

In this section, we explain the main ideas behind markability by focusing on complete histories with only global reads and writes. A history is complete if every transaction in it is either aborted or committed. A read R by a transaction T is global if T has no write to the same location before R. A write W by a transaction T is global if T has no write to the same location after W.

A transaction history is *markable* if and only if there exists a *marking* of it that is *write-observant*, *read-preserving*, and *real-time-preserving*. We explain each property in turn.

A marking of a transaction history is a relation on the union of the *transactions* and the *read operations* in the history. We can think of the marking as the union of a collection of orders: The *effect order*: The effect order is a total order of the transactions. The *access orders*: Consider an unaborted read operation R on a location i. Let us refer to the committed transactions that have write operation(s) to location i as *writers of i*. For each such R, the access order is an antisymmetric relation that orders R and every writer of i. The effect order represents the order in which the transactions appear to take effect. The access order of a read operation R from a location i represents where the access to i by R has happened between the accesses to i by the writers of i.

Note that marking not only recognizes the points where transactions take effect but also the points where reads take place. The effect point of a transaction captures the point where the whole transaction takes effect. But a transaction

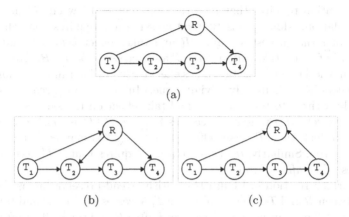

Fig. 1. Illustrations of Write-observation and Read-preservation

is split into multiple operations. Particularly, read operations observe values before the commit operation is even invoked. Any value that the TM algorithm returns in response to a read invocation should be justified at the point where the transaction takes effect. There is a point where each writer transaction writes the new value to the underlying shared objects. Every read operation reads the value that it returns at a certain point between the write points of the writer transactions. The access order captures this design decision. Having the access order in addition to the effect order makes it possible to decompose the consistency condition into two orthogonal invariants. Particularly, the read-preservation invariant makes sure that the read value is not overwritten in the interval between the point where a read happens and the point where the transaction takes effect. Next, we will explain write-observation and read-preservation invariants in turn.

At a high level, write-observation means that each read operation should read the most current value. Let us explain this idea in more detail. Consider an unaborted read operation R from a location i. Let *pre-accessors* be the writers of i that come before R in the access order for R. We can use the effect order to determine the *last* pre-accessor that is, the pre-accessor that is greatest in the effect order. Write-observation requires that the value that R reads be the same as the value written by the last pre-accessor.

Figure 1 illustrates the write-observation and read-preservation invariants. Each sub-figure shows a marking relation $\sqsubseteq$. In every sub-figure, the effect order is $T_1 \sqsubseteq T_2 \sqsubseteq T_3 \sqsubseteq T_4$ and the transaction T_3 performs the read operation R. In Figure 1(a), T_1 and $T4$ are writers of i and the access order for R is $\{T_1 \sqsubseteq R, R \sqsubseteq T_4\}$. T_1 is the last pre-accessor for R. Thus, by write-observation, R is expected to return the value that T_1 writes to i.

At a high level, read-preservation means that the location read by a read operation is not overwritten between the points that the read takes place and the transaction takes effect. Let us explain this idea in more detail. Consider an unaborted read operation R by a transaction T from a location i. Intuitively, read-preservation requires that no writer of i comes between R and T in the marking relation. More precisely, read-preservation requires that there is no writer T' of i that accesses i *after* R and takes effect *before* T and there is no writer T' of i that takes effect *after* T and accesses i *before* R. (Note that depending on whether a transaction takes effect earlier or later in its lifetime, one of these two conditions is usually trivially true.) In other words, read-preservation requires the writers to both access i and take effect on the same side of R and T. More precisely, if a writer T' accesses i *before* R (T' is marked before R in the access order), then T' takes effect *before* T (T' is marked before T in the effect order) too. Similarly, read-preservation requires that if T' accesses i *after* R, it takes effect *after* T too.

The marking relation in Figure 1(a) satisfies read-preservation as there is no writer between R and T_3. The transaction T_1 accesses i before R and takes effect before T_3 too. The transaction T_4 accesses i after R and takes effect after T_3 too. Figures 1(b) and 1(c) show markings that are not read-preserving. In Figure 1(b), T_1, T_2 and $T4$ are writers of i and the access order is $\{T_1 \sqsubseteq R, R \sqsubseteq T_2, R \sqsubseteq T_4\}$. The transaction T_2 is between R and T_3. Therefore, the marking is not read-preserving. In Figure 1(c), T_1 and $T4$ are writers of i and the access order is $\{T_1 \sqsubseteq R, T_4 \sqsubseteq R\}$. The transaction $T4$ is between T_3 and R. Therefore, the marking is not read-preserving.

The real-time-preservation condition requires that if all the events of a transaction T happen before all the events of another transaction T', then T is less than T' in the effect order.

Our marking theorem says that a history is opaque if and only if it is markable. So, to prove opacity, we can focus on proving markability. The algorithm designer can usually define the marking relation readily from the guarantees (such as linearization orders) of the used shared objects. In contrast to opacity, markability of the algorithm can be established by modular verification of the separate markability conditions that involve different aspects of the algorithm.

If a transaction history H is markable, we can show that H is opaque. We construct a justifying history by ordering the transactions in the effect order. Consider an arbitrary read R from i by T. We call the writers of i that take effect before T, pre-effectors. Let the last pre-effector be the pre-effector that is the greatest in the effect order. We need to show that the value that R returns is the value that the last pre-effector writes. We recall that we refer to the writers of i that access i before R as pre-accessors and refer to the pre-accessor that is greatest in the effect order as the last pre-accessor. First, we argue that pre-accessors are exactly pre-effectors. If a writer of i accesses before R, by read-preservation, it does not take effect after T. Thus, by totality of effect order, it takes effect before T. In the other direction, if a writer of i takes effect before T, by read-preservation, it does not access after R. Thus, as the access order orders R and every writer of i, T accesses before R. Second, from write-observation, we have that R returns the value written by the last pre-accessor. Thus, from the two above statements, we have that R returns the value written by the last pre-effector. This is the essence of the condition needed to prove opacity.

3   Marking TL2

Now, we look at the marking of the TL2 algorithm [11] as an example. TL2 is specified in Figure 2. The specification first declares the type of the used synchronization objects and then defines the methods of the TM interface.

In the $init$ method, each transaction t reads the current snapshot version from $clock$ at $I01$ and writes it to the read version register $rver[t]$ at $I02$. The read version is read at $R07$ and $C08$ to validate the read values. TL2 is a deferred-update TM algorithm. A value that a transaction t writes to a location is buffered in the write set $wset[t]$ at $W01$ and is written back to register $reg[i]$ at $C16_i$ while t is committing. TL2 records a version in the register $ver[i]$ for the value stored in the register $reg[i]$. The version register $ver[i]$ is updated to ascending numbers at $C17_i$ after new values are written back to $reg[i]$ at $C16_i$. The try-lock $lock[i]$ is used for exclusive access to the registers for location i. At commit, the lock $lock[i]$ of each location i in the write set $wset[t]$ is acquired at $C01$ to $C06$. (If a lock cannot be acquired, the previously acquired locks are released at $C05$ and the transaction is aborted at $C06$.) Then, a new snapshot number is read from $clock$ at $C07$. Then, for each location in the read set $rset[t]$, first $lock[i]$ and then $ver[i]$ are read at $C10_i$ and $C11_i$ and the read is validated. (If a read is not validated, the acquired locks are released at $C13$ and the transaction is aborted at $C14$.) Finally, the value buffered for each location i in $wset[t]$ is written back at $C15_i$ to $C18_i$. For each pair in the write set $wset[t]$, the following three operations are executed in order. First, the buffered value is written back to $reg[i]$, then $ver[i]$ is updated, and then $lock[i]$ is released. To read a location i, a transaction reads $ver[i]$, $reg[i]$, $lock[i]$ and again $ver[i]$ in order at $R03$ to $R06$ and then validates the read. (If the validation fails, the transaction is aborted.) Finally, i is added to the read set $rset[t]$ and the read value is returned.

Let us describe the marking relation for TL2. The $clock$ object numbers the snapshots. Every transaction reads an initial snapshot number at $I01$. A committing transaction makes a new snapshot at $C07$. The effect point of a TL2 transaction is $I01$, if it is live or aborted and, is $C07$, if it is committed. The effect order of transactions is the linearization order of $clock$ for their effect points. The access point of a read operation is at $R04$ where $reg[i]$ is read and the access point of a writer of i is $C16_i$ where $reg[i]$ is written. Consider a read R from i and a writer T' to i. If the access point of T' is executed before the access point of R, then T' is ordered before R in the access order of R. Otherwise, T' is ordered after R in the access order of R. The access and effect points for markability of a TM are reminiscent of the linearization points for linearizability of a concurrent data structure.

One of the two conjuncts of the read-preservation property requires that for every transaction T with an unaborted read operation R from a location i, there is no writer T' of i such that T' takes effect after T and accesses i before R. Let us see how TL2 preserves this property. We assume that there exists such a writer T' and show that the validation checks embodied in TL2 detect the existence of T' and abort R. We consider a transaction T with a read operation R from a location i and a writer T' of i. We assume that T' takes effect after

reg: **BasicRegister**$[\|I\|]$,	$rver$: **ThreadLocal BasicRegister**,
ver: **AtomicRegister**$[\|I\|]$,	$rset$: **ThreadLocal BasicSet**,
$lock$: **TryLock**$[\|I\|]$,	$wset$: **ThreadLocal BasicMap**,
$clock$: **SCounter**,	$lset$: **ThreadLocal BasicSet**

def $init_t()$	**def** $commit_t()$
$I01 \triangleright$ $snap = clock.read()$	$C01 \triangleright$ **foreach** $(i \in wset[t])$
$I02 \triangleright$ $rver[t].write(snap)$	$C02_i \triangleright$ $locked = lock[i].trylock()$
$I03 \triangleright$ **return** ok	**if** $(\neg locked)$
def $read_t(i)$	$C03_i \triangleright$ $lset.add(i)$
$R01 \triangleright$ $pv = wset[t].get(i)$	**else**
if $(pv \neq \bot)$	$C04_i \triangleright$ **foreach** $(j \in lset)$
$R02 \triangleright$ **return** pv	$C05_{ij} \triangleright$ $lock[j].unlock()$
	$C06_i \triangleright$ **return** $\mathbb{A}$
$R03 \triangleright$ $s_1 = ver[i].read()$	
$R04 \triangleright$ $v = reg[i].read()$	$C07 \triangleright$ $wver = clock.iaf()$
$R05 \triangleright$ $l = lock[i].read()$	
$R06 \triangleright$ $s_2 = ver[i].read()$	$C08 \triangleright$ $sver = rver[t].read()$
$R07 \triangleright$ $sver = rver[t].read()$	**if** $(wver \neq sver + 1)$
if $(\neg(\neg l \land s_1 = s_2 \land s_2 \leq sver))$	$C09 \triangleright$ **foreach** $(i \in rset[t])$
$R08 \triangleright$ **return** $\mathbb{A}$	$C10_i \triangleright$ $l = lock[i].read()$
	$C11_i \triangleright$ $s = ver[i].read()$
$R09 \triangleright$ $rver[t].add(i)$	**if** $(\neg(\neg l \land s \leq sver))$
$R10 \triangleright$ **return** v	$C12_i \triangleright$ **foreach** $(j \in lset)$
$\{R03 \rightarrow R04,\ R04 \rightarrow R05,\ R05 \rightarrow R06\}$	$C13_{ij} \triangleright$ $lock[j].unlock()$
def $write_t(i, v)$	$C14_i \triangleright$ **return** $\mathbb{A}$
$W01 \triangleright$ $wset[t].put(i, v)$	
$W02 \triangleright$ **return** ok	$C15 \triangleright$ **foreach** $((i, v) \in wset[t])$
def $abort_t()$	$C16_i \triangleright$ $reg[i].write(v)$
$A01 \triangleright$ **return** $\mathbb{A}$	$C17_i \triangleright$ $ver[i].write(wver)$
	$C18_i \triangleright$ $lock[i].unlock()$
	$C19 \triangleright$ **return** $\mathbb{C}$
	$\{C01 \rightarrow C07,\ C10 \rightarrow C11,\ C09 \rightarrow C15,$
	$C16 \rightarrow C17, C17 \rightarrow C18\}$

Fig. 2. $TL2$ Algorithm Specification

T and T' accesses i before R. For brevity, we consider only the case that T is a live or aborted (not a committed) transaction. Figure 3 depicts the two transactions. We use the binary operators $\prec_X$ to denote execution order, $\sim_X$ to denote concurrent execution and $\precsim_X$ to denote in-order or concurrent execution of method calls. We use the binary operators $\prec_{clock}$, $\prec_{ver[i]}$ and $\prec_{lock[i]}$ to denote the linearization order of $clock$, $ver[i]$ and $lock[i]$ respectively.[1] We recall that the

---

[1] We have formally proved the markability of TL2 using a novel program logic [27] that facilitates reasoning about execution and linearization orders. To keep the focus of this paper on markability, we use a simplified reasoning instead of the logic.

T		T'	
$I01 \triangleright$	$snap = clock.read()$	$C02_i \triangleright$	$lock[i].trylock()$
$I02 \triangleright$	$rver[t].write(snap)$		$\cdots$
		$C07 \triangleright$	$wver = clock.iaf()$
	$\cdots$		$\cdots$
		$C16_i \triangleright$	$reg[i].write(v)$
$R04 \triangleright$	$v = reg[i].read()$	$C17_i \triangleright$	$ver[i].write(wver)$
$R05 \triangleright$	$l = lock[i].read()$	$C18_i \triangleright$	$lock[i].unlock()$
$R06 \triangleright$	$s_2 = ver[i].read()$		
$R07 \triangleright$	$sver = rver[t].read()$		
	$\mathbf{if}\ (\neg(\neg l\ \wedge\ s_1 = s_2\ \wedge\ s_2 \leq sver))$		
	$\mathbf{return}\ \mathbb{A}$		

Fig. 3. TL2 Read-Preservation Example

real-time-preservation property of a linearizable object o states that if a method call m_1 on o is executed before another method call m_2 on o, then m_1 is linearized before m_2. Equivalently, if m_1 is linearized before m_2, then m_1 is executed before or concurrent to m_2. By the marking relation defined above, from the premise that T' takes effect after T, and that T is aborted and T' is committed, we have (1) $I01 \prec_{clock} C07$. Similarly, by the marking relation defined above, from the premise that T' accesses i before R, we have (2) $C16_i \prec_{reg[i]} R04$. The method calls $R05$ and $C18_i$ are on the object $lock[i]$. We consider two cases for the linearization order of them and show that R returns $\mathbb{A}$ in both cases. Case 1: (3) $R05 \prec_{lock[i]} C18_i$. From the execution, we have (4) $C02_i \prec_X C16_i$ and (5) $R04 \prec_X R05$. By the real-time-preservation property for $ver[i]$ on 2, we have (6) $C16_i \precsim_X R04$. By the transitivity of the execution order on 4, 6 and 5, we have $C02_i \prec_X R05$; thus, by the real-time-preservation property for $lock[i]$, we have (7) $C02_i \prec_{lock[i]} R05$. From 7 and 3, we have that $R05$ is executed when $lock[i]$ is acquired. Therefore, $R05$ returns $true$ i.e. $l = true$. Thus, the validation check fails and R returns $\mathbb{A}$.

Case 2: (8) $C18_i \prec_{lock[i]} R05$. By the real-time-preservation property for $lock[i]$, from 8, we have (9) $C18_i \precsim_X R05$. From the execution, we have (10) $C17_i \prec_X C18_i$ and (11) $R05 \prec_X R06$. By the transitivity of the execution order on 10, 9 and 11, we have (12) $C17_i \prec_X R06$. By the real-time-preservation property for $ver[i]$, from 12, we have (13) $C17_i \prec_{ver[i]} R06$. It is straightforward to separately prove that (14) The register $ver[i]$ is updated only to ascending numbers. From 14 and 13, we have that $R06$ reads a value that is greater than or equal to the value that $C17_i$ writes i.e. (15) $s_2 \geq wver$. From 1, and that iaf returns the incremented value, we have (16) $snap < wver$. The value of $sver$ is read at $R07$ from $rver$. The thread-local register $rver$ is only assigned at $I02$ to $snap$. Thus, we have (17) $snap = sver$. From 15, 16 and 17, we have $s_2 > sver$. Thus, the validation check fails and R returns $\mathbb{A}$ in this case too.

Please see the appendix [29] for the proof of markability of TL2 and also the marking relations for DSTM (visible reads) [23] and NORec [9] TM algorithms.

4   Markability

In this section, we first present preliminary definitions about execution histories and then, present the formal definition of markability and state its equivalence to opacity.

4.1   Histories

Strings. We use $\|s\|$ to denote the size of the string s. If s_1 and s_2 are strings, we write $s_1 \Subset s_2$ iff s_1 is a subsequence of s_2. For example, $bd \Subset abcde$. Let s be an isogram string (i.e. contains no repeating occurrence of the alphabet.) For any s_1, s_2, we write $s_1 \lhd_s s_2$ iff the last element of s_1 occurs before the first element of s_2 in s. For example, $ab \lhd_{abcde} de$.

Method Calls and Events. An *invocation event* is of the form $inv(l \rhd o.n_T(v))$ where l is a label, o is an object, n is a method name, T is a transaction identifier and v is a value. A *response event* is of the form $ret(l \rhd v)$ where l is a label and v is a value. A *completed* method call is the sequence of an invocation event and the matching response event (with the same label). We use $l \rhd o.n_T(v){:}v$ to denote the completed method call $inv(l \rhd o.n_T(v)) \cdot ret(l \rhd v)$.

Operations on Event Sequences. Let E and E' be *event sequences*. We use $E \cdot E'$ to denote the *concatenation* of E and E'. For a transaction T, we use $E|T$ to denote the subsequence of all events of T in E. A sequence of events is *sequential* if and only if it is a sequence of completed method calls possibly followed by an invocation event. A transaction T is *sequential* in a sequence of events E if $E|T$ is sequential.

Execution History. An *execution history* is an event sequence where invocation events have unique labels and every transaction is sequential. We say label l is in X and write $l \in X$ if there is an invocation event with label l in X. We use l, R and W to denote labels. As the labels are unique in a history, the following functions on labels are defined. The functions obj_X, $name_X$, $trans_X$, $arg1_X$, $arg2_X$, $retv_X$ map labels to the receiving object, the method name, the transaction identifier, the first and the second arguments, and the return value associated with the labels. Similary, iEv and rEv functions on labels map labels to the invocation and the response events associated with the labels.

Real-time Relations. For an execution history X, we define the *method call real-time* relations $\prec_X$ and $\preceq_X$ on labels as follows: First, $l_1 \prec_X l_2$ iff $rEv(l_1) \lhd_X iEv(l_2)$. Second, $l_1 \preceq_X l_2$ iff $l_1 \prec_X l_2 \lor l_1 = l_2$.

For an execution history X, we define the *transaction real-time* relations $\lll_X$ and $\lll\!\!\!\!{=}\,_X$ as follows. First, $T \lll_X T'$ iff $X|T \lhd_X X|T'$. Second, $T \lll\!\!\!\!{=}\,_X T'$ iff $T \lll_X T' \lor T = T'$.

Transactional Memory. The *transactional memory* is a singleton object *mem* that encapsulates a set of locations where each location, $i \in I$, $I = \{1, \ldots, m\}$ encapsulates a value v. The object *mem* has five methods $init_t()$, $read_t(i)$, $write_t(i, v)$, $commit_t()$ and $abort_t()$. The parameter t is the invoking transaction identifier. The method call $init_t()$ initializes t and returns ok. The method call $read_t(i)$ returns the value of location i or aborts t and returns $\mathbb{A}$. The method $write_t(i, v)$ writes v to location i and returns ok or aborts t and returns $\mathbb{A}$. The method $commit_t()$ tries to commit transaction t. If t is successfully committed, it returns $\mathbb{C}$; otherwise, it returns $\mathbb{A}$. The method $abort_t()$ aborts t and returns $\mathbb{A}$. The object *mem* can be implicit, that is $read_t(i)$ abbreviates $mem.read_T(i)$. The reserved values ok, $\mathbb{A}$, $\mathbb{C}$ denote successful completion of writes and, abortion and commitment of transactions respectively.

Transaction History. A *transaction history* H is an execution history such that $H|mem = H_{Init} \cdot H'$ with the following conditions. H_{Init} is the following history that initializes every location to v_0. $H_{Init} = l_{0i} \triangleright init_{T_0}() \cdot l_{00} \triangleright write_{T_0}(1, v_0):ok \cdot \ldots \cdot l_{0m} \triangleright write_{T_0}(m, v_0):ok \cdot l_{0c} \triangleright commit_{T_0}:\mathbb{C}$. For every $T \in H'$, the history $H'|T$ is a prefix of $E.E'$. The event sequence E is the initialization method call $l \triangleright init_T()$ (for some l), and then a sequence of reads $l \triangleright read_T(i):v$ and writes $l \triangleright write_T(i, v)$ (for some l, i, and v). The event sequence E' is one of the following sequences (for some l, i, and v): (1) $inv(l \triangleright read_T(i))$, $ret(l \triangleright \mathbb{A})$, (2) $inv(l \triangleright write_T(i, v))$, $ret(l \triangleright \mathbb{A})$, (3) $inv(l \triangleright commit_T())$, $ret(l \triangleright \mathbb{C})$, (4) $inv(l \triangleright commit_T())$, $ret(l \triangleright \mathbb{A})$, or (5) $inv(l \triangleright abort_T())$, $ret(l \triangleright \mathbb{A})$. Let $THistory$ denote the set of transaction histories. Let $Trans(H)$ denote the set of transactions of H. The projection of H on i, written $H|i$, denotes the subsequence of history H that contains exactly the events on location i. For a TM algorithm specification π, let $\mathbb{H}(\pi)$ denote the set of complete transaction histories that result from execution of transactions with π.

4.2   Formal Definition of Markability

First, we present some preliminary definitions in Figure 4. (We use the prefix T before some of the terms for transactions to avoid confusion with similar terms that are usually used for general concurrent objects.) A transaction T is *committed* or *aborted* in a transaction history H if there is respectively a commit or abort response event for T in H. A *completed* transaction is either committed or aborted. A *live* transaction is a transaction that is not completed. A *pending* transaction has a pending event and a *commit-pending* transaction has a commit pending event. An *extension* of a history is obtained by committing or aborting its commit-pending transactions and aborting the other live transactions.

A *local read* is a read that is preceded by a write by the same transaction to the same location. Intuitively, a local read should read a value that is previously written by the same transaction and hence the name. A *global read* is a read that is not local. A *local write* is a write that precedes a write by the same transaction to the same location. A local write is overwritten by the same transaction and

$$Committed(H) = \{T \mid \exists l \in H : obj_H(l) = mem \wedge trans_H(l) = T \wedge$$
$$retv_H(l) = \mathbb{C}\}$$
$$Aborted(H) = \{T \mid \exists l \in H : obj_H(l) = mem \wedge trans_H(l) = T \wedge$$
$$retv_H(l) = \mathbb{A}\}$$
$$Completed(H) = Committed(H) \cup Aborted(H)$$
$$Live(H) = Trans(H) \setminus Completed(H)$$
$$CommitPending(H) = \{T \mid T \in Live(H) \wedge \exists l \in H :$$
$$obj_H(l) = mem \wedge obj_H(l) = mem \wedge trans_H(l) = T\}$$
$$TExtension(H) = \{H' \mid H' \in THistory \wedge \exists H'' : H' = H \cdot H'' \wedge$$
$$Trans(H'') \subseteq Trans(H) \wedge \forall T : \|H''|T\| \le 1 \wedge$$
$$Live(H) \setminus CommitPending(H) \subseteq Aborted(H') \wedge$$
$$CommitPending(H) \subseteq Completed(H')\}$$
$$TReads(H) = \{R \mid R \in H \wedge obj_H(R) = mem \wedge name_H(R) = read \wedge$$
$$retv_H(R) \ne \mathbb{A}\}$$
$$TWrites(H) = \{W \mid W \in H \wedge obj_H(W) = mem \wedge name_H(W) = write \wedge$$
$$retv_H(W) \ne \mathbb{A}\}$$
$$LocalTReads(H) = \{R \mid R \in TReads(H) \wedge \exists W \in TWrites(H) :$$
$$trans_H(R) = trans_H(W) \wedge$$
$$arg1_H(R) = arg1_H(W) \wedge W \prec_H R\}$$
$$GlobalTReads(H) = TReads(H) \setminus LocalTReads(H)$$
$$LocalTWrites(H) = \{W \mid W \in TWrites(H) \wedge \exists W' \in TWrites(H) :$$
$$trans_H(W) = trans_H(W') \wedge$$
$$arg1_H(W) = arg1_H(W') \wedge W \prec_H W'\}$$
$$GlobalTWrites(H) = TWrites(H) \setminus LocalTWrites(H)$$
$$Writers_H(i) = \{T \mid T \in Trans(H) \wedge \exists l \in TWrites(H) : arg1_H(l) = i \wedge$$
$$trans_H(l) = T \wedge T \in Committed(H)\}$$

Fig. 4. Basic Definitions

hence the name. A *global write* is a write that is not local. The *writers of i* are the committed transactions that write to location i.

Markability is defined in Figure 5. A *marking* $\sqsubseteq$ of a transaction history is the union of the following relations on the set of transactions and the global reads. The *effect order*: The set of transactions is totally ordered by the marking relation $\sqsubseteq$. In other words, the marking relation $\sqsubseteq$ is total, antisymmetric and transitive on the set of transactions. The *access orders*: For each global read R from a location i, R and every writer of i are ordered by the marking relation $\sqsubseteq$. In other words, the marking relation $\sqsubseteq$ totally orders every global read R from a location i with respect to writers of i and is antisymmetric.

The *write-observation* property is comprised of the two properties: *local write-observation* and *global write-observation*. Local write-observation requires that every local read R from a location i returns the value written by the last write to i that is executed before R by the same transaction. As we defined before,

$Marking(H) = \{\sqsubseteq \mid$
$\quad \forall T1, T2, T3 \in Trans(H):$
$\qquad (T1 \sqsubseteq T2 \ \lor \ T2 \sqsubseteq T1) \land$
$\qquad (T1 \sqsubseteq T2 \ \land \ T2 \sqsubseteq T1) \Rightarrow (T1 = T2) \land$
$\qquad (T1 \sqsubseteq T2) \ \land \ (T2 \sqsubseteq T3) \Rightarrow (T1 \sqsubseteq T3) \land$
$\quad \forall R, T: Let \ i = arg1_H(R): (R \in GlobalTRead(H) \ \land \ T \in Writers_H(i)) \Rightarrow$
$\qquad (R \sqsubseteq T \ \lor \ T \sqsubseteq R) \land$
$\qquad (R \sqsubseteq T \Rightarrow \neg T \sqsubseteq R) \ \land \ (T \sqsubseteq R \Rightarrow \neg R \sqsubseteq T)\}$
$NoWriteBetween_H(W, R) \Leftrightarrow$
$\quad \forall W' \in TWrites(H): W' \preceq_H W \ \lor \ R \prec_H W'$
$LocalWriteObs(H) \Leftrightarrow$
$\quad \forall R \in LocalTReads(H): Let \ T = trans_H(R), i = arg1_H(R), H' = H|T|i:$
$\quad \exists W \in TWrites(H'):$
$\quad W \prec_{H'} R \ \land \ NoWriteBetween_{H'}(W, R) \ \land \ retv_{H'}(R) = arg2_{H'}(W)$
$NoWriterBetween_{H,i}(x, \sqsubseteq, x') \Leftrightarrow$
$\quad \forall T \in Writers_H(i): T \sqsubseteq x \ \lor \ x' \sqsubseteq T$
$LastPreAccessor_{H,\sqsubseteq}(T', R) \Leftrightarrow Let \ i = arg1_H(R), T = trans_H(R):$
$\quad T' \in Writers_H(i) \ \land \ T' \neq T \ \land \ T' \sqsubseteq R \ \land \ NoWriterBetween_{H,i}(T', \sqsubseteq, R)$
$GlobalWriteObs(H, \sqsubseteq) \Leftrightarrow$
$\quad \forall R \in GlobalTReads(H): \exists W \in GlobalTWrites(H): Let \ T' = trans_H(W):$
$\quad LastPreAccessor_{H,\sqsubseteq}(T', R) \land$
$\quad arg1_H(R) = arg1_H(W) \ \land \ retv_H(R) = arg2_H(W)$
$WriteObs(H, \sqsubseteq) \Leftrightarrow$
$\quad LocalWriteObs(H) \ \land \ GlobalWriteObs(H, \sqsubseteq)$
$ReadPres(H, \sqsubseteq) \Leftrightarrow$
$\quad \forall R \in GlobalTReads(H): Let \ i = arg1_H(R), T = trans_H(R):$
$\quad NoWriterBetween_{H,i}(R, \sqsubseteq, T) \ \land \ NoWriterBetween_{H,i}(T, \sqsubseteq, R)$
$RealTimePres(H, \sqsubseteq) \Leftrightarrow$
$\quad \preceq_H \subseteq \sqsubseteq$
$FinalStateMarkable = \{H \mid$
$\quad H \in THistory \ \land \ \exists H' \in TExtension(H): \exists \sqsubseteq \in Marking(H'):$
$\quad WriteObs(H', \sqsubseteq) \ \land \ ReadPres(H', \sqsubseteq) \ \land \ RealTimePres(H', \sqsubseteq)\}$

Fig. 5. *FinalStateMarkable*

pre-accessors of R are the writers of i that are ordered before R in the access order and the last pre-accessor of R is the one that is greatest in the effect order. Global write-observation requires that the value that every global read R from a location i returns is the value written by the global write to i by the last pre-accessor transaction of R.

The *Read-preservation* property requires that for every global read R from location i by transaction T, there is no writer transaction T' of i such that T' is marked between R and T (i.e. T' accesses i after R and takes effect before

T), or similarly, T' is marked between T and R (i.e. T' takes effect after T and accesses i before R).

The *real-time-preservation* property requires that if T is before T' in the transaction real-time order, then T takes effect before T' as well.

A transaction history is *final-state-markable* if and only if there exists a marking for an extension of it that is write-observant, read-preserving, and real-time-preserving.

The marking theorem states that a transaction history is final-state-opaque if and only if it is final-state-markable. The formal definition of opacity and the proofs are available in the appendix [29].

Theorem 1 (Marking). $FinalStateOpaque = FinalStateMarkable.$

5   Opacity of TL2

Now, we define the marking relation for the TL2 algorithm in Figure 2. We use the call string label $l_1{}'l_2$ to denote the method call labeled l_2 that is executed in the body of the method call labeled l_1. We use $initOf_H(T)$ and $commitOf_H(T)$ to denote the *init* and *commit* method calls of T in H.

Definition 1 (Marking TL2). *Consider an execution history $H \in \mathbb{H}(TL2)$. Let*

$$Eff(T) = \begin{cases} initOf_H(T)'I01 & if\ T \in Aborted(H) \\ commitOf_H(T)'C07 & if\ T \in Committed(H) \end{cases}$$
$$readAcc(R) = R'R04$$
$$writeAcc(T, i) = commitOf_H(T)'C16_i$$

The marking $\sqsubseteq$ for H is the reflexive closure of the relation $\sqsubset$ that is defined as follows:

$$\{(T, T') \mid T, T' \in Trans(H) \land Eff(T) \prec_{clock} Eff(T')\} \cup$$
$$\{(T, R) \mid Let\ i = arg1(R)\colon R \in GlobalTReads(H), T \in Writers_H(i) \land$$
$$writeAcc(T, i) \prec_H readAcc(R)\} \cup$$
$$\{(R, T) \mid Let\ i = arg1(R)\colon R \in GlobalTReads(H), T \in Writers_H(i) \land$$
$$readAcc(R) \precsim_H writeAcc(T, i)\}$$

The following theorems state the markability and the opacity of $TL2$.

Theorem 2 (Markability of TL2). $\forall H \in \mathbb{H}(TL2)\colon H \in FinalStateMarkable$

Corollary 1 (Opacity of TL2). $\forall H \in \mathbb{H}(TL2)\colon H \in FinalStateOpaque$

The appendix [29] presents the proofs. The above corollary states that every history of TL2 is final-state-opaque. As the set of histories of a TM algorithm is prefix-closed, a TM algorithm is opaque if and only if every history of it is final-state-opaque. (See [21], Observation 7.4.) Therefore, TL2 is opaque.

6   The Cost of Read Validation

The read-preservation invariant requires the TM algorithm to check that a read location is not overwritten between the point where the location is read and the point where the transaction takes effect. This requirement motivated us to study how read-preservation can influence the time complexity of TM operations and helped us construct client scenarios that exhibit lower bounds. We present a generalization of the seminal lower bound result presented in [20]. We first recall some definitions from previous works on the inherent complexity of TM [3, 19, 20, 34].

An aborted transaction that did not invoke an abort operation is said to be *forcefully* aborted. We say that two transactions *conflict* if they access the same location and one of them writes to the location. A TM algorithm is (weakly) *progressive* if and only if it forcefully aborts a transaction only when it conflicts with a live transaction. More precisely, it aborts a transaction only when there is a time t at which it conflicts with another concurrent transaction that is live at time t (not committed or aborted by time t). In addition to providing progress, progressive TM algorithms are expected to retry transactions less frequently and therefore, improve performance.

A TM algorithm is *invisible-reads* if and only if the read operation does not mutate (i.e. change the state of) any base object. Mutating base objects can potentially invalidate the caches and adversely affect performance. Thus, most high-performance TM algorithms are invisible-reads. A transaction is *read-only* if and only if it does invoke any write operations. We assume that the abort operation for a read-only transaction does not mutate any base shared object.

Two transactions *contend* on a base object o if and only if they access o and at least one of them mutates o. A TM algorithm is (strictly) *disjoint-access-parallel* if and only if two transactions contend on a base object only if they access a common memory location. Disjoint-access-parallelism can improve scalability as transactions that access disjoint memory locations access disjoint base objects.

A TM algorithm is *single-version* if and only if it stores a single value for each memory location in the base objects.

Theorem 3. *The time complexity of the commit operation of every opaque, progressive, disjoint-access-parallel and invisible-reads TM algorithm is $\Omega(|\mathcal{R}|)$ where $\mathcal{R}$ is the read set.*

This theorem shows that designers should pick at least one of the following sources of inefficiency in the design of every opaque TM algorithm: aborting non-conflicting transactions, sharing base objects between transactions that access disjoint locations, visible reads or linear-time complexity of the commit method. As an example, TL2 shares the *clock* object between all transactions and is, therefore, not disjoint-access-parallel. In addition, it has linear-time read-validation in the commit method.

Theorem 4. *The time complexity of the commit operation of every opaque, progressive, and invisible-reads TM algorithm that stores information about a* *constant number of locations in each shared object is $\Omega(|\mathcal{R}|)$ where $\mathcal{R}$ is the read set.*

The above theorem generalizes Theorem 3 of [20] by dropping the single-version requirement. Note that the assumption about limited capacity of shared objects is stated before the theorem in [20] and explicitly in the theorem here. We leave the proofs to the appendix [29].

7   Conclusion

We presented a decomposition of opacity called markability as a conjunction of separate invariants. We proved the equivalence of opacity and markability. We showcased the applicability of markability as a proof technique for opacity by stating the marking relation and proving the markability of the TL2 algorithm. In addition, we presented a lower bound for the time complexity of TM algorithms.

References

1. Ananian, C.S., Asanovic, K., Kuszmaul, B.C., Leiserson, C.E., Lie, S.: Unbounded transactional memory. In: HPCA (2005)
2. Attiya, H., Hans, S., Kuznetsov, P., Ravi, S.: Safety of deferred update in transactional memory. In: ICDCS (2013)
3. Attiya, H., Hillel, E., Milani, A.: Inherent limitations on disjoint-access parallel implementations of transactional memory. Theory of Computing Systems 49(4) (2011)
4. Baek, W., Bronson, N., Kozyrakis, C., Olukotun, K.: Implementing and evaluating a model checker for transactional memory systems. In: ICECCS (2010)
5. Cohen, A., O'Leary, J.W., Pnueli, A., Tuttle, M.R., Zuck, L.D.: Verifying correctness of transactional memories. In: FMCAD (2007)
6. Cohen, A., Pnueli, A., Zuck, L.D.: Mechanical verification of transactional memories with non-transactional memory accesses. In: Gupta, A., Malik, S. (eds.) CAV 2008. LNCS, vol. 5123, pp. 121–134. Springer, Heidelberg (2008)
7. Intel Corporation. Intel architecture instruction set extensions programming reference, tsx. 319433-012 (2012)
8. Dalessandro, L., Carouge, F., White, S., Lev, Y., Moir, M., Scott, M.L., Spear, M.F.: Hybrid norec: A case study in the effectiveness of best effort hardware transactional memory. In: ASPLOS (2011)
9. Dalessandro, L., Spear, M.F., Scott, M.L.: Norec: streamlining stm by abolishing ownership records. In: PPoPP (2010)
10. Damron, P., Fedorova, A., Lev, Y., Luchangco, V., Moir, M., Nussbaum, D.: Hybrid transactional memory. SIGPLAN Not. 41(11) (2006)
11. Dice, D., Shalev, O., Shavit, N.: Transactional locking II. In: Dolev, S. (ed.) DISC 2006. LNCS, vol. 4167, pp. 194–208. Springer, Heidelberg (2006)
12. Dice, D., Shavit, N.: TLRW: Return of the read-write lock. In: SPAA (2010)
13. Doherty, S., Groves, L., Luchangco, V., Moir, M.: Towards formally specifying and verifying transactional memory. Formal Aspects of Computing (2012)
14. Emmi, M., Majumdar, R., Manevich, R.: Parameterized verification of transactional memories. In: PLDI (2010)

15. Felber, P., Fetzer, C., Riegel, T.: Dynamic performance tuning of word-based software transactional memory. In: PPoPP (2008)
16. Guerraoui, R., Henzinger, T.A., Jobstmann, B., Singh, V.: Model checking transactional memories. In: PLDI (2008)
17. Guerraoui, R., Henzinger, T.A., Singh, V.: Software transactional memory on relaxed memory models. In: Bouajjani, A., Maler, O. (eds.) CAV 2009. LNCS, vol. 5643, pp. 321–336. Springer, Heidelberg (2009)
18. Guerraoui, R., Henzinger, T.A., Singh, V.: Model checking transactional memories. Distributed Computing (2010)
19. Guerraoui, R., Kapalka, M.: On obstruction-free transactions. In: SPAA (2008)
20. Guerraoui, R., Kapalka, M.: On the correctness of transactional memory. In: PPOPP (2008)
21. Guerraoui, R., Kapalka, M.: Principles of Transactional Memory. M&C (2010)
22. Hammond, L., Wong, V., Chen, M., Carlstrom, B.D., Davis, J.D., Hertzberg, B., Prabhu, M.K., Wijaya, H., Kozyrakis, C., Olukotun, K.: Transactional memory coherence and consistency. In: ISCA (2004)
23. Herlihy, M., Luchangco, V., Moir, M., Scherer, I.W.N.: Software transactional memory for dynamic-sized data structures. In: PODC (2003)
24. Herlihy, M., Moss, J.E.B.: Transactional memory: Architectural support for lock-free data structures. In: ISCA (1993)
25. Imbs, D., de Mendivil, J.R., Raynal, M.: Brief announcement: virtual world consistency: A new condition for stm systems. In: PODC (2009)
26. Kumar, S., Chu, M., Hughes, C.J., Kundu, P., Nguyen, A.: Hybrid transactional memory. In: PPoPP (2006)
27. Lesani, M.: On the correctness of transactional memory algorithms. Phd Dissertation (2014), http://www.cs.ucla.edu/~lesani/companion/dissertation
28. Lesani, M., Luchangco, V., Moir, M.: A framework for formally verifying software transactional memory algorithms. In: Koutny, M., Ulidowski, I. (eds.) CONCUR 2012. LNCS, vol. 7454, pp. 516–530. Springer, Heidelberg (2012)
29. Lesani, M., Palsberg, J.: Decomposing opacity, the companion page, http://www.cs.ucla.edu/~lesani/companion/disc14
30. Lesani, M., Palsberg, J.: Proving non-opacity. In: Afek, Y. (ed.) DISC 2013. LNCS, vol. 8205, pp. 106–120. Springer, Heidelberg (2013)
31. Matveev, A., Shavit, N.: Reduced hardware transactions: A new approach to hybrid transactional memory. In: SPAA (2013)
32. Minh, C.C., Trautmann, M., Chung, J., McDonald, A., Bronson, N., Casper, J., Kozyrakis, C., Olukotun, K.: An effective hybrid transactional memory system with strong isolation guarantees. In: ISCA (2007)
33. O'Leary, J., Saha, B., Tuttle, M.R.: Model checking transactional memory with spin. In: ICDCS (2009)
34. Perelman, D., Fan, R., Keidar, I.: On maintaining multiple versions in stm. In: PODC (2010)
35. Saha, B., Adl-Tabatabai, A.-R., Hudson, R.L., Minh, C.C., Hertzberg, B.: McRT-STM: A high performance software transactional memory system for a multi-core runtime. In: PPoPP (2006)
36. Shavit, N., Touitou, D.: Software transactional memory. In: PODC (1995)
37. Wang, A., Gaudet, M., Wu, P., Amaral, J.N., Ohmacht, M., Barton, C., Silvera, R., Michael, M.: Evaluation of blue gene/q hardware support for transactional memories. In: PACT (2012)

The Adaptive Priority Queue
with Elimination and Combining

Irina Calciu, Hammurabi Mendes, and Maurice Herlihy

Department of Computer Science
Brown University
115 Waterman St., 4th floor
Providence RI, USA
{irina,hmendes,mph}@cs.brown.edu

Abstract. Priority queues are fundamental abstract data structures, often used to manage limited resources in parallel programming. Several proposed parallel priority queue implementations are based on skiplists, harnessing the potential for parallelism of the add() operations. In addition, methods such as Flat Combining have been proposed to reduce contention, batching together multiple operations to be executed by a single thread. While this technique can decrease lock-switching overhead and the number of pointer changes required by the removeMin() operations in the priority queue, it can also create a sequential bottleneck and limit parallelism, especially for non-conflicting add() operations.

In this paper, we describe a novel priority queue design, harnessing the scalability of parallel insertions in conjunction with the efficiency of batched removals. Moreover, we present a new elimination algorithm suitable for a priority queue, which further increases concurrency on balanced workloads with similar numbers of add() and removeMin() operations. We implement and evaluate our design using a variety of techniques including locking, atomic operations, hardware transactional memory, as well as employing adaptive heuristics given the workload.

1   Introduction

A priority queue is a fundamental abstract data structure that stores a set of keys (or a set of key-value pairs), where keys represent priorities. It usually exports two main operations: add(), to insert a new item in the priority queue, and removeMin(), to remove the first item (the one with the highest priority). Parallel priority queues are often used in discrete event simulations and resource management, such as operating systems schedulers. Therefore, it is important to carefully design these data structures in order to limit contention and improve scalability. Prior work in concurrent priority queues exploited parallelism by using either a heap [6] or a skiplist [8] as the underlying data structures. In the skiplist-based implementation of Lotan and Shavit [8], each node has a "deleted" flag, and processors contend to mark such "deleted" flags concurrently, in the beginning of the list. When a thread logically deletes a node, it tries to remove

F. Kuhn (Ed.): DISC 2014, LNCS 8784, pp. 406–420, 2014.
© Springer-Verlag Berlin Heidelberg 2014

it from the skiplist using the standard removal algorithm. A lock-free skiplist implementation is presented in [11].

However, these methods may incur limited scalability at high thread counts due to contention on shared memory accesses. Hendler et al. [3] introduced Flat Combining, a method for batching together multiple operations to be performed by only one thread, thus reducing the contention on the data structure. This idea has also been explored in subsequent work on delegation [9,1], where a dedicated thread called a *server* performs work on behalf of other threads, called *clients*. Unfortunately, the server thread could become a sequential bottleneck. A method of combining delegation with elimination has been proposed to alleviate this problem for a stack data structure [2]. Elimination [4] is a method of matching concurrent inverse operations so that they don't access the shared data structure, thus significantly reducing contention and increasing parallelism for otherwise sequential structures, such as stacks. An elimination algorithm has also been proposed in the context of a queue [10], where the authors introduce the notion of *aging operations* - operations that wait until they become suitable for elimination.

In this paper, we describe, to the best of our knowledge, the first elimination algorithm for a priority queue. Only add() operations with values smaller than the priority queue minimum value are allowed to eliminate. However, we use the idea of aging operations introduced in the queue algorithm to allow add() values that are *small enough* to participate in the elimination protocol, in the hope that they will soon become eligible for elimination. We implement the priority queue using a skiplist and we exploit the skiplist's capability for both operations-batching and disjoint-access parallelism. RemoveMin() requests can be batched and executed by a server thread using the combining/delegation paradigm. Add() requests with high keys will most likely not become eligible for elimination, but need to be inserted in the skiplist, requiring expensive traversals towards the end of the data structure. These operations would represent a bottleneck for the server and a missed opportunity for parallelism if executed sequentially. Therefore, we split the underlying skiplist into two parts: a *sequential* part, managed by the server thread and a *parallel* part, where high-valued add() operations can insert their arguments in parallel. Our design reduces contention by performing batched sequential removeMin() and small-value add() operations, while also leveraging parallelism opportunities through elimination and parallel high-value add() operations. We show that our priority queue outperforms prior algorithms in high contention workloads on a SPARC Niagara II machine. Finally, we explore whether the use of hardware transactions could simplify our design and improve throughput. Unfortunately, machines that support hardware transactional memory (HTM) are only available for up to four cores (eight hardware threads), which is not enough to measure scalability of our design in high contention scenarios. Nevertheless, we showed that a transactional version of our algorithm is better than a non-transactional version on a Haswell four-core machine. We believe that these preliminary results will generalize to machines with more threads with support for HTM, once they become available. In summary, our main contributions are:

– We propose the first elimination algorithm for a priority queue, consisting of (1) *immediate elimination*, where suitable add() and removeMin() operations exchange arguments; and (2) *upcoming elimination*, where add() operations with small keys, yet not suitable for elimination, wait some time until either they become suitable or time out.
– We describe a scalable design for a priority queue based on our elimination algorithm and the delegation/combining paradigm introduced by prior work.
– We augment our priority queue design with an adaptive component that allows it to perform combining and elimination efficiently, while also allowing add() operations not involved in the elimination to insert in parallel.
– We analyze how hardware transactions could be used to simplify and improve our initial design and show performance results on a Haswell machine with transactional memory enabled.

2   Design

Our priority queue exports two operations: add() and removeMin() and is implemented using an underlying skiplist. The elements of the skiplist are buckets associated with keys. For a bucket b, the field b.key denotes the associated key. We split the skiplist in two distinct parts. The sequential part, in the beginning of the skiplist, is likely to serve forthcoming removeMin() operations of the priority queue (PQ::removeMin() for short) as well as add(v) operations of the priority queue (PQ:add() for short) with v small enough (hence expected to be removed soon). The *parallel part*, which complements the sequential part, is likely to serve PQ::add(v) operations where v is large enough (hence not expected to be removed soon). Either the sequential or the parallel part may become empty. Both lists are complete skiplists, with (dummy) head buckets called headSeq and headPar, respectively, with key $-\infty$. Both lists also contain (dummy) tail buckets, with key $+\infty$. We call the last non-dummy bucket of the sequential part lastSeq, which is the logical divisor between parts. Figure 1 shows the design.

When a thread performs a PQ::add(v), either (1) $v >$ lastSeq.key, and the thread inserts the value concurrently in the parallel part of the skiplist, calling the SL::addPar() skiplist operation; or (2) $v \leq$ lastSeq.key, and the thread tries to perform elimination with a PQ::removeMin() using an *elimination array*. A PQ::add(v) with v less than the smallest value in the priority queue can immediately eliminate with a PQ::removeMin(), if one is available. A PQ::add(v) operation with v bigger than minValue (the current minimal key) but smaller than lastSeq.key lingers in the elimination array for some time, waiting to become eligible for elimination or timeout. A *server thread* executes sequentially all operations that fail to eliminate.

This mechanism describes the first elimination algorithm for a priority queue, well integrated with delegation/combining, presented in more detail in Section 2.2. Specifically: (1) The scheme harnesses the parallelism of the priority

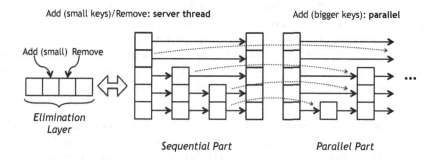

Fig. 1. Skiplist design. An elimination array is used for `removeMin()`s and `add()`s with small keys. A dedicated server thread collects the operations that do not eliminate and executes them on the sequential part of the skiplist. Concurrent threads operate on the parallel part, performing `add()`s with bigger keys. The dotted lines show pointers that would be established if the single skiplist was not divided in two parts.

queue `add()` operations, letting the ones with keys physically distant and large enough (bigger than `lastSeq.key`) execute in parallel. (2) At the same time, we batch concurrent priority queue `add()` with small keys and `removeMin()` operations that timed out in the elimination array, serving such requests quickly through the server thread – this latter operation simply consumes elements from the sequential part by navigating through elements in its bottom level, merely decreasing counters and moving pointers in the most common situation. While detaching a sequential part is non-negligible cost-wise, a sequential part has the potential to serve multiple removals.

2.1 Concurrent Skiplist

Our underlying skiplist is operated by the server thread in the sequential part and by concurrently inserting threads with bigger keys in the parallel part.

Sequential Part. The server calls the skiplist function `SL::moveHead()` to extract a new sequential part from the parallel part if some `PQ::removeMin()` operation was requested and the sequential part was empty. Conversely, it calls the skiplist function `SL::chopHead()` to relink the sequential and the parallel parts, forming a completely parallel skiplist, if no `PQ::removeMin()` operations are being requested for some time. In `SL::moveHead()`, we initially determine the elements to be moved to the sequential part. If no elements are found, the server clears the sequential part, otherwise separating the sequential part from the rest of the list, which becomes the parallel part. The number of elements that `SL::moveHead()` tries to detach to the sequential part adaptively varies between 8 and 65,536. Our policy is simple: if more than N insertions (e.g. N = 1000) occurred in the sequential part since the last `SL::moveHead()`, we halve the number of elements moved; otherwise, if less than M insertions (e.g. M = 100) were made, we double this number. After `SL::moveHead()` executes, a pointer called `currSeq` indicates the first bucket in the sequential part, and another called `lastSeq` indicates the final bucket. The server uses `SL::addSeq()` and `SL::removeSeq()` within the sequential part to remove elements or insert elements with small keys (i.e., belonging to the sequential part) that failed to eliminate. Buckets are not deleted at this time; they are deleted lazily when the whole sequential part gets consumed. A new sequential part can be created by calling `SL::moveHead()` again.

Parallel Part. The skiplist function `SL::addPar()` inserts elements into the parallel part, and is called by concurrent threads performing `PQ::add()`. While these insertions are concurrent, the skiplist still relies on a Single-Writer Multi-Readers lock with writer preference for the following purpose. Multiple `SL::addPar()` operations acquire the lock for reading (executing concurrently), while `SL::moveHead()` and `SL::chopHead()` operations acquire the lock for writing. This way, we avoid that `SL::addPar()` operates on buckets that are currently being moved to the sequential part by `SL::moveHead()`, or interferes with `SL::chopHead()`. Despite the lock, `SL::addPar()` is not mutually exclusive with the *head-moving operations* (`SL::moveHead()` and `SL::chopHead()`). Only the pointer updates (for new buckets) or the counter increment (for existing buckets) must be done in the parallel part (and not have been moved to the sequential part) after we determine the locations of these changes. Hence, in the `SL::addPar()` operation, we first try to get a *clean* `SL::find()`: a find operation followed by lock acquisition for reading, with no intervening head-moving operations. We can tell whether no head-moving operation took place since our lock operations always increases a timestamp variable, checked in the critical section. After a clean `SL::find()`, therefore now holding the lock, if a bucket corresponding to the key is found, we insert the element in the bucket (incrementing a counter). Otherwise, a new bucket is created, and inserted level by level using `CAS()` operations. If a `CAS()` fails in a certain level, we release the lock and retry a clean `SL::find()`.

Our algorithm differs from the traditional concurrent skiplist insertion algorithms in two ways: (1) we hold a lock to avoid head-moving operations to take place after a clean `SL::find()`; and (2) if the new bucket is moved out of the parallel section while we insert the element in the upper levels, we stop `SL::addPar()`, leaving this element with a capped level. This bucket is likely to be soon consumed by a `SL::removeSeq()` operation, resulting from a `PQ::removeMin()` operation.

2.2 Elimination and Combining

Elimination allows matching operations to complete without accessing the shared data structure, thus increasing parallelism and scalability. In a priority queue, any `SL::removeMin()` operation can be eliminated, but only `SL::add()` operations with values smaller or equal to the current minimum value can be so. If the priority queue is empty, any `SL::add()` value can be eliminated. We used an elimination array similar to the one in the stack elimination algorithm [4].

Each slot uses 64 bits to pack together a 32-bit value that represents either an opcode or a value to be inserted in the priority queue and a stamp that is unique for each operation. The opcodes are: EMPTY, REMREQ, TAKEN and INPROG. These are special values that cannot be used in the priority queue. All other values are admissible. In our implementation, each thread has a local count of how many operations it performed. This count is combined with the thread ID to obtain a unique stamp for each operation. Overflow was not an issue in our experiments, but if it becomes a problem a different algorithm for associating unique stamps to each operation could be used. The unique stamp is used to ensure linearizability, as explained in Section 3. All slots are initially empty, marked with the special value EMPTY, and the stamp value is zero.

A PQ::removeMin() thread loops through the elimination array until it finds a request to eliminate with or it finds an empty slot in the array, as described in Algorithm 1. If it finds a value in the slot, then it must ensure that the stamp is positive, otherwise the value was posted as a response to another thread. The value it finds must be smaller than the current priority queue minimum value. Then, the PQ::removeMin() thread can CAS the slot, which contains both the value and the stamp, and replace it with an indicator that the value was taken (TAKEN, with stamp zero). The thread returns the value found. If instead, the PQ::remove() thread finds an empty slot, it posts a *remove request* (REMREQ), with a unique stamp generated as above. The thread waits until the slot is changed by another thread, having a value with stamp zero. The PQ::removeMin() thread can then return that value.

Algorithm 1. PQ::removeMin()

1: **while true do**
2:    pos ← $(id + 1)\%$ ELIM_SIZE; (value, stamp) ← elim[pos]
3:    **if** IsValue(value) **and** (stamp > 0) **and** (value ≤ skiplist.minValue)) **then**
4:       **if** CAS(elim[pos], (value, stamp), (TAKEN, 0)) **then**
5:          **return** value
6:    **if** value = EMPTY **then**
7:       **if** CAS(elim[pos], (value, stamp), (REMREQ, uniqueStamp())) **then**
8:          **repeat**
9:             (value, stamp) ← elim[pos]
10:          **until** value ≠ REMREQ **and** value ≠ INPROG
11:          elim[pos] ← (EMPTY, 0); **return** value
12:    inc(pos)

A PQ::add() thread initially tries to use SL::addPar() to add its key concurrently in the parallel part of the skiplist. A failed attempt indicates that the value should try to eliminate or should be inserted in the sequential part instead. The PQ::add() thread tries to eliminate by checking through the elimination array for REMREQ indicators. If it finds a remove request, and its value is smaller than the priority queue minValue, it can CAS its value with stamp zero, effectively handing it to another thread. If multiple such attempts fail, the thread changes its behavior: it still tries to perform elimination as above, but as soon as an empty slot is found, it uses a CAS to insert its own value and the current stamp in the slot, waiting for another thread to match the operation (and change the opcode to TAKEN) returning the corresponding value.

The PQ::add() and PQ::removeMin() threads that post a request in an empty slot of the elimination array wait for a matching thread to perform elimination. However, elimination could fail because no matching thread shows up or because the PQ::add() value is never smaller than the priority queue minValue. To ensure that all threads make progress, we use a dedicated *server thread* that collects add and remove requests that fail to eliminate. The server thread executes the operations sequentially on the skiplist, calling SL::addSeq() and SL::removeSeq() operations. To ensure linearizability, the server marks a slot that contains an operation it is about to execute as *in progress* (INPROG). Subsequently, it executes the sequential skiplist operation and writes back the response in the elimination slot for the other thread to find it. A state machine showing the possible transitions of a slot in the elimination array is shown in Figure 2, and the algorithm is described in Algorithm 2.

Algorithm 2. Server::execute()

```
1: while true do
2:     for i: 1 → ELIM_SIZE do
3:         (value, stamp) ← elim[i]
4:         if value = REMREQ then
5:             if CAS(elim[i], (value, stamp), (INPROG, 0)) then
6:                 min ← skiplist.removeSeq(); elim[i] ← (min, 0)
7:         if IsValue(value) and (stamp > 0) then
8:             if CAS(elim[i], (value, stamp), (INPROG, 0)) then
9:                 skiplist.addSeq(value); elim[i] ← (TAKEN, 0)
```

---

3   Linearizability

Our design provides a linearizable priority queue algorithm. Some operations have multiple possible linearization points by design, requiring careful analysis and implementation.

Skiplist. A successful SL::addPar(v) (respectively, SL::addSeq(v)) usually linearizes when it inserts the element in the bottom level of the skip list with a CAS (respectively, with a store), or when the bucket for key v has its counter incremented with a CAS (respectively, with a store). However, a thread inserting a minimal bucket, whenever $v <$ minValue, is required to update minValue. When the sequential part is not empty, only the server can update minValue (without synchronization). When the sequential part is empty, a parallel add

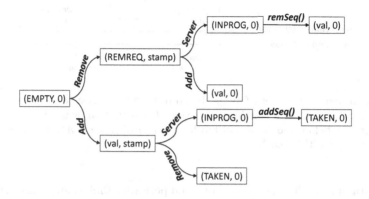

Fig. 2. Transitions of a slot in the elimination array

with minimal value needs to update `minValue`. The adding thread loops until a `CAS` decreasing `minValue` succeeds or another thread inserts a bucket with key smaller than v. Note that no head-moving operation is taking place (the `SL::addPar()` threads hold the `lock`). Threads that succeed changing `minValue` linearize their operation at the point of the successful `CAS`.

The head-moving operations `SL::moveHead()` and `SL::chopHead()` execute while holding the `lock` for writing, which effectively linearizes the operation at the `lock.release()` instant because: (1) no `SL::addPar()` is running; (2) no `SL::addSeq()` or `SL::removeSeq()` are running, as the server thread is the single thread performing those operations. Head-moving operations do not change `minValue`, in fact they preclude any changes to it. During these operations, however, threads may still perform elimination, which we discuss next.

Elimination. A unique stamp is used in each request posted in the array entries to avoid the "ABA" problem. Each elimination slot is a 64-bit value that contains 32 bits for the posted value (for `PQ::add()`) or a special opcode (for `PQ::removeMin()`) and 32 bits for the unique stamp. In our implementation, the unique stamp is obtained by combining the thread id with the number of operations performed by each thread. Each thread, either adding or removing, that finds the inverse operation in the elimination array must verify that the exchanged value is smaller than `minValue`. If so, the thread can `CAS` the elimination slot, exchanging arguments with the waiting thread. It is possible that the priority queue minimum value is changed by a concurrent `PQ::add()`. In that case, the linearization point for both threads engaged in elimination is at the point where the value was observed to be smaller than the priority queue minimum. See Fig. 3.

The thread performing the `CAS` first reads the stamp of the thread that posted the request in the array and verifies that it is allowed to eliminate. Only then it performs a `CAS` on both the value and the stamp, guaranteeing that the thread waiting did not change in the meantime. Because both threads were running at the time of the verification, they can be linearized at that point. Without the

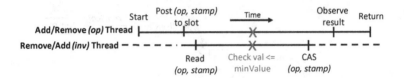

Fig. 3. Concurrent execution of an *op* thread posting its request to an empty slot, and an *inv* thread, executing a matching operation. The operation by the *inv* thread could begin anytime before the *Read* and finish any time after the *CAS*. The linearization point is marked with a red X.

unique stamp, the eliminating thread could perform a CAS on an identical request (i.e., identical operation and value) posted in the array by a different thread. The CAS would incorrectly succeed, but the operations would not be linearizable because the new thread was not executing while the suitable minimum was observed.

The linearizability of the combining operation results from the linearizability of the skiplist. The threads post their operation in the elimination array and wait for the server to process it. The server first marks the operation as *in progress* by CASing INPROG into the slot. Then it performs the sequential operation on the skiplist and writes the results back in the slot, releasing the waiting thread. The waiting thread observes the new value and returns it. The linearization point of the operation happens during the sequential operation on the skiplist, as discussed above. See Fig. 4.

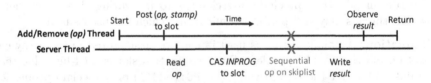

Fig. 4. Concurrent execution of a client thread and the server thread. The client posts its operation *op* to an empty slot and waits for the server to collect the operation and execute it sequentially on the skiplist. The linearization point occurs in the sequential operation and is marked with a red X.

4   Evaluation

In this section, we discuss results on a Sun SPARC T5240, which contains two UltraSPARC T2 Plus chips with 8 cores each, running at 1.165 GHz. Each core has 8 hardware strands, for a total of 64 hardware threads per chip. A core has a 8KB L1 data cache and shares an 4MB L2 data cache with the other cores on a chip. Each experiment was performed five times and we report the median. Variance was very low for all experiments. Each test was run for ten seconds to measure throughput. We used the same benchmark as flat combining [3]. A thread randomly flips a coin with probability p to be an PQ::add() and $1 - p$ to be a PQ::removeMin(). We started a run after inserting 2000 elements in the priority queue for stable state results.

Our priority queue algorithm (*pqe*) uses combining and elimination, and leverages the parallelism of PQ::add(). We performed experiments to compare against previous priority queues using combining methods, such as flat combining skiplist (*fcskiplist*) and flat combining pairing heap (*fcpairheap*). We also compared against previous priority queues using skiplists with parallel operations, such as a lock free skiplist (*lfskiplist*) and a lazy skiplist (*lazyskiplist*). The flat combining methods are very fast at performing PQ::removeMin() operations, which then get combined and executed together. However, performing the PQ::add() operations sequentially is a bottleneck for these methods. Conversely, the *lfskiplist* and *lazyskiplist* algorithms are very fast at performing the parallel adds, but get significantly slowed down by having PQ::removeMin() operations in the mix, due to the synchronization overhead involved. Our *pqe* design tries to address these limitations through our *dual* (sequential and parallel parts), *adaptive* implementation that can be beneficial in the different scenarios.

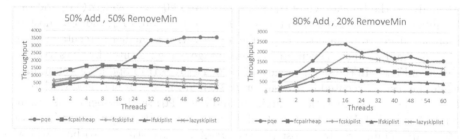

Fig. 5. Priority queue performance with 50% add()s, 50% removeMin()s

Fig. 6. Priority queue performance with 80% add()s, 20% removeMin()s

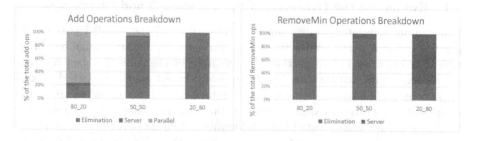

Fig. 7. add() work breakdown   **Fig. 8.** removeMin() work breakdown

We considered different percentages of PQ::add() and PQ::removeMin() in our tests. When the operations are roughly the same number, *pqe* can fully take advantage of both elimination and parallel adds, so it has peak performance. Figure 5 shows how for 50% PQ::add() and 50% PQ::removeMin(), *pqe* is much more scalable and can be up to 2.3 times faster than all other methods. When there are more PQ::add() than PQ::removeMin(), as in Figure 6 with 80% PQ::add() and 20% PQ::removeMin(), *pqe* behavior approaches the other methods, but it is still 70% faster than all other methods at high thread counts. In this specific case there is only little potential for elimination, but having parallel insertion operations makes our algorithm outperform the flat combining methods. The *lazyskiplist* algorithm also performs better than other methods, as it also takes advantage of parallel insertions. However, *pqe* uses the limited elimination and the combining methods to reduce contention, making it faster than the *lazyskiplist*. For more PQ::removeMin() operations than PQ::add() operations, the *pqe*'s potential for elimination and parallel adds are both limited, thus other methods can be faster. *Pqe* is designed for high contention scenarios, in which elimination and combining thrive. Therefore, it can incur a penalty at lower thread counts, where there is not enough contention to justify the overhead of the indirection caused by the elimination array and the server thread.

To better understand when each of the optimizations used is more beneficial, we analyzed the breakdown of the PQ::add() and PQ::removeMin() operations for different PQ::add() percentages. When we have 80% PQ::add(), most of them are likely to be inserted in parallel (75%), with a smaller percentage being able to eliminate and an even smaller percentage being executed by the server, as shown in Fig. 7. In the same scenario, 75% of removeMin() operations eliminate, while the rest is executed by the server, as seen in Fig. 8. For balanced workloads (50% − 50%), most operations eliminate and a few PQ::add() operations are inserted in parallel. When the workload is dominated by PQ::removeMin(), most PQ::add() eliminate, but most PQ::removeMin() are still left to be executed by the server thread, thus introducing a sequential bottleneck. Eventually the priority queue would become empty, not being able to satisfy PQ::removeMin() requests with an actual value anymore. In this case, any add() operation can eliminate, allowing full parallelism. We do not present results for this case because it is an unlikely scenario that unrealistically favors elimination.

4.1   Evaluating the Overhead of PQ::moveHead() and PQ::chopHead()

Maintaining separate skiplists for the sequential and the parallel part of the priority queue is beneficial for the overall throughput, but adds some overhead, which we quantify in this section. The number of elements that become part of the sequential skiplist changes dynamically based on the observed mix of operations. This adaptive behavior helps reduce the number of moveHead() and chopHead() operations required. Table 1 shows the percentage of the number of head-moving operations out of the total number of PQ::removeMin() operations for different mixes of PQ::add() and PQ::removeMin() operations. The head-moving operations are rarely called due to the priority queue's adaptive behavior.

Table 1. The number of head-moving operations as a percentage of the total number of `PQ::removeMin()` operations, considering different `add()` and `removeMin()` mixes

Add() percentages	% moveHead()	% chopHead()
80	0.24%	0.03%
50	0.32%	0.01%
20	0.00%	0.00%

5   Hardware Transactions

Transactional memory [5] is an optimistic mechanism to synchronize threads accessing shared data. Threads are allowed to execute critical sections speculatively in parallel, but, if there is a data conflict, one of them has to roll back and retry its critical section. Recently, IBM and Intel added HTM instructions to their processors [12,7]. In our priority queue implementation, we used Intel's Transactional Synchronization Extensions (TSX) [7] to simplify the implementation and reduce the overhead caused by the synchronization necessary to manage a sequential and a parallel skiplist. We evaluate our results on an Intel Haswell four core processor, Core i7-4770, with hardware transactions enabled (restricted transactional memory - RTM), running at 3.4GHz. There are 8GB of RAM shared across the machine and each core has a 32KB L1 cache. Hyperthreading was enabled on our machine so we collected results using all 8 hardware threads. Hyperthreading causes resource sharing between the hyperthreads, including L1 cache sharing, when running with more than 4 threads, thus it can negatively impact results, especially for hardware transactions. We did not notice a hyperthreading effect in our experiments. We used the GCC 4.8 compiler with support for RTM and optimizations enabled (-O3).

5.1   Skiplist

The Single-Writer-Multi-Readers lock used to synchronize the sequential and the parallel skiplists complicates the priority queue design and adds overhead. In this section, we explore an alternative design using hardware transactions. The naive approach of making all operations transactional causes too many aborts. Instead, the server increments a timestamp whenever a head-moving operation - `SL::moveHead()` or `SL::chopHead()` - starts or finishes. A `SL::addPar()` operation first reads the timestamp and executes a nontransactional `SL::find()` and then starts a transaction for the actual insertion, adding the server's timestamp to its read set and aborting if it is different from the initially recorded value. Moreover, if the timestamp changes after starting the transaction, indicating a head-moving operation, the transaction will be aborted due to the timestamp conflict. If the timestamp is valid, `SL::find()` must have recorded the predecessors and successors of the new bucket at each level i in `preds[i]` and `succs[i]`, respectively. If a bucket already exists, the counter is incremented inside the transaction and the operation completes. If the bucket does not exist, the operation proceeds to check if `preds[i]` points to `succs[i]` for all levels $0 \leq i \leq$ MaxLvl. If so, the pointers have not changed before starting the transaction and the new bucket can be correctly inserted between `preds[i]` and `succs[i]`. Otherwise, we commit the (innocuous) transaction, yet restart the operation.

Figures 9 and 10 compare the performance of the lock-based implementation and the implementation based on hardware transactions for two different percentages of `PQ::add()`s and `PQ::removeMin()`s. When fewer `PQ::removeMin()` operations are present, the timestamp changes less frequently and the `PQ::add()` transactions are aborted fewer times, which increases performance in the 80%-20% insertion-removal mix. In the 50%-50% mix, we obtain results comparable to the *pqe* algorithm using the lock-based approach, albeit with a much simpler implementation.

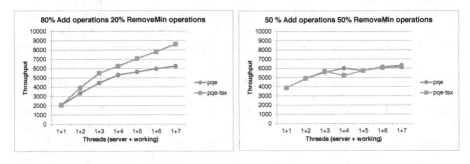

Fig. 9. Priority queue performance when we use a transaction-based dual skiplist; 80% `add()`s, 20% `removeMin()`s

Fig. 10. Priority queue performance when we use a transaction-based dual skiplist; 50% `add()`s, 50% `removeMin()`s

5.2   Evaluating the Overhead of Aborted Transactions

The impact of aborted transactions is reported in Tables 2 and 3. As the number of threads increases, the number of transactions per successful operation also increases, as does the percentage of operations that need more than 10 retries to succeed. Note that the innocuous transactions that find inconsistent pointers, changed between the `SL::find()` and the start of the transaction are not included in the measurement. After 10 retries, threads give up on retrying the transactional path and the server executes the operations on their behalf, either in the sequential part, using sequential operations, or in the parallel part, using `CAS()` for the pointer changes, but without holding the readers lock. The server does not need to acquire the readers lock because no other thread will try to acquire the writer lock.

Table 2. Transaction stats for varying # of threads, with 50% PQ::add()s and 50% PQ::removeMin()s

Working Threads	Transactions per successful operation	Fallbacks per total operations
1	1.01	0.00%
2	2.34	0.51%
3	3.21	1.73%
4	3.31	2.12%
5	3.46	2.74%
6	3.46	2.67%
7	3.61	3.25%

Table 3. Transaction stats for varying mixes, with 1 server thread and 3 working threads

Add percentage	Transactions per successful operation	Fallbacks per total operations
100	1.32	0.00%
80	1.77	0.01%
60	2.37	0.29%
50	3.22	2.01%
40	3.64	5.24%
20	3.92	10.34%
0	1.09	0.00%

The number of transactions per successful operation is at most 3.92, but 3.22 in the 50% − 50% case. The percentage of operations that get executed by the server (after aborting 10 times) is at most 10% of the total number of operations, but between 1.73% and 2.01% for the 50% − 50% case.

6   Conclusion

In this paper, we describe a technique to implement a scalable, linearizable priority queue based on a skiplist, divided into a sequential and a parallel part. Our scheme simultaneously enables parallel PQ::add() operations as well as sequential batched PQ::removeMin() operations. The sequential part is beneficial for batched removals, which are performed by a special *server thread*. While detaching the sequential part from the parallel part is non-negligible cost-wise, the sequential part has the potential to serve multiple subsequent removals at a small constant cost. The parallel part is beneficial for concurrent insertions of elements with bigger keys (smaller priority), not likely to be removed soon. In other words, we integrate the flat combining/delegation paradigm introduced in prior work with disjoint-access parallelism.

In addition, we present a novel priority queue elimination algorithm, where PQ::add() operations with keys smaller than the priority queue minimum can eliminate with PQ::removeMin() operations. We permit PQ::add() operations, with keys small enough, to linger in the elimination array, waiting to become eligible for elimination. If the elimination is not possible, the operation is delegated to the server thread. Batched removals (combining) by the server thread is well-integrated with both: (1) parallelism of add() operations with bigger keys; and (2) the elimination algorithm, that possibly delegates failed elimination attempts (of elements with smaller keys) to the server thread in a natural manner. Our priority queue integrates delegation, combining, and elimination, while still leveraging the parallelism potential of insertions.

References

1. Calciu, I., Dice, D., Harris, T., Herlihy, M., Kogan, A., Marathe, V., Moir, M.: Message passing or shared memory: Evaluating the delegation abstraction for multicores. In: Baldoni, R., Nisse, N., van Steen, M. (eds.) OPODIS 2013. LNCS, vol. 8304, pp. 83–97. Springer, Heidelberg (2013)
2. Calciu, I., Gottschlich, J., Herlihy, M.: Using delegation and elimination to implement a scalable numa-friendly stack. In: 5th USENIX Workshop on Hot Topics in Parallelism (2013)
3. Hendler, D., Incze, I., Shavit, N., Tzafrir, M.: Flat combining and the synchronization-parallelism tradeoff. In: Proceedings of the 22nd ACM Symposium on Parallelism in Algorithms and Architectures, SPAA 2010, pp. 355–364. ACM, New York (2010), http://doi.acm.org/10.1145/1810479.1810540
4. Hendler, D., Shavit, N., Yerushalmi, L.: A scalable lock-free stack algorithm. J. Parallel Distrib. Comput. 70(1), 1–12 (2010), http://dx.doi.org/10.1016/j.jpdc.2009.08.011
5. Herlihy, M., Moss, J.E.B.: Transactional memory: Architectural support for lock-free data structures. SIGARCH Comput. Archit. News 21(2), 289–300 (1993), http://doi.acm.org/10.1145/173682.165164
6. Hunt, G., Michael, M., Parthasarathy, S., Scott, M.: An efficient algorithm for concurrent priority queue heaps. Information Processing Letters 60(3), 151–157 (1996)
7. Intel Corporation: Transactional Synchronization in Haswell (September 8, 2012), http://software.intel.com/en-us/blogs/2012/02/07/transactional-synchronization-in-haswell/ (retrieved)
8. Lotan, I., Shavit, N.: Skiplist-based concurrent priority queues. In: Proc. of the 14th International Parallel and Distributed Processing Symposium (IPDPS), pp. 263–268 (2000)
9. Metreveli, Z., Zeldovich, N., Kaashoek, M.F.: Cphash: A cache-partitioned hash table. In: Proceedings of the 17th ACM SIGPLAN Symposium on Principles and Practice of Parallel Programming, PPoPP 2012, pp. 319–320. ACM, New York (2012), http://doi.acm.org/10.1145/2145816.2145874
10. Moir, M., Nussbaum, D., Shalev, O., Shavit, N.: Using elimination to implement scalable and lock-free fifo queues. In: Proceedings of the Seventeenth Annual ACM Symposium on Parallelism in Algorithms and Architectures, SPAA 2005, pp. 253–262. ACM, New York (2005), http://doi.acm.org/10.1145/1073970.1074013
11. Sundell, H., Tsigas, P.: Fast and lock-free concurrent priority queues for multithread systems. In: IEEE International Symposium on Parallel and Distributed Processing, p. 11 (April 2003)
12. Wang, A., Gaudet, M., Wu, P., Amaral, J.N., Ohmacht, M., Barton, C., Silvera, R., Michael, M.: Evaluation of blue gene/q hardware support for transactional memories. In: Proceedings of the 21st International Conference on Parallel Architectures and Compilation Techniques, PACT 2012, pp. 127–136. ACM, New York (2012), http://doi.acm.org/10.1145/2370816.2370836

Improving Average Performance by Relaxing Distributed Data Structures

Edward Talmage and Jennifer L. Welch

Department of Computer Science and Engineering
Texas A&M University, College Station, Texas, USA
etalmage@neo.tamu.edu, welch@cse.tamu.edu

Abstract. Linearizability is a powerful consistency condition but can be expensive to implement. Recently, researarchers have suggested gaining performance by relaxing the sequential specification of objects' data types. We consider, for the first time, linearizable *message-passing* implementations of relaxed Queues and prove upper and lower bounds on the elapsed time for *Dequeue* operations both in the worst case and on average.

Our results imply that worst-case time complexity does not indicate benefit from relaxation. In contrast, we present implementations of relaxed Queues for which the *average time complexity* of *Dequeue* is significantly smaller than both the worst-case lower bound for unrelaxed Queues and a newly-proved lower bound on the average time for unrelaxed Queues. We also prove lower bounds on the average time complexity of *Dequeue* for relaxed Queues that show our algorithms are asymptotically optimal and that there is an inherent complexity gap between different levels of relaxation.

Keywords: consistency conditions, distributed data structures, relaxed specifications, average cost, time bounds.

1   Introduction

The advent of cloud computing has rekindled interest in implementing shared data objects in message-passing distributed environments. Linearizability [9,7] has been the gold standard of consistency conditions for shared objects; for instance, the cloud storage system Windows Azure Storage provides linearizability (strong consistency) [5]. However, linearizability can be expensive to implement, in both message-passing [10,4] and shared memory [3], as processors must communicate in order to synchronize. One approach to circumventing this problem is to consider consistency conditions weaker than linearizability for "classic" data types; for instance, quasi-linearizability [1], sequential consistency [8], eventual consistency [11], and quiescent consistency [2]. Another approach, and the one we follow here, is to retain linearizability as the desired consistency condition but consider "relaxed" versions of classic data types. [1] and [6] introduced and formalized this concept. The relaxations typically allow nondeterminism in the return values of operations.

F. Kuhn (Ed.): DISC 2014, LNCS 8784, pp. 421–438, 2014.
© Springer-Verlag Berlin Heidelberg 2014

We explore the possible performance benefits of four kinds of relaxed data structures, originally proposed by Henzinger et al. [6]: out-of-order, lateness, restricted-out-of-order, and stuttering. We focus on the elapsed time for operations when the shared object is implemented in a message-passing system with bounded message delays and approximately synchronized clocks. In contrast, Henzinger et al. considered shared memory implementations of relaxed shared objects. To our knowledge, we are the first to consider message-passing implementations of these relaxations.

First, we prove that for a general class of operations, the worst-case elapsed time must be at least d, the maximum message delay. We then show that for three of the relaxations being considered (lateness, restricted-out-of-order, and stuttering), the *Dequeue* operation of the FIFO Queue data type falls into this class and thus must take at least d time. This lower bound indicates that, with respect to worst-case time for operations, there is marginal gain, at best, from these relaxations, as recent work [12] has shown that an unrelaxed FIFO Queue can be implemented with worst-case time for *Dequeue* at most $d + \epsilon$, where ϵ is the maximum skew between local clocks.

In light of this negative result regarding worst-case time for *Dequeues*, we next consider *average* time, in the hope that relaxed data types would require expensive synchronization less frequently. By average time, we mean the sum of the total time taken by all *Dequeues*, divided by the number of *Dequeues*, in the worst case. As a first step, we focus on shared Queues; analogous results hold for shared Stacks. We consider two relaxations from [6], each with an integer parameter $k \geq n$, where n is the number of processes. In an out-of-order k-relaxed Queue, the *Dequeue* operation can return any one of the k oldest elements in the Queue. In a restricted-out-of-order k-relaxed Queue, the *Dequeue* operation can return any one of the $k - \ell$ oldest elements in the Queue, where ℓ is the number of elements that were enqueued after the current top was enqueued but have already been dequeued. We present an algorithm for implementing an out-of-order k-relaxed Queue in which the average time for *Dequeue* is $d/\lfloor \frac{k}{n} \rfloor + \epsilon$. We also present an algorithm for implementing a restricted-out-of-order k-relaxed Queue in which the average time for *Dequeue* is $(2d + \epsilon)/\lfloor \frac{k}{n} \rfloor + \epsilon$. In both cases, the average time for the *Dequeue* operation is significantly below the worst-case lower bound of d, and decreases as k increases. In contrast, we show that the best possible average time for *Dequeue* in an unrelaxed Queue must be at least $d(1 - \frac{1}{n})$, indicating that relaxation does pay when considering average time.

We further show a lower bound of $d/\lfloor \frac{k}{n} \rfloor$ on the average time for *Dequeue* for the same two relaxations, still for $k \geq n$, which indicates that one of our algorithms is optimal while the other is within a factor of two of optimal. Our upper and lower bounds on average *Dequeue* time imply that there is an *inherent* performance benefit achievable by increasing k for these two forms of relaxation, as the lower bounds for any fixed value of k are larger than the corresponding upper bounds for sufficiently greater values of k. In contrast, the results in [1],[6] show performance improvements for shared memory implementations, based on experimental analyses of specific algorithms; no lower bounds are shown.

Unlike prior work that has proved lower bounds on the time complexity of operations (e.g., [10,4,3,12]), ours are for nondeterministic data types. Nondeterminism is harder to deal with, as one cannot always rely on some operation returning a certain value. In our proofs, we take care to argue that the object can be "boxed into a corner" under certain circumstances, so that there is only one possible right answer.

Table 1 summarizes the known bounds on the elapsed time for *Dequeue*. Section 2 contains our definitions and model assumptions. In Section 3, we prove lower bounds on the worst-case time for operations. Our two algorithms and their average-time analyses are presented in Section 4. Section 5 contains our lower bounds on the average time for *Dequeues*, and we conclude in Section 6.

Table 1. Bounds on *Dequeue* Time Complexity

	Worst Case Cost		Average Cost	
	Lower Bound	Upper Bound	Lower Bound	Upper Bound
FIFO Queue	$d + \min\{\epsilon, u, \frac{d}{3}\}$ [12]	$d + \epsilon$ [12]	$d(1 - \frac{1}{n})$ (Sec 5.1)	$d + \epsilon$ [12]
Out-of-Order	?	$d + \epsilon$ [12]	$\frac{d}{\lfloor k/n \rfloor}$ (Sec 5.2; $k < n^2$)	$\frac{d}{\lfloor k/n \rfloor} + \epsilon$ (Sec 4.2; heavily-loaded)
Lateness	d (Sec 3)	$d + \epsilon$ [12]	?	$\frac{d}{\lfloor k/n \rfloor} + \epsilon$
Restricted-Out-of-Order	d (Sec 3)	$d + \epsilon$ [12]	$\frac{d}{\lfloor k/n \rfloor}$ (Sec 5.3)	$\frac{2d+\epsilon}{\lfloor k/n \rfloor} + \epsilon$ (Sec 4.3; heavily-loaded)
Stuttering	d (Sec 3)	$d + \epsilon$ [12]	?	?

2 Model and Definitions

2.1 Specifying Data Types

We begin by defining abstract data types in the sequential case. We follow the definitions in [12] but modified to encompass nondeterminism (and thus relaxation).

A data type T provides a set of operations $OPS(T)$. Each *operation OP* has a set of possible invocations, which differ only in their possible arguments, and a set of possible responses, which differ only in their possible return values. An invocation of an operation followed immediately by a response for the same operation creates an *operation instance*. This can be denoted $OP_{inv}(arg)$-$OP_{resp}(ret)$, or, more concisely, $OP(arg, ret)$.

A data type T also provides a set of sequences of its operation instances, called the *legal* sequences and denoted $L(T)$. $L(T)$ must satisfy the following constraints:

- *Prefix-Closure:* If ρ is in $L(T)$, then every prefix of ρ is also in $L(T)$. Also, the empty sequence is in $L(T)$.
- *Completeness:* If ρ is in $L(T)$, then for every operation invocation $OP_{inv}(arg)$, there exists a response $OP_{resp}(ret)$ such that $\rho \cdot OP(arg, ret)$ is in $L(T)$.

Queue Specifications We give the definitions of a standard FIFO Queue and four different relaxed versions, which we will be using in this paper. The special value $\perp$ is assumed to not be a possible input. These relaxations were specified in terms of state machines in [6]. We here give equivalent definitions in terms of legal sequences of operation instances. These relaxations allow a bounded non-deterministic choice of return value for *Dequeue*.

Definition 1. *A* Queue *over a set of values V is a data type with two operations:*

- *Enqueue$(val, -)$, $val \in V$; intuitively, adds element val and has no return value*
- *Dequeue$(-, val)$, $val \in V \cup \{\perp\}$; intuitively, removes an element and returns it, and has no argument*

A sequence of operation instances is legal iff it satisfies the following conditions:

(C1) Every argument to an instance of Enqueue is unique[1].
(C2) Every return value of a Dequeue instance is unique.
(C3) Every non-$\perp$ value which an instance of Dequeue returns is the argument to a previous instance of Enqueue.
(C4) If ρ is a legal sequence of operation instances, then $\rho \cdot$ Dequeue$(-, val)$, $val \neq \perp$, is legal iff Enqueue$(val, -)$ is the first Enqueue in ρ which does not have a matching Dequeue$(-, v)$ in ρ. Furthermore, $\rho \cdot$ Dequeue$(-, \perp)$ is legal iff every Enqueue$(val, -)$ in ρ has a matching Dequeue$(-, val)$ in ρ.

The relaxed versions of Queue use some of conditions *(C1)-(C3)*, but each modifies condition *(C4)* to give a different set of legal return values for *Dequeue*, and one does not use *(C2)*. The altered versions of *(C4)* allow a larger set of possible return values.

The out-of-order relaxation, instead of requiring a *Dequeue* to return the oldest element, allows any of the k oldest elements as a return value for a *Dequeue*.

Definition 2. *An* Out-of-Order k-Relaxed Queue *satisfies (C1)-(C3) from Definition 1, and the following condition:*

(C4) If ρ is a legal sequence of operation instances, then $\rho \cdot$ Dequeue$(-, val)$, is legal iff there are fewer than k distinct val's such that Enqueue$(val', -)$ precedes Enqueue$(val, -)$ in ρ and there is not a matching Dequeue$(-, val')$ in ρ. Furthermore, $\rho \cdot$ Dequeue$(-, \perp)$ is legal iff there are fewer than k Enqueue$(val', -)$'s in ρ without matching Dequeue$(-, val')$'s in ρ.

The next relaxation, lateness, does not impose any restriction on how close to the true top an element which a *Dequeue* returns must be, but instead enforces that the oldest element *Enqueued* is returned by at most the kth *Dequeue* after it became the oldest element left in the structure. In effect, the structure tracks the lateness of the current top element (the number of other elements which have been returned by *Dequeues* since it became the top element). This lateness must always be less than k.

---

[1] This can easily be achieved by timestamping elements when they are added.

Definition 3. *A* Lateness *k*-Relaxed Queue *satisfies* (C1)-(C3) *from Definition 1, and the following condition:*

(C4) If ρ is a legal sequence of operation instances, then $\rho \cdot$ Dequeue($-$, val) is legal iff every Enqueue(val', $-$) preceding Enqueue(val, $-$) has a matching Dequeue($-$, val') in ρ or there are fewer than $k-1$ instances Dequeue($-$, val') that follow the first Enqueue(val'', $-$) which does not have a matching Dequeue($-$, val'') in ρ.
Further, $\rho \cdot$ Dequeue($-$, $\perp$) is legal iff there are fewer than $k - 1$ instances Dequeue($-$, val') that follow the first Enqueue(val'', $-$) without a matching Dequeue($-$, val'') in ρ or every val' such that Enqueue(val', $-$) is in ρ has a matching Dequeue($-$, val') in ρ.

The restricted out-of-order relaxation is effectively a combination of the previous two relaxations. It allows an instance of *Dequeue* to return any of the oldest *k* elements, as fixed in time when last the single oldest element was returned. Thus, at least once every *k* instances of *Dequeue*, the true top element must be returned.

Definition 4. *A* Restricted Out-of-Order *k*-Relaxed Queue *satisfies (C1)-(C3) from Definition 1, and the following condition:*

(C4) If ρ is a legal sequence of operation instances, $\rho \cdot$ Dequeue($-$, val), val $\neq \perp$, is legal iff, in the suffix ρ' of ρ which starts at the first Enqueue(val', $-$) which does not have a matching Dequeue($-$, val') in ρ, Enqueue(val, $-$) is among the first k instances of Enqueue.
$\rho \cdot$ Dequeue($-$, $\perp$) is legal iff there are fewer than k instances Enqueue(val', $-$) in ρ'.

The stuttering relaxation has a very different flavor than the other relaxations. Instead of requiring a return value to be one of the oldest left in the structure, it allows *Dequeues* to execute without actually changing the simulated state of the shared queue. Instead, up to *k* times, the same value may be returned to multiple instances of *Dequeue*, as if it were not actually removed from the shared queue.

Definition 5. *A* Stuttering *k*-Relaxed Queue *satisfies (C1) and (C3) from Definition 1, and the following condition:*

(C4) If ρ is a legal sequence of operation instances, then $\rho \cdot$ Dequeue($-$, val), val $\neq \perp$ is legal iff there is no Dequeue($-$, val') with val' $\neq$ val such that either Enqueue(val', $-$) is in ρ after Enqueue(val, $-$) or val' $= \perp$, and there are fewer than k copies of Dequeue($-$, val) in ρ.
$\rho \cdot$ Dequeue($-$, $\perp$) is legal iff every Enqueue(val', $-$) in ρ has at least one corresponding Dequeue($-$, val').

2.2   System Model

We consider a set $\Pi = \{p_0, \ldots, p_{n-1}\}$ of processes, each modeled as a state machine. There are three kinds of events that can trigger a transition of the state machine for a process: the receipt of a message, a local timer going off, or the invocation of an operation instance. A *step* of a process is a 6-tuple (s, T, C, M, R, s'), where s is a state of the process (the old state), T is a trigger event, C is the local clock value (a real number), M is a set of messages (to be sent), R is either $\emptyset$ or an operation instance response, and s' is a state of the process (the new state), such that M, R, and s' are the result of the transition function operating on s, T, and C.

A *view* of a process is a sequence of steps such that

- the old state of the first step is an initial state of the state machine;
- the old state of each step after the first one equals the new state of the previous step;
- each timer in the old state of each step has a value that does not exceed the clock time of the step;
- if the trigger of a step is a timer going off, then the old state of the step has a timer whose value is equal to the clock time for the step
- clock times of steps are increasing, and if the sequence is infinite then they increase without bound;
- at most one operation instance is pending at a time

A *timed view* is a view with a real number, called "real time", associated with each step. There must exist a real number c such that, for each step, the difference between the clock time and the real time is exactly c (the "offset" of the process' local clock from real time).

A *run* is a set of n timed views, one for each process, such that every message receipt has exactly one matching message send, and every message send has at most one matching message receipt. A run is *complete* if

- every message sent is received; and
- each timed view is either infinite or ends in a state in which no timers are set.

A run is *admissible* with respect to parameters d, u, and ϵ, if

- every received message has delay in the range $[d - u, d]$ and if a message is sent but not received, then the recipient's last step is at real time less than $t + d$, where t is the real time when the message is sent;
- for all processes p_i and p_j, $|c_i - c_j| \leq \epsilon$, where c_i is the clock offset of p_i and c_j is the clock offset of p_j.

We assume that any message from a process to itself is simulated as taking the minimum message delay $d - u$.

We consider only algorithms which are *Eventually Quiescent*: Every complete admissible run with a finite number of operations is finite (i.e., every view is finite).

2.3 Correctness Condition

We are interested in algorithms that run on the message-passing model described in Section 2.2 and provide a linearizable implementation of data types described in Section 2.1. We require such an algorithm to satisfy the following two conditions:

1. *Liveness:* In every complete admissible run, every operation invocation has a matching response and every response has a matching invocation.

Because of the Liveness property, in every complete admissible run, we can pair up matching operation invocations and responses to form operation instances in the run. We can now state our second requirement:

2. *Linearizability:* For every complete admissible run R, there is a permutation π of the set of operation instances in R such that (i) π is legal and (ii) if operation instance op_1 responds before operation instance op_2 is invoked, with respect to real time in R, then op_1 precedes op_2 in π. We call π a *linearization* of R.

The *worst-case time complexity* of operation OP, denoted $|OP|$, is defined as the maximum over every instance of OP in every complete admissible run, of the real time that elapses between the invocation of the instance and its response. Consider a run R, an operation OP, and a real time t. Let $avg\_time(R, OP, t)$ be the sum of the elapsed time taken by all instances of OP in R which complete by time t, divided by the number of such instances of OP. Then the *average time complexity* of OP is the least upper bound, over every complete admissible run R and every real time t, of $avg\_time(R, OP, t)$.

3   Worst-Case Lower Bound

First, we will show a lower bound on the worst case time complexity for a class of operations which includes some of the *Dequeues* defined in the previous section. This lower bound is nearly equal to the upper bound given in [12] for arbitrary data types. This shows that there is negligible, if any, benefit from relaxation, with regard to this complexity measure.

To show this bound, we consider runs carefully structured so that the sequential specification of the data type gives tight limits on what values are legal to return. By simultaneously invoking multiple operation instances, we can use an indistinguishability argument to show that at least one of the instances must delay returning long enough to learn about another instance.

Definition 6. *Define an operation OP to be* non-repeatable *with respect to ρ if there exists a sequence of operation instances ρ and an instance $op = OP(arg, ret) \in OP$ such that $\rho \cdot op$ is legal and no $ret' \neq ret$ is a legal return value for $\rho \cdot OP(arg)$, but $\rho \cdot op \cdot op$ is not legal.*

Theorem 1. *In any distributed shared memory implementation A, if there is an admissible run with linearization of its operation instances ρ and operation OP which is non-repeatable with respect to ρ, then $|OP| \geq d$.*

We next show that in several relaxations of Queues, *Dequeue* satisfies the hypothesis of Theorem 1.

Lemma 1. *For any algorithm implementing a lateness k-relaxed Queue, there is some admissible run with linearization ρ such that Dequeue is non-repeatable with respect to ρ.*

Corollary 1. *In any implementation of a lateness k-relaxed Queue, $|Dequeue| \geq d$.*

Lemma 2. *For any algorithm implementing a restricted out-of-order k-relaxed Queue, there is some admissible run with linearization ρ such that Dequeue is non-repeatable with respect to ρ.*

Corollary 2. *In any implementation of a restricted out-of-order k-relaxed Queue, $|Dequeue| \geq d$.*

Lemma 3. *For any algorithm implementing a stuttering k-relaxed Queue which has an admissible run R in which Dequeue stutters k times, Dequeue is non-repeatable with respect to the linearization of ρ, where $\rho \cdot op$ is the prefix of R's linearization ending with the kth stuttering instance op of Dequeue.*

Corollary 3. *For any algorithm implementing a stuttering k-relaxed Queue which in some admissible run has Dequeue stutter k times, $|Dequeue| \geq d$.*

The arguments used so far in this section to show a lower bound of d on the worst-case time complexity for relaxed versions of the *Dequeue* operation of relaxed Queues can be generalized to operations that remove elements from a set of elements. Consider any data type which maintains a set of current elements and has at least two operations, one to add elements and one to remove. Suppose further that the remove operation cannot remove any single element more than once. Finally, constrain the set of legal sequences of operation instances so that repeatedly invoking the remove operation must eventually remove every element in the set. Then we can show that the remove operation is non-repeatable with respect to some operation sequence, and thus the remove operation has worst-case time complexity at least d.

4 k-Relaxed Algorithms for Queues

We have shown that, with regard to the metric of worst-case operation time, there is no useful gain from relaxation of some common data types. This is due to the fact that distributed storage must still synchronize itself at times. But, in a relaxed data type, the required coordination may not be quite as close, so synchronization may not be required as often. We give two algorithms which exploit this lesser synchronization requirement to achieve better average operation cost, where the improvement scales with the degree of relaxation.

4.1   Local Variables

We specify the local variables our algorithms will use. Both algorithms use the same local variables, with the addition of *available* fields on *lQueue* elements and *tops$_j$* arrays for Algorithm 2. We will also use the parameter l, defined as $\lfloor \frac{k}{n} \rfloor$, throughout this section.

- *clean*: Boolean, initially true
- *lQueue*: Local copy of data structure, initially empty. Values have two associated fields: a *label* field which is initially *null* and can hold a process id and a Boolean *available*, initially true. Behavior is an extension of a local (non-distributed) FIFO Queue. Operations:
  - *enq(val)*: inserts *val*
  - *deqByLabel(p_j)*: removes and returns top (oldest) element labeled p_j, $\bot$ if none exists
  - *peekByLabel(p_j)*: returns, without removing, top element labeled p_j, $\bot$ if none exists
  - *deqBySet(S)*: removes and returns top element in *lQueue* which is also in the set S
  - *peekBySet(S)*: returns, without removing, the top element in both *lQueue* and S
  - *contains(val)*: returns true if *val* is in *lQueue*, false otherwise
  - *size()*: returns current number of elements
  - *sizeByLabel(p_j)*: Returns number of elements with label p_j
  - *unlabeledSize()*: returns current number of unlabeled elements
  - *tail()*: returns, without removing, the last element added
  - *remove(val)*: removes *val*
  - *label(p_j, val)*: label *val* with p_j
  - *labelOldest(p_j, x)*: labels the oldest x elements with p_j
- *Pending*: Priority queue to hold operation instances, keyed by timestamp; initially empty. Supports standard operations *insert(val, ts)*, *min()*, *extractMin()*
- *tops$_j$[]*, $0 \le j < n$: Arrays of data elements of size n, initially empty

4.2   Out-of-Order Relaxed Queues

First, we give an algorithm for an out-of-order k-relaxed Queue. This algorithm introduces the basic idea behind our later algorithm for restricted out-of-order k-relaxed Queues. This algorithm assumes $k > n$, and gives improved average performance over algorithms for unrelaxed Queues, increasing as k increases by multiples of n. The algorithm is designed to gracefully degrade performance as it runs out of elements, since a k-relaxed Dequeue on a Queue with fewer than k elements is not very meaningful. Instead, there will be an effectively lower k (down to a minimum of n) until the size of the Queue grows sufficiently. This also allows us to use fast Enqueues at all times.

The algorithm is inspired by the algorithm from [12]. To allow quick returns of most operation instances, giving good average performance, we distribute the top k elements of the Queue, which are legal to return at any given time, evenly among the processes. Each process can quickly return those elements assigned to it, then must synchronize to obtain more. When a process needs to return an element, due to a *Dequeue*, it returns the top element labeled with its own id. If there are no elements so labeled, then the process will not return until it has

Algorithm 1. Code for each process p_i to implement a Queue with out-of-order k-relaxed *Dequeue*, where $k \geq n$ and $l = \lfloor k/n \rfloor$, part 1.

```
 1: HandleEvent ENQUEUE(val)
 2:     send (enq, val, ⟨localTime, i⟩) to all
 3:     setTimer(ε, ⟨enq, val, ⟨localTime, i⟩⟩, respond)
 4: HandleEvent R-DEQUEUE
 5:     if lQueue.peekByLabel(pᵢ) ≠ ⊥ then
 6:         ret = lQueue.deqByLabel(pᵢ)
 7:         send (deq_f, ret, ⟨localTime, i⟩) to all
 8:         setTimer(ε, ⟨deq_f, ret, null⟩, respond)
 9:     else send (deq_s, null, ⟨localTime, i⟩) to all
10: HandleEvent EXPIRETIMER(⟨op, val, ts⟩, respond)
11:     if op == peek then return lQueue.peekByLabel(pᵢ)
12:     else if op == deq_f then return val
13:     else return ACK
14: HandleEvent RECEIVE (op, val, ts) FROM pⱼ
15:     Pending.push(⟨op, val, ts⟩)
16:     setTimer(u + ε, ⟨op, val, ts⟩, execute)
17: HandleEvent EXPIRETIMER(⟨op, val, ts⟩, execute)
18:     while ts ≥ Pending.min() do
19:         ⟨op', val', ts'⟩ = Pending.extractMin()
20:         executeLocally(op', val', ts')
21:         cancelTimer(⟨op', arg', ts'⟩, execute)
22: function EXECUTELOCALLY(op, val, ⟨*, j⟩)
23:     if op == enq then
24:         lQueue.enq(val)
25:         if clean == true and lQueue.size() ≤ k then
26:             let a = (lQueue.size() − 1) mod n
27:             lQueue.label(pₐ, lQueue.tail())
28:     else clean = false
29:         if op == deq_f then
30:             if j ≠ i then lQueue.remove(val)
31:         else
32:             if lQueue.peekByLabel(pⱼ) ≠ ⊥ then
33:                 ret = lQueue.deqByLabel(pⱼ)
34:             else ret = lQueue.deqByLabel(null)
35:             labelElements(j)
36:             if j == i then return ret
37:         if lQueue.size() == 0 then clean = true
38: function LABELELEMENTS(j)
39:     y = lQueue.unlabeledSize()
40:     lQueue.labelOldest(pⱼ, x), where x = min{l, ⌊lQueue.size()/n⌋, y}
```

waited long enough to learn about concurrent and recent operations at other processes, effectively synchronizing, as every operation in [12] did.

When a process tries to *Dequeue*, but has no local elements available and must synchronize, as part of its operation, it labels more elements for itself. No more than k elements are ever labeled, and for exactly k to be labeled, each process must have l elements labeled[2]. Thus, since the current process has no labeled elements, it is safe to claim more, up to a total of l. Then there will be at most k elements labeled, so every future operation returning a labeled element will return a legal element, according to the relaxation.

Before any elements are dequeued (while *clean* is true), *Enqueue* operations label up to k elements in round-robin fashion. This allows the first *Dequeue* invoked to return quickly, since it will find elements labeled with its invoking process. After a *Dequeue* is invoked, we mark the Queue as dirty (*clean* = *false*) and no longer label elements during *Enqueues*, because round-robin order may not be maintained if *Dequeues* are not invoked evenly across all processes. This maintains the good average performance in executions which may only perform a few *Dequeues*.

When there are fewer than k elements left in the Queue, a synchronizing *Dequeue* will act as if k were $lQueue.size()$, the number of elements which it knows are in the Queue. This means that it labels fewer elements for itself, allowing even performance across all processes. This behavior is adopted, as having a k larger than the current size of the Queue means that every element is legal to return.

Theorem 2. *Algorithm 1 is a correct implementation of an out-of-order k-relaxed Queue.*

Out-of-Order Relaxation Performance

Definition 7. *We will call a run R heavily loaded if for some linearization π of R, every prefix of π which is immediately followed by an instance of Dequeue has at least k more Enqueues than Dequeues.*

Theorem 3. *The average time complexity of Dequeue in any heavily-loaded complete, admissible run of Algorithm 1 is no more than $\frac{d}{l} + \epsilon$, where $l = \lfloor k/n \rfloor$.*

We can consider the more general case when the Queue is not necessarily heavily loaded.

Definition 8. *At each process p_i, the effective l is set when either (1) a Dequeue at the process is executed in a clean state or (2) when a slow Dequeue labels elements, to $\min\{l, \left\lfloor \frac{lQueue_i.size()}{n} \right\rfloor,$ $lQueue_i.unlabelled\_size()\}$ and remains until a new effective l is set.*

Thus, every instance in a linearization, except initial *Enqueues*, can be said to have an effective l determined by its invoking process and its location in the linearization. We show that each process' *Dequeues* maintain average performance determinedd by their effective l, which we call l'. The proof is very similar to the proof of Theorem 3, using the fact that there are at most l' elements labeled p_i at any time.

---

[2] Or $l + 1$ elements when k is not an exact multiple of n, and elements have been labeled by *Enqueues*.

Theorem 4. *Consider a complete, admissible run. For each process p_i, the average time complexity of Dequeues executed by p_i during a time interval in which its effective l is equal to l' is at most $\frac{d}{l'} + \epsilon$.*

4.3   Restricted Out-of-Order Relaxed Queues

We now present an algorithm for implementing a Queue with restricted out-of-order k-relaxed Dequeues, for $k \geq n$. This algorithm uses the idea of locally distributing the top elements of the Queue to allow processes to return quickly several times, before they must take time to synchronize their state with other processes. In addition, the algorithm uses the synchronizing operations to guarantee that the Queue's head is returned with sufficient frequency. Doing this imposes extra cost on some operations, because they effectively may be forced to "steal" the head element from another process. The algorithm still has good performance for sufficiently large k, and performance which improves monotonically as k increases.

The algorithm assigns elements to different processes by labeling them with process ids. The correctness argument depends on an invariant of the labeling: every element which has a label in the local state of a process is legal for an instance of *Dequeue* by that process to return. Further, labeled elements will only be returned by the process whose id they have, unless another process goes through an expensive synchronization process to steal it. Thus, if a process finds an element labeled with its own id, it can return it quickly without waiting to coordinate with other processes.

If a *Dequeue* does not find any elements labeled with its invoking process' id, then it must find another element to return, making it a slow *Dequeue*, since this will be expensive and require synchronization. A slow *Dequeue* ensures that the top element in the simulated queue is removed, either by itself or by another, concurrent slow *Dequeue*. When a process must return the top element, by the definition of a restricted out-of-order k-relaxed queue the top k elements in the simulated queue are now legal to return, so the process labels them. Thus, after a process executes a slow *Dequeue*, there will be more elements labeled with its id, if there are enough elements currently stored.

To ensure the top element is returned, a process p_i which invokes a slow *Dequeue* notifies all other processes of the operation instance. Each other process p_j will mark the element labeled p_j which is nearest the top of the simulated queue as unavailable for fast local return and broadcast it to all, marking it as being relevant to a slow *Dequeue* invoked at p_i. We call this element the local top for p_j. Timers in the algorithm are set such that every process will receive every other process' local top before it tries to execute the slow *Dequeue*. Since processes label elements from the top of the queue without skipping, if there are any labeled elements, then the top element in the simulated queue will be some process' local top. Then when a slow *Dequeue* is executed, it will return the top element in the entire queue, unless another, concurrent slow *Dequeue* has already returned it. In this case, the later slow *Dequeue* need not worry about returning the global top or labeling elements, and can return any of the local top elements, since they are reserved by their processes.

Since *Dequeues* synchronize as needed when the simulated queue empties, *Enqueues* do not need to synchronize. Thus, we always have fast *Enqueues*.

Theorem 5. *Algorithm 2 is a correct implementation of an out-of-order k-relaxed Dequeues.*

Restricted Out-of-Order Relaxation Performance We show the following upper bound on the average cost of *Dequeues* in Algorithm 2:

Theorem 6. *The average time complexity per Dequeue in any heavily loaded, complete, admissible run of Algorithm 2 is no more than $\frac{2d+\epsilon}{l}+\epsilon$, where $l = \lfloor k/n \rfloor$.*

We will later compare this to lower bounds on performance of an arbitrary algorithm for unrelaxed *Dequeues* to show that this relaxation gives better average performance. Further, our bound decreases with increasing k, which shows that stronger relaxation of the data type specification allow better performance.

4.4   Relaxed Stacks

Relaxed Stacks, with different semantics for *Pop* operations, can be defined analogously to relaxed Queues. The lower bounds from Section 3 all also apply to the equivalently-relaxed Stack.

The algorithms can be altered to implement Stacks with k-relaxed *Pops*. The only change required is that *Pushes* will be slow, taking $d + \epsilon$ or $2d + \epsilon$ time respectively for the out-of-order and restricted out-of-order relaxations. This extra cost is necessary because there is always contention between *Push* and *Pop*, since they interact with the same end of the data structure. This higher performance cost suggests that this algorithm, and possibly any implementation of a relaxed stack,is best used in scenarios with a long initialization time to add elements to the data structure, but which need high performance while only removing elements.

The upper bounds on average time complexity given by adapting our algorithms for out-of-order k-relaxed stacks will be $\frac{d}{l}$ for out-of-order relaxed *Pop* and $d + \epsilon$ for *Push*. For restricted out-of-order k-relaxed stacks, we will have $\frac{2d+\epsilon}{l} + \epsilon$ average time complexity for *Pop* and $2d + \epsilon$ for *Push*.

Algorithm 2. Code for each process p_i to implement a Queue with restricted out-of-order k-relaxed *Dequeues* for $k \geq n$, where $l = \lfloor k/n \rfloor$.

```
 1: HandleEvent ENQUEUE(val)
 2:     send (enq, val, ⟨localTime, i⟩) to all
 3:     setTimer(ε, ⟨enq, val, ⟨localTime, i⟩⟩, respond)
 4: HandleEvent R-DEQUEUE
 5:     if lQueue.peekByLabel(pᵢ) ≠ ⊥ then
 6:         x = lQueue.deqByLabel()
 7:         send (deq_f, x, ⟨localTime, i⟩) to all
 8:         setTimer(ε, ⟨deq_f, x, ⟨localTime, i⟩⟩, respond)
 9:     else send (deq_s, null, ⟨localTime, i⟩) to all
10: HandleEvent RECEIVE (op, val, ts) FROM pⱼ
11:     Pending.push(⟨op, val, ts⟩)
12:     if op = deq_s then
13:         clear topsⱼ
14:         top = lQueue.peekByLabel(pᵢ)
15:         top.available = false
16:         send (top, j) to all
17:     setTimer(d + u + ε, ⟨op, val, ts⟩, execute)
18: HandleEvent RECEIVE (val, k) FROM pⱼ
19:     topsₖ[j] = val
20: HandleEvent EXPIRETIMER(⟨op, val, ts⟩, respond)
21:     if op == deq_f then return val
22:     else  return ACK
23: HandleEvent EXPIRETIMER(⟨op, val, ts⟩, execute)
24:     while ts ≥ Pending.min() do
25:         ⟨op', val', ts'⟩ = Pending.extractMin()
26:         executeLocally(op', val', ts')
27:         cancelTimer(⟨op', arg', ts'⟩, execute)
28: function EXECUTELOCALLY(op, val, ⟨∗, j⟩)
29:     if op == enq then
30:         lQueue.enq(val)
31:         if clean == true and lQueue.size() ≤ k then
32:             let a = (lQueue.size() − 1) mod n
33:             lQueue.label(pₐ, lQueue.tail())
34:     else
35:         clean = false
36:         if op == deq_f then
37:             if j ≠ i then lQueue.remove(val)
38:         else if op == deq_s then
39:             if lQueue.peekBySet(topsⱼ) ≠ ⊥ then
40:                 ret = lQueue.deqBySet(topsⱼ)
41:             else if lQueue.peekByLabel(pⱼ) ≠ ⊥ then
42:                 ret = lQueue.deqByLabel(pⱼ)
43:             else
44:                 ret = lQueue.deqByLabel(null)
45:             if ∀x ∈ topsⱼ, lQueue.contains(x) == true then
46:                 labelElements()
47:             if ∄deq_s ∈ Pending and ∃topsⱼ[i] for some 0 ≤ j < n then topsⱼ[i].available = true
48:             if j == i then return ret
49:         if lQueue.size() == 0 then clean = true
50: function LABELELEMENTS
51:     while lQueue.unlabeledSize() > 0 and
             ∃j ∈ [0, n − 1] s.t. lQueue.sizeByLabel(pⱼ) < min{l, ⌈Queue.size/n⌉} do
52:         let m = minⱼ{lQueue.sizeByLabel(pⱼ)}
53:         lQueue.label(pₘ, lQueue.peekByLabel(null))
```

5   Lower Bounds on Average Time Complexity

Finally, we give lower bounds on the average time complexity of *Dequeue* operations in Queues. We show, first, that both of our algorithms give performance gains over unrelaxed Queues, when we consider average time per operation. This verifies our intuition that a relaxed data type can allow higher performance by reducing the required frequency of synchronization between processes.

Next, we give lower bounds on the average cost of *Dequeues* for algorithms implementing relaxed Queues. We show that our algorithm for Out-of-Order k-relaxed Queue is approximately optimal for *Dequeue* (with an extra term of ϵ, the clock skew bound), for reasonable values of k. We then show a lower bound for the Restricted Out-of-Order k-relaxed Queue which is approximately a factor of two less than the performance of our algorithm. Thus, we see that we have algorithms that are near-optimal for both of these intuitive relaxations, and implicitly for lateness-k relaxed Queues, as well, since a restricted out-of-order k-relaxed Queue is also lateness k-relaxed.

Our proofs rely heavily on the indistinguishability of runs, and the fact that no element can be returned more than once. We construct runs in which any algorithm with better performance than the lower bound we wish to show must have multiple processes behave in such a way that more than one will return the same element, based on the information they have. This contradiction allows us to conclude that algorithms performing faster than the proposed lower bounds are impossible.

Throughout this section, we assume $k \geq n$, the range where our algorithms are useful.

5.1   Strict Queue Lower Bound

We first consider implementations of unrelaxed Queues. Every *Dequeue* must return the unique top element in the structure. The proof for the average cost is very similar to the proof for the worst case cost. As we forced one operation instance to wait to make sure that it was not removing the top element a second time, so we can force multiple simultaneous operation instances to wait, giving a high average cost.

Theorem 7. *In any linearizable implementation of a (unrelaxed) Queue, Dequeue must take at at least $d\left(1 - \frac{1}{n}\right)$ time, on average.*

Our average operation times given by the algorithms for the two relaxations were $\frac{d}{l}$ and $\frac{2d+\epsilon}{l} + \epsilon$, respectively. We can see that for $l \geq 1$ and $n > 2$, the first algorithm gives better average performance per operation than the lower bound for unrelaxed queues, and for $l \geq 2, n > 2$ and sufficiently small ϵ, the second algorithm also performs better. Further, as l (and thus k) increases, the algorithms' performance will continue to increase, leaving the lower bound farther and farther behind. This shows that our algorithms give a benefit over prior algorithms for unrelaxed Queues, so we turn our attention to determining how close our algorithms are to optimal.

5.2   Out-of-Order Relaxation Lower Bound

Theorem 8. *Any algorithm implementing an out-of-order k-relaxed Queue with $k < n^2$ must have an average time complexity for Dequeue at least $\frac{d}{l}$, where $l = \lfloor \frac{k}{n} \rfloor$.*

This bound only holds for $l < n$, which is equivalent to $k < n^2$, but it is reasonable to think that at some point, having k significantly larger than the number of available processes ceases to be as useful in real-world systems, particularly if n is large. Another consideration is that this relaxation may not be the most useful in practice. When there are fewer than k elements in the structure, the specification allows returning $\perp$, indicating that the structure is empty, even though it may not be. Thus, there could be algorithms satisfying the specification of this relaxation which never return every element in the queue. Due to these limitations, we focus our attention next on the restricted out-of-order relaxation, which provides stronger guarantees and, as we have seen, is not asymptotically more costly to implement.

5.3   Restricted Out-of-Order Relaxation Lower Bound

Our last lower bound shows us that Algorithm 2 is less than a factor of two above the lower bound on average performance. Because a Restricted Out-of-Order k-Relaxed Queue satisfies the conditions of an Out-of-Order k-relaxed Queue, we could apply the previous lower bound to these operations as well. However, we next show a bound without the limitation of $k < n^2$.

Theorem 9. *Any algorithm implementing a restricted out-of-order k-relaxed Queue which guarantees an upper bound c on the average time complexity for Dequeue at all times during any complete, admissible run must have $c > \frac{d}{l}$.*

5.4   Relaxed Stacks

All three of the lower bounds in this section can be straightforwardly adapted to stacks, with the semantics of *Pop* altered analogously to those of *Dequeue*. Thus, we achieve analogous results for relaxed stacks as we have shown for relaxed queues.

6   Conclusion

We have made an introductory exploration into the benefits of relaxing data types to achieve higher performance in message-passing systems. Based on the intuition that non-determinism in a data type could make a lower degree of synchronization between processes sufficient, we have shown that there is a benefit to be gained by relaxing. First, we showed that the worst-case operation time is not affected by relaxation for a general class of operations. This follows from the fact that there are still times when we must have synchronization to enforce coherent behavior. Proceeding from there, we gave two algorithms for relaxed Queues which perform significantly better, on average for *Dequeues*, than the worst-case lower bounds for strict data types, for sufficient levels of relaxation ($k \geq n$). These algorithms exploit the non-determinism in the data type specification to assign different legal elements to different users in such a way that each user will be able to run locally, and thus quickly, for a time before they must resynchronize. Even with somewhat more costly synchronizing operations, as in one of the algorithms, the average cost per operation instance is significantly below the worst-case cost. To formalize this, we show a lower bound on average time complexity of *Dequeue* for unrelaxed Queues. This bound is higher than the performance our algorithms achieve, showing that there is a strict performance gain from relaxation. We then show lower bounds on average time complexity of *Dequeue* for relaxed Queues. We see that, for moderate relaxation, one of our algorithms is optimal, and for any level of relaxation, the other is less than twice the lower bound. Both algorithms have performance which improves as k increases, achieving greater performance gains from greater relaxation.

Looking forward, we would first like to tighten and complete the bounds given in this paper. Next, generalization of these results, both towards abstract data types and towards arbitrary relaxations, is of interest. It would also be interesting to see if there is any strong correlation between relaxations of data type specifications, as we consider here, and weaker consistency conditions, such as sequential consistency or eventual consistency. Some of our results, wherein processes operate quickly, merely maintaining a consistent local state for a time, feel as if they might correlate closely to such concepts.

Acknowledgment. This work was supported in part by NSF grant 0964696.

References

1. Afek, Y., Korland, G., Yanovsky, E.: Quasi-linearizability: Relaxed consistency for improved concurrency. In: Lu, C., Masuzawa, T., Mosbah, M. (eds.) OPODIS 2010. LNCS, vol. 6490, pp. 395–410. Springer, Heidelberg (2010)
2. Aspnes, J., Herlihy, M., Shavit, N.: Counting networks. J. ACM 41(5), 1020–1048 (1994)
3. Attiya, H., Guerraoui, R., Hendler, D., Kuznetsov, P., Michael, M.M., Vechev, M.T.: Laws of order: Expensive synchronization in concurrent algorithms cannot be eliminated. In: Ball, T., Sagiv, M. (eds.) Principles of Programming Languages (POPL), pp. 487–498. ACM (2011)
4. Attiya, H., Welch, J.L.: Sequential consistency versus linearizability. ACM Transactions on Computer Systems 12(2), 91–122 (1994)
5. Calder, B., Wang, J., Ogus, A., et al.: Windows Azure Storage: a highly available cloud storage service with strong consistency. In: Proceedings of the 23rd ACM Symposium on Operating Systems Principles, pp. 143–157 (2011)
6. Henzinger, T.A., Kirsch, C.M., Payer, H., Sezgin, A., Sokolova, A.: Quantitative relaxation of concurrent data structures. In: Giacobazzi, R., Cousot, R. (eds.) Principles of Programming Languages (POPL), pp. 317–328. ACM (2013)

7. Herlihy, M., Wing, J.M.: Linearizability: A correctness condition for concurrent objects. ACM Transactions on Programming Languages and Systems 12(3), 463–492 (1990)
8. Lamport, L.: How to make a multiprocessor computer that correctly executes multiprocess programs. IEEE Trans. Computers 28(9), 690–691 (1979)
9. Lamport, L.: On interprocess communication. Distributed Computing 1(2), 77–101 (1986)
10. Lipton, R.J., Sandberg, J.D.: PRAM: A scalable shared memory. Technical Report CS-TR-180-88, Princeton University, Department of Computer Science (1988)
11. Vogels, W.: Eventually consistent. Communications of the ACM 52(1), 40–44 (2009)
12. Wang, J., Talmage, E., Lee, H., Welch, J.L.: Improved time bounds for linearizable implementations of abstract data types. In: International Parallel and Distributed Processing Symposium (IPDPS), pp. 691–701 (2014)

Almost-Tight Distributed Minimum Cut Algorithms[*]

Danupon Nanongkai[1],[**] and Hsin-Hao Su[2],[***]

[1] Faculty of Computer Science, University of Vienna, Austria
[2] Department of EECS, University of Michigan, MI, USA

Abstract. We study the problem of computing the minimum cut in a weighted distributed message-passing networks (the CONGEST model). Let λ be the minimum cut, n be the number of nodes (processors) in the network, and D be the network diameter. Our algorithm can compute λ exactly in $O((\sqrt{n}\log^* n + D)\lambda^4 \log^2 n)$ time. To the best of our knowledge, this is the first paper that explicitly studies computing the exact minimum cut in the distributed setting. Previously, non-trivial sublinear time algorithms for this problem are known only for unweighted graphs when $\lambda \leq 3$ due to Pritchard and Thurimella's $O(D)$-time and $O(D + n^{1/2} \log^* n)$-time algorithms for computing 2-edge-connected and 3-edge-connected components [ACM Transactions on Algorithms 2011].

By using the edge sampling technique of Karger [STOC 1994], we can convert this algorithm into a $(1 + \epsilon)$-approximation $O((\sqrt{n}\log^* n + D)\epsilon^{-5} \log^3 n)$-time algorithm for any $\epsilon > 0$. This improves over the previous $(2 + \epsilon)$-approximation $O((\sqrt{n}\log^* n + D)\epsilon^{-5} \log^2 n \log \log n)$-time algorithm and $O(\epsilon^{-1})$-approximation $O(D + n^{\frac{1}{2}+\epsilon} \operatorname{poly}\log n)$-time algorithm of Ghaffari and Kuhn [DISC 2013]. Due to the lower bound of $\Omega(D + n^{1/2}/\log n)$ by Das Sarma et al. [SICOMP 2013] which holds for any approximation algorithm, this running time is *tight* up to a poly $\log n$ factor.

To get the stated running time, we developed an approximation algorithm which combines the ideas of Thorup's algorithm [Combinatorica 2007] and Matula's contraction algorithm [SODA 1993]. It saves an $\epsilon^{-9} \log^7 n$ factor as compared to applying Thorup's tree packing theorem directly. Then, we combine Kutten and Peleg's tree partitioning algorithm [J. Algorithms 1998] and Karger's dynamic programming [JACM 2000] to achieve an efficient distributed algorithm that finds the minimum cut when we are given a spanning tree that crosses the minimum cut exactly once.

---

[*] The full version of this paper is available at http://arxiv.org/abs/1408.0557. The preliminary versions of this paper appeared as brief announcement papers at PODC 2014 and SPAA 2014 [15,21].

[**] This work was partially done while at ICERM, Brown University USA and Nanyang Technological University, Singapore.

[***] This work is supported by NSF grants CCF-1217338 and CNS-1318294. This work was done while visiting MADALGO at Aarhus University, supported by Danish National Research Foundation grant DNRF84.

F. Kuhn (Ed.): DISC 2014, LNCS 8784, pp. 439–453, 2014.

1   Introduction

Minimum cut is an important measure of networks. It determines, e.g., the network vulnerability and the limits to the speed at which information can be transmitted. While this problem has been well-studied in the centralized setting (e.g. [5,9,6,7,14,13,2,20,8]), very little is known in the distributed setting, especially in the relevant context where communication links are constrained by a small *bandwidth* – the so-called CONGEST model (cf. Section 2).

Consider, for example, a simple variation of this problem, called λ-*edge-connectivity*: given an *unweighted* undirected graph G and a *constant* λ, we want to determine whether G is λ-edge-connected or not. In the centralized setting, this problem can be solved in $O(m + n\lambda^2 \log n)$ time [2], thus near-linear time when λ is a constant. (Throughout, n, m, and D denotes the number of nodes, number of edges, and the network diameter, respectively.) In the distributed setting, however, non-trivial solutions exist only when $\lambda \leq 3$; this is due to algorithms of Pritchard and Thurimella [19] which can compute 2-edge-connected and 3-edge-connected components in $O(D)$ and $O(D + n^{1/2} \log^* n)$ time, respectively, with high probability[1]. This implies that the λ-edge-connectivity problem can be solved in $O(D)$ time when $\lambda = 2$ and $O(D + n^{1/2} \log^* n)$ time when $\lambda = 3$.

For the general version where input graphs could be weighted, the problem can be solved in near-linear time [8,13,6,7] in the centralized setting. In the distributed setting, the first non-trivial upper bounds are due to Ghaffari and Kuhn [4], who presented $(2 + \epsilon)$-approximation $O((\sqrt{n} \log^* n + D)\epsilon^{-5} \log^2 n \log \log n)$-time and $O(\epsilon^{-1})$-approximation $O(D + n^{\frac{1}{2}+\epsilon} \operatorname{poly} \log n)$-time algorithms. These upper bounds are complemented by a lower bound of $\Omega(D + n^{1/2}/\log n)$ for any approximation algorithm which was earlier proved by Das Sarma et al. [1] for the weighted case and later extended by [4] to the unweighted case. This means that the running times of the algorithms in [4] are tight up to a polylog n factor. Yet, it is still open whether we can achieve an approximation factor less than two in the same running time, or in fact, in any sublinear (i.e. $O(D + o(n))$) time.

Results.   In this paper, we present improved distributed algorithms for computing the minimum cut both exactly and approximately. Our exact deterministic algorithm for finding the minimum cut takes $O((\sqrt{n} \log^* n + D)\lambda^4 \log^2 n)$ time, where λ is the value of the minimum cut. Our approximation algorithm finds a $(1 + \epsilon)$-approximate minimum cut in $O((D + \sqrt{n} \log^* n)\epsilon^{-5} \log^3 n)$ time with high probability. (If we only want to compute the $(1 + \epsilon)$-approximate *value* of the minimum cut, then the running time can be slightly reduced to $O((\sqrt{n} \log^* n + D)\epsilon^{-5} \log^2 n \log \log n)$.) As noted earlier, prior to this paper there was no sublinear-time exact algorithm even when λ is a constant greater than three, nor sublinear-time algorithm with approximation ratio less than two. Table 1 summarizes the results.

---

[1] We say that an event holds *with high probability* (w.h.p.) if it holds with probability at least $1 - 1/n^c$, where c is an arbitrarily large constant.

Table 1. Summary of Results

Reference	Time	Approximation
Pritchard&Thurimella [19]	$O(D)$ for $\lambda \leq 2$	exact
Pritchard&Thurimella [19]	$O(\sqrt{n}\log^* n + D)$ for $\lambda \leq 3$	exact
This paper	$O((\sqrt{n}\log^* n + D)\lambda^4 \log^2 n)$	exact
Das Sarma et al. [1]	$\Omega(\frac{\sqrt{n}}{\log n} + D)$	any
Ghaffari&Kuhn [4]	$O((\sqrt{n}\log^* n + D)\epsilon^{-5}\log^2 n \log\log n)$	$2 + \epsilon$
This paper	$O((\sqrt{n}\log^* n + D)\epsilon^{-5}\log^3 n)$	$1 + \epsilon$

Techniques. The starting point of our algorithm is Thorup's tree packing theorem [22, Theorem 9], which shows that if we generate $\Theta(\lambda^7 \log^3 n)$ trees $T_1, T_2, \ldots$, where tree T_i is the minimum spanning tree with respect to the loads induced by $\{T_1, \ldots, T_{i-1}\}$, then one of these trees will contain exactly one edge in the minimum cut (see Section 4 for the definition of load). Since we can use the $O(\sqrt{n}\log^* n + D)$-time algorithm of Kutten and Peleg [11] to compute the minimum spanning tree (MST), the problem of finding a minimum cut is reduced to finding the minimum cut that 1-*respects a tree*; i.e., finding which edge in a given spanning tree defines a smallest cut (see the formal definition in Section 3). Solving this problem in $O(D + \sqrt{n}\log^* n)$ time is the first key technical contribution of this paper. We do this by using a simple observation of Karger [8] which reduces the problem to computing the sum of degree and the number of edges contained in a subtree rooted at each node. We use this observation along with Garay, Kutten and Peleg's *tree partitioning* [11,3] to quickly compute these quantities. This requires several (elementary) steps, which we will discuss in more detail in Section 3.

The above result together with Thorup's tree packing theorem immediately imply that we can find a minimum cut exactly in $O((D + \sqrt{n}\log^* n)\lambda^7 \log^3 n)$ time. By using Karger's random sampling result [7] to bring λ down to $O(\log n/\epsilon^2)$, we can find an $(1 + \epsilon)$-approximate minimum cut in $O((D + \sqrt{n}\log^* n)\epsilon^{-14}\log^{10} n)$ time. These time bounds unfortunately depend on large factors of λ, $\log n$ and $1/\epsilon$, which make their practicality dubious. Our second key technical contribution is a new algorithm which significantly reduces these factors by combining Thorup's greedy tree packing approach with Matula's contraction algorithm [13]. In Matula's $(2 + \epsilon)$-approximation algorithm for the minimum cut problem, he partitioned the graph into *components* according to the *spanning forest decomposition* by Nagamochi and Ibaraki [14]. He showed that either a component induces a $(2 + \epsilon)$-approximate minimum cut, or the minimum cut does not intersect with the components. In the latter case, it is safe to contract the components. Our algorithm used a similar approach, but we partitioned the graph according to Thorup's greedy tree packing approach instead of the spanning forest decomposition. We will show that either (i) a component induces a $(1 + \epsilon)$-approximate minimum cut, (ii) the minimum cut does not intersect with the components, or (iii) the minimum cut 1-respect a tree in the tree packing. This algorithm and analysis will be discussed in detail in Section 4. We note that our algorithm can also be implemented in the centralized setting in $O(m + n\epsilon^{-7} \log^3 n)$ time. It is slightly worse than the current best $O(m + n\epsilon^{-3} \log^3 n)$ by Karger [6].

2 Preliminaries

Communication Model. We use a standard message passing network model called CONGEST [18]. A network of processors is modeled by an undirected unweighted n-node graph G, where nodes model the processors and edges model $O(\log n)$-*bandwidth* links between the processors. The processors (henceforth, nodes) are assumed to have unique IDs in the range of $\{1, \ldots, \text{poly}(n)\}$ and infinite computational power. We denote the ID of node v by $\text{id}(v)$. Each node has limited topological knowledge; in particular, it only knows the IDs of its neighbors and knows *no* other topological information (e.g., whether its neighbors are linked by an edge or not). Additionally, we let $w : E(G) \to \{1, 2, \ldots, \text{poly}(n)\}$ be the edge weight assignment. The weight $w(uv)$ of each edge uv is known only to u and v. As commonly done in the literature (e.g., [4,10,12,11,3,16]), we will assume that the maximum weight is $\text{poly}(n)$ so that each edge weight can be sent through an edge (link) in one round.

There are several measures to analyze the performance of distributed algorithms. One fundamental measure is the *running time* defined as the worst-case number of *rounds* of distributed communication. At the beginning of each round, all nodes wake up simultaneously. Each node u then sends an arbitrary message of $B = \log n$ bits through each edge uv, and the message will arrive at node v at the end of the round. (See [18] for detail.) The running time is analyzed in terms of number of nodes and the diameter of the network, denoted by n and D respectively. Since we can compute n and 2-approximate D in $O(D)$ time, we will assume that every node knows n and the 2-approximate value of D.

Minimum Cut Problem. Given a weighted undirected graph $G = (V, E)$, a *cut* $C = (S, V \setminus S)$ where $\emptyset \subsetneq S \subsetneq V$, is a partition of vertices into two non-empty sets. The *weight* of a cut, denoted by $w(C)$, is defined to be the sum of the edge weights crossing C; i.e., $w(C) = \sum_{u \in S, v \notin S} w(uv)$. Throughout the paper, we use λ to denote the weight of the minimum cut. A $(1+\epsilon)$-approximate minimum cut is a cut C whose weight $w(C)$ is such that $\lambda \leq w(C) \leq (1 + \epsilon)\lambda$. The (approximate) minimum cut problem is to find a cut $C = (S, V \setminus S)$ with the minimum or approximately minimum weight. In the distributed setting, this means that nodes in S should output 1 while other nodes output 0.

Graph-Theoretic Notations. For $G = (V, E)$, we define $V(G) = V$ and $E(G) = E$. When we analyze the correctness of our algorithms, we will always treat G as an *unweighted multi-graph* by replacing each edge e with $w(e)$ by $w(e)$ copies of e with weight one. We note that this assumption is used only in the analysis, and in particular we still allow only $O(\log n)$ bits to be communicated through edge e in each round of the algorithm (regardless of $w(e)$). For any cut $C = (S, V \setminus S)$, let $E(C)$ denote the set of edges crossing between S and $V \setminus S$

in the multi-graph; thus $w(C) = |E(C)|$. Given an edge set $F \subseteq E$, we use G/F to denote the graph obtained by contracting every edge in F. Given a partition $\mathcal{P}$ of nodes in G, we use $G/\mathcal{P}$ to denote the graph obtained by contracting each set in $\mathcal{P}$ into one node. Note that $E(G/\mathcal{P})$ may be viewed as the set of edges in G that cross between different sets in $\mathcal{P}$. For any $U \subseteq V$, we use $G \mid U$ to denote the subgraph of G induced by nodes in U. For convenience, we use the subscript $*_H$ to denote the quantity $*$ of H; for example, λ_H denote the value of the minimum cut of the graph H. A quantity without a subscript refer to the quantity of G, the input graph.

3   Distributed Algorithm for Finding a Cut That 1-Respects a Tree

In this section, we solve the following problem: Given a spanning tree T on a network G rooted at some node r, we want to find an edge in T such that when we cut it, the cut defined by edges connecting the two connected component of T is smallest. To be precise, for any node v, define $v^{\downarrow}$ to be the set of nodes that are descendants of v in T, including v. Let $C_v = (v^{\downarrow}, V \setminus v^{\downarrow})$. The problem is then to compute $c^* = \min_{v \in V(G)} w(C_v)$. The main result of this section is the following.

Theorem 1. *There is an $O(D + n^{1/2} \log^* n)$-time distributed algorithm that can compute c^* as well as find a node v such that $c^* = w(C_v)$.*

In fact, at the end of our algorithm every node v knows $w(C_v)$. Our algorithm is inspired by the following observation used in Karger's dynamic programming [8]. For any node v, let $\delta(v)$ be the weighted degree of v, i.e. $\delta(v) = \sum_{u \in V(G)} w(u, v)$. Let $\rho(v)$ denote the total weight of edges whose end-points' least common ancestor in T is v. Let $\delta^{\downarrow}(v) = \sum_{u \in v^{\downarrow}} \delta(u)$ and $\rho^{\downarrow}(v) = \sum_{u \in v^{\downarrow}} \rho(u)$.

Lemma 2 (Karger [8], Lemma 5.9). $w(C_v) = \delta^{\downarrow}(v) - 2\rho^{\downarrow}(v)$.

Our algorithm will make sure that every node v knows $\delta^{\downarrow}(v)$ and $\rho^{\downarrow}(v)$. By Theorem 2, this will be sufficient for every node v to compute $w(C_v)$. The algorithm is divided in several steps, as follows.

Step 1: Partition T into Fragments and Compute "Fragment Tree" T_F. We use the algorithm of Kutten and Peleg [11, Section 3.2] to partition nodes in tree T into $O(\sqrt{n})$ subtrees, where each subtree has $O(\sqrt{n})$ diameter[2] (every node knows which edges incident to it are in the subtree containing it). This algorithm takes $O(n^{1/2} \log^* n + D)$ time. We call these subtrees *fragments*

---

[2] To be precise, we compute a $(\sqrt{n} + 1, O(\sqrt{n}))$ *spanning forest*. Also note that we in fact do not need this algorithm since we obtain T by using Kutten and Peleg's MST algorithm, which already computes the $(\sqrt{n} + 1, O(\sqrt{n}))$ spanning forest as a subroutine. See [11] for details.

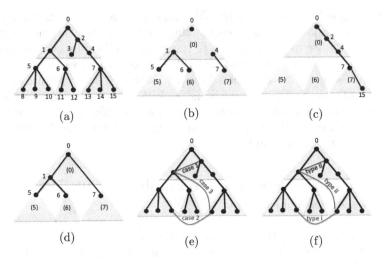

Fig. 1

and denote them by $F_1, \ldots, F_k$, where $k = O(\sqrt{n})$. For any i, let $\mathsf{id}(F_i) = \min_{u \in F_i} \mathsf{id}(u)$ be the *ID of F_i*. We can assume that every node in F_i knows $\mathsf{id}(F_i)$. This can be achieved in $O(\sqrt{n})$ time (the running time is independent of D) by a communication within each fragment. Figure 1a illustrates the tree T (marked by black lines) with fragments (defined by triangular regions).

Let T_F be a rooted tree obtained by contracting nodes in the same fragment into one node. This naturally defines the child-parent relationship between fragments (e.g. the fragments labeled (5), (6), and (7) in Figure 1b are children of the fragment labeled (0)). Let the *root* of any fragment F_i, denoted by r_i, be the node in F_i that is nearest to the root r in T. We now make every node know T_F: Every "inter-fragment" edge, i.e. every edge (u, v) such that u and v are in different fragments, either node u or v broadcasts this edge and the IDs of fragments containing u and v to the whole network. This step takes $O(\sqrt{n} + D)$ time since there are $O(\sqrt{n})$ edges in T that link between different fragments and so they can be collected by pipelining. Note that this process also makes every node know the roots of all fragments since, for every inter-fragment edge (u, v), every node knows the child-parent relationship between two fragments that contain u and v.

Step 2: Compute Fragments in Subtrees of Ancestors.   For any node v let $F(v)$ be the set of fragments $F_i \subseteq v^{\downarrow}$. For any node v in any fragment F_i, let $A(v)$ be the set of ancestors of v in T that are in F_i or the *parent* fragment of F_i (also let $A(v)$ contain v). (For example, Figure 1c shows $A(15)$.) We emphasize that $A(v)$ does not contain ancestors of v in the fragments that are neither F_i nor the parent of F_i. The goal of this step is to make every node v knows (i) $A(v)$ and (ii) $F(u)$ for all $u \in A(v)$.

First, we make every node v know $F(v)$: for every fragment F_i we aggregate from the leaves to the root of F_i (i.e. upcast) the list of child fragments of F_i. This takes $O(\sqrt{n} + D)$ time since there are $O(\sqrt{n})$ fragments to aggregate and each fragment has diameter $O(\sqrt{n})$. In this process every node v receives a list of child fragments of F_i that are contained in $v^{\downarrow}$. It can then use T_F to compute fragments that are descendants of these child fragments, and thus compute *all* fragments contained in $v^{\downarrow}$.

Next, we make every node v in every fragment F_i know $A(v)$: every node u sends a message containing its ID down the tree T until this message reaches the leaves of the child fragments of F_i. Since each fragment has diameter $O(\sqrt{n})$ and the total number of messages sent inside each fragment is $O(\sqrt{n})$, this process takes $O(\sqrt{n})$ time (the running time is independent of D). With the following minor modifications, we can also make every node v know $F(u)$ (the fragment that u is in) for all $u \in A(v)$: Initially every node u sends a message (u, F'), for every $F' \in F(u)$, to its children. Every node u that receives a message (u', F') from its parent sends this message further to its children *if* $F' \notin F(u)$. (A message (u', F') that a node u sends to its children should be interpreted as "u' is the lowest ancestor of u such that $F' \in F(u')$".)

Step 3: Compute $\delta^{\downarrow}(v)$. For every fragment F_i, we let $\delta(F_i) = \sum_{v \in F_i} \delta(v)$ (i.e. the sum of degree of nodes in F_i). For every node v in every fragment F_i, we will compute $\delta^{\downarrow}(v)$ by separately computing (i) $\sum_{u \in F_i \cap v^{\downarrow}} \delta(u)$ and (ii) $\sum_{F_j \in F(v)} \delta(F_j)$. The first quantity can be computed in $O(\sqrt{n})$ time (regardless of D) by computing the sum within F_i (every node v sends the sum $\sum_{u \in F_i \cap v^{\downarrow}} \delta(u)$ to its parent). To compute the second quantity, it suffices to make every node know $\delta(F_i)$ for all i since every node v already knows $F(v)$. To do this, we make every root r_i know $\delta(F_i)$ in $O(\sqrt{n})$ time by computing the sum of degree of nodes within each F_i. Then, we can make every node know $\delta(F_i)$ for all i by letting r_i broadcast $\delta(F_i)$ to the whole network.

Step 4: Compute Merging Nodes and T'_F. We say that a node v is a *merging node* if there are two distinct children x and y of v such that both $x^{\downarrow}$ and $y^{\downarrow}$ contain some fragments. In other words, it is a point where two fragments "merge". For example, nodes 0 and 1 in Figure 1a are merging nodes since the subtree rooted at node 0 (respectively node 1) contains fragments (5), (6), and (7) (respectively (5) and (6)).

Let T'_F be the following tree: Nodes in T'_F are both roots of fragments (r_i's) and merging nodes. The parent of each node v in T'_F is its lowest ancestor in T that appears in T'_F (see Figure 1d for an example). Note that every merging node has at least two children in T'_F. This shows that there are $O(\sqrt{n})$ merging nodes. The goal of this step is to let every node know T'_F.

First, note that every node v can easily know whether it is a merging node or not in one round by checking, for each child u, whether $u^{\downarrow}$ contains any fragment (i.e. whether $F(u) = \emptyset$). The merging nodes then broadcast their IDs to the whole network. (This takes $O(\sqrt{n})$ time since there are $O(\sqrt{n})$ merging nodes.) Note further that every node v in T'_F knows its parent in T'_F because its parent in T'_F is one of its ancestors in $A(v)$. So, we can make every node know T'_F in $O(\sqrt{n} + D)$ rounds by letting every node in T'_F broadcast the edge between itself and its parent in T'_F to the whole network.

Step 5: Compute $\rho^{\downarrow}(v)$. We now count, for every node v, the number of edges whose least common ancestors (LCA) of their end-nodes are v. For every edge (x, y) in G, we claim that x and y can compute the LCA of (x, y) by exchanging $O(\sqrt{n})$ messages through edge (x, y). Let z denote the LCA of (x, y). Consider three cases (see Figure 1e).

Case 1: First, consider when x and y are in the same fragment, say F_i. In this case we know that z must be in F_i. Since x and y have the lists of their ancestors in F_i, they can find z by exchanging these lists. There are $O(\sqrt{n})$ nodes in such list so this takes $O(\sqrt{n})$ time. In the next two cases we assume that x and y are in different fragments, say F_i and F_j, respectively.

Case 2: z is *not* in F_i and F_j. In this case, z is a merging node such that $z^{\downarrow}$ contains F_i and F_j. Since both x and y knows T'_F and their ancestors in T'_F, they can find z by exchanging the list of their ancestors in T'_F. There are $O(\sqrt{n})$ nodes in such list so this takes $O(\sqrt{n})$ time.

Case 3: z is in F_i (the case where z is in F_j can be handled in a similar way). In this case $z^{\downarrow}$ contains F_j. Since x knows $F(x')$ for all its ancestors x' in F_i, it can compute its lowest ancestor x'' such that $F(x'')$ contains F_j. Such ancestor is the LCA of (x, y).

Now we compute $\rho^{\downarrow}(v)$ for every node v by splitting edges (x, y) whose LCA is v into two types (see Figure 1f): (i) those that x and y are in different fragments from v, and (ii) the rest. For (i), note that v must be a merging node. In this case one of x and y creates a message $\langle v \rangle$. We then count the number of messages of the form $\langle v \rangle$ for every merging node v by computing the sum along the breadth-first search tree of G. This takes $O(\sqrt{n} + D)$ time since there are $O(\sqrt{n})$ merging nodes. For (ii), the node among x and y that is in the same fragment as v creates and keeps a message $\langle v \rangle$. Now every node v in every fragment F_i counts the number of messages of the form $\langle v \rangle$ in $v^{\downarrow} \cap F_i$ by computing the sum through the tree F_i. Note that, to do this, every node u has to send the number of messages of the form $\langle v \rangle$ to its parent, for all v that is an ancestor of u in the same fragment. There are $O(\sqrt{n})$ such ancestors, so we can compute the number of messages of the form $\langle v \rangle$ for every node v *concurrently* in $O(\sqrt{n})$ time by pipelining.

4   Minimum Cut Algorithms

This section is organized as follows. In Section 4.1, we review properties of the greedy tree packing as analyzed by Thorup [22]. We use these properties to develop a $(1 + \epsilon)$-approximation algorithm in Section 4.2. We show how to efficiently implement this algorithm in the distributed setting in Section 4.3. Due to the space limit, the implmentation in the sequential setting is deferred to the full version.

4.1   A Review of Thorup's Work on Tree Packings

In this section, we review the duality connection between the tree packing and the partition of a graph as well as their properties from Thorup's work [22].

A *tree packing* $\mathcal{T}$ is a multiset of spanning trees. The *load* of an edge e with respect to $\mathcal{T}$, denoted by $\mathcal{L}^{\mathcal{T}}(e)$, is the number of trees in $\mathcal{T}$ containing e. Define the *relative load* to be $\ell^{\mathcal{T}}(e) = \mathcal{L}^{\mathcal{T}}(e)/|\mathcal{T}|$. A tree packing $\mathcal{T} = \{T_1, \ldots, T_k\}$ is *greedy* if each T_i is a minimum spanning tree with respect to the loads induced by $\{T_1, \ldots, T_{i-1}\}$.

Given a tree packing $\mathcal{T}$, define its *packing value* $\mathtt{pack\_val}(\mathcal{T}) = 1/\max_{e \in E} \ell^{\mathcal{T}}(e)$. The packing value can be viewed as the total weight of a fractional tree packing, where each tree has weight $1/\max_{e \in E} \mathcal{L}^{\mathcal{T}}(e)$. Thus, the sum of the weight over the trees is $|\mathcal{T}|/\max_{e \in E} \mathcal{L}^{\mathcal{T}}(e)$, which is $\mathtt{pack\_val}(\mathcal{T})$. Given a partition $\mathcal{P}$, define its *partition value* $\mathtt{part\_val}(\mathcal{P}) = \frac{|E(G/\mathcal{P})|}{|\mathcal{P}|-1}$. For any tree packing $\mathcal{T}$ and partition $\mathcal{P}$, we have the weak duality:

$$\mathtt{pack\_val}(\mathcal{T}) = \frac{1}{\max_{e \in E} \ell^{\mathcal{T}}(e)}$$

$$\leq \frac{1}{\max_{e \in E(G/\mathcal{P})} \ell^{\mathcal{T}}(e)}$$

$$\leq \frac{|E(G/\mathcal{P})|}{\sum_{e \in E(G/\mathcal{P})} \ell^{\mathcal{T}}(e)} \qquad \text{(since max} \geq \text{avg)}$$

$$\leq \frac{|E(G/\mathcal{P})|}{|\mathcal{P}|-1}$$

(since each $T \in \mathcal{T}$ contains at least $|\mathcal{P}|-1$ edges crossing $\mathcal{P}$)

$$= \mathtt{part\_val}(\mathcal{P})$$

The Nash-Williams-Tutte Theorem [17,24] states that a graph G contains $\min_{\mathcal{P}} \lfloor \frac{|E(G/\mathcal{P})|}{|\mathcal{P}|-1} \rfloor$ edge-disjoint spanning trees. Construct the graph G' by duplicating $|\mathcal{P}|-1$ edges for every edge in G. It follows from the Nash-Williams-Tutte Theorem that G' has exactly $|E(G/\mathcal{P})|$ edge-disjoint spanning trees. By assigning each spanning tree a weight of $1/(|\mathcal{P}|-1)$, we get a tree packing in G whose packing value equals to $\frac{|E(G/\mathcal{P})|}{|\mathcal{P}|-1}$. Therefore,

$$\max_{\mathcal{T}} \mathtt{pack\_val}(\mathcal{T}) = \min_{\mathcal{P}} \mathtt{part\_val}(\mathcal{P}).$$

We will denote this value by Φ. Let $\mathcal{T}^*$ and $\mathcal{P}^*$ denote a tree packing and a partition with $\mathtt{pack\_val}(\mathcal{T}^*) = \Phi$ and $\mathtt{part\_val}(\mathcal{P}^*) = \Phi$. Karger [8] showed the following relationship between Φ and λ (recall that λ is the value of the minimum cut).

Lemma 3. $\lambda/2 < \Phi \leq \lambda$

Thorup [22] defined the *ideal relative loads* $\ell^*(e)$ on the edges of G by the following.

1. Let $\mathcal{P}^*$ be an optimal partition with part_val$(\mathcal{P}^*) = \Phi$.
2. For all $e \in G/\mathcal{P}^*$, let $\ell^*(e) = 1/\Phi$.
3. For each $S \in \mathcal{P}^*$, recurse the procedure on the subgraph $G|S$.

Define the following notations:

$$E_{o\delta}^X = \{e \in E \mid \ell^X(e) \circ \delta\}$$

where X can be $\mathcal{T}$ or $*$, and $\circ$ can be $<, >, \leq, \geq,$ or $=$. For example, $E_{<\delta}^*$ denote the set of edges with ideal relative loads smaller than δ.

Lemma 4 ([22], Lemma 14). *The values of Φ are non-decreasing in the sense that for each $S \in P^*, \Phi_{G|S} \geq \Phi$*

Corollary 5. *Let $0 \leq l \leq 1/\Phi$. Each component H of the graph $(V, E_{\leq l}^*)$ must have edge-connectivity of at least Φ.*

Proof. Accroding to how the ideal relative load was defined and Lemma 4, we must have $\Phi_H \geq \Phi$. By Lemma 3, $\lambda_H \geq \Phi_H \geq \Phi$.

Thorup showed that the relative loads of a greedy tree packing with a sufficient number of trees approximate the ideal relative loads, due to the fact that greedily packing the trees simulates the multiplicative weight update method. He showed the following lemma.

Lemma 6 ([22], Proposition 16). *A greedy tree packing $\mathcal{T}$ with at least $(6\lambda \ln m)/\epsilon^2$ trees, $\epsilon < 2$ has $|\ell^{\mathcal{T}}(e) - \ell^*(e)| \leq \epsilon/\lambda$ for all $e \in E$.*

4.2   Algorithms

In this section, we show how to approximate the value of the minimum cut as well as how to find an approximate minimum cut.

Algorithm for Computing Minimum Cut Value.   The main idea is that if we have a nearly optimal tree packing, then either λ is close to 2Φ or all the minimum cuts are crossed exactly once by some trees in the tree packing.

Lemma 7. *Suppose that $\mathcal{T}$ is a greedy tree packing with at least $6\lambda \ln m/\epsilon^2$ trees, then $\lambda \leq (2+\epsilon) \cdot$ pack_val$(\mathcal{T})$. Furthermore, if there is a minimum cut C such that it is crossed at least twice by every tree in $\mathcal{T}$, then $(2+\epsilon) \cdot$ pack_val$(\mathcal{T}) \leq (1 + \epsilon/2)\lambda$.*

Proof. By Theorems 3 and 6, $1/$pack_val$(\mathcal{T}) \leq 1/$pack_val$(\mathcal{T}^*) + \epsilon/\lambda \leq 2/\lambda + \epsilon/\lambda$. Therefore, $\lambda \leq (2 + \epsilon) \cdot$ pack_val$(\mathcal{T})$.

If each tree in $\mathcal{T}$ crosses C at least twice, we have $\sum_{e \in C} \ell^{\mathcal{T}}(e) \geq 2$. Therefore,

$$2/\lambda \leq \sum_{e \in C} \ell^{\mathcal{T}}(e)/w(C) \leq \max_{e \in C} \ell^{\mathcal{T}}(e) \leq 1/\text{pack\_val}(\mathcal{T}). \tag{1}$$

This implies that $(2 + \epsilon) \cdot$ pack_val$(\mathcal{T}) \leq (1 + \epsilon/2)\lambda$.

Using Theorem 7, we can obtain a simple algorithm for $(1 + \epsilon)$-approximating the minimum cut *value*. First, greedily pack $\Theta(\lambda \log n / \epsilon^2)$ trees and compute the minimum cut that 1-respects the trees (using our algorithm in Section 3). Then, output the smaller value between the minimum cut found and $(2 + \epsilon) \cdot$ pack_val$(\mathcal{T})$. The running time is discussed in Section 4.3.

Algorithm for Finding a Minimum Cut.   More work is needed to be done if we want to *find* the $(1 + \epsilon)$-approximate minimum cut (i.e. each node wants to know which side of the cut it is on). Let $\epsilon' = \Theta(\epsilon)$ be such that $(1 - 2\epsilon') \cdot (1 - \epsilon') = 1/(1 + \epsilon)$. Let $l_a = (1 - 2\epsilon')/$pack_val$(\mathcal{T})$. We describe our algorithm in Algorithm 4.1.

---

1. Find a greedy tree packing $\mathcal{T}$ with $(6\lambda \ln m)/\epsilon'^2$ trees in G.
2. Let C^* be the minimum cut among cuts that 1-respect a tree in $\mathcal{T}$.
3. Let $l_a = (1 - 2\epsilon')/$pack_val$(\mathcal{T})$.
4. **if** $(V, E^{\mathcal{T}}_{< l_a})$ has more than $(1 - \epsilon')|V|$ components **then**
5.   Let $C_{\min}$ be the smallest cut induced by the components in $(V, E^{\mathcal{T}}_{< l_a})$.
6. **else**
7.   Let $C_{\min}$ be the cut returned by APPROX-MIN-CUT$(G/E^{T}_{< l_a})$.
8. Return the smaller cut between C^* and $C_{\min}$.

Algorithm 4.1. APPROX-MIN-CUT(G)

The main result of this subsection is the following theorem.

Theorem 8. *Algorithm 4.1 gives a $(1 + \epsilon)$-approximate minimum cut.*

The rest of this subsection is devoted to proving Theorem 8. First, observe that if a minimum cut is crossed exactly once by a tree in $\mathcal{T}$, then C^* must be a minimum cut. Otherwise, C is crossed at least twice by every tree in $\mathcal{T}$. In this case, we will show that the edges of every minimum cut will be included in $E^{\mathcal{T}}_{\geq l_a}$. As a result, we can contract each connected component in the partition $(V, E^{\mathcal{T}}_{< l_a})$ without contracting any edges of the minimum cuts.

If $(V, E^{\mathcal{T}}_{< l_a})$ has at most $(1 - \epsilon')|V|$ components, then we contract each component and then recurse. The recursion can only happen at most $O(\log n / \epsilon)$ times, since the number of nodes reduces by a $(1 - \epsilon')$ factor in each level. On the other hand, if $(V, E^{\mathcal{T}}_{< l_a})$ has more than $(1 - \epsilon')|V|$ components, then we will show that one of the components induces an approximate minimum cut.

Lemma 9. *Let C be a minimum cut such that C is crossed at least twice by every tree in $\mathcal{T}$. For all $e \in C$, $\ell^{\mathcal{T}}(e) \geq (1 - 2\epsilon')/$pack_val$(\mathcal{T})$.*

Proof. The idea is to show that if an edge in $E(C)$ has a small relative load, then the average relative load over the edges in $E(C)$ will also be small. However, since each tree cross $E(C)$ twice, the average relative load should not be too small. Otherwise, a contradiction will occur.

Let $l_0 = \min_{e \in C} \ell^*(e)$ be the minimum ideal relative load over the edges in $E(C)$. Consider the induced subgraph $(V, E^*_{\leq l_0})$. $E(C)$ must contain some edges in a component of $(V, E^*_{\leq l_0})$, say component H. Notice that two endpoints of an edge in a minimum cut must lie on different sides of the cut. Therefore, $C \cap H$ must be a cut of H. By Corollary 5, $w(C \cap H) \geq \Phi$. Therefore, more than Φ edges in C have ideal relative loads equal to l_0. Since the maximum relative load of an edge is at most $\frac{1}{\Phi}$, $\sum_{e \in C} \ell^{\mathcal{T}^*}(e) \leq \Phi \cdot l_0 + (\lambda - \Phi) \cdot \frac{1}{\Phi} = \Phi \cdot l_0 + \frac{\lambda}{\Phi} - 1 < \Phi \cdot l_0 + 1$, where the last inequality follows by Lemma 3 that $\lambda < 2\Phi$.

On the other hand, since each tree in $\mathcal{T}$ crosses C at least twice, $\sum_{e \in C} \ell^{\mathcal{T}}(e) \geq 2$. By Lemma 6, $\sum_{e \in C} \ell^*(e) \geq 2 - \epsilon'$. Therefore, $\Phi \cdot l_0 + 1 > 2 - \epsilon'$, which implies

$$l_0 \geq (1 - \epsilon') \cdot \frac{1}{\Phi} > \frac{1}{\Phi} - \frac{2\epsilon'}{\lambda} \qquad\qquad \lambda < 2\Phi$$

$$\geq 1/\mathtt{pack\_val}(\mathcal{T}) - \frac{3\epsilon'}{\lambda} \qquad\qquad \text{By Lemma 6}$$

Therefore, by Lemma 6 again, for any $e \in E(C)$, $\ell^{\mathcal{T}}(e) \geq l_0 - \epsilon'/\lambda > 1/\mathtt{pack\_val}(\mathcal{T}) - 4\epsilon'/\lambda \geq (1 - 2\epsilon')/\mathtt{pack\_val}(\mathcal{T})$, where the last inequality follows from equation (1).

Lemma 10. *Let $C_{\min}$ be the smallest cut induced by the components in $(V, E^{\mathcal{T}}_{< l_a})$. If $(V, E^{\mathcal{T}}_{< l_a})$ contains at least $(1 - \epsilon')|V|$ components, then $w(C_{\min}) \leq (1 + \epsilon)\lambda$.*

Proof. Let $comp(V, E^{\mathcal{T}}_{< l_a})$ denote the collection of connected components in $(V, E^{\mathcal{T}}_{< l_a})$, and n', the number of connected components in $(V, E^{\mathcal{T}}_{< l_a})$. By an averaging argument, we have

$$w(C_{\min}) \leq \frac{\sum_{S \in comp(V, E^{\mathcal{T}}_{< l_a})} |E(S, V \setminus S)|}{n'}$$

$$= \frac{2|E(G/E^{\mathcal{T}}_{< l_a})|}{n'} \leq \frac{2|E(G/E^{\mathcal{T}}_{< l_a})|}{(1 - \epsilon') \cdot |V|} \qquad\qquad (2)$$

Next we will bound $|E(G/E^{\mathcal{T}}_{< l_a})|$. Note that for each $e \in E(G/E^{\mathcal{T}}_{< l_a})$, $\ell^{\mathcal{T}}(e) \geq (1 - 2\epsilon')/\mathtt{pack\_val}(\mathcal{T})$.

$$\sum_{e \in E(G/E^{\mathcal{T}}_{< l_a})} \ell^{\mathcal{T}}(e) \geq |E(G/E^{\mathcal{T}}_{< l_a})| \cdot (1 - 2\epsilon') \cdot \left(\frac{1}{\mathtt{pack\_val}(\mathcal{T})} \right)$$

$$\geq |E(G/E^{\mathcal{T}}_{< l_a})| \cdot (1 - 2\epsilon') \cdot \frac{2}{\lambda} \qquad \text{(by Equation (1)).} \quad (3)$$

On the other hand,

$$\sum_{e \in E(G/E^{\mathcal{T}}_{< l_a})} \ell^{\mathcal{T}}(e) \leq |V| - 1, \qquad\qquad (4)$$

since each tree in $\mathcal{T}$ contains $|V| - 1$ edges. Equations (3) and (4) together imply that

$$|E(G/E^{\mathcal{T}}_{<l_a})| \leq \frac{\lambda \cdot |V|}{2(1 - 2\epsilon')}.$$

By plugging in this into (Equation (2)), we get that

$$w(C_{\min}) \leq \frac{\lambda}{(1 - 2\epsilon')(1 - \epsilon')} \leq (1 + \epsilon)\lambda.$$

4.3 Distributed Implementation

In this section, we describe how to implement Algorithm 4.1 in the distributed setting. To compute the tree packing $\mathcal{T}$, it is straightforward to apply $|\mathcal{T}|$ minimum spanning tree computations with edge weights equal to their current loads. This can be done in $O(|\mathcal{T}|(D + \sqrt{n} \log^* n))$ rounds by using the algorithm of Kutten and Peleg [11].

We already described how to computes the minimum cut that 1-respects a tree in $O(D + \sqrt{n} \log^* n)$ rounds in Section 3. To compute l_a, it suffices to compute pack_val($\mathcal{T}$). To do this, each node first computes the largest relative load among the edges incident to it. By using the upcast and downcast techniques, the maximum relative load over all edges can be aggregated and boardcast to every node in $O(D)$ time. Therefore, we can assume that every node knows l_a now. Now we have to determine whether $(V, E^{\mathcal{T}}_{<l_a})$ has more than $(1 - \epsilon')|V|$ components or not. This can be done by first removing the edges incident to each node with relative load at least l_a. Then label each node with the smallest ID of its reachable nodes by using Thurimella's connected component identification algorithm [23] in $O(D + \sqrt{n} \log^* n)$ rounds. The number of nodes whose label equals to its ID is exactly the number of connected component of the subgraph. This number can be aggregated along the BFS tree in $O(D)$ rounds after every node is labeled.

If $(V, E^{\mathcal{T}}_{<l_a})$ has more than $(1 - \epsilon')|V|$ components, then we will compute the cut values induced by each component of $(V, E^{\mathcal{T}}_{<l_a})$. We show that it can be done in $O(D + \sqrt{n})$ rounds in the full version. On the contrary, if $(V, E^{\mathcal{T}}_{<l_a})$ has less than $(1 - \epsilon')|V|$ components, then we will contract the edges with load less than l_a and then recurse. The contraction can be easily implemented by setting the weights of the edges inside contracted components to be -1, which is strictly less than the load of any edges. The MST computation will automatically treat them as contracted edges, since an MST must contain exactly $n' - 1$ edges with weights larger than -1, where n' is the number of connected components. [3]

Time Analysis. Suppose that we have packed t spanning trees throughout the entire algorithm, the running time will be $O(t(D + \sqrt{n} \log^* n))$. Note that $t = O(\epsilon^{-3} \lambda \log^2 n)$, because we pack at most $O(\epsilon^{-2} \lambda \log n)$ spanning trees in each level of the recursion and there can be at most $O(\epsilon^{-1} \log n)$ levels, since the number of nodes reduces by a $(1 - \epsilon')$ factor in each level. The total running time is $O(\epsilon^{-3} \lambda \log^2 n \cdot (D + \sqrt{n} \log^* n))$.

---

[3] We note that the MST algorithm of [11] allows negative-weight edges.

Dealing with Graphs with High Edge Connectivity. For graphs with $\lambda = \omega(\epsilon^{-2} \log n)$, we can use the well-known sampling result from Karger's [7] to construct a subgraph H that perserves the values of all the cuts within a $(1 \pm \epsilon)$ factor (up to a scaling) and has $\lambda_H = O(\epsilon^{-2} \log n)$. Then we run our algorithm on H.

Lemma 11 ([6], Corollary 2.4). *Let G be any graph with minimum cut λ and let $p = 2(d+2)(\ln n)/(\epsilon^2 \lambda)$. Let $G(p)$ be a subgraph of G with the same vertex set, obtained by including each edge of G with probability p independently. Then the probability that the value of some cut in $G(p)$ has value more than $(1 + \epsilon)$ or less than $(1 - \epsilon)$ times its expected value is $O(1/n^d)$.*

In particular, let $\epsilon' = \Theta(\epsilon)$ such that $(1 + \epsilon) = (1 + \epsilon')^2/(1 - \epsilon')$. First we will compute λ', a 3-approximation of λ, by using Ghaffari and Kuhn's algorithm. Let $p = 6(d+2) \ln n/(\epsilon'^2 \lambda')$ and $H = G(p)$. Since p is at least $2(d+2) \ln n/(\epsilon'^2 \lambda)$, by Lemma 11, for any cut C, w.h.p. $(1 - \epsilon')p \cdot w_G(C) \le w_{H_i}(C) \le (1 + \epsilon')p \cdot w_G(C)$. Let C^* be the $(1 + \epsilon')$-approximate minimum cut we found in H. We have that w.h.p. for any other cut C',

$$w_G(C^*) \le \frac{1}{p} \cdot \frac{w_{H_i}(C^*)}{1 - \epsilon'} \le \frac{1}{p} \cdot \frac{(1 + \epsilon')\lambda_H}{1 - \epsilon'}$$

$$\le \frac{1}{p} \cdot \frac{(1 + \epsilon')w_{H_i}(C')}{1 - \epsilon'} \le \frac{(1 + \epsilon')^2}{1 - \epsilon'} \cdot w_G(C') = (1 + \epsilon)w_G(C') \quad (5)$$

Thus, we will find an $(1 + \epsilon)$-approximate minimum cut in $O(\epsilon^{-5} \log^3 n(D + \sqrt{n} \log^* n))$ rounds.

Computing the Exact Minimum Cut. To find the exact minimum cut, first we will compute a 3-approximation of λ, λ', by using Ghaffari and Kuhn's algorithm [4] in $O(\lambda \log n \log \log n(D + \sqrt{n} \log^* n))$ rounds.[4] Now since $\lambda \le \lambda' \le 3\lambda$, by applying our algorithm with $\epsilon = 1/(\lambda' + 1)$, we can compute the exact minimum cut in $O(\lambda'^4 \log^2 n(D + \sqrt{n} \log^* n))$ rounds.

Estimating the Value of λ. As described in Section 4.2, we can avoid the recursion if we just want to compute an approximation of λ without actually finding the cut. This gives an algorithm that runs in $O(\epsilon^{-2} \lambda \log n \cdot (D + \sqrt{n} \log^* n))$ time. Also, the exact value of λ can be computed in $O((\lambda^3 + \lambda \log \log n) \log n(D + \sqrt{n} \log^* n))$ rounds. Notice that the $\lambda \log \log n$ factor comes from Ghaffari and Kuhn's algorithm for approximating λ within a constant factor. Similarly, using Karger's sampling result, we can $(1 + \epsilon)$-approximate the value of λ in $O(\epsilon^{-5} \log^2 n \log \log n(D + \sqrt{n} \log^* n))$ rounds.

---

[4] Ghaffari and Kuhn's result runs in $O(\log^2 n \log \log n(D + \sqrt{n} \log^* n))$ rounds. However, without using Karger's random sampling beforehand, it runs in $O(\lambda \log n \log \log n(D + \sqrt{n} \log^* n))$ rounds, which will be absorbed by the running time of our algorithm for the exact minimum cut.

Acknowledgment. D. Nanongkai would like to thank Thatchaphol Saranurak for bringing Thorup's tree packing theorem [22] to his attention.

References

1. Das Sarma, A., Holzer, S., Kor, L., Korman, A., Nanongkai, D., Pandurangan, G., Peleg, D., Wattenhofer, R.: Distributed verification and hardness of distributed approximation. SIAM J. Comput. 41(5), 1235–1265 (2012)
2. Gabow, H.N.: A matroid approach to finding edge connectivity and packing arborescences. J. Comput. Syst. Sci. 50(2), 259–273 (1995)
3. Garay, J.A., Kutten, S., Peleg, D.: A sublinear time distributed algorithm for minimum-weight spanning trees. SIAM J. Comput. 27(1), 302–316 (1998)
4. Ghaffari, M., Kuhn, F.: Distributed minimum cut approximation. In: Afek, Y. (ed.) DISC 2013. LNCS, vol. 8205, pp. 1–15. Springer, Heidelberg (2013)
5. Karger, D.R.: Global min-cuts in RNC, and other ramifications of a simple min-cut algorithm. In: SODA, pp. 21–30 (1993)
6. Karger, D.R.: Random sampling in cut, flow, and network design problems. In: STOC, pp. 648–657 (1994)
7. Karger, D.R.: Using randomized sparsification to approximate minimum cuts. In: SODA, pp. 424–432 (1994)
8. Karger, D.R.: Minimum cuts in near-linear time. J. ACM 47(1), 46–76 (2000)
9. Karger, D.R., Stein, C.: An $\tilde{O}(n^2)$ algorithm for minimum cuts. In: STOC, pp. 757–765 (1993)
10. Khan, M., Pandurangan, G.: A fast distributed approximation algorithm for minimum spanning trees. Distributed Computing 20(6), 391–402 (2008)
11. Kutten, S., Peleg, D.: Fast distributed construction of small k-dominating sets and applications. J. Algorithms 28(1), 40–66 (1998)
12. Lotker, Z., Patt-Shamir, B., Rosén, A.: Distributed approximate matching. SIAM J. Comput. 39(2), 445–460 (2009)
13. Matula, D.W.: A linear time $2 + \epsilon$ approximation algorithm for edge connectivity. In: SODA, pp. 500–504 (1993)
14. Nagamochi, H., Ibaraki, T.: Computing edge-connectivity in multigraphs and capacitated graphs. SIAM J. Discret. Math. 5(1), 54–66 (1992)
15. Nanongkai, D.: Brief announcement: Almost-tight approximation distributed algorithm for minimum cut. In: PODC, pp. 382–384 (2014)
16. Nanongkai, D.: Distributed approximation algorithms for weighted shortest paths. In: STOC, pp. 565–573 (2014)
17. Nash-Williams, C.S.J.A.: Edge-disjoint spanning trees of finite graphs. J. London Math. Soc. s1-36(1), 445–450 (1961)
18. Peleg, D.: Distributed Computing: A Locality-Sensitive Approach. SIAM Monographs on Discrete Mathematics and Applications (2000)
19. Pritchard, D., Thurimella, R.: Fast computation of small cuts via cycle space sampling. ACM Transactions on Algorithms 7(4), 46 (2011)
20. Stoer, M., Wagner, F.: A simple min-cut algorithm. J. ACM 44(4), 585–591 (1997)
21. Su, H.H.: Brief annoucement: A distributed minimum cut approximation scheme. In: SPAA, pp. 217–219 (2014)
22. Thorup, M.: Fully-dynamic min-cut. Combinatorica 27(1), 91–127 (2007)
23. Thurimella, R.: Sub-linear distributed algorithms for sparse certificates and biconnected components. J. Algorithms 23(1), 160–179 (1997)
24. Tutte, W.T.: On the problem of decomposing a graph into n connected factors. J. London Math. Soc. s1-36(1), 221–230 (1961)

Distributed Algorithms
for Coloring Interval Graphs*

Magnús M. Halldórsson and Christian Konrad

ICE-TCS, School of Computer Science, Reykjavik University, Iceland
{mmh,christiank}@ru.is

Abstract. We explore the question how well we can color graphs in distributed models, especially in graph classes for which $\Delta + 1$-colorings provide no approximation guarantees. We particularly focus on interval graphs.

In the $\mathcal{LOCAL}$ model, we give an algorithm that computes a constant factor approximation to the coloring problem on interval graphs in O($\log^* n$) rounds, which is best possible. The result holds also for the $\mathcal{CONGEST}$ model when the representation of the nodes as intervals is given.

We then consider restricted beep models, where communication is restricted to the aggregate acknowledgment of whether a node's attempted coloring succeeds. We apply an algorithm designed for the SINR model and give a simplified proof of a $O(\log n)$-approximation. We show a nearly matching $\Omega(\log n / \log \log n)$-approximation lower bound in that model.

1   Introduction

In this paper, we study distributed algorithms for vertex coloring, especially on interval graphs. Given a set of intervals on the line $V = \{I_1, \ldots, I_n\}$ with $I_j = (a_j, b_j)$ and a_j, b_j being real numbers such that $a_j < b_j$, an interval graph G is obtained from V as follows: The vertex set of G are the intervals V, and two vertices $I_j, I_k \in V$ are adjacent if and only if I_j and I_k intersect. Interval graphs have a multitude of applications, appear naturally in scheduling problems, and can for instance be seen as one-dimensional projections of disk graphs that are often used for modeling wireless networks [1–3].

Graph Coloring. For an integer s, an s-coloring of a graph $G = (V, E)$ is an assignment $\gamma : V \to \{1, \ldots, s\}$ of colors to the vertices of a graph such that any two adjacent vertices have different colors. The chromatic number $\chi(G)$ of a graph G is the minimum number of colors that is needed to color G. It is well-known that determining $\chi(G)$ is NP-complete [4] in general graphs and it is even hard to approximate it within a $\Theta(n^{1-\epsilon})$ factor, for any $\epsilon > 0$ [5]. Sequentially, it is easy to find a coloring that uses at most $\Delta + 1$ colors where Δ is the maximal degree of a graph: Traverse the vertices of G in any order and assign the smallest

---

* Both authors are supported by Icelandic Research Fund grant-of-excellence no. 120032011.

F. Kuhn (Ed.): DISC 2014, LNCS 8784, pp. 454–468, 2014.

possible color to the current vertex. Since there are graphs for which $\Delta = \Theta(n)$ and $\chi(G) = \Theta(1)$ (for instance a star graph), such a coloring may be as bad as a $\Theta(n)$-approximation. An optimal coloring of an interval graph can be found by traversing the intervals with increasing left interval boundary and coloring them with the smallest possible color. Even if the intervals are traversed in arbitrary order, we obtain a *canonical* coloring, where a node colored $s(v)$ is adjacent to nodes colored $1, 2, \ldots, s(v) - 1$. It is known that such colorings of interval graphs yield a C-approximation, where $5 \leq C \leq 8$ [6].

Distributed Graph Coloring. Graph coloring has been extensively studied in the distributed setting (see [7–11] to name a few). In the distributed computational model, we assume a network of computational units modeled by a graph $G = (V, E)$ which is also the input graph of the problem. The computational units constitute the vertices of G, and two computational units can exchange messages if and only if an edge connecting them is included in E. Then, the runtime of a distributed algorithm is the number of communication rounds required to complete the algorithm. We assume that each vertex has a unique ID. In the $\mathcal{LOCAL}$ model, in each round, messages of unbounded size may be exchanged. In the $\mathcal{CONGEST}$ model, all message are of size at most $O(\log n)$ (n is the number of computational units). Due to the hardness of the graph coloring problem, the objective of most works on this topic in the distributed model is to find a coloring that uses $\Delta + 1$ or $O(\Delta)$ colors on general graphs. A $(\Delta + 1)$-coloring can be found by a distributed randomized algorithm in $O(\log n)$ communication rounds by a reduction to the maximal independent set problem that was first mentioned in [7] (a maximal independent set can be found in $O(\log n)$ time by Luby's algorithm [12]). An $O(\Delta)$-coloring can be computed by a distributed randomized algorithm in $2^{O(\sqrt{\log \log n})}$ rounds [13]. The best deterministic distributed coloring algorithm that finds an $O(\Delta)$-coloring performs $O(\Delta^\epsilon \log n)$ rounds, for any $\epsilon > 0$ [10]. Only few works consider more specialized graph classes for which better colorings can be obtained, and we reuse some of those works in this paper. In $O(\log^* n)$ rounds, Cole and Vishkin showed that a 3-coloring of a ring can be computed [14]. In [15], this technique has been extended to coloring *bounded-independence graphs* with $\Delta + 1$ colors (see Definition 1). Linial showed in [7] that coloring a ring with 3 colors requires $\Omega(\log^* n)$ rounds which renders the previous algorithms optimal.

Distributed Algorithms for Coloring Interval Graph. Our interest in coloring interval graphs in a distributed fashion stems from the following observation. As previously mentioned, most distributed coloring algorithms compute $(\Delta + 1)$-colorings which may be as bad as $\Theta(n)$ approximations. We are therefore interested in graph classes for which better approximation ratios can be obtained. Surprisingly, for interval graphs, we identify that in the $\mathcal{LOCAL}$ model, a constant factor approximation with runtime $O(\log^* n)$ can be obtained (**Theorem 4**). To this end, we identify that the subgraph $G_P \subseteq G$ of proper intervals (roughly those intervals that are not properly contained in other intervals) has a maximal degree of $O(\chi(G))$. Furthermore, G_P is of *bounded-independence* (**Theorem 2**) which is defined as follows:

Definition 1. *A graph* $G = (V, E)$ *is of* bounded-independence *if there is a bounding function* $f(r)$ *such that for each node* $v \in V$, *the size of a maximum independent set in the* r-*neighborhood of* v *is at most* $f(r), \forall r \geq 0$. *The* r-*neighborhood of a node* v *is the set of nodes at distance at most* r *from* v *(excluding* v*).*

Schneider and Wattenhofer present in [15] a distributed maximal independent set algorithm for bounded-independence graphs that runs in time $O(\log^* n)$. Using this algorithm, we compute an independent set in the subgraph G_P in $O(\log^* n)$ time, and we show how to extend it to a dominating set that dominates the whole graph G. Then, we use this dominating set to coordinate the coloring of all vertices. By construction, this coloring is a canonical one, and since every canonical coloring in an interval graph is at least an 8-approximation, the result follows.

Furthermore, we show that computing an $O(\log^* n)$-approximation to the coloring problem in interval graphs requires $\Omega(\log^* n)$ time by a reduction to a result of Linial [7]. Linial showed that obtaining a 3-coloring on a ring requires $\Omega(\log^* n)$ rounds. We show that any algorithm that colors interval graphs with fewer rounds would imply a faster 3-coloring algorithm of the ring contradicting the previous lower bound. This renders our algorithm tight. Moreover, we observe that if nodes are aware of their interval boundaries then the previous algorithm can even be implemented in the $\mathcal{CONGEST}$ where all messages are of size at most $O(\log n)$.

A Simple Coloring Scheme. We also consider a particular class of simple distributed coloring algorithms that have been successfully applied in the past to solve the coloring problem in the SINR (Signal to Interference plus Noise Ratio) model for wireless communication [16–18]. From a graph theoretical point of view, in the SINR model, a complete directed edge-weighted graph with vertex set L is given, where each vertex $l \in L$ represents a transmission link consisting of a sender and a receiver. The weights of the edges between transmission links determine the amount of relative interference that a transmitting sender has on the receiver of another link. The notion of independent sets and colorings are adapted as follows: A subset of nodes $L' \subseteq L$ is an independent set if the in-degree of every node $l \in L'$ from other nodes of L' is at most 1. An independent set corresponds here to a set of links that can successfully transmit simultaneously. Then an s-coloring is a decomposition of the vertex set into s independent sets. An s-coloring corresponds here to a schedule that permits the successful transmission of all links in s rounds. The algorithms for coloring SINR-instances of [16–18] are round-based, and they follow the scheme of Algorithm 1 (Algorithm 1 is stated for unweighted graphs $G = (V, E)$ which is the form we need in this paper).

The scheme of Algorithm 1 computes a coloring $\gamma : V \rightarrow \mathbb{N}$. In each round i, a probability p_i is determined in Line 4. Different Algorithms that follow this scheme such as the algorithms of [16–18] compute different sequences $(p_i)_i$. The sequence of probabilities p_i determine the efficiency of the scheme, and different graphs classes may require different sequences. Then, all not-yet colored nodes v

---

Algorithm 1. Simple coloring scheme

Require: $G = (V, E)$ {Input graph}
 1. $\gamma(v) \leftarrow \perp$ for all $v \in V$ {The coloring to be computed}
 2. $i \leftarrow 1$ {Current color}
 3. **while** $\exists v \in V$ with $\gamma(v) = \perp$ **do**
 4.   Determine p_i {Algorithms following this scheme have to implement this line}
 5.   **for all** $v \in V$ with $\gamma(v) = \perp$ **do**
 6. $T_v \leftarrow \text{coin}(p_i)$ {Pre-selection step: If $\text{coin}(p_i) = true$ then v is a candidate to be colored}
 7.   **end for**
 8.   **for all** $v \in V$ with $\gamma(v) = \perp$ and $T_v = true$ **do**
 9.   **if** $\bigvee_{u \in \Gamma_V(v) \text{ with } \gamma(u) = \perp} T_u = false$ **then** {Check whether a neighbor of v has been pre-selected}
10. $\gamma(v) \leftarrow i$ {Color node v}
11.   **end if**
12.   **end for**
13. $i \leftarrow i + 1$
14. **end while**
15. **return** γ

---

pre-select themselves as candidates to be colored with probability p_i in Line 6. We assume that we have a function coin: $[0, 1] \rightarrow \{true, false\}$ to our disposal such that $\text{coin}(p)$ returns *true* with probability p, otherwise *false*. Next, in Line 10, pre-selected nodes color themselves with color i if none of its not yet colored neighbors pre-selected themselves.

Algorithms that follow the scheme of Algorithm 1 are simple and easy to implement. They do not require a complicated mechanism for breaking ties as a pre-selected node is only colored if none of its neighbors is pre-selected, or, in other words, a node only has to learn the logical OR of the bits of its neighbors indicating whether a neighbor is pre-selected. As we will discuss in Section 5, exchanging this type of information does not put high demands on the distributed model in which this algorithm is implemented. This makes the algorithm a good candidate for being implemented in various models. We will show that an implementation of this scheme is possible in the very restrictive discrete beeping model [19] in which, among other things, nodes cannot distinguish between different neighboring nodes, and the number of neighbors of a node is unknown to the node itself. Algorithms of type Algorithm 1 are essentially the only type of coloring algorithms that can be implemented in this model.

This scheme of algorithms is referred to as *acknowledgement-only* (ack-only) algorithms [16–18] in the SINR community. As previously mentioned, in the SINR model, a set of communication links each consisting of a sender and a receiver is considered. Links are not aware of their neighborhood. In each round, a sender may either attempt to transmit (pre-select itself) and hope for a successful transmission, or it may remain silent and wait. Ack-only algorithms assume that senders receive an acknowledgment of whether their transmission was successful or whether it failed (check whether there are neighbors that pre-selected themselves). Successful links then remain silent until all links successfully transmitted (once a node is colored it does not attempt to color itself again). Since there is no information exchange between communication links, in each round, senders essentially can only flip a coin and transmit with a certain probability. Note that this situation is modeled by the scheme of Algorithm 1. While in the scheme of Algorithm 1 the identification of whether a communication attempt was success is checked in Line 9, this is achieved in the SINR model with explicit acknowledgments in a separate round that succeed with constant probability.

It is known that:

Theorem 1 ([20]). *There is an algorithm that follows the scheme of Algorithm 1 and colors a graph with $O(d\chi(G)\log n)$ colors w.h.p. where d is the inductive independence number of a graph.*

Inductive independence [21] is defined as follows:

Definition 2. *A graph $G = (V, E)$ is* inductive d-independent *if there exists an ordering π of the vertices V such that for every independent set $I \subseteq V$ and every vertex $v \in V$:*

$$|\{u \in \Gamma_G(v) \text{ with } \pi(u) > \pi(v)\} \cap I| \leq d.$$

The inductive independence number *of G is the smallest d such that G is inductive d-independent.*

Many interesting graph classes have bounded inductive independence, e.g., disc graphs are inductive 5-independent, planar graphs are inductive 3-independent, claw-free graphs are inductive 2-independent, and most importantly, chordal graphs (a superclass of interval graphs) are inductive 1-independent. It is well-known that chordal graphs are exactly those graphs that admit a *perfect elimination ordering*: A perfect elimination ordering in a graph $G = (V, E)$ is an ordering π of the vertices V such that, for each $v \in V$, $v \cup \{u \in \Gamma_G(v) \text{ with } \pi(u) > \pi(v)\}$ forms a clique. Note that this is equivalent to the definition of inductive 1-independence. In the context of SINR coloring, it is shown in [20] that many important SINR instances are inductive $O(1)$-independent, and by Lemma 1, an $O(\log n)$-approximation algorithm to the coloring problem in the SINR model is obtained. It is an open question whether there is an algorithm that follows the scheme of Algorithm 1 and computes an $O(1)$-approximation (in fact, for many instances no algorithm at all is known that computes an $O(1)$-approximation).

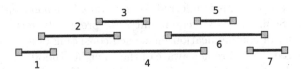

Fig. 1. Example of a perfect elimination ordering of an interval graph. For each interval with index i, the size of an independent set among its neighbors with larger index is at most 1.

In [18], an instance is provided that can be colored with 2 colors, while any such algorithm requires $\Omega(\log n)$ rounds. However, no hard instances are known with larger chromatic number.

In this paper, we settle this question for interval graphs up to a $\log \log n$ factor. As interval graphs are inductive 1-independent, we immediately obtain an $O(\log n)$-approximation by Theorem 1. We will show that every algorithm that follows the scheme of Algorithm 1 requires $\Omega\left(\frac{\log n}{\log \log n} \chi(G)\right)$ colors (**Theorem 6**), matching the upper bound up to a $\log \log n$ factor.

Furthermore, we provide an alternative proof of Theorem 1. We essentially identify that there is an algorithm following the scheme of Algorithm 1 that colors graphs G that have the property that any induced subgraph on α vertices has at most αk edges using $O(k \log n)$ colors (**Theorem 5**). We observe that inductive d-independent graphs have at most $d\chi(G)n$ edges, which allows us to conclude the statement of Theorem 1. Alternatively, our theorem can also be applied to k-*degenerate* graphs. A graph is k-degenerate if every induced subgraph has a node of degree at most k. Clearly, such a graph has at most kn edges.

While the lower bound does not carry over to the geometric SINR model, it shows that in the abstract SINR model, improved results for scheduling in terms of inductive independence are not possible by these types of algorithms.

Outline. In Section 2, we present necessary definitions and notations, and we prove a property about interval graphs that is required in the subsequent section. In Section 3, we present our upper and lower bound for a constant factor approximation in the $\mathcal{LOCAL}$ model and its adaption to the $\mathcal{CONGEST}$ model. Then, in the following sections, we consider the previously mentioned class of simple coloring algorithms. We revisit the result that an inductive d-independent graph can be colored by an algorithm of the previous scheme with $O(d\chi(G) \log n)$ colors in Section 4. Then, In Section 5, we underline the simplicity of algorithms that follows the scheme of Algorithm 1, and we show that they can be implemented in the very restrictive discrete beeping model. Finally, we prove in Section 6 that any algorithm of the previous scheme requires $\Omega(\frac{\log n}{\log \log n}\chi(G))$ colors on interval graphs.

Furthermore, we note that due to space restrictions, some proofs are omitted but can be found in the full version of this article.

2   Preliminaries

Definitions. An *independent set* in a graph $G = (V, E)$ is a subset $I \subseteq V$ of vertices such that for every pair of vertices $v_1, v_2 \in I : (v_1, v_2) \notin E$. An independent set I is *maximal* if $I \cup \{v\}$ is not an independent set for all $v \in V \setminus I$. A *dominating set* in a graph $G = (V, E)$ is a subset $D \subseteq V$ such that for any vertex $v \in V \setminus D$, v is adjacent to at least one vertex $u \in D$. Any maximal independent set is a dominating set, however, the converse is not true. For an integer k, a *distance-k-coloring* of a graph $G = (V, E)$ is an assignment

$\gamma : V \to \{1, \ldots, s\}$ of colors to the vertices of a graph such that any two vertices at distance at most k have different colors.

Interval Graphs. Let $V = \{v_1, \ldots, v_n\}$ be a set of intervals with $v_j = (a_j, b_j)$ for all $1 \leq j \leq n$ and real numbers a_j, b_j such that $a_j < b_j$. Let $G = (V, E)$ be the corresponding interval graph, i.e., there is an edge between vertices (intervals) v_j, v_k if the two intervals overlap. Let $m = |E|$. We assume that all a_i, b_i are distinct. For simplicity, we will assume that the input interval graphs are connected. The *neighborhood* of a vertex v in graph G is denoted by $\Gamma_G(v)$, and we define $\Gamma_G[v] = \Gamma_G(v) \cup \{v\}$. For a subset $V' \subseteq V$, we may write $\Gamma_{V'}(v)$ to denote $\Gamma_G(v) \cap V'$. Furthermore, the *k-neighborhood* of a vertex v is the set of nodes that are within distance at most k from v, and we denote it by $\Gamma_G^k(v)$. Then $\Gamma_G^1(v) = \Gamma_G(v)$. For a vertex $v \in V$, we denote by $\deg_G(v)$ the degree of v in G. For a subset $V' \subseteq V$, we may also write $\deg_{V'}(v)$ for the degree of v in the subgraph of G which is induced by the nodes V', that is, $\deg_{V'}(v) := \deg_{G|_{V'}}(v)$.

We say that an interval v is *proper* if there is no other interval u such that $\Gamma_G[v] \subsetneq \Gamma_G[u]$. For an interval graph $G = (V, E)$, we denote by $G_P = (V_P, E|_{V_P})$ the subgraph of G that is induced by the proper intervals of G. It is easy to see that the subgraph G_P of a connected interval graph is connected, too. Then the following degree bound holds (proof omitted).

Fact 1. *For all $v \in V_P$: $\deg_{G_P}(v) \leq 2\chi(G_P) - 2$.*

Distributed Algorithms. In the following, we will reuse existing distributed algorithms. The deterministic distributed algorithm of Wattenhofer and Schneider [15] colors a bounded-independence graph using $\Delta + 1$ colors in $O(\log^* n)$ time, and we will denote this algorithm by COLBI (BI stands for bounded independence). This algorithm can be implemented such that it returns a *canonical coloring*, i.e., a coloring such that no node could change its color to a smaller one. In the same work, Wattenhofer and Schneider show that in a bounded-independence graph, a maximal independent set can be deterministically computed in $O(\log^* n)$ time, and we denote this algorithm by MISBI. Both, COLBI and MISBI, can be implemented in the $\mathcal{CONGEST}$ model.

3 $O(1)$-approximation for Coloring Interval Graphs in the $\mathcal{LOCAL}$ Model

In this section, we show that an interval graph G can be colored in $O(\log^* n)$ time with $O(\chi(G))$ colors in the $\mathcal{LOCAL}$ model. Our algorithm makes use of the distributed algorithms COLBI and MISBI for computing a coloring and an independent set in bounded-independence graphs. We run these algorithms on the subgraph G_P of proper intervals. Unit disc graphs are of bounded independence [15]. Since the class of proper interval graphs is equivalent to the class of unit interval graphs, and unit interval graphs are a subclass of unit disc graphs, the following fact follows immediately:

Fact 2. *Proper interval graphs are of bounded independence.*

We present our algorithm in Subsection 3.1, its analysis in Subsection 3.2, and we discuss an implementation of the algorithm in the $\mathcal{CONGEST}$ model in Subsection 3.3.

3.1   Algorithm

1. **Identify the Subgraph G_P of Proper Intervals:** Each node v determines if $v \in G_P$ by checking if there is a neighbor $u \in \Gamma_G(v)$ such that $\Gamma_G[u] \supsetneq \Gamma_G[v]$. If no such neighbor exists then v is in G_P. This involves one round of communication where each node sends the list of its neighbors to all its neighbors.
2. **Compute a Maximal Independent Set J of G_P:** Using MISBI, we compute a maximal independent set J of the graph G_P in O($\log^* n$) rounds. J is needed for the computation of a dominating set in the next step.
3. **Compute a Dominating Set $N \cup J$:** Algorithm 2 computes a set N such that $N \cup J$ is a dominating set of the graph G. Ties are broken arbitrarily. In step one, every node communicated already its list of neighbors to its neighbors, and hence no further communication is required.

Algorithm 2. Computation of a dominating set

1. **for all** $v \in J$ **do**
2. $u_1 \leftarrow \arg\max_{u \in \Gamma_{G_P}(v)} |\Gamma_G(u) \setminus \Gamma_G(v)|$
3. $u_2 \leftarrow \arg\max_{u \in \Gamma_{G_P}(v)} |\Gamma_G(u) \setminus (\Gamma_G(v) \cup \Gamma_G(u_1))|$
4. $N \leftarrow N \cup \{u_1, u_2\}$
5. **end for**

---

4. **Find a Distance-3 Coloring of $G|_{N \cup J}$ and Obtain Color Classes $(I_i)_{i \geq 1}$:** We argue in the analysis that the maximal degree in the vertex induced graph $G|_N$ is 4, and hence the maximal degree in $G|_{N \cup J}$ is 5. Therefore, the size of the 4-neighborhood of every node is bounded by some constant C. We build the graph H on vertex set $N \cup J$ where nodes are adjacent if they are at distance at most 3 in G_P. This involves two additional rounds of communication to establish knowledge about the 3-neighborhood of each node. We run COLBI to color H in time O($\log^* n$) and we obtain a constant number of color classes $(I_i)_{i \geq 1}$. This coloring is a distance-3 coloring of $G|_{N \cup J}$.
5. **Coloring.** After each of the following iterations, in one round of communication, each node that has received a color notifies its neighbors about its own color. This guarantees that a not-yet colored node always knows the palette of still available colors that it may be colored with.
   Iterate over the sets $(I_i)_{i \geq 1}$ and do the following:
   Every node $u' \in I_i$ coordinates the coloring of not-yet colored nodes $u \in \Gamma_G[u']$ as follows: Nodes u send the palette of possible colors with which they may be colored to u'. The node u' is unique for u: As I_i is a color class of a distance-3 coloring, every other node $u'' \in I_i \setminus \{u'\}$ is at distance at least

2 from u. Then, u' determines a canonical coloring of all nodes u respecting the color restrictions of the nodes, and notifies the nodes u about their color.

3.2 Analysis

Due to space restrictions, the proof of the following lemma is omitted.

Lemma 1. *The following properties hold: (1) $J \cup N$ is a dominating set in G. (2) The maximal degree of a node in the graph $G|_N$ is 4.*

Concerning Item 1, note that for any node $u \in G \backslash G_P$ there is a node $v \in G_P$ that dominates u. Therefore, G_P contains a dominating set. J is an independent set. For each $u \in J$, Algorithm 2 basically selects the two intervals intersecting with u that reach out furthest to the left and the right, hence, dominating as many intervals of $G \setminus G_P$ as possible. It turns out that this is sufficient to dominate all nodes. Item 2 follows from the fact that G_P is a proper interval graph, and intervals do not include each other. Therefore, not too many intervals selected by Algorithm 2 may overlap.

Lemma 2. *For every $u \in V$ there is at least one set I_i s.t. $|\Gamma_G[u] \cap I_i| = |\Gamma_G[\Gamma_G[u]] \cap I_i| = 1$. That is, each node is dominated by a node in some I_i but has then no other node in I_i in its 2-neighborhood.*

Proof. Let u be a vertex in V. Since $J \cup N = \cup_i I_i$ is a dominating set, u is adjacent to at least one node u' of $J \cup N$. So, $|\Gamma_G[\Gamma_G[u]] \cap I_i| \geq |\Gamma_G[u] \cap I_i| \geq 1$. Let i be the index with $u' \in I_i$.

Suppose that $|\Gamma_G[\Gamma_G[u]] \cap I_i| \geq 2$. Then, there is a vertex v in V that is adjacent to both u and u'', for some u'' in $I_i \setminus \{u'\}$. There is a vertex $\hat{u}$ ($\hat{v}$) in G_P (not necessarily distinct from u (v)) corresponding to a proper interval that contains the interval of u ($\hat{v}$), and the neighbors of u (v) are also neighbors of $\hat{u}$ ($\hat{v}$), respectively. Thus, $u', \hat{u}, \hat{v}, u''$ is a path of length 3 in G_P, contradicting the distance-3 coloring property. $\square$

Lemma 2 shows that every node will be correctly colored in Step 5 of the algorithm. $|\Gamma_G[u] \cap I_i| = 1$ shows that all nodes will be considered in the coloring step of the algorithm, and $|\Gamma_G[\Gamma_G[u]] \cap I_i| = 1$ guarantees that the computed colorings of the different nodes of I_i do not interfere with each other. We conclude with the main theorem:

Theorem 2. *In the $\mathcal{LOCAL}$ model, there is a deterministic $O(1)$-approximation algorithm that computes a canonical coloring of an interval graph and runs in time $O(\log^* n)$.*

Proof. Concerning correctness of the algorithm, we showed in Lemma 2 that every node $v \in G$ will be colored in Step 5. By construction, the algorithm computes a canonical coloring, i.e., it always assigns the smallest color possible to a node. Therefore, the total amount of required colors can be bounded by the fact that any canonical coloring of an interval graph uses at most $8 \cdot \chi(G)$ colors [6]. The runtime of the algorithm is $O(\log^* n)$ since we essentially run a constant number of times the algorithms MISBI and COLBI whose runtimes are $O(\log^* n)$. $\square$

3.3 Adapting the Algorithm to the $\mathcal{CONGEST}$ Model

Suppose that every node $v_i \in V$ is aware of its interval representation and knows its interval boundaries a_i, b_i. We assume that the numbers a_i, b_i require space $O(\log n)$ to be written down. Then the previous algorithm can be implemented in the $\mathcal{CONGEST}$ model: Concerning Step 1, exchanging interval boundaries and the number of neighbors is enough to determine whether a node $v \in V$ is also in V_P. Step 2 remains unchanged. Since each node $v \in V_P$ knows the interval boundaries of its neighbors, Step 3 is simplified and v simply selects incident intervals that reach out furthest to the left and to the right. Step 4 remains unchanged. Since the maximal degree in H is bounded by a constant, all messages sent in order to compute the 3-neighborhood of every node are still of size $O(\log n)$. Concerning Step 5, note that it is impossible that every node u sends its palette of still available colors to the coordinator u' with a message of size $O(\log n)$. We therefore give up on obtaining a canonical coloring, and, instead, for each coloring round we use a set of new colors (for instance round i uses the colors $\{(i-1)n + 1, in\}$. Since, however, each coloring round uses $O(\chi(G))$ colors and there are only a constant number of sets I_i, we still obtain a constant factor approximation.

Theorem 3. *There is a deterministic $O(1)$-approximation algorithm that computes a coloring of an interval graph in the $\mathcal{CONGEST}$ model and runs in time $O(\log^* n)$ if each node knows its interval boundaries.*

3.4 Lower Bound for Coloring Interval Graphs in the $\mathcal{LOCAL}$ Model

Linial's lower bound shows that any distributed algorithm for coloring the n-cycle with three colors requires time $\Omega(\log^* n)$ [7]. By removing an arbitrary edge from an n-cycle, we obtain a path which in turn is an interval graph. We make use of this connection together with a well-known color reduction technique, and we obtain the following theorem (due to space restrictions, all details of this section are deferred to the full version of this paper).

Theorem 4. *Every (possibly randomized) distributed algorithm that colors an interval graph G on n vertices using $o(\log^*(n)\chi(G))$ colors requires time $\Omega(\log^* n)$.*

4 Simple Coloring Algorithm

We show now that an algorithm that follows the scheme of Algorithm 1 can be used to compute a $(k \log n)$-coloring on graphs G that have the property that every induced subgraph on α nodes has at most αk edges (Theorem 5). This property is fulfilled by k-degenerate graphs since clearly k-degenerate graphs have at most kn edges, and k-degeneracy inherits to induced subgraphs. Furthermore, it is easy to see that the degeneracy k of an inductive d-independent graph is bounded as $k \leq d\chi(G)$. Theorem 1 as stated in the introduction follows hence immediately from Theorem 5.

In order to color a graph with a limited number of edges in each induced subgraph with an algorithm of type Algorithm 1, we use the following sequence of probabilities: we start with probability $p_1 = 1$, and we repeat it $\frac{32e^2 \log n}{p_1}$ times. Then, we halve this probability, i.e., $p_2 = p_1/2$ and we repeat it $\frac{32e^2 \log n}{p_2}$ times. This procedure of halving the previous probability $p_{i+1} = p_i/2$ and repeating it $\frac{32e^2 \log n}{p_{i+1}}$ times continues until all nodes are colored. We will prove now Theorem 5. We note again that this type of proof was already used in [18] and [17], and we defer it therefore, and for space reasons, to the full version of this paper.

Theorem 5. *There is an algorithm that follows the scheme of Algorithm 1 and colors graphs $G = (V, E)$ that have the property that every induced subgraph on α vertices has at most αk edges with $\mathrm{O}(k \log n)$ colors and rounds w.h.p. Thus, the algorithm uses $O(d\chi(G) \log n)$ colors, where d is the inductive independence.*

5   Implementation in the Beep Model

In the discrete beeping communication model as introduced in [19], nodes of a network modeled by a graph $G = (V, E)$ communicate with each other via *beeps*. Nodes are not aware of their neighborhoods. In each round, a node $v \in V$ has the choice between two actions: Either v transmits a beep signal (v beeps), or v is in listening mode. If v is in listening mode, then v receives a signal only if at least one of its neighbors transmits a beep. The reception of a beep signal does not allow v to determine the number of its neighbors that transmitted it. Node v can only distinguish between the situation where none of its neighbors transmitted, or at least one of its neighbors transmitted. While in [19] asynchronous wake-up times of nodes are considered, we assume a synchronous model where all nodes are awake at time 0. Furthermore, we assume that nodes know a polynomial upper bound on n, the number of nodes. We assume that they have only $O(\log n)$ memory.

Despite the fact that the discrete beeping model is very restrictive, many non-trivial problems can be solved in this model. It models aspects of wireless networks (carrier sensing) and biological phenomena. Algorithms that can be implemented in this model can certainly be implemented in many other distributed models.

We will show now that the scheme of Algorithm 1 can be implemented in the discrete beeping model. In Line 9 of Algorithm 1, a pre-selected node has to determine whether either none of its neighbors pre-selected themselves, or whether there is at least one neighbors that pre-selected itself. Note that if we gave a node the ability to beep and listen at the same time, Line 9 of Algorithm 1 could be implemented in one communication round. The main difficulty for an implementation in the discrete beeping model stems from the fact that if a node decides to beep it cannot receive any information. Therefore, the pre-selected nodes cannot simply beep simultaneously in one round since the beep of a node wouldn't be heard by another beeping node. We will show, however, that this task can be computed in $O(\log n)$ rounds of communication. In the following, we denote by beep() the action that a node decides to beep, and by listen() the action that a node is in listening mode. The function listen() returns *true*, if at least one neighboring node beeped, otherwise it returns *false*. Algorithm 3 implements one round of Algorithm 1 in the discrete beeping model.

Algorithm 3. Iteration i in the beep model

Require: p_i {Probability p_i, integer $C \geq 4$}
1. **if** coin(p_i) **then**
2.   Select uniformly at random $S \subset \{1, 2, \ldots, C \log n\}$ such that $|S| = \frac{C \log n}{2}$
3. $B \leftarrow false$
4.   **for** $l = 1 \ldots C \log n$ **do**
5.   **if** $l \in S$ **then** beep() **else** $B \leftarrow B \vee$ listen() **end if**
6.   **end for**
7.   **if** $B = false$ **then** $\gamma(v) \leftarrow i$ **end if**
8. **end if**

Lemma 3. *Let $C \geq 4$ be an integer. The probability that a pre-selected node $v \in V$ colors itself in Line 7, despite having a pre-selected neighbor, is at most $\frac{1}{n^{C-3}}$ assuming that $n > 2C$.*

Since every node may get pre-selected at most $O(d\chi(G) \log n)$ times in the algorithm of Theorem 1, selecting a large enough value for C (for instance $C \geq 7$) guarantees that the overall error probability is small enough when implementing this algorithm in the discrete beeping model. From Lemma 3 and Theorem 1 we obtain the following corollary:

Corollary 1. *There is an algorithm that follows the scheme of Algorithm 1 that can be implemented in the discrete beeping model with $O(d\chi(G) \log^2 n)$ rounds and colors a graph with $O(d\chi(G) \log n)$ colors w.h.p. where d is the inductive independence number of a graph.*

6   Lower Bound for Algorithms of Type Algorithm 1

We discuss now a hard instance showing that no algorithm that follows the scheme of Algorithm 1 can achieve an approximation ratio of $o(\frac{\log n}{\log \log n})$ on interval graphs. We present the hard instance graph $G_{T,b} = (V, E)$ in its interval representation, where T and b are parameters as follows: As basic building blocks of our construction we use cliques of size $T = o(n)$ (we determine the precise value of T later). Their adjacency relations follow a tree structure with branching factor $\log^b n$ for an integer $b \geq 6$ (we set $b = 6$, but any constant $b \geq 6$ equally works), and we obtain a *containment interval graph* as in Figure 2, i.e., an interval graph where the set $\{\Gamma_{G_{T,b}}(v) \,|\, v \in V\}$ forms a laminar family. The vertex set V is decomposed into layers $V_0, \ldots, V_k$. We have $|V_i| = T \cdot (\log n)^{ib}$, and, therefore, $k = \Theta(\frac{\log n}{\log \log n})$ in order to have a total of n vertices. The chromatic number of this graph is $\chi(G_{T,b}) = Tk$. We aim to construct the hard instances for a given chromatic number, and we therefore set the parameter T to be $T = \chi(G_{T,b})/k$. Let us summarize the values of our parameters: We consider the n-vertex graph $G_{T,b}$ with chromatic number $\chi(G_{T,b})$ and we set $T = \chi(G_{T,b})/k = \Theta(\chi(G_{T,b}) \log \log n / \log n)$ and $b = 6$.

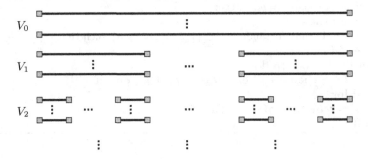

Fig. 2. Hard instance $G_{T,b} = (V, E)$. V_0 is a clique of size T, V_1 are $\log^b(n)$ cliques each of size T. This construction continues recursively until level $k = \Theta(\frac{\log(\frac{n}{T})}{\log \log n})$.

We shall prove now that any algorithm following the scheme of Algorithm 1 requires $\Omega(\chi(G_{T,b})k)$ iterations on graph $G_{T,b}$. However, due to space restrictions, all proofs of this section are omitted and can be found in the full version of this article. Our argument is as follows: Let $p_1, p_2, \ldots$ be the sequence of probabilities chosen by the algorithm, where p_i is the probability chosen in round i. We will argue that for any $k/2 \leq i < k$, layer V_{i+1} will be eliminated by the algorithm before the elimination of at most $1/10$ of the nodes of layer V_i since the presence of layer V_{i+1} induces high degrees to all nodes in layer V_i. For the nodes in V_i, this reduces the probability of being selected and colored. We show that the elimination of a layer takes time $\Omega(\chi(G_{T,b}))$ for any choice of probabilities. Since there are $k = \Theta(\frac{\log n}{\log \log n})$ layers, the result follows.

Denote by $V_i^j \subseteq V_i$ the set of not-yet colored nodes after iteration j. Then $V_i^0 = V_i$. Let $V^j = \bigcup_i V_i^j$. Denote by t_i the least number of iterations of the algorithm such that at least one clique of V_i lost at least $1/2T$ of its vertices, i.e., at least half of the vertices of at least one clique of layer i have disappeared. In any iteration j, any node $v \in V^j$ gets pre-selected with probability p_j. Then it is colored only if none of its neighbors have been preselected. Therefore, the probability of v being chosen and colored is $p_i(1 - p_i)^{\deg_{V^j}(v)}$.

Next, we show that it is very unlikely that a node of layer i is colored before iteration t_{i+1}.

Lemma 4. *Consider graph $G_{T,b}$. Let $0 \leq i < k$. For every iteration $j < t_{i+1}$, every $v \in V_i^j$, and large enough n:*

$$\mathbb{P}\left[v \text{ is colored in iteration } j\right] \leq \frac{1}{T \log^{b-2} n}.$$

This fact is then used in the following lemma. With high probability, all cliques of layer i are still of size at least $9/10$ of its initial size just after iteration t_{i+1}.

Lemma 5. *Consider graph $G_{T,b}$. Suppose that $t_{i+1} \leq T \log^2 n$. Then with probability at least $1 - O\left(\frac{1}{n^{\log^{b-5}(n)T-1}}\right)$ and n large enough, the size of the smallest clique in V_j after iteration t_{i+1} is at least $\frac{9}{10}T$ for any $j \leq i$.*

Using Lemma 5 we conclude that the number of rounds between t_{i+1} and t_i is $\Theta(\chi(G))$.

Lemma 6. *Suppose that $G_{T,b}$ is such that $\chi(G_{T,b}) \geq \log^5 n$. Then for any $i \geq k/2$, a small enough but constant c, and n large enough:*

$$\mathbb{P}\left[t_i - t_{i+1} \leq c\chi(G)\right] = O\left(\frac{1}{n^{\log n-1}}\right).$$

The previous lemma allows us to obtain our lower bound result.

Theorem 6. *Suppose that $G_{T,b}$ is such that $\log^5 n \leq \chi(G_{T,b}) \leq n^{1-\epsilon}$ for any $\epsilon > 0$ and let n be sufficiently large. Then any algorithm that follows the scheme of Algorithm 1 requires $\Omega(\chi(G_{T,b})\frac{\log n}{\log\log n})$ colors to color $G_{T,b}$ with high probability.*

References

1. Marathe, M., Breu, H., Hunt III, H.B., Ravi, S.S., Rosenkrantz, D.J.: Simple heuristics for unit disk graphs. Networks 25, 59–68 (1995)
2. Breu, H., Kirkpatrick, D.G.: Unit disk graph recognition is NP-hard. Comput. Geom. Theory Appl. 9(1-2), 3–24 (1998)
3. Halldórsson, M.M.: Wireless scheduling with power control. ACM Trans. Algorithms 9(1), 7:1–7:20 (2012)
4. Karp, R.M.: Reducibility Among Combinatorial Problems. In: Miller, R.E., Thatcher, J.W. (eds.) Complexity of Computer Computations, pp. 85–103. Plenum Press (1972)
5. Zuckerman, D.: Linear degree extractors and the inapproximability of max clique and chromatic number. In: Proceedings of the Thirty-eighth Annual ACM Symposium on Theory of Computing, STOC 2006, pp. 681–690. ACM, New York (2006)
6. Smith, D.A.: The First-fit Algorithm Uses Many Colors on Some Interval Graphs. PhD thesis, Tempe, AZ, USA, AAI3428197 (2010)

7. Linial, N.: Locality in distributed graph algorithms. SIAM J. Comput. 21(1), 193–201 (1992)
8. Kuhn, F., Wattenhofer, R.: On the complexity of distributed graph coloring. In: Proceedings of the Twenty-fifth Annual ACM Symposium on Principles of Distributed Computing, PODC 2006, pp. 7–15. ACM, New York (2006)
9. Kothapalli, K., Scheideler, C., Onus, M., Schindelhauer, C.: Distributed coloring in $\sqrt{\log n}$ bit rounds. In: Proceedings of the 20th International Conference on Parallel and Distributed Processing, IPDPS 2006, p. 44. IEEE Computer Society, Washington, DC (2006)
10. Barenboim, L., Elkin, M.: Deterministic distributed vertex coloring in polylogarithmic time. J. ACM 58(5), 23:1–23:25 (2011)
11. Métivier, Y., Robson, J.M., Saheb-Djahromi, N., Zemmari, A.: On the time and the bit complexity of distributed randomised anonymous ring colouring. Theor. Comput. Sci. 502, 64–75 (2013)
12. Luby, M.: A simple parallel algorithm for the maximal independent set problem. In: Proceedings of the Seventeenth Annual ACM Symposium on Theory of Computing, STOC 1985, pp. 1–10. ACM, New York (1985)
13. Barenboim, L., Elkin, M., Pettie, S., Schneider, J.: The locality of distributed symmetry breaking. In: Proceedings of the 2012 IEEE 53rd Annual Symposium on Foundations of Computer Science, FOCS 2012, pp. 321–330. IEEE Computer Society, Washington, DC (2012)
14. Cole, R., Vishkin, U.: Deterministic coin tossing with applications to optimal parallel list ranking. Inf. Control 70(1), 32–53 (1986)
15. Schneider, J., Wattenhofer, R.: An Optimal Maximal Independent Set Algorithm for Bounded-Independence Graphs. Distributed Computing 22 (2010)
16. Fanghänel, A., Kesselheim, T., Vöcking, B.: Improved algorithms for latency minimization in wireless networks. Theor. Comput. Sci. 412(24), 2657–2667 (2011)
17. Kesselheim, T., Vöcking, B.: Distributed contention resolution in wireless networks. In: Lynch, N.A., Shvartsman, A.A. (eds.) DISC 2010. LNCS, vol. 6343, pp. 163–178. Springer, Heidelberg (2010)
18. Halldórsson, M.M., Mitra, P.: Nearly optimal bounds for distributed wireless scheduling in the SINR model. In: Aceto, L., Henzinger, M., Sgall, J. (eds.) ICALP 2011, Part II. LNCS, vol. 6756, pp. 625–636. Springer, Heidelberg (2011)
19. Cornejo, A., Kuhn, F.: Deploying wireless networks with beeps. In: Lynch, N.A., Shvartsman, A.A. (eds.) DISC 2010. LNCS, vol. 6343, pp. 148–162. Springer, Heidelberg (2010)
20. Halldórsson, M.M., Holzer, S., Mitra, P., Wattenhofer, R.: The power of non-uniform wireless power. In: Proceedings of the Twenty-Fourth Annual ACM-SIAM Symposium on Discrete Algorithms, SODA 2013, pp. 1595–1606 (2013)
21. Ye, Y., Borodin, A.: Elimination graphs. ACM Trans. Algorithms 8(2), 14:1–14:23 (2012)

Distributed Symmetry Breaking in Hypergraphs[*]

Shay Kutten[1,**], Danupon Nanongkai[2,***], Gopal Pandurangan[3,†], and Peter Robinson[4,‡]

[1] Faculty of IE&M, Technion, Haifa, Israel
[2] Faculty of Computer Science, University of Vienna, Austria
[3] Department of Computer Science, University of Houston, USA
[4] School of Computing, National University of Singapore

Abstract. Fundamental local symmetry breaking problems such as Maximal Independent Set (MIS) and coloring have been recognized as important by the community, and studied extensively in (standard) graphs. In particular, fast (i.e., logarithmic run time) randomized algorithms are well-established for MIS and $\Delta + 1$-coloring in both the LOCAL and CONGEST distributed computing models. On the other hand, comparatively much less is known on the complexity of distributed symmetry breaking in *hypergraphs*. In particular, a key question is whether a fast (randomized) algorithm for MIS exists for hypergraphs.

In this paper, we study the distributed complexity of symmetry breaking in hypergraphs by presenting distributed randomized algorithms for a variety of fundamental problems under a natural distributed computing model for hypergraphs. We first show that MIS in hypergraphs (of arbitrary dimension) can be solved in $O(\log^2 n)$ rounds (n is the number of nodes of the hypergraph) in the LOCAL model. We then present a key result of this paper — an $O(\Delta^\epsilon \operatorname{polylog} n)$-round hypergraph MIS algorithm in the CONGEST model where Δ is the maximum node degree of the hypergraph and $\epsilon > 0$ is any arbitrarily small constant. We also present distributed algorithms for coloring, maximal matching, and maximal clique in hypergraphs.

To demonstrate the usefulness of hypergraph MIS, we present applications of our hypergraph algorithm to solving problems in (standard) graphs. In particular, the hypergraph MIS yields fast distributed algorithms for the *balanced minimal dominating set* problem (left open in

---

[*] The full version is available at http://arxiv.org/abs/1405.1649

[**] Research supported in part by the Israel Science Foundation and by the Technion TASP center.

[***] This work was partially done while at ICERM, Brown University USA and Nanyang Technological University, Singapore.

[†] This work was done while at Nanyang Technological University and Brown University. Research supported in part by the following research grants: Nanyang Technological University grant M58110000, Singapore Ministry of Education (MOE) Academic Research Fund (AcRF) Tier 2 grant MOE2010-T2-2-082, Singapore MOE AcRF Tier 1 grant MOE2012-T1-001-094, and a grant from the US-Israel Binational Science Foundation (BSF).

[‡] Research supported by the grant Fault-tolerant Communication Complexity in Wireless Networks from the Singapore MoE AcRF-2.

F. Kuhn (Ed.): DISC 2014, LNCS 8784, pp. 469–483, 2014.
© Springer-Verlag Berlin Heidelberg 2014

Harris et al. [ICALP 2013]) and the *minimal connected dominating set problem*.

Our work shows that while some local symmetry breaking problems such as coloring can be solved in polylogarithmic rounds in both the LOCAL and CONGEST models, for many other hypergraph problems such as MIS, hitting set, and maximal clique, it remains challenging to obtain polylogarithmic time algorithms in the CONGEST model. This work is a step towards understanding this dichotomy in the complexity of hypergraph problems as well as using hypergraphs to design fast distributed algorithms for problems in (standard) graphs.

1   Introduction

The importance, as well as the difficulty, of solving problems on hypergraphs was pointed out recently by Linial, in his Dijkstra award talk [24]. While standard graphs[1] model *pairwise* interactions well, hypergraphs can be used to model *multi-way* interactions. For example, social network interactions include several individuals as a group, biological interactions involve several entities (e.g., proteins) interacting at the same time, distributed systems can involve several agents working together, or multiple clients who share a server (e.g., a cellular base station), or multiple servers who share a client, or shared channels in a wireless network. In particular, hypergraphs are especially useful in modelling social networks (e.g., [33]) and wireless networks (e.g., [2]). Unfortunately, as pointed out by Linial, much less is known for hypergraphs than for graphs. The focus of this paper is studying the complexity of fundamental local symmetry breaking problems in *hypergraphs*[2]. A related goal is to utilize these hypergraph algorithms for solving (standard) graph problems.

In the area of distributed computing for (standard) graphs, fundamental local symmetry breaking problems such as Maximal Independent Set (MIS) and coloring have been studied extensively (see e.g., [26,23,5,30,20] and the references therein). Problems such as MIS and coloring are "local" in the sense that a solution can be *verified* easily by purely local means (e.g., each node communicating only with its neighbors), but the solution itself should satisfy a global property (e.g., in the case of coloring, every node in the graph should have a color different from its neighbors and the total number of colors is at most $\Delta + 1$, where Δ is the maximum node degree). Computing an MIS or coloring locally is non-trivial because of the difficulty of *symmetry breaking*: nodes have to decide on their choices (e.g., whether they belong to the MIS or not) by only looking at a *small* neighbourhood around it. (In particular, to get an algorithm running in k rounds,

---

[1] Henceforth, when we say a graph, we just mean a standard (simple) graph.

[2] Formally, a hypergraph (V, F) consists of a set of (hyper)nodes V and a collection F of subsets of V; the sets that belong to F are called *hyperedges*. The *dimension* of a hypergraph is the maximum number of hypernodes that belong to a hyperedge. Throughout, we will use n for the number of nodes, m for the number of hyperedges, and Δ for the degree of the hypergraph which is the maximum node degree (i.e., the maximum number of edges a node is in). A standard graph is a hypergraph of dimension 2.

each node v has to make its decision by looking only at information on nodes within distance k from it.) Some of the most celebrated results in distributed algorithms are such fast localized algorithms. In particular, $O(\log n)$-round (randomized) distributed algorithms are well-known for MIS [26] and $\Delta + 1$-coloring [5] in both the LOCAL and CONGEST distributed computing models [30].

Besides the interest in understanding the complexity of fundamental problems, the solutions to such localizable symmetry breaking problems had many obvious applications. Examples are scheduling (such as avoiding the collision of radio transmissions, see e.g. [13], [9], or matching nodes such that each pair can communicate in parallel to the other pairs, see e.g. [4]), resource management (such as assigning clients to servers, see, e.g. [3]), and even for obtaining $O(Diameter)$ solutions to global problems that cannot be solved locally, such as MST computation [14,22].

In contrast to graphs which have been extensively studied in the context of distributed algorithms, many problems become much more challenging in the context of hypergraphs. An outstanding example is the MIS problem, whose local solutions for graphs were mentioned above. On the other hand, in hypergraphs (of arbitrary dimension) the complexity of MIS is wide open. (In a hypergraph, an MIS is a maximal subset I of hypernodes such that no subset of I forms an hyperedge.) Indeed, determining the parallel complexity (in the PRAM model) of the Maximal Independent Set (MIS) problem in hypergraphs (for arbitrary dimension) remains as one of the most important open problems in parallel computation; in particular, a key open problem is whether there exists a polylogarithmic time PRAM algorithm [17,6,19]. As discussed later, efficient CONGEST model distributed algorithms that uses simple local computations will also give efficient PRAM algorithms.

1.1   Main Results

We present distributed (randomized) algorithms for a variety of fundamental problems under a natural distributed computing model for hypergraphs (cf. Section 2).

Hypergraph MIS. A main focus is the hypergraph MIS problem which has been the subject of extensive research in the PRAM model (see e.g., [17,18,19,6,27]). We first show that MIS in hypergraphs (of arbitrary dimension) can be solved in $O(\log^2 n)$ distributed rounds (n is the number of nodes of the hypergraph) in the LOCAL model (cf. Theorem 1). We then present an $O(\Delta^\epsilon \operatorname{polylog} n)$ round algorithm for finding a MIS in hypergraphs of arbitrary dimension in the CONGEST model, where Δ is the maximum degree of the hypergraph (we refer to Theorem 1 for a precise statement of the bound) and $\epsilon > 0$ is any small positive constant. In the distributed computing model (both LOCAL and CONGEST), computation within a node is free; in one round, each node is allowed to compute any function of its current data. However, in our CONGEST model algorithms, each processor will perform very simple computations (but this is not true in the LOCAL model). In particular, each step of any node v can be simulated in $O(d_v)$ time by a single processor or in $O(\log m)$ time with d_v processors. Here, d_v is the degree of the node in the *server-client* computation model — cf. Section 2; $d_v = O(m)$, where m is the number of hyperedges. From these remarks, it follows that our algorithms can be simulated on the PRAM model to within an $O(\log m)$ factor slowdown using $O(m + n)$ processors. Thus our CONGEST model algorithm also implies a PRAM algorithm for hypergraph MIS running in $O(\Delta^\epsilon \text{ polylog } n \log m)$ rounds using a linear number of processors for a hypergraph of arbitrary dimension.

Algorithms for Standard Graph Problems Using Hypergraph MIS. In addition to the importance of hypergraph MIS as a hypergraph problem, we outline its importance to solving several natural symmetry breaking problems in (standard) graphs too. For the results discussed below, we assume the CONGEST model.

Consider first the following graph problem called the *restricted minimal dominating set (RMDS)* problem which arises as a key subproblem in other problems that we discuss later. We are given a (standard) graph $G = (V, E)$ and a subset of nodes $R \subseteq V$, such that R forms a dominating set in G (i.e., every node $v \in V$ is either adjacent to R or belongs to R). It is required to find a *minimal* dominating set *in* R that dominates V. (The minimality means that no subset of the solution can dominate V; it is easy to verify the minimality condition locally.) Note that if R is V itself, the problem can be solved by finding a MIS of G, since a MIS is also a minimal dominating set (MDS); hence an $O(\log n)$ algorithm exists. However, if R is some arbitrary proper subset of V (such that R dominates V), then no distributed algorithm running even in sublinear (in n) time (let alone polylogarithmic time) is known. Using our hypergraph MIS algorithm, we design a distributed algorithm for RMDS running in $O(\min\{\Delta^\epsilon \text{ polylog } n, n^{o(1)}\})$ rounds in the CONGEST model (Δ is the maximum node degree of the graph) — cf., Section 4.

RMDS arises naturally as the key subproblem in the solution of other problems, in particular, the *balanced minimal dominating set (BMDS)* problem [16] and the *minimal connected dominating set (MCDS)* problem. Given a (standard) graph, the BMDS problem (defined formally in Section 4) asks for a minimal dominating set whose average degree is small with respect to the average degree of the graph; this has applications to load balancing and fault-tolerance [16]. It was shown that such a set exists and can be found using a *centralized* algorithm [16]. Finding a fast distributed algorithm was a key problem left open in [16]. In Section 4, we use our hypergraph MIS algorithm of Section 3 to present an $\tilde{O}(D + \min\{\Delta^\epsilon, n^{o(1)}\})$ round algorithm (the notation $\tilde{O}$ hides a polylog n factor) for BMDS problem (in the CONGEST model), where D is the diameter (of the input standard graph) and Δ is the maximum node degree.

The MCDS problem is a variant (similar to variants studied in the context of wireless networks, e.g. [10]) of the well-studied *minimum* connected dominating set problem (which is NP-hard) [8,11]. In the MCDS problem, we require a dominating set that is connected and is *minimal* (i.e., no subset of the solution is a MCDS). In contrast to the approximate minimum connected dominating set problem (i.e., finding a connected dominating set that is not too large compared to the optimal) which admits efficient distributed algorithms [12,15] (polylogarithmic run time algorithms are known for both the LOCAL and CONGEST model for the unweighted case), we show that it is impossible to obtain an efficient distributed algorithm for MCDS. In Section 4, we use our hypergraph MIS algorithm of Section 3 as a subroutine to construct a distributed algorithm for MCDS that runs in time $\tilde{O}(D(D\min\{\Delta^\epsilon, n^{o(1)}\} + \sqrt{n}))$. We also show that $\tilde{\Omega}(D + \sqrt{n})$ is a lower bound on the run time for any distributed MCDS algorithm.

Algorithms for Other Hypergraph Problems. Besides MIS (and the above related standard graph problems), we also study distributed algorithms for coloring, maximal matching, and maximal clique in hypergraphs in the full paper. We show that a $\Delta + 1$-coloring of a hypergraph (of any arbitrary dimension) can be computed in $O(\log n)$ rounds (this generalizes the result for standard graphs). We also show that maximal matching in hypergraphs can be solved in $O(\log m)$ rounds. Maximal clique is a less-studied problem, even in the case of graphs, but nevertheless interesting. Given a (standard) graph $G = (V, E)$, a maximal clique (MC) L is subset of V such that L is a clique in G and is maximal (i.e., it is not contained in a bigger clique). MC is related to MIS since any MIS in the complement graph G^c is an MC in G. For a hypergraph, one can define an MC with respect to the server graph (cf. Section 2). Finding MC has applications in finding a *non-dominated coterie* in quorum systems [28]. We show that an MC in a hypergraph can be found in $O(\text{DIM}\log n)$ rounds, where DIM is the dimension of the hypergraph and n is the number of nodes. All the above results hold in the CONGEST model as well.

1.2   Technical Overview and Other Related Work

We study two natural network models for computing with hypergraphs — the *server-client* model and the *vertex-centric* models (cf. Section 2). Our algorithmic results apply to both models (except the one on maximal matching).

The distributed MIS problem on hypergraphs is significantly more challenging than that on (standard) graphs. Simple variants/modifications of the distributed algorithms on graphs (e.g., Luby's algorithm and its variants [26,29,30]) do not seem to work for higher dimensions, even for hypergraphs of dimension 3. For example, running Luby's algorithm or its permutation variant [26] on a (standard) graph by replacing each hyperedge with a clique does not work — in the graph there can be only one node in the MIS, whereas in the hypergraph all nodes of the clique, expect one, can be in the MIS. It has been conjectured by Beame and Luby [6] that a generalisation of the permutation variant of an algorithm due to Luby [26] can give a polylog$(m + n)$ run time in the PRAM model, but this has not been proven so far (note that this bound itself can be large, since m can be exponential in n).

Our distributed hypergraph MIS algorithm (Section 3) consists of several ingredients. A key ingredient is the *decomposition lemma* (cf. Lemma 3) that shows that the problem can be reduced to solving a MIS problem in a low diameter network. The lemma is essentially an application of the *network decomposition* algorithm of Linial and Saks [25]. This applies to the CONGEST model as well — the main task in the proof is to show that the Linial-Saks decomposition works

for (both) the hypergraph models in the CONGEST setting. The polylogarithmic run time bound for the LOCAL model follows easily from the decomposition
lemma. However, this approach fails in the CONGEST model, since it involves
collecting a lot of information at some nodes. The next ingredient is to show how
the PRAM algorithm of Beame and Luby [6] can be simulated efficiently in the
distributed setting; this we show is possible in a low diameter graph. Kelsen's
analysis [19] of Beame-Luby's algorithm (which shows a polylogarithmic time
bound in the PRAM model for *constant* dimension hypergraphs) immediately
gives a polylogarithmic round algorithm in the CONGEST model for a hyper-
graph of *constant* dimension. To obtain the $\tilde{O}(\Delta^\epsilon)$ algorithm (for any constant
$\epsilon > 0$) for a hypergraph of *arbitrary* dimension in the CONGEST model, we
use another ingredient: we generalize a theorem of Turan (cf. Theorem 6) for
hypergraphs — this shows that a hypergraph of low average degree has a *large*
independent set. We show further that such a large independent set can be found
when the network diameter is $O(\log n)$. Combining this theorem with the analysis of Beame and Luby's algorithm gives the result for the CONGEST model
for any dimension. Our CONGEST model algorithm, as pointed out earlier, also
implies a $\tilde{O}(\Delta^\epsilon)$ round algorithm for the PRAM model. Recently, independently
of our result, Bercea et al.[7] use a similar approach to obtain an improved algorithm for the PRAM model. In particular, they improve Kelsen's analysis of
Beame-Luby algorithm to apply also for slightly *super-constant* dimension. This
improved analysis of Kelsen also helps us in obtaining a slightly better bound
(cf. Theorem 1).

We apply our hypergraph MIS algorithm to solve two key problems — BMDS
and MCDS. The BMDS problem was posed in Harris et al. [16], but no efficient
distributed algorithm was known. A key bottleneck was solving the RMDS problem (defined earlier) which appears as a subroutine in solving BMDS. We can view
RMDS as a hypergraph problem. To see this, it is useful to define a hypergraph using the following *server-client bipartite graph model* $B = (S, C)$: the server set S
represents the nodes of the hypergraph and the client set C represents the hyperedges; an edge is present between a server s and a client c if and only if node s
belongs to the hyperedge c. Given an instance of the RMDS problem, we take the
server set as R and the client set as V and an edge is present between a server and a
client if the server is adjacent to (or is the same as) the client in the given graph G.
Solving the RMDS problem now reduces to solving the *minimal hitting set (MHS)*
(same as the *minimal vertex cover(MVC)*) problem[3] in this hypergraph (cf., Section 4). Since a MHS is just the complement of the MIS (in the server set), this
reduces to solving MIS problem in a hypergraph.

The MCDS problem, to the best of our knowledge, has not been considered
before and seems significantly harder to solve in the distributed setting compared to the more well-studied approximate version of the connected dominating set problem [12,15]. The key difficulty is being *minimal* with respect to *both*

---

[3] A MHS (same as MVC) of a hypergraph is a minimal subset H of hypernodes that such
that $H \cap e \neq \emptyset$, for every hyperedge e of the hypergraph. Note that the complement
of a MHS is a MIS.

connectivity and domination. We use a layered approach to the problem, by first constructing a breadth-first tree (BFS) and then adding nodes to the MCDS, level by level of the tree (starting with the leaves). We also show a lower bound of $\tilde{\Omega}(D + \sqrt{n})$ for the MCDS problem by using the techniques of Das Sarma et al. [31]. This lower bound holds even when $D = \mathrm{polylog}\, n$. In this case, our upper bound is tight up to a $\mathrm{polylog}\, n$ factor. We also show that $\Omega(D)$ is a *universal* lower bound for MCDS as well as for maximal clique and spanning tree problems, i.e., it applies essentially to all graphs. These are shown in the full paper.

2 Preliminaries

A hypergraph $\mathcal{H}$ consists of a set $V(\mathcal{H})$ of n (hyper)nodes and a set family $E(\mathcal{H})$ of m hyperedges, each of which is a subset of $V(\mathcal{H})$. We define the *degree of node* u to be the total number of hyperedges that u is contained in. Furthermore, we define the *degree of the hypergraph*, denoted by Δ, as the maximum over all hypernode degrees. The size of each hyperedge is bounded by the *dimension* DIM of $\mathcal{H}$; note that a hypergraph of dimension 2 is a graph.

We now introduce our main model of computation. In our distributed model, $\mathcal{H}$ is realized as a (standard) undirected bipartite graph G with vertex sets S and C where $|S| = n$ and $|C| = m$. We call S the set of *servers* and C the set of *clients* and denote this realization of a hypergraph as the *server-client model*. That is, every vertex in S corresponds to a vertex in $\mathcal{H}$ and every vertex in C corresponds to a hyperedge of $\mathcal{H}$. For simplicity, we use the same identifiers for vertices in C as for the hyperedges in $\mathcal{H}$. There exists a (2-dimensional) edge in G from a server $u \in S$ to a client $e \in C$ if and only if $u \in e$. See Figure 1a for an example. Thus, the degree of $\mathcal{H}$ is precisely the maximum degree of the servers and the dimension of $\mathcal{H}$ is given by the maximum degree of the clients.

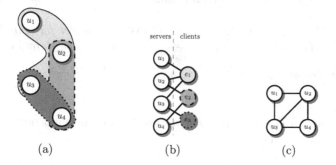

(a)   (b)   (c)

Fig. 1. Figure (a) depicts a hypergraph consisting of vertices $u_1, \ldots, u_4$ and edges $e_1 = \{u_1, u_2, u_3\}$, $e_2 = \{u_2, u_4\}$, and $e_3 = \{u_3, u_4\}$. Figures (b) and (c) respectively show this hypergraph in the bipartite server-client model and the vertex-centric model.

An alternative way to model a hypergraph $\mathcal{H}$ as a distributed network is the *vertex-centric* model (cf. Figure 1c). Here, the nodes are exactly the nodes of

$\mathcal{H}$ and there exists a communication link between nodes u and v if and only if there exists a hyperedge $e \in E(\mathcal{H})$ such that $u, v \in e$. Note that in this model, we assume that every node locally knows all hyperedges in which it is contained. For any hypergraph $\mathcal{H}$, we call the above underlying communication graph in the vertex-centric model (which is a standard graph) the *server graph*, denoted by $G(\mathcal{H})$.

We consider the standard synchronous round model (cf. [30]) of communication. That is, each node has a unique id (arbitrarily assigned from some set of size polynomial in n) and executes an instance of a distributed algorithm that advances in discrete *rounds*. To correctly model the computation in a hypergraph, we assume that each node knows whether it is a server or a client. In each round every node can communicate with its neighbors (according to the edges in the server-client graph) and perform some local computation. We do not assume shared memory and nodes do not have any a priori knowledge about the network at large.

We will consider two types of models — CONGEST and LOCAL [30]. In the CONGEST model, only a $O(\log n)$-sized message can be sent across a communication edge per round. In the LOCAL model, there is no such restriction. Unless otherwise stated, we use the CONGEST model in our algorithms.

Due to lack of space, the complete proofs can be found in the full paper.

3   Distributed Algorithms for Hypergraph MIS Problem

We present randomized distributed algorithms and prove the following for the hypergraph MIS problem:

Theorem 1. *The hypergraph MIS problem can be solved in the following expected time[4] in both vertex-centric and server-client representations.*

1. *$O(\log^2 n)$ time in the LOCAL model.*
2. *$O(\log^{(d+4)!+4} n)$ time[5] in the CONGEST model when the input hypergraph has constant dimension d.*
3. *$O(\min\{\Delta^\epsilon \log^{(1/\epsilon)^{O(1/\epsilon)}} n, \sqrt{n}\})$ time in the CONGEST model for any dimension, where ϵ is such that $1 \geq \epsilon \geq \frac{1}{\frac{\log\log n}{c \log\log\log n} - 1}$ from some (large) constant c. (In particular, $\Delta^\epsilon \log^{(1/\epsilon)^{O(1/\epsilon)}} n$ becomes $\Delta^{o(1)} n^{o(1)}$ when we use $\epsilon = \frac{1}{\frac{\log\log n}{c \log\log\log n} - 1}$.)*

In Section 3.1, we prove a *decomposition lemma* which plays an important role in achieving all the above results.

3.1   Low-Diameter Decomposition

First, we note that, for solving MIS, it is sufficient to construct an algorithm that solves the following *subgraph-MIS* problem on low-diameter networks.

---

[4] Our time bounds can also be easily shown to hold with high probability, i.e., with probability $1 - 1/n$.

[5] As is common, we use the notation $\log^f n$ which is the same as $(\log n)^f$.

Definition 2 (Subgraph-MIS Problem). *In the Subgraph-MIS problem, we are given an n-node network G. This network is either in a vertex-centric or server-client representation of some hypergraph $\mathcal{H}$. Additionally, we are given a subnetwork G' of G representing a sub-hypergraph[6] $\mathcal{H}'$ of $\mathcal{H}$. The goal is to find an MIS of $\mathcal{H}'$.*

Lemma 3 (Decomposition Lemma). *For any function T, if there is an algorithm $\mathcal{A}$ that solves subgraph-MIS on CONGEST server-client (respectively vertex-centric) networks G of $O(\log n)$ diameter in $T(n)$ time (where n is the number of nodes in G), then there is an algorithm for MIS on CONGEST server-client (respectively vertex-centric) networks of any diameter that takes $O(T(n)\log^4 n)$ time.*

The main idea of the lemma is to run the *network decomposition* algorithm of Linial and Saks [25] and simulate $\mathcal{A}$ on each cluster resulting from the decomposition. The only part that we have to be careful is that running $\mathcal{A}$ simultaneously on many clusters could cause a congestion. We show that this can be avoided by a careful scheduling. The details are as follows.

The network decomposition algorithm of [25] produces an $O(\log n)$-*decomposition with weak-diameter* $O(\log n)$. That is, given a (two-dimensional) graph G, it partitions nodes into sets $S_1, S_2, \ldots S_k$ and assigns color $c_i \in \{1, 2, \ldots, O(\log n)\}$ to each set S_i with the following properties:
- the distance between any two nodes in the same set S_i is $O(\log n)$, and
- any two neighboring nodes of the same color must be in the same set (in other words, any two "neighboring" sets must be assigned different colors).

This algorithm takes $O(\log^2 n)$ time even in the CONGEST model [25]. We use the above decomposition algorithm to decompose the server graph $G(\mathcal{H})$ (cf. Section 2) of the input hypergraph. The result is the partition of hypernodes (servers) into colored sets satisfying the above conditions (in particular, two nodes sharing the same hyperedge must be in the same partition or have differnet colors). In addition, we modify the Linial-Saks (LS) algorithm to produce low-diameter subgraphs that contain these sets with the property that subgraphs of the same color have "small overlap".

Lemma 4. *Let G be the input network (server-client or vertex-centric model) representing hypergraph $\mathcal{H}$. In $O(\log^3 n)$ time and for some integer k, we can partition hypernodes into k sets $S_1, \ldots, S_k$, produce k subgraphs of G denoted by $G_1, G_2, \ldots G_k$, and assign color $c_i \in \{1, 2, \ldots, O(\log n)\}$ to each subgraph G_i, with the following properties:*
1. *For all i, G_i has diameter $O(\log n)$ and $S_i \subseteq V(G_i)$.*
2. *For any S_i and S_j that are assigned the same color (i.e. $c_i = c_j$), there is no hyperedge in $\mathcal{H}$ that contains hypernodes (servers) in both S_i and S_j.*
3. *Every edge in G is contained in $O(\log^3 n)$ graphs $G_{i_1}, G_{i_2}, \ldots$*

---

[6] Given a subset $V' \subseteq V$, a sub-hypergraph of $\mathcal{H}$ is simply a hypergraph induced by V' — except hyperedges that contain vertices that do not belong to V', all other hyperedges of $\mathcal{H}$ (which intersect with V') are present in the sub-hypergraph.

Observe that the first two properties in Theorem 4 are similar to the guarantees of the Linial-Saks algorithm, except that Theorem 4 explicitly gives low-diameter graphs that contain the sets $S_1, \ldots, S_k$. The third property guarantees that such graphs have "small congestion".

Lemma 5. *MIS can be solved in $O(\log^2 n)$ rounds in the LOCAL models (both vertex-centric and server-client representations).*

Proof (Proof Sketch). Using Theorem 4, we partition the hypernodes of the input network into subgraphs each of which have $O(\log n)$ diameter and no two subgraphs assigned the same colour share a hyper edge. Note that there is no congestion in the LOCAL model when we simulate $\mathcal{A}$ (as specified in Lemma 3) on all graphs of color i. Thus, we need $O(T(n))$ time per color instead of $O(T(n) \log^3 n)$. Moreover, we can solve the subgraph-MIS problem on a network of $O(\log n)$ diameter in $O(\log n)$ time by collecting the information about the subgraph to one node, locally compute the MIS on such node, and send the solution back to every node. Thus, $T(n) = O(\log n)$. It follows that we can solve MIS on networks of any diameter in $O(\log^2 n)$ time.

3.2 $O(\log^{(d+4)!+4} n)$ Time in the CONGEST Model Assuming Constant Dimension d

Let $(\mathcal{H}, \mathcal{H}')$ be an instance of the subgraph-MIS problem such that the network G representing $\mathcal{H}$ has $O(\log n)$ diameter. We now show that we can solve this problem in $O(\log^{(d+4)!} n)$ time when $\mathcal{H}'$ has a constant dimension d, i.e. $|e| \leq d$ for every hyperedge e in $\mathcal{H}'$. By Theorem 3, we will get a $O(\log^{(d+4)!+4} n)$-time algorithm for the MIS problem in the case of constant-dimensional hypergraphs (of any diameter) which works in both vertex-centric and server-client representations and even in the CONGEST model. This algorithm is also an important building block for the algorithm in the next section.

Our algorithm simulates the PRAM algorithm of Beame and Luby [6] which was proved by Kelsen [19] to finish in $O(\log^{(d+4)!} n)$ time when the input hypergraph has a constant dimension d and this running time was recently extended to any $d \leq \frac{\log \log n}{4 \log \log \log n}$ by Bercea et al. [7][7]. The crucial part in the simulation is to compute a number $\zeta(\mathcal{H}')$ defined as follows. For $\emptyset \neq x \subseteq V(\mathcal{H}')$ and an integer j with $1 \leq j \leq d - |x|$ we define: $N_j(x, \mathcal{H}') = \{y \subseteq V(\mathcal{H}') \mid x \cup y \in E(\mathcal{H}') \wedge x \cap y = \emptyset \wedge |y| = j\}$, and $d_j(x, \mathcal{H}') = (|N_j(x, \mathcal{H}')|)^{1/j}$. Also, for $2 \leq i \leq d$, let[8] $\zeta_i(\mathcal{H}') = \max\{d_{i-|x|}(x, \mathcal{H}') \mid x \subseteq V(\mathcal{H}') \wedge 0 < |x| < i\}$ and $\zeta(\mathcal{H}') = \max\{\zeta_i(\mathcal{H}') \mid 2 \leq i \leq d\}$. We now explain how to compute $\zeta(\mathcal{H}')$ in

---

[7] The original running time of Kelsen [19] is in fact $O((\log n)^{f(d)})$ where $f(d)$ is defined as $f(2) = 7$ and $f(i) = (i-1)\sum_{j=2}^{i-1} f(j) + 7$ for $i > 2$. The $O(\log^{(d+4)!} n)$ time (which is essentially the same as Kelsen's time) was shown in [7]. We will use the latter running time for simplicity. Also note that the result in this section holds for all $d \leq \frac{\log \log n}{4 \log \log \log n}$ due to [7].

[8] A note on the notation: [6,19] use Δ to denote what we use ζ to denote here. We use a different notation since we use Δ for another purpose.

$O(\log^{(d+4)!} n)$ time. First, note that we can assume that every node knows the list of members in each hyperedge that contains it: this information is already available in the vertex-centric representation; and in the server-client representation, every hyperedge can send this list to all nodes that it contains in $O(d)$ time in the CONGEST model. Every node v can now compute, for every i, $\zeta_i(v, \mathcal{H}') = \max\{d_{i-|x|}(x, \mathcal{H}') \mid x \subseteq V(\mathcal{H}') \wedge 0 < |x| < i \wedge v \in x\}$. This does not require any communication since for any x such that $v \in x$, node v already knows all hyperedges that contain x (they must be hyperedges that contain v). Now, we compute $\zeta(\mathcal{H}') = \max\{\zeta_i(v, \mathcal{H}') \mid 2 \leq i \leq d \wedge v \in V(\mathcal{H}')\}$ by computing through the breadth-first search tree of the network representing $\mathcal{H}$ (this is where we need the fact that the network has $O(\log n)$ diameter).

Once we get $\zeta(\mathcal{H}')$, the rest of the simulation is trivial; we refer to the full paper for details.

3.3 $\Delta^\epsilon \log^{(1/\epsilon)^{O(1/\epsilon)}} n$ and $\Delta^{o(1)} n^{o(1)}$ Time in the CONGEST Model

We rely on a modification of Turán's theorem, which states that a (two-dimensional) graph of *low* average degree has a *large* independent set (see e.g. Alon and Spencer [1]). We show that this theorem also holds for high-dimensional hypergraphs, and show further that such a large independent set can be found w.h.p when the network diameter is $O(\log n)$.

Lemma 6 (A simple extension of Turán's theorem). *Let $d \geq 2$ and $\delta \geq 2$ be any integers. Let $\mathcal{H}$ be any hypergraph such that every hyperedge in $\mathcal{H}$ has dimension at least d, there are n hypernodes, and the average hypernode degree is δ. (Note that the diameter of the network representing $\mathcal{H}$ can be arbitrary.) If every node knows δ and d, then we can find an independent set M whose size in expectation is at least $\frac{n}{\delta^{1/(d-1)}}(1 - \frac{1}{d})$ in $O(1)$ time.*

Algorithm. We use the following algorithm to solve the subgraph-MIS problem on a sub-hypergraph $\mathcal{H}'$ of $\mathcal{H}$, assuming that the network representing $\mathcal{H}$ has $O(\log n)$ diameter. Let $n' = |V(\mathcal{H}')|$. Let d be an arbitrarily large constant. Let $\mathcal{H}'_d$ be the sub-hypergraph of $\mathcal{H}'$ where $V(\mathcal{H}'_d) = V(\mathcal{H}')$ and we only keep hyperedges of dimension (i.e. size) at least d in $\mathcal{H}'_d$. (It is possible that $\mathcal{H}'_d$ contains no edge.) We then find an independent set of expected size at least $\frac{n'}{\Delta^{1/(d-1)}}(1 - 1/d)$ in $\mathcal{H}'_d$, denoted by S; this can be done in $O(1)$ time by Theorem 6 (note that we use the fact that $\delta \leq \Delta$ here). Let $\mathcal{H}'_S$ be the sub-hypergraph of $\mathcal{H}'$ induced by nodes in S. Note that $\mathcal{H}'_S$ does not contain any hyperedge in $\mathcal{H}'_d$ and thus has dimension at most d, which is a constant. So, we can run the $O(\log^{(d+4)!} n)$-time algorithm from Section 3.2 to find an MIS of $\mathcal{H}'_S$. We let M'_S be such a MIS of $\mathcal{H}'_S$.

Our intention is to use M'_S as part of some MIS M' of $\mathcal{H}'$. Of course, any hypernode v in $V(\mathcal{H}'_S) \setminus M'_S$ cannot be in such M' since $M' \cup \{v\}$ will contain some hyperedge e in $\mathcal{H}'_S$ which is also a hyperedge in $\mathcal{H}'$. It is thus left to find which hypernodes in $V(H') \setminus S$ should be added to M'_S to construct an MIS M' of $\mathcal{H}'$. To do this, we use the following hypergraph. Let $\mathcal{H}''$ be the sub-hypergraph of $\mathcal{H}'$ such that $V(\mathcal{H}'') = V(\mathcal{H}') \setminus S$ and for every hyperedge $e \in E(\mathcal{H}')$, we add a hyperedge $e \cap V(\mathcal{H}'')$ to $\mathcal{H}''$ if and only if $e \subseteq M'_S \cup V(\mathcal{H}'')$; in other words, we keep edge e that would be "violated" if we add every hypernode in $\mathcal{H}''$ to M'. We now find an MIS M'' of $\mathcal{H}''$ by recursively running the same algorithm with $\mathcal{H}''$, instead of $\mathcal{H}'$, as a subgraph of $\mathcal{H}$. The correctness follows from the following claim (see the full paper for the proof).

Claim. $M' = M'_S \cup M''$ is a MIS of $\mathcal{H}'$.

We now analyze the running time of this algorithm. Recall that $E[|S|] \geq \frac{n'}{\delta^{(1/(d-1))}}(1 - 1/d)$. In other words, the expected value of $|V(\mathcal{H}'')| \leq (1 - \frac{c(d)}{\Delta^{1/(d-1)}})|V(\mathcal{H}')|$ where $c(d) = \frac{1}{2}(1 - 1/d)$ is a constant which is strictly less than one (recall that d is a constant). It follows that the expected number of recursion calls is $O(\Delta^{\frac{1}{d-1}})$. Since we need $O(\log^{(d+4)!} n)$ time to compute M'_S and to construct $\mathcal{H}''$, the total running time is $O(\Delta^{\frac{1}{d-1}} \log^{(d+4)!} n)$. By Theorem 3, we can compute MIS on any hypergraph $\mathcal{H}$ (of any diameter) in $O(\Delta^{\frac{1}{d-1}} \log^{(d+4)!+4} n)$ time. For any constant $\epsilon > 0$, we set $d = 1 + 1/\epsilon$ to get the claimed running time of $O(\Delta^\epsilon \log^{(5+1/\epsilon)!+4} n) = \Delta^\epsilon \log^{(1/\epsilon)^{O(1/\epsilon)}} n$. Moreover, by the recent result of Bercea et al. [7], we can in fact set d as large as $\frac{\log \log n}{4 \log \log \log n}$. If we set $d = \frac{\log \log n}{c \log \log \log n}$ for some large enough constant c, the term $\log^{(d+4)!} n$ can be bounded by $n^{o(1)}$ and thus the running time becomes $\Delta^{o(1)} n^{o(1)}$.

We obtain the $O(\sqrt{n})$ time by modifying the PRAM algorithm of Karp, Upfal, and Wigderson [18, Section 4.1]. This algorithm can be found in the full version.

4   Applications of Hypergraph MIS Algorithms to Standard Graph Problems

In this section we show that our distributed hypergraph algorithms have direct applications in the standard graph setting.

Restricted Minimal Dominating Set (RMDS).   We are given a (standard) graph $G = (V, E)$ and a subset of nodes $R \subseteq V$, such that R forms a dominating set in G (i.e., every node $v \in V$ is either adjacent to R or belongs to R). We are required to find a *minimal* dominating set that is a subset of R and dominates V. Since a minimal vertex cover is the complement of a maximal independent set, we can leverage our MIS algorithm (cf. Section 3). To this end, we show that the RMDS problem can be solved by finding a minimal hitting set (or minimal vertex cover) on a specific hypergraph H. The server client representation of H is determined by G and R as follows: For every vertex in V we add a client (i.e. hyperedge) and, for every vertex in R, we also add a server. Thus, for every vertex $u \in V$, we have a client e_u and, if $u \in R$, we also have a server s_u. We then connect a server s_u to a client e_v, iff either u and v are adjacent in G, or $u = v$. See the full paper for the complete pseudo code of this construction. Note that we can simulate this server client network on the given graph with constant overhead in the CONGEST model. We have the following result by virtue of Theorem 1:

Nodes compute the average network degree δ.

Every node u of degree $> 2\delta$ marks itself with probability $\frac{\log t}{t}$ where $t = \frac{2\delta \log \delta}{\log \log \delta}$.

Every node of degree $\leq 2\delta$ marks itself.

If a node v is not marked, and none of the neighbors of v are marked, then v marks itself.

Let MARKED be the set of nodes that are marked. Invoke the RMDS algorithm (cf. Section 4) on G where the restricted set is given by MARKED.

Every node that is in the solution set of the RMDS algorithm remains in the final output set.

Algorithm 4.1. A distributed BMDS-algorithm

Theorem 7. RMDS *can be solved in expected time* $\tilde{O}(\min\{\Delta^\epsilon, n^{o(1)}\})$ *(for any const.* $\epsilon > 0$*) on graph* G *in the CONGEST model and in time* $O(\log^2 n)$ *in the LOCAL model where* Δ *is the maximum degree of* G.

Balanced Minimal Dominating Set. We define the *average degree* of a (standard) graph G, denoted by δ, as the total degrees of its vertices (degree of a vertex is its degree in G) divided by the number of vertices in G. A *balanced minimal dominating set (BMDS)* (cf. [16]) is a minimal dominating set D in G that minimizes the ratio of the average degree of D to that of the graph itself (the average degree of the set of nodes D is defined as the average degree of the subgraph induced by D). A *centralized* polynomial time algorithm for computing a BMDS with (the best possible in general [9]) average degree $O(\frac{\delta \log \delta}{\log \log \delta})$ was given in [16]. A distributed algorithm that gives the same bounds was left a key open problem. We now present a distributed variant of this algorithm (cf. Algorithm 4.1) that uses our hypergraph MIS-algorithm as a subroutine.

Theorem 8. *Let* δ *be the average degree of a graph* G. *There is a CONGEST model algorithm that finds a BMDS with average degree* $O(\frac{\delta \log \delta}{\log \log \delta})$ *in expected* $\tilde{O}(D + \min\{\Delta^\epsilon, n^{o(1)}\})$ *rounds, where* D *is the diameter,* Δ *is the maximum node degree of* G, *and* $\epsilon > 0$ *is any constant.*

Minimal Connected Dominating Sets (MCDS). Given a graph G, the MCDS problem requires us to find a minimal dominating set M that is connected in G. We now describe our distributed algorithm for solving MCDS in the CONGEST model (see the full paper for the complete pseudo code) and argue its correctness. We first elect a node u as the leader using a $O(D)$ time algorithm of [21]. Node u initiates the construction of a BFS tree B, which has $k \leq D$ levels, after which every node knows its level (i.e. distance from the leader u) in the tree B. Starting at the leaf nodes (at level k), we convergecast the maximum level to the root u, which then broadcasts the overall maximum tree level to all nodes in B along the edges of B.

We then proceed in iterations processing two adjacent tree levels at a time, starting with nodes at the maximum level k. Note that since every node knows k and its own level, it knows after how many iterations it needs to become active. Therefore, we assume for simplicity that all leafs of B are on level k. We now describe a single iteration concerning levels i and $i - 1$: First, consider the set

---

[9] That is, there exists graphs with average degree δ, where this bound is essentially the optimal.

L_i of level i nodes that have already been added to the output set M in some previous iteration; initially, for $i = k$, set L_i will be empty. We run the $O(D+\sqrt{n})$ time algorithm of [32] to find maximal connected components among the nodes in L_i in the graph G; let $\mathcal{C} = \{C_1, \ldots, C_\alpha\}$ be the set of these components and let ℓ_j be the designated component leader of component $C_j \in \mathcal{C}$.

We now simulate a hypergraph that is defined as the following bipartite server client graph H: Consider each component in $\mathcal{C}$ as a *super-node*; we call the other nodes on level i *non-super-nodes*. The set C of clients contains all super-nodes in $\mathcal{C}$ and all nodes on level i that are neither adjacent to any super-node nor have been added to the output set O. The set S of servers contains all nodes on level $i - 1$. The edges of H are the induced inter-level edges of G between servers and non-super-node clients. In addition, we add an edge between a server $s \in S$ and a (super-node) client $C_j \in \mathcal{C}$, iff there exists a $v \in C_j$ such that $(v, s) \in E(G)$. Conceptually, we can think of the edges incident to C_j as pointing to the component leader node ℓ_j. Next, we find a MIS (cf. Section 3) on the (virtual) hypergraph H. We refer to the full paper for details.

Theorem 9. MCDS *can be solved in the CONGEST model in expected time* $\tilde{O}(D(D \min\{\Delta^{o(1)}, n^{o(1)}\} + \sqrt{n}))$.

References

1. Alon, N., Spencer, J.: The Probabilistic Method. Series in Discrete Mathematics and Optimization. Wiley (2008), http://books.google.co.jp/books?id=V8YgNioxF6AC
2. Avin, C., Lando, Y., Lotker, Z.: Radio cover time in hyper-graphs. Ad Hoc Networks 12, 278–290 (2014)
3. Azar, Y., Naor, J., Rom, R.: The competitiveness of on-line assignments. In: Frederickson, G.N. (ed.) SODA, pp. 203–210. ACM/SIAM (1992), http://dblp.uni-trier.de/db/conf/soda/soda92.html#AzarNR92
4. Balakrishnan, H., Barrett, C.L., Kumar, V.S.A., Marathe, M.V., Thite, S.: The distance-2 matching problem and its relationship to the mac-layer capacity of ad hoc wireless networks. IEEE Journal on Selected Areas in Communications 22(6), 1069–1079 (2004)
5. Barenboim, L., Elkin, M.: Distributed Graph Coloring: Fundamentals and Recent Developments. Synthesis Lectures on Distributed Computing Theory. Morgan & Claypool Publishers (2013)
6. Beame, P., Luby, M.: Parallel search for maximal independence given minimal dependence. In: SODA, pp. 212–218 (1990)
7. Bercea, I., Goyal, N., Harris, D., Srinivasan, A.: On computing maximal independent sets of hypergraphs in parallel. In: SPAA (June 2014)
8. Chen, Y.P., Liestman, A.L.: Approximating minimum size weakly-connected dominating sets for clustering mobile ad hoc networks. In: MobiHoc, pp. 165–172 (2002)
9. Chlamtac, I., Kutten, S.: Tree-based broadcasting in multihop radio networks. IEEE Trans. Computers 36(10), 1209–1223 (1987)
10. Dai, F., Wu, J.: An extended localized algorithm for connected dominating set formation in ad hoc wireless networks. IEEE Trans. Parallel Distrib. Syst. 15(10), 908–920 (2004), http://dx.doi.org/10.1109/TPDS.2004.48
11. Das, B., Bharghavan, V.: Routing in ad-hoc networks using minimum connected dominating sets. In: ICC (1), pp. 376–380 (1997)

12. Dubhashi, D.P., Mei, A., Panconesi, A., Radhakrishnan, J., Srinivasan, A.: Fast distributed algorithms for (weakly) connected dominating sets and linear-size skeletons. J. Comput. Syst. Sci. 71(4), 467–479 (2005)
13. Ephremides, A., Truong, T.V.: Scheduling broadcasts in multihop radio networks. IEEE Transactions on Communications 38(4), 456–460 (1990)
14. Garay, J.A., Kutten, S., Peleg, D.: A sublinear time distributed algorithm for minimum-weight spanning trees. SIAM J. Comput. 27(1), 302–316 (1998)
15. Ghaffari, M.: Near-optimal distributed approximation of minimum-weight connected dominating set. In: Esparza, J., Fraigniaud, P., Husfeldt, T., Koutsoupias, E. (eds.) ICALP 2014, Part II. LNCS, vol. 8573, pp. 483–494. Springer, Heidelberg (2014)
16. Harris, D.G., Morsy, E., Pandurangan, G., Robinson, P., Srinivasan, A.: Efficient computation of balanced structures. In: Fomin, F.V., Freivalds, R., Kwiatkowska, M., Peleg, D. (eds.) ICALP 2013, Part II. LNCS, vol. 7966, pp. 581–593. Springer, Heidelberg (2013)
17. Karp, R.M., Ramachandran, V.: Parallel algorithms for shared-memory machines. In: Handbook of Theoretical Computer Science, vol. A, pp. 869–942 (1990)
18. Karp, R.M., Upfal, E., Wigderson, A.: The complexity of parallel search. J. Comput. Syst. Sci. 36(2), 225–253 (1988), announced at STOC 1985 and FOCS 1985
19. Kelsen, P.: On the parallel complexity of computing a maximal independent set in a hypergraph. In: STOC, pp. 339–350 (1992)
20. Kuhn, F., Moscibroda, T., Wattenhofer, R.: Local computation: Lower and upper bounds. CoRR abs/1011.5470 (2010)
21. Kutten, S., Pandurangan, G., Peleg, D., Robinson, P., Trehan, A.: On the complexity of universal leader election. In: PODC, pp. 100–109 (2013)
22. Kutten, S., Peleg, D.: Fast distributed construction of small k-dominating sets and applications. J. Algorithms 28(1), 40–66 (1998)
23. Linial, N.: Locality in distributed graph algorithms. SIAM J. Comput. 21(1), 193–201 (1992)
24. Linial, N.: Dijkstra award talk Jerusalem (2013),
    http://www.cs.huji.ac.il/~nati/PAPERS/disc_2013.pdf
25. Linial, N., Saks, M.E.: Low diameter graph decompositions. Combinatorica 13(4), 441–454 (1993)
26. Luby, M.: A simple parallel algorithm for the maximal independent set problem. SIAM J. Comput. 15(4), 1036–1053 (1986), announced at STOC 1985
27. Luczak, T., Szymanska, E.: A parallel randomized algorithm for finding a maximal independent set in a linear hypergraph. J. Algorithms 25(2), 311–320 (1997)
28. Makino, K., Kameda, T.: Efficient generation of all regular non-dominated coteries. In: PODC, pp. 279–288 (2000)
29. Métivier, Y., Robson, J.M., Saheb-Djahromi, N., Zemmari, A.: An optimal bit complexity randomized distributed mis algorithm. Distributed Computing 23(5-6), 331–340 (2011)
30. Peleg, D.: Distributed Computing: A Locality-Sensitive Approach. SIAM, Philadelphia (2000)
31. Sarma, A.D., Holzer, S., Kor, L., Korman, A., Nanongkai, D., Pandurangan, G., Peleg, D., Wattenhofer, R.: Distributed verification and hardness of distributed approximation. SIAM J. Comput. 41(5), 1235–1265 (2012)
32. Thurimella, R.: Sub-linear distributed algorithms for sparse certificates and biconnected components. J. Algorithms 23(1), 160–179 (1997)
33. Wasserman, S., Faust, K.: Social network analysis: Methods and Applications. Cambridge University Press (1994)

On Streaming and Communication Complexity of the Set Cover Problem

Erik D. Demaine, Piotr Indyk, Sepideh Mahabadi, and Ali Vakilian

Massachusetts Institute of Technology (MIT)
{edemaine,indyk,mahabadi,vakilian}@mit.edu

Abstract. We develop the first streaming algorithm and the first two-party communication protocol that uses a constant number of passes/rounds and sublinear space/communication for logarithmic approximation to the classic Set Cover problem. Specifically, for n elements and m sets, our algorithm/protocol achieves a space bound of $O(m \cdot n^\delta \log^2 n \log m)$ using $O(4^{1/\delta})$ passes/rounds while achieving an approximation factor of $O(4^{1/\delta} \log n)$ in polynomial time (for $\delta = \Omega(1/\log n)$). If we allow the algorithm/protocol to spend exponential time per pass/round, we achieve an approximation factor of $O(4^{1/\delta})$. Our approach uses randomization, which we show is necessary: no deterministic constant approximation is possible (even given exponential time) using $o(mn)$ space. These results are some of the first on streaming algorithms and efficient two-party communication protocols for approximation algorithms. Moreover, we show that our algorithm can be applied to multi-party communication model.

1 Introduction

The Set Cover problem is one of the classic tasks in combinatorial optimization. Given a set of n elements $\mathcal{E}$ and a collection of m sets $\mathcal{S} = \{S_1, \ldots, S_m\}$, the goal of the problem is to pick a subset $\mathcal{I} \subset \mathcal{S}$ such that (i) $\mathcal{I}$ *covers* $\mathcal{E}$, i.e., $\mathcal{E} \subseteq \bigcup_{S \in \mathcal{I}} S$, and subject to this constraint, (ii) the number of sets in $\mathcal{I}$ is as small as possible. Set Cover is a well-studied problem with applications in many areas, including operations research [7], information retrieval and data mining [14], web host analysis [2], and many others.

Although the problem is NP-hard, a simple greedy algorithm is guaranteed to report a solution of size at most $O(\ln n)$ larger than the optimum. The algorithm is highly efficient and surprisingly accurate, with the reported solution size often within the 10% of the optimum on typical data sets [7]. However, it has been observed that, due to its sequential nature, the greedy algorithm is significantly less efficient when implemented on hierarchical, parallel and distributed architectures, which are commonly used nowadays for processing massive amounts of data. As a result, there has been considerable work on algorithms for Set Cover that are optimized for external memory [3], streaming [14,6], and cluster computing [2] architectures.

In this paper we consider Set Cover in three related computational models:

1. *Streaming Model:* In this model, the sets $S_1, \ldots, S_m$ are stored consecutively in a read-only repository. An algorithm can access the sets by performing sequential scans of the repository. However, the amount of read-write memory available to

F. Kuhn (Ed.): DISC 2014, LNCS 8784, pp. 484–498, 2014.

the algorithm is limited, and is smaller than the input size (which could be as large as mn). The objective is to design an algorithm that performs few passes over the data, and uses as little memory as possible.

2. *Two-Party Communication Model:* In this model, the sets are partitioned between two parties, Alice and Bob. Without loss of generality we can assume that Alice holds $S_1, \ldots, S_{m/2}$, while Bob holds $S_{m/2+1}, \ldots, S_m$. The parties communicate by exchanging messages, with Alice sending her messages to Bob during the odd rounds, and Bob sending his messages to Alice during the even rounds. The objective is to design a communication protocol to find a minimum cover of $\mathcal{E}$ that terminates in a few rounds such that the total length of the exchanged messages is as small as possible.

3. *Multi-party Communication Model:* In this model, the sets are partitioned among p parties that are not allowed to communicate with each other. However, there is a *coordinator* that communicates with each of the parties in rounds. In odd rounds, the coordinator performs some computation and broadcasts a single message to all of the parties; in even rounds, each party receives the message, performs some local computation, and sends a message back to the coordinator. Moreover, each party executes the same algorithm. The objective is to design a communication protocol to find a minimum cover of $\mathcal{E}$ that terminates in a few rounds and that the total size of the communication is as small as possible.

The first two models are intimately related. Specifically, any p-pass streaming algorithm that uses s bits of storage yields a $(2p - 1)$-round communication protocol exchanging at most $(2p - 1)s$ bits (see e.g., [8]). Thus, any efficient streaming algorithm induces a good communication protocol, while any lower bound for the communication complexity provides a lower bound for the amount of storage required by a streaming algorithm. Understanding the amount of communication necessary to solve problems in distributed communication complexity settings has been a subject of extensive research over the last few years, see e.g., [15] for an overview.

The Set Cover problem has attracted a fair amount of research over the last few years. The upper and lower bounds for the problem are depicted in Figure 1. Note that the simple greedy algorithm can be implemented by either storing the whole input (in one pass), or by iteratively updating the set of yet-uncovered elements (in at most n passes).

Our Results. Our main result is an $O(4^{1/\delta})$ pass, $O(4^{1/\delta}\rho)$-approximation streaming algorithm with $\tilde{O}(m \cdot n^\delta)$ space[1] for the Set Cover problem, where ρ denotes the approximation factor of an algorithm that solves Set Cover in off-line model. For example, the greedy algorithm yields $\rho = O(\log n)$, while an exponential algorithm yields $\rho = 1$. In particular, setting $\rho = 1$ and $1/\delta = \frac{1}{2} \log \log n - 1$ implies a $\frac{1}{4} \log n$-approximate communication protocol with complexity $mn^{O(1/\log \log n)}$. This matches the lower bound of Nisan [11] up to a factor of $n^{o(1)}$.

Furthermore, we show $\Omega(mn)$ lower bound for the communication complexity of any *deterministic* protocol approximating two-party Set Cover within a constant factor. Thus, the use of randomness is essential in order to achieve our result.

---

[1] $\tilde{O}(f(n, m))$ is defined as $O(f(n, m) \cdot \log^k f(n, m))$.

Result	Approximation	Passes/rounds	Space/communication	Type
Greedy	$O(\ln n)$	1	$O(m \cdot n)$	deterministic algorithm
	$O(\ln n)$	n	$O(n)$	deterministic algorithm
[14]	$O(\log n)$	$O(\log n)$	$O(n \log n)$	deterministic algorithm
[6]	$O(\sqrt{n})$	1	$\tilde{O}(n)$	deterministic algorithm
[11]	$\frac{1}{2}\log n$	any	$\Omega(m)$	randomized lower bound
This paper	$O(4^{1/\delta}\rho)$	$O(4^{1/\delta})$	$\tilde{O}(m \cdot n^\delta)$	randomized algorithm[2]
This paper	$O(1)$	any	$\Omega(m \cdot n)$	deterministic lower bound

Fig. 1. Summary of past work and our results. The algorithmic bounds are stated for the streaming model, while the lower bounds are stated for the two-party communication complexity model. We use ρ to denote the approximation factor of an off-line algorithm solving Set Cover, which is $O(\ln n)$ for the greedy algorithm and 1 for the exponential time algorithm. Furthermore, our result holds for any $\delta = \Omega(1/\log n)$.

We also show in Appendix A that our algorithm implies an $O(4^{1/\delta})$-round $O(4^{1/\delta}\rho)$-approximation communication protocol for multi-party communication model which communicates $\tilde{O}(m \cdot n^\delta + p \cdot n)$ bits per round.

Our Techniques. Our algorithms exploit *random sampling*. Two variants of sampling are used, depending on the size OPT of the minimum cover. If OPT is large, we use *set sampling*, i.e., we sample $O(\text{OPT})$ random sets and include them in the solution. This ensures that all universe elements contained in $(m \log n)/\text{OPT}$ sets are covered with high probability. Since each of the remaining elements is contained in at most $(m \log n)/\text{OPT}$ sets, the space needed to represent the input is reduced.

On the other hand, if OPT is small, the algorithm performs *element sampling*. Specifically, for a parameter $\alpha > 0$, the algorithm selects $O((\text{OPT} \cdot \log m)/\alpha)$ elements and computes a small cover of those elements. This task can be solved using only $O((m \cdot \text{OPT} \cdot \log m)/\alpha)$ space. We then show that any such solution in fact covers a $1 - \alpha$ fraction of the whole universe. Therefore, it suffices to cover the remaining αn elements, which can be done using less space since the universe size becomes smaller. The aforementioned process can be repeated recursively in order to reduce the space complexity to $O(mn^\delta)$ for any $\delta > 0$. A variant of the latter approach, element sampling, was previously applied in semi-streaming k-Max Coverage problem [9].

Preliminaries. In this paper we consider the Set Cover problem in the *set streaming* model which is based on the following setup appeared in [14].

Definition 1 (Set Streaming Model). *In set streaming model we are given $\mathcal{E}$ in advance and sets in $\mathcal{S}$ are revealed in a stream.*

---

[2] Our algorithms are randomized. Specifically, we assume that the streaming algorithm has access to a random oracle $r(i)$ such that the bits $r(1), r(2), \ldots$ are i.i.d. symmetric Bernoulli variables. The approximation guarantees offered by our algorithms are required to hold with high probability.

In the *off-line* Set Cover model, the universe of elements $\mathcal{E}$ and the collection of sets $\mathcal{S}$ are given all at once to the algorithm. In this paper, we assume that we are able to approximate off-line Set Cover within a factor ρ of its optimal solution. It is known that under $P \neq NP$, ρ cannot be smaller than $c \cdot \ln n$ where c is a constant [13,1]. At the same time, setting $\rho = 1$ (i.e., assuming an exact algorithm for set cover) provides space/approximation trade-offs without running time considerations. In particular, it establishes the "upper bounds on lower bounds", given that communicational complexity tools for proving lower bounds do not take the running time into account.

A trivial *one* pass streaming algorithm for the Set Cover problem is to read the whole stream and store all sets of $\mathcal{S}$ in memory. This leads to a ρ-approximation algorithm with $O(mn)$ space. We refer to this algorithm as Simple-Set-Cover algorithm which is shown in Figure 2 and will be used later in our algorithms. In Section 3, we show that any deterministic *constant* pass constant factor approximation algorithm for set streaming Set Cover requires $\Omega(mn)$ space (see Corollary 1). This implies that the trivial Simple-Set-Cover algorithm is tight. Thus to break the $\Omega(mn)$ space barrier of the constant pass algorithms for set streaming Set Cover, we should consider randomized approaches. In Section 2 we give a randomized constant pass algorithm for the problem that uses $o(mn)$ memory space. Moreover, Nisan proved that any randomized protocol of the Set Cover in two-party communication that achieves an approximation ratio better than $\frac{\log n}{2}$ requires $\Omega(m)$ memory space [11].

Simple-Set-Cover Algorithm   ⟨⟨Set Cover *Problem. Input:* $\langle \mathcal{E}, \mathcal{S} \rangle$⟩⟩

Store the projection of all sets in $\mathcal{S}$ over $\mathcal{E}$ in memory
Run the off-line algorithm to find a ρ-approximate cover sol
Return sol

Fig. 2. One pass algorithm for set streaming Set Cover$(\mathcal{E}, \mathcal{S})$ using $O(m \cdot n)$ space

2   A Constant Pass Algorithm

In this section, we give a randomized algorithm for set streaming Set Cover that has constant number of passes and consumes $\tilde{O}(m \cdot n^\delta)$ space where δ is an arbitrary *constant* greater than $4/\log n$. To this end, first in Section 2.1, we describe *set sampling* and *element sampling* approaches followed by a two pass randomized (2ρ)-approximation algorithm that uses $\tilde{O}(m \cdot n^{2/3})$ space to solve the Set Cover problem. Then, in Section 2.2, we extend the techniques further to obtain our main result as follows.

Theorem 1 (Main Theorem). *Suppose that there exists a ρ-approximation algorithm for the Set Cover problem in the off-line model. For $\delta = \Omega(1/\log n)$, there exists a randomized $O(4^{1/\delta}\rho)$-approximation algorithm to set streaming Set Cover with $O(4^{1/\delta})$ number of passes that consumes $O(m \cdot n^\delta \log^2 n \log m)$ bit of memory.*

Note that we can assume that $\delta = \Omega(1/\log n)$ because otherwise the approximation guarantee of Theorem 1 will be $\Omega(\sqrt{n})$ and there exists a single pass $4^{1/\delta}$ approximation algorithm in this case [6].

2.1 Sampling Approaches

In this section, we present two key modules in our algorithm: *element sampling* and *set sampling*.

Element Sampling. Let us assume that we are given k, the size of an optimal solution to Set Cover$(\mathcal{E}, \mathcal{S})$. Let $\mathcal{E}_{smp}$ be a subset of $\mathcal{E}$ of size $O(\rho \cdot \frac{k}{\varepsilon} \log m)$ picked uniformly at random where $\varepsilon < 1$. We claim that a ρ-approximate cover $\mathcal{C}_{smp}$ of $\mathcal{E}_{smp}$ is an ε-cover of $\mathcal{E}$ with high probability where ε-cover is defined as follows.

Definition 2. *A collection of sets $\mathcal{C}$ is an ε-cover of a set of elements $\mathcal{E}$ if $|\mathcal{E} \cap \bigcup_{S \in \mathcal{C}} S| \geq (1 - \varepsilon)|\mathcal{E}|$; in other words, $\mathcal{C}$ covers at least $1 - \varepsilon$ fraction of $\mathcal{E}$.*

Since we have assumed that an optimal cover of $\mathcal{E}$ is of size k, there exists a cover of size at most k for $\mathcal{E}_{smp}$ as well. Let $\mathcal{S}_{smp} = \{S \cap \mathcal{E}_{smp} \mid S \in \mathcal{S}\}$ be the collection of the intersections of all sets in $\mathcal{S}$ with $\mathcal{E}_{smp}$. By calling Simple-Set-Cover$(\mathcal{E}_{smp}, \mathcal{S})$, in one pass we can find a ρ-approximate cover of $\mathcal{E}_{smp}$, $\mathcal{C}_{smp}$, using $O(m \cdot |\mathcal{E}_{smp}|) = O(m\rho \cdot \frac{k}{\varepsilon} \log m)$ bits of memory. We say that $\mathcal{E}_{smp}$ is a **successful** *element sampling* if $\mathcal{C}_{smp}$ is an ε-cover of $\mathcal{E}$. The following lemma shows that if $\mathcal{E}_{smp}$ is picked uniformly at random, then with high probability $\mathcal{E}_{smp}$ is a successful *element sampling*.

Lemma 1 (Element Sampling Lemma). *Consider an instance of Set Cover with $\mathcal{E}$ and $\mathcal{S}$ as inputs. Let us assume that an optimal cover of Set Cover$(\mathcal{E}, \mathcal{S})$ has size at most k. Let $\mathcal{E}_{smp}$ be a subset of $\mathcal{E}$ of size $\rho \cdot \frac{ck}{\varepsilon} \log m$ chosen uniformly at random and let $\mathcal{C}_{smp} \subseteq \mathcal{S}$ be a ρ-approximate cover for $\mathcal{E}_{smp}$. Then $\mathcal{C}_{smp}$ is an ε-cover for $\mathcal{E}$ with probability at least $1 - \frac{1}{m^{(c-2)}}$.*

Proof: Since an optimal solution of Set Cover$(\mathcal{E}, \mathcal{S})$ has size at most k, an optimal solution of Set Cover$(\mathcal{E}_{smp}, \mathcal{S}_{smp})$ is also of size at most k. Thus a ρ-approximate cover $\mathcal{C}_{smp}$ for $\mathcal{E}_{smp}$ is of size at most $k\rho$.

Let $\mathcal{C}'$ be a subset of $\mathcal{S}$ covering less than $1 - \varepsilon$ fraction of $\mathcal{E}$. The probability that $\mathcal{C}'$ covers $\mathcal{E}_{smp}$ is at most $(1 - \varepsilon)^{\rho \frac{ck}{\varepsilon} \log m} < \frac{1}{m}^{ck\rho}$. Thus by union bound, the probability that $\mathcal{C}_{smp}$ covers $\mathcal{E}_{smp}$ and $\mathcal{C}_{smp}$ is an ε-cover of $\mathcal{E}$ is at least

$$1 - \left[\sum_{i=1}^{k\rho} \binom{m}{i} \right] \frac{1}{m^{ck\rho}} \geq 1 - \left[\sum_{i=1}^{k\rho} m^i \right] \frac{1}{m^{ck\rho}} \geq 1 - \frac{m^{k\rho+1}}{m^{ck\rho}}$$

$$\geq 1 - \frac{1}{m^{(c-2)k\rho}} \geq 1 - \frac{1}{m^{c-2}}.$$

Note that the term $\sum_{i=1}^{k\rho} \binom{m}{i}$ counts the number of all covers of size at most $k\rho$ which can be possibly returned as a solution to Set Cover$(\mathcal{E}_{smp}, \mathcal{S}_{smp})$. $\square$

Let $\mathcal{E}_{rem}$ be the set of elements remained uncovered after picking $\mathcal{C}_{smp}$ in the first pass. Lemma 1 showed that with high probability $|\mathcal{E}_{rem}| \leq \varepsilon n$. In the second pass, we cover the set $\mathcal{E}_{rem}$ by calling Simple-Set-Cover$(\mathcal{E}_{rem}, \mathcal{S})$ using $O(m \cdot \varepsilon n)$ space. These two steps together give a randomized two-pass (2ρ)-approximation for the problem that uses $O(m \cdot \frac{k\rho}{\varepsilon} \log m + m \cdot \varepsilon n)$ bits of memory which can be optimized by setting $\varepsilon = \sqrt{\frac{k\rho \log m}{n}}$. Thus the total required memory of element sampling is $O(m \cdot \sqrt{\rho k n \log m})$.

Theorem 2. *Let* $(\mathcal{E}, \mathcal{S})$ *be an instance of set streaming* Set Cover. *Assume that an optimal solution to* Set Cover$(\mathcal{E}, \mathcal{S})$ *has size at most* k. *Then there exists a two pass randomized* (2ρ)-*approximation algorithm for the problem that uses* $O(m \cdot \sqrt{\rho k n} \log m)$ *bits of memory.*

However, the required memory space of the described algorithm depends on k and it only performs well for small values of k. In the rest, we remove the dependency on k in the memory space of our algorithm by introducing another sampling module.

Set Sampling. In the *set sampling* module, in a single pass, the algorithm picks a subset of $\mathcal{S}$ uniformly at random. In contrast to *element sampling* technique, *set sampling* works effectively for large k. A *set sampling* $\mathcal{S}_{\mathrm{rnd}}$ of size $c\ell \log n$ is **successful** if $\mathcal{S}_{\mathrm{rnd}}$ covers all elements that appear in at least $\frac{m}{\ell}$ sets of $\mathcal{S}$. The following lemma shows that a subset of $\mathcal{S}$ of size $c\ell \log n$ picked uniformly at random is a successful *set sampling* with high probability.

Lemma 2 (Set Sampling Lemma). *Consider an instance* $(\mathcal{E}, \mathcal{S})$ *of set streaming* Set Cover. *Let* $\mathcal{S}_{\mathrm{rnd}}$ *be a collection of sets of size* $c\ell \log n$ *picked uniformly at random. Then,* $\mathcal{S}_{\mathrm{rnd}}$ *covers all elements of* $\mathcal{E}$ *that appear in at least* $\frac{m}{\ell}$ *sets of* $\mathcal{S}$ *with probability at least* $1 - \frac{1}{n^{c-1}}$.

Proof: Let e be an element of $\mathcal{E}$ that appears in at least $\frac{m}{\ell}$ sets of $\mathcal{S}$. The probability that e is not covered by $\mathcal{S}_{\mathrm{rnd}}$ is at most $(1 - \frac{1}{\ell})^{c\ell \log n} < e^{-c \ln n / \ln 2} = n^{-c/\ln 2}$. Thus the probability that there exists an element of $\mathcal{E}$ that appears in at least $\frac{m}{\ell}$ sets of $\mathcal{S}$ and is not covered by $\mathcal{S}_{\mathrm{rnd}}$ is at most $n \cdot n^{-c/\ln 2} \leq n^{-c+1}$. $\square$

Two Pass Algorithm. Now we describe a randomized *two-pass* (2ρ)-approximation algorithm for set streaming Set Cover problem that uses $\tilde{O}(m \cdot n^{2/3})$ space. Let k be a parameter to be determined later and let OPT be the size of an optimal solution of Set Cover$(\mathcal{E}, \mathcal{S})$. Consider the following two cases:

1. OPT $\leq k$. In this case we apply the *element sampling* approach to solve Set Cover$(\mathcal{E}, \mathcal{S})$ using $O(m \cdot \sqrt{\rho n k} \log m)$ bits (see Theorem 2).
2. OPT $\geq k$. In this case we apply the *set sampling* module. First, we pick a subset $\mathcal{S}_{\mathrm{rnd}}$ of $\mathcal{S}$ of size $ck\rho$ uniformly at random. By Lemma 2, each element e that is not covered by $\mathcal{S}_{\mathrm{rnd}}$ *with high probability* appears in $\frac{m}{\rho k} \cdot \log n$ sets of $\mathcal{S}$. Thus the required space to solve the problem over uncovered elements off-line is $O(n \cdot \frac{m}{\rho k} \log^2 n)$ bits; the total number of elements in projection of $\mathcal{S}$ over uncovered elements is $O(n \cdot \frac{m}{\rho k} \log n)$ and $O(\log n)$ bits is required for representing each of n elements.

Note that the algorithm does not really need to know OPT. It can run both cases in parallel and at the end, report the best solution of these two. Since each of these subroutines requires two passes, the whole algorithm can be done in two passes. Moreover, the total memory space is $O(m \cdot (\sqrt{n \rho k} \log m + \frac{n}{\rho k} \log^2 n))$ which is minimized by letting $k = \frac{1}{\rho} (\frac{n \log^4 n}{\log m})^{1/3}$. Thus it is a randomized two-pass (2ρ)-approximation algorithm for set streaming Set Cover using $O(m \cdot n^{2/3} (\log m \log^2 n)^{1/3})$ bits of memory.

Lemma 3. *There exists a randomized two-pass* (2ρ)-*approximation algorithm for set streaming* Set Cover *that uses* $\tilde{O}(m \cdot n^{2/3})$ *bits of memory.*

2.2   Our Algorithm

In this section we show that we can improve the result of Lemma 3 further in terms of required space by applying the sampling modules recursively. Our main claim is that the Recursive-Sample-Set-Cover algorithm described in Figure 3, achieves the guarantees mentioned in Theorem 1. More precisely, Recursive-Sample-Set-Cover($\mathcal{E}, \mathcal{S}, n, \delta$) finds an $O(4^{1/\delta}\rho)$-approximate cover of $\mathcal{E}$ in $O(4^{1/\delta})$ passes using $\tilde{O}(m \cdot n^\delta)$ bits of memory. We prove Theorem 1 at the end of this section.

In Recursive-Sample-Set-Cover($\mathcal{E}, \mathcal{S}, n, \delta$), first we check whether $|\mathcal{E}| \leq n^\delta$. If $|\mathcal{E}| \leq n^\delta$, we call Simple-Set-Cover($\mathcal{E}, \mathcal{S}$) to find a cover of $\mathcal{E}$ in one pass using $O(m \cdot n^\delta)$ bits. Otherwise, similar to the two pass algorithm, we combine *set sampling* and *element sampling* modules. However, here we recurse in *element sampling* module. In Recursive-Sample-Set-Cover($\mathcal{E}, \mathcal{S}, n, \delta$) we choose a threshold k to decide whether the size of an optimal cover is large or not. By the proper choice of k and the assumption that all sampling modules are successful, we show that **Case 1** in Recursive-Sample-Set-Cover returns an $O(4^{1/\delta}\rho)$-approximate cover if the size of an optimal cover of $\mathcal{E}$ is larger than or equal to k. Similarly, we show that in the case that the size of an optimal cover of $\mathcal{E}$ is smaller than k, **Case 2** of the algorithm returns an $O(4^{1/\delta}\rho)$-approximate cover. Moreover, in **Case 2** of the algorithm, which corresponds to the *element sampling*, we recursively invoke two instances of Recursive-Sample-Set-Cover on element sets of size at most $\frac{|\mathcal{E}|}{n^{\delta/2}}$. At the end, we return the best solution of these two cases.

Lemma 4. *Let $\mathcal{E}'_{\text{smp}}$ and $\mathcal{E}'_{\text{rem}}$ be subsets of $\mathcal{E}'$ as defined in* Recursive-Sample-Set-Cover($\mathcal{E}', \mathcal{S}, n, \delta$). *Then $|\mathcal{E}'_{\text{smp}}| = \frac{|\mathcal{E}'|}{n^{\delta/2}}$ and for large enough c, with high probability,* $|\mathcal{E}'_{\text{rem}}| \leq \frac{|\mathcal{E}'|}{cn^{\delta/2}}$.

Proof: Since k is chosen to be $|\mathcal{E}'|/(c^2\rho \cdot n^\delta \cdot \log m)$,

$$|\mathcal{E}'_{\text{smp}}| = c\sqrt{\rho|\mathcal{E}'|k \log m} = \frac{|\mathcal{E}'|}{n^{\delta/2}}.$$

We can rewrite $|\mathcal{E}'_{\text{smp}}|$ as

$$c\sqrt{\rho|\mathcal{E}'|k \log m} = c\rho k \log m / \sqrt{\frac{\rho k \log m}{|\mathcal{E}'|}}.$$

Thus by Lemma 1, a ρ-approximate cover of $\mathcal{E}'_{\text{smp}}$ is a ($\sqrt{\frac{\rho k \log m}{|\mathcal{E}'|}}$)-cover of $\mathcal{E}'$ with high probability. Hence, with high probability,

$$|\mathcal{E}'_{\text{rem}}| \leq |\mathcal{E}'| \cdot \sqrt{\frac{\rho k \log m}{|\mathcal{E}'|}} = \sqrt{\rho|\mathcal{E}'|k \log m} = \frac{|\mathcal{E}'|}{cn^{\delta/2}}.$$

$\square$

Next we define the **successful** invocation of Recursive-Sample-Set-Cover.

Definition 3. *An invocation of* Recursive-Sample-Set-Cover($\mathcal{E}', \mathcal{S}, n, \delta$) *is successful if either $|\mathcal{E}'| \leq n^\delta$; or $\mathcal{S}_{\text{rnd}}$ and $\mathcal{E}'_{\text{smp}}$ are respectively successful element sampling and set sampling, and both* Recursive-Sample-Set-Cover($\mathcal{E}'_{\text{smp}}, \mathcal{S}, n, \delta$) *and* Recursive-Sample-Set-Cover($\mathcal{E}'_{\text{rem}}, \mathcal{S}, n, \delta$) *are successful.*

Recursive-Sample-Set-Cover   ⟨⟨Set Cover *Problem. Input:* $\langle \mathcal{E}, \mathcal{S}, n, \delta \rangle$⟩⟩

Let $k = |\mathcal{E}|/(c^2 \rho \cdot n^\delta \log m)$

If $|\mathcal{E}| \leq n^\delta$

    sol $\leftarrow$ Simple-Set-Cover$(\mathcal{E}, \mathcal{S})$ ⟨⟨*In one pass*⟩⟩

    Return sol

⟨⟨**Case 1**: *handling* OPT$(\mathcal{E}, \mathcal{S}) \geq k$ *via "set sampling" module*⟩⟩

Let $\mathcal{S}_{\text{rnd}}$ be a collection of $ck\rho$ sets of $\mathcal{S}$ picked uniformly at random.   ⟨⟨*In one pass*⟩⟩

If each element of $\mathcal{E} \setminus \bigcup_{S \in \mathcal{S}_{\text{rnd}}} S$ appears in less than $\frac{m \log n}{k}$ sets of $\mathcal{S}$

    sol$_{\text{rnd}} \leftarrow$ Simple-Set-Cover$(\mathcal{E} \setminus \bigcup_{S \in \mathcal{S}_{\text{rnd}}} S, \mathcal{S})$ ⟨⟨*In one pass*⟩⟩

Else   ⟨⟨*Unsuccessful* set sampling⟩⟩

    sol$_{\text{rnd}} \leftarrow$ Invalid

⟨⟨**Case 2**: *handling* OPT$(\mathcal{E}, \mathcal{S}) < k$ *via "element sampling" module*⟩⟩

Sample a set of elements $\mathcal{E}_{\text{smp}}$ of size $c\sqrt{\rho|\mathcal{E}|k \log m}$ uniformly at random

sol$_{\text{smp}} \leftarrow$ Recursive-Sample-Set-Cover$(\mathcal{E}_{\text{smp}}, \mathcal{S}, n, \delta)$

Let $\mathcal{E}_{\text{rem}} = \mathcal{E} \setminus \bigcup_{S \in \text{sol}_{\text{smp}}} S$ ⟨⟨*In one pass*⟩⟩

If $|\mathcal{E}_{\text{rem}}| \leq |\mathcal{E}|/(cn^{\frac{\delta}{2}})$

    sol$_{\text{rem}} \leftarrow$ Recursive-Sample-Set-Cover$(\mathcal{E}_{\text{rem}}, \mathcal{S}, n, \delta)$

Else   ⟨⟨*Unsuccessful* element sampling⟩⟩

    sol$_{\text{rem}} \leftarrow$ Invalid

If any of sol$_{\text{rnd}}$, sol$_{\text{smp}}$ or sol$_{\text{rem}}$ is Invalid

    Return Invalid

Return the best of $(\mathcal{S}_{\text{rnd}} \cup \text{sol}_{\text{rnd}})$ and $(\text{sol}_{\text{smp}} \cup \text{sol}_{\text{rem}})$

Fig. 3. Recursive-Sample-Set-Cover for the Set Cover problem in set streaming model

Note that in Recursive-Sample-Set-Cover algorithm we only consider the result of successful invocations. To this end, we discard the run of the algorithm as soon as a sampling module fails.

Consider the *recursion tree* of Recursive-Sample-Set-Cover$(\mathcal{E}, \mathcal{S}, n, \delta)$. Each intermediate node in the tree has two children. Moreover, for each leaf of the tree, the number of elements in its corresponding Recursive-Sample-Set-Cover instance is at most n^δ. Thus, we have the following lemma.

Lemma 5. *The height the recursion tree of* Recursive-Sample-Set-Cover$(\mathcal{E}, \mathcal{S}, n, \delta)$ *is at most* $2/\delta$ *and the number of nodes in the tree is less than* $2 \cdot 4^{1/\delta}$. *Moreover, the number of nodes in the recursion tree is* $O(n)$.

Proof: In the root node of the tree, the element size is n and by lemma 4, the element size decreases by a factor of at least $n^{\delta/2}$ at each level of recursion. Thus, in level i we have at most 2^i instances of Recursive-Sample-Set-Cover with element size at most $n^{1-i\delta/2}$. Moreover, the element size of the corresponding instances of a leaf is at most n^δ. Thus, we can compute the height of the tree, h, as follows:

$$n^{1-\frac{h\delta}{2}} \leq n^{\delta} \implies (1 - \frac{h\delta}{2}) \leq \delta \implies h \leq \frac{2(1-\delta)}{\delta} \leq \frac{2}{\delta}$$

Since the height of the tree is at most $2/\delta$, the total number nodes in the tree is at most $2 \cdot 4^{1/\delta}$. Moreover since $\delta = \Omega(\log n)$, the number of nodes in the tree is $O(n)$.   □

The following lemma shows that an invocation of Recursive-Sample-Set-Cover is successful with high probability.

Lemma 6. *Consider an invocation of* Recursive-Sample-Set-Cover$(\mathcal{E}, \mathcal{S}, n, \delta)$. *For sufficiently large c, the invocation is successful with high probability.*

Proof of Lemma 6: Consider any particular node of the recursion tree. By Lemma 2 the probability that *set sampling* performed at that node is successful is at least $1 - \frac{1}{n^{c-1}}$ and by Lemma 1, the probability that the *element sampling* performed at that node is successful is at least $1 - \frac{1}{m^{c-2}}$. Therefore, by union bound over all the nodes in the recursion tree and using the fact that the number of nodes in the recursion tree is $O(n)$ (See Lemma 5), an invocation of the subroutine is successful with probability at least $1 - O(n) \cdot \frac{2}{n^{c-2}} \geq 1 - \frac{1}{O(n^{c-3})}$.   □

In the rest we compute the number of passes, approximation guarantee and the required space of Recursive-Sample-Set-Cover$(\mathcal{E}, \mathcal{S}, n, \delta)$.

Lemma 7. *The number of passes in* Recursive-Sample-Set-Cover$(\mathcal{E}, \mathcal{S}, n, \delta)$ *is* $O(4^{1/\delta})$.

Proof: We show that the number of passes the algorithm makes in each node of the recursion tree of Recursive-Sample-Set-Cover is at most 3. Therefore, by Lemma 5 the total number of passes of Recursive-Sample-Set-Cover is $O(4^{1/\delta})$.

In each leaf node which corresponds to an invocation of Recursive-Sample-Set-cover with element size at most n^{δ}, we call Simple-Set-Cover and it is done in one pass. For intermediate nodes, the algorithm has at most the following three passes.

- In the first pass, the algorithm picks $\mathcal{S}_{\text{rnd}}$. In the meantime, it maintains the set of uncovered elements by so far selected sets. Moreover, for each uncovered element e, it stores the number of sets in $\mathcal{S}$ containing e. These numbers are used to decide whether the *set sampling* is successful.
- Next, if $\mathcal{S}_{\text{rnd}}$ is successful, then the algorithm makes another pass to find a cover for the elements that are not covered by $\mathcal{S}_{\text{rnd}}$ via Simple-Set-Cover algorithm.
- Then the algorithm samples a set of elements $\mathcal{E}_{\text{smp}}$ and recursively finds a cover of $\mathcal{E}_{\text{smp}}$. Note that in Recursive-Sample-Set-Cover, we return the indices of the sets in the selected cover. Thus, to decide whether the *element sampling* is successful, the algorithm must make a pass to find the uncovered elements, $\mathcal{E}_{\text{rem}}$. If $|\mathcal{E}_{\text{rem}}| \leq \varepsilon n$, the module is successful and we recursively find a cover for $\mathcal{E}_{\text{rem}}$.

□

Lemma 8. *For sufficiently large c,* Recursive-Sample-Set-Cover$(\mathcal{E}, \mathcal{S}, n, \delta)$ *algorithm returns an* $O(4^{1/\delta}\rho)$-*approximate solution of* Set Cover$(\mathcal{E}, \mathcal{S})$ *with high probability.*

Proof: By Lemma 6, an invocation of Recursive-Sample-Set-Cover is successful with high probability. In the following we only consider successful invocations of Recursive-Sample-Set-Cover and compute the approximation factor for successful runs.

Consider a successful run of Recursive-Sample-Set-Cover($\mathcal{E}', \mathcal{S}, n, \delta$). If $|\mathcal{E}'| \leq n^\delta$, then the solution returned by the subroutine has size at most $\rho \cdot$ OPT where OPT is the size of an optimal cover of $\mathcal{E}$.

Otherwise, if an optimum solution for this instance has size at least $|\mathcal{E}'|/(c^2\rho \cdot n^\delta \log m)$ (**Case 1**), the size of the cover constructed by the subroutine is at most $c\rho \cdot (|\mathcal{E}'|/c^2\rho \cdot n^\delta \log m) + \rho \cdot$ OPT $\leq (c+1)\rho \cdot$ OPT, where the first term denotes the size of $\mathcal{S}_{\text{rnd}}$ and the second term denotes the size of the cover the algorithm picked for the elements that are not covered by $\mathcal{S}_{\text{rnd}}$.

If an optimum cover of the instance has size less than $|\mathcal{E}'|/(c^2\rho \cdot n^\delta \log m)$ (**Case 2**), then the union of the covers returned by Recursive-Sample-Set-Cover($\mathcal{E}'_{\text{smp}}, \mathcal{S}, n, \delta$) and Recursive-Sample-Set-Cover($\mathcal{E}'_{\text{rem}}, \mathcal{S}, n, \delta$) is a cover of $\mathcal{E}$ with small size (for precise value, see Equation 1). By Lemma 4, $|\mathcal{E}'_{\text{smp}}| \leq \frac{|\mathcal{E}'|}{n^{\delta/2}}$ and $|\mathcal{E}'_{\text{rem}}| \leq \frac{|\mathcal{E}'|}{cn^{\delta/2}}$. Since the size of an optimal cover of each of $\mathcal{E}'_{\text{smp}}$ and $\mathcal{E}'_{\text{rem}}$ is less than or equal to the size of an optimal cover of $\mathcal{E}'$, in this case

$$\text{Approx}(|\mathcal{E}'|, n, \delta) \leq 2 \times \text{Approx}(\frac{|\mathcal{E}'|}{n^{\delta/2}}, n, \delta). \tag{1}$$

Thus, we can write the following recursive formula for the approximation guarantee of Recursive-Sample-Set-Cover algorithm.

$$\text{Approx}(|\mathcal{E}'|, n, \delta) \leq \begin{cases} \max\{(c+1)\rho, 2 \times \text{Approx}(|\mathcal{E}'|/n^{\delta/2}, n, \delta)\} & \text{if } |\mathcal{E}'| > n^\delta \\ \rho & \text{if } |\mathcal{E}'| \leq n^\delta \end{cases}$$
$$\tag{2}$$

By Lemma 5, the height of the recursion tree of our algorithm is $2/\delta$. Hence, a successful run of the algorithm returns an $O(4^{1/\delta}\rho)$-approximate cover.   □

Lemma 9. *Consider a successful run of* Recursive-Sample-Set-Cover($\mathcal{E}', \mathcal{S}, n, \delta$). *After picking* $\mathcal{S}_{\text{rnd}}$, *the required memory space to call* Simple-Set-Cover($\mathcal{E}'\backslash\bigcup_{S\in\mathcal{S}_{\text{rnd}}} S, \mathcal{S}$) *is* $O(m \cdot n^\delta \log m \log^2 n)$ *bits.*

Proof: As defined in Figure 3, $\mathcal{S}_{\text{rnd}}$ is a collection of sets selected uniformly at random and $|\mathcal{S}_{\text{rnd}}| = ck\rho$ where $k = |\mathcal{E}'|/(c^2\rho \cdot n^\delta \log m)$. In a successful *set sampling*, $\mathcal{S}_{\text{rnd}}$ covers all elements that appear in at least $\frac{m}{k\rho} \cdot \log n$ sets of $\mathcal{S}$. Hence the required space to run Simple-Set-Cover($\mathcal{E}' \setminus \bigcup_{S\in\mathcal{S}_{\text{rnd}}} S, \mathcal{S}$) is $|\mathcal{E}'| \cdot \frac{m}{k\rho} \log n \cdot \log n = c^2 m \cdot n^\delta \log^2 n \log m$. Note that the additional $\log n$ in the memeory space is for representing the elements; $\log n$ bits is required to represent each element.   □

Lemma 10. Recursive-Sample-Set-Cover($\mathcal{E}, \mathcal{S}, n, \delta$) *uses* $O(m \cdot n^\delta \log m \log^2 n)$ *bits of memory to solve set streaming* Set Cover($\mathcal{E}, \mathcal{S}$) *where* $n = |\mathcal{E}|$.

Proof: We prove by induction that the space Recursive-Sample-Set-Cover($\mathcal{E}, \mathcal{S}, n, \delta$) requires is less than $c_1(m \cdot n^\delta + |\mathcal{E}|) \log m \log^2 n$ for a large enough constant c_1.

It is straightforward to see that the induction hypothesis holds for $|\mathcal{E}'| \leq n^\delta$. In this case we call Simple-Set-Cover$(\mathcal{E}', \mathcal{S})$ that can be executed using $m \cdot n^\delta$ bits. Lets assume that the induction hypothesis holds for instances with $|\mathcal{E}| < n'$. In the following we show that the induction hypothesis holds for $|\mathcal{E}'| = n'$ too.

In Recursive-Sample-Set-Cover$(\mathcal{E}', \mathcal{S}, n, \delta)$, first we perform the *set sampling* module and in this case the required space is bounded by the required space to store $\mathcal{S}_{\mathrm{rnd}}$ which is $|\mathcal{S}_{\mathrm{rnd}}| \cdot \log m$ plus the required space to run Simple-Set-Cover$(\mathcal{E} \backslash \bigcup_{S \in \mathcal{S}_{\mathrm{rnd}}} S, \mathcal{S})$ which is $O(m \cdot n^\delta \log m \log^2 n)$ (see Lemma 9). We assume that the required space for Simple-Set-Cover$(\mathcal{E} \backslash \bigcup_{S \in \mathcal{S}_{\mathrm{rnd}}} S, \mathcal{S})$ is $c_2 \cdot m \cdot n^\delta \log m \log^2 n$ (c_2 is computed in the proof of Lemma 9). Thus the total space to run *set sampling*

$$ck\rho \log m + c_2 \cdot m \cdot n^\delta \log m \log^2 n \leq n^{1-\delta}/c + c_2 \cdot m \cdot n^\delta \log m \log^2 n$$

$$\leq c_1 \cdot m \cdot n^\delta \log m \log^2 n$$

which holds for large enough c_1. After executing the *set sampling* module, we only need to keep the constructed cover which requires at most $|\mathcal{E}'| \log m$ bits (the size of the cover is at most $|\mathcal{E}'|$ and for each set in the cover we keep its index).

Then we perform the *element sampling* module. To this end, first we run Recursive-Sample-Set-Cover$(\mathcal{E}'_{\mathrm{smp}}, \mathcal{S}, n, \delta)$ using $c_1(m \cdot n^\delta + |\mathcal{E}'_{\mathrm{smp}}|) \log m \log^2 n$ bits (by induction hypothesis). After constructing a cover for $\mathcal{E}'_{\mathrm{smp}}$, we only keep the cover of $\mathcal{E}'_{\mathrm{smp}}$ which requires at most $|\mathcal{E}'_{\mathrm{smp}}| \cdot \log m$ bits. Next, if $\mathcal{E}'_{\mathrm{smp}}$ is a successful *element sampling*, we cover $\mathcal{E}'_{\mathrm{rem}}$ recursively; otherwise, we return `Invalid`.

Thus the required space of Recursive-Sample-Set-Cover$(\mathcal{E}, \mathcal{S}, n, \delta)$ is

$$\max\{c_1 \cdot m \cdot n^\delta \log m \log^2 n, \ |\mathcal{E}'| \log m + c_1 \cdot (m \cdot n^\delta + \frac{|\mathcal{E}'|}{n^{\delta/2}}) \log m \log^2 n, \quad (3)$$

$$(|\mathcal{E}'| + |\mathcal{E}'|/n^{\delta/2}) \log m + c_1 \cdot (m \cdot n^\delta + |\mathcal{E}'|/n^{\delta/2}) \log m \log^2 n\}$$

$$= (|\mathcal{E}'| + |\mathcal{E}'|/n^{\delta/2}) \log m + c_1 \cdot (m \cdot n^\delta + |\mathcal{E}'|/n^{\delta/2}) \log m \log^2 n$$

$$\leq c_1 \cdot (m \cdot n^\delta + |\mathcal{E}'|) \log m \log^2 n \quad \text{(for large enough } c_1)$$

In Equation 3, the first term denotes the required space while the algorithm is running the *set sampling* module. The second term denotes the required space for the case that the execution of the *set sampling* module is completed and the algorithm is running the first recursive call of the *element sampling* module. The last term is the required memory space while the algorithm is running the second recursive call of the *element sampling* module. Thus induction hypothesis holds for $|\mathcal{E}'| = n'$ and the proof is complete.
$\square$

Theorem 1 follows from Lemma 8, Lemma 7 and Lemma 10.

3   Lower Bounds

In this section, we give some lower bound results for the Set Cover problem in the set streaming model. Specifically, we discuss deterministic protocols and we show that one cannot give a constant pass algorithm with $o(mn)$ memory space that achieves a constant factor approximation for set streaming Set Cover. Our lower bound results follow from some results in the two-party communication model. In particular we consider the following variant of Set Disjointness problem in two-party communication model.

Definition 4 ((Sparse) Set Disjointness Problem). *In* Set Disjointness(n), *each of Alice and Bob receives a subset of* $\{1,\ldots,n\}$, S_A *and* S_B. *The goal is to determine whether* S_A *and* S_B *are disjoint or not. In* Sparse Set Disjointness(n,k), *each of two parties receives a subset of size at most* k *of* $\{1,\ldots,n\}$ *and the goal is to determine whether their sets intersect or not.*

Set Disjointness(n) is a well-studied problem in communication complexity and it is known that the best protocol (up to constant) in term of bits of communication is the trivial one in which Alice sends her entire input to Bob. Moreover, using the rank method, it has been shown that any deterministic protocol for Sparse Set Disjointness(n,k) requires $\Omega(m\log(n/k))$ bits of communication.

Nisan [11] proved that any *randomized* protocol approximating Set Cover in two-party communication with a factor better than $\frac{\log n}{2}$ has communication complexity $\Omega(m)$. In this section, exploiting the techniques of [11], we get $\Omega(mn)$ lower bound for the memory space of deterministic two-party protocols approximating Set Cover within a constant factor.

Definition 5 (r-covering property [10,11]). *Let* S *be a collection of subsets of* $\{1,\ldots, n\}$. *The collection* S *has the* r-*covering property if for every collection* $\mathcal{A} \subseteq \{S \mid S \in S \text{ or } \overline{S} \in S\}$ *of size at most* r, $\mathcal{A}$ *does not cover* $\{1,\ldots,n\}$ *unless a set* S *and its complement are both selected in* $\mathcal{A}$.

Lemma 11 (From [11]). *For any* $r \le \log n - O(\log\log n)$, *there exists a collection* S *of subsets of* $\{1,\ldots,n\}$ *that satisfies the* r-*covering property such that* $|S| \ge e^{n/(r2^r)}$.

Combining the known lower bound of Sparse Set Disjointness(n,k) with the r-covering property, we achieve the following lower bound result for deterministic protocols of Set Cover in two-party communication.

Theorem 3. *Any deterministic* α-*approximation protocol for* Set Cover($\mathcal{E}, S_A, S_B$) *in two-party communication requires* $\Omega(|S_A \cup S_B| \cdot |\mathcal{E}|)$ *communication if* $\alpha = O(1)$.

Proof: Given an instance (x_A, x_B) of Sparse Set Disjointness(n,k), we construct the following corresponding instance of two-party Set Cover($\mathcal{E}, S_A, S_B$).
Let $r = 2\alpha$ and let $S = \{S_1,\ldots,S_n\}$ be a collection of subsets of $\{1,\ldots,p\}$ satisfying r-covering property. By Lemma 11, it is enough to have $|S| = e^{p/(r2^r)}$ which implies that $p = r2^r \ln n$. Since $r = O(1)$, we have $p = O(\log n)$.
Define $\mathcal{E} = \{1,\ldots,p\}$. Let S_A be the collection of sets that Alice owns and let S_B denote the collection of sets owned by Bob. We define $S_A = \{S_i \mid x_A[i] = 1\}$ and $S_B = \{\overline{S_i} \mid x_B[i] = 1\}$.
The r-covering property of S guarantees that the size of an optimal cover of $\mathcal{E}, \mathcal{C} \subseteq S$, is either 2 (the case that $\mathcal{C}$ contains both S and $\overline{S}$ for a set $S \in S$) or at least r. Note that x_A and x_B intersect iff the size of an optimal cover of $\mathcal{E}$ is 2. Thus any protocol for two party Set Cover($\mathcal{E}, S_A, S_B$) with approximation ratio smaller than $r/2$ solves Sparse Set Disjointness(n,k) exactly.

It has been shown that Sparse Set Disjointness(n, k) has communication complexity $\Omega(k \log(2n/k))$. If we pick k such that $k = O(n^{1-\epsilon})$ for some constant ϵ, then $|\mathcal{E}| = p = O(\log n) = O(\log \frac{2n}{k})$. Thus by the known lower bound of Sparse Set Disjointness(n, k) in two party communication, two-party Set Cover$(\mathcal{E}, \mathcal{S}_A, \mathcal{S}_B)$ requires $\Omega(k \log(2n/k)) = \Omega(k \cdot p) = \Omega((|\mathcal{S}_A| + |\mathcal{S}_B|) \cdot |\mathcal{E}|)$ bits of communication. $\square$

Corollary 1. *Any deterministic constant factor approximation algorithm for set streaming* Set Cover *with constant number of passes requires* $\Omega(mn)$ *space.*

The following is based on the lower bound of [11].

Corollary 2. *Any randomized constant pass algorithm that approximates set streaming* Set Cover$(\mathcal{E}, \mathcal{S}_A, \mathcal{S}_B)$ *within a factor smaller than* $\frac{\log n}{2}$ *uses* $\Omega(|\mathcal{S}_A \cup \mathcal{S}_B|)$ *space.*

Acknowledgment. The work was supported in part by NSF grants CCF-1161626 and CCF-1065125, DARPA/AFOSR grant FA9550-12-1-0423, Packard Foundation, Simons Foundation and MADALGO — Center for Massive Data Algorithmics — a Center of the Danish National Research Foundation.

References

1. Alon, N., Moshkovitz, D., Safra, S.: Algorithmic construction of sets for k-restrictions. ACM Transactions on Algorithms 2(2), 153–177 (2006)
2. Chierichetti, F., Kumar, R., Tomkins, A.: Max-cover in map-reduce. In: Proc. of WWW, pp. 231–240. ACM (2010)
3. Cormode, G., Karloff, H., Wirth, A.: Set cover algorithms for very large datasets. In: Proceedings of the 19th ACM International Conference on Information and Knowledge Management, pp. 479–488. ACM (2010)
4. Dolev, D., Feder, T.: Multiparty communication complexity. In: Proc. of IEEE FOCS, pp. 428–433. IEEE (1989)
5. Ďuriš, P., Rolim, J.D.P.: Lower bounds on the multiparty communication complexity. Journal of Computer and System Sciences 56(1), 90–95 (1998)
6. Emek, Y., Rosén, A.: Semi-streaming set cover. In: Esparza, J., Fraigniaud, P., Husfeldt, T., Koutsoupias, E. (eds.) ICALP 2014. Part I. LNCS, vol. 8572, pp. 453–464. Springer, Heidelberg (2014)
7. Grossman, T., Wool, A.: Computational experience with approximation algorithms for the set covering problem. European Journal of Operational Research 101(1), 81–92 (1997)
8. Guha, S., McGregor, A.: Tight lower bounds for multi-pass stream computation via pass elimination. In: Aceto, L., Damgård, I., Goldberg, L.A., Halldórsson, M.M., Ingólfsdóttir, A., Walukiewicz, I. (eds.) ICALP 2008, Part I. LNCS, vol. 5125, pp. 760–772. Springer, Heidelberg (2008)
9. Kumar, R., Moseley, B., Vassilvitskii, S., Vattani, A.: Fast greedy algorithms in mapreduce and streaming. In: Proc. of SPAA, pp. 1–10. ACM (2013)
10. Lund, C., Yannakakis, M.: On the hardness of approximating minimization problems. Journal of the ACM 41(5), 960–981 (1994)
11. Nisan, N.: The communication complexity of approximate set packing and covering. In: Widmayer, P., Triguero, F., Morales, R., Hennessy, M., Eidenbenz, S., Conejo, R. (eds.) ICALP 2002. LNCS, vol. 2380, pp. 868–875. Springer, Heidelberg (2002)

12. Phillips, J.M., Verbin, E., Zhang, Q.: Lower bounds for number-in-hand multiparty communication complexity, made easy. In: Proc. of ACM-SIAM SODA, pp. 486–501. SIAM (2012)
13. Raz, R., Safra, S.: A sub-constant error-probability low-degree test, and a sub-constant error-probability pcp characterization of np. In: Proc. of ACM STOC, pp. 475–484. ACM (1997)
14. Saha, B., Getoor, L.: On maximum coverage in the streaming model & application to multi-topic blog-watch. In: SDM, pp. 697–708 (2009)
15. Woodruff, D.P., Zhang, Q.: When distributed computation is communication expensive. In: Afek, Y. (ed.) DISC 2013. LNCS, vol. 8205, pp. 16–30. Springer, Heidelberg (2013)

A   Multiparty Communication Algorithm for Set Cover

In this section, we describe how our algorithm can be applied in the *multi-party communication* model where the input is distributed among a set of p parties and the goal is to compute a function over the input, while minimizing the total amount of communication. It is assumed that there is *coordinator* which can communicate with each of the parties, however the parties do not communicate with each other directly. This model has been widely studied before (see for example [5,4,12]). Note that this model is an example of the *number-in-hand* model in which each party sees its own input, as opposed to the *number-on-forehead* model where each party can see the inputs of all the other parties except his own.

Our Model. In *coordinator* model there are p parties $P_1, \ldots, P_p$ and one coordinator. The coordinator can communicate with each of the parties, but the parties cannot communicate with each other. Also, only synchronous executions are considered: in even rounds, each party receives a message from the coordinator, performs some local computation, and sends a message back to the coordinator. In odd rounds, the coordinator receives messages from each party, performs some computation and broadcasts the same message to all of the parties. We consider a restricted variant of the coordinator model in which each party executes the same algorithm.

The Problem and Our Result. Let $\mathcal{E} = \{1, \cdots, n\}$ be the element set and let $\mathcal{S}$ be a collection of m sets and let $\mathcal{S}_1, \ldots, \mathcal{S}_p$ be a partitioning of $\mathcal{S}$ such that the party i only has the collection $\mathcal{S}_i$. The goal of the algorithm is for the coordinator to output the indices of the sets in $\mathcal{S}$ that constitute a minimum cover for $\mathcal{E}$.

We are interested in the total number of rounds, approximation factor and total amount of communication per round. Note that the communication of odd rounds is counted as the size of the single message broadcasted from the coordinator, and the communication of even rounds is counted as the total size of the messages from all the parties to the coordinator. Assuming the described model, we have the following theorem which mainly follows from Theorem 1.

Theorem 4. *There is a randomized $O(4^{1/\delta})$-round, $O(4^{1/\delta}\rho)$-approximation algorithm to* Set Cover$(\mathcal{E}, \mathcal{S})$ *with total communication of $\tilde{O}(m \cdot n^\delta + p \cdot n)$ in each round.*

Here ρ is the approximation ratio of the off-line Set Cover achieved by the coordinator.

Our Algorithm. We can show that it is possible for the coordinator to run the Recursive-Sample-Set-Cover such that its total communication with the parties is $\tilde{O}(m \cdot n^\delta)$ in each

round. The algorithm only needs to access the sets in one of the following three cases.
If $|\mathcal{E}| \leq n^\delta$:

1. First the coordinator broadcasts $\mathcal{E}$ to the parties using $O(n^\delta \log n)$ bits.
2. Each party P_i, sends the projection of it sets on $\mathcal{E}$ back to the coordinator, i.e., $\{S \cap \mathcal{E} \mid S \in \mathcal{S}_i\}$. This needs at most $O(mn^\delta \log n)$ bits of communication.

Set Sampling:

1. To choose a collection of $ck\rho$ sets uniformly at random, $\mathcal{S}_{\text{rnd}}$, the coordinator sends a constant size message to all parties to initiate the set sampling module.
2. Then each party P_i generates and sends a random number corresponding to each of its sets which is a vector of size $|\mathcal{S}_i|$ of random numbers. Note that it is enough for the random numbers to be in the range $(1, \ldots, m^c)$ for some constant c so that with high probability, the numbers for all the sets in $\mathcal{S}$ do not collide. This needs at most $O(m \log m)$ bits of communication.
3. The coordinator finds a threshold thr such that there are exactly $ck\rho$ numbers below thr among the received numbers and broadcasts thr. It requires $O(\log m)$ bits.
4. Each party P_i sends back a bit vector of size n showing which elements are covered by the sets in $\mathcal{S}_i$ whose assigned random number is less than thr. This needs at most $O(p \cdot n)$ bits of communication.
5. The coordinator broadcasts the set of uncovered elements $\mathcal{E}_{\text{rem}}$ using $O(n \log n)$ bits.
6. Each party P_i returns for each uncovered element e, the number of sets in $\mathcal{S}_i$ that contains e. This needs at most $O(p \cdot n \log m)$ bits of communication.
7. The coordinator checks whether $\mathcal{S}_{\text{rnd}}$ is successful. In the case of success, it sends "success" message using $O(1)$ bits.
8. In the case of success, each of the parties projects its sets on the uncovered elements and sends it back to the coordinator. Then coordinator solves the Set Cover problem over the uncovered elements off-line. By Lemma 9, this needs at most $O(mn^\delta \log m \log^2 n)$ bits of communication.

Element Sampling. The element sampling requires recursively invoking the algorithm for the instances of the Set Cover problem with smaller element size. The coordinator samples a set of elements $\mathcal{E}_{\text{smp}}$ and solves the problem recursively for $\mathcal{E}_{\text{smp}}$. Then the coordinator checks whether $\mathcal{E}_{\text{smp}}$ was successful and in this case of success, it solves the problem recursively for the set of uncovered elements $\mathcal{E}_{\text{rem}}$.

By the analysis of Recursive-Sample-Set-Cover in Section 2, it is straightforward to check that the total communication in each round is $\tilde{O}(m \cdot n^\delta + p \cdot n)$. Also the total number of rounds is constant per each recursive call of Recursive-Sample-Set-Cover. Therefore similar to the proof of Lemma 7, the total number of rounds of the algorithm is $O(4^{1/\delta})$. Hence the total communication of the algorithm is $\tilde{O}(4^{1/\delta}(m \cdot n^\delta + p \cdot n))$.

On the Communication Complexity of Linear Algebraic Problems in the Message Passing Model[*]

Yi Li[1], Xiaoming Sun[2], Chengu Wang[3], and David P. Woodruff[4]

[1] Max-Planck Institute for Informatics
yli@mpi-inf.mpg.de
[2] Institute of Computing Technology, Chinese Academy of Sciences
sunxiaoming@ict.ac.cn
[3] Google Inc.
wangchengu@gmail.com
[4] IBM Almaden Research Center
dpwoodru@us.ibm.com

Abstract. We study the communication complexity of linear algebraic problems over finite fields in the multi-player message passing model, proving a number of tight lower bounds. We give a general framework for reducing these multi-player problems to their two-player counterparts, showing that the randomized s-player communication complexity of these problems is at least s times the randomized two-player communication complexity. Provided the problem has a certain amount of algebraic symmetry, we can show the hardest input distribution is a symmetric distribution, and therefore apply a recent multi-player lower bound technique of Phillips *et al.* Further, we give new two-player lower bounds for a number of these problems. In particular, our optimal lower bound for the two-player version of the matrix rank problem resolves an open question of Sun and Wang.

A common feature of our lower bounds is that they apply even to the special "threshold promise" versions of these problems, wherein the underlying quantity, e.g., rank, is promised to be one of just two values, one on each side of some critical threshold. These kinds of promise problems are commonplace in the literature on data streaming as sources of hardness for reductions giving space lower bounds.

1 Introduction

Communication complexity, introduced in the celebrated work of Yao [30], is a powerful abstraction that captures the essence of a host of problems in areas as disparate as data structures, decision trees, data streams, VLSI design, and circuit complexity [11]. It is concerned with problems (or *games*) where an input is distributed among $s \geq 2$ players who must jointly compute a function $f : X_1 \times \cdots \times X_s \to Z$, each X_i and Z being a finite set: Player i receives

---

[*] Full version available at arXiv:1407.4755 [cs.CC].

F. Kuhn (Ed.): DISC 2014, LNCS 8784, pp. 499–513, 2014.
© Springer-Verlag Berlin Heidelberg 2014

an input $x_i \in X_i$, the players then communicate by *passing messages* to one another using a predetermined protocol $\mathcal{P}$, and finally they converge on a shared output $\mathcal{P}(x_1, \ldots, x_s)$. The main goal of the players is to minimize the amount of communication, i.e., the total length of messages communicated. Put $\mathbf{x} = (x_1, \ldots, x_s)$. We say that a deterministic protocol $\mathcal{P}$ computes f if $\mathcal{P}(\mathbf{x}) = f(\mathbf{x})$ for all inputs $\mathbf{x}$. In a randomized protocol, the players can flip coins and send messages dependent on the outcomes; we shall focus on the public coin variant, wherein the coin flip outcomes are known to all players.[1] We say a randomized protocol $\mathcal{P}$ computes f with error δ if $\Pr[\mathcal{P}(\mathbf{x}) = f(\mathbf{x})] \geq 1 - \delta$ for all inputs $\mathbf{x}$. In all cases, we define the *cost* of $\mathcal{P}$ to be the maximum number of bits communicated by $\mathcal{P}$ over all inputs. We define the *deterministic* (resp. δ-error *randomized*) communication complexity of f, denoted $\mathrm{D}(f)$ (resp. $\mathrm{R}_\delta(f)$) to be the minimum cost of a protocol that computes f (with error δ in the randomized case). It holds that $\mathrm{D}(f) \geq \mathrm{R}_\delta(f)$ for all f and $0 \leq \delta \leq 1$.

Most work in communication complexity has focused on the two-player model (the players are named Alice and Bob in this case), which already admits a deep theory with many applications. However, one especially important class of applications is *data stream* computation [8,16]: the input is a very long sequence that must be read in a few *streaming passes*, and the goal is to compute some function of the input while minimizing the memory (storage space) used by the algorithm. Several data stream lower bounds specifically call for *multi-player* communication lower bounds [1]. Moreover, several newer works have considered distributed computing problems with streamed inputs, such as the *distributed functional monitoring* problems of Cormode *et al.* [6]: in a typical scenario, a number of "sensors" must collectively monitor some state of their environment by efficiently communicating with a central "coordinator." Studying the complexity of problems in such models naturally leads one to questions about multi-player communication protocols.

In the multi-player setting, strong lower bounds in the message passing model[2] are a fairly recent achievement, even for basic problems. For the SETDISJOINT-NESS problem, a cornerstone of communication complexity theory, two-player lower bounds were long known [10,20] but an optimal multi-player lower bound was only obtained in the very recent work of Braverman *et al.* [3]. For computing bit-wise AND, OR, and XOR functions of vectors held by different parties, as well as other problems such as testing connectivity and computing coresets for approximating the geometric width of a pointset, optimal lower bounds were given in [19]. For computing a number of graph properties or exact statistics of databases, a recent work achieved optimal lower bounds [28]. There are also recent tight lower bounds for approximating frequency moments [27] and approximating distinct

---

[1] Though the private coin model may appear more "natural," our key results, being lower bounds, are *stronger* for holding in the more general public coin model. In any case, for the particular problems we consider here, the private and public coin models are asymptotically equivalent by a theorem of Newman [18].

[2] In contrast to the message passing model is the *blackboard* model, where players write messages on a shared blackboard.

elements [29]. Our chief motivation is to further develop this growing theory, giving optimal lower bounds for other fundamental problems.

Linear algebra is a fundamental area in pure and applied mathematics, appearing ubiquitously in computational applications. The communication complexity of linear algebraic problems is therefore intrinsically interesting. The connection with data streaming adds further motivation, since linear algebraic problems are a major focus of data stream computation. Frieze, Kannan and Vempala [7] developed a fast algorithm for the low-rank approximation problem. Clarkson and Woodruff [5] gave near-optimal space bounds in the streaming model for many linear algebra problems, e.g., matrix multiplication, linear regression and low rank approximation. Muthukrishnan [17] asked several linear algebra questions in the streaming model including rank-k approximation, matrix multiplication, matrix inverse, determinant, and eigenvalues. Sárlos [21] gave upper bounds for many approximation problems, including matrix multiplication, singular value decomposition and linear regression.

Our Results: Let us first describe the new two-player communication complexity results proved in this work. We then describe how to extend these to obtain our multi-player results.

Two-Player Lower Bounds: We start by studying the following closely related matrix problems. In each case, the input describes a matrix $z \in M_n(\mathbb{F}_p)$, the set of $n \times n$ matrices with entries in the finite field $\mathbb{F}_p$ for some prime p.

- Problem $\text{RANK}_{n,k}$: Under the promise that $\text{rank}(z) \in \{k, k+1\}$, compute $\text{rank}(z)$.
- Problem INVERSE_n: Under the promise that z is invertible, decide whether the $(1,1)$ entry of z^{-1} is zero.
- Problem $\text{LINSOLVE}_{n,b}$: Under the promise that z is invertible, for a fixed non-zero vector $b \in \mathbb{F}_p^n$, consider the linear system $zt = b$ in the unknowns $t \in \mathbb{F}_p^n$. Decide whether t_1 is zero.

There are two natural ways to split z between Alice and Bob. In the concatenation model, Alice and Bob hold the top $n/2$ rows and the bottom $n/2$ rows of z, respectively. In the additive split model, Alice and Bob hold $x, y \in M_n(\mathbb{F}_p)$ respectively, and $z = x + y$. The two models are equivalent up to a constant factor [25], see Section 5.3. All of this generalizes in the obvious manner to the multi-player setting.

Theorem 1. *Let f be one of* $\text{RANK}_{n,n-1}$, INVERSE_n, *or* $\text{LINSOLVE}_{n,b}$. *Then* $R_{1/10}(f) = \Omega(n^2 \log p)$.

The above immediately implies $\Omega(n^2 \log p)$ space lower bounds for randomized streaming algorithms for each of these problems, where the input matrix z is presented in row-major order. See the full version for details. Clearly these lower bounds are optimal, since the problems have trivial $O(n^2 \log p)$ upper bounds, that being the size of the input. We remark that Theorem 1 in fact extends to the *quantum* communication model, a generalization of randomized communication that we shall not elaborate on in this paper.

To prove these lower bounds, we use the *Fourier witness method* [25] for the promised rank problem, then reduce it to other problems. The reductions critically use the promise in the rank problem, for which establishing a lower bound was posed as an open question in [25]. Roughly speaking, the Fourier witness method is a special type of dual norm method [13,22,24]. In the dual norm method, there is a *witness* (a feasible solution of the dual maximization problem for the approximate norms). A typical choice of witness is the function itself (such as in the discrepancy method). In the *Fourier witness method* the witness is chosen as the Fourier transform of the function. This method works well for plus composed functions. For details, see Section 5.1.

We also consider the inner product and Hamming weight problems. Alice and Bob now hold *vectors* x and y.

- Problem IP_n: Under the promise that $\langle x, y \rangle \in \{0, 1\}$, compute $\langle x, y \rangle$. Here $x, y \in \mathbb{F}_p^n$.
- Problem $\mathrm{HAM}_{n,k}$: Under the promise that $\|x + y\| \in \{k, k + 2\}$, compute $\|x + y\|$. Here $x, y \in \mathbb{F}_2^n$ and $\|z\|$ denotes the Hamming weight of z, i.e., the number of 1 entries in z. Note that $x - y = x + y$.

We do not provide new two-player lower bounds for IP_n and $\mathrm{HAM}_{n,k}$, but state the known ones here for use in our s-player lower bounds. It is known that $\mathrm{R}_{1/3}(\mathrm{IP}_n) = \Omega(n \log p)$ [26] and $\mathrm{R}_{1/3}(\mathrm{HAM}_{n,k}) = \Omega(k)$ [9].

s-**Player Lower Bounds:** For each of the above problems, there are natural s-player variants. We consider the *coordinator model* in which there is an additional player, called the coordinator, who has no input. We require that the s players can only talk to the coordinator. The message-passing model can be simulated in the coordinator model since every time a Player i wants to talk to a Player j, Player i can first send a message to the coordinator, and then the coordinator can forward the message to Player j. This only affects the communication by a factor of 2. See, e.g., Section 3 of [3] for a more detailed description.

For the matrix problems, Player i holds a matrix $x^{(i)}$ and the computations need to be performed on $z = x^{(1)} + \cdots + x^{(s)}$. The Hamming weight problem is similar, except that each $x^{(i)}$ is a vector in $\mathbb{F}_2^n$. For the inner product problem, each $x^{(i)} \in \mathbb{F}_p^n$ and we consider the generalized inner product, defined as $\sum_{j=1}^n \prod_{i=1}^s x_j^{(i)}$.

We provide a framework for applying the recent *symmetrization* technique of Phillips *et al.* [19] to each of these problems. Doing so lets us "scale up" each of the above lower bounds to the s-player versions of the problems.

However, the symmetrization technique in [19] does not immediately apply, since it requires a lower bound on the *distributional* communication complexity of the two-player problem under an input distribution with certain symmetric properties. Nevertheless, for many of the two-player lower bounds above, e.g., those in Theorem 1, our lower bound technique does not give a distributional complexity lower bound. We instead exploit the symmetry of the underlying problems, together with a re-randomization argument in Theorem 3 to argue that the hardest input distribution to these problems is in fact a symmetric distribution; see Definition 1 for a precise definition of symmetric. We thus obtain a distributional lower bound by the strong version of Yao's minimax principle.

We obtain the following results. Here, $R_\delta^s(f)$ denotes the δ-error randomized communication complexity of the s-player variant of f. We give precise definitions in Section 3.

Theorem 2. *If* f *is one of* RANK$_{n,n-1}$, INVERSE$_n$, *or* LINSOLVE$_{n,b}$, *then* $R_{1/40}^s(f) = \Omega(sn^2 \log p)$. *Further,* $R_{1/12}^s(\text{IP}_n) = \Omega(sn \log p)$ *and* $R_{1/12}^s(\text{HAM}_{n,k}) = \Omega(sk)$.

We note that this has an application to the information-theoretic privacy of the RANK$_{n,n-1}$ problem. See the full version for details.

Related Work: Many linear algebra problems have been studied in both the communication complexity model and the streaming model. Chu and Schnitger [4] proved that $\Omega(n^2 \log p)$ communication is required by deterministic protocols for the singularity problem over $\mathbb{F}_p$. Luo and Tsitsiklis [14] proved that a deterministic protocol must transfer $\Omega(n^2)$ real numbers for the matrix inversion problem over $\mathbb{C}$, but Alice and Bob can only use addition, subtraction, multiplication and division of real numbers. Clarkson and Woodruff [5] proposed a randomized one pass streaming algorithm that uses $O(k^2 \log n)$ space to decide if the rank of an integer matrix is k and proved an $\Omega(k^2)$ lower bound for randomized one-way protocols in the communication complexity model via a reduction from the INDEXING communication problem. It implies an $\Omega(n^2)$ space lower bound in the streaming model with one pass. Miltersen et al. [15] showed a tight lower bound for deciding whether a vector is in a subspace of $\mathbb{F}_2^n$ in the one-sided error randomized asymmetric communication complexity model, using the Richness Lemma. Sun and Wang [25] proved the quantum communication complexities for matrix singularity and determinant over $\mathbb{F}_p$ are both $\Omega(n^2 \log p)$.

Compared to previous results, our results are stronger. For the rank problem, the matrix singularity problem in [25] is to decide if the rank of a matrix is n or less than n, but RANK$_{n,n-1}$ is to decide if the rank is n or $n-1$. This additional promise enables our lower bounds for INVERSE$_n$ and LINSOLVE$_{n,b}$. If we set $k = n$ in Clarkson and Woodruff's result [5], the result gives us an $\Omega(n^2)$ bound for randomized one-way protocols. However, our lower bounds work even for quantum two-way protocols. For the inverse problem, Luo and Tsitsiklis's result [14] is in a non-standard communication complexity model, in which Alice and Bob can only make arithmetic operations on real numbers. However, our lower bound works in the standard model of communication complexity. A result of Miltersen et al. [15] is to decide if a vector is in a subspace. Sun and Wang [25] studied the problem deciding whether two $n/2$ dimensional subspaces intersect at $\{\mathbf{0}\}$ or not, but we get the same bound in Corollary 1 even with the promise. The results are analogous to the difference between set disjointness [2] and unique set disjointness [10,20].

Corollary 1. *Alice and Bob each hold an* $n/2$-*dimensional subspace of* $\mathbb{F}_p^n$. *We promise that the intersection of the two subspaces is either* $\{\mathbf{0}\}$ *or a one-dimensional* *space. Any quantum protocol requires $\Omega(n^2 \log p)$ communication to distinguish the two cases.*

In the communication model, there is another way to distribute the input: Alice and Bob each hold an $n \times n$ matrix x and y, respectively, and they want to compute some property of $x + y$. This is equivalent to our model of matrix concatenation up to a constant factor [25], a fact we shall use in the paper.

Paper Organization: In Section 3 we present our framework of multi-party communication lower bound for a class of problems. In Section 4 we discuss the IP_n problem and in Section 5 the $RANK_{n,n-1}$ problem and related linear algebra problems.

2　Preliminaries

Communication Complexity: We briefly summarize the notions from communication complexity that we will need. For more background on communication complexity, we refer the reader to [11].

Let $f : X \times Y \to \{1, -1\}$ be a given function, which could be a partial function. Let $\mathrm{dom}(f)$ be the domain of f. Alice and Bob, with unlimited computing power, want to compute $f(x, y)$ for $(x, y) \in \mathrm{dom}(f)$. Alice only knows $x \in X$ and Bob $y \in Y$. To perform the computation, they follow a protocol Π and send messages to each other in order to converge on a shared output $\Pi(x, y)$. We say a deterministic protocol Π computes f if $\Pi(x, y) = f(x, y)$ for all inputs $(x, y) \in \mathrm{dom}(f)$, and define the *deterministic communication complexity*, denoted by $D(f)$, to be the minimum over correct deterministic protocols for f, of the maximum number of bits communicated over all inputs. In a randomized protocol, Alice and Bob toss private coins and the messages can depend on the coin flips. We say a randomized protocol Π computes f with error probability δ if $\Pr\{\Pi(x, y) = f(x, y)\} \geq 1 - \delta$ for all inputs $(x, y) \in \mathrm{dom}(f)$, and define the *randomized communication complexity*, denoted by $R_\delta(f)$, in the same way. When Alice and Bob share public random coins, the randomized communication complexity is denoted by $R_\delta^{\mathrm{pub}}(f)$. Let μ be a probability distribution on $X \times Y$. The *μ-distributional communication complexity* of f, denoted by $D_\delta^\mu(f)$, is the least cost of a deterministic protocol for f with error probability at most δ with respect to μ. Yao's principle states that $R_\delta^{\mathrm{pub}}(f) = \max_\mu D_\delta^\mu(f)$.

In the model for multiparty communication complexity, there are s players, each gets an input $x_i \in X_i$, and they want to compute some function $f : X_1 \times \cdots \times X_s \to \{-1, 1\}$ (which could be partially defined). We shall assume the coordinator model, in which there is an additional player called coordinator, who has no input. Players can only communicate with the coordinator but not each other directly. The coordinator will output the value of f. The private-coin, public-coin randomized communication complexity and μ-distributional communication complexity are denoted by $R_\delta^s(f)$, $R_\delta^{s,\mathrm{pub}}(f)$, and $D_\delta^{s,\mu}(f)$, respectively.

3   Reduction for Multi-player Communication

Let $(G, \otimes)$ be a finite group and f be a function on G (could be a partial function). Suppose that $G = \bigcup_i G_i$ is the coarsest partition of G such that f is a constant function (allowing the value to be undefined) over each G_i. For a subset $X \subseteq G$, let $\mathrm{pre}(X) := \{(g_1, g_2) \in G \times G : g_1 \otimes g_2 \in X\}$. Let $I(f) = \{i : G_i \subseteq \mathrm{dom}(f)\}$, where $\mathrm{dom}(f) \subseteq G$ is the set on which f is defined.

We say that a family $\mathcal{H}$ of functions $h : G \times G \to G \times G$ is a *uniformizing family* for function f if there exists a probability measure μ on $\mathcal{H}$ such that for any i and $(g_1, g_2) \in \mathrm{pre}(G_i)$, when $h \in \mathcal{H}$ is randomly chosen according to μ, the image $h(g_1, g_2)$ is uniformly distributed on $\mathrm{pre}(G_i)$.

Example 1 ($\mathrm{RANK}_{n,n-1}$). $G = M_n(\mathbb{F})$, the group of all $n \times n$ matrices over $\mathbb{F}$, with $\otimes$ being the usual matrix addition. In fact G is a ring, with the usual matrix multiplication. Define

$$f(x) = \begin{cases} 1, & \mathrm{rank}(x) = n; \\ 0, & \mathrm{rank}(x) = n - 1; \qquad x \in G. \\ \text{undefined}, & \text{otherwise}, \end{cases}$$

Then $I(f) = \{1, 2\}$ and $G_1 = \{x \in G : \mathrm{rank}(x) = n\}$ and $G_2 = \{x \in G : \mathrm{rank}(x) = n - 1\}$. The uniformizing family is $\mathcal{H} = \{h_{a,b}\}_{a \in G_1, b \in G}$ endowed with uniform measure, where $h_{a,b}(g_1, g_2) = (a(g_1 - b), a(g_2 + b))$.

Example 2 ($\mathrm{HAM}_{n,k}$). $G = \mathbb{F}_2^n$ with the usual vector addition. Define

$$f(x) = \begin{cases} 1, & w(x) = k; \\ 0, & w(x) = k + 2; \qquad x \in G. \\ \text{undefined}, & \text{otherwise}, \end{cases}$$

Then $|I(f)| = 2$. Let S_n denote the symmetric group of degree n. The uniformizing family $\mathcal{H} = \{h_{\sigma,b}\}_{\sigma \in S_n, b \in G}$ endowed with uniform measure, where $h_{\sigma,b}(g_1, g_2) = (\sigma(g_1 - b), \sigma(g_2 + b))$.

By reduction from the Disjointness problem, we know that $\mathrm{R}_{1/10}^{\mathrm{pub}}(\mathrm{HAM}_{k,k+2}) = \Omega(k)$.

As an auxiliary problem to the IP problem, we define
-   Problem IP'_n: Suppose that $p > 2$. Alice and Bob hold two vectors $x, y \in (\mathbb{F}_p^*)^n$ respectively. We promise that inner product $\langle x, y \rangle \in \{0, 1\}$. They want to output $\langle x, y \rangle$.

Removing 0 from the scalar domain gives us a group structure as below.

Example 3 (IP'_n). $G = (\mathbb{F}_p^*)^n$ associated with the multiplication $\otimes$ defined to be the pointwise product, i.e., $x \otimes y = (x_1 y_1, x_2 y_2, \ldots, x_n y_n)$. Let $f(x) = \mathbf{1}_{\{x_1 + x_2 + \cdots + x_n = 0\}}$.

The following problem was considered in [26].

– Problem CYCLE$_n$: Let π and σ be permutations in symmetric group S_n. Alice holds π and Bob σ, and they want to return 1 if $\pi \circ \sigma$ is exactly 1-cycle and return 0 otherwise.

Example 4 (CYCLE$_n$). $G = S_n$, the symmetric group of degree n, with the usual permutation composition. Define

$$f(x) = \begin{cases} 1, & x \text{ has exactly one cycle;} \\ 0, & \text{otherwise,} \end{cases} \qquad x \in G.$$

Then $|I(f)| = 2$. The uniformizing family is $\mathcal{H} = \{h_{\sigma,\tau}\}_{\sigma,\tau \in S_n}$ endowed with uniform measure, where $h_{\sigma,\tau}(g_1, g_2) = (\sigma^{-1} g_1 \tau^{-1}, \tau g_2 \sigma)$. Observe that $g \mapsto \sigma^{-1} g \sigma$ maps a cycle $(a_1, \ldots, a_k)$ of g to $(\sigma(a_1), \ldots, \sigma(a_k))$, it is easy to verify that $\mathcal{H}$ is a uniformizing family. It is known that $R_{1/3}^{pub}(\text{CYCLE}_n) = \Omega(n)$ [26].

We analyze the randomized communication complexity of problems that have a uniformizing family.

Definition 1. *A distribution ν on $G \times G$ is called* weakly sub-uniform *if*
1. *ν is supported on $\bigcup_{i \in I(f)} \text{pre}(G_i)$*
2. *$\nu|_{\text{pre}(G_i)}$ is uniform for all $i \in I(f)$*
In addition, if $\nu(\text{pre}(G_i)) = 1/|I(f)|$ for all $i \in I(f)$, we say ν is the sub-uniform *distribution.*

Theorem 3. *If there exists a uniformizing family for f and $\delta \cdot |I(f)| < 1$, then for the two-player game computing f it holds that*

$$R_{\delta|I(f)|}^{pub}(f) \leq D_\delta^\nu(f) \leq C \log_{|I(f)|\delta} \delta \cdot R_{|I(f)|\delta}^{pub}(f)$$

where $C > 0$ is an absolute constant and ν the sub-uniform distribution on $G \times G$.

Proof. Suppose the input is $(g_1, g_2) \in G \times G$. Next we describe a public-coin protocol Π'. With the public randomness, Alice and Bob choose a random h from the uniformizing family. They then run the optimal protocol Π_ν for input distribution ν (i.e., $\text{cost}(\Pi_\nu) = D_\delta^\nu(f)$) on input $h(g_1, g_2)$.

It is not difficult to see that the public-coin protocol Π' has error probability at most $\delta \cdot |I(f)|$. Therefore, $R_{\delta \cdot |I(f)|}^{pub} \leq \text{cost}(\Pi') = \text{cost}(\Pi_\nu) = D_\delta^\nu(f)$. On the other hand, by Yao's principle, $R_\delta^{pub}(f) \geq D_\delta^\nu(f)$. Note that $R_\delta^{pub}(f) \leq C \log_{|I(f)|\delta} \delta \cdot R_{|I(f)|\delta}^{pub}(f)$ for some absolute constant C, the conclusion follows. □

Now consider the following multi-player problem in coordinator model: There are s players and a coordinator. Each player receives an input $x_i \in G$. The coordinator will output the value of $f(x_1 \otimes x_2 \otimes \cdots \otimes x_s)$ with probability $\geq 1 - \delta$. Denote by $C_\delta^{s,pub}(f)$ the number of bits that must be exchanged by the best protocol. By the symmetrization technique from [19], we have the following lemma.

Lemma 1. *Suppose that f has a uniformizing family. Let ν be an arbitrary weakly sub-uniform distribution on $G \times G$ and Π_ν be a public-coin protocol that computes f with error probability δ on input distribution ν. Then $R_\delta^{s,pub}(f) \geq s\mathbb{E}[\mathrm{cost}(\Pi_\nu)]$.*

Proof. Let ν_s be the distribution over G^s such that ν_s is the uniform distribution over $\mathrm{pre}_s(G_i) := \{(x_1,\dots,x_s) \in G^s : x_1 \otimes \cdots \otimes x_s \in G_i\}$ when restricted onto it and $\nu_s(\mathrm{pre}_s(G_i)) = \nu(\mathrm{pre}(G_i))$. Let Π_s be an s-player (deterministic) protocol for input distribution ν_s with error probability δ.

Consider the following two-player protocol Π' on input $(g_1, g_2) \sim \nu$: First suppose that Alice and Bob have public randomness. They first use the public randomness to agree on an index j chosen at random uniformly from $\{1,\dots,s\}$. Alice also generates, using her own randomness, the input $\{x_i\}_{i\neq j}$ of other players uniformly at random conditioned on $\bigotimes_{i\neq j} x_i = g_1$. Then Alice and Bob run the s-player protocol, in which Bob simulates player j with input $x_j := g_2$, and Alice simulates all other players and the coordinator. The message sent in this protocol is just the message sent between the coordinator and player j in Π_s.

It is not hard to see that $(x_1,\dots,x_s) \sim \nu_s$. It follows from a symmetrization argument like the proof [19, Theorem 1.1] that $\mathbb{E}[\mathrm{cost}(\Pi')] \leq \mathrm{cost}(\Pi_s)/s$, where the expectation is taken over the public coins. The conclusion follows from taking the infimum over Π_s.

Theorem 4. *Suppose that f has a uniformizing family, then $R_\delta^{s,pub}(f) \geq \delta s\, R_{2|I(f)|\delta}^{pub}(f)$.*

Proof. Pick ν to be the sub-uniform distribution in the preceding lemma. By fixing the public coins and a Markov bound, one can construct a two-player deterministic protocol Π'' such that $\mathrm{cost}(\Pi'') \leq (1/\delta)\,\mathrm{cost}(\Pi_s)/s$ and Π'' succeeds with probability at least $1 - 2\delta$ when the input is distributed as ν. Hence $D_{2\delta}^\nu(f) \leq (1/\delta)\,\mathrm{cost}(\Pi_s)/s$. It then follows from Theorem 3 that $R_{2|I(f)|\delta}^{pub}(f) \leq (1/\delta)\,\mathrm{cost}(\Pi_s)/s$. Taking infimum over Π_s, we obtain that $R_{2|I(f)|\delta}^{pub}(f) \leq (1/\delta) \cdot D_\delta^{\nu_s}(f)/s \leq (1/\delta)R_\delta^{s,pub}(f)/s$. □

The following are immediate corollaries of the theorem above applied to our previous Example 2 and 4. We leave the results of Example 1 and 3 for later sections.

Corollary 2. $R_{1/12}^{s,pub}(\mathrm{HAM}_{k,k+2}) = \Omega(s\, R_{1/3}^{pub}(\mathrm{HAM}_{k,k+2})) = \Omega(sk)$.

Corollary 3. $R_{1/12}^{s,pub}(\mathrm{CYCLE}_n) = \Omega(sn)$.

4 The IP Problem

Let p be a prime. Sun *et al.* considered a variant of the IP problem, denoted by IP_n'', in which Alice has $x \in F_p^n$ and Bob $y \in (F_p^*)^n$, and showed that $R_{1/3}^{pub}(\mathrm{IP}_n'') = \Omega(n \log p)$ [26]. Via a simple reduction, we show that

Lemma 2. *When $p \geq p_0$ for some constant p_0, $R_{1/3}^{pub}(\mathrm{IP}_n') = \Omega(n \log p)$.*

Proof. For an input of IP″, Alice can send the indices of the zero coordinates to Bob using n bits; on the remaining coordinates, Alice and Bob have an instance of IP′ of size at most n. Hence $n + R_{1/3}^{\text{pub}}(\text{IP}'_n) \geq R_{1/3}^{\text{pub}}(\text{IP}''_n)$, whence the conclusion follows.   □

It is clear, by Yao's principle, that $R_\delta^{\text{pub}}(\text{IP}_n) \geq R_\delta^{\text{pub}}(\text{IP}'_n)$. Now, as an immediate corollary of Theorem 4, we have

Theorem 5. $R_{1/12}^{s,\text{pub}}(\text{IP}_n) = \Omega(sn \log p)$.

Proof. Let p_0 be as in Lemma 2. It follows from Lemma 2 and Theorem 4 that $R_{1/12}^{s,\text{pub}}(\text{IP}) \geq R_{1/12}^{s,\text{pub}}(\text{IP}') = \Omega(s R_{1/3}^{\text{pub}}(\text{IP}')) = \Omega(sn \log p)$. When $p < p_0$, the result is due to Braverman et al. in [3], who prove an $\Omega(sn)$ lower bound for IP over the integers with the promise that the inner product is 0 or 1. Note that this implies an $\Omega(sn \log p)$ lower bound for computing IP over $\mathbb{F}_p$ as well, since $p < p_0$ is a fixed constant.   □

5   The Rank Problem

We shall use the Fourier witness method to prove a lower bound on $\text{RANK}'_{n,n-1}$. We then use this result for $\text{RANK}_{n,n-1}$ to obtain lower bounds for the other problems. We review some basics of the Fourier witness method in Section 5.1 then give the proof of the lower bound in Section 5.2.

5.1   Fourier Witness Method

Fourier Analysis. For prime p, let $\mathbb{F}_p$ be the finite field of order p. We define the Fourier transformation on the group $(\mathbb{F}_p^n, +)$.

Definition 2 (Fourier transform). *Let $f : \mathbb{F}_p^N \to \mathbb{R}$ be a function. Then, the Fourier coefficient of f, denoted by $\hat{f}$, is also a $\mathbb{F}_p^N \to \mathbb{R}$ function, defined as $\hat{f}(s) = p^{-N} \sum_{x \in \mathbb{F}_p^N} \omega^{-\langle s,x \rangle} f(x)$, where $\omega = e^{2\pi i/p}$.*

Fact 6. $f = p^N \left(\left(\hat{f} \right)^* \right)^*$.

Approximate Norm and Dual Norm. The ℓ_p norm of a vector $v \in \mathbb{R}^n$ is defined by $\|v\|_p := \left(\sum_{i=1}^n |v_i|^p \right)^{1/p}$ and the ℓ_∞ norm by $\|v\|_\infty := \max_{i=1}^n |v_i|$. The trace norm of an $n \times n$ matrix F, denoted by $\|F\|_{\text{tr}}$, is defined as $\|F\|_{\text{tr}} := \sum_i \sigma_i$, where $\sigma_1, \cdots, \sigma_n$ are the singular values of F.

The matrix rank and some matrix norms can give lower bounds for deterministic communication complexity. For randomized lower bounds, we need the notions of approximate rank and norms.

Definition 3 (approximate norm). *Let $\rho : \mathbb{R}^X \mapsto \mathbb{R}$ be an arbitrary norm and $f : X \mapsto \mathbb{R}$ a partial sign function. The ε-approximate ρ norm of f, denoted*

by $\rho^{\varepsilon}(f)$, is defined as $\rho^{\varepsilon}(f) = \inf_{\phi} \rho(\phi)$, where the infimum is taken over all functions $\phi : X \mapsto \mathbb{R}$ that satisfy

$$\phi(x) \in \begin{cases} [1 - \varepsilon, 1 + \varepsilon] & \text{if } f(x) = 1; \\ [-1 - \varepsilon, -1 + \varepsilon] & \text{if } f(x) = -1; \\ [-1 - \varepsilon, 1 + \varepsilon] & \text{if } f(x) \text{ is undefined.} \end{cases}$$

The following lemma shows that the approximate trace norm gives lower bounds on quantum communication complexity, as well as on randomized protocols with public coins. The following lemma is a result in [12] combined with Neumann's argument for converting a public-coin protocol into a private-coin one.

Lemma 3. *For $\delta > 0$ such that $1/(1 - 2\varepsilon) \leq 1 + \delta$, it holds that*

$$R_{\delta}^{pub}(f) \geq \Omega \left(\log \frac{(\|F\|_{\text{tr}}^{\varepsilon})^2}{\text{size}(F)} \right) - O \left(\log n + \log \frac{1}{\delta} \right).$$

The approximate norms are minimization problems. We will consider the dual problems, which are maximization problems.

Definition 4. *Let ρ be an arbitrary norm on $\mathbb{R}^n$. The dual norm of ρ, denoted by ρ^*, is defined as $\rho^*(v) = \sup_{u : \rho(u) \leq 1} \langle v, u \rangle$.*

The following lemma characterizes the approximate norm as a maximization problem so that we can prove *lower* bounds more easily.

Lemma 4 ([23]). *Let f be a partial sign function and ρ an arbitrary norm. Then*

$$\rho^{\varepsilon}(f) = \sup_{\psi \neq 0} \frac{\langle f, \psi \cdot \text{dom}(f) \rangle - \|\psi \cdot \overline{\text{dom}(f)}\|_1 - \varepsilon \|\psi\|_1}{\rho^*(\psi)}, \quad \varepsilon > 0.$$

where

$$\text{dom}(f)(x) = \begin{cases} 1 & \text{if } f(x) \text{ is defined,} \\ 0 & \text{otherwise,} \end{cases}$$

$\overline{\text{dom}(f)}(x) = 1 - \text{dom}(f)(x)$, and $(\psi \cdot \varphi)(x) = \psi(x)\varphi(x)$.

We call a feasible solution in the dual problem the witness of the original problem. In particular, in Lemma 4, the function ψ is the witness. Any ψ gives a lower bound for $\rho^{\varepsilon}(f)$. It is difficult to find a useful witness. The first choice that comes to mind is to choose $\psi = f \cdot \text{dom}(f)$, because it makes $\langle f, \psi \cdot \text{dom}(f) \rangle$ large and $\|\overline{\text{dom}(f)}\|_1$ small. This is the discrepancy method. We use a different choice: $\psi = \widehat{(f \cdot \text{dom}(f))}$. We call it the *Fourier witness method*, introduced in [25], but used here for partial functions.

Definition 5 (approximate Fourier p-norm). *Let $f : \mathbb{F}_p^N \mapsto \mathbb{R}$ be a function and $p \geq 1$. The Fourier p-norm of f, denoted by $\|\hat{f}\|_p$, is the p-norm of $\hat{f}$. Furthermore, if f is a sign function, the approximate Fourier p-norm of f, denoted by $\|\hat{f}\|_p^{\varepsilon}$, is the approximate $\|\hat{\cdot}\|_p$ norm of f.*

Fact 7. *The dual norm of $\|\cdot\|_1$ is $\|\cdot\|_\infty$. The dual norm of $\||\hat{\cdot}\||_1$ is $p^N\||\hat{\cdot}\||_\infty$.*

The Fourier coefficients of a plus composed function are related to the singular values of the associated matrix, as shown by the following lemma, whose proof is omitted. Applied to approximate trace norm, it also builds a bridge between the approximate trace norm and the approximate Fourier ℓ_1-norm for a plus composed function. Similar results and additional background can be found in [12,25].

Lemma 5. *Suppose that $g : \mathbb{F}_p^N \mapsto \mathbb{R}$ is a function, and f is a plus-composed function $f(x,y) = g(x+y)$. Let F be the associated matrix of f. Then the singular values of F are p^N times the modulus of the Fourier coefficients of g, i.e. $\sigma_F = p^N \cdot |\hat{g}|$, where σ_F are the singular values of F and $|\hat{g}|(s) = |\hat{g}(s)|$. As a consequence, $\|F\|_{\mathrm{tr}}^\varepsilon = p^N \cdot \|\hat{g}\|_1^\varepsilon$.*

5.2   Rank$_{n,n-1}$

For a matrix $x \in \mathbb{F}_p^{n\times n}$, we define $\theta(x) = 1$ if x is of full rank and $\theta(x) = 0$ otherwise. We shall use θ as the witness in the proof of RANK$'_{n,n-1}$. The same function θ has been used to prove a communication complexity lower bound for the matrix singularity problem in [25].

Theorem 8. $R_{1/10}^{pub}(\text{RANK}_{n,n-1}) = \Omega(n^2 \log p)$.

Proof. Suppose that Π is a public-coin protocol for RANK$'_{n,n-1}$ with error probability $\leq 1/10$. Then Alice and Bob can build a public-coin protocol Π' as follows. They use the public coins to choose a random matrix r and run Π on input $(x - r, y + r)$. It is easy to see that Π' has error probability $\leq 1/10$ and $\text{cost}(\Pi') = \text{cost}(\Pi)$. Observe that the distribution of $\Pi'(x,y)$ is identical to the that of $\Pi'(a,b)$ whenever $x + y = a + b$.

Define the partial sign function $g(x) = 1$ if $\text{rank}(x) = n$, $g(x) = -1$ if $\text{rank}(x) = n - 1$, and $g(x)$ is undefined otherwise. Let $f(x,y)$ be the expected output of $\Pi'(x,y)$. Then f is a plus-composed function. By the correctness of Π, we know that $f(x,y) = g(x+y)$ whenever $g(x+y)$ is defined. We claim that $\|g\|_1^\varepsilon = \Omega(p^{n(n-3)/2})$ for $\varepsilon = 1/4$, following Lemma 4 (applied with witness θ as in the paragraph before the theorem statement) and Fact 7. See the full version for details. Finally, it follows from Lemma 3 that

$$R_{1/10}^{pub}(f) = \Omega\left(\log \frac{\|F\|_{\mathrm{tr}}^{1/4}}{\sqrt{\text{size}(F)}}\right) - O(\log n) = \Omega\left(\log \frac{p^{n^2}\|\hat{g}\|_1^\varepsilon}{\sqrt{\text{size}(F)}}\right) - O(\log n)$$

$$= \Omega\left(\log \frac{p^{n^2} \cdot 0.4 p^{n(n-3)/2}}{p^{n^2}}\right) - O(\log n) = \Omega(n^2 \log p). \quad \square$$

The lower bound for the multi-player RANK problem is an immediate corollary of Theorem 4.

Corollary 4. $R_{1/40}^{s,pub}(\text{RANK}_{n,n-1}) = \Omega(sR_{1/10}^{pub}(\text{RANK}_{n,n-1})) = \Omega(sn^2 \log p)$.

By padding zeros outside the top-left $k \times k$ submatrix, we obtain a lower bound for $\text{RANK}_{k,k-1}$.

Corollary 5. $R^{pub}_{1/10}(\text{RANK}_{k,k-1}) = \Omega(k^2 \log p)$.

5.3   Linear Algebra Problems

*Problem 1 (*INVERSE*).* Alice and Bob hold two $n \times n$ matrices x and y over $\mathbb{F}_p$, respectively. We promise that $x+y$ is invertible over $\mathbb{F}_p$. They want to determine if the top-left entry of $(x+y)^{-1}$ is zero (output -1) or non-zero (output 1).

*Problem 2 (*LINSOLVE*).* Alice and Bob hold two $n \times n$ matrices x and y over $\mathbb{F}_p$, respectively. We promise that $x+y$ is invertible over $\mathbb{F}_p$. b is a parameter of this problem. t is the vector of variables of the linear system $(x+y)t = b$. They want to determine if the first coordinate of t is zero.

Theorem 9. $R^{pub}_{1/20}(\text{INVERSE}) = \Omega(n^2 \log p)$ *for* $p \geq 3$.

Proof. We reduce RANK to INVERSE. Let $A = x + y$ and $\tilde{A}$ be the lower-right $(n-1) \times (n-1)$ block of A. Then $A^{-1}_{11} = 0$ iff $\text{rank}(\tilde{A}) < n-1$.

Now, suppose that A is an $(n-1) \times (n-1)$ matrix and $\text{rank}(A) \in \{n-1, n-2\}$. We augment A to A_1 by appending a random column. With probability $1 - 1/p$ it holds that $\text{rank}(A_1) = n-1$ when $\text{rank}(A) = n-2$. Now we augment A_1 to A_2 by appending a random row. With probability $1 - 1/p$ it holds that $\text{rank}(A_2) = n$ when $\text{rank}(A_1) = n-1$.

Run a protocol for INVERSE on A_2. We denote the communication complexity of the protocol by $c(n)$. When $\text{rank}(A) = n-1$, if the error probability of the protocol is at most $1/20$, then it outputs 1 with probability $\alpha \leq \frac{1}{20}\left(1 - \frac{1}{p}\right) + \frac{1}{p}$, while when $\text{rank}(A) = n-2$ it outputs 1 with probability $\beta \geq \frac{19}{20}\left(1 - \frac{1}{p}\right)^2$. Then $\beta - \alpha \geq \frac{19}{20}\left(1 - \frac{1}{p}\right)^2 - \frac{1}{20}\left(1 - \frac{1}{p}\right) - \frac{1}{p} \geq \frac{1}{18}$, $p \geq 3$, which implies that $\Theta(1)$ independent repetitions allow us to solve RANK on $(n-1) \times (n-1)$ matrices, i.e., to distinguish $\text{rank}(A) = n-1$ from $\text{rank}(A) = n-2$, with error probability $\leq 1/20$ and communication complexity $\Theta(c(n)) = \Omega((n-1)^2 \log p)$. Therefore $c(n) = \Omega((n-1)^2 \log p) = \Omega(n^2 \log p)$. $\square$

Theorem 10. $R^{pub}_{1/20}(\text{INVERSE}) = \Omega(n^2)$ *for* $p = 2$.

Proof. As before, we augment A to A_2. Here we further randomize A_2 by multiplying a random invertible matrix on both sides of A_2, that is, we form $B = G_1 A_2 G_2$ where G_1, G_2 are uniform over $n \times n$ non-singular matrices over $\mathbb{F}_p$. It is clear that $\text{rank}(B) = \text{rank}(A_2)$, and B is uniformly distributed over the $n \times n$ matrices with the same rank.

Run a protocol for INVERSE on B. Suppose that it outputs zero with probability p_0 when the input matrix has rank $n-1$. This probability can be calculated by Alice and Bob individually with no communication cost. When $\text{rank}(A) = n-1$, it outputs 1 with probability $\alpha = \frac{1}{20}\left(1 - \frac{1}{p}\right) + \frac{p_0}{p} = \frac{1}{40} + \frac{p_0}{2}$, while when $\text{rank}(A) =$

$n-2$ it outputs 1 with probability $\beta \geq \frac{19}{20}\left(1 - \frac{1}{q}\right)^2 + p_0 \cdot \frac{2}{p}\left(1 - \frac{1}{p}\right) = \frac{19}{80} + \frac{p_0}{2}$. Then, $\alpha - \beta \geq \frac{17}{80}$. The rest follows as in the proof for $p \geq 3$. $\qquad\square$

Now we reduce INVERSE to LINSOLVE$_b$.

Theorem 11. $R^{pub}_{1/20}(\text{LINSOLVE}_b) = \Omega(n^2 \log p)$ *for* $b \neq \mathbf{0}$,

Proof. We prove it by a reduction from INVERSE. Take an instance (x, y) from INVERSE. Since $b \neq 0$, there exists an invertible matrix Q such that $Qb = (1, 0, 0, \cdots, 0)^T$. Alice and Bob agree on the same Q, e.g. the minimal Q in alphabetical order. Then they run the protocol of LINSOLVE on input $(Q^{-1}x, Q^{-1}y, b)$. Then $t = (Q^{-1}x + Q^{-1}y)^{-1}b = (x+y)^{-1}QQ^{-1}(1, 0, \cdots, 0)^T = (x+y)^{-1}(1, 0, \cdots, 0)^T$ and thus $t_1 = ((x+y)^{-1})_{11}$. $\qquad\square$

Acknowledgements. We would like to thank Amit Chakrabarti for reading and helping with an earlier draft of this paper, and Troy Lee for giving us useful suggestions. D. Woodruff would also like to acknowledge the XDATA program of the Defense Advanced Research Projects Agency (DARPA), administered through Air Force Research Laboratory contract FA8750-12-C0323, for support for this project. X. Sun was supported in part by the National Natural Science Foundation of China Grant 61170062, 61222202 and the National Program for support of Top-notch Young Professionals.

References

1. Alon, N., Matias, Y., Szegedy, M.: The Space Complexity of Approximating the Frequency Moments. J. Comput. Syst. Sci. 58(1), 137–147 (1999)
2. Babai, L., Frankl, P., Simon, J.: Complexity classes in communication complexity theory. In: 27th Annual Symposium on Foundations of Computer Science, pp. 337–347 (1986)
3. Braverman, M., Ellen, F., Oshman, R., Pitassi, T., Vaikuntanathan, V.: A tight bound for set disjointness in the message-passing model. In: FOCS, pp. 668–677 (2013)
4. Chu, J.I., Schnitger, G.: Communication complexity of matrix computation over finite fields. Theory of Computing Systems 28, 215–228 (1995)
5. Clarkson, K.L., Woodruff, D.P.: Numerical linear algebra in the streaming model. In: Proceedings of the 41st Annual ACM Symposium on Theory of Computing, STOC 2009, pp. 205–214. ACM, New York (2009)
6. Cormode, G., Muthukrishnan, S., Yi, K.: Algorithms for distributed functional monitoring. In: Proc. 19th Annual ACM-SIAM Symposium on Discrete Algorithms, pp. 1076–1085 (2008)
7. Frieze, A., Kannan, R., Vempala, S.: Fast Monte-Carlo algorithms for finding low-rank approximations. In: Proceedings of the 39th Annual Symposium on Foundations of Computer Science, pp. 370–378. IEEE (1998)
8. Henzinger, M.R., Raghavan, P., Rajagopalan, S.: Computing on data streams. In: External Memory Algorithms: Dimacs Workshop External Memory and Visualization, May 20-22, vol. 50, p. 107. American Mathematical Soc. (1999)
9. Huang, W., Shi, Y., Zhang, S., Zhu, Y.: The communication complexity of the hamming distance problem. Inf. Process. Lett. 99(4), 149–153 (2006)

10. Kalyanasundaram, B., Schnitger, G.: The Probabilistic Communication Complexity of Set Intersection. SIAM J. Discrete Math. 5(4), 545–557 (1992)
11. Kushilevitz, E., Nisan, N.: Communication Complexity. Cambridge Univ. Pr. (1997)
12. Lee, T., Shraibman, A.: Lower Bounds in Communication Complexity. Foundations and Trends in Theoretical Computer Science 3(4), 363–399 (2009)
13. Linial, N., Shraibman, A.: Lower bounds in communication complexity based on factorization norms. Random Structures & Algorithms 34(3), 368–394 (2009)
14. Luo, Z.Q., Tsitsiklis, J.N.: On the communication complexity of distributed algebraic computation. J. ACM 40, 1019–1047 (1993)
15. Miltersen, P.B., Nisan, N., Safra, S., Wigderson, A.: On Data Structures and Asymmetric Communication Complexity. J. Comput. Syst. Sci. 57(1), 37–49 (1998)
16. Munro, J.I., Paterson, M.S.: Selection and sorting with limited storage. Theoretical Computer Science 12(3), 315–323 (1980)
17. Muthukrishnan, S.: Data streams: Algorithms and applications. Now Publishers Inc. (2005)
18. Newman, I.: Private vs. common random bits in communication complexity. Inf. Process. Lett. 39(2), 67–71 (1991)
19. Phillips, J.M., Verbin, E., Zhang, Q.: Lower bounds for number-in-hand multiparty communication complexity, made easy. In: Proceedings of the Twenty-Third Annual ACM-SIAM Symposium on Discrete Algorithms, SODA 2012, pp. 486–501 (2012)
20. Razborov, A.A.: On the distributional complexity of disjointness. Theoretical Computer Science 106(2), 385–390 (1992)
21. Sarlos, T.: Improved approximation algorithms for large matrices via random projections. In: 47th Annual IEEE Symposium on Foundations of Computer Science, pp. 143–152. IEEE (2006)
22. Sherstov, A.A.: The pattern matrix method for lower bounds on quantum communication. In: Proceedings of the 40th Annual ACM Symposium on Theory of Computing, STOC 2008, pp. 85–94. ACM, New York (2008)
23. Sherstov, A.A.: Strong direct product theorems for quantum communication and query complexity. SIAM Journal on Computing 41(5), 1122–1165 (2012)
24. Shi, Y., Zhu, Y.: Quantum communication complexity of block-composed functions. Quantum Information and Computation 9, 444–460 (2009)
25. Sun, X., Wang, C.: Randomized Communication Complexity for Linear Algebra Problems over Finite Fields. In: Dürr, C., Wilke, T. (eds.) 29th International Symposium on Theoretical Aspects of Computer Science (STACS 2012). Leibniz International Proceedings in Informatics, LIPIcs (2012)
26. Sun, X., Wang, C., Yu, W.: The relationship between inner product and counting cycles. In: Fernández-Baca, D. (ed.) LATIN 2012. LNCS, vol. 7256, pp. 643–654. Springer, Heidelberg (2012)
27. Woodruff, D.P., Zhang, Q.: Tight bounds for distributed functional monitoring. In: STOC, pp. 941–960 (2012)
28. Woodruff, D.P., Zhang, Q.: When distributed computation is communication expensive. In: Afek, Y. (ed.) DISC 2013. LNCS, vol. 8205, pp. 16–30. Springer, Heidelberg (2013)
29. Woodruff, D.P., Zhang, Q.: An optimal lower bound for distinct elements in the message passing model. In: SODA, pp. 718–733 (2014)
30. Yao, A.C.C.: Some complexity questions related to distributive computing (Preliminary Report). In: Proceedings of the Eleventh Annual ACM Symposium on Theory of Computing, pp. 209–213. ACM (1979)

Near-Constant-Time Distributed Algorithms on a Congested Clique⋆

James W. Hegeman, Sriram V. Pemmaraju, and Vivek B. Sardeshmukh

Department of Computer Science, The University of Iowa, Iowa City, IA 52242
{james-hegeman,sriram-pemmaraju,vivek-sardeshmukh}@uiowa.edu

Abstract. This paper presents constant-time and near-constant-time distributed algorithms for a variety of problems in the congested clique model. We show how to compute a 3-ruling set in expected $O(\log \log \log n)$ rounds and using this, we obtain a constant-approximation to metric facility location, also in expected $O(\log \log \log n)$ rounds. In addition, assuming an input metric space of constant doubling dimension, we obtain constant-round algorithms to compute constant-factor approximations to the minimum spanning tree and the metric facility location problems. These results significantly improve on the running time of the fastest known algorithms for these problems in the congested clique setting.

1 Introduction

The $\mathcal{CONGEST}$ model is a synchronous, message-passing model of distributed computation in which the amount of information that a node can transmit along an incident communication link in one round is restricted to $O(\log n)$ bits, where n is the size of the network [21]. As the name suggests, the $\mathcal{CONGEST}$ model focuses on *congestion* as an obstacle to distributed computation. In this paper, we focus on the design of distributed algorithms in the $\mathcal{CONGEST}$ model on a *clique* communication network; we call this the *congested clique* model. In the congested clique model, all information is nearby, i.e., at most one hop away, and so any difficulty in solving a problem is due to congestion alone.

Let $H = (V, E_H)$ denote the underlying clique communication network. In general, the input to the problems we consider consists of a $|V| \times |V|$ matrix M of edge-attributes and a length-$|V|$ vector of node attributes. M represents edge weights (or distances, or costs) and it is initially distributed among the nodes in V in such a way that each node $v \in V$ knows the corresponding row and column of M. In one typical example, M could simply be the adjacency matrix of a spanning subgraph $G = (V, E)$ of H; in this setting, each node $v \in V$ initially knows all the edges of G incident on it. A number of classical problems in distributed computing, e.g., maximal independent set (MIS), vertex coloring, edge coloring, maximal matching, shortest paths, etc., are well-defined in this setting. However, the difficulty of proving lower bounds in the congested clique model [7] means that it is not clear how quickly one should be able to solve any

---

⋆ This work is supported in part by National Science Foundation grant CCF-1318166.

F. Kuhn (Ed.): DISC 2014, LNCS 8784, pp. 514–530, 2014.
© Springer-Verlag Berlin Heidelberg 2014

of these problems in this model. Note that the input G can be quite dense (e.g., have $\Theta(n^2)$ edges) and therefore any reasonably fast algorithm for the problem will have to be "truly" distributed in the sense that it cannot simply rely on shipping off the problem description to a single node for local computation. In this setting, the algorithm of Berns et al. [3,2] that computes a *2-ruling set* of G in expected-$O(\log \log n)$ rounds is worth mentioning. (A *t-ruling set* is defined to be an independent set $I \subseteq V$ such that every node in V is at most t hops in G from some node in I.) In another important class of problems that we study, the input matrix M represents a metric space (V, d); thus each node $v \in V$ initially has knowledge of distances $d(v, w)$ for all $w \in V$. Nodes then need to collaborate to solve a problem such as *minimum spanning tree* (MST) or *metric facility location* (MFL) that are defined on the input metric space. In this setting, the deterministic MST algorithm of Lotker et al. [18] running in $O(\log \log n)$ rounds is worth mentioning.

Thus far the congested clique model has mainly served the theoretical purpose of helping us understand the role of congestion as an obstacle to distributed computation. However, recent papers [14,12] have made connections between congested clique algorithms and algorithms in popular systems of parallel computing such as MapReduce [6] and graph processing systems such as Pregel [19], thus providing a practical motivation for the development of fast algorithms on the congested clique.

1.1 Main Results

In this paper we present several constant-time or near-constant-time algorithms for fundamental problems in the congested clique setting.

- First, we present an algorithm that computes a 3-ruling set of G in expected $O(\log \log \log n)$ rounds, significantly improving the running time of the 2-ruling set algorithm of Berns et al. [3,2].
- Via a reduction presented in Berns et al. [3,2], this implies an expected $O(\log \log \log n)$-round algorithm for computing an $O(1)$-approximation for MFL. Again, this significantly improves on the running time of the fastest known algorithm for this problem.

Distributed algorithms that run in $O(\log \log n)$ rounds are typically analyzed by showing a doubly-exponential rate of progress; such progress, for example, is achieved if the number of nodes that have "successfully finished" grows by squaring after each iteration. The congested clique algorithms for MST due to Lotker et al. [18] and the above-mentioned MFL algorithm due to Berns et al. [3,2] are both examples of such phenomena. Our algorithm with triply-logarithmic running time, involves new techniques that seem applicable to congested clique algorithms in general. Our result raises the distinct possibility that other problems, e.g., MST, can also be solved in $O(\log \log \log n)$ rounds on a congested clique. In fact, our next set of results represents progress in this direction.

- We show how to solve the MIS problem on a congested clique in *constant* rounds on an input graph G_r induced by the metric space (V, d) in which every pair of nodes at distance at most r (for any $r \geq 0$) are connected by an edge. This result has two implications.
- First, given a metric space (V, d) of constant doubling dimension, we show that a constant-approximation to the MST problem on this metric space can be obtained in *constant* rounds on a congested clique setting.
- An additional implication of the aforementioned MIS result is that it leads to a *constant*-round constant-approximation to MFL in metric spaces of constant doubling dimension on a congested clique.

In order to achieve our results, we use a variety of techniques that balance bandwidth constraints with the need to make rapid progress. We believe that our techniques will have independent utility in any distributed setting in which congestion is a bottleneck.

1.2   Technical Preliminaries

Congested Clique Model. The underlying communication network is a clique $H = (V, E_H)$ of size $n = |V|$. Computation proceeds in synchronous rounds and in each round a node (i) receives all messages sent to it in the previous round, (ii) performs unlimited local computation, and then (iii) sends a, possibly different, message of size $O(\log n)$ to each of the other nodes in the network. We assume that nodes have distinct IDs that can each be represented in $O(\log n)$ bits.

MST and MFL problems. We assume that the input to the MST problem is a metric space (V, d). Initially, each node $v \in V$ knows distances $d(v, w)$ to all nodes $w \in V$. When the algorithm ends, all nodes in V are required to know a spanning tree T of V of minimum weight. (Note that here we take $d(u, v)$ to be the "weight" of edge $\{u, v\}$.) The input to MFL consists of a metric space (V, d) along with *facility opening costs* f_v associated with each node $v \in V$. The goal is to find a subset $F \subseteq V$ of nodes to *open* as facilities so as to minimize the facility opening costs plus connection costs, i.e., $\sum_{v \in F} f_v + \sum_{u \in V} D(u, F)$, where $D(u, F) := \min_{v \in F} d(u, v)$ is the *connection cost* of node u. Initially, each node $v \in V$ knows facility opening cost f_v and distances $d(v, w)$ for all $w \in V$. Facility location is a well-studied problem in operations research [1,4,9] that arises in contexts such as locating hospitals in a city or locating distribution centers in a region. More recently, the facility location problem has been used as an abstraction for the problem of locating resources in a wireless network [10,20].

t-ruling set problem. A *t-ruling set* of a graph $G = (V, E)$ is an independent set $I \subseteq V$ such that every vertex in G is at most t hops from some vertex in I. A t-ruling set, for constant t, is a natural generalization of an MIS and can stand as a proxy for an MIS in many instances. The input to the t-ruling set problem on a congested clique $H = (V, E_H)$ is a spanning subgraph $G = (V, E)$ of the underlying communication network H. Each node $v \in V$ is initially aware of all its neighbors in G. At the end of the t-ruling set algorithm, every node is required to know the identities of all nodes in the computed t-ruling set.

Metric spaces, doubling dimension, and growth-bounded graphs. If $M = (V, d)$ is a metric space then we use $B_M(v, r)$ to denote the set of points $w \in V$ such that $d(v, w) \leq r$. We call $B_M(v, r)$ the *ball of radius r centered at v*. A metric space $M = (V, d)$ has *doubling dimension* ρ if for any $v \in V$ and $r \geq 0$, $B_M(v, r)$ is contained in the union of at most 2^ρ balls $B_M(u, r/2)$, $u \in V$. In this paper, we work with metric spaces with constant doubling dimension, i.e., $\rho = O(1)$. Note that constant-dimensional Euclidean metric spaces are natural examples of metric spaces with constant doubling dimension. In distributed computing literature, metric spaces of constant doubling dimension have been investigated in the context of wireless networks [5,15]. For a graph $G = (V, E)$ and a node $v \in V$, let $B_G(v, r)$ denote the set of all vertices $u \in V$ that are at most r hops from v. A graph $G = (V, E)$ is said to have *bounded growth* (or said to be *growth-bounded*) if the size of any independent set in any ball $B_G(v, r)$, $v \in V$, $r \geq 0$, is bounded by $O(r^c)$ for some constant c. For any metric space (V, d) and $r \geq 0$, the graph $G_r = (V, E_r)$, where $E_r = \{\{u, v\} \in d(u, v) \leq r\}$ is called a *distance-threshold graph*. It is easy to see that if (V, d) has constant doubling dimension then a distance-threshold graph G_r, for any $r \geq 0$, is growth-bounded; this fact will play an important role in our algorithms. Distance-threshold graphs and more generally, growth-bounded graphs have attracted attention in the distributed computing community as flexible models of wireless networks [15]. Schneider and Wattenhofer [22] present a deterministic algorithm, running in $O(\log^* n)$ rounds, for computing an MIS on a growth-bounded graph.

Lenzen's routing protocol. A key algorithmic tool that allows us to design constant- and near-constant-time round algorithms is a recent deterministic routing protocol by Lenzen [16] that disseminates a large volume of information on a congested clique in constant rounds. The specific routing problem, called an *Information Distribution Task*, solved by Lenzen's protocol is the following. Each node $i \in V$ is given a set of $n' \leq n$ messages, each of size $O(\log n)$, $\{m_i^1, m_i^2, \ldots, m_i^{n'}\}$, with destinations $d(m_i^j) \in V$, $j \in [n']$. Messages are globally lexicographically ordered by their source i, destination $d(m_i^j)$, and j. Each node is also the destination of at most n messages. Lenzen's routing protocol solves the Information Distribution Task in $O(1)$ rounds.

2   3-Ruling Sets in $O(\log \log \log n)$ Rounds

In this section, we show how nodes in V can use the underlying clique communication network H to compute, in expected-$O(\log \log \log n)$ rounds, a 3-ruling set of an arbitrary spanning subgraph G of H. At a high level, our 3-ruling set algorithm can be viewed as having three steps. In the first step, the graph is decomposed into $O(\log \log n)$ degree-based classes and at the end of this step every node knows the class it belongs to. In the next subsection, we describe this *degree-decomposition step* and show that it runs in expected $O(\log \log \log n)$ rounds. In the second step, each vertex v of the given graph G joins a set S independently with probability p_v, where p_v depends on v's class as defined in the degree-decomposition step. This *vertex-selection step* yields a set S that will be shown to have two properties: (i) the expected number of edges in the induced subgraph $G[S]$ is $O(n \cdot \text{poly}(\log n))$; and (ii) with high probability, every vertex in G is either in S or has a neighbor in S. Given the degree-decomposition, the vertex-selection step is elementary and requires no communication. In the third step, we use the 2-ruling set algorithm of Berns et al. [3,2]. We show that, on an n-node graph with $O(n \cdot \text{poly}(\log n))$ edges, this algorithm runs in expected-$O(\log \log \log n)$ rounds. We will refer to this algorithm from [3,2] as the *2-ruling set algorithm*. Putting these three steps together yields a 3-ruling set algorithm that runs in $O(\log \log \log n)$ rounds in expectation.

2.1   Degree-Decomposition Step

Let $G = (V, E)$ be an arbitrary graph. For $k = 0, 1, 2, \ldots$, let $D_k = n^{1/2^k}$. The D_k's will serve as degree thresholds and will lead to a vertex partition. Let $k^* = \lceil \log \log n \rceil$. Note that $1 < D_{k^*} \leq 2$. Let $V_0 = V$, $G_0 = G$, and $U_1 = \{v \in V_0 \mid \text{degree}_{G_0}(v) \in [D_1, D_0)\}$. For $1 \leq k < k^*$, let

$$V_k = V_{k-1} \setminus U_k, \quad G_k = G[V_k], \qquad U_{k+1} = \{v \in V_k \mid \text{degree}_{G_k}(v) \in [D_{k+1}, D_k)\}$$

Let $V_{k^*} = V_{k^*-1} \setminus U_{k^*}$, $G_{k^*} = G[V_{k^*}]$, and $U_{k^*+1} = V_{k^*}$. See Figure 1 for an illustration of this decomposition. Let $N_G(v)$ denote the set of neighbors of vertex v in graph G. Here are some easy observations:

(i) For $0 \leq k \leq k^*$, $\Delta(G_k) < D_k$.
(ii) For $1 \leq k \leq k^* + 1$, if $v \in U_k$ then $|N_G(v) \cap V_{k-1}| < D_{k-1}$.
(iii) For $1 \leq k \leq k^* + 1$, if $v \in U_k$ then $|N_G(v) \cap U_j| < D_j$ for $j = 1, 2, \ldots k - 1$.

Now we describe algorithm to compute this degree-decomposition; in particular, we precisely describe how each node v computes an index $k(v) \in [k^* + 1]$ such that $v \in U_{k(v)}$. Below, we first describe at a high level a 2-phase approach that we use to compute the index $k(v)$ for each vertex v.

Lazy phase: Let $t = \lceil 1 + \log \log \log n \rceil$. The sets $U_1, U_2, \ldots, U_t$ are identified in a leisurely manner, one-by-one, in $O(\log \log \log n)$ rounds. At the end of this phase each vertex $v \in \cup_{i=1}^t U_i$ knows the index $k(v) \in [t]$ such that $v \in U_{k(v)}$.
Speedy phase: The set of remaining vertices, namely V_t, induces a graph G_t whose maximum degree is less than

$$D_t \leq n^{1/2^{1+\log \log \log n}} = n^{1/(2 \log \log n)}.$$

This upper bound on the maximum degree helps us compute the index values $k(v)$ for the remaining vertices at a faster rate. We first show that each vertex v in G_t can acquire knowledge of the graph induced by the ball $B_{G_t}(v, k^*)$ in

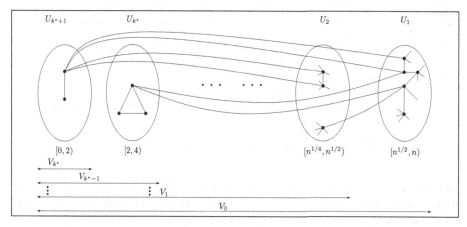

Fig. 1. Degree-Decomposition Step. U_1 is the set of all nodes in G with degrees in the range $[n^{1/2}, n)$ and V_1 is the remaining nodes. U_2 is the set of all nodes in V_1 with degrees in $G[V_1]$ belonging to the range $[n^{1/4}, n^{1/2})$. The decomposition continues in this manner until all nodes belong to some U_k. We use k^* to denote $\lceil \log \log n \rceil$. Assuming that $\log \log n = k^*$, we see that U_k^* is the set of nodes that have degree in $G[V_{k^*-1}]$ in the range $[2, 4)$. Note that a node v that belongs to U_{k+1} could have degree in G that is much larger than $D_k = n^{1/2^k}$.

$O(\log \log \log n)$ rounds via a fast *ball-growing algorithm*. (Recall that $k^* = \lceil \log \log n \rceil$.) We then show that $G[B_{G_t}(v, k^*)]$ contains enough information for v to determine $k(v) \in [k^*+1]$ via local computation. Therefore, after each vertex $v \in V_t$ acquires complete knowledge of the radius-k^* ball centered at it, it can locally compute index $k(v)$ and proceed to the vertex-selection step.

The Lazy-phase is straightforward and due to space restrictions we skip further discussion of this phase. We now present the *Speedy-phase algorithm* executed by vertex v. Note that the Speedy-phase algorithm is only executed at vertices v whose index $k(v)$ has not been established during the Lazy-phase algorithm. In other words, the Speedy-phase algorithm is only executed at vertices v in G_t, the graph induced by vertices not in $\cup_{j=1}^{t} U_j$. The key idea of the Speedy-phase algorithm is that once each node v in G_t has acquired knowledge of $G_t[B_{G_t}(v, r)]$, then in constant rounds of communication, each node v can "double" its knowledge, i.e., acquire knowledge of $G_t[B_{G_t}(v, 2r)]$. This is done by each node v sending knowledge of $G_t[B_{G_t}(v, r)]$ to all nodes in $B_{G_t}(v, r)$; the key is to establish that this volume of communication can be achieved on a congested clique in constant rounds. This idea has appeared in a slightly different context in [17].

The next two lemmas (whose proofs appear in the full version of the paper [13]) establish the running time and correctness of the Speedy-phase algorithm.

Lemma 1. *The Speedy-phase algorithm above runs in $O(\log \log \log n)$ rounds in the congested-clique model and when this algorithm completes execution, each vertex v in G_t knows $G[B_{G_t}(v, k^*)]$.*

Algorithm 1. Speedy-phase algorithm at vertex v

---

1. // *Growing the ball* $B_{G_t}(v, k^*)$
2. Each node sends a list of all of its neighbors in G_t to each of its neighbors (in G_t) // *After which each* $v \in V_t$ *knows* $G[B_{G_t}(v, 1)]$
3. **for** $i \leftarrow 0$ **to** $\lceil \log \log \log n \rceil - 1$ **do**
4.   Send a description of $G[B_{G_t}(v, 2^i)]$ to all nodes in $B_{G_t}(v, 2^i)$
5.   Construct $G[B_{G_t}(v, 2^{i+1})]$ from $G[B_{G_t}(u, 2^i)]$ received from all $u \in B_{G_t}(v, 2^i)$
6. Locally compute $k(v) \in [k^* + 1]$ such that $v \in U_{k(v)}$

Lemma 2. *For any graph H and a vertex v in H, suppose that v knows the graph induced by $B_H(v, k^*)$. Then v can locally compute the index $k(v) \in [k^* + 1]$ such that $v \in U_{k(v)}$.*

2.2 Vertex-Selection Step

As mentioned earlier, the vertex-selection step randomly and independently samples nodes in G, with each node v sampled with a probability p_v that depends on the class $U_{k(v)}$ it belongs to. Specifically, if v belongs to U_k then v is independently selected with probability $\min(2 \log n / D_k, 1)$. Let S be the set of vertices that are selected. Let $e(S)$ denote the set of edges in the induced graph $G[S]$.

Lemma 3. $E[|e(S)|] = O(n \cdot \log^2 n \cdot \log \log n)$.

Proof. Consider an arbitrary vertex $v \in V$ and let k, $1 \le k \le k^* + 1$ be such that $v \in U_k$. We will show that the expected number of edges between v and nodes in $\cup_{j \le k} U_j$ is less than $4k \cdot \log^2 n$.

In the graph G, node v has fewer than D_{k-1} neighbors in U_k. Thus, if $1 \le k \le k^*$, the expected number of edges in $e(S)$ between v and nodes in U_k is at most

$$\frac{2 \log n}{D_k} \cdot \sum_{u \in N_G(v) \cap U_k} \frac{2 \log n}{D_k} < \frac{4 \log^2 n \cdot D_{k-1}}{D_k^2} = 4 \log^2 n.$$

If $k = k^* + 1$, the number of edges between v and other nodes in U_{k^*+1} is at most 1.

In the graph G, node v has fewer than D_j neighbors in U_j, for $j < k$. Thus, if $1 \le k \le k^*$, the expected number of edges in $e(S)$ between v and nodes in U_j, $j < k$, is at most

$$\frac{2 \log n}{D_k} \cdot \sum_{u \in N_G(v) \cap U_j} \frac{2 \log n}{D_j} < \frac{4 \log^2 n}{D_k} \le 4 \log^2 n.$$

If $k = k^* + 1$, the expected number of edges in $e(S)$ between v and nodes in U_j, $j < k$, is

$$1 \cdot \sum_{u \in N_G(v) \cap U_j} \frac{2 \log n}{D_j} < 2 \log n.$$

Hence, summing over j, the expected total number of edges in $e(S)$ between v and $\cup_{j<k} U_j$ is less than $4k \cdot \log^2 n$. Using the fact that $k \leq 1 + \log \log n$, we see that the expected total number of edges in $e(S)$ between v and $\cup_{j \leq k} U_j$ is $O(\log^2 n \cdot \log \log n)$. The result follows.

We end our analysis with the following claim whose (straightforward) proof appears in the full version of the paper [13].

Lemma 4. *For any $v \in V$, $\Pr(v$ is in S or v has a neighbor in $S) \geq 1 - 1/n^2$.*

2.3   Putting It All Together

Now that we have a set S that induces a subgraph with $O(n \cdot \mathrm{poly}(\log n))$ edges, we rely on a 2-ruling set algorithm due to Berns et al. [3,2] to further sparsify $G[S]$. This 2-ruling set algorithm runs in expected-$O(\log \log n)$ rounds in general, but it is not too hard to show the following lemma (proof appears in full paper [13]) that is relevant when the number of edges in the input graph are bounded.

Lemma 5. *Given an n-vertex graph G with $O(n \cdot \mathrm{poly}(\log n))$ edges the 2-ruling set algorithm of Berns et al. [3,2] computes a 2-ruling set of G in expected-$O(\log \log \log n)$ rounds.*

We now combine the algorithm for degree-decomposition step algorithm, the vertex-selection step algorithm, and the 2-ruling set algorithm in order to obtain a 3-ruling set algorithm that runs in $O(\log \log \log n)$ rounds in expectation. Our final 3-ruling set algorithm is described below.

Algorithm 2. 3-Ruling Set Algorithm

---

1. Each node $v \in V$ uses the Lazy-phase and Speedy-phase algorithms to determine the index $k(v) \in [k^* + 1]$ such that $v \in U_{k(v)}$
2. Run the vertex-selection step to compute S
3. $I \leftarrow$ 2-RULINGSET$(G[S])$

---

3   MIS in Growth Bounded Graphs in Constant Rounds

Given a metric space (V, d) with constant doubling dimension, we show in this section how to compute an MIS of a distance-threshold graph $G_r = (V, E_r)$, for any real $r \geq 0$, in a *constant* number of rounds on a congested clique.

3.1   Simulation of the Schneider-Wattenhofer MIS Algorithm

Before we describe our MIS algorithm, we describe an algorithmic tool that will prove quite useful. We know that G_r is growth-bounded and in particular the size of a largest independent set in a ball $B_{G_r}(v, r)$ for any $v \in V$ is $O(r^\rho)$, where ρ is the doubling dimension of (V, d). Schneider and Wattenhofer [22] present a deterministic $O(\log^* n)$-round algorithm to compute an MIS for growth-bounded graphs in the $\mathcal{CONGEST}$ model. Suppose that f is a constant such that the Schneider-Wattenhofer algorithms runs in at most $f \log^* n$ rounds (note that f depends on ρ). We can *simulate* the Schneider-Wattenhofer algorithm in the congested clique model by (i) having each node $v \in V$ grow a ball of radius $f \log^* n$, i.e., gather a description of the induced graph $G[B_{G_r}(v, f \log^* n)]$ and then (ii) having each node v *locally simulate* the Schneider-Wattenhofer algorithm using the description of $G[B_{G_r}(v, f \log^* n)]$. Note that since the Schneider-Wattenhofer algorithm takes at most $f \log^* n$ rounds, it suffices for each node $v \in V$ to know the entire topology of $G[B_{G_r}(v, f \log^* n)]$ to determine if it should join the MIS. The "ball growing" step mentioned above can be implemented by using Lenzen's routing protocol as follows, provided Δ (the maximum degree of G_r) is not too large. Each node v can describe its neighborhood using at most Δ messages of size $O(\log n)$ each. Node v aims to send each of these Δ messages to every node w such that $d(v, w) \leq r \cdot f \log^* n$. In other words, v aims to send messages to all nodes in $B_M(v, r \cdot f \log^* n)$. Since $B_{G_r}(v, f \log^* n) \subseteq B_M(v, r \cdot f \log^* n)$, it follows that the messages sent by v are received by all nodes in $B_{G_r}(v, f \log^* n)$. We now bound the size of $B_M(v, r \cdot f \log^* n)$ as follows. Since M has doubling dimension ρ, the size of any MIS in $B_M(v, r \cdot f \log^* n)$ is $O((\log^* n)^\rho)$ and hence total number of nodes in $B_M(v, r \cdot f \log^* n)$ is $O(\Delta \cdot (\log^* n)^\rho)$. Therefore every node v has $O((\log^* n)^\rho \cdot \Delta^2)$ messages to send, each of size $O(\log n)$. Every node is the receiver of at most $O((\log^* n)^\rho \Delta^2)$ messages by similar arguments. Therefore, if $\Delta = O(\sqrt{n}/(\log^* n)^{\rho/2})$, we can use Lenzen's routing protocol to route these messages in $O(1)$ time. We refer this simulation of the Schneider-Wattenhofer algorithm [22] as Algorithm SW-MIS. The following theorem summarizes this simulation result.

Theorem 1. *If $\Delta(G_r) = O(\sqrt{n}/(\log^* n)^{\rho/2})$ then Algorithm* SW-MIS *computes an MIS of G_r in $O(1)$ rounds on a congested clique.*

3.2   Constant-Round MIS Algorithm

Our MIS algorithm consists of 4 phases. Next we describe, at a high level, what each phase accomplishes.

Phase 1: We compute vertex-subset $P \subseteq V$ such that (i) every vertex in V is at most one hop away from some vertex in P and (ii) $G_r[P]$ has maximum degree bounded above by $c \cdot \sqrt{n}$, for some constant $c > 0$.

Algorithm REDUCEDEGREE is the name we give to the algorithm that implements Phase 1. The algorithm consists of arbitrarily partitioning the vertex-set of G_r into $\sqrt{n}$ groups of size (roughly) $\sqrt{n}$ each and then separately and in parallel computing an MIS of each part. The algorithm simply returns the union of these MIS sets.

Phase 2: We process the graph $G_r[P]$ and compute two subsets W and Q of P such that (i) every vertex in P of degree at least $c \cdot n^{1/4}$ is either in W or has a neighbor in W and (ii) $Q \subseteq W$ is an independent set such that every vertex

---

Algorithm 3. LowDimensionalMIS

Input: $G_r = (V, E_r)$
Output: A maximal independent set $I \subseteq V$ of G_r
 1. $P \leftarrow$ ReduceDegree(G_r) // *Phase 1*
 2. $(W, Q) \leftarrow$ SampleAndPrune(G_r, P) // *Phase 2*
 3. $V' \leftarrow V \setminus (W \cup N(W))$; $R \leftarrow$ SW-MIS(G_r, V') // *Phase 3*
 4. $S \leftarrow Q \cup R$; $I \leftarrow$ RulingToMIS(S) // *Phase 4*
 5. **return** I

---

in W is at most 2 hops from some vertex in Q. Thus, if we delete W and all neighbors of vertices in W what remains is a graph of maximum degree less than $c \cdot n^{1/4}$. Let V' denote the set $P \setminus (W \cup N(W))$. Thus, at the end of Phase 2, Q is a 3-ruling set of $G_r[W \cup N(W)]$ and $\Delta(G_r[V']) < c \cdot n^{1/4}$.

Phase 3: We compute an MIS R of the graph $G_r[V']$ by simply calling SW-MIS.

Phase 4: Since Q is a 3-ruling set of $G_r[W \cup N(W)]$ and R is an MIS of $G_r[V']$, we see that $Q \cup R$ is a 3-ruling set of $G_r[P]$ and thus a 4-ruling set of G_r. In the final phase, we start with the 4-ruling set $S := Q \cup R$ and expand this into an MIS I of G_r.

While going from a constant-ruling set to an MIS seems as hard as computing an MIS from scratch on general graphs, on growth-bounded graphs, this is much more easy. For example, Gfeller and Vicari [11] convert a 3-ruling set into an MIS in $O(\log^* n)$ rounds. Algorithm MISToRuling, which implements Phase 4, uses a similar approach of constructing a cluster-graph of constant maximum degree and then vertex-coloring it so as to obtain a "schedule" using which we can process the clusters. We take advantage of the congested model to complete all this in constant rounds.

Phase 2 is randomized and runs in constant rounds w.h.p. The remaining phases are deterministic and run in constant rounds each. Algorithm LowDimensionalMIS summarizes our algorithm. We now describe Phase 2 in more detail; the remaining phases and their analyses appears in the full version of the paper [13].

3.3   Phase 2: Sample and Prune

Algorithm SampleAndPrune implements Phase 2 of our MIS algorithm. It takes the induced subgraph $G_r[P]$ as input and starts by computing a set $W \subseteq P$ using a simple random sampling approach. Specifically, for each $i = 1, 2, \ldots, \lceil 2 \cdot \log n \rceil$, each vertex in P simply adds itself to a set W_i independently, with probability $1/n^{1/4}$. We start by stating a useful property of W. (Proof of this lemma appears in the full version of the paper [13].)

Lemma 6. *Every node u with degree at least $n^{1/4}$ in $G_r[P]$ has a neighbor in W with probability at least $1 - \frac{1}{n^2}$.*

Algorithm 4. SAMPLEANDPRUNE (Phase 2)

Input: (G_r, P)
Output: (W, Q), $W \subseteq P$ such that $\{v \in P \mid \text{degree}_{G_r[P]}(v) \geq n^{1/4}\} \subseteq W \cup N(W)$;
   independent set $Q \subseteq W$ such that Q is a 2-ruling set of $G_r[W]$.
1. **for all** $v \in P$ **in parallel do**
2.   Vertex $v \in P$ adds itself to W_i with probability $1/n^{1/4}$ for $i = 1, 2, \ldots, \lceil 2 \cdot \log n \rceil$.
3. $W \leftarrow \cup_{i=1}^{\lceil 2 \log n \rceil} W_i$
4. **for all** $i \leftarrow 1$ **to** $\lceil 2 \log n \rceil$ **in parallel do**
5.   Send $G_r[W_i]$ to a vertex w_i, where w_i is the vertex of rank i in the sequence
   of vertices in V sorted by increasing ID
6.   Vertex w_i executes $X_i \leftarrow \text{LOCALMIS}(G_r[W_i])$
7. $Q \leftarrow \text{SW-MIS}(G_r[\cup_{i=1}^{\lceil 2 \log n \rceil} X_i])$
8. **return** (W, Q)

After using random sampling to compute W, Algorithm SAMPLEANDPRUNE then "prunes" W in constant rounds to construct a subset $Q \subseteq W$ such that Q is a 2-ruling set of W. In the rest of this subsection we prove that Algorithm SAMPLEANDPRUNE does behave as claimed here.

Lemma 7. *The number of edges in $G_r[W_i]$ is $O(n)$ w.h.p., for each $i = 1, 2, \ldots,$* $\lceil 2 \log n \rceil$.

Proof. We first bound the size of the set W_i and the maximum degree of $G_r[W_i]$ for any $i = 1, 2, \ldots, \lceil 2 \log n \rceil$. Observe that $\mathbf{E}[|W_i|] = n^{3/4}$ and since nodes join W_i independently, an application of Chernoff's bound [8] yields $\Pr(|W_i| \leq 6n^{3/4}) \geq 1 - \frac{1}{n^2}$. To bound $\Delta(G_r[W_i])$ we use the fact that degree of any node in $G_r[P]$ is at most $\sqrt{n}$ and therefore the expected degree of any node in $G_r[W_i]$ is at most $n^{1/4}$. Another application of Chernoff's bound yields $\Pr(\text{degree}_{G_r[W_i]}(v) \leq 6n^{1/4}) \geq 1 - \frac{1}{n^2}$ for each node v. Using the union bound over all nodes $v \in W_i$ yields that with probability at least $1 - \frac{1}{n}$ every node in $G_r[W_i]$ has degree at most $6n^{1/4}$. Hence, with high probability, the number of edges in $G[W_i]$ is at most $36n$. ∎

We end the analysis of Phase 2 by stating two lemmas (proofs appear in the full version [13]) that establish that Algorithm SAMPLEANDPRUNE runs on constant number of rounds.

Lemma 8. *The set $X := \cup_{i=1}^{\lceil 2 \log n \rceil} X_i \subseteq P$ is computed in constant rounds w.h.p. in Lines 4-6 of Algorithm* SAMPLEANDPRUNE. *Furthermore, Every vertex in W is at most one hop away from some vertex in X.*

Lemma 9. *W.h.p. it takes constant number of rounds to compute Q. Furthermore, Q is a 2-ruling set of $G_r[W]$.*

Remark: By diving into the details of the communication patterns of this MIS algorithm, it is possible to show that multiple instances (e.g., $O(\log n)$ instances) of this MIS algorithm, on graphs G_r, for different values of r can be executed in parallel. Details appear in the full version of the paper [13]. This will become useful for the MST algorithm described next.

4   Constant-Approximation to MST in Constant Rounds

For a metric space (V, d), define a *metric graph* $G = (V, E)$ as the clique on set V with each edge $\{u, v\}$ having weight $d(u, v)$. In this section we present a constant-round algorithm for computing a constant-factor approximation of an MST of given metric graph $G = (V, E)$ with constant doubling dimension. We start by showing how to "sparsify" G and construct a spanning subgraph $\hat{G} = (V, \hat{E})$, $\hat{E} \subseteq E$, such that $wt(MST(\hat{G})) = O(wt(MST(G)))$. Thus computing an MST on $\hat{G}$ yields an $O(1)$-approximation to an MST on G. The sparsification is achieved via the construction of a collection of maximal independent sets (MIS) *in parallel* on different distance-threshold subgraphs of G. Thus we have reduced the problem of constructing a constant-approximation of an MST on the metric graph G to two problems: (i) the MIS problem on distance-threshold graphs and (ii) the problem of computing an MST of a sparse graph $\hat{G}$. Using the fact that the underlying metric space (V, d) has constant doubling dimension, we show that $\hat{G}$ has linear (in $|V|$) number of edges. As a result, problem (ii) can be easily solved in constant number of rounds. In Section 3, we have shown how to compute an MIS of a distance-threshold graph in a constant doubling dimensional space on a congested clique in constant number of rounds. In fact, due to the rather "light-weight" bandwidth usage of our MIS algorithm, we can run all of the requisite MIS computations in parallel in constant rounds.

4.1   MST Algorithm

We now present our algorithm in detail. We partition the edge set E of the metric graph into two subsets E_ℓ (*light* edges) and E_h (*heavy* edges) as follows. Let $d_m = \max\{d(u, v) \mid \{u, v\} \in E\}$ denote the diameter of the metric space [1]. Define $E_\ell = \{\{u, v\} \mid d(u, v) \le d_m/n^3\}$ and $E_h = E \setminus E_\ell$. We deal with these two subsets E_ℓ and E_h separately.

First consider the set of light edges E_ℓ and note that $G[E_\ell]$ may have several components. We would like to select an edge set $\hat{E}_\ell$ such that (i) any pair of vertices that are in the same connected component in $G[E_\ell]$ are also in the same connected component in $G[\hat{E}_\ell]$, and (ii) $wt(\hat{E}_\ell) = O(wt(MST(G)))$. (Note that one can define $\hat{E}_\ell = E_\ell$ to have these two properties but we want to "sparsify" E_ℓ, ideally we would like to have $|\hat{E}_\ell| = O(n)$ and we show this for metric with constant doubling dimension.) The algorithm for selecting $\hat{E}_\ell$ is as follows. Let S be an MIS of the distance-threshold graph G_r, where $r = d_m/n^2$. (This MIS computation is not on graph induced by E_ℓ, notice the

---

[1] If the size of the encoding of distances is more than $O(\log n)$ bits then it is suffices to know only most-significant $\log n$-bits of encoding of d_m to act as "proxy" for d_m which will only increase the approximation factor by a constant.

Algorithm 5. MST-APPROXIMATION

Input: A metric graph $G = (V, E)$ on metric space (V, d)
Output: A tree $\hat{\mathcal{T}}$ such that $wt(\hat{\mathcal{T}}) = O(wt(MST(G)))$
1. $d_m = \max\{\{u,v\} \mid \{u,v\} \in E\}$
2. $E_\ell \leftarrow \{\{u,v\} \mid d(u,v) \leq \frac{d_m}{n^3}\}$ // *Processing light edges*
3. $S \leftarrow \text{COMPUTEMIS}(G[E_0])$ where $E_0 \leftarrow \{\{u,v\} \mid d(u,v) \leq \frac{d_m}{n^2}\}$
4. $\hat{E}_\ell \leftarrow \{\{u,v\} \mid u \in S \text{ and } d(u,v) \leq \frac{2 \cdot d_m}{n^2}\}$
5. $E_{\hbar} \leftarrow \{\{u,v\} \mid d(u,v) > \frac{d_m}{n^3}\}$ // *Processing heavy edges*
6. $h \leftarrow \left\lceil \frac{3 \log n}{\log c_1} \right\rceil$; $r_0 \leftarrow \frac{d_m}{c_1^h}$
7. **for** $i = 1$ **to** h **in parallel do**
8. $r_i \leftarrow (c_1)^i \cdot r_0$
9. $E_i \leftarrow \{\{u,v\} \mid d(u,v) \leq r_i\}$
10. $V_i \leftarrow \text{COMPUTEMIS}(G[E_i])$
11. $\hat{E}_i \leftarrow \{\{u,v\} \mid u,v \in V_i \text{ and } d(u,v) \leq c_2 \cdot r_i\}$
12. $\hat{E}_{\hbar} \leftarrow \cup_{i=1}^h \hat{E}_i$; $\hat{E} \leftarrow \hat{E}_\ell \cup \hat{E}_{\hbar}$
13. **return** MST-SPARSE$(G[\hat{E}])$

r. This is done to obtain certain properties of $\hat{E}_\ell$ described above.) Define $\hat{E}_\ell = \{\{u,v\} \mid u \in S \text{ and } d(u,v) \leq 2 \cdot d_m/n^2\}$. Note that $\hat{E}_\ell$ may not be a subset of E_ℓ.

Now we consider the set $E_{\hbar}$ of heavy edges. Let $c_1 > 1$ be a constant. Let h be the smallest positive integer such that $c_1^h \geq n^3$. Observe that $h = \left\lceil \frac{3 \log n}{\log c_1} \right\rceil$. Let $r_0 = d_m/c_1^h$ (note that for any heavy edge $\{u,v\}$, $d(u,v) > r_0$) and let $r_i = c_1 \cdot r_{i-1}$, for $i > 0$. We construct $\hat{E}_{\hbar}$ in *layers* as follows. Let $V_0 = V$ and V_i for $0 < i \leq h$ is an MIS of the subgraph $G[E_i]$ where $E_i = \{\{u,v\} \mid d(u,v) \leq r_i\}$. Let $c_2 > c_1 + 2$ be a constant. Define $\hat{E}_i$, the edge set at the layer i as: $\hat{E}_i = \{\{u,v\} \mid u,v \in V_i \text{ and } d(u,v) \leq c_2 \cdot r_i\}$. We define $\hat{E}_{\hbar} = \cup_{i=1}^h \hat{E}_i$ and $\hat{E} = \hat{E}_{\hbar} \cup \hat{E}_\ell$. A key feature of our algorithm is that a layer $\hat{E}_i$ does not depend on other layers and therefore these layers can be constructed in parallel. We then call an as-yet-unspecified algorithm called MST-SPARSE that quickly computes an exact MST of $\hat{G} = G[\hat{E}]$ in the congested clique model.

In the analysis that follows, we separately analyze the processing of light edges and heavy edges. We first show the *constant-approximation property* of $\hat{G}$ which doesn't require metric to be of constant doubling dimension. Later we show if the underlying metric has constant doubling dimension then Algorithm 5 runs in constant rounds w.h.p..

4.2   Constant-Approximation Property

Let $\mathcal{T}$ be an MST of graph $G = (V, E)$. Let $\hat{\mathcal{T}}$ be a MST of the graph $\hat{G} = (V, \hat{E})$. We now prove that $wt(\hat{\mathcal{T}}) = O(wt(\mathcal{T}))$. First we claim that the connectivity that edges in E_ℓ (i.e., the light edges) provide is preserved by the edges selected into $\hat{E}_\ell$ (Lemma 10) and the total weight of these selected edges is not too high

(Lemma 11). Later we make a similar claim for heavy edges (Lemma 12). Proofs of these lemmas appear in the full version of the paper [13].

Lemma 10. *For any vertices s and t in V, if there is a s-t path in $G[E_\ell]$ then there exists an s-t path in $G[\hat{E}_\ell]$.*

Lemma 11. $wt(\hat{E}_\ell) = O(wt(\mathcal{T}))$.

Consider an edge $\{u, v\} \in E(\mathcal{T})$. Let $C(u)$ and $C(v)$ be the components containing u and v respectively in the graph $\mathcal{T} \setminus \{u, v\}$.

Lemma 12. *If $\{u, v\} \in E(\mathcal{T}) \cap E_h$ then there exists an edge $\{u', v'\} \in \hat{E}$ such that (i) $d(u', v') \le c_2 \cdot d(u, v)$ and (ii) $u' \in C(u)$ and $v' \in C(v)$.*

This lemma implies that for every cut (X, Y) of G and an MST edge $\{u, v\}$ that crosses the cut, there is an edge $\{u', v'\}$ in $\hat{G}$ also crossing cut (X, Y) with weight within a constant factor of the weight of $\{u, v\}$. The following result follows from this observation and properties of $\hat{E}_\ell$ proved earlier.

Theorem 2. *Algorithm 5 computes a spanning tree $\hat{\mathcal{T}}$ of G such that $wt(\hat{\mathcal{T}}) = O(wt(MST(G)))$.*

4.3 Constant Running Time

The result of the previous subsection does not require that the underlying metric space (V, d) have constant doubling dimension. Now we assume that (V, d) has constant doubling dimension and in this setting we show that Algorithm MST-APPROXIMATION can be implemented in *constant* rounds. Even though the algorithm is described in a "sequential" style in Algorithm 5, it is easy to verify that most of the steps can be easily implemented in constant rounds in the congested clique model. However, to finish the analysis we need to show: (i) that COMPUTEMIS executes in constant rounds, (ii) that the $h = O(\log n)$ calls to COMPUTEMIS in Line 10 can be executed in parallel in constant rounds, and (iii) that MST-SPARSE in Line 13 can be implemented in constant rounds. We showed (i) in the previous section and for (ii) please refer to the full version [13]. In the following, we show (iii) by simply showing that $\hat{G}$ has linear number of edges.

We first claim that $|\hat{E}_\ell| = O(n)$ in Lemma 13 and then argue about heavy edges. Proof of this lemma appears in the full version of the paper [13].

Lemma 13. $|\hat{E}_\ell| = O(n)$.

Now we show $|\hat{E}_h| = O(n)$. We first state in the following lemma two useful properties of vertex-neighborhoods in the graph induced by $\hat{E}_i$. The proof of this lemma appears in the full version of the paper [13].

Lemma 14. *For each $u \in V_i$, (i) $|N_i(u)| \le c_3$ where $c_3 = c_2^{O(\rho)}$ and (ii) $N_i(u) \cup \{u\}$ induces a clique in $G[E_j]$ for all $i > 0$ and $j \ge i + \delta$ where $\delta = \left\lceil \frac{\log 2c_2}{\log c_1} \right\rceil$.*

The implication of the above result is that $|\hat{E}_i|$ is linear in size. Since we use $O(\log n)$ layers in the algorithm, it immediately follows that $|\hat{E}_h|$ is $O(n \log n)$. However, part (ii) of the above result implies that only one of the nodes in $N_i(u)$ will be present in V_j, $j \geq i + \delta$ since V_j is an independent set of $G[E_j]$. This helps us show the sharper bound of $|\hat{E}_h| = O(n)$ in the following.

Without loss of generality assume that h is a multiple of δ (if not, add at most $\delta - 1$ empty layers $\hat{E}_{h+1}, \hat{E}_{h+2}, \ldots$ to ensure that this is the case). Let

$$\beta(j) = \bigcup_{i=(j-1)\delta+1}^{j\delta} \hat{E}_i \qquad \text{for } j = 1, 2, \ldots, \frac{h}{\delta}$$

be a partition of the layers $\hat{E}_i$ into *bands* of δ consecutive layers. Let $\hat{E}_{odd} = \cup_{j:odd}\beta(j)$ and $\hat{E}_{even} = \cup_{j:even}\beta(j)$.

Lemma 15. $|\hat{E}_{odd}| = O(n)$, $|\hat{E}_{even}| = O(n)$ *and therefore* $|\hat{E}| = O(n)$.

Proof. We prove the claim for $\hat{E}_{odd}$. The proof is essentially the same for $\hat{E}_{even}$. We aim to prove the following claim by induction on k (for odd k): for some constant $C > 0$,

$$\left| \bigcup_{j:odd \geq k} \beta(j) \right| \leq C \cdot \left| \bigcup_{j:odd \geq k} V(j) \right|, \tag{1}$$

where $V(j)$ is the set of vertices such that every vertex in $V(j)$ has some incident edge in $\beta(j)$. Setting $k = 1$ in the above inequality, we see that $|\hat{E}_{odd}| = |\cup_{j:odd \geq k} \beta(j)| = O(n)$. To prove the base case, let k' be the largest odd integer less than or equal to h/δ. Then, $\cup_{j:odd \geq k'} \beta(j) = \beta(k')$ and $\cup_{j:odd \geq k'} V(j) = V(k')$. Consider a vertex $v \in V(k')$. By Lemma 14, there are at most c_3 edges incident on v from any layer. There are δ layers in $\beta(k')$ and therefore there are at most $c_3\delta$ edges from $\beta(k')$ incident on any vertex $v \in V(k')$. Hence, $|\beta(k')| \leq c_3\delta|V(k')|$. Therefore, for any constant $C \geq c_3\delta$, it is the case that $|\cup_{j \geq k'} \beta(j)| \leq C \cdot |\cup_{j \geq k'} V(j)|$.

Taking (1) to be the inductive hypothesis, let us now consider $|\cup_{j \geq k-2} \beta(j)|$. Then,

$$\left| \bigcup_{j:odd \geq k-2} \beta(j) \right| \leq \left| \bigcup_{j:odd \geq k} \beta(j) \right| + |\beta(k-2)| \leq C \cdot \left| \bigcup_{j:odd \geq k} V(j) \right| + c_3\delta \cdot |V(k-2)|. \tag{2}$$

The second inequality is obtained by applying the inductive hypothesis and the inequality $|\beta(k-2)| \leq c_3\delta|V(k-2)|$. By Lemma 14, at most half the vertices in $V(k-2)$ appear in $\cup_{j \geq k} V(k)$. Therefore, $|V(k-2) \setminus (\cup_{j \geq k} V(j))| \geq |V(k-2)|/2$. Hence,

$$\left| \bigcup_{j:odd \geq k-2} \beta(j) \right| \leq C \cdot \left| \bigcup_{j:odd \geq k} V(j) \right| + 2c_3\delta \cdot \left| V(k-2) \setminus \left(\bigcup_{j:odd \geq k} V(j) \right) \right|.$$

Picking $C \geq 2c_3\delta$, we then see that

$$\left| \bigcup_{j:odd \geq k-2} \beta(j) \right| \leq C \cdot \left(\left| \bigcup_{j:odd \geq k} V(j) \right| + \left| V(k-2) \setminus \left(\bigcup_{j:odd \geq k} V(j) \right) \right| \right)$$

$$= C \cdot \left| \bigcup_{j:odd \geq k-2} V(j) \right|.$$

The result follows by induction.

5 Constant-Approximation to MFL

Berns et al. [3,2] showed how to compute a constant-factor approximation to MFL in expected $O(\log \log n)$ rounds. (The algorithm presented in [2] runs in expected $O(\log \log n \cdot \log^* n)$ rounds, but this was subsequently improved to expected $O(\log \log n)$ in [3].) Analysis in [3,2] shows that if a t-ruling set of a distance threshold graph can be computed in T rounds on the congested clique, then it is possible to obtain an $O(t)$-approximation to MLF in $O(T)$ rounds. In [3] it is shown how to compute a 2-ruling set in expected $O(\log \log n)$ rounds on a This leads to a constant-factor approximation to MFL in expected $O(\log \log n)$ rounds. The 3-ruling set algorithm and the MIS algorithm in the present paper can replace the slower 2-ruling set and this yields the following result.

Theorem 3. *There exists a distributed algorithm that computes a constant-approximation to the metric facility location problem (w.h.p.) in the congested-clique model and which has an expected running time of $O(\log \log \log n)$ rounds. Additionally, if the input metric space has constant doubling dimension then a constant-approximation can be computed in constant rounds (w.h.p.)*

Acknowledgments. We would like to thank reviewers of DISC 2014 for their careful reading and thoughtful comments.

References

1. Balinski, M.L.: On finding integer solutions to linear programs. In: Proceedings of IBM Scientific Computing Symposium on Combinatorial Problems, pp. 225–248 (1966)
2. Berns, A., Hegeman, J., Pemmaraju, S.V.: Super-Fast Distributed Algorithms for Metric Facility Location. In: Czumaj, A., Mehlhorn, K., Pitts, A., Wattenhofer, R. (eds.) ICALP 2012, Part II. LNCS, vol. 7392, pp. 428–439. Springer, Heidelberg (2012)
3. Berns, A., Hegeman, J., Pemmaraju, S.V.: Super-Fast Distributed Algorithms for Metric Facility Location. CoRR, abs/1308.2473 (August 2013)
4. Cornuejols, G., Nemhouser, G., Wolsey, L.: Discrete Location Theory. Wiley (1990)

5. Damian, M., Pandit, S., Pemmaraju, S.V.: Distributed Spanner Construction in Doubling Metric Spaces. In: Shvartsman, M.M.A.A. (ed.) OPODIS 2006. LNCS, vol. 4305, pp. 157–171. Springer, Heidelberg (2006)
6. Dean, J., Ghemawat, S.: MapReduce: Simplified Data Processing on Large Clusters. Commun. ACM 51(1), 107–113 (2008)
7. Drucker, A., Kuhn, F., Oshman, R.: On the power of the congested clique model. In: Proceedings of the 2014 ACM Symposium on Principles of Distributed Computing, PODC 2014, pp. 367–376. ACM, New York (2014)
8. Dubhashi, D.P., Panconesi, A.: Concentration of Measure for the Analysis of Randomized Algorithms. Cambridge University Press (2009)
9. Eede, M.V., Hansen, P., Kaufman, L.: A plant and warehouse location problem. Operational Research Quarterly 28(3), 547–554 (1977)
10. Frank, C.: Facility location. In: Wagner, D., Wattenhofer, R. (eds.) Algorithms for Sensor and Ad Hoc Networks. LNCS, vol. 4621, pp. 131–159. Springer, Heidelberg (2007)
11. Gfeller, B., Vicari, E.: A Randomized Distributed Algorithm for the Maximal Independent Set Problem in Growth-bounded Graphs. In: Proceedings of the Twenty-sixth Annual ACM Symposium on Principles of Distributed Computing, PODC 2007, pp. 53–60. ACM (2007)
12. Hegeman, J.W., Pemmaraju, S.V.: Lessons from the congested clique applied to mapreduce. In: Halldórsson, M. (ed.) SIROCCO 2014. LNCS, vol. 8576, pp. 149–164. Springer, Heidelberg (2014)
13. Hegeman, J.W., Pemmaraju, S.V., Sardeshmukh, V.B.: Near-Constant-Time Distributed Algorithms on a Congested Clique. CoRR, abs/1408.2071 (2014)
14. Klauck, H., Nanongkai, D., Pandurangan, G., Robinson, P.: The Distributed Complexity of Large-scale Graph Processing. CoRR, abs/1311.6209 (2013)
15. Kuhn, F., Moscibroda, T., Wattenhofer, R.: On the Locality of Bounded Growth. In: Proceedings of the Twenty-fourth Annual ACM Symposium on Principles of Distributed Computing, PODC 2005, pp. 60–68. ACM (2005)
16. Lenzen, C.: Optimal Deterministic Routing and Sorting on the Congested Clique. In: Proceedings of the 2013 ACM Symposium on Principles of Distributed Computing, PODC 2013, pp. 42–50 (2013)
17. Lenzen, C., Wattenhofer, R.: Brief announcement: exponential speed-up of local algorithms using non-local communication. In: Proceedings of the 2010 ACM Symposium on Principles of Distributed Computing, PODC 2010, pp. 295–296 (2010)
18. Lotker, Z., Patt-Shamir, B., Peleg, D.: Distributed MST for Constant Diameter Graphs. Distributed Computing 18(6), 453–460 (2006)
19. Malewicz, G., Austern, M.H., Bik, A.J.C., Dehnert, J.C., Horn, I., Leiser, N., Czajkowski, G.: Pregel: A System for Large-scale Graph Processing. In: Proceedings of the 2010 ACM SIGMOD International Conference on Management of Data, SIGMOD 2010, pp. 135–146. ACM (2010)
20. Pandit, S., Pemmaraju, S.V.: Finding facilities fast. In: Garg, V., Wattenhofer, R., Kothapalli, K. (eds.) ICDCN 2009. LNCS, vol. 5408, pp. 11–24. Springer, Heidelberg (2008)
21. Peleg, D.: Distributed Computing: A Locality-Sensitive Approach, vol. 5. Society for Industrial Mathematics (2000)
22. Schneider, J., Wattenhofer, R.: A Log-Star Distributed Maximal Independent Set Algorithm for Growth-Bounded Graphs. In: Proceedings of the Twenty-seventh ACM Symposium on Principles of Distributed Computing, pp. 35–44. ACM (2008)

Brief Announcement: Replacement - Handling Failures in a Replicated State Machine

Leander Jehl, Tormod Erevik Lea, and Hein Meling

University of Stavanger, Norway
{leander.jehl,tormod.e.lea,hein.meling}@uis.no

1 Introduction

State machine replication is a common approach for building fault-tolerant services. A Replicated State Machine (RSM) typically uses a consensus protocol such as Paxos [1] to decide on the order of updates and thus keep replicas consistent. Using Paxos, the RSM can continue to process new requests, as long as *more than half of the replicas* remain operational. If this bound is violated, however, the current RSM is forced to stop making progress indefinitely. To avoid scenarios in which the number of failures exceeds the bound, it is beneficial to immediately instantiate failure handling, if this can be done without causing a significant disruption to request execution.

This can be done by reconfiguration, which is a general method to replace one set of replicas with another. Classical reconfiguration relies on the RSM to decide on a reconfiguration command [2]. For this, the old configuration must have a majority of operational replicas and a single correct leader. The latter can only be guaranteed if the replicas are sufficiently synchronized.

In this paper, we present Replacement [3], a reconfiguration algorithm specialized for replacing a faulty replica with a new one. Also Replacement requires a majority of operational replicas. However, different from traditional reconfiguration techniques, failure handling with Replacement does not rely on consensus. Thus, by using Replacement, faulty replicas can be replaced even during times of asynchrony, e.g. when clocks are not synchronized and the network experiences unpredictable delays, or when multiple replicas are competing for leadership. This is useful, since replacing slow or overloaded replicas can restore synchrony and replaced replicas can no longer compete for leadership.

In [4] we showed that reconfiguration without consensus is possible. However, the algorithm presented in [4] (ARec), has to stop the state machine during reconfiguration. Replacement, our new method, includes minor adjustments to the Paxos algorithm that allow the RSM to make progress, while replicas disagree on the current configuration. It thus avoids the increased client latency and temporary unavailability, caused by ARec.

2 Contribution

Replacement is similar to the round change in Paxos. A replacement request, specifying an old replica and its replacements, is propagated to all replicas, which

F. Kuhn (Ed.): DISC 2014, LNCS 8784, pp. 531–532, 2014.

then send PROMISE messages to the new replica. The new replica can determine a correct state and start running Paxos, after collecting a quorum of promises. The following ideas are key to Replacement.

New state only for the new replica. To ensure that no different values can get chosen before and after the replacement, we guarantee that a value, accepted by a majority before replacement, is still accepted by a majority after replacement. For this, it is enough if the new replica stores any possibly accepted value. Therefore, in Replacement, only the new replica needs to wait for promises, while the other replicas can continue to run Paxos.

Vector Timestamps. In Replacement, replicas use a vector clock to timestamp the current configuration. By attaching this vector clock to messages, we can detect and discard messages from replaced replicas. Thus Replacement can allow replicas, that are not replaced, to continue running Paxos in the same round. This is different from other reconfiguration methods [4,5] which enforce a round change in Paxos, and thus discard all messages from the previous round.

Combining Replacements. Every replacement has a unique timestamp and if two concurrent replacements are issued for the same replica, the one with the higher timestamp will be executed. However, if two concurrent replacements are issued for different replicas, both replacements will be executed, possibly in different orders. Thus, replacements for different replicas can be issued by different agents, without the risk that some replacement is lost due to concurrency with another, unrelated replacement.

Since replacements for different replicas are executed concurrently without any order or priority, concurrent replacements can block each other. We solve this with simple coordination among the replacing processes, which is only necessary if a majority of the replicas are replaced concurrently.

Evaluation. Our evaluation shows that using ARec causes longer repair times and temporary unavailability, compared to classical reconfiguration. Replacement performs on par with classical reconfiguration in a synchronous setting, but also allows failure handling in times of asynchrony.

References

1. Lamport, L.: The part-time parliament. ACM Trans. Comput. Syst. 16(2), 133–169 (1998)
2. Lamport, L., Malkhi, D., Zhou, L.: Reconfiguring a state machine. SIGACT News 41(1), 63–73 (2010)
3. Jehl, L., Meling, H.: Towards fast and efficient failure handling for paxos state machines. In: 2013 IEEE 33rd International Conference on Distributed Computing Systems Workshops (ICDCSW), pp. 98–102 (2013)
4. Jehl, L., Meling, H.: Asynchronous Reconfiguration for Paxos State Machines. In: Chatterjee, M., Cao, J.-N., Kothapalli, K., Rajsbaum, S. (eds.) ICDCN 2014. LNCS, vol. 8314, pp. 119–133. Springer, Heidelberg (2014)
5. Lamport, L., Malkhi, D., Zhou, L.: Vertical paxos and primary-backup replication. In: PODC, pp. 312–313 (2009)

Brief Announcement: The Power
of Scheduling-Aware Synchronization*

Panagiota Fatourou[1] and Nikolaos D. Kallimanis[2]

[1] FORTH-ICS & University of Crete, Greece
faturu@csd.uoc.gr
[2] FORTH-ICS, Greece
nkallima@ics.forth.gr

We present a new *combining-based* synchronization technique, called Hydra[1], that enables batching, on a single node, of the synchronization requests initiated by threads running on the same core. The technique results in highly-increased *combining degree* (which is the average number of requests that each *combiner* serves), and significantly reduces the number of expensive synchronization *primitives* (like CAS, Swap, Fetch&Add, etc.) performed. We prove that the performance power of Hydra is tremendous when employed in an environment supporting cheap context switching, like user-level threads. Hydra outperforms by far all previous state-of-the-art synchronization algorithms. We experimentally show that the throughput of Hydra is higher than that of CC-Synch, a state-of-the-art (blocking) synchronization protocol presented in PPoPP '12, by more than *an order of magnitude*. Hydra's throughput is surprisingly close to the ideal and this is achieved without increasing the average latency in serving each request.

We also study a simple variant of P-Sim [2], called PSimX, with highly upgraded performance; PSimX is wait-free. The performance of PSimX, albeit lower than that of Hydra, is also close to the ideal. By employing user-level threads in other synchronization protocols, the exhibited performance advantage is much lower than that of Hydra and PSimX. Based on PSimX, it is easy to implement useful *wait-free primitives* (e.g. multi-word CAS) at a surprisingly low cost.

Based on Hydra and PSimX, we implement and experimentally evaluate implementations of concurrent queues and stacks. These implementations outperform by far all current state-of-the-art concurrent queue and stack implementations, respectively. Although the current versions of Hydra and PSimX have been tested in an environment supporting user-level threads, they can also run on top of any threading library, preemptive or not (including kernel threads).

Protocol Description. Hydra maintains a linked list of nodes. Each node of this list stores announced requests of active threads running on the same core c. The first thread p among those running on c, that wants to apply a request,

---

* This work has been supported by the ARISTEIA Action of the Operational Programme Education and Lifelong Learning which is co-funded by the European Social Fund (ESF) and National Resources through the GreenVM project.

[1] Lernaean Hydra was an ancient monster of Greek mythology that possessed many heads. In Hydra, a processing core (the body) possesses a lot of user threads (the heads).

F. Kuhn (Ed.): DISC 2014, LNCS 8784, pp. 533–535, 2014.
© Springer-Verlag Berlin Heidelberg 2014

Alg	throughput	Variant's throughput	speedup
CC-Synch	4.18	4.60	1.10
DSM-Synch	4.10	4.58	1.12
P-Sim	3.90	23.2	5.94
Lock-Free	2.00	1.87	0.94
CLH	1.58	1.7	1.08
FC	2.99	5.51	1.84
OyamaAlg	1.72	2.8	1.63

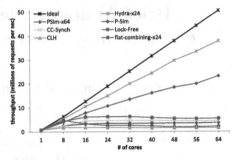

tries to store a pointer to a node nd in an array A. Other threads running on c may simultaneously compete on the same position of A, so CAS is used.

If p successfully stores nd in A, it records its request in nd, initiates a recording period by informing the other threads running on c that they can start recording requests in nd, and calls Yield. To apply a request, some other thread executing on c, discovers that a recording period is active and records its request in nd. Then, it calls Yield until some combiner serves its request.

Fair scheduling results in the reactivation of p at some later point. Then, p ends the current recording period, executes a Swap to append nd in the shared list, and decides whether it should become a combiner. If p does not become a combiner, it repeatedly calls Yield until a combiner either serves its request or informs p that it is the new combiner. Otherwise, it first serves its own request and then traverses the list and serves the requests recorded in the list nodes, in order, until either it has traversed all elements of the list or it has served up to some constant number of requests. Finally, p informs the process owning the next to traverse node in the list that it is the new combiner.

Performance Evaluation. We evaluated Hydra and PSimX in a 64-core machine consisting of four AMD Opteron 6272 processors (Interlagos). For our experiments, we consider the Fetch&Multiply benchmark used in [1,2]. The figure presents the throughput for the original versions of the evaluated algorithms and their variants where the best number of user level threads per core was employed for each algorithm; all algorithms other than P-Sim and flat-combining (FC) do not exhibit any serious performance gains when employing user level threads. We experimentally compare Hydra with CC-Synch [1], P-Sim [2], flat-combining (Hendler et. al, SPAA'10), OyamaAlg (Oyama et. al, PDSIA'99), a blocking implementation based on (CLH or MCS) spin-locks, and a simple lock-free implementation. Hydra outperforms CC-Synch by a factor of up to 11 without sacrificing the good latency ensured by CC-Synch. The performance advantages of Hydra over all other algorithms are even higher.

Although the current versions of Hydra and PSimX employ user-level threads, they can also run on top of any threading library, preemptive or not. Hydra and PSimX are *linearizable*. The full paper is provided in [3].

References

1. Fatourou, P., Kallimanis, N.D.: Revisiting the combining synchronization technique. In: Proc. of the 17th ACM Symp. on Principles and Practice of Parallel Programming, pp. 257–266. ACM (2012)
2. Fatourou, P., Kallimanis, N.D.: Highly-Efficient Wait-Free Synchronization. Theory of Computing Systems 53(4), 1–46 (2013)
3. Fatourou, P., Kallimanis, N.D.: The Power of Scheduling-Aware Synchronization. Technical Report TR 442, FORTH ICS, Hellas (2014)

Brief Announcement: Assignment
of Different-Sized Inputs in MapReduce*

Foto Afrati[1], Shlomi Dolev[2], Ephraim Korach[2],
Shantanu Sharma[2], and Jeffrey D. Ullman[3]

[1] National Technical University of Athens, Greece
[2] Ben-Gurion University of the Negev, Israel
[3] Stanford University, USA

Reducer Capacity. An important parameter to be considered in MapReduce algorithms is the "reducer capacity." A *reducer* is an application of the reduce function to a single *key* and its associated list of *values*. The *reducer capacity* is an upper bound on the sum of the sizes of the *values* that are assigned to the reducer. For example, we may choose the reducer capacity to be the size of the main memory of the processors on which the reducers run. We assume that all the reducers have an identical capacity, denoted by q.

Motivation and Examples. We demonstrate a new aspect of the reducer capacity in the scope of several special cases. One useful special case is where an output depends on *exactly* two inputs. We present two examples where each output depends on exactly two inputs and define two problems that are based on these examples.

Similarity-join. Similarity-join is used to find the similarity between any two inputs, *e.g.*, Web pages or documents. A set of m inputs (*e.g.*, Web pages) $WP = \{wp_1, wp_2, \ldots, wp_m\}$, a similarity function $sim(x, y)$, and a similarity threshold t are given, and each pair of inputs $\langle wp_x, wp_y \rangle$ corresponds to one output such that $sim(wp_x, wp_y) \geq t$. It is necessary to compare all pairs of inputs when the similarity measure is sufficiently complex that shortcuts like locality-sensitive hashing are not available. Therefore, it is mandatory to compare every two inputs (Web pages) of the given input set (*WP*).

Skew join of two relations $X(A, B)$ and $Y(B, C)$. The join of relations $X(A, B)$ and $Y(B, C)$, where the joining attribute is B, provides the output tuples $\langle a, b, c \rangle$, where (a, b) is in X and (b, c) is in Y. One or both of the relations X and Y

* More details appear in the technical report 14-05, Department of Computer Science, Ben-Gurion University of the Negev, Israel, 2014. This work was partially supported by the project Handling Uncertainty in Data Intensive Applications, co-financed by the European Union (European Social Fund) and Greek national funds, through the Operational Program "Education and Lifelong Learning," under the program THALES, the Rita Altura Trust Chair in Computer Sciences, Lynne and William Frankel Center for Computer Sciences, Israel Science Foundation (grant 428/11), the Israeli Internet Association, and the Ministry of Science and Technology, Infrastructure Research in the Field of Advanced Computing and Cyber Security.

F. Kuhn (Ed.): DISC 2014, LNCS 8784, pp. 536–537, 2014.
© Springer-Verlag Berlin Heidelberg 2014

may have a large number of tuples with the same B-value. A value of the joining attribute B that occurs many times is known as a *heavy hitter*. In skew join of $X(A, B)$ and $Y(B, C)$, all the tuples of both the relations with the same heavy hitter should appear together to provide the output tuples.

Problem Statement. We define two problems where exactly two inputs are required for computing an output, as follows: (i) *All-to-All problem.* In the *all-to-all* ($A2A$) problem, a set of inputs is given, and each pair of inputs corresponds to one output. Computing common friends on a social networking site and similarity join are examples. (ii) *X-to-Y problem.* In the *X-to-Y* ($X2Y$) problem, two disjoint sets X and Y are given, and each pair of elements $\langle x_i, y_j \rangle$, where $x_i \in X, y_j \in Y, \forall i, j$, of the sets X and Y corresponds to one output. Skew join and outer product or tensor product are examples.

The *communication cost*, *i.e.*, the total amount of data transmitted from the map phase to the reduce phase, is a significant factor in the performance of a MapReduce algorithm. The communication cost comes with tradeoff in the degree of parallelism however. Higher parallelism requires more reducers (hence, of smaller reducer capacity), and hence a larger communication cost (because the copies of the given inputs are required to be assigned to more reducers). A substantial level of parallelism can be achieved with fewer reducers, and hence, yield a smaller communication cost. Thus, we focus on minimizing the total number of reducers, for a given reducer capacity q. A smaller number of reducers results in a smaller communication cost.

Tradeoffs. The following tradeoffs appear in MapReduce algorithms and in particular in our setting: (i) a tradeoff between the reducer capacity and the total number of reducers, (ii) a tradeoff between the reducer capacity and parallelism, and (iii) a tradeoff between the reducer capacity and the communication cost.

Mapping Schema. A mapping schema is an assignment of the set of inputs to some given reducers under the following two constraints: (i) a reducer is assigned inputs whose sum of the sizes is less than or equal to the reducer capacity, and (ii) for each output, we must assign the corresponding inputs to at least one reducer in common. The following two problems are proved to be NP-compete:

The *A2A Mapping Schema Problem*. An instance of the *A2A mapping schema problem* consists of a set of m inputs whose input size set is $W = \{w_1, w_2, \ldots, w_m\}$ and a set of z reducers of capacity q. A solution to the *A2A mapping schema problem* assigns every pair of inputs to at least one reducer in common, without exceeding q at any reducer.

The *X2Y Mapping Schema Problem*. An instance of the *X2Y mapping schema problem* consists of two disjoint sets X and Y and a set of z reducers of capacity q. The inputs of the set X are of sizes $w_1, w_2, \ldots, w_m$, and the inputs of the set Y are of sizes $w'_1, w'_2, \ldots, w'_n$. A solution to the *X2Y mapping schema problem* assigns every two inputs, the first from one set, X, and the second from the other set, Y, to at least one reducer in common, without exceeding q at any reducer.

Brief Announcement: Scheduling Multiple Objects in Distributed Transactional Memory[*]

Costas Busch[1], Maurice Herlihy[2], Miroslav Popovic[3], and Gokarna Sharma[1]

[1] Louisiana State University, USA
[2] Brown University, USA
[3] University of Novi Sad, Serbia

Distributed Transactional Memory Model. We consider transactional memory implementations in distributed networked systems, where we provide several performance bounds and impossibility results. A network is modeled as a weighted graph G and each transaction resides at a node and requires one or more shared objects for read or write. We focus on the data-flow model where objects are mobile and the time for an object to traverse an edge is equal to the weight of the edge. In order to guarantee consistency, an object can have only one writable copy in the network at any moment of time. A transaction which is about to execute requires that all requested objects are available at its node.

An execution schedule specifies which transactions execute at any moment of time. The schedule also determines the network paths that the objects will follow while moving from one transaction node to another. We evaluate an execution schedule with two performance metrics: *communication cost*, which is the total distance traversed by all the objects, and *execution time*, which is the total time to execute all transactions. For simplicity, we assume that once a transaction has obtained all requested objects its actual computation time is instantaneous, which implies that the execution time for a set of transactions depends only on the edge traversal times of the requested objects along the followed paths.

Most of the previous works on distributed transactional memory focused on analyzing problem instances with only one shared object. Herlihy and Sun [1] provide a distributed directory approach and the first formal bounds for low doubling dimension metrics. Sharma *et al.* [3] generalize their approach for general network topologies. Zhang *et al.* [4] examine the special case of the work-conserving model with multiple objects and the relation to object TSP tours.

Contributions. We give a comprehensive set of bounds for problem instances where transactions require multiple objects. We assume batch problems where all transactions and their requested objects are known before execution starts. We provide offline schedules for the transactions that have near optimal communication cost. We also provide non-trivial bounds for the execution time, and explore trade-offs between communication cost and execution time. We continue with a description of our detailed contributions.

Communication cost. We first observe that the problem of minimizing the communication cost is NP-hard with a reduction from the graph TSP problem.

[*] This work is supported by the National Science Foundation grant CCF-1320835.

F. Kuhn (Ed.): DISC 2014, LNCS 8784, pp. 538–539, 2014.

We then give an upper bound for the communication cost. We use a universal TSP tour to schedule the transactions. A universal TSP tour [2] defines a traversal order for the network nodes so that any subsequence of nodes is also an approximate TSP tour for the respective nodes. By executing the transactions in the order according to the universal TSP tour we guarantee that each object follows an approximate TSP tour of the nodes with the transactions that request the object. The overall schedule has communication cost within $O(\log^4 n/\log\log n)$ factor from optimal, where n is the number of nodes. We obtain better bounds for planar graphs and networks with low doubling metrics.

Execution time. The problem of optimizing the execution time is NP-hard, and it is also hard to approximate it within any factor smaller than the number of transactions (reduction from vertex-coloring). We give an $O(\Delta)$ approximation algorithm for the execution time, where Δ is the maximum number of conflicts between transactions. This bound is obtained with a greedy coloring of a weighted conflict graph of transactions.

An interesting question is whether there are efficient schedules with execution time close to the optimal TSP tours of the objects. We answer this question to the negative, namely, there is a problem instance where each shortest object walk has length $O(n^{5/6})$, while any execution schedule requires time $\Omega(n)$. The same instance has $O(\log n)$ objects per transaction and $\Delta = O(n^{2/3}\log n)$; thus, the $\Omega(n)$ execution time does not follow trivially from other problem parameters. This problem instance demonstrates a significant asymptotic gap between the objects' optimal TSP tour lengths and the execution time.

Time and communication trade-offs. We give a problem instance where it is impossible to simultaneously optimize execution time and communication cost. In this problem instance a lower bound for the execution time is $\Omega(n^{2/3})$ and a lower bound for the communication cost is $\Omega(n)$. We provide two schedules, one with optimal execution time $O(n^{2/3})$, and another schedule with optimal communication cost $O(n)$. We observe that the first schedule has sub-optimal communication cost, while the second schedule has sub-optimal execution time. In fact, any schedule that achieves optimal execution time must have suboptimal communication cost $\Omega(n^{4/3})$. Furthermore, any schedule with optimal communication cost must have suboptimal execution time $\Omega(n)$.

References

1. Herlihy, M., Sun, Y.: Distributed transactional memory for metric-space networks. Distributed Computing 20(3), 195–208 (2007)
2. Jia, L., Lin, G., Noubir, G., Rajaraman, R., Sundaram, R.: Universal approximations for TSP, Steiner tree, and set cover. In: STOC, pp. 386–395 (2005)
3. Sharma, G., Busch, C., Srivathsan, S.: Distributed transactional memory for general networks. In: IPDPS, pp. 1045–1056 (2012), To appear in Distributed Computing
4. Zhang, B., Ravindran, B., Palmieri, R.: Distributed transactional contention management as the traveling salesman problem. In: Halldórsson, M.M. (ed.) SIROCCO 2014. LNCS, vol. 8576, pp. 54–67. Springer, Heidelberg (2014)

Brief Announcement: Relaxing Opacity in Pessimistic Transactional Memory

Konrad Siek and Paweł T. Wojciechowski

Institute of Computing Science
Poznań University of Technology
60-965 Poznań, Poland
{konrad.siek,pawel.t.wojciechowski}@cs.put.edu.pl

Since in the Transactional Memory (TM) abstraction transactional code can contain any operation (rather than just reads and writes), greater attention must be paid to the state of shared variables at any given time. Thus strong safety properties are important in TM, such as opacity [2], virtual world consistency [3], or TMS1/2 [1]. They regulate what values can be read, even by transactions that abort. In comparison to these, properties like serializability allow inconsistent views, so they are relatively weak. However, strong properties virtually preclude early release as a technique for optimizing TM. Early release is a mechanism that allows transactions to read from other transactions, even if the latter are still live. This can increase parallelism, and it is useful in high contention (see e.g., [4]). Thus, we introduce last-use opacity, a safety property that relaxes opacity.

Opacity consists of three core guarantees: serializability, preservation of real-time order, and consistency. We concentrate on the latter, which stipulates that non-local read operations (i.e. those that read values written by other transactions than the current one) must only read values from committed or commit-pending transactions. *Last-use opacity* relaxes this consistency criterion to only provide last-use consistency [7] and recoverability. Then, a transaction can read from another live transaction, if the latter will no longer access the variable in question. Plus, transactions must commit or abort in the order in which they access shared variables. These conditions are defined as follows:

Definition 1 (Commit-pending Equivalence). *Transaction T_i in history H is commit-pending-equivalent with respect to variable x if (a) T_i is live, and (b) there is a read or write operation op on x in $H|T_i$, s.t. for any history H_c for which H is a prefix ($H_c = H \cdot H'$) op is the last read or write on x in $H_c|T_i$.*

Definition 2 (Last-use Consistent Operation). *Given a history H, a transaction T_i and a read operation $op_r = r(x)v$ on variable x returning v in sub-history $H|T_i$, we say op_r is last-use-consistent as follows: (a) If op_r is local then the latest write operation on x preceding op_r writes value v to x; (b) If op_r is non-local then either $v = 0$ or there is a non-local write operation op_w on variable x writing v in $H|T_k$ ($k \neq i$) where T_k is committed, commit-pending, or commit-pending-equivalent with respect to x.*

Definition 3 (Recoverable Last-use Consistency). *History H is recoverable last-use-consistent if (a) every read operation in $H|T_i$, for every transaction*

F. Kuhn (Ed.): DISC 2014, LNCS 8784, pp. 540–541, 2014.

T_i in H is last-use–consistent, and (b) for every pair of transactions T_i, T_j such that $i \neq j$ and T_j reads from or writes after T_i, then T_i aborts or commits before T_j aborts or commit, and if T_i aborts, then T_j also aborts.

Relaxing consistency necessarily leads to some inconsistent views to be accepted. Hence, while last-use opacity prevents overwriting (releasing x and writing to it afterwards), it does not prevent zombie transactions—ones that view inconsistent state and are forced to abort. This happens if transaction T_i reads from T_j which, for whatever reason, later aborts. Even if T_i eventually aborts, it operates on stale data and, therefore, can behave unexpectedly. However, this can be rendered harmless by, e.g. sandboxing [5], or enforcing invariants.

On the other hand, using last-use opacity yields performance benefits, especially in high contention. In Fig. 1 we compare two variants of the same distributed TM [6]: last-use–opaque LSVA and opaque OSVA. In all benchmarks LSVA is able to process transactions faster, due to its ability to release early.

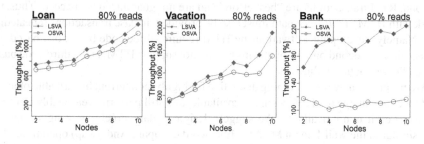

Fig. 1. Percentage improvement relative to a lock-based implementation

Acknowledgments. The project was funded from National Science Centre funds granted by decision No. DEC-2012/06/M/ST6/00463.

References

1. Doherty, S., Groves, L., Luchangco, V., Moir, M.: Towards formally specifying and verifying transactional memory. Formal Aspects of Computing 25 (September 2013)
2. Guerraoui, R., Kapałka, M.: On the Correctness of Transactional Memory. In: Proc. PPoPP 2008 (February 2008)
3. Imbs, D., de Mendivil, J.R., Raynal, M.: On the Consistency Conditions or Transactional Memories. Tech. Rep. 1917, IRISA (December 2008)
4. Ramadan, H.E., Roy, I., Herlihy, M., Witchel, E.: Committing Conflicting Transactions in an STM. In: Proc. PPoPP 2009(February 2009)
5. Scott, M.: Transactional Semantics with Zombies. In: Proc. WTTM 2014 (July 2014)
6. Siek, K., Wojciechowski, P.T.: Atomic RMI: A Distributed Transactional Memory Framework. In: Proc. HLPP 2014 (July 2014)
7. Siek, K., Wojciechowski, P.T.: Zen and the Art of Concurrency Control: An Exploration of TM Safety Property Space with Early Release in Mind. In: Proc. WTTM 2014(July 2014)

Brief Announcement: A Practical Transactional Memory Interface*

Shahar Timnat[1], Maurice Herlihy[2], and Erez Petrank[1]

[1] Computer Science Department, Technion
[2] Computer Science Department, Brown University

Transactional memory (TM) is becoming an increasingly central concept in parallel programming. Recently, Intel introduced the TSX extensions to the x86 architecture, which include RTM: an off-the-shelf hardware that supports hardware transactional memory. However, there are several reasons for a developer to avoid using hardware transactional memory. First, HTM is only available for some of the computers in the market. Thus, a code that relies on HTM only suits a fraction of the available computers. Second, RTM transactions are "best effort" and are not guaranteed to succeed. Thus, to work with HTM, a *fall-back* path must also be provided, in case transactions repeatedly fail. Namely, developing software using HTM requires three code bases: one based on transactions, a second one for platforms that do not support HTM, and a third code base to handle transaction failures.

We propose a new programming discipline for highly-concurrent linearizable objects that takes advantage of HTM when it is available, and still performs reasonably (around X0.6) when it is not available. We suggest designing data structures using an operation similar to the well-known MCAS(Multi-word Compare And Swap) operation. The MCAS operation executes atomically on several shared memory addresses. Each address is associated with an *expected-value* and a *new-value*. An execution of MCAS succeeds and returns true iff the data in all the addresses is equal to the expected value. In such a case, the data in each address is replaced with the new value. If any of the specified addresses contains data that is different from the expected value, then false is returned and the data in the shared memory remains unchanged. MCAS execution is not supported by common hardware, but there exists an algorithm that implements this operation using standard single-word CASes [4]. Alternatively, MCAS can be easily implemented using transactional memory or by locks.

We propose an extended interface of MCAS called MCMS (Multiple Compare Multiple Swap), in which we also allow addresses to be compared without being swapped. The extension may seem redundant, because, in effect, comparing an address without swapping it is identical to a regular MCAS in which this address' expected value equals its new value. However, when implementing the MCMS using transactional memory, it is ill-advised to write a new (identical) value to replace an old one, since this may cause unnecessary transaction aborts.

In order to study the usability of the MCMS operation, we designed two algorithms that use it. One for the linked-list data structure, and one for the binary search tree. The MCMS tree is almost a straightforward MCMS-based version of the lock-free binary

---

* This work was supported by the United States - Israel Binational Science Foundation (BSF) grant No. 2012171. Maurice Herlihy was supported by NSF grant 1331141.

F. Kuhn (Ed.): DISC 2014, LNCS 8784, pp. 542–543, 2014.

search tree by Ellen et al. [1]. But interestingly, attempting to design a linked-list that exploits the MCMS operation yielded a slightly new algorithm that turns out very efficient also when used with locks. The main idea is to mark a deleted node in a different and useful manner. Instead of using a mark on the reference (like Harris [3]), or using a mark on the reference and additionally a backlink (like Fomitchev and Ruppert [2]), or using a separate mark field (like the lazy linked-list [5]), we mark a node deleted by setting its pointer to be a back-link, referencing the previous node in the list. This approach works excellently with transactions, but can also be used with locks. In fact, a lock-based version of this new algorithm outperforms all known linked-list implementations.

We present three simple fall-back alternatives to enable progress in case RTM executions repeatedly fail. The simplest way is to use locks, in a similar manner to *lock-elision*. The second approach is to use CAS-based MCMS ([4]) as a fall-back. The third alternative is a copying scheme, where a new copy of the data structure is created upon demand to guarantee progress. Both the linked-list and tree algorithm outperform their lock-free alternatives when using either a lock-based fall-back path or a copying fall-back path. The list algorithm performs up to X1.8 faster than Harris's linked-list, and the tree algorithm performs up to X1.2 faster than the tree of Ellen et al. A fall-back path that relies on an MCMS fall-back path is at times a bit faster (up to X1.1) and at times a bit slower than the lock-free alternatives, depending on the specific benchmark and configuration.

Another important advantage of programming with MCMS is that the resulting algorithms are considerably simpler to design and debug compared to standard lock-free algorithms that build on the CAS operation. The stronger MCMS operation allows lock-free algorithms to be designed without requiring complicated "helping" operations typically of lock-free algorithms.

References

1. Ellen, F., Fatourou, P., Ruppert, E., van Breugel, F.: Non-blocking binary search trees. In: PODC (2010)
2. Fomitchev, M., Ruppert, E.: Lock-free linked lists and skip lists. In: PODC 2004, pp. 50–59 (2004)
3. Harris, T.L.: A pragmatic implementation of non-blocking linked-lists. In: Welch, J.L. (ed.) DISC 2001. LNCS, vol. 2180, pp. 300–314. Springer, Heidelberg (2001)
4. Harris, T.L., Fraser, K., Pratt, I.A.: A practical multi-word compare-and-swap operation. In: Malkhi, D. (ed.) DISC 2002. LNCS, vol. 2508, pp. 265–279. Springer, Heidelberg (2002)
5. Heller, S., Herlihy, M., Luchangco, V., Moir, M., Scherer III, W.N., Shavit, N.: A lazy concurrent list-based set algorithm. In: Anderson, J.H., Prencipe, G., Wattenhofer, R. (eds.) OPODIS 2005. LNCS, vol. 3974, pp. 3–16. Springer, Heidelberg (2006)

Brief Announcement: On Dynamic and Multi-functional Labeling Schemes

Søren Dahlgaard, Mathias Bæk Tejs Knudsen, and Noy Rotbart

Department of Computer Science, University of Copenhagen
Universitetsparken 5, 2100 Copenhagen
{soerend,knudsen,noyro}@di.ku.dk

1 Introduction

A labeling scheme is a method of distributing the information about the structure of a graph among its vertices by assigning short *labels*, such that a selected function on pairs of vertices can be computed using only their labels. In their seminal paper, Kannan et al. [1] introduced adjacency labeling schemes for trees using at most $2 \log n$ bits for each of the functions adjacency, siblings and ancestry. Alstrup, Bille and Rauhe [2] established a lower bound of $\log n + \log \log n$ for the functions siblings, connectivity and ancestry along with a matching upper bound for the first two. For adjacency, a $\log n + O(\log^* n)$ labeling scheme was presented in [3]. A $\log n + O(\log \log n)$ labeling scheme for ancestry was established only recently by Fraigniaud and Korman [4].

Cohen, Kaplan and Milo [5] considered *dynamic labeling schemes*, where the encoder receives n leaf insertions and assigns unique labels that must remain unchanged throughout the labeling process. In this context, they showed a tight bound of $\Theta(n)$ bits for any dynamic ancestry labeling scheme. In light of this lower bound, Korman, Peleg and Rodeh [6] introduced dynamic labeling schemes, where node re-label is permitted and performed by message passing. In this model they are able to maintain a compact labeling scheme for ancestry, while keeping the number of messages small. Additional results in this setting include conversion methods for static labeling schemes [7], as well as specialized distance [7] and routing [8] labeling schemes.

2 Our Contributions

In the full version [9] we first stress the importance of the lower bound achieved by Cohen et al. [5] by showing that it extends to routing, NCA, and distance. In contrast, we observe that for the dynamic setting, we can achieve efficient labeling schemes for the functions adjacency, sibling, and connectivity without the need of relabeling. More precisely, we observe that the original $2 \log n$ adjacency labeling scheme due to Kannan et al. [1] is in fact suitable for the dynamic setting. Moreover, the original labeling scheme also supports sibling queries and a slightly modified scheme is shown to work for connectivity. Our findings reveal an exponential gap between ancestry and the functions mentioned for the dynamic setting.

F. Kuhn (Ed.): DISC 2014, LNCS 8784, pp. 544–545, 2014.

We then present various families of insertion sequences for which labels of size $2\log n$ are required for each of the functions. This suggest that in the dynamic setting the original labeling schemes are in fact optimal, and contrast the static case, where adjacency labeling schemes requires strictly fewer bits than both sibling and connectivity. We prove the lower bound by showing a family of n insertion sequences that requires $O(n^2)$ distinct labels, as illustrated in Fig. 1.

Many other graph families enjoy (static) adjacency labeling schemes of size $O(\log n)$. Among those, we mention graphs with bounded arboricity, graphs of bounded treewidth and interval graphs. We show simple lower bounds of $\Omega(n)$ for dynamic adjacency labeling schemes for those families.

Multi-functional labeling schemes. In this context, we show the following results. First, we prove that $3\log n$ bits are necessary and sufficient for any dynamic labeling scheme supporting adjacency and connectivity. Interestingly, the same gap appears in the static setting where we prove that $\log n + 2\log\log n$ bits are sufficient and necessary for any unique labeling scheme supporting both connectivity and siblings/ancestry, in contrast to $\log n + \log\log n$ [2] for each function individually.

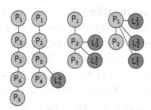

Fig. 1. The lower bound construction for adjacency dynamic labeling schemes. The red nodes are the ones that must be labeled with distinct labels.

References

1. Kannan, S., Naor, M., Rudich, S.: Implicit representation of graphs. SIAM Journal on Discrete Mathematics, 334–343 (1992)
2. Alstrup, S., Bille, P., Rauhe, T.: Labeling schemes for small distances in trees. SIAM J. Discret. Math. 19(2), 448–462 (2005)
3. Alstrup, S., Rauhe, T.: Small induced-universal graphs and compact implicit graph representations. In: FOCS 2002, pp. 53–62 (2002)
4. Fraigniaud, P., Korman, A.: An optimal ancestry scheme and small universal posets. In: STOC 2010, pp. 611–620 (2010)
5. Cohen, E., Kaplan, H., Milo, T.: Labeling dynamic xml trees. SIAM Journal on Computing 39(5), 2048–2074 (2010)
6. Korman, A., Peleg, D., Rodeh, Y.: Labeling schemes for dynamic tree networks. Theory of Computing Systems 37(1), 49–75 (2004)
7. Korman, A.: General compact labeling schemes for dynamic trees. Distributed Computing 20(3), 179–193 (2007)
8. Korman, A.: Compact routing schemes for dynamic trees in the fixed port model. In: Garg, V., Wattenhofer, R., Kothapalli, K. (eds.) ICDCN 2009. LNCS, vol. 5408, pp. 218–229. Springer, Heidelberg (2009)
9. Dahlgaard, S., Knudsen, M.B.T., Rotbart, N.: Dynamic and multi-functional labeling schemes, arXiv preprint arXiv:1404.4982

Brief Announcement: Update Consistency in Partitionable Systems

Matthieu Perrin, Achour Mostéfaoui, and Claude Jard

LINA – University of Nantes, 2 rue de la Houssinière, 44322 Nantes Cedex 3, France
{matthieu.perrin,claude.jard,achour.mostefaoui}@univ-nantes.fr,

Data replication is essential to ensure reliability, availability and fault-tolerance of massive distributed applications over large scale systems such as the Internet. However, these systems are prone to partitioning, which by Brewer's CAP theorem [1] makes it impossible to use a strong consistency criterion like atomicity. Eventual consistency [2] guaranties that all replicas eventually converge to a common state when the participants stop updating. However, eventual consistency fails to fully specify shared objects and requires additional non-intuitive and error-prone distributed specification techniques, that must take into account all possible concurrent histories of updates to specify this common state [3]. This approach, that can lead to specifications as complicated as the implementations themselves, is limited by a more serious issue. The concurrent specification of objects uses the notion of *concurrent events*. In message-passing systems, two events are concurrent if they are enforced by different processes and each process enforced its event before it received the notification message from the other process. In other words, the notion of concurrency depends on the implementation of the object, not on its specification. Consequently, the final user may not know if two events are concurrent without explicitly tracking the messages exchanged by the processes. A specification should be independent of the system on which it is implemented.

We believe that an object should be totally specified by two facets: its abstract data type, that characterizes its sequential executions, and a consistency criterion, that defines how it is supposed to behave in a distributed environment. Not only sequential specification helps repeal the problem of intention, it also allows to use the well studied and understood notions of languages and automata. This makes possible to apply all the tools developed for sequential systems, from their simple definition using structures and classes to the most advanced techniques like model checking and formal verification.

Eventual consistency (EC) imposes no constraint on the convergent state, that very few depends on the sequential specification. For example, an implementation that ignores all the updates is eventually consistent, as all replicas converge to the initial state. We propose *update consistency* (UC), a new consistency criterion in which the convergent state must be obtained by a total ordering of the updates that contains the sequential order of each process. Another equivalent way to approach it is that, if the number of updates is finite, it is possible to remove a finite number of queries such that the remaining history is sequentially consistent. Unlike Fig. 1a, Fig. 1b presents an eventually consistent history, as both processes read $\{1, 2\}$ once they have converged. However, it is not update

F. Kuhn (Ed.): DISC 2014, LNCS 8784, pp. 546–547, 2014.

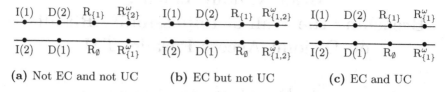

Fig. 1. Three histories for a set of integers, with different consistency criteria. An event labeled ω is repeated infinitely often.

consistent: in any linearization of the updates, a deletion must appear as the last update, so this history cannot converge to state $\{1, 2\}$. State $\{1\}$ is possible because the updates can be done in the order $I(2), D(1), I(1), D(2)$, so Fig. 1c, is update consistent. As update consistency is strictly stronger than eventual consistency, an update consistent object can always be used instead of its eventually consistent counterpart.

We can prove that update consistency is universal, in the sense that every object has an update consistent implementation in a partitionable system, where any number of crashes are allowed. The principle is to build a total order on the updates on which all the participants agree, and then to rewrite the history *a posteriori* so that every replica of the object eventually reaches the state corresponding to the common sequential history. Any strategy to build the total order on the updates would work. For example, this order can be built from a timestamp made of a Lamport's clock [4] and the id of the process that performed it. The genericity of the proposed algorithm is very important because it may give a substitute to composability. Composability is an important property of consistency criteria because it allows to program in a modular way, but it is very difficult to achieve for consistency criteria. A same algorithm that pilots several objects during a same execution allows this execution to be update consistent. This universality result allows to imagine automatic compilation techniques that compose specifications instead of implementations.

References

1. Gilbert, S., Lynch, N.: Brewer's conjecture and the feasibility of consistent, available, partition-tolerant web services. ACM SIGACT News 33, 51–59 (2002)
2. Vogels, W.: Eventually consistent. Queue 6, 14–19 (2008)
3. Burckhardt, S., Gotsman, A., Yang, H., Zawirski, M.: Replicated data types: Specification, verification, optimality. In: Proceedings of the 41st Annual ACM SIGPLAN-SIGACT Symposium on Principles of Programming Languages, pp. 271–284. ACM (2014)
4. Lamport, L.: Time, clocks, and the ordering of events in a distributed system. Communications of the ACM 21, 558–565 (1978)

Brief Announcement:
Breaching the Wall of Impossibility Results on Disjoint-Access Parallel TM

Sebastiano Peluso[1,2,3], Roberto Palmieri[1], Paolo Romano[2],
Binoy Ravindran[1], and Francesco Quaglia[3]

[1] Virginia Tech, Blacksburg, VA, USA
{peluso,robertop,binoy}@vt.edu
[2] IST/INESC-ID, Lisbon, Portugal
{peluso,romanop}@gsd.inesc-id.pt
[3] Sapienza University, Rome, Italy
{peluso,quaglia}@dis.uniroma1.it

Abstract. Transactional Memory (TM) implementations guaranteeing disjoint-access parallelism (DAP) are desirable on multi-core architectures because they can exploit low-level parallelism. In this paper we look for a breach in the wall of existing impossibility results on DAP TMs, by identifying the strongest consistency and liveness guarantees that a DAP TM can ensure while maximizing efficiency in read-dominated workloads. Along the path of designing this protocol, we report two impossibility results related to ensuring real-time order in a DAP TM.

Keywords: Transactional Memory, Disjoint-Access Parallelism, Real-Time Order.

1 Overview of the Achieved Results

A property that is deemed as crucial for the scalability of a TM is its ability to avoid any contention on shared objects, also called *base objects*, among transactions that access disjoint data sets – *disjoint-access parallelism* (or DAP) [1]. Also, since many real-world workloads are often read-dominated, another aspect with strong impact on performance of TM algorithms is optimizing the processing of read-only transactions. In this sense, two main properties are regarded as particularly important for read-only transactions: wait-freedom, i.e. transactions are never blocked or aborted (WFRO), and invisible reads, i.e. read operations never update any datum or base object (IRO). We succinctly denote their union as WFIRO.

Given the set of impossibility results related to implementing TM algorithms that guarantee different variants of the DAP property, as well as alternative consistency and liveness criteria [1,2,3], in this paper we find a breach in this wall of impossibility results, seeking an answer to the following question: what are the strongest *consistency* and *liveness* guarantees that a TM can ensure while remaining scalable — by ensuring DAP — and maximizing efficiency in read-dominated workloads — by having WFIRO? Our search space considers the Cartesian product of the consistency criteria specified by Adya's hierarchy [4]

F. Kuhn (Ed.): DISC 2014, LNCS 8784, pp. 548–549, 2014.

and of a set of liveness properties that comprises both TM-specific criteria [5], as well as classical progress criteria, i.e. obstruction-, lock- and wait-freedom.

Along the path that leads us to answer the above question, we also prove two novel impossibility results. If one selects *any* consistency criterion that ensures Real Time Order (RTO), i.e. by ensuring that transactions appear as executed without reversing the partial order defined by non-concurrent transactions, and independently of the isolation guarantees for concurrent transactions, it is impossible to ensure also WFRO, obstruction-free update transactions and the weakest form of DAP [1]. Further, even assuming weakly progressive update transactions [5], we are still faced with an impossibility result if we want IRO.

These results highlight the necessity of relaxing RTO to implement a scalable TM that maximizes the efficiency of read-only transactions by jointly guaranteeing DAP and WFIRO. This leads us to introduce a weaker variant of RTO, named *Witnessable Real Time Order* (WRTO), which demands that the RTO is enforced only among transactions exhibiting (transitive) data conflicts.

By adopting WRTO, we design a WFIRO TM that guarantees the strongest variant of DAP [2], strong progressiveness [5] and a consistency criterion whose semantics is very close to those provided by popular safety properties for TM, such as Opacity. This consistency criterion, known as Extended Update Serializability (EUS) [4,6] guarantees the serializability of the history of committed update transactions. Further, EUS ensures that all transactions (also transactions that eventually abort) observe a snapshot producible by some equivalent serialization of the history of (committed) update transactions.

Acknowledgments. This work is supported in part by US NSF under grant CNS-1217385 and by FCT via grants PEst-OE/EEI/LA0021/2013 and EXPL/ EEI-ESS/0361/2013.

References

1. Attiya, H., Hillel, E., Milani, A.: Inherent Limitations on Disjoint-Access Parallel Implementations of Transactional Memory. J. Theory Comput. Syst. 49(4), 698–719 (2011)
2. Guerraoui, R., Kapalka, M.: On Obstruction-free Transactions. In: 20th Annual Symposium on Parallelism in Algorithms and Architectures, pp. 304–313. ACM, New York (2008)
3. Bushkov, V., Dziuma, D., Fatourou, P., Guerraoui, R.: The PCL Theorem. Transactions cannot be Parallel, Consistent and Live. In: 26th Annual Symposium on Parallelism in Algorithms and Architectures, pp. 178–187. ACM, New York (2014)
4. Adya, A.: Weak Consistency: A Generalized Theory and Optimistic Implementations for Distributed Transactions. PhD Thesis. MIT (1999)
5. Guerraoui, R., Kapalka, M.: The Semantics of Progress in Lock-based Transactional Memory. In: 36th Annual ACM SIGPLAN-SIGACT Symposium on Principles of Programming Languages, pp. 404–415. ACM, New York (2009)
6. Peluso, S., Ruivo, P., Romano, P., Quaglia, F., Rodrigues, L.: When Scalability Meets Consistency: Genuine Multiversion Update-Serializable Partial Data Replication. In: 32nd IEEE International Conference on Distributed Computing Systems, pp. 455–465. IEEE Computer Society, Washington, DC (2012)

Brief Announcement: COP Composition Using Transaction Suspension in the Compiler

Hillel Avni[1] and Adi Suissa-Peleg[2]

[1] Ben Gurion University
hillel.avni@gmail.com
[2] Harvard University
adisuis@seas.harvard.edu

Abstract. Combining a number of transactions into a single atomic transaction is an important transactional memory (TM) feature supported by many software TM (STM) implementations. This composition, however, typically results in long transactions with an increased contention probability.

In consistency oblivious programming (COP), the read-only prefix of a data structure operation is performed outside of a TM transactional context. The operation is then completed by using a transaction that verifies the prefix output and performs updates. In STM, this strategy effectively reduces much of the overhead and potential contention.

In this work we emphasize the importance of *transaction-suspension*, which enables performing non-transactional memory accesses inside a transaction. Suspension not only simplifies the use of COP, but also enables the composition of a sequence of COP-based operations into a single transaction. We add transaction-suspension support to GCC-TM, and integrate COP into TM applications. We also support TM-Safe memory reclamation in transactions with COP operations, by adding privatization before a transaction abort to the GCC-TM library.

Introduction. Consistency Oblivious Programming (COP) [2], is a programming methodology for improving a TM-based data structure performance. In COP, the read-only prefix (ROP) of a data structure operation is performed in a non-transactional context. The operation is then completed by using a transaction that verifies the ROP output and performs updates. COP-based data structures effectively reduce much of the TM instrumentation overhead and potential contention.

The ROP may observe inconsistent states, and must avoid crashing as a result. It is the responsibility of the programmer to keep the ROP from hitting infinite loops or uninitialized pointers. Another type of crash may be caused by an ROP code segment that accesses a memory location after it was released by a concurrent transaction. To prevent this scenario we modified the privatization algorithm in the STM.

A useful feature supported by many STM implementations is transactions composability, the ability to combine a number of transactional atomic blocks

F. Kuhn (Ed.): DISC 2014, LNCS 8784, pp. 550–552, 2014.
© Springer-Verlag Berlin Heidelberg 2014

to be executed in a single transaction. This fosters the use of TM-based data structures, and facilitates the creation of non-trivial atomic transactions that access different data structures.

In this paper, we introduce a methodology that uses GCC-TM, the GNU C Compiler (GCC) [1] STM implementation, to support efficient and natural composition of COP operations. Our methodology is based on *transaction-suspension*, which enables executing non-transactional, non-instrumented instructions inside a transactional block. In order to support a suspension of a transaction in GCC-TM, we mark functions with the TM-Pure attribute[1] [4], that omits the instrumentation of these functions when called from transactions. We apply our methodology to the linked list and red-black tree, that are part of the data-structures library which is used by the STAMP applications. Our results show that this mechanism reduces 80% of the aborts caused by conflicts.

COP Composing Using Suspended Transactions. When using transaction-suspension, a COP operation, OP, embedded in a transaction T, goes through the following steps:

T_{start} →Any code→$T_{suspend}$ →OP_{rop} →T_{resume} →OP_{verify}→$OP_{updates}$ →Any code→T_{end}

OP_{verify} should verify the validity of the data gathered during the ROP code. This code is executed locally and must be concise, so that it does not introduce additional overhead.

In addition, note that OP_{rop} can be executed several times in non-transactional, suspended mode, and only if verification failure persists, it should fallback to transactional mode. If the transactional execution of the ROP, i.e., the fallback, aborts, the transaction naturally aborts.

The only way to compose COP operations without transaction-suspension, is the one proposed by [5], i.e., execute all ROP parts of the composed operations before starting the transaction, then, inside the transaction, verify their output and complete the transactions updates. This method allows composition only if an operation is not writing data that may later be accessed by another COP operation in the same transaction.

Safe Memory Reclamation. Two important functions that are TM-Safe [4], i.e., can be executed inside a transaction, are *malloc* and *free*. These functions are made safe by privatization. If transaction T wrote to memory, then before it commits, it waits for the termination of the transactions that started before its commit [3]. As a side effect of privatization, in case T detaches some memory block from a data structure and successfully commits, then T can free that block.

On the other hand, if T allocates some block of memory, M, and then aborts, it can free M without privatization. The reason is that the pointer to the tentative memory block is not exposed to other transactions.

---

[1] A function that is marked with the TM-Pure attribute is executed as a non-transactional code block. The TM-Pure attribute is supported by the GCC-TM implementation.

This is violated when COP is involved. If the non-transactional ROP code block traverses the data structure, it may acquire a pointer to a newly allocated memory block, and upon an abort of T and freeing M, the ROP may try to access unmapped memory. To prevent this scenario, we added privatization to writing transactions that are about to perform rollback. If a transaction is a read-only transaction, it can free its tentative memory blocks unconditionally. If, however, the transaction updated some memory location, it has to perform privatization as if it was successfully committed. Our evaluation showed that this privatization has a negligible impact on performance.

With the suspended mode, and rollback privatization, malloc and free become also COP safe. The reason is that memory is not recycled as long as there is a transaction in progress, and the COP operations are always encapsulated in transactions. One restriction is that allocation cannot take place in a ROP, because, in case the validation fails, the allocated memory will not be freed, as we do not abort the transaction in this case. However, as the ROP code typically avoids from writing to memory, it does not need to allocate or free memory.

References

1. Gcc version 4.7.0 (April 2012), http://gcc.gnu.org/gcc-4.7/
2. Afek, Y., Avni, H., Shavit, N.: Towards consistency oblivious programming. In: Fernàndez Anta, A., Lipari, G., Roy, M. (eds.) OPODIS 2011. LNCS, vol. 7109, pp. 65–79. Springer, Heidelberg (2011)
3. Dice, D., Matveev, A., Shavit, N.: Implicit privatization using private transactions. In: TRANSACT (2010)
4. Riegel, T.: Software Transactional Memory Building Blocks. PhD thesis, Technischen Universitat Dresden, geboren am 1.3.1979 in Dresden (March 2013)
5. Xiang, L., Scott, M.L.: Composable partitioned transactions. In: WTTM (2013)

Brief Announcement: Non-blocking Monitor Executions for Increased Parallelism[*]

Wei-Lun Hung, Himanshu Chauhan, and Vijay K. Garg

The University of Texas at Austin
{wlhung@,himanshu@,garg@ece.}utexas.edu

Motivation and Approach: Monitors are a prevalent programming technique for thread synchronization in shared-memory parallel programs. The current design of monitors uses the *wait/notification* mechanism that blocks threads from executing without exclusive access to critical sections. We explore the idea of allowing non-blocking executions of monitor methods to improve the collective worker thread throughput and cache-locality in multi-threaded programs.

Our proposed framework, called *ActiveMonitor*, uses the concept of *futures* [1,2] to provide non-blocking monitors by creating: (i) an *executor* for every monitor object (similar to remote-core-locking [3]), and (ii) *tasks* — equivalent to monitor methods — that are submitted to the executors. Our framework handles these steps automatically. The framework allows the programmer to use the keyword 'nonblocking' in signatures of monitor methods to make their execution non-blocking. Non-blocking methods return a *future* reference, which can be used to retrieve the result of method invocation. We re-interpret linearizability in this context, and enforce two rules to guarantee correctness: **(a)** all the tasks submitted to one monitor executor are processed in FIFO order. **(b)** tasks corresponding to a worker thread's invocations of methods on different monitors are processed in program order (of the worker thread). See [4] for details.

Evaluation: We present the performance evaluation of our approach for two monitor-based problems in Java. In our benchmark, each worker (thread) performs 512000 operations on shared data protected by monitors. We vary the number of workers from 2 to 24 on a 24-way machine, and measure the time required for all the workers to complete their operations.

1. Bounded-Buffer Problem: Every producer's put invocation is non-blocking, and every consumer's take is blocking. Items are plain objects. We also compare runtimes of Java's ArrayBlockingQueue based implementation (denoted by ABQ). We collect runtimes by varying: (a) number of workers for a fixed buffer-size (=4). (b) buffer-size for fixed number of producers/consumers (=16 each). (c) limit on non-blocking tasks allowed for fixed buffer-size (=4), and 16 producers and consumers each. Fig. 1 shows the results of these three experiments. Across all results, we use these legends for implementation techniques: LK: Java Reentrant locks, AS: *AutoSynch* [5], AM: *ActiveMonitor* (this paper).
2. Sorted Linked-List Problem: Worker threads insert or remove, with equal

---

[*] Supported in part by NSF Grants CNS-1346245, CNS-1115808, and Cullen Trust.

F. Kuhn (Ed.): DISC 2014, LNCS 8784, pp. 553–554, 2014.

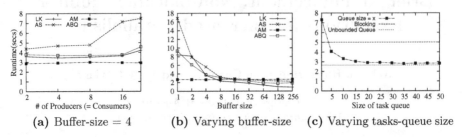

(a) Buffer-size = 4   **(b)** Varying buffer-size   **(c)** Varying tasks-queue size

Fig. 1. Runtimes (mean values across 25 runs) for bounded-buffer

probability, random integer values on a pre-populated linked-list of integers that is sorted in non-decreasing order. Both insert and remove operations are non-blocking. Each worker thread also performs some local operations outside the critical section (CS) between successive updates to the list. We collect the runtimes by varying: (a) number of workers, keeping local operations outside CS/worker fixed at 250. (b) number of workers as well as number of local operations outside CS. The results of these two experiments are shown in Fig. 2.

See [4] for extended evaluation on other monitor problems, details of CPU and memory consumption, and comparison with other implementation techniques.

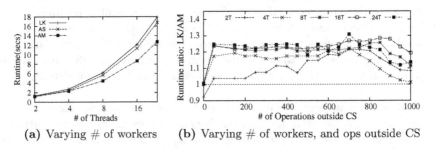

(a) Varying # of workers   **(b)** Varying # of workers, and ops outside CS

Fig. 2. Results (mean values across 25 runs) for sorted linked-list

References

1. Halstead, R.H.: Multilisp: A language for concurrent symbolic computation. ACM Trans. Program. Lang. Syst. 7(4), 501–538 (1985)
2. Kogan, A., Herlihy, M.: The future(s) of shared data structures. In: PODC (2014)
3. Lozi, J.-P., et al.: Remote core locking: Migrating critical-section execution to improve the performance of multithreaded applications. In: USENIX Annual Technical Conference, pp. 65–76 (2012)
4. http://arxiv.org/abs/1408.0818
5. Hung, W.-L., Garg, V.K.: AutoSynch: An Automatic-signal Monitor Based on Predicate Tagging. In: PLDI, pp. 253–262 (2013)

Brief Announcement:
Agreement in Partitioned Dynamic Networks

Adam Sealfon and Aikaterini Sotiraki

Massachusetts Institute of Technology
{asealfon,katesot}@mit.edu

Abstract. In the dynamic network model, the communication graph is assumed to be connected in every round but is otherwise arbitrary. We consider the related setting of *p-partitioned dynamic networks*, in which the communication graph in each round consists of at most p connected components. We explore the problem of k-agreement in this model for $k \geq p$. We show that if the number of processes is unknown then it is impossible to achieve k-agreement for any k and any $p \geq 2$. Given an upper bound N on the number of processes, we provide algorithms achieving k-agreement in $p(N-p-1)+1$ rounds for $k = p$ and in $O(N/\epsilon)$ rounds for $k = \lceil (1 + \epsilon)p \rceil$.

Keywords: distributed algorithms, dynamic networks, agreement, partitioned networks.

Dynamic graphs are a model for distributed algorithms which were introduced by Kuhn, Lynch and Oshman [1]. In this paper we explore the capabilities and limitations of a modification to the dynamic graph model addressing additional challenges arising in wireless communication.

In the dynamic graph model, the network is assumed merely to be connected in each round, with no additional assumptions about consistency from round to round. We weaken this assumption further, allowing the network to consist of more than one connected component. Formally,

Definition 1. *A dynamic graph $G = (V, E)$ is said to be p-partitioned if at each round t, it consists of at most p connected components.*

Processes communicate in synchronous rounds using local broadcast. The edges in each round are chosen by an adaptive adversary.

In this setting, many of the problems previously considered in the dynamic network model cannot be solved. In particular, tasks such as token dissemination, leader election and consensus which cannot be solved in partitioned static networks clearly are also impossible in partitioned dynamic networks. We consider the problem of k-agreement for constant k, which can be solved in static p-partitioned networks as long as $k \geq p$. The conditions for k-agreement are the following:

1. Agreement: All decision values are in W, where W is a subset of the initial values with $|W| = k$.

F. Kuhn (Ed.): DISC 2014, LNCS 8784, pp. 555–556, 2014.

2. Validity: Any decision value is the initial value of some process.
3. Termination: All processes eventually decide.

We show that k-agreement is not possible in the setting of p-partitioned dynamic networks if the number of processes is unknown, but that it can be achieved for any $k \geq p$ given an upper bound on the number of processes. Our results are qualitatively different from the case of ordinary dynamic networks, for which there are known consensus protocols which do not assume knowledge of the size of the network [2].

Theorem 1. *For all $p \geq 2$, $k \geq 1$ there is no algorithm which will solve k-agreement on p-partitioned dynamic graphs given no information about the size of the network.*

Theorem 2. *For any $p \geq 1$, we can solve p-agreement in $p(N - p - 1) + 1$ rounds on any p-partitioned dynamic graph, where N is a known upper bound on the number of vertices.*

Theorem 3. *For any $\epsilon > 0$, $p \geq 1$, we can solve $\lceil (1+\epsilon)p \rceil$-agreement in $O(N/\epsilon)$ rounds on any p-partitioned dynamic graph, where N is a known upper bound on the number of vertices.*

Our results apply to both undirected and directed graphs. More details and the complete proofs can be found in [3].

It would be interesting to consider whether it is possible to achieve agreement in fewer rounds in a p-partitioned dynamic network. Our algorithms solve $\lceil (1 + \epsilon)p \rceil$-agreement in $O(N/\epsilon)$ rounds and p-agreement in $p(N-p-1)+1$ rounds. It is unclear whether this dependence on p is intrinsic or whether p-agreement can be achieved in $O(N)$ rounds regardless of p. It would also be interesting to explore whether p-agreement can be achieved in fewer rounds with high probability against a nonadaptive adversary.

We have shown that it remains possible to solve nontrivial problems under the weaker assumption that the network at each round consists of at most p connected components. It remains open what additional problems can be solved in this model.

Acknowledgments. We would like to thank Mohsen Ghaffari and Nancy Lynch for helpful discussions. This material is based upon work supported in part by the National Science Foundation Graduate Research Fellowship under Grant No. 1122374.

References

1. Kuhn, F., Lynch, N., Oshman, R.: Distributed Computation in Dynamic Networks. In: Proc. 42nd ACM Symp. on Theory of Computing, STOC (2010)
2. Oshman, R.: Distributed Computation in Wireless and Dynamic Networks. PhD Thesis (2012)
3. Sealfon, A., Sotiraki, A.: Agreement in Partitioned Dynamic Networks. CoRR, abs/1408.0574 (2014)

Brief Announcement: The 1-2-3-Toolkit for Building Your Own Balls-into-Bins Algorithm

Pierre Bertrand[1] and Christoph Lenzen[2]

[1] Ecole Normale Suprieure Cachan
Avenue du prsident Wilson, 94230 Cachan
`pierre.bertrand@ens-cachan.fr`
[2] MPI for Informatics
Campus E1 4, 66123 Saarbrcken
`clenzen@mpi-inf.mpg.de`

Abstract. We examine a generic class of simple distributed balls-into-bins algorithms and compute accurate estimates of the remaining balls and the load distribution after each round. Each algorithm is classified by (i) the load that bins accept in a given round and (ii) the number of messages each ball sends in a given round. Our algorithms employ a novel ranking mechanism resulting in notable improvements. Simulations independently verify our results and their high accuracy.

1 Problem and Algorithm

Consider a distributed system of n anonymous balls and n anonymous bins, each having access to (perfect) randomization. Communication proceeds in synchronous rounds, each of which consists of the following steps.
1. Balls perform computations and send messages to bins.
2. Bins receive them, perform computations, and respond to received messages.
3. Each ball may commit to a bin, inform it, and terminate.

The main goals are to minimize the maximal number of balls committing to the same bin, the number of rounds, and the number of messages. This fundamental load balancing task has a wide range of applications, cf. [5].

Today, we understand the asymptotics of this problem very well [3,4,6]. However, lower and upper bounds have in common that they are not very precise. Arguably, with running time bounds like, e.g., $\Theta(\log \log n / \log \log \log n)$ or $\log^* n + \mathcal{O}(1)$, the involved constants are essential. In this work, we provide a simple, yet accurate analysis of a general class of algorithms. We introduce a novel *ranking* mechanism, resulting in superior performance.

Concretely, in each round $i \in \mathbb{N}$, the following steps are executed.
1. Each ball sends $M_i \in \mathbb{N}$ messages to uniformly independently random (u.i.r.) bins. These messages carry ranks $1, \ldots, M_i$.
2. A bin of current load ℓ responds to (up to) $L_i - \ell$ balls, where smaller ranks are preferred. Ties are broken by choosing u.i.r.
3. Each ball that receives a response commits to the responding bin to which it sent the message of smallest rank.

F. Kuhn (Ed.): DISC 2014, LNCS 8784, pp. 557–558, 2014.
© Springer-Verlag Berlin Heidelberg 2014

2   Techniques and Results

Applying Chernoff's bound, it is not hard to show that the number of bins with a given load and the number of remaining balls are strongly concentrated around the expected values. With high probability, the error resulting from assuming that these expected values are matched exactly is hence negligible. Using this argument (and the union bound) repeatedly, we can infer that it suffices to compute expected values, approximating the true distribution by expected values. We complement the derived analytical results by simulations, confirming that the deviations are indeed very small. Moreover, we use the simulations to compare to other algorithms from the literature.

Table 1. Evaluated specific scenarios (analytical and simulation results match)

goal	rounds	max. load	messages	exp. fraction of balls left	L	M
small load	3	2	$< 5.5n$	$< 6 \cdot 10^{-7}$	$(2,2,2)$	$(2,5,5)$
few rounds	2	3	$< 5.5n$	$< 6 \cdot 10^{-10}$	$(2,3)$	$(2,5)$
few messages	3	3	$< 3.5n$	$< 5 \cdot 10^{-8}$	$(2,3,3)$	$(1,2,2)$
safe termination	3	3	$< 3.85n$	$< 6 \cdot 10^{-19}$	$(2,2,3)$	$(1,4,5)$

Our simulations also show that the proposed algorithms compare favorably with all previous ones from the literature. The full paper, comprising a discussion of related work, the derivation of the analytical bounds, and details on the simulation results, is available on arxiv [2]. The used code can be found online [1].

Acknowledgements. Christoph Lenzen has been supported by the Deutsche Forschungsgemeinschaft (DFG, reference number Le 3107/1-1).

References

1. Bertrand, P.: Python scripts used for simulations and computations (2014), http://people.mpi-inf.mpg.de/~clenzen/babi/
2. Bertrand, P., Lenzen, C.: The 1-2-3-Toolkit for Building Your Own Balls-into-Bins Algorithm. Computing Research Repository abs/1407.8433 (2014)
3. Even, G., Medina, M.: Parallel Randomized Load Balancing: A Lower Bound for a More General Model. In: van Leeuwen, J., Muscholl, A., Peleg, D., Pokorný, J., Rumpe, B. (eds.) SOFSEM 2010. LNCS, vol. 5901, pp. 358–369. Springer, Heidelberg (2010)
4. Lenzen, C., Wattenhofer, R.: Tight Bounds for Parallel Randomized Load Balancing: Extended Abstract. In: Proc. 43rd Symposium on Theory of Computing (STOC), pp. 11–20 (2011)
5. Mitzenmacher, M., Richa, A., Sitaraman, R.: The Power of Two Random Choices: A Survey of the Techniques and Results. In: Handbook of Randomized Computing, vol. 1, pp. 255–312. Kluwer Academic Publishers, Dordrecht (2001)
6. Stemann, V.: Parallel Balanced Allocations. In: Proc. 8th Symposium on Parallel Algorithms and Architectures (SPAA), pp. 261–269 (1996)

Brief Announcement:
k-Selection and Sorting in the SINR Model

Stephan Holzer[1,*], Sebastian Kohler[2], and Roger Wattenhofer[2]

[1] Massachusetts Institute of Technology (MIT), Cambridge, USA
holzer@mit.edu
[2] ETH Zurich, Zurich, Switzerland
sebastian.kohler@alumni.ethz.ch, wattenhofer@ethz.ch

Abstract. We study algorithms and lower bounds for k-selection and sorting in the signal-to-interference-plus-noise-ratio (SINR) model. For the problem of finding the k-th smallest value in the network, we provide a $\mathcal{O}(\log^2 n)$ algorithm based on the aggregation trees presented in [2]. We argue that any algorithm using this approach has runtime $\Omega(\log^2 n/\log\log n)$. We show that sorting can be done in time $\Theta(n)$.

1 Model and Preliminaries

In the SINR model [1,5] we consider a set $V := \{v_1, v_2, \ldots, v_n\}$ of $n := |V|$ nodes in the Euclidean plane. Each node $v \in V$ has a unique ID $\mathrm{id}_v \in \{1, \ldots, n\}$ and is given an arbitrary input value $x_v \in [W]$ for some $W \in \mathcal{O}(poly(n))$. Time is slotted into discrete *time steps* of equal length and every node wakes up at the same time. Local computation does not count towards the complexity-measure as we are interested in communication complexity. Communication bandwidth is limited, only one message containing $\Theta(1)$ values from $[n]$ and $\Theta(1)$ values from $[W]$ can be sent/received by a node in a single time step. In each time step, each node $v \in V$ can choose an arbitrary *transmission power* $P_v \geq 0$. A message sent by a node s is received by node r if $P_r = 0$ and the received SINR at r exceeds a constant threshold $\beta > 1$, i.e., the SINR condition $\frac{P_s/d(s,r)^\alpha}{\sum_{s' \in V \setminus \{s\}} P_{s'}/d(s',r)^\alpha + N} \geq \beta$ is satisfied. Here, $\alpha > 2$ is the constant *path-loss exponent* and $N \geq 0$ is the *ambient noise*. The positions of the nodes, their IDs, n and W are known to all nodes. A probabilistic event A happens *with high probability* if $\Pr[A] \geq 1 - 1/n$.

2 Algorithms and Lower Bounds

We start with a sketch of an algorithm for k-selection (finding the k-th smallest value in the network). We use the construction of a minimum-latency aggregation schedule (MLAS) presented in Section 7.1 in [2], which is based on the fact that in our model $\Omega(n)$ links of a minimum spanning tree of V can be scheduled in a

---

* Part of this work has been done at ETH Zurich. At MIT the author is supported by the following grants: AFOSR Contract Number FA9550-13-1-0042, NSF Award 0939370-CCF, NSF Award CCF-1217506, NSF Award number CCF-AF-0937274.

F. Kuhn (Ed.): DISC 2014, LNCS 8784, pp. 559–561, 2014.
© Springer-Verlag Berlin Heidelberg 2014

single time step. While the tree in [2] is stated to be directed towards the root, we can also obtain such a tree with *bidirectional links* using the bidirectional version of the *amenability* in [2]. Using these trees and a canonically derived link scheduling technique we call *level schedule* we show how to shrink $O(\log n)$ times the range in $[W]$ that contains the kth-largest element by a constant factor, each time using $O(\log n)$ time steps to find a new range.

Theorem 1. *The k-selection problem can be solved in $\mathcal{O}(\log^2 n)$ time steps on an aggregation tree with a level schedule.*

Algorithm and proof of this theorem can be found in [3]. It has been shown in [2] that any distributive aggregation function can be computed in $\mathcal{O}(\log n)$ time steps in the SINR model with an MLAS. A matching lower bound [2] extends to k-selection, as finding the minimum is a special case of k-selection (i.e., k-selection with $k = 1$). Thus we could still hope for a quadratic speedup. However, this (if it is possible) requires new techniques since we show that by using a level schedule this can not be achieved.

Theorem 2. *The number of time steps required to solve the k-selection problem w.h.p. in an aggregation tree with a level schedule is in $\Omega(\log^2 n / \log \log n)$.*

The formal proof can be found in [3]. The theorem is proved with two reductions. First, solving the k-selection problem cannot be harder than solving the k-selection problem w.r.t. a subset of V. Second, it can be shown that in every MLAS aggregation tree as constructed in [2], there exist two disjoint subsets of V of size $\Omega(\sqrt{n})$ with the property that sending a message from one set to the other requires $\Omega(\log n / \log \log n)$ time steps. Any algorithm that solves the k-selection problem on an aggregation tree with a level schedule can therefore be used to build an algorithm that is $\Omega(\log n / \log \log n)$ times faster in the setting of the two-party k-selection problem (see [4]). This combined with a lower bound of $\Omega(\log n)$ for the two-party k-selection problem [4] proofs Theorem 2.

Finally we study sorting. We say that data in a network is sorted when each node $v \in V$ knows the id_v-th smallest input value in the network. An $O(n)$ algorithm and the full proof of Theorem 3 can be found in [3].

Theorem 3. *Assume $\alpha > 0$. Every (possibly randomized) algorithm in the SINR model for sorting has runtime $\Omega(n)$ in the worst case.*

Acknowledgements: We like to thank Magnus Halldórsson.

References

1. Gupta, P., Kumar, P.R.: The capacity of wireless networks. IEEE Trans. Inf. Theory 46(2), 388–404 (2000)
2. Halldórsson, M.M., Mitra, P.: Wireless connectivity and capacity. In: Proc. 23rd SODA 2012, pp. 516–526 (2012)

3. Kohler, S.: New algorithms for fundamental problems in wireless networks. Master's thesis, ETH Zürich, Department ITET, Zürich, Switzerland (2012)
4. Kuhn, F., Locher, T., Wattenhofer, R.: Tight bounds for distributed selection. In: Proc. 19th SPAA 2007, pp. 145–153 (2007)
5. Moscibroda, T., Wattenhofer, R., Weber, Y.: Protocol Design Beyond Graph-Based Models. In: Workshop on Hot Topics in Networks (2006)

Brief Announcement: Distributed 3/2-Approximation of the Diameter

Stephan Holzer[1,*], David Peleg[2,**],
Liam Roditty[3,***], and Roger Wattenhofer[4]

[1] Massachusetts Institute of Technology (MIT), Cambridge, USA
holzer@mit.edu
[2] Weizmann Institute, Rehovot, Israel
david.peleg@weizmann.ac.il
[3] Bar-Ilan University, Ramat-Gan, Israel
liamr@macs.biu.ac.il
[4] ETH Zurich, Zurich, Switzerland
wattenhofer@ethz.ch

Abstract. We present an algorithm to 3/2-approximate the diameter of a network in time $\mathcal{O}(\sqrt{n \log n} + D)$ in the CONGEST model. We achieve this by combining results of [2,6] with ideas from [7]. This solution is a factor $\sqrt{\log n}$ faster than the one achieved in [4] and uses a different approach. Our different approach is of interest as we show how to extend it to compute a $(3/2 + \varepsilon)$-approximation to the diameter in time $\mathcal{O}(\sqrt{(n/(D\varepsilon))} \log n + D)$. This essentially matches the $\Omega(\sqrt{(n/D)}\varepsilon + D)$ lower bound for $(3/2 - \varepsilon)$-approximating the diameter [1].

1 Model and Basic Definitions

The CONGEST model [5] is a message passing model with limited bandwidth. We are interested in the number of communication rounds required by a distributed algorithm to solve a problem in the CONGEST model. Thus we neglect internal computations subsequently. We denote the number $|V|$ of nodes of a network by n. The (hop-)distance of nodes u and v in G is denoted by $d(u,v)$. A k-dominating set for a graph G is a subset $\mathcal{DOM}$ of vertices with the property that for every $v \in V$ there is a node $u \in \mathcal{DOM}$ at distance of at most k to v. The diameter $D := \max_{u,v \in V} d(u,v)$ of a graph G is the maximum distance between any two nodes of the graph.

---

* Corresponding author. Part of this work has been done at ETH Zurich. Work at MIT supported by grants: AFOSR Contract Number FA9550-13-1-0042, NSF Award 0939370-CCF, NSF Award CCF-1217506, NSF Award number CCF-AF-0937274.
** Supported in part by grants from the Israel Science Foundation, the United-States - Israel Binational Science Foundation and the Israel Ministry of Science.
*** Work supported by the Israel Science Foundation (grant no. 822/10).

F. Kuhn (Ed.): DISC 2014, LNCS 8784, pp. 562–564, 2014.
© Springer-Verlag Berlin Heidelberg 2014

2 Results

Theorem 1. *Algorithm 1 computes a 3/2-approximation of the diameter w.h.p. in $\mathcal{O}(\sqrt{n \log n} + D)$ time.*

We present Algorithm 1 which is inspired by [7] and can be implemented in a distributed way. Details of this implementation and a proof of Theorem 1 will appear in a journal version that merges [2] and [6]. Here, $C_k(w)$ denotes the set of k closest vertices to w visited by a (partial) breadth first search (BFS) starting in w that stops after visiting k nodes (ties are broken arbitrarily, e.g. by lexicographical order in the tree's topology).

Algorithm 1. Computes a 3/2-approximation to the diameter of G

1: **each** node v **joins** set S with probability $\sqrt{\log(n)/n}$;
2: **compute** a BFS from **each** node in S;
3: **for every** $v \in V$, **compute** $p_S(v) :=$ the closest node in S to v;
4: $w := \arg \max_{v \in V} d(v, p_S(v))$;
5: **compute** a BFS tree from w as well as $C_s(w)$;
6: **for every** $v \in C_s(w)$, **compute** a BFS tree from v;
7: **return** the maximum depth of any BFS tree that was computed;

Theorem 2. *For any $0 < \varepsilon \leq 1/3$, a $(3/2 + \varepsilon)$-approximation of the diameter can be computed w.h.p. in $\mathcal{O}\left(\sqrt{n/(D\varepsilon)\log n} + D\right)$ time.*

Details of the algorithm and a proof of Theorem 2 will appear in a journal version that merges [2] and [6]. We only sketch the main insight, which is to modify Algorithm 1 by using ideas of an algorithm to $(1 + \varepsilon)$-approximate the diameter presented in [2]. First we obtain a 2-approximation D' of D by computing the depth of a BFS from the node with smallest ID. Next we compute a $\Theta(\varepsilon D')$-dominating set $\mathcal{DOM}$ of size $\mathcal{O}(n/(\varepsilon D'))$ using [3]. Now we execute Algorithm 1 restricted to the nodes in $\mathcal{DOM}$, where 1) nodes join S with a probability $\sqrt{\log(n)/|\mathcal{DOM}|}$ instead of $\sqrt{\log(n)/n}$, and 2) nodes not in $\mathcal{DOM}$ implicitly participate in the algorithm (mainly by forwarding messages). Executing Algorithm 1 on this $\Theta(\varepsilon D')$-dominating set affects the approximation ratio only by $\Theta(\varepsilon)$. This reduction of the number of vertices to $\mathcal{O}(n/(\varepsilon D'))$ yields the speedup.

References

1. Frischknecht, S., Holzer, S., Wattenhofer, R.: Networks Cannot Compute Their Diameter in Sublinear Time. In: Proc. 23rd SODA 2012, pp. 1150–1162 (2012)
2. Holzer, S., Wattenhofer, R.: Optimal distributed all pairs shortest paths and applications. In: Proc. 31st PODC 2012, pp. 355–364 (2012)
3. Kutten, S., Peleg, D.: Fast distributed construction of small k-dominating sets and applications. Journal of Algorithms 28(1), 40–66 (1998)

4. Lenzen, C., Peleg, D.: Efficient distributed source detection with limited bandwidth. In: Proc. 32nd PODC 2013, pp. 375–382 (2013)
5. Peleg, D.: Distributed computing: A locality-sensitive approach. Society for Industrial and Applied Mathematics, Philadelphia (2000)
6. Peleg, D., Roditty, L., Tal, E.: Distributed algorithms for network diameter and girth. In: Czumaj, A., Mehlhorn, K., Pitts, A., Wattenhofer, R. (eds.) ICALP 2012, Part II. LNCS, vol. 7392, pp. 660–672. Springer, Heidelberg (2012)
7. Roditty, L., Williams, V.V.: Fast approximation algorithms for the diameter and radius of sparse graphs. In: Proc. 45th STOC 2013, pp. 515–524 (2013)

Brief Announcement: Space-Optimal Silent Self-stabilizing Spanning Tree Constructions Inspired by Proof-Labeling Schemes

Lélia Blin[1,*] and Pierre Fraigniaud[2,**]

[1] LIP6-UPMC, University of Evry-Val d'Essonne, France
[2] CNRS and University Paris Diderot, France

Abstract. We present a general roadmap for the design of space-optimal polynomial-time silent self-stabilizing spanning tree constructions. Our roadmap is based on sequential greedy algorithms inspired from the design of proof-labeling schemes.

Context and Objective. One desirable property for a self-stabilizing algorithm is to be *silent*, that is, to keep the individual state of each process unchanged once a legal state has been reached. Silentness is a desirable property as it guarantees that self-stabilization does not burden the system with extra traffic between processes whenever the system is in a legal state. Designing silent algorithms is difficult because one must insure that the processes are able to collectively decide *locally* of the legality of a global state of the system, based solely on their own individual states, and on the individual states of their neighbors. This difficulty becomes prominent when one takes into account an important complexity measure for self-stabilizing algorithms: *space complexity*. Keeping the memory space limited at each process reduces the potential corruption of the memory, and enables to maintain several redundant copies of variables (e.g., for fault-tolerance) without hurting the efficiency of the system.

Our objective is to compute some spanning tree T of G. Typically, the tree T is rooted at some node r, and it is distributedly encoded at each node v by the identify of v's parent $p(v)$ in T. (The root r has $p(r) = \bot$). We are interested in all kinds of spanning trees, but will mostly focus our attention to two specific kinds of spanning trees: minimum-weight spanning trees (MST), and minimum-degree spanning trees (MDST). Constructing MSTs is a classical problem in the distributed computing setting. In the case of MDSTs, we aim at designing an algorithm which, for any given (connected) graph G, constructs a spanning tree T of G whose degree is minimum among all spanning trees of G. Our interest in MDSTs is motivated by resolving issues arising in the design of MAC protocols for sensor networks under the 802.15.4 specification. It is also worth pointing out that MDSTs arise in many other contexts, including electrical circuits, communication networks, as well as in many other areas. Since HAMILTONIAN-PATH is NP-hard, we actually slightly relax our task, by focussing on the construction

---

* Additional supports from ANR project IRIS.
** Additional support from ANR project DISPLEXITY, and INRIA project GANG.

F. Kuhn (Ed.): DISC 2014, LNCS 8784, pp. 565–566, 2014.

of spanning trees whose degree is within +1 from the minimum degree OPT of any spanning tree in the given graph.

It is known that, for every task with a proof-labeling scheme on k-bit labels, there is a silent self-stabilizing algorithm for that task using registers on $O(k + \log n)$ bits in n-node networks [2]. However, the convergence time of the generic algorithm in [2] may be exponential.

Our Results. We present a general roadmap for the design of *space-optimal polynomial-time* silent self-stabilizing constructions of spanning trees optimizing different kinds of criteria, under the state model[1]. Following our roadmap, we were able to design space-optimal algorithms for both MST and MDST constructions. Our MST algorithm uses registers of size $O(\log^2 n)$ bits in n-node networks, which is known to be optimal. While there exists more compact MST algorithms, these algorithms designed for minimizing the size of the memory are not silent. Our MDST algorithm is an additive approximation algorithm. It returns a spanning tree with degree at most OPT + 1. It uses registers of $O(\log n)$ bits, which is know to be optimal. It exponentially improves the previous best known (OPT + 1)-approximation algorithm, which is not silent, yet is using $\Omega(n \log n)$ bits of memory per node, and is converging in the same number of rounds. Both our algorithms converge in a number of rounds polynomial in n, and perform polynomial-time computation at each node. In fact, our MDST algorithm constructs a special kind of trees, named *FR-trees* after Fürer and Raghavachari. Indeed, we show that verifying whether a given tree is an arbitrary trees of degree $\leq$ OPT + 1 cannot be done in polynomial time, unless NP = co-NP. Instead, we show that there is a proof-labeling scheme for FR-trees using labels on $O(\log n)$ bits.

Our roadmap relies on a collection of ingredients. The first ingredient is the design of sequential *greedy* algorithms guided by *proof-labeling schemes*. The second ingredient is a *redundant* proof-labeling scheme for spanning trees, enabling the design of silent *loop-free* self-stabilizing algorithms for permuting tree edges with non-tree edges. The third ingredient is the design of a silent algorithm for the construction of the $O(\log n)$-bit label informative-labeling scheme for nearest common ancestor (NCA) from the literature, in order to identify the fundamental cycles. The two latter ingredients are used for implementing the sequential algorithms of the first ingredient in a distributed silent self-stabilizing manner.

More details are available in [1,2].

References

1. Blin, L., Fraigniaud, P.: Polynomial-Time Space-Optimal Silent Self-Stabilizing Minimum-Degree Spanning Tree Construction. Tech. Rep. arXiv 1402.2496 (2014)
2. Blin, L., Fraigniaud, P., Patt-Shamir, B.: On Proof-Labeling Schemes versus Silent Self-Stabilizing Algorithms. In: 16th SSS (2014)

---

[1] Recall that, in the state model, every node has read/write access to its own public variables, and read-only access to the public variables of its neighbors in the network G connecting the node.

Brief Announcement:
Secure Anonymous Broadcast

Mahnush Movahedi, Jared Saia, and Mahdi Zamani

Dept. of Computer Science, University of New Mexico, Albuquerque, NM, USA 87131
{movahedi,saia,zamani}@cs.unm.edu

Consider a network of n parties, where there is a private and authenticated communication channel between every pair of parties. In anonymous broadcast, one or more of the parties want to anonymously send messages to all parties. This problem is used in many applications such as anonymous communication, private information retrieval, distributed auctions, and multi-party computation. To the best of our knowledge, known techniques for solving this problem either scale poorly with n or are vulnerable to jamming attacks [2,4], collisions [9], or traffic analysis [3].

We propose a decentralized algorithm for anonymous broadcast whose communication and computation scale linearly (up to a polylogarithmic factor) with the number of parties and is not vulnerable to jamming, collision, and traffic analysis. Our protocol is information-theoretically secure, does not require any trusted party, and is load-balanced. The protocol can tolerate up to a $(1/6 - \epsilon)$ fraction statically-scheduled *Byzantine* parties, for some positive constant ϵ. We assume the communication is *synchronous*, and we do *not* require reliable broadcast channels.

Similar to DC-Nets [2,4,9], we use *Multi-Party Computation (MPC)* for achieving anonymity with traffic analysis resistance. In MPC, a set of n parties, each having a secret input, compute a known function over their inputs without revealing the inputs to any party. In DC-Nets, all parties participate in a multi-party sum protocol with a zero input except one that participates with an input equal to a message it wants to broadcast. At the end, the sum result, which is equal to the nonzero input, is revealed to all parties anonymously.

Unlike DC-Nets, we let parties participate in a *multi-party shuffling* protocol, where the parties collaborate with each other to randomly shuffle their inputs. To achieve scalability, we perform local communications and computations in logarithmic-size groups of parties called *quorums*, where we ensure that the fraction of dishonest parties in each quorum is guaranteed not to exceed a certain value. We create a set of quorums using the polylogarithmic Byzantine agreement protocol of Braud-Santoni et al. [1]. We prove the following theorem in [7].

Theorem. *For any $\epsilon > 0$, there exists an unconditionally-secure n-party protocol tolerating $t < (1/6 - \epsilon)n$ dishonest parties such that, with high probability, each honest party sends its message to all parties anonymously. The protocol has $O(\log n)$ rounds of communication and requires each party to send $\tilde{O}(1)$ bits and compute $\tilde{O}(1)$ operations for delivering one anonymous bit.*

Protocol Overview. To perform multi-party shuffling, we assign to each message a uniform random value, and then obliviously sort the messages according to the random values. We implement this in a decentralized fashion by evaluating

F. Kuhn (Ed.): DISC 2014, LNCS 8784, pp. 567–568, 2014.

the sorting circuit of [6] over secret-shared[1] inputs. A sorting circuit consists of *comparator* gates each with two inputs and two outputs, where the outputs are determined by comparing the inputs. Our protocol first builds a set of quorums in a one-time setup phase and then, assigns each comparator to a quorum that is responsible for computing the functionality of the comparator over secret-shared values using the secure comparison protocol of [8]. Then, the circuit is evaluated level-by-level, passing the outputs of one level as the inputs to the next level. Once the local computation is finished in each quorum, the result is forwarded to the next quorum via one-to-one communication with parties of the next quorum. Finally, at the highest level, the shuffled messages are reconstructed and sent back to all parties via a binary tree structure.

When forwarding a secret-shared value from one quorum to another, we need to ensure that no coalition of dishonest parties from the quorums involved can learn anything about the secret value. To this end, we first generate a random polynomial that passes through the origin, and then add it to the polynomial that corresponds to the shared secret. The result is a new polynomial that represents the same secret but with *fresh* random coefficients (see [7] for a formal definition).

One issue with the *shuffling-via-sorting* technique described above is that if the random values are not distinct, then the resulting distribution can deviate from the uniform distribution. In [7], we show that by choosing the random values from a sufficiently large domain, we can prevent such collisions with high probability. Namely, we prove that a domain of size $\Omega(kn^2 \log n)$ elements guarantees a uniform random shuffle with probability $1 - 1/n^k$, for any constant $k > 0$.

References

1. Santoni, N., Guerraoui, R., Huc, F.: Fast Byzantine agreement. In: PODC 2013, pp. 57–64 (2013)
2. Chaum, D.: The dining cryptographers problem: Unconditional sender and recipient untraceability. Journal of Cryptology 1, 65–75 (1988)
3. Dingledine, R., Mathewson, N., Syverson, P.: Tor: The second-generation onion router. In: USENIX Security Symposium 2004, p. 21 (2004)
4. Golle, P., Juels, A.: Dining cryptographers revisited. In: Cachin, C., Camenisch, J.L. (eds.) EUROCRYPT 2004. LNCS, vol. 3027, pp. 456–473. Springer, Heidelberg (2004)
5. Katz, J., Koo, C.-Y., Kumaresan, R.: Improving the round complexity of VSS in point-to-point networks. In: Aceto, L., Damgård, I., Goldberg, L.A., Halldórsson, M.M., Ingólfsdóttir, A., Walukiewicz, I. (eds.) ICALP 2008, Part II. LNCS, vol. 5126, pp. 499–510. Springer, Heidelberg (2008)
6. Leighton, T., Plaxton, C.G.: A (fairly) simple circuit that (usually) sorts. In: FOCS 1990, pp. 264–274 (1990)
7. Movahedi, M., Saia, J., Zamani, M.: Secure Anonymous Broadcast. ArXiv e-prints, 1405.5326 (May 2014)
8. Nishide, T., Ohta, K.: Multiparty computation for interval, equality, and comparison without bit-decomposition protocol. In: Okamoto, T., Wang, X. (eds.) PKC 2007. LNCS, vol. 4450, pp. 343–360. Springer, Heidelberg (2007)
9. Zamani, M., Saia, J., Movahedi, M., Khoury, J.: Towards provably-secure scalable anonymous broadcast. In: USENIX Free and Open Comm. on Internet, FOCI (2013)

---

[1] We use the verifiable secret sharing scheme of [5] that builds upon Shamir's scheme.

Brief Announcement:
Privacy-Preserving Location-Based Services

Mahnush Movahedi and Mahdi Zamani

Dept. of Computer Science, University of New Mexico, Albuquerque, NM, USA 87131
{movahedi,zamani}@cs.unm.edu

Nowadays, mobile users frequently ask *Location-Based Services (LBS)* to find points of interest near them, to receive information about traffic along their route, or to receive customized advertising. Unfortunately, shared location data can be used by others (e.g., providers and governments) for precise surveillance and hence, compromising user privacy. As far as we know, current privacy-preserving LBS protocols have at least one of the following drawbacks: (1) assumption of trusted third parties [2,6], (2) vulnerability to global attacks such as traffic analysis [5,6], (3) inaccurate query results due to spatial cloaking [2,5,6], and (4) insecurity against malicious behaviors [2,5,6].

In this paper, we propose an efficient protocol for privacy-preserving LBS that is secure against malicious attacks as well as global attacks. Our protocol scales well with the number of clients and is load-balanced. Load-balancing is crucial since mobile devices usually have very limited resources. Moreover, unlike the majority of previous work which rely on centralized trusted servers, our construction is fully-decentralized. Our protocol provides polylogarithmic per-client communication and computation costs with respect to the number of clients and achieves the highest location accuracy by avoiding location cloaking.

Theorem. [1] *Consider n clients in a fully-connected synchronous network with private channels, where each client has a locational query to send to a server. There exists an n-party cryptographic protocol tolerating up to $t < (1/6 - \epsilon)n$ malicious clients such that, with high probability, each honest client sends its query to the server anonymously. The protocol requires each client to send $\tilde{O}(1)$ bits and compute $\tilde{O}(1)$ operations in $O(\log n)$ rounds of communication.*

Protocol Overview. Consider n parties $P_1, P_2, ..., P_n$ each having a locational query x_i, for all $i \in [n]$. The parties want to anonymously send their queries to a location-based server and receive the query results back. Our high-level idea is to perform a *multi-party shuffling* among all clients ensuring that their inputs remain private, and no adversary can trace the messages to their corresponding senders. To this end, we adopt and implement the distributed shuffling technique of [7] with cryptographic assumptions for achieving location privacy. This protocol first builds a set of *quorums*[1] in a one-time setup phase, and then uses the quorums in an online phase for shuffling client queries: a uniform random value is assigned to each message, and then the messages are sorted obliviously according to the random values using a sorting circuit [7]. Figure 1 (left) depicts

---

[1] A quorum is a group of $O(\log n)$ parties, where the fraction of malicious parties in each quorum is guaranteed not to exceed a certain value.

F. Kuhn (Ed.): DISC 2014, LNCS 8784, pp. 569–571, 2014.
© Springer-Verlag Berlin Heidelberg 2014

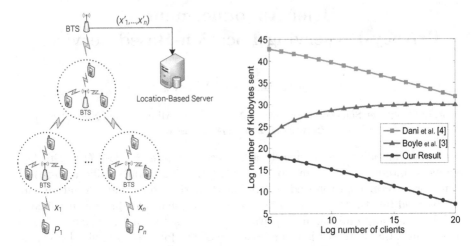

Fig. 1. Our architecture (left) and our simulation results (right)

our protocol architecture based on the algorithm of [7]. Each circle depicts a quorum of mobile users who connect to their local base station. Once the local computation is finished in each quorum, the result is forwarded to the next quorum via one-to-one communication with clients of the next quorum. Finally, at the highest level, the shuffled queries are reconstructed and sent to the LBS. Once the queries are processed, the server broadcasts the results to the parties (see [1] for a precise protocol description).

To study the feasibility of our scheme and compare it to previous work, we implemented a simulation of our protocol and two other protocols [3,4] that can be used for shuffling n queries randomly in a similar setting. As far as we know, these protocols have the best scalability with respect to the network size among other works. Figure 1 (right) shows the simulation results obtained for various network sizes between 2^5 and 2^{20} (between 32 and about 1 million). We observe that our protocol performs significantly better than others (see [1] for a complete simulation setup and discussion on the results).

References

1. Full version of this paper, http://cs.unm.edu/~zamani/papers/lbs-full.pdf
2. Bamba, B., Liu, L., Pesti, P., Wang, T.: Supporting anonymous location queries in mobile environments with PrivacyGrid. In: WWW 2008, pp. 237–246 (2008)
3. Boyle, E., Goldwasser, S., Tessaro, S.: Communication locality in secure multi-party computation: How to run sublinear algorithms in a distributed setting. In: Sahai, A. (ed.) TCC 2013. LNCS, vol. 7785, pp. 356–376. Springer, Heidelberg (2013)
4. Dani, V., King, V., Movahedi, M., Saia, J.: Quorums quicken queries: Efficient asynchronous secure multiparty computation. In: Chatterjee, M., Cao, J.-N., Kothapalli, K., Rajsbaum, S. (eds.) ICDCN 2014. LNCS, vol. 8314, pp. 242–256. Springer, Heidelberg (2014)

5. Ghinita, G., Kalnis, P., Skiadopoulos, S.: Prive: Anonymous location-based queries in distributed mobile systems. In: WWW 2007, pp. 371–380 (2007)
6. Mokbel, M.F., Chow, C.-Y., Aref, W.G.: The new casper: Query processing for location services without compromising privacy. In: VLDB 2006, pp. 763–774 (2006)
7. Movahedi, M., Saia, J., Zamani, M.: Secure Anonymous Broadcast. ArXiv e-prints, 1405.5326 (May 2014)

Author Index